Egypt is like no other place. She mystifies and confounds. She awes and aggravates. She humbles and horrifies. What you see depends on which eyes you choose to look through; but no matter the lens, you will find paradox everywhere.

When you first arrive, the sounds keep you awake at night. Donkeys shriek. Horns honk. People shout a lot, whether they're haggling over the price of something, hollering their destination to a microbus driver or telling a joke. Stay long enough and the sounds lull you to sleep. There's always laughter; and the fury of hot blood. Everyone feels strangely like family and consequently gets too involved in everyone else's business. God, too, seems ubiquitous and every other phrase reveals the spirit of Egypt: *hamdulil'allah* (thank God), we have what we have; *insha'allah* (God willing), it will be better tomorrow; *hamdulil'allah* (Egypt is blessed).

This page Karnak's towering pillars and mighty pylons hint at the vastness of the ancient city of Thebes.

Previous page Of the Seven Wonders of the ancient world, only the Pyramids are left standing.

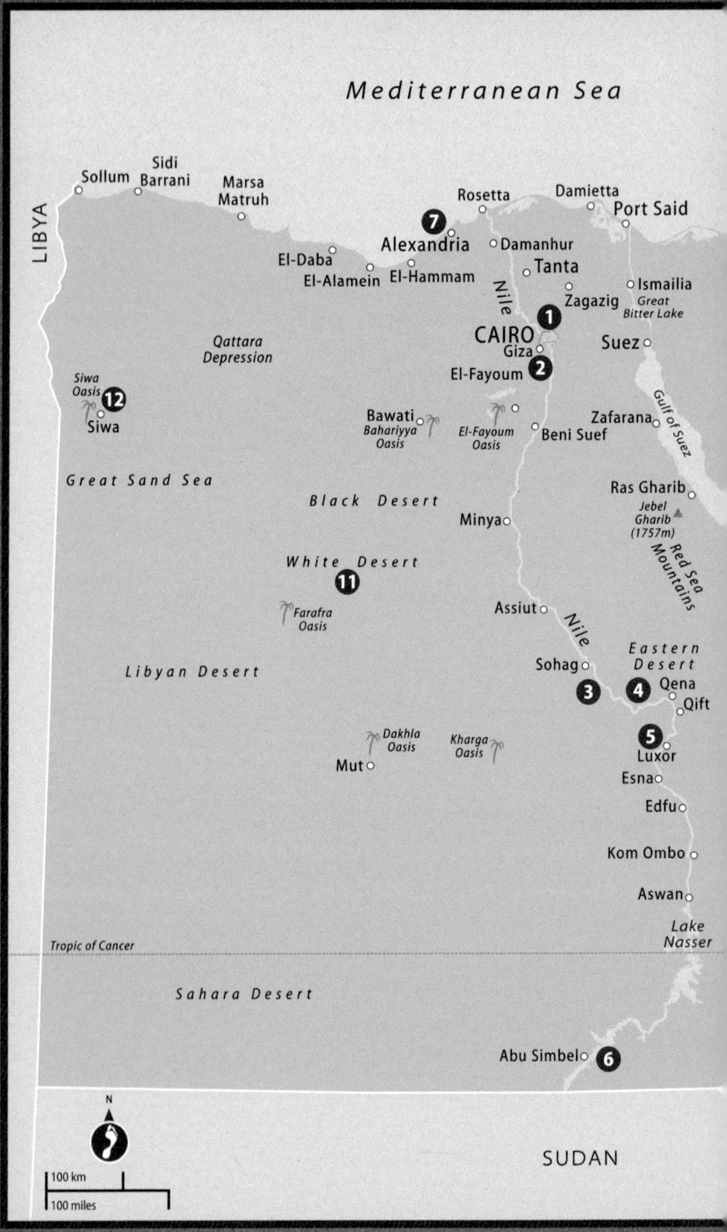
Mediterranean Sea
LIBYA
Sollum
Sidi Barrani
Marsa Matruh
Rosetta
Damietta
Port Said
7
Alexandria
Damanhur
El-Daba
El-Alamein
El-Hammam
Tanta
Ismailia
Zagazig
Great Bitter Lake
Nile
1
CAIRO
Giza
Suez
Qattara Depression
2
El-Fayoum
Siwa Oasis
12
Siwa
Bawati
Bahariyya Oasis
El-Fayoum Oasis
Beni Suef
Zafarana
Gulf of Suez
Great Sand Sea
Black Desert
Ras Gharib
Minya
Jebel Gharib (1757m)
Red Sea Mountains
White Desert
11
Farafra Oasis
Assiut
Nile
Eastern Desert
Libyan Desert
Sohag
3
4
Qena
Qift
5
Luxor
Dakhla Oasis
Kharga Oasis
Mut
Esna
Edfu
Kom Ombo
Aswan
Lake Nasser
Tropic of Cancer
Sahara Desert
Abu Simbel
6
SUDAN
N
100 km
100 miles

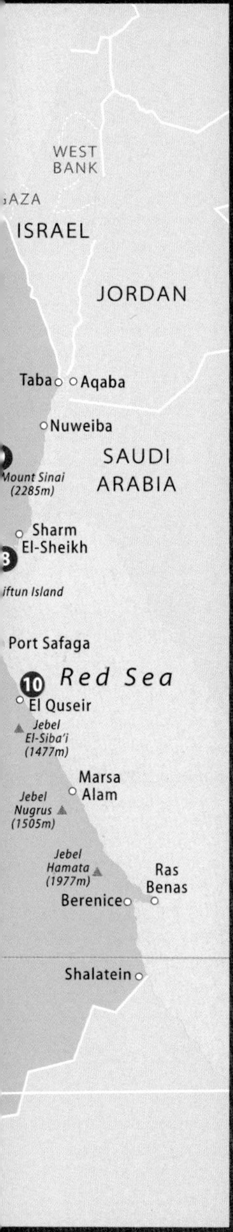

Highlights

See colour maps at the end of book

1 Cairo
Minarets, museums and markets, plus the electrifying energy of 17 million people, make up Africa's largest city. » page 53

2 Pyramids of Giza
The world's oldest and greatest tourist attraction. » page 117

3 Abdyos
The most beautiful and finely carved reliefs in Egypt adorn the walls of Seti I's magnificent temple. » page 213

4 Dahabiya cruises
The most luxurious and elegant way to travel between the ancient monuments that dot the riverbank. » page 252

5 Luxor's West Bank
Marvel at the Theban Necropolis and crumbling temples nestled in the moutainside. » page 254

6 Lake Nasser & Abu Simbel
The Sun Temple of Ramses the Great looks out over the vast lake, where crocodiles lurk. » pages 323 & 330

7 Alexandria
Great seafood, Roman remains, quirky bars and a flourishing cultural scene. » page 342

8 Ras Mohammed National Park
Where the land is barren and the water an explosion of colour, a scuba diver's dream. » page 407

9 St Catherine's
Visit the fabled monastery and climb Mount Sinai. » pages 445 & 448

10 El-Quseir
A sleepy coastal village dominated by an old fortress, where daytime swimming and snorkelling is followed by an evening sheesha on the beach. » page 480

11 White Desert
Watch the sun rise through eerie wind-sculpted white rock formations. » page 502

12 Siwa Oasis
Boutique hotels, ancient ruins, Berber culture and the silence of the Great Sand Sea. » page 528

Drifting up the Nile in a *felucca* is one of the quintessential Egyptian experiences.

The Red Sea sustains one of the world's most impressive coral reef systems.

Contents

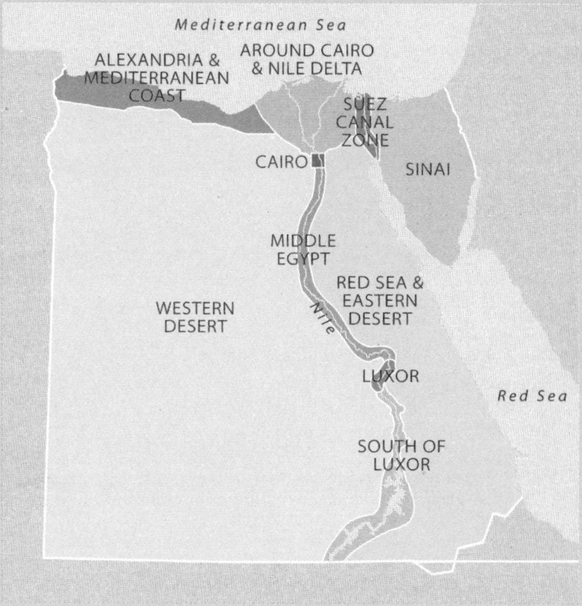

Mediterranean Sea
ALEXANDRIA & MEDITERRANEAN COAST
AROUND CAIRO & NILE DELTA
SUEZ CANAL ZONE
CAIRO
SINAI
MIDDLE EGYPT
RED SEA & EASTERN DESERT
WESTERN DESERT
Nile
LUXOR
Red Sea
SOUTH OF LUXOR

Essentials

Contents

Footprint features

Planning your trip

Where to go

As the Cradle of Civilization, the monuments and mystique of the pharaohs have lured tourists to Egypt since Thomas Cook organized the first tours in the 1860s. Now equal numbers come just for the beaches and the diving, while the desolate wastes of the Gilf Kebir and the lonely sacred peaks of Sinai beckon those who enjoy the most adventurous safaris and treks. Egypt really has it all, whatever sort of holiday you prefer: rich culture, inspiring landscapes, luxurious cruises, ancient history, underwater worlds and the crazy culture shock of Cairo. What often stands out is the famed hospitality of the people, so allow time to be spontaneous, accept some of the constant offers of tea, then sit back and watch the endlessly fascinating circus of Egyptian life.

Most people arrive in **Cairo**, where they've come to experience the legendary pyramids and the treasures of the Egyptian Museum. Often, however, the most lasting impressions are made in Islamic Cairo, which seethes with humanity, is packed with mausoleums, mosques and markets – the most famous being the maze of the Khan El-Khalili – and bewilders your every sense. Cairo has fantastic shopping, diverse restaurants and a range of nightlife to suit everyone – from backstreet bars and midnight *felucca* trips, to all-night coffee shops and belly-dancing shows.

A world away from the frenetic pace of the capital city is **Siwa**, an oasis that time forgot until tarmac linked it to the north coast in the 1980s. Berber culture is hanging on in the dusty hamlets, where women swathed in blue blankets are ferried around in donkey carts by small boys and men maintain the verdant palm gardens. Every year the Siayha Festival draws people from far and wide to dance, feast and worship by the mountain of Jebel Dahkhrur. Some of the most attractive accommodation in Egypt is found in Siwa, where eco-friendly lodges provide exquisitely sophisticated bedrooms and fabulous cuisine. Just 60 km from the Libyan border, Siwan safaris delve into the Great Sand Sea where unexpected hot springs, perfect sand dunes and star-filled nights around a camp fire are an intrinsic part of the experience.

The **Great Desert Circuit** links the oases of Bahariyya, Farafra and Dakhla – literal springs of life in the barren Sahara. The oasis atmosphere is totally laid-back and the people exceedingly welcoming. Notable old ruins, medieval villages and extraordinary desert safaris cause Western civilization to fade into the background; the White Desert, with its meringue-like chalky rock formations, is like nowhere else on earth.

Along the **Nile Valley**, pharaonic monuments reign supreme. Abydos and Dendara defy all logic with their perfect engravings and reliefs, while Luxor and the Karnak Temple have been mesmerizing travellers for millennia. The Valley of the Kings on the West Bank is surely the zenith of tomb art, and the gloriously colonial Winter Palace hotel transports guests back to Howard Carter's time.

Nile **cruises**, best done on an old-style *dahabiya*, steam down from Luxor to Aswan, passing through emerald green and turquoise blue landscapes that clash with apricot sands, down to Nubia. The temples of Philae and Abu Simbel are unmissable (particularly at night), *feluccas* sail around the islands in the Nile, and Nubian villages are colourfully painted with traditional designs.

Beyond the mountains of the Eastern Desert, the **diving** is supreme. Hurghada attracts the bulk of tourists to party and play, but further south are pristine reefs and swathes of

Packing for Egypt

Generally, travellers tend to take more than they need. At the moment, you can find most things you might require in Egypt, though choices of products may be more limited. Laundry services are generally cheap and speedy.

A travelpack – a hybrid backpack/suitcase – rather than a rigid suitcase, covers most eventualities and survives bus boots and roof racks with ease. Serious trekkers will need a framed backpack, but most safaris are by jeep or camel so you won't be carrying your luggage. The desert climate throughout the year means hot days and cool nights. Bring loose-fitting light cotton shirts and trousers and a sweater or light jacket for evenings and cooler regions. Layers are always a good idea. Avoid tank tops and other clothing that bares cleavage or legs above the knee if travelling beyond coastal areas. Bring sandals and comfortable shoes with socks for long walks. Women may also wish to bring a headscarf and everyone should bring a sunhat.

Those intending to stay in budget accommodation or take a desert safari might also want to include: cotton sheet sleeping sack and pillow case; sleeping bag; padlock (for hotel room and pack); student card; toilet paper; and a universal bath plug.

Checklist Sunhat or headscarf; sun cream; sunglasses; bathing suit; flip-flops or sandals; money belt; earplugs; eye mask; insect repellent and/or mosquito net; contraceptives; tampons; International Driving Licence; photocopies of essential documents; spare passport photographs; Swiss Army knife; torch; wet wipes or hand-sanitizer; zip-lock bags.

untouched coastline dotted with appealing and environmentally aware campsites and guesthouses. Tribal communities have a part in tourism here, and there are opportunities to sip bitter coffee with nomads and visit the bizarre camel market at Shalatein.

Over the water is **Sinai**, a haven for chilling by the beach and providing easy access to some of the world's best dive sites. Dahab is the traditional place to get properly laid-back, though it's more of a town these days than a village. For palm-reef huts, candle-light and cheap rooms, backpackers head a little further north to the unspoiled beaches that are a stone's throw away from Saudi Arabia.

Little visited is the **Canal Zone**, and – besides the mellow atmosphere, tree-lined streets and plethora of top-class fish restaurants – that's the appealing aspect of it. Here, and in the Delta, real Egypt exists and tourists are welcome to fit in, whether it's at a folk concert in Port Said or a moulid in Tanta.

Itineraries

One week Egypt offers a range of short-trip possibilities, but you have to be selective and not try to cram too much in. In one week, it's best to take internal flights otherwise you will lose precious time on the bus or train. Start with one night/two days in Cairo to explore the Egyptian Museum, the *souks* of Islamic Cairo and the Pyramids of Giza. Then, depending on your focus, either fly to Sinai or the east coast for diving, relaxing and day safaris, or if you're after pharaonic splendours travel south to Luxor and the Valley of the Kings.

If you want to save Cairo for another trip, international flights will take you straight to your point of interest allowing you to tag on a couple of days in Aswan from Luxor, or the chance of a live-aboard diving safari from Hurghada or Sharm El-Sheikh.

Two weeks With two weeks, plan to spend at least two to three days in Cairo to visit the desolate pyramids of Saqqara and Dahshur, the museum and churches of Coptic Cairo and enjoy sunset views of the city from Al-Azhar Park. Then go by plane or train to Luxor and spend a couple of days around the ancient capital of Thebes and biking round the West Bank. Funds permitting, book a cruise and sail down the Nile exploring temples on the way to Aswan, where you can enjoy time relaxing on the beautiful banks of the Nubian city and experience the mystique of Philae at night. Take a day trip to Ramses the Great's temple at Abu Simbel before flying back to Cairo from Aswan.

If you're on a tight budget, take a train from Cairo straight to Aswan and enjoy a two- to three-day *felucca* trip up the Nile to Edfu. From there, carry on up to Luxor to enjoy the splendours of Karnak and the pharaohs' tombs and, if you've time left, the most beautiful of all temples at Abydos.

Alternatively, focus on Egypt's natural wonders. After exploring Cairo, travel to the Red Sea coast for world-class diving around Marsa Alam and the austere realms of the Eastern Desert. Or head for the enchantment of Sinai for a few days' lounging in Dahab's seaside dens followed by a hike through dramatic mountains in the company of Bedouin, before heading back to Cairo. If the Sand Sea is of greater interest, plan a safari around the oases of the Western Desert. It's a nine-hour bus ride to remote Siwa, a unique oasis where three days won't feel like enough for the hotsprings, sandbaths, ruins and tranquillity. From there you can cross the desert to Bahariyya, camp in the psychedelic White Desert and move on to the medieval mud-brick villages of Dakhla, taking six days, with another gruelling bus ride back to Cairo at the end.

One month With a month, you could see most of Egypt's main attractions, but this depends on how fast you like to move and how extensively you intend to explore. After some time in Cairo, take the train to Alexandria to spend a day or two eating great fish and checking out the cultural scene, before moving on for a few days in Siwa. Do the Desert Circuit, stopping off in the oases en route to Dakhla or Kharga, where you will have Graeco-Roman temples and monasteries to yourself. From either place you can hire a car to Luxor to save time, or travel via Assiut on public transport. Explore the vast temples of Thebes before heading south to Aswan and, if funds allow, take a luxurious and unforgettable Lake Nasser cruise to Abu Simbel, or a cheaper (but still magical) *felucca* back to Edfu.

From Luxor there is an arduous bus direct to Dahab to enjoy snorkelling, sands and days to unwind. It is possible to squeeze in a visit to St Catherine's Monastery and a walk up Mount Sinai before taking a bus back to Cairo. Or from Luxor, you may wish to strike off east over the desert via Qift to isolated El-Quseir and the desert monasteries, or even further south to where the road almost ends at Wadi El-Gemal and tribal hospitality is at its warmest.

When to go

Temperature-wise, the best time for travelling in Egypt, except possibly Alexandria, is between October and April and especially November to February. The sun shines the whole year round and even if winter nights get cold in Cairo, daytime temperatures are almost always above 20°C though there's a risk of cloudy haze. In Alexandria, stiff breezes make it unpleasant at the beginning of the year, but it's also a place to be avoided during the summer holidays (June to mid-September) when rich Cairenes descend and take over the coastal resorts and public beaches become unbearably crowded. During the winter months, the mountains of Sinai and the sands of the desert are freezing at night, and while sleeping under the stars is still possible you have to be very well prepared for the cold.

The temperature increases as you travel south, Luxor is always about 10°C warmer than Cairo, and it can hit 50°C in Aswan between June and August. The desert is intolerably hot in the summer and barely any safaris are undertaken, while in April be prepared for the *khamseen* wind – the wind of 50 days – which blows sand and heat that are totally blinding. Relative humidity can be high (over 70%) on the coast and the Delta. Inland, humidity is never a problem and at the height of summer it falls to less than 20% in many places.

Another factor to take into account is Islamic festivals, most of which add to anyone's enjoyment of Egypt, but if you want a smooth and comfortable travelling experience then Ramadan is a month to avoid. During this time, the vast majority of the population will be fasting and it can be almost impossible in small places to find food during the day. To eat, drink or smoke in public is definitely insensitive and alcohol is only available to foreigners in tourist strongholds or Westernized bars and hotels. Transport also becomes more difficult as the streets of Cairo are gridlocked for three hours before sunset with commuters hurrying to get home, long journeys are broken by halts for *iftar* (breakfast) and drivers push all limits for speed. Despite all the inconveniences, however, overlapping with a few days of Ramadan can be atmospheric and fun, as cities stay up the whole night and hospitality is extended even more than usual. Dependent on the lunar calendar, it is predicted Ramadan will start on 1 August 2011, 20 July 2012 and 9 July 2013.

What to do

The possibility for adventure and sport in Egypt is surprisingly varied. In addition to more standard forms of entertainment like swimming and golf, you can ride a horse or camel in the desert, snorkel or dive among some of the most pristine coral reefs on the planet, or leisurely sail on an age-old *felucca*, a vessel that has been floating on the Nile for centuries. Also, in Sinai and the Western Desert, there are extensive hiking and trekking opportunities. Local tour operators are listed in each town's individual Activities and tours sections.

Balloon flights

Several companies in Luxor specialize in flights, try www.dream-balloons.com and www.sindbadballoons.com. A few budget hotels also organize flights at a cheaper rate.

Competition and popularity has brought the price of balloon flights in Luxor down to the point where budget hotels now arrange trips for their guests. Normally collection is from your hotel, the flight lasts around 45 minutes and takes place on the West Bank over the Valley of the Kings and Valley of the Queens. It is a surreal experience – the fact the sky is thick with other balloons only adds to the spectacle – as the pink dawn sweeps over waking villages and the push of people and noise and crush of traffic are left far behind.

These trips are subject to weather conditions over which there is no control – make sure your tour agent offers a refund in case of cancellation. Agility is required to climb into the basket and children under 138 cm (4'6") are not accepted.

Birdwatching

ⓘ *UK operator Sunbird Tours, T01767- 262522, www.sunbirdtours.co.uk, offers birdwatching trips to Egypt.*

As Egypt is at the crossroad of three continents and central to the migration routes of many birds, opportunities for birdwatching abound. In Sinai, Ras Mohammed National

Park is home to a wide range of bird species. Nearer to Cairo, Wadi Rayan, a picturesque man-made lake, is a good spot. Also popular is the huge natural salt lake of Qarun, by El Fayoum Oasis. There are several books on ornithology in Egypt, all available at the **AUC** bookshop in Cairo.

Cruising on the Nile

Cruise boats A long meander down the ancient and enchanting Nile is a highlight for many. Cruise boats are often lavish affairs with fabulous buffets, sumptuous cabins and large swimming pools on deck. It's an easy and comfortable means of seeing a lot of historic monuments over a short period of time while still having plenty of opportunity for more indulgent holiday pursuits, such as sun-tanning or being entertained by belly-dancers or Egyptian folk music with a glass of wine in your hand.

Dahabiyas A relatively recent, utterly perfect and rather expensive option for cruising on the Nile are the magnificent old-style *dahabiyas*. When the French invaded Egypt, the sultans watched the battle from their *dahabiyas* and Napoleon later had his own vessel. In the days of the monarchy in the 1920s to 1940s, *dahabiyas* were the provenance of the aristocracy. Wood-panelled cabins, brass fittings, double lateen sails and colonial interiors recall the elegance of past days, while modern comforts and amenities are all provided. The food is spectacularly fresh and entertainments avoid the tacky to focus more on quiet and leisurely pursuits. Traditional sailing boats can moor at places the cruise ships can't reach and are less tied by rigid itineraries, meaning that visits to temples can be timed for quieter periods.

Feluccas For travellers on a budget or in search of a more rugged Nile cruise, a great way to get a taste of the river in all her splendour and take in the temples between Aswan and Esna is on a *felucca*. These traditional sailing boats have been plying the river since time immemorial, with their fresh white paint and bright orange and blue trims. Being in the hands of a competent crew, working the sails and tacking to-and-fro to catch the breezes, allows the centuries to slip away. Days are spent enjoying the passing scenery, reading, and talking to fellow passengers. Nights range from lively partying around bonfires on sandy island shores to quiet sky-gazing.

Desert safaris

Almost every hotel or camp in the oasis towns organizes safaris by jeep or camel. For a wide range of expeditions (up to 40 days), check **Badawiya Expedition Travel** ⓘ *T02-2526 0994, www.badawiya.com*, and **Khaset Expeditions** ⓘ *www.khaset-xp.com*, an Egyptian-French partnership.

Nearly 45,000 people visit Egypt each year to make an expedition into the desert. The two regions most commonly explored are Sinai with its vibrant-coloured canyons and ancient sacred peaks, and the Western Desert, where oases sprout amid endless dunes, bubbling hot springs and weird limestone rock formations. The Eastern Desert is also becoming more popular, where the stern grey mountains hide unexpected and magical wadis, and nomadic tribes still roam. Jeep tours are usually cheaper than camel safaris, some tour companies and local desert guides provide absolutely everything for as little as US$30 per person per day (and, depending on what you want, up to US$150 per person per day). Trips generally include food, sleeping bags/blankets and transport (whether it's camel or jeep) and give you the freedom to create your own adventure. Trips are enhanced by the company of local Bedouin guides who can share their knowledge of the environment and find their way through dune scapes and mountains by their wits alone. Tea is a ritual, drunk incredibly strong from tiny glasses. Campfires are a must for warming the bones on desert nights, and invariably a *tabla*, *mismar* (flute) or *simsameya* will be produced and someone will have a beautiful singing voice.

The sandy plateaux of the Sinai are best seen from the back of a camel. Excursions can be as short as a half day, but with a few days it's possible to cross the interior between St Catherine and the east coast, to Dahab or Nuweiba, visiting dramatic canyons and skirting rugged peaks on the way. Shorter camel trips that explore rarely visited areas in the western region of Sinai can be arranged in Wadi Feiran. Options for trips in the Western Desert are manifold. A thorough exploration of the Gilf Kebir area requires 14-19 days (by jeep) and takes in the numerous rock-art sites, incredible valleys, the silica glass field and rusty wreckage of Second World War vehicles. If you are short on time, one-day jeep tours can be made from Siwa (to the Great Sand Sea), from Bahariyya (to the Black Desert), from Farafra (to the White Desert) or from Dakhla (through immense dunes little visited by tour groups). Of these, the White Desert is the most extraordinary visually and is thus the most popular, but it is still possible to find an overnight spot with no other campfires in sight. Travelling by camel instead of jeep allows more time for contemplation, plus the sense of being at one with the land is far more intense – although it is physically quite gruelling. The ideal times of year to take a safari are spring or autumn, to avoid the freezing winter nights and the unbearably hot summer days. April is best avoided, however, when there's a high chance of sandstorms as the khamsin winds blow over the Sahara.

Diving and snorkelling

To get an idea of dive sites and prices, see **Emperor Divers**, www.emperordivers.com, or **Oonasdivers**, www.oonasdivers.com, who have diving centres at all the main destinations in Sinai and on the Red Sea coast.

Climatic and geographic features make the Red Sea the place to scuba-dive and snorkel and many tourists come to Egypt with no intention whatsoever of seeing the monuments on land. Scores of dive shops in Sharm El-Sheikh, Hurghada and Dahab offer relatively affordable dive courses that can have you certified in five days. If you lack the funds or inclination, snorkelling can be just as fulfilling. In most places along the Red Sea coast, you can rent everything you'll need to breathe underwater for about E£20 a day. Sinai highlights include Ras Mohammed National Park and the shoreline wonders of Dahab, Sharm El-Sheikh and Basata. From Sharm El-Sheikh, El-Gouna and Hurghada, you can also hop on a boat for more remote diving and snorkelling opportunities, while the southerly reaches of the Eastern Coast allow divers to easily access reefs and islands such as Elphinstone and Zabargad – an experience not to be missed.

A mixture of deep-water fish and surface coral give a total of more than 1000 species of fish to observe, some 500 species of coral and thousands of invertebrate reef dwellers. The clear waters ensure that the fish can be 'caught' on film. Sites to visit include sheer drop-offs, sea-grass meadows, coral-encrusted wrecks, gullies and pinnacles: a new world. Water temperatures vary. A 3 mm or 5 mm wetsuit is recommended for most of the year but something thicker is required for winter (18°C) or a prolonged series of dives.

Live-aboards This method of accessing the dive sites permits divers to reach more remote locations in smaller groups so, in theory, less disturbance is caused. It provides the diver with accommodation and the opportunity for unlimited daily dives but with limited need to travel.

Most live-aboard agents extend all year round over the northern waters from Sharm El-Sheikh and Hurghada to Ras Mohammed, Gulf of Suez, Tiran Straits and Port Sudan. In summer they chart south from Marsa Alam to the more isolated reefs and islands. Summer is the best time to dive in the south when the winds and currents are not so strong and the water temperature (here at the Tropic of Cancer) reaches about 30°C. Boats from Hurghada tend to head northwards to Abu Nawas and Thistegorm, eastwards to Ras Mohammed or southwards to Safaga.

Daily dives Diving costs €40-65 per day (€30-55 per day if booking five days or more), depending on the season and whether you are booking from Hurghada or Sharm El-Sheikh (which are cheaper) or Marsa Alam, further south.

PADI diving courses The prices quoted for PADI courses should include all diving equipment and materials. The Open Water course takes five days – three days of theory and work in confined water/deep swimming pool to put the theory into practice and two days in the ocean completing four open-water dives. Courses requiring certification are an extra €35 per certificate for which you will require two passport photographs. You will also need a log book (on sale in diving resorts) to record your dives.

Other qualifications Open Water Certification: €300-400. Advanced Open Water Certification (two days): €220-240. Medic First Aid (one day): €70. Rescue Diver Certification (three-four days): €350. Dive Master Certification: €550-700. Under Water Naturalist: €110-120. Night Diver: €150-180. Multi-level Diver: €150. Reef Diver: €120. Wreck Diver: €230.

Fishing

ⓘ *The African Angler, T/F097-230 9748, www.african-angler.net, has a good range of trips that run regularly. Lake Nasser Adventure, www.lakenasseradventure.com, based in Aswan, is an Egyptian/Swiss-British partnership, which provides fishing safaris and boat-trekking cruises.*

Fishing is becoming a very popular sport, especially on Lake Nasser where there are over 32 species of fish. The immense body of water has allowed 'big game' fish to develop and thrive, and a day's catch can be spectacular. Specialist operators organize camping/fishing safaris, usually one to six days, with accommodation either on board 'mother-ships' from where anglers set out each day on smaller vessels, camping on the shore, or afloat small crafts sleeping one to three people. The total isolation and uniqueness of the destination, plus plenty of crocodiles and other wildlife to look out for, makes for a satisfying adventure – ideal for anyone who loves the outdoor life. A permit is required to both fish and visit the lake, which takes about three weeks to process prior to departing on a safari and will be arranged by the tour operator. There are also deep-sea fishing trips on the Red Sea starting from Hurghada.

Horse riding

ⓘ *AA Stables, T012-153 4142, in Giza have horses that are properly looked after and can arrange riding lessons.*

Galloping around the sands surrounding the pyramids at Giza is an exhilarating and breathtaking way to get a bit of exercise. Avoid the mangy beasts that hang around the entrances to the site and choose a reputable stable in the area past the entrance to the Sphinx. The West Bank of Luxor has a couple of stables in Gezira village just up from the ferry landing, and it's a wonderful way to explore the landscape with lots of scope for detours and flexibility. In Sinai, you can go horse riding from Sharm El-Sheikh and Dahab.

Trekking

ⓘ *With an emphasis on ecotourism, Sheikh Sina Bedouin Treks, T069-347 0880, www.sheikhsina.com, and www.sheikmousa.com, focus on mountain treks in Sinai.*

The best place for trekking in Egypt is the interior of Sinai. Options range from an afternoon or late-night meander up Mount Sinai to treks of several weeks through the mountainous interior. Scaling majestic summits and camping in lush wadis and gardens, treks are led by local Bedouin tribesmen who also do the cooking and share their knowledge of the local flora and fauna. A good linear route goes from St Catherine's to El-Tur on the western coast, scaling Jebel Umm Shomar (the second-highest peak in Egypt) on the way, but there are countless other options and circular routes, which can be tailored to suit trekkers' preferences. For those who prefer flatter terrain, the Western Desert is the best bet. Trips are led by guides and camels are used to transport all the camping equipment, water and luggage necessary for an expedition. Food can be brought out by jeep to the designated camping spot in the evenings, meaning you are guaranteed a fresh dinner each night.

Watersports

ⓘ *Moon Beach, 40 km south of Ras Sudr, T069-340 1501, www.moonbeachretreat.com, has a wide sandy beach, excellent windsurfing school and is just a short journey from Cairo. (Moon beach is closed Jan-Feb).*

In addition to underwater pursuits, Egypt offers excellent spots for windsurfing, kitesurfing and waterskiing. Ras Sudr on the western coast of the Sinai and Safaga on the Red Sea coast are both known for their reliable year-round gusts. The lagoon and bay south of Dahab is also a popular spot for learning to windsurf or kitesurf.

Getting there

Air

It is possible to fly direct to Egypt from Europe, the Middle East, the USA and most adjacent African countries.

Airfares vary according to season. They peak from June to September and around other holiday times (Christmas and New Year). The cheapest times to travel are during November and January. As a rule, the earlier you buy a ticket, the cheaper it will be. It's worth checking in with a few travel agents to see if any special promotions are available and sometimes tour companies offer cheaper fares as they buy them in big numbers. Return tickets are usually a lot cheaper than buying two one-way tickets or opting for an open-ended return, unless you fly with a charter airline. Round-the-World tickets don't include Cairo on their standard itineraries and you will have to go through a company that will custom-build trips.

From Europe

From London, **BMI**, www.flybmi.com, **British Airways**, www.ba.com, and **EgyptAir**, www.egyptair.com, offer daily flights to Cairo International airport. Flight time is about five hours and ticket prices range from £350 in the off-season to £450 during peak tourist season. You can save a bit of money if you fly indirect via a European capital (see below), usually in Eastern Europe, Germany or Greece. There are also consistent charter flights to Hurghada, Luxor and (especially) Sharm El-Sheikh, some of which leave from regional airports. Have a look at www.thomsonfly.com, www.firstchoice.co.uk, www.jet2.com and www.fly thomascook.com, as there are some great deals (as low as £50 one way if you get lucky) if you don't mind starting your journey outside Cairo.

There are no direct flights from Ireland and most people fly via London. **Air France**, www.airfrance.com, offers direct flights to Cairo via Paris. From Germany, **Lufthansa**, www.lufthansa.com, via Frankfurt, and **TUIfly**, www.TUIfly.com, are a good budget choice from Berlin, Munich and Cologne. **KLM**, www.klm.com, flies to Cairo from Amsterdam. **Austrian Airlines**, www.aua.com, **Czech Airlines**, www.czechairlines.com, **Malev**, www.malev.hu, and **Olympic Airways**, www.olympic-airways.com, have services too, often at competitive prices.

From North America

From New York **EgyptAir** offers an 11-hour daily direct flight to Cairo, ticket prices range from US$1000 in the off-season up to US$1500 during peak travel times. Most European carriers offer flights from major North American cities to Cairo via their European hubs. **British Airways** and **KLM** serve the bigger cities on the west coast. From Canada, there are direct flights with **EgyptAir** from Montreal two or three times a week, taking about 11 hours. Some European airlines also have connecting services from Montreal and Toronto that do not necessitate overnight stays in Europe.

From Australia and New Zealand

There are no direct flights from Australia or New Zealand, but many Asian and European airlines offer services to Cairo via their hub cities. Tickets can be expensive, so it may be worth opting for a Round-the-World ticket, which could be comparable in price or even cheaper than a round-trip flight. From Australia to Egypt tickets range from about AUS$1750 during the off-season to AUS$2500 in the peak season. **Qantas**, www.qantas.com, **Austrian Airlines**, www.aua.com, and **Alitalia**, www.alitalia.com, in addition to a few Asian carriers, offer competitive prices.

Discount flight agents

Using the web to book flights, hotels and other services directly is becoming an increasingly popular way of making holiday reservations. You can get some good deals this way. Be aware, though, that cutting out the travel agents is denying yourself the experience that they can give, not just in terms of the best flights to suit your itinerary, but also advice on documents, insurance and other matters before you set out, safety, routes, lodging and times of year to travel. A reputable agent will also be bonded to give you some protection if arrangements collapse while you are travelling.

In the UK and Ireland

STA Travel, T0870-160 5524, www.sta travel.co.uk. 65 branches in the UK, including many university campuses. Specialists in low-cost student/youth flights and tours, also good for student IDs and insurance.

Trailfinders, 194 Kensington High St, London W8 7RG, T020-7938 3939, www.trailfinders.com. 18 branches in London and throughout the UK. Also one in Dublin.

In North America

Air Brokers International, 685 Market St, Suite 400, San Francisco CA 94105, T01-800-883 3273, www.airbrokers.com. Consolidator and specialist on RTW and Circle Pacific tickets.

Discount Airfares Worldwide On-Line, www.etn.nl/discount.htm. A hub of consolidator and discount agent links.

STA Travel, T1-800-781-4040, www.sta travel.com. Branches all over the USA and Canada.

Travel CUTS, in all major Canadian cities and on university and college campuses, T1-866-246-9762, www.travelcuts.com. Specialists in student discount fares, IDs and other travel services. Also in California, USA.

Travelocity, www.travelocity.com. An online consolidator.

In Australia and New Zealand

Flight Centre, T133-133, www.flightcentre.com.au. With offices throughout Australia and other countries.

STA Travel, T134-STA, www.statravel.com.au; 208 Swanston St, Melbourne VIC 3000, T03-9639 0599; 5 travel centres in Australia. In NZ: T0800-474400, www.statravel.co.nz, 130 Cuba St, Wellington, T04-385 0561. Also in major towns and university campuses.

Travel.com.au, T1300-130482, 80 Clarence St, Sydney NSW 2000, T1300-130482, www.travel.com.au.

Airport information

Departure tax is included in the price of airline tickets. Confirm airline flights at least 48 hours in advance. Most airports require that travellers arrive at least two hours before international departure times. Have all currency exchange receipts easily available, though it is unlikely you will be asked for them. Before passing into the departure lounge it is necessary to fill in an embarkation card. Only a limited amount of currency can be reconverted before you leave, which is a tedious process and not possible at Luxor airport. Sometimes suitable foreign currency is not available. It is better to budget with care, have no excess cash and save all the trouble.

Baggage allowance

General airline restrictions apply with regard to luggage weight allowances before a surcharge is added; normally 30 kg for first class and 20 kg for business and economy class. If you are travelling with a charter flight or budget airline, you might have to pay for even one item of luggage to go in the hold. Carry laptops in your hand luggage, and check the airline's website to see what the restrictions are on hand luggage as this varies between different carriers.

Road and sea

Egypt has land and sea borders with neighbouring countries, see Border crossings box, page 23, for more information.

Getting around

From camel to plane to *felucca*, Egypt is equipped with numerous transport options. Congestion and chaos can be a bit anxiety-inducing on long road ventures, but with a bit of courage and flexibility, you can access most areas without too much effort. As for timetables and infrastructure, the country seems to run on magic. There are few regulations and little consistency, but somehow, people always seem to get where they want to go.

Restricted areas Potentially risky are Egyptian border areas near Libya and Sudan, as well as off-road bits of Sinai, where landmines (usually marked by barbed wire) may exist.

Air

The national airline is **EgyptAir**, www.egyptair.com, who have rebranded and became the first Middle Eastern member of Star Alliance in July 2008. In the past, foreigners paid a different (and much more expensive) price for internal flights than Egyptian residents or nationals, but now there is one ticket price for all and flying has become an affordable option for many travellers. In peak seasons, demand can be high and booking ahead is essential. You can buy E-tickets on the EgyptAir website, though it doesn't always accept the final payment. In this case, you'll have to go to an EgyptAir office or travel agent.

There are daily flights from Cairo to Alexandria, Luxor, Aswan, Abu Simbel, Sharm El-Sheikh and Hurghada and less frequently to Marsa Matruh (in season) and Taba. Example flight times: Cairo to Luxor one hour, Cairo to Aswan two hours, Aswan to Abu Simbel 40 minutes, Cairo to Hurghada, one hour.

Rail

Rail networks are limited, but travel by train can be delightful, especially to a few key destinations along the Nile. First class is most comfortable in that it tends to be the quietest with air conditioning and a waiter service, but second-class air-conditioned is very similar and almost half the price. Third class never has air conditioning and can be quite cramped and dirty, and a foreigner travelling on main routes would not be sold a ticket anyway. There are daily sleeper trains to Luxor and Aswan, which are pricey but mean you can actually lie horizontally. A 33% discount is given to those with an ISIC student card on all trains, except the sleeper cars to Aswan and Luxor. Carriages are non-smoking but people tend to collect and smoke in the corridor by the toilets. Long-distance trains generally have food and beverages available.

The rail network extends west to Salloum on the Libyan border, south along the Nile from Alexandria and Cairo to Luxor and Aswan. There are links to Port Said and Suez. For detailed train information, contact the **Cairo information office**, T02-2575 3555, or check their useful website, www.egyptrail.gov.eg. Approximate journey times from Cairo by train: Alexandria two hours; Aswan 12 hours; Luxor nine hours; Port Said four hours.

Restricted travel Though there are a dozen daily trains travelling south from Cairo to Middle and Upper Egypt, foreigners are technically only permitted to ride on one, which are guarded by policemen. For train travel once in Upper Egypt, the tickets visitors can purchase are still restricted, but it's sometimes possible to board the train and pay the conductor once in motion. It's highly unlikely you will be kicked off.

Border crossings

The main entry points into Egypt on land are as follows:
From Israel Eilat–Taba crossing in Sinai, see page 438.
From Jordan Via Israel overland, or Aqaba–Nuweiba on the ferry, see page 436.
From Libya Al-Bardia–Sollum, 12 km east of the border, see page 374.
From Sudan Boat from Wadi Halfa–Aswan leaves once a week, see page 322.

See page 51 for passport and visa information.

River and sea

Ferry

Ferries connect Hurghada on the Red Sea coast to Sharm El-Sheikh in the Sinai five times a week. The boats are fast catamarans so the journey takes just 90 minutes. There are daily ferries between Nuweiba and Aqaba, in Jordan.

Nile cruises, feluccas and dahabiyas

Heading up the Nile on a cruise boat, *felucca* or *dahabiya* is one of the quintessential Egyptian experiences. Cruise boats travel from Luxor or Esna to Aswan, while *dahabiyas* go between Esna and Aswan, and on Lake Nasser. *Feluccas* go downstream from Aswan to finish at Kom Ombo (one night) or Edfu (two nights) though the actual distance covered depends on the wind. River trips are a great way to get around Egypt and see some wonderful sights along the way. For more information see page 16. For more detailed descriptions of trips see page 250 (cruise boats), page 252 (*dahabiyas*) and page 300 (*feluccas).*

Road

Bicycles and motorcycles

Bicycle hire is available in any town where there are tourists, but the mechanical fitness of the machines is often dubious. Take a bike for a test ride first to check the brakes and tyres are OK. It is feasible to cycle long-distance through Egypt but the heat is punishing, and in between towns and cities along the Nile Valley cyclists find they are accompanied by their own personal police convoy. In urban areas, traffic conditions make cycling a very dangerous sport. Motorcycles can also be hired, though it's less common. The problems regarding cycles apply also to motorcycles – only more so.

Bus

Buses, the main mode and cheapest means of transport, link nearly all towns in Egypt. Air-conditioned coaches ply the major routes and keep to a timetable. It's advisable to book tickets 24 hours in advance, though this is not possible in some oasis towns or from Aswan. **Upper Egypt**, **East Delta** and **West Delta** are the three main operators covering the whole country and are cheapest, usually with air conditioning and assigned seats. **Superjet** and **GoBus** also offer buses to/from most towns to Cairo, with newer and more luxurious buses that are about 30% more expensive. The downside is they play videos half the night. There are usually night buses that can save you losing a day on long journeys,

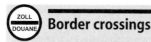

Hazardous journeys

Bear in mind that Egypt currently tops the statistic charts for the highest mortality rate due to motor accidents in the world. You are taking your life in your hands on many road journeys and this is particularly true at night, when driving without headlights is the norm and buses seem to career wildly into the unknown blackness. Long-distance service taxis are the most dangerous, at any time of day, and should be taken only when there are no other options. Drivers push all limits to get there as fast as they can, so as to be able to start filling up with passengers again and complete as many return journeys as possible per day.

and drivers always make a couple of tea-and-toilet stops at roadside coffee shops. Inner-city buses are usually dirty and crowded, and there's a jostle when the bus arrives. In the larger cities, buses often fail to come to complete stops so prepare to run and jump if you do not get on from a route's hub point. Ask a Cairene for an intra-city bus schedule and they'll laugh. The easiest thing to do is ask which bus is going to your desired destination. Using buses to travel from one city to another is a good way to get around but sorting out the routes of most inner-city buses makes taking the tram, subway, or a cheap taxi, a better option. Example fares: Cairo to Dahab E£80, Cairo to Bahariyya E£30. **Note** Buses in Middle and Upper Egypt, if carrying more than four foreigners, are a bit wary. It is essential, therefore, if travelling by bus, that you purchase your ticket in advance (where possible) to ensure a seat. Because of these restrictions, travel by train offers the most flexibility and reliability in the region. It's also generally faster, more consistent and comfortable.

Car hire

Vehicles drive on the right in Egypt. An international driving licence is required. Petrol (super) is E£2-3 per litre. Road signs are in Arabic, with most offering the English transliteration. Cairo and Alexandria have street signs in Arabic and English on all the major thoroughfares. Road conditions vary from new dual carriageways to rural tracks only one-vehicle wide to far flung roads that are a rough, unsurfaced *piste*. Problems include encroaching sand, roads that end with no warning and lunatic drivers. Driving at night is especially hazardous as people only put their headlights on to flash at oncoming vehicles. Likewise, driving in the major cities can be nightmarish with no margin for error and constant undertaking. If you are going to give driving a shot, make sure that you are well insured as the road accident rate is one of the highest in the world. For information on Safety in the Desert, see page 496.

Car hire cost varies greatly relative to the quality of the vehicle and the location of the rental agency. The minimum is about US$40 per day, and a large deposit is generally required. Some companies place restrictions on areas that can be visited. Be aware that there are many police check points for cars in Egypt and they often request to see your papers, so have them on hand or be prepared for a hefty fine on the spot. The problems of driving your own or a hired car are twofold – other drivers and pedestrians.

The main car hire firms are **Avis**, www.avis.com and **Hertz**, www.hertz.com. See listings in each individual town transport section. Approximate **journey times** from Cairo by road: Alexandria three hours; Sharm El-Sheikh six hours; Aswan 16 hours; Luxor 10 hours; Port Said three hours.

Tourist numbers waver

The number of tourists visiting Egypt fell dramatically after the massacre at Luxor in November 1997. After a very difficult time for the industry in Egypt, with the flow of visitors down to less than one million in 1998, the tourists began to flood back and over four million came in 2000.

Then 9/11 hit the country hard, along with the Al-Aqsa Intifada in Palestine – again, tourism plummeted. More recently, bomb blasts in Cairo and the Sinai in 2004, 2005 and 2006 put off thousands more visitors again. Another area to suffer has been the Western Desert with the fallout from the September 2008 kidnapping of 19 tourists and Egyptians in the Gilf Kebir. Restrictions on travel have been tightened up on some routes, preventing complete freedom of movement for the 45,000 annual visitors who want to explore the oases or take a desert safari.

The momentous events of 2011 with the overthrow of the Mubarak regime will doubtless cause tourism to decrease yet again while the situation stabilizes. Since Egypt is in the centre of one of the world's hotbeds of unrest, tourism will continue to rise and fall. But history indicates that no matter how far it falls, tourists do eventually come back.

Hitchhiking

This is only really a consideration in outlying places not well-served by public transport. Rides are often available on lorries and in small open trucks but payment is often expected. Hitchhiking has a measure of risk attached to it and is not normally recommended, but in out of the way places it is often the only way to travel. Solo women travellers are strongly advised not to hitchhike.

Taxis and service taxis

Private vehicles, often Toyota Hiaces (called microbuses or service taxis, pronounced *servees*), cover the same routes as buses and usually cost less. They and the large stationwagon-like long-distance service taxis (Peugeots), sometimes following routes not covered by buses run on the 'leave when full' principle, which can involve some waiting around. For more space or a quicker departure the unoccupied seats can be purchased. However, the drivers can be some of the most reckless in the country (particularly in the nippier Toyotas) and it is probably only worth taking them if you've missed the bus and are stuck somewhere. Inner-city taxis are smaller, rarely have a working meter, and can also be shared. In Cairo you will immediately note the hordes of aging black and white taxis decorated with tasselled fringes, mirrors, and a Koran on the dash. Newer taxis in Cairo are white with black checks on them. They should have functioning meters which start with E£2.50 on the clock and go up in increments of 25pt. In Alexandria, they are yellow/orange and black, and equally ubiquitous. In such urban centres taxis are unquestionably the easiest way to get around, and extraordinarily cheap (particularly outside of Cairo).

Note Until very recently service taxis in Upper Egypt would not accept foreigners when travelling between towns so they could avoid the confines of the convoys. Though the convoys (with the exception of Aswan to Abu Simbel) no longer function, some drivers remember the problems of the past and are reluctant to take foreigners. Be calmly persistent and you should get on in the end.

Mine peril

Thirty people die from land mine explosions in Egypt each year on average. There are estimated to be as many as 21 million land mines still in place dating from the Second World War or the several Arab-Israeli wars in more recent years. Some 16.7 million lie in the Western Desert, a damaging legacy of the long campaigns in that area in the years 1940-1943. Most of the remaining 5.7 million mines are in the Canal Zone and the adjacent battlefields of Sinai.

Most mines are anti-tank devices but, as they deteriorate with age, become unstable and are quite capable of detonating under the pressure of a human foot. Clearances and minefield marking (often merely rusty barbed wire) are going ahead slowly but meanwhile tread with care in the following areas:

1. For 30 km either side of the Alexandria–Marsa Matruh highway and all areas around the El-Alamein battlefields.
2. The open country to the west of the Red Sea such as in the deserts surrounding Safaga and Hurgada.
3. Gulf of Suez.
4. The remote areas of the Gulf of Aqaba/Sinai hinterlands.
5. North Sinai around sites such as El-Arish.
6. The Sinai passes at Mitla and Giddi.

The best advice is to stay away from locations where there are no signs of previous recent entry and always heed warning markers (posted in both Arabic and English).

Sleeping

Hotels

As tourism is one of Egypt's major industries, accommodation is widely available at the main sites and in all the major cities. With prices to suit all pockets, this varies from de luxe international hotels to just floor or roof space for your sleeping bag. There has also been a recent influx of eco-establishments popping up in Sinai and the Western Desert, a couple of which are mega-luxurious while others offer a more rustic experience. Most quality hotel chains are represented and offer top-class facilities in their rooms and business centres. There are also many cheap hotels with basic and spartan rooms ranging from the clean to the decidedly grimy. Mid-range accommodation is a bit more limited, though the occasional gem exists. There is a pronounced seasonality to demand for accommodation and in the spring, autumn and winter holiday months the main tourist areas can be very busy and the choicest hotels fully booked. Advanced reservations are recommended, especially for luxury hotels. Finding cheap accommodation is easy throughout the country, even in high season. Make sure you ask to see the room first.

Prices for the top-class hotels are on a par with prices in Europe while mid-range hotels are generally cheaper in comparison. Note that while price is a reasonable reflection of the type of hotel and service you can expect, some hotels are expensive but very ordinary while others are wonderful and quite cheap. International hotels have an uncomfortable habit of changing owner and name. Be prepared for this and if confused ask for what it was called before.

With friends like the tourist police

Those travelling around Egypt in private cars will often find themselves in the bear hug of the police authorities – mainly the tourist police. This is especially the case in Middle Egypt and Upper Egypt outside of the tourist bubbles of Luxor and Aswan. You may also come upon the free escort service when travelling between the Red Sea coast and the Nile Valley, or when exploring the Western Desert and central Sinai. Individual or small groups of foreigners find their transport under close official guard that can be uncomfortable, despite the good intentions. Officers may suggest they ride in the car with you, and if you refuse or there's not enough room, a police vehicle may follow you.

There is little that can be done to gain liberty. The Egyptian government is determined in the wake of the 1997 massacre at Luxor and bomb blasts in the Sinai that no further tourist lives will be lost to terrorist attacks. Police chiefs know that any publicized tourist deaths by Islamists in their district will mean instant transfer to an isolated village in the deep south! The best way to handle the problem is to create as profound a cordon sanitaire around your vehicle as possible; keep well out of sight line of the weapons of your watchdogs and keep as great a distance between your own car and that of your escort so as to avoid a collision. Approach the game with a sense of humour.

In almost every case, the advertised room price (that charged to the individual traveller) is higher than that paid by the package tourist. Bargaining is common, especially when tourism is scarce. The categories used in this book are graded as accurately as possible by cost converted to American dollars. Our hotel price range is based on a double room in high season and includes any relevant taxes and service. We try to note when a meal is included. Please be aware that prices for hotels are constantly shifting, sometimes significantly, depending on the season and the political climate. As we have quoted high season prices, expect to find costs equal to, or less than, the prices indicated. When in doubt, always ask as prices can literally be sliced in half in the hot summer months. At hotels of three-stars and higher, credit cards are almost always accepted.

Normally the facilities indicated in the box above will be available and are therefore not repeated in the descriptions.

Note Tax and a service charge will be added to your accommodation bill, apart from in budget hotels or unless it is clearly stated as inclusive.

Youth hostels

Information from **Egyptian Youth Hostels Association** ⓘ *1 El-Ibrahimy St, Garden City, Cairo, T02-2796 1448, www.iyhf.org*. There are 17 hostels (in Egypt's main historic and tourist towns) that are open year round. Overnight fees range from US$1.5-9 and often include breakfast. Visitors may stay more than three consecutive nights if there's space. Although cheap meals are available, all the big hostels have a members' kitchen where guests can prepare meals for themselves (use of the kitchen is free). Rules generally include no alcohol or gambling, single sex dormitories, and lights out between 2300-0600. Booking is recommended during peak travel times. They can be a good way to meet Egyptians, but are generally a couple of kilometres out of the centre of town and are horribly busy during student holidays.

Sleeping price codes

LL over US$250	L US$150-249	AL US$100-149
A US$66-99	B US$46-65	C US$31-45
D US$21-30	E US$12-20	F US$7-11
G under US$7		

Price of a double room in high season. During the low season, when many places may be half empty, it's often possible to bargain the room rate down.

LL **5 star** Luxury hotels. All facilities for business and leisure travellers are of the highest international standard. Mostly chain hotels but a few privately owned gems.

L **4-5 star** Central heated, air-conditioned rooms with WC, bath/shower, TV, phone, mini-bar, clean linen daily. Usually have a choice of restaurants, coffee shop, shops, bank, travel agent, swimming pool, parking, sport and business facilities.

AL **4 star** As L but without the luxury, reduced number of restaurants, smaller rooms, limited range of shops and sports facilities.

A **3 star** Air conditioning, TV, private bath/shower and WC. Usually comfortable, and with bank, shop, and pool.

B **2-3 star** Expect clean rooms with private bath, air conditioning and satellite TV. Depending on management, will have room service and a choice of cuisine.

C-D **2 star** Simpler provision. Air conditioning is probable, fan is certain. May not have restaurant. Most rooms with private bath/shower and WC.

E-F **1 star** Basic accommodation, some rooms with shared toilet facilities, variable in cleanliness, perhaps noisy and sometimes in dubious locations.

G Very basic, probably with shared toilet facilities, perhaps fans, often dormitory beds. The range of cheap accommodation is extreme. It's possible to find great deals in lovely environs, as well as some real dives. If you're on a tight budget, your best bet is to shop around, if you have the time.

Camping

There are only a few official campsites with good facilities and guards. It's possible to stake out an unofficial campsite in the oases of the Western Desert, but always ask if you appear to be on someone else's land, and offer them a tip before you leave. Beware of veering too far off road in regions that are desolate as landmines are still widely scattered around some regions, especially near El-Alamein, Sinai and along the Red Sea coast. Camping Bedouin-style under unpolluted sky in the pristine Western Desert is a highlight of many travellers' journeys.

A few popular destinations, Dahab (Sinai) and Bahariyya (Western Desert) among them, have what are misleadingly called 'camps'. These are generally very cheap and sometimes have charming grounds that offer small concrete rooms or simple bamboo huts for a few dollars per night. They often include bedding and a shared bath.

Eating

Forget the stories of sheep's eyes and enjoy the selection of filling, spicy and slightly unusual meals. Less adventurous, Western-style food (other than pork) can be found in many restaurants, and high-end hotels have fantastic international cuisine (but for the price you would pay at home). Basic street-stall food can be delicious, but if you are wary or they look a bit grungy, a multitude of cheap restaurants also serve local favourites often brought out *mezze*-style with a basket of bread so you can enjoy tasting a bit of everything. Alexandria and the Canal Zone cities offer the freshest seafood in the country.

Do bear in mind the suggestions in the Health section on food best avoided in uncertain conditions, see page 39.

Food

Egyptian food is basically a mixture of Mediterranean cuisines, containing elements of Lebanese, Turkish, and Greek cooking, with few authentic local dishes.

Breakfast is usually *fuul*, fava beans simmered slowly overnight, the national dish and a cheap meal at most stalls. These are served in a thick spicy sauce, sometimes with an egg, and usually in a sandwich. When it's fresh and when it's been done well, it is a mouth-watering savoury delight. Some of the best *fuul* comes from the colourful carts on wheels, which station themselves in the same places every day so hungry customers can gather round. The *fuul* is ladled out of a vast pot, hidden in the depths of the cart and heated from below, before being mashed with spices, oil, lemon, salt and pepper. Tourists rarely stop and sample a plate, but the vendors will be pleased and surprised if you do, while other customers will be highly entertained. It's probably best to avoid the chopped salad that comes with the dish, but the *ai'ish* (bread) is certainly safe enough. Equally cheap and popular is *taamiyya*, deep fried balls of ground fava beans spiced with coriander and garlic, again often served in a sandwich garnished with *tahina* (sesame seed dip) and *torshi* (brightly coloured pickled vegetables such as turnips, carrots, and limes). These constitute Egyptian fast food with the addition of *shawarma*, sliced lamb kebab sandwiches, and *fatir*, which is sold in special *fatatri* cafés, where the thin dough pancake is made to order with either sweet or savoury fillings.

Bread is the staple of the Egyptian diet, its Arabic name *ai'iish* means life. The local *ai'iish baladi*, a brown flat loaf similar to pita, tastes good fresh and should only be eaten on the day of purchase. The white flour *ai'iish shami* is less common.

Lunch is the main meal of the day, eaten anytime between 1300 and 1700. Carbohydrates, usually rice and bread, form the bulk of the meal accompanied by fresh seasonal vegetables and either meat or fish. *Mezzas*, a selection of small salads, are served at the beginning of the meal and include *tahina*, *babaghanoug* (*tahina* with mashed aubergines), olives, local white fetta-style cheese, *warra einab* or stuffed vine leaves, and *kobeiba*, deep fried bulgar wheat stuffed with meat and nuts. Like most Middle Eastern countries, *kebab*, lamb pieces grilled over charcoal on a skewer, and *kofta*, minced lamb, are common main dishes. Chicken and pigeon are also widely available, the latter considered a local delicacy when stuffed with rice and nuts. Fish is commonly eaten in coastal regions and often superb. Try the sea bass or red snapper but watch the bones in the latter. Lobster and shrimp are relatively cheap.

Fuul for all

Fuul has been an important dish for Egyptians since banqueting scenes were painted on the pharaonic tombs. It is nutritious and cheap and is the staple diet for low-income and strong-stomached locals. In Cairo a meal from one of the 25,000 (illegal) street vendors will start the day. At E£1 per sandwich it fills an empty hole and provides protein and carbohydrates.

Fuul is also considered 'in' by the Cairo smart set, who frequent luxury outlets such as Akher Saa, El-Tabei and El-Omda to buy it with onions, pickles, lemon and fresh bread – to eat in or take away.

The *fuul* bean is grown in most agricultural areas of Egypt, as an accompaniment to a major crop – the best is said to come from Minya. Nevertheless, imports are still necessary to supply consumption demands.

Variants on *fuul* dishes include: *fuul bil zeit el harr* – with oil; *fuul bil samna* – with ghee (clarified butter); *bisara* – with oil, onion, garlic and coriander. *Fuul* is also the main ingredient in *ta'ameya* and *felafel.*

Egyptian **main dishes** include *molokhia*, finely chopped mallow leaves, prepared with garlic, spices and either rabbit or chicken, and a good deal more tasty than its glutinous texture suggests; *fatta*, layers of bread, rice, chunks of lamb or beef, yogurt, raisins and nuts, drenched in a vinegar garlic broth; *koshari*, a poor man's feast that will fill a belly for at least four hours, is composed of macaroni, rice and brown lentils covered with fried onions and a spicy tomato sauce; and *mahshi*, vegetables, typically black or white aubergines, tomatoes, green peppers, cabbage leaves or courgettes, stuffed with rice, herbs and vegetables.

Fruits, like vegetables, are seasonal although there is a wide variety available all year round. Produce is picked when it's ripe and so generally fruit and vegetables are absolutely delicious. Winter offers dates of various colours ranging from yellow to black, citrus fruits, small sweet bananas, pears, apples, and even strawberries. Summer brings plums, peaches, figs, pomegranates, guava, mangoes, grapes, melons and a brief season, for a few weeks in May, of apricots.

Traditional Egyptian **desserts** are sweet, sticky, fattening, and delicious. The best of all is *Om Ali*, or Mother of Ali, a warm pudding of bread or pastry covered with milk, coconut, raisins, and nuts. Also try the oriental pastries including *atayef*, deep fried nut-stuffed pancakes; *baklava*, honey-drenched filo pastry layered with nuts; *basbousa*, a syrupy semolina cake often filled with cream and garnished with pistachio nuts and *konafa*, shredded batter cooked with butter and stuffed with nuts. Cold rice pudding is on offer at most *koshari* restaurants, and is much better than it sounds.

Vegetarianism is not a concept with which Egyptians are familiar. While vegetable dishes are plentiful, and the majority of Egyptians only rarely eat any large quantity of meat, it is difficult to avoid tiny pieces of meat or meat stock in vegetable courses. Even the wonderful lentil soup, like most Egyptian soups a meal on its own, often has the addition of a chicken stock cube. Fortunately, basic staples such as *koshari*, *fuul* and *taamiyya* are omnipresent in any town and true life-savers for vegetarians. In the smaller oases, a diet of rice, salad and potatoes or courgettes stewed in tomato sauce is tasty though repetitive.

Eating price codes

ΨΨΨ over US$20 ΨΨ US$5-20 Ψ under US$5

Prices for a two-course meal for one person, excluding drinks or service charge.

Drink

Tea (*shai*) is the essential Egyptian drink, taken strong without milk but with spoonfuls of sugar. Tea is also prepared with mint, *shai bil na'ana*, and said to be good for the digestion. Instant **coffee**, just called 'Nescafé', is available. If you want it with milk, ask for *laban* and if you want sugar separately request *sucre burra*. The thick Turkish coffee known as *ahwa*, which is usually laced with cardamom or occasionally cinnamon, should be ordered either *saada*, with no sugar; *arriha*, with a little sugar; *mazbut*, medium; or *ziyada*, with extra sugar. Leave the thick mud of coffee grains in the bottom half of the cup. The *mazbut* is the most popular.

Other hot drinks include a cinnamon tea, *irfa*, reportedly good for colds; and the less common *sahleb*, a milk drink with powdered arrowroot, coconut, and chopped nuts.

Cold drinks include the usual soft drink options of Coca-Cola, Pepsi, 7-Up, and Fanta. Of more interest are the traditional *ersoos* (liquorice juice); *asir limon*, tangy and delicious but highly sweetened lemon juice; *karkade*, made from the dried petals of the red hibiscus, drunk both hot and cold; and *tamarhindi*, from the tamarind. Freshly squeezed juice stands are located throughout all cities, and mean you can drink seasonal pomegranate, mango, or orange juice for just E£2-3 a glass.

Bottled water is sold widely. Check that the seal is intact and that the bottle has not been refilled. Be prepared for shortage or restriction of water in more rural areas. Tap water in the urban centres is generally safe to drink, but so chlorinated it's intolerable for a lot of travellers. It's better to opt for bottled water which is cheap and easily available.

Although Egypt is a Muslim country, **alcohol** is available in bars and some restaurants. While five-star hotels are beginning to import beer in barrels, the local 'Stella' beer is the most popular sold, with the better-quality 'Stella Export', in half litre bottles. There are a few local wines, the reds and rosés are very drinkable and the whites less so. Most commonly found are Omar Khayyam, Obelisque, Cape Bay and Sherazad (who do a good rosé). The local spirits are bottled to resemble international brands, and include an ouzo called *zibib*, a rum 'Zattos', and a 'Big Ben' gin. Beware of local liqueurs that don labels and names resembling Western brands such as 'Jhony Wakker' and the like, they have been known to contain alcohol so strong that they can cause blindness if drunk to excess.

Festivals and events

The Islamic year (*Hejra/Hijra/Hegira*) is based on 12 lunar months that are 29 or 30 days long depending on the sighting of the new moon. The lengths of the months vary therefore from year to year and from country to country depending on its position and the time at sunset. Each year is also 10 or 11 days shorter than the Gregorian calendar. The Islamic holidays are based on this Hejarian calendar and determining their position is possible only to within a few days.

The important festivals that are also public holidays (with many variations in spelling) are *Ras El-Am*, the Islamic New Year; *Eïd Al-Fitr* (also called *Aïd Es Seghir*), the celebration at the end of Ramadan; *Eïd Al-Adha* (also called *Aïd El-Kebir*), the celebration of Abraham's willingness to sacrifice his son and coinciding with the culmination of the *Hajj* in Mecca; *Mouloud* (also called Moulid An-Nabi), the birthday of the Prophet Mohammed.

The day of rest for Muslims is Friday. Observance of Friday as a religious day is general in the public sector, though privately owned shops may open for limited hours. The main exception is tourism where all systems remain operative. Holy days and feast days are taken seriously throughout the country.

Ramadan, the ninth month of the Muslim calendar, is a month of fasting for Muslims. The faithful abstain from eating between dawn and sunset for about one month until an official end is declared to the fast and when *Eïd Al-Fitr*, a three-day celebration, begins. During the fast, especially if the weather is hot or there are political problems affecting the Arab world, people can be depressed or irritable. The pace of activity in official offices slows down markedly, most closing by 1400. You may want to stay out of the area during Ramadan and particularly the *Eïd Al-Fitr*, but for the patient and curious traveller, it can be a fascinating time. As the sun sets during the holy month and everyone rushes homeward to break fast, it offers a rare and delightful occasion to wander through barren Cairo streets. *Iftar* (breaking the fast) in the company of local people is an interesting experience, and anyone is welcome to join a communal meal at one of the mercy tables that encroach on to the street each sunset. The country's poor are looked after by the mosques and the wealthy, who provide set meals every day for whoever is in need; this can involve feeding hundreds of people. Although you shouldn't expect true culinary delights, you might get dates, bird's tongue (a kind of pasta) soup, hearty stews and traditional sweets. For the rushed or impatient traveller, note that travel facilities immediately before and after Ramadan are often very congested since families like to be together especially for the *Eïd Al-Fitr*.

Islamic festivals

These are approximate dates for 2011/2012:

15 Feb/4 Feb Prophet's Birthday.

1 Aug/20 Jul Beginning of Ramadan.

30 Sep/19 Aug End of Ramadan (Eid El-Fitr).

6 Nov/26 Oct Eid El-Adha.

26 Nov/15 Nov Islamic New Year.

Coptic celebrations

These are approximate dates for 2011/2012:

19/20 Jan Epiphany.

7 Apr Annunciation.

24 Apr/15 Apr Easter.

Cultural and sporting events

Jan Cairo International Book Fair, Nasr City.
22 Feb Sun Festival of Ramses II, Abu Simbel.
Mar Cairo International Fair; Spring Flower Show, Orman Gardens, Giza, Cairo.
Apr Sham El-Nessim (Sniffing of the Breeze, or the first day of spring) is celebrated with family picnics.
Jul International Festival of Documentary Films, Ismailia.
Aug Arab Music Festival, Opera House, Cairo; Nile Festival Day (Wafaa El-Nil), Giza, Cairo.
Aug/Sep International Folklore Dance festival, Ismailia.
Sep Alexandria Mediterranean Biennale (every 2 years); International Festival for Vanguard Theatre, Cairo; Alexandria Film Festival, Alexandria; World Tourism Day; Nile Festival.
Oct Pharaoh's Rally, 3100-km motor vehicle race across the desert, Cairo.
22 Oct Sun Festival of Ramses II, Abu Simbel.
24 Oct Commemoration of Battle of El-Alamein, El-Alamein.
Nov Luxor National Day; International Children's Book Fair, Nasr City, Cairo.
Nov/Dec International Film Festival, Cairo.
Dec Festival for Arab Theatre, Cairo; Festival for Impressionist Art (every 2 years), Cairo.

Public holidays

1 Jan New Year's Day.
7 Jan Coptic Christmas.
15 Mar El Fayoum National Day.
25 Apr Liberation of Sinai.
1 May Labour Day.
18 Jun Evacuation Day – the day the British left Egypt in 1954.
23 Jul Anniversary of 1952 Revolution.
26 Jul Alexandria National Day.
6 Oct Armed Forces' Day – parades and military displays.
13 Oct Suez Day.
23 Dec Victory Day.

Shopping

There are department stores and malls in Cairo and Alexandria but the most interesting shopping is in the bazaars and *souks*. The process can take time and patience, but bargains abound. The main bazaar in Cairo, Khan El-Khalili, has a wide selection of ethnic items. It attracts tourists by the hoards, though wandering far off the main alleys will lead to shops and corridors rarely visited. For a truly off-the-beaten-track shopping experience, visit one of the many fruit and vegetable *souks* scattered throughout the country. You'll find chickens milling about, people singing songs about their wares and dead cows hanging from storefront windows. Prices are clearly marked in Arabic numerals, usually indicating the cost of a kilogram. Bargaining is not appropriate in this context but learn the numerals so that nobody takes advantage of you.

What to buy

Egypt is well known for its **cotton and textiles**. Higher-end stores in luxury hotels and shopping malls around Cairo and Alexandria (as in World Trade Centre, First Residence Mall, Nile City Towers, and Marriott) have stores that sell linens and new clothes. For colourful tapestries, scarves and bags, Khan El-Khalili is a good place to start. Also of interest may be the Tent Makers' Bazaar, south of Bab Zuweila in Islamic Cairo, where it's possible to commission the making of a bedcover or a Bedouin tent. Lengths of printed

The art of bargaining

Haggling is a normal business practice in Egypt. Modern economists might feel that bargaining is a way of covering up high-price salesmanship within a commercial system that is designed to exploit the lack of legal protection for the consumer. But even so, haggling over prices is the norm and is run as an art form, with great skills involved. Bargaining can be fun to watch between a clever buyer and an experienced seller but it is less entertaining when a less-than-artful buyer such as a foreign traveller considers what he/she has paid later! There is great potential for the tourist to be heavily ripped off. Most dealers recognize the wealth and gullibility of travellers and start their offers at an exorbitant price. The dealer then appears to drop his price by a fair margin but remains at a final level well above the real local price of the goods.

To protect yourself in this situation be relaxed in your approach. Talk at length to the dealer and take as much time as you can afford to inspect the goods and feeling out the last price the seller will accept. Do not belittle or mock the dealer – take the matter very seriously but do not show commitment to any particular item you are bargaining for by being prepared to walk away empty-handed. Never feel that you are getting the better of the dealer or feel sorry for him. He will not sell without making a profit. Also it is better to try several shops if you are buying an expensive item such as a carpet or jewellery. This will give a sense of the price range. Walking away – regretfully of course – from the dealer normally brings the price down rapidly but not always. Do not change money in the same shop where you make your purchases, since this will be expensive.

tent fabric cost E£20 per metre, or the appliqué wall-hangings depicting sufi dancers and abstract Arabic motifs cost E£100 and above. If you want a *gallabiyya*, formal or otherwise, wander around the shops surrounding Al-Azhar mosque in Cairo. For handmade rugs, check out the many stores lining Sharia Saqqara, near the Giza Pyramids. Or if you are visiting the oases, wait till then to buy Bedouin designs woven in camel wool either in natural colours or bright with geometric designs.

Jewellery, in particular, gold, silver and some precious stones, are cheap in Egypt. In the centre of Khan El-Khalili, as well as places scattered about Islamic Cairo, you will find exquisite gold jewellery. Sold by weight, with a bit of money tacked on for craftsmanship, you can have pieces made to order. Particularly popular are cartouches bearing your name or the name of a friend. Siwa oasis is known for beautiful Berber silver jewellery, and although the world-renowned antique pieces were sold long ago, modern pieces are made to the traditional designs.

Papyrus can be found, albeit of varying quality, everywhere. Ensure when you are shopping around for papyrus that it is real, not the increasingly common imitation banana leaf. Real papyrus is not chemically treated, a process which causes the picture to disintegrate after three or four years. You can tell chemically treated papyrus by its homogenous surface and pliability. Thick and unmalleable, real papyrus can't be rolled or folded. Authentic papyrus also has variants of colour as the stalks have lighter and darker patches, which you can see in the meshwork when you hold it up to the light. Rest assured that the papyrus sellers you will trip over at every major tourist site are not selling the real thing, though if you just want to pick up some cheap presents then they have their uses.

Dr Ragab's Papyrus Institute in Cairo is a bit pricey, but offers good-quality trustworthy papyrus art.

You'll probably smell the **perfume** stalls before you see them. They're all over Khan El-Khalili and most carry an extraordinary variety of smells – ranging from rose to Egyptian musk to replicas of famous scents. Prices range from E£20-50. Ask around at different stalls for the going price before purchasing. Also fragrant and incredibly colourful are the abundance of stalls that sell **spices** displayed in large burlap sacks. You will find everything from dried hibiscus to thyme, cumin to saffron, which is priced higher per kilo than gold, but still comparatively cheap. For an alternative spice experience, check out **Harraz Medicinal Plants Co** ⓘ *Sharia Ahmed Marhir St, east of Midan Bab Al-Khalq*, a store in Cairo specializing in ancient remedies and medicinal plants. Upstairs you can consult with the resident herbalist if anything ails you.

Other things of interest you will find in larger *souks* and bazaars: kitsch souvenirs galore, *sheesha* pipes, musical instruments (drums in particular) copper and brass ware, wooden boxes inlaid with intricate designs and backgammon and chess sets.

Bargaining

Haggling is expected in the *souks*. Most shop owners site the start price at two to three times the amount they hope to make. Start lower than you would expect to pay, be polite and good humoured, enjoy the experience and if the final price doesn't suit, walk away. There are plenty more shops. Once you have gained confidence, try it on the taxi drivers and when negotiating a room. The bargaining exchange can be a great way to meet people and practise your Arabic.

Interestingly, a barter exchange system still exists in some rural weekly markets, where goods such as seeds, eggs or beans can be exchanged for a haircut or access to education. This is unlikely to be something you will get involved with as a traveller, however.

Essentials A-Z

Accident and emergencies

Ambulance T123. **Fire** T125. **Police** T122 (from any city). **Tourist Police** T126.

Report any incident that involves you or your possessions. An insurance claim of any size will require the backing of a police report. If involvement with the police is more serious, for instance as a result of a driving accident, remain calm and contact the nearest consular office without delay. Some embassies advise leaving the scene of an accident immediately and heading straight to your embassy.

Children

Family is everything in Egypt and people are incredibly warm and receptive to children. They are welcome pretty much anywhere, many hotels will provide an extra bed and there is no resentment of noisy toddlers in restaurants (though only higher-end hotels will have highchairs to hand). Sensible precautions that you would take in any hot place, such as sunhats, sun-cream, mosquito repellent, and awareness of dehydration apply all the more in the extreme heat of Egypt. It's also wise to be careful where you eat as children are more liable to get food poisoning. There is plenty to keep them occupied in the way of swimming, snorkelling and camel rides. However, pushchairs are not really practical in the big cities and the noise and filth can make walking around with children a fraught experience. Hazards to watch out for include the traffic, pollution and dust, and lack of safety barriers in high monuments (particularly in Islamic Cairo). Avoid excessive heat by travelling during autumn and spring, and take rehydration sachets with you in case of outbreaks of diarrhoea. Food children will like includes *shish tawouq* kebabs, *fiteer* pizzas, *kushari* noodles and a whole range of *mezze* dishes.

Customs and duty-free

On arrival you may be asked to declare if you have more than one of any electrical item with you (video cameras, computers) on the D form. In case of theft, report to police or they will assume you have sold them and will charge you duty.

Goods may be imported into Egypt as follows: 200 cigarettes or 250 g of tobacco, 2 litres of alcohol, 1 litre of perfume, gifts up to the value of E£500. In addition to this, foreigners are permitted 48 hrs from arrival to buy a further 3 litres of alcohol at duty-free shops. Duty-free export of purchases can be arranged through the larger shops and tourist agencies.

Disabled travellers

Though many people in Egypt live with disabilities, there are few provisions for the disabled. Most budget hotels require clambering up flights of stairs and using public transport is pretty much an impossibility; although new metro stations are being built with disabled access, the older central stations were not. Newer museums have ramps and most modern buildings have lifts, as do all 5-star hotels. Access to many sites, particularly tombs, is limited not only by there being steep steps inside but by the necessity of walking up a cliff or negotiating sand to get to them. With temples it is easier as many are built largely on the flat, though stone floors are uneven. There is access to the Sound and Light show at the Sphinx, and the Giza Pyramids plateau is being upgraded and made more user-friendly.

On the streets of central Cairo, high and frequent kerbs make walking on the pavement difficult for anyone, but some main alleyways of Islamic Cairo are being repaved and shouldn't be a problem

Family travel in Egypt

Got yourself an infant Indiana Jones or little Lara Croft? If your kids are into adventure and hidden treasure, Egypt makes an exciting and educational destination where you can combine the mysteries of the pharaohs with some beach time on the Red Sea coast. Many parents get DDS (Disney Dithering Syndrome) when it comes to Egypt, constantly asking themselves: "Are our kids too young? Will they get much out of it?" Obviously, school-age children who have covered ancient Egypt in the classroom will be blown away by seeing the real thing, but that doesn't mean younger travellers will find it boring. The secret is to combine fact with fun. Don't make your trip an endless procession of museums and adult-focused tours, instead build itineraries around mini-adventures, like sailing on a *felucca* or riding a camel. Many families avoid the summer meltdown by visiting Egypt over Christmas or during half-term breaks in spring and autumn. However, without the luxury of long summer holidays you do have to pack a lot in and follow a fairly well-established route.

(although crossing roads in between will be). Hiring a taxi for the day to take you around is the most sensible option, and doubtless the driver will assist where possible. In the Sinai, there are some dive companies that accept students with disabilities and disabled people have been known to camel ride up the face of Mt Sinai. The best bet may be to book a tour with a company that caters to the needs of disabled travellers. Check out the following: Society for the Accessible Travel & Hospitality, www.sath.org; www.egyptforall.net and www.access-able.com.

Drugs

Though there is no shortage of drugs in Egypt, drug-enforcement policies are strict. The death penalty or life-imprisonment may be imposed for those convicted of smuggling or selling narcotics. Possession of even small quantities may lead to a prison sentence, and certainly to heavy fines and immediate deportation. Marijuana use goes back a long way in Egypt and *bango* is still grown in the Sinai. The most unlikely looking people seem to be smokers, and you will probably be offered it at some point. The best advice is to avoid all illegal narcotics and don't presume that places like Dahab are still places to relax with a joint, as much has been done to stamp it out.

Electricity

The current in Egypt is 220V, 50Hz. Sockets are for 2-pin round plugs, so bring an appropriate adapter. If you have US-made appliances that use 110V it's a good idea to bring a converter. Power cuts do not happen that frequently, but in remote hotels be aware that generators are usually switched off at night and for a few hours during the day.

Embassies and consulates

Australia, 1 Darwin Av, Yarralumla, ACT 2600 Canberra, T61-2-9281 4844, www.egypt.org.au.
Austria, 1190 Wien, Kreindll Gasse 22, Vienna 1190, T31-378 0104-5, www.egyptembassyvienna.at.
Belgium, Av de l'Uruguay, 19 1000 Bruxelles, T32-2-663 5820.
Canada, 1 Place Ville Marie, Montréal, Quebec, H3H 7V6, T1-514-866 8455.

Denmark, Kristianiagade 19, DK - 2100, Copenhagen, Denmark, T45-3543 7070.
France, 56 Av d'Iena, 75116 Paris, T33-1-5367 8830.
Germany, 6-7 Stauffenberg Str, 10785 Berlin, www.egyptian-embassy.de.
Ireland, 12 Clyde Rd, Dublin 4, T353-1-660 6566, www.embegyptireland.ie.
Israel, 54 Rehov Basel, Tel Aviv, T972-3-546 4151/2.
Japan, 154 Aobadai, Meguro-ku, Tokyo, T081-3-3770 8022.
Jordan, 14 Riyad Mefleh St, Amman, T962-6-560 5175/6.
Libya, El-Shatt St, Tripoli, T218-21-444 8909; and consulate at El-Awarsi St, Western Fuwaihat, T218-61-223 2522.
Morocco, 31 El-Gazaer St, Sawmaat Hassan, Rabat, T212-7-731834.
Netherlands, Bad Huis Weg 92, PO Box 2587 CL, The Hague, T31-70-354 4535/354 2000.
Norway, Drammensveien 90A, 0244 Oslo 2, T47-2308 4200, www.egypt-embassy.no.
Palestinian Territories, Thawra St, Gaza, T972-8-282 4374.
Spain, Velázquez 69, Madrid 28006, T34-91-577 6308.
Sudan, Sharia Al-Gomhoriya, PO Box 1126, Khartoum, T03-1182 3666.
Sweden, Strandvagen 35, Stockholm, T46-8-660 3145.
Switzerland, 61 Elfenauweg, 3006 Berne, T41-31-352 8055.
UK, 2 Lowndes St, London, SW1X, T020-7235 5684, www.MFA.gov.eg. Open 1000-1200, Mon-Fri, for visas.
USA, 1110 2nd Av, New York, NY10022, T1-212-7597120; 3001 Pacific Av, San Francisco, CA 94115, T1-415-3469700, www.egy2000.com.

Gay and lesbian travellers

Though there are as many gay people in Egypt as anywhere else, being openly gay as an Egyptian male is almost unheard of.

While not actually illegal in Egypt, homosexuality is forbidden in the Koran and the Bible and gay foreign men should exercise caution when in the country. The authorities veer away from persecuting foreigners, but Egyptian partners will not be immune – as the infamous raiding of the **Queen Boat** in 2001 proved. Since then, the scene has gone more underground and we are not going to recommend venues to meet people here. But it's common knowledge that Cairo, Aswan and especially Luxor have a reputation that the tourist board do nothing to promote.

Interestingly, men are strikingly open with each other. It's not uncommon to see them embracing, kissing on the cheeks or walking down the street arm in arm. Don't be misled, such public gestures are indicative of friendship and brotherhood, and rarely indicate anything else. Meanwhile, lesbian culture is so subdued that women on the look out will have to look hard. For more information about gay holidays in Egypt, check out www.gayegypt.com. But do not access gay websites from Egypt, as the authorities are known to monitor some (if not all) of them.

Health

The local population in Egypt is exposed to a range of health risks not usually encountered in the western world. Many of the diseases are major problems for the local poor and destitute and though the risk to travellers is more remote, they cannot be ignored. Obviously 5-star travel is going to carry less risk than backpacking on a minimal budget.

The health care in the region is varied. There are many excellent private and government clinics/hospitals. But as with all medical care, first impressions count. If a facility looks grubby then be wary of the general standard of medicine and hygiene. It's worth contacting your embassy or consulate on arrival and asking where the recommended (ie those used by diplomats) clinics are. (Providing embassies with information of your whereabouts can be also useful if a friend/relative gets ill at home and there is a desperate search for you around the globe.) You can also ask them about locally recommended medical dos and don'ts. If you do get ill, and you have the opportunity, you should also ask your medical insurer whether they are satisfied that the medical centre or hospital that you have been referred to is of a suitable standard.

Ideally, you should see your GP or travel clinic at least 6 weeks before your departure for general advice on travel risks, malaria and vaccinations. Make sure you have travel insurance, get a dental check (especially if you are going to be away for more than a month), know your own blood group and if you suffer a long-term condition such as diabetes or epilepsy make sure someone knows or that you have a Medic Alert bracelet/necklace.

Vaccinations

Vaccinations are not required unless you are travelling from a country where yellow fever or cholera frequently occurs. You are advised to be up to date with the following: **Polio** if none in last 10 years; **Tetanus** again if you haven't had one in the last 10 years (after 5 doses you have had enough for life); **Diphtheria** if none in last 10 years; **Typhoid** if none in last 3 years; **Hepatitis A** as the disease can be caught easily from food/water. **Rabies** is not generally a risk in Egypt but it has been reported in a few rural areas off the tourist trail.

Health risks

Bites and stings

It is a very rare event indeed for travellers, but if you are unlucky (or careless) enough to be bitten by a venomous snake, spider, scorpion or sea creature, try to identify the creature, without putting yourself in further danger.

Snake bites in particular are frightening, but in fact rarely poisonous – even venomous snakes bite without injecting venom. Reassure and comfort the victim frequently. Immobilize the limb with a bandage or a splint and get the person to lie still. Do not slash the bite area and try to suck out the poison because this sort of heroism does more harm than good. If you know how to use a tourniquet in these circumstances, you will not need this advice. If you are not experienced, do not apply a tourniquet. Victims should be taken to a hospital or a doctor without delay.

Do not walk in snake territory in bare feet or sandals – wear proper shoes or boots. If you encounter a snake stay put until it slithers away and do not investigate a wounded snake. Spiders and scorpions may be found in the more basic hotels. If stung, rest and take plenty of fluids and call a doctor. The best precaution is to keep beds away from the walls and always look inside your shoes and under the toilet seat.

Certain sea fish when trodden upon inject venom into bathers' feet. This can be exceptionally painful. Wear plastic shoes if such creatures are reported. The pain can be relieved by immersing the foot in hot water (as hot as you can bear) for as long as the pain persists or citric acid juices in fruits such as lemon is reported as useful.

Dengue fever

This is a viral disease spead by mosquitos that tend to bite during the day. The symptoms are fever and often intense joint pains, also some people develop a rash. It should all be over in 7 to 10 unpleasant days. Dengue is endemic in patches around the border area with Sudan. Unfortunately there is no vaccine against this. Employ all the anti-mosquito measures that you can.

Diarrhoea

Diarrhoea can refer either to loose stools or an increased frequency; both of these can be a nuisance. It should be short lasting but persistence beyond 2 weeks, with blood or pain, require specialist medical attention.

Ciproxin (Ciprofloaxacin) is a useful antibiotic for bacterial travellers' diarrhoea. It can be obtained by private prescription in the UK. You need to take one 500 mg tablet when the diarrhoea starts and if you do not feel better in 24 hrs, the diarrhoea is likely to have a non-bacterial cause and may be viral (in which case there is little you can do apart from keep yourself rehydrated and wait for it to settle on its own). The key treatment with all diarrhoeas is rehydration. Try to keep hydrated by taking the right mixture of salt and water. This is available as Oral Rehydration Salts (ORS) in ready-made sachets or can be made up by adding a teaspoon of sugar and a half teaspoon of salt to a litre of clean water. Drink at least 1 large cup of this drink for each loose stool. You can also use flat carbonated drinks as an alternative. Immodium and Pepto-Bismol provide symptomatic relief.

The standard advice to prevent problems is to be careful with water and ice for drinking. Ask yourself where the water came from. If you have any doubts then boil it or filter and treat it. There are many filter/treatment devices now available on the market. Food can also transmit disease. Be wary of salads (what were they washed in, who handled them), re-heated foods or food that has been left out in the sun having been cooked earlier in the day. There is a simple adage that says 'wash it, peel it, boil it or forget it'. Also be wary of unpasteurized dairy products, these can transmit a range of diseases from brucellosis (causing fevers and constipation), to listeria (meningitis) and tuberculosis of the gut (obstruction, constipation, fevers and weight loss).

Hepatitis

Hepatitis means inflammation of the liver. Viral causes of the disease can be acquired anywhere in the world. The most obvious symptom is a yellowing of your skin or the whites of your eyes. However, prior to this all that you may notice is itching and tiredness.

Pre-travel hepatitis A vaccine is the best bet. Hepatitis B (for which there is also a vaccine) is spread through blood and unprotected sexual intercourse. Unfortunately there is no vaccine for hepatitis C or the increasing alphabetical list of other hepatitis viruses. The prevalence of hepatitis C is unusually high in Egypt.

Leptospirosis

Various forms of leptospirosis occur throughout the world, transmitted by a bacterium that is excreted in rodent urine. Fresh water and moist soil harbour the organisms, which enter the body through cuts and scratches. If you suffer from any form of prolonged fever consult a doctor.

Malaria

Not widespread. Minimal risk exists in the El-Fayoum area only. Risk is highest from Jun-Oct. Check with your doctor before you go about which prophylactic (if any) you should take if travelling in this region. Remember that it is risky to buy medicinal tablets abroad because the doses may differ and there may be a trade in false drugs.

Use insect repellent. Remember that DEET (Di-ethyltoluamide) is the gold standard. Apply the repellent every 4-6 hours but more often if you are sweating heavily. If a non-DEET product is used check who tested it. Validated products (tested at the London School of Hygiene and Tropical Medicine) include Mosiguard, Non-DEET Jungle formula and non-DEET Autan. If you use citronella remember that it must be applied very frequently (ie hourly) to be effective.

Prickly heat

This very common intensely itchy rash can be avoided by frequent washing and wearing loose clothing. It is cured by allowing skin to dry off (through use of powder and spending 2 nights or so in an a/c hotel).

Rabies

Be aware of the dangers of the bite from any animal. Rabies vaccination before travel can be considered but if bitten always seek urgent medical attention – whether or not you have been previously vaccinated – after first cleaning the wound and treating with an iodine-based disinfectant or alcohol.

Schistosomiasis (bilharzia)

This infection is caused by a parasite, released from fresh water snails. Infected humans contaminate the water by their urine or stools. The form that penetrates the skin after you have swum or waded through water can cause a local itch soon after, fever after a few weeks and much later diarrhoea, abdominal pain and spleen or liver enlargement.

A single drug cures this disease. Avoid infected waters and check the CDC, WHO websites and a travel clinic specialist for up-to-date information.

Sexual health

The range of visible and invisible diseases is incredible. Unprotected sex can spread HIV, hepatitis B and C, gonorrhea (symptoms: green discharge), chlamydia (symptoms: nothing to see but may cause painful urination and later female infertility), painful recurrent herpes, syphilis and warts, just to name a few. You can cut down the risk by using condoms or avoiding sex altogether.

Sun

Take good heed of advice regarding protecting yourself against the sun. Over- exposure can lead to sunburn and, in the longer term, skin cancers and premature skin aging. The best advice is simply to avoid exposure to the sun by covering exposed skin, wearing a hat and staying out of the sun if possible, especially between late morning and early afternoon. Apply a high-factor sunscreen (greater than SPF15) and also make sure it screens against UVB. A further danger in tropical climates is heat exhaustion or more seriously heatstroke. This can be avoided by good hydration, which means drinking water past the point of simply quenching thirst. Also when first exposed to tropical heat take time to acclimatize by avoiding strenuous activity in the middle of the day. If you cannot avoid heavy exercise it is also a good idea to increase salt intake.

Underwater health

If you plan to dive make sure that you are fit to do so. The **British Sub-Aqua Club** (BSAC), Telford's Quay, South Pier Rd, Ellesmere Port, Cheshire CH65 4FL, UK, T01513-506200, www.bsac.com, can put you in touch with doctors who will carry out medical examinations. Check that any dive companies you use are reputable and have the appropriate certification from the **Professional Association of Diving Instructors** (PADI), with centres worldwide, www.padi.com.

Water

There are a number of ways of purifying water. Dirty water should first be strained through a filter bag and then boiled or treated. Bring water to a rolling boil for several minutes. There are sterilizing methods that can be used and products generally contain chlorine or iodine compounds. There are a number of water sterilizers now on the market available in personal and expedition size. Make sure you take the spare parts or spare chemicals with you and do not believe everything the manufacturers say.

Further information

Websites

British Travel Health Association (UK), www.btha.org. This is the official website of an organization of travel health professionals.
Fit for Travel (UK), www.fitfortravel.scot.nhs.uk. This site from Scotland provides a quick A-Z of vaccine and travel health advice requirements for each country.
Foreign and Commonwealth Office (FCO) (UK), www.fco.gov.uk. This is a key travel advice site, with useful information on the country, people, climate and lists the UK embassies/consulates.
The Health Protection Agency (UK), www.hpa.org.uk. Up-to-date malaria advice guidelines for travel around the world. It gives

specific advice about the right drugs for each location. It also has useful information for those who are pregnant, suffering from epilepsy or planning to travel with children.
Travel Screening Services (UK), www.travelscreening.co.uk. The clinic gives vaccine, travel health advice, email and SMS text vaccine reminders and screens returned travellers for tropical diseases.

Books

Lankester, Dr Ted, *The Travellers' Good Health Guide*, ISBN 0-85969-827-0.
Warrell, David, and Sarah Anderson, eds, *Expedition Medicine*, The Royal Geographic Society, ISBN 1 86197 040-4.
International Travel and Health World Health Organisation Geneva, ISBN 92 4 158026 7.
Young Pelton, Robert, *The World's Most Dangerous Places*, ISBN 1-566952-140-9.

Insurance

Always take out comprehensive insurance before you travel. Consider a plan that offers immediate repatriation for illness or accident, as well as for cancellation or curtailment of your trip. If you have to make a medical claim, make sure you keep all receipts for treatments, doctor's fees, etc. You may need to get extra cover for any activities (scuba-diving, hiking, safaris). Claims for lost or stolen items must be backed up by a police report, obtaining which can be difficult with language problems and officials not wanting to accept responsibility. Keep details of your policy and the insurance company's number with you at all times.

Internet

Internet facilities are found in many of the budget and mid-range hotels in tourist centres, and all large hotels have (expensive) services. Even the smallest and most far-flung of places will have internet cafés where local youth congregate for gaming and these can charge as little as E£2 per hr, while in hotels or traveller-orientated cafés it costs between E£5-10. Many 'posher' cafés in Cairo, Alexandria and the Red Sea resorts have Wi-Fi, which is often free to use if you're having a drink.

Language

The official language is **Arabic**. Colloquial Arabic (*omayya*) differs significantly from the written, classical form (*fos-ha*) derived from the Arabic of religious texts. Spoken Arabic in Egypt has a dialect that varies slightly from the Arabic of other countries. For example, what is usually pronounced 'j' in other Arab countries is pronounced with a hard 'g' in Egypt. However, because of Egypt's once- acclaimed film industry and the significant on-screen presence of Egyptian actors, most people around the Arab world understand the Egyptian dialect and foreigners wanting to study Arabic often learn the Egyptian dialect. In addition to Arabic many Egyptians speak, or at least dabble in, foreign languages. Younger generations tend to be more proficient in **English** whereas older generations (particularly in Alexandria) might know **French**. As tourism is such a foundation of Egypt's economy hotel staff, and people generally in touristy places, are quite fluent in English. Outside of the big cities, however, you will find that including the occasional Arabic word in your speech will facilitate communication quite a bit. It's also helpful to learn some basic direction words, as getting around and finding the right bus often depends more on asking rather than reading a schedule. Learning to read Arabic numerals and how to say them is easy and certainly worthwhile, then you can recognize bus numbers or prices, and have a bit more sway when it comes to bargaining.

Local customs and laws

Though Egypt is among the more liberal and 'Westernized' of the Arab countries, it is still an Islamic country where religion is deeply embedded in daily life. While Islam is similar to Judaism and Christianity in its philosophical content and the 3 revealed religions are accepted together as the religions of the book (*Ahl Al-Kitab*), it is wise for travellers to recognize that Islamic practices in this traditional society are a sensitive area. Public observance of religious ritual and taboo are important, just as is the protection of privacy for women and the family. Islam of an extremist kind is on the wane in Egypt but bare-faced arrogance by visitors will engender a very negative response even among normally welcoming Egyptians who generally have no tendencies towards fundamentalist views.

Islam has a specific code of practices and taboos but most will not affect the visitor unless he or she gains entry to local families or organizations at a social level. In any case a few considerations are worthy of note by all non-Muslims when in company with Muslim friends or when visiting particularly conservative areas. (1) Dress modestly. Women in particular should see the dress code, below, for further explanation. (2) If visiting during the holy month of Ramadan where Muslims fast from sunrise to sunset, dress particularly conservatively and avoid eating, drinking and smoking in public places. (3) If offering a gift to a Muslim friend, be aware that pork and alcohol are forbidden. If you choose to offer other meat, ensure it is *hallal*, killed in accordance with Muslim ritual. (4) If dining in a traditional Bedouin setting or context, do not use your left hand for eating since it is ritually unclean. (If knives and forks are provided, then both hands can be used.) Do not accept or ask for alcohol unless your host clearly intends to imbibe. Keep your feet tucked under your body away from food.

Class discrepancies and the *khawagga* (foreigner)

Compared with other developing countries, there are particularly great discrepancies among Egyptians with regard to their experience, openness, education and worldliness. Some are extremely sophisticated, knowledgeable and well travelled while others (widely known as *fellaheen* – peasants) are markedly conservative and parochial. Class is often a delineating factor, as is education and the urban/rural divide. For the traveller, maintaining awareness of social context is essential for positive and culturally sensitive interchanges with locals.

Another evident discrepancy is the cost of services for Egyptians and foreigners. If you have not yet stumbled upon the word *khawagga* (foreigner), you soon will, as it holds similar implications to the word gringo in many Latin American countries. Taxi fares, entries to many attractions, even the price of luxury accommodation all cost foreigners more. Bear in mind that the average Egyptian makes about US$1500 per head per year; the average foreign tourist lives on approximately US$32,000.

Courtesy

Politeness is always appreciated. You will notice a great deal of hand shaking, kissing, clapping on backs on arrival and departure from a group. There is no need to follow this to the extreme but handshakes, smiles and thank yous go a long way. Shows of affection and physical contact are widely accepted among members of the same sex. Be more conservative in greeting and appreciating people of the opposite sex. Do not show the bottom of your feet or rest them on tables or chairs as this gesture is regarded as extremely rude in Egypt. Be patient and friendly but firm when bargaining for items and avoid displays of anger. However, when it comes to getting onto public transport, forget it all – the description 'like a Cairo bus' needs no explanation.

Dress code

Daily dress for most Egyptians is governed by considerations of climate and weather. Other than labourers in the open, the universal reaction is to cover up against heat or cold.

For males other than the lowest of manual workers, full dress is normal. Men breaching this code will either be young and regarded as being of low social status or very rich and Westernized. When visiting mosques, *madresas* or other shrines/tombs/religious libraries, Muslim men wear full and normally magnificently washed and ironed traditional formal wear. In the office, men will be traditionally dressed or in Western suits and shirt sleeves. The higher the grade of office, the more likely the Western suit. At home people relax in a loose *gallabiyya*. Arab males will be less constrained on the beach where swimming trunks are the norm.

For women the dress code is more important and extreme. Quite apart from dress being a tell-tale sign of social status among the ladies of Cairo or Alexandria or of tribal/regional origin, decorum and religious sentiment dictates full covering of body, arms and legs. The veil is increasingly common for women, a reflection of growing Islamic revivalist views. There are still many women who do not don the veil, including those with modern attitudes towards female emancipation, professional women trained abroad and the religious minorities – Copts in particular. Jewellery is another major symbol in women's dress, especially heavy gold necklaces.

The role of dress within Islamic and social codes is clearly a crucial matter. While some latitude in dress is given to foreigners, good guests are expected to conform to the broad lines of the practice of the house. Thus, except on the beach or 'at home' in the hotel (assuming it is a tourist rather than local establishment), modesty in dress pays off. This means jeans or slacks for men rather than shorts together with a shirt or T-shirt. For women, modesty is slightly more demanding. In public wear comfortable clothes that at least cover the greater part of the legs and arms. If the opportunity arises to visit a mosque or *madresa*, then a *gallabiyya* and/or slippers are often available for hire at the door. Most women do not swim in public and if they do, they tend to dive in fully clad. If you choose to swim outside a touristy area, wear shorts and an opaque T-shirt. Offend against the dress code – and most Western tourists in this area do to a greater or lesser extent – and you risk antagonism and alienation from the local people who are increasingly conservative in their Islamic beliefs and observances.

Mosque etiquette

Do not enter mosques during a service and take photographs only after asking or when clearly permissible. Visitors to mosques and other religious buildings will be expected to remove their shoes. Men should never enter the area designated solely for women, but foreign women are tolerated in the main prayer halls of most mosques unless it is actually a time of prayer. If you are wandering somewhere you aren't supposed to be, someone will point it out to you soon enough.

Photography

Photographs of police, soldiers, docks, bridges, military areas, airports, radio stations and other public utilities are prohibited. Photography is also prohibited in tombs where much damage can be done with a flash bulb. Photography is unrestricted in all open, outdoor historic areas but some sites make an extra charge for cameras. Flashes are not permitted for delicate relics such as the icons in St Catherine's Monastery. Many museums have now banned photography completely to avoid any accidental use of flash. This includes the Egyptian Museum. Taking photographs of any person without permission is unwise, of women is taboo, and tourist attractions like water sellers, camels/camel drivers, etc, may require *baksheesh* (a tip). Even the goat herder will expect an offering for providing the goats. Always check that use of a video camera is permitted at tourist sites and be prepared to pay a heavy fee (E£100+) for permission.

Media

Newspapers and magazines

Quite a lot of English-language publications have popped up in Egypt over the last few years. The *Egyptian Gazette* is a fairly poor daily paper in English. The *Middle East Times* does a decent job of keeping readers informed of the political, social and cultural goings on of Cairo and can be accessed online at www.metimes.com. The most influential Egyptian daily is *Al-Ahram*. It also publishes an English-language paper, *Al-Ahram Weekly*, out on Thu, which has a good listings section for Cairo. There are a few English monthly glossies including *Egypt Today*, which offers an extensive up-to-date listing of hotels, businesses, restaurants and attractions around Egypt. The *Croc* is a pocket-sized free guide that you can pick up in cafés, restaurants and clubs with good listings for cultural events, restaurants, bars, etc, and is updated quarterly.

Radio and television

The BBC World Service (London) and Voice of America (VOA) broadcast throughout the region. Reception quality varies greatly: as a general rule lower frequencies give better results in the morning and late at night and the higher ones in the middle of the day. Nile FM (104.15 FM) plays bad Western pop in case you've been missing it. TV is thriving in Egypt and nowadays, more people have access to a screen than a refrigerator. Nile TV offers consistent French and English-language programming, with news broadcasts and analysis. Satellite TV is increasingly available even in mid-range hotels, featuring British and American primetime, MTV and movies as well as CNN, BBC World and Al-Jezeera.

Money

Currency

Exchange rates Feb 2011, E£1 = US$0.17, €0.12 or GB£0.10. For up-to-the-minute exchange rates visit www.xe.com.

You will see prices throughout this guide listed in either **US dollars**, **euro** or **Egyptian pounds** depending on how they're quoted in different parts of the country and for different activities. Due to recent fluctuations in the value of the US dollar, many upmarket hotels and tourist centres in Egypt (such as Hurghada and Sharm El-Sheikh) now quote their prices in euro rather than dollars. However, Egyptian pounds are used for the vast majority of everyday transactions and hotels are generally happy to accept the equivalent value in local currency.

The Egyptian pound is divided into 100 piastres (pt). Notes are in denominations of E£5, E£10, E£20, E£50, E£100, E£200, while the old 25 and 50 piastres notes and E£1 notes are being phased out. Newer E£1 coins are in circulation, and other denominations (which are almost not worth carrying) are 10, 25, and 50 piastres. It's a good idea to always have lots of pound coins to hand so you don't get short changed the odd extra pound or 2 when taking a taxi.

Regulations and money exchange

Visitors can enter and leave Egypt with a maximum of E£10,000. There are no restrictions on the import of foreign currency provided it is declared on an official customs form. Export of foreign currency may not exceed the amount imported. Generally, it's cheaper to exchange foreign currency in Egypt than in your home country. It's always wise to change enough money at home for at least the first 24 hrs of you trip, just in case. The bank counters on arrival at Cairo airport are open 24 hrs. A small amount of foreign cash, preferably US$, although sterling and euro are widely accepted, is useful for an emergency.

Banks

There is at least one of the national banks in every town plus a few foreign banks (such as HSBC and Citibank) in the big cities and Barclays have recently started operating in all major towns. Banking hours are 0830-1400

Sun-Thu (0930-1330 during Ramadan); some banks have evening hours. Changing money in banks can be a bit time-consuming, though commission is not usually charged. **ATMs** are widely available (but not in all the oases) but require a surcharge of between US$3-5, and often have a daily withdrawal limit of around E£2500-4000. They are also known to munch on the occasional card, so beware. Still, using an international credit or debit card is the easiest and quickest way to access your money and means you receive trade exchange rates which are slightly better than rates given by banks. Maestro, MasterCard, Plus/Visa and Cirrus are all widely accepted.

Credit cards

Access/MasterCard, American Express, Diners Club and Visa are accepted in all major hotels, larger restaurants and shops, and tend to offer excellent exchange rates. Outside of the tourist industry, Egypt is still a cash economy.

Traveller's cheques

Traveller's cheques are honoured in most banks and bureaux de change. US$ are the easiest to exchange particularly if they are well-known brands like Visa, Thomas Cook or American Express. There is always a transaction charge so a balance needs to be struck between using high-value cheques and paying one charge and carrying extra cash or using lower-value cheques and paying more charges. Egypt supposedly has a fixed exchange rate – wherever the transaction is carried out.

Cost of travelling

Depending on the standards of comfort and cleanliness you are prepared to accept for accommodation, food and travel, it is still possible to survive on as little as US$10-15 per person per day. However, prices for everything in Egypt are rising all the time with inflation soaring (basic foods have increased by 50%, gasoline 90%); tourists should be aware that hotel prices and transport costs continue to rise, and that the ticket prices for monuments are put up every Oct/Nov. Accommodation runs from about US$8-15 for a basic double in a liveable hotel to well over US$200 for 5-star luxury comfort. Basic street food can fill you up for less than US$1, or you can opt for a more Western-style meal, still affordable at US$6-10 a plate. Transport varies according to mode, but distances between the major cities can be covered for around US$15-20. The Cairo metro is less than US$0.25 and local buses are around the same. Renting a car is a significantly more expensive option at around US$60 per day.

There are costs often not accounted for in other parts of the world that you will inevitably encounter in Egypt. Most sit-down restaurants include a 12% tax (after the service charge, which is 10%) on the bill and it is common practice to tip an additional 10%. Another kind of tipping, known as *baksheesh*, occurs when you are offered a small service, whether or not you ask for it. If someone washes the windows of your car or looks after your shoes in a mosque, they will expect a modest offering. Carry around a stash of E£1 coins and take it in your stride, it's part of the culture.

Opening hours

Banks Sat-Thu 0830-1400.
Government offices 0900-1400 every day, closed Fri and national holidays.
Museums Daily 0900-1600 but generally close for Fri noon prayers, around 1200-1400.
Shops Normal opening hours are summer 0900-1230 and 1600-2000, winter 0900-1900, often closed on Fri or Sun. Shops in tourist areas seem to stay open much longer.

Post

All post offices are open daily except Fri, supposedly from 0800-2000 though these times may not strictly adhered to in small towns and certainly not during Ramadan. The **Central Post Office** in Cairo is open

24 hrs. All airmail letters cost E£3, postcards E£1.50, and take about 5-10 days to get to Europe and about 2 weeks to get to North America, New Zealand and Australia. You can pay a bit more to send letters registered delivery. Postage stamps can be purchased from post offices, cigarette kiosks and from hotels (from where you can also post mail).

Parcels for abroad may only be sent from a main post office. Do not seal any package until it has been examined. Shops will sometimes arrange to send items you purchase. Receiving any parcel involves paying import duty upon collection from the post office (they will inform you if something has arrived).

Safety

The level of petty crime in Egypt is no greater than elsewhere. It is very unlikely that you will be robbed but take sensible precautions. Put your valuables in a hotel deposit box or keep them on your person rather than leave them lying around your room. Avoid carrying excess money or wearing obviously valuable jewellery when sightseeing. External pockets on bags and clothing should never be used for carrying valuables, pickpockets do operate in some crowded tourist spots. It is wise to stick to the main thoroughfares when walking around at night.

Trading in antiquities is illegal and will lead to confiscation and/or imprisonment. Should you need to buy currency on the black market do so only when it is private and safe. Be careful as Egypt, like most countries, has tight laws against currency smuggling and illegal dealing.

Keep clear of all political activities. Particularly in light of the recent events where foreign journalists have been targeted. By all means keep an interest in local politics but do not become embroiled as a partisan. The *mokharbarat* (secret services) are singularly unforgiving and unbridled in their action against political interference.

Following the war on Iraq, there was a fairly widespread anti-American and anti-Anglo sentiment, but for the most part the disillusion is not mis-targeted. Egyptians seem to separate their disdain for foreign governments from individual travellers. Nonetheless, with such a volatile political climate, it's wise to check with your national authorities before departure for Egypt. If coming from the UK, for travel advice, check the Foreign and Commonwealth Office at www.fco.gov.uk; from the US, check the Dept of State at www.travel.state.gov.

9/11, the war on Iraq and the attacks on foreigners in the Sinai in 2004-2006 brought about a new set of challenges for the tourist industry and reinforced the government's attempts at ensuring safety for foreign visitors. Part of the system required most Western tourists travelling in private cars, hired taxis and tourist buses to travel in police-escorted convoys when journeying between towns in certain regions. This still applies in Upper Egypt, where scheduled convoys travel between Aswan and Abu Simbel. In 2010, restrictions were eased in other areas of Upper Egypt and now tourists are permitted on public transport. However, not all drivers are aware of the change in the rules and it can be a headache getting a ride in certain areas (such as Luxor to Dendara and Abydos, and along the east coast). Independent travellers are better off using trains where possible. If you want to drive through, inquire with the tourist authority. See box, page 27.

Confidence tricksters

The most common 'threat' to tourists is found where people are on the move, at airports, railway and bus stations, offering extremely favourable currency exchange rates, selling tours or 'antiques', and spinning hard-luck stories. Confidence tricksters are, by definition, extremely convincing and persuasive. Be warned – if the offer seems too good to be true, it probably is.

Student travellers

Student identification cards

Full-time students are entitled to obtain an International Student Identity Card (ISIC), which is distributed by student travel offices and travel agencies in 77 countries. The ISIC card gives you more economical prices on many forms of transport (air, sea, rail) and substantial discounts (up to 50%) at most Egyptian ancient sights and museums. Before you leave, contact: **ISIC**, www.istic.com, for details. Note that although student IDs from specific schools suffice in some places, it is worth getting the ISIC card because it is easily identified by most establishments. In Cairo, ISIC cards can be obtained from **Egyptian Student Travel Services (ESTS)**, 23 Sharia Al-Manial, Roda, T02-2531 0330, www.estsegypt.com, with proof of student status (student ID or letter from university or school). Bring a photograph and E£93.

Tax

Departure tax is included in the price of airline tickets. Tax and a service charge will be added to your hotel bill, apart from in budget hotels or unless it is clearly stated as inclusive.

Telephone

Country code +20.

Directory enquiries T140. If the operators don't speak English, they'll usually find someone who can help you.

The cheapest time to telephone is between 2000-0800. Local calls can be made from some shops (tip the shop keeper), cigarette kiosks and hotels (which normally add a premium in any case). You will also find yellow and green **Menatel** phone booths scattered throughout urban areas; buy a card at any kiosk where you see a Menatel sign. Calls to England and North America cost about E£5 per min; to call Australasia, it's a bit more expensive. Long-distance and international calls can also be made from *telephon centraals*, most of which are open 24 hrs and print you a receipt. Business centres at better hotels also facilitate international phone calls, for a price.

Mobile phones are very widely used in Egypt and local rates are cheap. Like Europe, they run on the GPS system. If you have roaming service, you should be able to use your phone, though be aware that if people call you from outside Egypt you will probably incur long-distance charges. If you are going to be in the country a while and make a lot of national calls, it is best to get either a **Vodaphone** or **Mobinil** sim card. These cost around E£50 and there are outlets in every town and city. Top-up cards are sold in kiosks (where you often pay a small mark-up of E£1) or you can buy more credit in Vodaphone/Mobinil shops. You may need to get your phone unlocked, which can prove a hassle as they are reluctant to do it in official retail outlets.

Time

GMT + 2 hrs.

Tipping

Tipping, or *baksheesh*, a word you will fast learn, is a way of life – everyone except high officials expects a reward for services actually rendered or imagined. Many people connected with tourism get no or very low wages and rely on tips to survive. The advice here is to be a frequent but small tipper. The principal of 'little and often' seems to work well. Usually 12% is added to hotel and restaurant bills but an extra tip of about 10% is normal and expected. In hotels and at monuments tips will be expected for the most minimal service. Rather than make a fuss, have some small bills handy. Tips may be the person's only income.

Alms-giving is a personal duty in Muslim countries. It is unlikely that beggars will be too persistent. Have a few small bills ready and offer what you can. You will be unable to help everyone and your donation may be passed on to the syndicate organizer.

Tour operators

UK and Ireland

Baobab Travel, Old Fallings Hall, Old Fallings Lane, Wolverhampton WV10 8BL, T0121-314 6011, www.baobabtravel.com. Group and tailor-made eco-tours and safaris, mainly in the Sinai. Has an ethical slant. Also do yoga holidays.

Crusader Travel, 57 Church St, Twickenham, T020-8744 0474, www.crusadertravel.com. Concentrate on diving and watersports but also do Nile Cruises and fishing safaris.

Discover Egypt, T0844-880 0462, www.discoveregypt.co.uk.

Exodus Travel, Grange Mills, Weir Rd, London SW12 0NE, T020-8675 5550, www.exodus.co.uk. Diving, desert and pharaonic tours.

Explore Worldwide, Nelson House, 55 Victoria Rd, Farnborough GU14 7PA, T0845-013 1539, www.explore.co.uk. For hotels/camping in oases of Siwa and Western Desert, also Nile cruises, Abu Simbel, *felucca* sail-trek, Red Sea and Sinai.

Explorers Tours, Explorers, 8 Minster Court, Tuscam Way, Camberley GU15 3YY, T0845-094 3379, www.explorers.co.uk. Hotel and liveaboard diving holidays in Sharm El-Shiek and Dahab.

The Imaginative Traveller, 1 Betts Av, Martlesham Heath, Suffolk IP5 3RH, T01473-667337, www.imaginative-traveller.com. You get a lot for your money.

On The Go Tours, 68 North End Rd, West Kensington, London W14 9EP, T020-7371 1113, www.onthegotours.com. Varied tours including diving courses and sightseeing.

Oonas Divers, 16 Gildredge Rd Eastbourne, East Sussex BN21 4RL, T01323-648924, www.oonasdivers.com. Quality liveaboard accommodation, also a fascinating Red Sea Diving Safari, involving camping and diving off the southern Red Sea coast.

Peltours Ltd, Sovereign House, 11/19 Ballards Lane, Finchley, London N3 1UX, T0844-225 0120, www.peltours.com. Nile cruises, diving and other watersports.

Regal Holidays, 58 Lancaster Way, Ely, Cambs CB6 3NW, T01353-659999, www.regal-diving.co.uk. Diving specialists for the Red Sea.

Soliman Travel, 162 Hammersmith Rd, London W6 7JP, T0870-027 5230, www.solimantravel.co.uk. Specialist tours to famous battlefields of Western Desert.

Sunbird, PO Box 76, Sandy, Bedfordshire SG19 1DF, T01767-262522, www.sunbird tours.co.uk. A variety of locations in Egypt with emphasis on birdlife and history.

Tailor Made Holidays, 5 Station Approach, Hinchley Wood, Surrey KT10 0SP, T020-8398 7424, T020-8398 4464, www.tailormade holidays.co.uk. Offer 'Hooked on the Nile' and 'Fishing on Lake Nasser' trips. They have 6 boats fed by a supply boat on Lake Nasser, a civilized safari in a steel-hulled boat, with ample opportunities to fish.

Violet Ultra Travel, Edge Bank, Skelsmergh, Kendal LA8 9AS, T0161-408 0078, www.violetultratravel.com. Red Sea diving specialists, with livea-boards and shore-diving, they sort out military expeds.

Rest of Europe

USIT, 19 / 21 Aston Quay, Dublin 2, Ireland, T01-602 1904, www.usit.ie. Specialist student travel services.

North America

Abercrombie and Kent, T1800-554 7016, www.abercrombiekent.com.

Bestway Tours, Canada, T604-264 7378, www.bestway.com. Tours combining Egypt with neighbouring countries.

Egypt Tours, T1800-573 4978, www.egypttours.com.

Australia and New Zealand

Abercrombie and Kent, Australia, T1300-851800, www.abercrombiekent.com.au; New Zealand, T0800-441638.

Explore Worldwide , Australia, T02-8913 0700; New Zealand, T09-524 5118, www.explore.co.uk.

Intrepid Traveller, T1300-364512, www.intrepidtravel.com. Egypt-wide tours aiming to take you to less touristed places.

Peregrine Adventures, T1300-854444, www.peregrine.net.au.

Trailfinders, T1300-780212, www.trailfinders.com. Good for flights.

Tourist information

Depending on where you are in Egypt the provision of tourist information is variable, as is the usefulness of information provided. The offices in bigger cities tend to be quite well equipped and at least have an English speaker on duty. They're worth a visit if you are nearby. The particularly helpful tourist offices are noted in the relevant chapter sections. When the tourist offices fall short, hotels, pensions and other travellers are often even better resources to access reliable travel information.

Egyptian state tourist offices abroad

Austria, Elisabeth Strasse, 4/Steige 5/1, Opernringhof, 1010 Vienna, T43-1-587 6633, aegyptnet@netway.at.

Belgium, 179 Av Louise 1050, Brussels, T32-2647 3858, touregypt@skynet.be.

Canada, 1253 McGill College Av, Suite 250, Quebec, Montreal, T1-514-861 4420.

France, 90 Champs Elysées, Paris, T33-1-4562 9442/3, Egypt.Ot@Wanadoo.Fr

Germany, 64A Kaiser Strasse, Frankfurt, T49-69-252319.

Italy, 19 Via Bissolati, 00187 Rome, T39-6-482 7985.

Spain, Torre de Madrid, planta 5, Oficina 3, Plaza de España, 28008 Madrid, T34-1-559 2121.

Sweden, Dorottningatan 99, Atan 65, 11136 Stockholm, T46-8-102584, egypt.Ti.Swed@alfa.telenordia.se

Switzerland, 9 rue des Alpes, Geneva, T022-732 9132.

UK, Egyptian House, 170 Piccadilly, London W1V 9DD, T020-7493 5283.

USA, 630 5th Av, Suite 1706, New York 10111, T1-212-332 2570, egyptourst@ad.com.

Egypt on the web

www.bibalex.gov.eg Detailed information and up-to-date news on the new Alexandria Library, and has a calendar of events.

www.touregypt.net A comprehensive site put together by the Ministry of Tourism. Detailed listings include online shopping from Khan El- Khalili, maps of most cities, walking routes of national parks, hotel and tour guide index and general information on life in Egypt.

www.weekly.ahram.org.eg Online version of the weekly English-language sister paper to the national daily *Al-Ahram*, extensive archive with search engine.

Visas and immigration

Passports are required by all and should be valid for at least 6 months beyond the period of your intended stay in Egypt. Visas are required by all except nationals of the following countries: Bahrain, Jordan, Kuwait, Libya, Oman, Saudi Arabia and the UAE. Cost varies between different embassies in different countries but payment must be in cash or by postal order, cheques are not accepted. It can take up to 6 weeks for some embassies to process a postal application, or they can be issued in 1 day if you turn up in person. They are valid for 3 months from date of arrival and for 6 months from date of issue and cannot be post-dated. Visas issued from embassies are either single-entry or multiple entry (which allows you to re-enter Egypt twice). Most Western tourists find it easiest to buy a renewable 30-day tourist visa (US$15 or equivalent in euro or sterling) on arrival at all international airports – but this is not possible when you are entering via an overland border crossing or a port.

For south Sinai visits, including St Catherine's Monastery, a Sinai-only visa permits a stay of up to 14 days. You can obtain a Sinai-only visa free of charge when entering through Sinai entry points of Taba, Sharm el-Sheikh airport, Nuweiba and Sharm el-Sheikh seaports. Note that Sinai-only visas are not valid for Ras Mohammed or trekking in Central Sinai.

Visa extensions can be obtained in 1 day (turn up early) at the Mogamma, Midan Tahrir, Cairo; Sharia Khaled Ibn El-Walid in Luxor; and 28 Sharia Talaat Harb in Alexandria. Some governorate capital cities, such as Ismailia and El-Tor, also have passport offices with extension facilities and these can be quite efficient places to renew (check the information under the appropriate section in the text). You will need your passport, 2 new photographs, cash to pay for renewal (cost varies depending what sort of visa, single- or multiple-entry, you require) and possibly bank receipts to prove you have exchanged or withdrawn enough hard currency to warrant your travels. Overstaying by 15 days does not matter, but after 2 weeks, be prepared for an E£153 fine and some hassle.

Entry into Israel, Palestine, Jordan, Libya and Sudan

Obtaining visas to travel in **Libya** and **Sudan** can be quite a lengthy process, and not always a sure bet, try to do this paperwork before entry to Egypt.

You can get a 1-month visa to **Jordan** on the ferry from Nuweiba to Aqaba, prices vary slightly according to nationality but it is around US$15. Crossing into **Israel**, most Western citizens can obtain a free entry visa on the border between Taba and Eilat that lasts for 3 months. However, if you intend to travel onward to Syria or Lebanon (or any Arab country apart from Jordan), you will experience problems if you have travelled through Israel first. Though Israeli border authorities will stamp a separate piece of paper, the Egyptians insist on stamping passports with an exit stamp that clearly shows which border you have crossed. For access to the current border situation, consult the respective embassy.

Weight and measures

Metric.

Women travellers

Travelling alone as a woman can be a challenging experience in Egypt. Young Muslim women rarely travel without the protection of a male or older female, and so to Egyptians unschooled in Western culture, a single woman may automatically be regarded as strange (at best) or considered of easy virtue (at worst). Exposure to some of the ways of the Western world hasn't helped, with plentiful tales of easy sex to be had with foreigners in Hurghada and Sinai. Harassment can take many forms, from hissing and catcalls to fervent invites and inappropriate touching. In fact, the majority of Egyptian women will also admit to being verbally or physically harassed so the problem is well entrenched. However, with smart and sensible behaviour, it's possible to be adventurous without taking unsafe risks. See box, page 52, for more information on avoiding hassle. See also information on page 44.

Working in Egypt

In order to work as a foreigner in Egypt, you need a special work permit. This requires evidence of a job offer and some form-filling, which is processed through the Mogamma. Many places of work also require that you

Avoiding hassle

Here are some general hints to minimize the pestering that will certainly occur on some level as a woman travelling in Egypt. Try to walk with confidence and at least pretend that you know where you're going. Dress modestly – the less bare flesh the better (especially avoid revealing your shoulders, cleavage and legs). In conservative areas, don't reveal your legs at all and consider tying long hair up. Always carry a thin shawl or scarf to wrap around you in case you suddenly feel over-exposed. When swimming pretty much anywhere outside of the Red Sea resorts, wear leggings and a opaque T-shirt rather than a bathing suit. Ignore rude and suggestive comments and most importantly, avoid looking onlookers in the eye. In general, try not to react in a way that may aggravate a situation – it's best not to react at all.

When riding public transport, if possible sit next to women (on the Cairo subway the first car is reserved for women only) and avoid late-night transport if alone. If seeking advice or directions outside of hotels and other touristy places try to ask a woman or an older businessman-type. If you feel exceptionally uncomfortable, deliberate embarrassment of the man in question can be a powerful weapon – shout *haram* ('it's forbidden'). You may want to don a wedding band to dissuade potential suitors. If you're travelling with a man, you can avoid a lot of interrogations and confusion by saying that you're married. Absolutely avoid going into the desert or solitary places alone with a man you don't know.

Note that men and women in Egypt relate to one another differently from men and women in many Western countries. The Western concept of 'friendship' can be misunderstood. Opt to be conservative in the way you interact and engage with Egyptian men, as a mere smile can be misinterpreted as an expression of more than platonic interest. Most importantly, trust your instincts, be smart and keep a sense of humour. The rewards of travelling alone as a female in Egypt far outweigh any of the hassle. If you cloak yourself in baggy clothes and try to look as androgynous as possible, you'll be able to go wherever you want and be treated as a man would be, with the added bonus of everyone looking out for you just because you are a 'woman on your own'. Remember, the consequences for serious violations against foreigners in Egypt are so dire that the incidence of rape and other forms of extreme harassment and violation is significantly less than in most other countries.

undergo a medical examination, which will probably include blood tests.

There is no shortage of foreigners working in Egypt, but most of them are recruited from outside for specific projects. Opportunities for casual work are limited to journalism, teaching and diving. There are a handful of English newspapers and magazines in Cairo that employ foreigners with journalistic inclinations, but it's easiest to organize this once you've arrived. If you are TEFL certified and interested in teaching English, you may find informal employment with the private sector and if you work in a school they will arrange a work permit for you. Those interested in diving jobs should try the Red Sea coast or Sinai. It's best to ask around and check with dive shops to see what's available. If you plan to be around for a while, check with your respective embassy to see if there are any longer term projects available.

Cairo

Contents

Footprint features

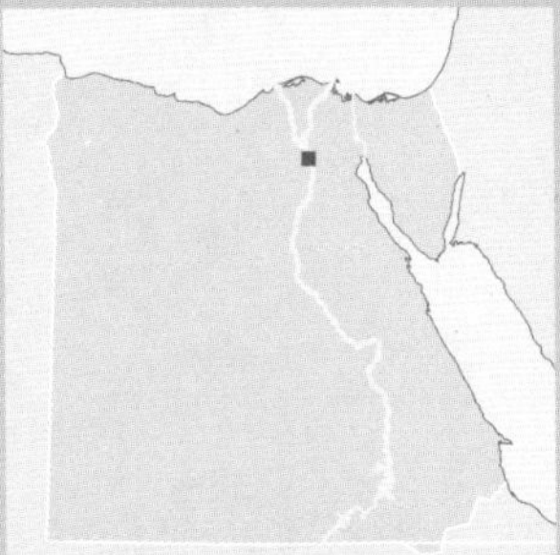

At a glance

Getting around Taxis are both inexpensive and plentiful, while the metro is useful for longer journeys. Buses and micros are crowded but cheap.

Time required Allow a minimum of 3 days.

Weather Very hot Jun-Sep. Winter days are beautiful, but the nights are surprisingly cold.

When not to go It's only the summer heat that makes sightseeing hard work. Avoid Ramadan if eating street food and drinking alcohol are a crucial part of your holiday experience.

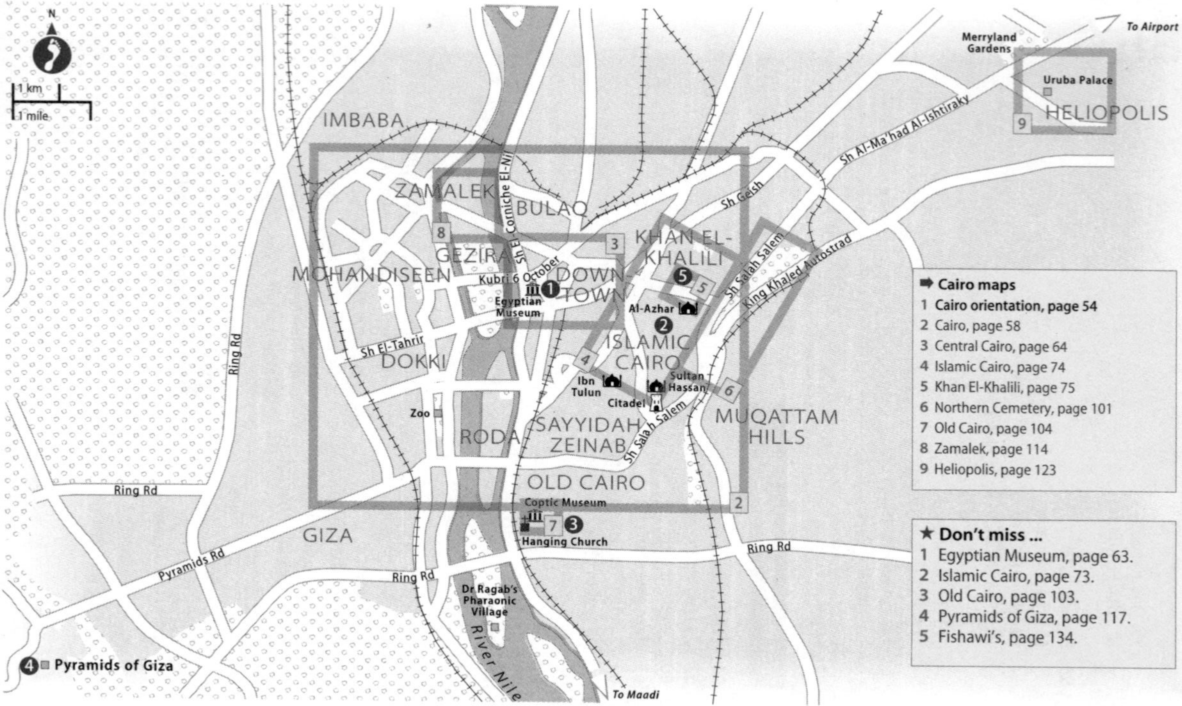
N
1 km
1 mile
To Airport
Merryland Gardens
Uruba Palace
HELIOPOLIS
9
IMBABA
Sh Al-Ma'had Al-Ishtiraky
ZAMALEK
Sh El Corniche El-Nil
BULAQ
Sh Geish
8
3
KHAN EL-KHALILI
GEZIRA
Sh Salah Salem
King Khaled Autostrad
MOHANDISEEN
Kubri 6 October
DOWN-TOWN
5
Egyptian Museum
Al-Azhar
Sh El-Tahrir
ISLAMIC CAIRO
DOKKI
4
Ibn Tulun
Sultan Hassan
6
Citadel
Zoo
MUQATTAM HILLS
RODA
SAYYIDAH ZEINAB
Sh Salah Salem
OLD CAIRO
Ring Rd
2
Coptic Museum
7
Hanging Church
GIZA
Ring Rd
Pyramids Rd
Ring Rd
Dr Ragab's Pharaonic Village
River Nile
Pyramids of Giza
To Maadi
Cairo maps
1 Cairo orientation, page 54
2 Cairo, page 58
3 Central Cairo, page 64
4 Islamic Cairo, page 74
5 Khan El-Khalili, page 75
6 Northern Cemetery, page 101
7 Old Cairo, page 104
8 Zamalek, page 114
9 Heliopolis, page 123
Don't miss ...
1 Egyptian Museum, page 63.
2 Islamic Cairo, page 73.
3 Old Cairo, page 103.
4 Pyramids of Giza, page 117.
5 Fishawi's, page 134.

At the crossroads of Asia, Africa and Europe stands the metropolis of Cairo, the largest city in the Middle East and Africa and one of the most populous in the world. With more than 25,000 inhabitants per square kilometre, Cairo has an estimated 16 million souls living in a place designed for two million. The Nile runs like a vein through the centre, sustaining hearts and bellies as it has for millennia. On either bank extraordinary remains of civilizations past – thousands of years of pharaonic, Coptic and Islamic history – commingle with the dwellings and lives of modern Egyptians.

Cairo has more than one face. Part of the city wants to hold hands with the most cosmopolitan world cities and boast the splendours of its past; the other just wants to get by. Mega-malls and manicured *midans* sprout up with an air of contrived sophistication, but the rubble of failed building projects and the bulk of the population that concerns itself more with finding food and housing simply doesn't care about the absence of rubbish bins.

Testimony to Cairo's multiple faces is everywhere. A walk around the city is a walk through thousands of years: from the colossal Pyramids of Giza at the edge of the Western Desert to the Old Coptic Quarter on the east bank; through the alleys of Islamic Cairo, gushing with life and hundreds of ancient monuments to the downtown quarter where the stunning façades of 19th-century buildings remind onlookers of the profound influence of European occupiers. And in between the ancient monuments and modern buildings, *souks* and *ahwas* (coffee houses), bazaars and *falafel* stalls fill every crevice where the contagious energy of Cairo, perhaps the city's greatest attraction of all, looms on as it always has.

Ins and outs → *Colour map 2, B2. Population: 17,000,000. Altitude: 75 m.*

Getting there

As one of the world's most crowded and noisy cities, arriving in Cairo can be a daunting experience. Authorities have worked hard to eliminate the once all-pervading hustle on arrival at the airport, taxi drivers are no longer permitted to pick up rides from the curb and other would-be hustlers are left outside if they don't flash the necessary identification. Still, upon reaching the pavement outside the airport, independent travellers may encounter a barrage of unsolicited offers from self-declared tour guides, drivers, hotel vendors, and the like, seeking to take advantage of an unschooled newcomer. Breathe deeply, avoid eye contact, firmly say *la'a shukran* (no, thank you), and stick to your plans. Bear in mind that Cairo is an exceptionally safe city and violent crime is virtually non-existent. The greatest thing to fear is getting severely overcharged for a taxi ride or being lured to a dingy hotel room. With a day or two meandering around the city, you'll figure out how things work soon enough. The easiest way to dodge such happenings from the outset is to work out in advance where you're going and how you intend to get there.

The **airport**, www.cairo-airport.com, is 22 km (about 45 minutes) northeast of Cairo. **Terminal 1** ⓘ *T02-2265 5000/1* caters for all **EgyptAir** flights, and some international airlines. The newer **Terminal 2** ⓘ *T02-2265 2824 (departure information), T02-2265 2077 (arrival information)*, is 3 km away and takes all other international flights. (Terminal 3 is being built, and will handle both domestic and international flights, just to confuse the matter further). In both terminals, there are tourist information booths in the departure hall but they are not overly helpful. Also on site are ATM machines and several banks that remain open through the night as flights arrive. Visas are on sale just before passport control at the bank counter (US$15 or equivalent in euro or sterling).

Taxi drivers will assuage you upon exiting, they ask for E£80-100 to transport you to the centre, locals usually pay E£50. If you can bargain down to around E£60, you've done well. Taxis get cheaper the further you head out of the car park, and if you can pick one up outside the precincts of the airport they are cheaper still. Another good option is the **Shuttle Bus** ⓘ *T02-2265 3937, available from the limousine counter on arrival or leaving every half hour*, who have seven-seater minibuses with set prices to various districts of Cairo.

Despite what any taxi driver at the airport will tell you, it is possible to take public transport into the city. However, it is a big hassle and not really recommended. Buses and minibuses gather by the bus stop, about 300 m in front of Terminal 1, visible as you exit. If you're heading Downtown or to Giza, the most comfortable option is to take one of the air-conditioned buses (E£2). Between 0700-2300, bus No 356 goes from the airport to **Midan Ramses** and on to **Midan Tahrir**. Further public buses, a little cheaper and a bit more uncomfortable, run from Terminal 1 through the night: minibus No 27 (E£1.50) runs from the airport to **Midan Tahrir**; bus No 948 (E£1) runs to **Midan Ataba** (on the outskirts of central Cairo). If you arrive at Terminal 2 and want to take public transport, a free 24-hour shuttle bus connects the two terminals. These line up outside arrivals and, about three minutes after setting off, reach a roundabout by a parking lot where a bus stop has been constructed. Get off here and catch an onward bus to Cairo. There is also a bus direct from the airport to **Alexandria**. » *For listings, see pages 125-154.*

Getting around

Considering its size, getting around Cairo is quite easy. The centre, known as Downtown, is a condensed area and walking is a good way to see the heart of the city. There is a local

24 hours in the city

First stop, the **Egyptian Museum**. Be there when it opens and head straight to the Tutankhamen galleries in an attempt to beat the crowds. After a couple of hours, hop on the metro down to **Old Cairo** and visit the Hanging Church and the Coptic Museum; the Ben Ezra Synagogue (Egypt's oldest) is an optional extra. The Nilometer is easily accessible from here, if you haven't seen one elsewhere.

Take a metro back **Downtown** and head to Felfela's for a filling taste of local food for lunch, before taking a taxi to the Northern Gates and a walk through **Islamic Cairo**. Going south down Sharia Al-Muizz allows you to visit the spectacular Qaloun complex and have a wander around the Khan El-Khalili, Cairo's main *souk* since 1382. Stop for mint tea and *sheesha* at the famed Fishawis coffee shop, before continuing south past the Al-Ghuri's magnificent mosque and mausoleum. Pass through the huge gate of the Bab Zuweila and on through the tentmakers bazaar all the way down to the mosque of Ibn Tulun, where you can climb the spiralled minaret, visit the Gayer-Anderson House and do a bit of souvenir shopping in the Khan Misr Toulun. Take a taxi to Al-Azhar Park to enjoy sunset views over the whole city, before having dinner on a floating restaurant or one of Zamalek's swanky restaurants.

Join the crowds **Downtown** for an evening of window shopping, before having drinks in the rowdy Horiyya coffee shop or (if you've still got the energy) splash out at the Mena House bar with the Pyramid's a mere stone's throw away.

bus service, metro system, and a profusion of cheap taxis. A few air-conditioned buses that run on the major thoroughfares connect the main *midans* (squares) to Heliopolis and the airport. They are a bit more expensive than the public buses (E£2), but more pleasant to use. For the truly adventurous traveller, the inner-city buses and minibuses (50 pt-1.50 pt) cover every inch of Cairo. They are generally so crowded that people literally hang out of doors, and as they rarely come to complete stops, courageous riders must run and jump to hop on. There are also microbuses that are private van-like vehicles that transport passengers through the maze of Cairo (E£1). There is usually a driver and a navigator that shouts the destination out of a moving van. When it suits you, motion to the van and they'll stop. You can also shout out where you want to go and if it's en route, they will enthusiastically let you on. If you see a large collection of people at what looks like a bus stop, just tell someone where you want to go and they will go out of their way to put you on the right bus/micro or at least point you in the right direction.

The metro is excellent – clean, cheap, and efficient, but with only two lines (and a third in construction), it doesn't cover the entire city. For cheaper and quicker transport, you may want to traverse the city by metro and then take a taxi or microbus for the final leg of your trip. Taxis are so inexpensive, abundant and easy, they really are the most convenient way of getting around. The relatively new white cabs have made life for Cairenes and tourists much easier, as they have working meters which start at E£2.50 and go up in 25 pt increments. The older black and white cabs are everywhere but they don't have working meters so as a newcomer it's best to agree a price before you get in, or when you've got to grips with fares pass the money through the window after getting out of the cab. Less plentiful are **yellow cabs** ⓘ *they can be prebooked by calling T16516 or T19155*, that have air conditioning and working meters; these are cheaper for longer journeys around Cairo but work out more for short dashes. » *See Transport, page 147.*

2 Cairo

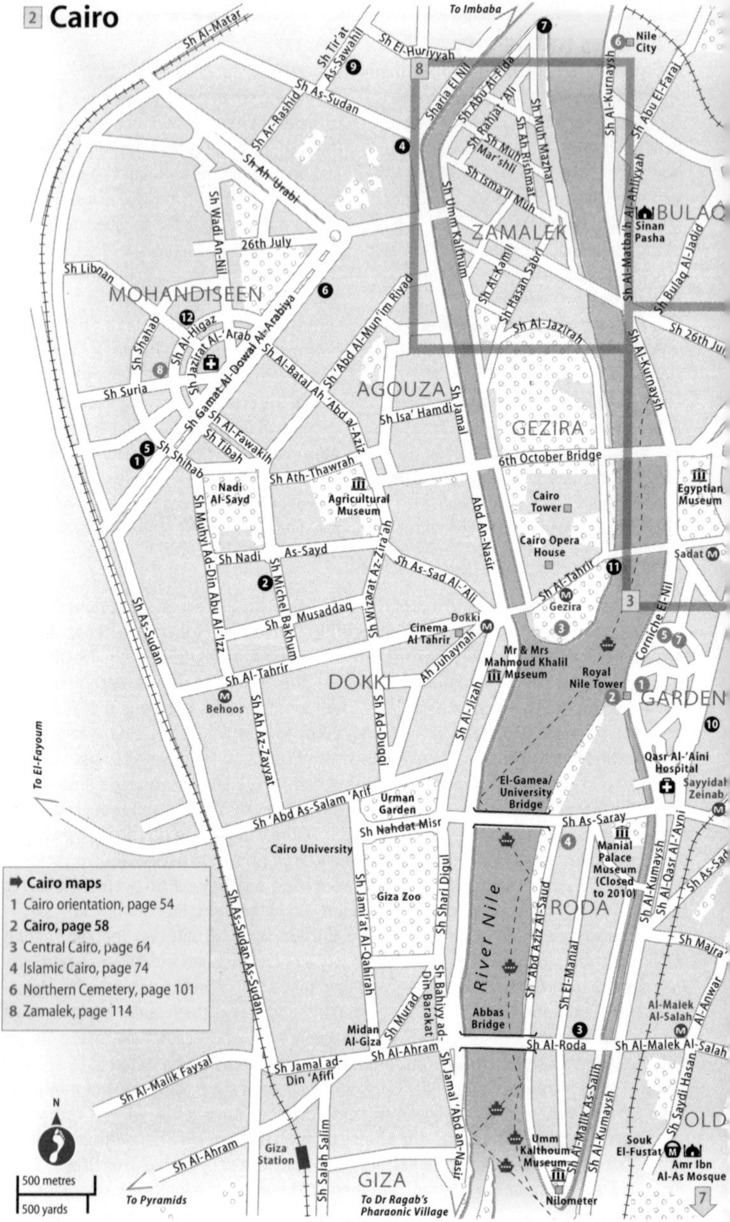
To Imbaba
Sh Al-Matar
Sh El-Huriyyah
Sh Tir'at As-Sawahil
Sh As-Sudan
Sh Ar-Rashid
Sh Ah 'Urabi
Sharia El Nil
Sh Abu Al-Fida
Sh Rahjat 'Ali
Sh Muh Mar'shli
Sh Ah Rishmat
Sh Muh Mazhar
Sh Isma'il Muh
Sh Al-Kurnaysh
Nile City
Sh Abu El-Faraj
BULAQ
Sinan Pasha
Sh Bulaq Al-Jadid
Sh Al-Matba'h Al-Ahliyyah
ZAMALEK
Sh Umm Kalthum
Sh Al-Kamil
Sh Hasan Sabri
Sh Al-Jazirah
Sh 26th July
Sh Wadi An-Nil
26th July
Sh Libnan
MOHANDISEEN
Sh Gamat Al-Dowal Al-Arabiya
Sh 'Abd Al-Mun'im Riyad
Sh Shahab
Sh Al-Higaz
Sh Jazirat Al-'Arab
Sh Al-Batal Ah 'Abd al-'Aziz
AGOUZA
Sh Jamal
Sh Suria
Sh Isa' Hamdi
GEZIRA
Sh Al-Fawakih
Sh Tibah
Sh Shihab
6th October Bridge
Sh Ath-Thawrah
Nadi Al-Sayd
Agricultural Museum
Cairo Tower
Egyptian Museum
Abd An-Nasir
Cairo Opera House
Sh Muhyi Ad-Din Abu Al-'Izz
Sh Nadi As-Sayd
Sh Michel Bakhum
Sh Wizarat Az-Zira'ah
Sh As-Sad Al-'Ali
Sadat
Sh Al-Tahrir
Gezira
Sh Musaddaq
Cinema Al Tahrir
Dokki
Ah Juhaynah
Corniche El-Nil
Sh As-Sudan
Mr & Mrs Mahmoud Khalil Museum
Royal Nile Tower
Sh Al-Tahrir
DOKKI
GARDEN
Behoos
Sh Ah Az-Zayyat
Sh Ad-Duqqi
Sh Al-Jizah
To El-Fayoum
Qasr Al-'Aini Hospital
Sayyidah Zeinab
El-Gamea/ University Bridge
Sh 'Abd As-Salam 'Arif
Urman Garden
Sh Nahdat Misr
Sh As-Saray
Cairo University
Manial Palace Museum (Closed to 2010)
Sh Al-Qasr Al-'Ayni
Sh Al-Kumaysh
Sh As-Sad
Giza Zoo
Sh Shari Digul
River Nile
Sh 'Abd Aziz Al-Saud
RODA
Sh Jami'at Al-Qahirah
Sh Majra'
Sh As-Sudan As-Sudan
Sh El-Manial
Sh Bahiyy ad-Din Barakat
Sh Murad
Abbas Bridge
Al-Malek Al-Salah
Sh Al-Anwar
Midan Al-Giza
Sh Al-Ahram
Sh Al-Roda
Sh Al-Malek Al-Salah
Sh Al-Malik Faysal
Sh Jamal ad-Din 'Afifi
Sh Jamal 'Abd an-Nasir
Sh Al-Malik As-Salih
Sh Al-Kumaysh
Sh Saydi Hasan
OLD
Sh Al-Ahram
Giza Station
Sh Salah Salim
Umm Kalthoum Museum
Souk El-Fustat
Amr Ibn Al-As Mosque
GIZA
To Pyramids
To Dr Ragab's Pharaonic Village
Nilometer
500 metres
500 yards
N
Cairo maps
1 Cairo orientation, page 54
2 Cairo, page 58
3 Central Cairo, page 64
4 Islamic Cairo, page 74
6 Northern Cemetery, page 101
8 Zamalek, page 114

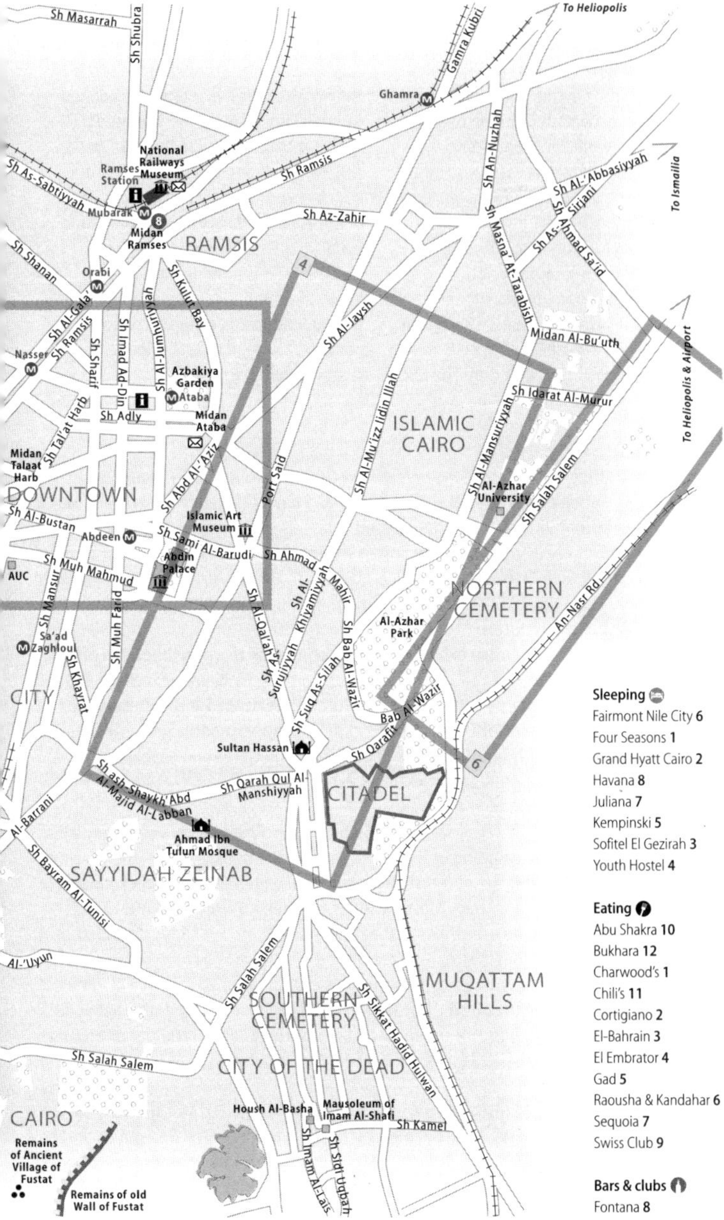

Sleeping
Fairmont Nile City **6**
Four Seasons **1**
Grand Hyatt Cairo **2**
Havana **8**
Juliana **7**
Kempinski **5**
Sofitel El Gezirah **3**
Youth Hostel **4**

Eating
Abu Shakra **10**
Bukhara **12**
Charwood's **1**
Chili's **11**
Cortigiano **2**
El-Bahrain **3**
El Embrator **4**
Gad **5**
Raousha & Kandahar **6**
Sequoia **7**
Swiss Club **9**

Bars & clubs
Fontana **8**

Cairo with kids

Divide your time between the Pyramids of Giza and the Egyptian Museum. At the latter, don't expect much in the way of interactive exhibits or even English interpretation. However, what you do get are the dazzling treasures of teenage pharaoh Tutankhamen, including his famous gold funerary mask. Another must-see is the grizzly and engrossing Royal Mummy Room, displaying the remains of 11 Egyptian queens and rulers. Talking above a 'hushed whisper' is forbidden – good luck with that! The last surviving Ancient Wonder of the World, the Pyramids of Giza, is often bemoaned by adult visitors as being 'swamped by Cairo's suburbs' or 'spoilt by touts'. Most children, however, will simply be struck with innocent wonder at the sheer size of these extraordinary monuments. Kids' initial impulse is to climb the things. However, this is a definite 'no-no', so quash any disappointment by exploring the pyramid's long, cramped 'secret' passages that lead to mysterious subterranean chambers.

Information

Main tourist office ⓘ *5 Sharia Adly, near Midan Opera, T02-2391 3454, daily 0900-1800 (closed during Fri prayers)*. The staff speak English and have a decent map of Cairo plus a few colourful pamphlets, but they have little to offer in the way of useful information. There are tourist offices at the airport, open 24 hours, and at **Ramses Train Station** ⓘ *T02-2579 0767*; **Giza Train Station** ⓘ *T02-3570 2233, 0800-2200*; and by the **Pyramids of Giza** ⓘ *T02-3383 8823, 0800-1700*. Often more helpful than the tourist offices is the information available in hotels.

If you are interested in a more exhaustive explanation than this handbook can offer for the Islamic area of the city, pick up a copy of Caroline Williams' excellent *Islamic Monuments in Cairo* (available in the AUC Bookstore). The Society for the Preservation of the Architectural Resources of Egypt (SPARE) publishes superb and extremely detailed maps of Islamic Cairo with brief accounts of each monument (also available at the AUC Bookstore, Diwan or Lenhert & Landrock, E£13 each).

Opening times In the last few years, the **Historic Cairo Restoration Programme** has exploded in Islamic Cairo resulting in the temporary closure of many monuments, those closed at the time of writing are noted. It also means that sights that have been closed for decades are at last reopening again. Most mosques are open from around 0800 until 2000. All the mosques in Cairo are accessible to the public except those of **Sayyidnah Hussein** and **Sayyidnah Nafisah**. Note that many of the mosques in Islamic Cairo are active places of worship and shouldn't be entered by non-Muslims during times of prayer. The times of prayer vary depending on the season, but are vaguely dawn, midday, mid-afternoon, dusk and mid-evening. Churches are open Monday-Saturday 0800-1700, and Sundays 1200-1700. The Pyramids of Giza are open 0900-1700, but last entry is at 1600.

Admission charges The **Ministry of Tourism**, in response to agitated Muslims who did not want to pay admission to pray, have deemed all mosques free to enter. Exceptions are the mosques of Sultan Hassan and Sultan Al-Rifai, which have entry charges. The Citadel, museums and other secular sights have admission charges that vary from E£10-50 and hand out official tickets. For students with ID, there is a 50% discount. Cameras sometimes

Take a deep breath

According to UN figures lead pollution in the atmosphere in Cairo is equivalent to one tonne per car per year and Cairo now has over 1.5 million cars.

Egypt's Environmental Affairs Agency has reported that lead pollution and other suspended particles in the air over Cairo, which tend to manifest every autumn like a black cloud over the capital reducing visibility down to a few metres and breathing to a desperate struggle, is responsible for between 15,000 and 20,000 additional deaths annually.

USAID has funded a programme, now in its fifth year, that is addressing the problem by moving significant lead smelters out of the city, sponsoring vehicle emissions testing and tune-ups and promoting the use of natural gas (an abundant natural resource in Egypt and a much cleaner burning fuel) in public and private transport. Improvements have already been detected, but lead levels in the air are still well above the World Health Organisation's acceptable levels.

require an additional fee of E£10-20, videos E£100. There are a few sly touts left lingering about the more touristed mosques who will insist there is an entry fee. There is not. If someone asks you for an admission charge, ask for a ticket, their inability to find one usually facilitates passage. *Baksheesh* is still expected for guides (who may offer to lead you up a minaret), an acceptable amount is E£5 or a bit more for large parties, and it is common courtesy to tip the shoe caretaker E£1.

Background

Since the Arab conquest in AD 641 Egyptians have called both the city and the whole country 'Misr' (pronounced *masr*), the ancient Semitic name for Egypt and also mentioned in the Koran. 'Al-Qahira' ('the Victorious') is the city's official but less commonly used name, derived from Al-Qahir (Mars), because the planet was in ascendance when the Fatimids (see page 549) started the construction of their new city in AD 971. In medieval times, this became corrupted by Europeans to Cairo, the Latin version of the name.

Although Cairo itself is younger than Alexandria, the surrounding region has a very ancient and impressive past. **Memphis**, 15 km south of Cairo across the Nile, was established as the first pharaonic capital in 3100 BC and during this period huge necropoli were developed, starting with **Saqqara** and culminating with the largest of all pyramids at modern-day Giza. During the New Kingdom, another cult centre known as On, or **Heliopolis** to the Greeks, and later Aïn Shams (Spring of the Sun) by the Arabs, was developed further north when a canal was cut between the Nile and the Red Sea. It took the Roman occupation to subdue the influence of Memphis and Om, when Emperor Trajan (AD 98-117) recognized the strategic importance of the east bank fortress town of **Babylon-in-Egypt** and a thriving community soon sprang up around its walls. During the subsequent Christian era Memphis was completely abandoned never to rise again, while Babylon became the seat of the bishopric and the west bank village of **Giza** grew into a large town.

When the Arabs conquered Egypt in AD 641, they were given specific instructions by Khalifa Omar in Damascus to establish their administrative capital in Babylon rather than at the Christian stronghold of Alexandria. The general Amr ibn Al-As built his encampment (or Fustat) in the middle of a deserted triangular plain bounded by Babylon

Flinders Petrie: beginnings of systematic archaeology

Flinders Petrie applied the first systematic excavation techniques to archaeological sites in Egypt. He was born in 1853 in Scotland and arrived in Egypt in 1880 in search of measurements of the pyramids. He excavated many sites, recording in detail each item and layer of his work with consistency and accuracy – in sharp contrast to the acquisitive and unscientific digging of this and earlier periods. It was he who set the chronological framework within which most archaeologists and their colleagues later worked.

Petrie had the reputation, even as a young man, for wanting his own way and there were constant skirmishes between him and his financing committee in London. In 1886 Petrie left his employment with the Egypt Exploration Fund but remained in Egypt for a further 37 years, actively excavating and recording his finds. He eventually left Egypt in 1923 when the law on the division of archaeological finds was changed after the discovery of the tomb of Tutankhamen by Howard Carter. He died in 1942.

in the south, Aïn Shams (ancient Heliopolis) to the northeast and Al-Maks (the Customs Point), now the site of Ramses Station, to the northwest. The Amr mosque was the first of a number of new and permanent buildings that were erected as the plain was developed and the city rapidly grew in size and importance. It is thought that the name Misr was used in order to distinguish it from the many other towns called Fustat in the Arab world.

By the time the Fatimid heretical Shi'a invaders arrived from North Africa in AD 969, only the south of the plain had been developed. Their military commander, Gohar, therefore chose to build a new walled city (which included the Al-Azhar mosque, palaces, pavilions and gardens for the sole use of the khalifa, his family and retainers), about 1.5 km north of the Fustat complex and called it Al-Qahira. Two centuries later in AD 1168 calamity struck Fustat when, fearing occupation by the invading Crusaders, the vizier Shawar set fire to the city. Over 54 days the fire almost totally destroyed Fustat whose inhabitants fled to Al-Qahira and constructed temporary housing. Three years later the last Fatimid khalifa died and his vizier, the Kurdish-born **Salah Al-Din**, assumed control of the country and founded the Sunni Muslim orthodox Ayyubid Dynasty (AD 1171-1249). He expelled the royal family from Al-Qahira, which he then opened up to the populace, and soon it became the commercial and cultural centre.

Salah Al-Din actually only spent one-third of his 24-year reign in Cairo. Much of his time was spent fighting abroad where he recaptured Syria and eventually Jerusalem from the Crusaders in 1187, finally dying in Damascus in 1193. Yet he still found time to expand the walls surrounding the Fatimid city and built the huge **Citadel** on an outcrop of the Muqattam Hills, which became the city's nucleus and remains the focal point of the Islamic city to this day.

Under Mamluk rule (AD 1250-1517) the city grew rapidly to become the largest city in the Arab world. As the east bank of the Nile continued to silt up, the newly elevated areas provided additional space that was developed to house the expanding population.

Under the **Ottomans** (AD 1517-1798) both Cairo and Alexandria were relegated to the position of mere provincial cities with little in the way of public building undertaken in the whole of the 17th and 18th centuries. This changed, however, with the combination of the arrival of the French in 1798 and the coming to power in 1805 of the Albanian-born Ottoman officer Mohammed Ali. As part of his ambitious plan to drag Egypt into the modern world by introducing the best that Europe had to offer, he embarked on a project that included a huge public building programme in Cairo and turned it into a large modern capital city.

The combination of very rapid population growth and extensive rural migration to the city, particularly since the Second World War, has completely overwhelmed Cairo. It has totally outgrown its infrastructure and today a city, intended to house only two million people, is home to perhaps 16 million, with at least a million more commuting in every day. The result is that the transport, power, water and sewage systems are completely inadequate and hundreds of thousands live wherever they can find shelter including the infamous 'Cities of the Dead' cemeteries. What is amazing is that, despite all its problems, this ancient city actually functions as well as it does and that in adversity the Cairenes are so good natured and friendly.

Sights

There is never enough time to see all the sights that Cairo has to offer, particularly in the two or three days that most visitors have at their disposal. First on the majority of agendas (and what any day-tour of the city will include) are the Pyramids of Giza, the Egyptian Museum and the Khan El-Khalili. With more time, the churches of Old Cairo, the Citadel and Mosque of Mohamed Ali, plus the outlying pyramids and tombs at Saqqara are key destinations. The streets of Islamic Cairo are dense with mosques, mausoleums and Ottoman houses, all (or any) of which are worth exploring, while the Cities of the Dead contain some of the finest Islamic architecture in the city. The modern Egyptian capital has developed on both sides of the river, spreading in all directions, where interesting and eclectic museums can be found. Get a feel for Cairo by cruising down the Nile on a felucca *at sunset, as the skyline comes alive with city lights, and spend an afternoon or evening in a local* ahwa. *To see Cairo from up high, there are stellar lookout points over the city's labyrinthine sprawl from the Cairo Tower and the top of the Grand Hyatt Hotel.* ▸▸ *For listings, see pages 125-154.*

Central Cairo

Egyptian Museum

ⓘ *The museum takes up the north side of Midan Tahrir (entry is from the sculpture garden fronting the building), T02-2578 2448, www.egyptianmuseum.gov.eg. Daily 0830-1645 (the museum remains open until 1815, last entry at 1645), except on Wed, when the museum closes at 1200 for maintenance. In 2011, it is hoped that the museum will also be open in the evenings, daily, until 2200. Ramadan opening hours: 0900-1600. It is strongly recommended to visit the museum either early in the day or last thing in the afternoon, as it is taken over by coach parties most of the time. The Tutankhamen exhibit is particularly in demand and it might even be necessary to queue for entry. Tickets cost E£60, E£30 for students, cameras and video are not permitted, there is an additional fee of E£100 (students E£60), for the Royal Mummy Room. It may be worth buying a detailed guide to the rooms, in which case the AUC Press'* Guide to the Egyptian Museum *(E£150) is the best and has a picture index to help you find what you are looking for. Tour guides wait around outside the ticket booth, some are more entertaining than others, but most seem to be quite well-informed. The going rate is E£60-80 per hr, it's possible to bargain, a tour lasts about 2 hrs. The museum is overwhelming and you need to allow at least 4 hrs for a full initial viewing of both floors. A shortened tour of about 2 hrs will give you enough time to take in the ground floor followed by a visit to the Tutankhamen Gallery. There is a souvenir shop outside the museum on the right of the*

3 Central Cairo

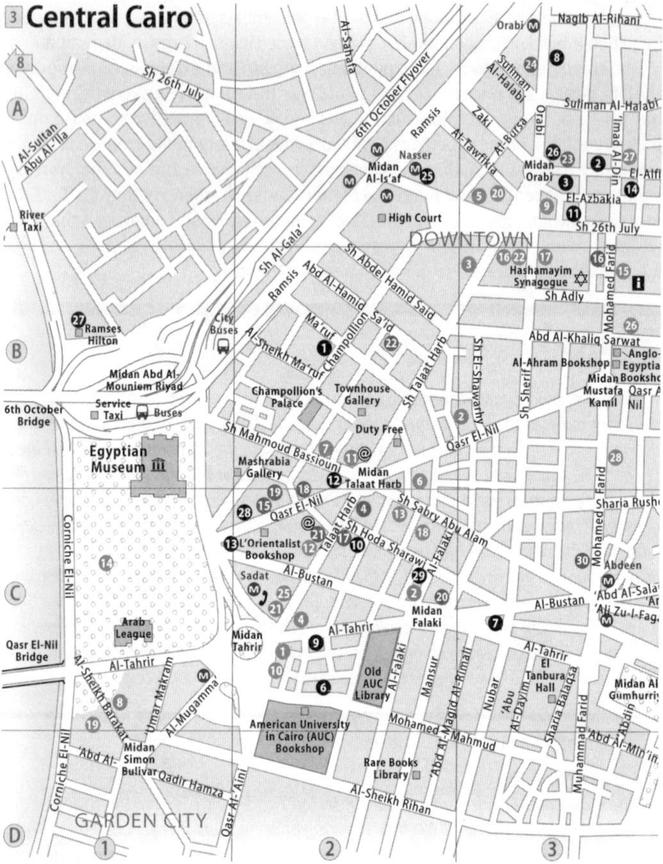

N

200 metres
200 yards

Sleeping

African Hostel **27** *A3*
Akram Inn **1** *C2*
Alexander **28** *B3*
Amin **2** *C2*
Bluebird **3** *B3*
Canadian Hostel **4** *C2*
Cairo Inn **11** *B2*
Carlton **5** *A3*
Cosmopolitan **6** *B2*
Dahab **7** *B2*
Dina's Hostel **26** *B3*
Garden City House **8** *C1*
Grand **9** *A3*
Ismailia House **10** *C2*
Lialy Hostel **11** *B2*
Lotus **12** *C2*
Meramees **13** *C2*
Nile Hilton **14** *C1*
Paris **25** *C2*
Pension Roma **15** *B3*
Ramses II **16** *B3*
Richmond **17** *B3*
Safari **20** *A3*
Sara Inn Hostel **18** *C2*
Semiramis Intercontinental **19** *C1*
Suisse **7** *B2*
Sultan **20** *A3*
Sun **21** *C2*
Talisman **22** *B3*
Venice **20** *A3*
Victoria **23** *A4*
Windsor **24** *A3*

Eating

Abu Tarek **1** *B2*
Akher Sa'a **2** *A3*
Alfi Bey **3** *A3*
Arabesque **28** *C1*
Cilantro's **6** *C2*
El-Nil Fish **7** *C3*
El-Tabei **8** *A3*
Fatatri El-Tahrir **9** *C2*

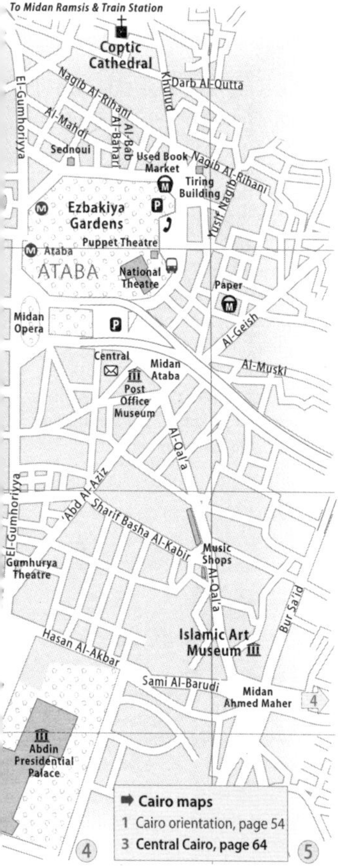

Felfela **10** *C2*
Gad **11** *A3*
Greek Club **12** *B2*
Groppi's **12** *B2*
Kowloon at Cleopatra Hotel **13** *C1*
Le Bistro **29** *C2*
Maharaja **27** *B1*
Peking **14** *A3*
Sayed Hanafi **26** *A3*
Shabrawi **25** *A2*

Bars & clubs
After Eight **15** *C2*
Café Riche **4** *C2*
Cafeteria Honololo **16** *B3*
Cafeteria Irabi **24** *A3*
Cafeteria Stella **17** *C2*
Carrol Restaurant **18** *C2*
El-Horriya **20** *C2*
Estoril **21** *C2*
Happy City **30** *C3*
Le Grillon **19** *C2*
New Arizona **23** *A3*
Odeon Rooftop **22** *B2*

entrance and an official sales area on the left inside the main building. Café and restaurant facilities are available on the 1st floor, via the souvenir shop, and there is a new high-class restaurant to the left of the museum, where there is also a courtyard coffeeshop.

The Egyptian Museum (called in Arabic *El-Mathaf El-Masri* and sometimes, mistakenly, referred to as the Cairo Museum), is one of the wonders of the country. Its most famous exhibits are the spectacular Tutankhamen displays and the world-renowned Mummy Room, but the enormous wealth of other pharaonic materials numbers a staggering 136,000. Unrivalled even by the grand museums of Berlin, London, New York and Paris, for tourists and scholars alike the museum is a must if only for a few hours.

The setting-up of a museum to house the Egyptian national collection was the brainchild of Auguste Ferdinand François Mariette, a distant relation of Champollion, the decipherer of Egyptian hieroglyphics. He himself was a great scholar of Egyptology and, after winning the confidence of the crown prince Sa'id Pasha, was appointed to oversee all excavations in Egypt and to establish a museum in which to protect the treasures that had been uncovered. The museum that he succeeded in establishing in Bulaq in 1858 was, however, flooded 20 years later, and after a soujourn in Giza, the artefacts were rehomed in 1902 in the dusty pink landmark you visit today. It remains well planned for its age, despite the confusing labelling and numbering system, but it's simply not large enough for the sheer volume of treasures it holds, many of which are stored in the basement and never seen by anyone at all. A new purpose-built Grand Museum is being constructed at Giza to overcome these inadequacies, the foundation stone was laid in January 2000 on a site of 600,000 sq m. Costing an estimated US$500 million it will be the world's largest historical gallery, displaying the hundreds of priceless monuments that now lie gathering dust in store rooms. However, progress is slow and the opening date is tentatively set for 2013, though in reality this is unlikely. The statue of Ramses the Great, which stood for decades in the midan that bears his name, has already been moved to the site of the Grand Museum of Egypt. After years cloaked in scaffolding, when he finally proceeded at a snail's pace through the main streets of Downtown to his new home, crowds to rival the funeral of Umm Khalsoum waved him off from bridges and buildings. Now he casts a sad and lonely figure dumped on the desert sands near the site of the new museum.

A visit to the museum begins with a look at the **sculpture garden**, where the tomb of Mariette, a number of sphinx-headed statues and a sarcophagus lie under the sun. At the time of writing, the outside area was being renovated into an **Open Air Museum**, and the statues will be better displayed and lit up at night. The museum building has two floors, plus a new little **Childrens' Museum** in the basement. This is entered from the left side of the main building and is uncrowded as well as free. There are some beautiful pieces inside, displayed thematically, interspersed with huge Lego models of the Sphinx, amongst others. Interesting are the blue faiance shabti figures, jewellery and mask (with a stripey turquoise beard) from the Tomb of Hor in Dahshur, two striking copper statues of Pepi I, and children will certainly enjoy the case of bird and animal figurines,

Egyptian Museum – ground floor

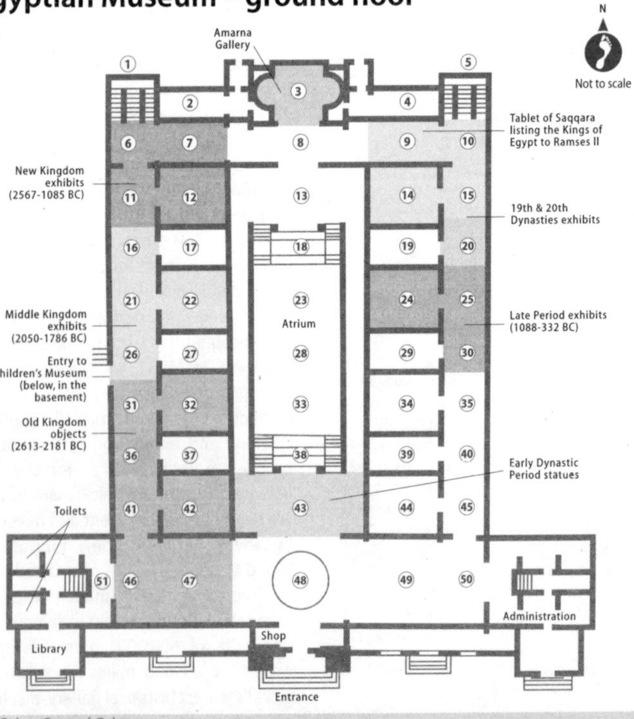

Note In the main museum, rooms are (confusingly) numbered the same on both the ground and upper floor. In the description below, GF = ground floor; UF = upper floor. Rooms and galleries are both described as 'Rooms'.

Touring the museum The ground floor arranged chronologically when starting in a clockwise direction in the hallway (Room 48-GF).

In the foyer (**48-GF**, display unnumbered) are recent additions to the museum's collection out of chronological sequence. The chief object to note is the limestone statue of **Zoser**, orchestrator of the Step Pyramid at Saqqara, whose eyes have been gouged out. Room **43-GF** holds a number of Early Dynastic period statues, but most significant is the **Narmer Palette** which, for the first time, shows the unification of Upper and Lower Egypt. Old Kingdom (2613-2181 BC) objects take up **GF Rooms 47, 46, 41, 42, 36, 31** and **32**. In Room **42-GF** there is a notable standing wooden statue of the priest Ka-aper and a beautifully preserved statue of King Chephren, whose pyramid stands in Giza. In Room **32-GF**, display 39 is a painted effigy of **Seneb the dwarf** and his family. He was keeper of the royal wardrobe in the fifth Dynasty. A well-sculpted, painted statue of Ti (display 49), a noble of the same period and other figures such as Prince Ra-hotep and his wife Nofert are also to be found in Room **32** (display 73).

The Middle Kingdom period (2050-1786 BC) is represented in **GF Rooms 26, 21, 22** and **16**. The painted statue of Menutuhotep II in Room **26-GF**, with enormous feet and calves

Egyptian Museum – upper floor

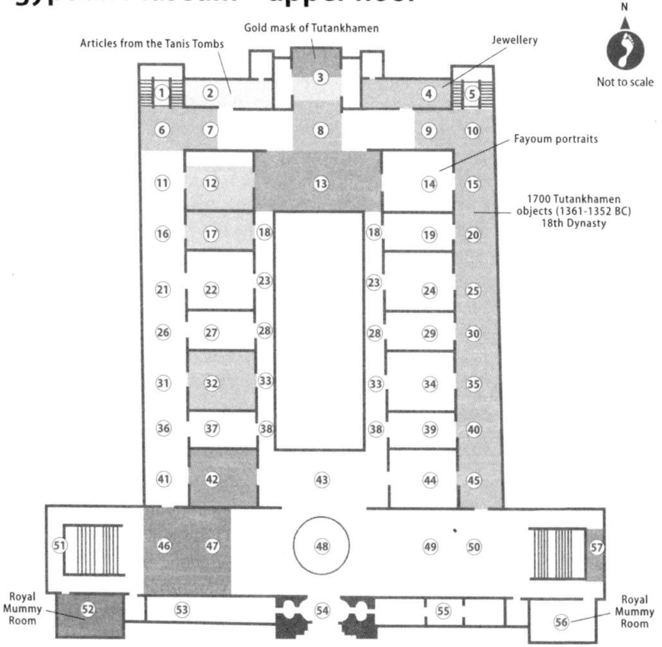

Mummy come home

An elegant tomb (Room **56**) was constructed in the museum in 2006 to provide a final resting place for some of the most famous pharaohs. Dimmed lighting, a vaulted ceiling and individual glass cases equipped with dehumidifiers protect the neatly wrapped desiccated remains. President Sadat banned the public display of mummies as improper shortly after his inauguration, and it was only in 1994 that the dead pharaohs went back on show.

The mummies have suffered many indignities. Take Merneptah, grandson of Seti I. Having survived a spectacular first burial with all the pomp and splendour due to Egyptian royalty, tomb robbers flung his mummy aside and 21st Dynasty priests rewrapped him and placed him with eight other displaced corpses in a side chamber in the Tomb of Amenhotep II. Rediscovery in 1898 was followed by transport to Cairo where he was put on view. Queen Nedjemet, another resident, was slashed by the knives of those who unwrapped her. The great Ramses II, unwrapped in public in 1886 in an unseemly 15-minute strip, has also found a decent home here. Among the 11 who have found, hopefully, a final resting place here beside Ramses II are Merytamum his queen and his father Seti I.

and a sour expression, was found at Deir El-Bahari by Howard Carter. Room **26-GF** also houses a series of sarcophagi including the unmissable **Tomb of Harhotpe** that beautifully illustrates objects in everyday use such as sandals and linen items together with hieroglyphs of magic spells and offerings. King Senusert I is depicted in 10 seated limestone statues in Room **22-GF** though these are outshone for visual impact by his 56-cm wooden statuette (display 88) carrying sceptres in both hands to denote his royal authority. A singular double-headed statue of **Amenemhat III** as the Nile god (display 104), and lion-headed sphinxes of the same provenance are in Room **16-GF** (display 102). The four sphinxes are in grey granite and come from the find by Auguste Mariette at Tanis.

The New Kingdom ran from 2567-1085 BC. The exhibits in the set of galleries **11**, **12**, **6** and **7** are mainly from the 18th Dynasty, and present more complex garments and headgear than in previous eras. Room **12-GF** is well endowed with notable objects, chiefly the **Shrine to Hathor** from the Temple of Tuthmosis III at Deir Al-Bahri, which contains a life-sized statue of the goddess in the form of a cow. Also of importance are the statues of Senenmut, steward of Queen Hatshepsut and tutor to her daughter, and the mastermind behind the design of the Hatshepsut's Temple at Deir El-Bahri. The figures in Room 12-GF include his block statue with his pupil, Princess Neferure, peering below his chin.

Recently refurbished Room **3-GF** is given over to objects from the **reign of Akhenaten** (Amenhotep IV), who set up his capital at Tell El-Amarna (south of Minya) and altered the mode of public art and architecture in Egypt to one of realism. The ultra-refined, elongated style of the paintings and sculpture of the period is unmistakable from all other pharaonic art, as the objects in this room clearly demonstrate. There are stunning sandstone statues of Akhenaten, and several heads of women are on display, with the quartzite unfinished head of beautiful Nefertiti (display 161) being the most famous. Also on show is the foil and inlay from the KV55 coffin, discovered in 1907 in the Valley of the Kings. It contained a mystery mummy that some archaeologists believe to be that of Akhenaten, in part due to the elongated skull that is clearly apparent on the stone statues displayed around the room. DNA testing is to be carried out to try and determine whose the badly preserved body really is.

Never smile at a crocodile

In the Ancient Egyptian Agricultural Museum the 5-m-long crocodile complete with wicked grin is fortunately very dead, as are the many other animals on display. A dog lies on its side, prostrate, seemingly sleeping in the sun and a baboon sits back resting on its haunches, huge hands hanging over its knees.

These were the animals worshipped, pampered, hunted and bred by the Ancient Egyptians: fat cats; even fatter Apis bulls; domesticated sheep and horses; birds ranging in size from the falcon and duck to the ostrich and the venerated ibis. The animals depicted in the hunting scenes on the countless reliefs and tomb paintings have not, fortunately, come to life, but their skeletal and mummified remains are on display here.

The central atrium of the museum (Rooms **13**, **18**, **23**, **28**, **33** and **38-GF**) is used to exhibit mega-statues from a mixture of periods, most eye-catching of which is a 7 m high representaton of Amenhotep III and his wife Queen Tiy (Room **18**).

Objects of the 19th and 20th Dynasties are displayed in Rooms **9**, **10**, **15**, **14** and **20-GF**. Room 9-GF contains the **Tablet of Saqqara** (display 660), which lists the kings of Egypt to Ramses II. The crystalline limestone head of General Nakhtmin (display 195) is in Room 15-GF and shows fine workmanship. The painted bust of **Meryut-Amun**, daughter of Ramses II and queen in succession to Nefertari, is also in Room 15-GF.

Best of the Late Period (1085-332 BC) is concentrated in Rooms **25, 24** and **30-GF**. Key items include the Psametik group of statues in greenstone of which those of the Psametik, a head jeweller, with Hathor (display 857) and of Isis, wife of Osiris (display 856), are particularly well executed. A statue of Princess Amenartais in alabaster (display 930 in the centre of Room 30-GF) is a beautiful example of 25th Dynasty sculpture.

On the Upper Floor, the pride of the museum is contained in the **Tutankhamen collection** in rooms **3, 4, 6, 7, 8, 9, 10, 15, 20, 25, 30, 35, 40** and **45-UF** with 1700 objects on exhibition. The remarkable treasures, found intact by the Englishman Howard Carter in 1922, were saved from grave-robbers by the tomb's position low in the valley hidden under that of Ramses VI and by the construction of workmen's huts across its entrance. Unlike most other archaeological finds before 1922, the Tutankhamen treasure was retained in Egypt and considering that he only reigned for nine years, between the ages of nine and 18, the mind boggles to imagine what Seti I's tomb must have contained. You should look at the entire set of Tutankhamen displays, but if time is short at least look at the following items. The two life-size **Ka statues of Tutankhamen**, which flank the entrance to Room 45, are executed in black bitumen-painted wood and were found in the antechamber guarding his tomb. The king holds a mace in his right hand and a staff in his left, and wears a khat headdress and gilded kilt. **The gold mask of Tutankhamen** (Room 3-UF), garnished with cornelian, coloured glass, lapis lazuli, obsidian, quartz, and turquoise. The 54-cm-high mask wears a ceremonial beard and a headdress knotted at the back of the neck. The blue stripes are in lapis lazuli, and there is a gold ureaus and vulture head above the brow. **The innermost coffin of Tutankhamen** (Room 3-UF) is rendered in gold and semi-precious stones with coloured glass. Some 187.5 cm long and weighing 110.4 kg, the coffin is in the Osiride form of a mummy with crossed arms carrying divine emblems. The body is covered by carved feathers and the representations of Upper and Lower Egypt – the vulture and cobra. The outer two sarcophagi were fashioned from wood, one is on display

Not just the Egyptian Museum

There is a lot to be said for visiting small, eclectic museums in Cairo. Not only are they compact enough to only take up an hour of your time, often they are quirky and kitsch, or set in lush and quiet gardens, plus a visit takes you into areas you wouldn't necessarily explore otherwise. Some are full of dusty treasures that in any other country would be highlights of a national collection. Just be prepared for some nonsensical labelling – but then you even get that in the Egyptian museum, and it somehow adds to their charm. Good places to start include:

Agricultural Museum, Dokki – for bizarrely eclectic displays and the princess' art collection, see page 115.
Islamic Ceramics Museum, Zamalek – for exquisite colours and marble interiors, see page 113.
Mahmoud Khalil Museum, Dokki – to have Impressionist masterpieces all to yourself in a grand villa, see page 115.
Manial Palace Museum, Roda – for botanical gardens and glorious royal residence, see page 111.
National Railways Museum, Ramses – for tranquillity amid the chaos of the city's main station, see page 72.

here while the other lies in situ in his tomb at Thebes. The golden **Canopic chest** (Room 9/10-UF, display 177) was in the antechamber of the king's tomb and is made of wood gilded with gold and with silver, and is ornately decorated with family and hunting scenes. The chest was protected by four statues of Seket, the water goddess, displayed in gilded and painted wood about 90 cm high. The lids of the alabaster **Canopic jars**, containing the remains of the king's entrails, are formed in the king's image and lightly painted. Tutankhamen's **wooden funerary beds** (Room 9/10-UF) are made of stuccoed wood, gilded and painted. The most remarkable is the couch in the image of the goddess Mehetweret with cow's heads and lyre-like horns set about sun disks. The extraordinary **Throne of Tutankhamen** (Room 35-UF, display 179) is 102 x 54 cm, coated with sheets of gold and ornamented with semi-precious stones. In addition to the winged serpent arms of the throne, the seat back carries a scene in which Tutankhamen's wife anoints him with oil. The finely inlaid ebony and ivory **ceremonial chair** (Room 25-UF, display 181) of Tutankhamen is regarded as among the best examples of Egyptian cabinet-making ever found. It is decorated with uraeus snakes and divinities. The tomb of Tutankhamen contained 413 small, approximately 50 cm high, **'shawabti' statues**, some of which are on display here (Room 35-UF). The curious figures would perform tasks the gods set for the pharaoh in the afterlife. Jewellery, cups and amulets were kept in the **Anubis chest** (Room 45-UF, display 185) made in stuccoed wood and ornamented with black resin, gold, silver and varnish. Anubis as a jackal sits on the chest ready to guide Tutankhamen in the afterworld. Adjacent to the Tutankhamen galleries, and well worth looking out for, are the touchingly realistic **Fayoum portraits** in Room **14-UF**. For the most part encaustic (wax) painted on wooden bases by Greek artists in the second century AD to leave a likeness of the deceased for his family (see box, page 168).

In the opposite wing **(Rooms 27** and **32-UF)** is the wonderful 25-piece collection of Meketra's models, found in the tomb of Meketra, a noble of the Middle Kingdom (2000 BC), at a site south of Deir El-Bahari. The miniatures show the form, dress, crops, vessels and crafts of the period. The best known is the offerings bearer (display 74), 123 cm high and made of painted wood, showing a servant, carrying a basket of vases on her head and a duck in her right hand. There are also models of fishermen, cattle, weavers and carpenters in displays 75, 76, 77 and 78 respectively.

Last but not least, if you can afford it, the **Royal Mummy Room** (Room **56-UF**) contains what is left of some of the most famous pharaohs of them all. Eleven mummies are on display, some still shrouded in their wrappings, but most have had at least their faces unwrapped and seem to rest peacefully in the climate-controlled cases. Best preserved are Seti I and Ramses II, whose hair appears to have been tinted, while the mummies of queens Hodjmet and Henttawy are still wearing their wigs.

Downtown

Most independent travellers to Cairo stay in Downtown, the non-stop pulsing heart of the modern city that radiates out from the central Midan Talaat Harb. Laid out in the 1860s when Khedive Ismail sought to replicate the boulevards of Paris, gracious five-and six-level buildings still predominate on the main streets although their street-level windows contain a distracting mass of gaudy signage, spangled displays of shoes and arrays of risqué underwear. Shops and restaurants stay open late into the night, while streams of traffic and consumers pack the streets way into the small hours. It's also the chief hunting-ground (particularly around midans Tahrir and Talaat Harb) of the *kherti*, pesky touts – usually young men – who make it their business to approach foreigners with predictable lines such as 'are you looking for something?' and 'is it me?' Anyone who comes up to you, asking random questions and being overly helpful, is best avoided as there will always be an ulterior motive, even if it's just something as tedious as 'look in my shop' rather than anything sinister.

There are many characterful and ethereal turn-of-the-century buildings dotted around Downtown that are worth looking out for as you traverse between museums, Islamic Cairo and the other sights. Especially atmospheric and decrepit is the former palace of Prince Said Halim, usually (and wrongly) referred to as **Champollion's Palace**. Dating from 1896, it is a pink-marble mix of Baroque and Belle Époque themes, adorned with the Ottoman logo, the prince's initials and numerous stone angels. Now in a state of complete disrepair and infested by bats, the gates are locked and the awaited restoration project shows no sign of materializing. The palace is on Sharia Mimaar Hussein Pasha off Sharia Champollion (a tree-lined street nice for walking) and adjacent to the Townhouse Gallery and a couple of locally famed outdoor *ahwas* that are worth stopping into.

On Sharia Adly, is the stern and imposing **Hashamayim Synagogue** ⓘ *open 0800-1700 (except Sun), entrance US$5/E£30 (no student discount), no photo/video allowed, bring your passport*, which, though it appears to be art deco judging from the wonderful exterior adorned with palm trees, is actually significantly earlier, dating from 1905. The grey edifice would be better placed in Gotham City, an aura that is compounded by the heavy police presence outside. Inside, the enormous dome and stained glass windows are most impressive.

Abdin Presidential Palace Museum ⓘ *Just east of Midan El-Gumhurriya, entered from the rear of the palace, T02-2391 0130. Sat-Thu 0900-1500. E£10, students E£2, cameras E£10.*
This imposing building, completed in 1872, became the official royal residence when Khedive Ismail relocated the seat of state here as part of his schemes to modernize Cairo. For the previous 700 years the rulers had occupied the Citadel, but Abdin was not to know such longevity and King Farouk was deposed when the Egyptian republic was born in 1952. The rooms of the actual palace are not for viewing, being still used on official state

occasions, but 21 halls contain exhibits. The first section, President Mubarak's Hall, contains a selection of the gifts he has received – a varied collection of medals, portraits, clocks and plaques. Crossing the courtyard, where there is a shrine to Sidi Badran, brings you to the Military Museum, which takes up 13 of the halls. Here are displayed a host of weaponry and suits of armour, as well as unusual items such as Rommel's dagger and two guns belonging to Napoleon Bonaparte. The final section is of silverware, porcelain and crystal owned by the descendants of Mohammed Ali Pasha, indicating a very luxurious lifestyle. Who lifted the 125-kg silver tray when it was laden?

National Railways Museum ⓘ *north of Downtown, next to Ramses station, T02-2576 3793, daily 0800-1400 E£10, Fri E£20.*
A silent haven away from the madness of Ramses. A couple of gleaming steam locomotives are the highlights unless you are a signalling enthusiast, but the old Egypt tourist posters fading on the walls, amber lighting and industrial architecture make it a gratifying half hour or so. It's recommended to pop in if you have time to kill when waiting for a train.

Midan Ataba, Midan Opera and Ezbakiya Gardens

The old heart of colonial Cairo (the original Shepheard's Hotel stood on Ezbakiya Gardens), this area is now full of crowded markets among the European-style buildings. The **Post Office Museum** ⓘ *on Midan Ataba, T02-2391 0001, Sat-Thu 1000-1400, E£10, students E£5*, is a quaint diversion in an attractive building. Also worthy of a visit is the **Sednaoui** department store, which has a glorious atrium with art nouveau glasswork, creaking wooden staircases up three storeys and gigantic chandeliers – but practically no goods for sale. It was owned by Nazarenes from Syria until 1961, when nationalization meant that Parisian hats and foreign cosmetics came to an end. Another classic piece of architecture is the **Tiring Building**, designed by Oscar Horowitz, which opened as a department store in 1912. Look up to see its landmark cupola upon which four figures of Atlas support the globe.

Bulaq

The cacophony of car horns, lines of fruit carts, and endless rails of clothes spilling off the pavement make a walk down Sharia 26th July in Bulaq something of a mission. A separate suburb in the 19th century, Bulaq used to be the commercial port of Cairo when Sharia 26th July was an avenue lined with flowering trees leading tourists to Shepheard's Hotel. It was also visited by soldiers from the canal zone who frequented the prostitutes in the 'seven houses' of Bulaq, as they were the cheapest in the city and easily linked to the barracks by train. The women had to have regular medical check-ups and would first visit the hammams, singing songs on the way from the brothels as they rode along in carts. At one time the Egyptian Antiquities Museum was situated in Bulaq, and the locale is still worth a visit for a taste of *baladi* Cairo, a couple of interesting mosques, and some of the cities last-remaining functioning hammams. Public baths were generally found near market areas serving workers who couldn't get home to bathe, with the water heated by burning rubbish.

Mosque of Sinan Pasha The Albanian-born Sinan Pasha was recruited for service as a boy at the Sublime Porte in Istanbul and rose to become Sulayman the Magnificent's chief cupbearer. He was governor of Cairo between 1571-1572 and is best remembered for his building activities rather than political events. He erected buildings in Alexandria and re-excavated the canal between the Nile and Alexandria, but the major buildings he initiated in Egypt were at Bulaq and included this mosque, essential as the focal point of the community, a *sabil*, a *maktab*, commercial buildings, a hammam, residential houses, shops, a mill and a bakery. The small, square Ottoman mosque stands in a scruffy garden, with entrances from three sides into the large central domed chamber with two tiers of stained glass windows. While most of the Sinan Pasha complex has long since disappeared, the adjacent public bath (men only) is still in operation. It is a beautifully peaceful place.

Islamic Cairo

As noted in the history of Cairo (see page 61), the city initially developed as a series of extensions and walled mini-cities that radiated in a northeast direction from the original encampment of Fustat outside the walls of the Babylon-in-Egypt fortress. Built with defence purposes in mind, the streets of the Islamic city are narrow and, in addition to looming Mamluke mausoleums and age-old mosques on every corner, the feeling of having stepped back in time is deepened by the ceaseless trading, shouting and everyday life all around. Congested with hissing men pushing hand-carts and shuffling shoppers laden with bags, scented with spices and criss-crossed by cats, getting lost in the ancient alleyways is what this city is all about. It's a pity that the ambiance on some of the main streets (notably near the Khan on Sharia Muski and Sharia Al-Muizz) is being eradicated by the concerted restoration efforts that are in effect. The streets of Gamaliya are being repaved with slippery cobbles and pavements have taken the place of onion and garlic stalls, resulting a more artificial air that long-time visitors to Cairo will find upsetting. Designated a pedestrian zone between 0600-2400, shopkeepers can now only receive deliveries in the depths of night and the chaos that defined Islamic Cairo might be dimmed as palm trees are planted and faux-Arabesque street lighting takes the place of swinging single light-bulbs. Fortunately, these changes haven't encroached too far into the mayhem as yet, and south of Al-Azhar the streets are still an absorbingly dirty labyrinth filled with the rickety tables of vendors and hoardes of people browsing in the shadows of Mamluke mosques.

There are literally hundreds of mosques in Cairo – the city of 1000 minarets – and it is difficult for any visitors to know where to begin. Broadly speaking, the most important sights to visit in Islamic Cairo lie in a wide belt to the east of the main Sharia Port Said. Take as much small change with you as you can gather as, although entry to almost all mosques is free, a bit of *baksheesh* is expected if you climb minarets. People might demand E£10 or even E£20, but E£3 is acceptable (E£5 if you have taken a particularly long time). It can also enable you to wheedle your way into sights that are not yet officially open to the public.

Ins and outs

The easiest way to get to Islamic Cairo is by taxi or microbus. Taxis from the centre should cost around E£5. Public bus services around Al-Azhar have essentially ceased with the government's attempt to lessen congestion in the area. Walking from Downtown is interesting and easy. From **Midan Ataba**, there are two routes. You can either stroll along **Sharia Al-Azhar** (under the flyover) or wander down the fascinating, jam-packed and narrow **Sharia Muski**, which eventually winds up in the **Khan El-Khalili** (both routes take 15-20 minutes).

Etiquette Islamic Cairo is a particularly conservative area so it's wise to dress especially modestly. Women should wear clothes that cover their legs and arms and should bring along a headscarf for use in mosques. Men should avoid shorts and sleeveless T-shirts. Shoes must be removed for entry into mosques.

4 Islamic Cairo

N
200 metres
200 yards
Sleeping
Le Riad 1
Eating
Gad 1
Mohamed Ali's 2
Zizo 3
Bab Al-Futuh
Mosque of Al-Hakim
Bab Al-Nasr
Galal
North Wall
Al-Mansuriya
Al-Gamaliya
Mosque & Sabil-Kuttab of Suleyman Agha Al-Silahdar
Galal
Amir Al-Guyush
Al-Khaliq Al-Masri
Beit Al-Suhaymi
Khanqah of Beybars Al-Gashankir
Darb Al-Asfur
Mosque of Al-Aqmar
Sabil-Kuttab of Abd Al-Rahman Kutkhuda
Medresa & Mausoleum of Tatar Al-Higaziya
Site of Musafirkhana Palace
Palace of Amir Bashtak
Barquq Complex
Textile Museum
Fatimid Tower
Al-Nasir Complex
House of Uthman Kathuda
Qalaoun Complex
Madresa & Mausoleum of Sultan Al-Salih Ayyub
Al-Geish
Sharia Port Said
5
Sayyidnah Hussein Mosque
KHAN EL-KHALILI
Midan Al-Hussein
Guhar Al-Qa'id
Al-Muski
Al-Muski
Madresa of Sultan Al-Ashraf Barsbay
Sh Al-Azhar
Al-Azhar University
Al-Azhar Mosque
Ghuriyya
Wikala & Sabil-Kuttab of Sultan Qaitbay
Sh Al-Azhar
Wikala of Sultan Al-Ashraf Qansuh Al-Ghuri
Ayyubid Walls
Sh Salah Salem
6
Beit El-Zeinab Khatun, Beit Al-Harawi & Beit El-Set Wasela
House of Gamal Al-Din Al-Dhahabi
3
Sh Al-Muizzli Din Allah
Fakahani Mosque
Sabil-Kuttab of Tusun Pasha
Sharif Basha Al-Kabir
Al-Qal'a
Mosque of Sultan Al-Muayyad Sheikh
Hammam As-Sukariyah
Gate
Museum of Islamic Art
Hammam Al-Muayyad
Bab Zuweila
Mosque of Vizier Al-Salih Tala'i
Mosque of Qijmas Al-Ishaqi
Al-Azhar Park
Midan Ahmed Mahir
Ahmad Mahir
Zawiya & Sabil of Sultan Al-Nasir Farag
Sami Al-Barudi
Sh Darb Al-Ahmar
Mosque & Tomb of Ahmed Mihmandar
Mosque & Tomb of Amir Aslam Al-Silahdar
Gate
Tentmakers'
Mosque of Altunbugha Al-Maridani
Mohammad Ali
Mosque of Amir Aqsunqur/Blue Mosque
Abdin Presidential Palace
Mosque of Malika Safiya
Mosque of Gani-Bak Al-Ashrafi
Beit Ar-Razzaz
Madresa of Sultan Al-Ashraf Sha'ban II
Sh Bab Al-Wazir
Al-Ganbakiya
Al-Sheikh Rihan
Sh Suq As-Silan
Madresa & Mausoleum of Amir Khayrbak
Bab Al-Wazir
Sh Al-Manjar
Sh Qarafet
Midan Al-Khidawiye
Al-Hilmiya
Maristan of Al-Muayyad
Al-Rifai
Al-Rifai Mosque
Sultan Hassan Mosque
Mausoleum & Medresa of Sunqur El-Sadi & Mevlevi Sufi Theatre
Muhammad 'Ali
Qani Bey As-Sayfi
Citadel
Midan Salah Al-Din
Palace of Amir Taz
Sh Saliba
Sh Salah Al-Din
Mosque of Amir Shaykhu
Sabil-Kuttab of Sultan Qaitbay
Sabil-Kuttab of Um Abbas
Mosque of Qanibai Al-Muhammadi
Mosque of Amir Taghri Bardi
Khanqah of Amir Shaykhu
Al-Sayyida 'Aisha
Midan Sayyida Zeinab
Qadri
Khan Misr Touloun
Sh Al-Ashraf
Al-Sayyida 'Aisha
Madresa & Tombs of Salar & Sangar Al-Gawli
Beit Al-Kritliyah (Gayer-Anderson House)
'Abd Al-Magid Al-Labban
Mosque of Ahmed Ibn Tulun
To Mosque of Sayyidnah Nafisah
Cairo maps
1 Cairo orientation, page 54
4 Islamic Cairo, page 74
5 Khan El-Khalili, page 75

Khan El-Khalili

ⓘ *Most shops are shut on Sun, and some shut on Fri.*

Although it also refers to a specific street, Khan El-Khalili is the general name given to the vast maze of individual *souks* that are an essential ingredient of any visit to Cairo. The ultimate market experience, it is a labyrinthine criss-crossing of hundreds of covered alleys and tiny stalls, manned by sharp-witted merchants adept at spotting what catches your eye. The Arab/Islamic system of urban planning traditionally divided the *souks* by professions or guilds and while the system is less rigid than formerly there is still a concentration of one particular trade in a particular area. Khan El-Khalili includes streets that almost exclusively sell

5 Khan El-Khalili

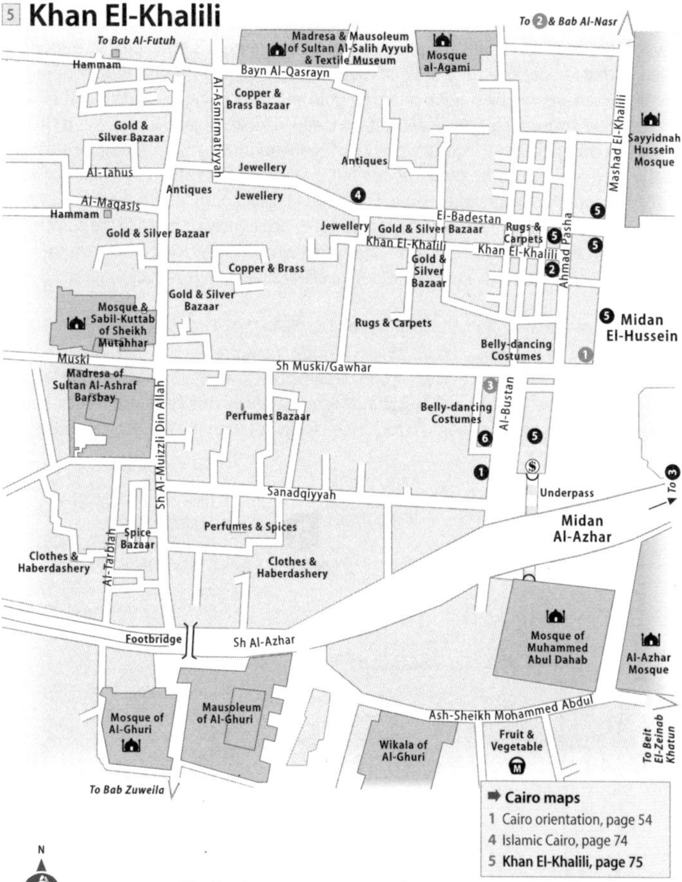

N
20 metres
20 yards

Sleeping
El Hussein **1**
El-Malky **2**
Radwan **3**

Eating
Egyptian Pancake House **1**
Fishawi's **2**
Gad **3**
Naguib Mafouz Coffee Shop & Khan El-Khalili **4**
Taj Al Sultan **5**
Tea/Cafés **6**

gold, silver, copper, perfume, spices, cloth or any one of a number of particular products. Many of the products are manufactured within the *souk*, often in small workshops behind or on top of the shops. If you're lucky or courageous enough to enquire, someone may welcome you in for a look around to see how things are made.

Known to locals simply as 'the Khan', this has been the main *souk* in Cairo since 1382 when it was first created around a caravanserai by Amir Jarkas Al-Khalil, the Master of Horse to the first of the Burji Mamluk Sultans, Al-Zahir Barquq (1382-1389). The caravanserai attracted many foreign and local traders and expanded rapidly to become a base for the city's subversive groups and was consequently frequently raided. Much of the area was rebuilt by Sultan Al-Ashraf Qansuh Al-Ghuri (1501-1517) but it still maintained its role as Cairo's main area for traders and craftsmen. It is essential to bargain because the traders will always start at about double the price they actually expect. It is traditional to respond by offering them about one third of what they originally quoted. This is not so for precious metals, which are sold by weight, prices for gold and silver being given daily in the paper. On a bracelet for example a small percentage is added for workmanship, and this is the only thing that is negotiable. Antique jewellery is of course more expensive. Today the main area of the *souk* is occupied by tourist shops but a few of the streets to the west are more authentic and much more interesting. For a more baladi (local) feeling there's the Muski: leading west away from the Khan, Sharia Muski gets increasingly crowded to the point where pedestrian traffic has to shuffle along in lanes, cramming sideways to let hand-carts towering with bundles trundle past, while the wares on offer range from pyramids to plastic goods.

Mosque of Al-Azhar ⓘ *See plan page 76, Sat-Thu 0900-1500, Fri 0900-1100 and 1300-1500. Tip any guides. No bare legs allowed, shawls provided for women.*
On the southwest of Midan El-Hussein, an underpass below busy Sharia Al-Azhar leads to the famous and very influential **Al-Azhar Mosque and University** whose leader, known as the Sheikh Al-Azhar, is appointed for life and is Egypt's supreme theological authority.

Mosque of Al-Azhar

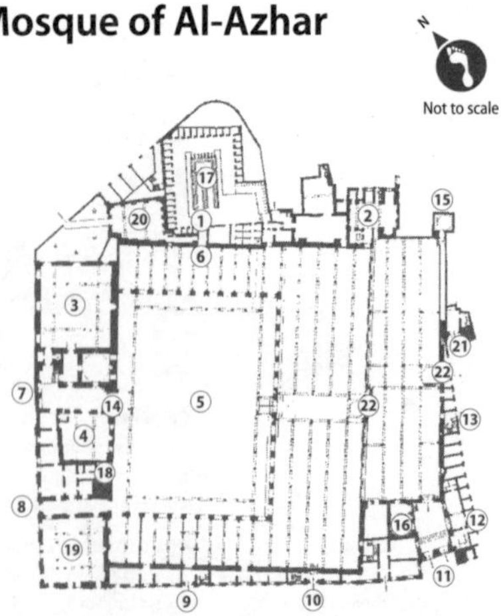

1 Entrance
2 Gawhar Medersa
3 Aqbugha Medersa
4 Taybars Medersa
5 Sahn
6 Bab Qaitbai (Barber's Gate)
7 Bab al-Muzayyinin
8 Bab al-Abbas
9 Bab al-Maghariba
10 Bab al-Shawam
11 Bab al-Saayidal
12 Bab al-Haramayn
13 Bab al-Shurbah
14 Bab and minaret of Qaitbai
15 Tomb of Sitt Nafisa
16 Tomb of Abdel al-Rahman Karkhuda
17 Toilets
18 Minaret of Qahnsuh al-Ghawri
19 Riwaq of Abbas II
20 Riwaq Al-Hanafiyyah
21 Qibla
22 Mihrab

The mosque was built in AD 970 and established as a university in AD 988 which, despite a counter-claim by Fes' Qarawiyin Mosque in Morocco, may make it the world's oldest university. With the exception of the main east *liwan*, however, little remains of the original building because additions and modifications were made by successive rulers, including modern buildings to the north, designed to house the university's administration block. The latest addition is an unsightly fence around the outside that seems to serve no purpose at all.

During the Shi'a Fatimid era (AD 969-1171), the university was used as a means to propagate the Shi'a faith in a predominantly Sunni city, but it fell into disrepair under Salah Al-Din and his successor Ayyubids (Sunni Muslim rulers), before being reopened by the Bahri Mamluks (1250-1382) and eventually becoming a bastion of Sunni orthodoxy. Later, during the rise in Arab nationalism in the late 19th and early 20th centuries, Al-Azhar became a stronghold for independent thinkers and it was from here that in 1956 President Nasser made his speech against the Suez invasion.

The entrance to the mosque is through the **Barber's Gate** (where students traditionally had their hair shaved), which was built in the second half of the 15th century by Qaitbay. This opens out on to the 10th-century Fatimid *sahn* (courtyard) overlooked by three minarets. With the exception of the Mamluk *madresa* (theological schools) surrounding the *sahn*, most of the buildings date back to the Fatimid period. Take the opportunity to climb one of the five minarets for an excellent view over the surrounding area.

North of Al-Azhar

On the north side of Midan El-Hussein, opposite the Al-Azhar complex, is the **Sayyidnah Hussein Mosque**, Cairo's official mosque where some 10,000 people pray daily and where dignitaries worship on important occasions. This is closed to non-Muslims. This mosque is named after, and contains the head of, the Prophet Mohammed's grandson Hussein. The rest of his body is perhaps in Iraq. He was killed at Karbala in AD 680 at the climax of the struggle that led to the early schism in the Muslim world between the orthodox Sunni (followers of the way) and the Shi'a (party) followers of Ali. Hussein, son of Mohammed's daughter Fatima, was the father of the Prophet's only direct descendants, who revere Hussein as a martyr and a popular saint like his sister Zeinab. His mosque is the focus of his annual *moulid*, one of Cairo's most important, chaotic and intense festivals that is held over a fortnight during the month of Rabi El-Tani, attracting thousands who camp in the streets.

Midan Hussein to Bayn Al-Qasrayn From Midan Hussein, walking 200 m west along Sharia Muski brings you to the intersection with Sharia Al-Muizzli Din Allah. On the southwest corner of the crossroads is the **Madresa of Sultan Al-Ashraf Barsbay** (1422-1437). This liberal and enlightened Mamluk Sultan, originally from the Caucasus, financed his capture of Cyprus in 1426 by turning the spice trade (which is based just to the south of his *madresa*) into a state monopoly. The *madresa* is cruciform in plan with the *sabil-kuttab* near the entrance, marked by a splendid onion-shaped dome. An offset corridor leads into the courtyard containing two marble tombs, those of the wife and the son of the sultan who is himself buried in the Northern Cemetery. Though not remarkable architecturally, the exterior is splendidly striped and the interior a peaceful haven, heady with the scent of spices – still intoxicating from the top of the minaret.

At the northwest corner is the **Mosque and Sabil-Kuttab of Sheikh Mutahhar**, erected in 1744. Turn right at the crossroads and head north along Sharia Al-Muizz passing some of the many goldsmiths and coppersmith shops. These are concentrated in

Islamic Cairo: suggested routes

- North from Al-Azhar via the concentration of buildings in the **Qalaoun/Al-Nasir/Barquq complex**, to the **Al-Hakim Mosque** at the north gates of the old city. See page 77.
- South from Al-Azhar to the **Al-Muayyad Mosque** that stands at the **Bab Zuweila** gate at the south edge of the old city and the buildings on Sharia Darb Al-Ahmar to the **Sultan Hassan Mosque** and the modern **Al-Rifai Mosque**. See page 84.
- West from the Citadel, continuing to the mosques and museums in the imposing fortress and the huge ancient **Ahmed Ibn Tulun Mosque**. See page 97.
- To the mosques and tombs in the **City of the Dead**, which lies in the 'Northern Cemetery' to the east of Islamic Cairo. See page 100.

The ancient **Al-Azhar Mosque** and the nearby *souqs* in the **Khan El-Khalili** district are at the centre of modern-day Islamic Cairo.

the alleys to the right, including the actual Sharia Khan El-Khalili. If you have time and want to get away from other tourists, strike off into the warren of goldsmiths' stalls on the left of the street where you will happen upon ash-coloured mosques and monumental houses that are not yet part of the restoration programme. If you get lost, just ask anyone to point you back in the direction of Muski or the Khan.

On the right-hand side of the Sharia Al-Muizz, on the site of the former slave market, is the **Madresa and Mausoleum of Sultan Al-Salih Ayyub** (1240-1249) who was the last of the Ayyubid Sultans and the first to introduce the foreign Mamluk slave-soldiers. Look for the minaret set back behind the shops, which at first glance looks as though the top has fallen off but is in fact the only remaining example of an Ayyubid 'pepperpot' or 'incense-burner' crown left in Cairo. The **Sabil-Kuttab of Khesruw Basha** protudes from the restored outer wall, and is free to enter. Further on is Ayyub's mausoleum, a serene final resting place for his wooden cenotaph, with walls enhanced by two beautifully painted and embossed Koranic borders. The domed ceiling contains stained-glass windows and is hung with lamps, and the columns and *mihrab* are of striped black, white and ruby-coloured marble. The *madresa* is special because it was the first to include all four of Egypt's schools of law, while the tomb was the first of any sultans to be placed next to the *madresa* of its founder. Previously, all tombs were built inside the necropolis so this marks the beginning of what was to become the standard Mamluk mosque-*madresa*-mausoleum formula, initiated by Ayyub's wife Shagarat Al-Durr (Tree of Pearls).

Housed in the restored *sabil-kuttab* of Mohamed Ali is the **Textile Museum** ⓘ *daily 0900-1930 (winter), 0900-2200 (summer), entrance E£20, students E£10, no photos*, which illuminates the 7000-year history of weaving in Egypt. The museum is uncrowded and crammed with beautiful and colourful pieces, ranging from pharaonic times to the last days of the royal family. The ground floor starts by displaying linens from ancient Egypt, including gloves from a mummy, a baby's nappy found at Deir Al-Medina in Luxor, and shrouds bearing the image of Osiris. One of the earliest-known textiles is a fragment of linen from Fayoum, dating to 4400 BC, two millennia older than the Giza Pyramids. The ancient weavers also embroidered and decorated the cloths with faience beads, gold and pieces of coloured glass. In the second room, look up to see the restored ceiling. The rich tradition of Coptic weaving is well-represented, with bold colours depicting human figures and stylized leaves and flowers. Look out for the 18th century priest's vestements, decorated with images of the apostles and the virgin and child. The Coptic displays continue on the upper level, and it is clear to see how their traditions were incorporated by the Umayyad weavers, though Christian symbols were replaced by Islamic motifs and scripts. The sultans brought weaving under government control, and commissioned lavish clothing, while Byzantine emperors, Roman popes and the European courts all dressed in Egyptian-made fabrics. Impressive are the pieces of the *qiswa*, the cloth which covers the *ka'aba* in Mecca and was produced in Egypt until the 20th century. These black curtains of embroidered silk could weigh up to half a tonne.

Opposite, with a wonderful unbroken 185-m-long façade, stands an amazing complex of *madresas* founded by three of the most influential medieval sultans, Qalaoun, Al-Nasir and Barquq. This section of the street is known as **Bayn Al-Qasrayn** (Between Two Palaces) because in the Fatimid period the magnificent great Western Palace and Eastern Palace stood on either side. Nothing is left of these now except the name, which also inspired the title of Naguib Mahfouz's first book in his *Cairo Trilogy*, usually translated as 'Palace Walk'. The three buildings have recently opened to the public after a successful restoration process, and are open from 0900-2100 daily (entrance free).

Qalaoun Complex ⓘ *a bit of baksheesh gets you up the minaret*. The earliest and most impressive *maristan-madresa-mausoleum* was built by Sultan Al-Mansur Qalaoun Al-Alfi (1280-1290). Like so many other Mamluk ('possessed') slave-soldiers he was a Kipchak Turk who used the name Al-Alfi because he was originally bought for the high price of 1000 (or *alf*) dinars. He subsequently diluted the influence of his own Kipchaks amongst the Mamluks by importing Circassians whom he billeted in the Citadel. These Burgis Mamluks (*burg* meaning 'tower') were rivals to the Bahri Mamluks (1250-1382) stationed on Roda Island and eventually created their own dynasty (1382-1517). Qalaoun was a constant headache to the Crusaders and eventually died of a fever in 1290 aged 79, on an expedition to recapture Acre.

The complex, built on the site of the Fatimid's Western Palace, only took just 13 months to complete in 1284-1285. It includes a *madresa* and mausoleum to the left and right, respectively, of a 10-m-high corridor that led to the *maristan*. Visit the mosque/*madresa* first, which has Syrian-style glass mosaics on the hood of the *mihrab* and is a beautifully proportioned and impressive space. But save yourself for the beauty of the mausoleum as it's like stepping inside a jewellery box. The restored ceilings are brilliantly coloured and gilded, tinted glass casts subtle light, ancient granite pillars and marble inlays all ornament the interior, while the dome soars 30 m above. The tomb of Qalaoun and his son Al-Nasir Mohammed is in the middle of the room surrounded by a beautifully carved *mashrabiya* screen.

Al-Nasir Complex To the north is the Sultan Al-Nasir Mohammed complex that was started by Sultan Kitbugha in 1295 and finished by Al-Nasir during his second reign in 1304, an era commemorated by over 30 mosques and other public buildings throughout the city. The nine-year-old Mohamed was elected Sultan when Qalaoun's eldest son Khalil was assassinated in 1294, only to be deposed a year later by the Mongol regent Kitbugha. Lajin (1297-1299) forced Kitbugha into exile, but he didn't last long either and was assassinated while playing chess. Following this chapter of 'accidents', Mohammed was restored to the throne, but was kept in terrible conditions by his regent until he escaped to Jordan 10 years later. He eventually returned with a large army the following year, executed his enemies, and ruled unchallenged for another 30 years until his death in 1341.

The complex consists of a mosque, *madresa* and tomb. It is worth going in to see the *qibla* wall, which still has its original decoration and Kufic inscriptions. The fabulous Gothic doorway was filched from one of the Crusader churches at Acre by Al-Nasir's elder brother, Khalil.

Barquq Complex This is followed to the north by the *madresa* and tomb that make up the Sultan Barquq complex, built in 1384-1386. The marble entrance and the silver-encrusted bronze-plated door are very impressive and lead through an offset corridor to the *sahn*, which has four *liwans* arranged in a cruciform shape. The *qibla liwan*, to the east, is divided into three aisles by four massive pharaonic columns that support beautifully carved ceilings painted blue and gold. Upstairs there are cells for the Sufi monks who once inhabited the building. From the *madresa* a door leads to the marble-walled mausoleum where Sultan Barquq was originally buried before being transferred to the mausoleum specially built by his son Al-Nasir Farag in the city's Northern Cemetery (see below).

Sultan Al-Zahir Barquq (1382-1389 and 1390-1399), whose name means 'plum', reigned twice and was the founder of the dynasty of Circassian slave-soldiers who became the Burgis Mamluk rulers of Egypt. He was reportedly an enlightened ruler, who admired piety and intelligence and surrounded himself with learned scholars, before dying of pneumonia aged 60 in 1399.

Palaces and madresas Besides the Qalaoun/Al-Nasir/Barquq complex, there are a number of other interesting, if less important, buildings on and near the east side of the street on the route north to the Al-Hakim mosque. This area, which is the heart of Islamic Cairo, is definitely worth exploring if you have a full day.

Directly opposite the Qalaoun complex is Sharia Beit Al-Qadi. About 40 m down on the left-hand side stands the modern-looking house, No 19, marked with a green plaque. Visitors should knock to be shown around in return for a little *baksheesh*, someone will find the key if it is not open. This is the remains of a palace built in 1350 but better known as the **House of Uthman Kathuda** who restored it during the 18th century.

Further north opposite Barquq's complex are the remains of the **Palace of Amir Bashtak** (Al-Nasir's son-in-law) built in 1334-1339 and a fine example of the domestic architecture of the time. The original five-storey structure has been reduced to two and the windows in the rather plain façade are covered with *mashrabiyya*. Access is via an offset courtyard to the left of the complex. After you have had a peek at the courtyard, continue down the alley through the door at the end, where Mohamed Ali's *fuul* cart lies waiting in case you need some sustenance (see Eating, page 134).

Sabil-Kuttab of Abd Al-Rahman Kutkhuda ⓘ *Daily 0830-1730, tickets E£10, students E£5.* There used to be many of the these Ottoman-influenced *sabil-kuttab* throughout Cairo, which combine a water supply for the public at street level and a Koranic school in the building above. A fair few remain but this is a particularly elegant example, built in 1744 by a powerful *amir* seeking absolution for his former sins. Standing on a triangular piece of land where the road forks in two, the building is tall and slim. A beautifully carved timber screen on the upper storey protects the *kuttab* on its three open sides and the balcony (now unfortunately glassed in) permits a good view. Below, the double arches are supported by delicate columns. The *sabil* is entirely faced with gorgeous aquamarine and turquoise Syrian tiles, including a depiction of the *Kaba'a* at Mecca. The circular well from which the water supply was drawn is tucked away in the little room to the back of the sabil.

Sugar and spice and all things nice

A visit to the spice market (Souk Al-Attarin) is highly recommended both for the visual impact and the tremendous aromas. Anything that could possibly be wanted in the way of herbs, spices, henna, dried and crushed flowers and incense are on display, piled high on the ancient pavements in massive burlap bags or secreted away in tin boxes in various drawers inside. Ask if what you want does not appear to be in stock but do not be fobbed off with old merchandise, fresh spices are always available. Prices are extremely low by Western standards and shopkeepers are prepared to sell small amounts, weighing out the purchase into a little paper cornet. Saffron is the best buy, far cheaper than at home, but sometimes only the local rather than higher-quality Iranian saffron is available. The main street of the spice market runs parallel to Sharia Al-Muizzli Din Allah beginning at the Ghuriyya. Here, many of the shops have been in the same family for over 200 years. Some of the owners are also herbalists (*etara*), practising traditional medicine and offering cures for everything from bad breath to rheumatism. Cairo's most famous herbalist, however, is Abdul Latif Mahmoud Harraz, 39 Sharia Ahmed Maher, near Bab El-Khalq. Founded in 1885, the shop attracts a devoted following throughout the Middle East.

The Arabic names for the more common herbs and spices are:

Allspice	*kebab es-seeny*
Arabic gum	*mystica*
Bay leaf	*warra randa*
Basil	*rihan*
Cardamon	*habbahan*
Cayenne	*shatta*
Celery salt	*boudra caraffs*
Chervil leaves	*kozbarra*
Chilli	*filfil ahmar*
Cinnamon	*erfa*
Cloves	*orumfil*
Coriander	*kosbara*
Cumin	*kamoon*
Fennel	*shamar*
Ginger	*ginzabeel*
Horseradish	*figl baladi*
Mace	*bisbassa*
Marjoram	*bardakosh*
Mint	*naanaa*
Oregano	*zaatar*
Paprika	*filfil ahmar roumi*
Peppercorns	*filfil eswed*
Rosemary	*hassa liban*
Saffron	*zaa'faran*
Sage	*maryameya*
Savory	*stoorya*
Sesame	*semsem*
Tarragon	*tarkhoun*
Turmeric	*korkom*

If you don't feel like paying, you can squint through the glass from the street to get an idea, but then you'll miss out on the exquisitely painted ceilings in the *kuttab* above.

Mosque of Al-Aqmar About 75 m further north on the right up the main road is the Mosque of Al-Aqmar that was built in 1121-1125 by the Fatimid Vizier of Khalifa Al-Amir (1101-1131). It was originally at the northeast corner of the great eastern Fatimid palace. It is particularly important for three reasons: it was the first Cairo mosque with a façade following the alignment of the street, rather than the *qibla* wall, so that its ground plan was adjusted to fit into an existing urban environment; it was the first to have a decorated stone façade, the colour giving it its name, which means moonlight; and it introduced the shell motif and the stalactite, which subsequently became favourites in Cairo, into architectural styles.

The mosque has been restored over the centuries. Amir Yalbugha Al-Salami restored the *minbar*, *mihrab* and ablution area in 1393 and added the minaret in 1397. The minaret was apparently removed in 1412 because it had started leaning, but the current structure includes the original first storey, which is made of brick covered with unusual carved stucco decorated with chevron patterns. Because the street level has risen since the mosque was built there are steps down to the entrance, which is offset from the main part of the mosque. Despite its importance and unique features, the original interior of the mosque is unspectacular. Around the base of the almost square *sahn* the arches bear Koranic verses in the early angular and unpointed Kufic script on an arabesque background.

Beit Al-Suhaymi ⓘ *Daily 0900-1700 or until 1500 during Ramadan, E£30, students E£15, entrance includes 2 other buildings: the Beit Kharazati next door and the Beit El-Gaafar nearby.* Take the next right-hand turn for a detour to Darb Al-Asfar, a highly renovated street that presumably gives an idea of what the whole of Gamaliya will look like once the restorers have finished their job. Here is the Beit Al-Suhaymi, built in 1648 and 1796 and inhabited until 1961, one of the finest examples of a luxurious Mamluk mansion in the whole of the city. Beautifully restored, it has a lovely courtyard and a *haramlik* (harem) for the women with superb tiling and a domed bathroom. It is the wonderfully atmospheric venue for weekly folk music and songs, plus occasional special events and performances particularly during Ramadan.

Returning to the main street and continuing north, one reaches the **Mosque and Sabil-Kuttab of Suleyman Agha Al-Silahdar** ⓘ *0900-1700, during Ramadan 0800-1500*, built in 1837-1839 by one of Mohammed Ali's ministers who also built many other *sabils* throughout the city. The style of the building is very much influenced by the contemporary style in Istanbul including the minaret with an Ottoman-style cylindrical shaft and pointed conical top. It is now being restored.

Mosque of Al-Hakim ⓘ *Entrance free, but aggressive demands for* baksheesh *to climb the minarets. Almost as good views can be had from the top of the Northern Walls.* At the north end of Sharia Muizz is the giant Mosque of Al-Hakim, named after the third Fatimid caliph, abutting the **North Wall** of the old city of Fustat and commemorating its most notorious ruler. It was begun in AD 990 by the Shi'a Muslim Fatimid Khalifa Al-Aziz and was eventually finished some 23 years later by his son who took the name **Al-Hakim bi-Amr Allah** (Ruler by God's Command) and ruled between AD 996-1021.

Possibly having a Christian wife was the reason why his reportedly tolerant and humane father Al-Aziz had been more forbearing towards Christians and Jews than towards the indigenous Sunni Muslim population. In contrast his son was intolerant of everyone (see box, page 85). With such a colourful history, the enormous mosque itself is actually rather plain. It is organized around a large central *sahn* and built of bricks with a large porch in the traditional Fatimid style. It has been restored many times throughout the centuries, notably after the major earthquake in 1302 and by Sultan Al-Hassan in 1359. Originally the two minarets stood separate from the walls; the huge salients, added in 1010 to strengthen them, are in fact hollow shells. After the 14th century it was converted to house Crusader prisoners-of-war, then was used as a stable by Salah Al-Din, during the French occupation it was a fortified warehouse, and in the mid-19th century it stored items destined for the Museum of Islamic Art. Since 1980 the mosque has been practically rebuilt in white marble by the Indian-based Bohra sect of Ismaili Muslims, who claim direct spiritual descent from the Fatimid imams whom they worship.

The Northern Walls ⓘ *Keys and a 'guide' can be found if you enquire by Bab Al-Nasr, at the wooden shack just south of the gate. E£5* baksheesh *should cover things.* The northern walls and gates of the Fatimid city are a masterpiece of military architecture (although they were were never actually put to the test by a siege) and are monumentally impressive when viewed from the main street beyond. At present, access is through the square-towered **Bab Al-Nasr** (Gate of Victory), where French troops that were garrisoned here during Napoleon's occupation renamed the towers – 'Tour Juien', 'Courbin' and 'Pascal' are neatly engraved above the doorways. From the towers there are views out to the Bab Al-Nasr cemetery opposite, an organic mixture of tombs and ramshackle houses. Walking the dark 200-m-long stretch of wall between Bab Al-Nasr to Bab Al-Futuh you appreciate how soldiers could move between the two towers under cover, stealthily firing arrows through slits in the walls. Towards the end of the tunnel, a block of masonry on the right is carved with pharaonic inscriptions and there are more on the stairs showing processions of oxen and a hippopotamus, pieces of Memphis being reused. The round towers of **Bab Al-Futuh** (Open Gate) are a mirror of Bab Zuweila at the southern boundary of the Fatimid City, just discernable in the distance from the top of the gate. Walk back to Bab Al-Nasr along the top of the wall, noting holes in the floor through which boiling oil could be poured on enemies, and to get a good look at Al-Hakim's mosque and minarets.

Sharia Al-Gamaliya Taking you south back to Midan Al-Hussein, Sharia Al-Gamaliya has several fine old buildings but many of them are works in progress and will be open to the public later in 2011. The **Khanqah of Beybars Al-Gashankir**, on the left side, is the oldest sufi monastery in Cairo dating from 1310. Beybars was sultan for only a year, and when Al-Nasir Mohammed came back to power he had him flogged and strangled, and obliterated his name from the façade of the khanqah. If you can get inside, the marbling is particularly beautiful, otherwise look for the bulbous dome of the exterior and the rare turquoise tiles on top of the minaret.

The **Madresa-Mausoleum of Tatar Al-Higaziya** is in a small street that connects Sharia Al-Gamalia with Midan Beit Al-Qadi. Tatar was the daughter of Sultan Al-Nasir Mohammed, the sister of Sultan Hassan and the wife of the Amir Baktimur Al-Higazi. Little else is known about her except that she died of the plague in 1360, yet her tomb is still visited by women seeking her blessing. Built in two phases, the mausoleum for her murdered husband dates from 1347 and the palace itself was converted into a *madresa* in 1360, which explains the irregular shape.

Entrance to the building leads via a porch with a lovely ceiling into the *sahn*. The octagonal minaret to the southwest of the *sahn* has been missing its top for over a century. Access to the minaret, the ablution area and storage areas are all via doors off the *liwans*. The ribbed stone dome over the mausoleum, one of the earliest in Cairo, is on the corner of two streets and passers-by can solicit a blessing or invoke a prayer via the open windows. The restoration work carried out in the 1980s was done with care and consideration.

At the next crossroads are a couple of towering *wikalas*, and standing beneath them gives a sense that this alley was indeed once the second-most major thoroughfare of the medieval city. On the west side, the **Wikala Al-Bazara** ⓘ *daily 0900-1700, E£20, students E£10*, though largely rebuilt, is a good example of the layout of the caravanserai. Downstairs, the animals were stabled and goods stored, while the merchants slept on the upper floors. Further east is the void where once stood the Ottoman **Musafirkhana Palace** (House of Guests). What used to be a rather fine rambling building, constructed between 1779 and 1788 by the merchant Mohammed Muharram, burnt to a crisp in 1998. There is talk of rebuilding it, but it probably won't happen for at least another decade.

South of Al-Azhar

The lanes south from Al-Azhar mosque have a number of very interesting buildings including the **Mosque of Sultan Al-Muayyad Sheikh** at the medieval **Bab Zuweila**. Further to the south of Fustat is the **Sultan Hassan Mosque** and the much more modern **Al-Rifai Mosque**, which stand side by side below the mighty **Citadel** (see page 94). One can then head west to the huge and very old **Mosque of Ahmed Ibn Tulun** and the nearby **Gayer-Anderson House**. Allow a minimum of half a day to take in all the sights on a tour of the southern part of Islamic Cairo.

Butneya Immediately to the south of Al-Azhar is an area known as **Butneya**, once notorious as the base for Cairo's underworld where drugs were openly traded by powerful and locally popular gangsters. After a major crackdown in 1988 most of them left, but the area is still home to minor local gangs who tend to prey on shops, restaurants and middle-class Egyptians rather than on tourists. Directly behind Al-Azhar mosque is the **Wikala and Sabil-Kuttab of Sultan Qaitbay**, the first of two hostels founded by this sultan, found along the alley that terminates in a little square where three houses are open to the public. The most rewarding is first on the left, the **Beit El-Zeinab Khatoun** ⓘ *daily 0900-1700, E£20, students E£10*, which dates from 1468, was rebuilt in 1713, and restored in 1996. It is worth visiting for its excellent views over Al-Azhar and to appreciate the function of *mashrabiya* windows, designed to let the breezes cool water in earthenware pots placed in the screens. Opposite, across the square, is the **Beit Al-Harawi** ⓘ *daily 0900-1700, E£20, students E£10*, with a grand ground-floor reception room, handsomely decorated and adorned with Koranic inscriptions. Concerts are frequently held here, check www.weekly-ahram.org.eg. The adjoining **Beit El-Set Wasela** has recently opened to the public after being largely rebuilt. It is now a cultural venue used for performances of Arabic poetry; it is free to wander around the warren-like structure, and although most rooms are empty there is a beautiful painting on the interior walls. Also on the square is a very chic homeware and interiors shop, while back on the alley behind Al-Azhar are the most famous book-binders in the city, both worth having a browse through on the way past (see Shopping, page 143).

The Wikala, Mosque-Madresa and Mausoleum of Al-Ghuri ⓘ *Wikala 0900-1800, E£15 students E£8; Mosque-Madresa 0900-2000, entrance free although* baksheesh *very much expected; Mausoleum and Sabil-Kuttab, 0900-1700, E£20 students E£10.* Immediately to the south of the Al-Azhar complex are a few of the 20 remaining *wikalas* (hostels for merchants that were usually above a bonded warehouse for their goods), which numbered over 200 in the 1830s. The restored **Wikala of Sultan Al-Ashraf Qansuh Al-Ghuri**, originally built in 1504, is down the backstreet off the southwest corner of Al-Azhar. Four floors high, the façade has an impressive array of windows and the rooms upstairs where traders from around the world would have slept, have now been converted into workshops for artisans; a selection of handicrafts made by artisans in for sale in the building next door. It is best to come on a Monday, Wednesday or Saturday night when it's the venue for a free Sufi concert.

Back on Sharia Al-Azhar, next to the footbridge, is the Ghuriyya, the magnificent complex of Sultan Al-Ashraf Qansuh Al-Ghuri (1501-1517), which is bisected by a continuation of Sharia Al-Muizzli Din Allah. The complex is made up of the **mausoleum and sabil-kuttab** to the east of the street and the **mosque-madresa** to the west. Built in 1504-1505, this was the last great Mamluk public building before the Ottoman conquest. Al-Ghuri died of a stroke, aged about 76, during a battle near Aleppo against the Turks,

Al-Hakim – the vanishing despot

In AD 996 at the age of 11 Al-Hakim succeeded his father as the second Egyptian Fatimid Khalifa and began a despotic reign. At the age of 15 he had his tutor assassinated and started his extremely cruel and relentless persecution of Christians, Jews, Sunni Muslims, women and dogs. He prohibited any Christian celebrations and had the Church of the Holy Sepulchre in Jerusalem demolished. He also prohibited Sunni ceremonies and tried to established Shi'a Islam as the only form of Islam. Women were forbidden to leave their homes and, in order to enforce this, cobblers were not permitted to make or sell women's shoes. At one time all of Cairo's dogs were exterminated because their barking annoyed him. Merchants who were found to have cheated their customers were summarily sodomized by his favourite Nubian slave while Al-Hakim stood on their head. Wine, singing, dancing and chess were also prohibited and the punishments for disobeying these laws were very severe and usually resulted in a gruesome death.

His erratic rule, with laws often changing overnight, led to tensions within Fustat/Cairo, particularly between the various religious communities. In 1020, the news that Al-Hakim was about to proclaim that he was a manifestation of Allah provoked serious riots to which he responded by sending in his Sudanese troops to burn down the city where they clashed not only with the civilians, but also the Turkish and Berber soldiers. An alternative story is that one particular quarter of Fustat was torched because he thought that was where his favourite sister Sitt Al-Mulk (Lady of Power) took her lovers, but when she was proved to be a virgin by the midwives he examined the ruins and asked: "Who ordered this?" Whatever the truth, he then sent his chief theologian Al-Darazi to Syria for safety where he is believed to have originated the theology of the Druze who consider Al-Hakim to be divine.

Despite his ruthless public acts Al-Hakim's personal life was very abstemious and he was a very generous alms-giver. He took to riding around the city and surrounding countryside on a donkey with only a couple of servants but disappeared in February 1021. Following the discovery of his knife-slashed robe, it is believed he was murdered, possibly on the instructions of Sitt Al-Mulk with whom he apparently argued because of her refusal to begin an incestuous marriage with him. The fact that his body was never discovered led the Druze to believe that he had retreated from the world to return at a later date, while the Copts believe that he had a vision of Jesus, repented and became a monk.

who then immediately invaded and captured Egypt to begin their lengthy rule from 1517 to 1805. Because Al-Ghuri's body was never found he could not be buried in his magnificent and hugely expensive tomb and his successor, Tumanbey, who was hanged to death from the Bab Zuweila, occupied it in his place. The mausoleum's interior of black and white marble appears almost art deco, the floor is a patchwork of patterns, and the walls are carved in an arabesque design. Open the wooden doors in the walls to reveal the rich green and red paintwork on the insides. The dome up above was the crux of the restoration process. Having already collapsed three times since it was first built, the current project opted for a flat drum-topped solution that can be seen from the roof but not from below. The adjacent room, now also used for concerts, has an impressive

The hammam

A visit to the hammam or Turkish bath is still part of life for many Egyptians. Some Egyptian families have no bathing facilities at home and rely on the public hammam. A ritual purification of the body is essential before Muslims can perform prayers, and even for the well-off classes in the days before bathrooms, the 'major ablutions' were generally done at the hammam. Segregation of the sexes is of course the rule at the hammam: some establishments are open only for women, others only for men, while others have a shift system (mornings and evenings for the men, all afternoon for women). In the old days, the hammam, along with the local *zaouia* or saint's shrine, was an important place for women to gather and socialize, and even pick out a potential wife for a son.

In the older parts of the cities, the hammam is easily recognizable by the characteristic colours of its door. A passage leads into a large changing room-cum-post-bath rest area, equipped with masonry benches for lounging on and (sometimes) small wooden lockers. Here one undresses under a towel.

This is the procedure. First into the hot room: 5-10 minutes with your feet in a bucket of hot water will see you sweating nicely, and you can then move back to the raised area where the masseurs are at work. After the expert removal of large quantities of dead skin, you go into one of the small cabins or *mathara* to finish washing. (Before doing this, catch the person bringing in dry towels, so that they can bring yours to you when you're in the *mathara*.) For women, in addition to a scrub and a wash, there may be the pleasures of an epilation with *sokar*, an interesting mix of caramelized sugar and lemon. Men can undergo a *taksira*, which involves much pulling and stretching of the limbs. And remember, allow plenty of time to cool down, while reclining in the changing area.

In Cairo, you can visit the 18th-century **Hammam El-Malatili**, 40 Sharia Amir El-Gyushi (0700-1900) or the back alley **Hammam El-Tabbali**, 1 km east of Ramses on Bayn El-Haret. There are also a few hammams around the Bab Zuweila. Women can visit the **Hammam Beshtak**, a cleaner public bath, at Sharia El-Silah (1000-1700; men 1800-0800).

wooden *khankah* dome where stained-glass windows allow light onto the astonishing cedar wood ceilings. From the *sabil-kuttab* you can climb up to the roof to look at the clothes market below and admire the mosque opposite, which gives a real sense of passing back through the centuries.

After restoration, the stripy exterior of the mosque-*madresa* is stunning and once again looks like David Roberts' iconic painting from 1839. Inside the mosque (women have to cover their heads), the original stained-glass windows and exquisite marbles are a feast for the eyes. It's possible to watch prayer-time from the balcony above the women's section at the rear, and from the minaret (*baksheesh* will be expected to unlock the door) the views over Al-Azhar and all the way to the Citadel are fantastic.

Between Ghuriyya and Bab El-Zuweila The stretch of **Sharia Al-Muizz li-Din Allah** between the massive monuments of Al-Ghuri has been re-roofed in accordance with its original appearance when it was the site of the exotic silk market. Today mainly household goods and women's clothes are sold in the shops and stalls, throngs of ladies peruse underwear and crockery while motorbikes weave in between. Each section of this thoroughfare, Islamic Cairo's main street, was named after the merchandise sold in that particular stretch. For example the fruit-sellers had their own mosque, the **Fakahani Mosque** (rebuilt in 1735), about 200 m down the street on the left-hand side. Make a detour by walking left from its northwest corner and then left again where, 70 m to the east at No 6, is the **House of Gamal Al-Din Al-Dhahabi** ⓘ *daily 0900-1700, E£10, students E£5*, Cairo's richest gold merchant in 1637 when this beautiful house was built. After restoration, you can now visit the peaceful courtyard with a central fountain and see the finely painted wooden ceilings and magnificent inlaid marble dadoes of the interior rooms. Back to the south of the mosque, is the ornate **Sabil-Kuttab of Tusun Pasha** ⓘ *daily 0900-1700, E£10, students E£5*, built in his name by his father Mohammed Ali Pasha in 1820. From here the south gates of the ancient city are just ahead. Before going through the gates turn left at the *sabil-kuttab*. About 75 m along the side street is an old 18th-century men's bath-house known as **Hammam As-Sukariyah,** which was originally owned by a rich woman who also owned the nearby *wikala* and *sabil* of Nafisah Bayda. Although, like the other remaining bath-houses in the city, it is no longer a den of vice, it is still an interesting place to visit and relax. Today it helps the local community by allowing its fire for heating the water to be used to cook *fuul mudammas* (beans) for the locals' breakfast.

Bab Zuweila ⓘ *Daily 0830-1700, E£15, students E£8*. The Bab Zuweila, built by Badr Al-Gamali in 1092 when Fatimid fortifications were being reinforced, was one of the three main gates in the city walls. At 20 m high, with a 4.8-m-wide multi-storey arch between two solid stone towers topped by twin minarets, it presents a beautiful and impressive sight particularly from the south. It is named after mercenaries from the Al-Zuweila tribe of Berbers who were stationed in the nearby barracks. The gate was soon inside the city following the successive expansions and Salah Al-Din's construction of larger walls further out from the centre. Cairo was in effect divided into two with the inner walls still in existence and both sets of gates locked at night.

Bab Zuweila also has a more popular history linked to the annual caravans departing both to Mecca and the south, which the caliph used to watch depart from his window. It was not only the location of street performers including snake-charmers, storytellers and dancers, but after the 15th century it also became the site of grisly public executions. Common criminals were beheaded, garrotted or impaled, while cheating merchants were hanged from hooks or rope. Defeated Mamluk Sultans, including the last one in 1517, were hanged and sometimes nailed to the doors. Well into the 20th century, sick people came to Bab Zuweila to be cured by miraculous healings worked by the spirit of a saint. They would tie bits of clothing or an offending tooth to the knobs of the gate and rub their foreheads and chests against it, while praying to the saint, Zuweila. From the top of the minarets there is an excellent view over the surrounding area and the adjacent mosque.

Mosque of Sultan Al-Muayyad Sheikh Immediately to the west of the gate is the Mosque of Sultan Al-Muayyad Sheikh (1412-1421) built on the site of the old Kazanat Al-Shamaii prison. Al-Muayyad had been incarcerated here on a number of occasions because of his love of alcohol when he was a Mamluk slave-soldier. On being released after one particularly long and unpleasant stretch, he vowed to replace the prison with a mosque, which he began in 1415 after becoming Sultan.

The mosque, now repaired and restored, is sometimes known as the Red Mosque because of the colour of its external walls. It was one of the last to be built in the ancient large enclosure style before the Turkish style was adopted as the norm. The superb

Adhan – the call to prayer

Listening to the first call to prayer just before the sun begins to rise is an unforgettable experience. This is known as the *adhan* and is performed by the *muezzin*, originally by the strength of his own voice from near the top of the minaret but today is probably a recording timed to operate at a particular hour.

There is no fixed tune, but in Egypt there is one particular rhythm used all over the country for the *adhan*. The traditional Sunni *adhan* consists of seven phrases, with two additional ones for the morning prayer. There are some variations that the well-tuned ear will pick up.

1 **Allahu Akbar** (Allah is most great) is intoned four times. This phrase is called *al takbir*.

2 **Ashhadu anna la ilah ill'-Allah** (I testify that there is no god besides Allah) is intoned twice.

3 **Ashhadu anna Muhammadan rasul Allah** (I testify that Mohammed is the apostle of Allah) is intoned twice. This and the preceeding phrase are called the *shihada*, a confession of faith.

4 **Hayya 'ala 'l-salah** (come to prayer) is intoned twice.

5 **Hayya 'ala'l-falah** (come to salvation) is intoned twice. This and the preceeding phrase are called *tathwib*.

6 **Allahu Akbar** is intoned twice.

7 **La ilah ill'Allah** (there is no god besides Allah) is intoned once.

The two additions to the morning prayer are: **Al-salatu khayr min Al-nawm** (Prayer is better than sleep), which is intoned twice between the fifth and sixth phrases, and **Al-salatu wa'l-salam 'alayka ya rasul Allah** (Benediction and peace upon you, Oh Apostle of Allah) intoned after the seventh phrase.

bronze-plated wooden entrance doors leading to the mosque were originally intended for the Sultan Hassan Mosque but were purchased by Al-Muayyad and installed here. The entrance leads into a vestibule with an ornate stalactite ceiling. From the vestibule, the door on the left leads to Al-Muayyad's mausoleum and marble tomb with Kufic inscription, while nearby is the tomb of his son, Ibrahim, who died in 1420.

Down a little alley behind the mosque is a large and elegant building that looks like a small palace but is in fact the **Hammam Al-Muayyad** bath-house, built in 1420. This has fallen into disrepair and is now often flooded. The area between the two is known as Bab El-Khalq after a medieval gate that has long since vanished, and in the weeks before the start of Ramadan the shops here display row upon row of shiny lanterns in every possible size, shape and colour. The iconic *fanous* (lantern) is an Egyptian traditon that goes back to the time of the Fatamids and, while a large proportion are now imported from China and play absurd tunes and 'dance', traditional metal and glass designs are still hand-fashioned from old tin cans in tiny workshops.

From here a 20-minute walk or a five-minute taxi west of Bab Zuweila along Sharia Ahmed Maher brings you to the Museum of Islamic Art.

The Museum of Islamic Art ⓘ *Junction of Sharia Port Said and Sharia Qala'a equidistant between Midan Ataba and the Bab Zuweila, Daily 0800-1700, entrance E£50, students E£25, T02-2364 7822, T02-3390 9390. No photography; bags must be left at the entrance.*

This museum underwent lengthy renovations (various upsets delayed the restoration, from electrical fires to the collapse of its foundations when an ill-conceived extra floor was built) and reopened in October 2010. It contains the rarest and most extensive collection of

Islamic works of art in the world. It was originally established in the courtyard of the Mosque of Al-Hakim (see page 82) in 1880 but it was moved to the present building in 1903.

The recently re-opened Islamic Art Museum is a triumph. Carefully chosen exhibits from the museum's extensive store are displayed in a tasteful, uncluttered environment. The walls are a muted grey with white accents and pierced metal lamps resembling bird cages are hung in profusion. There has been great attention to detail in the refit, even the modern blinds echo traditional Islamic design.

From the ticket barrier, steps lead up to a small display area where a beautiful eighth-century Quran in Kufic script is on show. Around the walls are well-written information panels putting the periods in Egypt's history that are represented in the museum into context. The right side of the museum showcases items in chronological order, in rooms which encircle a 15th-century sunken fountain and an intricately decorated wooden ceiling panel. Passing a display case of enamelled glass mosque lamps leads you into a room of Umayyad and Abbasid items. Look out for the deeply carved stucco and wood friezes showing birds and a ninth-century coffin fragment inlaid with bone and ebony. Three rooms of Fatimid artefacts follow, with intricately decorated wood panels. In the final Fatimid room are two wonderfully carved 12th-century *mihrabs* (niches which show the direction of Mecca) and on the end wall is the original stucco *mihrab* from Ibn Tulun mosque. From here, you can exit to the courtyard, passing between a pair of elaborate door panels, to view the superb collection of *mashrabiyya* attached to the side of the building and perhaps visit the courtyard café.

Re-enter to rejoin galleries dedicated to the art of the Mamluks. Here, glass cases gather together colourful potsherds, brass ewers and small items of furniture. Most striking is a 14th-century Quran box/table inlaid with ivory and ebony. On the walls are framed panels of vivid, blue tiles decorated with plants, flowers and geometric shapes. The next Mamluk room contains fragments of ceramic bowls and tiles with designs including a bird and a deer. The two curved steel swords with gilt inlay and intricate calligraphy on the blades belonging to Al-Ghouri and Tumanbey are a highlight of this room. The final room on this side of the museum showcases carved wooden pieces, including an elaborate 14th-century *minbar* (pulpit) inlaid with ivory and bone. Leave here, passing a marble door which was a gift from the King of Afghanistan and more exquisitely coloured tile panels, to return to the central gallery.

The second half of the museum is arranged thematically. After the collection of Ottoman ceramics and gold coins, turn left to follow the rooms in a clockwise direction. The first room is dedicated to science and medicine; beautiful pages from illuminated Arab manuscripts on herbs are displayed, among other medical paraphernalia. Look out for the Iranian paper-thin cotton shirt covered with Quranic talismans, and a rich blood-red agate bowl. The next room is also science-related and showcases three complicated 18th-century Ottoman sundials, intricate astrolabes, compasses and hour glasses. Some stained-glass windows are backlit to reveal their true complexity, while an enormous stucco facade in the shape of a *mihrab* hangs over the sunken fountain. In the next room look for sections from a fountain decorated with highly realistic catfish. A glass case of metal flasks leads to a room exhibiting a profusion of ewers, mosque lamps and *mashrabiyya*. Wood and marble panels show examples of both Kufic and Cursive script, including deeds of ownership, carved on panels over 2 m long. Two rooms of delicate and exquisite textiles from Iran, Turkey, Yemen, Iraq and Egypt follow. Wool, cotton, silk, linen and silver thread are all used in the collection of carpets and tapestries. A large 17th-century Persian carpet made of wool lies under a finely-carved ceiling panel. In the room to the left carved tombstones show extraordinarily-skilled calligraphy. The majority of the stones are made of marble, but two striking basalt blocks from the 12th-century stand out. A giant wooden cenotaph from the Mosque of Al-Hussein is also on show. Complete Mamluk and Ottoman tombs are surrounded by cases of beautifully gilded manuscripts. Also notable are the 17th-century ceramic panels showing the Haram Al-Sharif in Mecca. Vibrant panels of rich blue-green, 14th-century Iranian tiles are on the wall. Exit this gallery and walk past a huge, ornate carved wooden panel with a built-in Quran niche to your right. This is from Rashid (Rosetta) and dates from the 17th century. On your left four exquisite, 18th-century jewellery boxes from India inlaid with ivory can be seen. They have many tiny drawers and compartments and show such a high level of craftsmanship that in any other museum they might be the highlight. Finally, walk through the long gallery (leading back to the entrance), which is dedicated to works of art from Iran. Highlights include exquisitely inlaid 17th-century door panels, metal lamps, coffee pots and mirrors, alongside bird-shaped incense burners. Particularly fetching are the bowls decorated with animals, depicting lifelike camels and delicately painted human figures. A large 13th-century, hammered and inlaid copper alloy candlestick is decorated with a line of ducks around its top and lions round the base.

Bab Zuweila to the Tentmakers From the south of Bab Zuweila there are two routes you can take to reach the **Sultan Hassan** and **Al-Rifai mosques** that stand north of the Citadel. One is to continue straight along what is officially known as Sharia Al-Muizzli Din Allah but which, like so many other long roads, changes its name in different sections and at this point is also known as Sharia Al-Khiyamiyya, or the Tentmakers' bazaar because of its colourful fabrics market. After about 1 km you reach a major crossroads where you should turn left (southeast) along Sharia Al-Qala'a, which leads to the rear of the two mosques. A much more interesting route includes a few nearby sites on Sharia Al-Khiyamiyya before heading east along Sharia Darb Al-Ahmar, after which the whole area is named, towards the Citadel.

Immediately south of the gates are two buildings that are bisected by Sharia Al-Khiyamiyya. To the west is the *zawiya* (Sufi monastery) and *sabil* (public fountain) of **Sultan Al-Nasir Farag** (1405-1412) who was Barquq's son and successor (now open to the public). To the east is the much more magnificent **Mosque of Vizier Al-Salih Tala'i**, which was both the last Fatimid mosque and, when it was built in 1160, was the country's first suspended mosque resting on top of a series of small vaulted shops which, with the rise in the street level, are now in the basement. Tala'i reportedly died regretting the construction of the mosque because, being directly outside the walls of the city, it could be used as a fortress by an enemy.

The great earthquake of 1303 destroyed the minaret, which was restored together with the rest of the mosque by Amir Baktimur Al-Gukandar (Polo-Master) and subsequently in 1440, 1477 and lastly and very badly in the 1920s after the minaret had collapsed yet again.

The entrance porch, with its large portico and an arcade of keel-arches raised on ancient columns with Corinthian capitals, is unique in Cairo. The decoration around the entrance is, however, similar in style to the earlier Al-Aqmar mosque. The porch's *mashrabiyya* dates from the first restoration and the bronze facings on the exterior door are also from 1303 while the carvings on the inside of the door are a copy of the original that is now in the Islamic Museum.

The highlight of the interior is the exquisite *minbar*, the fourth oldest in Egypt and a very fine example of Mamluk wood carving, above which is the first appearance in a Cairo mosque of a wind vent (*malqaf*), which was an ingenious early Islamic form of air conditioning. In the northeast *qibla liwan* the tie-beams, which are inscribed with Koranic inscriptions in floriated Kufic script, are original although the ceiling is modern.

Tentmakers' bazaar to Safiya Mosque Further south down the street is what is probably the city's best preserved example of a **roofed market** which, because of the multitude of coloured printed fabrics sold here, is known as the **Tentmakers' bazaar**. Slightly further along the street is the **Madresa-Mosque of Amir Gani-Bak Al-Ashrafi**, which was built in 1426 and is named after a favourite of Sultan Al-Ashraf Barsbay. Gani-Bak's meteoric rise to *amir* in 1422 naturally created many enemies, who poisoned him at the age of 25. He was such a favourite that the Sultan had his body transferred to a tomb in his own Eastern Cemetery complex. Although the mosque has similarities to a number of other Mamluk mosques of the same period and despite the loss of both a coloured marble lintel over the portal door and the windows, its decoration even now is more ornate than other examples. Nearby is what little remains of the **Souk Al-Surugiyyah** (saddle-makers' market).

The Turkish-style **Mosque of Malika Safiya**, built in 1610, lies to the west in a small street off Sharia Mohammed Ali. It is one of the few mosques in Cairo to bear a woman's name although Queen Safiya acquired it deviously rather than constructing it herself. Safiya, who was from the noble Venetian family of Baffo, was captured by pirates along with a large party of other women in 1575 while on their way to Corfu. Because of her beauty she was presented to the Sublime Porte where she became chief consort of Sultan Murad III. He made her his *Sultana Khasski* (favourite) which gave her considerable power and influence, increased further when she produced Murad's first-born son. At her son's death Safiya was exiled to a harem where she lived in obscurity until she died in 1618.

Darb Al-Ahmar Returning to Bab Zuweila and turning right (east) into Sharia Darb Al-Ahmar (Red Road) there is an fascinating and unspoilt 1.25-km walk to the Citadel. The street gets its name from the incident in May 1805 when the Mamluks were tricked into going to discuss their grievances with Mohammed Ali Pasha. He had them slaughtered as they travelled 'Between the Two Palaces' and their heads sent to Istanbul as a demonstration of his power and independence. In March 1811, they fell for a similar trick on the same street when 470 Mamluks and their retainers were persuaded into going to a banquet at the Citadel and were slaughtered on their return near Bab Zuweila.

About 150 m after the Bab Zuweila, on a corner of the fork in the road is the beautiful late-Mamluk era **Mosque of Qijmas Al-Ishaqi** who was Sultan Qaitbay's Viceroy of Damascus. Although the mosque was built in 1480-1481, it is now known locally as the **Mosque of Abu Hurayba** after the 19th-century sheikh who occupies the tomb.

At this point you can make a detour off the main road east up Sharia Abu Hurayba where the left-hand fork leads 250 m to the **Mosque and Tomb of Amir Aslam Al-Silahdar** built in 1344-1345 and then follow the road around southwest and back to the main Sharia Darb Al-Ahmar.

Alternatively, forget about the detour and just continue south from the Mosque of Qijmas Al-Ishaqi along Sharia Darb Al-Ahmar. About 50 m on the right is the **Mosque and Tomb of Ahmed Al-Mihmandar**, built in 1324 but restored in 1732, but much more interesting is the beautiful, relaxing and very peaceful **Mosque of Altunbugha Al-Maridani** (1339-1340), which is 100 m further along the street. This is one of the most impressive 14th-century buildings in Cairo. Altunbugha (Golden Bull), originally from the Turkish town of Mardin, rose through the ranks to become *amir* and then married one of Sultan Al-Nasir Mohammed's daughters and became his cupbearer. After the sultan died in 1340 his successors imprisoned Altunbugha until 1342, when he was made governor of Aleppo only to die the following year at the age of 25.

Altunbugha's courtyard mosque, which was extensively restored in 1895-1903, is one of the oldest remaining buildings in this area. The minaret, to the right of the entrance, was the first in Cairo with an entirely octagonal shaft. It was built by Mu'allim Al-Suyufi, the chief royal architect, who also built the minaret of Aqbugha at Al-Azhar. The shafts of both are decorated by two-coloured inlaid stonework. Fortunately the restoration work followed the original plans so that the bulb-crowned canopy supported on stone pillars, the earliest existing example, was retained. The courtyard is particularly beautiful, with trees growing and cats aplenty.

Another 200 m further south past a small Turkish mosque, by which time the road is now called Sharia Bab Al-Wazir, is the large **Madresa of Sultan Al-Ashraf Sha'ban II**. It was built in 1368 when he was only 10, for his mother who was one of Al-Nasir Mohammed's concubines, which is why it is known locally as *Umm Sultan Sha'ban* (mother of Sultan Sha'ban). However, she outlived him as the Sultan was murdered in 1378 and ended up being buried here himself. The *madresa* and prayer area have recently reopened after being restored. Next door to the mosque is the large and well-restored **Beit Ar-Razzaz**, a palace complex which contains at least 180 rooms, dating from between the 15th to 18th centuries. Some remarkable examples of Islamic decoration, such as *mashrabiyya*, exist here and it is worthy of a visit.

On the road south is the **Mosque of Amir Aqsunqur** who was the son-in-law of Al-Nasir Mohammed and later became Viceroy of Egypt. It is sometimes known as the **Mosque of Ibrahim Agha** by locals and the **Blue Mosque** by Europeans because of both the exterior's blue-grey marble and the beautiful indigo and turquoise tiling of the *qibla* wall. In the 1650s Ibrahim Agha usurped the mosque, started in 1346, and it was he who decorated it with imported tiles.

The **Madresa-Mausoleum of Amir Khayrbak** was built in stages with the earliest, the mausoleum, being erected in 1502. Khayrbak, the Mamluk governor of Aleppo, betrayed his master Sultan Al-Ghuri at the Battle of Marj Dabiq in 1516 where the Turks routed the Mamluks. He was rewarded for his treachery by being appointed the first Ottoman governor of Egypt, and became renowned for his cruelty and greed. Squeezed between existing buildings the complex is best viewed from the Citadel end from where one can see the minaret (which has just had its missing upper storey replaced) and the intricately carved dome of the tomb raised above arched windows. To the left of the entrance corridor is the *sabil-kuttab* and to the right the portal entrance to the mosque, which one enters by stepping over a piece of pharaonic stone. From the windows of the tomb it's possible to get a good view of the ruined Alin Aq palace and Salah Al-Din's city walls.

The *madresa* became a Friday mosque in 1531 when the *minbar* was added. Documents show that the staff included one imam, six *muezzins*, 23 *qari* (Koran readers) – nine of whom recited the Koran at the windows – and a sufi sheikh.

The mosques of Sultan Hassan and Rafai ⓘ *Entrance to each E£25, students E£15, open Sat-Thu 0800-1630, Fri 0800-1100 and 1500-1630, during Ramadan until 1430.* Directly below the Citadel on Midan Salah Al-Din, these two adjacent mosques present themselves best at dusk when the atmosphere becomes charged with the call to prayer and the very air seems to shimmer around their colossal forms. The Sultan Hassan Mosque was started in 1356 by Sultan Al-Nasir Hassan and finished seven years later, but not before his assassination in 1361. It is one of the largest mosques in the world and was at times used as a fortress, being conveniently placed for hurling roof-top missiles at enemies in the Citadel.

The building is a masterpiece of Islamic art and is of incomparable simplicity and beauty; it is said that the Sultan ordered the hand of the architect to be cut off, in order that the building would remain unique. The main entrance is through a large, impressive doorway decorated with stalactites and finely sculpted ornaments. This leads into an antechamber connected to the magnificent cruciform courtyard where an ablutions fountain is covered by a large dome, originally painted blue. Each of the vaulted *liwans* served as a place for the teachings of one of the four doctrines of Sunni Islam. The *liwan* containing the *mihrab* has richly decorated marble-lined walls and a Koranic frieze in Kufic writing carved in the plaster work. The marble *minbar* here is one of the finest in Cairo, its height accentuated by hanging lamp-chains. The original glass lamps from these chains can be found in the Museum of Islamic Art in Cairo and in the Victoria and Albert Museum in London. A bronze door with gold and silver motifs leads to the mausoleum of Sultan Hassan, again a room of grand proportions, dominated by a 21-m-diameter dome that was actually built later, during the Turkish period. As Sultan Hassan was murdered and his body never recovered, two of his sons are buried here in his place.

The three-section 86-m minaret by the mausoleum is the highest in Cairo, with each new section decorated at its base with stalactites. Another smaller 55-m minaret on the east side of the mosque was built in 1659 to replace the existing one that was decaying.

Despite its appearance, the Al-Rifai Mosque, directly to the east of Sultan Hassan Mosque, was only started in the late 19th century and finished in 1912. However, the mosque, which is named after Sheikh Ali Al-Rifai who was the founder of the Sufi order of *tariqa* bearing his name, blends remarkably well into the surroundings. It was begun by the Dowager Princess Khushyar, the mother of Khedive Ismail who died in 1885 before it was finished, and was intended to contain the tombs of her descendants. Besides Al-Rifai and herself it contains the tombs of Khedive Ismail (1863-1879), his sons Sultan Hussein Kamil and King Ahmed Fouad I, and King Farouk who died in exile and was initially buried in the Southern cemetery. It is also the last resting place of the last Shah of Iran (Mohammed Reza Pahlavi), who died in exile in 1980 and, on President Sadat's instructions, was buried with great ceremony in a tomb made of green marble imported from Pakistan.

Mosque of Sultan Hassan

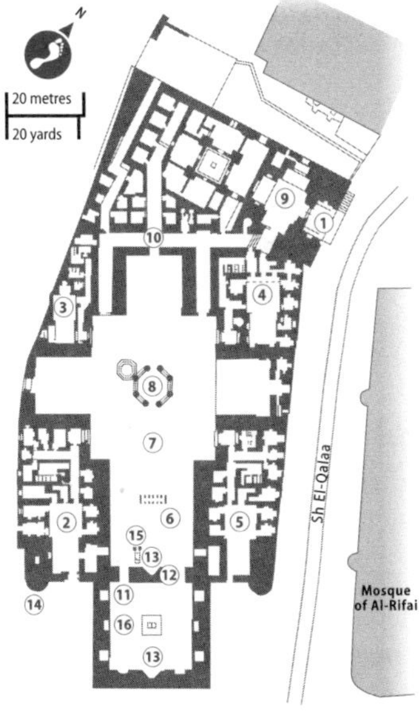

1 Entrance
2 Hanifi medersa
3 Hanabali medersa
4 Malaki medersa
5 Shafi'i medersa
6 Sanctuary/liwan
7 Sahn
8 Water for ablutions
9 Antechamber (domed)
10 Corridor
11 Bronze-faced door with gold and silver inlay
12 Qibla
13 Mihrab
14 Base of minaret
15 Minbar
16 Tomb chamber/ mausoleum

The Citadel ⓘ *T02-2512 1735, daily 0800-1600 winter, 0800-1430 summer, E£50, students E£25, tips might be necessary for guides in the museums and shoe attendants in the mosques, entrance into the museums ends 1 hr before closing time, enter via Bab Al-Gebel. The Citadel can be reached direct from Midan Abdel Mounim Riyad (near Midan Tahrir) by taking bus No 72 or minibus No 154; a taxi from the centre costs about E£10. Tell the taxi driver to take you to 'Al-Qala'a', with a guttural 'q'.*

The **Citadel** (also known as *Al-Qala'a Al-Gebel* – Citadel of the Mountain – or *Al-Burg*) perches on the steep slopes of the Muqattam Hills, its multiple minarets piercing the skyline and the silver (tin) dome of the Mosque of Mohamed Ali glinting in the sun. It was begun by **Salah Al-Din** in 1176 as part of an ambitious general fortification plan that included enclosing the whole city with a new wall that could be controlled from the main fort. The original fortress and remaining fortifications were strongly influenced by the architecture of castles built in Palestine and Syria by the Crusaders, and incorporate pieces of demolished Fatimid mosques and tombs as well as blocks of casing stone from the Pyramids of Giza. It was built in two walled enclosures, linked by their shortest walls, with the military area to the northeast and the residential quarters in the southwest. Every 100 m or so along the walls there is a tower connected to its neighbours by upper ramparts and by internal corridors that run the full circuit of the

The Citadel

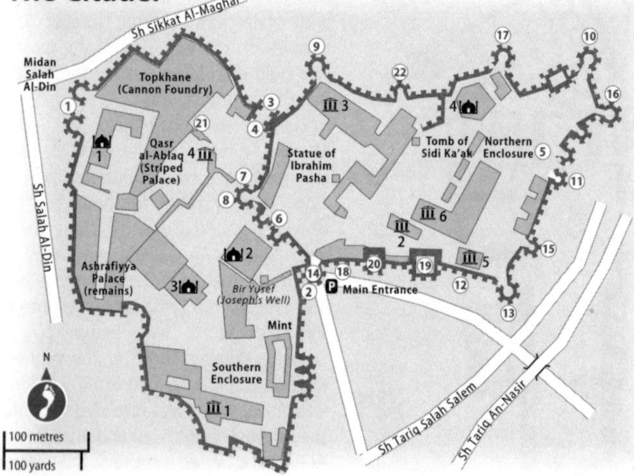

Gates & Towers ◯

Bab Al-Azab **1**
Bab Al-Gabal **2**
Bab Al-Gadid **3**
Bab Al-Mudarrag **4**
Bab Al-Qarafah **5**
Bab Al-Qullah **6**
Bab Al-Wustani **7**
Burg Al-Wustani (Middle Tower) **8**
Burg Al-Ahmar (Red Tower) **9**
Burg Al-Haddad (Blacksmith's Tower) **10**
Burg Al-Imam (Imam's Tower) **11**
Burg Al-Matar (Flight Tower) **12**
Burg Al-Muballat (Paved Tower) **13**
Burg Al-Muqattam **14**
Burg Al-Muqusar (Concave Tower) **15**
Burg Ar-Ramia (Sand Tower) **16**
Burg As-Sahra (Desert Tower) **17**
Burg As-Suffa (Alignment Tower) **18**
Burg At-Turfa (Masterpiece Tower) **19**
Burg Kirkilyan (Tower of the 40 Serpents) **20**
Lion's Tower **21**
Tower of Muh 'Ali **22**

Museums

Qasr Al-Gawhara **1**
Carriage Museum **2**
Harim Palace Military Museum **3**
National Police Museum **4**
Seized Museum **5**
Archaeological Garden Museum **6**

Mosques

Ahmed Katkhuda Al-Azab **1**
Sultan Al-Nasir Mohammed **2**
Mohammed Ali Pasha **3**
Suleyman Pasha **4**

walls. The whole complex is still under military control and there are large areas that are closed to the public.

Later the Citadel was abandoned until the Mamluks' arrival, when it became the Sultan's residence and the base of the *Burgi Mamluks* (1382-1517). In the 14th century Sultan Al-Nasir Mohammed (1310-1340) added a number of buildings including a mosque and later, because of the development of warfare and the use of canons, the Turks undertook major reinforcements. The most recent modification to the Citadel was by Mohammed Ali Pasha (1805-1840) who built an impressive mosque on the site of the original palaces. Today the most interesting features of the Citadel are the **Mosque of Mohammed Ali Pasha**, which provides an amazing view west over Cairo and the restored **Sultan Al-Nasir Mohammed Mosque**.

Walls, towers and gates The Ayyubid walls and towers (1176-1183) around part of the northern enclosure are from the time of Salah Al-Din. The dressed stone walls are 10 m high, 3 m thick and 2100 m in circumference interspersed with half-round towers. The **Bab Al-Azab**, enclosed by a pair of round-headed towers, stands on the west side of the Citadel. It was the original entrance to the Southern enclosure and has brass-bound wooden doors dating from 1754. **Bab Al-Qullah** (16th century) connects the two separate parts of the Citadel. The original Mamluk gate was replaced after the Ottoman conquest and was widened in 1826 to allow Mohammed Ali's carriage to pass through. **Bab Al-Gadid** (New Gate) was built in 1828 and is in reality a large tunnel with a vaulted ceiling,with guard rooms on either side. Built in 1207 by the Mamluk Sultan Baybars, the **Burg As-Siba** (Lions' Tower) is so called because it is decorated with a frieze of stone lions, the sultans' heraldic symbol. **Burg Al-Muqattam** (16th-century) is the largest tower in the citadel, over 25 m high and 24 m in diameter, with 7-m-thick walls built to withstand artillery attack.

Mosque of Mohammed Ali Pasha The Mosque of Mohammed Ali Pasha, was started in 1824 but only finished eight years after his death in 1857. The architecture was strongly influenced by the Ottoman mosques of Istanbul with the characteristic high, slender, octagonal minarets and an imposing dome that had to be rebuilt in the 1930s. The marble-floored courtyard is very finely proportioned, with a beautiful central ablutions fountain. To the northwest is a small square tower for a clock that was a gift from King Louis-Philippe of France in 1846 in exchange for the obelisk now in the Place de la Concorde in Paris, but the clock has never worked. The mosque is covered by a large dome with four half-domes on each side. Once inside, it takes some time to become accustomed to the dim lighting. The white marbled tomb of Mohammed Ali is to the right after the entrance, behind a bronze grille. This mosque is unusual, having two *minbars*. The large wooden construction, carved, painted and gilded, was installed by Mohammed Ali. It was too large to erect in the conventional space by the *mihrab* and was placed under the central dome making the weekly sermon inaudible to most of the congregation. In 1939 King Farouk installed a smaller alabaster *minbar* carved with a geometric pattern – to the right of the *mihrab*.

Sultan Al-Nasir Mohammed Mosque The Sultan Al-Nasir Mohammed Mosque was built between 1318 and 1335. It is certainly the best preserved Mamluk building in the Citadel and is claimed to be one of the finest arcade-style mosques in Cairo, the arches being supported by pharaonic and classical columns plundered from elsewhere. The two distinctive minarets, one above each entrance, are covered in the upper part with green, blue and white ceramic tiles attributed to craftsmen from Persia as are the onion-shaped bulbs on the tops of the minarets. The magnificent marble that covered the floors and lined the walls was unfortunately removed on instructions of the Ottoman ruler Selim I, although the *mihrab* remains in good condition.

The little-visited **Mosque of Suleyman Pasha** (1528), in the northern enclosure of the Citadel, was the first domed mosque to be built in Cairo during the Ottoman period. Its stalactite portal leads not directly into the paved courtyard like most Ottoman mosques but into the prayer hall on its southwest side. This is due to its cramped position by the Citadel's walls. The minaret is typical of the style common in Istanbul, a tall slender cylinder with a conical top, but like the Mamluk minarets it has two galleries. The minaret's pointed cap is covered with green tiles, as are the surrounding mosque and prayer hall, similar to a number found in Cairo's mosques of the period.

The mosque interior comprises a richly painted domed central area flanked on three sides by three supported semi-domes. The frescoes on the walls were restored in the 19th century and it is uncertain how faithful they are to the original Ottoman decoration. There was insufficient space adjacent to the *mihrab* for the *minbar*, which had to be placed under the central dome. The conical top of the marble *minbar* is decorated with a Mamluk-inspired geometric pattern based on the stars and polygon forms, similar to the Ottoman minarets.

Citadel museums The **Carriage Museum** was housed in the dining hall used by British officers stationed in the Citadel. At the time of research it was closed to the public, and is supposed to reopen in a restored building in Bulaq, when it will display eight carriages once used by the Egyptian royal family and some painted wooden horses.

The **Prison Museum** contains the cells where prisoners were detained, which you can view through the bars, the most famous convict being Anwar Sadat who was held here by the British for his revolutionary activities.

The **Military Museum** is in the **Harim Palace** built in 1827 as the private residence of Mohammed Ali. There are three extensive wings with many halls and side rooms, all decorated in lavish style. It is a splendid spectacle, well worth a visit. King Farouk ordered its conversion into a museum, which traces the history of the Egyptian army from pharaonic times to the present day. There are military uniforms, rifles and cannons on display, while the tanks captured in the October 1973 conflict are in the courtyard and make a popular photo spot.

The **National Police Museum** has some strange and interesting exhibits of policing problems ranging from assassination attempts to the protection of Egyptian antiquities. Note the sensational crimes of the serial killer sisters from Alexandria who murdered 30 women prior to being captured in 1921. It is constructed on top of Burg as-Siba and the view from the terrace takes in the Pyramids on the left through to the minaret of the Mosque Al-Fath in Midan Ramses to the right. It's absolutely breathtaking – on a clear day. The adjacent terrace café is an excellent place to relax, with equally amazing views and amazingly high prices to match.

The **Seized Museum** is unfortunately closed, with no indication of when it might reopen. Inside two small rooms exhibits items confiscated from dealers in the antiquities black market, spanning the history of Egypt. The first room is set aside for pharaonic items including a painted wooden sarcophagus and funerary beads in excellent condition. The second room is cramped with an assortment of treasures, including a collection of Byzantine, Islamic and European gold coins, a small group of beautiful books in the Arabic script, seven stunning Coptic icons and a set of official seals from the reign of the Mohammed Ali.

The **Qasr Al-Gawhara** (Palace of Jewels) stands on the site of the palace of the Circassian Mamluk sultans. It was built in 1814 as the first of two palaces with French-style salons that Mohammed Ali erected in the Citadel, and contains an impressive audience hall and guest rooms. Having been the residence of Egypt's rulers since the 12th century he predicted that his descendants would rule Egypt as long as they lived in the Citadel: sure enough, Ismail's move to the Abdin Palace foreshadowed the decline in their fortunes. At the time of writing the museum was closed for restoration, but should reopen with displays of portraits, costumes, furniture and ornaments that belonged to King Farouk.

The **Archaeological Garden**, in the Northern Enclosure, contains a small collection of bits and pieces – pieces of columns and monuments – as well as welcome benches. It is a very quiet and attractive place to take a rest.

Just south of the Mosque of Sultan Al-Nasir Mohammed, covered by a tower and locked at the time of writing, stands **Joseph's Well**. Also known as the Well of the Snail, an enclosed spiral staircase leads down some 87 m through solid rock to the water level of the Nile. Two platforms with pumps operated by oxen raised the water, which was then carried to the surface by donkeys. It was built between 1876 and 1182 by Crusader prisoners and provided a secure supply of drinking water for all of the Citadel.

Qasr Al-Ablaq (Striped Palace) was built in 1315 by Al-Nasr Mohammed for official receptions. Mohammed Ali Pasha had the building torn down but a remaining portion of outer wall shows its alternating bands of black and yellow marble.

West from the Citadel

From Midan Salah Al-Din it's a 15- to 20-minute walk west along Sharia Saliba to the Mosque of Ibn Tulun. On the left you'll soon see the second decorated **Sabil-Kuttab of Sultan Qaitbay** (1477), which is now gorgeously restored and home to a library. Continue west past the small **Mosque of Qanibai Al-Muhammadi** to the imposing architectural buildings with matching minarets that face each other across the street. On the right is the **Mosque of Amir Shaykhu** (1349) and on the left his **Khanqah** (1355). Amir Shaykhu was the Commander-in-Chief of the Mamluk army during the reign of Sultan Hassan. The *khanqah* had small cells for up to 70 sufis around the inner courtyard and in the northeast corner of the arcaded prayer hall is Amir Shaykhu's tomb.

There is an option to turn right here, up Sharia Suyufiya, for a worthy detour to the hugely impressive **Palace of Amir Taz** ⓘ *T02-2514 2581, free*. One of the last great Mamluk palaces, and the most intact, it was built in 1352 by Amir Taz to celebrate his marriage to the daughter of Sultan Al-Nasir Mohamed. He never really got the chance to enjoy his magnificent abode as conspiracies and intrigues against him pursuaded him to flee Cairo, despite the fact he was described as being tall and courageous. A mainstay of the Historic Cairo Programme, the restoration of the palace is regarded as a great success, with positive effects on the local area in the provision of a community centre, a space for art exhibitions, and as the venue for music events (check the listings on www.weekly-ahram.org.eg). Enclosed by high stone walls, the central courtyard and gardens are a peaceful and austere space, while inside the decoration becomes more flamboyant. The main *qa'ah* has traces of the original paint and gilding, in the Bahri Mamluk style, and the stunning vaulted ceilings in the ground-floor bathrooms are pierced with coloured glass. The *maqad* looks onto the courtyard through four soaring arches, resting on marble columns topped with Corinthian capitals. Wooden waterwheels, cisterns and aquaducts were revealed during the restoration process, these and the *haramlik* fountain have now been excavated. A small museum traces the history of the Mamluks and displays choice artefacts and alabaster ornaments.

Just over the crossroads, on the right, is the **Mevlavi Sufi Theatre** ⓘ *T02-2510 7806, open 0900-1800*, also known as the Cairo Tikiyya, lovingly and painstakingly restored over many years by a joint Italian-Egyptian team. Part of the Rumi sect, the 'whirling dervishes' who lived and practised here came to Egypt just after the Ottoman conquest, and were the last of the sect to be dissolved in 1945. The polished circular wooden floor (scuffed by the feet of devotees) of the main *sama-khana*, or Hall of Listening, is overlooked by two galleries supported on slender pillars. The *minrab* serves as an anchor point of a horizontal axis that symbolically divides the space into the known and unknown worlds. The interior is decorated with botanic designs, while the flying birds on the dome represent the liberation of the soul from a materialist life. It's the perfect place to reenergize, as is the peaceful Turkish garden outside. A small museum displays uniforms and belongings of the Sufis, as well as pottery and porcelain. The adjacent **mausoleum-madresa of Sunqur El-Sadi** has some of most sensational carved stucco in Cairo on its dome, with beautiful arabesque designs and inscriptions relating to death from a popular medieval text. Look for the unusually shaped crescent upon atop its minaret.

Retrace your steps and and turn right onto Sharia Saliba at the cross roads, with the **Sabil-Kuttab of Um Abbas** on the corner, passing the small but impressive **Mosque of Amir Taghri Bardi** (1440) with a carved stone dome. While the structure of this building follows the east-west line of Sharia Saliba, the interior is aligned southeast to Mecca.

Mosque of Ibn Tulun ⓘ *Daily 0800-1700. Bus No 72 or minibus No 154 go from Midan Abdel Mounim Riad to to the Citadel, via the Saiyyida Zeinab area and then past the mosque. A taxi from Downtown costs E£5-10*. The largest mosque in Cairo and the oldest to retain its original features is the Mosque of Ahmed Ibn Tulun, built between AD 876-879. The cosmic proportions and austere interior make it stand out among a million other mosques in Cairo, while the captivating Gayer-Anderson house next door and tasteful souvenirs in the shop opposite make it an excellent place to start a day's wanderings. Ahmed Ibn Tulun, the son of a Turkish slave, was made governor of Egypt but then proceeded to declare independence from the Baghdad-based Abbasid Khalifas. He thereby became the first of the Tulunids (AD 868-905) at the new town of Al-Qata'i (the Concessions or the Wards), northeast of Fustat and near the foothills of Muqattam. When the Abbasids regained power in Egypt in AD 905 they destroyed much of the town except for the mosque, which fell into decay until it was restored in 1296 by Sultan Lagin. He had hidden there after being implicated in an assassination attempt against his predecessor (at which time the mosque was believed to be haunted) and vowed he would restore the place.

The mosque was originally designed by a Syrian Jacobite Christian architect, which probably explains the presence of many designs and motifs inspired by Coptic art. Legend says that the sycamore beams were brought from Mount Ararat and were part of Noah's ark. External measurements are 140 x 122 m making it the largest place of worship in Cairo. The central courtyard is 92 sq m yet despite its huge size, the overall impression is of harmony, simplicity and sobriety. The walls have been plastered but the ornamentation is sculpted rather than moulded. Kufic inscriptions, almost 2 km long, circle the mosque several times below the roof and relay about 20% of the Koran. The marble-plated *mihrab*, added in the 13th century, is surrounded by a glass mosaic frieze. Directly above is a small wooden dome. The *minbar*, presented by Sultan Lagin in 1296, is a fine work of art. The minaret has an unusual outside spiral staircase, which appears to be a copy of the one at Samarra in Iraq; the view from the top over the surrounding area is excellent and worth the climb. You'll have to tip E£1 for shoe-covers to wear inside the mosque, but it's fine to keep footwear on for climbing the minaret.

Gayer-Anderson House ⓘ *T02-2364 7822, daily 0900-1600, E£35, E£20 for students, E£20 video cameras.* The **Gayer-Anderson House** should be given priority over other restored houses if you have limited time in Cairo, as it is exquisitely detailed and full of Orientalist period pieces. Also known as the **Beit Al-Kritliyah** (House of the Cretan Woman), it's actually two adjoining houses that abut the southeast corner of Ibn Tulun's mosque. Originally one house was for men's accommodation (*salamlik*) and the other for women (*haramlik*). The roof area was solely for the women who crossed from one building to the other by a small bridge on the second floor. A *mashrabiyah*-screened balcony overlooks the large two-storey sitting room (*qa'ah*) with its marble floor and ornately tiled fountain, permitting the women to see the male visitors and the entertainments without being seen themselves.

In 1934, the government allowed Major Robert Gayer-Anderson (1881-1945), a retired British doctor and member of the Egyptian Civil Service, to restore and refurnish the houses with Ottoman-era furniture and fittings. A passionate collector, the major filled the rooms with curios gathered from around the region, resulting in differently themed rooms including the Damascus room, Persian room, Turkish room and Byzantine room. Gorgeous carpets cover the floors, you can wander amongst the furniture while light comes in through fine *mashrabiyah* windows, ceilings have been faithfully restored and are bright with colour, and the rooftop provides awesome views over Ibn Tulun. Other rooms include a library containing historical books, a writing room and a display room for the Major's collection of pharaonic antiquities. Guides will take you on a tour, if you wish, and they'll expect tips afterwards.

Sayyidah Zeinab The area to the west of the Ibn Tulun Mosque is known as Sayyidah Zeinab after the Prophet Mohammed's granddaughter Zeinab (AD 628-680) who settled in Fustat in AD 679 with her five children and the son of her brother Hussein who was murdered at Karbala in the Sunni-Shi'a conflict. Because of her position as closest kinswoman to the martyred Ali and Hussein the area has become a site of pilgrimage for foreign Shi'a Muslims. This is focused on the mosque built, and continuously rebuilt, over her tomb, located off Sharia Bur Said but closed to non-Muslims. Her *moulid* (saint's day) between 13-27 Ragab attracts up to half a million revellers who come to watch the wild Sufi parades and evening festivities.

The **Madresa and Tombs of Amirs Salar and Sangar Al-Gawli** was once a much larger set of buildings than what you see today, but even so the remaining tombs and the *madresa* indicate some of the original grandeur. The domes over the tombs are of varying sizes, that to the east being the largest. The slender minaret stands about 45 m high, with a square first storey, octagonal second storey and a cylindrical third that culminates in a cornice of stalactites capped with a ribbed dome. Passing through the stalactite arch, steps lead you up to the vaulted corridor and to the tombs. The most ornate is the Tomb of Amir Salar, 7 m sq, encircled by a wooden frieze and with a fine marble *mihrab*. Note the design of the windows in the dome. Turning east from the stairs leads to the mosque. The larger courtyard had small rooms for students (the grills over the doors need some explanation) and a smaller courtyard off which is the *mihrab*.

Cities of the Dead

ⓘ *The easiest way to the Southern Cemetery from Sultan Hassan Mosque, is to head south towards Sharia Imam Al-Shafi for about 1.5 km, more pleasant by taxi than on foot, E£3-4. The easiest way to the Northern Cemetery is either by taking a taxi direct to Qarafat Al-Sharqiyyah, or by walking east along Sharia Al-Azhar from the Al-Azhar mosque for about 15 mins until you reach the roundabout junction with the north-south dual carriageway of Sharia Salah Salem and then north for 250 m. Then cut into the cemetery and head for the dome and minaret, which are clearly visible.*

The Cities of the Dead is the name given by Europeans to Cairo's two main cemeteries that spread north and south from the Citadel. Half a million people are thought to live among the mausoleums and tombs of the sprawling necropoli, and the communities here have shops, electricity and even schools. In Egypt there has long been a tradition of living close to the dead but the very large numbers are a relatively recent trend caused by an acute scarcity of housing. Consequently the people who live in the cemeteries tend to be comparatively poor and, although certainly not dangerous, it is obviously advisable not to flaunt your wealth, to dress modestly and remember that these are people's homes. The Cities of the Dead are one of few intimidating places in Cairo (lone women will certainly feel conspicuous, either sex will feel more comfortable with company) and somewhere you can get very lost after dark. The vast majority of people are as welcoming as all other Egyptians, but if anyone in Cairo is likely to throw stones at you, it will be the children here.

The **Southern Cemetery** (*Al-Qarafa Al-Kubra*) is older and spreads to the southeast but there are relatively few monuments to see. The **Mausoleum of Imam Al-Shafi** is the focus of a visit here, with splendid marbling and a quite astounding dome, gilded and painted red and blue, and topped by a metal boat. Remember this is an active shrine and be very respectful when visiting (see box, page 102, for more about the sights in the Southern Cemetery). The **Northern Cemetery**, which is known locally as Al-Qarafa Al-Sharqiyyah (the Eastern Cemetery) because it was east of the old city, is more interesting and has been the burial place of the sultans since the 14th century. It contains a number of the most beautiful mausoleums in the city, including those of Barquq and Qaitbay.

Muslim graveyards have no flowers unless they grow wild by chance. Instead of buying flowers to decorate family graves on their routine weekly visit, relatives will, instead, often give a simple dish to the poor to provide a meal for their children.

Mausoleums in the Northern Cemetery

In the Northern Cemetery the **Mausoleum of Sultan Al-Zahir Barquq** ⓘ *daily 0900-2000*, was built over a 12-year period in 1398-1411 by his son Al-Nasir Farag. It was the first royal tomb to be built in the necropolis after Barquq had expressed a wish to be interred alongside a number of pious Sufi sheikhs already buried there. Therefore his body was moved from his *madresa* on Sharia Al-Muizzli Din Allah once the 75-sq-m complex had been completed. It is square with two minarets symmetrically placed on the façade. The entrance in the southwest corner leads along a corridor to the *sahn*, which has an octagonal fountain in the centre and is surrounded by four *liwans*. The east *liwan* has three very simple *mihrabs* and an extraordinarily finely sculpted stone *minbar*. Doors lead from either side of the *liwan* into mausoleums. The north mausoleum contains Barquq's own marble cenotaph, which is richly decorated with Koranic inscriptions, together with the tombs of an unknown person and another intended for Farag whose body was left in Damascus after he had been assassinated on a military campaign in Syria. The mausoleum to the south holds the tombs of Barquq's wife and two granddaughters.

A little to the south is the **Madresa and Mausoleum of Sultan Al-Qaitbay** ⓘ *daily 0900-1700*, built in 1472-1474, which is a magnificent example of 15th-century Arab art and one of Egypt's most beautiful monuments from the Arab era. From the outside, the building's proportions are pleasingly harmonious, with boldly striped masonry, and a dome finely decorated with polygonal motifs. The minaret is also remarkable for its square base, octagonal middle section and cylindrical top tier, all finely inscribed. Seventeen steps climb to the cruciform *madresa* with narrow side *liwans* and a covered *sahn* with an exquisite octagonal lantern ceiling. The sheer volume and complexities of the marble decoration that seems to coat every surface is breathtaking. The east *liwan*, where the ceiling is modern, still has a very well preserved and finely encrusted *minbar*. A door in the south corner of the *qibla liwan* leads to the mausoleum, which is decorated with an equal wealth of marbling, however its high dome is simply decorated in contrast with the highly ornate walls. Sultan Qaitbay's tomb is enclosed behind an elaborate wooden *mashrabiyya* while the other tomb is that of one of his sisters.

6 Northern Cemetery

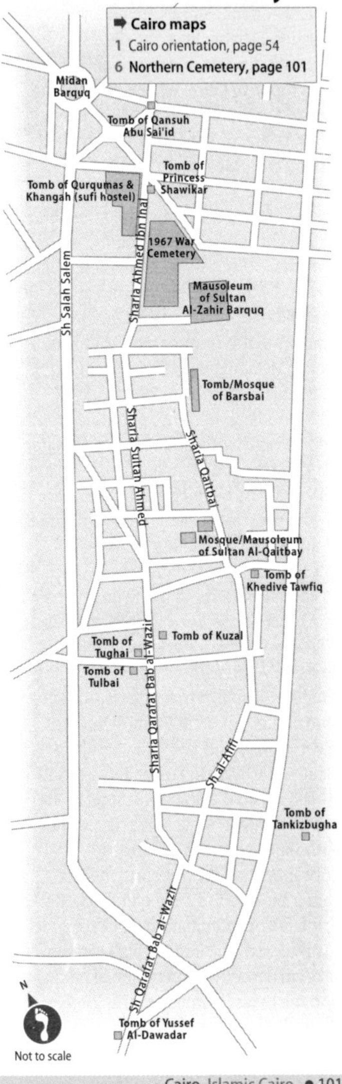

Al-Azhar Park ⓘ *Sharia Salah Salem, T02-2510 3868, www.alazhhzarpark.com, daily 0900-2300 (0900-2200 on Wed), E£5, the entrance gate is on Salah Salem, a taxi from Downtown costs about E£10*. Called in Arabic *Hadiyka Al-Azhar* (which will help taxi drivers), the Al-Azhar Park is an emerald-green success story built on top of the immense mound of the Islamic city's rubbish dump. For centuries, waste matter was thrown over the historic wall east of Darb Al-Ahmar, eventually submerging the wall and piling into a veritable mountain. An impressive 1300-m stretch of the **Ayubbid wall** has been excavated, and the Darb Al-Ahmar buildings flanking it have been spruced up to give a much-needed boost to a poor and deprived neighbourhood. The epic project to transform this into a pleasure garden took over a decade and was funded by the Aga Khan Trust for Culture, who have negotiated an

Muslim cemeteries

One of the lasting monuments in Islam is the *qarafah* or graveyard. All are different, ranging from undefined rocky areas near villages, where unnamed head and foot stones are barely distinguishable from the deserts surrounding them, to the elaborate necropoli of Cairo, where cities for the dead are established. In all cemeteries bodies are interred with head towards the *qibla* – Mecca.

In Egypt, graveyards often contain a series of simple whitewashed mud brick tombs of holy men (*marabouts*), around which his disciples and their descendants are laid. More grandly, in Cairo at the City of the Dead is the Eastern Cemetery, known as the Tombs of the Mamluks, a set of Muslim graveyards, developed particularly from the 15th century. It contains large numbers of notable tombs, most importantly that of Tomb of Sultan Al-Zahir Barquq. A second and even more elaborate cemetery is Cairo's Southern Cemetery. This ancient graveyard includes a number of the earliest examples of Muslim funerary architecture in Egypt and is home to the Tomb of the Imam Shafa'i, the most significant mausoleum in Cairo. The Imam Shafa'i was born in Palestine in AD 767 and was the originator of the Shafi'ite School of Islamic jurisprudence, one of the four great Sunni Schools of Law. He spent his last years (until his death in AD 820) in Fustat in Cairo. Salah Al-Din set up the Shafa'i Mosque in 1180, which included the Imam's new tomb. Although subject to numerous subsequent reconstructions, the last under the Khedive Tawfiq in 1891, the tomb is in an adequate state of repair to justify a visit. The large Shafa'i complex takes in a mosque, a ceremonial gateway and the mausoleum itself. The tomb is simple but decorated at various times with silver and paintings. The mausoleum has some fine beams and a wooden cupola together with much of the inscriptions and ornamentation undertaken by Salah Al-Din's builders. Shafa'i's tomb lies to the north of the building. Its religious focus is a delicate 20th-century sandalwood screen or *maqsurah* and a marble stela. These are kissed by visiting Muslims as a sign of faith. Also entombed at the site are Mohammed abd Al-Hakim and Princess Adiliyyah, mother of Sultan Al-Kamel, while the Sultan himself (interred elsewhere) is commemorated by an uninscribed tomb in the south of the chamber. A walk along Sharia Sidi Uqbah and Sharia Imam Shafa'i takes you past a wide variety of funerary constructions, many in a sad state of decay. Also worth a visit is the Al-Basha *Housh* (house) which backs onto the Shafa'i tomb on a parallel road (Shariyah Imam Al-Lais) to the west. This is the 19th-century mausoleum of the family of Mohammed Ali Pasha.

Death and funerals are times for noisy outbreaks of wailing and crying. In traditional families, the approach of a person's death is signalled by wailing, increased on actual death by the addition of the mourning neighbours and relatives. Occasionally in villages the body is laid in a large room where funeral dances are performed by mourning women, singing the praises of the deceased. Corpses are washed and wrapped in a simple shroud for interment. Mourners follow the cortege to the cemetery often in large crowds since every person who walks 40 paces in the procession has one sin remitted. At the grave side a *shedda* or declaration of Islamic faith is recited.

agreement with the government that will allow them to manage the park for at least 20 years. The next phase is underway to create an 'urban plaza' with extra car parking, a café, a small retail area and a new museum. This **Museum of Islamic Cairo** (projected to open in 2011) will prepare visitors for the experience to come in the lanes of the old city and has opened up a western exit into Darb Al-Ahmar. The remains of the original mud-brick Fatimid wall that were uncovered during the park's construction will also be displayed in the future, near the museum.

The park is amazingly lush, with shrubs, trees and flowers in abundance, and full of Cairene families enjoying the palm-lined walkways and children's play area. Come to the park for sunset and you will get sweeping views across the city as monuments are lit up and the green neon lights of minarets glow. The high vantage point provides one of Cairo's best views over the mausoleums of the Cities of the Dead, past the skyscrapers of Downtown and over the Nile to the pyramids in Giza. The fabulous Citadel View Restaurant (see Eating, page 134) on the northern hill is worth splashing out on, or the outside café is a delightful place to sit with a cool drink (although there's a minimum charge and painfully slow service).

Old Cairo and Roda Island

This settlement was constructed by the Persians in about 500 BC to guard the junction of the Nile and the canal linking it to the Red Sea. During the Christian period the fortified settlement of Babylon-in-Egypt grew into a large town. It was perhaps named by the fort's homesick building workers from modern-day Iraq or from the name for Gate of Heliopolis (Bab-il-On). Later the Arabs called it Qasr Al-Sham'ah (Fortress of the Beacon). Whatever its origins, it is now commonly known as Old Cairo (Masr Al-Kadima) or identified, not entirely correctly, by some as Coptic Cairo.

Old Cairo is located on the east bank of the Nile, opposite the southern tip of Roda Island to which it was connected by a pontoon bridge. Leaving Mar Girgis station, you are confronted by two circular Roman towers some 33 m in diameter which comprised the west gate of the fortress. Built on what was at that time the east bank of the Nile, now 400 m further west, the towers sit on foundations now smothered beneath 10 m of Nile silt and rubble. Between them is the Coptic Museum, while the Hanging Church is entered to their right and the modern Church of St George to their left. The other main churches and synagogue of Ben Ezra are accessed via the little flight of sunken steps to the left of the metro exit.

Ins and outs

The easiest and cheapest way to get to Old Cairo is via the metro, E£1, which drops you right in front of the Coptic quarter. Get off at **Mar Girgis** (St George), four stops from **Sadat** in the Helwan direction. For more of an adventure, river-taxis leave Maspero Dock between 0700-0800, E£1, and call at Mar Gigis five stops later. Alternatively, a taxi from Downtown costs E£10. The churches do not charge admission, but most have donation boxes. To get a taste of Coptic culture and see heaps of Coptic Cairenes milling about from holy sight to holy sight, come on Sunday; if you are in search of a peaceful stroll through Old Cairo, it is best to avoid it on Wednesday, Friday and Sunday.

The Coptic Museum

ⓘ T02-2362 8766, www.copticmuseum.gov.eg and www.coptic-cairo.com, daily 0900-1700 (last entrance at 1600), during Ramadan supposedly until 1500 though it might shut earlier, E£50, students E£25, cameras are not permitted and must be deposited by the turnstiles. Recently restored and reorganized, the Coptic Museum is among Egypt's principal displays of antiquities and houses an outstanding collection of Coptic treasures. It was founded in 1908, with the support of the royal court, as a means of preserving Coptic artefacts and Egypt's Christian heritage against the acquisitive activities of local and foreign collectors. There was an expansion programme in 1947 that enabled the collection to include a number of small but very valuable objects and items from Coptic churches and monasteries throughout Egypt.

The museum gives an interesting insight into the evolution of Christian (and to some extent secular) art and architecture in Egypt in the period AD 300-1800. As well as demonstrating the interchange of ideas with the larger Islamic community, earlier pieces show how the transition from paganism to Christianity was a gradual process with many Graeco-Roman myths incorporated in proto-Coptic art and sculpture. The displays are arranged thematically across two floors in the New and Old Wings; reckon on about three hours for a thorough viewing or an hour to just whip round. It's a good idea to go over

Old Cairo

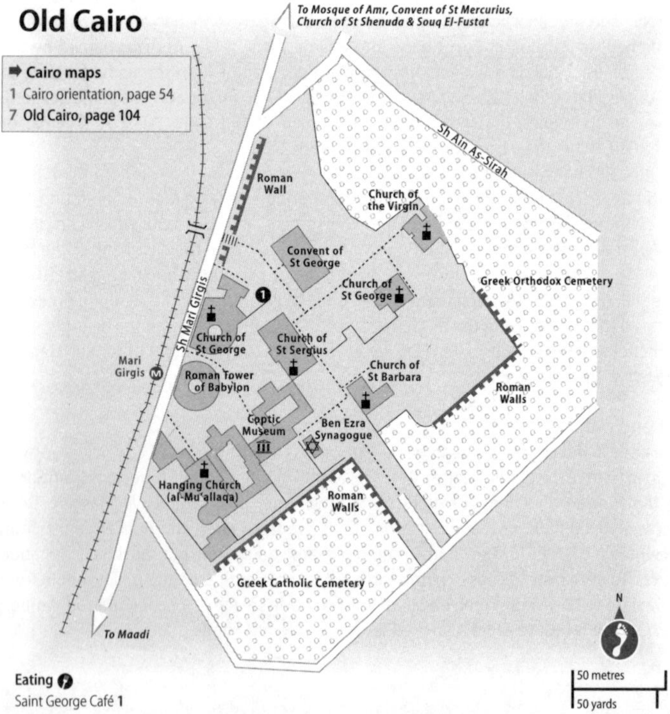

lunchtime, when the museum is virtually empty. The enclosed garden is neatly laid out with benches and large pieces of old stonework. There is also a gift shop, library and a small café, though the nearby Saint George Café (next to the church of the same name; see map page 104) is a nicer place to relax.

Beginning on the ground floor of the New Wing, go in an anticlockwise direction through the museum. Among the chunky Ahnas sculptures in **Room 3** look out for the pediment on the right-hand wall showing the nymph Daphne in the laurel leaves, with pudding-bowl haircut and classic almond-shaped eyes, and further along a frieze containing the faun Pan, both from the third or fourth century. **Room 4** is devoted to early Christian reliefs, which give weight to the suggestion that the Christian cross developed from the pharaonic *ankh*. **Room 5** contains stylized friezes of uniform acanthus and vine leaves from the fifth-century monastery of St Jeremiah in Saqqara (see page 161), barely eroded either by the desert or by time. In the courtyard is a splendid array of column capitals individually carved into lotus leaves, vines, palm fronds and acanthus (a couple still have traces of paint) and a six-step limestone pulpit (the earliest recorded). Treasures from St Jeremiah continue in **Room 6** where a perfectly preserved and fresh-painted niche depicting Christ floating above a seated Virgin Mary steals the show. Pieces from the Monastery of St Apollo in Bawit, probably the richest hoard of church sculpture ever discovered in Egypt, are in **Rooms 7**, **8** and **9**. The lintels, door jambs, panels and dados from Bawit are all exquisite but the highlight is an unusually bright oratory apse showing Christ enthroned by the mythological creatures of the Apocalypse; below, on either side of the virgin and child, the apostles are personalized by their differing facial hair and expressions. Note also the magnificent remains of an arch in **Room 9**, supported by columns carved with modernistic geometrical designs.

Upstairs in **Room 10-11** religious and thematic elements, portrayed through various media, are grouped together. Look in the first case for the weaving of a centaur surrounded by medallions containing baskets of fruit and animals – it is hard to believe that it's over 1500 years old. The Old and New Testaments are of equal importance in the Coptic faith, and both sets of Biblical stories are represented in the rest of Room 11. At the end of the left wall, particularly impressive is the 11th-century Fayoumi painting showing Adam and Eve among the fruit and foliage of the Garden of Eden, before and after their fall from grace. **Room 12** contains liturgical vestments, and then a display of the famed skill of Coptic weavers starts in earnest in **Room 13**. Remarkably, nothing in the room is newer than the eighth century and some remnants are as old as third century. Floral designs, agricultural scenes, human figures, animals and birds are prominent subjects, giving Coptic textiles a personal feel as well as divulging detailed information about the society that created them. **Room 15** displays the Nag Hammadi Codices. Only two pages are on show, plus some leather book-bindings, but this is the primary source for study of Gnosticism and early Christian mysticism. The theme of writing continues in **Room 16** with some marvellous illuminated manuscripts, a variety of writing accoutrements and some messages on ostracon (pot-shards) that deal with grain sales, health enquiries and other matters of daily life. **Room 17** is devoted to the 1600-year-old Psalter found near Beni Suef, then it's a quick dash through the tube linking the New Wing to the Old, via a small display about the hermitages found at Kellia. It's worth looking at the diagram of a reconstructed hermitage, which is very far removed from any previous notions you might have had of a hermit's cell.

In the Old Wing, the building itself is as rewarding as the artefacts. The ceiling carvings throughout this section are from Coptic houses in Old Cairo and have been incorporated into the building along with panels and tiles. Coptic woodwork was very varied and ornate, heavy work being executed in acacia and palm and finer work in imported cedar, pine and walnut. Ebony too was very popular. A frieze in **Room 18** depicts a large crocodile and further on in **Room 19** look for the pull-along wooden toys, fashioned into horses, an elephant and birds, which are presumed to come from children's graves. **Rooms 20-22** require you to have saved some energy and are a true highpoint of the museum. They contain the icons, spanning a huge range of iconographic styles – Byzantine, Greek, Cretan, Syrian and more. Seek out the icon of St Barbara, from the

Coptic Museum

New wing - ground floor

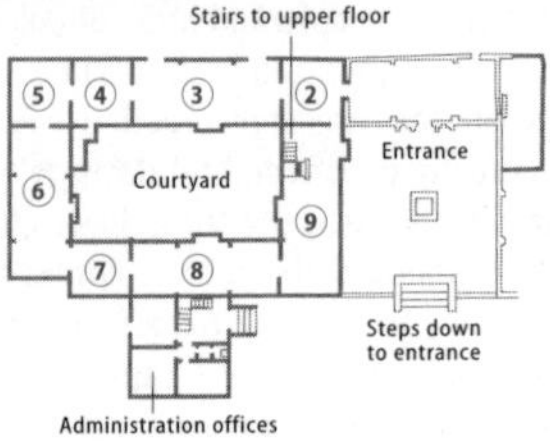

2 Masterpieces
3 Sculpture from Ahnas
4 Ankhs
5, 6 & Courtyard Objects from the Monastery of St Jeremiah at Saqqara
7-9 Pieces from the Monastery of Apollo at Bawit

New wing - upper floor

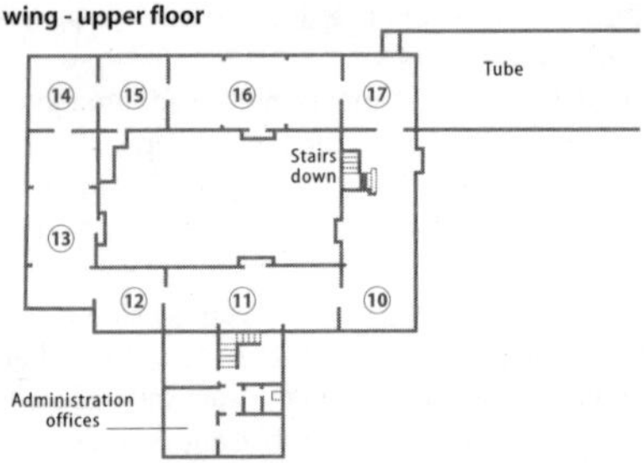

10 Coptic culture
11 Religious themes
12 Liturgical vestments
13 & 14 Textiles
15 Nag Hammadi Codices
16 Writing
17 Psalter
Tube Kellia Monasteries

Old wing - upper floor

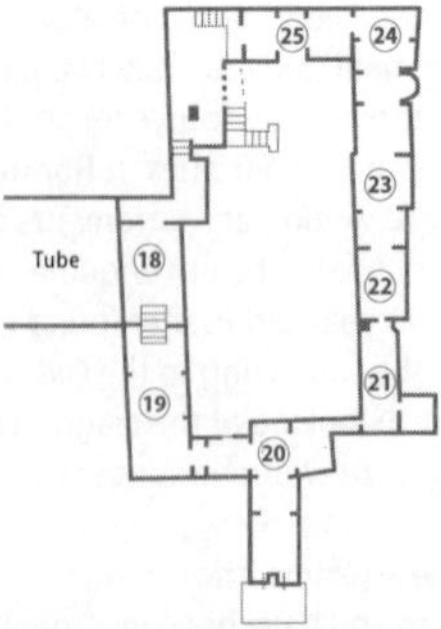

18 Nilotic scenes
19 Daily life & saints
20-22 Icons
23 Metalwork
24 & 25 Ceramics & glass

Not to scale

nearby church dedicated to her, leaning on a Rapunzel-esque tower and dressed in the Western medieval style. **Room 23** has some unimaginably heavy and ornate keys from the monastery doors of Middle Egypt, plus jewellery, intriguing lamps fashioned into animal shapes, and a wealth of incense censers – so important in the Coptic liturgy – swinging on chains. The pottery in **Room 24** is arranged according to decoration and size. There are red clay jugs, small pots for make-up, and beautifully painted urns and bowls. You might feel by now that the collection of ceramics and glass in **Room 25** is mercifully small, but it's worth lingering over the two-handled miniature flasks that pilgrims used to take holy water back from Abu Menas, depicting the martyred saint between two camels, and marvel at the unbelievably fiddly designs on the base of water jugs used to filter out impurities. After exiting down the stairs, it's possible to see the old Roman Water Gate that is signed down some steps in the courtyard.

The Hanging Church

ⓘ *Daily 0800-1700. Coptic Masses held on Fri 0800-1100 and Sun 0700-1000, photography permitted. There are often volunteers about who will give a free guided tour – enquire with staff by the church door to see if anyone is available.*

Beside the Coptic Museum, the other main attraction in Old Cairo is the Hanging Church (*Al-Mu'allaqah* or 'The Suspended One'). It is so called because it perches on top of the three stone piers of the semi-flooded Roman **Water Gate** from where the Melkite bishop Cyrus, the last Byzantine viceroy, fled by boat as the Muslim army arrived. The original church, built in the fourth century, was demolished in AD 840 by Ali Ibn Yahya who was the Armenian Governor. It was rebuilt in AD 977 and modified several times, most recently in 1775. The church is approached through a narrow courtyard from which steep steps lead, via a 19th-century vestibule, to the church's entrance. The painting of the Virgin on the right-hand wall on entering is known as the Coptic Mona Lisa, as her eyes and face follow you when you move from side to side. Against the left-hand wall are relics of saints contained in cylindrical vessels wrapped in red cloth: it is to these you should appeal for blessings. The church is divided into a wide nave and two narrow side aisles by two rows of eight columns with Corinthian capitals. Look out for the

Church of Al-Mu'allaqah (The Hanging Church)

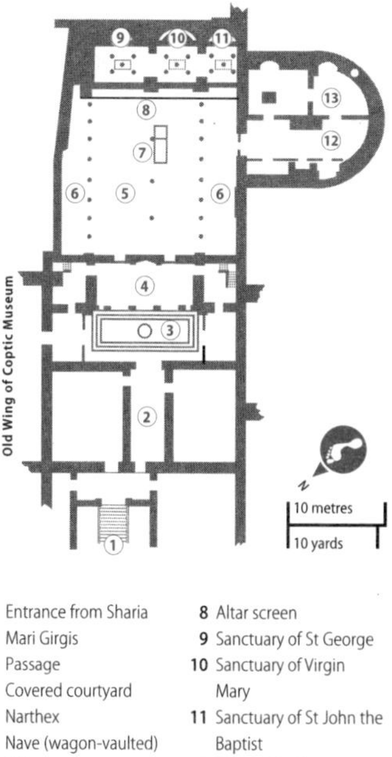

1 Entrance from Sharia Mari Girgis
2 Passage
3 Covered courtyard
4 Narthex
5 Nave (wagon-vaulted)
6 Aisle
7 Marble pulpit
8 Altar screen
9 Sanctuary of St George
10 Sanctuary of Virgin Mary
11 Sanctuary of St John the Baptist
12 Shrine of Takla Hamanout
13 Baptistry with basin

odd-one-out black basalt capital. The vaulted roof is of timber, and echoes the hull of the upturned ark. There are three supporting columns in the centre of the nave and an 11th-century marble pulpit supported by 15 delicate columns. On examination each pair of columns is identical but no two pairs are the same. One of the columns is black, representing Judas, and another is grey, representing either Doubting Thomas or Peter, who denied Christ. The 13th-century *iconostasis*, which separates the congregation from the three *haikals* (altar areas), is an incredible feat of fine woodwork and appears virtually transparent. To the right of the altar is a room that is built over the eastern tower of the southern gateway of the old fortress – there is a cordoned-off hole in the floor, through which you can see 13 m down to appreciate the fact there are no foundations – just date palm trunks holding the church up. The screen dividing this room from the main church is of very delicate woodwork – the mother of pearl inlay is enhanced by holding a candle or torch behind. To its left and right, two secret passageways lead down to the foundations. These recent discoveries are thought to be escape routes used by the Christians during times of persecution.

The Convent of St George

ⓘ *Access down the sunken steps in front of the exit of Mar Girgis metro, 1000-1600.* St George was a Roman soldier and one of the many Christians who fell foul of Diocletian. His body was brought to Egypt in the 12th century. Although you cannot enter the actual convent you can descend into the soaring main hall, a remarkable feature of which are the 8-m-high wooden doors studded with nails. Within are some beautiful icons while the windows are *mashrabiya*, as this was once a Fatimid house. In the small room at the left hangs a chain which, it is claimed, was used to secure early martyrs.

The Church of St Sergius

ⓘ *Turn left out of the convent, then turn right at the end of the lane, open 0800-1600.* The fifth-century Church of St Sergius is dedicated to two soldiers, St Sergius and St Bacchus, who were martyred in Syria in AD 303. The earliest pieces of the building date from the fifth century. It lies some 3 m below street level and was rebuilt in the Fatimid period after having been virtually destroyed by fire in the eighth century. The architecture of the church, which contains many antiques recovered from ancient monuments, follows the style of a traditional basilica with the nave divided from the side aisles by two rows of six marble pillars. Eleven of these monolithic columns are marble and one is of red granite. The remains of illustrations on these pillars represent the apostles or saints. Some of the series of icons found here are 17th century and show scenes from the lives of Christ, the Virgin Mary and some of the saints. The partially flooded crypt, to the left of the sanctuary, the only remaining vestige of the original church, is intriguing because it is claimed that the Holy Family sought refuge here during their flight to Egypt and the places where they sat are still visible. It has always been a popular place of pilgrimage and a special Mass is held annually on the 24th day of the Coptic month of Bechens (1 June) to commemorate the flight.

The Church of St Barbara

ⓘ *0800-1600.* Just behind the church of St Sergius is the very similar 11th-century Church of St Barbara standing on the site of an older church dedicated to St Cyrus and St John in AD 684 that was destroyed during an Arab assault. It is said that when some Christians from Damanhur, including Cyrus and John, confessed to their faith they were shot with arrows,

No peace for the holy either

In the grim, barren desolation of the Moqattam hills to the south of Cairo were a number of abandoned windmills. These had been used by the British army during the First World War to produce flour supplies and were no longer required.

In 1936 a monk called Mina obtained one to use as a place of retreat and prayer. With the door replaced and the roof made safe he constructed a small living area downstairs and an even smaller chapel above. His intention to devote himself to peaceful contemplation proved impossible. The monk in the windmill was good news to those needing a release from their mental and physical problems. The number of visitors increased and set times were allocated for services each day.

The area was declared unsafe during the Second World War and Mina moved, with some reluctance, to the neighbouring churches of Archangel Michael and St Mary in Old Cairo, just 3 km away.

After the hostilities Mina purchased the land adjacent to the former windmill site and built a church dedicated to St Mina the martyr. To this was added a large monastic complex complete with accommodation where he stayed until he was elected patriach in 1971 and became Pope Shenuda III.

Whereas the monasteries in Egypt had suffered from serious decline, the influence of a Pope who had spent so many years in retreat caused a revival of interest in monasticism among the Coptic community. Buildings have been restored, visitors welcomed and the number of monks has increased.

burned in a furnace, tied to a horse's tail and dragged through the streets and survived – to be beheaded. The remains of these two martyrs are in the side chapel approached from the left of the altar. The third-century relics of St Barbara were brought to the church and are now contained in a lovely little chapel to the left of the altar. St Barbara was an attractive young woman from Nicomedia in Asia Minor. In one version of her history she tried to convert her father to Christianity and he killed her. In the second version she was denounced by her family when she decided to become a nun – then tortured and finally put to death by the Romans along with her faithful attendant St Juliana.

The Ben Ezra Synagogue

ⓘ *0900-1600, photography strictly forbidden.* South of the Church of St Barbara is the Ben Ezra Synagogue in the former sixth-century Church of St Michael the Archangel, which itself had been built on the site of a synagogue destroyed by the Romans. This is the oldest surviving synagogue in Egypt. In the 12th century it was sold back to the Jews by the Copts in order to pay taxes being raised to finance the Ibn Tulun mosque. The synagogue is built in the basilica style with three naves and an altar hidden by doors, which are wonderfully worked and encrusted with ivory. When the synagogue was extensively repaired in the 19th century, medieval Hebrew manuscripts, known collectively as the **Geniza documents** and providing details of the history of the 11th-16th centuries, were discovered. These are now kept in libraries around Western Europe.

Church of St George

ⓘ *Via the first door on the left of the main entrance to the museum, 0800-1600.* The Church of St George is a modern construction from 1904 and the only circular church in Egypt, so shaped because it is actually built on top of the north tower of the old fortress. Part of the Monastery of St George, which is the seat of the Greek Orthodox Patriarchate of Alexandria, the church is nevertheless the scene of one of the largest Coptic *moulids* in Egypt on 23 April (St George's Day). It is worth a quick look for the brightly stained glass, enormous chandelier, heady scent of incense and a few nice icons. The adjacent Café Saint George is a bit expensive but the best place to re-group after seeing so many churches, with alfresco wicker seating, whispering trees, good lemon juice (*asir lamoon*) and passable coffee.

If you are going to walk from the main Coptic sights to the mosque and monasteries to the north, you will pass by the **Souk Al-Fustat**, about 400 m north of the metro station, on the right-hand side of Sharia Saydi Hassan Al-Anwar, before the Mosque of Amr. You can't miss the freshly constructing building, which provides workspaces for local artisans (metal workers, leather workers, glass blowers, etc) in an attempt to keep traditional crafts alive. Well-priced high-quality goods are on sale in the chic shops on the ground floor (see Shopping, page 145).

Other sacred sights

Mosque of Amr Ibn Al-As The original Mosque of Amr Ibn Al-As (Gama Amr), 500 m north of Mari Girgis metro station, was built in AD 642 by the commander of the Arab army that captured Egypt in that year. Built near to both Babylon-in-Egypt and the Arabs' encampment (Fustat), it is the oldest mosque in Egypt and one of the oldest in the entire Islamic world. Because of the continual enlargements, which began in AD 673 only 10 years after Amr's death aged 93, and included major restoration work in the 15th and 18th centuries and the most recent work in the 1970s, nothing of the original mud-brick thatched-roof mosque still exists. Recently repainted and cleaned, its aspect today is virtually modern. As is often the case in the older mosques the interior includes many pillars taken from ancient Egyptian monuments. As a result the whole mosque is a hybrid with parts of the fabric dating from before the conquest of Egypt until the 19th-century alterations. In the north corner under the dome and surrounded by a bronze screen, on the site of Amr's house in Fustat, is the tomb of his son Abdullah who was born when Amr was only 13, became a Muslim before him and was a close companion of the Prophet.

Convent of St Mercurius ⓘ *10-min walk north of the central Coptic area, past the Mosque of Amr Ibn Al-As and on the left, 0700-2000.* This walled complex of churches is worth visiting to escape the presence of the soldiers, tourists and shops that infiltrate the main sights of Coptic Cairo. After a vision in which St Mercurius was presented with a luminous sword (hence his Arabic name *Abu Seifein* – Mr Two Swords) in order to fight for the cause of Christianity, he was persecuted and killed for his faith. Relics are said to be here in the convent and also in the adjacent church. The convent has its origins in the sixth century but has gone through many stages of rebuilding especially in the 10th century. The **Church of St Mercurius**, the largest church here, is actually a church and four large chapels, the chapel on the ground floor dedicated to St Jacob (containing the font used for adult baptism) (at the time of writing this chapel was closed for restoration) and those upstairs (only reliably open on Fridays) dedicated to St George, John the Baptist and the children killed by Herod.

In the church itself steps lead down to a damp cellar room which is the cell of the Great Hermit Saint Barsoun. You need to take your shoes off if you want to enter this cell. In the courtyard behind the church is a small, very basic café and some toilets. In the same complex is the **Church of St Shenuda**. This church, noted for its 18th-century icons, is adjacent to the church of St Mercurius. There are seven icons in the ebony and cedarwood screen, the central one shows the Virgin and the others each have pictures of two apostles. Shenuda is associated with the Red and White monasteries (see page 212). Nearby, the **Church of the Virgin** is thick with icons and hanging lanterns which, as shafts of sunlight pierce the gloom, create an intensely spiritual atmosphere.

If you have ventured this far, you can avoid backtracking by exiting the convent by the door next to the blue bridge over the Metro tracks. Turn right out of the convent, keep the tracks to your left and walk along the road for 300 m to pick up the Metro at Malek El-Salah station. On your right as you walk away from the convent are four vast cemeteries. Apart from the Commonwealth War Graves Commission cemetary (open 0800-1430) there are no set opening times, but there is often a man with a key who is happy to let you wander around for a small amount of *baksheesh*.

Coptic Orthodox Cathedral There are more than 100 Coptic Orthodox churches in Cairo but the special pride is the **Coptic Orthodox Cathedral** (1965) dedicated to St Mark. This is just off Sharia Ramses. It can seat 5000 worshippers, houses the patriarchal library and accommodates the patriarch Pope Shenuda III.

Roda Island

An island south of Zamalek, accessible by bridge from Garden City at the northern end and from Old Cairo at the bottom, Roda has a couple of interesting sights, the eccentric Manial Palace being chief among them. Strolling the 2 km between the palace in the north and the Nilometer to the south along mainly post-1950s streets is something few tourists find time to do, but offers plenty of scope for a relaxing *sheesha* and *ahwa* in shady streets that are more peaceful than most.

The Manial Palace ⓘ *Daily 0900-1630, E£20, E£10 for students. Currently closed for restoration and scheduled to reopen in 2011.* An oasis of tranquillity in noisy Cairo and well worth visiting, the palace was built in 1903 and is now a museum. It was the home of King Farouk's uncle Prince Mohammed Ali and comprises a number of buildings in various styles including Moorish, Ottoman, Persian, Rococo and Syrian. The first is the **Reception Palace** at the gate, beautifully decorated with polychrome tiles and stained glass. Upstairs are a number of luxurious rooms, of which the **Syrian Room** is the finest, and a mother-of-pearl scale model of Sultan Qaitbay's mausoleum. To the right is a mosque with a tall mock Moroccan minaret and then a macabre yet curious **Trophies Museum** with tatty and poorly stuffed animals including a hermaphrodite goat and a table made of elephant's ears. The **Royal Residence** in the middle of the garden is a mixture of Turkish, Moroccan, Egyptian and Syrian architectures and contains a number of rooms, nearly all of which are decorated with blue earthenware tiles. The **Throne Hall** behind the residence contains impressive royal portraiture and the **Private Museum** includes a varied collection of Korans, manuscripts, carpets, plates and glassware, and is fascinating. The palace gardens are 5500 sq m and contain a rare collection of trees brought back to Egypt by Mohammed Ali.

The Nilometer and Umm Khalsoum Museum On the southern tip of Roda island stands a small kiosk containing the **Nilometer** ⓘ *daily 0900-1600, E£15, students E£8*, originally built in the ninth century BC. There has probably been a nilometer here since ancient times but this one was constructed in AD 861 and is considered the second oldest Islamic structure in

Umm Khalsoum, Egypt's Mother Diva

The taxi driver has put his favourite cassette on. Who does that forceful voice, rising above the slithering quarter tones of the violins, belong to? It could well be that of Umm Khalsoum, the best known Egyptian of this century after Gamal Abd Al-Nasser and still the most popular Arab singer. There was nothing in her background to suggest that Umm Khalsoum was to become the greatest diva produced by the Arab world.

Born in 1904 in a small village in the Nile Delta region, Umm Khalsoum became interested in music through listening to her father teach her brother Khalid to sing religious chants for village weddings. One day, when Khalid was ill, Umm Khalsoum accompanied her father and performed instead of her brother. The guests were astonished at her voice. After this, she accompanied her father to sing at all the weddings. In 1920, the family headed for Cairo. Once in the capital, Umm Khalsoum's star rose fast. She met the poet Ahmad Ramzi and made her first commercial recordings. In 1935, she sang in her first film. She subsequently starred in numerous Hollywood-on-the-Nile productions.

In 1946, personal and health problems made Umm Khalsoum abandon her career, temporarily as it turned out. Due to her illness, she met her future husband, the doctor Hassan El-Hafnawi, whom she married in 1954. She then resumed her career. Songs such as *Al awal fil gharam wal hubb* ('The first thing in desire and love'), *Al hubbi kullu* ('Love is all') and *Alf layla wa layla* ('A Thousand and One Nights') made her name across the Arab lands. In the 1960s, her Thursday-evening concert on the Cairo-based Radio Sawt Al-Arab ('Voice of the Arabs') became an Arab-wide institution. During the Yemeni civil war, the Monarchist troops knew that Thursday evening was the best time to attack the Egyptian troops supporting the Republicans as they would all be clustered round their radio sets listening to their national diva. So massive was her fame that she was dubbed 'the Fourth Pyramid'.

Umm Khalsoum's deep, vibrant voice was exceptional, of that there is no doubt. Nevertheless, the music may be difficult for Western ears. Though the lyrics are often insufferably syrupy, the diva's songs continue to enjoy wide popularity and her films, subtitled in English or French are often shown on Egyptian satellite channel Nile TV. If there is one piece of modern Arab music you should try to discover, it has to be the Umm Khalsoum classic love song, *Al Atlal* ('The remains of the camp fire'). The theme, a lament sung over the ashes of the camp fire for the departed lover, goes way back to the origins of Arab poetry.

Umm Khalsoum died in 1975, and her funeral cortège filled the streets of Cairo with hundreds of thousands of mourners. Her voice lives on, played in cafés and cars, workshops and homes all over the Arab world.

Cairo, after the Amr Ibn Al-Aas Mosque. The original measuring gauge remains today and there is exquisite Kufic calligraphy on the interior walls and an elaborately painted dome. The **Umm Khalsoum Museum** ① *Sharia Al-Malek Al-Salah, Roda, daily 1000-1600, E£2,* contains memorabilia from the life of Egypt's ultimate diva (see box, above). It's a small and well-curated museum set in pleasant grounds next to the Manasterli Palace (an impressive Rococco structure where concerts are infrequently held). In the museum are Umm Khalsoum's famous sunglasses and ubiquitous pink scarf, alongside photos, press cuttings and audiovisuals – most poignant of which shows her funeral procession that brought the streets of Cairo to a standstill in 1975. You can listen to her songs and if they appeal to you there is an enterprising stall outside selling her CDs. There is also an impressive display of aged audio equipment that was no doubt once state-of-the-art.

Zamalek and Gezira

This island in the Nile was unoccupied until the middle of the 19th century when Khedive Ismail built a magnificent palace and landscaped its surrounds into sprawling royal gardens populated by exotic animals. These days, the palace is part of the Marriott hotel and **Zamalek**, the northern part of the island, is a leafy, upmarket residential area popular with expats and the Egyptian elite. There are many decent restaurants (some of them floating), welcoming places for a drink, excellent shopping (books, art and souvenirs) and the delightful Islamic Ceramics Museum. **Gezira** occupies the southern half, mostly taken up by the grounds of the Gezira Club and the Opera House complex, plus there are some attractive gardens along the river and the landmark Cairo Tower.

Islamic Ceramics Museum

ⓘ *1 Sharia Sheikh Al-Marsafy, next to the Marriott, Zamalek, Sat-Thu 1000-1400 and 1700-2100, entrance E£25, students E£12.50. Photos permitted upon application.*

The palace of Prince Amr Ibrahim is a cool, marbled haven and provides a beautiful home for exquisite ceramics dating from the seventh century to the modern day. The soft tints, hues and glazes bring out the designs on vessels and dishes collected from countries stretching from Morocco to Persia. The garden contains some pieces of sculpture, while in the basement there's an art gallery (free) that has interesting displays by contemporary Egyptian artists.

Cairo Tower

ⓘ *Sharia Hadayek Al-Zuhrey, Gezira, T02-2736 5112, daily 0900-0100 (-2400 in winter), E£70.*

The 187-m tower with a lotus-shaped top is a prominent icon of the Cairo skyline, especially at night when it is lit with waves of neon lights that constantly change colour. It was built with Soviet help in 1957-1962 and has recently undergone a revamp. Although the Sky Garden revolving restaurant at the top and cafeteria are very decent, it is the viewing platform that is most impressive. Providing the pollution is not too bad, you can look east across the modern city centre to the minarets and mosques of Islamic Cairo and the Muqattam Hills beyond; to the west the Pyramids and desert sprawl out on the horizon. It's a great view of the city at night.

The west bank

The newer suburbs on Cairo's west bank are chiefly comprised of concrete blocks built post-1960, interspersed with the occasional grand villa, crumbling mansion and pleasant green square. There are a few smaller, less frequented museums that have a great deal of charm as well as some good restaurants, which may draw you over this side of the river. **Dokki** (pronounced *Do'ii*, with a glottal stop in the middle) is home to the **Agricultural Museum** and the **Mr and Mrs Mahmoud Khalil Museum**, but not much else that would interest a tourist. **Mohandiseen**, further inland, is a middle-class enclave of swanky boutiques, fast-food joints and decent international and Egyptian cuisine. It is about the only district in Cairo that looks and feels Western (but just on the main drags) with strings of American coffee shop chains, wide palm-lined boulevards, luminous billboards and sleekly fashionable shoppers. In sharp contrast is **Imbaba** to the north, a gritty suburb with great *baladi souks* and where a string of 30 or so picturesque houseboats remain moored along the Nile at Midan Kit Kat. The attractions of **Giza**, apart from the obvious, are the child-friendly **Pharaonic Village** and the **zoo**, which has attractive botanical gardens adjacent to it.

8 Zamalek

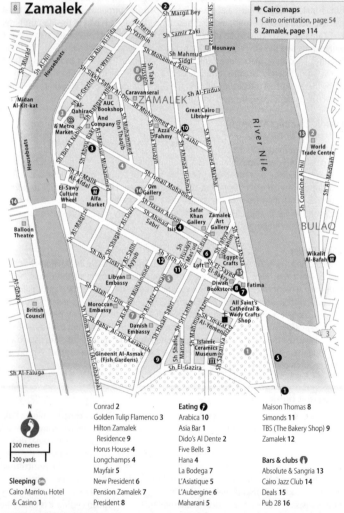

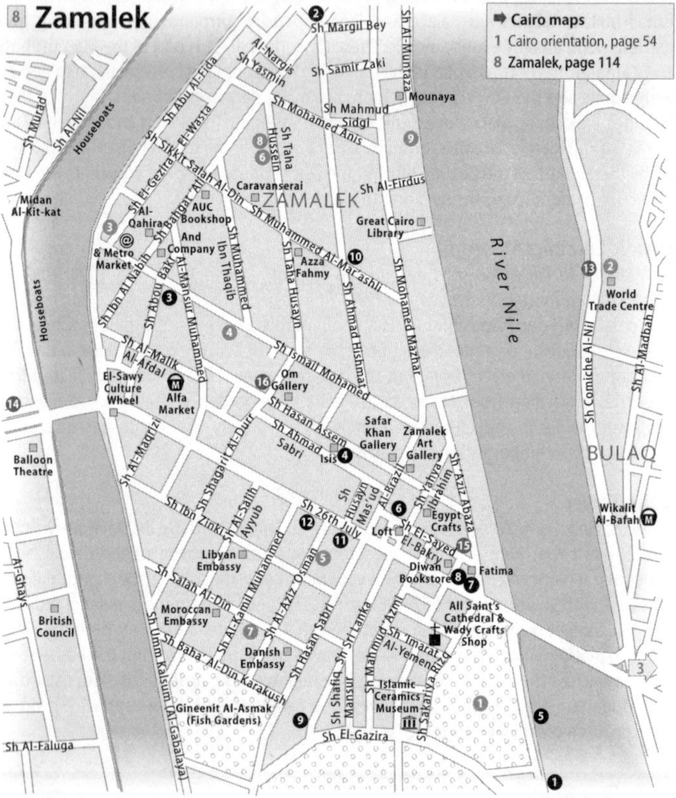

Sleeping
Cairo Marriott Hotel & Casino **1**
Conrad **2**
Golden Tulip Flamenco **3**
Hilton Zamalek Residence **9**
Horus House **4**
Longchamps **4**
Mayfair **5**
New President **6**
Pension Zamalek **7**
President **8**

Eating
Arabica **10**
Asia Bar **1**
Dido's Al Dente **2**
Five Bells **3**
Hana **4**
La Bodega **7**
L'Asiatique **5**
L'Aubergine **6**
Maharani **5**
Maison Thomas **8**
Simonds **11**
TBS (The Bakery Shop) **9**
Zamalek **12**

Bars & clubs
Absolute & Sangria **13**
Cairo Jazz Club **14**
Deals **15**
Pub 28 **16**

Agricultural Museum

ⓘ *Adjacent to the Ministry of Agriculture in Dokki at end of 6th October Bridge, T02-3761 6874, Tue-Sun 0900-1400, E£3, cameras 20 pt.*

This has the distinction of being the oldest agricultural museum in world (dating from 1930), with stuffed animals, racks of luminescent birds, Egyptian farming practices and photos of medical anomalies. It might sound tedious, but it is a slice of unspoilt history – the museum itself ought be in a museum – full of waxy wooden display cabinets and housed in glorious buildings engraved with decorative flora and fauna. Downstairs in the main Scientific Museum, countryside scenes are brought to life by statues of farmers at work and gruesome pictures of rural diseases (pay the guard a bit of *baksheesh* to gain entry to the side galleries). The many animals that were worshipped, hunted or eaten – cats, ostrich, Apis bulls and falcons – are here, as mummies or skeletons. Unfortunately the labels, in a variety of languages, give little information if they exist at all.

The ticket price includes entrance to several museums in the grounds, some of which are closed for maintenance and due to reopen in 2011. The strangely beautiful **Bread Halls** reveal the story of bread in Egypt, with plaster-casts of the various forms of this staple food and interesting old photographs. The **Cotton Museum** surveys cotton-growing in Egypt and the **Ancient Egyptian Agriculture Museum** contains quite a choice range of pharaonic artefacts; both are housed in Soviet-style edifices but are currently closed for renovation. Also on site is the **Palace of Princess Fatma**, daughter of Khedive Ismail, which is accessible to those with special interest. Meticulously maintained on two levels, the museum displays her ornate furniture, many beautiful works of art, and collections of ivory curios, old cameras and Persian carpets. The gardens surrounding the museum are a peaceful place to relax, full of dusty old palms and flowering trees.

Mr and Mrs Mahmoud Khalil Museum

ⓘ *1 Sharia Kafour, off Sharia Giza, Dokki, T02-3748 2142, www.mkm.gov.eg, Wed-Mon 0900-1730, E£25, students E£12, photo ID required for entry.*

The sumptuous villa of the Khalil's hides a wonderful collection of Impressionist paintings by the likes of Renoir, Monet and Toulouse-Lautrec. It also used to house a Van Gogh, but this was stolen in broad daylight in 2010 prompting a nationwide overhaul of museum security facilities and the imprisonment of the curators of museum. Despite the loss, there are also some fine sculptures, including works by Rodin, and the fact very few visitors make it here mean it's a pleasurably personal experience.

Giza Zoo

ⓘ *T02-3570 1552, daily 0900-1700 in winter, 0800-1800 in summer, E£20.*

The zoo has many claims to fame. In particular it is the biggest exhibitor in Africa, having on display the largest number of endangered species. Its situation near the west bank of the Nile at Giza makes it easily accessible over El-Gamea Bridge. The zoo is organized into five huge grottos, one holding statues of rare Egyptian mammals. There are over 6000 animals and birds on display from around 40 species. Features include the Reptile House and the Lion House. The zoo is proud of its record in breeding and returning to the wild barbary sheep, nubian ibex, dorcas gazelle and sacred ibis. **Note** Visitors used to Western zoos may find a visit here very distressing, particularly the lion cages.

Step into the salon

Beauty parlours provide all sorts of treatments. Foot massages and pedicures are lengthy and often public, enjoyed by both men and women; ladies then go on to choose from an array of gaudy nail polish.

Men should head to the barbers, not to risk a radical haircut but for a cut-throat close shave. Not only do they double- shave customers the smoothest they've ever been, there's an invigorating head, face and neck massage afterwards that sets the teeth tingling. Be warned, though, the barber might take it upon himself to start threading your face to remove all stray wisps above the cheekbones, plus eye-wateringly removal of any nasal hairs and shaping of eyebrows. Make sure you are happy with the hygiene standards of the establishment before you let them take a razor to you.

While it's not recommended for women to chance going for a haircut in Egypt (unless it's for bizarre feathering or 'trims' that take 15 cm off) there are other ways to indulge yourself for a small sum. Hair removal is cheap and relatively painless, with lumps of cool sticky melted sugar (*helawa*) being pressed and smeared onto the skin then worked off in jerky tugs. Egyptian women get virtually every hair plucked from their body, and though you might not want a full body wax, lots of foreigners living in Cairo follow the custom to some degree and get their arms sugared. Face 'threading' is an interesting process to watch but not necessarily to participate in, with a stretch of twisted cotton held between the mouth and fingers and drawn across the skin to magically remove the tiny hairs with a pinging sound. *Baladi* women perform these tasks for each other at home, but if you don't have that option, a good places to go is Tarek Nail Centre, 47 Sharia Michel Bakoum, Mohandiseen, T02-3748 7422, quite a public experience for pedicures (but privacy for other things), full leg wax E£50. They also have a salon in Maadi, 73 Road 9, T02-2358 3385.

Dr Ragab's Pharaonic Village

ⓘ *On Jacob's Island, Giza, 3 km south of the city centre, T02-3572 2533 or T02-35718675/6/7, www.pharaonicvillage.com, daily Sep-Jun 0900-1800, Jul-Aug 0900-2100, E£201, children under 4 years free.*

Numerous actors on floating amphitheatres perform the daily activities of the ancient Egyptians as you cruise and view from a pharaonic boat. The pace is set by the boat tour through the village on the bullrush-fringed Nile so be sure to allow at least two hours. There are 12 museums relating the history of Egypt, plus demonstrations of papyrus-making – it's possible to purchase quality papyrus copies of illustrations and writing found in tombs at the on-site Papyrus Institute. The Nefertari yacht takes you on a one-hour cruise along a scenic stretch of the Nile as part of the ticket price. It's a great place for children who will enjoy the Tut Land amusement park, and a quite bizarre experience for anyone.

Pyramids of Giza

ⓘ T02-2391 3454, daily 0800-1700 winter, 0800-1800 summer, E£80 (students E£40) to enter the area, additional E£200 (students E£100) to enter the Pyramid of Cheops. The number of tourists who can enter Cheops is limited in order to preserve the monument so arrive early (morning session 0800, then another batch at 1300; 250 at one time in winter, 150 people in summer), additional E£60/30 to enter the second and third pyramids. No cameras permitted inside the pyramid, they have to be left with the guards on entering, and claustrophobics should avoid going inside. For Sound and Light performances, see page 141. A camel ride around the pyramids can be a fun way to take in their splendour, offer no more than E£20 for a short ride – to be paid after your meander. AA and MG stables (past the entrance to the Sphinx) are among the more notable in Giza.

One of the first things that visitors to the Pyramids will notice is their unexpected proximity to Cairo. The second is the onslaught of hustlers that bombard the awe-struck onlooker. Despite the increased police presence that tries in earnest to subdue the camel and horse hustlers, water and soda hawkers and papyrus and postcard vendors, they still get through. Be firm with your 'no' and they'll get the point, eventually. To get the best out of the experience, it's definitely recommended to be first through the gate or the last person in before the gates close, and strike off into the desert around to view their majesty from afar.

Of the Seven Wonders of the ancient world only the Pyramids are left standing. Those at Giza are by no means the only ones in Egypt but they are the largest, most imposing and best preserved. When Herodotus, chronicler of the Ancient Greeks, visited them in 450 BC they were already more ancient to him than the time of Christ is to us today. That the huge blocks were quarried, transported and put into place demonstrates how highly developed and ordered the Old Kingdom was at its peak. Herodotus claimed that it would have taken 100,000 slaves 30 years to have constructed the great **Pyramid of Cheops**, but it is more likely that the pyramid was built by peasants, paid in food, who were unable to

Pyramids of Giza

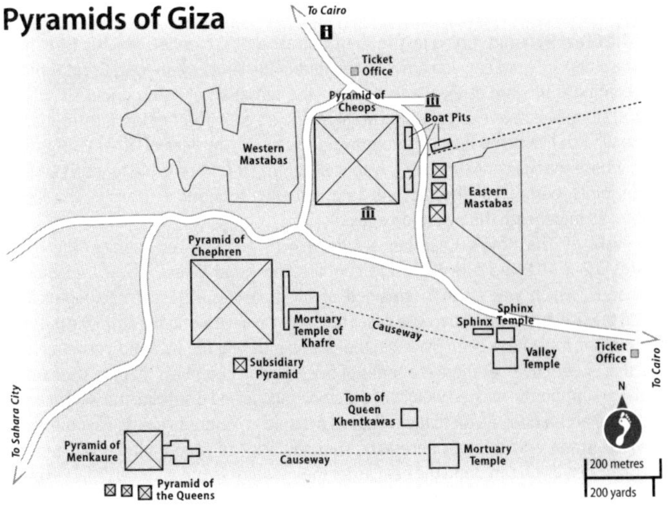

work the land while the Nile flooded between July and November. Happily, the high waters also made it possible to transport the casing stone from Aswan and Tura virtually to the base of the pyramids. The enormous Pyramid of Cheops, built between 2589-2566 BC out of over 2,300,000 blocks of stone with an average weight of two and a half tonnes and a total weight of 6,000,000 tonnes to a height of almost 140 m, is the oldest and largest of the pyramids at Giza. Maybe not surprisingly, it can be seen from the moon. The **Pyramid of Chephren** and **Pyramid of Menkaure** date from 2570-30 BC. There is a theory that the odd plan of the three Pyramids of Giza, progressively smaller and with the third slightly offset to the left, correlates to the layout of the three stars of Orion's Belt. Highly controversial, it suggests that the Ancient Egyptians chose to reproduce, on land and over a great distance, a kind of map of the stars.

A breakdown in the structure of society, and the reduction of wealth, have been proposed as reasons why other pyramids were not constructed on the same scale later in the Old Kingdom. The first thefts from tombs occurred relatively soon after the Pyramids' construction, which was undoubtedly an important factor in the preference for hidden tombs, such as in The Valley of the Kings, by the time of the New Kingdom.

The Great Pyramid of Cheops (Khufu)

Very little is known of Cheops. His tomb, which could have provided some answers, was looted long before any archaeologists arrived. He is believed to have been the absolute ruler of a highly stratified society and his reign must have been one of great wealth in order to afford so stupendous a burial site. Although he was buried alone, his wives and relations may have merited smaller *mastabas* nearby.

Originally the 230 x 230 m pyramid would have stood at 140 m high but 3 m has been lost in all dimensions since the encasing limestone was eroded or removed by later rulers who used the cemeteries like a quarry to construct the Islamic city. The entrance, which was at the centre of the north face, has been changed in modern times and access is now 15 m lower via an opening created by the plundering Khalifa Ma'mun in AD 820.

Inside the Great Pyramid Going up the 36-m long ascending corridor, which is 1.6 m high and has a steep 1:2 gradient, you arrive at the start of the larger 47-m-long **Great Gallery**, which continues upward at the same incline – the sensation of being under six million tonnes of stone becomes overpowering at this point; it's definitely not for claustrophobics or those who dislike being hustled into moving too quickly by lines of other visitors. The gallery, whose magnificent stonework is so well cut that it is impossible to insert a blade into the joints, narrows at the top end to a corbelled roof and finishes at the King's Chamber, 95 m beneath the pyramid's apex.

The walls of **The King's Chamber** are lined with polished red granite. The room measures 5.2 x 10.8 x 5.8 m high and contains the huge lidless Aswan red granite sarcophagus, which was all that remained of the treasures when archaeologists first explored the site. It was saved because it was too large to move along the entrance passage and, therefore, must have been placed in the chamber during the pyramid's construction. Above this upper chamber there is a series of five relieving chambers that are structurally essential to support the massed weight of the stones above and distribute the weight away from the burial chamber. A visit to the collapsed pyramid at Maidoum (see El-Fayoum, page 173) will illustrate why this was necessary. You may want to wait around a while in the King's Chamber, if you can stand the heat, to let the crowds thin out and you'll start to get a sense of the mystique of the place that prompts some visitors to start chanting.

One of the great mysteries of the massive Pyramid of Cheops is the four tiny meticulously crafted 20-cm-sq shafts, which travel, two from the King's Chamber and another two from the Queen's Chamber, at precisely maintained angles through the body of the pyramid to the outer walls. Obviously serving a significant function, they were originally thought to be ventilation shafts. However, Egyptologists are now more inclined to believe that they are of religious significance and relate to the Ancient Egyptians' belief that the stars are a heavenly counterpart to their land, inhabited by gods and souls of the departed.

The main feature of the ancient night sky was the Milky Way, the bright band of stars that was believed to be the celestial Nile. The most conspicuous of the stars were those of Orion's Belt, whose reappearance coincided with the yearly miracle of the Nile flood and was associated with Osiris, the protector god. The brightest star in the sky (Sirius) was his consort, the goddess Isis, because it was glitteringly beautiful and followed Osiris across the sky. Linked to the creation myth, the texts on the great pyramid's walls repeatedly tell of the dead Pharaoh, seen as the latest incarnation of Horus, the son of Isis and Osiris, travelling in a boat between various star constellations. At an angle of exactly 45°, the southern shaft of the King's Chamber points directly at where Orion's Belt would have been in the sky in ancient times. Meanwhile, the southern shaft of the Queen's Chamber points to Sirius, his consort Isis. The northern shaft of the King's Chamber is directed at the circumpolar stars, important to the Ancient Egyptians as the celestial pole because these stars never disappear or die in the sky. The 'star shafts' thus appear to be directed so that the spirit of the dead Pharaoh could use the shafts to reach the important stars with pinpoint accuracy.

Around the Great Pyramid of Cheops

In accordance with the pharaonic custom, Cheops married his sister Merites whose smaller ruined pyramid stands to the east of his, together with the pyramids of two other queens, both of which are attached to a similarly ruined smaller sanctuary. Little remains

Pyramid of Cheops (section)

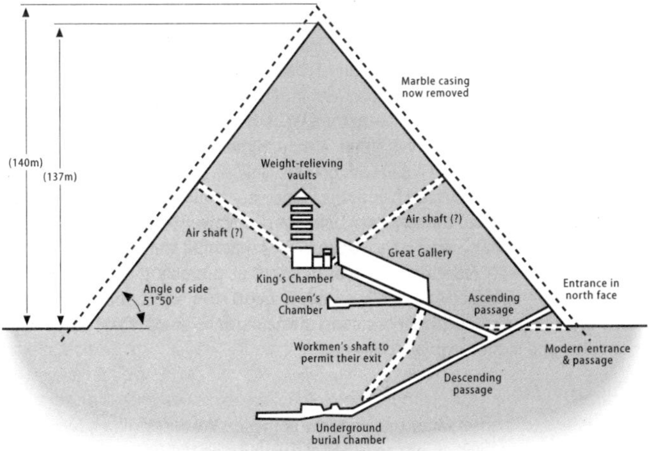

of **Cheops' Mortuary Temple**, which stood to the east of the pyramid. It was connected by a causeway, which collapsed only in the last 150 years, to the Valley Temple that stands near the modern village of **Nazlat Al-Samman**. The temples and causeway were built and decorated before Cheops' Pyramid was completed.

West of the Cheops Pyramid is an extensive **Royal Cemetery** in which 15 *mastabas* have been opened to the public after having been closed for over 100 years. A 4600-year-old female mummy, with a unique internal plaster encasement unlike that seen anywhere else, was discovered at the site.

The **Sun Boat Museum** ⓘ *daily 0900-1600, E£60, students E£30*, is at the base of the south face of the Cheops Pyramid where five boat pits were discovered in 1982. The boat on display, painstakingly reassembled over 14 years and an amazing 43 m long, is held together with sycamore pegs and rope. The exact purpose of these buried boats is unclear but they may have been a means of travelling to the afterlife, as can be seen in the 17th to 19th Dynasty tombs at Thebes, or possibly a way of accompanying the Sun God on his diurnal journey. It may not sound like much and is yet another expense in an already expensive day, but the scale and antiquity of the vessel is impressive and makes real the engravings of boats you so often see on temple walls around Egypt.

Pyramid of Chephren ⓘ *E£20, students E£10*, or Khafre as he is sometimes known, was built for the son of Cheops and Hensuten and stands to the southwest of the Great Pyramid of Cheops. Although, at 136.5 m high and an estimated weight of 4,880,000 tonnes, it is actually a few metres smaller than the Cheops Pyramid and its construction on a raised limestone plateau was a deliberate attempt to make it appear larger than that of his father. The top of the pyramid still retains some of the casing of polished limestone from Tura that once covered the entire surface, providing an idea of the original finish and how the pyramid would have appeared to the earliest travellers – gleaming and white as they approached from the desert. The entrance to the tomb was lost for centuries until 1818 when Belzoni located it and blasted open the sealed portal on the north side. Although he believed that it would still be intact, he found that it had been looted many centuries earlier. As with the Pyramid of Cheops there is an unfinished and presumed unused chamber below the bedrock. The entrance passageway now used heads downwards before levelling out to a granite-lined passageway that leads to the burial chamber. To the west of the chamber is the red granite sarcophagus, built into the floor, with the lid lying nearby.

The **Mortuary Temple of Khafre** lies to the east of the pyramid and is more elaborate and better preserved than that of his father. Although the statues and riches have been stolen, the limestone walls were cased with granite, which is still present in places. There are still the remains a large pillared hall, a small sanctuary, outhouses and a courtyard.

A 500-m causeway linked the Mortuary Temple to the **Valley Temple**, which is better preserved than any other because it lay hidden in the sands until Mariette rediscovered it in 1852. It is lined with red granite at roof height that protects the limestone. Two entrances to the temple face east and lead to a T-shaped hall supported by enormous pillars. In front of these stood 23 diorite statues of Khafre. The only one that has remained intact can be found in the Egyptian Museum.

The Sphinx

The Sphinx is next to Khafre's Valley Temple to the northeast. We are extremely lucky that it still exists because it was built of soft sandstone and would have disappeared centuries ago had the sand not covered it for so much of its history. Yet it is equally surprising that it was ever carved because its sculptor must have known that such soft stone would quickly decay. The Arabs call it the Father of Terror (*Abu'l-Hawl*). Nobody can be certain who it represents but it is possibly Khafre himself and, if this is the case, would be the oldest known large-scale royal portrait. Some say that it was hewn from the remaining stone after the completion of the pyramid and that, almost as an afterthought, Khafre set it, as a sort of monumental scarecrow, to guard his tomb. Others claim that the face is that of his guardian deity rather than Khafre's own. The Sphinx was first uncovered by Tuthmosis IV (1425-1417 BC) thereby fulfilling a prophecy that by uncovering the great man-lion he would gain the throne. Recent efforts to conserve the Sphinx are now complete but the rising water table threatens to accelerate its decay. Earlier attempts to restore it caused more harm than good when the porous sandstone was filled, totally inappropriately, with concrete. The Sphinx suffered at the hands at Mamluke and Napoleonic troops who used him for target practice, and a piece of the missing 'beard' is exhibited in the British Museum.

The name 'sphinx', which means 'strangler', was given first by the Greeks to a fabulous creature that had the head and bust of a woman, the body of a lion and the wings of a bird. The sphinx appears to have originated in Egypt in the form of a sun god with whom the pharaoh was associated. The Egyptian sphinx is usually a lion with the head of a king wearing the characteristic wig-cover. There are, however, ram-headed sphinxes associated with the god Amun.

Pyramid of Menkaure (Mycerinus)

This is the smallest of the three Giza Pyramids and marks the beginning of a steep decline in the standards of workmanship and attention to detail in the art of pyramid-building. At the time of Menkaure's death (who was Chephren's successor and later known by the Greek name of Mycerinus) the pyramid was unfinished and the granite encasement intended to cover the poor quality local limestone was never put in place by his son Shepseskaf. The base is 102 x 104 m (the original measurements much reduced by removal of stones) and rises at 51 degrees to 66.5 m high, considerably lower than the earlier pyramids. It also differs from those of Khufu and Khafre in that the lower chamber was used as the burial tomb. The walls are lined with granite hewn into the rock below the level of the Pyramid's foundations. A fine basalt sarcophagus was discovered in the recessed floor but unfortunately lost at sea en route to Britain.

East of the Pyramid of Menkaure lies the **Mortuary Temple**, which is relatively well preserved. The walls were not encased with granite or marble but with red mud bricks and then lined with a thin layer of smoother limestone. It is connected to the Valley Temple via a 660-m mud-brick causeway that now lies beneath the sand.

Subsidiary pyramids

South of the Pyramid of Menkaure are three smaller incomplete pyramids. The largest, to the east, was most likely intended for Menkaure's principal wife. The granite sarcophagus of the central tomb was recovered and was found to contain the bones of a young woman.

The **Tomb of Queen Khentkawes**, who was an obscure but intriguing and important figure, is to the south of the main Giza pyramids. Although she appears to have been married to Shepseskaf, who was the last Fourth Dynasty pharaoh, she subsequently married a high priest of the sun god Re at a time when the male dynastic line was particularly weak. By going on to bear a number of later kings who are buried in Saqqara and Abu Sir, she acted as the link between the Fourth and Fifth Dynasties. Her tomb is an enormous sarcophagus and is linked to a Mortuary Temple cut out of the limestone.

The **Zawiyat Al-Aryan Pyramids** are roughly halfway between Giza and North Saqqara and one has to ride through the desert to see them. A visit would probably only be rewarding to the devoted Egyptologist. There are two pyramids of which the southernmost one is probably a Third Dynasty (2686-2613 BC) step pyramid. The granite of the more northerly suggests that it is Fourth Dynasty (2613-2494 BC) but it would appear to have been abandoned after the foundations had been laid.

Other excursions around Cairo

Birqash Camel Market

ⓘ *35 km northwest of Cairo: getting there via public transport is quite a confusing affair, as there are no direct routes, but if you want to try, take a taxi or minibus to the old camel market in Imbaba (near Imbaba Airport), from there, minibuses run to the the 'souk al-gamal'. Alternatively, hire a taxi for the morning or go with one of the organized tours from a budget hotel. Ismailia and Sun Hotel, in Midan Tahrir, both have weekly trips for E£50 per person, they usually leave around 0630 and return at 1130, the earlier you arrive at the market, the more action you'll see. Tourists are expected to pay a E£20 fee to enter the market.*

Cairo's Friday camel market (there is a smaller version on Mondays) makes an interesting and bewildering morning trip. Shortly after the sun rises, camel traders mill about the smelly grounds in search of the biggest humps and healthiest gums they can find. Larger camels are generally used for transport and farming; smaller ones land up on the dinner table. As the camels have walked from Sudan to Aswan (taking a month) and then been trucked to Cairo, some of them are in a poor state and all of them are hobbled. It is worth bearing in mind an excursion to the market can be distressing as well as fascinating.

Heliopolis

ⓘ *By a/c airport bus from Midan Abdel Moniem Riad (E£2) or by tram from Midan Ramses (50pt), 30 mins.*

Heliopolis (*Masr Al-Gedida*) is a charming and beautiful suburb 12 km northeast of central Cairo, designed in 1905 by the Belgian-born industrialist Baron Empain. He dreamt of creating the perfect garden city, a true oasis in the desert, and he succeeded – the tree-lined boulevards of fantastical Oriental architecture became the secluded choice of colonialists and affluent Egyptians in the early years of the 20th century. Today Heliopolis is still a desirable address, with a pervasive air of prosperity and sophistication throughout (and the added enticement of the new City Stars complex), but it is happily totally Egyptian and, come evening, shoppers go crazy and life takes off on the streets. Tiered and arcaded buildings, decorated with ornamental minarets and Islamic emblems, make up much of Heliopolis' whimsical architecture. Particularly fine are the neo-Mamluk buildings along Sharia Ibrahim Al-Laqqany and Sharia Baghdad, and on the residential square behind the Basilica. Though the sprawl of the metropolis has long since encompassed the Baron's little enclave, if you arrive by tram you still get the sense of arrival in another city.

Baron Empain built himself a palace on raised ground with exotic gardens, from which he viewed the construction of Heliopolis below. Known locally as the **Qasr El-Baron**, the palace is a bizarre medley of Hindu and Buddhist architectural styles and motifs. The grounds have recently been cultivated by the Ministry of Tourism, with palm trees and grass being sprinkled around the clock; however, it's off-limits to the public and you'll have to be content with views of Shiva, gargoyles and dragons from behind the railings.

From the palace you can see the landmark building of the **Basilica of Notre Dame**. The interior of the Basilica is unspectacular, but its 'jelly mould' exterior is a miniature replica of St Sofia in Istanbul and the remains of Baron Empain and his son are interred within. The Basilica marks the end of Helipolis' main drag, Sharia Al-Ahram (so-called because at one time the pyramids of Giza could be seen from here), which leads up to another key landmark, the **Uruba Palace**. A monumental and beautiful structure, completed in 1910, the former Palace Hotel was once the most lavish of all the hotels in the region. It became a military hospital during World War II and was for many years the offices of President Mubarak; entry (and even scrutiny) is forbidden.

While a visit to Heliopolis will not be at the top of the list if you've only a few days in Cairo, it is perfect for an afternoon of pleasant yet stimulating strolling followed by good food and drinks, especially if you are tiring of mosque visits and museums.

Heliopolis

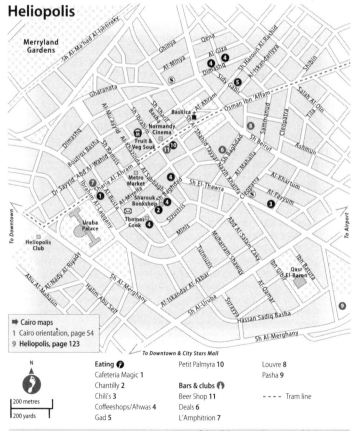

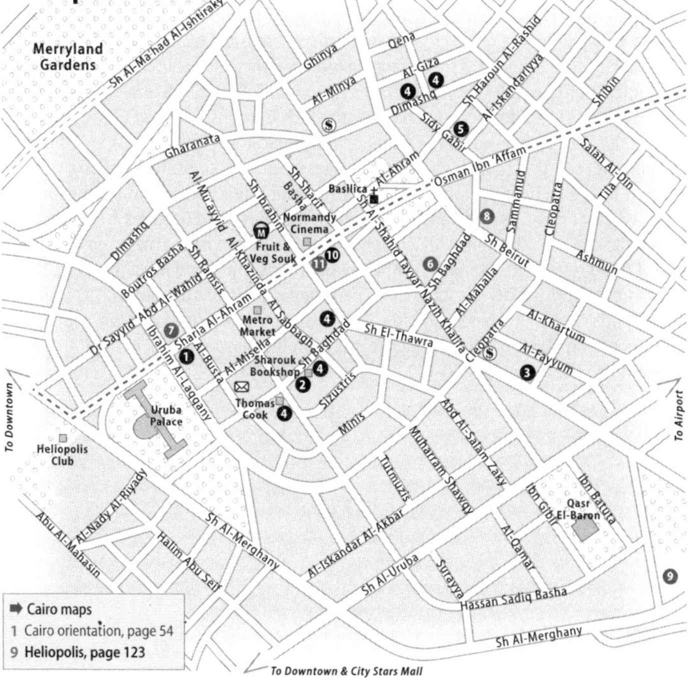

N

200 metres
200 yards

Eating
Cafeteria Magic **1**
Chantilly **2**
Chili's **3**
Coffeeshops/Ahwas **4**
Gad **5**
Petit Palmyra **10**

Bars & clubs
Beer Shop **11**
Deals **6**
L'Amphitrion **7**
Louvre **8**
Pasha **9**

---- Tram line

Trips down the Nile

A trip to Egypt would be remiss without at least an hour's meander on the Nile on an age-old *felucca*. Even if you are planning to go to Luxor or Aswan where *feluccas* are an essential ingredient of any visit, it's still mesmerizing to have a night-time sail while in Cairo when the city is at its most beautiful. Most *feluccas* accommodate up to eight people, and some have seats for far more – the greater number of passengers, the cheaper the fare. Bargaining is the norm, be prepared for a battle, but a standard price is around E£70 per hour. Tips are expected. *Feluccas* for hire dock in front of the Nile Hilton, Downtown, and near the Four Seasons in Garden City.

If you want to sail on a greener part of the Nile, past pastoral islands and away from the city, take a taxi to the nearby suburb of **Maadi** (E£15-20) and ask for the *felucca* dock. Or, an alternative trip closer to the city can be taken around the island of Zamalek on one of the motorboats moored past the houseboats north of Midan Kit Kat. These have neon lights and blare out Egyptian pop; a circuit can be done in about an hour; try to bargain for E£60.

Gardens

Apart from the pinnacle that is Al-Azhar Park (see page 101) the gardens of Cairo are likely to be a disappointment, being criss-crossed with concrete and big on 'Keep Off The Grass' signs. But if you are in need of some tranquillity away from the city bustle, you could try the **Zoological Gardens** ⓘ *0900-1700, but avoid Fri and public holidays*, in Giza, where there are many rare and beautiful trees. In Zamalek, the **Fish Gardens** ⓘ *Sharia Geziret al-Wusta, daily 0900-1630*, has several large aquaria with tropical fish housed in a weird grotto, popular with courting couples strolling the rather scrubby grounds. There's also a string of gardens in Gezira, running north along the river from Tahrir Bridge towards the Marriott Hotel, which cost between E£2 and E£10 to enter. The **Merryland Gardens** in Heliopolis are a splendid place for children, with a dolphin on site, a pedalo lake, a merry-go-round and lots of good restaurants. **Kanatir Al-Khaireya Gardens** (the Good Barrage) about 20 km downstream from the city has some shady parks and is good for a day out with a picnic (but not on Fridays when it is hideously crowded). The journey there is a lot of fun, with a party atmosphere on board the ferry, which leaves from the Maspero Dock in the front of the television building, hourly 0800-1000, returning 1400-1600.

Cairo listings

Hotel prices
LL over US$250 **L** US$150-249 **AL** US$100-149
A US$66-99 **B** US$46-65 **C** US$31-45
D US$21-30 **E** US$12-20 **F** US$7-11
G under US$7

Restaurant prices
🍴🍴🍴 over US$20 🍴🍴 US$5-20 🍴 under US$5

Sleeping

As the largest city in Africa and the Middle East, and one of the world's great tourist destinations, Cairo has hundreds of hotels ranging from the premier de luxe accommodation of major international chains to some really rugged local dives. The listings below, which have sought to avoid the worst and include the extraordinary, provide options to suit varied budgets, though higher end mid-range accommodation is somewhat lacking in Central Cairo. Nearly all the notable budget and mid-range accommodation centres around Downtown (the City Centre) and Zamalek. The most exceptional expensive hotels are also in the City Centre or near the Pyramids. Be sure to check online for discount rates and promotions at mid- and top-range hotels, significantly cheaper than the rack rate.

Credit cards are accepted in higher-end establishments, and some mid-range places. Take into account that the prices of accommodation in Cairo and all over Egypt fluctuate significantly depending on the season and number of tourists in the country, so use the price codes indicated here as a guide.

For travellers on a budget, Cairo has loads of interesting and decent cheap hotels, which means fierce competition, and brutal hotel touts. Lies are part of the game. You will be told hotels are full, or closed, or have doubled in price. Take control of the situation by choosing a place in advance, or assertively spend some time wandering around the centre exploring your options. Also remember that bargaining is the norm in Egypt, especially if it's summertime or you have plans to stay for a while. Where possible, we have included specific costs for the most budget of choices.

Camping Because Cairo has very little undeveloped earth on which to pitch a tent and since there are so many budget hotels, there is little demand for camping. The only decent real campground is **Salma Camping**, T02-2381 5062. It can be reached by turning off from Harraniya village on the road between the Pyramids and Saqqara. It offers cabins, a camping ground, hot showers, a buffet and a bar. E£30 to pitch a tent; E£100 for a simple double cabin.

Central Cairo *p63, maps p58 and p64*

LL Four Seasons, 1089 Corniche El-Nil, Garden City, T02-2791 7000. Some of the classiest rooms in town and faultess restaurants – famed for their Fri brunches, E£200 for all you can eat. There is another **Four Seasons** in Giza, 35 Sharia Giza, T02-3573 1212, opposite the zoo, which is somewhat brasher but a hot-spot for belly-dancing, Sufis and entertainments.

LL Kempinski, 12 Sharia Ahmed Rageb, Corniche El-Nil, Garden City, T02-2798 0000, www.kempinski.com. Plush new place, with a level of personalised service equal to that of a boutique hotel despite having 191 rooms (including 54 suites). Interiors are classic modern, blending Egyptian and European styles, with marble bathrooms and expensive fittings. Floor 10 has a champagne balcony, **Jazz Bar**, exclusive restaurant and rooftop pool (which becomes a bar/club at weekends). The other top-quality restaurant, **Osmanly**, serving Turkish food, and the de luxe spa make it a perfect choice if you have money to spend.

LL Nile Ritz-Carlton, Corniche El-Nil, Midan Tahrir, www.ritzcarlton.com. On the Nile adjacent to the Egyptian Museum, this Cairo landmark was opened in 1959 by President Nasser and is currently being fully renovated. It's due to reopen in 2011, check the website for the latest dates.

LL Semiramis Intercontinental, Corniche El-Nil, Garden City, T02-2795 7171. Masses of rooms in an ugly pink building and expensive, but excellent service all around and good views of the Nile overlooking the end of Gezira Island. Outdoor pool. People come for the belly-dancing at the weekends, and the **Bird Cage** Thai restaurant, which achieves absolute perfection in terms of food, service and atmosphere.

LL-L Fairmont Nile City, Corniche El-Nil, Bulaq, T02-2461 9356, www.fairmont.com. One of the newest additions to the 5-star scene, the **Fairmont** is utterly luxurious with rooms that combine contemporary chic with art nouveau styling. The wealth of restaurants and uber-cool bars are a plus point, as is the fabulous spa. It is 10 mins in a taxi from Downtown.

L Conrad, 1191 Corniche El-Nil, Bulaq, T02-2580 8000. What appears to be a fairly uneventful location is actually an interesting mix of teeming markets, old mosques and hammans in the lanes of Bulaq behind the hotel, contrasted with the grandeur of the **Nile City Mall** shops and cafés just north along the river. There's a pool and good healthclub, notable restaurants, and **Sangria** restaurant/ **Absolute** nightclub is directly opposite.

AL Talisman, 39 Sharia Talaat Harb, T02- 2393 9431, www.talisman-hotel.com. This gem of a hotel is hidden down an alley parallel to Sharia 26th July. Look for the **New Minerva** hotel sign and once inside take the left-hand elevator up to rich, warm colours and tasteful Arabesque decor throughout. Each room is unique and the lounge area is festooned with artefacts. This is the only almost-boutique hotel in Downtown, and it's a good idea to book in advance. Free Wi-Fi or broadband.

AL-A Cosmopolitan, 1 Sharia Ibn Taalab, Qasr El-Nil, T02-2392 3956. In the centre of Downtown in a quiet side street, the elegant building has a fabulous chandelier in the foyer, yet some rooms are pokey for the price – ask for one with a balcony. All have a/c, fridge and TV. The restaurant serves reasonable food, the **Kings Bar** is a good hangout, plus there's a café and nightclub next door. Breakfast included.

A-B Grand Hotel, 17 Sharia 26 July, T02-2575 7700, www.grandhotelcairo.com. In a crowded but central location, it retains a few original art deco fixtures among a mixture of parquet and plastic veneers. Rooms are clean with new mattresses and spotless marble bathrooms. Breakfast included, TV and fridge in rooms, but there's no bar. Staff are very friendly and helpful.

B Victoria Hotel, 66 Sharia El-Gumhoriyya, T02-2589 2290, www.victoria.com.eg. A large pink hotel that's been around since the 1930s, but long red carpets, wooden floors and loads of chandeliers make it feel almost Victorian. High-ceilinged a/c rooms have all amenities, en suites are roomy and have tubs as well as showers. There's an internet café, cosy darkened bar and a pleasant open-air coffee shop with lots of foliage. The best deal for a 3-star in the city, and although not in the 'heart' of Downtown it's an easy walk to Islamic Cairo. Breakfast included.

B Windsor, 19 Sharia Alfi Bey, T02-2591 5277, www.windsorcairo.com. Historic and atmospheric, well-run, family-owned hotel with clean a/c rooms. Look at a few as they vary greatly, the de luxe rooms are stacked with antique furniture while others have drawers hanging off. Bathrooms are definitely on the small side, some cheaper rooms have toilet outside. Breakfast included. One of the classiest and cosiest bars in the city, with barrel chairs, plenty of memorabilia and an interesting history. Michael Palin stayed here while going around the world in 80 days. Show your *Footprint Handbook* to receive a 15% discount.

B-C Cairo Inn, 1st floor, 6 Midan Talaat Harb, T02-2575 9213, cairoinn44@hotmail.com. Offers 7 spotlessly clean rooms with bath. Free Wi-Fi and breakfast. An excellent central location, but noisy.

C Carlton, 21 Sharia 26 July, T02-2575 5181, www.carltonhotelcairo.com. 60 airy a/c rooms with high ceilings, dark waxy furniture and wooden floors. Bathrooms need revamping. Near the bustling *souk* El-Tawfiqa and Sharia Alfi with its bars and cheap eats.

Hotel has laundry service, restaurant and a nice rooftop *ahwa*. Breakfast is extra. A good place to escape other tourists.

C Garden City House Hotel, 23 Sharia Kamal El Dinn Salah, Garden City, T02-2794 8400, www.gardencityhouse.com. On the edge of Midan Tahrir yet this place feels well out of any backpacker scene. Large rooms have plenty of furniture and share huge balconies with a bit of a view. There's a sociable breezy restaurant area and general air of nostalgia throughout. Doubles cost E£130/205 with or without a/c and bathroom (which are clean but old-fashioned), breakfast included. Friendly staff. Long-stay discounts are possible.

C Paris Hotel, 15 Sharia Talaat Harb, T02-2395 0921, T012-400 7126, parishotel_2006@hotmail.com. 8 simple, clean rooms with tiled floors, immaculate (but small) en suites. All with a/c and balconies. Free tea and coffee. Slightly dark public areas. Breakfast is extra. (Sister hotel **Le Paris** is 2 buildings away and is a bit pricier but includes breakfast, T02-2390 3815.)

C-D Sun Hotel, 9th and 10th floor, 2 Sharia Talaat Harb, T02-2579 7977. An old-timer on the budget scene, Sun has had a refit and the new rooms with a/c, satellite TV and fridge are often booked up. Located in a convenient spot, but with annoyingly infrequent elevators, necessitating walking down 10 floors (and possibly up 2). Rooms are cleaned and sheets changed daily, breakfast included, internet (E£5 per hr). A good place to come for trips to nearby sights like Saqqara or the Camel Market, even if you're not staying here.

C-E Pension Roma, 169 Sharia Mohamed Farid, T02-2391 1088, www.pensionroma.com.eg. Among the classiest of budget options, this old-world hotel is impeccably clean with hardwood floors, original fittings and furnishings and high ceilings and fans (pay more for a/c in the new annex). The staff is friendly and informative, lounge has TV, and it attracts an international and age-diverse group of travellers. Doubles start at E£104 with shared bath, with private bath E£170-250, they can accommodate 3 or 4 people in larger rooms, and the singles are the best value in Cairo. Some excellent balconies look down on the mayhem, breakfast included. Highly recommended, you should book ahead. Free Wi-Fi.

C-E Sara Inn Hostel, 21 Sharia Yousef El-Guindi, Bab El-Louq, T02-2392 2940, www.sarainnhostel.com. A quiet, intimate recently renovated hotel, centrally located with friendly staff. Good location as quiet at night and bustling during the day. Rooms have TV and most have balconies. Warmly decorated, communal lounge with TV and internet access. Can pick up from airport if pre-book 2 nights in a double room.

C-F Meramees Hotel, 32 Sharia Sabry Abu Alam, near Midan Talaat Harb, T02-2396 2518. Recommended for no hassle and good *felucca* trips, it's a low-key place where single women will feel comfortable. Pleasant airy a/c rooms have either complete bathrooms or shower cubicles only. Beds in nicer-than-average dorms are E£30. Cleaned daily, breakfast included, internet.

D Alexander Hotel, 165 Sharia Mohamed Farid, T02-2390 1844, alexander.hotel@hotmail.com. 10 smallish rooms all with a/c and bath are very clean but slightly cramped. A bit overpriced at $22 for a double. Public areas are kitsch with faux leopard skin cushions. Staff are friendly and the location is spot on. Free Wi-Fi and breakfast.

D Bluebird Hotel, 42 Sharia Talaat Harb, 6th floor, T02-2575 6377. Small family set-up in a top-floor hideaway with extremely clean rooms, all with fans. Choice of bathroom (very much) inside the room or spotless shared showers, and a communal kitchen, breakfast included. A cute little place.

D Canadian Hostel, 5 Sharia Talaat Harb, T02-2392 5794. Recommended for the super-friendly staff who offer good travel advice. Clean airy rooms are a little stark and gloomy, but breakfast is included, there's reliably hot water, cheap laundry (E£10), communal fridge, internet (E£6 per hr) and free Wi-Fi. Double rooms with standing fans are E£130, E£20 more for a/c.

D Juliana Hotel, 8 Sharia Ibrahim Naguib, Garden City, T012 4249 896, www.juliana-hotel.com. With just 9 simple, immaculate, quiet en suite rooms all with satellite TV, a great place to stay. The only problem may be finding it, but they provide excellent directions on their website. There's free Wi-Fi and use of the kitchen. A good central location that feels peaceful and away from it all.

D Lialy Hostel, 8 Midan Talaat Harb, 2nd floor, T02-2575 2802. Right in the heart of everything, spotless, private, and homely – though rooms are very simple. The staff is young, well-informed and friendly. Hearty breakfast included, there's a great view over Midan Talaat Harb from the lounge. Internet, laundry (E£1 per piece) and free use of the kitchen. All bathrooms are shared.

D Lotus Hotel, 12 Sharia Talaat Harb, T02-2575 0966, www.lotushotel.com. 50 rooms, some with bath and a/c, in a drab but clean and centrally located hotel run by the same family as **Windsor**. Some rooms have balcony. Breakfast included. Restaurant is OK and the uneventful **Polo Bar**, which is a real blast from the past, has a small balcony way above Talaat Harb. Reception is on the 7th floor. Show your *Footprint Handbook* for a 15% discount.

D Ramses II Hotel, 37 Sharia Talaat Harb, Downtown, T02-2395 0745. All 18 rooms have private bath, a/c, satellite TV, some have glimpses of the silver dome of the Citadel but all have good views as it's on the 12th floor. Rooms are new and staff are friendly, not bad for E£160 a double. Breakfast is on the terrace with superb views across the city, it feels more Egyptian than some backpacker haunts. Free Wi-Fi. Internet E£4.

D-E African Hostel, 3rd floor, 15 Sharia Emad El-Din, T02-2591 7220, T02-2591 1744, www.africanhousehostel.com. 12 clean, simple rooms located in an elegant 1860s building have wooden floors and clean bedding. Rooms on 4th floor have balconies. Public areas are brightly-painted but a bit tired looking. Free internet, free Wi-Fi and tea. Super-friendly staff. Doubles with shared bath E£100, private bath E£120. A good choice.

D-E Richmond, 41 Sharia Sherif, T02-2393 9358. The glossy orange and green paint is a little startling, but 4 front rooms have good balconies and get lots of light. You won't see many other tourists there. Smells a bit smoky. Breakfast included and friendly management.

D-F Ismailia House, 8th floor, 1 Midan Tahrir, T02-2796 3122. A classic budget hotel in the middle of Midan Tahrir, entrance hidden in an alley behind the book stand. It's a friendly place with good management, clean rooms but grubby shared baths, reliable cheap tours (available to non-guests), and an absolutely flabbergasting view of Midan Tahrir. News crews film from the balconies when there's action in the main square. Laundry, internet, shared kitchen, lounge with CNN always on. Some rooms have a/c, all others have fans. Request one with a balcony. Breakfast included. Dorms E£35, doubles E£90, with bath and fan.

D-F Venice Hotel, 4 Sharia Souk El-Tawfikia, T02-2773 5307, www.venicehosokawaya.net. Venice has undergone a re-vamp in the last year, and all rooms are freshly painted with new mattresses and bedding, and consequently higher prices. Clean dorm beds are E£35. Run by Japanese and Egyptians. Kitchen, washer and dryer.

D-G Dina's Hostel, 5th floor, 42 Sharia Abdel Khalek Sarwat, T02-2396 3902, T010-3025 346, dinahostel@gmail.com. A welcome new arrival on the Cairo hotel scene. Bright spacious rooms have wooden floors and crisp, clean bedding. Free Wi-Fi. Internet E£5. Standard breakfast but the hard-boiled eggs are fresh and warm. An 8-bed dorm offers the cleanest budget accommodation around. (E£40 per bed). The 2 bathrooms are pristine and beautifully tiled. (More are being planned.) No a/c or fans yet. If arriving at night there's a buzzer downstairs.

E Hotel Suisse, 8th floor, 26 Sharia Mahmoud Bassiouni, T02-2574 6639. Rooms here are spacious and bright, have sinks and fans, some have balconies. Staff are very pleasant, it's an all-round winner in terms of atmosphere, location and value for money.

E-G Akram Inn, 5 Midan Tahrir, T02-2794 4353, akramsafir@hotmail.com. 4-bed dorms are E£25 a bed Climbing up 3 floors of stairs is painful with luggage, but the location is undeniably top and one room has balcony views over the Midan. No breakfast but there's a kitchen, fridge, internet (E£5 per hr).
E-G Dahab Hotel, 7th floor, 26 Sharia Mahmoud Bassiouny, T02-2579 9104. One of the cheapest beds in town, this rooftop hotel is amazingly successful in offering a little taste of Dahab in the middle of downtown Cairo madness. Small, very simple rooms on the rooftop, some with fans, have clean sheets and decent pillows. Bathrooms are clean and newly tiled. It's the garden that's special; a little oasis overflowing with flowers and plants, you can even hear birds chirping. Pure backpacker vibes, it's a good place to meet people. Breakfast E£8 extra.
F Amin Hotel, 38 Midan Falaky, Bab El Louk, T02-2393 3813. Dingy double rooms with acceptable shared baths are about the cheapest in town at E£39, or E£44-49 with private bathroom. Come here for a proper Egyptian vibe, lack of hassle, excellent balcony views and proximity to the Horiyya coffee shop – but not for comfort or good facilities.
G Safari Hotel, 4 Sharia Souk El-Tawfikia, 5th floor, T012-446 9010. The funk and flavour of the colourful *souk* outside makes up for the filth of the building, meaning the Safari and **Sultan** are perennially popular with backpackers. Dorm beds going for E£20 (men and women separate), using 2 shared but clean showers, but don't expect clean sheets. Safari has plenty of bustle, is friendly and popular with Japanese backpackers.
G Sultan Hotel, 4 Sharia Souk El-Tawfikia, T02-2577 2258. This is where it's at for backpackers on the tightest of budgets. Cheap dorm beds for E£20 on the 1st floor (separate for men and women), shared baths are rather grimy, but many folk make it home for a while. Kitchen facilities and laundry, plus gaudy murals to welcome you in the reception area.

Islamic Cairo *p73, maps p74 and p75*
If you like things noisy and crazy, stay in the immediate vicinity of the Khan and get properly immersed in Islamic Cairo. If you're here during the Moulid of Al-Hussein (booking imperative) don't expect to get any sleep and bear in mind that multiple mosques and the call to prayer are literally on the doorstep in all events.
LL Le Riad, 114 Sharia Muizz li-Din il-Allah, T02-2787 6074/5, www.leriad-hoteldecharme.com. With a lovely roof garden and tea shop, this new 'boutique' hotel has 17 spacious themed rooms (Umm Khalsoum, pharaonic, etc) with flagged stone floors, artwork on the walls, rich colours and modern amenities. The bathrooms are fabulous. It's just a shame that it is so expensive. Breakfast included and free internet.
C-D El Hussein Hotel, Midan El-Hussein, T02-2591 8089. In the heart of Khan El-Khalili, entry via an alley at the front (right-hand side) of the Khan. A gloomy old-fashioned hotel but, if you can handle the noise, the location makes it worthwhile. The large rooms with private bath have great balconies overlooking Midan Hussein. It's worth shelling out to avoid the shared bathrooms, though the private ones are on the dank side too. Rooms with a/c are a bit more expensive (double E£180). Great view from the cafeteria.
D El-Malky Hotel, 4 Sharia El-Hussein, T02-2589 0804, www.elmalky.com. Unquestionably the best value of the 3 hotels around Midan Hussein, at E£110-130 per room. You'll definitely need to book in advance. Except for the El-Hussein mosque, which sounds periodically, street noise isn't a problem. Rooms and baths are reasonably clean and include TV, telephone and fan, some with a/c. Breakfast included. Make sure you request a room with a balcony, as some have no windows, and check out the view from the roof.
D Radwan, 83 Sharia Gawhar El-Kaaid, Midan Al-Azhar, T02-2590 1311. Though rooms are pretty scuffed they are clean, as are the private baths. The hotel has quite a nice vibe and there are seating areas on each floor. Go

between 1000-1200 to view a few rooms, and check the a/c works (a few have balconies). Noisy but vibrant location. No breakfast. Friendly staff.

Roda Island *p111*

LL Grand Hyatt Cairo, Corniche El-Nil, Garden City, T02-2365 1234. Excellently located on the north tip of Roda Island, looking down on *feluccas* circling on the river. There's a range of restaurants, and an adjacent **Hard Rock Café**, plus one of the best views of Cairo from the revolving restaurant bar. They are serving alcohol again (but only in the restaurant) after the furore caused in May 2008 when the Saudi owner turned the hotel dry and up to US$1 million of liquor was poured into the Nile.

G Youth hostel, 135 Sharia Abdul Aziz Al-Saud, El-Manial, Roda Island, near University Bridge, T02-236 0729, T02-2362 4593. Location is inconvenient, though connected to the city via public transport. Stunning Nileside views.There's a shared kitchen with prepared meals available, family rooms and laundry. E£16-25, depending on if you share a room with 3 beds or 8-10. Doors closed 2400-0800. Book in advance. Places for disabled. Handy ATM outside.

Zamalek and Gezira *p113, maps p58 and p114*

LL Cairo Marriott Hotel and Casino, 16 Sharia Saray El-Gezira, Zamalek, T02-2728 3000, www.cairomarriotthotel.com. Over 1000 rooms, mainly in 2 high-rise towers, around a lavish 19th-century Gezira Palace built to commemorate the opening of the Suez Canal and still retaining much of its splendour. Restaurants are average, but the garden terrace is simply perfect for a drink, **Harry's Bar** is reassuringly familiar, and there's the **Omar El-Khayyam** casino. Also has own sporting facilities – tennis court, health club, etc – and though day-use of the pool is very expensive, it has possibly the nicest settings in the city. Classic and palatial, the **Marriott** makes a good place to unwind from the bustle of Cairo.

LL Sofitel El Gezirah, 3 Sharia El Thawra Council, Gezira, T02-2737 3737, www.sofitel.com. Ignore the uninspiring exterior because the **Sofitel** has been stylishly revamped by a French interior designer and is now worthy of its prime location at the southern tip of the island. Luxurious and tasteful rooms, truly high-class restaurants, a decadent spa and a bar floating on decking over the Nile.

L Hilton Zamalek Residence, 21 Sharia Mohamed Mazhar, Zamalek, T02-2737 0055, www1.hilton.com. Due to open in 2011, this Hilton Zamalek Residence has a perfect location next to the Nile in a quiet area of the city. Lovely new pools, fresh furnishings, oriental and international restaurants – it will be worth looking into.

L-AL Golden Tulip Flamenco Hotel, 2 Sharia El-Gezira El-Wasta, Zamalek, T02-2735 0815/6, www.goldentulipflamenco.com. Most rooms have a good view of houseboats on the Nile and are of a decent standard. There's a 24-hr café, **Carmen** lounge bar is quiet and friendly, and a beer in the 10th floor Spanish restaurant affords marvellous sunset views (though it is not open air). Doubles are US$140, US$20 more for a Nile view, some suites, it's always busy with businessmen so best to book ahead.

AL Horus House Hotel, 21 Sharia Ismail Mohammed, T02-2735 3634, www.horushousehotel.4t.com. 1 floor under **Longchamps**, this is a marginally cheaper and less appealing choice. Rooms have all the extras and have been freshly decorated, the staff are friendly and there's a (very cheap, 24-hr) bar and restaurant but, compared to its bright upstairs neighbour, the hotel feels old and dreary. However, you are guaranteed to meet some interesting long-stay residents over breakfast (which is included).

A Longchamps, 21 Sharia Ismail Mohammed, T02-2735 2311, www.hotellongchamps.com. Long-standing family-run hotel that is about the quirkiest in Cairo. Always popular, it's imperative to book in advance. 2 shaded terraces offer peace, greenery and a cold beer, the restaurant is pleasant, the breakfast buffet highly recommended and there is a library.

Rooms (standard, superior, executive) are very comfortable with new furniture, a/c, TV, fridge and a hint of the colonial flavour that permeates the public areas.

A President Hotel, 22 Sharia Taha Hussein, T02-2735 0718. Awesome views over the island, new bathrooms and huge rooms with good facilities compensate for the shabby public areas and generic decor. Some rooms have enormous balconies overlooking the Nile, and the **Cellar Bar** down in the basement is delightfully dark and atmospheric. The French patisserie is famed. The adjacent **New President Hotel**, 20 Sharia Taha Hussein, T02-2737 2780. Has some rooms that have been tastefully renovated, standard ones are dated though clean and spacious. It's not a bad mid-range option, and slightly cheaper than the original President.

C Mayfair Hotel, 9 Sharia Aziz Osman. T02-2735 7315, www.mayfaircairo.com. Unspectacular but clean rooms (try for one with a balcony) in a quiet location. Breakfast included, served on the pleasant flowery balcony with free Wi-Fi. Show your *Footprint Handbook* for a 10% discount. Doubles are around E£250, with a/c and bath, it's always busy so call ahead.

C Pension Zamalek, 6 Sharia Salah Al-Din, T02-2735 9318. Spacious, warm old-fashioned rooms, some with a/c and heater, most with balconies, in very tranquil nook off Zamalek's main drag. A family-run super-friendly hotel, every 2 rooms share a spotless bath. Laundry service and TV in the eerie salon. Breakfast included. Phone ahead as they're often booked up with long-stayers (who get a discount).

The west bank *p113, map p58*

Most tourists staying in Giza will have been pre-booked into one of the many high-end hotels as part of a package deal. With the obvious exception of the pyramids, Giza is too much out on a limb to be convenient for main attractions of the city.

LL Mena House Oberoi, 6 Sharia Pyramids, El-Ahram, T02-3377 3222, www.oberoi hotels.com. An exquisite old-style hotel built in 1869, with sublime views of the Pyramids and set in luxuriant gardens. Excellent Indian (and other) restaurants, disco, casino, largest outdoor pool in Cairo (you can see the Pyramids as you float around), tennis, a nearby 18-hole golf course, horse and camel riding with experienced instructors. Take a room in the renovated older part for preference. If out of your budget, it's still a delightful place to enjoy breakfast opposite the Pyramids.

A Havana Hotel, 26 Sharia Syria, Mohandiseen, T02-3749 0758, www.havanahotelcairo.com. Modest, friendly Anglo-Egyptian hotel, breakfast included.

A-B Saqqara Country Club & Hotel, Saqqara Rd, Abu El-Nomros, T02-3381 1307. 20 rooms outside the city near the Saqqara pyramids, well run with good food and excellent horse-riding facilities. Temporary club membership available. Day use, including a drink, is E£120.

Trips down the Nile *p124*

Maadi

LL Villa Belle Epoque, Near Rd 9, T02-2516 9656, Maadi, www.villabelleepoque.com. A 1920s villa with 13 period rooms, delightful gardens, pool, excellent restaurant and charming bar. It is a true boutique hotel, in a residential suburb 8 km south of the city centre.

Eating

Cairo is a cosmopolitan city with an increasingly diverse and eclectic population. The cuisine reflects huge variety. You can find Japanese, vegetarian, Chinese, Italian, Indian and French, in addition to superb Middle Eastern cuisine. At the most chic restaurants (often found in the chicest of hotels), expect to pay what you would at home for a classy meal. It's also possible to dine deliciously on the cheap. You can fill up on tasty local fare (*fuul*, *taameyya* and *koshari*) for less than a dollar. Do pay attention, though, especially when buying food on the street. If things don't seem too clean and there isn't a quick turnover of custom, it's better to move on and find some establishment where the flies and the heat are less menacing. Opening times and menus may change during Ramadan as some restaurants focus on providing a slap-up *iftar* meal, and *koshari* also becomes impossible to find during this period. Most restaurants home-deliver, which also applies to hotels.

Central Cairo *p63, maps p58 and p64*

ΨΨΨ The Bird Cage, Semiramis Intercontinental, Corniche El-Nil, Garden City, T02-2795 7171. Open 1230-2400. Thai cuisine complete with live (caged) birds, neo-feng shui design and sheer curtains separate tables for privacy. Ask for 'spicy' otherwise you might find dishes toned down, all the entrees are excellent, and so is the service. Very expensive and very good.

ΨΨΨ Maharaja, Ramses Hilton, 1115 Corniche El-Nil, T02-2577 7444. Open 1300-1600 and 1900-2400. Modern decor within a small space, the Maharaja serves up some marvellous Indian cuisine, specializing in tandoori. There's a non-smoking section.

ΨΨΨ Pane Vino, Semiramis Intercontinental Hotel, Corniche El-Nil, T02-2795 7171. Open 1300-0100. Serves top-notch antipasta and pizza (the Da Vinci is recommended), in modern metal and glass surroundings. A lively place with music and lots of shouting coming from the show kitchen.

ΨΨΨ Paprika, 1129 Corniche El-Nil, T02-2578 9447. Open 1200-0100. Paprika-based dishes of mixed Egyptian and Hungarian food. Near the TV and Radio Building, it's not uncommon to spot local Egyptian celebrities on the premises.

ΨΨΨ-ΨΨ Alfi Bey, 3 Sharia El-Alfi, Downtown, in pedestrian precinct, T02-2577 1888. Open 1300-0100. Authentic Egyptian food since 1938, especially kebabs, koftas, lamb chops and shank, grilled and stuffed pigeon with pastas and rice. Smart waiters provide an efficient and friendly service, but custom is declining as the place feels dated and no alcohol is served.

ΨΨΨ-ΨΨ Kowloon, Cleopatra Hotel, 1st floor, Midan Tahrir, T02-2575 9831. Open

1100-2300. Authentic Korean cuisine that delights even Korean patrons, with some Chinese dishes thrown in. The place feels retro in a good way.

ΨΨΨ-ΨΨ Peking, behind Diana Cinema, 14 Sharia Saraya El-Azbakia, T02-2591 2381. Open 1200-0100. Warm atmosphere and friendly service with a mix of Asian and Oriental decor, extensive Chinese menu though not the most authentic. Some say ketchup is the secret ingredient of the sweet and sour sauce. It's reliable, however, and there are a few vegetarian options. Several chains around Cairo, they also home deliver.

ΨΨΨ-ΨΨ Taboula, 1 Sharia Latin America, Garden City, T02-2624 5722. Open 1200-0130 daily. Romantic subterranean lounge space, with dim lighting and faithfully Lebanese decorations, cushions, and pictures all around. The hot and cold *mezza* suit vegetarians and meaty mains are as authentic as the interior and the menu vast. Highly recommended. Serves alcohol.

ΨΨ Abu Shakra, 69 Sharia Qasr El-Eini, Downtown, T02-2531 6111. Open 1200-0200. Among the most reputable and oldest of all local grills in Egypt (since 1947), pigeon, leg of lamb and grilled chicken all to be recommended. Vegetarians limited to delicious soups and salads. The late-lamented Muslim missionary Mohammed Mitwalli El-Shaarawi was said to order here frequently. A recent refit has left it rather soulless and with TVs in the main dining area.

ΨΨ Arabesque, 6 Sharia Qasr El-Nil, Downtown, T02-2574 8677, www.arabesque-eg.com. Open 1200-0200 daily. A chance to try less common Egyptian dishes: *mezza* includes *besara* (a tasty bean dip) and mains include tagines and stuffed pigeon. Old tiled floors, stella bottle lampshades, lit alabaster on the bar, Orientalist art and very dim lighting make it a cool hideaway. It's a handy location just off Tahrir.

ΨΨ El-Bahrain, 123 Sharia El-Roda, by the Fatima Hamada Cinema, Manial, T02-2532 2175, daily 1300 until late. Their grandfathers were fishermen, and for the last 4 years this restaurant has been serving up the freshest of the day's catch. Pick your fish from the ice (ask for it to be cooked *mistakawi* style), accompanying salads are excellent and the shrimps some of the best you'll ever taste. The 1st-floor restaurant is nothing flash, the usual marble and plastic surrounds, but it's great value. They will feed large groups for E£25 per head.

El-Nil Fish Restaurant, 25 Sharia Al-Bustan, near Midan Falaki. Open 1200-0100. Fish fresh off the ice is grilled or fried, either to take away or eat upstairs. Served with the standard salads, it's always delicious and is very reasonably priced.

Felfela, 15 Sharia Hoda Sharawi, Downtown, T02-239 2833. Open 0830-0130. One of Downtown's most popular tourist restaurants, serves good, clean, local food and beer in a dimly lit, strangely funky cave-like environment. A good place for a first experiment with Egyptian food on arrival, there is also a branch in Giza near the pyramids and others around the country. Also see page 133, for **Felfela Takeway**.

Greek Club, 3 Sharia Mahmoud Bassiouni, Downtown, T02-2575 0822. Open 0700-0200. Above **Groppis** on Midan Talast Harb, this is a deserved classic of the Cairo scene. Grand neo-classical interior, complete with moose head, there's no menu but dishes are standard kebab, salad, soups, nothing truly special, but the terrace (only open in summer) is a splendid vantage point over the Midan. Beer is reasonable at E£12.

Le Bistro, 8 Sharia Hoda Sharawy, T010-507 0078. Open 1200-2400, their bar (next door) is open till 0200. Good French food in a modern little blue and white space, intimate tables, no pretensions. Fillet steaks (E£55), chops, fish and chicken are all done to a high standard.

Abu Tarek, 40 Sharia Champollion, corner of Sharia Maarouf, T02-2577 5935. Open 0800-2400. Serving up what is arguably the best *koshari* in town since 1950. A good place to land with an empty belly after hours of aimless wandering. If you've been worried about trying it on the street for fear of stomach upsets, rest assured that Abu Tarek is among the cleanest of *koshari* establishments. It's more expensive than your average *koshari* joint with a small dish starting at E£E5.

Akher Sa'a, 8 Sharia El-Alfi. Open 24 hrs. An all-Egyptian vegetarian's heaven. Lentil soup is excellent, as is *shakshouka* and all other local favourites. Eat-in or take-out.

El-Tabei el-Domiati, 31 Sharia Orabi, T02-2575 4391. Open 0700-0100. Another cheap and famed local favourite serving up *mezze* galore and, of course, *fuul* and *tameyya*. Especially recommended for its trustworthy salad bar, though there is less choice in recent years.

Fatatri El-Tahrir, 166 Sharia Tahrir, 1 block east of Midan Tahrir. Serves delicious *fatir* both sweet and savoury; favoured with locals and travellers alike for being cheap, filling and open all night long.

Felfela Takeaway, 15 Sharia Talaat Harb, T02-2392 2833. Near to the Downtown restaurant of the same name, this takeaway joint also has a few seats inside. A great, cheap introduction to local flavours, the lentil soup is delicious, but there's also *koshari*, grilled meats, salads and sandwiches.

Gad, several locations across the city, but most convenient Downtown is 13 Sharia 26th July, T02-2576 3583. Open 24 hrs. Always heaving; tasty, cheap local grub includes excellent *fuul*, *taamiyya*, and acclaimed liver sandwiches. Seating upstairs and deliver almost anywhere.

Sayed Hanafi, 5 Midan Orabi, on Sharia El-Alfi, T02-2576 9162. Constantly packed with Egyptians. Serves excellent, authentic, cheap staples.

Shabrawi, Sharia 26 July. Near the junction with Sharia Ramses, look for the crowd milling around outside waiting to be served with the freshest, juiciest *shawarma* sandwiches in town.

Ahwas and cafés

Arabica, 1st floor, 20 Sharia Marashly, corner of Sharia Ahmed Heshmat, Zamalek T02-2735 7982. Open daily 1000-0200. One of few cafés still to offer free Wi-Fi, this place has a large selection of *fatir*, decent Western breakfasts, omelettes on toast (try the goat's cheese), salads and OK juices. Prices are more reasonable than most and it's popular with students from the nearby AUC residence. Walls are decorated by customer's artwork – there are crayons for sketching on the paper tablecloths.

Cilantro's, 31 Sharia Mohammed Mahmoud, opposite the old AUC campus. For a Western-style coffee Downtown, the most pleasant environment is still upstairs at **Cilantro's** despite the competition from **Costa** and **Beano's** nearby. There are a couple of tables out on the balconies and velvet 'snugs' for couples, it's unpretentious and has a clean toilet. They charge for Wi-Fi, however.

Groppi's, Midan Talaat Harb, Downtown. This landmark used to be the place to meet, but renovations have dimmed the classic café's former charm. The coffee isn't great but the pastries are OK, and it's handy when you're ready for a break. A more agreeable location is the branch on Sharia Adly, which has a garden terrace that is genuinely peaceful.

Islamic Cairo *p73, maps p74 and p75*

Citadel View Restaurant, Al Azhar Park, Salah Salem, T02-2510 3868, www.alahzarpark.com. Daily 1200-0100. A little expensive, but the views are so worth it and it's an ideal way to round off a day in Islamic Cairo. An excellent mix of Oriental and Western mains, or on weekend evenings there's an all-you-can-eat buffet.

Naguib Mafouz Coffee shop and Khan El-Khalili Restaurant, 5 Sikkit El-Badestan, Khan El- Khalili, T02-2593 2262. Open 1000-0200. The classiest place to relax after a day's wander through Islamic Cairo, has a/c, serves Western and Egyptian *mezze* and meals. Prices for tea and coffee are inflated, but the surroundings justify going. Live Oriental music is featured on occasion. Minimum charges apply.

Egyptian Pancake House, 7 Midan Al-Azhar. *Fiteer* galore, savoury and sweet. Tuna, cheese, eggs, meat, chicken, cream, and even turkey cock are available fillings. Price range from E£15-25 depending on size and filling.

Taj Al Sultan, Al-Hussein, T02-2787 7273/5, www.tajalsultan.com. Open 1000-0200. Strange to find an Indian restaurant in the heart of Islamic Cairo, but typical British-Indian dishes (*rogan josh*, *murg masala*, *sag aloo*) are done very well. There is also an extensive Arabic menu plus a couple of international dishes. The old building, with a rooftop with great views, decorated in Orientalist style is pleasing, the coffee shop is attractive, and the prices are not outrageous considering the location.

Gad, Sharia Al-Azhar. Open daily 0900-0200. The famous fast-food chain is perfect for tasty soup and staples if you're hungry round the Khan but don't want to pay tourist prices. There is seating upstairs.

Mohamed Ali's *fuul* cart, behind the Palace of Amir Bashtak, Sharia Al-Muizz, Midan Hussein. Undoubtedly some of the best *fuul* going, as the queues further testify. Handy for basic refuelling north of the Khan, and an interesting place to take a break among dilapidated mansions.

Zizo, Midan Bab El-Futuh. Open 1200-0700. Facing the north wall of Islamic Cairo. Said to have the best liver sausage and fried brain in town, if that's your thing. This tiny takeaway joint is a local landmark, very cheap and open through the night.

Ahwas and cafés

Fishawi's, smack bang in the middle of Khan El-Khalili. Open all the time. **Fishawi's** is Cairo's longest standing *ahwa*, claiming never to have closed since it first opened in 1773. If you only go to one coffee shop in Egypt, let it be this one. The place is filled with atmosphere, dangling chandeliers, mottled mirrors and characters that have been here for decades. Plus heaps of tourists and hawkers adding to the cacophony of noise. *Sheesha*, fresh juice, tea and Turkish coffee are all good, but at a steep price.

Zamalek and Gezira *p113, maps p58 and p114*

ŸŸŸ **Abu El-Sid**, 157 Sharia 26th July, in an alley behind **Maison Thomas**, T02-2735 9640. Open 1300-0200. Intimately lit sumptuous decor makes you feel like you've entered a harem, the cuisine is authentically Egyptian and it's a rare chance to smoke *sheesha* and drink alcohol at the same time. Egyptian men admit that Abu El-Sid is as close as it gets to their mum's cooking, try the *molokhia*, a unique slimy green soup. However, it's not great for vegetarians and can get annoyingly busy (when the staff try to hurry you along; essential to book a table at weekends).

ŸŸŸ **Asia Bar**, **Blue Nile Boat**, Sharia Saraya El-Gezira, T02-2735 3112. This floating restaurant is a recommended haunt, for sushi and a beer you can't go wrong. There's a very cool bar to hang out in.

ŸŸŸ **Hana**, 25 Sharia Hassan Asem Sayed Bakri, T02-2738 2972. Open 1200-0030. Recently reopened in a new venue, this is an authentic Korean restaurant that also serves some Chinese dishes. The *kimchi* and hot-and-sour soup are good, and the beef *bartogi* (cook up the slices on your own personal hot plate) comes recommended. One of the few restaurants in town that makes edible tofu. Serves beer and other alcohol, and has a very loyal clientele.

ŸŸŸ **L'Asiatique**, **Le Pacha 1901**, Sharia Saraya El-Gezira, T02-2735 6730. Open 1900-0200. Superb sushi and Thai cuisine on the floating, not cruising, **Pacha**, a delightful, albeit pricey dining experience.

ŸŸŸ **La Bodega**, 157 Sharia 26th July (1st floor), T02-2735 0543. Open 1200-0200. Arty international in a venue that's as chic and spot-on as it gets in Cairo. There's a choice between the mustardy and colonial room or the newly refurbished cuisine 'Aperitivo' section that specializes in Italian for dining, plus a separate lounge with plush leather chairs as well as private rooms. The bar is lively, dark and well-stocked with quite a mixed clientele, and it's one of the few places that serves alcohol during Ramadan.

ŸŸŸ **Maharani**, Le Pacha 1901, Sharia Saraya El-Gezira, T02-2735 6730. Open 1400-2400. A 5-star Indian floating restaurant set to the sound of sitars. Something for everyone on the menu, a decent vegetarian section, the yellow dahl is strongly recommended.

ŸŸŸ **Sequoia**, 3 Sharia Abou El-Feda, T02-2736 6379. A beautiful setting on the northern tip of Zamalek makes this a good place for sunset nibbles and a drink, overlooking houseboats and Imbaba bridge. The food has improved greatly in recent years, although the service can still be slow, but it's more the location and stylishly spacious outdoor setting that make it. No minimum charge before 1700.

ŸŸŸ-ŸŸ **Chili's**, **Nile City Boat**, Sharia Saray Al-Gezira, T02-2735 3122, delivery T19002. True, it's purely a Tex-Mex restaurant that serves up American-style food, but the setting on the **Nile City Boat** with outdoor seating on deck is just superb. Meals are reliable, vegetarians will find things of interest on the menu, and the prices are not outrageous.

ŸŸŸ-ŸŸ **Five Bells**, corner of sharias Ismail Mohamed and El Adel Abu Bakr, Zamalek, T02-2735 8635. Indoor and garden seating in an old villa with old-style atmosphere, serves tasty dinners though vegetarians will be limited to soups and *mezza*. Be prepared for persistent attention from neighbourhood cats.

ŸŸŸ-ŸŸ **Maison Thomas**, 157 Sharia 26 July, T02-2735 7057. Open 24 hrs, and good for home delivery. Continental-style deli atmosphere, serving pretty authentic Italian pizza. The caramel chocolate cake and cheesecake are scrumptious if you have room for dessert. The place can use a better ventilation system, but the decor works and it's a real institution. Good for breakfast. Branches also open in Heliopolis, Maadi and Mohandiseen.

ŸŸ **Crave**, 22a Sharia Taha Hussein, T02-2736 3870. Open 1100-0200. A café/restaurant with cool decor, slouchy leather sofas and good food if you're craving something Western. The sort of place that suits a leisurely breakfast or when you need a/c.

ŸŸ **Dido's Al Dente**, 26 Sharia Bahgat Ali, Zamalek, T02-2735 9117, www.didospasta.com. Open 1300-0500. This little pasta place can use more space, but if you're in the mood for tasty cheap Italian fare, it's worth the cram: the penne arrabiatta is a winner, the pizzas are great and portions are generous. However, the service can be abominable if they're busy. Popular with AUC students who live in the hostel nearby. They also home deliver.

ΨΨ **L'Aubergine**, 5 Sharia Sayed El-Bakry, T02-2738 0080. A mellow little restaurant, with a wide drinks menu, and vaguely Italian food that's very acceptable. A good selection for vegetarians, one of the best in the city. Upstairs is a bar/club that gets going at around 2200 which is quite fun.

Ψ **TBS (The Bakery Shop)**, 4D, Sharia Gezira, T02-2736 0071/3. A surprisingly good Western-style sandwich bar, with paninis, German bread, ciabatta, etc, all freshly made, plus some good pastry items. Choose from a great mix of sandwich fillings, and they can toast the end product for you. Takeaway only.

Ψ **Zamalek Restaurant**, 118 Sharia 26 July, near intersection with Sharia Al Aziz Osman. Open 0600-0200. A sit-down meats and grills joint on Zamalek's main drag.

Ahwas and cafés

Mandarin Koueider, 17 Sharia Shargarat Al-Dor, Zamalek. This place has the best ice cream and sorbets in Cairo. Mango and mandarin flavours come out on top.

Simonds, Sharia 26 July, Zamalek, T02-2735 9436. Open 0730-2130. One of the oldest stand-up coffee shops in Cairo, it unfortunately underwent a soulless refit in 2008 and little of the 1898 charm remains. Even so, it is still a good place to read the paper, observe classic Cairo characters, and have decent cappuccino. The mini-pizzas and OJ are a great pick-me-up.

The west bank *p113, map p58*

Mohandiseen

There are several good restaurants in Mohandiseen that can make the trip to the concrete suburbs worthwhile, but bear in mind most do not serve alcohol.

ΨΨΨ **Bukhara**, 5 Sharia Lebnan (entry from Sharia Hegaz), T02-3302 5669. Great Indian cuisine, many people reckon it's the best in Cairo. There's also a branch in Maadi (43 Sharia Misr Helwan, T02-2380 5999) and they deliver.

ΨΨΨ **Charwood's**, 53 Sharia Gamat El-Dowel El-Arabiya, T02-3749 0893. Open 1300-0030. Recommended for a laid-back atmosphere, quality steaks and great oven-baked pizzas. Faultless service. A good little hideaway, though the decor is spartan, it's tasteful. Serves alcohol.

ΨΨΨ **Raousha & Kandahar**, 3 Sharia Gamat El-Dowal, T02-3303 0615. Open 1200-2400. An Oberoi-owned restaurant split in 2 to serve excellent Lebanese or Indian cuisine. Overlooks one of the busiest streets in Cairo. Attentive service.

ΨΨΨ-ΨΨ **Ataturk**, 20 Sharia Riyadh, T02-3347 5135. Open 1000-0200. Turkish food, all the *mezzas* are fab, it's worth getting the mixed platter, served with fresh bread. No alcohol.

ΨΨΨ-ΨΨ **Cortigiano**, 44 Sharia Michel Bakhum, T02-3337 4838. Open 1300-0100. Pizzas, soups and Italian specialities continue to delight customers. Hefty portions and a good choice of desserts. No alcohol. Has a branch in Heliopolis (T02-2414 2202).

ΨΨ **Maroush**, 64 Midan Lebanon, T02-3345 0972. Open 0900-0200. Restaurant and *ahwa*. Large comfortable outdoor seating area overlooking the midan. Authentic Lebanese cuisine. Most people come here for *sheesha* and tea, and order some *mezza* to accompany. A very local place. No alcohol served.

ΨΨ-Ψ **El Omda**, 6 Sharia El-Ghazza, behind Atlas Hotel, T02-3336 7596. Open 1200-0200. Famed for traditional Egyptian food, especially *fuul* and *koshari*, served very speedily. For carnivores, try the kebab, *kofta* and *shish tawook*.

Imbaba

ΨΨΨ-ΨΨ **The Swiss Club**, Villa Pax, 90 Sharia El Gehad, off Sharia Sudan, Midan, Kit Kat, T02-3314 2811, www.swiss-club-cairo.com. Palm trees and banyans surround grassy lawns, a children's play area, and a pseudo-Swiss villa. It's an odd but delightful enclave in the heart of Midan Kit Kat's back-alleys. The cuisine encompasses rosti and fondues, but there's plenty of other decent Western choices and a kid's menu. Entrance is E£10 (children under 6 free), open 0900-2000 for food and drinks (alcohol served), though private parties often continue in the hired rooms late into the night. The service, however, is mediocre.

Ÿ **El Embrator**, before the post office on Sharia Sudan, Midan Kit Kat. Possibly the best *koshari* chain in town and they're extremely generous with their toppings. Finish with *ros bi-laban* (rice pudding) if you've got room. Worth stopping in if you've come this way to look at the houseboats.

Giza

ŸŸŸ **Moghul Rooms**, Mena House Oberoi, T02-3383 3222. Open 1200-1445 and 1930-2345. Authentic Indian food, sophisticated atmosphere, live Indian entertainment every evening. A fabulously plush experience in a historic hotel, but does serious damage to your wallet.

ŸŸŸ-ŸŸ **Barry's Oriental Restaurant**, 2 Sharia Abu Aziza, T02-3388 9540. Follow the road (Sharia Abu El-Houl) past the entrance to the Sphinx (on your right) to the very end, Barry's is above **AA Stables**, just ring the bell. Go for drinks, meat grills or *mezza* (if you're vegetarian, great *besara*) and the best view of sunset behind the pyramids in the world. You can even just about hear the Sound and Light show from the roof terrace. It's best to check the price of Saqqara and juices before you order them. There's also a shop with some old and interesting curios.

ŸŸŸ-ŸŸ **Christo**, 10 Sharia El-Haram, T02-3383 3582. Open 1100-0300. A choose-your-own-seafood restaurant with a view of the pyramids. Often busy at lunchtimes with tour groups, the service is good but the decor is getting scruffy.

ŸŸ **Andrea**, 59 Mariuteya Canal Rd, T02-3383 1133. Known for its pigeon dishes and still the best place for grilled chicken. Outdoor eating on a plant-filled patio shaded by awnings. A family-friendly place with lots of open space for children to play.

Heliopolis *p122, map p123*

ŸŸŸ **Chantilly**, 11 Sharia Baghdad, Korba, T02-2414 5620. Open 0700-2400. In the centre of Heliopolis, a long-standing Swiss establishment popular with wealthier locals and expats, Chantilly has a nice atmosphere and good patisserie at the front. Continental mains are heavy and very meat orientated (vegetarians are restricted to soup or salads) but their cheese fondue is excellent for a splash out (E£165). Serves alcohol, and has a pleasant shady terrace out the back.

ŸŸŸ **City Stars**, Sharia Omar Ibn Al-Khatab, T02-2480 0100. Restaurants generally open 1100-2400. For a massive choice of every kind of food you could be missing, trek out to **City Stars**: **Wagamama**, **Eatalian**, **Shogun**, **Bellini Cocktail Lounge** and plenty more.

ŸŸŸ-ŸŸ **Chili's**, 18 Sharia El-Thawra, T02-2418 8048. Open 1100-0100. Spicy Tex-Mex food served up in huge portions, try their fajitas and awesome black beans. The large outdoor patio with cooling fans make it a popular hangout in Heliopolis after the sun sets. Extensive dessert menu, including banana splits and brownies. No alcohol. Branches in Mohandiseen and Gezira.

ŸŸŸ-ŸŸ **Petit Palmyra**, 27 Sharia Al-Ahram, T02-2417 1720, www.palmyragroups.com. Open daily 1100-0100. This piano restaurant has been operating since 1949, and has a mix of Lebanese, oriental, and international food (pigeon, veal, chops) plus a separate vegetarian selection. Old-fashioned ambiance. Alcohol served, piano music from 2030.

Ÿ **Cafeteria Magic**, 131 Sharia Al-Ahram (El-Nouzah). Reliable *fuul*, *taamiyya*, *shwerma* and other staples, either to eat in or take away. Handily opposite L'amphitrion.

Ÿ **Gad**, Sharia Haroun Al-Rashid. Super-cheap takeaway Egyptian sandwich favourites from the countrywide chain. A safe bet for those with sensitive stomachs.

Trips down the Nile *p124*

Maadi

Red Onion, 27A Road 276, T02-2520 0240.

Villa 55, 55 Road 9, T02-2380 9592. The quiet garden setting seems a million miles away from the hustle of Cairo, while there is a tastefully decorated a/c interior for those steamy days. Food is international.

Bars and clubs

Central Cairo *p63, map p64*

Cairo has plenty of intriguing and diverse places to go for a drink, from strictly functional via classic vintage to bijou expensive. Some of the upmarket bars have room to dance and they morph into discos later on, plus there are plenty of 'nightclubs' that put on a floorshow or belly dancing. Some 5-star hotels also have discos that appeal to a range of affluent and Westernized Egyptians. Bear in mind most places don't serve alcohol during Ramadan, only top-end hotels and a couple of bars in Zamalek. Look out for Drinkies beverage shops, which also deliver (T19330).

Absolute, Casino El-Shargara, Corniche El-Nil, Maspero, Bulaq, T02-2579 6512, www.deyafa.net. Weekend nights see hectic club music, and there are chiller nights during the week. It's a cool-looking venue on the river, with the excellent **Sangria** bar upstairs for pre-party drinks and Italian/Lebanese food.

After Eight, 6 Sharia Qasr El-Nil (past a kiosk down an unlikely-looking alley), T010-339 8000. Open 1200-0300, sometimes later. A real hotspot on the Downtown scene, this smoky little dive is one of few places in Cairo to hear good live music. Currently *Sahra* play *rai* favourites and originals you can dance to on a Thu to a packed house, other nights have a swingtime thing going on, and DJ Dina (a woman) is on the decks on Tue, or Bashir and his band on a Nubian vibe on Sun. There is a cover charge of E£100 on Thu and E£50 on Sun. Fully stocked bar, standard menu serving variety of meats and pastas through the night.

Café Riche, 17 Sharia Talaat Harb, T02-2392 9793, www.caferiche.com. Open 1000-2400. Classic café that has seen the face of virtually every Arab intellectual and artist of the last century. Renovations have altered the feel of the place and now it's less of a revolutionary den, but it's still worth a visit, especially if you can get the story from an old timer, and the beer is reasonably priced.

Estoril, 12 Sharia Talaat Harb, T02-2574 3102. Cold beer, nibbles, and surprisingly good food – vegetarians should try the *fattah*. A place where artists and intellectuals still gather to work and play.

Fontana Hotel, Midan Ramses, T02-2592 2321, has an open-air bar on the top floor looking down on the mayhem of the Midan far below with *sheesha* and Stella at reasonable prices. There's also a 24-hr disco – one of the kitschiest you will ever see.

Grand Hyatt Hotel, Garden City, has spectacular views over the city from the lounge bar on the 40th floor. There is no minimum charge before 1900, or E£95 per person after that. You can stop for a drink or just have a wander round, and there's also a revolving restaurant upstairs open from 1900.

Happy City Hotel, 92C Sharia Mohamed Farid, T02-2395 9333. This bar on the rooftop has views over a busy Downtown street, reasonably priced booze, decent food is available, plenty of seating to accommodate big groups or lone drinkers having a beer over their book.

Hard Rock Café, by the **Grand Hyatt Hotel**, Corniche El-Nil, T02-2532 1277/81/85. Open 1200-0400. Provides all you expect from the place: standard tex-mex specials, celebrity guitars, funky costumes, live shows, karaoke, and theme nights. The dance floor gets kicking after midnight. No minimum for foreigners.

Kings Bar, **Cosmopolitan Hotel**, 1 Sharia Ibn Taalab. Open 1000-0200. A fairly salubrious, relaxing yet local-feeling choice, warmly lit by yellow lanterns, generally peopled with *pasha* types shooting the breeze. It's a good place to snack or dine while you're drinking, with grills, salad, fish and steaks at quite reasonable prices. Stella E£13, all in.

Le Bistro, 8 Sharia Hoda Sharawy, T012-849 1943. A nice little bar open 1900-0200, with a restaurant of the same name next door.

Le Grillon, 8 Sharia Qasr El-Nil, Downtown; T02-2576 4959. Open 1100-0200. Pleasing indoor garden, restaurant, bar and *ahwa*, very popular spot for local intellectuals and artists. Conversations about revolutions and poetry continue into the wee hours over excellent *sheesha* and beer. The food is mid-priced and quite good, lots of meats, soups and salads, fairly standard Egyptian fare. It's a local place that is comfortable for single women and somewhere you will see Egyptian women enjoying a drink.

Odeon Rooftop Bar, **Odeon Palace Hotel**, 6 Sharia Abdel Hamid Said. Open 24 hrs and offers a great view of the city. A nice place to come to wind down after a rowdy evening, or where the hardcore carry on past dawn.

Tamarai, **Nile City Towers**, www.tamarai-egypt.com. This rooftop restaurant morphs into a club as the night wears on. It is genuinely chic, a high-society spot and place to glimpse celebrities. People get properly dancing. Every Tue is Nostalgia Night.

Windsor Hotel Barrel Lounge, 19 Sharia Alfi Bey, T02-2591 5277, is a truly delightful place for a drink, although the prices are a bit steep these days. The ambience is charming despite, or perhaps because of, the fading Anglo decor of polished wood, antlers and mottled mirrors.

Local drinking holes

Locals' bars are generally patronized by men only, and women on their own will probably feel uncomfortable although should be perfectly safe. As the government forbids the word 'bar' in the names of establishments, most go under the guise of 'cafeteria'.

Cafeteria Honololo, Sharia Mohammed Farid across the street from **Pension Roma**, Downtown. A taste of Cairo's seediest: Stella, *sheesha*, Heinekein, and bar girls.

Cafeteria Irabi, Sharia Orabi, Downtown. A miniature Stella-themed den that is friendly and allows glimpses of the world through the open door.

Cafeteria Stella, next to **Felfela** restaurant, Downtown. This tiny hole-in-the-wall of a bar is as local as it gets. On offer: basic *mezza*, E£9.50 Stella, and rum and brandy that is probably best avoided.

Carrol Restaurant, 12 Sharia Qasr El-Nil, Downtown. The food is expensive and the ambience extraordinarily gaudy. After midnight, there's a live show, performed by the only women who frequent the place.

El-Horriya, Midan Falaki, Bab El-Louk, Downtown. About the only local *ahwa* that serves beer, Horriya is a true Cairo institution. Everyone comes here, old and young, foreign and local, to spew thoughts on the state of the country, play chess, and get rowdy as the night wears on. It's become a bit over-run with AUC youth in recent years, but still should feature on any Cairo itinerary.

New Arizona, Sharia Alfi Bey, Downtown. They have removed the wallpaper of Swiss mountain posters, but this is about as local as it gets. Probably best not venture into the nightclub upstairs.

Zamalek *p113, map p114*

Buddha Bar, Sofitel El Gezirah, T02-2737 3737. Dominated by a gargantuan gold Siddhartha, the decor is plush (dark red velvet) great food downstairs (terrace with amazing Nile views, Asian and sushi) and upstairs gets into a dancing groove later on, good music and environment. Take plenty of cash.

Cairo Jazz Club, 197 Sharia 26 July, Mohandiseen, T02-3345 9939. Many rate it as the best place in town for live local music. Each night has a theme or regular act, check www.icroc.com for what's on. Loungey feel with a small dance floor that doubles as a stage. On occasion there's real jazz, and it's often quite good.

Deals, 2 Sharia El-Sayed El-Bakry, Zamalek. Closes at 0200. A noisy buzzing basement-like bar with cheapish beer and lots of Western food on the menu (try their shrimp provençale if you find yourself here at dinnertime). Also have branches in Mohandiseen and Heliopolis, but this one's the busiest.

Marriott Hotel, 16 Sharia Saray El-Gezira. Offers the drinking choices of **Harry's Pub** and the **Garden Promenade**. The first is a British-style wood-panelled pub with karaoke some nights, while the garden terrace is people-watching central and surrounded by shady trees and birds. Both serve OK continental food.
Pub 28, 28 Sharia Shagar Al-Durr, Zamalek. One of the oldest pubs in Zamalek, it attracts a more matured expat crowd as well as *pashas* quaffing large quantities of whisky in the smoky darkness. Cheap-ish beer and bar food (great French onion soup) means it's always crowded.
Purple Lounge, 6 Imperial Boat, Saray El-Gezira, Zamalek, T02-2736 5796. Highly expensive and plush club playing house and retro sounds. If you're planning on dropping a lot of cash, it's worth it to be in one of very few places where people really get dancing.

Restaurants that double as late-night bars (see Eating, page 135) include: **La Bodega**, a cool yet not too pretentious, place for a drink, and **L'Aubergine**, a black box bar popular with students and local expats, which starts kicking around 2200 and is heaving on a Thu.

Heliopolis *p122, map p123*
Deals, 40A Sharia Baghdad, T02-2291 0406. Open 1600-0200. Very dim, cosy and functional, this is a more laid-back version of the **Deals** in Zamalek. The food (steaks, pasta, *mezza*) is tasty enough and there's a DJ every night from 2000.
L'Amphitrion, Sharia Al-Ahram, T02-2258 1379. Open 0800-0100. Nothing remains of the original 1922 fixtures but, now the Palmyra nightclub down the road has been turned into a Starbucks, this is the only place left in Heliopolis to have a beer in the outdoors and remember the allied forces who did likewise. Stella is E£20 and good *sheesha tuufah* E£8.50. Alcohol has to be drunk in the back courtyard with a curious water feature, complete with a Buddha statue. Plus there's an interesting clientele of higab-ed ladies, lone drinkers and old-school gentlemen. Slow service despite the plentiful cheery waiters. Food is available in the adjacent restaurant.
The Louvre, in the **Beirut Hotel**, 43 Sharia Baghdad, T02-2415 2347. Open 1200-0100. Feeble reproductions of the Mona Lisa don't really justify the name, but this is a stalwart for local expats. Serves acceptable food.
Pasha Bar, **Baron Hotel**, T02-2291 5757, www.baronhotels.com. With an attempt at oriental decor and views to the Baron's Palace, it's not a bad spot for a quiet drink before the DJ comes on at 2230.

Entertainment

Cairo *p63, maps p58, p64, p74, p75, p101, p104, p114 and p123.*

Belly-dancing shows
For a slick belly-dancing performance by one of the famous stars, head to one of the ritzy 5-star hotels. There's usually a cover charge (E£300-600, depending on the venue), which includes the show and a multi-course meal. Otherwise, progressively cheaper venues exist in floating restaurants (particularly the **Nile Maxim**, in front of the Marriott, T012-738 8888), in the strip of dodgy nightclubs along Pyramids Rd and tucked away in seedy alleyways Downtown. Of the latter, the **Palmyra**, and the **Miami**, both down an alley at 16 Sharia 26th July, are as sleazy as they come and give a taste of Cairo's underworld. Women are fine to visit these places but only when accompanied by men, and everyone must be wary about being ripped-off for drinks or snacks and should query the price of anything and everything before consuming it.
Semiramis Intercontinental, T02-2795 7171, at present hosts Dina, one of the most acclaimed dancers in town, every Thu night at 2330-0300, entrance includes dinner and taxes E£500-740 depending on proximity to stage.

Casinos
Found in the following hotels, see Sleeping, page 125; make sure you bring your passport with you:

Cairo Marriott, Mena House Oberoi, Nile Hilton, Ramses Hotel, Semiramis Inter-continental and Sofitel El Gezirah.

Cinemas

Current information on cinema performances can be found on www.icroc.com, in *Al-Ahram Weekly*, www.weekly-ahram.org.eg, the *Egyptian Gazette*, and the monthly glossy *Egypt Today* magazine. Commercial cinemas change their programmes every Wed and screenings are generally at 1030, 1330, 1530, 1830 and 2130 and sometimes at 2400, especially on weekends. Cultural centres have 1 or 2 screenings per week. Arabic films rarely have subtitles.

The following cinemas show films in English:

Al Tahrir, 122 Sharia Al-Tahrir, Dokki, T02-2335 4726.

Cairo Sheraton, Midan Galaa, Dokki, T02-3336 9700.

Cosmos, 12 Sharia Emad El-Din, Downtown, T02-2574 2177.

Family Land, Osman Towers, Corniche El-Nil, next to Maadi Hospital, Maadi, T02-2524 8100.

French Cultural Centre, 1 Sharia Maddraset El-Huquq El-Faransiya, Mounira, T02-2794 7679.

Galaxy, 67 Sharia Abdel Aziz Al-Seoud, Manial, T02-2532 5745, www.galaxycairocinema.com.

Goethe Institute, 5 Sharia El-Bustan, Downtown, T02-2575 9877.

Good News First Mall, Sharia Giza (opposite Giza Zoo), T02-3571 7803.

Karim, 15 Sharia Emad El-Din, Downtown, T02-2592 4830.

Metro, 35 Sharia Talaat Harb, Downtown, T02-2393 7566.

Odeon, 4 Sharia Dr A Hamid Said, Downtown, T02-2576 5642.

Ramses Hilton, 7th floor of the hotel's shopping annexe, Corniche El-Nil, Downtown, T02-2574 7435.

Renaissance Nile City, Nile City Towers, Corniche El-Nil, T02-2461 9101/2/3.

Stars/Golden Stars, City Stars Mall, Sharia Omar Ibn Al-Khatab, Heliopolis, T02-2480 2012/3, www.citystarscinema.com.

Townhouse Gallery, 10 Sharia Nabrawi, off Sharia Champollion, Downtown, T02-2576 8086, www.thetownhouse gallery.com, occasionally has programmes screening foreign films.

Villa Grey, 24 Sharia Abdallah Al Kateb, Dokki, T02-3338 2184. A cine-club showing art-house and foreign films, Wed at 2030.

Galleries

Cairo Opera House Art Gallery, Gezira, T02-2739 8132. Sun-Thu 1000-1430 and 1630-2030.

French Cultural Centre, 1 Sharia Maddraset El-Huquq El-Faransiya, Mounira, T02-2794 7679. Also at 5 Sharia Chafik El-Dib, Ard El-Golf, Heliopolis, T02-2417 4824, F02-2419 9143.

Gezira Art Centre, 1 Sharia El-Marsafy, Zamalek, T02-2737 3298. Interesting exhibitions by contemporary artists.

Hannager Arts Centre, Opera House Grounds, T02-2735 6861. Daily 1000-2200.

Khan El-Maghraby Gallery, 18 Sharia El-Mansour Mohammed, Zamalek, T02-2735 3349. Mon-Sat, 1200-2200.

Mashrabia Gallery, 8 Sharia Champollion, T02-2578 4494, www.mashrabiagallery.com. Exhibitions by foreign and Egyptian artists. Daily, except Fri and Mon 1100-2000. Contemporary art.

Safar Khan Gallery, 6 Sharia Brazil, Zamalek, T02-2735 3314. Sat-Thu, 1000-1300, 1700-2000.

Townhouse Gallery of Contemporary Art, 10 Sharia Nabrawi, off Sharia Champollion, Downtown, T02-2576 8086, www.thetown housegallery.com. Sat-Wed 1000-1400 and 1800-2100, Fri 1800-2100, closed Thu. Probably the best space in town to see interesting and adventurous exhibitions. Gift and bookshop opposite.

Zamalek Art Gallery, 11 Sharia Brazil, T02-2735 1240.

Sound and Light show

2 performances daily at the Sphinx and pyramids, Giza, www.soundandlight.com.eg at 1830 and 1930 in winter; 2030 and 2130

in summer. E£75, no student discounts. The voice of the Sphinx narrates the story of the pyramids in the following languages: Arabic, English, French, German, Italian, Japanese, Russian and Spanish. Call for specific schedules, T02-3383 8823/3587 6767.

Theatre, music and dance

Current information for performances is given in the *Egyptian Gazette* and *Al-Ahram Weekly*, www.weekly-ahram.org.eg. Apart from the *Opera House*, all theatrical performances are likely to be in Arabic.

Arab Music Institute, 22 Sharia Ramses, Downtown, T02-2574 3373. Classical Arabic music performances, twice a week.

Balloon Theatre, Sharia Corniche El-Nil, El-Agouza, nr Al-Zamalek Bridge, T02-2347 1718.

Beit Al-Suhaymi, Darb Al-Asfar, Al-Hussein, Islamic Cairo, T02-2591 3391. Folk music and songs every Sun at 2000, free, for 2 hrs, and occasional special events and performances, particularly during Ramadan.

El-Genena Theatre, Al-Azhar Park, Salah Salem, T02-2362 5057. Great venue to hear music, sometimes international.

El-Gomhouriya Theatre, 12 Sharia El-Gomhouriya, Abdin, T02-2390 7707.

El Mastaba Center for Egyptian Folk Music, El Tanbura Hall, 30A Sharia Balaqsa, Abdin, T02-2392 6768. Performances every Thu by Rango and on Fri by El Tanbura at 2130, cost E£20 and last around 1½ hrs. A visit is strongly recommended, particularly on a Thu when Rango get people out their seats and perform some haunting ensembles.

El-Sawy Culture Wheel, Sharia 26 July, Zamalek, T02-2736 6178, www.culturewheel.com. Bands and concerts most nights in a great venue under 15th May bridge, varying from Bedouin folk, to Arab rap, to Ghanaian flutes.

Makan, 1 Sharia Saad Zaghloul, Al-Mounira, T02-2792 0878. *Zar* performance by the Mazaher band every Wed, involving drumming and chanting (traditionally to drive out evil spirits), and Nass Makan every Tue at 2100, which is folk music from around Egypt. An essential night out and best on Wed. Tickets can be reserved by phone 48 hrs in advance, which gives a E£10 discount (or buy for E£30 on the night). Performances last about 2 hrs.

The National Theatre, Midan Ataba, T02-2591 7783.

Opera House, Gezira, info T02-339 8144, box office T02-2739 0132, www.cairoopera.org. Has a hall with 1200 seats for opera, ballet and classical music performances, a 2nd hall with 500 seats for films and conferences and an open-air theatre. For grandeur, get tickets to the main hall show; advance booking recommended. Men must wear jacket and tie.

Puppet Theatre, Ezbakiah, El-Ataba, T02-2591 0954, traditional puppetry shows which might appeal, Thu and Fri 1930, Fri 1030.

Whirling dervishes On Mon, Wed and Sat, 2030, during Ramadan 2100, in Wikala El-Ghuri, near Midan Hussein, Islamic Cairo. Tickets are given out at 1830 and it is advisable come at that time to collect one; least busy on a Mon night. Free. Cameras (but not video) permitted. Sponsored by the Ministry of Culture, the **El-Tanoura Dance Troupe** puts on a spectacular show in the restored *wikala*, which makes a great setting. Just hearing the vibrant music and staring at the colourful spinning can put you into a trance. The performance lasts about 1½ hrs and is a Cairo must-see (if you suspend any desire for authenticity for a while).

Festivals and events

Cairo *p63, maps p58, p64, p74, p75, p101, p104, p114 and p123*

Jan International Book Fair at the Exhibition Grounds in Nasr City, 0900-1900. **Christmas**, Coptic Church. **Epiphany**, Coptic Church.

Mar International Fair: Annual Spring Flower Show.

Apr **Easter**, Coptic Church. **Annunciation**, Coptic and Roman Catholic.

Jun **Pentecost**, Coptic Church.

Jul International Festival of Documentary Films.
Aug International Song Festival. Nile Festival Day at Giza.
Sep International Festival of Vanguard Theatre. Nile Festival Day in Cairo.
Nov International Children's Book Fair at Nasr City.
Dec Festival for Arab Theatre. Festival of Impressionist Art (alternate years). International Film Festival.

Shopping

Cairo *p63, maps p58, p64, p74, p75, p101, p104, p114 and p123*

Bookshops

As the largest publisher of Arabic books in the world, Cairo is a haven for Arabic literature enthusiasts. For second-hand books (some of which are in English) try the book market in the northeast corner of Ezbekiya Gardens, by Midan Ataba. The following are shops selling books and periodicals in European languages:

Al-Ahram, 165 Sharia Mohammed Farid, Downtown. Sat-Thu 0900-1700.

American University in Cairo (AUC) Bookstore, Sharia Kasr El-Aini, Downtown, on the old campus, T02-2797 5929, www.aucpress.com. Open Sat-Thu 1000-1800 (-1500 in Ramadan). On 2 floors, Cairo's biggest and best collection of fiction and books on Egypt (and everywhere else). They no longer stock textbooks, which have been moved to the campus in New Cairo. There's also a store next to the AUC Hostel, Zamalek, T02-2739 7045, open Sat-Thu 0900-1800, Fri 1300-1800. Note that it's 20% off everything the first Sat of the month.

Anglo-Egyptian Bookshop, 165 Sharia Mohammed Farid, Downtown, T02-2391 4337. Mon-Sat 0900-2000. Fairly intellection selection, classic fiction but better for non-fiction, plus some guidebooks.

Dar El-Bustan, 29 Sharia Faggala, Downtown. Open 0900-1700, Fri 1000-1500, closed Sun.

Diwan, 159 Sharia 26 July, Zamalek, T02-2736 2578, www.diwanegypt.com. Open 0900-2330. Coffee shop inside, children's books section. French, English and Arabic books on offer, occasional cultural events in the evenings, definitely one of the best selections in the city. Also has a branch in Maadi, 45 Rd 9, T019-8887 326, and Heliopolis at 105 Sharia Abou Bakr El-Seddik, T02-2690 8184.

L'Orientalist, 15 Qasr El-Nil, Downtown, T02-2575 3418, www.orientalebooks.com. Rare books and maps, original David Roberts lithographs, and other beautiful antique items.

Lehnert & Landrock, 44 Sharia Sherif, T02-392 7606, daily 1000-1900, and in the mall next to Naguib Mahfouz Coffeeshop in the Khan el-Khalili. Also has branches at Giza and in the Egyptian Museum. Books in German and English, but best known for the black and white prints by Lehnert & Landrock who documented the Middle East in the early 20th century.

Librairies Renaissance, 20 Sharia El-Sawra, Mohandiseen, T02-3761 5835. Best for French books. They also have branches in Heliopolis (T010-1662012) and Maadi (T02-25199684).

Livres de France, 17 Sharia Brazil, Zamalek, T02-2735 1148. Open 1000-1900, Sat 1000-0130, closed Sun. Ma'adi branch at 2 Road 23, near Ma'adi Grandmall, opens Mon-Sat 1100-1900.

Madbouli, 6 Midan Tala'at Harb, Downtown, T02-2575 6421, www.madboulybooks.com. Open 0900-2300. Down in the basement they have a decent selection of books in various European languages.

Shorouk, 1 Midan Talaat Harb, Downtown, T02-2393 0643. Open 0900-2200. Has a good fiction section. Also in Heliopolis at 15 Sharia Baghddad, Korba, and in City Stars Mall.

Virgin Megastore, City Stars Mall, Heliopolis, T02-2480 2244. One of the biggest book departments in Cairo.

Crafts and souvenirs

Among the most attractive areas to shop is the Khan El-Khalili Bazaar and Sagh comprising an array of shops dating from the

14th century. Renowned for craftsmanship in silver and gold, embroidered cloth, copperware, leather and mother-of-pearl inlaid goods. (Remember that the import of ivory is forbidden into most Western countries.) **The Kerdassa village**, east of Giza, is noted for its embroidered cotton and silk dresses, and good-quality carpets at a cheaper price than you will find in the bazaars (E£120 for simple organic colours, up to E£300 for more complex and colourful designs). Haraneya, west of Giza, is another main centre for quality carpets. See page 33 for more information on shopping. Listed below are fixed-price shops in Cairo selling good-quality crafts and souvenirs from around Egypt.

Abd El-Zaher Book Binders, 31 Sharia Sheikh Mohamed Abdou, behind Al-Azhar Mosque, T02-2511 8041, www.abdel-zaher.com. Open 1000-2200. Notebooks, photo albums, folders, etc, are beautifully bound in leather and handmade paper. They can cover books or diaries to order, and can initial them in gold, though it might take a few days. Also has a small selection of books on Egypt.

Al Ain Gallery, 73 Sharia El-Hussein, Dokki, T02-3749 3940. Bedouin textiles, cushions, ceramics, and 1000 filigree and metalwork lanterns.

Al-Khatoun, 3 Sharia Mohamed Abdou, Islamic Cairo, T02-2514 7164, www.al khatoun.com. Open 1100-2100 (1200-2300 in Ramadan). Fabulous swathes of cloth, pots, beaten copperware, iron lamps, old film posters, cushions, pop art and other items of homeware that are all in impeccable taste. Their new branch in Zamelek is called

Al Qahira, 1st floor, 6 Bahgat Ali, T011-3133 932, www.alqahiracrafts.com. Open 1100-2100 except Sun. Housed in an attractive apartment.

And Company, 3 Sharia Bahgat Ali, Zamalek, T02-2736 5689. Open 0900-2300, daily. This is where to come for superior Egyptian cotton, specializing in clothing, sheets, etc of a contemporary rather than ethnic bent. Also sells quality jewellery, pottery, candles and the like, plus works by local artists.

Atlas, near Nagib Mahfouz Café in Khan El-Khalili, T02-2590 6139. Moiré silk handmade shoes.

Azza Fahmy Boutique, 15C Sharia Taha Hussein (corner of Sharia Mohamed Marashli), T02-2735 8351, www.azzafahmy.com. Open 1000-2200. Celebrated jewellery designer.

Caravanserai, 16 Sharia Marashly, Zamalek, T02-2735 0517. Open Mon-Sat 1000-2000, Sun 1000-1730. Well-known for its fabulous lighting, which remains unique among all the pretenders. They also have some mirrors, ornaments and ceramics. A visit here could result in a major purchase to take home.

Egypt Crafts, 1st floor, 27 Sharia Yahia Ibrahim, Zamalek, T02-2736 5123, www.fairtradeegypt.org. Sat-Thu 0900-2000, Fri 1000-1800. Helping to revive traditional crafts throughout Egypt, this non-profit fairtrade shop has a good selection of pottery, basketry, hand-woven scarves and rugs, jewellery and much more. A very stress-free as well as worthy place to indulge yourself.

Fatima, 157 Sharia 26 July, Zamalek, T02-2736 9951, in an alley of the main road next to Abu El-Sid restaurant. A cubby-hole selling intricate embroidered textiles and clothing from Egypt and central Asia.

Khan Misr Touloun, Sharia Touloun, facing the main entrance of Ibn Touloun Mosque T02-2265 3337. Daily 1000-1700, except Sun. Handicrafts from the villages and oases of Egypt (and countries further afield). They pretty much have something for everyone – books, glassware, textiles, clothes, pots, woodwork – although some shoppers feel the selection is not as attractive as it once was.

Loft, 12 Sharia Sayed El-Bakri, Zamalek, T02-27366931, www.loftegypt.com. Open 1000-1500. An eclectic selection of oriental furniture, metalwork, friezes, over-the-top lighting, icons and antiques are displayed in a boudoir-like setting – worth visiting in itself.

Markaz, 1b Road 199 (entrance on Road 233), Maadi, T02-2754 7026, T010-240 5858. Open 1000-2100, daily. Working with NGOs and small enterprises all over Egypt, exquisite crafts, rugs, drapes, cushions, scarfs and more are discerningly selected and worth paying a bit more for.

Mounaya Gallery, 14 Sharia Montazah, Zamalek, T02-2737 7726, www.mounaya.com. Stocks an interesting range of textiles, metalwork and ornaments.

Morgana, Road 9, Maadi, T010-125 0441. Fabulous antique colonial and Egyptian furniture plus a smattering of nick-nacks, pictures, old clocks, etc.

Nagada, 13 Sharia Refa'a, Dokki, T02-3748 6663, www.nagada.net. Open 1000-1830. An exquisite selection of fabrics, textiles, clothing, and ornaments, as well as exclusive pottery creations from their workshop in Tunis in Fayoum (see page 177), High-quality goods at high-end prices.

Nomad, 1st floor, 14 Saraya Al-Gezira, Zamalek, T02-2736 1917. Open 1000-2100. Tasteful goods from all over Egypt, the original jewellery made to traditional designs is especially good. They also have a smaller branch in the **Marriott**.

Om Gallery, 14 Sharia Hassan Assem, Zamalek, T02-2736 3165. This small gallery has an eclectic array of handmade leather and wrought-iron artworks, alabaster lamps and curios.

Oum El-Dounia, 1st floor, 3 Sharia Talat Harb, just off Midan Tahrir, T02-2393 8273. This delightful shop keeps getting bigger and better, with goods selected from all over Egypt at reasonable prices. If you can't find anything in here then something's wrong. Large selection of books, mainly in French. Open 7 days a week, 1000-2100. There's also a branch in Maadi on Rd 23 (off Sh El-Nadi), T02-2753 0483, daily 0930-2030.

Shahira Mehrez and Companions, 3rd floor, 12 Sharia Abi Emama, Dokki, T02-3748 7814. Open Sat-Thu 1000-2000. An intriguing shop with some lovely antiques (rugs, pots, calligraphy, etc) and faboulous *galabiyyas* made by seamstresses from around Egypt to the owner, Shahira's, designs.

Souk Al-Fustat, Sharia Saydi Hassan Al-Anwar, Old Cairo. Open 1000-2200. A bit pricey, but it showcases traditional crafts (some of which are made in the workshops of the complex). Sadly, this exceptionally high-quality *souk* doesn't have the air of being the great commercial success that was hoped for, with shop units sitting empty, but it's a good place to get handmade metal lanterns with arabesque motifs in all sizes and designs, curios, unique jewellery, handwoven fabrics and such like. Haggling is still possible in many shops.

Swellams, 30 Sharia Adly, T02-2393 9470, *the* place to buy cotton pyjamas in Cairo. Family-run for 55 years, **Swellams** has made clothes for former presidents and still sells beautifully made garments and, in addition to their classic pyjamas, can tailor shirts and suits.

Wady Craft Shop, All Saint's Cathedral, 5 Sharia Michel Lutfalla, Zamalek, T02-2735 4350, www.wadycrafts.com/shop. Open 0930-1700, Sun and Fri 1100-1600. Handicrafts made by disadvantaged and disabled persons, as well as Sudanese refugees, all proceeds go to these charitable causes.

Supermarkets

Metro markets are scattered around Cairo and have a good variety of stock, hotline T19619. There are branches of **Carrefour** in 6th October City and Maadi. **Alfa Market**, 4 Sharia El-Malek El-Afdal, Zamalek, T02-2736 6265, which is good for toiletries as well as groceries, and **El Tamimi** supermarket, 116 Sharia 26th July, Zamalek, T02-2738 0274, are open 24 hrs and seem to be able to produce almost anything out of their storerooms. **Isis**, 8 Ahmed Sabry, Zamalek, T02-2738 2724, is a small health food store that might be helpful for those with specific dietary requirements.

Activities and tours

Cairo *p63, maps p58, p64, p74, p75, p104, p114*

Bowling

Cairo Land, 1 Sharia Salem. 1000-0100.

Maadi Family Land, Corniche El-Nil. 1000-0200.

MISR Bowling Centre, 9th floor, Al Bustan Centre, Bab El-Louk.

Diving

Maadi Divers, 18 Road 218, Maadi, T02-2519 8644, www.maadi-divers.com. The 1st PADI dive centre in Cairo.

Nautilus Diving, 4 Sharia Omar Shabban, off Sharia El-Nozha, Ard El-Golf, Heliopolis, T02-2417 6515, www.nautilusdiving.com.

Seascapes Diving and Safari, 1/2 Sharia Lasilky, New Maadi, T02-2519 4930. Mon-Fri 0900-1700. PADI courses, diving trips and desert safaris.

Golf

Katameya Heights Golf Course, 23 km southeast of Cairo, www.katameyaheights.com. 2 courses, 1 with 18 holes and another with 9 holes.

Mena House Oberoi, Gezira Sporting Club and the Marriott Hotel at Mirage City also have 18-hole courses.

Gym and health clubs

Cairo Sheraton Health Club, Galaa Sq, Giza, T02-3336 9700/800 ext 599/177. Fully equipped gymnasium and other facilities.

Golden Tulip Flamenco Hotel Health Club, 2 Sharia El-Gezira El-Wosta, Zamalek, T02-2735 0815. Mon-Sat 0800-2200. Gymnasium, sauna, jacuzzi and massage.

Gold's Gym, 8th and 9th floor, Maadi Palace Mall, T02-2378 5592. 3000 sq m including a mixed-gender gym, a ladies-only gym and 2 pools.

Samya Alloubah Dance and Fitness Centre, 6 Sharia Amr, off Sharia Syria, Mohandiseen, T02-3302 0572. Gym, steam room, gymnastics, martial arts and dance and fitness classes for both adults and children.

Spa and Wellness Centre, Four Seasons Hotel Cairo at the First Residence, T02-2567 2040. Full-service spa, 8 treatment rooms and extensive facilities. Specializes in Cleopatra milk baths, Nefertiti facials, papyrus wraps and private spa for couples.

Horse riding

It's very pleasant to ride in the desert by the pyramids, particularly for sunrise or sunset. Avoid the haggard-looking horses lined up for tourists by the pyramid's gate and head for the stables in Kafr El-Gebel (straight on past the entrance to Sound and Light show). **AA Stables**, T012-153 4142, and **MG Stables**, T02-3385 1241 are the most highly recommended, have regular Western clients, and offer a variety of excursions from the standard hour-long ride around the pyramids (E£50), riding lessons, to a trip to Saqqara. More elaborate excursions and night rides need to be booked in advance. See also Saqqara Country Club, below.

Swimming

Heliopolis, and **Gezira** sporting clubs have pools that you can pay daily or monthly memberships to use. The **Mohamed Ali Club**, on the banks of the Nile, by Mounib metro stop, has a great pool, day use is E£60 or on Fri E£80. It's possible to use the pools at some hotels, those in the 5-star establishments obviously cost more. The **Atlas Hotel**, Mohandiseen (E£35 minimum charge, enough for a couple of drinks as well) and the **Fontana**, Midan Ramses (E£25) both have small and unappealing pools.

Other hotels with good pools include: **Grand Hyatt**, Garden City, for E£200 per day 0700-1900; **Marriott**, Zamalek, which has hiked its prices to E£240 per day, or Thu-Sat E£305; the **Nile Hilton** charges E£150 and the pool is large though the surroundings a bit tacky; **Semiramis Intercontinental** is good for E£137 per day. The **Saqqara Country Club**, at the end of Saqqara Rd, Giza, T02-3381 1307, costs E£120 per person including lunch and a drink, day-use of a room E£220. If you go early at the weekend it will be mostly empty, later on it gets crowded with Egyptians. Plus there is horse riding, tennis courts, a restaurant and bar lounge. It's a great place to get away from it all.

Tennis

Katameya Tennis Resort, www.katameyaheights.com, 23 km southeast of Cairo. Has 10 clay and 2 grass courts but you have to know a member.

Marriott Hotel, has hard courts for rent by the hr, and adequate racquets.

Tour operators

Abercrombie and Kent, 18 Sharia Youssef El-Guindy, El Bustan Centre, Downtown, T02-2393 6255, www.akegypt.com.
American Express, 21 Sharia Giza, Nile Tower Building, T02-574 3656.
Astra Travel, 11 Midan El-Missaha, Dokki, T02-3749 1469, www.astratravel.com. Also have branches in Heliopolis and Maadi.
Egypt Rays, 18 Sharia Hassan Shawi, Nasr City, www.egyptrays.com. Can cut your costs by booking budget accommodation, entry tickets to all sites included.
Isis Travel, 48 Sharia Giza, Orman Bldg, T02-3749 4325, www.isistravel.com.
Mena Tours, El-Nasr Bldg, Sharia El-Nil, Giza, T02-3574 0864, and 14 Sharia Talaat Harb, T02-2396 2497, www.mena-tours.net.
Misr Travel, 1 Sharia Talaat Harb, T02-2393 0010, and 7 Sharia Talaat Harb, T02-2393 0168, www.misrtravel.net.
See Real Egypt, El Obour Building, Sharia Salah Salem, Nasr City, T018-305 0677, www.seerealegypt.com. Customized or standard tours, mainly visiting the big sights in Cairo and down the Nile Valley.
Spring Tours, 11 Sharia Talaat Harb, T02-392 2627, and 3 Sharia Sayyid El-Bakry, Zamalek, T02-2393 2573, www.springtours.com. Open 0900-1800.
Travco, 12 Sharia Mahmoud Azmi, Zamalek, T02-2736 2024, www.travco.com.
Thomas Cook, 7 Sharia Baghdad, El-Korba, Heliopolis, T02-2416 4000; 17 Sharia Mahmoud Bassiouny, Downtown, T02-2574 3955/67/776, daily 0800-1700; 10 Sharia 26 July, Mohandiseen, T02-3346 7187, www.thomascookegypt.com.

Transport

Cairo *p63, maps p58, p64, p74, p75, p104, p114*

Air

Cairo International Airport, is about 22 km northeast of downtown Cairo. **EgyptAir**, www.egyptair.com, which operates from Terminal 1, offers regular flights to the following domestic destinations: **Abu Simbel**, **Alexandria**, **Assuit**, **Aswan**, **Hurghada**, **Luxor** and **Sharm El-Sheikh**.

Airline offices Air Canada, 26 Sharia Mahmoud Bassiouny, T02-2575 8402, www.aircanada.com. **Air France**, 2 Midan Talaat Harb, T02-2770 6250, www.airfrance.com, Sun-Thu 0830-1630. **Austrian Airlines**, 6 Sharia El-Sheikh El-Marsafi, Zamalek, T19404, www.austrian.com, Sun-Thu 0800-1600. **British Airways**, Intercontinental Residence Suites, City Stars Complex, Sharia Al Forsan, Heliopolis, T02-2480 0380, Sun-Thu 0900-1700. **CSA Czech Airlines**, 9 Sharia Talaat Harb, T02-2393 0395, www.csa.cz. **Cyprus Airways**, 4th Floor, 17 Sharia Qasr El-Nil, T02-2395 4770, www.cyprusair.com. **Delta**, 17 Sharia Ismail Mahmoud, Zamalek, T02-2736 2039, www.delta.com. **EgyptAir**, 9 Sharia Talaat Harb, T02-2393 2836, 6 Sharia Adly, T02-2392 7649. **El-Al**, 5 Sharia El-Makrizi, Zamalek, T02-2736 1795, www.elal.co.il. **Emirates**, 18 Sharia El-Batal Ahmed Abdel Aziz, Mohandiseen, T19899, www.emirates.com. **Lufthansa**, 6 Sharia El-Sheikh El-Marsafi, Zamalek, T19380, Sun-Thu 0800-1700, www.lufthansa.com. **Saudi Arabian Airlines**, 5 Sharia Qasr El-Nil, T02-2574 1200, www.saudiairlines.com. **Singapore Airlines**, 22nd Floor, Infinity Towers, 8 Sharia Geziret Al-Arab, Mohandiseen, T02- 3749 2879, www.singaporeair.com. **Swiss**, 6 Sharia El-Sheikh El-Marsafi, Zamalek, T19380, www.swiss.com, Sun-Thu 0800-1700. **Syrianair**, 25 Sharia Talaat Harb, Downtown, T02-2393 6232, www.syriaair.com. **Turkish Airways**, 17 Sharia Sabri Abu Alem, Midan Taalat Harb, Downtown, T02-2396 0454, www.turkishairlines.com, daily except Fri 0900-1800.

Bus

Local Only recommended for the truly adventurous or extremely broke traveller, public buses in Cairo guarantee an experience to write home about. That said, the public bus network succeeds surprisingly well in connecting the labyrinth of streets that make up Cairo's many boroughs. Before setting off, beware: except for the main hubs in **Midan Abdel Mouneim Riad** (by MidanTahrir), behind **Midan Ramsis** and next to **Midan Ataba** where the lines start and stop, the buses often fail to come to complete stops and require extraordinary agility to mount and descend. However, when the driver sees a foreigner flagging down the bus he may make a special exception and come to a halt. When mounting a bus, get on from the back, pay your ticket to the attendant and plan to descend from the front. Since they're so cheap and the way most Cairenes get around, buses are always crowded – especially during commuting hours from 0700-1000 and 1500-1900. Be mindful of yourself and your belongings as pickpockets and groping may occur. Note that bus numbers are generally posted above the dashboard or on a plate in the window. Do not confuse the vehicle identification number (sometimes in English) with the route number. As bus numbers are not in English, it's a good idea to learn the numerals (read as in English from left to right). Some bus routes have slashes through the digits, which indicate a wholly different route. The slightly smaller and newer public buses are a bit more manageable since there is no standing room and only 1 door (not to be confused with the even smaller private microbuses that look more like vans). Buses operate daily from 0530 to 0030 with extended hours during Ramadan and cost 50 pt, minibuses cost E£1-2. If in doubt, just ask the person next to you how much it costs to your destination.

The **CTA** a/c buses are more comfortable and a good way to get to the airport, though they take a detour through Heliopolis, which can mean a journey time of well over an hour. They cost a flat E£2, no matter how far you ride. When in doubt, ask a station chief located in a box in the middle of all main bus hubs. They may not speak English, but state your destination and they'll point you in the right direction.

Long distance Cities in Egypt are well connected by buses that are quite comfortable and inexpensive. When tourist season is high, it's wise to buy tickets in advance, especially to key destinations like the Sinai, Siwa or Hurghada. You must buy tickets at the bus station; phone reservations are still not possible. The following schedules are for your reference. Do not rely too heavily on them as times and prices change constantly in Egypt depending on the number of tourists and a million other variables. You can always call the respective bus station to enquire about departure times – try to have an Arabic speaker nearby as few operators are proficient in English. Note that some prices are quoted in ranges because later buses tend to be a few pounds more expensive than early morning buses. There are several bus stations in Cairo that cover different regions of Egypt.

Turgoman/Cairo Gateway is the main terminal, on Sharia Shanan in Bulaq, now signed as the 'Cairo Gateway' although no one calls it that. Recently rebuilt and modernized, there are electronic boards above the ticket counters showing destinations and times. It's huge and offers services to virtually everywhere in Egypt (except El-Fayoum). Ironically, though, it's not readily connected to public transport, but is within walking distance of Midan Ramses (500 m). By taxi, it's a E£5 ride from Midan Tahrir. 4 bus companies operate from Turgoman:

East Delta, T02-2577 8347, have daily buses to the following destinations in Sinai: **Taba**, then on to **Nuweiba** 0600, 0930, 2300 (E£70-E£80, 7 hrs); **St Catherine** 1100 (E£45, 8 hrs) via **Wadi Feiran** (E£40, 7 hrs); **Sharm El-Sheikh** 0630, 1030, 1630, 2300, 0145 (E£60-80, 8-9 hrs); **Dahab**, 0715, 1330, 1930, 1215 (E£90, 8 hrs); **El-Arish** 2 daily (E£27-37, 5-6 hrs); **Ras Sudr** 0715, 0815, 1930 (E£30, 3 hrs). The Sinai-bound buses also pick up passengers at **Abbasiya** terminal, 3 km north of Ramses, 30 mins after leaving Turgoman, and at **Al-Maza** terminal past Heliopolis,

15 mins after Abbasiya. Buses leave for **Ismailia** and **Suez** every ½ hr from 0600-2000 (both destinations E£9, 1½-2 hrs); for **Port Said** buses leave every hour from 0545-2130 (E£17, 3 hrs). The Canal Zone buses also pick up passengers from Al-Maza.

West & Middle Delta, T02-2575 2157/ 2415 6597, operates buses every hour to **Alexandria** 0430-0100 (E£30-35, 3 hrs); **Marsa Matruh** at 0615, 0630, 0730, 0830, 1100, 1515, 1945, 2130 (E£50-60, 6-7 hrs); **Salloum** at 2330 (E£65, 9-10 hrs); **Siwa** 1 bus daily at 1945 (E£65, 7-8 hrs). They also have buses to destinations in the Delta: **Tanta** and **Mahalla** every hour between 0700-2000 (E£8-10, 2-2½ hrs).

Upper Egypt Travel, T02-2576 0261, operates buses to the **Western Desert**: **Bahariyya** daily at 0800 (E£30, 5 hrs); **Farafra** (E£55, 8-9 hrs) and **Dakhla** at 0700, 1800 (E£75, 12 hrs), via **Bahariyya**; **Kharga** 2130, 2230 (E£65, 10-11 hrs). The **Red Sea Coast**: daily to **Hurghada** at 0800, 1200,1330, 1700, 1830, 2100, 2200, 2330, 0100 (E£70-75, 6 hrs). The 1700 continues to **Aswan** (E£100, 14 hrs) and the 2100 continues to **Luxor** (E£100, 11 hrs), both go via **Safaga** (E£80-85); the 1330, 1830 and 2330 continue to **El-Quseir** (E£81, 8 hrs) and **Marsa Alam** (E£91, 11 hrs) and to **Shalatein** (E£96). Buses to **Wadi Natrun** (E£7, 2 hrs) leave from bus station on Sharia Shubra, call first at **Sadat City** (E£6, 1½ hrs).

Tickets for international buses to **Saudi Arabia** (3 per week) can be bought from the same office, though the staff who deal with these are only present on Sat.

Superjet, T02-2579 8181, operates buses to prime tourist destinations and are a step above others in terms of quality and price. To **Hurghada** at 0730, 1430, 2315 (E£65, 6 hrs); **Sharm El-Sheikh** at 0730, 1515, 2345 (E£85, 6 hrs); **Luxor** at 2345 (E£100, 9-10 hrs); **Port Said** every hour from 0645-2000 (E£23, 3 hrs). Also runs international buses 4 times a week to **Libya**, **Jordan**, **Syria** and **Saudi Arabia**. Buses for international destinations leave from the Al-Maza terminal, T02-2290 9013, at the far end of Heliopolis except for the Libya bus, which starts at Turgoman. buses to **Alexandria** leave from Shari Al-Galaa near Midan Abdel Mounim Riy every hour from 0600-2300 (E£25, 3 hrs).

Aboud Station is on Sharia Ahmed Hel 3 km north of Ramses – a E£5 taxi ride from Ramses, E£10 from Downtown, or a quick microbus hop. From here, 3 companies operate daily buses at least once an hour from 0600 to 2000 to **El-Fayoum**, the **Delta**, **Middle and Upper Egypt**, and **Alexandria** (Specific cities: **Alexandria**, **Damanhur**, **Tanta**, **Benha**, **Mansura**, **Damietta**, **Zagazig**, **Fayoum**, **Minya**, **Assiut**, **Sohag**, **Luxor** and **Aswan**). Note that those going to Middle and Upper Egypt may want to opt for the comparably cheap and significantly more comfortable and convenient train.

Calèche
Horse-drawn carriages are generally found south of the Marriott hotel on Zamalek. Not a way to get around, but nice for an evening's exploration. Expect to pay about E£30 per hr.

Car hire
Al Arabia, 13-71 Sharia Ahmed Orabi, Mohandiseen, T02-3304 9776. Avis, 16A Sharia Ma'amal El-Soukkar, Garden City, T02-2794 7081. Hertz, www.hertzegypt.com, at the airport, T02-2265 2430.

Ferry
Small ferries cross between Imbaba on the west bank of the Nile and Zamalek, at the north end of the island. The fare is 50 pt and it's a pleasant 10-min trip. The boats don't operate on a Fri.

Metro
Marked with big red 'M' around the city. Signs are clearly marked in both English and Arabic. There are 2 functioning lines: **El-Marg–Helwan** and **Shobra–Giza**, with a 3rd still in construction that will link the airport to the west bank of the city. It's easy, efficient, relatively clean and cheap (E£1 to go anywhere). Every train has a women-only

of particular interest

wntown.

an Ramses; Ramses Train Station.

osest stop to Islamic Cairo, can walk to Al Azhar and Khan El-Khalili here.

Mar Girgis: in the heart of Old Cairo, definitely the best way to get here.

Maadi: lots of expats live in this accessible suburb, some good restaurants and access to services not as available in other parts of Cairo; good library and prettiest part of the Corniche with lots of Nile-side restaurants and coffee shops; also a good spot to commence a *felucca* ride (take a taxi from the metro stop – about E£4 to the Nile).

carriage, where children are of course also permitted. Make sure you hold on to your ticket, you'll need it to exit. During rush hours (0700-1000, 1500-1900) it can be uncomfortably crowded, hot and pushy. Still, the metro is more manageable and reliable than the buses and often quicker than a taxi.

Taxi

There is a profusion of the black and white taxis in Cairo. They're ramshackle, but easy to use and by Western standards, extraordinarily cheap. There are now newer white and black cabs (mainly white with small black checks on the side). These should all have a/c and functioning meters, which start with E£2.50 on the clock and go up in increments of 25pt. They are a real life-changer for tourists, taking much of the stress and arguments out of travelling by taxi. To hail a taxi, simply wait on the side of the street, extend your arm, and say 'tax!'. But you will find they pull up alongside you beeping and shouting 'tax' at you anyway, whenever you walk along the side of the road. Before entering, tell the driver your desired destination and establish that they know the way. The older black and white cabs never have a functioning meter, or if it does function the price is so antiquated it is completely irrelevant. If you want to avoid a haggling fuss, agree on a fare before entering the taxi. Otherwise, be prepared for a struggle. Most locals know the fair charge from one place to another. It's best to enquire at your hotel or with the tourist authority to get an idea of the standard rates. In general, travelling from one point of the centre to another shouldn't cost more than E£5. From one borough to another, E£10-15. To the **Giza Pyramids**, from Downtown expect to pay at least E£20 and to the airport, E£30-40. In general, taxis waiting outside hotels expect more money so it's best to walk 100 m and hail a taxi from the street.

There are a few yellow cabs and blue cabs circulating Cairo that have a/c and working meters. These can be booked by calling T16516 or T19155, and are good for travelling longer distances (say to the airport, which is around E£35 in a yellow cab) but they work out more expensive for short hops.

Note In Egypt, there is basic etiquette when riding in a taxi. Single women always sit in the back seat, at a diagonal to the driver. If a man is present, he generally sits in the front, next to the driver. Note that it is not uncommon for people going to different destinations to share taxis. If you do not want to share, simply notify your driver if he slows to pick someone up, bearing in mind he may expect more money.

As well as private and shared private taxis, there are service taxis (pronounced *servees*), which follow specific routes and carry up to 7 passengers. They function in the same way as microbuses and can be flagged down from anywhere en route. Fares range from E£1-2.

Trains

The main railway station in Cairo, **Ramses Station**, T02-2575 3555, in Midan Ramses, is a E£4-5 taxi ride from Tahrir and easily accessible via **Mubarak** metro station. Train timetables and fares can be checked online at www.egyptrail.gov.eg, although it's not yet possible to book online. Ramses Station is a bit confusing, with several different ticket counters selling tickets for different destinations. There is a tourist office at the back of the station (T02-2579 0767, open 0830-2000) who can advise on train schedules and ticket counters. There are plenty of tourist police hanging around who are willing to point you in the right direction. There are ATMs inside the station.

In short, if you're facing the main platforms, tickets to **Alexandria** are purchased in the back left corner; to **Middle** and **Upper Egypt**, from the counters by platform 11 outside to the left, via the underpass; to **Port Said/Ismailiya**, outside the main door behind you.

Trains go to **Alexandria** almost once an hr, first departure at 0600 and last departure at 2230 taking around 2½ hrs. So-called express trains, which have fewer stops, leave at 0800, 0900, 1200, 1400, 1800, 1900 and 2230, costing E£50 1st class, E£35 2nd class; slower trains at 0815, 1100, 1510, 1600, 1700 and 2000 cost E£35/E£19. There are 3 trains daily to **Port Said** (E£22, 2nd class a/c) at 0615, 1445 and 1915, via **Ismailia** (E£16, 2nd

Cairo Metro

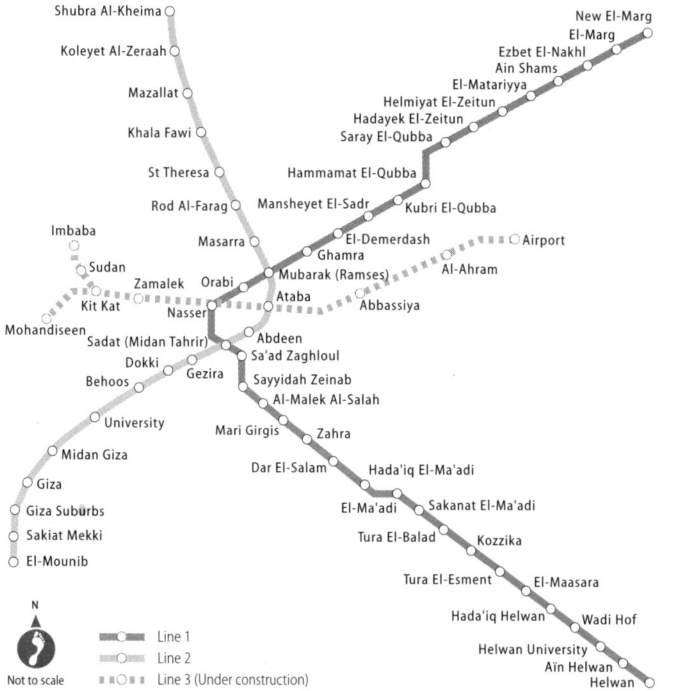

class a/c), plus 3 to Ismailia only at 1300, 1845 and 2100, but they are slow and the journey is far quicker by bus. For **Suez**, trains leave from Ain Shams Station rather than Ramses, but the journey is easier by bus or service taxi. Trains also cover **Delta** destinations (daily, at least once an hr),

Travel to **Upper Egypt** is restricted for foreigners to 1 train per day, leaving at 2200 from Ramsis (2210 from Giza). Foreigners will only be sold 1st-class tickets which cost E£167 for either **Luxor** and **Aswan**. Tickets can be booked up to 1 week in advance, and it's recommended to book at least 48 hrs in advance. It might be possible to board other trains for destinations in Middle and Upper Egypt, but this is best attempted from Giza rather than Ramsis station; it is better to pay on board than trying to buy a ticket in advance, when authorities will be alerted to your presence. **Sleeping Trains**, T02-2576 1913, also travel to **Luxor** and **Aswan** daily at 2000 and 2130, departing from Giza station. The central booking office is in Ramsis station, however, open 0900-2300, where they demand payment in US$, euro or pounds sterling only (credit cards and Egyptian pounds are not accepted). During peak season, it's wise to buy your ticket in advance, which can be done up to 2 weeks before travel. Price US$60 per person; US$45 for children aged 4-9 years – prices include dinner and breakfast. The sleepers are a clean, comfortable way to travel. Each train has a 'club' area (a very smoky but kitsch bar) and restaurant. They also run trains in the summer (Jul and Aug, but not during Ramadan), to **Marsa Matruh**.

Directory

Cairo *p63, maps p58, p64, p74, p75, p104, p114*

Banks

The vast majority of banks are in Downtown, or in more affluent districts such as Mohandiseen, Zamalek, Dokki or Heliopolis Most have ATMs that accept foreign cards, as do all high-end hotels. 5-star hotels are also a good place to change TCs or foreign currency, and you will see plenty of money-changing shops in any commercial area. **Barclays**, **Citibank**, and **HSBC** all have a presence in the city, with branches in Downtown, Mohandiseen, Garden Ctiy and Zamalek. **Western Union** (Money Transfers), 8 Sharia El-Slamlek, Garden City, T02-792 0741, T02-792 1691.

Cultural centres

American, US Embassy, 5 Sharia America Al-Latiniya, T02-2794 9601. Open Sun-Thu.
British, British Council, 192 Sharia El-Nil, Agouza, T19789, www.britishcouncil.org.eg. Open Mon-Sat. Has an excellent library that can be joined for a minimum of 6 months, E£120, plus 1 photo and ID.
Cervantes, 20 Sharia Adly, Kodak Passage, Downtown, T02-2399 04639.
CSA, 4 Road 21, Maadi, T02-2358 5284, www.livinginegypt.org. Open Sun-Wed 0900-2100, Thu 0900- 1700. Provides information and support for the expat community in Egypt. Gym, library, outings, courses and coffee shop.
Egyptian Centre for International Cultural Cooperation, 11 Sharia Shagaret El-Dor, Zamalek, T02-2736 5419.
French, 1 Sharia Madraset El-Hoquq El-Faransia, Mounira, T02-2794 4095, T02-2794 7679 and 5 Sharia Sharfiq El-Dib, Heliopolis, T02-2417 4824.
German, Goethe Institute, 5 Sharia Bustan, Downtown, T02-2575 9877.
Indian, 23 & 37 Sharia Talaat Harb, Downtown, T02-2393 9152. Has yoga classes, a library and screens Bollywood movies.
Italian, 3 Sharia Sheikh El-Marsafi, behind Marriott Hotel, Zamalek, T02-2735 8791. Open Sun-Thu.
Japanese, 3rd Floor, Cairo Centre Building, 106 Sharia Qasr El-Aini, Garden City, T02-2792 5011.
Swiss Club, Villa Pax, Sharia Gehad, off Sharia Sudan, Imbaba, T02-3314 2811.

Embassies and consulates

Most consulates take a 2-day weekend, between Thu and Sun. **Australia**, World Trade

Centre, Sharia Corniche El-Nil, Bulaq, T02-2575 0444; **Austria**, 5 Sharia Wisa Wasef, El-Riad Tower, Giza, T02-3570 2975; **Belgium**, 20 Sharia Kamel El-Shenawi, Garden City, T02-2794 7494; **Canada**, 26 Sharia Kamel El-Shenawi, Garden City, T02-2794 3110/9; **Denmark**, 12 Sharia Hassan Sabri, Zamalek, T02-2735 6490; **Eritrea**, 6 Sharia El-Fellah, Mohandiseen, T02-3303 3503; **Ethiopia**, 2 Midan Al-Misaha, Dokki, T02-3335 3696; **France**, 29 Sharia Morad, Giza, T02-3570 3919; **Germany**, 8B Sharia Hassan Sabri, Zamalek, T02-2735 0283; **India**, Consulate (visa services, applications from 0830-1130 and collections between 1230-1330), 37 Sharia Talaat Harb Downtown, T02-2392 5162; **Israel**, 6 Sharia Ibn Malek, near El-Gamaa Bridge, Giza, T02-3761 0548; **Jordan**, 6 Sharia El-Basem El-Kateb Off Sharia El-Tahrir, Dokki, T02-3749 9912; **Kenya**, 29 Sharia El-Qods El-Sharif, off Sharia Shehab, Mohandiseen, T02-3345 3628; **Kuwait**, 12 Sharia Nabil El-Waqqad, Dokki, T02-3760 2661; **Lebanon**, 22 Sharia El-Mansour Mohamed, Zamalek, T02-2738 2823; **Libya**, 7 Sharia El-Saleh Ayoub, Zamalek, T02-2735 1269; **Morocco**, 10 Sharia Salah El-Dein, Zamalek, T02-2735 9849; **Netherlands**, 18 Sharia Hassan Sabri, Zamalek, T02-2739 5500; **Saudia Arabia**, 5 Sharia El-Gehadya, Garden City, T02-2795 8111; **South Africa**, 55 Road 18, Maadi, T02-2359 4365; **Spain**, 41 Sharia Ismail Mohammed, Zamalek, T02-735 3652, 7355813; **Sudan**, 3 Sharia El-Ibrahimi, Garden City, T02-2794 9661 (you may need a letter of recommendation from your own embassy); 1-month single-entry tourist visas cost US$100 and can be paid in E£, processing takes at least 1 day, longer for US citizens; **Switzerland**, 10 Sharia Abdel Khalek Sarwat, Downtown, T02-2575 8284; **Syria**, 18 Sharia Abdel Rehim Sabri, Dokki, T02-3749 5210; **Tunisia**, 26 Sharia El-Gezira, Zamalek, T02- 2736 8962; **UK**, 7 Sharia Ahmed Raghab, Garden City, T02-2794 0852; **USA**, 5 Sharia America Al-Latiniya, Garden City, T02-2797 2301.

Emergencies

Ambulance: T123. **Fire**: T125. **Police**: T122. **Major police offices**: at Railway Station, Cairo Airport, Midan Tahrir, Sharia 26 July/Mansour Mohammed, Pyramids. **Tourist Police**: T126. **Tourist Police Head Office**: T02-390 6027.

Immigration

Visa extensions can be obtained at the grey monstrosity of the Mugamma building on Midan Tahrir, Downtown, Sat-Thu 0800-1700. This generally involves taking your documents in 1st thing in the morning and collecting in the afternoon around 1300 (or the next day before 1200). You need a photocopy of the last page of your passport, a copy of the last stamp of entry, 1 passport photo (photocopying and photo booths available in the foyer of the Mugamma). For a 6-month tourist visa it currently costs E£11, to add multiple entry is E£60. If you overstay your visa, there is a 15-day grace period during which you can pay a fine at the Mugamma of E£153 or the same amount is payable at the airport on leaving the country. To extend your visa go up to the 1st floor, walk down the long corridor after the X-ray machine, head for window 12 to collect a form. Go to window 44 to pay and take the stamps you will be given back to number 12. You leave everything there and collect it when they tell you from window 38.

Internet

The vast majority of hotels have internet services, and in budget hotels they are as cheap as going to an internet café. **4U Internet Café**, 6 Midan Talaat Harb, Downtown, open 0830-1300, E£5 per hr; **Café Internet**, 8 El-Mamar El-Togary, Sour Nady El-Zamalek, Mohandiseen, open 1000-2400, E£6 per hr; **Hany Internet Café**, 16 Sharia Abdel Khaleq Tharwat, Downtown, E£2 per hr; **Int@net**, 36 Sharia Sherif, Downtown, T02-2393 9740; **Sigma Net**, above Metro supermarket, Sharia Ismail Mohamed, Zamalek, E£8 per hr, open 24 hrs and they are quite clued up; **Starnet Cyber Café**, 18 Sharia Youssef El-Guindy, El-Bostan Centre, Downtown, open 1000-2400,

E£6 per hr; **Sun Cafe**, off Souk Tawfiqaya, Downtown, open 24 hrs.

Language schools

Arabic classes available at: **International Language Institute**, 4 Sharia Mahmoud Azmy, off Ahmed Orabi, Mohandiseen, T02-3346 3087, www.arabicegypt.com; **Kalimat Language & Cultural Centre**, 22 Sharia Mohamed Mahmoud Shaaban, Mohandiseen, T02-3761 8136, www.kalimategypt.com, very well regarded, set up a few years ago by former teachers at the British Council; **Egyptian Centre for International Cultural Cooperation**, 11 Sharia Shagarat El-Dor, Zamalek, T02-2736 5419, cheapest (48 hrs for E£950) but not the best.

Medical services

Hospitals and clinics **Anglo-American Hospital**, by Cairo Tower, Gezira, T02-2735 6162. **As-Salam International Hospital**, Corniche El-Maadi, T02-2524 0250; **Cairo Medical Centre**, 4 Sharia Abou Obeida El-Bahr, Midan Roxy, Heliopolis, T02-2258 1003/0566; **Dar al-Fouad Hospital**, Sixth of October City, has excellent facilities though it is a E£50/45-mins ride in a taxi from central Cairo, T02-3835 6030/40; **El-Salam Hospital**, 3 Sharia Syria, Mohandiseen, T02-3302 9091-5, also the place to go if you need an X-ray; **Dr Neveen El-Hafnawy Clinic**, 10 Sharia Souria, Mohandiseen, T02-3761 6905, for gynaecological issues; **Shaalan Surgicenter**, 10 Sharia Abd El-Hamid Lotfi, Mohandiseen, T02-37485479, Sat-Thu 0900-2200.

Pharmacies **El-Esaaf Pharmacy**, next to Nasser metro, Sharia Ramses, T02-2574 3369, open 24 hrs, no delivery; **Seif**, 76 Sharia Qasr Al-Ainy, Downtown, T02-2794 2678, open 24 hrs, delivery; **New Universal Pharmacy**, 12 Sharia Brazil, Zamalek, T02-2735 4896, 0900-2400, delivery; **Zamalek Tower Pharmacy**, 134 Sharia 26 July, Zamalek, T02-2736 1338, 1030-1530, 1800-2300, delivery.

Post office

Cairo's main post office is in **Midan Ataba**, open Sat-Thu 0800-2100 (Ramadan 0900-1600). The post office at **Midan Ataba** also has a *poste restante* office that will hold mail for a month, free. Enter via Sharia El-Badek and look for the 'private boxes' counter. There are other branches, but they tend to be more crowded. Major hotels often provide the same services. If you have an American Express card, you can send mail via AmEx on Shari Qasr El-Nil. Stamps are available at post offices and from hotel shops and cigarette kiosks. Postcards cost E£1.50 to send anywhere in the world and letters E£3.

Packages are best sent off from the **Midan Ramses** post office (counter open Sat-Thu 0800-1500). Bring your parcel unsealed so it can be searched. Packaging is possible in the post office for a few extra E£.

Couriers: Aramex, T02-3338 8466; **DHL**, 38 Sharia Abdel Khaliq Sarwat, Downtown, T02-2302 9801 plus offices in Garden City; **Federal Express**, 16 Sharia Khaled Ibn El-Walid, Masaken Sheraton, Helipolis, T02-2268 7888/999, and 3 Sharia Salah Jahin, Mohandiseen, T02-3302 7656.

Telephone

Mobile sim cards are cheap and easy to buy in Cairo, available from Vodaphone, Etisalat and other companies who have stores all over the city. Re-charge cards can be bought at any kiosk or you can top-up your credit in the official stores. Besides the international telephone and fax services at all major hotels, there are several public telecom centres where it's possible to make international phone calls for cheaper, but the wait can be long. Main offices are at **Sharia Adly**, near the tourist office, **Sharia Ramses**, near Sharia Tawfiqia, and **13 Midan Tahrir**. To avoid the hassle of the telecomm-unication centres, you can buy a phone card from many kiosks and supermarkets. Most pervasive around Egypt are the yellow and green **Menatel** booths. Cards range in price from E£5-20. A E£10 card will cover about 20 mins of local calls. International calls can cost up to E£10 per min.

Around Cairo & the Nile Delta

Contents

Footprint features

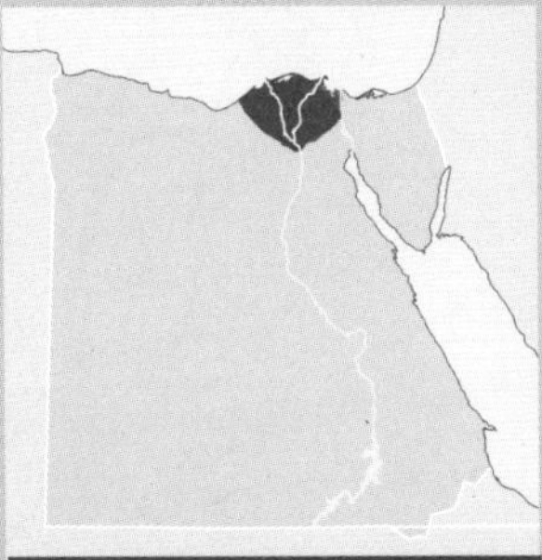

At a glance

Getting around Microbuses are frequent and convenient.

Time required 2-3 days will give you a taster. El-Fayoum alone can be thoroughly explored in a couple of days.

Weather Much like Cairo, but slightly cooler in the Delta and slightly hotter in El-Fayoum.

When not to go El-Fayoum can be affected by sandstorms in Apr.

★ Don't miss ...

1 Saqqara and Dahshur, pages 158 and 165.
2 El-Fayoum and Lake Qaroun, page 166 and 170.
3 Tanta's eight-day moulid, page 178.
4 Rosetta, page 180.

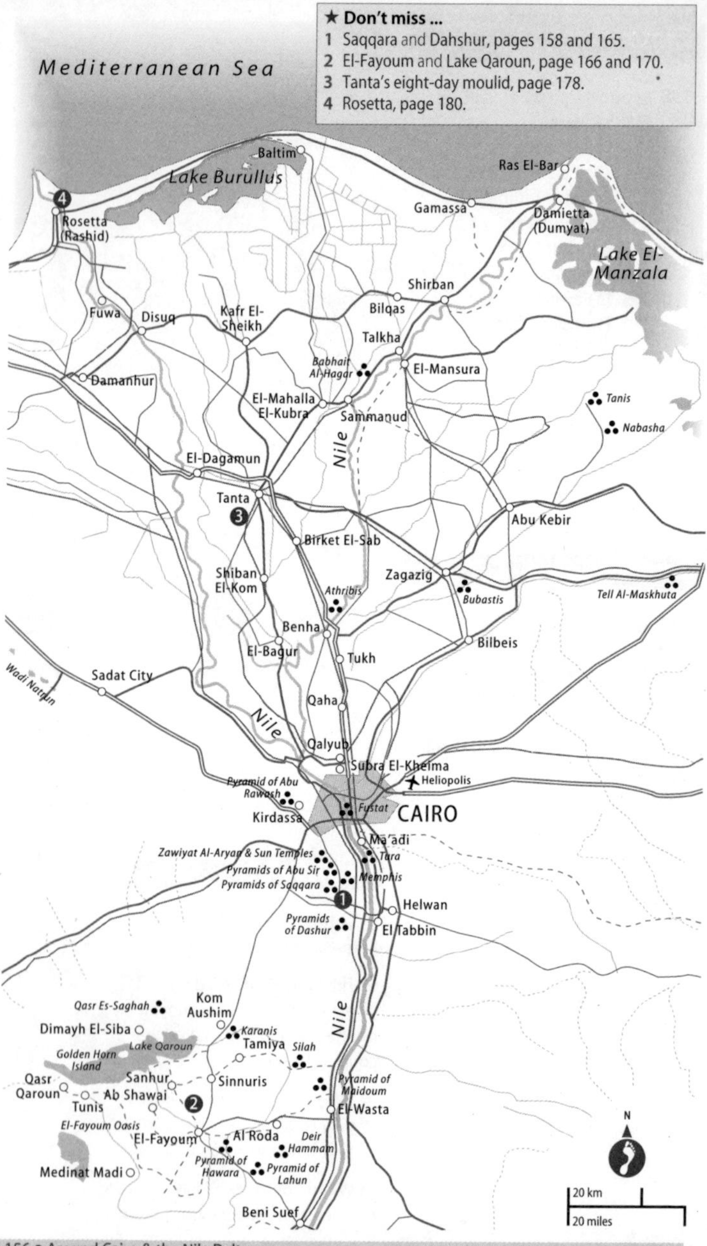

The region surrounding Cairo is full of both ancient sites and communities typical of contemporary rural life. Pyramids in romantically ruinous states are scattered around the south, the north is dotted with the desolate remains of pharaonic cities, while in between spread the fertile flatlands of the Delta, Egypt's most heavily populated region. The famous Step Pyramid of Saqqara in the vast necropolis of the early pharaohs is worth visiting before going on to Giza, to see the development from the simple underground tomb to the audacious concept of the Pyramid of Cheops. Further south, the harsh desert gives way to the beautiful pseudo-oasis of El-Fayoum, a lush expanse of fields and palms offering sanctuary to some of the richest birdlife in Egypt as well as respite from the pollution and heat of Cairo. Ptolemaic temples, the artists' enclave of Tunis, and the ultramarine waters of Lake Qaroun all nestle on the edge of the arid western desert only an hour and a half away from the city.

Beyond Cairo, the two main tributaries of the Nile continue northwards to meet the Mediterranean near Damietta and Rosetta, where Ottoman houses, winding medieval lanes full of *calèches*, and the picturesque expanses of the Nile are a pleasant surprise. On either side, and between the two branches, the green and fertile plains fan out to create – with the help of some of the world's oldest and most efficient irrigation systems – the agricultural heartland of Egypt. Because of the lack of hard stone in the Delta, successive generations plundered the remains of pharaonic cities' ancient sites, leaving atmospheric and isolated remnants for the adventurous few to rediscover. Beyond agriculture, the Delta is known for its many *moulids* – popular religious festivals and the best night out you can have in Egypt.

Around Cairo

There are several interesting day- or half-day trips that can be made from Cairo. South of the city lie a series of pyramids which, due to their desert location, many visitors find more rewarding and evocative than a visit to the great pyramids at Giza. Peace and tranquility can be found around Lake Qaroun in El-Fayoum oasis, where village life is easily accessible. To the north of Cairo, the living monasteries at Wadi Natrun allow insight into the Coptic tradition and have beautiful paintings on the interior walls. ▸▸ *For listings, see pages 175-177.*

Saqqara → *Colour map 2, B2.*

ⓘ *Open daily 0800-1600, E£60, students E£30, camera/video free, parking E£2.*

Saqqara, which faces Memphis (the oldest known imperial city on earth) across the Nile, was the enormous necropolis for the first pharaohs. With many tombs believed to be still undiscovered it is Egypt's largest archaeological site, spanning more than 7 sq km. From its inception it expanded west into the desert until the Fourth Dynasty (2613-2494 BC) when the Giza plateau superseded it. At the end of the Fifth Dynasty (2494-2345 BC) a more systematic construction of pyramids and *mastabas* began, which resulted in many splendid monuments around Saqqara and some of the most gorgeously decorated private tombs in Egypt. The approach through a forest of date palms and the sweep of the desert beyond are as breathtaking as the multitude of hidden *mastabas*, ruinous courts and causeways, and the sand-strewn rungs of the step pyramid itself.

Ins and outs

Getting there Given the relative proximity to Cairo, and the distance between tombs in Saqqara, it is worth hiring a taxi for the day (E£130-180 for Giza and Saqqara; E£180-200 if you include Dahshur). Most travel agencies book tours to the area for about E£100 or more per person and budget hotels often transport groups for less. Tours generally do not include ticket prices. Public transport can be a bit fiddly, though very cheap – and you are left with the problem of how to get between the various sites within the area of Saqqara itself. If you choose to brave public transport, take any microbus going to Giza from Sharia Gala'a (Downtown), change at Midan Giza to a microbus headed for the Pyramids (in Arabic, 'Haram') and ask to get down at the Marioteya canal. Cross the Pyramids Road and walk down the side street to the south. From there you can get a micro to Saqqara. Get off on the main road by the sign for Saqqara antiquities and walk the remaining 1.5 km to the site. (Getting back is less complicated. Once you get to the Pyramids Road you can very likely catch something all the way to Midan Tahrir without changing in Giza). Giza to Saqqara by camel or horse can be a rewarding journey. A round trip with waiting time costs around E£300-400 per person, but one way is usually more than enough as it takes two to four hours (horses are faster) plus a good couple of hours at Saqqara. Bring water and food for the day, as the restaurants surrounding the area tend to be overpriced and bare in their offerings and if you are walking between tombs you won't get much time for a proper meal break. Soft-drink sellers operate around the main attractions.

The journey to Saqqara, though short in terms of actual distance, can be like stepping back in time. On the far side of the Marioteya Canal rural life goes on as it has for centuries. Early in the morning, the fields and palm groves are partially obscured by a romantic mist and in the afternoon you will see donkeys and water buffalo being led home, indifferent to the passing cars and microbuses after a hard day's work. If you have no plans to visit anywhere else outside Cairo, then the road to Saqqara can show you a different side to life in the city.

Note Saqqara can be easily visited as a day trip from Cairo. See page 125 for Cairo accommodation. Public transportation can sometimes be difficult to come by late at night, so plan your trip accordingly.

Imhotep Museum

A ticket includes entrance to the excellent new Imhotep Museum (past the ticket booths), which should not be missed. Building blocks and artefacts are put into context using scale diagrams, the main hall being dominated by an impression of how Zoser's tomb would have looked in its heyday. Stunning green-blue faience tiles, textured to resemble reeds, line the walls. Vessels, statues (some so detailed that the pleats in the fabric can be seen) and friezes have been intelligently selected. On display is the mummy of King Merenre I; the oldest, most complete royal mummy known. Simply wrapped, the king's bare toes protrude from the linen strips. A decorated block from the causeway of Unas shows emaciated figures, with their ribs clearly outlined, during a time of famine. There is a fascinating room detailing the life and work of Jean-Philippe Lauer, who spent 75 years working and restoring the site. This room also houses his library of marvellous volumes on early exploration of Egypt's antiquities. Sadly, these are too precious to be handled.

Zoser's Funerary Complex

This complex, the largest in Saqqara, is an example of some of the world's most ancient architecture. The whole complex, including but not confined to the **Step Pyramid**, was designed and built for Zoser (2667-48 BC), the second king in the Third Dynasty, under the control of his chief architect Imhotep who many regard as the world's first architect. At its heart is the **Step Pyramid**, the first of its kind, which can be seen as a prototype for the Giza Pyramids. This marked the evolution of burial tombs from *mastabas* with deep shafts for the sarcophagus to imposing elevated mausoleums. Although the external fine white limestone casing, brought from quarries across the Nile at Memphis, has disappeared over time the step structure is still clearly visible. The pyramid eventually reached a height of 62.5 m on a base 109 m by 121 m, which, although small by comparison with those at Giza, is still an amazing feat. The advances represented by Zoser's Pyramid were not in the building techniques or materials, which were already established, but the concept, design and calculations involved that made such a monument possible.

The shaft, leading 28 m vertically down to the Royal Tomb, was sealed with a three-tonne granite block but this still did not prevent the tomb from being looted. Another 11 shafts were found, 32 m deep, under the east side of the Pyramid, which led to the tombs of the queens and royal children. Unfortunately these are no longer open to the public and the area is currently under restoration.

The whole funerary complex was completely surrounded by buttressed walls over 544 m long, to deter intruders and thieves and to provide space for the Pharaoh's *ka* (spirit) to live in the afterlife. Although 14 fake doors were built, only the one in the southeast corner, which leads into the colonnaded **Hypostyle Hall** actually gives access to the site. Before entering the colonnade, observe the fake door complete with hinges and sockets in the vestibule on the right. The Colonnade leads through to the **Great Court**, on the south side of which there is a frieze of cobras similar to the one found in the museum. This represents the fire-spitting goddess of destruction Edjo who was adopted as the Uraeus, the emblem of royalty and of protection, and worn on the pharaonic headdress (see box on cobras, page 329).

Further along this south wall is a deep shaft at the bottom of which lies **Zoser's Southern Tomb**, which some believe held the king's entrails. More importantly there is a relief, depicting the king running the Heb-Sed race, which illustrates the purpose of the surrounding buildings and monuments. Some of them are mere façades like a Hollywood film-set, simply representing a pastiche of this crucial ceremony for the afterlife. Their intended purpose was to eternalize the symbol of the unification of a greater Egypt and the power of the pharaoh even in death.

This symbolism is echoed in the lotus and papyrus capitals on top of the columns fronting the **House of the South** and the **House of the North**, which represent the heraldic emblems of Upper and Lower Egypt, respectively. The House of the South is interesting because its columns, precursors of the Greek Doric style, and its New Kingdom graffiti offer a fascinating reminder of the continuity of human civilization.

On the north side of the Step Pyramid there is a stone casket, known as the **Serdab** (cellar), containing a copy of a life-size statue of Zoser. The original is in the Egyptian Museum in Cairo. The Serdab has two cylindrical holes to enable the statue to communicate with the outside world and to preserve the Pharaoh's *ka*. To the west of the Serdab the **Funerary Temple** is in ruins but some of the walls and the entrance can still be seen. A tunnel originally linked it with the royal tomb. At the time of writing this was closed for restoration.

South of Zoser's Funerary Complex

The Pyramid of Unas, which was built for the last pharaoh of the Fifth Dynasty (2494-2345 BC), appears from the outside to be a heap of limestone rubble but the inside of the burial chamber has a star-covered ceiling and the passage has beautiful green hieroglyphs of magic formulae for the pharaoh to ease his passage into the afterlife. These are the first decorations ever made inside a tomb and formed the basis for the *Book of the Dead* (see Valley of the Kings, page 257). The pyramid was opened as a tourist attraction in 1881 by the director of antiquities Gaston Maspero with financial sponsorship from Thomas Cook & Son, but is now permanently closed to prevent greater deterioration. To the east, a few remnants of the **Funerary Temple** can be seen, some granite columns with palm capitals and pieces of granite floor. Beyond this the remains of a causeway linking the Funerary Temple to the Valley Temple 700 m away has been uncovered, which conjures up a real feeling of walking back in time.

North and south of the causeway are a sprinkling of tombs worth looking into, as well as two 45-m-long troughs of Unas' boat pits. The fascinating and well preserved **Mastaba of Queen Nebet**, Unas' wife, contains some rare scenes of Nebet in the women's quarters, or harem, in the palace. The **Mastaba of Princess Idout** has 10 rooms, of which five are decorated to give a glimpse of life in Idout's day with many rural and domestic scenes. The **Mastaba of Merou** contains some exceptionally well-preserved tableaux; in the Grand Offerings Room the paint scarcely seems to have faded at all. The **Saqqara New Tombs** ⓘ *requires a separate ticket, E£30, students E£15, either purchased from the main ticket office or from the shed near the car park by the Step Pyramid,* are equally vivid and include the adjoining tombs of **Niankhkhnum and Khnumhotep** and the **Mastaba of Irukaptah**, with deeply colourful depictions of the royal manicurists at work, scenes of fishing, and activities at the dairy – look out for the cow giving birth.

The remains of the **Pyramid of Sekhemkhet**, which was at the centre of an unfinished and unused funerary complex very similar to that of his predecessor Zoser, were only discovered in 1950 and there is no public access. To the east of the Pyramid of Sekhemkhet can be seen the remains of the **Monastery of St Jeremiah**, which was founded in the fifth century but destroyed by the Arabs five centuries later. Following its discovery in 1907 many of the paintings and extraordinary carvings were removed and are now on display in the Coptic Museum in Cairo.

North of the Funerary Complex

The **Pyramid of Teti**, the founder of the 6th Dynasty (2345-2181 BC), was discovered by Mariette in 1853 but is now little more than a pile of rubble in constant danger of being submerged by sand. It is possible to enter up the steep pathway leading to the funerary chamber, where the ceiling is decorated with stars.

To the north are a number of well-preserved *mastabas*. The most outstanding of which is **Mereruka**, who was Teti's vizier, chief judge and inspector – an important person in Sixth Dynasty society. This is one of the largest Old Kingdom *mastabas* to have been found and its 32 rooms are divided into three parts for Mereruka (21 rooms), his wife (six rooms) and his son (five rooms). In the main entrance passage Mereruka is depicted at an easel, painting the three seasons. The following room contains interesting hunting scenes, revealing the types of animal they stalked and the techniques that they used. Scenes of everyday life are beautifully depicted throughout the tomb, giving a valuable

North Saqqara

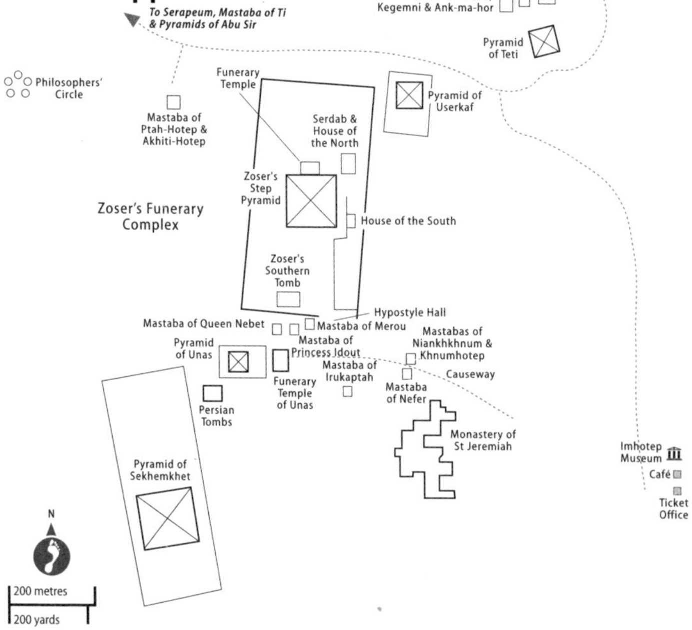

The sacred scarab

Scarabaeus sacer, a dung beetle, is the celebrated beetle held sacred by the ancient Egyptians. They were fascinated by the beetles' strange habit of fashioning perfectly round balls from animal droppings. (These balls, larger than the insect itself, are moved backwards using the rear legs, the head being thrust against the ground to give purchase. The balls are then buried with newly laid eggs and provide food for the developing larvae.)

The scarab was used as a symbol of the sun god as Egyptians thought the sun was pushed around the heavens just as the beetle pushed the ball of dung.

The dung beetle is called *Kheper* in the Egyptian language and is associated with the verb *kheper*, which means to come into being. Models of the beetle made in clay were supposed to have healing powers while live beetles, secured by a small chain through the wing-case, were actually worn as decoration.

The scarab seal was used to stamp letters into the clay seal on letters, bottles, wine jars, and so on, with the owner's mark.

insight into contemporary life. The largest room, with six pillars, has a statue of Mereruka to the north and some unusual mourning scenes, while on the left are scenes of him being carried by his son and surrounded by dwarfs and dogs.

To the east, the **Mastaba of Kagemni**, also a vizier and judge of the Sixth Dynasty, has some excellent reliefs and paintings of a much a higher standard, but unfortunately less well preserved. Further east is the **Mastaba of Ankh-ma-hor**, also known as the Doctor's Tomb because of paintings depicting circumcision and an operation on a broken toe. Other rooms show the usual scenes of the preparation and transportation of the offerings and various representations of hunting and daily life. Look on the south wall for the mourners fainting at the burial ceremony.

One of the finest of all the *mastabas* is the double **Mastaba of Ptah-Hotep and Akhiti-Hotep**, which contains some of the finest Old Kingdom art and some fascinating unfinished work clarifying the techniques used in painting reliefs. Ptah-Hotep was a priest of Maat in the reign of Djedkare, Unas' predecessor, while his son Akhiti-Hotep was vizier, judge, and the overseer of the treasury and the granaries.

The red paint of the unfinished agricultural scenes in the entrance corridor reveals how preliminary drawings were made before the wall was carved and painted. The outstanding masterpiece, however, is in the **Sanctuary** dedicated to Ptah-Hotep. On the walls behind the entrance Ptah-Hotep is seated watching a concert while his servants wash and manicure him. Other walls bear scenes of Ptah-Hotep receiving offerings. On the left wall, which is the most interesting and impressive, the figure in the first boat is being given water by a boy. The inscription describes him as the Chief Artist, who is thought to have been Ankhen-Ptah, and this scene may well represent the first known example of an artist's signature.

The Serapeum The bizarre Serapeum was a burial place for the sacred Apis Bulls, believed to be manifestations of Ptah's blessed soul and were identified with Osiris after his death. They were given full honours in a ceremony worthy of any pharaoh, embalmed, and then the mummified body placed in a sarcophagus and sealed off from the main gallery by means of a richly decorated wall. The high priests would then start searching for the new

Apis Bull within the sacred herd. It had to be the only calf of its mother, black in colour except for a white diamond-shaped marking on the forehead, and have a scarab symbol on its tongue. The cult of the Apis Bulls was significant enough to last well into the Ptolemaic period, and the gloomy passageways of the Serapeum are in fact two and a half millennia younger than the Step Pyramid of Zoser – an interval as long as that which separates the Serapeum burials from our own time.

The long, sloping path down to the Serapeum leads to the three galleries, where 24 surviving sarcophagi are set in small galleries on either side of the main one. Each sarcophagus, from the quarries of Aswan, was made from a single piece of rock and weighed around 65 tonnes. Only three of the enormous basalt or granite sarcophagi bear inscriptions, and these are marked with the cartouches of different pharaohs, Amasis, Cambyses and Khababash. The Serapeum was discovered in 1851 but, with the exception of one tomb, most had already been looted. The artefacts discovered are now displayed in the Musée du Louvre, Paris. At the time of writing the Serapeum was closed for restoration.

The Mastaba of Ti One of the wonders of the Old Kingdom, the beautiful reliefs in Ti's *mastaba* provide fascinating insights into life at the time. Ti was a Fifth Dynasty royal hairdresser who married well and became steward of the sun temples of Neferikare and Nouserre and whose children later bore the title of 'royal descendant'. The reliefs in the courtyard have been damaged but their representations of daily life – breeding birds (north wall left), Ti on his litter with dogs and dwarfs (east wall, centre), and Ti with his wife (west wall centre) – are still worth seeing. In the centre of the courtyard an undecorated shaft leads to the tomb. On the left of the corridor joining the tomb to the main shrine, just after the door, servants are depicted bringing offerings while on the right are musicians and dancers. The main hall of offerings and shrine have an abundance of scenes depicting daily life, from the brewing of beer and the baking of bread to illustrations of boat construction (note the extreme simplicity of the tools used). You can't miss Ti's immense sarcophagus filling the recess in which it stands.

The south wall holds the **Serdab**, where a copy of Ti's statue, the original being in the Cairo Museum, can be peeped at through the slit. Around the two slits there are scenes of daily market life, carpenters, tanners, and various other artisans. Around the second slit, Ti is entertained by musicians while servants burn incense. These paintings should be taken on one level as literal depictions of Egyptian life but it is also important to realize the importance of symbolism and allegory. The north walls show Ti in a boat observing a hippopotamus hunt in the Delta region, but as the hippopotamus was symbolic of evil there is probably more to the picture than meets the eye.

Nearby is the Ptolemaic **Philosophers' Circle**, a collection of seven badly degraded statues arranged in a semi-circle and protected by a concrete enclosure.

South Saqqara

This completely separate necropolis, founded by the pharaohs of the Sixth Dynasty (2345-2181 BC), is about 1 km south of the Pyramid of Sekhemkhet in North Saqqara. Currently this whole area is off limits to casual tourists and can only be visited by written permission from the Supreme Council of Antiquities in Cairo. Should that situation change, or if you choose to scope out the area without official permission, there are stupendous pyramid views of Saqqara to the north and Dahshur to the south. Downsides are a lot of wading through sand, and the relative lack of impressive remains. It has a few interesting tombs, based on the Pyramid of Unas as an architectural model, but sadly has been plundered by unscrupulous stone masons or their suppliers. The pyramids of **Pepi I** and **Merenre** are in ruins.

To the east of the latter lies the **Pyramid of Djedkare**, known in Arabic as the Pyramid of the Sentinel, which is 25 m tall and is open to visitors. The entrance is on the north side through a tunnel leading into the funerary chamber but there is comparatively little to see.

The most important and interesting tombs are further south. The **Pyramid of Pepi II** is surrounded by an entire funerary complex. The inside chamber is decorated with stars and funerary inscriptions. Within the complex are a number of other smaller pyramids belonging to his queens. They are all based on the same design as Pepi's pyramid and contain a miniature funerary complex. The **Pyramid of Queen Neith** has some wonderful inscriptions and decorations.

To the east is the **Mastaba Faraoun**, the tomb of **Shepseskaf**, the last pharaoh of the Fourth Dynasty (2613-2494 BC). The inside is interesting but undecorated and the walls are made from large blocks of granite. From the outside the tomb looks like a gigantic sarcophagus and the exterior was originally covered in a thin layer of limestone. About 1 km further south are two more pyramids. The first is the brick **Pyramid of Khendjer**, which has a funerary chamber made out of quartzite. The second is larger, but unfinished, and bears no inscriptions or signs of use. It has impressive underground white stone chambers and a quartzite funerary chamber.

The Pyramids of Abu Sir and Sun-Temples of Abu Ghura

Pyramids of Abu Sir

ⓘ *Due to reopen to tourists in 2011 after several years of closure. Daily 0800-1600 winter, and until 1800 summer. A pain to access by public transport, you can pass by on your way to Saqqara either by taxi or camel from Giza.*

The site originally contained 14 Fifth Dynasty pyramids but only four are still standing, and are worth visiting for their isolated beauty more than any impressive scale or their state of preservation. The **Pyramid of Neferefre** was never finished and is now in very poor condition. The next (also unfinished) pyramid to the north was built for **Neferikare** and towering over the others is, at 68 m, the tallest of the group. To the northeast, the **Pyramid of Nouserre** is worth noting for its **Funerary Temple** which, although originally built for the Neferikare, was used by Nouserre because of Neferikare's premature death. About 100 m to the northeast lies the tomb of **Ptah-Cepses**. The *mastaba* is not in good condition but from outside the columns with lotus capitals (which are the oldest so far discovered) can still be seen. Inside is a huge granite sarcophagus and the remains of a few decorated columns.

Sahure's Pyramid, is directly north and its **Funerary Temple** is not too severely damaged. Excavation work around it has led to the discovery of the remains of a 240-m ramp that connected it to the **Valley Temple**. Sahure was brother to Userkaf whose pyramid is at Saqqara. The ceilings are decorated with yellow stars on a blue background and the reliefs carved on the limestone walls showed the king's defeat of his neighbours in the desert and those from Asia. Some have been removed and placed in museums, but a few remain and are quite well preserved.

Sun-Temples of Abu Ghurab

A short distance northwest of Abu Sir's pyramids, the sun-temples were built in the Fifth Dynasty when the solar cult had been declared the state religion. Unlike earlier temples their purpose was solely devotional and the pharaohs who built them were not buried here. Originally twin temples, only the **Sun-Temple of Nouserre** remains with the **Sun-Temple of Userkaf** being little more than rubble. Fortunately because they were identical little is lost.

At the western end of an enclosed courtyard a massive 70-m obelisk once stood. The obelisk was the symbol of the primordial mound, the sun's resting place at the end of the day. An alabaster altar stands in the centre of the courtyard, and animals were sacrificed at the northeast corner from where channels cut in the paving carried the blood to 10 alabaster basins, nine of which survive.

Dahshur → *Colour map 2, B2.*

ⓘ *Daily 0800-1600 winter, until 1700 summer, E£30, E£15 for students. Microbuses run from the Marioteya Canal off Pyramids road, direct to Dahshur village 7 km south of Saqqara (or you can change microbuses at the turn off for Saqqara). From the village you can find transport to take you the final 2 km to the site. However, as it's a further 1 km between the sites and public transport gets trickier late in the day, it is easier to hire a taxi there and back from Cairo (E£120).*

If you were surprised by the proximity of Cairo to the Giza Pyramids, or annoyed by the crowds of tourists and hawkers, come to Dahshur. Here, surrounded by nothing but the grey and gold desert, are two sublimely shaped looming monoliths and no one in sight but a few bored policemen. This is how pyramids appear in one's imagination. In the middle of the desert, miles away from civilization, free from tour buses and weighty with a sense of history. A sunset overlooking the pyramids, where there's a small shimmering lake that appears in winter and disappears in summer, is enhanced by the striking separation of the desert landscape and the linear agricultural fields around. Snefru (2575-2551 BC), first ruler of the Fourth Dynasty at the time of great pyramid construction, built the two pyramids in Dahshur and was perhaps responsible for the pyramid at Maidoum. His constructive tendencies were continued by his son Cheops. The monoliths of the Red Pyramid and the Bent Pyramid loom mightily at Dahshur,

After the ticket office, you arrive first at the **Red Pyramid** to the north, named after the reddish local limestone used in the core. It is thought to be the first true pyramid to be constructed with sloping sides rather than steps, and is second in size only to the Great Pyramid of Cheops at Giza. Some of the original Tura limestone facing stones remain on the eastern side and limestone fragments of the monolithic pyramidion still exist. A 28-m climb leads to the entrance, from where you plunge down a shaft to two corbelled antechambers, their sides as smooth as if they were built yesterday. A wooden staircase takes you up to the burial chamber, which was unused by Snefru or anyone else. Claustrophobics who balked at the thought of entering the Great Pyramid should give it a go, as there are no other bodies pushing and shoving to induce anxiety on the descent.

Scheduled to open the public in 2011, the **Bent Pyramid** (also known as the Southern Shining Pyramid) was constructed of local limestone with a casing of polished Tura limestone; the casing blocks slope inwards making them more stable and also more difficult to remove. At the base the pyramid measures 188.6 m and the height is 97 m (originally 105 m). If construction had continued at the original angle it would have been 128.5 m high.

The pyramid is unique on two counts. First, the obvious change in angles giving the pyramid its unusual shape, for which there are a number of theories put forward. Some think that the builders got tired and changed the angle to reduce the volume and so complete it sooner, others suggest that the change in slope indicated a double pyramid – two pyramids superimposed. It is further hypothesised that the architect lost his nerve, as this pyramid was being built when the pyramid at Maidoum collapsed. That too had an angle of 52° so a quick rethink was necessary. The pyramid is also unique in having two entrances. The first entrance in the middle of the north face is about 12 m above the ground and leads to the upper chamber. The second in the west face is only just above ground and leads to the lower chamber. Both chambers are corbelled and the floors of both were built to a depth of 4 m with small stone blocks.

There are three other pyramids here (from north to south) belonging to the 12th Dynasty Kings, Amenemhat II, Senusert III and Amenemhat III, of which only the latter is more than a pile of rubble.

Memphis → *Colour map 2, B2.*

ⓘ *Daily 0800-1600, E£35, students E£20, camera/video free. Reaching Memphis by public transport can be a confusing and time-consuming affair, as is moving on from here to sites nearby. Much better to make a whistle-stop here as part of a taxi-tour to the other sites.*

Just 15 km south of Cairo, Memphis was founded in the First Dynasty (3100-2890 BC) by Menes. The pharaohs' capital city throughout the Old Kingdom (2686-2181 BC), it was inhabited for four millennia. Eventually the old city was abandoned by the Moors and has now returned to the Nile silt from which it was originally constructed. Very little remains today, just some odd bits of statuary and stelae dotted about a garden. Most notable are a giant alabaster sphinx weighing 80 tonnes and a prostrate limestone **Colossus of Ramses II**, both of which may have stood outside the huge Temple of Ptah. He is a much photographed and beautifully preserved Ramses; Murray's guidebook from 1900 recommends visitors stand on his chest to appreciate his expression fully, though today there's a raised walkway around him to facilitate viewing. Also in evidence are the remains of the Embalming House, where there are several alabaster tables, weighing up to 50 tonnes, used to embalm the sacred Apis Bulls before burial at Saqqara (see page 596). Beyond these, Memphis's former glories can now only be imagined.

El-Fayoum → *For listings, see pages 175-177. Colour map 2, C2.*

Although usually described as an oasis, El-Fayoum is not fed by underground water like the Western Desert oases, but by Nile water transported to this natural triangular depression by a series of canals. The water comes from the Ibrahimeya Canal at Assiut, via the Bahr Yusef, which itself feeds into a number of smaller canals west of Fayoum City. Having irrigated the oasis the water runs into **Lake Qaroun** which, despite having dramatically shrunk over the past few thousand years, is still Egypt's largest natural salt-water lake. About 70,000 years ago the Nile flood first broke through the low mountains that surround El-Fayoum to form Lake Qaroun and the surrounding marshes. This is believed to be one of the first, if not *the* first, sites of agriculture in the world as plants that grew around the lake were collected, land was fenced in, and dry and guarded storage areas were built. Even today El-Fayoum is still famous for fruit, vegetables and chickens and to describe food as *fayoum* means that it is delicious.

Ins and outs

Getting there Fayoum City is the main town in the oasis and the province's capital, 103 km southwest of central Cairo and 85 km from Giza, a one- to 1½-hour journey along the four-lane carriageway. Buses leave from Aboud Terminal in Cairo every 15 minutes from 0600-2000 or from El-Mouneeb every 30 minutes, from 0600-1900. Tickets cost E£10-12 and can be purchased in advance, though this isn't necessary. Service taxis bound for Fayoum (E£10-12) congregate around Midan Ramses, Midan Orabi and Midan Giza. There are three daily trains from Ramses to Fayoum City, but only third class and it can take up to four hours. Another option is to hire a private taxi from Cairo to chauffeur you around, which is definitely the best idea for day trips if you can afford it, as the sights are quite spread out. Private taxis to Fayoum City should cost around E£350 per day.

Getting around The Bahr Yusef canal bisects Fayoum. Buses and taxis from Cairo terminate at the main bus station on the southwest side of the city. Service taxis to Ab Shawai, from where you can travel on to Tunis, are found at the Ab Shawai terminal to the south of the Bahr Yusef canal. Services to Beni Suef leave from the station 1.5 km northeast of the city centre. If you don't want to walk, you can hire a *hantour* (horse-drawn carriages, E£10-15, depending on where you're going) to your destination. Private taxis cost about E£30 per hour. Taxis around Fayoum city centre are a E£2 flat rate.

Information The **main office** ⓘ *T084-634 2313, 2 km north of town,* is accessible by minibus No 5, where the head of staff can help with arranging tours of the oasis. There's also a **small office** ⓘ *next to the 4 waterwheels in the city centre,* but the staff's English is somewhat lacking, and at present all they offer is a fairly useless map and the usual glossy pamphlet.

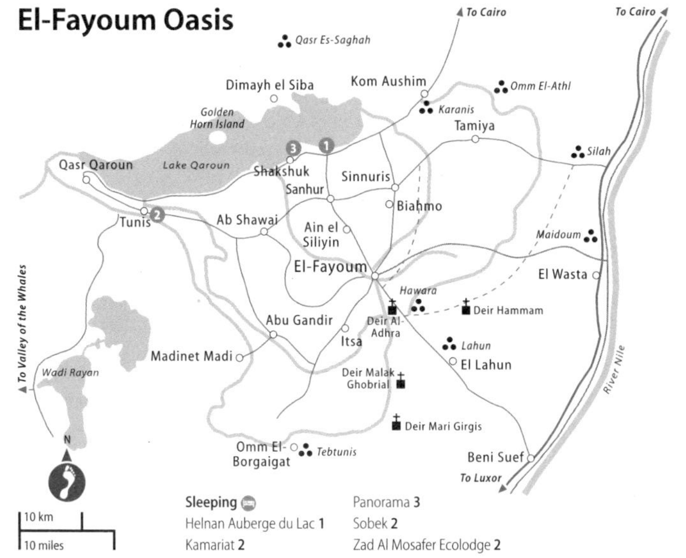

Fayoum portraits

While excavating in a cemetery in the vicinity of the Hawara pyramid Sir Flinders Petrie found 146 quite remarkable hand-painted portraits varying in quality of style and preservation. These funeral masks, or portraits, were executed in tempera, or encaustic – a mixture of paint and wax – on slices of cedar or other wood. They were of children, men and women of all ages. They date from Graeco-Roman times, 30 BC to 395 AD, and are among the earliest portraits known. It is assumed that they were commissioned during the person's lifetime and used as decoration in the home until required. When the deceased was embalmed the portrait would be attached to the coffin or mummy case. Examples can be seen in the Egyptian Museum in Cairo.

Background

The 12th Dynasty pharaoh Amenemhat I (1991-1962 BC) first drained part of the marshes to develop the area for agriculture and also dug a large canal from the Nile. The result of this and further developments by Amenemhat III (1842-1797 BC), who showed great interest in the area and built a pyramid at Hawara (see page 172), was Lake Moeris (Great Lake), twice the present size and teeming with fish, and an agricultural area to the south renowned for its rich and varied crops.

The Romans, who called the area Crocodilopolis (because of the ever-present crocodiles) changed Fayoum's previous system of crop rotation and forced the area to supply grain exclusively to the Roman market. Muslims believe that the prophet Joseph developed the area during his captivity in Egypt through the canalization of the Bahr Yusef River and by building the world's first dam. And although Fayoum's national strategic importance diminished with the canalization of the Nile Delta it remains one of the most productive agricultural areas in the country.

The water level in Lake Qaroun had been falling for about 2000 years until the construction of the Aswan High Dam led to far greater stability in the level of the Nile. Indeed, by medieval times the lake had become far too salty to sustain freshwater fish and new species had to be introduced. It appears that the water table is rising again as houses and fields at the lakeside have been flooded in recent years, and guests have to step up to raised sills to gain access to hotels along the lake shore.

Despite its stagnant and polluted water the beach resorts around Lake Qaroun still attract affluent visitors, mainly Egyptian, to the region. The oasis is declared free from bilharzia (schistosomiasis), a recommendation in itself. The season runs all year round, but from January to April it is considered too cold to swim. The summers are not as hot as Luxor/Aswan and the winters are not as cool as Cairo or the Delta. In the quieter areas there is a rewarding amount of wildlife to observe. While the fox is common in the town, the wolf is found only on the desert periphery. Sightings of wild cat are very rare. Thousands of egrets roost in the oasis, herons are common and many migrating birds take a rest here in spring and autumn.

Fayoum City

The majority of the oasis' population of 1.8 million people are not Nile Valley Egyptians but settled and semi-nomadic Berber people who are related to the Libyan Arabs. There is comparatively little to see in Fayoum City itself, and visitors are not advised to stay in the city for long but rather to enjoy the peace and tranquillity of the oasis' gardens and the lake. Two kilometres north of the town centre is the 13-m red granite **Obelisk of Senusert I**, estimated to weigh over 100 tonnes, standing in the middle of a traffic roundabout. The covered *Souk Al-Qantara* and the adjacent street of goldsmiths, **Es-Sagha**, found across the fourth bridge to the west of the central tourist office, are refreshingly authentic and well worth visiting. A little further west is the attractive **Mosque of Qaitbay/Khawand Asal-Bey**, possibly the oldest in the oasis, often – and erroneously – attributed to the Mamluk Sultan Qaitbay (1468-1498) who was noted as a warrior, a builder and a torturer. It was built for Asal-Bay, his favourite concubine. Remains of its impressive structure, most of which fell into the Bahr Yusef in 1892, include the dome supported by ancient pillars, some with Corinthian capitals, the rather plain *mihrab* and the gilded teak *minbar* elaborately carved and inlaid with ivory from Somalia.

Other mosques nearby are also worth visiting, particularly during the *moulids* (see box, page 179). The **Mosque and Mausoleum** in honour of local sheikh **Ali El-Rubi** is the scene of his birthday feast (around the middle of *Shabaan*). It attracts crowds from around the

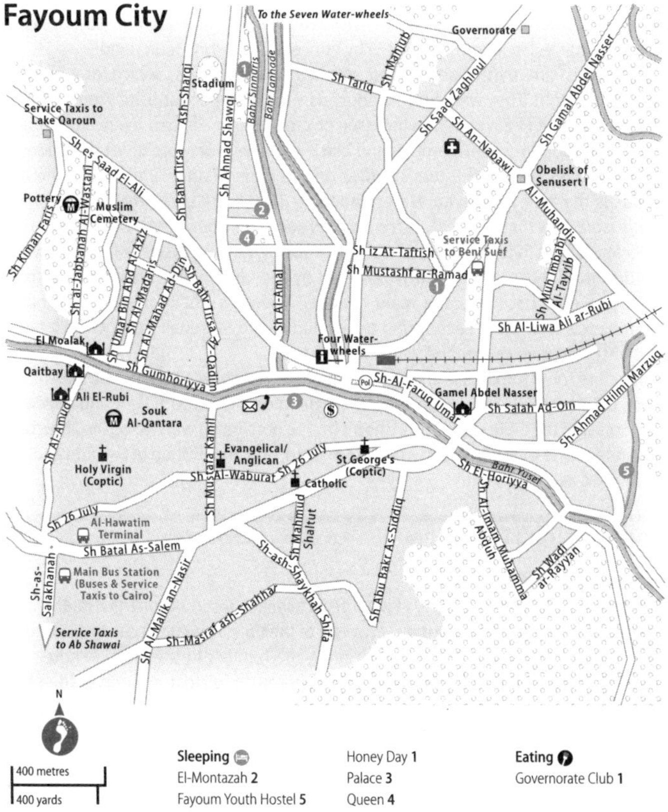

The groaning waterwheels of El-Fayoum

Because the land in the El-Fayoum oasis varies from +26 m to -42 m in three main steps, self-powered waterwheels were essential and the construction of one particular type, which is exclusive to El-Fayoum, began in pharaonic times.

There are often whole series of these *sawaqih al-Hadir* (roaring waterwheels), which produce a perpetual groaning noise. There are over 200 in the oasis, which has adopted the waterwheel as its official symbol.

In January each year every canal is cleaned and repaired. The sluices are shut, silt is dredged, walls are strengthened and the waterwheels, now white with dead algae, are lifted and overhauled. Although the wheels are considered to be ancient, in fact no part is more than about 10 years old.

oasis who sleep in the streets, perform *zikrs* in the courtyard, and revel in the funfairs around. Up a small street north of Bahr Yusef is the **El-Moalak Mosque** or **Hanging Mosque**, so-called because it is built above five arches each of which housed a workshop. It was constructed in limestone in 1375 by Prince Soliman Ibn Mouhamed.

The locals are particularly proud of their **waterwheels**, which are indeed a magnificent sight. They were first introduced by the Ptolemies and are used now as the official symbol of El-Fayoum province (see box, page 170). There are over 200 to see in the region, about 4-5 m in diameter and black with layers of protective tar. Besides the four large ones behind the tourist office on the main Sharia Gumhoriyya, the most famous is the series of **Seven Waterwheels** ⓘ *3 km north along the Bahr Sinnuris, a 30-min walk, take the west bank on the way there and come back along the east.* A solitary wheel at a farm is followed by a spectacular group of four and then the final two wheels by a bridge. They are continuously powered by the fast-flowing water of the stream, which just runs back into the main channel when it's not required for irrigation. Maintenance takes place each spring but should an urgent repair be required it takes a team of strong men to stop the wheel rotating.

There are four **churches** in the town, that of the Holy Virgin (Coptic Orthodox) is the oldest, dated at 1836. Notice the large altar screen decorated with light and dark wood inlay work and the Bible stand and Bishop's throne both inlaid with ivory. The church also contains a shrine to Anba Abram who died in 1914, one time Bishop of Fayoum and Giza, and revered as a local saint.

Excursions from El-Fayoum → *For listings, see pages 175-177.*

Lake Qaroun and Tunis

Lake Qaroun,'Lake of the Horn', is a favourite local beach resort despite the stagnant and salt-encrusted water. Although it is calm much of the time, in winter it can be quite rough and teeming with ducks and geese that bring the hunters to the lakeside hotels. It is possible to negotiate a rowing boat from the Auberge du Lac to the barren **Golden Horn Island** or to the north shore. There lie the ruins of **Dimayh El-Siba**, which would have been on the edge of the lake but, due to the retreat of the waters, are now almost 3 km away. This old Ptolemaic city with ruins of a small temple dedicated to Soknopaios (crocodile) was once the starting point of a camel trade route to the oases of the Western Desert. The goods first crossed the lake by boat, which still a good way to reach the site.

On the southwest corner of Lake Qaroun is **Tunis** village, a picturesque little enclave and now the heart of the Fayoum potting community whose designs are frequently displayed in Cairo's shops. It is an idyllic place to relax and enjoy lovely walks to absorb rural life, with a couple of charming eco-lodges (see Sleeping, page 176), which are perfect getaways. It's interesting to visit the pottery workshops, where local artists create traditional vessels and homewares under the tutorship of skilled pottery artists. Prices are considerably lower than in the shops and it's possible to commission special orders that take about a week to deliver.

Qasr Qaroun ⓘ *daily 0900-1600, E£32 students E£16*, to the west end of the lake, has the remains of the Graeco-Roman city of Dionysias, and a well-preserved limestone Ptolemaic temple dedicated to a crocodile god and decorated with a symbol of a winged sun. The date is not certain as there are no inscriptions. It is a compact structure but inside there are many small rooms, corridors, cellars and tunnels. It is fun to explore – take a torch. Watch out for scorpions. There are two spiral staircases to the roof, which provide a superb view.

Wadi Rayan and the Valley of the Whales

ⓘ *Entrance US$3, overnight camping E£10, vehicles E£5. Accessible only by private vehicle; a taxi from Fayoum City costs E£200-300 depending on whether or not you include the Valley of the Whales.*

A protected area since 1989, Wadi Rayan contains rare wildlife, 169 species of bird, ancient Roman and pharaonic ruins, plus the surreal Valley of the Whales. The dramatic landscape, with three blue man-made lakes contrasting against golden sand and mountains, mean it's a beauty spot popular with Cairo's ex-pats and Egyptians. Hiking in the hills is possible, where you can see churches engraved into the mountains and gain momentous views of the lake and desert beyond. Also here are Egypt's only waterfalls, rather piddling affairs, but an extremely crowded destination on public holidays and Fridays (best avoided). As well as the wealth of birdlife (mostly spotted during winter), the wadi is home to the world's smallest fox, the Fennec Fox, and a small population of the threatened Docras Gazelle. A visitor centre provides a background to the area, while several lodges and restaurants accommodate for basic needs.

A recently constructed road leads to the **Valley of the Whales**, now making access by non-4WD vehicles possible from Wadi Rayan. Designated a World Heritage Site by UNESCO in 2005, the hulking skeletons of 40-million-year-old marine mammals lie scattered over the desert floor. The fossils validate the evolution of whales from land-based animals to ocean-going mammals, and new remains are still being uncovered. A wilderness campsite is available, with fire pits and toilet facilities, and trails have been marked out for vehicles and walkers in order to protect the area from degradation.

Karanis

ⓘ *Daily 0900-1600 in winter and 0900-1700 in summer, E£32, students E£16. Museum: T084-501825, Tue-Sun 0900-1600 in winter and 0900-1700 in summer, E£16.*

To the east of the lake and 25 km from the city on the main road towards Cairo, the modern village of **Kom Aushim** is adjacent to the site of the ancient city of **Karanis**. Karanis, founded in the third century BC and inhabited by mercenaries of Ptolemy II, was once the centre of a large agricultural area exporting cereals to Rome via Alexandria. Of the two Roman temples, the **Temple of Pnepheros and Petesouchos** (yet more crocodile gods) is bigger and more interesting. Look for the oil/wine presses, tank for crocodiles, Roman baths with evidence of heating pipes, a row of headless sphinxes and the former residence of British High

Commissioner Sir Miles Lampson. The results of excavations carried out in the 1920s by the University of Michigan are displayed, together with exhibits from other sites around the Fayoum, in a small circular **museum**. The most interesting exhibits are the carefully restored pottery and glassware, two of the famed Fayoum portraits, the central mummy, the necklaces and the minute statues. Trips to **Qasr Es-Saghah**, a small limestone temple containing seven shrines, and the ruins of the Ptolemaic settlement of Soknopaious Nesos, which used to be on the lakeside but is now 11 km away, 65 m above water level, can be arranged from the museum but it's best to phone a day in advance.

Omm El-Athl, east of Karanis is the ruins of Bachias city, 700 mud brick houses and a small mud-brick temple dedicated to a crocodile god. The Pedestals of **Amenenhat** – two 6-m-high crumbling stone pedestals that once supported a seated colossus of Amenemhat III, can be seen in Biahmo village, 7 km north of Fayoum. Records suggest that each statue of red quartzite was 13 m above the top of its pedestal and each colossus and pedestal was surrounded by a huge solid wall. However, the scant remains are only really of interest to enthusiasts with a lot of imagination.

Madinet Madi

ⓘ *Access is by car, or the El-Qasmiya bus/micro departing from Al-Hawatim southwest of Fayoum city centre can drop you off.*

Madinet Madi, about 30 km southwest of Fayoum City, contains the ruins of a 12th Dynasty temple, built by Amenemhat III and Amenemhat IV dedicated to Sobek the crocodile god and Renenutet the serpent goddess. This site retains an attractive avenue of lions and winged sphinxes. The walls are constructed of limestone, a soft medium for the many reliefs including one of Sobek on the outside wall at the back. The cartouches of both Amenemhats are in the sanctuary with the elegant feet and ankles (all that remains) of several statues. Ongoing excavations have uncovered many new finds, and mean that the site will soon be charging an entrance fee.

Omm El-Borgaigat, with the ruins of **Tebtunis**, is 30 km south of Fayoum. This temple was dedicated to Sobek and was constructed of locally quarried coarse limestone. Little remains of the walls though some paving remains. A cache of mummified crocodiles was found here at the beginning of the last century.

The pyramids of El-Fayoum

There are four separate pyramid sites in the vicinity. **Hawara** ⓘ *daily 0900-1600, E£32, students E£16*, about 10 km southeast from Fayoum, is a mud-brick pyramid 58 m high with a base measuring 100 m, all the decorative casing long since removed. Contrary to normal practice the entrance was positioned on the south side in an unsuccessful attempt to confuse looters. Adjacent to this pyramid is the legendary **Labyrinth**, a mortuary temple also built by Amenemhat III, covering an area of 105,000 sq m. It was half carved into the interior of the rock and was composed of over 3000 rooms but today few traces remain of this spectacular construction. Nearby is the tomb of his daughter Princess Sobek-Nefru Ptah, which was discovered intact in 1956. The poorly preserved necropolis at Hawara are where the famous Fayoum Portraits were discovered.

The ruined **Pyramid of Senusert II** (1897-1878 BC) ⓘ *daily 0900-1600, E£32, students E£16* near **Lahun** was built by Amenemhat III's grandfather. It was built on a rocky outcrop on which limestone pillars were constructed and then covered over with mud-brick and finally encased in stone. A 'sponge' made of sand and flint was placed around the base in order to prevent any flooding. Once again the unusual south-facing entrance did not deter the tomb robbers who looted Senusert's sarcophagus but left some wonderful jewellery that's now in the Egyptian Museum and New York's Metropolitan Museum. The walled pyramid complex also includes the ruins of a subsidiary pyramid for the queen, the mortuary temple and the *mastaba* tombs of other members of the royal family.

The collapsed **Maidoum Pyramid** ⓘ *daily 0900-1600, E£32, students E£16, to the northwest of El-Wasta on the Nile, and most easily reached from there by a 1-hr early morning train journey followed by a 15-min taxi ride to the village of Maidoum and a short walk,* was originally 144 m sq and 42 m high. However, over the centuries this imposing pyramid, which is built on the edge of an escarpment above the cultivated area, has collapsed leaving only a central three-stepped core of stone standing 65 m high that looks rather like a medieval fort. The difficult entry is up a 30-m stairway on the north side from which visitors descend into a long 57-m sloping passage that levels out to reach a short vertical shaft leading to the limestone-lined and corbel-roofed burial chamber on the same level as the pyramid's foundations.

While it is generally agreed that the Maidoum Pyramid housed the first Fourth Dynasty (2613-2494 BC) pharaoh Snefru, because he also had two other pyramids at Dahshur, it is now believed that it was started by his father Huni and completed by Snefru. The theory as to why it collapsed is that, unlike the pyramids at Giza, which distributed the stresses inwards, it has incorrectly calculated outward stresses – part of the trial and error evolution from the early step-pyramid to the later standard pyramid.

Slightly further north are the rubble remains of the **Seila/Silah** step pyramid of limestone from Second Dynasty and adjacent rock tombs, thought to be Christian. This excursion requires 4WD, a guide and a short walk.

The monasteries of El-Fayoum

Saint Anthony (AD 251-356) acted as an inspiration for hermits and there were soon numerous monasteries throughout the country including the Fayoum depression. A number still stand today. The 12th-century **Deir Al-Adhra** (Monastery of the Virgin), just off the road to Beni Suef about 6 km outside Fayoum City, is the most accessible. It was inhabited until the 18th century then fell into disuse. Bishop Anba Abram was buried here in 1914. The *moulid* of the Virgin is celebrated here each August and the number of pilgrims, already large, is increasing each year. Further south is the beautiful seventh-century Coptic **Deir Malak Ghobrial** (Monastery of the Angel Gabriel) on the desert escarpment at Naqlun above the cultivated lowlands. There is a large number of cells in the area – cut into the hillside – which were accommodation for the monks. The last rebuilding/refurbishment took place this century, so today pilgrims to the annual celebration find more comfortable places to stay in the monastery buildings that surround the church. The church is of a simple classic design. Elements of older buildings have been incorporated giving an impression of greater antiquity. There are icons from the 19th century. **Deir Hammam**, which was originally built in the sixth or eighth century, is 6 km northeast of Lahun and Coptic **Deir Mari Girgis** (Monastery of St George) can be reached by boat from Sidmant Al-Gabal which is 15 km southwest of Lahan. Even more isolated is **Deir Anba Samwail** (Monastery of St Samuel) which is about 30 km south of the rim of the Fayoum depression and can only be reached by pack animal or 4WD.

Wadi Natrun → *Colour map 2, B1.*

Wadi Natrun is a natural depression of salt lakes and salt flats lying in the desert west of the Nile Delta, situated off the Giza–Alexandria desert road at approximately Km 100. It is a birdwatchers' paradise brimming with age-old Coptic monasteries, and makes for an excellent day trip from Cairo. Wadi Natrun became the centre of a series of monastic groups principally in the fourth century AD. Insecurity, the plague and attacks by Bedouin led to the decline of some scattered communities but also led to some centralization of Christians into monasteries, four of which remain populated to the present day.

Ins and outs

Getting there A taxi from Cairo for the day should cost around E£200-250, depending on your itinerary. You can hop on a **West Delta** bus to the village of Bir Hooker from Cairo's Turgoman station (hourly 0600-1800, E£5); from the village, you can either hire a taxi to take you around the monasteries (around E£50) or you can hitch a pickup bound to the monastery Deir Anba Bishoi (E£1). Alternatively, service taxis leave from Aboud Terminal and stop at the resthouses and petrol stations located at Km 105, where you will need to charter a taxi or you may be able to hitch a ride with Coptic pilgrims passing though.

Note Fasting days and feasts make the opening days of the monasteries rather erratic, and it is definitely best to check the website, www.copticpope.org, to see what is open and when. Deir Anba Bishoi is the only one of the four to open every day.

Sights

The **Deir Abu Maqar** (Monastery of St Makarios) ⓘ *only open to visitors who have a letter of introduction from the Coptic Patriarchate in Cairo or Alexandria*, lies 3 km off the highway. Its significance is linked to the importance of St Makarios, the son of a village priest who arrived at Wadi Natrun in AD 330 and became the spiritual leader of the Christian hermits and monks in the area and was known for his rigourously ascetic way of life. He was buried at the monastery, and a further nine patriarchs of the Church are also interred at the site.

The site itself is made up of several **churches**, frequently destroyed and rebuilt. The main church, that of St Makarios, is basically a much-restored building on ancient foundations with some small survivals like the 11th-century dome and vestiges of the side chapels from the seventh to the ninth centuries. Those of St Benjamin and St John are among the most ancient of the original fabric. The main site contains the Cell of the Chrism, the fluid used to embalm Jesus Christ, and there is a belief that some of this original material was stored here at Deir Abu Maqar. A small bakery for making the host is located in a room still standing in its original form on the north wall. Behind the churches, there's an 11th-century three-storey defensive tower. Note the religious paintings in the tower's smaller chapels.

To the northwest lie two other living monasteries – **Deir Anba Bishoi** (Pschoi) and **Deir El-Suriani**. Deir Anba Bishoi was

Wadi Natrun

named after the patron saint who went to the wadi following a divine revelation and lived there in solitude. These two sites are easily reached and offer no problems for visitors who wish to walk around. The mainly 20th-century buildings at Deir Anba Bishoi are run by a thoroughly modern community of monks. The layout of the ancient church is cruciform, with a central nave leading to a choir, through doors to the altar sanctuary. Small side chapels (Chapel of the Virgin to the left and Chapel of St Istkhirun or Ischyrion to the right) lie on either side of the sanctuary.

Deir El-Suriani (Monastery of the Syrians) is thought to be an 11th-century foundation by orthodox monks who resisted a schismatic movement at Deir Anba Bishoi. The site was acquired by a devout Syrian Christian in the eighth to ninth centuries and thus took its now popular name since the schism had ended and the monks had returned to their centre at Bishoi. Built over the cave used by St Bishoi, the Church of the Virgin Mary, two main sections – the nave and the choir-sanctuary separated by buttresses and a doorway. The nave has a basin for the washing of feet, a stone screen and houses some religious relics, reputedly including hair from the head of Mary Magdalene, in a niche where St Bishoi lived in ascetic contemplation. In a semi-dome above the west door there is a picture of the Ascension. The altar is of very dark marble.

It is the choir that is most famous, however, for its wonderful 10th-century black, wooden doors with their ivory inlays. Note the paintings in the semi-domes, the death of the Virgin to the left and the Annunciation and the Nativity to the right. There is a library of over 3000 books and many valuable manuscripts. There is also a small museum on site which contains a large selection of 16th and 17th century icons. Check before visiting, as the monastery is closed to the public at times of important religious ceremonies.

Deir El-Baramous, also known as the Monastery of the Romans, is the fourth monastery of the group and the oldest of the sites. It is somewhat isolated to the north end of Wadi Natrun, among lush cultivation and orchards. Legend has it that Maximus and Domitius, two sons of the Roman Emperor Valentinian, died young of self-imposed fasting at this place and that St Makarios set up the new monastery to commemorate them. The five churches are dedicated to the Virgin Mary, St Theodore, St George, St John the Baptist and St Michael. The church of St Michael is on the second floor of the keep, to which there is a drawbridge held in position by an unusual key/pin known as an Egyptian lock. The now unused refectory has a special 6-m-long stone table, carved all in one piece.

Around Cairo listings

For Sleeping and Eating price codes and other relevant information, see pages 26-31.

Sleeping

Fayoum City *p168, map p169*

B-C Queen, Sharia Manshat Luftallah, T084-634 6189. Clean, carpeted rooms are comfortable if rather gaudy, with private bath, fridge, a/c and TV. Corridors and public areas are the most dimly lit of any hotel in Egypt. Breakfast included, restaurant with Egyptian dishes, free Wi-Fi and kindly staff. A quiet and pleasant place to stay, particularly if you're in town for a while.

C Honey Day Hotel, 105 Sharia Gamal Abdel Nasser, T084-634 0205, T010-521 7090. A bit of a walk from the town centre en route to the Obelisk of Senusert, but a clean 2-star hotel that is small and friendly with its own restaurant. Rather blank carpeted rooms have a/c, TV and fridge, while public areas are a crazy hotch-potch of styles. Free Wi-Fi and use of the PC.

D Palace Hotel, Sharia El-Horiyya, T084-631 1222. Good central location overlooking the

Bahr Yusef. Reasonable and clean rooms, older ones E£100 per double, or newly refurbished on the upper levels for E£200. All have private bath, TV, fridge and a/c. Breakfast included. Owner speaks English and is a good source of information. Cars, motorbikes and bicycles for hire.

E El-Montazah, Manshat Lutfallah, T084-634 8662. Near the Bahr Sinnuris canal in a quieter area north of the town centre, run by Copts. A decent budget hotel and, though rooms have seen better days, they are clean. Cheaper small rooms share bathrooms (E£60), others have a/c and en suites (E£120).

F Fayoum Youth Hostel, Flat No 7, Housing Block No 7, Hadaka, ask for '*Beit El-shebab*' to find it. 46 beds, self-catering facilities. Breakfast included. Inconveniently located and often empty. Still, at E£12 per person, the price is the cheapest in town.

Lake Qaroun and Tunis *p170, map p167*

LL-L Helnan Auberge du Lac, Lake Qaroun, T084-698 1200, www.helnan.com. Built by King Farouk as a hunting lodge in 1937, most old black and white Egyptian movies were shot at the Auberge and King Ibn Saud and Winston Churchill met here in 1945 to carve up to Middle East. The Helnan have recently brought back some of the former glory, and rooms have been refurbished in a classical style including King Farouk's old bedrooms, which are now a duplex suite complete with jacuzzi. There are restaurants, bars, pool, facilities for the disabled and a fishing pier. The view from the more expensive rooms is blocked by the cheaper chalets built in the gardens beside the lake.

A Panorama, Shakshuk, Lake Qaroun, T084-683 0746. 66 a/c chalet rooms with balcony and lake view, TV room, small pool, water sports, fishing, duck shooting, garden, restaurants inside and out – seafood's their speciality.

A-D Kamariat, Lake Qaroun, Tunis, (Cairo office) T02-3302 5428. An environmentally friendly set-up with bright and simple rooms built mainly from natural materials, and including TV. You have to cook your own meals, but can also request a typical Fayoumi meal including duck or fish and *feteer*. Rooms at the back are E£100, or with a lake view E£300. They offer horse-riding as well as birdwatching trips.

D-E Zad Al Mosafer Ecolodge, Tunis, T084-682 0180, T010-639 5590, abdogobair@maktoob.com. Built from natural materials and encircling scented herbal gardens, appealing rooms have plastered walls, pottery lamps and rush - they are great value, but don't expect luxury. Some rooms share large bathrooms, other have en suites, plus there are chalets sleeping up to 5 persons. Rooms are E£80-150 for a double, or more for those with a better view and a/c. There are panoramic views of Lake Qaroun from the rooftop and the upstairs lounge, and lovely outdoor areas where you can slouch around. It is a short walk up the hill to Tunis village. Good restaurant, children's play area and little swimming pool (open to outside guests for a small charge). The owner, writer Abdou Gobair, also arranges birdwatching trips and excursions to Wadi Rayan, plus horse-riding (E£50 per hr) and camel-riding (E£40) is available. The gift shop has an excellent selection of crafts and pottery.

D-F Sobek, Tunis, T016-888 5423. A new little guesthouse with a distinctly hippyish vibe, has stone-built chalets of varying sizes and simplicity around a rustic garden. Some rooms share bathrooms, others are more comfortable and can sleep up to 4, There's a wicker gazebo for relaxing with views over olive groves and farmland towards the lake. Camping is possible for E£20. Traditional Fayoumi cooking is available, or guests are welcome to use the kitchen. Desert tours, boat trips and pottery workshops can all be arranged.

Eating

Fayoum City *p168, map p169*

Dining out is not great in Fayoum City, there are several local eateries around the central

Bahr Yusef canal and market areas, which tend to be better at grilled meats and chicken than *koshari* or *fuul*. None stands out enough to recommend.

Governorate Club, on the grounds of Nadi Al-Muhafzah, reached by *hantour* or minibus No 9. There's a small entrance fee to the club. Food is cheap and tasty, with kebab, chicken, and steak, spaghetti, and standard local *mezzas*.

Lake Qaroun and Tunis *p170*

Auberge du Lac, Lake Qaroun. Provides decent international food in attractive and historic surroundings.

Café Gabal El-Zinah, Lake Qaroun. Play areas for children, boat landing, fish is main item on menu as well as duck from the lake.

Lake Plage Café, Lake Qaroun. Has 1.5 km of beach, play areas for children, adequate but unimaginative.

Zad Al Mosafer Ecolodge, Tunis. A lovely place for a decent dinner in the quaint restaurant, with Stella for E£18. As well as typical Egyptian grills and some international meals, they do Fayoumi pigeon and duck dishes and use organic produce from the garden.

Shopping

Fayoum City *p168, map p169*

Fayoum chickens, fresh fruit and straw baskets are available in the city Souk Al-Qantara.

Lake Qaroun and Tunis *p170*

The village of Tunis, a farming community transformed into an artist's haven, is renowned for its exquisite local pottery. Several small workshops can be visited, and it is a relaxing place to shop. The **Fayoum Pottery School**, T084-682 0405, T018-111 515, T1010-331 0813. Daily 1000-2000, are the most well established and teach local children (they also have a showroom in Cairo, www.nagada.net). **Rawya's**, T010-631 7840 is another good place to start, or just wander the lanes and see who is open.

Transport

Fayoum City *p168, map p169*

Bus

To **Cairo**'s Ahmed Helmi and Giza stations, buses leave every 30 mins between 0630-1830 from the main bus station (*'mowaf autobis'*) southwest of the town centre. There are also regular buses south to **Beni Suef** (from where you can change for onward journeys the to the Nile Valley and East Coast) from nearby Al-Hawatim terminal.

Microbuses to **Beni Suef** leave from a terminal 1 km north of the centre.

Service taxi

Service taxis are quicker than buses and leave the depot next to the bus station for **Cairo** to **Midan Giza** or **Midan Ramses**, 1-1½ hrs, E£10-12. To get to **Tunis**, services leave from *'mowaf Ab Shawai'* in Fayoum to Ab Shawai, from where you change to another service to Mafarit Tunis or Yousef el-Sedik.

Train

There are daily trains to **Cairo/Giza** at 0730, 1230 and 1700 and to **Al-Wasta** at 0520, 0830, 1600, 1900 and 2130, but the service is slow and limited to 3rd-class travel.

Directory

Fayoum City *p168, map p169*

Banks Bank of Alexandria, Banque du Caire, Banque Misr and National Bank of Egypt, are in the town centre and have ATMs. **Medical services** Hospital: Sharia Saad Zaghoul, T084-634 2249. **Post office** On the south side of the Bahr Yusef canal, Sat-Thu 0800-2000.

The Nile Delta

Throughout the Delta, countless branches of the River Nile cut through cities, villages and fields that see few tourist visitors. The fertility of the area has enabled this scorched desert country, of which just 4% of the land is cultivatable, to support its huge population and to export large quantities of fruits and vegetables. Travelling around is easiest and quickest by microbus and service taxi. *➡ For listings, see pages 187-190.*

Western Delta → *For listings, see pages 187-190. Colour map 2, A1/2.*

Across the wider Rosetta branch of the Nile is the Western Delta. The main attractions are the port of Rashid (Rosetta) and some of Egypt's biggest annual *moulids* held in and around Tanta and Damanhur. This route, like most in the Delta, goes through an interesting mixture of scenery: fields of cotton, sugar cane and patches of vegetables, tiny clusters of houses, and old-fashioned water-lifting devices. The area bustles with carts, donkeys, men perched on lawnmower-like contraptions chugging through the streets, and people working in the fields. It is an ever-changing scene of rural Egypt, yet most travellers rush straight on to Alexandria. The taming of the Nile in the late 19th century, allowing perennial irrigation, enables the cultivation of three or four crops a year in this extremely fertile region.

Tanta

This town maintains its rural atmosphere despite being one of the largest cities in Egypt and having a major university. Although it is an interesting and quite charming city, where you can enjoy a taste of contemporary Egyptian life without the glories of past eras and masses of tourists, there is little or nothing to see in Tanta itself for most of the year. Plenty of stunning neglected colonial-era buildings remain, but probably not for much longer as no one seems to recognize their beauty or historical value and modern high-rises are gradually replacing them. Tanta really comes alive, however, in late October at the end of the cotton harvest, during the eight-day festival or **Moulid of Sayid Ahmed El-Badawi** when the population swells to nearly three million as pilgrims pour in from throughout Egypt and the Muslim world. Until the *moulid* was forced into a decline in the mid-19th century because it was so overly riotous and dangerous it was the largest *moulid* in the Muslim world, and in the early years of the 20th century important officials from both the Ottoman and British hierarchy attended the celebrations. It is still the largest *moulid* in Egypt even though in recent years festivities have been further calmed down, and any local can tell you tales of their youth when the crushes in the streets resulted in death on a daily basis. The day after the Big Night (*Leila Kebir*), the *khalifa* which in the past was a riot of camels, drums and circuses as the mounted sheikh leads the procession, these days is merely a crush outside the mosque as the sheikh exits to his car.

Sayid Ahmed El-Badawi (1199-1276) was the founder of one of Egypt's largest Sufi brotherhoods/orders (*tariqas*), which is known as the Badawiya. Born in Fes, Morocco, he emigrated to Arabia and then travelled to Iraq where he joined the Rifaiyah brotherhood. After being sent to Tanta in 1234 as its representative, he received permission to establish his own *tariqa*, which soon flourished. Although the mosque built by his successor and containing his tomb was demolished in the mid-19th century, a large, new, rather

Moulids – festivals in the Delta

Officially, *moulids* are festivals in commemoration of a specific saint when pilgrims obtain their *baraka*, or blessing, by visiting their shrine. There is usually a parade of devotees, carrying banners and dressed in turbans and sashes in the colours of their saint, sometimes led by floats or camels. Chanting and dancing goes on for hours, led by charismatic singers (*munshi*). There is nothing more moving and uplifting than witnessing a *zikr* at a moulid. As the *munshi* sings and chants, he transports the swaying devotees into another realm and all inhibitions are lost as young and old, rich and poor, men and women, move together in praise of Allah. It's a real eye-opener to a side of Egyptian society that is hidden far beneath the layers of everyday life, a chance for people to cut loose and express intense spiritual joy. Women wearing *higab*, uniformed street cleaners, *felaheen* in *galabiyyas* and muscled T-shirted youths all sway and turn in harmony to the music making a truly hypnotic sight. In addition, the most important *moulids* are like a giant medieval fair where pilgrims meet their friends and eat, drink and celebrate. They stroll among the stalls and rides watching the magicians, acrobats, snake charmers, animal trainers, stick fighters, terrifying stunts on the wall of death and other traditional entertainments.

undistinguished one was built by pasha Abbas I (1848-1854) and is the focus of Badawi's annual *moulid*. Another *moulid* in July is held in honour of the female saint Sheikha Sabah.

El-Mahalla El-Kubra

The industrial city of El-Mahalla El-Kubra is 25 km northeast of Tanta and 120 km north of Cairo. It is a particularly scruffy and unattractive place that, unsurprisingly, sees few tourists. To the west of the hospital in the nearby riverside town of **Sammanud** lie the remains of the red and black granite **Temple of Onuris-Shu** ⓘ *Sun-Thu 1000-1300*, rebuilt by Nectanebo II (360-343 BC) for Tjeboutjes, the capital of the 12th Nome of Lower Egypt. Now surrounded by apartment blocks, the small enclosure of dusty stone blocks, some adorned with hieroglyphs, is far from impressive. Further northeast some 10 km from Sammanud along the main H8 highway towards **Talkha** there is the modern town of **Bahbait Al-Hagar** and what little remains of the great **Temple of Isis** in the ancient town of **Iseum** (or **Pr-Hebeit** as it was known to the ancient Egyptians).

Damanhur

Midway between Tanta and Alexandria, Damanhur lies in the middle of the Western Delta, 160 km northwest of Cairo. This sleepy provincial capital and textile town, which was once the site of the ancient city of Tmn-Hor dedicated to Horus, has little to offer the visitor. In November, however, there is the **Moulid of Sheikh Abu Rish**, which follows the more important one in Tanta. Extending over two days in January is Egypt's only **Jewish moulid** at the shrine of a 19th-century mystic called **Abu Khatzeira**. For security, non-Jewish Egyptians are denied entrance to the festival; most attendees are Europeans and Israelis who bring sick relatives or bottled water to be blessed at the shrine.

The Hoopoe

The Hoopoe (*Upupa epopsis*) is like no other bird – it is the only one in its species. It is a resident breeder, fairly common especially in the Delta area. The sexes are similar, both 28 cm in length. You will see it on lawns and in parks and oases where it disturbs the ground searching for grubs. It also eats locusts, moths, spiders and ants. It nests in holes in old trees or ruins (plenty of scope in Egypt) laying up to six eggs.

In general the colouring is buff/pink with distinctive black and white bars in a striped pattern on the wings and tail. It has a long down-curving bill with a black tip, a square tail and broad rounded wings, striped with black tips. A distinctive crest runs from front to back of the head, the feathers having quite marked black tips. This crest is raised when it alights and is evident in mating displays. The call is a distinct 'Hoo-poo-oo'.

Rashid (Rosetta)

ⓘ *There's no direct transport from Cairo. The easiest way to arrive by public transport is to travel either via Damanhur or Alexandria, from where you can catch a service taxi to Rashid (1 hr, E£3.50).*

Rashid (Rosetta to Europeans), formerly known as 'the city of a million palms and dates', used to be the principal port in Egypt. Since ancient times its fortunes have been linked with the ebb and flow of those of its neighbour Alexandria, 64 km to the west. When one waxed, the other would wane. Mohammed Ali's Mahmudiya Canal project linking the Nile to Alexandria marked the end of Rosetta's significance as a port. And while Alexandria is now Egypt's second city, Rosetta is little more than a fishing village. However, its location on the brink of the Nile estuary is an especially scenic one and it's possible to hire bicycles to explore the outlying countryside (and take them across the river on the ferry to the rowdy villages on the east bank). There is still a medieval feel to the cobbled narrow winding streets, with *ahwas* on every corner and masses of horse-drawn carriages and donkey carts ferrying vegetables to market, while in terms of the number of Islamic monuments in town Rosetta is second only to Cairo. For most people, however, the town is synonymous with the 1799 discovery of the **Rosetta Stone**, the key to our understanding of hieroglyphics and, consequently, much of what we know of Egypt's ancient civilization. The stone is inscribed in Greek, hieroglyphics and demotic Egyptian with a proclamation by Ptolemy V Epiphanes. Today it rests in the British Museum of London.

There is some striking architecture in the town from the Ottoman period, recently renovated or under restoration, that offers a taste of Rosetta's splendid past. Many of Rosetta's 22 Ottoman houses are made of distinctive red and black brick and incorporate recycled stones and columns from earlier eras. Many too have delicately carved *mashrabiya* windows and screens. At the time of writing, the majority of these houses were not open to the public as much restoration work is still ongoing; however the exteriors are still impressive. Buildings which can be accessed include the **Beit Kili**, on Midan El-Gumhoriyya by the Corniche, which dates from 1879 and is now a museum ⓘ *T045-292 1733, E£25, students E£15, daily 0900-1700*. The building is noted for its delicately handcrafted woodwork, while on display are a few pieces of glassware, Ottoman period swords, manuscripts, costumes, tiles and armour. The upper rooms contain some lovely inlaid furniture and the overall effect is pleasing. The museum ticket

Breaking the code

Jean-François Champollion was born in the village of Figeac in France in 1790. He was a precocious learner of difficult foreign languages and from an early age became involved with studies of Greek, Latin and the Coptic languages.

Like other scholars before him, in the 1820s he began deciphering Egyptian hieroglyphs and by 1822 evolved a virtually complete set of hieroglyphic signs and their Greek equivalent, using the information on the Rosetta Stone.

The Rosetta Stone was found near Rashid in 1799 by soldiers of Napoleon's expedition to Egypt. The huge, irregularly shaped piece of granite weighing 762 kg was embedded in the wall of El-Rashid fort, a piece of recycled fortification. It is thought to have been written by one of the high priests of Memphis in the ninth year of Ptolemy V's reign (196 BC) and is originally a decree of Ptolemy V declaring the benefits he, as a monarch, conferred on Egypt. Its importance was not in its content – though it did establish, among other things, that Ptolemy reunited the country – but in its presentation of three scripts: Greek script below and hieroglyphs; demotic and cursive Egyptian languages above.

The Swede Akerblad and the Englishman Thomas Young had made some progress in deciphering the Rosetta Stone but it was Champollion, using his knowledge of Egyptology, Greek and Coptic languages, who finally broke the code. He was the first to understand that individual Egyptian hieroglyphs stood for individual letters, groups of letters and even for entire objects.

Champollion undertook archaeological work in Egypt in 1828 with the Italian Ippolito Rosellini, recording a series of sites in the Nile Valley. He died in 1832 aged 42 years having been curator of the Egyptian collection of the Louvre and professor of Egyptian antiquities at the Collège de France. His brother Jacques-Joseph prepared and published his works after Jean-François's death.

also gives entry to the Museum Garden opposite, although there is nothing to see save a few fragments of columns. The **Abu Shahim Mill** and adjacent **Amasyali House** ⓘ *E£15, students E£8, daily 0900-1600*, are worth a visit. The mill was built in 1760 and contains two huge millstones that would have been turned by horses to grind flour and rice. The Amasyali House, dating from 1880, has an impressive facade with a fine mashrabiya doorway, painted ceilings and incorporates ancient columns into the building. This ticket also includes entry to the 19th-century bathhouse, **Hammam Azouz**, which gives a sense of the splendour of traditional marbled *hammams*. Some rooms have deteriorated, despite restoration, giving a quite spooky effect.

Of the 12 Ottoman mosques, a couple are worth a visit for their coloured tilework. The huge **Zaghloul Mosque**, built around 1600, a block north of the main road to Alexandria, is a double mosque. The brighter and smarter half to the west is noted for its arched courtyard while the other half, with over 300 columns, sadly suffers from partial submersion. The **Mohammed Al-Abassi Mosque** (1809) standing to the south of the town by the Nile, has a distinctive minaret. The **Ali Maladi Mosque** is being restored, and has many columns looted from Graeco-Roman sites and a beautiful doorway.

Near Rosetta, there is the Mamluk **Qaitbay Fort (Fort St Julien)** ⓘ *E£15, students E£8, daily 0900-1600 (closes at 1500 in Ramadan), 7 km out of town, most easily accessed by taxi (E£30-35 round trip) or taxi boat slightly more (E£50).*

Herodotus: the historian

Herodotus lived in Greece in the fifth century BC. His great achievement was his history of the Greek wars against the Persian Empire. His origins are obscure but it is believed that he was a Greek born in Asia Minor in approximately 485 BC. He developed the great tradition of Greek historical research in which questions were asked and answers to them sought in the available written evidence. He became an avid collector of information – stories and travel data – which he eventually assembled into his *History*, writings on the wars against the Persians. He travelled widely in Asia Minor, the Black Sea region and the Mediterranean islands.

Perhaps his most famous journey was to Egypt. He began in the Nile Delta and voyaged to Memphis, Thebes and the first cataract. He was deeply interested in the topography of the Nile Valley and in the nature of the Nile flood. He is attributed with the saying that, "Egypt is the gift of the Nile". Like all geographer-historians of the early period, he mixed scientific evidence and serious observation with myths, fables and tall tales. His readers were given all the excitement of the grotesque and supernatural wonders of the world, though he rarely entirely gave up rational explanations for historical events. His works were widely accepted in Athenian society and today are regarded as an important development in the establishment of history as an academic study (he was a contemporary and companion of Sophocles). In his later life he moved to a new Greek city colony in Thurii, Italy, where he is buried.

The 18th-century mosque of **Abu Mandur**, 5 km upstream, is accessed by boat taxi or felucca (E£30).

Eastern Delta → *For listings, see pages 187-190. Colour map 2, A/B 2/3.*

The branching of the Nile divides the Delta into three interlocking areas. The main road (H1) from Cairo to Damietta runs north through the Central Delta via Tanta before striking northeast through El-Mansura but there are other more interesting routes. Turning east in Benha, a road goes through Zagazig and the ruins of Bubastis to the ancient sites of Nabasha and Tanis, from which a minor road continues north through intensive cultivation to El-Mansura. Damietta gives access along the coast either east to Port Said (see page 392) at the northern end of the Suez Canal or west to the coastal resorts of Ras El-Bar, Gamassa and even the isolated Baltim.

The main road is normally very busy with a mixture of agricultural traffic and vehicles bound for the ports. On Fridays and holidays it can be even busier with private cars. Shamut Oranges between Tukh and Benha is a very popular spot for picnics. Pigeon towers of varying designs are common in the Delta region, resembling enormous holey beehives and even crowning the roofs of multi-storey buildings in the centre of towns. The pigeons provide free fertilizer and are the main ingredient in 'pigeon sweet and sour', a speciality Delta dish.

Benha

About 48 km north of Cairo, Benha is the first major town on the H1 highway. It's a stop on the Cairo–Alexandria train line, and accessible by bus every 20 minutes (0600-2100) from

Sacred cats

Cats were first domesticated by the Egyptians and it seems probable that the breed they domesticated was the Kaffir cat, a thin, striped, grey cat common all over Africa. Numerous tomb drawings and mummified bodies have been discovered which date from the very early Egyptian dynasties.

The cat was held in great awe and worshipped in the form of the cat-headed goddess Bast (or Pasht) from which it has been suggested the word 'puss' is derived. Egyptians believed that all cats went to heaven: there was a choice of two heavens, the more aristocratic creatures having a better-class destination. If a family cat died the household members would all go into mourning and shave off their eyebrows.

Cairo's Aboud terminal, where it's also possible to catch a service taxi. Close by lie the remains of the ancient town of **Athribis**, which was once the capital of the 10th Nome and associated with the worship of the black bull. Although it pre-dates the Greeks, its greatest importance was during the Roman period. Its orderly layout, like that of many Delta towns, was built around two intersecting roads. Little remains of the town today except traces of 18th to 26th Dynasty temples and an extensive Graeco-Roman cemetery. A cache of 26th to 30th Dynasty silver ingots and jewellery from the site is now in the Egyptian Museum in Cairo.

Zagazig

ⓘ *Reached by frequent buses or service taxis from Aboud Terminal in Cairo (E£4-6, 1½ hrs). Trains also run from Cairo each day, taking the same amount of time.*

The provincial capital, 36 km northeast of Benha, 80 km from Cairo, was founded in 1830 and its main claim to fame is as the birthplace of the nationalist Colonel Ahmed Orabi who led the 1882 revolt against the British. The town itself has little to recommend it, especially in terms of accommodation, but is lively due to the huge student population and very friendly to the rare independent traveller who winds up here. Most tourists come to Zagazig to see the jumbled ruins of **Bubastis** that lie 1 km southeast of the town, or (less frequently) to attend the **Moulid of Abu Khalil**, which happens during the month of Shawwal.

Bubastis

ⓘ *To reach the site, go through the underpass below the train tracks, then walk the km south along Sharia Farouq, or hail a taxi (E£1) or microbus (35 pt). A taxi from the central station square costs E£3. A museum and tourist bazaar are being constructed at the entrance to the site; daily 0830-1600, E£15, students E£10.*

Bubastis, also called **Tell Basta**, was the capital of the 18th Nome of Lower Egypt and was known to the Ancient Egyptians as Pr Bastet (House of Bastet). The name is derived from the worship of the Egyptian cat goddess Bastet who was believed to be the daughter of the sun-god Re. During the Old Kingdom she was originally associated with the destructive forces of his eye and was symbolized as a lion. Later, during the Middle Kingdom, this image was tamed and she was represented with a brood of kittens and carrying the sacred rattle. The ancient Egyptians worshipped cats and mummified them at a number of sites including Bubastis because they believed that they would be protected by Bastet.

The pied kingfisher

The pied kingfisher (*Ceryle rudis*) is very common in Egypt – wherever there is water. Like all kingfishers it is recognized by its larger than expected head with a rather insignificant crest, a long, sturdy, sharp beak and by its short tail and short legs. The bird, 25 cm long, is found in both salt and fresh water. It is a superb diver, fishing from a hovering position over the water or from a perch on a convenient branch. The sexes are similar in sizes in colouring, being black and white – a white band over the eye reaching to the back of the head, a mottled crest and a white throat and neck. The back is mottled, the feathers are black with white edges. The wings are mainly black with a white central band. It has a white breast and under surface except for two black bands (only one black band on the female). It nests in holes in the river bank.

The town was begun during the Sixth Dynasty (2345-2181 BC) with the granite **Temple of Bastet**, which was enlarged over the centuries up until the 18th Dynasty (1567-1320 BC) and excavated in the 19th century. Herodotus described it as the most pleasing in the whole of Egypt but also criticised the antics of up to 700,000 pilgrims who attended the licentious festivals here and quaffed wine to great excess. Nowadays, the site resembles a field of rubble yet the lack of tourists, shadowy granite statues poking out of the grass, and blocks of masonry strewn about can make you feel like an early archaeologist piecing together a temple plan. Inspection of fallen blocks reveals hieroglyphs and hidden reliefs of Bastet, while hoopoes perch on top of the crumbled columns of the Hypostyle Hall. Look out for Ramses' torso – his decapitated head and feet and arms are scattered nearby. You won't miss the standing statue of Queen Meryut Amun, though her features are clumsy in comparison the beauty of her statue at Akhmim in Middle Egypt (see page 213). An underground **cat cemetery** where many statues of Bastet have survived, lies beyond. You may (if you're lucky) get a guide to let you in, otherwise you can peer through the windows at the baby-sized remains.

Tanis

ⓘ *Daily 0800-1600, E£16, students E£5. Public transport from Zagazig involves changing at the villages of Faqos and Hassaneya before reaching San El-Hagar, from where you can take a tuk-tuk or walk 0.5 km to the site. It's a pretty lengthy process but incredibly cheap, totting up to just E£4.50. Bring a torch to explore the underground tombs.*

While most travellers from Zagazig head north to El-Mansura, those going east towards the Suez Canal might make a detour to the ruins of the Old Kingdom city of Djane, better known by its Greek name Tanis, located near the modern village of San El-Hagar 167 km from Zagazig.

Until earlier this century it was believed that Tanis was Avaris, the capital of the Hyksos Kingdom during the 15th Dynasty, but Avaris has now been discovered further to the southwest at the modern day site of Tell El-Dab'a. French archaeologists are hard at work at Tanis, as they have been since the 1860s, and what they are establishing now is that it is in fact much newer than was previously thought, certainly post-21st Dynasty, one of three 'capitals' that existed in the area. Like other ancient Delta sites, the limestone blocks were pillaged and ground down to make lime leaving only the strong granite foundations, too big and heavy to be removed. What at first glance appears as a desolate wasteland dotted with ruins, broken statues and stone, inhabited solely by shimmering emerald birds swooping and beeping, becomes increasingly impressive close up. When confronted by countless immense stelae, some cleanly broken where they fell, and deeply carved sunken reliefs sharp in the sun, it is actually quite easy to imagine the grandeur that must once have been Tanis.

The layout of the city would have been very similar to Thebes, and in fact the temples to Amun and Mut found here exactly mimic those at Karnak. They are, of course, in a much more ruinous state, and only the remnants of the **Temple of Amun** are worth investigating. Tanis differed to Thebes, however, in that the **Royal Necropolis** was housed inside the Temple of Amun where six royal tombs have been uncovered, almost intact. Some of these can be entered, necessitating much scrambling and leaping as it's not very tourist-friendly. The Tomb of Usurkon II has remains of paint, portraying Nut and the Underworld in addition to various cobras, baboons, bulls and dogs. Sheshank III's tomb still contains his sarcophagus though his mummy is now in the Egyptian Museum.

Tell Al-Maskhuta

Another ruined site on the eastern edge of the Delta is **Tell Al-Maskhuta**, which lies just south of the main Zagazig (70 km) to Ismailia (11 km) road. It has been identified as the site of the ancient town of Tjehu which was the capital of the 8th Nome of Lower Egypt and was often known by its Biblical name of Pithom. Archaeological excavations have revealed the foundations of the ancient city, a temple structure and brick chambers for single and multiple burials together with children's bodies buried in amphorae. A well preserved sphinx and a statue of Ramses II were also uncovered and are now in the gardens of the Ismailia Museum.

El-Mansura

About 55 km north of Zagazig, El-Mansura is an attractive Nile city that was founded comparatively recently (AD 1220) by the great Salah Al-Din's nephew during the Siege of Damietta by the Crusader forces. Despite its name, which means 'the Victorious', the Crusaders reoccupied Damietta in 1249 and then, following the death of Sultan Ayyub (1240-1249), which was concealed by his widow in order not to demoralise his troops, the Crusaders recaptured the town. However, when the Crusaders were weakened by a vicious bout of food poisoning, the Muslims counter-attacked and captured not only El-Mansura but also France's King Louis IX.

Today Mansura is better known as the centre of the cotton industry. During harvest time it is interesting to see the activity in the fields, but the incredibly overladen carts bring road traffic to a standstill. If you do wind up here, visit the **Mansura National Museum** ⓘ *on Sharia Bur Said, T050-224 3763, Tue-Sun, 1000-1800, E£3,* where Louis IX was held prisoner before he was eventually ransomed for the return of Damietta. The museum maps out the warring and bloodshed of the battles with the Crusaders and displays the odd bit of armour and weaponry from the time.

Monastery of St Damyanah

Continuing further along the H8 highway 25 km past Talkha, is the town of **Shirban**, which has a bridge to the east bank of the Rosetta branch of the Nile. Leaving H8 and travelling 12 km west along H7 is **Bilqas** where, 3 km to the north, is the Monastery of St Damyanah (Deir Sitt Damyanah). St Damyanah was put to death, along with another 40 maidens, under Diocletian's purges against the Christians. Normally it is isolated and difficult to reach

High Noon at Damyanah – Martyrs' Calendar

Damyanah, who was the daughter of Rome's regional governor in the time of Diocletian (AD 284-305), chose celibacy rather than marriage and took refuge with 40 other virgins in a palace built for her by her father. When her father renounced the worship of the Roman gods and converted to Christianity both he and all of the women were executed on the orders of Diocletian. His persecution of the Christians was so great that the Copts date their era, known as the Martyrs' Calendar, from the massacres of AD 284.

The first shrine to Damyanah is believed to have been built by St Helena who was the mother of emperor Constantine (AD 306-337).

except during the annual **Moulid of Damyanah** between 15-20 May, which is one of the country's largest Christian *moulids*. Thousands of pilgrims flock to the four 19th- and 20th-century churches on the site in the hope of being healed. Women praying for increased fertility and those who have lost young children are common visitors here.

Dumyat (Damietta)

Back near the Nile the easiest way north from El-Mansura is to cross the river to the Central Delta town of Talkha and head up the main H8 highway to the coastal town of Damietta (known to Egyptians as Dumyat). Furniture-making is a vitally important craft, with 'Louis Farouk' gilted chairs lining the streets and being exported throughout the Gulf from the new port, while production of confectionery and fresh fruit and vegetables adds to the economy.

The town is in many ways similar to Rosetta (see page 180), but has a much more modern facade and a significantly larger population. Damietta flourished as a trading port throughout the Middle Ages but suffered greatly during the Crusades. The Christian forces occupied the town in 1167-1168 and again in 1218-1221 when St Francis of Assisi accompanied the invaders. Worse was yet to come, for the Mamluks destroyed the city in 1250 and made the river impassable as a punishment for suspected disloyalty and to prevent further invasions. The Ottomans revived and rebuilt the town though, unlike Rosetta, many of their attractive buildings have been engulfed and you will be lucky to spot the occasional *mashrabiyya* balcony jutting from an otherwise modern edifice. The last Ottoman Pasha here surrendered to the Beys in 1801 before the time of Mohammed Ali, and the construction of the Suez Canal shifted trade to Port Said, 70 km to the east.

Though not unpleasant, being on a wide curve of the river lined with well-kept gardens, Damietta has little to attract visitors. Look out for remnants of the Ottoman buildings, and in particular the **Ma'ini Mosque** which has just been restored from utter dereliction. Microbuses can drop you at Midan Sorour very close to the mosque, which is now an active place of worship again, with a wonderful inlaid marble floor, *mashrabiyya* windows, octagonal, soaring internal arches and classic Delta-style brickwork. You may be allowed to climb the stairs to the roof and explore further interior rooms decorated with much *mashrabiyya*. Nearby, visit the **Greek Orthodox church of St Niklas and St George**, full of ancient icons and precious gifts from orthodox communities worldwide. Also close by is the new **Coptic church of St Mary** opened by Pope Shenuda in 1992, where the remains of the cleric Sidhum Bishai lie in a glass casket (reminiscent of the mummies of the pharaohs in the Egyptian Museum) plus a supposed relic of the true cross.

About 1 km from the bus station, the **Mosque of Amr Ibn el-Ars** has been rebuilt and revamped, with innumerable newly-cut marble pillars filling the aisles around the central courtyard. Just outside remain fragments of the original ancient columns and the warden will be happy to show you the adjacent shrine of Abu Mouvy. Out of town is the huge **Lake El-Manzala** which in winter teems with migrating birds including flamingos, spoonbills and herons. On the other side of the branch of the Nile there are three beach resorts, **Ras El-Bar**, **Gamassa** and **Baltim** which, although technically in the Central Delta, are most easily reached from Damietta.

Nile Delta listings

For Sleeping and Eating price codes and other relevant information, see pages 26-31.

Sleeping

Tanta *p178*

Unless you are visiting specifically for the *moulid* (when it is essential to book well in advance), there should be no problem in finding a room.

B Green House, Sharia El-Borsa, off Midan Gumhoriyya about 500 m east of the train station, T/F040-333 0320. 30 good a/c rooms with TV and fridge, restaurant, almost central location. Worth trying if **New Arafa** is full.

B New Arafa Hotel, Midan Al-Mahatta, T040-340 5040, F335 7080. Decent mid-range hotel with spacious rooms that have comfy beds, a/c, TV, fridge and adequate bathrooms. There's a restaurant, coffeeshop and alcohol available. Breakfast included. Directly outside the train station and only 250 m from the mosque at the centre of the *moulid* celebrations. Single/double E£260/380.

B-C Kafr Shishda village, past Mahala El-Kobra village, 17 km outside of Tanta. It's a pain to get to (you'll need to phone for directions) but this private residence which sleeps up to 18 people could come in handy around *moulid* time if you plan to attend for more than 1 day. 3 apartments, 2 very basic but 1 (that sleeps 4) with huge terraces and marbled bathrooms, is the attractive get-away of the artist owner whose works decorate the walls. Orange and mango trees grow in the garden, the complex backs onto the river (though it's too near the bridge to be scenic), and you can self-cater or ask for meals to be supplied.

El-Mahalla El-Kubra *p179*

C-D Omar El-Khayyam, Midan 23 July, T/F040-223 4299. The only decent hotel in town has large good-value rooms with a/c, TV and clean private showers, plus some suites. The restaurant is OK and breakfast is included.

Rashid (Rosetta) *p180*

Rashid is just 45 mins from Alexandria, so you may be better of visiting as a day trip from there (unless you have a penchant for hanging out in traditional *ahwas*, of which Rashid is crammed).

D Rasheed International Hotel, Midan Al-Horiyya, T/F045-293 4399, rasheedhotel@yahoo.com. Far and away the best hotel in Rashid, though that's not saying much. Rooms are spacious, with balcony, TV, fridge and small bathrooms. Expect curtains to be hanging off and the gloomy restaurant to be empty. However, breakfast is included and the staff kindly. Get a top floor room for amazing views over the midan to the river.

E-F El-Nile Hotel, on the Corniche, T045-2922382. The only place actually on the Corniche, some rooms are passable but others not (they won't even let you see them!), all are basic, a few have views of the river. Little English spoken, singles are E£50.

E-F Mecca Hotel, just around the corner from the El-Nile down a lane off the Corniche, Cheaper rooms on the lower levels are often full, but the recently renovated upper floor is much preferable with fresh paint and new tiles. Pay more for private bath, though shared are about acceptable. No English spoken by the irritating manager.

Zagazig *p183*

You are better off venturing here from Cairo or Alexandria on a day trip. If you do get stuck in town, you can try:

B Marina, 58 Gamal Abdel Nasser, T055-231 3934. A 3-star option that is by far the nicest place to stay. Anyone who is not watching their purse-strings should immediately head here.

E Opera, opposite the train station, no English sign, T055-230 3718. Out of the 2 budgets options, this fills up first, and it's not surprising as the **El-Zaf** next door is completely filthy, if marginally cheaper.

El-Mansura *p185*

B Marshal El-Gezirah, Sharia Gezirah El-Ward, T/F050-221 3000. About 2 km west of the town centre on the Corniche, it is the poshest in town. All rooms have balconies with nice views over gardens and the river, furnishings a bit gloomy in comparison with the marble lobby. Breakfast included. Single/double E£274/357

D Marshal, Midan Mahatta il-Atr, T/F050-223 3920-2. 57 rooms that are very cosy if slightly old fashioned, with TV, fridge, a/c and little balconies, There's a nice patisserie and coffeeshop downstairs, with free Wi-Fi. A well above average buffet breakfast is included. Singles are E£90, doubles E£150.

E Macca Touristic, 1 Sharia El-Abbasy, near the Corniche, T050-224 9910. 54 rooms, very decent for the price (doubles E£70), clean, good river views from top floors, TV, private bathrooms, pay extra for a/c, kitsch posters in the hallways, breakfast included. Bang next door to a mosque.

Dumyat (Damietta) *p186*

There are a couple of hotels near the Corniche, best of which are:

B-C Soliman Inn, 5 Sharia Galaa (just off the Corniche), T/F057-2377050. Old fashioned but not unattractive rooms with fridge, a/c, TV and decent bathrooms. Balconies have good views, though it's on a noisy road. They also have 'suites' for a silly E£500. Breakfast included, worth haggling on the price.

D-E El-Manshy, 5 Sharia El-Nokrashy, T057-232 3308. Pinky-peach paint dominates in these 20 rooms, which have depressing carpets but are clean and comfortable, with TV, a/c and small bathrooms. Down a lane off Sharia Galaa, near the Corniche, There's no lift so it feels like a lot of stairs with heavy bags and the restaurant is not appealing. Single E£80, double E£120.

Eating

Tanta *p178*

Besides the acceptable restaurants in the aforementioned hotels, there are cheap stalls around town. For fantastic stuffed pigeon (*hammam*), a Delta speciality, try **Um El-Mohamed** restaurant on Sharia Fatah. The best sweet shop in town is on Midan Sa'ha. During the *moulid* special sweets fill the shops and stalls around the central mosque and in abundance are dried chickpeas (*hummus*) sold by weight.

Rashid (Rosetta) *p180*

There are a few local eateries around the market area (Abu Youssef is good for *fuul*, *tamayia* and has OK *kushari*), plus a few stalls that grill the day's catch until the fish is positively blackened – yet delicious.

Andrea Park, 2.5 km north along the Corniche, T010-709 8595. For somewhere more salubrious, take a taxi (E£1.50) to 'Andrea Bark' (as the sign says), where a fish meal (*bouri*, rice, salads) costs E£35 per 500 g. Meals are served lunchtime only (until 1500), but the cafeteria is open until late (0400 in season) and it's a pleasant location on the river.

Mansura *p185*

There's a **Metro** supermarket where Sharia El-Gomhoriya meets the Corniche, 2.5 km west of the town centre.

🍴🍴 **Giardino**, 117 Sharia El-Gomhoriya, T050-222 2097. Closes at 0100. The 'only' place to eat in town has a restaurant upstairs (open from 1300) and café downstairs with very reasonably priced fish and chicken dishes, sandwiches, and good juices. It's near the Gamat el-Mansura (university) about 2.5 km along the Corniche.

🍴🍴-🍴 **Abou Shama**, Sharia El-Sawra, T050-225 5811. Open 0730-0100. Lots of kebabs, chickens, clay-pots and *kushari*, in a modern and inviting fast-food/take-away restaurant. Located half-way down Mansura's main shopping street, which links the railway station and Sharia Bur Said.

Festivals and events

Tanta *p178*

Oct Moulid of Sayid Ahmed El-Badawi. See page 178.

Damanhur *p179*

Jan **Jewish moulid**, at the Shrine of 19th-century mystic Abu Khatzeira.

Nov Moulid of Sheikh Abu Rish.

Zagazig *p183*

The **Moulid of Abu Khalil** takes place during the month of Shawwal (around Oct/Nov).

Transport

Tanta *p178*

Bus

Gomla bus station, 2 km north of the city centre, has hourly service (0600-2100) to all the towns mentioned in this section, plus 3 morning buses to **Port Said**. Buses to **Cairo** leave every 30 mins from 0600-2200.

Taxi

Service taxis run regularly from the bus station to **Cairo** and **Alexandria**, and to other Delta destinations. Leaving when full.

Train

There are 8 trains daily to **Cairo** calling at **Benha** and to **Alexandria** (1 hr) calling at **Damanhur**, preferable to the bus, and less frequent services to **Mansura**, **Damietta** and **Zagazig**.

El-Mallaha El-Kubra *p179*

Buses and service taxis

Superjet buses and service taxis for **Cairo** and **Tanta** leave from Midan Shown on Sharia 23rd July, while services for western Delta destinations (Kafr El-Sheikh, Disuq) leave from Zahra station. Local minibuses which can take you to either Shown or Zahra are easily picked up from Midan 23rd July. Services to Mansura, Sammanud, Alexandria and Dumyat leave from Midan Talat Harb, which is close to the railway station.

Train

There are trains to **Cairo** at 0600, 0700, 0815, 1530, 1830 and 2130 (2½ hrs) and **Alexandria** at 0900 and 1800 (2½ hrs), plus trains to Mansura every hour.

Zagazig *p183*

Bus

Buses leave from the terminal on the far side of the train tracks for **Tanta**, **El-Mansura**, **Benha**, **Alexandria**, **Ismailia** and **Port Said**.

Taxi

Service taxis congregate by the railway station. They go all over the **Delta** as well as to **Cairo** and the **Canal region**.

Train

Trains from Zagazig run daily to **Cairo**, (26 daily, 1 hr), via **Benha** (45 mins). Also to **Ismailia** (13 daily, 1½ hrs), and **Port Said** (7 daily, 2½ hrs).

El-Mansura *p185*

Bus

Buses run hourly (0800-2100) to **Cairo** (E£10) and **Alexandria** from the bus station on the west side of Midan Umm Khalsoum. It's also possible to take a bus directly to the **Sinai** and the **Canal Zone** cities.

Service taxi

Service taxis for **Cairo** also leave from Talkha service depot, which is the hub for destinations such as Mahalla, Kafr El-Sheikh, Tanta, Dumyat, Port Said and Alexandria.

Train

From Mansura, there are trains to **Cairo** at 0530, 0630, 0730, 1500 and 1800 (2½-3 hrs, 1st class E£40), **Zagazig**, **Damietta** and **Tanta**.

Dumyat (Damietta) *p186*

Bus and service taxis

From the bus station (*mauwaff*) on Sharia Galaa, there are buses every 45 mins from 0630-1930 to **Cairo** either down the main H8 highway via **Tanta** and **Benha** or the east route via **El-Mansura** and **Zagazig**. Buses to **Alexandria** leave at 0630, 0800, 1400 and 1600 (2 ½ hrs, E£20) and buses for **Port Said** leave at 0730, 0800, 0830 and 0900 (1 hr, E£3). Nearby, service taxis to **Port Said** go when full (E£3.50), as they do for **Cairo**, **Alexandria** (E£16), **El-Mansura** and other Delta towns.

Train

Although they are slower, there are trains to **Cairo**, **Alexandria**, **Tanta** and **Zagazig**.

Directory

Dumyat (Damietta) *p186*

Banks Banque du Caire and Bank of Alexandria on Sharia Galaa have ATMs and there is a branch of Barclays on the Corniche.

Middle Egypt

Contents

Footprint features

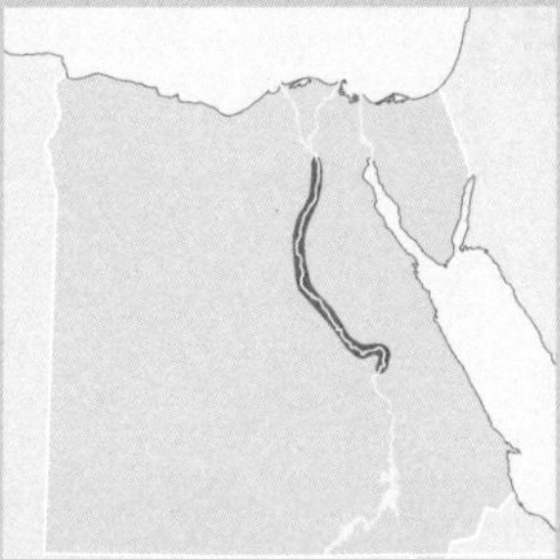

At a glance

Getting around Tourists are encouraged to travel by train, but local minibuses are an incredibly cheap way of getting around.

Time required 4-6 days.

Weather Winter is extremely pleasant. Summers are a little cooler than in Luxor and furthur south.

When not to go If you don't like crowds avoid the Moulid of the Virgin (15-30 Aug) when a million pigrims descend on the Convent of the Virgin near Assiut.

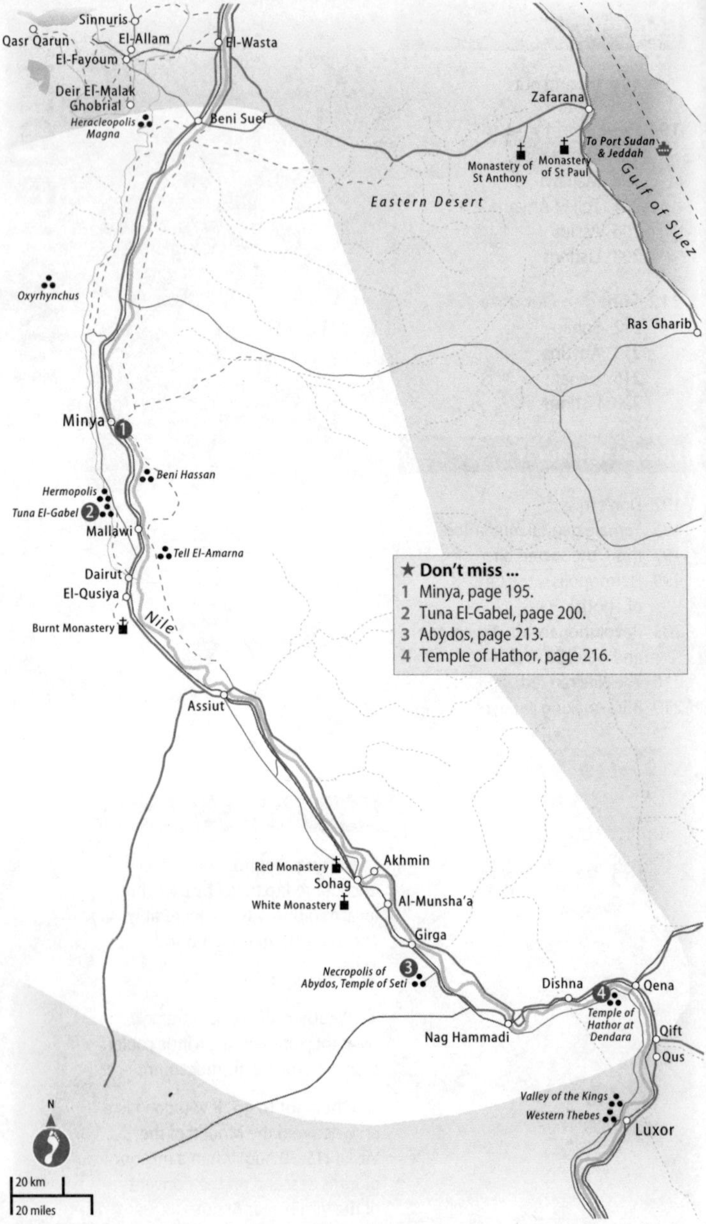
Sinnuris
Qasr Qarun
El-Allam
El-Wasta
El-Fayoum
Deir El-Malak Ghobrial
Heracleopolis Magna
Beni Suef
Zafarana
To Port Sudan & Jeddah
Monastery of St Anthony
Monastery of St Paul
Gulf of Suez
Eastern Desert
Oxyrhynchus
Ras Gharib
Minya
1
Beni Hassan
Hermopolis
Tuna El-Gabel
2
Mallawi
Tell El-Amarna
Dairut
El-Qusiya
Burnt Monastery
Nile
★ Don't miss ...
1 Minya, page 195.
2 Tuna El-Gabel, page 200.
3 Abydos, page 213.
4 Temple of Hathor, page 216.
Assiut
Red Monastery
Akhmin
Sohag
White Monastery
Al-Munsha'a
Girga
3
Necropolis of Abydos, Temple of Seti
Dishna
4
Qena
Temple of Hathor at Dendara
Nag Hammadi
Qift
Qus
Valley of the Kings
Western Thebes
Luxor
N
20 km
20 miles

Most travellers cross the stretch of land between Cairo and Qena gazing out at the striking contrast of verdant Nile Valley and stark gold desert from the window of a train or plane, wholly bypassing the heartland and its scenic and archaeological treasures. But if you're keen to get a taste of the way most Egyptians live, Middle Egypt is the place to be. Small-time farmers work the land using traditional techniques and age-old tools. Women wash clothes and pots in the river and canals. Buffalo sleep under drooping date palms and donkeys carry children through the mud-brick villages. The provincial pace is slow and the frenzy of Cairo far away. So unfrequented a destination is this region that one can easily go days without seeing another foreign face.

The area known as Middle Egypt, so dubbed by 19th-century archaeologists, is tangibly distinct from Upper Egypt to the south. It has a large Coptic Christian population (at 20%, it's twice the national average), and an economy that is based more on sugar cane than tourism. Though the security policies of the government (see page 194) may suggest otherwise, the threat of Islamist militants has largely abated, and the people are among the friendliest you will meet.

One of the prettiest cities in the whole country is Minya, the provincial capital hailed as the 'the Bride of Upper Egypt', where majestic colonial buildings have stood the test of time and a relaxing Corniche is the locals' pride and joy. Though she's matured a bit, Minya is still a sleepy, romantic place with many of Middle Egypt's most notable ancient sights all within range. Climbing the cliff to the tombs of Beni Hassan or crossing the desert plains to the necropolis of Tuna El-Gabel has a mystique that harks back to the time of 19th-century exploration. Further south, the unquestionable highlights of the region are the magnificent temples of Abydos and Dendara, containing the most perfectly preserved and perfectly executed reliefs of any pharaonic structure in the land.

Ins and outs

Warning

Since the terrorist attacks that began in Middle Egypt in 1992 and climaxed with the 1997 massacre at the Hatshepsut Temple in Luxor, Middle Egypt and, for a brief time, Egypt at large, was on the travel advisory lists of the US State Department and Britain's Foreign Office. In order to remedy the tourism slump, the government trampled on the Islamist uprising and developed a security system to ensure tourists' safety. As a result, visitors to the region will find themselves under the constant eye of the tourist police. Though the extent of this protection is highly variable, you may find yourself escorted around some towns by a guard and confined to your hotel after nightfall. It can be quite an annoyance and a bit of patience and humour go a long way. Luxor and Aswan (see pages 225 and 299) are security 'bubbles' in the Nile Valley, and as such do not require the perpetual presence of tourist police. Since the temples of Dendara and Abydos, the most significant sights in Middle Egypt, are a day trip from Luxor, it is easiest to stay in Luxor and take the a tour to the sights, however this means you have to share the space with coach-loads of others.

Restricted travel

Though there are more than a dozen daily trains travelling from Cairo to the provincial capitals of Middle Egypt, foreigners are technically only permitted to ride on the 2200, which is guarded by policemen. However, with insistence and persistence you can board any train at Giza or Ramses stations and pay on board. There are frequent buses from Cairo that will probably let you on, but you never know. Therefore, travelling by train offers the most reliability to Middle Egypt, and is also faster, more consistent and comfortable. For train travel once in Middle Egypt, purchasing tickets is easy or again just board the train and pay the conductor once in motion. Service taxis around Middle Egypt are sometimes reluctant to accept foreigners when travelling between towns, as until recently travel on microbuses by foreigners was restricted (not all drivers are aware of the easing of restrictions). Services/micros are a flexible and very cheap option. If you want to drive, inquire with the tourist authority.

Beni Suef to Assiut

→ *Colour map 1, A1-B2.*

About 130 km south of Cairo, with a population of 86,000, Beni Suef is the northernmost provincial capital in Middle Egypt. There's no reason to visit this uneventful and somewhat rickety town, especially since the few nearby sights can be seen on day trips from Cairo or the Fayoum. But if you get stuck for a night en route elsewhere, you can explore Beni Suef on foot in less than an hour.

▸▸ *For listings, see pages 208-211.*

Beni Suef

Except for the **Maidoum Pyramid** ⓘ *see page 173, from Beni Suef a private taxi costs around E£100,* which is easily seen on a trip from the Fayoum Oasis or Cairo, there is little to see save a small museum and the ancient, poorly preserved cities of **Heracleopolis** and **Oxyrhynchus** ⓘ *15 km west of Beni Suef and 9 km west of Beni Mazar on the route to Minya. Expect to pay a taxi around E£80 for the round trip, depending on how long you intend to visit.*

Female genital mutilation

Though the practice is illegal, Egypt has one of the highest female genital mutilation (FGM) rates in the world. In 2000, USAID funded a health survey in Egypt that found 97% of women of reproductive age have undergone the practice. Some progress was shown in terms of percentage of the women's daughters (78% of whom had undergone circumcision in 2000; 83% in 1995). There is no doctrinal basis for FGM in either Islam or Christianity, and it is as common a practice among Copts as it is Muslims. Furthermore, many Egyptians believe circumcision helps to maintain female chastity and cleanliness. However, following the FGM-related deaths of two girls in 2007, the first lady, Suzanne Mubarak, has spoken out and announced the launch of a national campaign to tackle the issue. Plus the Ministry of Health and Population has issued a decree banning medical personnel from performing FGM operations in any clinic or hospital, and the supreme religious authorities at Al-Azhar have made a statement denouncing any basis for FGM in the Islamic Sharia law.

Agree on the price before setting off to avoid a struggle. Excursions can also be made from here to the **monasteries** of **St Anthony** and **St Paul** (see pages 463 and 464).

Minya → *For listings, see pages 208-211. Colour map 3, B1.*

Minya, 110 km south of Beni Suef and 245 km from Cairo on the west bank of the Nile, is among the most picturesque and charming cities in Egypt. People are warm and relaxed, and the large Christian population is very much in evidence. There's a wide green patch that runs alongside the river, and at night and on weekends locals flood the Corniche with their families to picnic and play. Though Minya and nearby Mallawi were at the centre of militant Islamist attacks in the mid-1990s, the last 10 years have seen relative peace. Happily, security efforts have relaxed slightly in the last year, although some hotels are still off-limits to foreign visitors and security guards insist on accompanying independent travellers to nearby sites. Around town, however, you are free to explore without a police escort – just write and sign a declaration that states you wish to be alone and will take responsibility for anything that might happen to you.

Ins and outs

Getting there and around All trains running between Cairo and Luxor stop in Minya. At Ramses and Giza stations you will be encouraged to take an official tourist train, but it is possible to board any other train if you insist. Minya train station is in the town centre, on Sharia Gumhoriyya, the main street, which runs northeast to the riverfront about 1 km away. Buses stopping at Minya depart from Cairo's Turgoman station daily (five hours). Service taxis to Minya leave Cairo from Midan Giza (four hours). The main service taxi depot and bus terminals are five minutes' walk to the right (south) of the railway station along Sharia Sa'ad Zaghloul. It is possible to take service taxis to some sites around Minya, though with a police escort this can be stressful. Hiring a private taxi costs around E£175-200 (to see some/all of the sites on the east bank) and E£220-250 to visit Tell El-Amarna and Tuna El-Gabel for the day. Minya is small enough to easily explore on foot. It's also possible to take short trips around town with a *hantour* (horse-drawn carriage).

No in-town trip should cost more than E£10. Expect to pay around E£25 for an hour's meander. ▸▸ *See Transport, page 210.*

Information The Minya provincial government is now keen to promote tourism and the **ETA office** ⓘ *T086-237 1521, Sat-Thu 0900-1400*, on the Corniche is worth a visit and has OK maps of the town. There is also an **information office** ⓘ *daily 0800-2300*, at the train station but they are short on facts.

Sights

The centre of Minya is bounded on the east by the Nile; the railway line and the Ibrahimiya Canal run parallel to the west, giving it the feel of an island. Across the river lie fields of farmland running up to a small mountain chain announcing the desert beyond. On this east bank 'New Minya' is being developed, which includes the Akhenaten Museum – an eye-catching and out-of-place pyramid structure. Although there are no ancient sites in the town itself, the Corniche is charming and you can hire the *felucca* ferry to the rural island in the middle of the Nile richly cultivated with crops. There are numerous old villas and apartments romantically crumbling, elegant streets and squares lined with local coffee shops, and active markets where shopping is relaxing and stress-free. Worth visiting are the **El-Lowmati Mosque**, just south of the ETA office, which utilizes marble and granite Graeco-Roman pillars in its peaceful courtyard, and the **El-Amrowi Mosque** (a further 100 m south), which has fine floral designs painted on the old wooden ceiling. Both date from the Fatamid era.

Deir Al-Adhra, Tehna Al-Gebel and the Frazer Tombs

ⓘ *Deir Al-Ahdra on the east bank, about 25 km north of Minya, is reached via service taxi to Samalut, then a pickup to a car ferry across the Nile. Then either hire a service, or walk through the fields and up the steps in the mountain to the church. A time-efficient alternative is to include it in a full-day excursion to all sites on the east bank for E£200.*

The monastery of **Deir Al-Ahdra** is an evocative place, set atop a hill with views across the lush farmlands to the Nile. Founded by Empress Helena in the fourth century, the niche to the right of the altar is supposedly the site of a cave that sheltered the Holy Family during their flight to Egypt. In the tranquil central nave, one of the 12 columns contains a hollowed-out baptismal font. Forty days after Coptic Easter, the church comes alive when thousands of pilgrims arrive for the week-long Feast of the Assumption. About 5 km south, **Tehna Al-Gebel** is a dramatic walk among fallen columns and over huge slabs to a crag containing some roughly hewn tombs. In one, a capital of Hathor's head hangs from the ceiling, in another a crocodile mummy with vicious teeth gathers dust, while Graeco-Romans in togas guard the entrance to a pharaonic chamber. A further 5 km south, the **Frazer Tombs** ⓘ *0800-1700, a crazy E£15, students E£10*, are a short walk up the cliff from pretty pastoral lowlands. Three are worth investigating to view larger-than-life defaced statues and clear hieroglyphs. Take a torch, and look for the man and wife who've been holding each other's hand since the days of the Old Kingdom.

Zawiyyet Al-Mayyeteen

ⓘ *7 km south of Minya on the east bank, behind the village of Al-Sawada, a pleasant walk through villages if the police don't spot you. Or stop in a taxi en route to Beni Hassan.*

This extraordinary cemetery, one of the largest in the world, stretches for miles. The endless domes of mud-brick Islamic mausoleums defy description when viewed from

Ibis – the sacred bird

This bird has been held in great esteem by man for over 5000 years and was considered sacred by ancient Egyptians as a representation of Thoth. It is depicted in coronation scenes listing the years of the king's rule. The bird's 'ability' to write is traced to the movements of the beak in the water and the resemblance of that beak to a held writing implement.

The main cult centre of the ibis-god Thoth was Hermopolis Magna, but mummies of the sacred ibis have been found all over the country (though now the bird is rare in Africa north of the Sahara). They were found in tombs of kings and queens and in cemeteries set aside just for ibis mummies. A simple explanation equates the annual flooding of the Nile with the arrival of this bird and its disappearance as the water receded. Ceremonies to greet the rising water incorporated large flocks of these migrating birds.

above, and present a challenging maze to wander through. Among the jumble of alleyways lies the tomb of Hoda Sharawi, pioneer of the Egyptian feminist movement, who dared to unveil herself at Cairo Railway Station in 1923. At the southern end of the cemetery, the Tomb of Nefersekheru, a royal scribe from the 18th to 19th Dynasty, contains remnants of statues and wall reliefs. Little else remains of the pharaonic city of Hebenu, save the debris of a pyramid.

Beni Hassan

ⓘ *Daily 0800-1700, E£25, students E£15, photographs not permitted. You will encounter many guards who will unlock the tombs for you, all of whom expect a tip of E£2 or so. Have lots of* baksheesh *on hand to facilitate this. To reach Beni Hassan, you should be permitted to take a service taxi to the small town of Abu Qirkus on the main Minya–Mallawi road, from where you can find a pickup to the banks of the Nile. From here a ferry costs E£10 per person, less if you are in a group. The easier option is to take a private taxi from Minya across the bridge to the east bank and south to Beni Hassan. Depending on how long you intend to stay and how good your bargaining skills are, it should cost E£60-80 (or, if you plan to include it in a full-day excursion to all sites on the east bank, E£200).*

Named after an ancient Arab tribe, Beni Hassan is the site of a neat row of 11th and 12th Dynasty (2050-1786 BC) tombs dug into the barren rock face of hills overlooking the River Nile. They mark a stage in the evolution of tomb design from the lateral Old Kingdom (2686-2181 BC) style *mastabas* to the deep New Kingdom (1567-1085 BC) royal tombs of the Valley of the Kings (see page 257). Of the 39 tombs, only 12 were decorated and only four can currently be visited (although *baksheesh* can yield entry into others). These were not royal tombs but built for regional rulers and military leaders, and are the first to show illustrations of sports, games and the daily life of the people of the Middle Kingdom (rather than those of offerings and magic formulae for reaching the afterlife that are more commonly associated with the royal tombs). Dean Arthur Penrhyn Stanley, who visited in 1852, rightly noted how the tombs reveal how "gay and agile these ancient people could be... there is nothing of death or judgement here". Beautiful tableaux of muscular wresters, artistic depictions of colourful birds and animals, and an almost total lack of other visitors make Beni Hassan a mesmerizing and memorable experience.

Tomb of Amenemhat (No 2) Regional governor and commander-in-chief at the time of Senusert I (1971-1928 BC), Amenemhat's tomb has a columned portico façade and a lintel bearing a list of his titles. The texts inside the door relate to his numerous military campaigns south to Kush and praise his administrative skills. Particular reference is made to a year when there was heavy flooding of the Nile but taxes were not increased. The main chamber has a vaulted roof that was supported by four columns (three remain) and is decorated with an orange chequered pattern. To the back of the chamber the niche contains the remnants of statues of Amenemhat, his wife and his mother. The walls are finely decorated with a cooking scene on the right of the south wall. In the middle Amenemhat is seated during an offering ceremony, while the north wall has scenes of hunting and military preparations. On the east wall are startlingly lucid illustrations of wrestling poses, plus an attack on a fortress and boats sailing towards Abydos. Look for the delicate depiction of gazelles on their hind legs nibbling at a bush on the west wall, to the left on entering the tomb.

Tomb of Khnumhotep (No 3) The tomb of Amenemhat's successor Khnumhotep has a proto-Doric columned portico leading into a central chamber with a niche for his statue at the far end. Inscriptions of great historical importance about feudal life in the 12th Dynasty were discovered in the tomb. Below the scene of desert hunting on the north wall is a lower register showing the arrival of an Asian caravan, which offers gifts to the governor. Their foreign clothing and features are described in minute detail. On the east wall, Khnumhotep and his wife are shown fishing and fowling in the marshes, on punts using harpoons; above the niche are exquisitely painted species of birds in flight. On the south wall he inspects boat building and then sails to Abydos while other registers show dyers, weavers, carpenters and other artisans.

Tomb of Baqet III (No 15) The tomb of the governor of the Oryx Nome dates back to the 11th Dynasty (2050-1991 BC). On the north wall are scenes of a desert hunt with four mythological animals in the midst of the normal animals (including some copulating gazelles). On the east wall there is a tableaux of 200 wrestling positions, seemingly between two different races, while the south wall reveals events from Baqet's turbulent life including an attack on a fortress.

Tomb of Kheti (No 17) Baqet's son and heir's tomb is quite similar to that of his father. The same close-encounter wrestling scenes are to be found on the east wall and there are representations of craftsmen and desert hunts. On the south wall Kheti is shown watching agricultural scenes (note the spotty and colourful breeds of cattle) and receiving offerings from under a sunshade attended by his servants and a dwarf. In the chamber, two columns with lotus capitals remain of the original six.

Mallawi → *Colour map 3, B1.*

Not the most prepossessing of places, Mallawi is somewhere people merely stop off when using public transport to reach archaeological sites such as Tel El-Amarna, Tuna El-Gabel and the Meir Tombs. Replaced by Minya as the regional capital in 1824, Mallawi has been in a state of decline ever since. Today its littered streets make it a town most people avoid, particularly because Minya is just up the road. At present there are no hotels that accept tourists so it's not possible to stay overnight. There is, however, a good **museum**

Hermopolis – the City of Thoth

Hermopolis was the City of Thoth, the gods' scribe and vizier, the reckoner of time, the inventor of writing and, following his association with Khonsu, a moon-god with mastery of science and knowledge. Thoth is depicted either with a man's body and the head of a sacred ibis or as a white and very well-endowed baboon. Although his cult originated further north in the Nile Delta, its greatest following was in Middle Egypt.

In the city's complex creation myth, known as the Hermopolitan cosmogony, the chaos before the world's creation was thought to have had four characteristics: water, infinity, darkness and invisibility, each represented by a male and a female god who collectively are known as the Hermopolitan Ogdoad (company of eight). A primordial mound and the cosmic egg arose from the chaos and hatched the sun god who then began to organize the world from the chaos. While most people believed the Ogdoad itself produced the cosmic egg, Thoth's devotees credited him alone with having laid it and therefore having been connected with the creation of the world. A modern interpretation of the link between his representation as a baboon and his role in the Creation is associated with baboons' habit of shrieking at sunrise and thus being the first to welcome the sun. The baboon was also connected with the moon and there are often statues of baboons with moons on their heads. This is probably because of the ancient Egyptians' love of puns and word-play because the word for 'to orbit' was apparently similar to that for 'baboon'. Although by the New Kingdom this Hermopolitan version of the Creation myth had been supplanted by the Heliopolitan cosmogony, Thoth's cult continued until the later Ptolemaic era.

ⓘ *Sat-Thu 0800-1500, E£6, students E£3, cameras E£10,* which displays some beautiful and unusual findings from Tuna El-Gabel and Hermopolis. Among the many mummified ibis and animals on display is a baboon with amulets still embedded in the linen wrappings, as well as the mini-sarcophagi that housed their remains. Painted plaster death masks from Hermopolis individualize the deceased, and decorative coffins made from a variety of materials are in an excellent state of preservation. Upstairs look out for the coins minted with the profiles of tousle-haired Roman emperors and 2000-year-old palm baskets identical to those still woven today.

Antinopolis

ⓘ *It is necessary to travel north from Mallawi to take the ferry east across the Nile to visit the village of Sheikh Abada, neighbouring the ruined Roman town of Antinopolis.*

Construction started here in AD 130 in memory of the beautiful Antonius, a favourite who was accompanying Emperor Hadrian on an official visit to the area. It is said that he drowned himself in the Nile to prevent a danger prophesied for the Emperor. (It had been foretold that someone of importance would drown in the Nile on this visit.) Early travellers described the splendid columns and archways, now dismantled and dispersed, but the plan of the town can still be traced. When Flaubert visited in 1850, he saw "the ruin *par excellence*, of which one says, 'And yet this was a city' ".

Hermopolis Magna and Tuna El-Gabel

The ruined seventh Dynasty (2181-2173 BC) city of Hermopolis Magna was the ancient city of Khmunu, the capital of the Hare Nome. Ruled by the High Priest, it had a dual function as both a secular and religious centre. It was once quite large, extending to both sides of the Nile's banks, with a temple surrounded by a 15-m-thick wall at its centre. The town regained importance under the Ptolemies, who associated the ibis-god Thoth with their god Hermes and gave the town its name. Today, little remains of the city except a large mound of rubble, mud-brick foundations and some emotive rose-granite columns, many still standing while others languish among the ruins. An open-air museum nearby contains grimy findings from the old city, as well as two massive sandstone baboons (with defaced phalluses) that once held up the ceiling of the temple of Thoth.

In the same period, a vast necropolis, now known as **Tuna El-Gabel** ⓘ *daily 0800-1600, E£20, students E£10, cameras not permitted (without* baksheesh*)*, was established 6 km west across a very hot, empty and dramatic desert road from the small town of that name and 10 km southwest of Hermopolis. There is comparatively little to see above ground because most of the tombs lie below the sand dunes that would cover the whole site if it were not for the lonely workers' constant efforts to keep them at bay. To the right, on the way to the necropolis, is a stele, one of 14 that marked the borders of the kingdom of Tell El-Amarna. Set behind glass, it's worth climbing up the long flight of steps to see the clearly preserved inscriptions.

Tuna El-Gabel is best known for its sacred animal necropolis set in catacombs that are thought to stretch as far as Hermopolis. Many mummified remains of baboons and ibises, which were formerly bred here, were discovered, but the best preserved among them have been relocated to museums around the country. These were deemed sacred animals because they represented the two living images of Thoth. By the entrance to the catacombs you'll be shown some decrepit examples of ibis mummies and baboon skulls, before descending to a spooky chamber with a niche containing Thoth in his baboon form. Passageways lead off, lined with loculi for ibis and scattered with tiny sarcophagi, past bits of bones and bandages and huge piles of battered amphorae lying in side chambers. Stairs lead enticingly into the dark, and one flight descends to a limestone sarcophagus belonging to a high priest of mummification. Take a torch for this subterranean expedition.

A few hundred metres south is the main part of the **City of the Dead**, modelled on a real city with streets and some tombs that resemble houses. Egyptians traditionally went to visit their dead relatives and took a meal or spent the night in the mausoleum. Some of the tombs therefore have more than one chamber and a few have an additional storey or even a kitchen. The City of the Dead's most interesting building is the splendid **tomb-chapel of Petosiris** who was the High Priest of Thoth at Hermopolis. His exquisite inlaid wooden coffin is on display in the Museum in Cairo. Built in 350 BC, the chapel's wall decorations are a blend of pharaonic and Greek artwork, evident in the Greek togas. The vestibule has illustrations of traditional activities: farming, brick-making, wood-working and jewellery-making. The winemaking process is beautifully detailed, from the harvesting of grapes off elaborate vines, then trodden by muscular youths, to the vatting process in urns. Every inch of the main chamber is covered with colourful reliefs, particularly complex and complete are the bottom friezes showing a procession adorned with lotus flowers, birds and palm fronds. Look on the right-hand wall to see a frieze of nine stoic baboons, their brown fur and pink faces still bright. The mausoleum was a family tomb, and the inner shrine is dedicated to the father and brother of the tomb owner. On either side of the door

Footprint Mini Atlas
Egypt

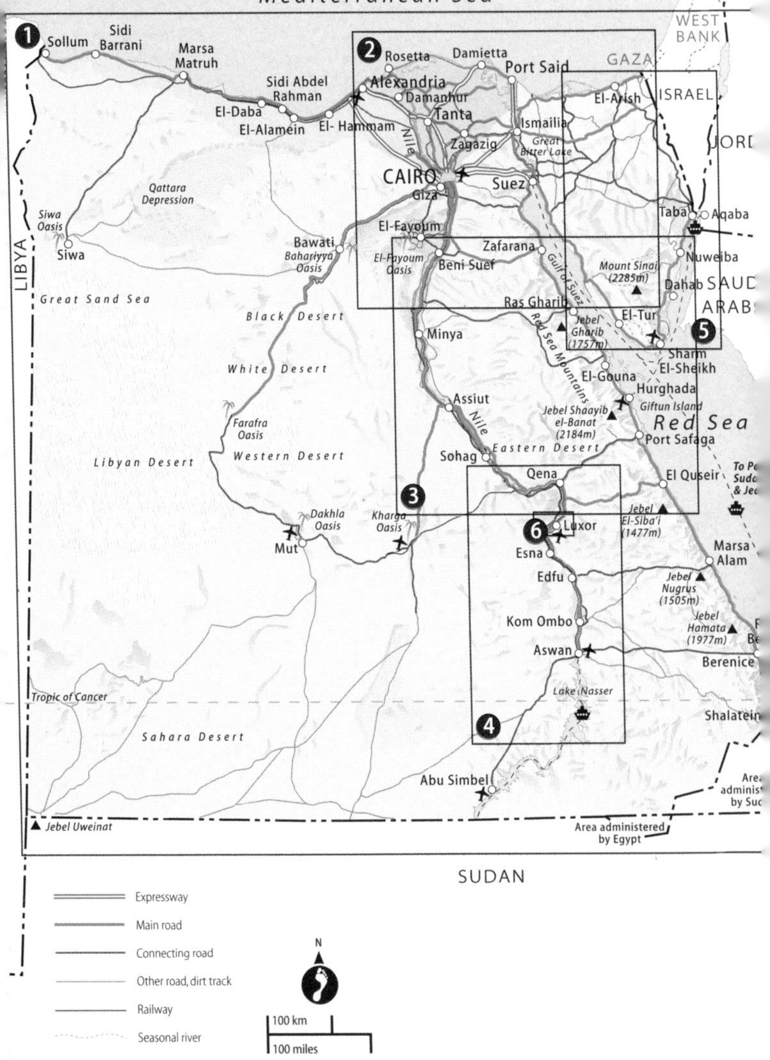

Map 1

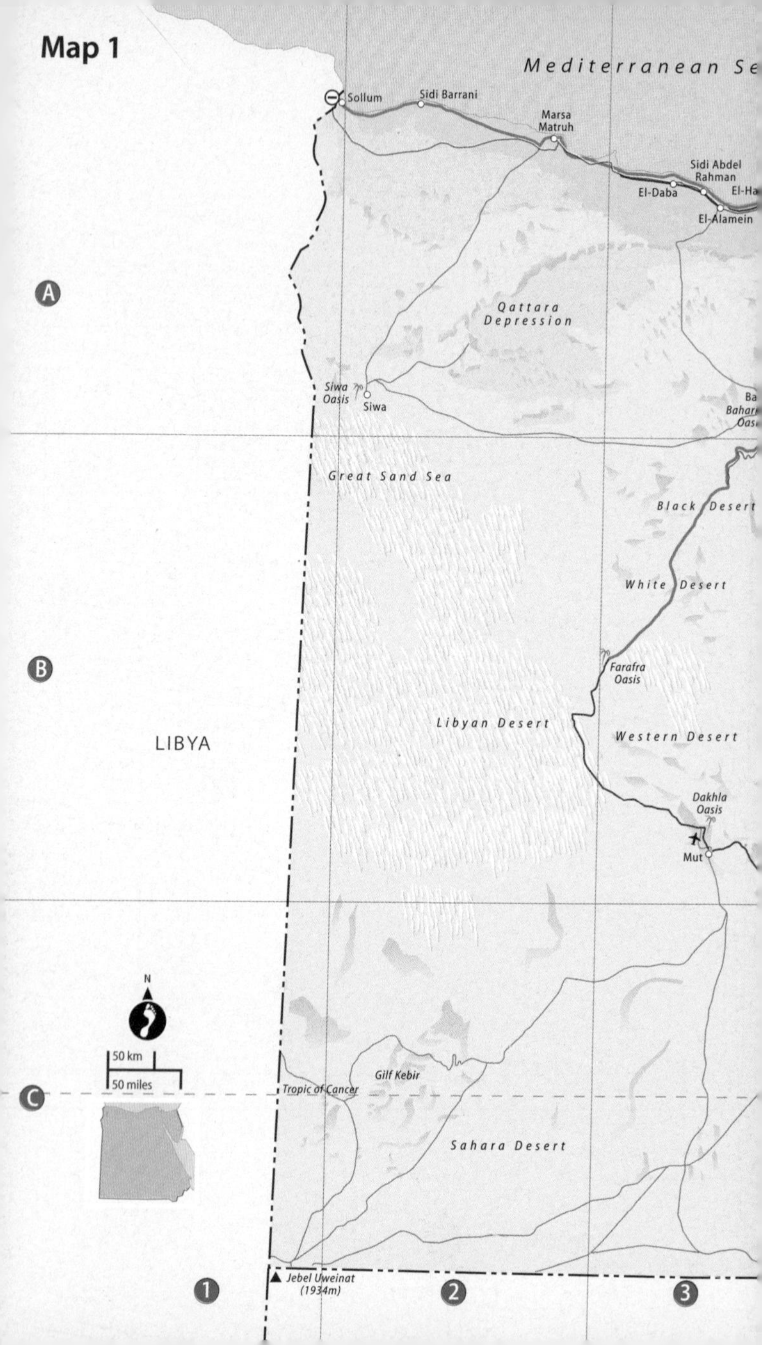
Mediterranean Se
Sollum
Sidi Barrani
Marsa Matruh
Sidi Abdel Rahman
El-Daba
El-Ha
El-Alamein
A
Qattara Depression
Siwa Oasis
Siwa
Ba
Bahar
Oas
Great Sand Sea
Black Desert
White Desert
B
Farafra Oasis
Libyan Desert
LIBYA
Western Desert
Dakhla Oasis
Mut
N
50 km
50 miles
Gilf Kebir
C
Tropic of Cancer
Sahara Desert
Jebel Uweinat (1934m)
1
2
3

WEST BANK
GAZA
JORDAN
ISRAEL
A
Damietta
Port Said
Alexandria
Nile
Great Bitter Lake
CAIRO
Suez
Taba
Aqaba
El-Fayoum
El-Fayoum Oasis
Beni Suef
Zafarana
Nuweiba
Gulf of Suez
SAUDI ARABIA
Mount Sinai (2285m)
Dahab
Ras Gharib
Red Sea Mountains
Jebel Gharib (1757m)
Minya
Sharm El-Sheikh
El-Gouna
Hurghada
Giftun Island
Assiut
Nile
Jebel Shaayib el-Banat (2184m)
B
Port Safaga
Red Sea
Eastern Desert
Sohag
Qena
Qift
El Quseir
To Saudi Arabia
Jebel El-Siba'i (1477m)
Luxor
Kharga Oasis
Esna
Marsa Alam
Edfu
Jebel Nugrus (1505m)
Kom Ombo
Jebel Hamata (1977m)
Aswan
Berenice
Ras Benas
Lake Nasser
C
Shalatein
Area administered by Sudan
Abu Simbel
Jebel Elba
Area administered by Egypt
SUDAN
4
5
6

Map 2

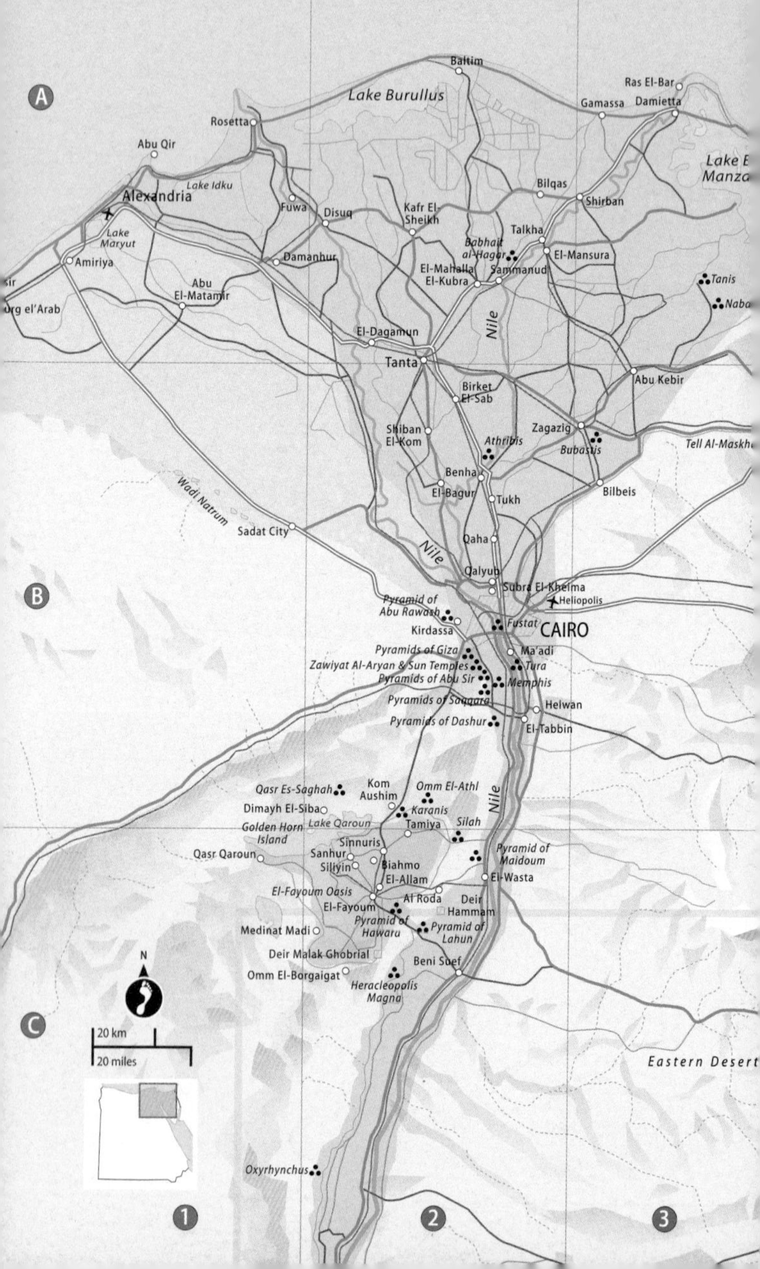

A
B
C
1
2
3
Baltim
Ras El-Bar
Lake Burullus
Gamassa
Damietta
Rosetta
Abu Qir
Lake Idku
Alexandria
Fuwa
Disuq
Kafr El-Sheikh
Bilqas
Shirban
Lake Maryut
Amiriya
Damanhur
Talkha
Babhait al-Hagar
El-Mansura
El-Mahalla El-Kubra
Sammanud
Tanis
Abu El-Matamir
Nile
El-Dagamun
Tanta
Abu Kebir
Birket El-Sab
Shiban El-Kom
Zagazig
Athribis
Bubastis
Wadi Natrum
Benha
El-Bagur
Tukh
Bilbeis
Sadat City
Qaha
Qalyub
Subra El-Kheima
Heliopolis
Pyramid of Abu Rawash
Kirdassa
Fustat
CAIRO
Pyramids of Giza
Ma'adi
Zawiyat Al-Aryan & Sun Temples
Tura
Pyramids of Abu Sir
Memphis
Pyramids of Saqqara
Helwan
Pyramids of Dashur
El-Tabbin
Qasr Es-Saghah
Kom Aushim
Omm El-Athl
Dimayh El-Siba
Karanis
Golden Horn Island
Lake Qaroun
Tamiya
Silah
Qasr Qaroun
Sinnuris
Sanhur
Siliyin
Biahmo
Pyramid of Maidoum
El-Allam
El-Wasta
El-Fayoum Oasis
Al Roda
Deir Hammam
El-Fayoum
Pyramid of Hawara
Pyramid of Lahun
Medinat Madi
Deir Malak Ghobrial
Beni Suef
Omm El-Borgaigat
Heracleopolis Magna
N
20 km
20 miles
Eastern Desert
Oxyrhynchus

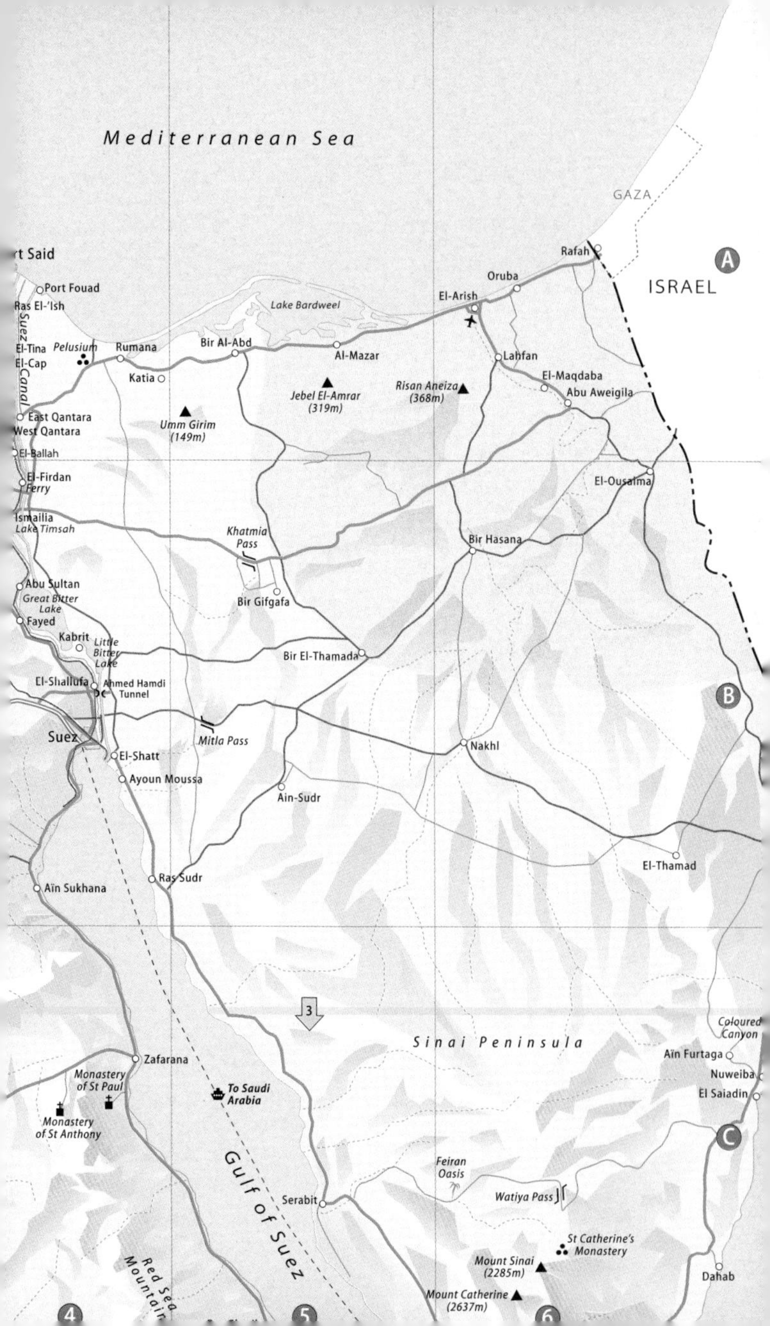

Mediterranean Sea
GAZA
rt Said
Rafah
A
ISRAEL
Oruba
El-Arish
Port Fouad
Ras El-'Ish
Lake Bardweel
Suez Canal
El-Tina
Pelusium
Rumana
Bir Al-Abd
Al-Mazar
Lahfan
El-Cap
Katia
Jebel El-Amrar (319m)
Risan Aneiza (368m)
El-Maqdaba
Abu Aweigila
Umm Girim (149m)
East Qantara
West Qantara
El-Ballah
El-Firdan Ferry
El-Ousaima
Ismailia
Lake Timsah
Khatmia Pass
Bir Hasana
Abu Sultan
Great Bitter Lake
Bir Gifgafa
Fayed
Kabrit
Little Bitter Lake
Bir El-Thamada
El-Shallufa
Ahmed Hamdi Tunnel
B
Suez
Mitla Pass
Nakhl
El-Shatt
Ayoun Moussa
Ain-Sudr
El-Thamad
Ras Sudr
Aïn Sukhana
3
Sinai Peninsula
Coloured Canyon
Aïn Furtaga
Nuweiba
El Saiadin
Zafarana
Monastery of St Paul
To Saudi Arabia
Monastery of St Anthony
C
Gulf of Suez
Feiran Oasis
Serabit
Watiya Pass
St Catherine's Monastery
Mount Sinai (2285m)
Dahab
Red Sea Mountains
Mount Catherine (2637m)
4
5
6

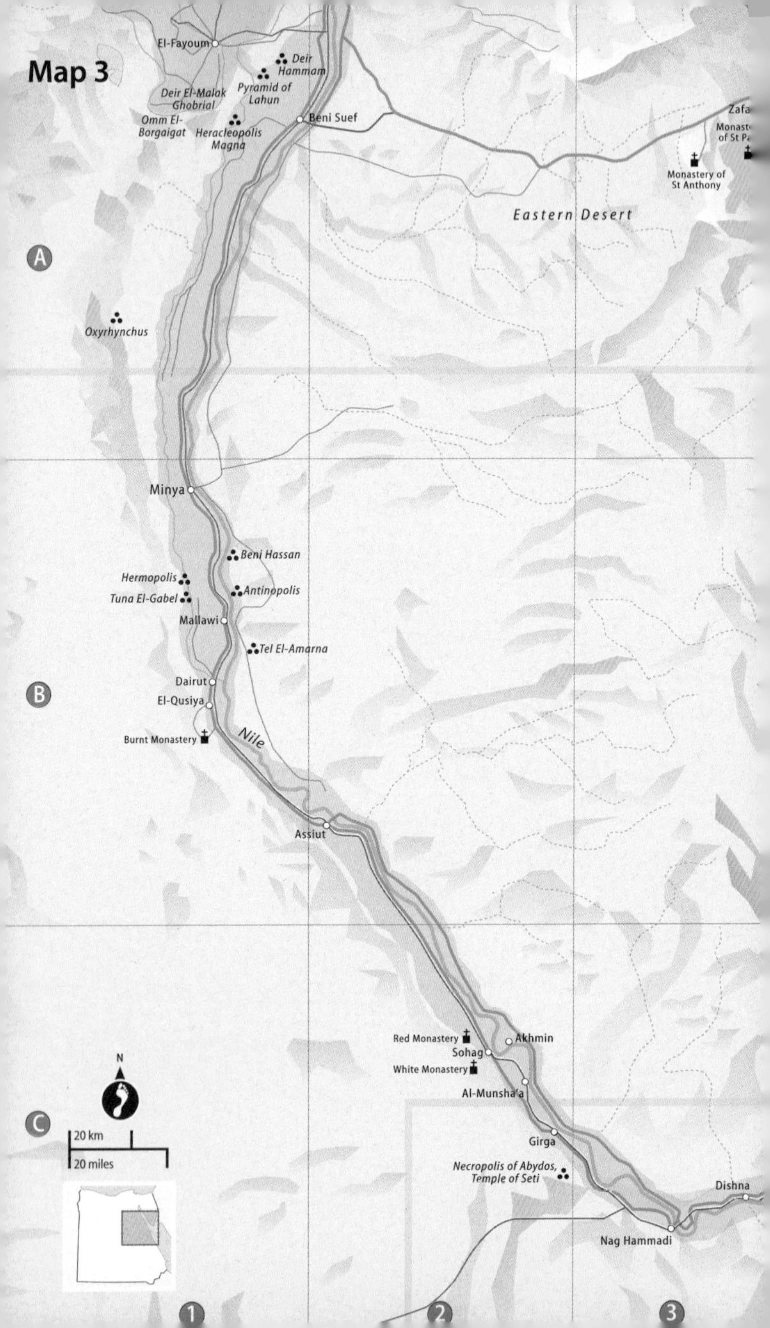

Map 3
El-Fayoum
Deir Hammam
Pyramid of Lahun
Deir El-Malak Ghobrial
Omm El-Borgaigat
Heracleopolis Magna
Beni Suef
Zafa
Monast of St Pa
Monastery of St Anthony
Eastern Desert
A
Oxyrhynchus
Minya
Beni Hassan
Hermopolis
Antinopolis
Tuna El-Gabel
Mallawi
Tel El-Amarna
Dairut
B
El-Qusiya
Burnt Monastery
Nile
Assiut
Red Monastery
Akhmin
Sohag
White Monastery
N
Al-Munsha'a
C
20 km
Girga
20 miles
Necropolis of Abydos, Temple of Seti
Dishna
Nag Hammadi
1
2
3

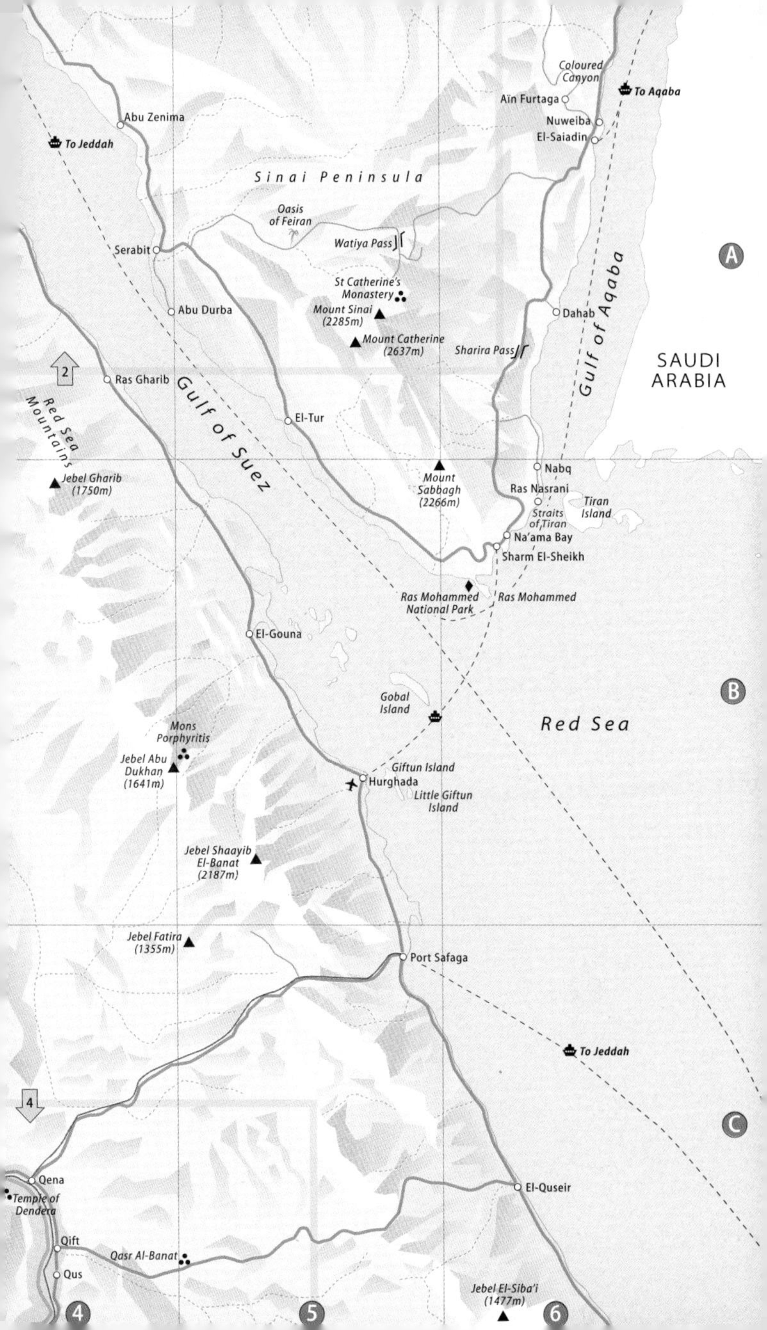
Coloured Canyon
To Aqaba
Aïn Furtaga
Nuweiba
El-Saiadin
Abu Zenima
To Jeddah
Sinai Peninsula
Oasis of Feiran
Watiya Pass
Serabit
A
St Catherine's Monastery
Mount Sinai (2285m)
Abu Durba
Dahab
Gulf of Aqaba
Mount Catherine (2637m)
Sharira Pass
SAUDI ARABIA
2
Ras Gharib
Gulf of Suez
Red Sea Mountains
El-Tur
Mount Sabbagh (2266m)
Nabq
Jebel Gharib (1750m)
Ras Nasrani
Tiran Island
Straits of Tiran
Na'ama Bay
Sharm El-Sheikh
Ras Mohammed National Park
Ras Mohammed
El-Gouna
B
Gobal Island
Red Sea
Mons Porphyritis
Jebel Abu Dukhan (1641m)
Giftun Island
Hurghada
Little Giftun Island
Jebel Shaayib El-Banat (2187m)
Jebel Fatira (1355m)
Port Safaga
To Jeddah
4
C
Qena
Temple of Dendera
El-Quseir
Qift
Qasr Al-Banat
Qus
Jebel El-Siba'i (1477m)
4
5
6

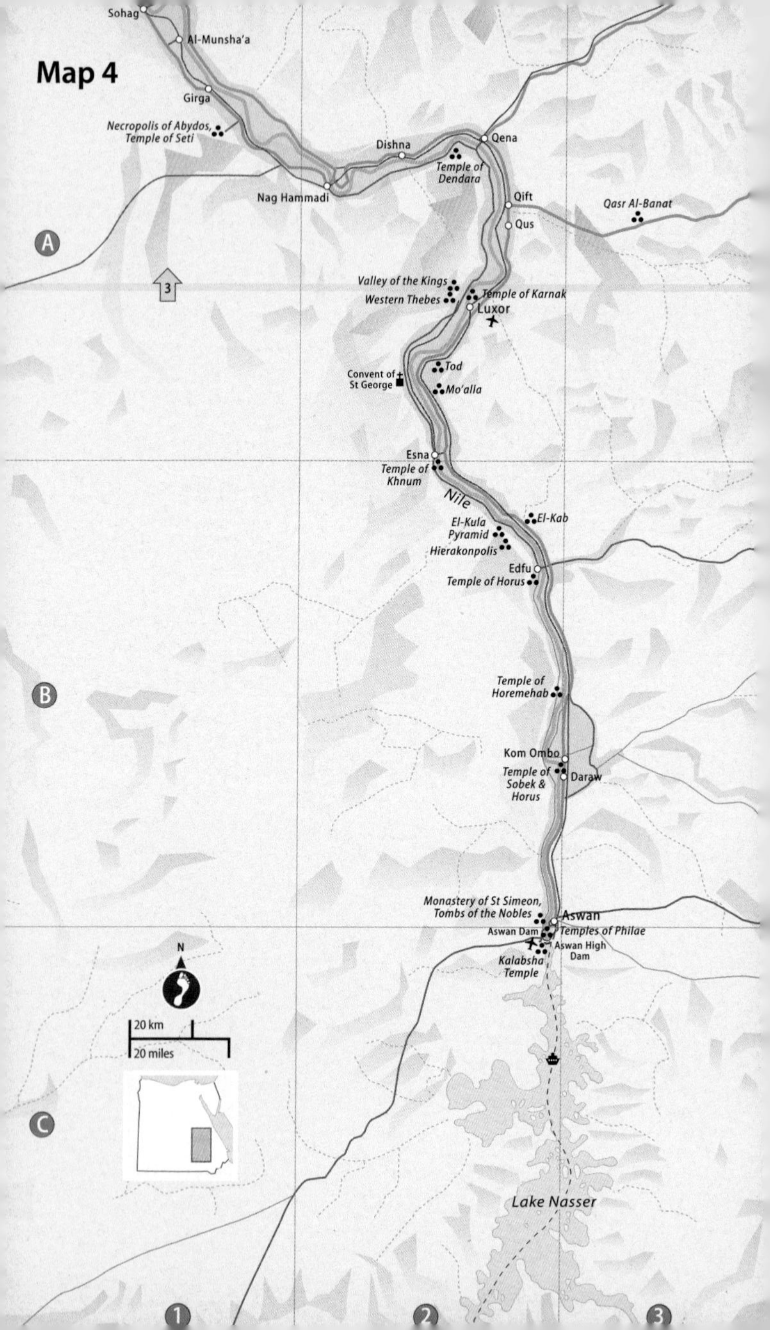

Map 4
Sohag
Al-Munsha'a
Girga
Necropolis of Abydos,
Temple of Seti
Dishna
Qena
Temple of
Dendara
Nag Hammadi
Qift
Qus
Qasr Al-Banat
A
3
Valley of the Kings
Western Thebes
Temple of Karnak
Luxor
Tod
Convent of
St George
Mo'alla
Esna
Temple of
Khnum
Nile
El-Kab
El-Kula
Pyramid
Hierakonpolis
Edfu
Temple of Horus
B
Temple of
Horemehab
Kom Ombo
Temple of
Sobek &
Horus
Daraw
Monastery of St Simeon,
Tombs of the Nobles
Aswan
Aswan Dam
Temples of Philae
Aswan High
Dam
Kalabsha
Temple
N
20 km
20 miles
C
Lake Nasser
1
2
3

Map 5
GAZA
Rafah
Oruba
El-Arish
Lake Bardweel
Al-Abd
Misfaq
Al-Mazar
Lahfan
Jebel El-Amrar (319m)
Risan Aneiza (368m)
El-Maqdaba
Abu Aweigila
El-Ousaima
N
20 km
20 miles
A
ISRAEL
atmia Pass
Bir Hasana
Bir Gifgafa
Giddi Pass
Bir El-Thamada
tla Pass
Nakhl
2
Ain-Sudr
JORDAN
El-Thamad
Ras en Naqb
Eilat
Aqaba
Taba
B
Gez Fara'un
Coloured Canyon
Sinai Peninsula
Aïn Furtaga
Nuweiba
3
Abu Zenima
To Saudi Arabia
Gulf of Suez
Feiran Oasis
Watiya Pass
Gulf of Aqaba
SAUDI ARABIA
Serabit
St Catherine's Monastery
Mount Sinai (2285m)
Abu Durba
Dahab
Mount Catherine (2637m)
Ras Gharib
C
El Tur
Mount Sabbagh (2266m)
Nabq
Jebel Gharib (1757m)
Ras Nasrani
Straits of Tiran
Tiran Island
Naama Bay
4
5
Sharm El-Sheikh
6
Red Sea
Ras Mohammed National Park
Ras Mohammed

Map 6 Luxor/Thebes

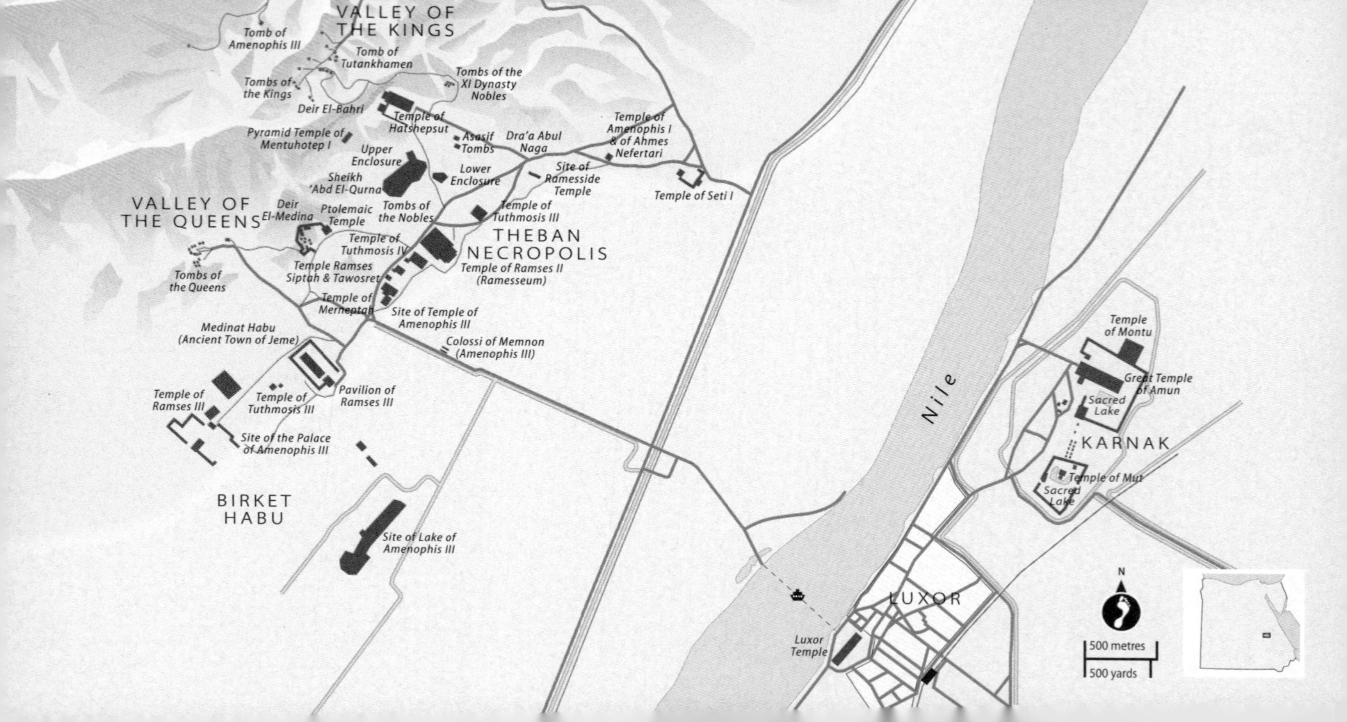

Map symbols

Capital city
Other city, town
International border
Regional border
Customs
Contours (approx)
Mountain, volcano
Mountain pass
Escarpment
Glacier
Salt flat
Rocks
Seasonal marshland
Beach, sandbank
Waterfall
Reef
National highway
Paved road
Unpaved or *ripio* (gravel) road
Track
Footpath
Railway
Railway with station
Airport
Bus station
Metro station
Cable car
Funicular
Ferry
Pedestrianized street
Tunnel
One way-street
Steps
Bridge
Fortified wall
Park, garden, stadium
Sleeping
Eating
Bars & clubs

Building
Sight
Cathedral, church
Chinese temple
Hindu temple
Meru
Mosque
Stupa
Synagogue
Tourist office
Museum
Post office
Police
Bank
Internet
Telephone
Market
Medical services
Parking
Petrol
Golf
Archaeological site
National park, wildlife reserve
Viewing point
Campsite
Refuge, lodge
Castle, fort
Diving
Deciduous, coniferous, palm trees
Mangrove
Hide
Vineyard, winery
Distillery
Shipwreck
Historic battlefield
Related map

Index

to the shrine are offering and sacrifice scenes, plus a large scarab beetle and superb sun-discs. In the shrine are illustrations from traditional Egyptian funerary texts with the east wall depicting a funerary procession. The actual burial chambers, where three generations of high priests were buried, are 8 m below the shrine.

The nearby two-storey tomb-chapel of **Isadora** dates from 120 BC and still contains the well-preserved petrified mummy of a young woman. Legend tells of a beautiful girl, forbidden by her father to marry her lover. Her death by drowning in the sacred Nile as she rowed to meet her beloved led to the brief establishment of a cult for her. Also worth a visit is the tomb known as the **House of Graffiti** that has been restored and contains a kitchen, various rooms and a chamber where the deceased was exposed before being buried in the funerary shaft. A huge dilapidated **waterwheel**, a short walk further on, has a shaft 70 m deep that can be accessed if you so desire, although hundreds of bats hang about in here.

Note Much of the important material found at these two sites is in the museum in Cairo but the Mallawi museum (open mornings only) also features a number of items from here.

Tell El-Amarna → *Colour map 3, B1.*

Midway between Minya and Assiut, 12 km south of Mallawi, Tell El-Amarna is the East Bank city founded by Pharaoh Amenhotesp IV (1379-1362 BC). Better known as Akhenaten, he left Thebes (Luxor) to establish a totally new and heretical monotheistic religion. Little remains today because most of the temples and palaces were destroyed by subsequent pharaohs, who reverted back to a polytheistic religion and used the masonry of Tell El-Amarna to construct their own buildings elsewhere. Clouds of sand obscure the remnants of the fabled city, tomb murals have been defaced and obliterated, potsherds and mud-bricks stand in piles where once there were temples. Yet the site still has plenty of atmosphere, perhaps because of its utterly harsh bleakness.

Ins and outs

Getting there Though tour groups are returning to the area, independent travellers are rare, in part because of the restrictions around public transport. Unless you have your own car, you will probably have to hire a private taxi and be escorted by a policeman from Minya or Assiut. Independent drivers, who will also almost certainly require a police escort, should head south from Mallawi to the village of Deir El-Mawas and then east to the ferry crossing. The river can easily be accessed by catching any southbound bus or pickup from the depot just south of the Mallawi train station at the bridge between the canal and the railway tracks. You can cross the river by motorboat, car ferry (E£2 for tourists, E£16 for a vehicle), *felucca* or tourist boat (E£4 round trip). There is a tourist information office on the west bank next to the ferry.

History

Amenhotep IV (1417-1379 BC) and his dark-skinned and possibly Nubian 'chief wife', Queen Tiy, still inspire more speculation than any other pharaonic dynasty. Early in his reign, Amenhotep espoused the worship of the cult of Aten, an aspect of the sun god depicted as human and mentioned in early texts. Some scholars suggest the belief was adopted from his father who may have privately subscribed to such ideas. Amenhotep IV, however, espoused it so strongly, at the expense of Amun and the other gods, that it upset the high priests of Amun in Thebes. As a result, in the fifth year of his reign in 1374 BC, he and his wife Nefertiti moved the capital to Akhetaten ('Horizon of Aten') halfway between Thebes and Memphis at Tell El-Amarna in order to make a clean break with previous traditions. For those of a romantic disposition the large gully or river *wadi* cutting through the eastern cliffs has been likened to the Egyptian symbol for the horizon. It has been suggested that it was because the sun rose from behind these cliffs that Amenhotep IV chose this as the site for his new city of Akhetaten.

On arrival, he changed his name to Akhenaten or 'Servant of Aten' while Nefertiti became Nefernefruaten or 'Beautiful are the Beauties of the Aten'. In the 12th year of his reign he adopted a more confrontational approach to the old cults and his decision to close down all the old temples probably led to unrest because of the detrimental economic effect caused by the temple being closed. There is some evidence that Akhenaten was criticized for not defending Egypt's borders and for jeopardizing the territories previously won by his expansionist father.

How Akhenaten's reign ended is still a mystery. One theory is that Akhenaten rejected his wife Nefertiti and made his son-in-law Smenkhkare the co-regent. Some have interpreted the fact that the two men lived together, and some of their poses in the murals, suggest proof of a homosexual relationship. Smenkhkare, who was both the husband of Akhenaten's eldest daughter and his half-brother, is thought to have continued ruling for a year after Akhenaten's death in 1362 BC but soon died himself. The other, more contentious, interpretation of events is that, far from splitting with Nefertiti, the pharaoh actually made her co-regent and his equal. She may then have adopted Smenkhkare as her official name and been illustrated in a different way. However, only the cartouches can be used to identify the figures, which makes the theory a suitably interesting alternative. The reality is that no one knows the truth.

Worship of Aten did not long outlive its creator. In 1361 BC Smenkhkare was succeeded by Tutankhamen (1361-1352 BC), another of Amenhotep III's sons and Akhenaten's half-brother, who returned to the Thebes-based cult of Amun. He and his successors attempted to eradicate all traces of Akhenaten and the city of Akhetaten was subsequently destroyed and pillaged by Seti I (1318-1304 BC) so that nothing was known of the city or its cult until the second half of the 20th century.

Apart from the romantic story of Akhenaten, the importance of the city lies in its short history. Although about 5 km long, the city was built and occupied for no more than 25 years. When abandoned, a record of late 18th-Dynasty life remained, depicting everything from peasants in small houses to the official buildings and palaces. Most urban sites in Egypt have

Tell El-Amarna

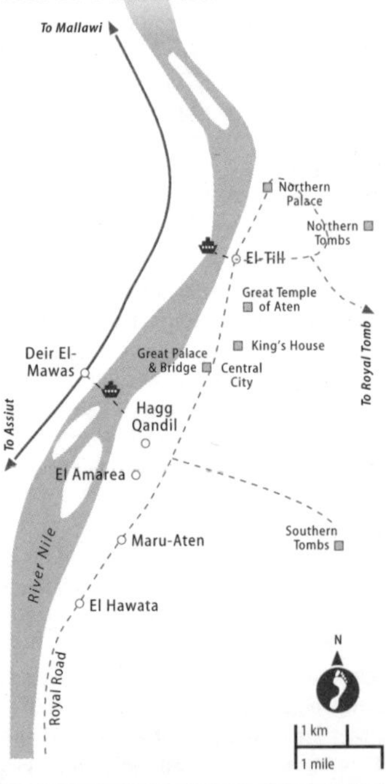

Revolutionary art: Akhenaten and Nefertiti

The new settlement of Akhetaten was not only revolutionary in its religion but also in the arts. A number of craftsmen and artists were recruited to work on the decoration of the new city. Rather than focusing almost exclusively on the theme of resurrection and the afterlife they also depicted daily life and nature in greater detail than before. There were two main art styles with the first depicting Akhenaten with an elongated face, protruding stomach, and feminine thighs (as demonstrated by the famous colossi from his temple at Karnak, which are now in the museum in Cairo) while the later style is much less distorted. It has been suggested, although not proven, that the earlier distortions were partly due to the difficulties that the artists had in radically altering their style. Alternatively it may have been that the decoration was undertaken too hastily using inferior limestone and varying quality carvings. It has been suggested that Akhenaten intended that the depictions of himself and his family, which appear in the shrines of private houses in Tell El-Amarna, should be worshipped and that only he could directly mediate with the god. The Aten disc is only shown when he or the royal family are present. While the pharaoh was always, at least nominally, accepted as a god or the gods it appears that Akhenaten may have been particularly literal about this convention.

Unusually, in scenes of royal dinners, both the pharaoh and his wife were depicted and the presence of both their cartouches almost as co-rulers demonstrated the difference in Amenhotep IV's approach. Wives had never previously been portrayed as equal and their names had never appeared side by side.

either been lost under modern towns and villages or have been badly damaged and so Tell El-Amarna offers a unique record.

The site

ⓘ *Oct-May 0700-1600, Jun-Sep 0700-1700, there is a E£1 per person fee to be paid at the office on exiting the ferry landing, the main ticket office is about 2 km further where there is a café and small shop, E£45, students E£25. Separately, the Northern and Southern tombs are E£25/15 each, and the Royal tomb an overpriced E£20/10. The ticket office also sells bus rides to the sites, E£5 to each site if there are 8 or more people, or E£50 for the whole bus.*

The huge site is made up of a number of different areas – the city ruins to the south of El-Till; the Northern Tombs, 5 km to the east; the Royal Tomb, further away up a hidden valley; the rarely visited Southern Tombs, southeast of El-Till; and the Northern Palace near the riverbank north of the village. Plan at least half a day for a thorough taste of the site. If you want to know more about current excavation work at Tell El-Amarna, especially regarding occupation of the tombs by early Coptic monks, visit www.armanaproject.com.

The Northern Tombs

The most interesting site at Tell El-Amarna is the necropolis for the nobles, many of whom were not originally from Thebes but were elevated to their position by Akhenaten after he arrived here. Most of the tombs devote more space and decoration to Akhenaten himself than to the occupant. It's advisable to bring a torch if you want to examine the elevated reliefs, though tombs do now have lighting.

Tomb of Huya (No 1) Huya was the superintendent of the Royal Harem and Steward of Akhenaten's mother Queen Tiy. At the entrance he is pictured praying next to a hymn to Aten and on either side of the door are highly unusual scenes of Queen Tiy drinking wine with Akhenaten, Nefertiti and princesses. On the left wall is a scene showing Akhenaten in a procession being carried on his litter towards the Hall of Tribute where ambassadors from Kush and Syria await his arrival. To the left and right of the entrance to the shrine are somewhat damaged scenes of Huya being decorated by Akhenaten from the Window of Appearances. On the right-hand wall Akhenaten leads Queen Tiy to see the temple he has built for his parents while the staff who worked on the temple are displayed below. The shrine is undecorated but the niche has some scenes of funerary offerings, mourning, and a curious representation of the funerary furniture.

Tomb of Mery-Re II (No 2) This tomb of the Royal Scribe, Overseer of the Two Treasuries and Overseer of the Harem of the Great Royal Wife Nefertiti, was started during Akhenaten's reign but finished by Smenkhkare and follows a similar plan to Huya's tomb. After the now destroyed Hymn to the Aten at the entrance, Mery-Re is shown worshipping the Aten and then to the left Nefertiti offers Akhenaten a drink next to three young princesses. Further along, the upper register depicts Mery-Re receiving a golden collar from Akhenaten, while foreigners look on, and then being acclaimed by his household. On the right wall Akhenaten, Nefertiti and their daughters are at the centre of a scene divided into three subjects. The first shows black slaves, with their faces painted red, carrying gold bars and coins. The tables are heaped with piles of gold and a number of slaves are shown carrying their children. In the second scene, Asian people pay homage to Akhenaten and bring him treasures and a number of female slaves. The last scene shows a double procession with the empty royal litter and the royal guard while treasures are offered to the Pharaoh. The rest of the tomb was never finished except for a defaced scene on the back wall of Mery-Re being rewarded by Smenkhkare and his wife.

Tomb of Ahmose (No 3) The tomb of Akhenaten's fan bearer, who therefore had the right to a noble's tomb, is with another group of four tombs just beyond the next valley. The tomb was unfinished and some of the scenes are damaged. Most of them depict aspects of the palace including the throne room, the royal apartments and some of Akhenaten's army preparing for battle.

Tomb of Mery-Re I (No 4) The tomb of the High Priest of Aten and the father of Mery-Re II has three chambers and is one of the best preserved. On the entrance wall he is shown in adoration before Aten while in the columned and flower-decorated vestibule Mery-Re and his wife Tenro are shown in prayer. On the left-hand wall of the main chamber, which now only has two of the original four columns, Mery-Re is invested with the High Priest's gold collar by Akhenaten. The royal family and escorts are then portrayed in an important scene (because it shows the height of the buildings), leaving the palace for the Great Temple in chariots. There are hymns to Aten and offering scenes above the entrance to the unfinished inner chambers. On the right of the main chamber Akhenaten, accompanied by Nefertiti and two of their daughters, is in the Great Temple making sacrifices to Aten. Other scenes show Akhenaten after the sacrifice with his daughters playing musical instruments while beggars await alms in the corner. Below is a scene that has given archaeologists a rare insight into the original appearance of the city. Mery-Re is seen showing the Pharaoh the stocks in the temple with views towards the port, a stable and the royal boats on the Nile.

Tomb of Pentu (No 5) and Tomb of Panehsi (No 6) The nearby tomb of the royal scribe and chief physician, is badly disfigured and it is better to see the Tomb of Panehsi, which is 500 m to the south. This High Priest's tomb, which has four columns in each of the two chambers, was later transformed by the Copts into a chapel but many of the original decorations are still in place. In the first chamber are scenes of Akhenaten decorating Panehsi. On the left-hand wall, the royal family worship Aten in front of their household. There are further scenes of Akhenaten including one on the far wall on the left behind a Coptic baptistry and one by the stairs leading down to the funerary chamber, showing him with Nefertiti and their daughters in their chariots surrounded by troops.

The Royal Tomb This tomb, which was closed from 1934 until recently, lies in a hidden valley where the sun is seen to rise each dawn. Now connected by a road, the journey is worth it as much for the romantic approach to the ravine as what lies inside. Deeply cut sun reliefs in the main chamber are the main eye-catcher, precious little else remains but for realistic depictions in a side chamber of the family worshipping the Aten. It is unclear whether Akhenaton was actually buried here, as any body would have presumably been destroyed in the aftermath of his reign. Currently the Supreme Council of Antiquities are promoting the mummy found in tomb KV55 in the Valley of the Kings as being that of the rebel pharaoh; DNA-tests that may shed light on the mystery are still pending.

The Northern Palace, about 1.5 km north of El-Till, was recleared years ago by the Egyptian Antiquities Service. Although it is really only for enthusiasts it is possible to walk around and enter this large mud-brick ruin where a section of mosaic can still be seen.

Other sites Leaving El-Till you pass the remains of the massive **Great Temple of Aten** on the right, which is now partly covered by the modern cemetery. There are then the vague ruins in the sand of a mixture of administrative and residential buildings until one reaches the **Small Temple of Aten**. Just before the temple there is a large mud-brick structure on either side of the road. This is the remains of the bridge that crossed the road and connected the **King's House** to the east with the so-called **Great Palace**. It was also where Akhenaten and Nefertiti bestowed gifts on the populace from the Window of Appearances, as depicted in so many of the tomb reliefs. This area, including the palace, temple and ancillary buildings is the **Central City** that was the administrative and religious centre of the ancient city.

The Southern Tombs

Visitors to the Southern Tombs usually travel on the north–south road along the edge of the cultivated area that almost exactly follows the ancient 'royal road' linking all Akhetaten's official buildings. The tombs are spread over seven low hills in two groups but only about five of the 18 tombs are of any real interest. Among them is the **Tomb of Ay (No 25)** (1352-1348 BC), Akhenaten's maternal uncle and vizier to Amenhotep III, Akhenaten and Tutankhamen whom he succeeded as pharaoh when he died. There are unproven theories either that his wife Tiyi was Nefertiti's wet-nurse or that the couple conceived Tutankhamen. Bright red paint remains on the ceiling, and pillars half-hewn from the rock create the impression of a mini-temple. On the right-hand wall of the vestibule, every kink of the couple's beautiful braided hair is meticulously reproduced. On the left of the entrance is a fine relief of Akhenaton and Nefertiti bestowing gifts from the Window of Appearances. Despite this being the finest tomb in the necropolis, the southern tombs are rarely visited by tourists.

Assiut → *For listings, see pages 208-211. Colour map 3, B2.*

Assiut, 109 km south of Minya, is the largest city south of Cairo and infamous for being one of the Islamic fundamentalist strongholds and the scene of some of Egypt's worst and longest standing communal violence. The fighting has for the most part subsided and a new attraction since appeared. In autumn of 2000, the local church of St Mark became the chosen site of the regular apparition of the Virgin Mary. Witnesses claimed the miracle manifested itself as an ethereal light above the church tower. Beyond that, Assiut has little to offer the tourist save a few interesting monasteries, proximity to the Meir tombs, and Nile Valley access to the Western Desert oases. But neither is it an unpleasant place, there are lively bazaars (in the area known as Al-Qasreya on the southwest of town), some attractive spots by the Nile, decent hotels and some magnificent rambling old villas in varying states of decrepitude. Should you wish to break a journey south, it is a more appealing town than Sohag.

Ins and outs

Getting there and around There is a small **tourist office** ⓘ *T088-230 5110, Sat-Thu, 0830-2000,* in the Governorate building on the Corniche with helpful staff.

Note In Assiut, police protection is usually provided – whether you want it, or not. In an emergency contact the **police** ⓘ *T088-232 2225*, or **hospital** ⓘ *T088-232 3329.*

The train, bus and northern service taxi stations are all on Sharia El-Geish and most of the best hotels are on or near the same street. Roads in front of the stations run to the Nile; roads behind the railway station lead to the *souks*. The airport, 10 km northwest of the city, has no bus connection. » *See Transport, page 211.*

Sights

The Convent of the Virgin ⓘ *12 km west of Assiut, a taxi costs E£30-40 with waiting time.* The convent (*Deir El-Ahdra*), incorporating a huge smoke-blackened cave, was originally built by Empress Helena in AD 328. The main cave was originally a pharaonic quarry. Copts believe the Holy Family sought refuge from Herod in the caves at Dirunka. Every year in August, up to 1 million pilgrims come to witness the icons paraded around the cave-church during the Moulid of the Virgin. In all there are seven churches in the complex and a service is performed in a different one every day of the week. It is claimed that the Church of the Blessed Virgin Mary was the first church built in Egypt, although the current church was constructed in 1964 and badly damaged by Islamic extremists in 1988. Extremely gentle, enthusiastic and friendly nuns will show you around. There is dormitory accommodation for pilgrims. A gift shop sells photos showing the various miracles that have been witnessed in the area including the one in the cave itself when a brilliant white dove, which nobody saw with their own eyes, was captured on film during the annual August procession with the icon of the Virgin. On the other side of the main road are a number of Catholic buildings also dedicated to the Virgin Mary. Though they lack the character of the Convent they could be worth a quick visit if you have a patient taxi driver. The pink church with two towers has some extravagant dioramas and grottoes in its crypt.

The Burnt Monastery ⓘ *Further afield, 42 km north of Assiut, 5 km out of El-Qusiya. A monk will provide a guided tour of the monastery and surrounds, which are open to visitors 24 hrs a day except on feast days. A taxi to here and the nearby Meir Tombs costs E£80-100 with waiting* *time*. The Burnt Monastery *(Deir El-Muharraq)* dates back to the fourth century and gets its name from its location on the edge of the burning desert. Given the attacks on Coptic churches by the area's Islamic fundamentalists, it's an apt name. The Burnt Monastery is the largest and wealthiest in Middle Egypt and the location of the **Feast of Consecration**, an annual *moulid* involving up to 50,000 pilgrims. The heart of the monastery is the old church next to the square keep, as it is here that the Holy Family apparently spent over six months during the flight from Herod. It was their longest hiding place anywhere in Egypt as logically it was the safest being so far from the Nile, the main means of travel and communication. The immaculate compound also contains an 1882 church with an Italian marble iconostasis, the Abbot's enviable mansion, and a seventh-century keep where monks took sanctuary in times of siege. The bodies of any who died during these times had to be stashed in a gap between the top floor and the roof. The monastery is considered a place of healing and has had a continuous community of monks since its foundation, now numbering around 120. Until the mid-20th century, there were a number of Ethiopian mendicants residing here who left an iconostasis in the old church as their legacy.

The Meir Tombs ⓘ *50 km northwest of Assiut, 6 km north of the village of Meir, 0800-1700, E£20 students E£10*. In a barren limestone ridge reached via steps swamped by sand drifts, the Meir Tombs are a place for those who like to have antiquities to themselves. Six of the tombs can be visited and are notable for the lively naturalist paintings within, although statutory discovered inside has been re-homed in museums. **Tombs 1** (Niankh-Pepi) and **2** are linked. Every wall is covered with paintings of 720 deities and smoke-blackened by the cooking fires of early Copts who used the tombs as monastic cells. It is interesting to see the grid patterns and line drawings of incomplete murals that give a clear demonstration of how the process of decoration was achieved. **Tomb 3** shows yawning hippos bathing in the river and a cow giving birth. In **Tomb 4** (Senbi) look out for the emaciated wild-haired man on the right-hand wall and lions copulating, while the left-hand wall shows boat-building before a ferocious battle on water commences. Women play a prominent role in **Tomb 6** (Ukhhotep III), perhaps because of the local cult of Hathor, and the soft pastel colourings of peach, mint, ochre and azure are particularly beautiful.

Beni Suef to Assiut listings

For Sleeping and Eating price codes and other relevant information, see pages 26-31.

Sleeping

Beni Suef *p194*

B Semiramis, Sharia Safir Zaghloul, Midan El-Mahat, T082-232 2092. 30 rooms, a poor-quality hotel just north of the train station, but with 2 official stars it's the best in town. No gastronomic delights, but for safety and comfort eat here.

C Bakri Palace, Al-Riyadhi St, next to Banque Misr, T082-233 2329. Equipped with glass lift, the hotel offers decent a/c rooms with private bath. The restaurant has an extensive menu of reasonable fare, including seafood.

Minya *p195*

Minya has a good range of hotels to suit most budgets. Some prefer to tell foreigners that they are full (even when plenty of keys are dangling behind the receptionist's head), but the ones listed should be accommodating.

AL Grand Aton Hotel, 2 km north of the train station, Corniche El-Nil, T086-234 2993-5. Large, fairly attractive chalets with terraces next to the river have good bathrooms and amenities. There's a pleasant garden, pool and coffee shop (meals can be eaten indoors or out). It was being refurbished at the time of writing.

A Nefertiti/MG Hotel, Corniche El-Nil, T086-234 1515/6/8. Opposite the **Aton** across the tree-lined Corniche, this is where most tour groups head. Rooms in the main building have balconies overlooking the Nile, but garden chalets without a river view are slightly cheaper, larger and more appealing. The **Greenhouse** restaurant serves up meals for E£40-50 and there's a bar and small swimming pool. Efficient and friendly staff. Still commonly known by locals as the **Etap**, if the taxi driver is failing to understand you. The hotel is due to be refurbished in the near future and will reopen as the 'MG', so call ahead to check prices.

B Cleopatra, Sharia Taha Hussein, T086-237 0800. One block back from the Corniche, about 1.5 km north from the town centre, this spotless hotel has some kitsch styling, with plenty of mirrors, heavy patterns and pharaonic images. However, staff are well-trained and rooms well-equipped with small balconies, there are 2 restaurants with beer and views, free Wi-Fi in the public areas or internet cable in the rooms. Singles E£150, doubles E£250 with breakfast.

B Horus Resort, Corniche El-Nil, T086-2316 660/1, www.horusresortmenia.com. Cheerfully decorated modern rooms have good mid-range facilities, chalet-style with nice bathrooms, while public spaces are grandiose and sterile. Don't expect everything to work perfectly, but there's a large inviting Nile-side pool and beer is served on the spacious terraces to compensate. Kids play-area, retailers, free Wi-Fi, all in all it's a good deal. Breakfast buffet included. Singles E£225, doubles E£275.

C King Akhenaten Hotel, Corniche El-Nil, a 15-min walk from the train station, T086-236 5917/8, www.kingakhenaton.8m.com. Clean, comfy rooms, a bit out-dated (brown is the theme) but fairly easy on the Western eye. Some corner rooms have huge balconies with great Nile and mountain views. Excellent breakfast buffet, the top-floor restaurant also serves reasonably priced meals (no alcohol), Wi-Fi is E£20 per day. A popular choice.

E Lotus, 1 Sharia Port Said, T086-236 4541/00. 1 km from both the station and the river, rooms are clean, if gloomily decorated, with rather noisy a/c, private bath, TV, fridge. There's a kitsch but cheerful restaurant on the top floor that sells cheap alcohol (Stella E£10.50). Breakfast included. It is worth booking ahead, the reasonable rates mean it gets busy (singles E£85, doubles E£100).

E-F El-Shata (Beach) Hotel, 31 Sharia El-Gumhoriyya, T086-236 2307. Bright, clean but shabby rooms are small though acceptable, some have side views of the Nile from balconies, all are pretty noisy. Staff are amenable and it's good value at E£60-80 for a double, depending on whether you have a/c and private bath.

F Savoy Hotel, just across from the train station in Midan Mahatta, T086-326 3270. In a classic building, some rooms equipped with private bath, TV and fridge. Management says they will only take groups of tourists, and always seem to be full in any case, but it's worth a try as it's convenient and atmospheric (rooms E£50).

F-G Hotel Majestic, 5 Sharia El-Gumhoriyya, T086-236 4212. Bare and basic rooms with high ceilings in an old building have clean sheets and fans. And not much else. Shared bathrooms with peeling paint are pretty grim. The manager is kind and professional though very little English is spoken, it's the best of the real budget choices (doubles with shared bath E£30, dorm beds E£10) and handy for the train station.

Assiut *p206*

Several hotels in Assiut are reluctant to accept foreigners (such as the Reem and the Tahrir, immediately next to the station) but the ones below should be amenable. All serve an inclusive breakfast unless otherwise stated.

A Assiutel Hotel, 146 Sharia Nile, T088-231 2121. Comfy rooms with big beds have a/c, TV and fridge. There's a choice between standard (US$66) and lux (US$86) doubles, standard are more faded but have balconies while lux are freshly refurnished and have flat-screen TVs and minibar. Nile views from the (enclosed) rooftop coffee shop, public areas with antique furniture and wooden walls, and there's a mock-Tudor restaurant that doubles up as the only bar in town. Friendly staff. Wi-Fi throughout, decent breakfast buffet, it's still the best hotel in Assiut.

A-B Badr Hotel, Sharia El-Thallaga, behind the train station, T088-232 9811/2. Has plain but well-equipped rooms, with a/c, TV and fridge, although curtains are beginning to hang off and there are no balconies. Top-floor rooms are quiet, even so near the station, and public areas are attractive in a kitschy kind of way.

A-B El Madina Hotel, behind the bus station, T088-232 2730. A colourful new plate-glass edifice with excellent fresh rooms and spotless baths (tubs). Good *sheesha* on the rooftop, nice staff, not much soul as yet.

B Casa Blanca, Sharia Mohammed Tawfik Khashaba, T088-233 7662. Lacks the views of the Assiutel and is only marginally cheaper. However it is handier for town and the station, plus staff are pleasant. Worth checking out a few rooms, as there are many configurations.

D Akhenaten Hotel, Sharia Mohammed Tawfik Khashaba, T088-232 7723. An unspectacular hotel, but bright clean rooms are spacious and come with private bath, a/c and TV making it a good deal for the price (doubles E£150 with breakfast).

E Al-Nahr Hotel, 41 Shari Mohammed Ali Makarem, T088-233 4253. Cosy double rooms with a/c, TV and private bath are a bargain for E£85. Away from the train tracks, the streets here are quieter and more interesting. Take a front-facing room, as they have balconies and are larger than ones at the side. No breakfast.

F YMCA, Sharia Mimase, off Sharia El-Gumhoriyya, about 10 mins' walk from the train station, T010-348 2952. Bottom of the rung price-wise, but clean and quiet, a/c, no breakfast. Gets booked out so call ahead.

Eating

Beni Suef *p194*

Outside of the hotel restaurants, have a stroll along Sharia Riyadhi. The centre of the Beni Suef's bustle, it's lined with lots of shops, pharmacies, juice joints, and *fuul*, *taamiyya* and *koshari* stalls. For a *sheesha* or pastry, try Coffee Shop Si Omar, near the Bakri Palace.

Minya *p195*

Nefertiti Port, across from the end of Sharia El-Gumhoriyya (on the Corniche) is a stationary boat with a restaurant on the upper deck that has decent kebab and *kofta* for about E£40.

Koshari El-Nigma, off Midan Mahatta, has the best *koshari* in town.

Pizza Suezi, just off Midan Tahrir, does delicious *fatir* (sweet or savoury) for E£5-10 and will provide chairs so you can sit outside.

Savoy, off Midan Mahatta. Open 24/7. Has *koshari* and a wealth of salads, kebabs, *fuul* and *taamiyya*.

Seven Eleven, on the Corniche about 200 m north of El-Gumhoriyya, T086-232 1045. Open 1200-0300. Does chicken, pizza and coffees in a more American vein.

A beer is cheap in the **Ibn Khassib Hotel**, on Sharia Rageb, on the dark and dusty terrace. The **Lotus Hotel** cafeteria is more frequented and salubrious.

Assiut *p206*

The various clubs offer decent food and usually admit better-dressed tourists. There are a number of good cheap and cheerful restaurants between the back of the station and the *souk* in the main commercial district. Cheap restaurants that offer a fairly similar local menu of the usual grilled chicken and stewed vegetables include: **Express Restaurant** and **Mattam Al-Azhar**. There is a good juice bar directly opposite the El Madina Hotel.

Assiutel, of the hotel restaurants this is the best with quite a varied menu, but there is little competition.

Sunshine Restaurant, 48 Sharia El-Corniche, south of the **Assiutel**, T088-231 4907, has a good salad selection and does excellent mixed grills and seafood in clean and sterile environs.

Shopping

Minya *p195*

While the more upmarket shops are on Sharia Taha Hussein, the best and main shopping streets bisect Midan Tahrir halfway between the station and the river. These extend south, where they transform into a busy and interesting *souk*. There has been a Mon animal market (Souk El-Itnayn) since Ottoman times, on the Western side of the canal, about 4 km south of the bridge. Go early, as it starts winding down after 1000.

Transport

Beni Suef *p194*

Bus

Buses run to **Cairo** and **Fayoum** every 30 mins throughout the day. There is a less frequent direct service to **Alexandria** and a few major destinations in the Delta. The bus station is south of the railway station, across the canal.

Taxi

Service taxis congregate at the depot by the bus station. They run regularly north to **Cairo**, west to **Fayoum**, south to **Minya** and east to **Zafarana** on the Red Sea. Whether or not they will transport you is unpredictable, but it's worth a shot.

Train

It is easy to make a quick getaway from Beni Suef because virtually every express and standard train travelling north and south through the Nile Valley stops at the station in the city centre.

Minya *p195*

Bus

Upper Delta, T086-232 6820, have 10 daily buses from the terminal on Sharia Sa'ad Zaghloul to **Cairo** between 0730 and 0130 (E£23, 4-5 hrs) and 3 per day south to **Assiut** at 0600, 0900 and 1200 (E£6, 3 hrs). **EUT** (United Transport), T086-233 5452, also on Sa'ad Zaghloul, have buses to **Cairo** at 0400, 0500, 0600 and 1530 (E£20); **Mallawi** at 0700, 1000 and 1230 (E£2, 45 mins); **Sharm El-Sheikh** at 1730 (E£61, 10 hrs); and **Hurghada** at 1000 and 2300 (E£40, 4-5 hrs).

Taxi

Service taxis, which are quicker and ludicrously cheap, can go to Beni Suef and northern destinations in between from the nearby depot under the railway arch. Those for **Abu Qirkus** (30-45 mins), the jumping-off point for **Beni Hassan**, can only be caught 250 m further south just across the railway and the canal bridge, also the starting point for services to **Mallawi** (45 mins, E£1.50) and **Assiut** (2 hrs, E£5).

Train

Intercity trains stop at Minya so it is easily possible to travel north to **Cairo** (4 hrs) via **Beni Suef** or south to **Luxor** (5 hrs) via **Assiut** (1 ½ hrs) and **Sohag** (3-3 ½ hrs).

Assiut *p206*

Air

Internal flights to **Cairo** (2 per week) and **Kharga** (2 per week) from the airport, 10 km northwest of the town.

Bus

7 daily buses **Cairo** (7 hrs); 5 to **Kharga Oasis** (5 hrs) that go on to **Dakhla** (8-9 hrs); 4 to **Qena** (4 hrs); as well as buses every 2 hrs (0600-1800) north to **Minya** (2 hrs) and south to **Sohag**.

Taxi

Service taxis run to every town between **Minya** and **Sohag**, as well as to **Kharga** (5 hrs), and if accepting foreign travellers, are easy to catch from the depots in the mornings but are less frequent later in the day. They also run frequently to **Cairo** in case the trains are full. Ask for Mowgaf El-Azhar to get to the service taxi station for Cairo and the north. To head south by service taxi ask for the 'Mowgaf' followed by the name of the place you want to reach. A taxi should cost E£3 from the train station.

Train

Run almost hourly to **Cairo** (7 hrs) via **Mallawi** (2 hrs), **Minya** (3 hrs), and **Beni Suef** (5 hrs); 12 per day to **Luxor** (6-7 hrs) and **Aswan** (10-12 hrs) via **Sohag** (2 hrs) and **Qena** (4-5 hrs).

Directory

Beni Suef *p194*

Banks Bank of Alexandria in Midan El-Gumhoriyya. Banque Misr and Banque du Caire are next to each other on Sharia Riyadhi, each has ATM, open Sun-Thu, 0830-1400. **Post office** Opposite the Semiramis Hotel in Midan El-Mahat. **Telephone** At railway station.

Minya *p195*

Banks Bank of Alexandria and National Bank of Egypt on the Corniche at the end of Sharia El-Gumhoriyya, where you can find ATMs, open Sun-Thu 0800-1400, and near the train station is Banque du Caire with an ATM. **Immigration** Above the post office, T086-236 4193, Sat-Thu 0800-1400, visa extensions. **Internet** Zuma, half-way down Sharia El-Gumhoriyya, is open 24 hrs, E£2 per hr. **Medical services** University Hospital, on the Corniche 500 m south of Sharia El-Gumhoriyya, T086-237 2261. **Post office** Off the Corniche, open Sat-Thu 0830-2100.

Assiut *p206*

Banks There are a number of banks, including the Alexandria Bank (open Sat-Thu 0830-1400 and 1800-2100, Fri 0900-1230 and 1800-2100) in the commercial district around Talaat Harb. Banque du Caire on Sharia Nemis has an ATM. **Internet** Cafés are scattered all over the city. Maro on Sharia Yusri Ragheb is recommended. E£2 per hr. **Post office** Behind the railway station, open Sat-Thu 0830-2000. **Telephone** There is a Central beside the railway station.

Sohag to Dendara

➔ Colour map 3, C2-4, A2. Phone code: 093.

An agricultural and university west bank city, 97 km south of Assiut on the widest point of the Nile, Sohag (pronounced 'Sohaj') has a large Coptic community among its 500,000 population. Although it has a few minor sites it is not geared toward tourists (who used to be escorted by police on all excursions, although this restriction has softened of late) but it does have the advantage of being relatively close to the beautiful temple at Abydos and within a half-day journey from Dendara. Bear in mind, though, that it's possible to visit both these sites on a day trip from Luxor. A new museum is due to open in 2011, in Medinat Nasr on the east bank right next to the Nile, which will showcase the wealth of finds from Akhmim and the surrounding area. It is hoped that around 5000 artefacts will be displayed, including mummies. On the east bank of the Nile, across from Sohag proper, is the village of Akhmim where a towering statue of the ancient queen Meryut Amun was uncovered in 1981. A pleasant two-three hour trip can be made to the nearby Red and White monasteries, where exceptional paintings are being restored in the apse of the Red Monastery. Sohag itself is not an appealing city, nor particularly friendly. However, the souk is wonderfully authentic and worth a wander if you are in town. ▸▸ *For listings, see pages 220-222.*

Sohag ➔ *For listings, see pages 220-222. Colour map 3, C2.*

The **tourist office** ⓘ *T093-461 0093, Sat-Thu 0800-1400*, is on the first floor of the governorate building in Medinat Nasr, on the east bank near the bridge. They will help arrange a taxi to the monasteries and provide a couple of brochures, but English is not their strong point.

The White Monastery and the Red Monastery

ⓘ *6 km west of Sohag, a taxi costs E£40-50,with waiting time, for a visit to both monasteries. Entrance is free, open 24 hrs (supposedly).*

Deir Al-Abyad, the **White Monastery**, has light-coloured limestone walls and was founded in the fifth century by St Pjol although it is attributed to his nephew St Shenute, one of the most prominent figures in the history of the Coptic church. It once had a population of over 2000 monks but today only four permanent mendicants remain. St Shenute worked in the White and Red Monasteries for over 80 years – he is believed to have lived until well over 100 – and introduced both spiritual and social support for the local community as well as medical help. He documented a great deal of Coptic literature on papyri, using the Akhmimic dialect, some examples of which can be seen in the Coptic Museum in Cairo. Stone to build the monastery was brought from ancient sites nearby, especially Arthribis, and hieroglyphs and Hellenistic decoration can be seen engraved on blocks in the walls. The layout echoes that of a pharaonic temple, and in fact the imposing building resembles a temple more than a church. Remove your shoes before entering the soaring interior, which is divided with decorated columns into a central nave and two aisles. A faded image of Christ Pantokrator looks down from above. The three altars are dedicated to St Shenute (in the centre), St George and The Holy Virgin. It is possible to follow the stairs, from the left side of the central nave, to the upper level where the relics of a saint are shrouded in red behind a mashribiya screen. There is a *moulid* every July that climaxes on the 14th. Drinks, snacks and souvenirs can be bought at the shop within the monastery walls.

Three and a half kilometres to the north, on the edge of the village of Awlad Nusayr, is the smaller Deir Al-Ahmar, **Red Monastery,** founded in the mid-fifth century by St Bishoi, a disciple of Shenute. It is built of burnt red brick, hence the name and is said to have been the centre of a monastery of 3000 monks. The nave is open to the sky, with only the eastern end still roofed. The church of St Bishoi has some extraordinary frescoes inside the triconch sanctuary that are being painstakingly restored. The Italian-run project, which began in 2002, is due for completion in 2012, but you should be able to view their progress among the scaffolding. Almost every interior surface is covered with paint, mostly dating from the fifth to 10th centuries, including the pillars that are decorated with floral and abstract patterns. As a millennium's worth of soot is removed, glorious images of the virgin and child and the apostles are being slowly revealed on the three apses. In particular, note the rare image of Mary suckling Jesus on the domed ceiling of the left-hand apse; below them, portraits of St Bishoi, St Shenute and St Pjol adorn the niches. Also look out for the images of deer and peacocks, and the pop-eyed rendition of St Basilicus on the far lower niche on the right-hand side.

Akhmim

Across the Nile from Sohag is the interesting ancient town of Akhmim once, though it seems unbelievable now, the capital of the Ninth Nome. Unfortunately, police desperately urge you to leave as soon as you have seen the designated sights and are reluctant to let you wander off down the enticing medieval laneways.

Here stands an imposing statue of **Queen Meryut Amun** ⓘ *daily 0800-1700, E£20, students E£10; if the fees seem a bit steep you can get a good view through the railings*, which was uncovered in 1981 when foundations were being dug for a school. At 11 m tall, she is the tallest statue discovered in Egypt of an ancient queen and was the daughter of Ramses II (who she also ended up marrying). In her left hand she carries a flail and the details of her wig, earrings and necklace are sharply sculpted. Across the road among chaotic excavations lies a massive but neglected and dusty bust of her father, with traces of paint on his headdress and a gorgeously intact beard. His seated legs lie nearby and give a sense of how colossal the complete figure would have been.

Akhmim also has a long and famed history as a centre of weaving going back to the time of the pharaohs, whose palaces were adorned by the fabrics created here while tradition holds that their shrouds were make of Akhmim silk. In the Coptic era, it remained the most prominent centre of weaving and during Roman times local turnips provided the purple hues that dyed the robes of the emperors. Some of this tradition is preserved by a weaving factory, opposite the entrance to Meryut Amun through the green gates, although the designs for sale are 1950s and created on mechanical looms. Fabulous vintage cars (*fuuljahs*) ply the route between Sohag and Akhmim, 50 pt to share (though it's hard to get a seat) or E£7 to hire the whole thing.

Abydos

→ *For listings, see pages 220-222. Colour map 3, C2.*

Ins and outs Most people come to Abydos on an organized trip from Luxor in a convoy. If you want to take public transport (and thus arrive alone rather than with masses of others on a fixed schedule) is possible to take a service taxi to the nearby village of El-Balyana, halfway between Sohag and Qena, from Sohag (one hour, E£2) or take a train to Qena from Luxor so the police don't stop you, and change there. The turn-off from El-Balyana to Abydos is marked by a police checkpoint, where officers will insist you take a private taxi the remaining 12 km southwest to the temple (E£10). You might want to negotiate a return trip with waiting time, so as not to be at the mercy of the taxis at the other end. If you then want to hire a private taxi on to Dendara, it costs around E£130-150.

Sights Abydos is home to the stunning **Temple of Seti I** ⓘ *daily 0800-1700, E£30, students E£15*. It contains some of the most exquisitely carved reliefs of any monument in Egypt, and the detail in faces, jewellery and hairstyles can be utterly transfixing, particularly on the unpainted reliefs. Meanwhile, blocks of white light coming through the holes in the ceiling allow you to admire the extensive colours of ochre, turquoise, umber and colbalt still clinging to the interior walls. As the holiest town of all for the ancient Egyptians, pilgrims were making the journey to Abydos from the Seventh Dynasty (2181-2173 BC) until well into the Ptolemaic era (323-30 BC), and it is still a spiritual visit for many people.

It was the cult centre for **Osiris**, the god of the dead who was known as 'Lord of Abydos' because, according to legend, either his head or his whole body was buried at the site (see Temple of Isis, Aswan, page 311). Abydos, which looked out over the Western Desert, was considered the door to the afterlife. Initially, in order to achieve resurrection it was necessary to be buried at Abydos but the requirement was later changed to a simple pilgrimage and the gift of a commemorative stela. There are cemeteries and tombs scattered over a very wide area in Abydos but there are only a few buildings left standing that aren't too far apart: the Temple of Seti I, the Osirieon (Cenotaph) and the Temple of Ramses II.

The **Temple of Seti I** was constructed in fine white marble by Seti I (1318-1304 BC) as an offering in the same way that lesser mortals would come on a pilgrimage and make a gift of a stela. Most of the work on the temple and its convex bas-reliefs, among the most beautiful of all New Kingdom buildings, was carried out by Seti I, but when he died his son Ramses II (1304-1237 BC) completed the courtyard and façade. This can be seen from the quality of workmanship, which changes from Seti I's beautiful bas-reliefs to Ramses II's much cheaper, quicker, and therefore cruder, sunken reliefs. It is unusual in being L-shaped rather than following the usual rectangle design and because it has seven separate chapels rather than a single one behind the hypostyle halls.

The theme of the seven separate chapels is evident in the **First Hypostyle Hall**, built and decorated by Ramses II's second-rate craftsmen, where the columns with papyrus capitals depict Ramses with the god represented in the corresponding sanctuary. In the much more impressive **Second Hypostyle Hall**, built by Seti, the first two rows of columns also have papyrus capitals but the last row have no capitals at all. On the right-hand wall Seti is pictured before Osiris and Horus who are pouring holy water from vases and making offerings in front of Osiris' shrine as five goddesses look on. The quality of the work in this hall contrasts sharply with the rougher decoration in the outer hall – probably because Ramses had ordered all the most skilled craftsmen to concentrate on his own temple.

Behind the inner hypostyle hall there are seven separate **sanctuaries** that are dedicated to the deified Seti I, the Osiris triad of Osiris, Isis and Horus, and the Amun triad of Amun, Mut and Khonsu. Many of the wonderful bas-reliefs are still coloured, which gives a good idea of the temple's original decoration, but some of the finest are unpainted and show the precision and great artistry used in the moulding. The sanctuary furthest to the left is dedicated to Seti and contains a beautiful scene of the Pharaoh being crowned by the goddess of Upper and Lower Egypt. His plaited sidelocks of hair symbolize childhood and are utterly beautiful.

Each of these sanctuaries would have contained the god's barque as well as his stela placed in front of a false door. The sanctuary was locked and only High Priests had access because the Ancient Egyptians believed that the gods lived in their sanctuaries. The daily rituals that were carried out included a sacrifice as well as the dressing and purification of the stelae. Unlike the others, the **Sanctuary of Osiris** does not have a false door at the back of the chapel but connects with the pillared **Suite of Osiris**. It is decorated with scenes from the Osiris myth and has three shrines on the west wall dedicated, with magnificent and incredibly vivid paintings, to Seti, Isis and Horus. The Mysteries of Osiris miracle play would have been performed in the hall and in the unfinished and partially destroyed Sanctuary of Osiris, which is reached through a narrow entrance on the opposite wall.

Back in the Second Hypostyle Hall the temple changes direction on the left-hand or southeast side with two entrances leading to a number of other halls. The nearest is the three-columned **Hall of Sokar and Nefertum**, northern deities subsequently integrated into the Osirian cult, with the separate **Chapel of Sokar** and **Chapel of Nefertum** at the back. Through the other entrance is the narrow star-decorated **Hall/Gallery of Ancestors/Lists** which, very usefully for archaeologists, lists in rows the names of the gods and 76 of Seti's predecessors although, for political reasons, some, such as Hatshepsut, Akhenaten and his heirs, are omitted. The gallery leads on to the **Hall of Barques** where the sacred boats were stored, the **Hall of Sacrifices** used as the slaughterhouse for the sacrifices, and other storerooms: they are currently closed to visitors. Instead it is best to follow the side **Corridor of the Bulls**, where Ramses II is shown lassoing a bull before the jackal-headed 'Opener of the Ways' Wepwawet on one side and driving four dappled calves towards Khonsu and Seti I on the other, before climbing the steps to the temple's rear door and the Osirieon.

The **Osirieon**, built earlier than the main temple and at water level, which has led to severe flooding, is sometimes called the Cenotaph of Seti I because it contains a sarcophagus. Although it was never used by Seti I, who is actually buried in the Valley of the Kings in Luxor (see page 257), it was built as a symbol of his closeness to Osiris. Many other pharaohs built similar 'fake' tombs, which were modelled on the tombs at Luxor, in Abydos but were eventually buried elsewhere. The Osirieon is the only

Temple of Seti I, Abydos

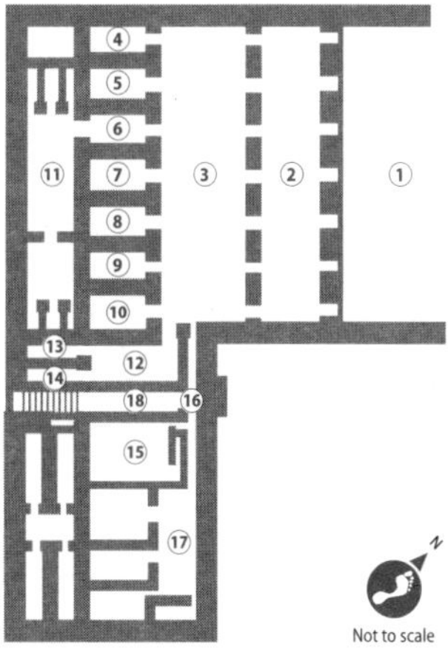

1 First & second court (destroyed)
2 First hypostyle hall
3 Second hypostyle hall
4 Chapel/Sanctuary of Horus
5 Chapel/Sanctuary of Isis
6 Chapel/Sanctuary of Osiris
7 Chapel/Sanctuary of Amun-Re
8 Chapel/Sanctuary of Re-Harakhiti
9 Chapel/Sanctuary of Ptah
10 Chapel/Sanctuary of Seti I
11 Suite of Osiris
12 Suite of Sokar & Nefertum
13 Chapel of Sokar
14 Chapel of Nefertum
15 Hall of the Books
16 Gallery of the Lists
17 Hall of Sacrifice
18 Corridor of the Bulls

remaining visible tomb but is unfortunately largely inaccessible because of the inundation of sand and the flooding caused by the rise in the water table.

The small **Temple of Ramses II** (accessed via the track to the right of Seti I's temple, someone will fetch the key), is naturally an anticlimax after the scale and sheer beauty of the Temple of Seti I. However, it was originally a very finely built shrine, erected in 1298 BC for Ramses' *Ka* or spirit in order to give him a close association with Osiris. The workmanship is better than in most of Ramses II's monuments because it was probably decorated by craftsmen trained in his father's era. Although the temple was reportedly almost intact when first seen by Napoleon's archaeologists, it has since fallen into ruin except for the lower parts of the limestone walls which are still surprisingly brightly coloured. Ramses' chunky feet and calves are all that remain of the statutory in the main courtyard.

Qena → *For listings, see pages 220-222. Colour map 4, A2.*

The town of Qena, just 58 km north of Luxor, despite being the provincial capital, is not very welcoming to foreign visitors. Services are lacking, and often unavailable to tourists. Though the town has undergone a makeover at the hands of a progressive governor (complete with rubbish bins), it's not particularly friendly and police escorts can't be dodged for long. The main reason for stopping in Qena is to see the magnificent temple at Dendara about 8 km from the centre of town but also worth a look if you make it here is the lovely Abdur Rahim mosque on the main road in town.

Ins and outs

Getting there and around From the train station, the adjacent bus station and the southbound service taxi depot, on either side of the main canal, Sharia El-Gumhoriyya leads southeast to a major roundabout and the town's main street, to the west end of which is the northbound service taxi depot, near the River Nile. To get to Dendara from the centre of Qena, tourist police generally insist that independent travellers hire a private taxi to take them to the temple and back. If you can dodge security, service taxi pickups (50 pt) bound for Dendara converge at a depot by the large intersection near the Nile. » *See Transport, page 221.*

Dendara → *Colour map 4, A2.*

ⓘ *Summer 0700-1800, winter 0700-1700 but they stop admitting visitors an hour before closing time, E£35, students E£20, use of cameras and video recorders free.*

Dendara was the cult centre of Hathor from pre-dynastic times and there are signs of earlier buildings on the site dating back to Cheops in the Fourth Dynasty (2613-2494 BC). Hathor, represented as a cow or cow-headed woman, was the goddess associated with love, joy, music, protection of the dead and, above all, of nurturing. Her great popularity was demonstrated by the huge festival held at Edfu when her barque symbolically sailed upstream on her annual visit to Horus to whom she was both wet-nurse and lover. As they reconsummated their union the population indulged in the Festival of Drunkenness, which led the Greeks to identify Hathor with Aphrodite who was their own goddess of love and joy.

The **Temple of Hathor**, built between 125 BC and AD 60 by the Ptolemies and the Romans, is the latest temple on a site begun by Pepi I in the Sixth Dynasty (2345-2181 BC). The enclosing wall around the temple is of unbaked bricks laid alternately convex and concave, like waves of a primeval ocean – an extraordinary sight in itself. The huge, well-preserved temple dominates the walled Dendara complex which also includes a number of smaller buildings. Even though it was built by non-Egyptian foreign conquerors it copies the earlier pharaonic temples with large hypostyle halls leading up, via a series of successively smaller vestibules and storerooms, to the sanctuary at the back of the temple. There are also two sets of steps leading up to and down from the roof sanctuaries.

Temple at Dendara

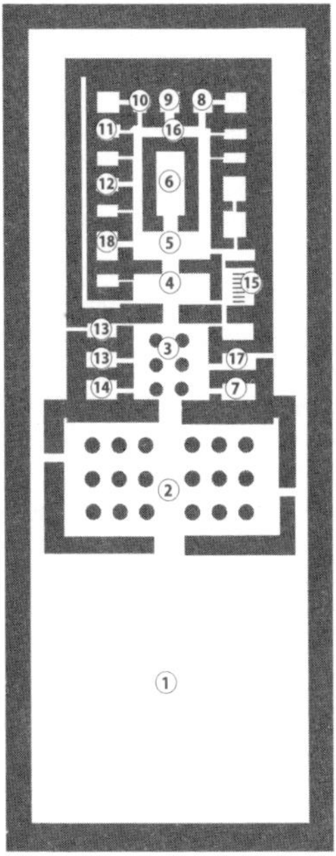

N

Not to scale

1 Court
2 Pronaos/First Hypostyle Hall
3 Second Hypostyle Hall/ Hall of Appearances
4 First Vestibule/ Hall of Offerings
5 Second Vestibule/ Hall of Ennead
6 Sanctuary of the Golden One
7 Treasury
8 Per-Neser Chapel/ House of Flame
9 Per-Ur Chapel/ Shrine of Egypt
10 Per-Nu Chapel
11 Sacred Serpent
12 Seat of Repose
13 Harvest Rooms
14 Laboratory
15 Stairs to roof
16 Stairs to crypts
17 Nile Room
18 Hathor's Wardrobe

At the front, the pylon-shaped façade is supported by six huge Hathor-headed columns with blue painted head-dresses, and reliefs showing the Roman emperors Tiberius and Claudius performing rituals with the gods. Through in the **Hypostyle Hall** there are 18 Hathor-headed columns, capitals of which are sistra-rattles associated with music and dance. The magnificent ceiling, which is illustrated with an astronomical theme showing the mystical significance of the sky, has retained much of its original colour. It is divided between day and night and illustrates the 14 days' moon cycle, the gods of the four cardinal points, the constellations, the zodiac, and the elongated goddess Nut who swallows the sun at sunset and gives birth to it at dawn. It is currently being restored and is, therefore, slightly obscured by scaffolding; intense blue and white colours are being revealed.

The next room, which is known as the **Hall of Appearances** and is supported by six columns, is where the goddess appeared from the depths of the temple as she was transported on her ritual barque for the annual voyage to Edfu. On either side of the doorway there are scenes of offerings and the presentation of the temple to the gods.

Around this Hall are six small rooms (all lit by sunlight from holes in the roof). The first on the left was the laboratory, used for the preparation of balms and the nine oils used to anoint the statues. It has several inscriptions, with the recipes and instructions for their preparation. The next two rooms were used as store-rooms for offerings such as flowers, beer, wine and poultry. The second room, called the Nile Room, has an exit to the back corridor and the well outside. Next is the first vestibule,

The Nile ran red

As the story goes – Re, the sun-god, creator of all men and all things, began to grow old and the men he had so carefully created began to mock him. They criticized his appearance and even complained about his neglect of them. Re was angry at their lack of reverence due to his position; after all, he was their creator. He called a secret council of gods and goddesses (Geb, Shu, Tefnut, Nut and Hathor), where it was agreed that they would destroy all mankind.

The task of destruction was handed to Hathor, the daughter of Re. She seems to have been happy in her work, 'wading in blood' as the story goes. The gods realized, almost too late, that without the men the tasks on earth in the temples would not be performed. It was essential, therefore, to protect those who remained. The drug mandrake was mixed with freshly brewed beer and the blood of the already slain making 7000 vessels in all. This liquid was poured across the land (symbolic of the Nile floods) and Hathor, waking, mistook this liquid for blood, drank it all and was too stupefied to complete her gruesome task.

which was known as the **Hall of Offerings** because it was there that the priests displayed the offerings for the goddess on large tables. The food and drink was then divided among the priests once the gods had savoured them. On the left a stairway leads to the roof sanctuary. The second vestibule, called the **Hall of the Ennead**, contained the statues of the kings and gods that were involved in the ceremonies for Hathor while her wardrobe was stored in the room on the left. This leads on to the **Sanctuary of the Golden One**, which contained Hathor's statue and her ceremonial barque that was carried to the river each New Year to be transported on a boat upstream to the Temple of Horus at Edfu. The south and north walls of the independently roofed sanctuary depict the pharaoh in various phases of the ceremony. The so-called **Corridor of Mysteries** around the outside of the sanctuary has nine doors that lead to 11 small shrines with 32 crypts, including the crypt where the temple's valuables would have been stored. Make sure to enter the **Per-Neser Chapel** where a trapdoor gives access to one of these crypts, consisting of a two-pronged corridor covered with delicate carvings.

The walls of the stairway from the left of the Hall of Offerings to the **Roof Sanctuaries** (which, unlike anywhere else, have been completely preserved), depict the New Year ceremony when the statue of Hathor was carried up to the roof to the small open **Chapel of the Union with the Disk** to await the sunrise. The scenes on the left of the stairs represent Hathor going up while those on the right show her returning down. In the northwest corner of the roof terrace is **Osiris' Tomb**, where ceremonies commemorating Osiris' death and resurrection were carried out. In the east corner there are two rooms with the outer one containing a blackened plaster-cast copy of the original **Dendara Zodiac** ceiling that was stolen and taken to the Louvre in Paris in 1820. The Zodiac was introduced to Egypt by the Romans and, although Scorpio's scorpion is replaced by a scarab beetle and the hippo-goddess Tweri was added, this circular zodiac held up by four goddesses is virtually identical to the one used today.

The views from the uppermost level of the roof terrace are superb, however the area is now cordoned off since an American tourist toppled over the side when taking a photograph a few years ago. However, if you express enough interest and there aren't any other people around, police/guardians may allow you up. From the roof, the overall scale

Brick-making in Egypt

Sun-dried bricks were made from the dried Nile mud. This mud shrinks a great deal when it dries and has to be protected from the sun and the wind to prevent the brick collapsing even before it is used. To reduce the breakage rate the mud was mixed with chopped straw or reeds.

The Bible tells of the Israelites being forced to make bricks while in captivity in Egypt. Each brick-maker had a daily target with only whole bricks being counted. Making bricks without straw meant more journeys to collect mud as it was then the only ingredient and the bricks were fragile and more frequently broken.

and layout of the temple buildings, the extensive outer walls and the intensively cultivated countryside surrounding Dendara can really be appreciated. From the northern edge of the upper terrace there are good views looking down on to the sanatorium, the two birth houses and the Coptic basilica (see below).

Back downstairs and outside the temple, on the exterior south wall, there are two giant damaged reliefs depicting Cleopatra (the only surviving relief depicting Cleopatra VII in the whole of Egypt) and her son Caesarion, and beyond a number of small ruined buildings surrounding the main temple. At the back is the **Temple of Isis** that was almost totally destroyed by the early Christians because of the fear that the worship of Isis as the universal Egyptian goddess might spread (a custodian will appear to magically open up the two rooms). At the front of the main temple to the right is the **Roman Birth House**, or Mammisi, which has some particularly beautiful carvings covering its façade and south walls. The **Sanatorium**, between the Mammisi and the main temple, was where pilgrims who came to Dendara to be healed by Hathor were treated and washed in water from the sunken stone-lined **Sacred Lake**, now drained of water and with date palms poking out the top. Between the two birth-houses is a ruined fifth-century **Coptic Basilica**, one of the earliest Coptic buildings in Egypt, which was built using stone from the adjacent buildings.

Sohag to Dendara listings

For Sleeping and Eating price codes and other relevant information, see pages 26-31.

Sleeping

Sohag *p212*

Sohag is not a particularly appealing town and sees few foreigners, but it's recommended to phone ahead as hotels are tend to be very busy.

L-AL Hotp Hotel, Medinat Nasr (on the east bank), T019-992 7332/3. By far the swankiest choice in Sohag, the Hotp (or 'Hotep') is a cruise boat permanently moored on the east bank of the Nile. Unfortunately, a bridge dominates the view, but the 48 rooms (doubles US$130) are attractively furnished in a modish style with black wood, bright fabrics and modern facilities. Bathrooms are tiny, as you would expect on a boat, but most rooms are quite spacious (except for the standard singles, US$70). Suites (US$180) are very similar to the doubles and not worth the extra money.

B Al-Safa Hotel, on the west bank 1 km north of the station, T093-230 7701. Western-style clean rooms, those at the rear have balconies overlooking the Nile, with TV, a/c and fridge. Nothing spectacular but comfortable and not bad value, has popular patio coffeeshop by the water, decent restaurant and good breakfast is included. Free Wi-Fi.

B Nile Hotel, Medinat Nasr (on the east bank), T093-460 6253-5. Sohag's newest hotel (they are still building the upper storeys) has an ornate exterior, spacious public areas and decent rooms with the amenities you would expect for the price (single E£200, double E£300). Furniture is a bit dark and they have a propensity to cover the light wood floors with unattractive rugs, but the rooms with balconies to the Nile are pleasant as is the riverside garden coffeeshop. The restaurant is very reasonable. Breakfast included.

D Andalos, opposite the train station, T093-233 4328. Rooms are clean with private bath, hot water, towels and soap. Noisy, but still the best choice near the station. The manager is nice, with limited English.

D Cazalovy Hotel, on the east bank, T093-460 1185. Includes breakfast, but rooms could be cleaner.

D Merit Amoun Hotel, on the east bank, T093-460 1985. 30 rooms, being renovated at the time of writing so should be a better alternative.

D Sara Plaza, no English sign, it's the tall orange and blue building with a neon sign on top, to the left on exiting the train station. Fairly sanitary rooms have a/c and private bath, breakfast included. Hot water is not reliable, but quite quiet because rooms are so high up.

F Youth hostel, 7 Sharia Port Said 1.5 km from station, T093-232 4395. Not much English spoken, a bed is E£15. Parking.

Abydos *p213*

It is possible to stay close by the temple at Abydos if you want to imbibe some of Seti I's spirit and its promised 'high energy'.

B House of the Companions, to the right of Ramses II's temple, T010-331 2188 (Amir). Large airy rooms for rent with all meals included, singles E£150 or doubles E£240. Various healing, meditation and purification programmes are available. Worth phoning ahead, there is a genuinely intense atmosphere and you get to experience the beauty of the temple at all hours if you can deal with a dose of mumbo-jumbo.

Qena *p216*

Visitors are discouraged from staying in Qena, not so much by the police these days but more by the poor choice of hotels. If you are determined, the best bet is:

D-E New Palace, Midan Mahata, Qena, T096-532 2509. 75 rooms, far from palatial, it's still the best of the options. Rooms are overpriced and depressing, but clean enough, all have TV and some have balcony. With a/c, en-suite and breakfast, singles are E£120, doubles E£150, or with a/c, shared bath and no breakfast E£80/100 (women won't be enamoured by these bathrooms, which have urinals in). There are also 5 small singles with en-suite but no a/c for E£60. Staff are kindly. Located behind the Mobil garage near the train station.

Eating

Sohag p212

Finding decent food is an issue in Sohag.

Safa hotel has a pretty decent restaurant and serves up good fish soup.

Nile Hotel, the restaurant is quite pleasant and meals are very reasonably priced, with grills, chicken, fish and plenty of salads and soup.

There's also a decent kebab place in Midan Aref, not far from the station as well as the usual scattering of *fuul*, *taameyya* and *koshari* stands around the train station.

Abydos p213

Cafeteria Hadika Al-Pharoni, in front of the temple. OK meals are served up for between E£10-20, if you negotiate.

Qena p216

Besides *koshari* and *fuul* stalls, there are a few small cheap restaurants, including: **El-Prince**, **Hamdi** and **Maradona** and **Omar Kyam** (which is probably the best), all located on the main street in town.

Shopping

Akhmim p213

Hussein El-Khatib & Sons. Sat-Thu 0800-2000. Produce silk and cotton textiles that are for sale in their showroom beneath the weaving factory. For sale by the metre (E£75 for silk/cotton mix) or pre-packaged as place settings, or bed covers (E£100-150). Worth stopping by, the designs are unusual.

Transport

Sohag p212

Bus

The bus depot, T093-233 2021, is a 5-min walk south from the train station. There are daily buses to **Cairo** (8 hrs, E£40-45) at 0900, 1000, 1100 and 1830. There are also buses to **Assiut** at 0630, 0900, 1200 and 1300 (2 hrs, E£5).

Taxi

Service taxis run north as far as **Assiut**, from the depot near Midan Opera, on the north side of town. Services for the south leave from the southern end of Midan Al-Aref, going to **Qena** (3 hrs) via **El-Balyana** (for Abydos, 1 hr, E£2) and **Nag Hammadi**. Some also go direct to **Luxor** and **Aswan**, though it's an uncomfortable journey. Be forewarned that bus and taxi travel for foreign visitors may be restricted.

Train

Travel by train is preferable, and offers the least restrictions. All trains travelling between **Cairo** and **Luxor** stop in Sohag. You should be allowed to get on any train and then pay on board, which costs a bit extra, but if you try to buy a ticket in advance you will only be sold ones for the tourist trains.

Qena p216

Bus

There are 2 a/c **Superjet** buses to **Cairo**, via **Hurghada** and **Suez**, as well as service to other Red Sea destinations like **Safaga** and **El-Quseir**. Though buses also go to Nile Valley hub towns like **Assiut**, **Sohag** and **Minya**, they are more easily accessed by train.

Taxi

Service taxis, if open to foreign travellers, make a quick and easy way to travel. South-bound service taxis to **Luxor** and all points in between depart from the square just across the canal behind the railway station. 500 m away there are service taxis to **Safaga** and **Hurghada**. Northbound service taxis along the west bank to **Sohag** via **Nag Hammadi** and **El-Balyana**, can be caught from the depot near the river in the southwestern part of town. Microbuses circulate around town, passing the train station on route.

Train

At least 6 daily trains northbound to **Cairo** via **Sohag**, **Assiut**, **Minya** and **Beni Suef**, and south to **Luxor** (40 mins) and **Aswan**.

Directory

Sohag *p212*
Banks National Bank of Egypt and Barclays (T093-2230 2178), both on Sharia El-Gomhuriyya (the Corniche), have ATMs. **Internet** Salem Net, next to the Andalos Hotel, has a speedy connection for E£1 per hr, open 24 hrs, though it's full of youths 'gaming'. **Post office** On the Corniche, Sat-Thu 0800-2000, with the telephone exchange next door.

Qena *p216*
Post office At the canal end of the main street, open Sat-Thu 0800-2000.

Luxor

Contents

Footprint features

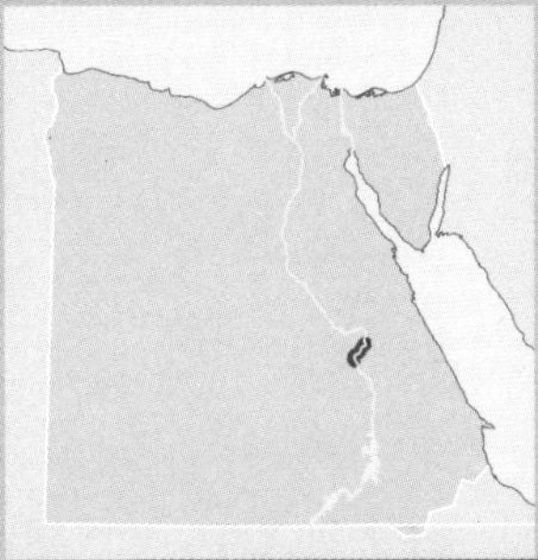

At a glance

Getting around *Calèches* and microbuses will get you to Karnak. Bikes are great for the West Bank.

Time required Possible in 2 days, but better to spend at least 4.

Weather Winter is perfect climatically. May-Sep is hot but still busy with tour groups.

When not to go European school holidays are always crowded, Christmas in particular.

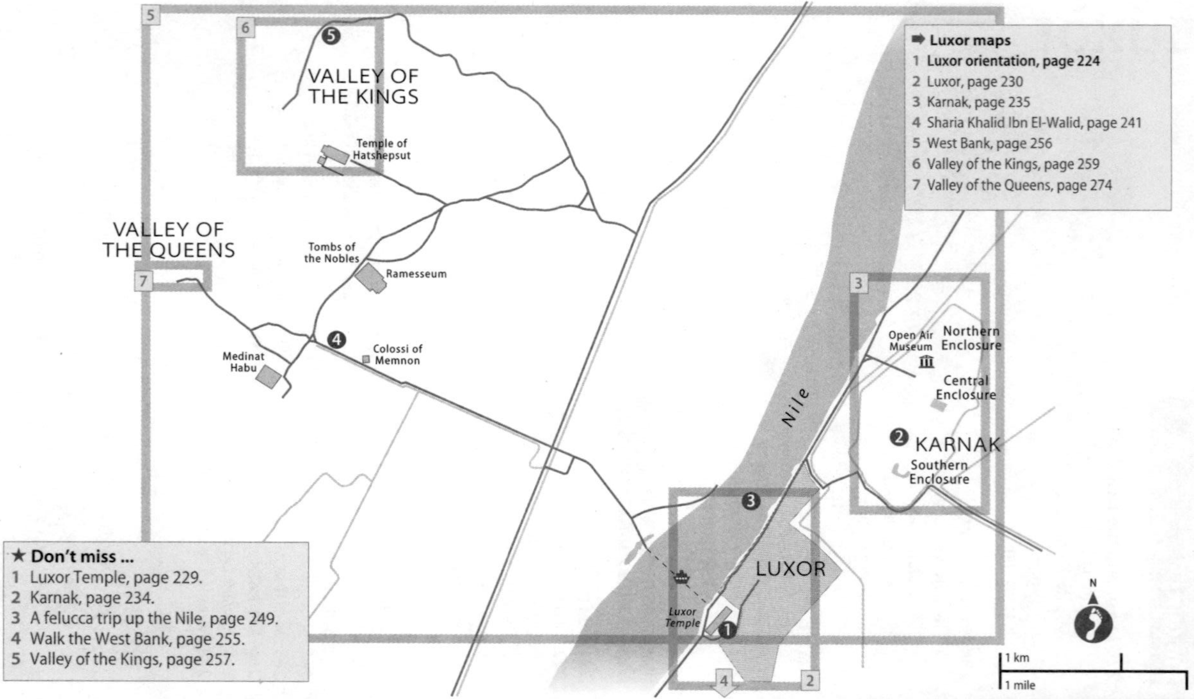

➡ Luxor maps

1 **Luxor orientation, page 224**
2 Luxor, page 230
3 Karnak, page 235
4 Sharia Khalid Ibn El-Walid, page 241
5 West Bank, page 256
6 Valley of the Kings, page 259
7 Valley of the Queens, page 274

★ Don't miss ...

1 Luxor Temple, page 229.
2 Karnak, page 234.
3 A felucca trip up the Nile, page 249.
4 Walk the West Bank, page 255.
5 Valley of the Kings, page 257.

In Luxor, the ancient exists amid the contemporary like nowhere else. Life has thrived in villages scattered about mounds of Theban tombs for untold centuries. Colossal temples loom over the Nile with bustling streets a few steps away. Evident in the architecture, the food, the clothes people wear, the things they sell and the games they play, Luxorians are remarkably capable of integrating layers of history with the present and future.

Second only to the Pyramids as Egypt's most visited attraction, the ancient capital of Thebes (1567-1085 BC) is among the world's oldest tourist destinations. A city built upon cities of millennia past, the area has been inhabited for at least 6000 years. With an overwhelming number of well-preserved sandstone temples and elaborate tombs, many deem Luxor the world's greatest open-air museum. The remains of Karnak Temple, a vast and beautifully preserved complex built over the span of more than 1000 years, are a highlight of any trip if you time your visit right. Luxor Temple, once a refuge for every great religion that thrived in ancient Egypt, rises gracefully alongside the Nile and at night is splendidly lit and open to visitors.

Across the river is the West Bank, spotted with tombs and magnificent mortuary temples, where the Valley of the Kings yields a taste of the profound and vital journey to the next life. Nearby, the intimate and little-visited Tombs of the Nobles reveal in glorious technicolour how everyday life was lived over 3000 years ago. Even for the most avid of Egyptologists, it's wise to be selective about what you choose to visit and intersperse tomb and temple hopping with a bit of repose. A sunset *felucca* ride or sailing to nearby Banana Island, a meander through the colourful tourist *souk* in the centre of town, or just an exploration of the West Bank villages are vital ingredients for a good experience in this tourist-trap town. Luxor also serves as a convenient base for day trips to the temples of Dendara and Abydos to the north, and the temples of Esna and Edfu, to the south.

Luxor and the East Bank

➔ *Colour map 4, A2. Population: 45,000.*

There is a reason Luxor is deemed the world's biggest open-air museum: it brims over with extraordinary sights. In brief, on the East Bank, the Luxor Temple (see page 229), and Karnak Temple complex (see page 234) are the two essential stops. Large tour parties on day trips from Hurghada tend to arrive at Karnak Temple at 1100-1230 and 1600-1730, and these times are definitely best avoided. Karnak at dawn, being first through the gate, is the best way to do it. Visit Luxor Temple at night – it's beautifully lit and easily accessible as it's right in the middle of town. ▸▸ *For listings, see pages 241-253.*

Ins and outs

Getting there

Luxor is 676 km south of Cairo, 65 km south of Qena and 223 km north of Aswan. The airport is 7 km east of the town centre. Visas are on sale just before passport control. From the airport, a taxi to the town centre should cost E£30-40. The airport is not well connected by public transport so taxis are unquestionably the easiest way to go. The new bus terminal is also a fair trek out, and taxis from here demand E£30 for a ride into the centre or there are microbuses into town for E£1. Arrival at the train station is easier as it's in the middle of Luxor and it's possible to walk to most budget hotels, or if you're hauling a lot of luggage you can take a *calèche* (horse-drawn carriage) or taxi anywhere in town for E£10.

Getting around

Luxor is small enough to be explored on foot (depending on how you tolerate the heat), large enough to feel like there's always something happening and full enough to need a week to really see it; but with so much to see, a visit can be overwhelming. But besides the ubiquitous hassle that can make even the most rugged traveller weary, Luxor is a comfortable place, easy to get around and impossible to get lost in with the Nile as a marker. Most of the main hotels, shops, tour offices, museums and temples are adjacent to the river on the eastern side. Most budget hotels are scattered around Sharia Mohamed Farid and Sharia Televizion, south of Sharia Al-Mahatta. Karnak temple is about 2 km north of town. Access to the West Bank is provided by public ferries and private hire motorboats or *feluccas* along the Corniche. There is also a bridge, 7 km from town that gives access to West Bank-bound vehicles. ▸▸ *See Transport, page 250.*

Information

The main **Egyptian Tourist Authority (ETA) office** ⓘ *T095-237 3294, open daily 0800-2000, English-speaking staff tend to turn up around 1000*, is directly opposite the train station. It is good for checking bus and train times and current official prices for everything including *calèches* and taxis, and for checking the Sound and Light schedule at Karnak. There are further offices in the train station, T095-237 0259, and the airport, T095-237 2306, which work the same hours. The **Tourist Police** ⓘ *T095-237 0750*, are next to the railway station.

Warning Bear in mind that as tourism sustains the bulk of the city's economy, the hustle and hassle in Luxor is among the most intense in the country. Expect to be bombarded by horse-drawn carriages, *felucca* captains, souvenir peddlers and hotel touts. And expect to

24 hours in Luxor

At first light, take a *calèche* to **Karnak** and spend a couple of hours in Egypt's best-preserved and most impressive temple. Then, if you haven't booked a tour already, catch the ferry across the river and book a taxi for a half day at the West Bank sights. Start with either **Medinat Habu** or the **Ramesseum**, followed by **Deir El-Bahri** and three of the **Nobles' Tombs**. Try to be in the **Valley of Kings** at lunchtime when it's least busy, then enjoy some hearty local food at one of the small restaurants near Medinat Habu or by the riverbank.

In the afternoon, visit the cool interiors of the **Luxor Museum** and follow it with an hour on a *felucca* for sunset. Have an aperitif at the **Windsor Hotel**, before dinner and a meander through the *souk*. Visit **Luxor Temple** at night (before 2200), beautifully lit, before a nightcap of *karkade* and *sheesha* in a coffee shop.

be ripped off at least once. Hotel touts congregate to meet all tourist trains coming in, making arrival at the station quite stressful. It is even worse on arrival at the bus station, where young guys who meet the incoming buses are quite aggressive in their activities. It is best to know exactly where you're going before arriving. You may be told your hotel of choice has closed, is full, or the price has changed. These tales are unlikely to be true, as the accommodation situation doesn't really change that much in Luxor. If a driver tries to take you to his brother's hotel instead, adamantly insist to be dropped where you want to go and don't pay until you get there. Try to inform yourself about fair prices and the games people play, and remember that everyone is just trying to make a living. With a bit of patience and a sense of humour, you'll come to find that behind the frenzy lie a warm, welcoming people.

Best time to visit

Tourist season extends from October to March, peaking around Christmas and the New Year, when the weather is sunny and sublime. Most monuments and museums are open 0600-1800 in winter, 0500-1900 in summer, take note that offices will stop selling tickets 45 minutes or one hour before closing times. In the thick of summer, it's best to visit tombs and temples in the early morning hours, although the heat of the mid-afternoon, if you can bear it, does wonders to drive away the hordes of tourists and touts.

Background

On the site of the present-day town of Luxor stood the ancient city that the Greeks called **Thebes** and which was described in Homer's *Iliad* as the "city of a hundred gates". Later the Arabs described it as '*el-Uqsur*' or 'city of palaces' from which it gets its current name.

The town and the surrounding limestone hills had been settled for many centuries but during the Old Kingdom (2616-2181 BC) it was little more than a small provincial town called Waset. It first assumed importance under Menutuhotep II who reunited Egypt and made it his capital, but it was during the 18th-20th Dynasty of the New Kingdom (1567-1085 BC) that Thebes really reached its zenith. Except for the brief reign of Akhenaten (1379-1362 BC), it was the capital of an Egyptian Empire that stretched from Palestine to Nubia for nearly 500 years, and at its peak the population reached almost one million. Besides being the site of the largest and greatest concentration of monuments in the world it was, for the ancient Egyptians, the prototype for all future cities.

Luxor with kids

Luxor has the potential to both amaze and daze. Don't be tempted to try and squeeze in dynasty after dynasty of tomb sightseeing, but focus instead on a few of the most enigmatic sites. Highlights include the tombs of Ramses I and Ramses VI – both of which have burial chambers with elaborately painted scenes of animal-headed gods. Older children may enjoy the challenge of reaching the tomb of Tuthmosis III with its steep shafts and challenging passageways designed in an (unsuccessful) attempt to thwart tomb robbers. You'll find that a series of early-morning excursions to the West Bank has less 'whinge potential' than a single, long, hot day trip. Spend the afternoons relaxing by a pool and then set off again when it's cooler to visit local Luxor beauties like the Great Hypostyle Hall – a forest of 134 towering pillars at Karnak. A great way to reach this spectacular complex is to take one of the local horse-drawn carriages.

When the capital later shifted elsewhere it remained a vibrant city and the focus for the worship of Amun ('the Supreme Creator'). Although there is no obvious connection with the Greek city of Thebes the name was subsequently given to the city by the Greeks. It was a shadow of its former self during the Ptolemaic (323-30 BC) and Roman (30 BC-AD 640) periods but, unlike ancient Memphis to the south of Cairo, it was never abandoned and it became an important Christian settlement. In the Luxor region a number of temples became Coptic monasteries. For example, at both Deir El-Medina and Deir El-Bahri Egyptian monuments were taken over and converted for Christian use.

After the Muslim conquest in AD 640, the town continued to decline and it was not until the beginning of the 19th century, during Napoleon's expedition to Egypt, that its historical importance began to be recognized. The display of some of its treasures in Paris's Louvre museum sparked off considerable interest from the world's archaeologists – who continue to make important discoveries even today. Since 1869, when Thomas Cook took his first party of travellers to Egypt for the opening of the Suez Canal, Luxor has become the foremost tourist destination in Upper Egypt. Today, although it has become an important administrative town, the economic livelihood of Luxor is (as the sudden collapse in business during the 1990-91 Gulf war and as the mass exodus of thousands of tourists in November 1997 demonstrated) almost totally dependent on the tourist industry.

Modern-day Luxor is undergoing a transformation, as the current governor has initiated a series of radical schemes in an effort to expose more of the ancient past and to make the most of the monuments. Some of these initiatives are regretted by locals and tourists alike, as the organic nature of the city is being altered and many homes lost as the layers of buildings are stripped back. Not only has Sharia Al-Mahatta been widened to allow a view of Luxor Temple on arrival at the station, but the gritty old *souk* has been sanitized and is now strictly a tourist bazaar. A tunnel is being constructed beneath the Corniche between the Mummification Museum and Luxor Museum, in order to allow the road to be pedestrianised and become a waterside promenade. The village of Old Gurna on the West Bank used to delight the eye on the approach to Thebes, with its colourful *hajj* paintings on buildings clustering below the ridge. Now the vast majority of houses have been demolished, only a few remain (which are being kept as a model of how life was in Old Gurna), to enable proper excavation of the Tombs of the Nobles and protect them from water drainage from the village. Further long-term plans, which will take

10-15 years to complete, include the relocation of all the cruise boats to a new mooring beyond the bridge 7 km to the south (not many people will complain about this one), to protect Luxor Temple from pollution. Already in full swing is an ambitious scheme to reconnect Luxor and Karnak temples via the Avenue of the Sphinxes, which involves demolishing every building and home that stands in the way. What will happen to any mosques that have grown up over the ancient passage is still being debated. Probably every person you meet in Luxor will have a tale to tell about their parents, uncle or daughter-in-law being re-homed as a consequence and the inadequate compensation they have been paid.

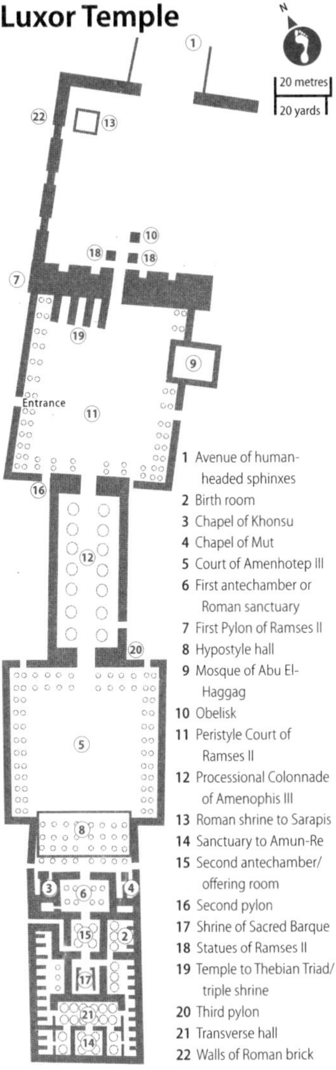

Sights

Luxor Temple

ⓘ *The temple, in the centre of town on the Corniche, is open daily 0600-2030 in winter, 0600-2130 in summer, E£50, students E£25, cameras free. Allow a couple of hours. It is particularly striking at night; a ticket permits re-entry, but only on the same day. Entrance is from Sharia Karnak (not from the Corniche, as was previously the case).*

Like the much larger Karnak Temple, Luxor Temple is dedicated to the three Theban gods Amun, Mut and Khonsu. **Amun** is usually depicted as a man wearing ram's horns or a tall Ostrich-feathered Atef crown. His wife **Mut** was considered to be the mistress of heaven and **Khonsu** was their son who was believed to travel through the sky at night assisting the scribe god.

Because it is smaller, quite compact and fewer pharaohs were involved in its construction, Luxor Temple is simpler and more coherent than Karnak Temple. Although the 18th Dynasty pharaoh Amenhotep III (1417-1379 BC) began the temple, his son Amenhotep IV, better known as Akhenaten, concentrated instead on building a shrine to Aten adjacent to the site. However, Tutankhamen (1361-1352 BC) and Horemheb (1348-1320 BC) later resumed the work and decorated the peristyle court and colonnade. Ramses II (1304-1237 BC) completed most of the

2 Luxor

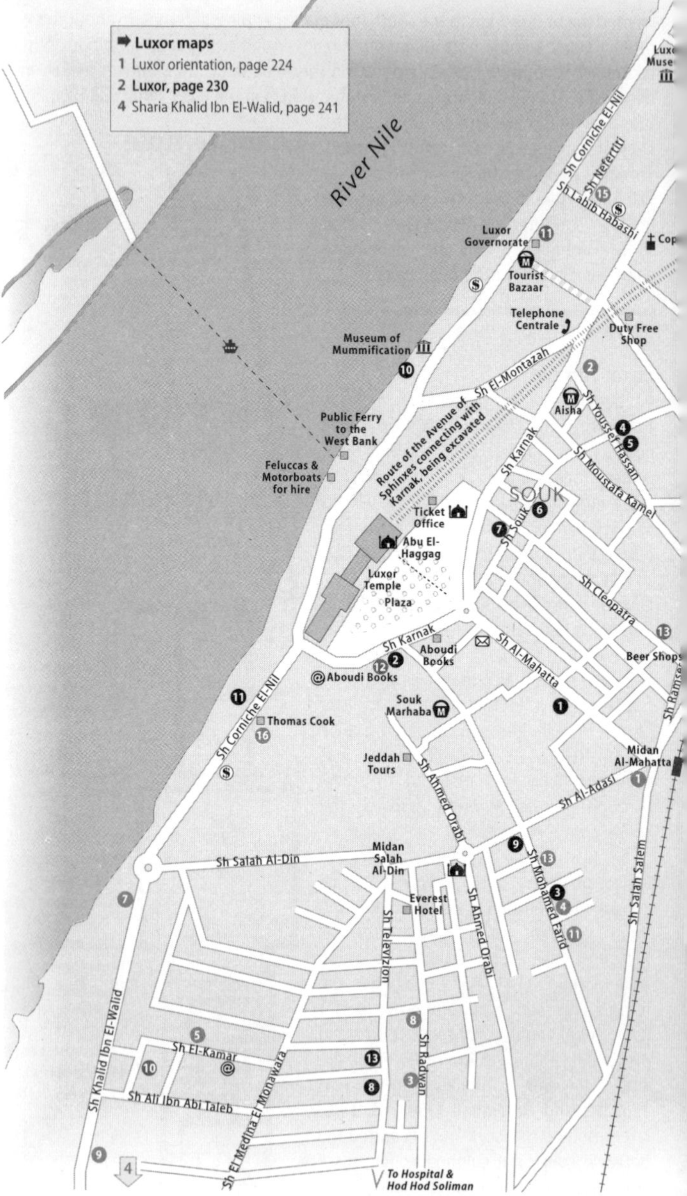
Luxor maps
1 Luxor orientation, page 224
2 Luxor, page 230
4 Sharia Khalid Ibn El-Walid, page 241
River Nile
Sh Corniche El-Nil
Sh Nefertiti
Sh Labib Habashi
Luxor Governorate
Tourist Bazaar
Telephone Centrale
Duty Free Shop
Museum of Mummification
Sh El-Montazah
Aisha
Sh Youssef Hassan
Public Ferry to the West Bank
Feluccas & Motorboats for hire
Route of the Avenue of Sphinxes connecting with Karnak, being excavated
Sh Karnak
Sh Moustafa Kamel
SOUK
Ticket Office
Sh Souk
Abu El-Haggag
Luxor Temple
Plaza
Sh Cleopatra
Beer Shops
Aboudi Books
Sh Al-Mahatta
Souk Marhaba
Thomas Cook
Jeddah Tours
Sh Ahmed Orabi
Midan Al-Mahatta
Sh Al-Adasi
Midan Salah Al-Din
Sh Salah Al-Din
Sh Mohamed Farid
Sh Salah Salem
Everest Hotel
Sh Televizion
Sh Khalid Ibn El-Walid
Sh El-Kamar
Sh Radwan
Sh Ali Ibn Abi Taleb
Sh El Medina El Monawara
To Hospital & Hod Hod Soliman

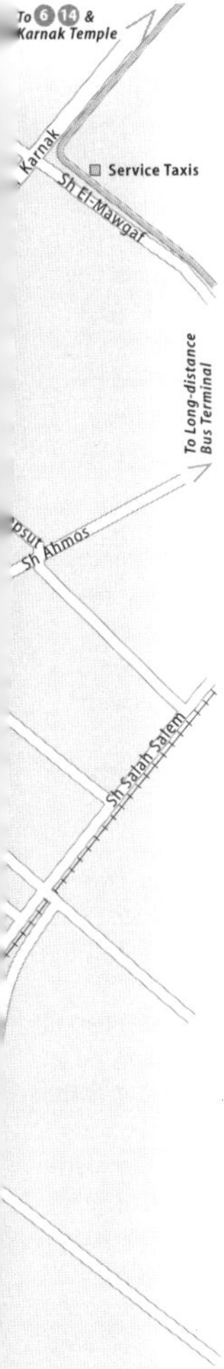

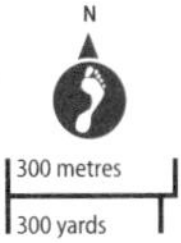

Sleeping
Anglo 1
Boomerang 4
Domina Inn Emilio 2
Fontana 3
Happy Land 5
Iberotel Luxor 7
Little Garden 8
Luxor Hilton Resort & Spa 6
New Pola 9
Nubian Oasis 12
Oasis 13
Philippe 15
Rezeiky Camp 14
Seven Heaven 11
Sofitel Winter Palace 16

Eating
Abu Ashraf 1
Abu El-Hassan El-Shazly 9
Ali Baba 2
El Zaeem 5
Jamboree 6
Kebabgy 11
Lotus 7
Metropolitan 10
Mish Mish 8
Quick 13
Sofra 3

Bars & clubs
Esquire 10
Mercure 11
Saint Mina Hotel 13
Sinbad 12

building by adding a second colonnade and pylon as well as a multitude of colossi. The Temple subsequently became covered with sand and silt which helped preserve it, although salt encrustation has caused some damage. Because the ground level has risen 6 m since its construction the temple now stands at the bottom of a gentle depression. The avenue of sphinxes lining the approach, a 30th Dynasty (380-343 BC) addition, once stretched all the way to the Karnak Temple complex. Though at first glance they all appear identical, actually each face (that of Amenhotep III) is subtly different, some a little plump and others very serious, but all with the mysterious secret smile of the sphinx. Excavation and demolition work is underway to uncover this avenue, buried under the modern city for countless centuries, and it's estimated it will take until 2030 to reconnect the two temples and realign any ruinous sphinxes which lie in fields and backyards.

In front of the gigantic First Pylon are the three remaining colossi of Ramses II and to the left stands a single obelisk towering 25 m high. A 22.8-m-high second obelisk was given to France by Mohammed Ali Pasha in 1819 and re-erected in the Place de la Concorde in Paris, where it still stands. The **First Pylon** gives a powerful and immediate impression of how awe-inspiring the temple must have looked in its prime. Its reliefs depict Ramses' supposed victory at the Battle of Kadesh, with later embellishments by Nubian and Ethiopian kings.

Passing through the pylon, the **Peristyle Court** is set at a slight angle to the rest of the temple to encompass earlier shrines built by Tuthmosis III (1504-1450 BC), on the right, dedicated to the Theban triad. The double row of columns surrounding the court are shaped into the classic representation of papyrus reeds bound together to form a bud at the top. The east end of the court has not been fully

The hassle, haggle and hustle

Luxor is as synonymous with 'hassle' as it is with the 'Valley of the Kings'. Many visitors get frustrated and depressed by the constant pesterings of *felucca* men and *calèche* drivers, the harsh battles when bargaining in the *souk*, the need to be mistrustful of friendly overtures and of the locals' conspiracy in the overcharging of all foreigners. But before getting too irate, it's as well to remember the other side.

The effects of terrorist attacks in Egypt, 9/11 and the war in Iraq have meant the number of tourists in Luxor has fluctuated wildly in recent years. In a town where most people's bread is connected to tourism, the impact has been dire. As a result, everyone does everything they can to get as much as they can. Sometimes it means budget hotels cut their rates in half just to earn a few pounds, or guides offer the same tour to one hard haggler for 100 pounds less than to another. This is how people get by. Especially when the season is slumping, every tourist counts. Most tour guides and *felucca* captains will make a chunk of money in a day and not see another chunk for a long spell. When bargaining for a cheaper deal, bear in mind that less is not always best and the quality of your experience may suffer if you take advantage of this situation. Be fair and realistic and try to maintain a sensitivity to the people on your back. They are used to seeing the vast majority of Western tourists paying to stay in five-star hotels, eat international cuisine (in restaurants locals would not be allowed into), and have two-week holidays with their children every year. It's not surprising that they try to take advantage.

excavated because it is the site of the **Mosque of Abu El-Haggag**, which can be entered from the other side. At the south end of the court, the portal flanking the entrance to the colonnade supports two black granite statues bearing the name of Ramses II, but the feathers of Tutankhamen.

The daunting **Colonnade** of 14 columns with papyrus capitals leads to the older part of the temple. The walls are detailed with the procession of the **Opet Festival**, following an anticlockwise direction, decorated by Tutankhamen and Horemheb. Beyond it is the **Court of Amenhotep III**, a second sweeping peristyle court with double rows of columns flanking three of the sides. None of the original roof remains, and the floor and 22 massive columns have had to be relaid because the rising water table was undermining the foundations. It leads to the **Hypostyle Hall** with 32 papyrus columns that were taken over by Ramses IV and Ramses VII, who took no part in their erection but still added their cartouches. Look out for the chamber that was converted into a Coptic church during the fourth century. The pharaonic reliefs were plastered over and early Christian paintings covered the whitewash, their colour and detail just recently exposed by a restoration project. In other areas the stucco is crumbling away to reveal the original reliefs.

Beyond is a smaller second vestibule, the **Offerings Chamber**, with its four columns still in place. Further on, in the **Sanctuary of the Sacred Barque**, the doors were made of acacia and inlaid with gold. Alexander the Great (332-323 BC) rebuilt the shrine in accordance with Amenhotep III's original plans, and left reliefs of himself on the outer wall. Also look out for the depiction of a virile Amun, whose erect phallus has been weathered over the centuries by the touch of women who want to conceive. The east passage leads to the **Birth Room** built because of Amenhotep's claim that he was the son of the god Amun, who is depicted as entering the queen's chamber disguised as

Tuthmosis IV and breathing the child into her nostrils. The furthest hall has 12 poorly maintained papyrus-bud columns and leads on to the small **Sanctuary of Amenhotep III** where the combined god Amun-Min is represented.

Mosque of Abu Haggag

This mosque, built atop the ruins of Luxor Temple, contains the tomb of Abu Haggag, the patron saint of Luxor who died in 1243. Although another mosque with the same name has been built nearby, this one is still preferred by locals. After a fire in 2009, the mosque has been renovated and many of the pharaonic elements that were incorporated into the building have been re-exposed. Stucco that had been covering columns carved with hieroglyphs was removed revealing, among others, the cartouche of Ramses II. While most of the present-day mosque is 19th-century, the northern minaret is very much older. As well as the small grave of Abu Haggag, there are shrines containing the remains of his uncles and family. The atmospheric mosque is worth a visit: the prayer hall is beautiful and there are views down to the temple; generous *baksheesh* will be expected by the mosque attendants.

Luxor Museum

ⓘ *The museum is on the Corniche halfway between Luxor and Karnak temples, daily 0900-1400 and 1600-2100 (last tickets 1230 and 2030) winter, 0900-1500 and 1700-2100 summer, Ramadan 1300-1600. Entrance E£80, students E£40, no cameras/video permitted.*
The exhibits in this modern museum, ranging from pharaonic treasures to the Mamluk period, are tastefully displayed after a relatively recent reorganization and the opening of a new wing. A seven-minute documentary is shown in the small cinema behind the ticket booth, which helps put the artefacts in context, and it is worth looking at the statues in the small garden at the front before entering the museum proper.

On entering, visitors are greeted by a statue of Amun, taking the facial features of King Tutankhamun. Close by is a splendid gilded head of Hathor (the cow-goddess) and a huge sloe-eyed head of Amenhotep III in pink granite. Down the steps to the right are the New Kingdom statues that were found in a cache at Luxor Temple in 1989, probably the most important items in the museum. Twenty-four statues were unearthed, though not all can be seen here; of particular note is the red quartzite statue of Amenhotep III, preserved in complete perfection down to his sandalled feet, and a smooth grey granite Hathor. Back on the ground floor, equally striking is a calcite crocodile-headed Sobek, cradling Amenhotep III in his arms, and an exquisite votive statue of Mayi offering a crocodile to Sobek carved from black granite.

The new wing presents 'Thebes Glory', the centrepieces of which are the unwrapped mummies of Ahmose I and (possibly) Ramses I (whoever he was, his face is extraordinary). Ahmose I was one of several pharaohs unearthed among a stash of royal mummies discovered in 1881, hidden in a communal grave by the priests of the 21st Dynasty – an attempt to keep the remains safe that proved successful for nearly 3000 years. Nearby, look out for the military decoration belonging to Ahmose's mother, an incredible necklace comprising three giant flies made of solid gold. Also of interest in the main Thebes Glory room is a relief of Amenhotep III making war on his chariot, as well as Tutankhamun's royal bows. From here, as you move to the upper level, note the statues of doleful slaves prostrate with their hands behind their back or held by their hair by Ramses VI. The upper level is dedicated to scribes and the art of writing, and includes the architect's original plans for the tomb of Ramses IX.

Mummification

The ritual of mummification reached its zenith during the New Kingdom at the same time as the Luxor and Karnak temple complexes were being built. It was developed because the ancient Egyptians believed that in order for a person to reach their heavenly aspect or *Ka* in the afterlife, it was essential that both their name and body survived thereby sustaining their cosmic double or *Ka*, which was transported from one life to the next. In order to achieve this, the mummification ritual developed into an extremely complex means of preserving bodies. The dead were placed in tombs together with any food and utensils thought necessary to accompany the person's *Ka* for the journey to the underworld.

Although we know quite a bit about the most commonly used New Kingdom mummification methods, others are still being revealed. For example, a recently opened princess' tomb in Giza revealed that the body had been hollowed out and lined with very fine plaster.

The mummification method found in and around the Valley of the Kings, however, usually involved removing the brain through the nose (it was discarded because the heart was thought to be the centre of intelligence). The entrails and organs were then extracted and stored in jars, known as Canopic jars, while the corpse was soaked in natrun salts for 40 days until it was dehydrated, at which point the embalming process began. In an attempt to recreate its original appearance the body was packed and then painted red if male and yellow if female. Artificial eyes, made of polished stone or jewels were inserted into the eye sockets and the face was made up before the body was wrapped in gum-coated linen bandages and placed in its coffin.

On the highest floor, between three memorable busts of Akhenaten, is the Wall of Akhenaten, 283 sandstone blocks found inside the middle of the Ninth Pylon at Karnak. Here Akhenaten and Nefertiti are shown worshipping Aten, amid scenes of life in the temple. Also on display on this floor are a few choice exhibits from Tutankhamen's tomb including funerary bed and two model barques.

Museum of Mummification

ⓘ *Daily 0900-1400, 1600-2100 winter, 0900-1400, 1700-2200 summer; Ramadan 1300-1600 only. E£50, students E£25. Cameras not permitted.*

Right on the banks of the Nile this museum tells the story of mummification, as practised by the ancient Egyptians, as an integral part of their religious belief in the afterlife. This museum, considered to be the first of its kind in the world, contains a comprehensive display. Exhibits include several human, reptile and bird mummies as well as stone and metal tools used in the mummification process. A well-preserved mummy of a 21st Dynasty high priest of Amun is of interest. It is well set out and worth a short visit. Note the examples of canopic jars for storing the liver, lungs, stomach and intestines.

Karnak Temple complex

ⓘ *Daily 0600-1730 (last tickets sold an hr before closing, but it's recommended to get there by 1600 at the latest), E£70, students E£35. Cameras free. Tickets are purchased by the new visitor centre (which has some interesting old photos on display) on the south side of the vast plaza in front of the temple. To get to Karnak, you can walk or bike the 2.5 km north along Sharia Karnak, but it is probably better to save your energy for the site itself. Microbuses (50 pt) with Karnak en route are found around the train station (look for the yellow signs on the dashboard, yell out 'Karnak', if they're going, they'll stop for you).* Calèches *and private taxis from town officially cost E£20-25. If they wait (2 hrs) and bring you back, it's E£45 and some* baksheesh. *Expect to bargain hard. If you can face it, it is worth getting up early to be first there and avoid the big tour parties. Allow half a day to see in detail. If possible return in the evening for the Sound and Light show (E£100, students E£60, children aged 6-15 E£75, under 6 free). There are 3 shows daily with a late-night slot for a fourth to accommodate large tour groups. In winter, shows happen daily at 1830, 1945, 2100 (and 2215). In summer, 2000, 2115, 2230 (and 2345). Check at the tourist office, www.soundandlight.com.eg or T095-238 6000 for the latest schedules as the languages vary.*

Karnak Temple, the largest pharaonic monument in the country after the Giza Pyramids covering almost half a square kilometre, is a rambling complex of towering pillars and mighty pylons. Known in earlier times as Iput-Isut 'the most esteemed of places', the extent, scale and quality of the remains is astonishing. And they presumably would have been even more impressive, had not many of the blocks been filched by 19th-century *pashas* to be used in the construction of sugar cane factories nearby. Still, as Flaubert said, Karnak gives 'the impression of a life of giants', and as you stand dwarfed by the massive masonry it becomes easy to believe in the vastness of the ancient city of Thebes. The complex's temples vary greatly in style because they were constructed over 1300 years and every great pharaoh made his mark. Their only common theme is worship of Amun, Mut and Khonsu, who make up the Theban Triad of gods.

Temple of Amun At the heart of the complex is the enormous Temple of Amun, which was altered, extended and added to by successive rulers. Although the heretical Akhenaten, who converted to the world's first monotheistic religion and moved the capital from Thebes to Tell El-Amarna (see page 201), replaced the images of Amun with representations of Aten, these were

3 Karnak

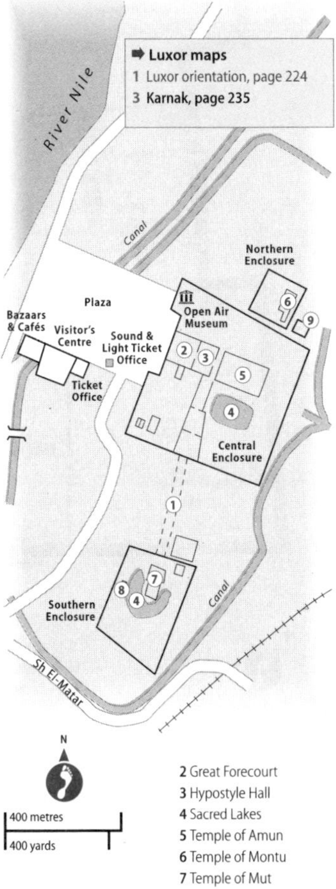

1 Avenue of Ram Headed Sphinxes
2 Great Forecourt
3 Hypostyle Hall
4 Sacred Lakes
5 Temple of Amun
6 Temple of Montu
7 Temple of Mut
8 Temple of Ramses III
9 Treasury of Tuthmosis I

later erased by his successors and Amun's images were restored. The Temple of Amun is approached via the **Avenue of Ram-Headed Sphinxes (1),** which used to link it to the Temple at Luxor. The imposing **First Pylon (13)** is 130 m wide and each of the two unfinished towers are 43 m high and, although incomplete, nothing else quite matches its

Karnak central enclosure - Temple of Amun

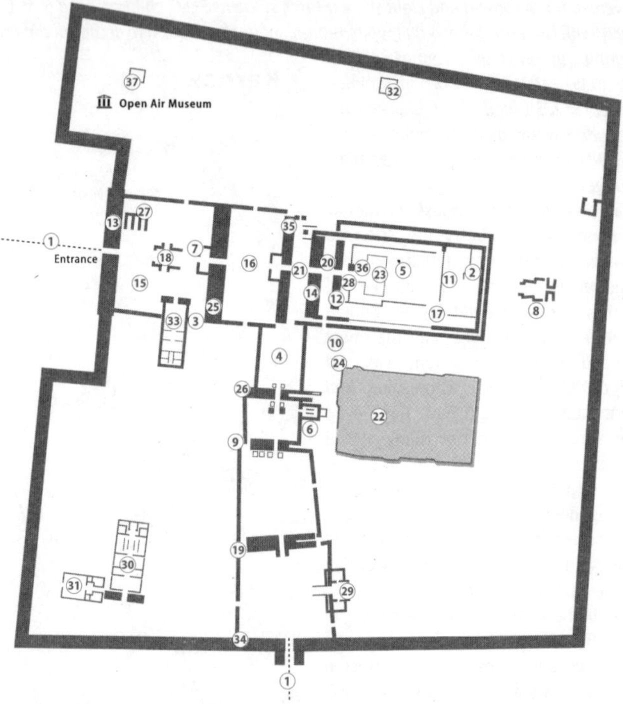

1 Avenue of ram-headed Sphinxes
2 Botanical vestibule
3 Bubastite portal
4 Cachette court
5 Central court
6 Chapel of Tuthmosis III
7 Colossus of Ramses II
8 Eastern Temple of Ramses II
9 Eighth pylon
10 Fallen Obelisk of Hatshepsut
11 Festival Hall of Tuthmosis III
12 Fifth pylon
13 First pylon
14 Fourth pylon
15 Great forecourt
16 Hypostyle hall
17 Karnak Table of Kings
18 Kiosk of Taharqa
19 Ninth pylon
20 Obelisk of Hatshepsut
21 Obelisks of Tuthmosis
22 Sacred lake
23 Sanctuary of sacred boats
24 Scarab statue
25 Second pylon
26 Seventh pylon
27 Shrine of Seti II
28 Sixth pylon
29 Temple of Amenhoptep II
30 Temple of Khonsu
31 Temple of Opet
32 Temple of Ptah
33 Temple of Ramses III
34 Tenth pylon
35 Third pylon
36 Vestibule
37 White Chapel of Sesostris

enormous scale. Moving towards the inner core of the temple, which is the oldest section, one is moving back in time through successive dynasties. The entry towers are thought to have been constructed by the Nubian and Ethiopian kings of the 25th Dynasty (747-656 BC) while recent work has revealed that several levels were built during the later Greek and Roman eras.

Arriving through the First Pylon, you come to the **Great Forecourt (15)**, begun in the 20th Dynasty (1200-1085 BC) but completed some time later. Immediately on the left is the very thick-walled rose-coloured granite and sandstone **Shrine of Seti II (27)** (1216-1210 BC) which was a way-station for the sacred barques of Amun, Mut and Khonsu as they were taken on ritual processions. The outer façade portrays Seti II making offerings to various deities. In the middle of the Great Forecourt are the 10 columns of **Taharga**, which once supported a 26.5 m high kiosk or small open temple.

To the right of the forecourt is the small **Temple of Ramses III (33)**, which would have stood in solitary splendour in front of the **Second Pylon (25)** when it was first built in honour of Amun. Like the Shrine of Seti II, it was used as another way-station for the sacred barques. Part of an inscription in the interior reads: "I made it for you in your city of Waset, in front of your forecourt, to the Lord of the Gods, being the Temple of Ramses in the estate of Amun, to remain as long as the heavens bear the sun. I filled its treasuries with offerings that my hands had brought."

To the left of the Second Pylon is the 15 m high **Colossus of Ramses II (7)** with his daughter Benta-anta standing in front of his legs. On the right of the pylon is the **Bubastite Portal (3)** named after the 22nd-Dynasty kings from the Delta town of Bubastis. Inside the Second Pylon, blocks and statues from the destroyed temple to Aten were discovered, which are now centrepieces of the Akhenaten displays in Luxor and Cairo museums.

Passing through the Second Pylon brings you to the immense and spectacular **Hypostyle Hall (16)**, which is probably the most overpowering part of the whole Karnak complex. Its 134 giant columns were once topped by sandstone roof slabs, the 12 largest are a gigantic 23 m high and 15 m round and make up the central processional way to the chambers. The other 122 smaller columns, which have papyrus bud capitals and retain some of their original colour at the higher levels, cover the rest of the hall. They are decorated by dedications to various gods, but particularly to the many different guises of Amun and the Theban Triad, and are also inscribed with the cartouches of the pharaohs who contributed to the hall. The south side was decorated by Ramses II with vivid but cheap and simple concave sunk-reliefs, while the north is attributed to Seti II whose artists painstakingly carved delicate convex bas-reliefs on the walls. Ramses is shown, on the south side of the internal wall of the Second Pylon, making offerings before the gods and seeking their guidance, while on the left is a beautiful representation of Thoth inscribing Seti's name on a holy tree.

Seti II is depicted on both sides of the Third Pylon but the south wall running along the right of the hall was mainly decorated by Ramses II. He is shown being crowned by Horus and Thoth and then being presented to Amun. The **Third Pylon (35)** was constructed by Amenhotep III on the site of several earlier shrines that were moved to the Open Air Museum within the walls of Karnak. On the inner east face is a text of tribute and a scene showing the gods' sacred boats. Amenhotep III built a small court to enclose four **Tuthmosid Obelisks (21)** in the narrow gap between the Third and Fourth Pylon, which at that time represented the entrance to the Temple. Of the four, only one pink granite obelisk (23 m high, weighing 143 tonnes and originally tipped with electrum) built by

Tuthmosis II now remains and the stone bases and some blocks from two other obelisks built by Tuthmosis III are scattered nearby.

Moving towards the earlier centre of the temple is the limestone-faced sandstone **Fourth Pylon (14)**, built by Tuthmosis I. Texts describing later restorations are recorded on both sides by Tuthmosis IV to the left and Shabaka to the right. Just inside is a small **Transverse Hall** that was originally a hypostyle hall before the temple was extended outwards. Only 12 of the original papyrus bud columns and one of two 27 m and 340 tonne rose-granite **Obelisk of Hatshepsut (20)**, which once stood at the entrance, now remain. In the 16th year of the reign of Hatshepsut (1503-1482 BC), the only woman to rule Egypt as pharaoh, these two obelisks were transported from Aswan where a third unfinished one still lies in the quarry (see The Unfinished Obelisk, page 304). The tip of the second obelisk, which fell to the ground, is now lying near the Sacred Lake. The surviving erect obelisk is decorated along its whole length with the following inscription – "O ye people who see this monument in years to come and speak of that which I have made, beware lest you say, 'I know not why it was done'. I did it because I wished to make a gift for my father Amun, and to gild them with electrum." Her long-frustrated and usurped infant stepson Tuthmosis III, who had plotted against her during her reign, took his revenge by hiding the obelisks behind walls almost to the ceiling, which actually preserved them from later graffiti.

The east wall of the Transverse Hall is the **Fifth Pylon (12)**, which has been attributed to Hatshepsut's father Tuthmosis I. Beyond is another hall and then the badly damaged sandstone **Sixth Pylon (28)**. The world's first imperialist, Tuthmosis III, inscribed it on both sides with details of his vanquished enemies and his victory at the Battle of Megiddo or Armageddon. Past the pylon is a **Vestibule (36)**, which is flanked by two courts and is dominated by two granite pillars with carvings showing Tuthmosis III being embraced by Amun, and the lotus and papyrus symbols of Upper and Lower Egypt. A seated statue of Amenhotep II is against the west wall and on the north side are two colossi of Amun and Amunet, although their faces resemble Tutankhamen who had them built. The Vestibule leads to the Granite Sanctuary built by Alexander the Great's moronic half-brother and successor Philip Arrhidaeus (323-317 BC). The ceiling is covered with golden stars on a dark base while the walls depict scenes of Philip with the god Amun. The exterior walls are decorated in a similar fashion.

North of the Sanctuary beyond the granite door is a series of small chambers built by Hatshepsut but later altered by Tuthmosis III. Some of the rooms were walled up by her son to conceal Hatshepsut's influence and consequently the bright colours have been very well preserved, although Hatshepsut's face has been cut away whenever it appeared.

Further to the east is Tuthmosis III's **Festival Hall (11)** which, with its central tentpole-style columns symbolizing the tents used during his campaigns, is unlike any other Egyptian building. It was built for his jubilee festivals that were intended to renew the pharaohs' temporal and spiritual authority. Access is via a small vestibule that leads to the central columned hall. The columns in the central aisle are taller than the side ones and would have supported a raised section of the roof thereby permitting sunlight to enter. The hall was later used as a Christian church and early paintings of the saints can still be seen on some of the columns.

Off to the southwest is a small chamber where the original stela known as the **Karnak Table of Kings (17)**, minus Hatshepsut, was found. The original is in the Louvre in Paris, the one on display here a replica. The series of interconnecting chambers beyond is dedicated to the Theban Triad and further north is an attractive chamber known as the

Botanical Vestibule (2). Its four columns have papyrus capitals and are carved with the unfamiliar plants and shrubs discovered by Tuthmosis III during his Syrian campaign. Surrounding the small chamber on the far east wall is the small and badly decayed **Sanctuary of Amun**, built by Hatshepsut and originally decorated with two raised obelisks on either side of the entrance – only the bases now remain. The nearby **Chapel of Sokar**, which is dedicated to the Memphite god of darkness, is better preserved.

To the south of the main temple, the **Sacred Lake (22)** (200 m x 117 m) has been restored to its original dimensions but has become stagnant since the inundation that used to feed the lake by underground channels from the River Nile ceased after the construction of the Aswan Dam. Today the lake is totally uninteresting but it has the Sound and Light Show grandstand at the far end and a café on the north side. A Nilometer is attached to the lake and there is a statue of a giant scarab beetle that childless women walk around five times in order to ensure that they soon bear children.

While the main temple runs from west to east there is a secondary axis running south from the area between the third and fourth pylons. It begins with the **Cachette Court (4)**, which received its name after the discovery between 1903 and 1906 of 17,000 bronze statues and 780 stone ones that had been stored in the court during the Ptolemaic period, the best of which are now in the Egyptian Museum in Cairo. The reliefs on the outside wall of the Hypostyle Hall, northwest of the court, depict Ramses II in battle starting with the second Battle of Kadesh. Facing this, on the outer (western) wall of the Cachette Court, is a copy of the earliest known international peace treaty. The **Treaty of Kadesh** was drawn up between the Egyptians and the Hittites in 1258 BC, when both sides needed to stop warring with each other in order to focus on fighting more immediate threats. Ramses II promises King Hattusilis III that he will not "gouge out their eyes, kill his children, destroy his house, cut off his tongue, ears, feet or any other part of his body". Other less gory agreements still form the foundations of peace treaties today, such as the sanctity of messengers, repatriation of refugees, and the promise of mutual assistance should either be threatened by a third party. On the east walls, close to the **Seventh Pylon (26)**, is a replica of a stela now in the Egyptian Museum showing the only reference to Israel during pharaonic times. The Seventh Pylon was built by Tuthmosis III and shows him massacring his prisoners before Amun. In front of the façade are parts of two colossi of Tuthmosis and in the courtyard to the left is the small chapel of Tuthmosis III.

Although restoration work continues on the nearby **Eighth Pylon (9)** and others further along, it may be possible to have a quick look in return for a small tip to the guard, either early or late in the day when there are fewer people. The Eighth Pylon was built by Tuthmosis II and Hatshepsut and contains extensively restored reliefs and cartouches. As in many other places, Hatshepsut's name has been erased and replaced by that of Tuthmosis III, while Akhenaten's name was erased by Seti I. The south side of the pylon has four of the original six **Seated Colossi**, two of which are Tuthmosis II and one is Amenhotep I.

The **Ninth Pylon (19)** and the **Tenth Pylon (34)** were built by Horemheb (1348-1320 BC) using materials from the demolished Aten Temple. The Tenth Pylon has two colossi of Ramses II and his wife Nefertari usurping the original colossi of Amenhotep III. On the south side of the pylon there are two quartzite colossi of Amenhotep III. The pylon is part of the outer enclosure and marks the start of the ram-headed sphinx-lined road to the southern enclosure.

In the far southwest corner of the central enclosure are two fairly well preserved temples, but they are of limited interest. The **Temple of Khonsu (30)** was built by Ramses III and Ramses IV and dedicated to the son of Amun and Mut. Many of the reliefs show

Herihor, high-priest of Amun, who ruled Upper Egypt after Ramses XI (1114-1085 BC) moved his capital to the Delta and delegated power to the high-priest. In the courtyard Herihor's name is inscribed on every pillar and all the scenes depict him venerating the gods and making offerings to them. The **Temple of Opet (31)**, the hippopotamus-goddess, is normally closed to the public as excavations are ongoing.

Southern Enclosure To the south, enclosed by a mud-brick wall are the much over-grown remains of the Temple of Mut and associated buildings. They are worth a quick visit. The entrance is in the centre of the north wall. Outside the enclosure and to the east are the ruins of a temple and to the west remains suggested as a barque sanctuary. Inside the enclosure, in a central position between the entrance and the Sacred Lake, and orientated north-south, stands the **Temple of Mut (5)**, consort of Amun. Little remains of this construction accepted as the work of Ptolemies II and VII except a number of diorite statues of the lioness-headed god, Sekhmet. To the northeast is the **Temple of Amenhotep III (4)**, later restored by Ramses II. Little remains except the bases of the walls and pillars and the feet on wall decorations. To the west of the Sacred Lake stands the **Temple of Ramses III (6)** with some military scenes on the outer walls and a headless colossus on the west side.

Northern Enclosure On the north side of the central enclosure, the **Temple of Ptah (32)** (currently closed for excavation) leads on to Karnak's northern enclosure, which includes two temples, a sacred lake (now dry) and some chapels. The **Temple of Montu**, the god of war, was built by Amenhotep III, some of whose cartouches survive, and restored by Ramses IV. He left his mark too. Also in this small enclosure (150 sq m) to the west is a

Karnak southern enclosure - Precinct of Mut

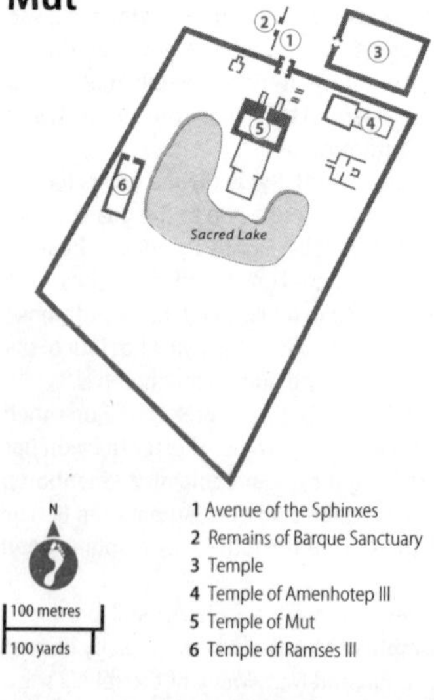

1 Avenue of the Sphinxes
2 Remains of Barque Sanctuary
3 Temple
4 Temple of Amenhotep III
5 Temple of Mut
6 Temple of Ramses III

Karnak northern enclosure - Precinct of Montu

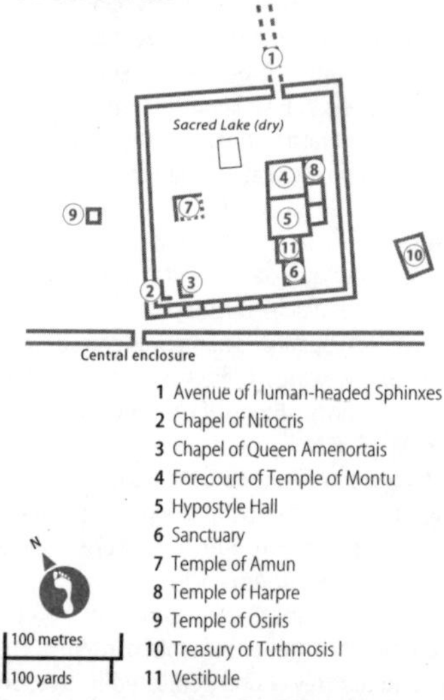

1 Avenue of Human-headed Sphinxes
2 Chapel of Nitocris
3 Chapel of Queen Amenortais
4 Forecourt of Temple of Montu
5 Hypostyle Hall
6 Sanctuary
7 Temple of Amun
8 Temple of Harpre
9 Temple of Osiris
10 Treasury of Tuthmosis I
11 Vestibule

temple to Amun (7). At the southern wall, six small gateways give access to six small chapels of which the **chapels of Amenortais and Nitocris (2 and 3)** are the best preserved.

To the east outside the enclosure is the **Treasury of Tuthmosis I (10)**, while to the west stand the remains of a **Temple of Osiris (9)**.

4 Sharia Khalid Ibn El-Walid

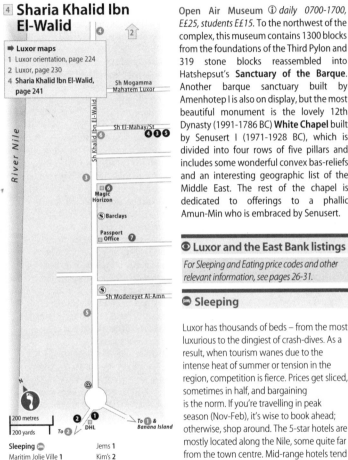

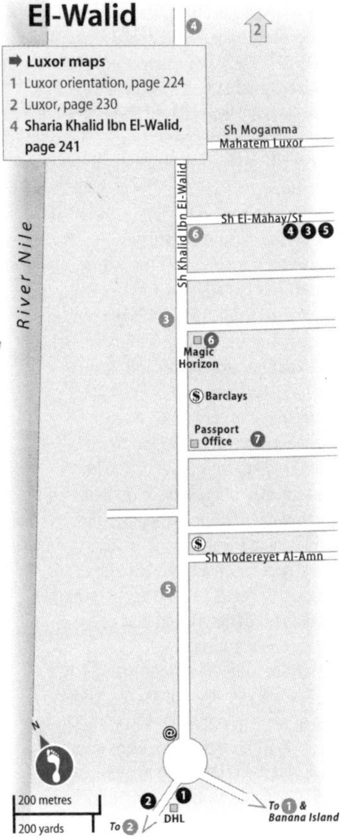

Sleeping
Maritim Jolie Ville **1**
New Pola **4**
Luxor Sheraton **2**
Pyramisa Isis **5**
Sonesta St George **3**
St Joseph **6**

Eating
A Taste of India **3**
Jems **1**
Kim's **2**
Oasis Café **4**
Pizza Roma.it **5**

Bars & clubs
Kings Head Pub **6**
Murphy's Irish Bar **7**

Open Air Museum *daily 0700-1700, E£25, students E£15.* To the northwest of the complex, this museum contains 1300 blocks from the foundations of the Third Pylon and 319 stone blocks reassembled into Hatshepsut's **Sanctuary of the Barque**. Another barque sanctuary built by Amenhotep I is also on display, but the most beautiful monument is the lovely 12th Dynasty (1991-1786 BC) **White Chapel** built by Senusert I (1971-1928 BC), which is divided into four rows of five pillars and includes some wonderful convex bas-reliefs and an interesting geographic list of the Middle East. The rest of the chapel is dedicated to offerings to a phallic Amun-Min who is embraced by Senusert.

Luxor and the East Bank listings

For Sleeping and Eating price codes and other relevant information, see pages 26-31.

Sleeping

Luxor has thousands of beds – from the most luxurious to the dingiest of crash-dives. As a result, when tourism wanes due to the intense heat of summer or tension in the region, competition is fierce. Prices get sliced, sometimes in half, and bargaining is the norm. If you're travelling in peak season (Nov-Feb), it's wise to book ahead; otherwise, shop around. The 5-star hotels are mostly located along the Nile, some quite far from the town centre. Mid-range hotels tend to be scattered both north and south of Sharia Mahatta, the central vein that runs perpendicular to the Nile from the train station. Most offer swimming pools and rooftop terraces with bars. Budget hotels are concentrated around the town centre, and virtually all include breakfast and most breakfasts consist of the same thing: bread, jam, cheese, tea or coffee, and a boiled egg. In the listing that follows, it is only noted if breakfast is extraordinary or not included. Note that there are some lovely budget to mid-range hotels on the West Bank, so also see the listings on page 281.

East Bank *p226, maps p230 and p241*

LL Luxor Hilton Resort & Spa, New Karnak, north of town with free courtesy bus, T095-237 4933, www.hiltonworldresorts.com. Reopened late 2008, after a 2-year multi-million-dollar refurbishment, the Hilton offers a truly de luxe experience. Decor is contemporary chic, there are 7 bars and restaurants to indulge at, and 2 Nile-side pools (1 with submerged sun-loungers). Undoubtedly the most glamorous and modern place to stay on the East Bank.

LL Sofitel Winter Palace, Corniche El-Nil, T095-238 0422/5, www.sofitel.com. The oldest (from 1886), and most famous luxury hotel in Luxor whose guests have included heads of state, Noel Coward and Agatha Christie. Classic rooms are rather small (for the price) in the old building, either overlooking the Nile or the verdant garden full of towering old palms, and there are magnificent suites (top price almost €2000). But what you're paying for really is the history and the exquisite public spaces, such as the Victorian lounge with its creaky parquet floor, chandeliers and Orientalist art. Rooms by the luxuriant garden are cheaper in the adjacent **Pavilion Winter Hotel** and a new building modelled in the colonial style is being built, but won't be finished until 2012 at least. The terrace bar is in splendid position overlooking Corniche and river, plus there are numerous other dining and drinking options, and a terribly chic pool. Breakfast costs extra and is expensive.

LL-L Sonesta St George Hotel, Corniche El-Nil, T095-238 2575, www.sonesta.com. A modern 7-storey building, the interior is all marble and glittering lights, generally bustling and busy. The lower level terrace overlooks the Nile and there's a fabulous pool for guests' use only. 10 restaurants and bars to choose from, of which the **Mikado** Japanese restaurant comes highly recommended for its food if not its atmosphere. Quality sport and fitness centre and all the 5-star amenities you desire.

L Iberotel Luxor, Sharia Khalid Ibn El-Walid, T095-238 0925, www.iberotelegypt.com. With an emphasis on friendly service, this upscale hotel feels relaxed and has good restaurants and pleasant terraces. Essential to get a Nile-view room unless you want to look down on the foyer. The pool floating on the Nile is an added bonus and there are good recreational facilities. They have a floating restaurant every Thu with an Oriental show from 1930-2200 (E£200) or 3 day trips a week to Dendara for E£425 per person on Sun, Tue and Fri (Tue is the quietest).

L Luxor Sheraton Hotel and Resort, Sharia El-Awameya, T095-237 4544, www.sheraton.com/luxor. A well-managed hotel with 298 rooms in main building with views of Nile (more expensive) or bungalows in garden (very comfortable). Shopping arcade, disco, tennis courts, heated pool, *feluccas* to rent. The service is consistently excellent and although it caters mainly to tour groups, it's possible to get a good deal as an independent traveller.

L Maritim Jolie Ville, Kings Island, T095-227 4855, www.jolieville-hotels.com. Enormous and deservedly popular resort with 326 rooms in 21 bungalow pavilions (more being built, which will take it up to 645 rooms). Currently being renovated to 5-star status but it remains homely, among lush flowering gardens and a wealth of birdlife on a beautiful island 4 km south of Luxor. A good choice for families, under 12s sleep free. Connected to mainland by bridge where the taxis to town line up or there's a free shuttle bus. Good restaurants, infinity pool and separate relaxing pool (children not allowed), spa, fitness centre and tennis.

L Pyramisa Isis, Sharia Khalid Ibn El-Walid, T095-237 0100, www.pyramisaegypt.com. Large hotel with high standard rooms and public areas that are quite slick. Rear rooms have good balconies looking onto the river and pool, the Italian restaurant comes recommended, there's also Chinese dining, plus 2 decent swimming pools by the Nile. Much better room rates online can make it a great deal.

AL-A El-Luxor, Corniche El-Nil, T095-238 0944, www.el-luxor-hotel.com. A popular choice that has an especially convenient location, with good facilities in the airy rooms and an excellent breakfast. Rooms overlook the Nile or the garden. The attractive pool is open to non-guests and there's a good choice of restaurants and bars. There is an extra charge for the gym.

B Domina Inn Emilio Hotel, Sharia Youssef Hassan, T095-237 6666, emiliogroup@emiliotravel.com. Refurbished rooms all have satellite TV, music system, a/c, minibar and inoffensive white-wood furnishings. Most have balconies, and those on the upper floor have views over the Avenue of the Sphinxes. There's a small bar in the foyer and by the pool, 2 restaurants, disco, and a real bonus is the clean and popular pool on the roof. In winter, it's wise to make reservations as the place swarms with European groups.

B-C Philippe Hotel, Sharia Dr Labib Habashi, T095-237 2284, www.philippeluxorhotel.com. Another Luxor hotel that has undergone a renaissance, and the lobby and refitted rooms are now almost swanky. Some have slight Nile views (which you pay more for), some look onto **Windsor's** pool next door, all include TV, a/c, and fridge. Some rooms have remodelled bath, some have balcony. They vary significantly in size so look around before booking if possible, and a few of the singles contain so much huge furniture you can hardly open the door. Pool is only OK, but the terrace and bar surrounding it are attractive for a sunset drink.

C New Pola, Sharia Khalid Ibn El-Walid, T095-236 5081, www.newpolahotel.com. A blank rather unappealing tower from the outside, however rooms are much larger than average, freshly tiled with plain and inoffensive furnishings, balcony, fridge, a/c and TV. Good value at E£200 per double. Nicer at the front, but bear in mind that Nile views are across the busy road. There's a small square rooftop pool with plenty of sun-loungers and folks enjoying a beer.

C St Joseph, Sharia Khalid Ibn Walid, T095-238 1707, www.xanga.com.stjos. A mid-range and somewhat tacky hotel that attracts Brits and groups. That said, it is social and fun with a busy rooftop pool area covered with Astroturf, with good views and rooms that are priced right at US$35 per double. Free Wi-Fi, good amenities and located near Luxor's nightlife.

C-G Boomerang, Sharia Mohamed Farid, T019-136 1544, www.boomerangluxor.com. Excellent new hostel with high standards, close to the railway station in the little traveller enclave that's formed on Mohamed Farid. Clean rooms with quality beds (mattresses steam-cleaned regularly) all have their own bathrooms (often across the corridor), a/c, satellite TV and balconies. There are some suites; dorm beds cost E£30. Tours offered, free Wi-fi or use of PC is E£5 per hr. Very pleasant Australian-Nubian management and a family atmosphere also makes it suitable for those travelling with children. Smoking permitted only on the rooftop, where there is also a sun-deck. Good buffet breakfast. Highly recommended.

D Little Garden Hotel, Sharia Radwan, off Sharia Televizion, T095-227 9090, littlegardenlxregy@hotmail.com. A quaint yet modern hotel that has the slight aura of a villa, popular with Egyptian couples. Rooms are simple and clean, bathrooms fresh, beds large and comfy. The pricier suites have huge terraces, but don't go for the traditional-style domed rooms on the roof, which are stale in comparison. The garden is more of a patio, but lovely, with fruit trees and flowers.

Rooftop restaurant serves Oriental food and has party nights with dancing and dinner (call for timings as there's no set schedule). Internet E£10 per hr for guests.

D Nefertiti, Sharia El-Sahaby, off Sharia Karnak in the tourist bazaar, T/F095-237 2386, www.nefertitihotel.com. Doubles with a/c, TV, fridge and private bath (E£160) are very clean, with towels and linens replaced daily. Attractively refurbished throughout in an Arabesque style, this centrally located hotel offers a great rooftop (sun-lounging area) with an awesome view of the avenue of the sphinxes and the Nile. At night, the surrounding streets are filled with lively local *ahwas*, including the famed Oum Koulsoum with great *sheeshas*. Breakfast buffet is a step above most and food from their street-side restaurant is also available in the room or on the roof, there's a pool table, *tawla* (backgammon), free Wi-Fi and basic weight room equipment. Family-like warm atmosphere offers a nice respite for weary travellers; this place is highly recommended.

E Anglo Hotel, Midan Al-Mahatta, T095-238 2133. If you want to be bang next to the station this is an old-style hotel that's decent value. Rooms are simple, furniture the bare minimum, soft pillows, some have inside bathrooms, all have a/c and TV, only 1 has both private bath and balcony. There's a basement bar, open 2000-0200, or they'll bring beer to your room for E£10. It does have a dubious reputation, however, perhaps not the best choice for lone women. Breakfast is E£5 extra per person.

E-F Happy Land, Sharia El-Kamar, near Sharia Televizion, T095-227 1828, www.luxorhappyland.com. With doubles from E£55-80, singles E£40-70 (dependent on location, a/c, minibar, private bath, etc) the Happy Land remains a stalwart of the backpacker scene. Rooms really are spotlessly clean, sheets and towels are changed daily, and bathrooms have toilet paper. 8 of the 24 rooms have balconies and it's a quiet area. Free Wi-Fi and use of washing machine, nice rooftop terrace where an excellent breakfast is served, there's even a jacuzzi tucked away up there. Luggage storage and use of facilities for guests after check-out. Note that they don't have touts at the station, so ignore people there who claim to work for Happy Land.

F Fontana, Sharia Radwan, off Sharia Televizion, T095-228 0663, www.fontanaluxorhotel.com. Doubles with private bath E£45, singles E£30, subtract E£5 for shared bath. Rooms are simple and clean, ones at the front have balconies, some have a/c. Clean spacious bathrooms include toilet paper and towels. Loquacious Mr Magdy Soliman and his staff are helpful, though they get on some people's nerves, there's free use of the washing machine and Wi-Fi. If you're getting a night train, you can store bags and have a shower before departing at no extra charge. Good in that the breakfast is served as early as 0500 or as late as 1100, lunch is available, and there are bikes and motorbikes for rent. If you call ahead they will arrange a free taxi for you from the station.

F-G Oasis Hotel, Sharia Mohamed Farid, T010-380 5882, www.luxoroasis.com. Blue is the theme throughout this cheap option, which has a lovely rooftop perfect for a relaxing breakfast (included), or the free 'sunset tea'. They also have extremely cheap meals and beer. Unfortunately, many rooms are rather cell-like (particularly the singles), but some have private bath and a/c. Wi-Fi free and tours available, balloon rides are E£400.

F-G Seven Heaven 3, Sharia Mohamed Farid, T095-236 2671, www.sevenheavenhotel.com. Previously the **Nubian Oasis**, now managed by the family who own the popular Seven Heaven in Dahab. All rooms have private bath and it's cheap with a/c rooms for E£50 or with fan for E£20 (pay per room, not per person). The recently renovated rooftop terrace is a good spot to hang out, use of the washing machine is E£1 per item, breakfast is E£5-10, free Wi-Fi/internet and use of the kitchen. If you don't mind a few murals and want to meet other travellers, come here.

Camping

Rezeiky Camp, Sharia Karnak, T095-338 1334. Offers cheap tent sites and not-so-cheap a/c rooms. On site, there's a swimming pool, internet café, washing machine and garden with bar and restaurant, serving different Egyptian meals nightly at reasonable prices. It's a bit of a hike to town.

Eating

East Bank *p226, maps p230 and p241*
Luxor has plenty of fairly cheap Middle Eastern restaurants that have virtually identical menus (kebab, chicken, moussaka) concentrated on Sharia Al-Mahatta and nearby Sharia Al-Adasi. They tend to be inexpensive, safe and pretty good. There's also a growing European expatriate community that has introduced some delicious new mid-range eateries to Luxor in recent years; these places are found on or around Sharia Khalid Ibn El-Walid and are likely to serve alcohol.

Expensive restaurants and fine-dining seem to be generally confined to 5-star hotels. Try the **Sonesta St George** for Japanese, the **Sheraton** for Italian, and the **1886** in the Old Winter Palace for French (formal dress compulsory, men must wear jacket and tie).

ΨΨΨ **Le Lotus Boat**, at Iberotel Hotel. Well-organized dinner cruises every Thu offering international cuisine and an Oriental show from 1930-2200 (E£200), book to get a good seat. Also day cruises with a high-quality lunch while travelling to Dendara for E£425 per person on Sun, Tue and Fri (Tue is the quietest).

ΨΨΨ-ΨΨ **Kim's**, Sharia Khalid Ibn El-Walid, T095-238 6742. An unprepossessing canteen environment, but chock-full of Koreans enjoying authentic dishes that really hit the mark. Go early as everyone clears out by 2100. Efficient service and generous portions, you will struggle to eat your main after snacking on all the *kimchee*.

ΨΨΨ-ΨΨ **Metropolitan/Kebabgy**, Corniche El-Nil (on the river, near the Winter Palace), T095-236 9994. Very much geared towards tourists, and the setting by the Nile with outdoor tables and plenty of shade pushes the price up. That said, they are always busy and you can enjoy a good range of dishes both Egyptian and Western along with an alcoholic beverage. Kebabgy has more of a cosy evening feel, with feluccas around, whereas Metropolitan is more café-style and close to the cruise boat moorings.

ΨΨΨ-ΨΨ **Sofra**, 90 Sharia Mohammed Farid, T095-235 9752, www.sofra.com.eg. Daily 1000-2330. A sweet restaurant with a largely Egyptian menu that incorporates some Mediterranean influences. Housed in an old period building with Arabesque decor and antiquey tiled floors, most people choose to dine on the rooftop but there is also a little downstairs garden and interior. It not only has class but the food is excellent and comes highly recommended by all-comers and local ex-pats. Perfect for a guaranteed good meal out, and feels pretty special for Egypt.

ΨΨ **Ali Baba Café**, Sharia Karnak, enter on side street. Simple rooftop restaurant that offers a lovely view of Luxor temple, particularly at sunset and in the early evening when the temple is lit up. The food is standard Egyptian fare, but the servings are quite small. Stella and local wine are cheap.

ΨΨ **A Taste of India**, Sharia St Joseph Hotel, T095-228 0892. For the last 10 years, they've been serving up decent Indian and international cuisine in an Asian-style setting. British management means you are going to be familiar with the dishes and the helpful waiters are accurate with their descriptions of the menu. It's as good as Indian food is going to get in Luxor and makes a nice change.

ΨΨ **Chez Omar**, Midan Youssef Hassan, near the *souk*, T095-236 7678. Open 0800-0300. This place offers decent food and fast, friendly service alongside Bob Marley prints, a/c and even tablecloths. Lit up with green lights at night, it's a good place to breathe after a long day. Considering the alternatives and the fact it is tourist-oriented, it's still pretty cheap, for example E£45 gets you a 5-course dinner including soup, salad, rice, vegetable, dessert and a meat of your choice.

¥¥ **Jamboree**, Sharia El-Souk, T012-781 3149, www.jamboreerestaurant.com. Open 0800-2300. In pleasing new premises above the *souk*, with an outdoor terrace, the menu features omelettes, soups and sandwiches as well as traditional Egyptian food, plus fish, chicken, steaks and a good vegetarian selection. Sunday roast available if you pre-book. Entrées include an excellent salad bar. The food is tasty and good for unsettled stomachs. Also on offer are milkshakes and Movenpick ice cream, but no alcohol.

¥¥ **Jems**, Sharia Khalid Ibn El-Walid, T012-226 1697, on the 2nd floor. The atmosphere isn't quite as quaint as neighbouring restaurants but guests love the food and keep coming back. The policy is, if you return more than once in the course of the week, you are offered a modest discount that gets bigger every time you return. There are set vegetarian meals, a hodgepodge of Middle Eastern and British fare and an extensive bar. The *shish tawook* comes highly recommended. Tables by the window offer good views of the action on the street.

¥¥ **Lotus**, in the heart of the *souk* on the 2nd floor. Serves a selection of Middle Eastern and European dishes including spinach cannelloni, fish and chips and a variety of vegetarian options. Large windows look down on thriving alleyways. 15% discount for students. The service is good and the chocolate mousse delicious.

¥¥ **Oasis Café**, ShariaSt Joseph, T017-595 4667, www.oasiscafeluxor.com. A hip café and gallery is an unusual find in Luxor, the Oasis has attractively painted walls adorned with lovely paintings. Unfortunately the food is not quite as special as the surroundings, but if you crave Western-style sandwiches and salads it fits the bill. Otherwise just go for a coffee to absorb the refined yet causal ambiance.

¥¥ **Pizza Roma.it**, Sharia St Joseph, T011-879 9559, www.pizzaroma-it.com. Open 1200-2300. For an authentic pizza or other Italian dish, this bright modern café-style establishment is where you should head. Italian-Egyptian run, it's on a street where many of Luxor's 'foreign' food restaurants are found.

¥¥-¥ **Abou El-Hassan El-Shazly**, Sharia Al-Adasi (corner with Mohamed Farid), T016-342 9164. Open 0900-0400. Great value local food in a sanitary setting that appeals more to Egyptians than tourists. Outdoor seating on the street corner or a/c interior, recognisable by the painted green chairs and maroon tablecloths. Excellent tagines (E£15-25), chicken and fish meals (E£25) and lots on the BBQ (E£25-45). Surprisingly good for vegetarians, ask about options (which change daily and aren't on the menu).

¥¥-¥ **Mish Mish**, Sharia Televizion. Serves up tasty cheap pizza with fluffy crust, although the local cheese doesn't melt like mozzarella a medium should fill you up. Also serves pastas, sandwiches and standard Middle Eastern dishes. A longtime popular eatery among backpackers.

¥¥-¥ **Quick Restaurant**, Sharia Televizion, T095-227 2970, www.quickpizzaluxor.com. Open 1000-0400, also delivers. Next door to **Mish Mish**. Pies, pizza, burgers, fish, chicken and grills in a fast-food style environment, all very reasonably priced (from E£20-70).

¥¥-¥ **Abu Ashraf**, Sharia Mahatta, halfway between the station and the *souk*. Open 0900-0200. Sells tasty *koshari*, *shish kebab*, roasted chicken, and lots of cheap salads. Nothing on the printed menu exceeds E£20 (and you can further negotiate the price though some of staff are a bit sniffy) and the place is clean.

¥ **El Zaeem**, Sharia Yousseff Hassan. Open 24 hrs. Egyptian staples are either taken away or eaten upstairs in an a/c marble setting. Tourist prices apply on the written menu (at least double what locals pay) though you can try and argue it out with the man on the till. Then you might get a *fuul* sandwich or *koshari* for E£1-4.

Bars and clubs

East Bank *p226, maps p230 and p241*
The Nile Terrace at the **Winter Palace** will always beckon for a historic sunset drink, or the **Royal Bar** inside the hotel has plenty of period atmosphere. In the winter, all 5-star and most 4-star hotels have some kind of 'live' music, belly dance or disco. In the summer, they're less frequent, it depends how many people are in town. Quite a few 'authentic' pubs have sprung up over the last few years, generally British-themed, which are mostly centred around Sharia Khalid Ibn El-Walid and are close enough to one another to warrant an evening tour of Luxor pub life. In addition to pubs, a few hotels have rooftop bars offering great views of the town and Nile, particularly at sunset. Besides the bars, Luxor is a lovely town to stroll around at night. There are dozens of *ahwas* scattered around where local men smoke *shisha*, sip tea, watch loud Arabic movies and play dominoes and *towla* (backgammon) into the wee hours, and don't frown at the presence of a tourist.

Esquire, Sharia Ali Ibn Abi Taleb, T012-332 8563. This place has more class than most and is easily walkable from the centre of town. Waxy wood and brass, a huge bar to prop up, quite a diverse menu with English traditionals such as cottage pie as well as Egyptian dishes. Beer is E£12-15 or there's a range of spirits on offer, happy hour daily 1700-1900 when beer goes down to E£10, quiz nights on Tue and Thu at 2030, and premier league matches shown. Food is served until 2300 and the bar stays open till 0100.

The King's Head Pub, Sharia Khalid Ibn El-Walid, T095-228 0489. The king in question is Akhenaten in the most longstanding and happening pub in town. It's a true taste of England except that the place stays open until people are ready to go home (at least until 0200) and serves dozens of cocktails with specials like 'Sex on a felucca'. There's a free pool table in the back. The menu is extensive and includes a wide variety of hot and cold *mezza* (E£15), curries, sandwiches and English standards (fish and chips E£47). Stella E£13, cocktails E£29.

Murphy's Irish Bar, Sharia El-Gawazat, near the passport office off Sharia Khalid Ibn El-Walid, T095-238 8101, www.murphyirishpub.com. Open 1000-0230. Huge 2-floor pub with pool table and football on the TV upstairs. 1980s music wafts in the background quiet enough to hear yourself speak, comfy chairs and lots of wood, not too pricey with Stellas going for E£14. Several whiskies are available and there's an extensive pub menu that includes a veggie burger, a variety of jacket potatoes and loads of soups, salads and pastas. The disco in the basement gets going at about 2230 and feels more like a regular Western club than most in town.

Saint Mina Hotel bar, Sharia Cleopatra, T095-237 5409. Open 1900-0200. Down in the dingy cellar of the Christian-run hotel, this functional bar has a very local vibe and some of the cheapest Stella in town.

Sinbad, Sharia Al-Karnak, in front of the (now closed) **Luxor Wena Hotel**, T010-302 9523. Great for an garden drink under the trees decked with fairy lights and there's always a few people around, everyone is welcome in this friendly spot. The food is very average (Western pretenders mix with Egyptian dishes) but nothing is too pricey and beer is cheap (E£8). Good apple sheesha E£5.

Festivals and events

East Bank *p226, maps p230 and p241*
The **Egyptian International Marathon** happens on 14 Feb each year, on the West Bank.

The **Moulid of Abu El-Haggag** happens during the first 2 weeks of the month before Ramadan (*Shabban*). Luxor's biggest *moulid* has parades, processions, stick-fighting, *zikrs* and all the other traditional entertainments that you don't get to see very often as a tourist.

The **Opet Festival**, which recreated the ancient festival celebrating the pharaoh's rebirth as the son of Amun when barques (boats) were carried along the Avenue of the Sphinxes from Karnak to Luxor temple, used to happen on 4 Nov each year. It was unsure whether this would continue to occur at the time of research; best to check with the tourist office.

O Shopping

East Bank *p226, maps p230 and p241*
Shopping in Luxor can be stressful. A leisurely meander through the *souk* is almost impossible when countless kitschy souvenirs are being thrown in your face and everyone is hollering at you to have a look. But there is a lot to look at. Spices, dried herbs and nuts and lots of colourful scarves are all over the place. Local alabaster carved into vases (E£40, small), clay pots and tagine are cheap (E£5, medium size).

Aisha, on Sharia Youssef Hassan, opposite the Emilio Hotel, www.aisha-crafts.com. Open daily 1030-1500, 1800-2230. A wide array of tasteful crafts, scarves, throws, lamps and glassware, as well as Bedouin jewellery. A good place to start, without any hassle, and although the prices are 'fixed', significant discounts will be offered as you browse.

Fair Trade Center, Sharia Karnak, by Luxor Temple, T010-034 7900. Open from 0900-2230 every day. This non-profit organization with an excellent range of tasteful goods from all over Egypt is also very worthwhile.

Habiba, in the *souk*, Sharia Sidi Mahmoud (near Lotus restaurant), T095-235 7305, www.habibagallery.com. Open 1000-2200 daily. Some lovely pieces including cotton goods, jewellery, scarves and lighting.

There are duty-free shops near the Emilio Hotel and by the plaza at Karnak Temple. On the southern end of the Corniche around the strip of 5-star hotels, there are some upscale stores that promise no hassle and sell beautiful gold jewellery and high-quality Egyptian cotton clothing. For the independent traveller, there's an abundance of fresh fruit and vegetables around the *souk* in the **Sharia Televizion market** on Tue. Those who crave Western food and snacks should head to **Arkwrights** food store, Sharia St Joseph, T095-228 2335, which is "open all hours" and has plenty of treats that you might be missing. Generally the further away from the river, the lower the prices and the less the hassle.

Bookshops

Aboudi Bookshop, by Luxor Temple. Open 0930-2330. May be the best bookshop for non-Arabic readers outside Cairo. It offers an extensive collection of fiction and historical books in English, German and French. It also has lots of maps and guidebooks to specific areas in Egypt and a decent selection of cards and gifts.

Al-Ahram, by the Museum of Mummification on Corniche El-Nil. Open 0800-2200. Has a good selection of books, also maps and cards and newspapers.

Gaddis Bookshop, by the **Winter Palace** on Corniche El-Nil, T095-372142. Open 0800-2130. Books in English, French and German plus lots of gift items, in an intriguingly olde-worlde environment.

Foreign newspapers are sold in a kiosk in the middle of the street outside the **Old Winter Palace Hotel**. There is a high chance that these will also be offered for sale by street vendors along the Corniche where the cruise ships are moored.

Activities and tours

East Bank *p226, maps p230 and p241*

Balloon flights

Becoming an ever more popular activity as competition brings down prices, making it an option even for budget travellers. These days the skies over the West Bank are thick with balloons each dawn, a spectacular sight in itself. Actual flight time is a maximum of 45 mins, but drifting over the Valley of the Kings and Theban temples is a truly memorable experience in the magical morning light. You can also spy down on the farmers starting work in the fields, women cooking on fires, and rooftops where washing and dates lie drying. The mountains are positively glowing by the time the trip comes to an end and the blue of the Nile is unbelievable. All companies will pick you up from your hotel on the morning of your flight at 0500-0530, most include a breakfast on the boat as you cross the Nile in the dark. Then you ascend into the gloom to a height of 300 m. If you chose to take a trip organized through one of the budget hotels it would be wise to check that the operating company has insurance, certification and offer a full refund if the flight is cancelled due to unsuitable weather conditions. There are a few companies with offices on Sharia Khalid Ibn Walid, or pick up a flyer in any high-end hotel. Budget hotels, such as those on Sharia Televizion and Mohamed Farid, offer balloon tours for around E£400 per person.

Calèche

Horse-drawn carriages are all over the place (you can't avoid them if you try), often in queues. Go to the one in front, when he's done, he will return to the end of the queue. E£10 should be enough to get you across town; the official rate is E£30 for an hour's ride, but you'll be lucky to get this.

Feluccas

Feluccas are numerous on this most beautiful stretch of the Nile. Travel is limited to the southward direction, but this also has the most attractive scenery. Sunset is the best time to ride but bring a sweater and protection against mosquitoes (E£40 per hr if you're a hard bargainer). It is a lovely journey to nearby **Banana Island**, where you can stroll through the papaya and orange plantations (give the owner of the island E£5), it's about a 2-hr round trip. Longer *felucca* trips start from Aswan and head north with the current, see box page 300.

Seaplane flights

Get an even higher view of Luxor in the early morning from a small seaplane, contact T010-079 3310/010-070 7429, flights last about 25 mins and cost US$85 per person including a drink.

Swimming

An exceptionally important activity after a hot day's temple exploring, especially in the summer. Some hotels with pools offer day use for a fee. At the cheaper end of the spectrum, the pool on the roof of the **Emilio Hotel** is largest and cleanest with plenty of sunbathers, E£30. The best deal in town is at the **El-Luxor**, which has a splendid pool with lots of loungers in a palm garden, day use E£50 per person. The pool at the **Iberotel**, E£75, is a bit blank and functional but scores points for actually floating on the Nile.

Tour operators

You can buy ISIC (student) and ITIC (teacher) cards from **Jeddah Tours**, 1st floor, Sharia Ahmed Orabi, T095-238 2163, for E£95; take 2 photos and a copy of your passport. To obtain an ISIC card you will need a letter from your place of study; for a teacher's card you will just have to sign a form. Open daily 0900-2300 (half-hr break from 1600-1630), on Fri from 1030. The process takes less than 10 mins and can save you a fortune.

Travel agencies and tour operators are concentrated on the Corniche by the **Winter Palace**. The lesser-known agencies often offer the best deals. Half- or full-day tours include Dendara, Aswan and Abu Simbel, Abydos, *felucca* and camel trips, and West Bank tours.

Carlson Wagonlit Travel, Corniche El-Nil, Old Winter Palace, T095-2371, alaa_luxor5@yahoo.com. Wide range of tours, discounts given on the advertised prices which are already cheaper than most.

Cruise boats

Regular Nile cruises operate between Luxor and Aswan for two to five days (standard tour) or seven days (extended tour). The quality of operator and cruise ship will, of course, be largely dependent on the price paid. If the cruise is taken as an all-inclusive package, it is recommended that, if possible, one is chosen where the overall itinerary is under the day-to-day control of a tour manager who is a direct employee of the cruise company. The local management of cruises can be sub-contracted to Egyptian travel agents who, should difficulties arise with the tour, may consider themselves primarily as guides and show marked reluctance to take on any wider responsibility or be fully accountable for solving problems of a more challenging nature.

It is easy to arrange a cruise on arrival in Luxor if you don't like planning things too much in advance. There are scores of agents along the Corniche. Enquire at a few, try to see the actual boat if possible, and check their programmes – bottom-end cruises probably won't include all the sights.

Most cruises go from Luxor to Aswan, with the journey sometimes in reverse, or a trip both ways. Starting from Aswan you are travelling with the current so the trip will be shorter, and it has the disadvantage of being against the wind which can make relaxing on the top deck almost an impossibility.

An typical itinerary will offer the following popular features:
Luxor: visits to the West Bank (Valley of the Kings, Valley of the Queens, Colossi of Memnon, Temple of Queen Hapshetsut), Luxor and Karnak Temples (plus at least one alabaster factory shop!). Option of Sound and Light show at Karnak. **Esna**: Temple of Khnum. **Edfu**: Temple of Horus – access by *calèche*. **Kom Ombu**: Temple of Horus and Sobek. **Aswan**: *Felucca* boat outing to Kitchener Island, trip to Nubian village on Elephantine Island, Unfinished Obelisk, High Dam, Temple of Philae (plus at least one papyrus factory shop!). Option of Sound and Light show at Philae. **Dendara**: Temple of Hathor (this may not be on all itineraries).

Nawas Tours, Souk Marhaba, Sharia Ahmed Orabi, T095-237 0701/2. A cheaper agency selling Hurghada–Sharm ferry tickets, and day cruises to Dendara.
Thomas Cook, Corniche El-Nil, next to the Winter Palace Hotel, T095-237 2402, www.thomascookegypt.com. Has a wide variety of quality tours around Luxor and all Egypt.

Transport

East Bank *p226, maps p230 and p241*
Note Check all times – timetables are often a printed figment of someone's imagination.

Air

EgyptAir, next to the Winter Palace Hotel, T095-238 0581/2, open 0800-2000 and at the airport, T095-238 0588, offers frequent daily flights, particularly in the winter high season, to **Cairo**, **Aswan**, and **Abu Simbel** via **Aswan**. 3 flights a week go to **Sharm El-Sheikh**. Fares change depending on the season. Book your tickets well in advance. **Luxor Airport** : T095-237 4655.

Bus

Tourists are no longer restricted to convoys in order to travel between **Luxor** and **Aswan**. You can now negotiate microbuses in order to reach the temples of Esna, Edfu and Kom Ombo, but **do not** leave Luxor after 1800 as it

Esna lock closures Cruises from Luxor to Aswan can be disrupted by the twice-yearly closure of the lock at Esna for maintenance. Closures usually occur for two weeks in June and December and prospective travellers are strongly advised to check these dates beforehand. When the lock is closed, ships are moored at Esna and passengers are transported by coach to those points on the itinerary inaccessible by river. This can significantly reduce the pleasure of a cruising holiday. A second lock has opened at Esna that does much to ease the pressure of cruise traffic. Passage through is now a speedier process – in the past, boats were sometimes waiting up to 20 hours to get through during peak tourist periods.

Meals Expect three good meals per day, often buffet style. Some meals are served on a covered deck. Meal times are likely to operate to a fairly inflexible timetable. Free tea, coffee and soft drinks are available at any time. The bar will be open most of day as this is where they make most of their money. Special menus can usually be organized.

Social life and entertainment Almost inevitably at some stage during the cruise there will be an evening dinner at which travellers will be encouraged to dress in local Egyptian costume – a *gallabiya* party. Other evening entertainment may include discos, live Egyptian/Nubian music and performances by belly dancers, jugglers and acrobats.

Cabin accommodation Cabins at water level will offer limited views and, depending on position, may be more affected by engine noise and fumes than others. A supplement can be paid for a cabin on an upper deck. Top-level cabins may have a sun deck as their roof. It's best to obtain a plan of the vessel before you book your cabin. Bear in mind that when the ship is moored there may not be a view from the cabin whatever its level. Ships can often be berthed six or seven abreast and access to the shore is gained by walking through one ship after another. Expect to be issued with a boarding pass when going ashore.

officially requires a private convoy (arranged through a travel agent).

Local Microbus: a cheap (50 pt) and easy way to get around town and to the Karnak Temple. Callout your destination to microbuses passing by. A popular route, Sharia Karnak–Sharia Mahatta–Sharia Televizion, includes the train station to Karnak temple.

Long distance Buses at 0830, 1030 and 1430 leave from Zanakta terminal, T095-232 3218, a 50 pt micro ride from the town centre or E£30 in a taxi. Buses leaving at 1630, 1830 and 1930 also depart from next to the railway station, before calling at the bus terminal. Reserve tickets in advance if possible, or buy at least 30 mins before departure. Currently, there is 1 bus daily to **Cairo** at 1830 (10 hrs, E£100). 1 bus daily to **Dahab** at 1630 (14-17 hrs, E£130) via **Sharm El-Sheikh** (13-16 hrs, E£120). 1 bus daily to **Port Said** at 1930, via the **Red Sea Coast** (E£75). 5 buses per day go to **Suez** (8 hrs, E£60-70) via **Qena** (1 hr, E£5) and **Hurghada** (4 hrs, E£35-45).

Cycle hire

Cheap and fairly roadworthy cycles can be found at plenty of budget hotels, and along Sharia Mahatta or Sharia Televizion for E£10-15 per day.

Motorcycle hire

Motorcycles (around E£100-150 per day) are available for hire from bike shops and

Dahabiya trips

These traditional sailing boats, some of which are renovated original crafts, are a fantastic, if pricey, way to cruise the Nile. It's advisable to book a *dahabiya* cruise before arriving in Egypt, as they are often chartered by private groups and spaces are in any case limited by the small size of the vessels. Below is information on several recommended boats:

Assouan, **El-Nil**, **Meroe** and **Malouka**, www.nourelnil.com. Some of the largest *dahabiyas* on the Nile, these replica vessels are perfect down to the finest detail, while plumbing and conveniences are state of the art. The highly personalised service, charming crew members and utterly tasteful decor are especially noted by past guests. Departing from Esna for Aswan on Mondays, for five nights, the *Assouan* and *El-Nil* have a few standard rooms that are slightly more affordable (€1100-1500 per person in a double room).

El Bey, **El Hanem**, **Zahra**, **Nesma**, **Amber** and **Musk**, www.dahabiya.com. These small boats each measure 38 m by 6 m and accommodate up to 12 people. Each two-person air-conditioned cabin has been individualized with colonial finishes, and themed to match the name of the ship. There's no alcohol licence but guests are welcome to bring their own on board so they can enjoy cocktails on the top deck. Sailings are every Saturday from either Luxor or Aswan and last seven days.

Royal Cleopatra, www.nubiannile cruises.com. Resembling a yacht, the *Cleopatra* is in fact a converted *sandale*, a *felucca* that used to carry cargo along the Nile. Sleeping up to six guests in two gorgeous wood and white staterooms, some meals are eaten al fresco on shore. An Egyptologist guides you through the sites between Esna and Aswan, and cruising can be four, five or seven-days. A five-day cruise costs US$2225/2695/3650 per person, depending whether it's triple/double/single occupancy.

Vivant Denon, www.dahabeya.net. Built in 1889, this vessel has been beautifully restored by Didier Caille to sleep six passengers in four cabins. Cruises generally run between October and April, and though it is possible to charter for summer sailings the fact there is no air conditioning on board has to be considered. In-depth tours are given of all the sites, with the itinerary and destinations tailored to group requests. Cabins are not sold separately, the boat is rented in its entirety. *Vivant Denon* is only available for a few weeks per year; sailings are on Saturdays and last one week.

Lazuli, www.lazulinil.com. Three boats with five or six cabins, some rooms have private balconies. Mod-cons such as air conditioning, internet and TVs are provided and decor is slightly more contemporary.

Royal House Boat, www.royalhouse boat.com. With only two cabins and one suite, the Royal House boat is certainly exclusive. Rooms have plasma screens, satellite TV and fancy bathrooms with jacuzzis. Excursions are guided and there is 24-hour butler service. High season price is €500/650 for a standard/suite cabin. Sailings are from Esna every Tuesday for five nights.

hotels on the East Bank, ask around or try the **Fontana** or **Everest** (T016-1331 5443) hotels. It is a fantastic way (probably the best) to head off and explore the West Bank and gives you a chance to explore outlying areas of Luxor town.

Taxi

Local Taxis congregate around the train station and can easily be hailed from all major thoroughfares; E£5-10 around town; E£30-40 to the airport.

Long distance Private taxi: sample charges: E£325 direct to **Aswan**; E£350 round trip to **Dendara** and **Abydos**. To **Kharga** should cost a maximum of E£600.

Service taxi from the terminal just off Sharia El-Karnak, halfway between the Luxor town centre and Karnak temple, these are quicker and more convenient than trains or buses.

Train

Foreigners are technically restricted in their choice of trains, and you will not be allowed to pre-book tickets for the majority of trains (although you can just turn up at the station and pay on board). To **Cairo**, there is now only 2 'secure' trains, with a/c and restaurants on board, though a further 9 trains make the journey each day (the tourist office, opposite the station, has a list of the times). 1st/2nd-class trains to **Cairo** (10 hrs, E£167/90) leave daily at 2230 and 2330. If you are travelling as a family or group, you can buy 4 seats (E£167 each) in a Nefertiti Cabin (which seats 6 privately) and the other 2 won't be sold. It is essential, particularly in the high winter season, to reserve your seat at the station a few days before you travel (it is possible to reserve up to 15 days in advance).

Privately run **sleeper** trains depart daily to **Cairo** at 1940, 2040 and 2230 (9-10 hrs, US$60 per person, US$45 children 4-9 yrs, payable in US$ or euro only). There is 1 daily 2nd-class direct train to **Alexandria** at 1530 (16 hrs) but it stops absolutely everywhere en route; better to take a train to Cairo and switch as trains run almost every hour between Alexandria and Cairo. 1st/2nd-class 'secure' trains to **Aswan** (3 hrs) leave daily at 0735, 0935, 1810 and stop in **Esna** (45 mins), **Edfu** (1½ hrs) and **Kom Ombo** (2 hrs). To get to **El-Quseir** or **Marsa Alam** it's best to take a train to **Qift** from where buses leave for the East Coast at 1100, 1430 and 1700 (on to El-Quseir, 2 hrs, E£15; Marsa Alam, 3 hrs, E£30). There are also regular service taxis from Qift, which you will have no problem boarding if you miss the bus.

Directory

East Bank *p226, maps p230 and p241*

Banks There are numerous banks and 5-star hotels in Luxor with ATMs. Banks are generally open Sun-Thu 0830-1400 and 1700-1800. **Immigration** Passport Office: Sharia Khalid Ibn El-Walid, opposite Hotel Steinberger, T095-238 0885, visas extended, Sat-Thu, 0800-1500, come around 0900 to get a visa processed same day.

Internet Cafés are dotted around town, the going rate at present is around E£5-10 per hr. However, almost all the budget hotels offer free Wi-Fi or use of PC for E£5 per hr.

Medical services Hospital: **General Hospital**, Corniche El-Nil, T095-237 2025. **Luxor International Hospital**, Sharia Televizion, T095-238 7192-4, best in town.

Post office Main post office (Sat-Thu 0900-2100) is on Sharia Al-Mahatta. Hotels sell stamps.

West Bank and Theban Necropolis

On the West Bank, depending on your interest, if you hire a car it takes a day to cover the major highlights or up to two full days to visit in its entirety. Obviously, it takes longer if you are on foot (using microbuses to get around where possible) or by bike. Although the West Bank is dominated by the Theban Necropolis and the Valley of the Kings, there are also some fascinating temples and monuments above ground worth exploring, in particular the Ramesseum and Medinat Habu, which are not on the standard itineraries of large tour companies. In addition, the Tombs of the Nobles have fewer visitors but some of the most colourful and interesting paintings and they really shouldn't be missed. *▸▸ For listings see pages 281-284.*

Ins and outs

Getting there and around

Direct road access from Luxor to the West Bank is possible for coaches, minibuses and cars via the Nile Bridge, about 7 km south of town. It takes 30-40 minutes to get from the centre of Luxor to the Valley of the Kings via the bridge. The quicker and easier way for independent travellers to get to the West Bank is by public ferry (E£1 for foreigners, 25 pt for Egyptians), which leaves from in front of Luxor temple. The ferry runs 24 hours a day, although you will be waiting a while for it to fill up if it's late at night. Alternatively, you can hire a private motorboat or *felucca* (E£5) to take you across.

Bike Bikes (E£15-20 per day) are readily available on the West Bank, someone will probably offer you one on exiting the ferry or just head to the couple of hire places on the main street, past the minibus station. Or you can rent one on the East Bank, where it's slightly cheaper, and take it on the ferry with you. It is probably the best way to see the West Bank (apart from motorbike), allowing you to visit the major sites in a full-day and have time to relax as well. Be aware that it's a steady uphill gradient all the way to the Valley of the Kings, a bit tough and definitely not recommended in the thick of summer, though coming back down is a breeze. Guards at the various sights will keep an eye on your bike for you. You may want to offer a couple of pounds of *baksheesh* for the favour, but it's not strictly necessary.

Donkey Travelling by donkey can be memorable, if a bit hard on the bum. A short excursion is fun, but it is not a serious means of transport for sightseeing. It does afford some amazing views as you climb up to the Valley of the Kings. For a morning meander, expect to pay about E£50. It's best arranged through one of the budget hotels and usually involves taking the public ferry across the Nile and meeting your donkey there.

Organized tours Many tourists and travellers alike opt to explore the West Bank with an organized tour. Most tours also include a certified guide who can elucidate some of the mysteries and secrets of the ancients and their civilization. In the summer, the pricier tours offer the respite of an air-conditioned coach. The disadvantage is that you're being trucked along with a herd of other folk and your time in each place is dependent on your guide and group rather than your own inclination. Tours can be booked from any of the countless travel agents along the Corniche on the East Bank (there is a dense handful near the Winter Palace, see tour operators, page 249 for listings). For a tour of the West Bank's highlights from a reputable travel agent expect to pay E£250-350 per person. West Bank tours are also offered (sometimes aggressively) by virtually every budget and mid-range hotel in town, with transport in minibuses (generally not air conditioned). Cost fluctuates significantly with the season and is always negotiable. Aim to pay about E£150-200 per person (excluding tickets) for a guided tour of the highlights. If you want to hire a private guide, everyone has a brother who's a tour guide. Ask for leads at the tourist office or try your hotel, and make sure whoever you end up with is licensed.

Taxi If you want to see the sights at your own pace and have a ride, you can hire a taxi for a few hours. Rather than hailing one from the East Bank, it's a lot cheaper and faster to take the public ferry across the Nile and pick one up from the landing. You will be bombarded with offers. Expect to pay about E£180 to be shuttled around the major sights for four to five hours, or E£50-60 to take in three sights (eg the Valley of the Kings, Deir El-Bahri and Medinat Habu). Bargain hard.

Walking If it's cool enough, walking around the West Bank sights is just about feasible. Public transport, in the form of pickups or microbuses, can get you from the ferry to the main ticket booth for 50 pt. Except for the Valley of the Kings, which is 8 km from the Colossi by road, all main sights are within 3 km of the Colossi, which are about 1.6 km from the ferry landing. Getting back can be harder, and you might have to wait a while for a passing vehicle. It's tough to find a pickup that will get you all the way to the Valley of the Kings (unless it is early morning and the locals are on their way to work), but you could hire a taxi for that leg of the trip for E£15-20. Otherwise, it is a breathtaking walk over the mountain to the Valley of the Kings from Deir Al-Medina (one hour, take the stairs to the left of the car park for a steep ascent past the police post, then follow the track to the right) or from Hatshepsut's Temple (45 minutes, just head up the track behind the temple). Obviously this can be done in reverse, starting up the valley slopes above the tombs where would-be guides hang around and insist you'll get lost (you won't, dismiss them harshly if you are not interested). The walk is worth doing for the stunning views of the valley, tombs and temples.

Tickets and visiting information

Although 63 tombs have been discovered so far, many are closed to the public, some for restoration and others for rest. A system has been devised to reduce wear and tear on the more popular tombs – by closing them at intervals. The changes happen so often that the guards who work in the Valleys have a hard time keeping up. A list of open tombs is displayed by the ticket booth at the Visitor Centre. There are always at least 11-12 tombs open in the Valley of the Kings and three open in the Valley of the Queens. The Ministry of Tourism tries to ensure at least a few of the more remarkable tombs are always open. Expecting to see every single tomb and temple on the West Bank is impractical unless you intend to visit every day for a week. If you don't have a guide and want to know which open tombs are most worth seeing, ask at the ticket booth. Make sure you bring a supply of water and snacks, as they are expensive around the sights.

Tickets to the Valley of the Kings, the Valley of the Queens, and Deir El-Bahri (Hatshepsut Temple) can all be bought outside the sites. Tickets for Tutankhamen's, Ramses VI's and Ay's tombs are also bought at the Valley of the Kings, though from a separate booth after the Visitor Centre. Tickets to everything else, including the Tombs of the Nobles, Deir El-Medina, Medinat Habu and the Ramesseum must be bought in advance at the 'old' ticket booth 200 m after the Colossi of Memnon. Booths are open from 0600-1600. Sites are open 0500-1600 winter, 0600-1700 summer. There are discounts for those with ISIC or ITIC cards of up to 50% to all sights, the last window at the old ticket booth is reserved for students. Photography of all sorts is prohibited inside all

5 West Bank

➡ Luxor maps
1 Luxor orientation, page 224
2 Luxor, page 230
3 Karnak, page 235
5 The West Bank, page 256
6 Valley of the Kings, page 259
7 Valley of the Queens, page 274

N
500 metres
500 yards

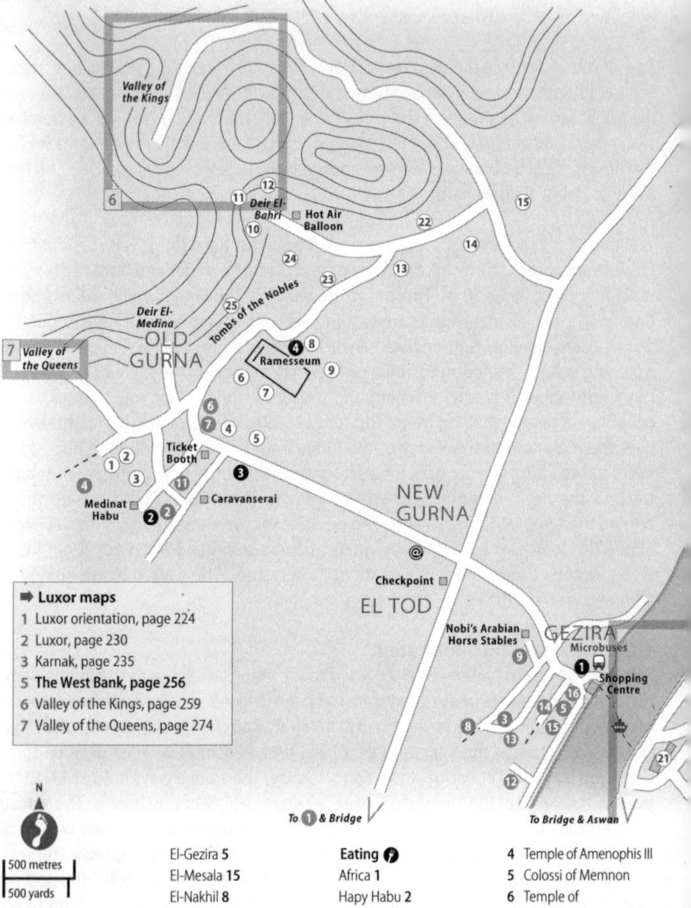

Sleeping 🛏
Al-Moudira 1
Amenophis 2
Amon & Kareem 9
Beit Sabee 4
Desert Paradise Lodge 10
El Fayrouz 3

El-Gezira 5
El-Mesala 15
El-Nakhil 8
Gezira Gardens 12
Habou 11
Marsam 6
Nile Valley 16
Nour El-Gourna 7
Ramses 14
Sheherazade 13

Eating 🍴
Africa 1
Hapy Habu 2
Memnon 3
Ramesseum Resthouse 4

Sites ○
1 Temple of Ramses III
2 Temple of Tuthmosis III
3 Pavillion of Ramses III

4 Temple of Amenophis III
5 Colossi of Memnon
6 Temple of Tuthmosis IV
7 Temple of Merneptah
8 Temple of Tuthmosis III
9 Temple of Amenophis II
10 Temple of Mentuhotep
11 Temple of Tuthmosis III
12 Temple of Hatshepsut

tombs. Note that flash photography can seriously damage the pigment in the tombs. Resist all temptation. There is no charge to see the Colossi of Memnon.

Tourists from cruise ships tend to congregate at the Valley of the Kings between 0700-1000, so avoid this period if at all possible. Lunchtime is definitely the quietest time, although it is the hottest time of the day it is recommended to time a visit for 1300-1400. It can't be stressed enough that the difference between a magical experience and one where you don't notice any tomb art because you are trying to survive being jostled by bus-loads of people hangs on what time you go.

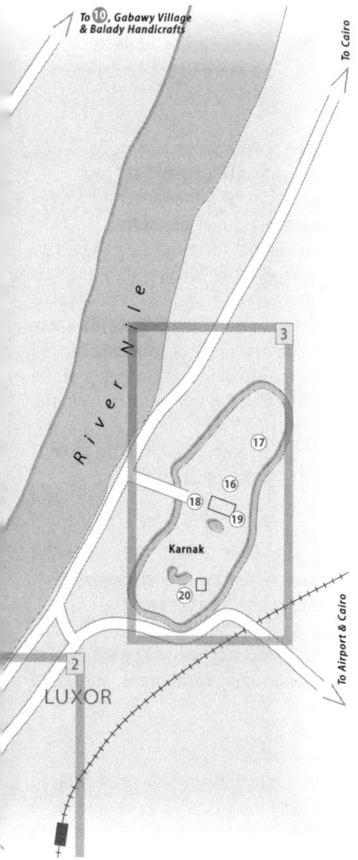

13 Site of Ramesside Temple
14 Temple of Amenophis I & Ahmes Nefertari
15 Temple of Seti I
16 Great Temple of Amun
17 Temple of Montu
18 Temple of Ramses III
19 Temple of Amenophis II
20 Temple of Mut
21 Luxor Temple
22 Nobles' tombs at Dra'a Abul Naga
23 Nobles' tombs at El-Khokha
24 Nobles' tombs at El Asasif
25 Nobles' tombs at Sheik Abd El-Gurna

Colossi of Memnon

These two gigantic sandstone colossi, which are located on the main road 1.6 km from the river 200 m before the 'old' ticket booth, represent Amenhotep III (1417-1379 BC). Although the faces and crowns have been eroded the two colossi make a strange spectacle seated in splendour on the edge of the fields and it's worth stopping on your way past. They are particularly mesmerising at dusk, when a couple of little eateries opposite provide the perfect spot for a sunset drink. The Colossi once stood in front of Amenhotep III's mortuary temple, which collapsed and was plundered for stone long ago. However, excavations begun in the last few years are now uncovering a wealth of statutory hidden beneath the earth. This temple site is strictly off-limits while work continues, but you can observe some of the megaliths from the roadside (many remain cloaked in protective sheeting).

Valley of the Kings

ⓘ *www.valleyofthekings.org, entry is E£80, students E£40, and gives you access to 3 tombs of your choosing, except for Tutankhamen's tomb, which costs E£100/50 extra (closed between 1300-1400) and Ramses VI's which is E£50/25. The visitor centre has film footage, running on a loop, showing the emptying of Tutankhamen's tomb and a scale model of the valley, which is quite*

The singing colossus of Memnon

The northern gigantic sandstone colossus was broken off at the waist by the earthquake in 27 BC after which it was reputed to sing at dawn. This phenomenon, which was most likely caused by the wind or the expansion of the broken stone in the morning sunlight, attracted many visitors including the Roman emperors Hadrian in AD 130 and Septimus Severus (AD 193-211). The latter decided it should be repaired, after which it never sang again.

useful for getting your bearings. Video cameras must be left in the cloakroom (free). The tuf-tuf train from here (cost E£4 per ride) saves the tiresome 300-m walk up the valley in the heat.

Also known as Wadi Biban El-Muluk, the Valley of the Kings is one of many necropoli in the limestone hills on the West Bank. The area first became a burial site during the New Kingdom rule of Tuthmosis I (1525-1512 BC) in the hope that the tombs would be safe from looters. The kings' tombs are not actually confined to the single valley and it is believed that there may be others still waiting to be discovered. Those already discovered are numbered in the chronological order of their discovery rather than by location. Although some are simple and comparatively crude the best are incredibly well preserved, stunningly decorated and a testament to the intricate craftsmanship of the workers. Most of the discovered tombs are in the east valley but the Tomb of Ay in the west valley (Valley of the Monkeys) is worth a visit, see page 265.

The tombs generally follow two designs. The early 18th Dynasty (1567-1320 BC) tombs are a series of descending galleries followed by a well or rock pit that was intended both to collect any rain water and deter thieves. On the other side of the pit there were sealed offering chambers and then the rectangular burial chamber built at right angles to the descending galleries. The later tombs, from the late 18th to the 20th Dynasties (1360-1085 BC), were built in the same way but the galleries and burial chambers were on the same axis, being cut horizontally but deeper, straight into the rock face.

Note There was obviously no need, originally, for light in the tombs and today the authorities maintain the lowest possible light levels. Take a torch, it will enable you to read this book, admire the outstanding wall decorations and illustrations, and avoid tripping on the uneven ground!

Ramses VII 1148-1141 BC (1)

This later style, single horizontal plane, and poorly preserved tomb lies in a small valley to the right after the entrance gate and is seldom visited by tourists. Above the outer door Ramses VII's names are displayed with a scabbard and disc. The walls are lined with scenes from the *Book of Gates*. The most interesting area is the Burial Chamber with its granite sarcophagus still in place. The picture on the ceiling portrays the constellations and calendar of feasts while the sky goddess Nut spans the area. The inner chamber contains scenes of Ramses making offerings to the gods.

Ramses IV 1166-1160 BC (2)

Nearer is the tomb of Ramses IV; although his huge sarcophagus was reburied in Amenhotep II's tomb by the priests, it has been returned. Do not be discouraged by the Coptic and Greek graffiti (note the saints with halos by the entrance on the right side) because the colours of the inner tomb are truly fantastic. The first two corridors contain poorly preserved reliefs of the *Litany of Re*, while the Hall and Burial Chamber are decorated with parts of the *Book of the Dead* and a golden Nut spans the bright blue ceiling. The sarcophagus lid shows Ramses IV protected by images of Isis and Nephthys and the pink granite sarcophagus is inscribed with magical texts. This is the only tomb for which the original plans, drawn on papyrus, still survive (now in the Turin Museum).

Prince Mentuherkhepshef (19)

Discovered by Belzoni in 1817 in the southeastern extremity of the east valley is a tomb that rarely receives visitors. Intended as a final resting place for a king (Ramses VIII) but truncated and occupied by Prince Mentuherkhepshef, one of the sons of Ramses IX, there is no burial chamber as such. The entrance is remarkable for its width (3.6 m), while the door jambs are decorated with serpents. The glass-covered walls of the 3-m-wide corridor each bear seven images of Prince Mentuherkhepshef making offerings to the gods, including Khonsu, Osiris and Ptah. The paintings, particularly of Prince

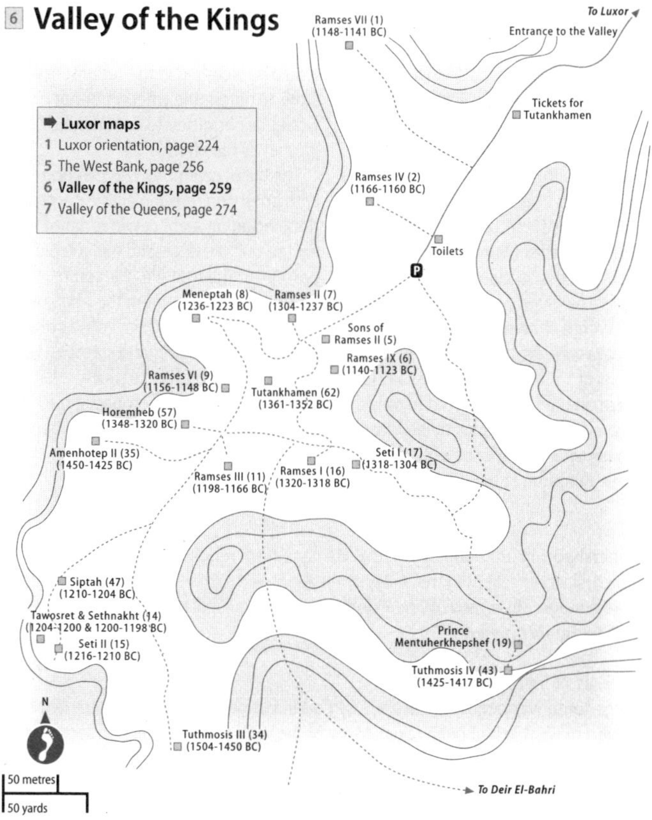

Theban Death Rites and the Book of the Dead

In order to fully appreciate the Theban Necropolis in the soft limestone hills opposite Luxor it is important to understand a little about the celebration and rituals of death in Ancient Egypt.

The *Book of the Dead* (see box, page 261) is the collective name given to the papyrus sheets that were included by the ancient Egyptians in their coffins. The sheets contained magic spells and small illustrations to assist the deceased in the journey through the underworld to afterlife. In total there are over 200 spells though no single papyrus contained them all. Some of the papyrus strips were specially commissioned but it was possible to buy ready-made collections with a space left for the relevant name.

Some of these spells came from the Pyramid texts. They were the oldest references to this passage from one life to the next. They were found on the walls of pyramids constructed during the fifth to seventh Dynasties (2494-2170 BC). Later the text and descriptions of the rituals that were involved were written on the actual coffins of commoners, not kings. The spells were written in vertical columns of hieratic script. Eventually lack of space on the sarcophagi led to only the ritual prayers and offerings being listed. When papyrus began to be used during the New Kingdom (1567-1085 BC) written texts were enclosed in the coffin and they became known as the *Book of the Dead*. Many copies of the writings, including the *Book of the Caverns* and the *Litany of Re*, were subsequently discovered.

The ancient Egyptians believed that at sunset the sun-god Re descended into the underworld and voyaged through the night before emerging at dawn to sail his barque across the heavens until sunset when the whole cycle began again. This journey was believed to be replicated by the dead pharaoh who descended through the underworld and whose heart, which was believed to be the centre of intelligence (see box, page 234), would be weighed in the Judgment of Osiris to determine whether or not he would be permitted to continue his journey to the afterlife.

The burial ceremony was elaborate with priests performing all the necessary rites, including sacrifices, in order to ensure that the deceased had a rapid passage to the next life. The tomb, together with everything the pharaoh might need, including slaves, was then closed, plastered over and stamped with the royal seal. In order to protect the royal tombs from graverobbers, they were fitted with false burial chambers and death-traps most of which, unfortunately, did not work.

Mentuherkhepshef although now rather damaged, are renowned for being among the most technically excellent in the Valley of the Kings and exhibit the Ramsesian school to great advantage. His wraps of linen clothing create transparent layers and he wears a forelock to signify his youth.

Tuthmosis IV 1425-1417 (43)

This large tomb was discovered in 1903 by Carter, but others had been there before and everything moveable had been taken. Many of the walls and pillars are undecorated and the impression is rather austere. The well room has scenes of Tuthmosis paying homage to to the gods and receiving the key of life from various deities including Hathor. The antechamber has illustrations of a similar theme and both have a ceiling of yellow stars on a dark blue sky.

Books of the afterlife

The Egyptians believed that the journey to the afterlife was through *Duat*, the underworld, and to combat the monsters and other evils there, a series of prayers and some magic spells were necessary. These were written in the *Book of the Dead*, which also contained a map of *Duat*.

Book of the Dead Called *The Book of Coming Forth by Day* by the Egyptians. This is a collection of mortuary texts, spells or magic formulas that were placed in tombs and intended to be of help in the next world. They are thought to have been compiled and perhaps edited during the 16th century BC. They included texts dating back to around 2000 BC (Coffin Texts) and 2400 BC (Pyramid Texts). Selected sections were copied on papyrus by scribes (illustrated versions cost more) and sold for inclusion in one's coffin. Many selections have been found and it is estimated that there were approximately 200 chapters. Extracts appear on many of the antechamber walls of the Ramessid tombs. Nearly 12 chapters are given over to special spells – to turn the deceased into any animal shape.

Book of Am-Duat Called *The Book of the Secret Chamber* by the Egyptians. It deals with the sun's journey through the underworld during the 12 hours of the night. Selections are found in many tombs. Full versions are inscribed on the walls of the burial chambers of Tuthmosis III and Amenhotep II.

Book of Gates Refers to the 12 gates that separate the hours of the night and first appears on tombs of the 18th Dynasty. The inscriptions in the tomb of Ramses VI give the most complete version. This has the same journeying theme as the *Book of Am-Duat* but the *Duat* is not comparable other than for the fact that is has 12 segments.

Book of Caverns A full version of this is found in the tomb of Ramses VI.

Litany of Re This deals with Re (see page 602) in all his 75 different forms.

Books of the Heavens Describes the passage of the sun through the 24 hours of the day and includes the *Book of the Day*, the *Book of Night* and the *Book of the Divine Cow*. These texts were first used during the New Kingdom and there are several pieces inscribed in the tomb of Ramses VI.

For further details refer to *The Ancient Egyptian Book of the Dead* by RO Faulkner.

Ramses IX 1140-1123 BC (6)

Immediately to the left of the barrier, this tomb is typical of the later long, deep style that became the established style by the end of the New Kingdom. The reliefs on the corridor walls depict Ramses before the gods and the four pillared Offerings Chamber leads to the richly decorated Burial Room, but the sarcophagus is missing. The ceiling in yellow on a dark blue background depicts a scene from the *Book of the Night* with jackals, watched by Nut, drawing the barque through the skies to the afterlife.

Meneptah 1236-1223 BC (8)

Set back against the cliff face on the other side of the road is a long steep 80-m tomb with a wonderfully preserved false Burial Chamber. The ceilings of the five corridors are decorated with flying vultures and other forbidding reliefs. Looters abandoned the sarcophagus lid here, which portrays scenes taken from the *Book of Gates* and the *Book of Am-Duat* similar to those in the antechamber. Steep steps lead down to the Burial Chamber where the rest of his pink granite sarcophagus lies, decorated with intricate designs from the *Book of Gates*. It is claimed that Meneptah was pharaoh during the time of the Exodus.

Ramses VI 1156-1148 BC (9)

Note – A separate entry ticket is required.

The discovery of this tomb, which was usurped from his predecessor Ramses V and enlarged to become one of the longest in the valley, shed light on some aspects of pharaonic beliefs that were not previously understood. The corridor displays reliefs from unknown and long-since lost *Books*. Egyptologists were fascinated at their revelation of pharaonic concepts, more usually associated with India, of reincarnated birth into a new life. One does not, however, have to be an expert to appreciate the graphic designs and the colours beyond the graffiti drawings in the first two corridors.

The themes on the corridor ceilings are predominantly astronomical while the walls are largely devoted to the *Book of Gates* and the entire version of the *Book of Caverns*. In the Offerings Hall there is a relief of Ramses making libations before Osiris, while the pillars are devoted to the pharaoh making offerings to other gods including Amun. Descending deeper within the tomb, the passage leading to the Burial Chamber is guarded by serpents of Nekhbet, Neith, Meretseger and Selket. Further on illustrations from the *Book of the Dead* predominate. Just before the entrance to the Burial Chamber, cryptographic texts adorn the ceiling. Astronomical scenes from the *Book of Day* and the *Book of Night* cover the ceiling and the sky goddess Nut observes from above. The sarcophagus, shattered by grave robbers centuries ago, lies broken in the centre of the room.

Ramses III 1198-1166 BC (11)

Also known as 'Tomb of the Harpists', this particularly beautiful and exceptionally large tomb is unusual because, unlike those of most pharaohs, it contains scenes from everyday life. It was originally intended for Sethnakht (1200-1185 BC), but the angle of digging was such that it coincided with another tomb and was abandoned. Later Ramses III restarted the work by digging into the rock face from a different angle. The lintel with a disc and Re shown with a ram's head accompanied by Isis and Nephthys can be seen at the entrance. Ten side chambers, which were for storing objects that the pharaoh would require after his death, lead off from the entrance corridor. In the last on the left is the famed depiction of the two harpists, the lyrics of the song are carved into the entrance wall. The final section of the tomb is closed because of a collapsed ceiling.

Tomb of Ramses VI (9)

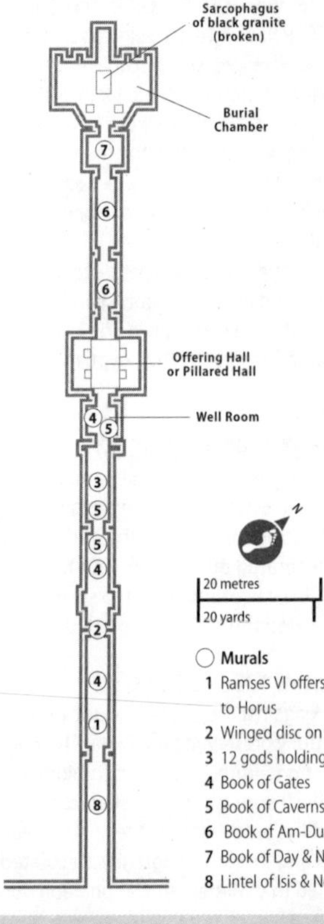

◯ **Murals**

- **1** Ramses VI offers lamp to Horus
- **2** Winged disc on lintel
- **3** 12 gods holding a rope
- **4** Book of Gates
- **5** Book of Caverns
- **6** Book of Am-Duat
- **7** Book of Day & Night
- **8** Lintel of Isis & Nephthys

Ramses I 1320-1318 BC (16)

Despite being the founder of the 19th Dynasty, his short reign meant that this Ramses did not merit a larger tomb but it still has beautifully ornate and sophisticated designs that are preserved on the blue-grey foundation. The granite sarcophagus in the burial chamber is decorated with yellow while the wall relief depicts scenes of the pharaoh with local deities and divisions from the *Book of Gates*. The eastern wall of the entrance corridor is decorated with 12 goddesses depicting the hours of the night. This is one tomb not to be missed if open when you visit.

Tomb of Tuthmosis III 1504-1450 BC (34)

Hidden away high up a side valley furthest from the main gate this is one of the oldest tombs, and its distinctive location makes it feel quite special and different. Though it is particularly stuffy and sweaty after the long ascent and descent, there is a pleasing spacious lightness to the chambers and its simple design is balanced by the interesting layout. After the second steep corridor, it veers sharply to the left into the antechamber. The walls here are lined with lists of 741 deities who are portrayed as tiny stick figures. The burial chamber, shaped, unusually, like a cartouche, is entered down a set of oval shaped steps. The walls here are dominated by sections of the *Book of Am-Duat* with an abridged version also inscribed on two pillars. Tuthmosis III is depicted on one of the pillars with his mother standing behind him in a boat. A beautiful carving of Nut, effectively embracing the mummified Tuthmosis with her outstretched arms, lines the inside of the red granite sarcophagus. His mummy is in the museum in Cairo.

Siptah 1210-1204 BC (47)

The interesting tomb of Siptah, a monarch of the late 19th Dynasty, was discovered by Edward Ayrton in 1905. The stair entry leads to a long corridor plastered and painted with formal scenes of the Litany of Re on the right and left, with images of Mut and a fine representation of Siptah before Re-Horakhte. The intermediate corridors leading, via the antechamber, to the Burial Chamber are undecorated. Inside the burial chamber are four rough-hewn pillars and a red granite sarcophagus bearing jackal and demon figures. The tomb was disturbed at one time – possibly during the 21st Dynasty – and the mummified body of Siptah was found in a cache of royal mummies in the tomb of Amenophis II (35) in 1898, the withered left foot of the King clearly visible.

Tawosret 1204-1200 and Sethnakht 1200-1198 BC (14)

Sited close by the tomb of Tuthmosis I, this is one of the longest (112 m) axial tunnels in the Valley of the Kings – belonging to Tawosret, wife of Seti II from the 19th Dynasty. The monument was taken over by Sethnakht, the first ruler of the 20th Dynasty, who lengthened the tomb and removed the remains of Tawosret, it is suggested, to the cache in Tomb KV35. The original ownership of the tomb is still apparent in the first corridor, with male deities bearing female designations, but many scenes of Tawosret before the gods were usurped by Sethnakht. In the barrel-domed burial chamber of Tawosret itself there are scenes from the *Book of the Dead*, the ceremony of the opening of the mouth and the *Book of the Gates*, together with a finely drawn scene of facets of the Sun God Re as a disc and ram-headed eagle from the *Book of the Caverns*. Beyond is the extended royal tomb of Sethnakht along broad corridors decorated with unpainted scenes from the *Book of the Secret Chamber*. In the blank burial chamber of Sethnakht his reconstructed granite sarcophagus lies in place.

Seti II 1216-1210 BC (15)

The tomb of Seti II has been open since antiquity. It was a hastily completed monument but is important in that it has a number of innovations that became standard practice in subsequent tomb building. The wall niches in the antechamber to the first pillared hall are much more pronounced than in earlier tombs while the entrance is cut into the hill face lacking the previously used wall and stairway. The burial chamber is crudely adapted from what was to have been a passage to a larger room that was never excavated. There are conventional decorations on the entrance doorway of Ma'at, the goddess of truth and beauty (see page 599), and scenes from the *Litany of Re* are shown in a variety of reliefs on both the left hand wall of the first and second corridors. Beyond the first corridor the walls are unplastered and generally painted in an attractive but peremptory fashion. The antechamber has an unusual format of figures of deities among which the king is shown riding on a panther and hunting in a papyrus boat. In the pillared hall itself there are formal scenes from the *Book of the Gates* and above the damaged sarcophagus is a fine picture of Nut, goddess of the sky, with outreaching wings. The mummy of Seti II was among the kings found in the cache of royal mummies at the tomb of Amenophis II (**35**).

Amenhotep II 1450-1425 BC (35)

When this tomb, one of the deepest in the valley, was opened up again by Victor Loret in 1898 a trove of grisly and invaluable treasure was found. Here for once the tactics of building false chambers and sunken pits actually worked and the pharaoh's mummified body was found inside the sarcophagus, along with another nine royal mummies that had been removed from their original tombs for safety's sake. Amenhotep's mummy was originally kept in the tomb but after a nearby theft it was removed to the Egyptian Museum in Cairo. Ninety steep steps and a descending corridor lead into a pillared chamber where the tomb's axis shifts 90° to the left, after which the walls and ceiling are decorated. The ceiling is coloured blue with an astronomical star design in yellow and the walls delicately illustrated with passages from the *Book of the Secret Chamber*. Columns show pictures of the king with deities – Anubis, Hathor and Osiris. Further stairs (the air gets hotter and thicker with each one) and a short passage lead to the enormous two-level Burial Chamber. Amenhotep's sarcophagus sits in a sunken area with storage chambers around, the second on the right being where the cache of mummies was discovered. Look in particular for the beautiful image of Isis in sunk relief at the end of the decorative quartzite sarcophagus, still with its lid in place.

Horemheb 1348-1320 BC (57)

After the long, steep and undecorated descent is the Well Room where beautifully detailed reliefs begin. Colourful scenes portray General Horemheb who, despite lacking royal blood later became pharaoh, was the powerful regent behind Tutankhamen's short rule and leader of the Theban counter-revolution against Akhenaten's monotheistic religion. The scenes of Horemheb being introduced to the gods are repeated in the antechamber, which is dominated by the huge red granite sarcophagus. Point a torch inside the sarcophagus for a glance at some bones. Some guides suggest that the base black lines in the sanctuary indicate the first draft of the decorating, while the marks are corrections, as Horemheb died too young for the artists to finish.

The curse of Tutankhamen

Tutankhamen's tomb's fame and mystery was enhanced by the fate of several of those who were directly connected with its discovery. The expedition's sponsor Lord Carnarvon, who had first opened the tomb with his chief archaeologist Howard Carter, died shortly afterwards in April 1923 from an infected mosquito bite. Howard Carter supposedly protected himself by not entering the tomb until he had performed an ancient ritual. A subsequent succession of bizarre deaths added weight to British novelist Marie Corelli's unproven claim that "dire punishment follows any intruder into the tomb". However, such alleged curses have done nothing to deter the tens of thousands of visitors who still visit the site despite the fact that most of the treasures are now in the Egyptian

Tutankhamen 1361-1352 BC (62)

The tomb owes its worldwide fame not to its size or decoration, being on the whole rather small and ordinary, but to the multitude of fabulous treasures that were revealed when it was opened in November 1922. Even the burial chamber is relatively limited in size, so when Carter broke through the rooms were crammed with an abundance of artefacts. In fact, the scale of the discovery was so vast that it took 10 years to fully remove, catalogue and photograph all of the 1700 pieces. Considering that the boy king reigned for a mere nine-10 years and was a comparatively minor pharaoh, the lavish funeral objects found seem all the more extraordinary.

The short entrance corridor leads to four chambers but only the Burial Chamber, which is the second on the right, is decorated. Around the room from left to right glassed-in murals display Tutankhamen's coffin being moved to the shrine by mourners and officials after which his successor Ay (1352-1348 BC) performs the ceremony of the Opening of the Mouth and makes sacrifices to sky-goddess Nut. Tutankhamen is then embraced by Osiris and is followed by his black-wigged *Ka* or spirit. A scene from the *Book of Am-Duat* on the left-hand wall depicts the pharaoh's solar boat and sun-worshipping baboons. The quartzite sarcophagus is still in place, with its granite lid to one side, and inside the innermost solid-gold coffin, containing his mummified remains.

Seti I (17)

Seti I's is regarded as the most developed form of the tomb chambers in the Valley of the Kings. At some 120 m it is the longest, but it is permanently closed for conservation purposes since its decorations suffer from condensation produced by visitors. Throughout the tomb there are paintings/reliefs of fine workmanship on nearly every surface, though not all were completed. Seti's mummy can be viewed in the museum in Cairo while the sarcophagus is in Sir John Soane Museum in London.

Tomb of Ay

ⓘ *E£25, students E£15, you need a car to get there or by foot allow 2 hrs there and back.*

This monument **(23)** in the west valley dates from the 18th Dynasty and was opened up by Bellzoni in 1816, cleared by Schaden in 1972 and opened to the public in recent years. The entry shaft at first has a shallow incline but then after a second flight, steps become very steep. Flat shoes are a necessity here.

The 'lost' tomb

Explored and looted decades ago, dismissed as uninteresting by Egyptologists, and used as a dump for debris from the excavation of Tutankhamen's tomb, Tomb 5 in the Valley of the Kings was about to become a car park. However, the final exploration in May 1995 unearthed a major discovery, certainly the largest and most complex tomb ever found in Egypt and possibly the resting place of up to 50 sons of Ramses II. Excavations are expected to take at least another five years, but the tomb's unusual design is already apparent. Instead of plunging down into the steep hillside, Tomb 5 is more like an octopus with at least 62 chambers branching off from the central structure. There may be more chambers on a lower level and it is hoped that some of the mummies may still be entombed.

No treasure is expected: robbery of the tomb was documented as early as 1150 BC, but the elaborate carvings and inscriptions along with the thousands of artefacts littering the floor, including beads and fragments of jars used to store the organs of the deceased, nevertheless offer a wealth of information about the reign of one of ancient Egypt's most important kings.

Egyptologists have never before found a multiple burial of a pharaoh's children and in most cases have no idea what happened to them. This find thus raises the question of whether Ramses buried his children in a unique way or that archaeologists have overlooked a major type of royal tomb. And where are Ramses' dozens of daughters? Are they buried in a similar mausoleum, perhaps in the Valley of the Queens?

Ay (1352-1348) was the counsellor of Tutankhamen and his successor to the throne. The tomb had probably been built for King Tutankhamen but was incomplete at the time of his sudden death. Ay had no claims to royal descent and was not even high-ranking in the priesthood, but his tomb is celebrated for its unusual pharaonic hunting scene in the Burial Chamber.

Only the Burial Chamber is decorated but even here there has been extensive damage to the paintings and the roof is just rough-hewn rock without decoration. Throughout almost all of the tomb the cartouches have been defaced. On the entry wall to the left of the door is the famous hunting scene with the deceased shown clubbing birds and plucking reeds as if he was an ordinary being rather than a deity. On the north wall is a painting representing 12 baboons (hence the name Tomb of the Monkeys) or hours of the night from the *Book of the Secret Chamber*. On the west wall look for the image with Ay before the gods, including Osiris, Nut and Hathor. A well worked but slightly damaged boating scene is shown on the south wall above passages from the *Book of the Secret Chamber*. On the lintel area above the door to the canopic chamber is a fine representation of the four sons of Horus, which you will not see anywhere else in the Valley of the Kings. The sarcophagus, made out of quartzite and nicely tooled in reliefs of deities, was formerly in the museum in Cairo but was transported back to the tomb in 1994. Its lid is intact and there are wings of four goddesses – one at each corner, with wings protectively wrapped round the sarcophagus.

Howard Carter's House

ⓘ *Open 0600-1800 (-1700 in winter), entrance E£20, students E£10, T012-145 2501.*
The most famous of all Egyptian archaeologists lived on site when excavating in the Valley of the Kings, and his house, located by the entrance to the valley, has recently been opened as a museum. Information panels fill you in on the discovery and cataloguing of the tomb, while a 3D hologram of 'Carter' describing his work is a nice feature. Period furniture has been used to reconstruct his bedroom, darkroom, study and other rooms, and facsimiles of his notes and diaries lie around. There is also a lovely garden café, the perfect place for a rest, although it is very expensive.

Deir El-Bahri

ⓘ *E£30, students E£15, cameras and videos free of charge. A tuf-tuf train runs tourists to the temple for E£2, but it's a short walk.*
Meaning 'Northern Monastery' in Arabic, Deir El-Bahri derives its name from the fact that during the seventh century the Copts used the site as a monastery. It is now used as the name for both the magnificent **Mortuary Temple of Hatshepsut** and the surrounding area.

Queen Hatshepsut was not just the only female pharaoh to reign over ancient Egypt (1503-1482 BC) but also one of its most fascinating personalities. She was Tuthmosis I's daughter and was married to his successor Tuthmosis II but was widowed before she could bear a son. Rather than give up power to the son of one of her husband's minor wives she assumed the throne, first as regent for the infant Tuthmosis III but then as queen. Tuthmosis III, who later hugely expanded the Egyptian Kingdom and was the first imperialist, was only able to assume office when Hatshepsut died 21 years later in 1482 BC. He naturally resented her usurping his position and went on to remove all traces of her reign including her cartouches. Consequently the full truth about her reign and the temples she built both here and at Karnak was only fully appreciated by archaeologists relatively recently. As a woman she legitimized her rule by being depicted with the short kilt and the false beard worn by the male pharaohs.

Hatshepsut's imposing temple, which was only dug out of the sand in 1905, was designed and built in the Theban hills over an eight-year period by Senenmut who was her architect, steward, favourite courtier and possibly the father of her daughter Neferure. Against the rocky cliffs of the Theban hills, the stark clean planes of the terraces, surfaces and ramps appear as brand-new rather than just reconstructed – it is almost impossible to comprehend that the temple is 3500 years old. The temple's three rising terraces, the lower two of which were lined with fountains and myrrh

Temple of Hatshepsut

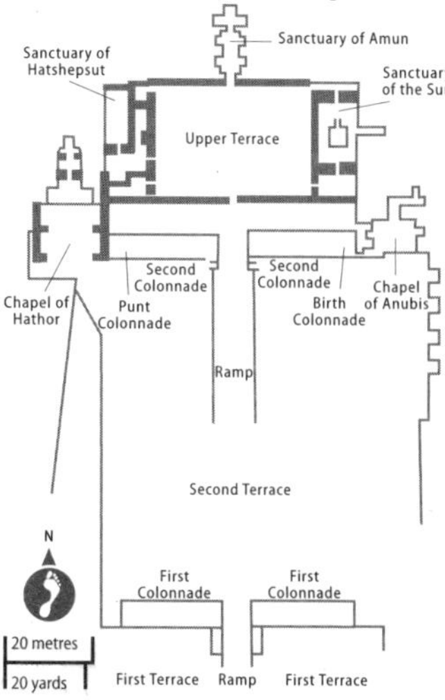

Howard Carter

Howard Carter was born at Swaffham in Great Britain in 1873. When he was only 17 years old he was taken on by the Archaeological Survey of Egypt under Flinders Petrie and became Inspector General of Antiquities in Upper Egypt in 1899 for the Antiquities Service. Carter was responsible for excavation of the Valley of the Kings and discovered the tombs of Hatshepsut and Tuthmosis IV in 1902 for the American Theodore Davis. After a dispute with Davis he moved to Saqqara in 1903 but then left the Archaeological Service to open a studio in Luxor where, in 1907, he met and began his archaeological association with the wealthy Earl of Carnarvon, whose own efforts at excavation had failed. When Theodore Davis gave up his concession to excavate in the Valley of the Kings in 1914, Carter, backed by the Earl of Carnarvon, took it up and continued digging, locating six more royal tombs. In 1922, Carter's last year of sponsorship by Lord Carnarvon, he came across a set of remains of workmen's houses built across a stairway to a tomb. Carter waited for Lord Carnarvon to arrive at the site and then dug away the remaining rubble to reveal the entrance to the Tomb of Tutankhamen. Eventually Carter's men cleared the way to the anteroom, which was full of interesting cloths, furniture and other materials. The burial chamber that Carter found was again packed with valuable objects but none more so than the gold-laden coffins and mummy of Tutankhamen. Carter remained at the site for a further 10 years supervising the cataloguing activity of so great a find. The nearby house that he lived in has recently been opened as a small museum. He died in London in 1939.

Howard Carter will always be known principally as the discoverer of the Tomb of Tutankhamen. But his imprint on Egyptology went far deeper. He was among the first archaeologists, following Flinders Petrie, to apply scientific principles to the recording of his excavations. Remarkably, the treasure trove of objects found in 1922 has still to be studied in full and, to Carter's great disappointment, there were in any case no parchments or manuscripts to explain historical events surrounding the boy king and the court politics of the day.

trees, were originally linked to the Nile by an avenue of sphinxes that aligned exactly to Karnak. A pair of lions stood at the top and bottom of the ramp, which leads from the ground level terrace over the first colonnade to the large second terrace.

The scenes on the left-hand side of the first colonnade columns depict the transportation of the two obelisks from Aswan to Karnak temple. Behind its columns on the right-hand side is a relief in which Amun can be seen receiving an offering of four calves from Hatshepsut, whose face has been erased by her son. The original stairs from the second terrace to the second colonnade have now been replaced by a ramp. Hatshepsut's famous voyage to **Punt**, which was known as 'God's Land' by the ancient Egyptians, and various texts to Amun are depicted on the left-hand side of the second colonnade. Voyages to Punt, now believed to be modern-day Somalia, had been undertaken since the Old Kingdom in order to find the incense and myrrh that was required for temple rituals.

Further to the left is the **Chapel of Hathor** where the goddess is depicted both as a cow and as a human with cow's ears suckling Hatshepsut. This area is badly damaged because Tuthmosis removed most traces of Hatshepsut and later Akhenaten came along and erased Amun. The reliefs on the colonnade to the right-hand side of the ramp portray Hatshepsut's apparently divine conception and birth. She claimed that her father was the supreme god Amun who visited her mother Ahmose disguised as Tuthmosis I, just as Amenhotep III made similar claims later on (see Luxor Temple, page 229). Further to the right is the fluted colonnade and the colourfully-decorated **Chapel of Anubis**, who is portrayed in the customary way as a man with a jackal mask, but the images of Hatshepsut are once again defaced. Note, however, the frieze of cobras, the colourful bird in the top left-hand corner and the bright blue starred ceiling.

The ramp leading to the smaller and recently restored upper terrace is decorated with emblems of Upper and Lower Egypt with vultures' heads guarding the entrance. The columns were originally round, but were squared off by Tuthmosis III in an attempt to replace her name with his own and that of his father. Beyond the Osiride portico (a line of reconstructed statues of Hatshepsut in Osiride form) to the left is the **Sanctuary of Hatshepsut** with its enormous altar and to the right is the **Sanctuary of the Sun**. In the middle at the back of the whole temple is the **Sanctuary of Amun**, which is dug into the cliff-face and aligned with Hatshepshut's tomb in the Valley of the Kings on the other side of the hill. A huge granite doorway carved with hieroglyphs marks the entrance, but the area is cordoned off. A further burial chamber for Hatshepsut's lies underneath the Sanctuary, but it is unclear whether she was ever actually interred in either place.

Tombs of the Nobles

ⓘ *The tombs are divided into groups, a ticket to each group costs E£12. It's wise to bring a torch to look at shadowy corners and lots of small notes to offer as* baksheesh *(either to take advantage of a guard's knowledge or to be left alone).*

Nobles' tombs are found at a variety of sites throughout Egypt but none are better preserved than those on the West Bank. While the pharaoh's tombs were hidden away in the Valley of the Kings and dug deep into the valley rock, those of the most important nobles were ostentatiously built at surface level overlooking the temples of Luxor and Karnak across the river. Their shrines were highly decorated but the poor quality limestone made carved reliefs impossible so the façades were painted on plaster. Freed from the restricted subject matter of the royal tombs, the artists and craftsmen dedicated less space to rituals from the Books and more to representations of everyday life and their impressions of the afterlife. Because, unlike the royal tombs, they were exposed to the elements many of the nobles' shrines have deteriorated badly over time. Although some were subsequently used as store rooms and even accommodation, others are still in relatively good condition and give a clear impression of how they must originally have looked. They are worth visiting for their wealth of vernacular paintings – quite as interesting as the formal sculptures of the great tombs of the Kings and Queens.

The most frequented are the tombs located in the area known as Sheikh Abd El-Gurna (commonly known simply as 'The Tombs of the Nobles'), where a ticket gains entry into three sets of tombs: **Ramoza (55)**, **Userhat (56)** and **Khaemhet (57)**; **Nakht (52)** and **Mena (69)**; and those of **Rekhmire (100)** and **Sennofer (96)**. Further tombs belonging to nobles are open for viewing at **El-Asasif**, **El-Khokhah** and **Dra'a Abul Naga**. The tombs of **Sennedjem**, **Peshdu** and **Inherkhau** are just above Deir El-Medina (see page 276), an archaeological site where the housing of the workmen on the West Bank has been excavated.

Tomb of Ramoza (55)

Ramoza was Vizier and Governor of Thebes at the beginning of the Akhenaten's heretical rule in 1379 BC and the tomb illustrates the transition in style between the worship of Amun and Aten (see Tell El-Amarna, page 201). The impressive and excellent workmanship of the shrine is probably because it was built by Ramoza's brother Amenhotep who was the chief of works at the family's home town of Memphis. Only the main columned hall can be entered, the inner hall and false sarcophagus area are separated off. This is one of the few tombs where the forecourt is still preserved and the central entrance leads into a broad columned hall. The tomb was carved out of solid limestone and all the decoration carved on polished rock. On the wall to the right are depictions of Ramoza with his wife and opposite on the back wall Akhenaten and Nefertiti stand at their palace windows giving a golden chain to Ramoza. On the left-hand wall are scenes of Ramoza and his wife worshipping Osiris. Beyond is an undecorated inner hall with eight columns and the shrine at the far end. There is a second gap on the left of the end wall leading to the actual sarcophagus chamber. Within each hall are entrances to dark tunnels that end with a dangerous 15-m drop to the burial chamber.

Tomb of Userhat (56)

Userhat who, in the reign of Amenhotep II, was a royal tutor and scribe, was buried in a small tomb that was partially damaged by early Christian hermits. At the extremity of the outer hall on the left is a stela showing the purification by opening of the mouth. At the opposite end of this hall look out for the representation of the double python, a symbol of protection. **Note** The interesting representation of rural life on the left on the way into the hall, the façade of the snake-headed harvest goddess Renehat on the right of the back wall, and a realistic hunting scene in the desert on the left of the inner hall.

Tomb of Khaemhet (57)

Khaemhet, another royal scribe and overseer of the granaries in the period of Amenhotep III in the 18th Dynasty, adopted a raised relief system for the carved and painted decoration of his tomb-chapel, which is worth seeing for its variety. The tomb is entered through a courtyard off which there two other blocked off tomb entrances. The Khaemhet tomb is made up of two transverse chambers joined by a wide passage. In the outer chamber there are rich reliefs depicting rural scenes, some of the originals now only to be seen in Berlin. The passage has funeral scenes and the voyage to Abydos, while both the transverse chambers have statue niches of Khaemhet and his family.

Tomb of Nakht (52)

Set in the entrance of the tomb is an interesting display including a plan of the tomb, sketches of the reliefs and a replica of the statue of Nakht. Unfortunately the original was lost in 1917 when the SS Arabia, which was transporting it to the USA, was torpedoed by the Germans in the Atlantic. Inside, the tomb is well lit and the decoration protected by glass screens.

Nakht was Tuthmosis IV's astronomer, vineyard keeper and chief of his granaries. He and his wife Tawi were buried in this small shrine with a well-preserved and colourful antechamber which depicts the harvest in intricate detail. On its west wall in the centre is a painting illustrating parts of Nakht's life together with the goddess of the west. On the left of the far wall is a depiction of a funeral banquet at which Nakht (the top half has been badly defaced), is shown seated beside his wife, a cat at his feet is eating a fish and he is being entertained by a blind harpist and beautiful dancing girls. Opposite is an unusual painting of peasants treading grapes while empty wine jars await filling. Here the ceiling is brightly decorated with designs representing woven mats. The marshland scenes on the right-hand (south-facing) section of the antechamber are exceptionally fine – the fish are wonderfully depicted. In the inner chamber there is a deep shaft leading to the inaccessible burial chamber.

Tomb of Mena (69)

This tomb has undergone restoration and, although Mena's eyes have been gouged out by rivals to prevent him seeing in the afterlife, the paintings are in good condition. He was an 18th Dynasty scribe or inspector of the estates in both Upper and Lower Egypt. On the end wall on the right-hand side of the outer hall is a depiction of a series of gods, notably Hathor and Isis. On the adjacent wall is a fine painting of Mena and his wife giving flowers. Opposite is a vignette of the younger members of the family making gifts to their father. In the left-hand limb of the outer hall note the depiction of Mena's wife in an elegant dress and jewellery as she stands with her husband before Osiris. In the inner hall there is a niche for a statue of Mena and his wife. In the inner hall, look out for the finely executed paintings of hunting and fishing scenes on the right-hand wall close to the statue niche, showing crocodiles, wild cats and fish. The brightly coloured ceilings represent woven cloth.

Tomb of Sennofer (96)

At the time of Amenhotep II (1450-1425 BC), Sennofer was, among other things, Mayor of Thebes, overseer of the granaries and gardens, and chief vintner. In the antechamber of this tomb there is an excellently clear set of diagrams etched on the glass showing the layout of the tomb and its decorations, accompanied by explanations. The ceiling is covered in illustrations of grapes and vines, thus the tomb is known as the 'Tomb of Vines'. Within the four-pillared hall Sennofer is shown making offerings to the deities and on his journey into the afterlife, accompanied by his wife Meryt. A double figure of the jackal-headed Anubis looks down on the whole chamber from above the entrance. There is a false door painted on the right-hand wall with the god Anubis and the goddess Isis. Facing the entrance arch look to the right for a depiction of Sennofer's wife, son and daughters. On the north (end) wall Sennofer and his wife cross to the west bank of the river by boat, accompanied by a funeral offering of wine, flowers and food. On the west wall are the goddess Hathor and Osiris in the dark colours of the dead. On the same wall to the left is the funeral furniture for use in the afterlife. Above, note the vultures with wings spread for protection of the tomb. On the pillars are formal representations of mummification, cleansing rites and offerings.

Tomb of Rekhmire (100)

This crucifix-shaped tomb should not be missed because its highly decorative paintings and inscriptions reveal some of the secrets of Ancient Egypt's judicial, taxation and foreign policy. Rekhmire, who came from a long line of viziers and governors, was the vizier at the time of Tuthmosis III's death in 1450 BC when he then served his successor Amenhotep II. Walking left or clockwise around the whole tomb from the entrance wall of the transverse corridor you can see: Egyptian taxes, Rekhmire being installed as vizier, foreign tributes being received from Punt, Crete, Nubia, Syria and Kush; then along the main corridor the inspection of the various workshops, the voyage to Abydos, the various gods of the dead, and the end niche that would have contained a statue of Rekhmire. The ceiling has deteriorated but some of the original plaster work remains, with a continuous line down the centre of the main north-pointing chamber. Look out too for the splendid marsh/woodland scene which, with a small lake and trees, has a warmth and realism that contrasts nicely with the formal and predictable decoration in praise of the gods (notably Osiris) and Tuthmosis III. On the way out along the other corridor wall are pictures of the afterworld and then, back in the transverse hall, illustrations of hunting and fowling, winemaking, Rakhmire's wives and ancestors, and finally more taxes being collected.

Tombs at El-Asasif

ⓘ *Between Deir El-Bahri and the Tombs of the Nobles are the El-Asasif tombs. Tickets are bought at the Deir El-Bahri ticket office, a ticket for the Asasif tombs, E£25, student E£15, gives entrance to Kheruef and Anch-hor's tombs and a separate ticket is required for Pasaba's tomb, E£25/15. The turn-off to the tombs is signed to the left, off the road to Deir El-Bahri, 100 m before the ticket office.*

Kheruef (192) Kheruef's, the Steward of Amenhoptep III's wife Queen Tiye, is one of few tombs at El-Asasif that survived the rapacious activities of tomb robbers, largely because it was filled with compacted debris. Added importance arises from its decoration, which is not only good quality but also unusually illustrates the festivals of the Jubilee, an affirmation of a king's power in the land towards the close of the 18th Dynasty.

The architecture of the tomb is sophisticated, with a short entry tunnel leading into a large open courtyard at the side of which is a four-pillared portico over a decorated wall. In the centre of the west wall there is an entrance (with locked gate) to the 30-pillared hall, where only one fluted column is left standing. This remnant does, however, give some idea of the original grandeur of this chamber before its ceiling collapsed. A doorway leads to an extension to an unfinished second hall, where two pillars are in place.

The decoration of the tomb is worth some attention. To the right, after the entrance under a picture of Amenhotep, are nine vignettes of nations conquered by the pharaoh, each representative of a different race and city. On the portico wall is a set of scenes of stick fighting, sports, dancing and men driving cattle as part of the festival of the pharaoh's jubilee in which Kheruef is keen to show his important role. At the left-hand end of the portico is another set of images showing the king and queen sailing at the end of the jubilee festival and decorated, large-scale figures of Amenhotep III and his queen. There are wonderful impressions of ladies clapping, musical instruments such as flutes being played, and ladies dancing during the jubilee celebrations – all very beautifully and graphically done. Look out for Nubian dancing ladies though the colouring is now faded. These figures are mainly on the bottom two registers, the high levels being scraped and broken and in very bad condition.

At the very end of the blue-ceilinged access tunnel to the pillared hall, on the right-hand side, is a large panel of the king and queen in a boat crossing to Abydos but it is badly damaged. On the right of the corridor, about 2-3 m from the end and about 1 m from ground, is a small cartoon in black of Sinmootè, one of the great craftsmen of the period, and it leads specialists to suspect that this area was used as a trial ground for the workers who built the main Hatshepsut temple.

Anch-hor (414) This 26th Dynasty tomb in El-Asasif was prepared for the chief steward of the divine votaress of Amun, and Overseer of Upper Egypt. A long flight of stairs leads down to a set of 10 rooms and an open courtyard. The main chamber has eight square columns and leads to a deep antechamber, and then to a small burial chamber with a niche in the west end. The engravings are uncoloured and often unfinished, but look out for a beautiful gazelle and a heron, plus a unique scene of the art of bee-keeping.

Pabasa (279) Nearer the entrance to Hatshepsut's Temple is the tomb of this 26th Dynasty official. On the lintel above the doorway is a relief of a barque, after which a hall leads to the pillared first court where six pillars are carved with scenes of daily life, such as catching birds, bee-keeping and fruit-picking. The granite sarcophagus of Pabasa is now in the Kelvingrove Art Gallery and Museum in Glasgow.

Tombs at El-Khokah

ⓘ *There are some 60 tomb chapels from the Ramessid period at El-Khokha, about 500 m south of the El-Asasif tombs.*

Nefersekhru (296) Nefersekhru, whose tomb was discovered in 1915 by Mond, was the scribe of the divine offerings of all of the gods. He married three wives who are all represented in the tomb.

Inside, the single chamber has a ceiling of highly coloured panels in geometric designs probably representing a carpet. To the south of the door on the entrance wall is a formal picture taken from the *Book of the Gates* and scenes of Nefersekhru before the deities. Beautiful paintings on the left of the back wall show the deceased sporting a leopard-skin outfit. The middle panel has three registers, of which the left one, which is more or less intact, shows a wife. Two things of which to take special note are the dominating image of Osiris, the king of the dead – sadly scarred – and the statues of Nefersekhru set in niches in the middle section.

On the right wall at the end is well-executed sculpture of two wives and the deceased sitting on a bench. On the back wall under a lintel is a scene of feasting with the deceased and one of his wives handing out gifts, including flowers, to visitors. There are agricultural scenes on the left-hand side of door on entry to the chamber.

The western side chamber leads to another Ramessid tomb chapel (**295**) of unknown ownership with a shaft in its north eastern extremity. The ceiling of this side room has a spectacular carpet design.

Neferrompet (178) This small but famous tomb temple to the Scribe of the Treasury lies to the right at the bottom of the stairs leading to Nefersekhru's tomb. Also discovered in 1915 by Mond, it dates from the time of Ramses the Great. Made up of two chambers joined by a narrow doorway, lighting in the tomb is good and the walls are protected by glass.

Decoration is typical of the Ramessid tomb type, and in both rooms the friezes portray Hathor's face and Anubis. The first hall has a ceiling with beautiful carpet-like paintings bearing geometrical designs with flowers. The most interesting decoration is a representation of 14 scenes from the *Book of the Gates* with Neferrompet and his wife drinking from the pool, a weighing scene led by Anubis, a harpist singing, and his wife playing draughts. She wears beautiful hair styles and attractive dresses – in places the garment appears so fine that the outline of her arm shows through the cloth. Look for the cat with a bone in the far left-hand corner.

In the second chamber are five panels showing adoration of the gods. There is a much-noted panel showing Neferrompet keeping a tally of offerings given to the temple, which is in excellent condition and illustrates life in the treasury at that time. On the end wall is a series of four statues cut from the rock and decorated, showing perhaps Mutemwia and daughters or possibly priestesses.

Tombs at Dra'a Abul Naga

ⓘ *Opened to the public in 1999, the tombs at Dra'a Abul Naga are about 1 km south of the El-Khokha tombs by road. Some 48 tombs from the 18th Dynasty have been located here, in valleys scattered over a wide area of the desert, of which 2 are open.*

Roy (255) This finely decorated tomb was prepared for Roy, the royal scribe and steward of the estates of Horemheb. It is one of the most beautiful of the all nobles' tombs with remarkable scenes and colouring still intact. The southern wall is decorated with ploughing scenes, flax-pulling and a funeral procession showing grieving friends and mourners led by Anubis. The northern wall is decorated by offering scenes and libations before the deceased and his wife. There is a niche containing stelae with the barque of Re adorned with baboons. On the left side, the deceased is worshipping Hathor in the form of a tree goddess with Ba (the soul) drinking. On the right Roy's wife is worshipping.

Shuroy (13) Also north of the road at Dra'a Abul Naga is the tomb of Shuroy, the head of the brazier bearers. The tomb is worth a visit since the entry chamber is brightly coloured with many scenes in a good state of preservation – as bright as the day they were drawn. The first hall is decorated with sketches of the deceased and his wife adoring divinities, and look on the right side for the gates decorated with demons. The door jambs of the second hall carry sketches of the Shuroy on the right and his wife on the left. The left side of the chamber is decorated with offerings-bearers and a funeral procession, including a child mourner before a mummy, and the deceased kneeling with braziers before Hathor on a mountain. On the right side there are scenes representing offering-bearers before the deceased and his wife and a banquet with clappers and bouquets.

Valley of the Queens

ⓘ *Nefertari's tomb is closed to the general public, due to the disintegration of the paintings as a result of exposure. It can only be viewed these days by VIPs or corporate groups, at enormous expense (E£20,000 plus E£100 per person). A visit to the other tombs in the valley costs E£35/20.*

The 'Valley of the Queens' is a bit of a misnomer, as it is in fact chiefly the burial site of the princes. It was originally known as the 'Place of Beauty' but is now called in Arabic the 'Gates of the Harem' (Biban El-Harem). It was used as a burial site for officials long before the queens and their offspring, who had previously been buried with their husbands, began to be buried here in the 19th Dynasty (1320-1200 BC). It contains more than 80 tombs but many are still unidentified. The tombs are generally quite simple with a long

7 **Valley of the Queens**

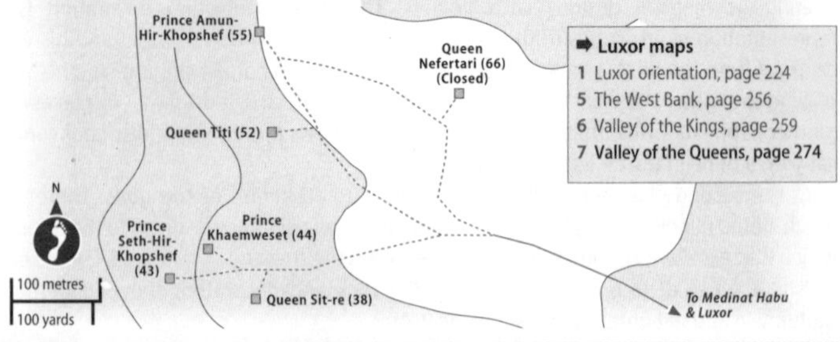

corridor, several antechambers branching off and the burial chamber at the end. The most famous tomb is that of Ramses II's wife Nefertari, the best preserved and most colourful of any tomb in any valley in Egypt. However, now that this is permanently closed except to VIPS and only three other tombs are open, the Valley of the Queens has fallen off most tour bus agendas. Which can make a visit refreshingly quiet, if you have the time, though the appeal of the tombs is certainly more subtle.

Prince Khaemweset (44)

Although the tomb is dedicated to one of Ramses III's young sons, who died of smallpox, it is dominated by the pharaoh himself. The reliefs depict the young boy being led to the underworld by his father who is offering sacrifices and helping his son through the judgement of Osiris to the Fields of Yaru. The side chambers are well preserved, with pastel colours beautiful against a chalk background, and the detail in their clothing (down to the patterns on their sandaled feet) quite exquisite.

Queen Titi (52)

Queen Titi was the daughter, wife and mother of a succession of 20th Dynasty pharaohs called Ramses, but it is uncertain to which one she was married. A corridor leads to a square shrine that branches into three antechambers with the badly preserved burial chamber on the left being dedicated to the four sons of Horus and Osiris. The central chamber features the Queen before the gods and the shrine is dominated by animal deities with pictures of jackals, baboons and guardian lions. The right-hand chamber depicts the tree goddess and Hathor as a cow (now defaced) rejuvenating the Queen with Nile water.

Prince Amun-Hir-Khopshef (55)

Prince Amun-Hir-Khopshef was the eldest son of Ramses III and, again, he died young, but this time possibly in battle at the age of nine. Descent to the tomb is via a stairway into the main hall from which there is a corridor to the burial chamber. The tomb is elaborately decorated with fine illustrations which remain in good condition. The scenes show excerpts from the *Book of the Gates* and Ramses III leading his son in a course around the stations of the gods. An oddity is the sarcophagus which contained the remains of a foetus, now displayed in a glass cabinet in one corner of the burial chamber.

Private tombs

Qurnat Murai

Amenhoptep (Huy) Amenhoptep (Huy) was the Viceroy of Kush in the reign of Tutankhamen. The tomb-chapel is cruciform with a transverse chamber and an incomplete inner chamber with four irregular pillars. The decoration of the transverse chamber is fascinating, showing Nubian royalty in procession delivering rings of gold to Tutankhamen, feathers adorn their bleached hair and they drive a chariot pulled by a cow. Almost all the worthwhile decorations are in the west wing of the transverse chamber, although sections of Hymn to Ptah occur in the small corridor between the two chambers.

Deir El-Medina

ⓘ *Tickets available at the main ticket office, E£30, students E£15 for Sennedjem and Inherkhau tombs and the Hathor Temple, and note that there is a separate ticket for the tomb of Peshedu, E£15 student E£8. Cameras must be left outside the tombs.*

The original occupants of this village were the workers who excavated and decorated the tombs in the Valley of the Kings. The neat remains of the 18th-Dynasty town comprise a narrow street, in places little more than a metre wide, with the houses tightly packed on either side. The foundations show how small these dwellings were, and often they were subdivided, but remains of stairs indicate an upper storey and sometimes a cellar. Some houses were a little larger and contained a kitchen.

Above the site of Deir Al-Medina are three tombs open at present, those of Sennedjem, in the 19th Dynasty, Peshedu and Inherkhau, foreman of a construction team in the 20th Dynasty. All are beautifully preserved and have outstanding paintings. Normally guides are not allowed to conduct their groups into the comparatively small chambers, and relatively few visitors in any case makes it a worthwhile visit.

Sennedjem (217) Sennedjem's tomb was found undamaged in 1886 by Gaston Maspero, then head of the Antiquities Service. It is a small, simple, rectangular burial chamber, 6 m by 3 m, with narrow stairs leading into it – note the bare-breasted Mut on the underside of the lintel. On discovery it held intact the mummies of Sennedjem, his wife, son and two daughters-in-law, plus a handsome range of funeral materials – now unfortunately dispersed across the museums of the world. The wall decorations, protected by glass, are first-rate in style and condition, while the domed ceiling is wonderfully decorated with snakes, pictures of the gods and very fetching black and white cow. Clockwise round the chamber are hunting/forest scenes in the lower register and, above, a mummy on a bier with the goddesses Isis and Nephthys protecting it. Also look out for the priest who is clad in a wonderfully detailed leopard skin ensemble. On the side wall Sennedjem and his wife stand before the gods and, on the back wall is the masterpiece of the tomb: the body of Sennedjem lying on an ornamental bier being embalmed by Anubis. On the east wall is a painting of the barque of Re flanked by blue baboons and, below, a view of the afterworld (where the Nile seems to be the centre of life also). The south wall shows Sennedjem and his wife, Iyneferty, facing the Deities of the Gates, their frilly hair is just lovely. Of great appeal is the depiction of the tree of life on the ceiling, from which a goddess is appearing bearing an offering table.

Inherkhau (219) This is another brilliantly painted tomb, accessible down two steep flights of steps to a low-ceilinged anteroom with plastered walls bearing coloured paintings and a ceiling covered with abstract designs, now damaged by efflorescence and exfoliation of the limestone rock. An exit leads down steps under a low lintel to the main vaulted chamber, approximately 5 m by 2 m. On the left-hand side is a painting of a scarab an elegant stork, several Anubis, and a fine depiction of the family with hair left down in funeral form. Also, note the cat of Heliopolis (with the head of a ferocious hare) killing a serpent beneath the holy tree. At the north end, slightly damaged, is a full-scale representation of Inherkhau and his family with offerings. The right-hand side wall also carries more pictures of Inherkhau's family, the children naked and with hair curled round their ears to denote immaturity. The ceiling is vaulted and painted in bright ochre, yellow and gold, bearing cartouches and a detailed list of events in the life of Inherkhau.

Peshedu (3) A short toil uphill brings you to Peshedu's tomb, which is highly decorated and in very good condition. It celebrates the life of the 'servant in the place of truth' and is very light and airy, with the coloured scenes protected by transparent screens. It is entered down a very steep flight of stairs, with a low roof – beware. Eventually, an entrance leads into the first large chamber, which narrows down into a low gateway just 1.5 m high. This is where the wonderful decorations begin – all in good condition on panels on both sides with hieroglyphics above. On the sides of the entry corridor are images of Anubis lying on an altar. Within the burial chamber, the wealth of decoration begins above the doorway where the god Ptah-Sokaris is shown as a winged falcon under the eye of Horus. The two human figures are Peshedu on the right and his son on the left. Inside to the left the upper register shows a beautiful image of a female (probably the goddess of the sycamore) carrying water up the tree and below right are rows of Peshedu's attendants in fine detail. The long left-hand wall carries an image of Peshedu and his wife with two children standing before Horus with passages of *Book of the Dead* around them.

The right wall of the burial chamber shows Peshedu and his child before Re-Horakhte and three other gods. Surrounding these images are passages from the *Book of the Dead*. Inside the burial chamber to the left is the now famous scene of Peshedu beneath a date palm in fruit by the side of the water.

Hathor Temple The Ptolemaic Hathor Temple stands just to the north of the workers' village and gives its name, Deir El-Medina (Monastery of the Town) to the area, as in the early Christian era it was inhabited by monks. Dedicated to Maat and Hathor, whose head atop the square pillars still has blue painted hair, the temple is a peaceful spot. The three shrines to the rear are white-washed and colourful decoration remains on the depictions from the Book of the Dead. Ask if you can go on the roof, via the damaged stairway.

Other temples and sites

The Ramesseum

ⓘ *Tickets available at the main ticket office, E£25, students E£15.*

While most tourists confine themselves to the Valley of the Kings and Hatshepsut's temple, there are a number of other interesting West Bank ruins closer to the river. Of these, among the most impressive was the Ramesseum, a 19th-century name for what was effectively a state cult-temple, on the opposite side of the road near the Tombs of the Nobles. Today, only scattered remains and faded reliefs are left of the great temple, which once stood there and reportedly rivalled the splendours of the temples at Abu Simbel. It is still an extremely worthwhile stop that fires the imagination and you will be alone but for the cooing and fluttering of the pigeons. There a sleepy little resthouse where you can get a cool drink, handily near the exit of the temple (see Eating, page 284).

Ramses II (1304-1237 BC) built this mortuary temple, on the consecrated site of Seti I's (1318-04 BC) much smaller but collapsing temple, in order to impress his subjects. But he failed to take into account the annual flooding of the Nile. The result was that this enormous tribute to Amun and himself was less eternal than he expected. The first two pylons collapsed and only a single colonnade remains of what would have been the **First Courtyard**. On its south side is a palace where Ramses stayed when he attended religious festivals on the West Bank. In front of the ruins of the Second Pylon is the base of the enormous colossus of Ramses, which was originally over 17 m high but it is now much eroded and various parts of his anatomy are scattered throughout the world's museums.

Ramses The Great (1304-1237)

Known by the Egyptians as Ramses Al-Akbar (The Great), a name that would no doubt have pleased him, the achievements of Ramses II, arguably Ancient Egypt's most famous king, were majestic. During his 67-year reign, the pharaoh presided over an empire stretching west from present-day Libya to Iraq in the east, as far north as Turkey, and south into Sudan. While his military feats were suitably exaggerated for posterity in the monuments of his day, Ramses also engineered a peace treaty with Egypt's age-old northern rivals, the Hittites, by a strategic marriage to a daughter of the Hittite king in 1246 BC that ended years of unrest. The peace lasted for the rest of the pharaoh's lengthy reign. Ramses II is believed to be the pharaoh of the biblical 'exodus', although Egyptian records make no mention of dealings with Israelite slaves. His massive fallen statue at the Ramesseum inspired Shelley's romantic sonnet *Ozymandias*, a title taken from the Greek version of Ramses' coronation name *User-maat-re*. Egypt's most prolific pharaoh (siring at least 80 children), he was also a prodigious builder. He began building soon after ascending the throne at the age of 25, having discovered that the great temple his father Seti I had begun at Abydos was a shambles. During the rest of his reign he erected dozens of monuments including a temple to Osiris at Abydos, expansions of temples at Luxor and Karnak, and the awe-inspiring cliff temples at Abu Simbel. In an age when life expectancy was 40 years at most, Ramses, who lived to 92, must truly have appeared to be a god.

The forefinger alone measures more than 1 m in length. The upper part of the body crashed into the second court where the head and torso remain. Next to the three stairways leading to the Hypostyle Hall stood three smaller colossi stood but only a single fragmented one has stood the test of time.

Although it is now roofless, 29 of the original 48 columns still loom tall in the **Hypostyle Hall**. The centre of the roof would have been higher than the sides in order to allow shafts of sunlight to enter. To the left of the entrance is the famous relief of the Egyptian victory over the Hittite city of Dapur during the Battle of Kadesh. Around the base of the west walls some of Ramses' many sons are depicted. At the far end of the hall a central door leads into the Astronomical Room, renowned for its ceiling illustrated with the oldest-known 12-month calendar. Because the temple was dedicated to Amun it is thought to represent a solar year. Two other vestibules, a library and a linen room, lead to the ruined sanctuary, which is the temple's highest point.

Medinat Habu

ⓘ *Tickets available at the main ticket office, E£30, students E£15.*

The Mortuary Temple of Ramses III (1198-1166 BC), which lies west of the Colossi of Memnon at a place known in Arabic as **Medinat Habu**, was modelled on that built by his forefather Ramses II nearby. It is second only to Karnak in terms of its size and complexity and within the enormous enclosing walls are a palace, a Nilometer and several smaller shrines with some pre-dating the temple itself. When Thebes was threatened, as it was during the 20th Dynasty's Libyan invasions, the enclosing walls of the complex were large enough to shelter the entire population. The immensity of the structures that remain are still quite overwhelming and the temple is a true highlight, uncluttered by visitors and a good place to finish a day on the West Bank as the sun goes down.

Although Ramses III named his temple the 'House of a Million Years', the smaller shrine that already occupied the site next to the south enclosure walls was in use long after the main temple shrine had fallen into disuse.

To the north, the **Small Temple**, which was constructed by Hatshepsut but later altered by Tuthmosis III who, as ever, erased her cartouche, was built on a platform from which there are good views in all directions. Until the 18th century a grove of acacia trees led to the Colossi of Memnon. The site, known as Jeser Ast or 'Sacred Place', was venerated because it was thought that the waters of chaos had divided and the primeval mound erupted here. During Akhenaten's rule, Amun's images were destroyed but they were later replaced by those of Horemheb and Seti I.

The whole temple complex is entered via the three-storey southeast gatehouse, which is built like a fortified Syrian pavilion and was originally 22 m high. Arriving through it into the large forecourt you can see the small temple to the right, the huge main temple directly ahead, and the small Chapels of the Votressess, dating from the 25th Dynasty (747-656 BC) kings of Kush, just to the left.

The remarkable homogeneity of the main temple's structure reflects the fact that it was designed and built by Ramses III alone rather than being expanded by successive pharaohs. The wonderfully preserved **First Pylon** was originally dedicated to Amun but was also used by Ramses II as a memorial to his Libyan and Asiatic campaigns. It would originally have been larger than the one at Luxor, standing 27 m high and 65 m long, but now the north corner and cornice are missing. The images on the left of the Pylon show Ramses slaying Nubian prisoners watched by Amun and Ptah while Syrians are slain on the right. The illustrations are based on genuine wars Ramses III never actually fought either nation.

On the left of the entrance way through the First Pylon, before arriving in the great 48 x 34 m **First Court**, Ramses III is shown worshipping the deities Ptah, Osiris and Sokar. The west of the court is flanked by eight columns and the east by seven Osiride pillars. On the **Second Pylon** the pharaoh is depicted marching rows of prisoners, the third row being Philistines (or Palestinians) wearing feathered headdresses, towards Amun and Mut. The **Second Court** is also made up of a combination of Osiride pillars and columns, and here the intensity of the colours on pillars and on ceiling slabs are especially breathtaking and well-preserved. One scene depicts the Feast of Sokar while the lower register of the back wall is dedicated to the Ramses III's sons and daughters. At the far right end of the hall is a small entrance that has two interesting illustrations. One shows the pharaoh before Seth, but this was later defaced to change him into Horus, while above the door Ramses is shown kneeling on the symbol of the united Upper and Lower Egypt.

The west door connects to the ruins of the severely damaged **Hypostyle Hall**. Above the door the pharaoh can again be seen kneeling over the symbol of Upper and Lower Egypt and at the base of the entry wall are 13 princesses and 10 princes. The central aisle of the hall would have been raised, in the same way as at Karnak, to allow Re's sunlight to enter.

A multitude of side rooms would originally have led off from the Hypostyle Hall but little now remains because of the severe damage caused by the major earthquake in 27 BC. The best-preserved room is the **Treasury** to the north where the walls are adorned with scenes of the pharaoh making offerings of gold to Amun. Another small room shows him wearing the Osiride symbols of the Atef feathered crown, a crook and flail.

The outer walls are better preserved and some of the reliefs are clearly visible. At the far end of the south wall is a calendar of religious feasts that is believed to be the longest such inscription. Further along is a portrayal of all the benefits with which Ramses III was blessed by Amun, while the rear west wall is dedicated to the pharaoh's victories in battle. In the northeast corner of the enclosure, near the Small Temple, is a small sacred lake where childless women came to bathe at night and pray to Isis that they might conceive. Close by stand the remains of the Nilometer that was originally fed by a canal that branched off from the Nile.

On a more modern theme – the **Monastery of St Theodore** lies to the southwest of the Temple of Medinat Habu and is within easy reach. The religious pictures are quite modern. Theodore was one of the many Christian soldiers who fell foul of Diocletian's oppression.

West Bank and Theban Necropolis listings

For Sleeping and Eating price codes and other relevant information, see pages 26-31.

Sleeping

West Bank *p254, map p256*

In recent years, several charming hotels have sprung up on the West Bank. Though the area has a lot less action than the East Bank, services are completely adequate and for people in search of a more tranquil Luxor experience it is an appealing place to be. Egyptophiles who return frequently to Luxor would not dream of staying anywhere else. The cheap public ferry makes transport across the Nile easy, and runs all night. Prices below include breakfast, unless stated otherwise. Most hotels don't offer TV in the rooms as they are aiming for a more rustic experience.

LL Al-Moudira, Hagar Dabaiyya (5 km from the bridge), T012-325 1307, www.moudira.com. An Arabesque hotel that is palatial, exquisite and far away from everything except serenity. Built with natural materials, each unique room is furnished with antiques, equipped with full amenities and with a divine terrace. Bathrooms are lavish (particularly in the suites) while the pool (heated in winter), courtyards, restaurant and gardens are simply perfect. They can arrange pick-up from the airport (45 mins, E£100), Luxor downtown (E£70) or the ferry (E£30), as well as driver/guide for the sights. Free Wi-Fi in the lobby and a most tasteful gift shop. Probably the loveliest hotel in all Egypt, at prices that are below what you would expect for such a wonderful experience.

AL-B Beit Sabee, Medinat Habu, T010-632 4926, www.nourelnil.com. A beautiful traditional mud-brick house with glorious views of the Theban mountains and an outlook onto Medinat Habu (now sadly marred by the wall that the government has built to enclose the West Bank sites). The 8 rooms are of varying sizes, very rustic-chic, all en suite with unique furnishings and colour schemes. Attracts a mix of nationalities and age-groups, there is a wonderful rooftop terrace, good-value vegetarian meals are possible, and they can help arrange transport and advise on interesting local excursions. This maison d'hotel is one of those special places.

A Desert Paradise Lodge, New Gabawy village, north of the Valley of the Kings, T095-231 3036/T016-997 7720, contact@desertparadiselodge.com. This marvellous little enclave with Swiss-Egyptian owners has 10 raised rooms around a relaxing courtyard of trees. Each large, domed suite has a front and back door, Western-standard bathrooms and wooden furniture. 2 rooms on the upper level have a/c (others not, for environmental reasons) and enjoy a glorious sun terrace. The little pool, upstairs indoor lounge, and restaurant are very homely – it is just a shame that new housing surrounding them has encroached on the fabulous mountain views. Stay for 7 nights and get 1 night free.

C Amon, Gezira, T095-231 0912, www.amonhotel.com. The tropical garden is a major plus point, the restaurant pleasing and modern, balconies lovely, rooftop has loungers. Rooms are boring yet well furnished and feel homely. Single women travellers repeatedly recommend this place.

C El Fayrouz Hotel, Gezira El-Bairat, T095-231 2709, www.elfayrouz.com. This is a great hotel all round, but it's the secluded garden restaurant that really makes it (see Eating, page 283). Rooms are neutral with sizable baths, 1 roof terrace has Bedouin seating, staff are excelllent and free Wi-Fi. Conveniently located on the edge of Gezira El-Bairat village, singles/doubles are E£95/115 or (in the newer rooms, which are nicer and have a/c) it's E£150/180. Many guests have been coming back every year since they opened and wouldn't dream of staying anywhere else, which speaks for itself.

C El-Nakhil Hotel, Gezira El-Bairat, T095-231 3922, T012-382 1007. Beautiful spacious rooms have brick-domed ceilings, dark red walls and quality furnishings, lit by filigree lanterns, plus high-spec bathrooms (some with tubs). There is an air of peace and refinement throughout, a pleasant garden and Luxor Temple is visible from the rooftop restaurant. Far more chi-chi than other similarly priced options, there is also 1 room with disabled facilities and free Wi-Fi throughout. The only problem is the manager, who can be overbearing (especially with lone women) and you will need to be firm.

C El Mesala Hotel, Gezira, T012-351 4523, www.elmesalahotel.com. Opened in summer 2010, this hotel has 8 rooms, 2 suites and 1 flat, all with a/c, fridge and TV. 3 have excellent big balconies overlooking the Nile and Luxor Temple directly in front. Nicely furnished, the bathrooms are particularly good. Shady roof terrace and little front garden, all very well maintained (so far!). The owners (brothers) can help arrange apartments for those who want to spend a week or more on the West Bank.

C Gezira Gardens, T095-231 2505, www.el-gezira.com. A well-established place that is of a good standard, the exterior is painted a cheerful white and blue though interior furnishings feel a bit dark and gloomy. Rooms have fridge, TV, a/c, balcony/terrace, plus 8 apartments (sleeping 4, €60). There's a good pool which outside guests can use for E£15, a nice bar and rooftop restaurant. Free Wi-Fi, internet E£15 per hr.

C Kareem, Gezira, T095-231 3530, www.hotelkareemlxr.com. A particularly clean and freshly decorated hotel with 12 rooms (4 more to come), some have a/c and most have balconies, but there are no fridges, TV or Wi-Fi (PC costs E£2 per half hr). Wonderfully lush views from the shady rooftop (from where you can take dinner). Come here not for Egyptian atmosphere but for quality furnishings and a clean modern feel. Doubles E£210.

C Nile Valley, Gezira, T095-231 1477/ T012-796 4473, www.nilevalley.nl. Deservedly popular place, rooms here are bright white with touches of colour, nice new showers, daily cleaning, refurbishments are frequently carried out which keeps things fresh. Decent-sized pool (with bar stools in the water! Non-guests can use for E£50), the usual rooftop restaurant, as well as poolside and a/c dining. Upstairs rooms have balconies.

C Nour El-Gourna Hotel, Gurna, opposite the ticket office, T095-231 1430, T010-295812, www.nourelgournahotel.com. Mud-brick and simple, this small hotel is quite charming and has excellent food. The 7 rooms have spotless linens and rustic furnishings, 2 upstairs have balconies (and are more expensive), all are individual. There are views from the upstairs terrace to the Colossi of Memnon, and a village atmosphere. Internet is available (not Wi-Fi). No alcohol served.

C Sheherazade, Gezira, T010-611 5939, www.hotelsheherazade.com. There are 2 main differences at this hotel when compared to other West Bank offerings: 1 being the extensive garden-restaurant which has actual grass, and the other the unusual architecture with domed public areas that soar to the sky. Garish paintings from the 1001 Nights adorn some walls, there is a honeymoon suite and private rooftop. They charge for Wi-Fi (E£10 per day), most rooms have a/c, the breakfast is superb, and the decor Egyptian.

D Amenophis Hotel, near Medinat Habu Temple, T095-206 0078, hussein amonphis17@yahoo.com. A good choice in the upper-budget category, doubles are E£150 and although they're not huge or atmospheric they are certainly fresh and attractive with especially comfy beds and pillows. Go for a corner room at the front for great views of the fields stretching east and windows and balconies on 2 sides. The location near Medinat Habu is utterly peaceful and rural. They also have an apartment that sleeps 4 for E£300 per night. Free use of PC.

D El-Gezira Hotel, Gezira, T/F095-231 0034, www.el-gezira.com. This popular hotel is a long-timer on the West Bank scene, rooms are looking slightly dated but have fridges, a/c and balconies (on the upper level). Singles are E£100, doubles E£150. The sociable rooftop (where you can have dinner) and garden with water feature are a bonus, and they serve alcohol (beer E£12). They also own the Gezira Gardens nearer the river (see above), where El-Gezira guests can use the pool for free.

D Marsam Hotel, Gurna, T095-237 2403, T010-3426471, marsam@africamail.com. Popular with archaeologists during the season, austere rooms have reed furniture and are cool, calm, dark retreats. The smaller rooms without bath are one of the cheapest deals on the West Bank (single E£65, double E£130 with breakfast), there are also high-ceiling rooms with private bath (E£80/170). Unfortunately the pillows are rock hard, but otherwise all is perfect. The rooftop looks out over fields to the Colossi of Memnon or back to the hills and the garden is a shady relaxing place to be. Bikes are available for hire. An excellent choice with a very special atmosphere.

D Ramses Hotel, Gezira, T/F095-231 2748, www.ramsesshotel.net, Good value rooms are somewhat garishly decked out but the colourful walls are attractive, all have a/c, TV and fridge (single E£80, double E£120, triple E£160). Tall building means great views from most balconies, there's a sun-deck above the rooftop restaurant, and nice patio out the front. Family-run.

E Habou Hotel, Medinat Habu, T095-231 1611, habouhotel@hotmail.com. Rooms are fairly basic with outside bathrooms, fans, no mossie nets – really it's just a bed with clean sheets. But the upstairs terrace views directly onto the 1st pylon of Medinat Habu at unbeatable (only worth staying on the upper level) and worth some discomfort. Internet available.

Eating

West Bank *p254, map p256*

A number of restaurants have sprung up on the West Bank, and all the hotels have attractive roofs or gardens where you can dine.

🍴 **Africa Restaurant**.

🍴 **African Garden**, opposite the ferry landing, T095-231 1488, T012-365 8722. Open 0800-2400. Serves up the standard Luxor menu of rice, salad, meat/fish and veg for E£35 in a delightful outside courtyard. Surrounded by fruit trees and mint that the friendly staff will pick to accompany your tea. As the menu differs somewhat for English speakers, if there's a local dish you want that you don't see, ask for it. Serves a good traditional Egyptian breakfast. Beer available. Good bathrooms.

🍴 **El Fayrouz Hotel**, Gezira El-Bairat, T095-231 2709, www.elfayrouz.com. Sociable seating among flower and shrubs, varied menu to choose from, pizzas are particularly recommended although everything is reliably good. It's also a great place hang out and have a beer.

🍴 **Hapy Habu Restaurant**, T095-206 0718. About 50 m beyond the entrance to Medinat Habu, this well-maintained little place offers a range of Western dishes as well Egyptian food – great when you fancy a pancake, quiche or light lunch rather than a hot rich stew. The location is idyllic and the garden terrace most relaxing. Recommended.

🍴 **Nour El Gourna Hotel & Restaurant**, Old Gurna, opposite the ticket office, T095-231 1430, T010-295812, www.nourel gournahotel.com. Delicious tagines and stews come in substantial portions – in fact, it's a good idea to negotiate sharing 1 meal between 2. They can accommodate vegetarians, while meat eaters will be treated to duck and pigeon delicacies. A lovely spot under shady reed awnings, and the staff are extremely nice.

ΨΨ-Ψ **Memnon Restaurant**, next to the Colossi of Memnon, T012-327 8747. A good resting place for a chilled drink as the sun sets on the Colossi (though they might have to dash out on a motorbike to get more beer, it comes with an iced glass). The food is recommended by ex-pats who live on the West Bank, with all sorts on offer from pasta to fish, plus great soups and salads (they pride themselves on their *fattoush*), all reasonably priced. You can't fault the view or the tiny flowery garden.

ΨΨ-Ψ **Ramesseum Resthouse**, by the entrance to the Ramesseum, is perfect for a post-temple drink either inside the cool interior or outside in the shade (beer E£15). Meals are good too, groups occasionally come at lunchtime. Owned by the Abdel Rasoul family – see the articles inside which feature the grandfather who was part of Howard Carter's team.

Shopping

West Bank *p254, map p256*

For chic and well-selected items from Egypt and further afield head to **Heavenly Blue**, in the new shopping centre by the ferry, T016-634 7582, open daily 1000-2200. Ingeborg Unseld is an interior designer and her impeccable taste is evident: elegant clothes, great Ramaḍan lanterns, throws, bags, Lenhert & Landrock photos, and much more. She also showcases local artists and supports West Bank craft initiatives. Just behind her shop is **Nour El Nil Boutique**, which has an eclectic selection of goods from the flea markets of Alexandria and Paris, alongside other quirky items from Egypt.

A good place to buy Egyptian handicrafts is **Caravanserai**, near Medinat Habu, T012-327 8771, www.caravanserai.luxor.com, where the owner Khairy sells glassware, pottery, Bedouin embroidery, ethnic jewellery and more. He tries to promote local village industries, in particular. Open daily 0800-2200.

Very worthwhile is a visit to **Balady Handicrafts**, Gurna, T010-543 6085, www.baladyhandicraft.com. A project started by a local family to find gainful employment for kids no longer allowed to tout postcards to tourists on the West Bank. Children are trained in potting, weaving and embroidery (after school hours; you can see them at work from 0700-1330 and 1500-1700). The shop sells the attractive products of their labour; each pot carries the name of the child-artist, who receives payment accordingly.

Activities and tours

West Bank *p254, map p256*

Cycle hire

Cheap and fairly roadworthy cycles are available in Al-Gezira village on the West Bank for slightly more than on the East Bank.

Horse riding

Horse riding on West Bank has become popular, usually passing through villages and some monuments towards the mountains (E£30 per hr). Camel and donkey excursions are also possible (E£30). Try **Nobi's Arabian Horse Stables**, Al-Gezira, West Bank, T095-231 0024, T010-504 8558, or **Pharaoh's Stables**, T095-231 2263; probably best to call in advance.

Tour operators

QEA, Al-Gezira, West Bank, T095-231 1667, T010-294 3169, www.questforegyptian adventure.com. Tailor-made tours of Luxor's East or West Banks (1 day) and further afield around Egypt.

South of Luxor

Contents

Footprint features

At a glance

Getting around Cruise boats are popular between Luxor and Aswan. You can also cruise on Lake Nasser. *Feluccas* sail from Aswan to Edfu and flights head to Abu Simbel.

Time required Allow 2-3 days for Aswan.

Weather Perfect for winter sun. Stiflingly hot between May and Sep.

When not to go The Sun Festival at Abu Simbel attracts hoards of people on 22 Feb and 22 Oct. Avoid if you dislike crowds.

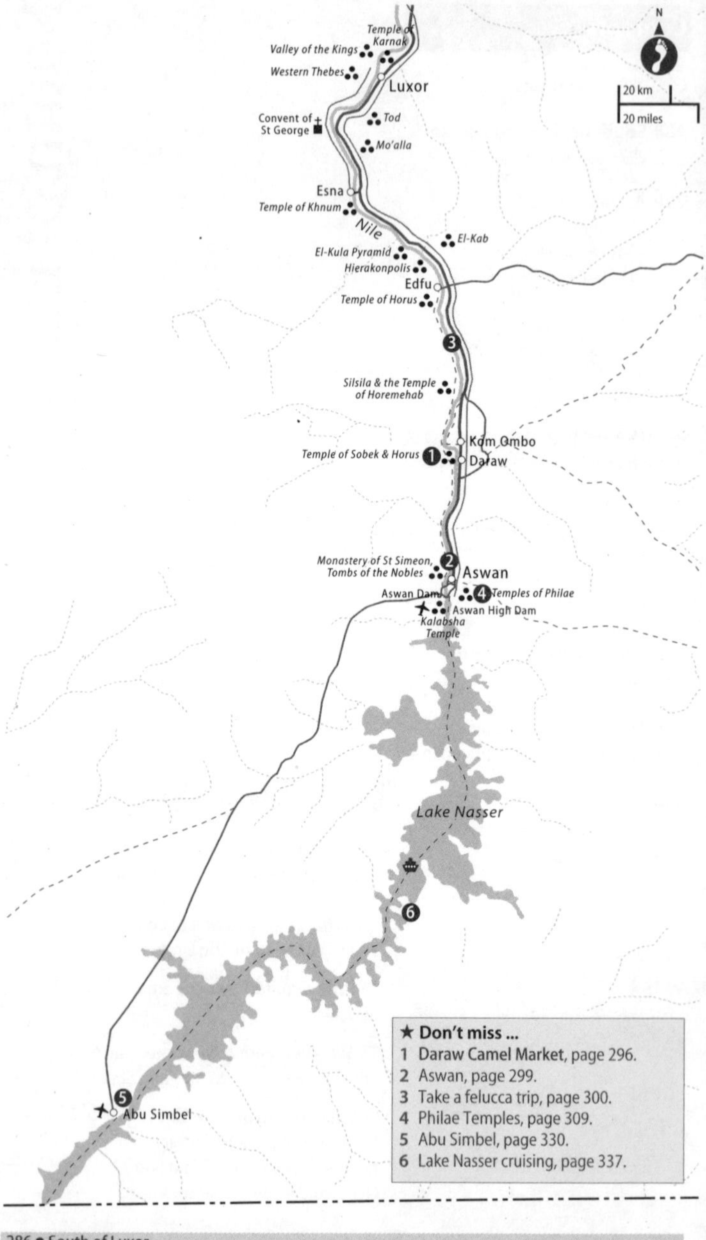

★ Don't miss ...

1 **Daraw Camel Market**, page 296.
2 Aswan, page 299.
3 Take a felucca trip, page 300.
4 Philae Temples, page 309.
5 Abu Simbel, page 330.
6 Lake Nasser cruising, page 337.

The Nile Valley between Aswan and Luxor is home to some of the world's most stunning monuments, but in this region it is the Nile that is the luminary and the central vein. For 228 km, the ancient river languidly meanders along past the stripes of crops with ibis paddling in their watery furrows, farmers wearing every colour of *gallabiyya*, ancient sandstone quarries, donkeys turning wooden waterwheels and sheep among the sugar cane. The area is best explored by boat – from the deck of a cruiser or more intimately in a *felucca* or *dahabiya*, with the Nile so close you can feel it mumbling and sighing, still as glass in the morning and raging like a rough sea by midday. Placed at strategic and commercial centres near the river, the striking Graeco-Roman monuments of Edfu and Kom Ombo are among the most colourful and complete pharaonic structures in the country.

The further south one ventures, the more apparent the melding of Africa and Arabia. Aswan, the provincial capital, is populated largely by Nubians, a taller and darker-skinned people with a unique language and tradition. Although the city itself has become as commercial as Luxor, endless time can be lost wandering around nearby islands, walking amid Nubian villages and reclining on *feluccas* watching birds soar overhead. Close by, the island temple of Philae is a spiritual place, especially after dark – if you see just one sound and light show on your travels, let it be this one. After the Pyramids and the Sphinx, Abu Simbel, adorned with four enormous colossi of Ramses II, is the defining image of Egypt. Just 40 km north of the Sudanese border, the temple was erected as testimony to the Pharaoh's might for anyone who dared approach from the south. Three millennia later, the monument's sheer size still inspires awe. A night spent in laid-back Abu Simbel on the brim of Lake Nasser gives the opportunity to enjoy a peaceful dawn at the temple, a memorable experience as profound as the monument itself.

Ins and outs

Getting around Travel in Upper Egypt, at present, is fairly straightforward. With no terrorist attacks since 1997, there is little to worry about. The last surviving tourist convoy in Egypt operates between Aswan and Abu Simbel and this is expected to be dispensed with in the near future. Despite this local authorities prefer foreigners travelling overland in Upper Egypt to travel in groups when venturing between the major sights. As such, accompanying a tour (which is sometimes just a ride) is often the easiest and most hassle-free way to go. There are many options, catering to both piaster-pinching backpackers as well as tourists with more resources, see pages 321 and 337. However, if you are few in number and take a chance boarding buses, service taxis and trains, the benefits of not arriving at a temple with hundreds of other tourists makes the extra effort worthwhile. While there should be no problem getting out of smaller towns on microbuses (such as Kom Ombo, Edfu, and so on), problems may arise when drivers remember the restrictions of the past. Generally speaking, calm persistence will get you onto your chosen form of transport. For information on *felucca* trips on the Nile, see page 300.

Best time to visit Most people visit the area between October and March, and around Christmas in particular. There is a running joke in Aswan, 'we have the best weather in the world ... in the winter.' And it's true. In December, temperatures average a lovely 30°C. Come July, though, they rise to a scorching 40°C. Be prepared.

South of Luxor to Aswan

→ Colour map 4, A2-B2.

The main road follows the Nile along its east bank from Luxor, past Edfu (115 km) on the west bank, before continuing via Kom Ombo (176 km) to Aswan (216 km). There is an alternative, less crowded and less scenic route along the west bank from the Valley of the Kings to Esna (55 km) and Edfu before having to cross the river to continue the journey along the east bank to Aswan. Most visitors make this journey by river in one of the many floating hotels that moor at the sites along the way (see boxes on Nile Cruisers and felucca *trips, pages 250 and 300). Egyptian village life, often obscured from the road and not easily appreciated from the window of a speeding car, can be seen on this relaxing journey that many deem the highlight of their trip though Egypt.* *▸▸ For listings, see pages 297-298.*

Ins and outs

Getting there There are no longer official restrictions on foreigners travelling in this area so any form of available transport can be used to get around. Coming from Luxor it is possible to take the train or bus, hire a private taxi (about E£300-400 to go from Luxor to Aswan) or even take microbuses (though note that these are few and far between on a Friday). *▸▸ See Transport, page 297.*

Mo'alla Cemetery

ⓘ Before visiting this site buy your tickets at the kiosks on Luxor's West Bank, at the Luxor Museum kiosk or be prepared to pay an informal fee of some E£20 to the guardian. Travelling from Luxor, after the Nagga Abu Said station take the first turning left, cross the bridge over the canal then take the unsurfaced track that swings left towards the cliffs and the cemetery.

There are rock-cut tombs in the cemetery of Mo'alla on the east bank 40 km south of Luxor dating from the First Intermediate period. Four tombs are located here, cut into the cliffs. All entrances face the west and the Nile.

The tomb of Ankhtifi (1) Ankhtifi was one time governor of the area between Edfu and Armant. He was a very important man in his time and noted for feeding the people in neighbouring areas during a time of famine. The tomb is of a slightly irregular shape and cut directly into the rock, shaped to fit in with the harder veins in the rock strata. On entry there is a rectangular chamber that originally had 30 pillars in three rows of 10, some round and others hexagonal in form. Most pillars are decorated with fine plasterwork and those pillars near the doors carry the best examples of coloured hieroglyphs. An amusing scene on the wall immediately to the right of the entrance door shows a huge fish being caught by spear, and there is a small picture of the deceased and his beautiful wife in very good condition, about 50 cm sq. Other interesting scenes of daily life include lines of animals carrying food to relieve a local famine and a row of spotted cattle to indicate Ankhtifi's wealth. The burial chamber lies at a lower level at the rear of the main hall.

Tombs 2 and 3 These comprise small chapels cut into the rock, but very little decoration remains – mind your head as you go down into the chambers.

The tomb/chapel of Sobekhotep (4) This monument to another regional governor lies a short way to the north in the cemetery. It is entered (or seen into) via a metal door. There are vestiges of decoration on the door jamb but the best known decoration is on the back wall where there are representations of trees and a man taking animals as offerings. The three pits inside the grill have over them a picture of the owner in full size carrying a staff and on the right a scene with eight women.

Esna

This small market town lies about 55 km south of Luxor on the west bank of the Nile, and (as with any Egyptian town) feels like a bustling place. Besides its Temple of Khnum, it's mainly known for the sandstone dam across the river, built in 1906 at about the same time as the first Aswan dam. Cruise ships and barges usually have to queue a while for their turn to pass through the barrages, though waiting time has been considerably reduced by the building of a second lock. It's a typical dusty town, not geared towards tourists save for the souvenir-sellers, and there is not much to keep you here once you've finished at the temple. The narrow lane ways around the back of the temple, away from the 'souvenir street' do, however, afford an insight into the life of a typical Upper Egyptian town and are worth a short stroll. There are also a few attractive but crumbling villas by the side of the Nile. Have a look for the 600-year-old doorway to a *caravanserai*, to the right of the entrance down to the temple, set slightly back from the street. You can be in and out in under two hours, which will keep the local police force happy. If you do stop off to see the temple after a *felucca* trip (most of which finish 30 km south of Esna), you'll find stalls serving simple food in the *souk*. Service taxis and buses stop about 10 minutes' walk from the temple, which is in the centre of town, walk to the river and then south along the Corniche to the ticket kiosk.

The **Temple of Khnum** ⓘ *daily 0600-1700 winter, 0600-1800 summer, E£20, students E£10,* lies partially exposed in a deep depression in the centre of town. The excavation began in the 1860s but could not continue because the area above was covered in

Horus – the first living god-king

Horus, who was originally the Egyptian sky-god and falcon-god, was later identified as the son of Osiris and his sister Isis. He subsequently avenged his father's murder by his uncle Seth in an epic fight at Edfu in which Horus lost an eye and Seth his testicles. It was not until Isis intervened that Horus prevailed as good triumphed over evil. Osiris pronounced his judgment by banishing Seth to the underworld and enthroning Horus as the first living god-king.

Each pharaoh claimed to be an incarnation of Horus and the annual Festival of the Coronation, at Edfu's now-destroyed Temple of the Falcon in front of the main temple's grand pylon, followed by a crowning ceremony in the temple's main forecourt, symbolized the renewal of royal power.

houses. Also, over the centuries since its construction, the annual Nile flood has deposited 10 m of silt over the temple site so that in fact all that is visible today is the **Hypostyle Hall**. This comes as a disappointment to some visitors, and consequently many tours no longer include Esna on their itineraries. The only part of the temple that can be seen is Ptolemaic/Roman, built on the foundations of a much older shrine which was also dedicated to the ram-headed deity Khnum. He was believed to have created man by moulding him from River Nile clay on a potter's wheel. Later, when Amun became the principal deity, Khnum had an image change and, in conjunction with Hapy, came to be regarded as the guardian of the source of the Nile.

The hypostyle hall's **Outer Facade** is decorated from left to right with the cartouches of the emperors Claudius, Titus and Vespasian Inside the lofty hall 18 columns with capitals of varying floral designs support the **Astronomical Ceiling** which, although once a beautiful and complex spectacle, is barely visible today because it was blackened by the wood fires of a Coptic village once housed within the temple. In places various deities and animals, including winged dogs, two-headed snakes and the pregnant hippo-goddess Taweret can be seen intermingled with signs of the zodiac. The hall's columns are inscribed with texts detailing the temple's various festivals. On the right side (as you enter the temple), look out for the cross-legged pharaoh, frogs on top of a capital representing the goddess Heqet and the square pillar engraved with countless crocodiles. Around the northern outer walls at the back of the temple are texts to Marcus Aurelius while Titus, Domitian and Trajan slay their Egyptian enemies on the eastern and western outer walls.

Al-Kab

ⓘ *0800-1700 summer, E£30, student E£15.*

Al-Kab, 32 km south of Esna, was known in antiquity as Nekheb – home of the vulture goddess Nekhbet. It was a pre-dynastic settlement, although the remains that you see today are mostly from the New Kingdom era. A series of tombs of the high priests/scribes are dug into a hillside close to the road, while the ruins of the temple are enclosed within a huge 5000-year-old mud-brick wall found across the railtracks near to the river. Four of the tombs are open to the public and some rich colouring remains in a couple of them, while the scenes of daily life (fishing, fowling, fixing nets, etc) mingle with the graffiti of early travellers (Belzoni made his mark here in 1817).

Temple of Horus

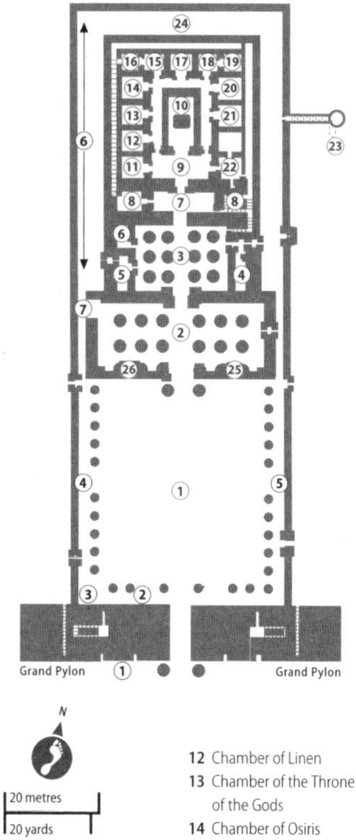

1 Court of offerings
2 First hypostyle hall
3 Second hypostyle hall/ festival hall
4 Offering hall: liquid offerings
5 Offering hall: solid offerings
6 Laboratory
7 First vestibule/hall of offerings
8 Stairs to roof
9 Second vestibule/ Sanctuary of Horus
10 Main sanctuary dedicated to Horus with altar
11 Chapel of Min
12 Chamber of Linen
13 Chamber of the Throne of the Gods
14 Chamber of Osiris
15 Tomb of Osiris
16 Chamber of the West
17 Chamber of the Victor (Horus)
18 Chapel of Khonsu
19 Chapel of Hathor
20 Chapel of the Throne of Re
21 Chapel of the Spread Wings
22 Sun Court
23 Nilometer & well
24 Passage of victory/ ambulatory
25 Library
26 Chamber of Ungents

◯ **Murals** see text

Edfu and the Temple of Horus

ⓘ *0700-1800 winter, 0700-2000 summer, E£50, student E£25. Sunset is a good time to visit, when the crowds vanish and you also have the option to stay for the Sound and Light Show (at 2000, 2100 and 2200). The temple is west or inland from the river along Sharia Al-Maglis and can be reached by* calèche *(10 mins, E£30), some of which are drawn by bony and badly treated horses, which await the arrival of the tourist cruise ships. Taxis and pickups linger around the train station on the east bank, quite close to the Nile bridge; the service taxi terminal at the town-side west end of the bridge is a 20-min walk or short ride to the temple. Intercity buses drop their passengers on Sharia Tahrir or the parallel Sharia El-Gumhoriyya about halfway between the bridge and the temple.*

Edfu, 60 km south along the west bank almost equidistant from Luxor (115 km) and Aswan (106 km), is the site of the huge, well-preserved Ptolemaic cult Temple of Horus – the most complete in the whole of Egypt. The almost-intact ceilings and wealth of carvings make it more immediately impressive than many older pharaonic cult temples and, as it replicates their architectural design in any case, gives a strong impression of what they would have looked like in their prime. Edfu Temple (as it is generally known) was the focus of the ancient city of Djeba. It was begun in August 237 BC by Ptolemy III and took 25 years – and several Ptolemies – to complete. The decoration took another five years and then a revolt in Upper Egypt meant it was not until February 176 BC that the opening ceremony actually took place under Ptolemy VII. Further additions were still being made into Ptolemy XIII's reign. Like Esna's Temple of Khnum, it was completely buried (except for its huge pylons) under silt and sand and its top was covered with houses until the 1860s but, unlike Esna, the whole site has been excavated. It had been severely damaged by the town's inhabitants and it was not until 1903 that the excavation work was finally completed.

The complex is entered from the ticket office at the south end of the Great Pylon. Just to the southwest is the small east-west axis birth house called the **Mammisi of Horus**, which was built by Ptolomy VII and VIII. The inner sanctuary is surrounded by a peristyle of foliage-capped columns, topped by pilaster capitals showing the grotesque figures of Bes, god of joy and birth. His frightening appearance was thought to dispel evil and to protect women in labour (see page 596). Each year there was a performance of the miracle play that represents Horus' birth at the same time as the birth of the divine heir to the throne of Egypt. At the southwest corner of the birth house there are reliefs of Isis suckling Horus (in infancy) and an erect Amun. On the pillars of the colonnades in the forecourt Hathor beats a tambourine, plays the harp and suckles Horus (in adolescence).

The main temple is entered through a gateway in the huge **Grand Pylon** on either side of which are grey granite statues of the hawk-god Horus. A tiny Ptolemy stands in front of the left-hand statue. On the left outer wall of the pylon Ptolemy XIII (88-51 BC), who was also known as Neos Dionysus and had usurped the pylon from its original builder Ptolemy IX (170-116 BC), is shown killing his enemies before Horus and Hathor **(1)**. The right wall has the same illustration in mirror image. On its inner wall the barge of Horus tows the barque of (no sails are required as the waterborne procession is downstream.) Celebrations for the gods' arrival are seen at **(3)**. The pylon also contains the usual guardians' quarters and stairs up to the roof.

The giant **Court of Offerings** is lined with 32 columns with paired capitals behind which, on the west side, Ptolemy IX makes offerings to Horus, Hathor and Ihy, their son **(4)**, and on the right (east) Ptolemy X appears before the same three **(5)**. At the north end of the court is the **First Hypostyle Hall**, built by Ptolemy VII (180-145 BC), with its 18 once brightly painted columns supporting the roof. There are three different types of capital, repeated on either side of the hall. Before the entrance of the Hall stand two further statues of Horus, in grey granite, the larger on the left being a popular spot for photographs. At the entrance to the Hypostyle Hall is the small Chamber of Unguents to the left with reliefs of flowers and recipes for consecrations (you will need a torch to examine the interior) and a small library, where the names of the guests for the day's festival would be kept, to the right. Here many rolls of papyrus were found. The foundation ceremonies are illustrated on the walls of the hall.

Leading north from the hall is a narrower 12 slender columned hypostyle hall, known as the **Festival Hall**, the oldest part of the building dating back to Ptolemy III (246-222 BC) and completed by his son, where offerings entered the temple and were prepared. Recipes for offerings are found on the walls of the laboratory. These were then carried through into the **Hall of Offerings** where the daily offerings would have been made at the many altars and tables bearing incense, juices, fruit and meat. From here there are steps to the roof that were used for the procession up to where the **Chapel of the Disc** once stood. The stairs are illustrated with pictures of the priests carrying the statues of the gods to the roof to be revitalized. The roof offers an excellent view of the surrounding area, but the gates are permanently locked and baksheesh will not gain access.

The Offerings Hall leads to the inner vestibule called the **Sanctuary of Horus**, where engravings show Ptolemy IV making offerings to the deities while others show Horus and Hathor in their sacred vessels. Within is a low altar of dark syenite on which stood the sacred barque (a replica is now in place) and behind is the large upright shrine of Aswan granite where the statue of the god was placed. The sanctuary is virtually a separate temple, surrounded by a series of 10 minor chambers, which are intricately carved.

Not to be missed is the ambulatory, where you can access a sunken well and Nilometer below the eastern wall. Horus' defeat of Seth, who is portrayed as a hippopotamus, is illustrated in the middle of the west wall of the ambulatory **(6)**. Note how the hippo gets smaller and smaller as the tale is repeated to the north. On the same side where the ambulatory narrows to the south the pharaoh helped by gods pulls close a clap net containing evil spirits portrayed as fish, birds and men (**7**). There are some interesting water spouts jutting from the top of the interior wall, some in better repair than others, carved as lions' heads.

Silsila

In between Edfu and Kom Ombo as limestone gives way to sandstone and the river narrows, the ancient quarries of Silsila come into sight on the West Bank of the river. In use from the 16th to the first century BC, the quarries were the source of tonnes of sandstone used in temple building. Convicts were used to cut the huge blocks from the cliffs then they were transported on the Nile to sacred sights around Egypt. You can still see holes carved into the rock where the ancient boats were moored. The cliffs are decorated with graffiti and stelae, and small temples with false doors and statues were also hewn into the surrounding rock. The cliffs of Silsila are particularly beautiful around sunset and attractively lit up at night. The colourful **Temple of Horemheb** ⓘ *open 0700-1600 winter, 0700-1700 summer, entry into the temple E£25, students E£15*, has some interesting carvings, note the slaves tied up on the left side of the entrance hall and Horemheb being suckled by the gods on the side wall. If you're on a boat and have the chance to stop, it's definitely worth exploring, even after hours. As the cruise boats cannot dock here, *felucca* and *dahabiya* travellers get the place to themselves. Arriving by land is a bit more of a challenge, it's really only worth the trek if you have a lot of time and a lot of interest: the closest town is Faris, from there, you will need to take a ferry to west bank where you can hire a private taxi for E£20 to bring you to the temple.

Silwa

About 30 km south of Edfu is the small but colourful Nubian village of Silwa. Many of the houses are decorated with unusual paintings depicting stick-fighting and men riding horses. The residents are friendly and welcoming, and if you are in a taxi or private car it is well worth a photo stop here.

Kom Ombo

Kom Ombo was the ancient crossroads where the Forty Days Road caravan route from western Sudan met the route from the eastern desert gold mines. It was also the place where African war elephants were trained up for use in the Ptolemaic army. Sixty-six kilometres south of Edfu and only 40 km north of Aswan, today this small east bank town is known for its sugar refinery, which processes the cane grown in the surrounding area. It is also now home to many of the Nubians who were displaced by the flooding following the construction of the Aswan High Dam. Tourists stop here to visit the Temple of Sobek and Horus that stands directly on the banks of the Nile, 4 km south of the town. If you are staying overnight in Edfu, the temple is particularly attractive at dusk when it is floodlit and many of the beautiful reliefs are shown at their best, especially in the first and second hypostyle halls. Taking a torch with you at this time of day is wise. There is a café on the bank in front of the temple, where you also find the ticket booth. A new museum displaying mummified crocodiles found at Kom Ombo has been built, but was not yet open at the time of research, and beyond this there are few shops and restaurants.

Kom Ombo Temple, is the more usual name given to the small but beautiful **Temple of Sobek and Horus** ⓘ *daily 0700-1900 winter, 0700-2000 summer, E£30, students E£15.* To reach the temple, leave the service taxi to Aswan at the turn-off 2 km south of Kom Ombo town from where the signposted 'tembel' is only 1.5 km away. In the town itself, buses and service taxis stop on the north–south Sharia 26th July, 300 m apart. Cheap pickups to the temple can be caught from behind the white mosque, one block away from the Luxor–Aswan road on Sharia El-Gomhoriyya, for E£10. These days most visitors arrive by *felucca, dahabiya* or cruiser.

The temple faces the Nile at a bend in the river and is unusual because it is dedicated to two gods rather than a single deity. The left-hand side is devoted to a form of Horus the Elder or Haroeris known as the 'Good Doctor', his consort Ta-Sent-Nefer ('Good Sister') and his son Horus the Younger, who was known as Pa-Heb-Tawy ('Lord of the Two Lands'). The right-hand side of the temple is dedicated to the crocodile-god Sobek-Re (here identified with the sun), his wife in another form of Hathor, and their moon-god son Khonsu. Sobek was an appropriate choice, given the fact that the nearby sandbanks were a favourite basking ground for crocodiles until the construction of the Aswan Dam. A healing cult developed here and pilgrims who came to be cured would fast for a night in the temple precinct before participating in a complex ceremony with the priest of Horus in the heart of the temple.

Temple of Sobek & Horus at Kom Ombo

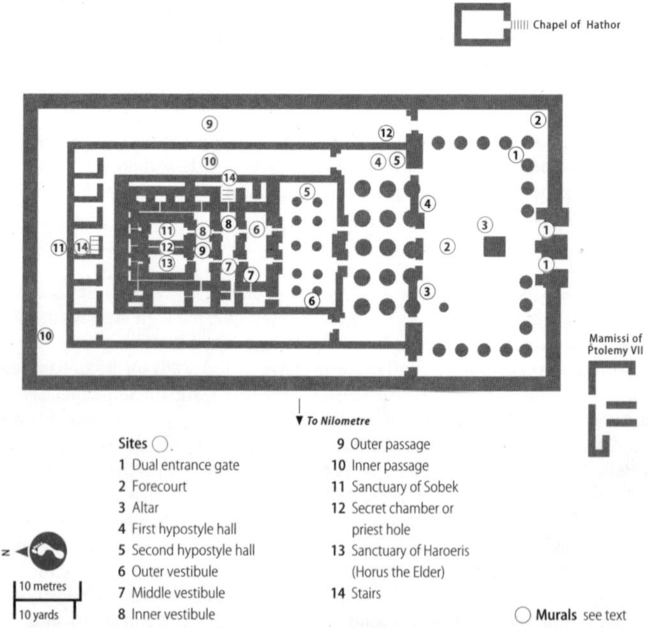

The present temple, like many others along this stretch of the Nile, is a Graeco-Roman construction, built of sandstone. Ptolemy VI started the temple, Neo Dionysus oversaw most of the construction while Emperor Augustus added some of the finishing touches. Its proximity to the Nile was a mixed blessing because, while its silt assisted in preserving the building, the flood waters eroded the First Pylon and Forecourt. In front of the temple to the left is the **Mamissi of Ptolemy VII**, which has been virtually destroyed by flooding, and to the east is the **Gate of Neos Dionysus**, who was the father of Cleopatra, and the **Chapel of Hathor**, which is impressively carved and has a central panel covered by the key of life.

With the Pylon and much of the **Forecourt** now destroyed by water erosion, only the stumps of the colourful columns, with a high-water mark clearly visible at about 2.5 m, and a few pieces of its walls now remain. Continuing the theme from the rest of the temple the twin deities are divided so that the left-hand columns are dedicated to Horus the Elder and the right-hand ones to Sobek-Re. In the centre of the forecourt is the base of a huge square altar. On the column in the far corner **(1)** note the eye socket in the relief of Horus, which was inlaid for greater decoration. Behind this column, right in the corner **(2)**, a staircase rose up to the roof level. At the north end is the double entrance of the **First Hypostyle Hall**, on the left wall of which **(3)** Neos Dionysus undergoes the purification ritual overseen by Horus and on the right **(4)** the same ritual is overseen by Sobek. The capitals are brightly decorated with floral arrays and the bases decorated with lilies. The reliefs on the lintel and door jambs show the Nile gods binding Upper and Lower Egypt together.

The five entrance columns and the 10 columns inside the Hypostyle Hall and its wall reliefs are especially decorative and the curious mixture of the two deities continues. Part of the roof has survived on the east side of the Hall and flying vultures are clearly depicted on the ceiling **(5)**. The rear walls leading to the older **Inner Hypostyle Hall**, which has two entrances and 15 columns, show Ptolemy VII holding hymnal texts before the Nile gods. The most striking relief is adjacent on the left of the north wall where Horus the Elder presents the *Hps*, the curved sword of victory to Ptolemy VII, while Cleopatra II and Cleopatra III, his wife and sister respectively, stand behind him **(6)**.

This is followed by three double **Entrance Vestibules**, each progressively smaller and higher than the last, also built by Ptolemy VII. The outer vestibule shows the goddess of writing Sheshat measuring the layout of the temple's foundations **(7)**, while the middle chamber served as an **Offering Hall** to which only priests were allowed entrance. Look for the long list or calendar detailing the temple gods' various festivals, one for each day **(8)**. Two small side rooms served as the library for the sacred texts and the other as a vestry for the altar clothes and the priests' robes. As in Edfu, a staircase originally led to the now-destroyed Chapel of the Disk on the roof.

The inner vestibule has two doors leading to the two separate **Sanctuaries of Horus and Sobek** and between the doors the gods give a Macedonian-cloaked Ptolemy a notched palm branch from which the Heb Sed, or jubilee sign displaying the number of years of his reign, is suspended **(9)**. Khonsu, who is wearing a blue crescent around a red disk, is followed by Horus in blue symbolizing the air, and Sobek in green representing the water. Beneath the sanctuary are the crypts, which are empty and usually closed to the public. Visible is a small **secret chamber**, from where the priests spoke to the gods. It lies between the two sanctuaries, in what would have appeared as a very thick wall.

On the inner wall of the **outer corridor (10)** is the first known illustration of medical instruments, including bone-saws, scalpels, suction caps and dental tools, which date from the second century AD. While your guide may tell you that complicated operations were carried out 1800 years ago, it is most probable that these were instruments used in

What colour is a camel?

With some imagination it is possible to distinguish five different colours of camel. The white camel is the most beautiful and the most expensive as it is claimed to be the fastest runner. The yellow version is second best – and slightly cheaper. Looking for a solid, dependable beast to carry the baggage? Choose red. A blue camel, which is really black but is called blue to avoid the problems of the evil eye, is not high in the popularity stakes. And a creature that is a mixture of white, red, yellow and black is just another unfortunate beast of burden.

the mummification process. Adjacent to the left is a repeated relief of Isis on a birthing stool. Nearby the temple corridor floor is marked with graffiti, drawn by patients and pilgrims who spent the night there before the next day's healing ceremonies. Also in the outer corridor, at the back of the temple **(11)**, Horus and Sebek stand either side of a small panel surrounded by mystic symbols of eyes, ears and animals and birds each sporting four pairs of wings. Continue round the corridor to **(12)** where the traditional killing of the enemies scene, much eroded, this time includes a lion.

In the northwest corner of the temple complex is a large circular well that has a stairway, cistern and rectangular basin that are believed to be connected in some ways with the worship of the crocodile god Sobek.

Daraw Camel Market (Souk El-Jamaal)

ⓘ *8 km south of Kom Ombo. The camel market is on Tue from 0700-1400, and occasionally on Sun or Mon in winter. It's most lively in the early morning. The livestock market is also on Tue, where hundreds of cows, chickens, sheep, and goats mill about as their proud owners try to strike up a good deal (there's another one in Kom Ombo on Thu, same hours). To get there, take a train (45 mins, buy ticket on board, all trains stop at Daraw) or bus (hourly) from Aswan, they will drop you on the main road, from there, walk north across the tracks (take a right as you exit the train station, walk 200 m, and take another right to cross the tracks), follow the road for about 3 km, after you pass the open fields and see houses, turn right and follow the sounds and scents, if you want to take a private taxi from Aswan the trip should cost around E£200 return. If you're on a* felucca*, ask the captain to drop you in Daraw and hire a pickup to take you to the market and back (about E£20-25 per group).*

An easy stop if you're sailing a *felucca* up the Nile is the village of Daraw. Except for one of the most interesting and unforgettable camel markets in the world, there's not much to see in the dusty little town. Sudanese merchants and Bishari tribesmen wrangle and haggle with Nubian farmers and Egyptian peasants (*fellaheen*) over camels that have walked for weeks by caravan along the Forty Days Road to be showcased. When they reach Abu Simbel, trucks usually bring the camels to the veterinarian in Daraw where they receive the necessary inoculations to ensure good health before heading to the market. Once in the market, camels go for over E£5000 depending on their age, sex, and general well being. Strong healthy females tend to be worth the most, for their reproductive capabilities. Only the males are killed for their meat. After being sold in Daraw, many camels end up at the camel market in Birqash, about an hour north of Cairo. In addition to milk and meat, camels are used for working the fields and carrying tourists around.

South of Luxor to Aswan listings

For Sleeping and Eating price codes and other relevant information, see pages 26-31.

Sleeping

Esna *p289*

Esna is so close to Luxor, that most visit it on a day trip or on a cruise.

F Haramin, about 1 km south of the ticket kiosk along the Corniche. It's very basic but probably the best of 3 not very nice options. There's also **F Al Medina** in the central square and **F Dar as Salaam** closer to the temple.

Edfu *p291*

There are no good hotels in town and most tourists are either only passing through or staying on cruise ships. You could try:

E El-Medina, just off the main roundabout on Sharia El-Gumhoriyya, T097-471 1326, friendly but shabby.

Kom Ombo *p293*

Kom Ombo is so close to Aswan, it is not worth staying there.

F Cleopatra Hotel, near the service taxi depot on Sharia 26th July. Probably the best bet if you're desperate.

Eating

Esna *p289*

There are a few cafés and stalls sprinkled around the central square.

Edfu *p291*

In addition to the standard food stalls, there is a pricey café by the temple.

Zahrat El-Medina Restaurant, on the Corniche across from El-Medina. Cheaper place to sit down for a bite.

Kom Ombo *p293*

Besides the small stalls that serve *fuul*, *taamiyya* and *kebab*, there are a couple of cafés by the Nile serving meat standards.

Shopping

Esna *p289*

When the cruise ships reach the locks here the traders appear in a flotilla of small rowing boats and attempt to sell a wide variety of clothing, etc. Goods are hurled from the boats in a polythene bag onto the top deck of the ship for the purchaser to examine and then barter over the price. Rejected goods are thrown back (although these are not always dispatched with the same accuracy as they were received!). If a price is agreed and a purchase made, a small garment to act as ballast, again in a bag, is then thrown up on deck with the expectation that payment will be placed inside the package and returned to the sender.

Edfu *p291*

The main tourist bazaar is next to the Edfu temple complex and offers a colourful selection of cheap goods, particularly *gallabiyas*, scarves and other local souvenirs. However, as t is impossible to enter the temple without walking past the stalls, here you find some of the most aggressive sales techniques in the country.

Transport

Esna *p289*

Bus

From **Luxor** to Esna and further south buses are cheap and frequent but crowded in the morning, and they stop a lot, which makes service taxis a quicker option.

Service taxi
Service taxis to **Luxor** (1 hr, E£3), **Edfu** (1 hr) and **Aswan** (2-3 hrs). From the service taxi drop-off point in Esna, you can either walk the 1 km to the temple, take a pick up or hire a carriage.

Train
Virtually all trains heading south from **Alexandria** and **Cairo** to **Aswan** stop at Esna, as do northbound trains from Aswan. The station is an awkward 5 km out of town on the opposite bank of the Nile.

Edfu *p291*
Bus
Buses arriving in Edfu sometimes stop on the east bank opposite town, which requires further transport into town with pickups. You can catch a bus out of town north to **Luxor** through **Esna** (2 hrs) or south to **Aswan** via **Kom Ombo** (1 hr) from Sharia Tahrir halfway between the bridge and the temple. There is also a daily morning bus to **Marsa Alam** that is supposed to leave at 0800 (3 hrs). **Aswan** to **Luxor** at 0800 and stop at Kom Ombo and Edfu for about 1 hr. The 1100 convoy goes directly to Luxor.

Service taxi
If foreigners are permitted to ride in them, service taxis are the quickest option. Find them at the west end of the bridge. Prices are comparable to the public buses. North to **Esna** (1 hr) and **Luxor** (2 hrs), or south to **Kom Ombo** (45 mins) and **Aswan** (1 hr).

Train
Trains to and from **Luxor** and **Aswan** stop at Edfu, but the station is 4 km from town on the other side of the Nile.

Kom Ombo *p293*
Bus
Buses running between **Aswan** and **Luxor** usually stop in town on Sharia 26th July about 350 m south of Sharia El-Gumhoriyya.

Service taxi
Service taxis north to **Edfu** (1 hr) and Luxor (2 ½ hrs, E£11) or south to **Aswan** (45 mins) are at the terminal on Sharia 26 July just south of Sharia El-Gumhoriyya.

Train
To/from **Luxor** and **Aswan** stop at Kom Ombo station just across the highway.

Directory

Esna *p289*
Banks One bank open Sat-Thu 0830-1400, Sun 1800-2100, and Wed 1700-2000.

Edfu *p291*
Banks Sharia El-Gumhoriyya in the centre.
Post office Near the temple on Sharia Tahrir on the south side of the main roundabout.

Kom Ombo *p293*
Banks Next to the mosque, open Sun-Thu 0830-1400 and 1000-1330 during Ramadan.

Aswan

→ *Colour map 4, B2. Population: 350,000. Altitude: 193 m.*

Aswan, Egypt's southern frontier town, in its delightful river setting, is a highlight of any Nile cruise. It is stunningly beautiful, charmingly romantic, and the sunniest city in Egypt, hence its popularity. However, the city's undoubted attractions are helping to send it the same way as Luxor and the ever-growing tourist scene has all the accompanying downsides of increased hassle, clean-ups of the souk, felucca *captains waiting on every corner and hideous buildings springing up. But though the sense of ancient enchantment that used to pervade the very air of Aswan is hard to find now, it is still here – you just might have to look on the west bank or in one of the villages to find it. The city itself is not too large to walk around in the cooler part of the day and the pace of life is slow and relaxing. From the cool and inviting Corniche you can watch tall-masted* feluccas *handled masterfully by a tiny crew and listen to Nubian musicians. Across the river, dramatic desert cliffs merge with palm-lined Nile waters, and huge apricot-coloured sandbanks appear startling against the cloudless blue sky. In the late evening you can watch the flocks of egrets skimming the surface of the Nile as they go to roost before you feast on freshly caught Nile fish. In the early morning you can watch the sun rise behind the city and hear the call of the* muezzin. *With the outstanding Nubian museum, colourful west bank villages and islands to explore, as well as proximity to several notable temples and the nearby High Dam, the city is much more than a stopover en route to Abu Simbel.*
▸▸ *For listings, see pages 315-322.*

Ins and outs

Getting there and around The railway station is at the north end of the town, about two minutes' walk from the Corniche, or 10 minutes' walk from the heart of the *souk* heading south. Most mid-range and higher-end hotels are by the Nile. Budget hotels are scattered around the railway station and in the *souk*. The inter-city bus station and service taxi station are about 4 km out of town. To get to town from the bus station, take a microbus (50 pt) or a private taxi (E£5-10). *Feluccas* and cruise boats moor along the Corniche. Aswan's desert airport is 24 km south of town. There is no bus service connecting the airport and town. A taxi costs about E£40-50 for a hard bargainer. Bicycles are becoming very popular for covering short distances. There are several hire shops around the *souk* and Corniche and an especially reliable one behind the train station. Cross the railway station via the bridge, walk ahead and you'll find the bike shop on the first corner to the right, near the mosque. The going rate is E£15 per day. ▸▸ *See Transport, page 321.*

Note If arriving at the station on one of the official tourist trains, you will be met by hotel touts, taxi drivers and *felucca* men keen to push tours and misinformation upon you. It's best to politely ignore them, and either head straight to the tourist information centre next door for help and advice, or get a taxi to the hotel of your choice with a driver that isn't loitering in the immediate vicinity of the station (a maximum of E£10 to any hotel in town). Don't be tempted to agree to a tour with any middleman or taxi driver who is touting at the station. For *felucca* trips, it is best to visit the main tourist office who can recommend trustworthy captains. Use your hotel (or a tour operator) to arrange trips to Abu Simbel only, and not for *felucca* voyages. As well as cutting out any middlemen, this allows you to establish exactly what you want and what you are paying for, and means the crew are directly responsible for providing what was agreed in the first place.

Felucca trips

Due to the direction of the river's flow, wind conditions and the problematic locks at Esna, extended *felucca* trips start in Aswan and go north towards Luxor. Most common are the one-day/one-night trips to nearby Kom Ombo (where the *felucca* stops immediately in front of the temple) and the three-day/two-night trips to Edfu. From there, it's possible to carry on overland to other significant sights between Aswan and Luxor.

Often, captains who come from villages en route will invite you to visit their home. There are also a scattering of interesting stops on the Nile (such as Silsila); if the wind is pushing you on fast enough, you may want to ask your captain to dock so you can have a look around. *Feluccas* don't go all the way to Luxor and you will have to take a microbus or taxi the final leg of the journey. It's easy to hire a taxi back to Aswan or north to Luxor from your destination and captains will be keen to arrange it for you (bear in mind it will be more expensive than what you could find on your own). This is where you are often at the mercy of unscrupulous drivers (probably related to your *felucca* captain) who insist that there is no way of travelling on by public transport, and certainly won't aid you in locating where it leaves from. In fact, a very common problem are captains who make the final stop before the actual town of Edfu and force passengers to take a taxi onwards, refusing to sail any further. Be assured that from both Kom Ombo and Edfu there are microbuses going north and south, though you might have to take a taxi to the microbus station and wait a while for the vehicle to fill up. Travellers are also frequently disappointed by the locations chosen to moor for the night, when there are scores of other boats around and it's too near a town. Try to establish a good relationship with the crew and push for peaceful moorings, if that's the experience you are seeking. The boat will stop if you need to use the 'bathroom' on shore, which is a bit traumatic, especially at night.

The standard number of passengers is between six and eight. It's better to aim for six if you want a bit of space to move about. The government has established fixed prices for *felucca* trips. If there are at least six passengers, it should cost about E£50 per person for one night (to Kom Ombo), E£75 for two nights and E£95 for

Information There are two tourist offices in Aswan, quite close to one another. The primary **tourist office** ⓘ *T097-231 2811, T010-576 7594, daily 0800-1500 and 1800-2000 winter, 1900-2100 summer, Ramadan 1000-1400 and again after iftar*, is next to the train station in a little domed building. It's worth stopping off here immediately on arrival at the station, as manager Hakeem Hussein offers possibly the best and most informative tourist office in the country. He will happily assist you in navigating the area, giving you the most recent of the ever-changing schedules and prices of transport, tours and entertainment. He can be contacted on his mobile (T010-576 7594) outside office hours. They can also help in booking trustworthy and suitable accommodation and advising on *felucca* trips and tours.

Background

Aswan's indigenous inhabitants are the ethnically, linguistically and culturally distinct **Nubians** who are more African than Arab. A robust civilization had flourished on the southern banks of the Nile since the time of the first pharaohs, and despite being three nights (to Edfu town itself). The tourist office in Aswan can advise you on the latest figures. The price does not include the cost of the necessary 'permission' (an additional E£5), or the cost of food and bottled water (an additional E£35-45, per day for three meals). If you want beer or other extras, plan to bring it yourself, or ask for it and pay extra. Whether or not demand for *felucca* cruises is high, captains will ask for more; bargaining is the norm. Beware of a captain who accepts a price lower than the ones cited, chances are the money you save is coming out of the amount allotted for your food or you run the risk of being deposited somewhere south of your desired destination. If there are fewer than six people in your group, pay more to accommodate for the captain's loss.

With more than 500 *feluccas* and at least that many sailors based in Aswan, it can be a stressful experience choosing a captain, but incredibly worthwhile once you're lazily meandering down the Nile. You will be bombarded by offers, and most hotels organize trips (from which they'll most likely receive a commission that comes out of the money allotted to your supplies). When you're considering who you intend to share a few days with, find a captain who speaks English and has a few years' experience behind him. Be mindful that perverts and thieves thrive among good honest sailors. It is strongly recommended to check in with the tourist office for a list of recommended captains, and you can leave a note with them if you're looking for other passengers to share a boat with. Also, lots of *felucca* captains and prospective passengers tend to mill about the Aswan Moon restaurant and the *felucca* docks a bit further down in the evening. If you're only opting for a *felucca* because you're on a budget and would rather be cruising down the Nile in more luxurious style, bear in mind that it's possible to get a four-star cruise ship for US$40-50/night – even less in summer. Ask at the tourist information office if they have any leads or take a wander down the Corniche and speak to the managers of the boats. If there are spare berths it is possible to negotiate a decent rate and bypass the travel agents.

Note As well as regular Nile cruises you can also start *dahabiya* trips from Aswan, for more information on these options see pages 250 and 252.

frequently invaded and conquered by their northern neighbours who were dependent on their gold mines, the Nubian kings actually controlled all Egypt during the 25th Dynasty (747-656 BC). Many favoured Nubians became noblemen and administrators throughout ancient times, and Cleopatra was from the modern-day Sudanese town of Wadi Halfa. Indeed, the term 'Nubian' today is equally applicable to the Sudanese who live along the Nile as far south as Khartoum. The later Nubian kingdom of Kush, whose capital was the Sudanese town of Merowe and which included Aswan, remained largely independent from Egypt. Having been the last region to adopt the Christian faith, Nubia became a stronghold of the faith and a sanctuary for Coptic Christians fleeing the advance of Islam.

For many centuries a sleepy backwater, Aswan assumed national importance when it became the headquarters for the successful 1898 Anglo-Egyptian re-conquest of Sudan. With the 1902 construction of the first **Aswan Dam** the town became a fashionable winter resort for rich Europeans who relished its dry heat, luxury hotels and stunning

The souk

The *souk* or bazaar economy of North Africa has distinctive characteristics. In Egypt a series of large *souks* continues successfully to exist while bazaar economies elsewhere are faltering. In Egyptian cities as a whole, such as Aswan, Islamic ideas and traditional trading habits have remained strong.

The bazaar originally functioned as an integral part of the economic and political system. Traditional activities in financing trade and social organizations were reinforced by the bazaar's successful role in running international commodity trade. The bazaar merchants' long-term raising of credits for funding property, agricultural and manufacturing activities was strengthened by this same trend.

There is a view among orientalists that Egyptian/Islamic cities have a specific social structure and physical shape. The crafts, trades and goods were located in accordance with their 'clean' or 'unclean' status, and whether or not these goods could be sold close to the mosque or *madresa*. Valuable objects were on sale near to the main thoroughfares, the lesser trades, needing more and cheaper land, were pushed to the edge of the bazaar. There was a concentration of similar crafts in specific locations within the bazaar so that all shoe-sellers, for example, were in the same street. These ground rules do not apply in all Egyptian bazaars but in many cases they are relevant in different combinations. Thus, there is a hierarchy of crafts, modified at times by social custom and Islamic practice, which gives highest priority to book-making, perfumes, gold and silver jewellery, over carpet-selling, and thence through a graded scale of commodities through metal-work, ceramics, sale of agricultural goods and ultimately low-grade crafts such as tanning and dyeing.

views, particularly from the *feluccas* sailing on the Nile at sunset. But the dam also caused many Nubian villages to the south of Aswan to be submerged by the rising waters. With no decent agricultural land left to farm, menfolk headed to the cities leaving the women in charge, and Cairo's population of *bawabs* (doorkeepers) is still predominantly Nubian today. With the building of the Aswan High Dam in 1970, the swamping of Nubia was complete and many of those who were displaced joined in swelling the populations of Aswan and Kom Ombo. Despite the subsequent construction of a number of heavy industries in Aswan, to take advantage of the cheap hydroelectric power generated at the dam, the town has retained its attractive charm and relaxed atmosphere.

Sights

The **Nubia Museum** ⓘ *T097-231 9111, 0900-2100 summer, E£50, students E£25*, stands on a granite hill to the south of the town on the road past the Old Cataract Hotel.

The UNESCO-sponsored Nubia Museum is regarded as a great success, and most visitors to Aswan feel that an hour or so here is well spent. The building incorporates features of Nubian architecture and showcases some 5000 artefacts tracing the area's culture from prehistoric to modern times. The colossal statue of Ramses, the remaining part of a temple at Gerf Hussein, dominates the entrance, a reminder of his positive presence in Nubia. The prehistoric cave depicts the first attempts at rock carvings and the use of tools. The pharaonic period demonstrates the importance of this region to the rulers of Egypt as a gateway to the south. There are sections devoted to Graeco-Roman, Coptic and Islamic influences in Nubia, and of course a section about the UNESCO project to save the monuments threatened by the creation of Lake Nasser. The colourful

1 Aswan

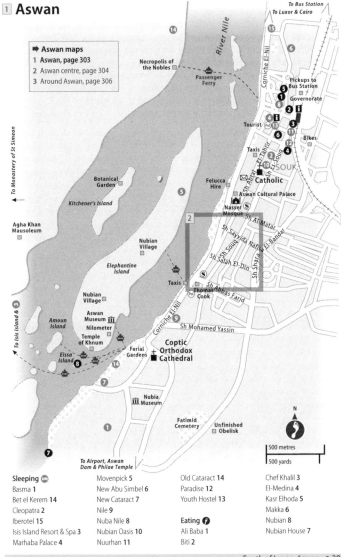

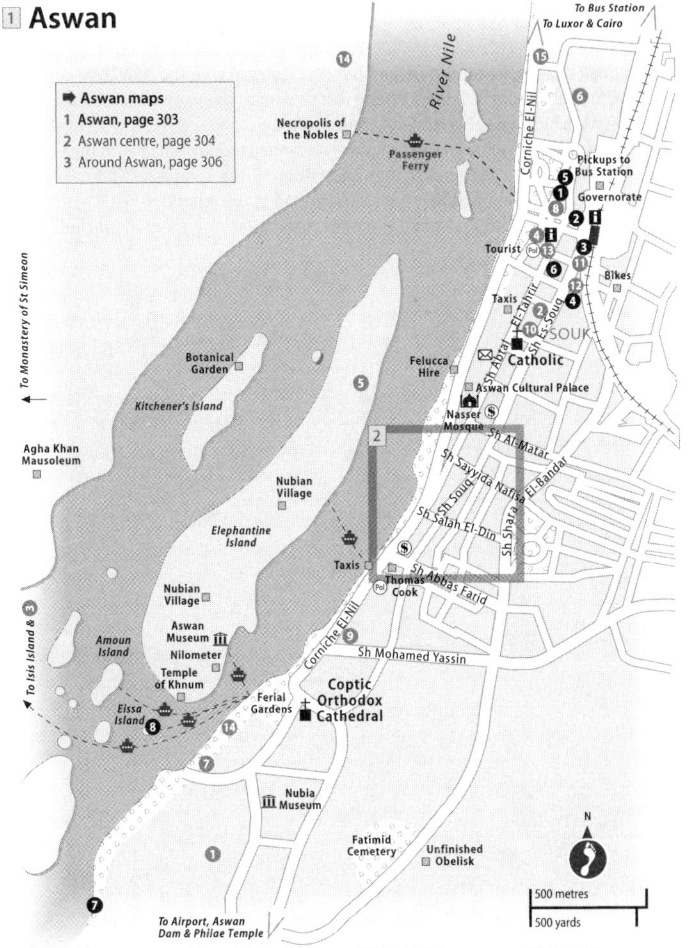

Sleeping
Basma **1**
Bet el Kerem **14**
Cleopatra **2**
Iberotel **15**
Isis Island Resort & Spa **3**
Marhaba Palace **4**
Movenpick **5**
New Abu Simbel **6**
New Cataract **7**
Nile **9**
Nuba Nile **8**
Nubian Oasis **10**
Nuurhan **11**
Old Cataract **14**
Paradise **12**
Youth Hostel **13**

Eating
Ali Baba **1**
Biti **2**
Chef Khalil **3**
El-Medina **4**
Kasr Elhoda **5**
Makka **6**
Nubian **8**
Nubian House **7**

exhibition of folk heritage emphasizes the individuality of Nubian culture. The most common crafts are pottery and the weaving of baskets and mats from palm fronds.

On the hill on the way to the Nubia Museum are the **Fryal Gardens** ⓘ *daily 0900-2200, E£5*, popular with courting couples, and a good place to stop off for a *haga saah* (something cold) under the shady trees and enjoy views down onto the first cataract.

On the outskirts of Aswan about 2 km along the highway south, is the **Unfinished Obelisk** ⓘ *daily 0600-1600 winter, 0600-1700 summer, E£25, students E£15*, in the quarries that provided red granite for the ancient temples. You can walk the 2 km, hire a bike, or take a taxi for E£25 return. The huge obelisk, which would have weighed 1168 tonnes and stood over 41 m high, was abandoned before any designs were carved when a major flaw was discovered in the granite. It was originally intended to form a pair with the **Lateran Obelisk**, the world's tallest obelisk that once stood in the Temple of Tuthmosis III at Karnak but is now in Rome. When it was discovered in the quarry by Rex Engelbach in 1922 the unfinished obelisk shed light on pharaonic quarrying methods, including the

2 Aswan centre

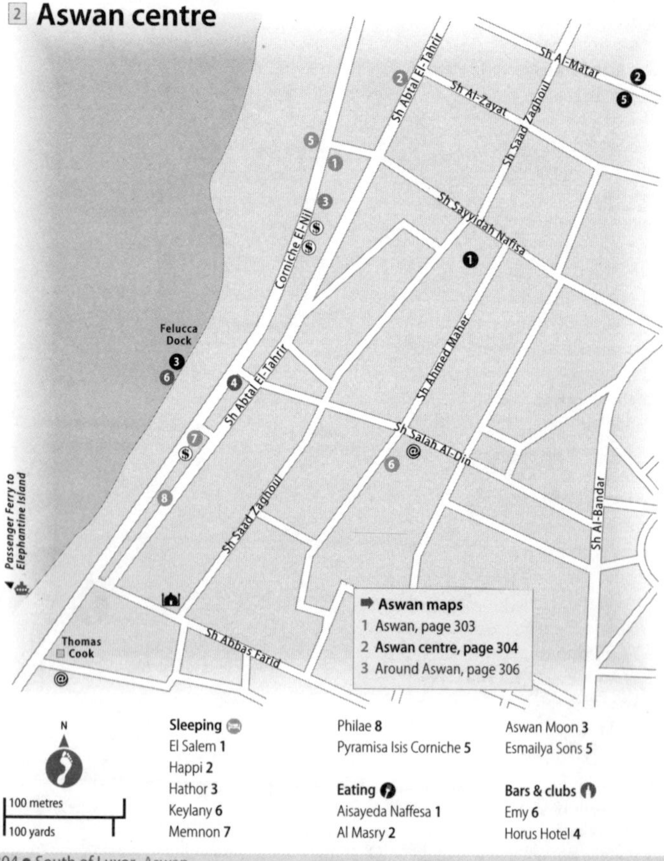

Sleeping
El Salem **1**
Happi **2**
Hathor **3**
Keylany **6**
Memnon **7**
Philae **8**
Pyramisa Isis Corniche **5**

Eating
Aisayeda Naffesa **1**
Al Masry **2**
Aswan Moon **3**
Esmailya Sons **5**

Bars & clubs
Emy **6**
Horus Hotel **4**

soaking of wooden wedges to open fissures, but shaping and transporting them remains an astounding feat.

Note It's easy to combine a visit to the Unfinished Obelisk with a trip to the High Dam or the Philae Temples, see pages 309.

Elephantine Island

ⓘ Felucca *to Elephantine Island E£25 per hr as your captain waits; E£30 per hr to sail around; or a local ferry (E£1) runs from 0600 until 2400, leaving from in front of the EgyptAir office and landing in front of the Aswan Museum.*

Opposite the Corniche and only a short ferry ride away in the middle of the Nile is sultry Elephantine Island. Measuring 2 km long and 500 m at its widest point, the island gets its name from the bulbous grey rocks off its south tip that resemble bathing elephants. There are a couple of Nubian villages and some interesting ruins that are well worth a visit, and meandering to the far side for an unimpeded vista of the the Aga Khan Mausoleum (see page 306) and the amber sands of the west bank is a timeless interlude from life. Also, the hideous tower of the Movenpick Hotel on the island is somehow less noticeable close up than it is from the Corniche, from where it impedes every view.

The **Aswan Museum** ⓘ *daily 0800-1600 winter, 0800-1700 summer, E£30, students E£15 and E£10 for camera, price includes entrance to the museum, the ruins of the Yebu and the Nilometer*, was closed for restoration at the time of writing; the Nilometer and ruins can still be visited, although there is no reduction in the ticket price. Established in order to display relics salvaged from the flooded areas behind the Aswan dams, which is ironic because the villa and its sub-tropical gardens originally belonged to Sir William Willcocks, designer of the first Aswan Dam. It offers a spread of pharaonic material, Roman and Islamic pottery, jewellery, and funerary artefacts. The ground floor is arranged in chronological order with items from the Middle and New Kingdoms, including pottery, combs and some jewellery, while the basement displays a series of human and animal mummies and an impressive gold-sheathed statue of Khnum.

You can see the **Roman Nilometer** if you take the pathway southwards to the left of the museum entrance. This fascinating device, rediscovered on the southeast tip of Elephantine Island in 1822, was designed to measure the height of the annual Nile flood. This enabled the coming season's potential crop yield to be estimated and the level of crop taxation to be fixed. Besides Roman and very faint pharaonic numerals, there are also more recent tablets inscribed in both French and Arabic on the 90 walled stairs that lead down to a riverside shaft.

Long before Aswan itself was occupied, Elephantine Island's fortress town of **Yebu** (the word for both elephant and ivory in ancient Egyptian) was the main trade and security border post between the Old Kingdom and Nubia. It was reputed to be the home of Hapy, the god of the Nile flood, and the goddess of fertility, Satet, both of whom were locally revered, and the regional god Khnum, who was represented by a ram's head. The ruined **Temple of Khnum** (30th Dynasty), at the south end of the island, boasts a gateway portraying Alexander II worshipping Khnum, which suggests that the Greeks added to this temple complex. The island has a number of less impressive ruins, and temples have been built here for four millennia. Make time when visiting to take advantage of an outstanding high viewpoint to enjoy the beautiful panorama of the Aswan Corniche to the east, including the picturesque Old Cataract Hotel, the islands and the Nile itself.

In addition to the museum, Nilometer and temple ruins, there are two small Nubian villages on Elephantine Island. A wander here gives a taste of contemporary life, albeit not much changed in centuries. You will almost certainly be invited into someone's home, most likely by Mohammed who has a beautiful Nubian House (aka the crocodile house) next to the museum (signed). Decorated with traditional Nubian handicrafts, you can enjoy a cup of tea or a cold drink on his colourful roof. Be forewarned that this rooftop operates as a commercial café/bazaar so that a wrangle over the price of your drink doesn't spoil your experience.

Kitchener's Island

ⓘ *Daily from 0800 until sunset, E£10, accessible by* felucca.

Kitchener's Island lies north of the larger Elephantine Island and, originally known as the 'Island of Plants', it has a magnificent **Botanical Garden**. The beautiful island was presented to Lord Kitchener, who had a passion for exotic plants and flowers from around the world, in gratitude for his successful Sudan campaign and the gardens have been maintained in their original style. The atmosphere on the island, which is almost completely shielded from the bustle of Aswan by Elephantine Island, is very relaxed and its lush vegetation, animals and birds make it an ideal place to watch the sunset. There is an expensive café at the south end of the island.

The west bank

Aga Khan Mausoleum

The beautiful **Aga Khan Mausoleum** ⓘ *closed to the public*, on a hill on the west bank of the Nile opposite the town, was built of solid marble for the third Aga Khan (1877-1957) who was the 48th Imam of the Ismaili sect of Shi'a Muslims. He was renowned for his wealth and was given his body weight in jewels by his followers for his 1945 diamond jubilee. As an adult he visited Aswan every winter for its therapeutic climate, having fallen in love

3 Around Aswan

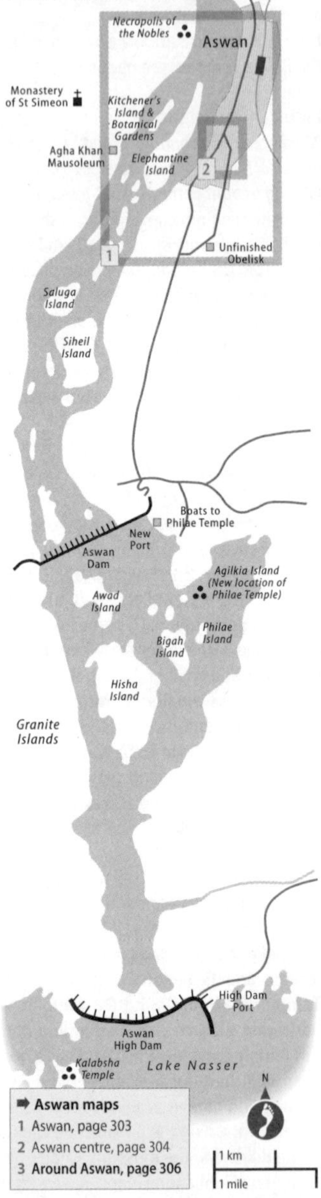

with its beauty and built a villa on the west bank. Until her death, his widow lived in the villa every winter, and erected the mausoleum on the barren hill above the villa. It is a brilliant white marble building, closely resembling a miniature version of the Fatimids' mausoleums in Cairo, the only hint of colour being the fresh red rose that was placed daily on the sarcophagus by his wife.

Necropolis of the Nobles

ⓘ *The tombs are open from 0700-1600 winter, 0700-1700 summer, E£25, students E£15, access by* felucca *or ferry (E£1-E£5) from the dock slightly to the south of the Governorate building in the northern part of town. Go down the only steps with no cruise ship sign above them, the ticket office is above the ferry landing. Wear a strong pair of shoes and take a torch. There is a guide on duty to show the way, unlock the tombs and turn on the electric lights, his services are part of the entry fee but a small tip is also a good idea.*

The Necropolis of the Nobles at Qubbet Al-Hawwa (Dome of the Wind) is further north along the west bank of the Nile (west being the world of the dead and east the world of the living). The riverside cliff is lined with tombs from various periods that have been discovered during the last century. Just above the waterline are the Roman tombs, and higher up in the more durable rock are those of the Old and Middle Kingdoms. The majority of the dead are believed to have been priests or officials responsible for water transport between Egypt and Nubia. Most tours begin at the southern end with the tombs of Mekhu and Sabni. Most of the tombs are numbered in ascending order from south to north. Only the more interesting ones are mentioned here.

The necropolis is illuminated at night by hidden spotlights – magnificent when viewed from the Aswan side of the Nile.

Tomb of Mekhu (No 25) Mekhu was a chief overseer in Upper Egypt at the time of the Sixth Dynasty and was killed while on official duties. His son Sabni mounted an expedition to reclaim his father's body and successfully returned to Aswan to give Mekhu a ceremonial burial. The main chamber is cut out of solid rock leaving 18 slightly tapering columns, decorated with reliefs of the family and fragments of other funeral scenes. The inner wall to the left carries a series of false doors inscribed to Mekhu. Also accessed from here (the original entry is blocked) is a memorial to Mekhu's son **Sabni (No 26)**. To the right of the main chamber is a large false door and a depiction of fishing and fowling from river craft.

Tomb of Sarenput II (No 31) Sarenput, who was governor or Guardian of the South at the height of the Middle Kingdom, has the largest, most elaborate and best preserved tomb in this necropolis. The first hall, containing a small granite offering table, has a decorated ceiling and distinctive striped door lintel. Steps lead to a narrow connecting corridor that has six niches with statues of Sarenput II. In the inner chamber, four pillars represent the deceased on their inward-facing sides. In a small recess at the rear of the tomb there is an elaborate relief portraying him with his wife, son and mother in a beautiful garden.

Harkhuf (No 34) Harkhuf was Guardian of Southern Egypt and a royal registrar in the Sixth Dynasty. Though he achieved great fame as a noble of Elephantine and leader of diplomatic and military expeditions, his tomb-temple is modest. On the right side of the entrance wall to the main chamber are the remains of a verbatim copy of a letter from Pepi II commending Harkhuf and, around the doorway, offering scenes. Inside the small rock-cut chamber, the four columns carry pictures of the deceased and biographical texts.

On the inner wall there are two niches, the left-hand one with a false door bearing offering scenes and the right-hand one with a small offering table below a painted stela. An inclined shaft leads to the burial chamber. Adjacent, lies the tomb-temple of **Pepinakht (No 35)**, who led military campaigns to Asia and the south which are described by wall texts inside.

Tomb of Sarenput I (No 36) The grandfather of Sarenput II was both Guardian of the South and also the overseer of the priests of Khnum and Satet during the 12th Dynasty (1991-1786 BC). The tomb is one of the largest, but unfortunately many of the reliefs are badly decayed. Those carved on the polished limestone doorway, however, are wonderfully clear, through which you enter into an antechamber with six columns close to the inner wall, which originally carried a finely decorated portico. On the right column there are carvings on all faces of a likeness of Sarenput. The inner wall carries important scenes in good condition. On the left is a scene of the deceased spearing fish, his wife clutching him, lest he should fall, and his son on the adjacent bank. Above are farming scenes with oxen. An inner hall is entered through a narrow doorway, a modest room where the pillar decorations and the paintings on the plaster of the walls have all but disappeared. Fragments show scenes of fowling, boating and women at work. A narrow corridor has been cut into the west wall rising to the small burial chamber with two columns and a niche and shrine for Sarenput.

Tomb of Ka-Gem-Em-Ahu To the north of these tombs is a separate tomb-temple, to Ka-Gem-Em-Ahu, reached by a sandy path. Ka-Gem-Em-Ahu was the high priest of Khnum in the late New Empire. His tomb was discovered by Lady William Cecil in 1902. Most of the plaster work has been lost from the six-pillared outer courtyard but scenes of boats on the Nile can still be made out with one or two residual depictions of funeral scenes, such as the weighing of the heart. Enter the low entrance to the main tomb where the ceiling is quite ornately decorated with flowers, birds and geometric designs. Although the walls are quite plain, the left-hand side inner pillar carries painted plaster with a representation of the deceased and his wife. A sloping passage leads from the main chamber to the burial chamber below, which is difficult to access.

Monastery of St Simeon

ⓘ *Daily from 0700-1600 winter, 0700-1700 in summer, E£25, students E£15, accessible by ferry from just south of the Governorate building (should be E£1 but foreigners may struggle to get it for less than E£5), and then either by a 30-min walk through soft sand or a 10-min camel ride (which can carry 2, aim for E£40) hired near the landing stage, or hire a pick up to take the back road and wait for you (E£30-40).*

This desert monastery, which lies on the west bank inland from the Aga Khan's Mausoleum, was founded and dedicated in the seventh century to a fourth-century monk Anba Hadra, who was later ordained bishop.

Following an encounter with a funeral procession on the day after his own wedding Anba Hadra decided, presumably without consulting his wife, to remain celibate. He became a student of St Balmar, rejected urban life and chose to become a desert hermit living in a cave. The fortress monastery stands at the head of a desert valley looking towards the River Nile and from where the dramatic sunsets appear to turn the sand to flames. Until Salah Al-Din destroyed the building in 1173 it was used by monks, including Saint Simeon about whom little is known, as a base for proselytizing expeditions first south into Nubia and then, after the Muslim conquest, north into Egypt.

Although the monastery is uninhabitable its main feature the surrounding walls, the lower storeys of hewn stone and upper ones of mud-brick, have been preserved and the internal decorations are interesting. At intervals along the walls there are remains of towers. Visitors are admitted through a small gateway in the east tower that leads to a church with a partially collapsed basilica but the nave and aisles are still accessible. There is a painting of the ascended Christ near the domed altar recess and four angels in splendid robes. The walls of a small cave chapel, which can be entered via the church, are richly painted with pictures of the Apostles which were partially defaced by Muslim iconoclasts. The cave chapel leads to the upper enclosure from which the living quarters can be entered. Up to 300 monks lived in simple cells with some hewn into the rock and others in the main building to the north of the enclosure, with kitchens and stables to the south.

Nubian village

One of the most accessible and colourful of Aswan's Nubian villages lies here on the west bank just 200 m north of the ferry landing. Not visited as often as those on Elephantine Island this village remains a peaceful place to wander around either before or after visiting the Monastery of Saint Simeon or the Necropolis of the Nobles.

Aswan Dams

ⓘ *Cross the High Dam between 0700-1600 winter, 0700-1700 summer, E£20, students E£10. A taxi here from Aswan costs E£35 return, if the taxi takes you and waits at the unfinished obelisk and Philae temple (around a 3-hr trip), it should cost around E£70. Note that you will also have to pay for the motorboat to transport you to and from the island of Philae, an additional E£40 for the boat or E£5 per person.*

There are in fact two Aswan Dams but it is the so-called **High Dam**, just upstream from the original 1902 British-built Aswan Dam, that is Egypt's pride and joy and which created Lake Nasser, the world's largest reservoir. In fact the High Dam is so big (111 m high, 3830 m long, 980 m wide at its base and 40 m at its top) that it is almost impossible to realize its scale except from the observation deck of the lotus-shaped Soviet-Egyptian Friendship tower or from the air when landing at nearby Aswan airport. It is claimed that the structure of stones, sand, clay and facing concrete give it a volume 17 times that of the Pyramid of Cheops. To help appreciate the scale and consequences of the dam's construction, the visitors' pavilion, which includes a 15-m-high model of the dam and photographs of the relocation of the Abu Simbel temple, is worth a visit. Occasionally, crossing the dam is prevented for security reasons. The contrast, however, between the view of the narrow river channel looking towards Aswan on the downstream side of the dam and the vast area of Lake Nasser, almost like an open sea, as you look upstream, could not be more marked.

Philae temples

ⓘ *0700-1600 winter, 0700-1700 summer, E£50, students E£25, permit for commercial photography E£10, no charge for video recorders. The easiest way to get to Philae is to join one of the many organized tours from Aswan, although this means you will have to follow a schedule. Or take a taxi to the dock (E£30-35 return) and then a motorboat to the temple. The boats seat 8 people and should cost E£5 per person (although the boat men will demand E£20) or E£40 per private boat for the return journey including a 1-hr wait. Make sure you state a 2-way trip or you will have problems later when they try to charge double.*

The great dams of Aswan

Although it has since become a cliché, the Nile really is 'the lifeblood of Egypt' and the combination of a restricted area of agricultural land and an ever-expanding population has necessitated the very careful management of what limited water is available. The theory behind the construction of the Aswan dams was that, rather than years of low water levels, drought and famine being followed by years when the Nile flooded and washed half the agricultural soil into the Mediterranean, the flow of the Nile could be regulated and thereby provide a much more stable flow of water. Unfortunately, although the two dams did control the Nile waters and thereby boost both hydroelectric power and agricultural production, the mushrooming population outstripped the gains and Egypt now imports almost half of its cereal requirements. At the same time it is now recognized that the High Dam was planned and built when the level of the Nile was particularly high. Whether it is because of climatic change or simply part of an apparent 20- to 30-year cycle the volume of water reaching Aswan is decreasing and if the trend continues it may be necessary to pipe natural gas from the Gulf of Suez to generate the electricity at the giant 2100 mw power station at Aswan.

The original Aswan Dam was built by the British between 1898-1902 and was then raised twice in 20 years to make it the largest dam in the world. Although no longer used for storage or irrigation, the dam, which is crossed by the road to the airport, is now mainly used to provide local power. After the 1952 Revolution, the new leaders recognized that massive population pressure meant that a more radical solution was required both to control the waters of the Nile and generate sufficient electricity for the new industrial sector and bring power to every Egyptian village. To finance the construction of the planned High Dam, following the withdrawal of a World Bank loan under US pressure, Nasser nationalized the Suez Canal and persuaded the USSR to help build the dam. Construction started in 1960 and was completed in 1971 after Nasser's death in September 1970.

Although it took a number of years to fill, the most visible effect of the dam was the creation of Lake Nasser. This has enabled Egypt, unlike Sudan or Ethiopia, to save water during times of plenty and have an adequate strategic reserve for times of shortage. The extra water from the dam significantly increased the area of land under permanent irrigation and allowed over one million feddans (about 400,000 ha) of desert to be reclaimed. In addition, the extra electric power facilitated the expansion of the industrial sector not only around Aswan but throughout the country.

There were, however, major environmental implications of the dam's construction because the rise of Lake Nasser flooded the homeland of the Nubians who were forced to migrate north to other towns and cities (to date they have been offered negligible compensation). Another drawback is that the lake accumulates the Nile's natural silt that used to fertilize the agricultural land downstream from Aswan. Consequently farmers in Lower Egypt are now having to rely heavily on chemical fertilizers, destabilizing the whole food chain. In view of its expanding population, however, Egypt would be in an absolutely hopeless situation without the dams.

David Roberts – painter of Egypt

David Roberts was a remarkable man whose oriental paintings brought to life Egypt and its heritage for many people in the Western world. His pictures are full of atmosphere and wonderful colour. Among the most famous are the *Temple of Dendara, Island of Philae, Nubia* and *A Street in Cairo* together with his paintings of the Temple of Ramses II at Abu Simbel.

Roberts, born in 1796, had a difficult childhood as the son of an impecunious Edinburgh cobbler. He eventually became known as a painter of theatrical scenery at the Old Vic and Covent Garden before making his name as a picture painter with items such as *The Israelites leaving Egypt* and scenes of his travels in Spain.

David Roberts arrived in Egypt in 1838 and spent 11 months travelling through the Nile Valley and visiting the Holy Land. He was a prolific sketcher of sites and left six volumes of lithographs of this visit, including several scenes of Cairo. Many of these and other scenes were later translated into oil paintings.

Roberts returned to Great Britain where, in his absence, he had been made an associate of the Royal Academy. He lived to 69 years and produced many masterpieces based on his travels in Egypt, incidentally providing a wonderful record of the state of Egyptian monuments of the time.

There are many inexpensive cards and books with copies of his illustrations. It is useful to have one with you when visiting the major sites. They show very clearly parts that have disappeared, parts that are now too high to view and give an excellent idea of the coloured decorations.

Few would dispute that among the most beautiful and romantic monuments in the whole of Egypt are the Philae temples, which were built on Philae Island in the Ptolemaic era (332-30 BC) as an offering to Isis. In fact, the Temple of Isis and the rest of the monuments were moved to the neighbouring **Agilkia Island** by UNESCO in 1972-1980 when the construction of the High Dam threatened to submerge Philae forever. They were then reconstructed to imitate the original as closely as possible but the new position no longer faces neighbouring Bigah island, one of the burial sites of Osiris and closed to all but the priesthood, which was the raison d'être for the location in the first place.

Temple of Isis Although there are other smaller temples on the island it is dominated by the Temple of Isis. Isis was the consort of her brother Osiris and eventually became the 'Great Mother of All Gods and Nature', 'Goddess of Ten Thousand Names', and represented women, purity and sexuality. Isis is attributed with having reconstructed Osiris' dismembered body and creating his son Horus, who became the model of a man and king. In the third to fifth centuries the worship of Isis became Christianity's greatest rival throughout the Mediterranean. There have even been claims that the early Christians developed the cult of the Virgin Mary to replace Isis in order to attract new converts.

Different parts of the Temple of Isis, which occupies over a quarter of the new island, were constructed over an 800-year period by Ptolemaic (332-30 BC) and Roman (30 BC-AD 395) rulers. At the top of the steps where the motorboats arrive is the **Kiosk of Nectanebo (1)**, from where runs a Roman colonnaded Outer Court leading to the main temple. Its irregular shape gives the impression of greater length. On the west or lake side of the court the **Colonnade of Augustus and Tiberius (3)** is well preserved and contains

Philae temples

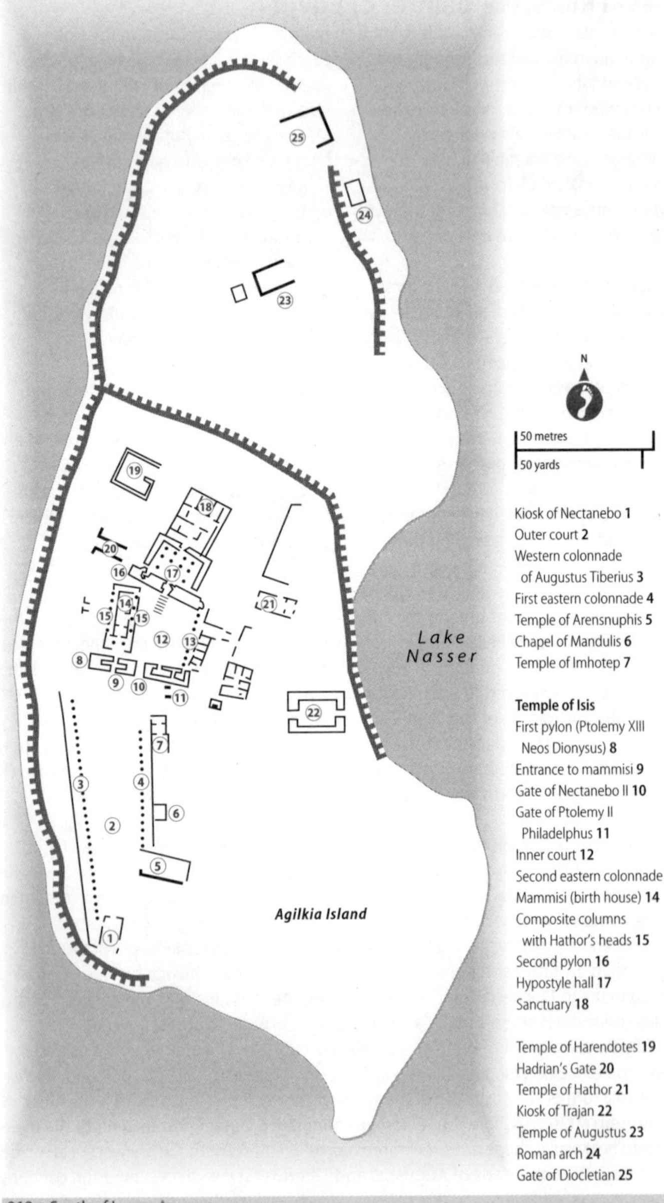

Kiosk of Nectanebo **1**
Outer court **2**
Western colonnade of Augustus Tiberius **3**
First eastern colonnade **4**
Temple of Arensnuphis **5**
Chapel of Mandulis **6**
Temple of Imhotep **7**

Temple of Isis
First pylon (Ptolemy XIII Neos Dionysus) **8**
Entrance to mammisi **9**
Gate of Nectanebo II **10**
Gate of Ptolemy II Philadelphus **11**
Inner court **12**
Second eastern colonnade **13**
Mammisi (birth house) **14**
Composite columns with Hathor's heads **15**
Second pylon **16**
Hypostyle hall **17**
Sanctuary **18**

Temple of Harendotes **19**
Hadrian's Gate **20**
Temple of Hathor **21**
Kiosk of Trajan **22**
Temple of Augustus **23**
Roman arch **24**
Gate of Diocletian **25**

31 columns with individual capitals, plant shaped – papyrus in various stages of bud. There are still traces of paint on some of the columns and on the starred ceiling. On the right is the plainer **First Eastern Colonnade (4)** behind which are the foundations of the **Temple of Arensnuphis (5)** (Nubian God), the ruined **Chapel of Mandulis (6)** (Nubian God of Kalabsha), and the **Temple of Imhotep (7)** (the architect of Zoser's step pyramid at Saqqara who was later deified as a healing God).

The irregular plan of the temple is due to the terrain. A huge granite intrusion has been incorporated into the right-hand tower of the First Pylon and steps to this pylon are also to accommodate hard rock. You enter the temple through the **First Pylon of Ptolemy XIII Neos Dionysus (8)** with illustrations showing him slaying his enemies as Isis, Horus and Hathor look on. The pylon was originally flanked by two obelisks, since looted and transported to the UK, but today only two lions at the base guarding the entrance remain. The **Gate of Ptolemy II Philadelphus (11)**, just to the right of the pylon's main **Gate of Nectanebo II (10)**, is from the earlier 30th Dynasty (380-343 BC). On its right is graffiti written by Napoleon's troops after their victory over the Mamluks in 1799.

Arriving in a large forecourt to the left is the colonnaded **Mammisi (14)**, used for mammisi rituals. It was originally built by Ptolemy VII and expanded by the Romans, which explains why images of Isis with Horus as a baby are intermingled with the figures of contemporary Roman emperors. In the inner sanctum of the Mammisi itself are historically important scenes of Isis giving birth to Horus in the marshes and others of her suckling the child-pharaoh. A curiosity to note on the outer western wall of the Birth House is a memorial to men of the Heavy Camel Regiment who lost their lives in the Sudanese Campaign of 1884-1885. The tablet commemorates the nine officers and 92 men who were killed in action or died of disease. Look carefully at the Hathor-headed columns facing into the Inner Court from the walls of the Mammisi – at the far end her face is straight but at the near end she is smiling. On the opposite side of the forecourt from the Mammisi is the late Ptolemaic **Second Eastern Colonnade (13)** behind which are a number of attractive reliefs and six small function rooms including a library.

The axis of the temple is changed by the **Second Pylon (16)**, set at an angle to the first, which was built by Ptolemy XIII Neos Dionysos and shows him presenting offerings to Horus and Hathor on the right tower (some of the scenes on the left tower were defaced by the early Christians). Beyond the Pylon a court containing 10 columns opens onto the **Hypostyle Hall (17)**, much reduced in size due to lack of space. These columns have retained few traces of their original colour although the capitals are better preserved. The ceiling in the central aisle has representations of vultures that were symbolic of the union of Lower and Upper Egypt. The rest of the ceilings have astronomical motifs and two representations of the goddess Nut. On either side of the wall, backing onto the Second Pylon, Ptolemy VII and Cleopatra II can be seen presenting offerings to Hathor and Khnum. The crosses carved on pillars and walls here provide evidence of the Coptic occupation. From the entrance at the far end of the Hypostyle Hall is a chamber that gives access to the roof. The interconnecting roof chambers are all dedicated to Osiris and lead to his shrine. Vivid reliefs portray the reconstruction of his body.

Continuing upwards and north from the chamber, linked to the Hypostyle Hall, are three rooms decorated with sacrificial reliefs representing the deities. The central room leads to a further three rooms linked to the **Sanctuary (18)** in which is a stone pedestal dedicated by Ptolemy III, which formerly supported the holy barque of Isis. Reliefs portray Isis and her son surrounded by Nubian deities. The temple's exterior was decorated at the direction of the Emperor Augustus.

Hadrian's Gate (20) has some very interesting reliefs on the north wall depicting Isis, Nephthys, Horus and Amun in adoration before Osiris in the form of a bird. Behind is the source of the Nile emerging from a cavern while Hapy, a Nile god in human form with a headdress of papyrus, is shown pouring water from two jars, indicating the Egyptians' knowledge that the Nile had more than one source. The south wall depicts a mummified Osiris lying on a crocodile together with another image of the reconstructed Osiris seated on his throne with his son Horus.

Smaller shrines can be seen throughout the island dedicated to both Nubian and local deities. East of the temple of Isis is the small **Temple of Hathor (21)**. Two columns have Hathor-capitals while, in a famous relief, the local deities play musical instruments. Much of the later additions to the buildings on Philae were Roman due to its position as a border post (such as extension of walls, huge gates and kiosks). **The Kiosk of Trajan (22)**, built in AD 167 has 14 columns with floral motifs and stone plaques on the lintels that were intended to hold sun discs, though these were never completed. Only two walls have been decorated and these depict Osiris, Horus and Isis receiving offerings from the Emperor Trajan. It is thought that the Kiosk originally had a wooden roof. From here, looking southeast towards the original Philae Island, it is possible to see the remains of the coffer dam that was built around it to reduce the water level and protect the temple ruins before they were moved to Agilkia. At the northeast end of the island is the ruined **Temple of Augustus (23)** and the **Gate of Diocletian (25)**. These were next to a mud-brick Roman village that had to be abandoned by the archaeologists when Philae was moved because the water had already caused such severe erosion.

Sound and Light show ⓘ *Usually there are shows daily at 1830, 1945 and 2100 in winter and 2000, 2115 and 2230 in summer. These change during Ramadan and the show can be totally booked out by private tour companies, so check with the tourist office, call T097-230 5376 or see www.soundandlight.com.eg for the latest schedule. Mon English/French; Tue French/English; Wed French/English; Thu French/Spanish/English; Fri English/French/Italian; Sat English/Arabic; Sun German/French/ English. Cheap tours from Aswan abound, but if you want to go alone tickets cost E£75 (no student discount), you'll have to pay for a taxi (E£30-35 return) and the motorboat (E£5 if you share with a group, E£40 on your own). Give yourself at least 45 mins to get there from Aswan.*

Like most big temples in Egypt, Philae has its own Sound and Light Show. This one is an informative and melodramatic hour-long floodlit tour through the ruins. Some find it kitchy, and others majestic. Arriving before sunset in time for the first show can be especially memorable. Travelling out from the harbour in a small flotilla of boats, watching the stars come out and tracing the dark shapes of the islands in the river silhouetted against the orange sunset sky is a stunning prelude to the beauty of the ancient floodlit ruins.

Soheel Island and West Soheel village.

Soheel Island is near the First Cataract, about 4 km upriver from Aswan. It is reachable by *felucca* (haggle to get it for E£50-60) or you can take a micro or taxi from the Corniche and ask to go to the stadium area ('stad'). When you get there ask for the Tameem Il Sahi (a clinic), and on the riverbank near the clinic there are boats with which you can negotiate to go across to Soheel Island. It's a very short distance so you should get it for E£10-20. From the ferry landing you can visit the Nubian village (free) and the **Famine Stela** ⓘ *E£25, student E£15. The stela area is a little overpriced and you may be able to get in just for* *a donation.* The granite boulders of the hill here are decorated with Ptolemaic designs. Following the scratchings to the summit, you get a wonderful view over the First Cataract area and see the Famine Stela itself. This dates to Zoser's reign and describes how a lengthy period of famine was ended by the building of a new temple on Soheel Island.

To see a slightly different style of Nubian village, an interesting trip can be made to West Soheel. This is close to the Old Dam and can be easily reached by taxi and perhaps incorporated into a trip to the Unfinished Obelisk and Philae. By public transport, take a micro from the Corniche going south. Ask for the 'khazan' and get off after you have crossed the dam. There is a traffic circle with an obelisk in the centre. A sign clearly points north along the bank to 'Gharb Sohail' (West Soheel), wait by the sign to get a pickup to the village. There are numerous houses vividly decorated with colourful Nubian designs, dead crocodiles nailed over the doorways and some live (caged) crocs too. From the village you can see over to Soheel Island where the Famine Stela is. It is possible to get a boat to row you over and wait for you for an hour, but from this side of the island you need to ford a stream and scramble through acacia thicket to reach the site. Much easier to access from the other bank. Going back to Aswan you may be lucky enough to get one micro all the way from West Soheel to the Corniche.

Aswan listings

For Sleeping and Eating price codes and other relevant information, see pages 26-31.

Sleeping

Aswan *p299, maps p303, p304 and p306*
Although it's a primary destination for visitors to Egypt, the hotel scene in and around Aswan is rather stagnant as increasing numbers of tourists stay on cruise boats or *dahabiyas*. Some classic budget options are dotted around the *souk* and you can also find surprisingly cheap rooms on the Corniche with stunning views of the Nile. It is possible to stay in houses on Elephantine Island – spend a few hours there and someone is sure to suggest it to you – but it will be very basic accommodation.

Note that the prices for accommodation fluctuate significantly. In the summer, prices can decrease up to 50%. Use the following price codes to get a general idea, but definitely enquire further. Plan to bargain. Even in mid-range and more expensive hotels, you can strike a deal. Note that when booking online it is vital to be clear about what exactly you expect to be included in the price. For example, get in writing that you have a Nile view, that breakfast and taxes are included, etc, to ensure there are no arguments when it comes to paying your bill.

LL Iberotel,Corniche El-Nil, T097-232 8824, aswan@jaz.travel, www.iberotel.com. Formerly the **Army Hotel**, this spotless 151-room hotel has undergone a major refit. The main building east of the Corniche has an imposing lobby decorated with pharaonic-style lotus columns and Orientalist paintings. There are all the usual amenities as well as a small shopping mall and adjacent bowling complex. The views from the 7th-floor **Panorama** restaurant are so good that bookings must be made before 1500 if non-residents want to dine there. A gleaming tiled tunnel runs under the Corniche to the pool area where there are 44 tastefully appointed Nile-side chalets. Inside the rooms is non-smoking, but smokers can request a room with a terrace to indulge their habit.

LL Movenpick, Elephantine Island, T097-230 3455, www.moevenpick-hotels.com. Fabulous balconied rooms, excellent location in middle of river, reached by a free ferry, the hideous tower that spoils most views in Aswan is less of an obstruction from the confines of the hotel. Stunning views particularly at sunset, **Orangerie Restaurant** and the **Lounge Bar** are chic, and the pool and grounds are superb. Recommended as the only place for pure luxury in Aswan.

LL Old Cataract Hotel, Sharia Abtal El-Tahrir, T097-231 6000, www.sofitel.com. An Edwardian Moorish-style hotel, probably Egypt's most famous, the **Old Cataract** featured in Agatha Christie's *Death on the Nile* and has been *the* place to stay in Aswan since it opened in 1899. Unfortunately, since May 2008 it has been closed for renovation and is due to reopen in Sep 2011, so check the website for the current status. Connected by a series of gardens is the cheaper, modern **New Cataract**, in an unfortunate slab of a building (also closed for refurbishment).

L Isis Island Resort and Spa, T097-231 7400. Presumably designed to blend in with the surroundings (which it almost does at sunset) this pink monstrosity is spread over its own island to the south of town at the first cataract, it's a picturesque setting and relaxing atmosphere. Rooms are constantly being refurbished and many cannot be called truly 5-star. But the pool is great, their terrace is a marvellous place to watch the sun go down and it's still an excellent place to get away from it all. Frequent free boats shuttle residents back and forth.

L-A Philae Hotel, 79 Corniche El-Nil, T097-231 2090, T010-222 9628, hanan-attiatallah@web.de. Newly refurbished to a very high standard, this Egyptian-German enterprise offers a range of pristine en suite rooms with double glazing so you can enjoy your Nile view without the accompanying noise. Chic locally sourced ornaments and lamps blend harmoniously with ultra clean comfortable modern fittings. An excellent choice.

AL Marhaba Palace Hotel, Corniche El-Nil, T097-233 0102-4, www.marhaba-aswan.com. Rooms are spotless and well furnished, some have huge terraces, but bathrooms are a bit squashed. The roof cafeteria has a great view across the river thick with *feluccas* to the Tombs of the Nobles, unblemished by the Movenpick tower. There's a decent pool and restaurant, but it's pricey; try to negotiate a discount.

AL Pyramisa Isis Corniche Hotel, Corniche El-Nil, T097-231 5200, www.pyramisaegypt.com. Chalet rooms are a bit overpriced for the quality, but this is the only hotel actually on the riverbank facing Elephantine Island. Offers a/c bungalows in a small garden with a pool and all the usual 4-star amenities, riverside terrace and restaurant with superb sunset views. Don't expect anything very grand, and look for a good deal online.

AL-A Basma Hotel, Sharia El-Fanadek, T097-231 0900/1, www.basmahotel.com. Perched on Aswan's highest hill, commanding breath-taking views of the west bank and Aga Khan's mausoleum, the **Basma** is a generic 4-star hotel with all the usual amenities. However, the large pool is welcoming, staff are friendly and the terrace good for a sunset beer until the **Old Cataract** reopens. It is handily located for the Nubian Museum.

A Cleopatra, Sharia Saad Zaghloul, Aswan, T097-231 4001-4. Located in the heart of the *souk*, the lobby is quite chic in a modern-Orientalist kind of way but carpeted rooms are decidedly retro and could do with a lick of paint. Balconies overlook town and there are all the usual 3-star facilities though bathrooms are nothing special. Pool on top floor is clean but small.

A Nile Hotel, 15 Corniche El-Nil, T097- 231 4222, www.nilehotel-aswan.com. A pleasant, bright hotel that is deservedly popular. Rooms all have Nile views, side-view rooms have balconies while front-facing don't (though they are bigger). Subtle decor, rag rugs, TV, fridge, minibar, a/c, safety boxes and the dining room is more attractive than most. There is also a suite, more expensive$81, but very spaciouswith an immense terrace.

B Cleopatra, Sharia Saad Zaghloul, Aswan, T097-231 4001-4. Located in the heart of the *souk*, the lobby is quite chic in a modern-Orientalist kind of way but carpeted rooms are decidedly retro and could do with a lick of paint. Balconies overlook town and there are all the usual 3-star facilities though bathrooms are nothing special. Pool on top floor is clean but small.

B-C Bet El-Kerem, Nagh El-Kuba, West bank, T012-384 2218, www.betelkerem.com, on the west bank 200 m north of the ferry landing for the Necroplois of the Nobles. This tranquil hotel offers a chance to get away from the bustle of Aswan. Nine double rooms are simply furnished and decorated with bright Nubian artwork. The rooftop cafeteria with its comfy benches, rag-rugs and outstanding views across the Tombs of the Nobles and the Nile is the undoubted highlight. Soft drinks are free and the (slightly overpriced) food is freshly-cooked and tasty. Very friendly, welcoming staff.

C-D Paradise Hotel, Saad Zaghoul, 2 mins from the railway station, T097-232 9690/1. Opened in 2008, this is a good-value choice if you can rise above some bad-taste fixtures and fittings. New mattresses, large beds, breakfast included, and the staff make every effort to please. Rooftop coffee shop has a panoramic view of the Nile and there's an Italian restaurant. Front-facing rooms are the more spacious pool at Cleopatra Hotel.

D Happi Hotel, Sharia Abtal El-Tahrir, T097-231 4115/6. Closed for refitting at the time of writing, but has Nile views from rather cramped singles and more spacious double rooms. Bathrooms are notably clean, beer and decent food are available, the Happi is perennially popular.

D Keylany Hotel, 25 Sharia Keylany,(known by locals as Sharia Gedid) at the southern end of the *souk*, T097-231 7332, www.keylany hotel.com. Spotless white painted rooms, attractive tiled floors and a lovely rag-rug-and-reeds chill-out café on the roof make the Keylany a nice place to be. There are also older, slightly scruffier rooms with shared bath that are more backpacker affordable. A/c, fridge, safety box, and plans for a pool on the roof. The internet café in the basement is effective but expensive, though Wi-Fi is free for hotel residents.

D Nuba Nile Hotel, Sharia Abtal El-Tahrir, T097-231 3267, info@nubanile.com. This is a good deal (doubles E£180) and can get pretty busy; it's wise to book ahead. Rooms have large comfortable beds, some touches of *mashrabiya*, a/c (2 installations in some rooms), though vary in size – look at a few if you have the chance. The teeny pool on the roof is more for dangling your feet than swimming, internet in the foyer café is E£4 per hr, no seasonal discounts. Breakfast included.

E El Salam Hotel, 101 Corniche El-Nil, T097-230 2651. Slightly cheaper than the **Hathor** next door, rooms are pristine, linens fresh, those at the front have huge balconies (but shared bath) while side-view rooms have private bath. If you ignore the gloomy corridors and faded prints of England circa 1970, this is a fine hotel in a good location. The rooftop's a bit shabby but the view more than makes up for this. Staff are friendly and there's no hassle.

E Hathor, Corniche El-Nil, T097-231 4580. Has an excellent location and great rooftop with loungers, though the pool is very small. Decent rooms have a/c (controlled from downstairs) and baths are clean and tiled, if a bit cramped. Soft pillows rather than bolsters, bigger than average beds and a nice atmosphere make it the best choice in this price bracket (doubles E£100, including breakfast). Wi-Fi is E£10 for your whole stay.

E Memnon Hotel, Corniche El-Nil (entrance is from the back street), T097-230 0483, www.memnonhotel-aswan.com. The a/c rooms are clean, if a bit tatty, some have superior bathrooms, others better views – look at a few. Rooms at the back (no view) or those on the 1st floor (carpeted) are marginally cheaper. Again, the rooftop pool doesn't beckon but the view is panoramic. There are plans for a rooftop restaurant. The lift is only for the fearless – watch out for the gap in the floorboards.

E New Abu Simbel Hotel, Sharia Abtal El-Tahrir, T097-230 6096. On the northern side of town, the hotel's selling point is its pleasant garden where breakfast is served and the staff are mellow. Rooms are clean but getting jaded with a/c, private bath, and balcony views (over a school yard) to the Tombs of the Nobles. Across the street from a few local *ahwas*, it's still a good place to escape any bustle and hassle.

F Nubian Oasis Hotel, 234 Sharia Saad Zaghloul, T097-231 2123/6. A budget hotel located in the middle of the *souk*, fairly basic rooms have grubby paintwork but clean linen and a/c. Some rooms on higher floors have good views of town and beer is available on the rooftop terrace with impressive vistas for E£10. Free internet for 30 mins then E£5 per hr after that. Breakfast served from 0300 onwards – handy for early starts to Abu Simbel. Doubles E£50, singles E£30. Hassle from touts has been reported.

F Nuurhan, Sharia Saad Zaghloul, T097-231 6069. Another cheap option in the middle of the *souk*. Reasonably clean and comfy rooms with drab furniture (some don't have curtains), price varies depending on whether you have a/c and private bath (doubles E£45), although shared baths are actually newer and preferable. Expect *felucca* tours to be pushed on you.

G Youth Hostel, 96 Sharia Abtal El-Tahrir, entrance from the alley on the right of the **October Hotel**, T097-230 2313. Dorms with fans, 8 beds (bunks) and nothing else cost E£12 or triples are E£17 per bed. Usually empty, except when universities let out and then it becomes a popular spot for Egyptian college students. Open all year, midnight curfew casually imposed. It's only really worth staying here if you're on the tightest of budgets, but the sheets are clean, staff welcoming and you won't be pestered to go on a tour.

Eating

Aswan *p299, maps p303, p304 and p306*
For expensive and exceptionally chic dining options, there's nothing outside the resort hotels. There are, however, a number of mid-range and cheap restaurants that serve good food. There are also a couple of notable *fatir* pizza joints, and of course the sit-down cafeterias, some floating on the Nile where the setting can be better than the food. Tourists often get charged double local prices in smaller places, so it might be worth brushing up on Arabic numerals so you can read the menu and get a better price.

TTT 1902 Restaurant, in the **Old Cataract Hotel**. If the **Cataract** has opened again after refurbishments, the 1902 will be serving international food spiced with Nubian dancers in classic decor. Even budget-conscious visitors may want to indulge in a cup of tea or a glass of wine at sunset on the terrace. It really is an institution.

TTT Darna Restaurant, New Cataract Hotel. Impressive buffet in a restaurant resembling an Egyptian house.

TTT-TT Nubian Restaurant, on Issa Island south of Elephantine, T097-230 0307, T012-216 2379. Set Nubian meals for about E£75. Wine and beer are available, but pricey. The restaurant offers a free boat that leaves from the dock in front of EgyptAir. The setting is romantic, but the folkloric show is clichéd and doesn't happen if tour groups aren't around.

TT Al Masry Restaurant, Sharia Al-Matar. Spotless a/c restaurant popular with locals and tourists alike. Offers standard meals of fish, chicken, kebab and pigeon.

TT Aswan Moon, on the Corniche, T097-231 6108. The most acclaimed of the floating restaurants, the food is OK, but it's better to come here for the Nile-side setting and colourful atmosphere plus it's 10° cooler by the river than on the street. More lively at night, sometimes there's entertainment in the summer and it's a good place to meet other travellers and/or *felucca* captains.

Ÿ **Biti**, in the main Midan in front of the train station, T097-230 0949. Cute pizza restaurant on 3 levels, the 2nd floor has a/c, the 3rd is on the roof. Excellent *fatir* costs E£35 for 5 toppings, good service and they also home deliver between 1900-0100; most delightful is the view over the square. Open 1000-0330, good place to people watch once the sun sets.

Ÿ **Chef Khalil**, in the *souk*. Serves tasty seafood by the weight. Choices include lobster, prawns and sole, and various fillet of other locally caught fish. All meals accompanied by *tahina*, salad and chips or rice. Entrées are E£35-60. If this tiny restaurant is full, hang out, it's worth the wait.

Ÿ **El-Medina**, in the heart of the *souk*. Clean, renowned local joint that serves up good homemade cooking. Mostly meat dishes, but they will prepare you a veggie plate.

Ÿ **Makka**, Sharia Abtal al Tahrir, T097-230 3232. Open 1200-0100. On the tour group circuit, but therefore clean and comfortable with good food. Stuffed pigeon and a wealth of kebabs all come with salads, rice and veg.

Ÿ **Nubian House**, on the hill behind the Basma Hotel, T097-232 6226. A popular intimate restaurant serving authentic and delicious Nubian food for E£20-30 per entrée. *Sheesha* also on offer, but no alcohol. Outdoor seating with stunning panoramic views over all of Aswan make it worth the trek from the centre of town, especially around sunset. When there are groups in for dinner a Nubian troupe provides music, so call ahead if you wish to join or avoid this.

Ÿ **Panorama**, on the Corniche, T097-230 6169, an old-timer on the Aswan restaurant scene. Known for good-quality, traditional Egyptian food and an eclectic collection of Nubian artefacts. Serves reliable tasty tagines, has an extensive menu of herbal teas and non-alcoholic cocktails and delicious Nubian coffee to finish. Service can be slow but food is cooked to order and is worth the wait.

Ÿ **Pharaohs**, on the west bank south of the Aga Khan's Mausoleum, T012-791 9895. Accessible only by boat, good Nubian home cooking for E£50-60 per person, something a bit different and beautiful boat trip to get there. Call ahead, don't just turn up.

Ÿ-Ÿ **Aisayeda Naffesa**, Sharia Ahmed Maher, T097-231 7152. This place has been around for years and serves up tasty Egyptian dishes, however their juices are a let down. They have a few tables under the awning outside and, though you will typically be charged more than locals, it is still cheap and recommended for ambiance and flavour.

Ÿ-Ÿ **Esmailya Sons Restaurant**, Sharia Al-Matar, has standard meat, soup, rice, salad and veg meals, though the fish option is most popular. It's opposite Al Masry restaurant and is significantly cheaper, there's a menu displayed outside in Arabic and English.

Ÿ **Ali Baba**, Sharia Abtal al Tahrir, has the best *koshari* in town but at annoyingly inflated tourist prices. The right-hand half of the building has takeaway Egyptian staples.

Ÿ **Kasr Elhoda**, Sharia Abtal al Tahrir, north of the station. Open 1000-0200. Has cheap (E£15-40) *fatir* and is always packed with Egyptians. It's a typical marble interior with a/c and no English menu. There's also a good bakery next door.

Entertainment

Aswan *p299, maps p303, p304 and p306*

There are nightclubs in the big hotels that offer Nubian and Western floorshows when enough tourists are in town. During the winter, except on Fri, there are nightly performances (from 2130-2300) by the Nubian Folk Troupe at the Cultural Palace, T097-232 3344, at the north end of the Corniche. The Horus Hotel, 89 Corniche El-Nil, T097-230 3323 has female singers accompanied by *oud* and *tabla* on the rooftop every night from 2200, which can make for a surreal Aswan experience. Beer is E£20 and *sheesha* E£5, the distant west bank lights glowing orange while city minarets glow green sets the atmosphere.

Emy, next to Aswan Moon, the best place for an evening drink. The top floor of the floating restaurant picks up a nice breeze and most of the clientele wear *galabiyas* and turbans. **Oscar Hotel** on Sharia El Baraka. The basic basement bar is actually open-air and quite friendly to tourists, although other drinkers invariably start arguing amongst themselves later on.

An evening in Aswan is also well spent wandering through the ever-thriving *souk*, puffing on a *sheesha* in a local *ahwa*, or strolling by the Nile. Families tend to congregate in the midan across from the train station, where there are plenty of cafés.

A night time *felucca* sail is always a romantic way to spend an evening, especially in Aswan where the riverbanks are among the most beautiful. Keep your ears open for celebratory sounds as you may well run into a wedding party – which you will very likely be invited to join.

Shopping

Aswan *p299, maps p303, p304 and p306*
Aswan used to have perhaps the most colourful and exotic *souk* in all of Egypt outside of Cairo. Sadly, the huge patchwork of umbrellas and narrow alleys that made up the maze of the *souk* have been swept away during a misguided beautification initiative and what is left is a sterile pedestrianized thoroughfare that lacks any soul. However, though locals buying and selling fresh produce and doing their daily shopping all seem to have migrated to the laneways radiating from the main *souk* street, there is still good tourist shopping to be done while the odd traditional *ahwa* or butchers shop remain lodged in between the alabaster and papyrus. Musical instruments, spices and nuts from the depths of Sudan, tempting baked goods moved along by eager boys on carts, shimmering scarves and embroidered *gallabiyyas*, ancient stereos and local music to play in them – all of it can be found along the endless Sharia Souk. Aswan is a good place to look for acclaimed Nubian music, most music merchants blare tunes from their humble sound systems at all hours. If you want to listen to a particular album, just ask. CDs should cost E£30. There is also a duty-free shop on the Corniche (near the EgyptAir office), as well as a large departmental store on Sharia Abtal El-Tahrir. The best bookshop is **Nubia Tourist Book Center** in the rowing club building (El Nadi el-Tagdeef) on the Corniche, T097-231 9777, open 0800-2300, which stocks AUC titles and books in different European languages, as well as good postcards and Lehnert & Landrock prints. There is also another branch on Sharia Saad Zaghloul, near the Paradise Hotel.

Activities and tours

Aswan *p299, maps p303, p304 and p306*
The major hotels have good sports facilities but remember that with temperatures as high as 50°C (122°F) in summer this is not the place to be engaging in a lot of movement.

Felucca trips

Official prices, regulated by the government, are E£35 per hr though you may struggle to get this. For example, if you sail to Kitchener's Island, Aga Khan Mausoleum and Elephantine Island, and spend a couple of hours wandering around, a 3-hr trip with 1 hr of sailing time should cost around E£90. If there are more passengers, prices usually go up. Haggle hard. For longer *felucca* trips along the Nile, see box, page 300. *Feluccas* can be found on Corniche El-Nil, although the men with the *feluccas* will probably find you first.

Public ferries run to Elephantine Island (E£1, from 0600-2200) from the dock by the EgyptAir office, and another from near the station to the Tombs of the Nobles. Foreigners aren't supposed to use them after sunset, although if you're staying on Elephantine or at Bet El Kerem it shouldn't be a problem to head home late.

Hiking

Plenty of good walks. A walk around Elephantine Island is a good place to start (about 2 hrs depending on your pace).

Swimming

The best and biggest pool in town available to outside guests is at the **Basma Hotel**, where day use costs US$10. More conveniently located (and right on the Nile) but more expensive is the pool at the **Isis Pyramisa** where a day-use room will set you back US$50 but can be used by up to 3 people. The pool at the **Iberotel** is also US$50 for day use, or there's the very affordable **Cleopatra** rooftop pool, for E£20.

Tour operators

All hotels organize transport to Abu Simbel and other sites. Be aware that most hotels pool their guests. What that means is 1 person may pay E£60 for a ride to Abu Simbel in 1 hotel and someone else may pay E£80 in another to wind up on the exact same bus. Shop around a bit and bargain hard, especially when the season is low. However, some hotels will only book their guests on their tours. Cheaper places tend to book cheaper trips and are more open to haggling.

For people with more money, there are numerous travel agencies and guide companies around town who are all touting for your booking. Tours and treatment don't differ much. Half-day tours usually include a trip to the **Unfinished Obelisk**, the **High Dam** and the **Temple of Philae**. Expect to pay around E£180. Travel agencies can also organize *felucca* trips to the nearby islands if you have a group of at least 3 (about E£50-80 per person). Try **Eastmar Travel**, Corniche El-Nil, T097-232 3787; **Misr Travel**, 1 block behind Corniche on way to railway station, adjacent to tourist information; or **Thomas Cook**, Corniche El-Nil, T097-230 4011, daily 0800-1400 and 1700-2000.

Transport

Aswan *p299, maps p303, p304 and p306*

Air

EgyptAir, southern end of the Corniche, T097-231 5000-5, www.egyptair.com, open 0800-2000. There are 4-5 regular daily flights to **Luxor** (30 mins) and **Cairo** (1 hr). There are 1-3 daily flights to **Abu Simbel** – often booked out by tour groups (see Transport, Abu Simbel, page 338). Taxis to the airport cost around E£50.

Bus

The bus station is 3.5 km north of the town centre, **Upper Egypt**, T097-230 0454, office open 0700-1600. A taxi there will cost you E£5-10, or you can grab a covered pickup by the train station or on the Corniche for 35 pt. If heading to Abu Simbel by bus, rules stipulate that only 4 foreigners are permitted per bus, or else they have to join a convoy, although this isn't strictly enforced. Add to that the fact that bus tickets can only be purchased 1 hr in advance necessitating an early start. Currently, there are 3 buses a day to **Abu Simbel** at 0800, 1100 (less reliable) and 1600 (4 hrs, E£25). 2 buses go to **Cairo**, the 1530 takes 12-14 hrs, and stops at **Hurghada** (6-7 hrs, E£50) while the other leaves at 1700, is a bit cheaper, and stops in **Suez**; both should have a/c and TV. If the 1530 bus to **Hurghada** is leaving too late for you, take an early train to Luxor where you can change to a bus (0815, 1030, 1430, 4 hrs, E£25-32). There's a bus to **Marsa Alam** at 0630 every day, 4-5 hrs, E£25, which you should have no problems boarding. There are frequent buses heading north to **Kom Ombo** (1 hr, E£2), **Edfu** (2 hrs, E£4) and **Esna** (3 hrs, E£6), arriving in **Luxor** (4 hrs, E£10). You can also reach **Sohag** and **Assiut** by bus. Hours, prices and even routes change constantly. For the most current bus schedule, check with the tourist office or your hotel. Be prepared for stops at several checkpoints when travelling by bus. Have your passport ready and don't worry, it's standard procedure.

Ferry

There is 1 ferry per week to Wadi Halfa in **Sudan** run by the **Nile Valley Company**, T018-3160 926, www.takourny.free-boards.net, beside the Marhaba Hotel. Currently these are scheduled to leave on Mon from Aswan at 1200 (though expect delays, and turn up at least 2 hrs early), returning from Wadi Halfa on Wed. The journey takes between 18-24 hrs (1st class E£500, 2nd class E£322, children aged 4-10 E£193).

Taxi

Service taxis now have no security restrictions and are permitted to carry foreigners from Aswan. They will get stopped at police checkpoints on the way out. Some drivers remember the problems of the past and are reluctant to take foreign passengers. Remain calm and persist and they should take you. It's also possible to hire a private taxi for long-distance journeys. For a trip to **Luxor**, stopping at all the major sights along the way, expect to pay E£400.

Train

Trains are definitely the easiest, most comfortable option, though there are some restrictions. Technically, foreigners are only permitted to travel on 3 'secure' trains bound for **Cairo** (0600, 1800, 2000, 12-14 hrs). 1st class E£165. All have a/c and a restaurant on board. There is also a private company that runs sleeper cars to **Cairo** (1600, 1900; US$60, payable in US$ or euro only). For all trains to Cairo, it's wise to book your tickets at least 1 day in advance. 2nd-class trains to Cairo (13 hrs; E£55) via Luxor (3 hrs; E£18) leave at 0730, 1600, 1900, 2100. They usually stop in **Kom Ombo**, **Daraw**, **Edfu**, and **Esna**. As these trains are not supposed to carry foreigners, plan to buy your ticket on the train. Check with the tourist office or train station for the most current schedule.

Directory

Aswan *p299, maps p303, p304 and p306*

Banks Besides the major hotels, there are numerous Egyptian banks on the Corniche or Sharia Abtal El-Tahrir. **Embassies and consulates** Passport Office: T097-231 2238, Sat-Thu 0830-1300. **Internet** The going rate is E£6 per hr. It's much cheaper to get CDs and DVDs burnt in Luxor than Aswan. **Medical services** Hospitals: German Hospital, on the Corniche, T097-302176. **Post office** On the Corniche, open Sat-Thu 0800-2100. It is best to post outgoing mail from the major hotels as they seem to get priority. **Telephone** 2 doors south of EgyptAir across from public ferry.

Lower Nubia

➔ *Colour map 1, C4/5.*

Upon seeing the mighty statues of Abu Simbel, it's difficult to believe that they were buried for centuries by desert sands. Johann Burckhardt (see box, page 331) finally happened upon them in 1813. Their grandiosity is surely the ultimate testimony to Ramses II's sense of self. The giant pharaonic statues are absolutely spectacular and well worth the detour south to the largest man-made lake in the world, that surrounds Abu Simbel. The juxtaposition of crystalline blue water teeming with life and the harsh dry desert outlining it is striking and makes Lake Nasser a treat to explore. Besides the wide variety of migrating birds, there are fox, gazelle and huge crocodiles that live off the shallows and shores of the lake. Fishermen travel from afar to partake in extraordinary fishing (the rich silt that once nourished the riverbank of the Nile now nourishes the bellies of the lake's inhabitants). There is also a magnificent collection of Nubian temples scattered around Lake Nasser's shores and the Lake Nasser cruise, while expensive, is incredibly rewarding. ▸▸ *For listings, see pages 335-338.*

Lake Nasser Temples

ⓘ *These monuments were previously almost inaccessible to most tourists, but some new roads now allowed overland access via private convoy to the majority of sites.*

Originally spread along the length of the Nile, the important Nubian antiquities saved by UNESCO from the rising waters of Lake Nasser were clustered in groups of three to make for easier visiting. Many of the Nubian monuments do not have the magnificence of those north of the High Dam though their new sites are more attractive. A number were erected in haste in ancient times, with little concern for artistic merit, but for the sole reason of inspiring awe in the conquered people of Nubia.

Kalabsha

ⓘ *Daily 0800-1600 winter, 0800-1700 summer, tickets E£35, students E£20. The easiest way to reach it is by taxi (E£40 round trip) from Aswan or possibly as part of a half-day tour including the Unfinished Obelisk, the Aswan Dams and Philae. You'll need to be firm in negotiations with the boatmen at the west end of the High Dam to get them to take you for E£60. Pay at the end of the return trip after about an hour on the site.*

The Temple of Mandulis The original site of the temple, built in the 18th Dynasty (1567-1320 BC) in honour of Marul (Greek *Mandulis*), was about 50 km south of Aswan at Talmis, which was subsequently renamed Kalabsha. Mandulis was a Lower Nubian sun god of fertility equated with Horus/Isis/Osiris and usually shown in human form with an elaborate headdress of horns, cobras and plumes all topped off with a sun disc. Over the centuries the later Temple of Mandulis, a Ptolemaic-Roman version of the earlier one, developed a healing cult as did those of Edfu and Dendara. It is the largest free-standing Nubian temple and was relocated by West German engineers in 1970 to now stand semi-marooned on an island or promontory (depending on the water level). It is rarely visited by tourists, although so easily accessible from Aswan, and the lake setting and harsh surrounds provide a good backdrop to the remains.

Leading up to the First Pylon is an impressive 30-m causeway used by pilgrims arriving by boat. It is not known why the causeway and first pylon are set at a slight angle to the temple, but in order to align the structure the first court is in the shape of a trapezium, with the pillars on the south side grouped closer together. At either end of the pylon a staircase leads up to the roof and the thickwalls contain four storage rooms, two at each side.

The left portico, beside the entrance to the Hypostyle Hall, portrays the pharaoh being purified and anointed with holy water by Thoth and Horus, while on the right is inscribed a decree ordering the expulsion of pigs from the temple precincts. The column capitals are ornate and flowered, the paintings having been preserved with their original colours. On either side of the doorway leading to the vestibule is a relief of Trajan making offerings to Isis, Osiris and Mandulis on the left and Horus, Mandulis and Wadjet on the right.

Beyond the hall are the vestibules, each with two columns and south access to the roof (now locked). Most of the decoration has survived and on the entrance wall the pharaoh can be seen offering incense to Mandulis and Wadjet, and milk to Isis and Osiris. The south wall depicts the emperor making libations to Osiris, Isis, Horus, Wadjet and Mandulis. The statue of Mandulis has long since vanished, though he is pictured on the walls among the other deities.

Lake Nasser temples

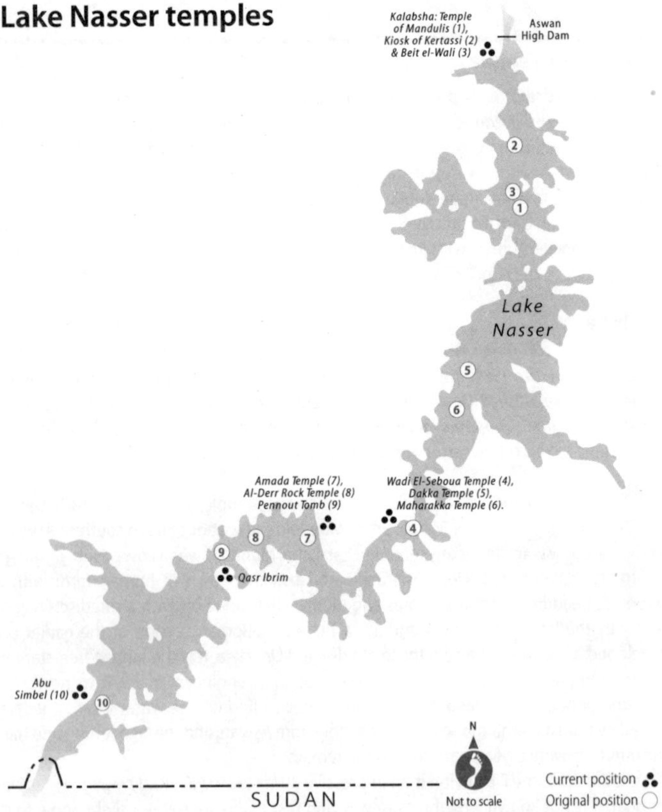

The Kiosk of Kertassi Near the lakeside just south of the Temple of Mandulis is the Ptolemaic-Roman Kiosk of Kertassi rescued by UNESCO from its original site 40 km south of Aswan. Described by the photographer Francis Frith in 1857 as a "bonnie little ruin", the single chamber has two Hathor-headed columns and other lotus-topped columns sharply decorated with foliage and flowers. Dedicated to Isis, the temple is undecorated except for one column in the northwest whose reliefs on the upper part depict the pharaoh standing before Isis and Horus the child.

Beit El-Wali In the hillside behind stands a small rock temple, Beit El-Wali (House of the Governor), again part of the UNESCO rescue mission. It was originally situated northwest of Kalabsha when it possessed a long causeway to the river. The reliefs and residual colours are well preserved and bright, making it worth the short walk. Built during Ramses II's youth by the Viceroy of Kush, it is believed to have been erected in honour of Amun-Re as he is depicted most frequently. The reliefs in the temple's narrow forecourt depict Ramses II victorious against the Nubians and Ethiopians (south wall) and defeating the Asiatics, Libyans and Syrians (north wall). In fact a great deal of smiting and defeating is illustrated. In particular the tribute being offered on the east wall of the entrance courtyard is well worth examination, while on the wall opposite look out for the dog biting a Libyan's leg. The two columns in the vestibule are unusual in a Nubian monument – being fluted. When this building was used as a Christian church the entrance forecourt was roofed over with brick domes.

Temple of Mandulis

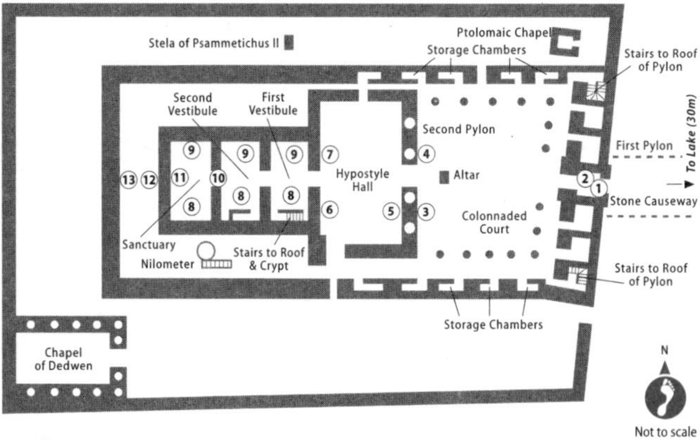

Murals ○

1 Lintel with sundisc
2 Emperor Augustus with Horus
3 King being purified with sacred water by Horus & Thoth
4 Decree in Greek regarding expulsion of pigs from temple
5 Coptic crosses carved on wall
6 Second register - a pharaoh offers a field to Isis, Mandulis & Horus
7 Second register - Amenophis II offers wine to Mandulis & another
8 Procession of gods, the King in the lead, before Osiris, Isis & Horus
9 Procession of gods, the King in the lead, before Mandulis, a juvenile Mandulis & Wadjet
10 Lintel with sundisc
11 King with various gods
12 King with deities - double picture
13 King before Mandulis

Fishing on Lake Nasser

Lake Nasser is the result of flooding 496 km of the Nile Valley with the construction of the Aswan Dam. The extraordinarily rich silt that once coated the valley during the seasonal flood is now at the bottom of the lake, sustaining the marine environment. As a result of the extreme nourishment, the fish have grown to huge sizes and Lake Nasser has become a popular destination for keen fishermen from around the world. There are over 6000 sq km to fish in and 32 species to catch (the two most popular being Nile perch and tiger fish).

Nile perch (*Lates niloticus*) are found in the Nile and other rivers, but grow to their greatest size in large bodies of water such as Lake Nasser. They are large-mouthed fish, greeny-brown above and silver below. They have an elongated body, a protruding jaw, a round tail and two dorsal fins. They are one of the largest freshwater fish in the world and can be over 1.9 m in length and 1.5 m in girth. The record catch in Lake Nasser was a massive 176 kg.

The most common of the tiger fish caught is *Hydrocynus forskaalii*. They have dagger teeth that protrude when their mouths are closed. They resemble a tiger in both appearance (they have several lengthwise stripes) and in habit (they are swift and voracious). They can grow to 5.5 kg.

Catfish are represented by 18 different species in the lake but the two of interest to anglers are *Bagrus* and *Vundu* of which the largest caught in Lake Nasser to date was 34 kg.

The main methods of fishing are trolling – restricted on safari to six hours a day, which covers a wide area and can result in a bigger catch of bigger fish; or spinning or fly fishing from the shore, generally in the cool of the morning, which is a delight and a challenge as it requires more skill as well as a strong line and heavy-duty gloves.

All fishing on Lake Nasser is on a catch and release policy, except those needed for the evening meal.

Wadi El-Seboua

ⓘ *Daily 0800-1600 winter, 0800-1700 summer, tickets E£25, students E£15. These temples were inaccessible by road until recently, and are not on the programmes of most big tour operators so normal convoy is not an option. But if you want to get there overland it is possible to take a private convoy with a police escort. Enquire at the tourist office in Aswan for help and for up-to-date information about prices. Most people will be visiting as part of a Lake Nasser cruise, during which the boats often moor to see the temples illuminated at night.*

The isolated oasis of Wadi El-Seboua, 135 km from the High Dam, contains the Temple of Wadi El-Seboua, the Temple of Dakka and the Temple of Maharakka. The giant **Temple of Wadi El-Seboua** (Valley of the Lion) is named after the two rows of sphinxes that line its approach. Unfortunately, a number of the sphinxes have been decapitated and the heads illegally sold to treasure hunters. It was constructed between 1279 BC and 1212 BC under Setau, the supervisor of the Viceroy of Kus and is dedicated to Amun, Re-Harakhte and the deified Ramses II. A huge statue of Ramses II and a sphinx stand on either side of the entrance, the base of each decorated with bound prisoners as a reminder of Egyptian supremacy. There are six human-headed sphinxes wearing the double crown in the First Courtyard and four falcon-headed sphinxes in double crown in the Second Courtyard. Again the bases have illustrations of bound prisoners. Steps lead up to the main part of the temple, where the massive statue on the left of the First Pylon is of the wife of

Worship of the Nile crocodile – Crocodylus niloticus

These huge creatures, the largest reptile in Africa, were worshipped as the god Sobek (see page 603), who was depicted as a man with a crocodile's head. The Ancient Egyptians kept them in lakes by the temples, which were dedicated to crocodile gods, and fed them the best meat, geese and fish and even wine. Special creatures were decked with jewels, earrings, gold bracelets and necklaces. Their bodies were embalmed after death (which for some came after more than 100 years). It is suggested that they were worshipped out of fear, in the hope that offerings and prayers would make them less vicious and reduce the dangers to both man and beast.

The problem was these cold-blooded creatures needed to come out of the river to bask in the sunshine and feed – and they could move at a surprising speed on land. The long muscular tail was used as a rudder and on land could be used to fell large animals at a single blow. Small humans were easy prey.

In other regions they were hunted, eaten and considered a protector as they prevented anyone from swimming across the Nile.

It is fortunate that today these 900-kg creatures can no longer reach the major part of Egypt. They cannot pass the Aswan dam but they exist to the south of this barrier in large numbers.

Ramses II and behind her leg their daughter Bint-Anath. The corresponding statue from the right of the entrance now lies in the sand outside, damaged when the temple was converted into a church.

The carved reliefs by local artists in poor quality sandstone are crude but much remains of their original colour. Around the court are roughly hewn statues of Ramses II unusually portrayed as a Nubian, holding the crook and flail scepters displayed against the 10 pillars – but most have been damaged. Along the lower register appear a procession of princes and princesses, estimated at a total of over 50 of each, all the offspring of the mighty Ramses. From the far end of the First Pillared Hall the temple is cut into the rock and this inner section has decorations better preserved and with better colours. The Christians who used this as a church covered the reliefs with plaster to permit their own decoration, thus preserving the earlier work. In the Sanctuary a relief on the wall shows Ramses II presenting a bouquet to the godly triad, but early Christians have defaced the figures and Ramses II now appears to be offering lotus flowers to St Peter.

The Temple of Dakka A painful 1500-m walk uphill is the Ptolemaic-Roman Temple of Dakka, reconstructed on the site of an earlier sanctuary. In fact several rulers contributed to its construction and decoration. Started by the Meroitic King Arqamani, it was adapted by the Ptolemies Philopator and Euergetes II and changed yet again by Emperors Augustus and Tiberius.

Like many temples it was used for a time by the Christians as a church and in some places fragments of their decorations remain. This is the only temple in Egypt facing north, an orientation preserved by UNESCO, pointing to the home of Thoth but more probably an error by the foreign-born Ptolemaic builders. The pylon is still in good condition, standing an imposing 13 m in height. The gateway has a curved cornice with a central winged sun disc on either side and a high level niche at each side intended to hold a flag pole, while on the left of the doorway is graffiti in Greek, Roman and Meriotic (ancient Nubian). Stairs in either side of the pylon lead to the roof, from which a fine view is obtained. Look for the deep incisions in the inner pylon wall, probably made by locals convinced that the stone possessed healing properties.

The main temple building is across an open courtyard, but before you enter turn back and admire the vista to the north. There are four interconnecting rooms, many of the decorations being of deities receiving assorted offerings. A staircase leads off the vestibule on the west side up to the roof – again the views are staggering. Off the sanctuary is a small room to the east side leading, it is thought, to a now-choked crypt. Here the decorations are in quite good condition – two seated ibises, two hawks and two lions. The lioness being approached by the baboons needs some interpretation. As an animal could approach a lioness without danger except if she was hungry, if a human was in danger at any time they assumed animal form to worship in safety. The king is seen worshipping gods including Osiris and Isis, and Horus and Hathor. The large pink granite casket in the sanctuary once held the cult statue of Thoth.

The Temple of Maharakka Less impressive is the unfinished Roman Temple of Meharakka, dedicated to Isis and Serapis. This stood on the southern border of Egypt in Ptolemaic and Roman times, but is now a short walk down hill from the Temple of Dakka. Rather plain inside, bar the Roman graffiti from travellers and soldiers fighting Nubian troops in 23 BC, the temple illustrates the union of Egyptian and Roman styles. Isis is depicted full frontal, instead of the more common profile, while her son Horus wears a toga. Other surviving carvings depict Osiris, Thoth and Tefnut. The temple consists of one room – six columns on the north side, three columns on the east and west side and six on the south side joined by screen walls. The capitals of the columns were never completed. For stair access to the roof, from which there are spectacular views, enter the temple and turn right. This is the only known spiral staircase in an Egyptian building. Look east to the pharaohs' gold mines.

Temple of Amada

ⓘ *Daily 0800-1600 winter, 0800-1700 summer, tickets E£45, students E£25. Accessible to cruise boats only, whose passengers are ferried to the site on motor launches.*

Some 40 km further south in the Amada Oasis is the oldest temple in Nubia, the sandstone Temple of Amada, dedicated to Amun-Re and Re-Harakhte. It was built by Tuthmosis III and Amenhotep II, with the roofed pillared court added by Tuthmosis IV, which accounts for the many scenes of Tuthmosis IV with various gods and goddesses on the walls and pillars. At the left of the entrance hieroglyphics detail the victorious campaigns of Meneptah against the Libyans. Before entering the next doorway look up at the Berber grafiti of animals high on the wall at both sides. Inside, reliefs on the right show the Pharaoh running the Heb-Sed race, cattle being slaughtered and presented as offerings as heads and haunches. Opposite are the foundation ceremonies, an interesting depiction of the way a site for a building was marked out, foundations dug, bricks manufactured and the construction eventually completed and handed over to the owner. In the central section are more offerings of pomegranates, very realistic ducks and cakes. The stela at the back of the sanctuary tells of the temple's foundation during Amenhotep II's time. The holes in the roof allow light in so one can see, on the back wall, Amenhotep dispensing justice to six Syrian captives: a prisoner is turned upside down and crucified; a grisly reminder to his remote Nubian subjects of the pharaoh's treatment of enemies.

Cobras

The Egyptian cobra occurs on every kingly brow. The *Uraeus*, the cobra's head and the neck with the hood spread, as worn in the head dress of Egyptian divinities and sovereigns, is a sign of supreme power.

Fortunately this is the only place you are likely to see an Egyptian cobra (although Cleopatra conveniently found one in the environs of her palace).

All cobras are potentially very dangerous although the venom is used to catch prey rather than eliminate humans. These creatures, though infrequently seen, are not considered in danger of extinction.

There are other cobras in Egypt. The smaller black-necked spitting cobra sprays venom up to the eyes of its attacker – causing temporary blindness and a great deal of agony. The black refers to the distinctive bands round the neck. Sightings are confined to the region south of Aswan. The Innes cobra is exceedingly rare, recorded in particular around St Catherine's Monastery.

The Rock Temple of Al-Derr Here too is the Rock Temple of Al-Derr, built in honour of Amun-Re, Re-Harakhte and the divine aspect of the pharaoh, notable for the excellent colour and preservation of its reliefs. It is the only temple on the east bank of the Nile in Nubia. In the first Hypostyle Hall the temple's builder Ramses II stands in the Tree of Life and presents libations to Amun. Ibis, the eternal scribe, behind, records the pharaoh's years and achievements. The decorations here are, however, very damaged and only small pieces of these scenes can now be made out. The four large statues of Ramses II as Osiris, incorporated in the last row of columns, are reduced to legs only. The majority of the reliefs on the outer walls boast of the pharaoh's military triumphs and warn the Nubians that his might is unassailable. However, inside the second Hypostyle Hall, the pharaoh, depicted as a high priest, becomes a humble servant of the gods. On the right-hand wall he gives flowers, offers wine, escorts the barque, receives jubilees from Amun-Re and Mut and further along the Heb-Sed emblem is produced nine times. On the opposite wall he has his name recorded on the leaves of a tall acacia tree. Entering the sanctuary, on the left, Ramses is putting in a plea to live forever. In the sanctuary on the back wall there were originally four statues as in the larger temple at Abu Simbel (see page 330), now nothing, but on the wall decorations the king continues to offer perfumes, cake and flowers.

The Tomb of Pennout The rock-cut tomb of the Chief of the Quarry Service, Steward of Horus and viceroy of Wawat (northern Nubia) under Ramses VI, is a rare example of a high official buried south of Aswan. The ancient Egyptians believed that their souls were only secure if their bodies were carried back and buried in Egyptian soil. The tomb's wall paintings rather poignantly reflect this conviction, expressing Pennout's desire to be laid to rest in the hills of Thebes. The walls are decorated with traditional themes, including the deceased and his family. Before entering on the left are the deceased and his wife Takha in adulation, on the main wall is the judgement scene with the weighing of the heart against a feather and below the traditional mourners pouring sand on their heads. On the end wall Horus leads the deceased and wife to Osiris, Isis and Nephthys for a blessing but the lower register has all disappeared. To the left of the inner chamber is a representation of the solar cult. There is no entry into the inner chamber but the three badly mutilated statues of Pennout, and his wife with Hathor between can be viewed. The actual burial chamber lies

3 m below. Above on the lintel is the sun-god barge and howling baboons. What is left of the decoration on the wall to the right shows Pennout with his wife and six sons while on the end wall Pennout in golden colours is in his illustrated biography that continues on toward the exit. It is very disappointing to note that almost all the wall decorations were intact when this temple was moved here and even more disappointing to note that the damage had been caused by illegal removal from the monument.

Qasr Ibrim

ⓘ *Daily 0800-1600 winter, 0800-1700 summer, tickets E£30, students E£15, accessible to cruise boats only.*

The fortress of Qasr Ibrim, 40 km north of Abu Simbel, is the only Nubian monument to inhabit its original site, once a plateau but now an island. It is noted for an exceptional length of continuous occupation, from 1000 BC to AD 1812. The ancient city included seven temples to Isis and a mud-brick temple built by the Nubian king Taharka, ruins of which are visible in the centre of the island. In the pre-Roman period construction of a massive stone temple, similar to the structures at Kalabsha, turned the garrison city into a major religious centre. A healing cult developed and Qasr Ibrim became 'the Philae of the south'. Footprints, carved by pilgrims to commemorate their visit, are still visible in the temple floor. A tavern, 400 BC, on the north side of the island is recognizable by the large piles of pottery shards. The temple was destroyed by early Christians who built an orthodox cathedral on the site in the 10th century AD in honour of the Virgin Mary, the Christian version of Isis, three walls of which remain standing. By the steps to the burial crypt are numerous fragments of red (Roman) and glazed (Ottoman) pottery. Bosnian troops loyal to the Ottoman Sultan invaded the site in 1517 whereupon the cathedral was converted into a mosque, and their descendants inhabited the site for the next 300 years. The fortress was brought under central control in 1812.

Abu Simbel →

For listings, see pages 335-338. Colour map 1,C4.

Abu Simbel, 280 km south of Aswan and only 40 km north of the Sudanese border is the site of the magnificent **Sun Temple of Ramses II** and the smaller **Temple of Queen Nefertari**. With the exception of the temples, hotels and the homes of tourist industry employees, there is almost nothing else here. That is part of its charm, as is the immediate warmth of the locals that's so refreshing after the cut-and-thrust of Aswan. The village is centred around a couple of little eateries-cum-*ahwas* where the bus drops people off, with a modern *souk* to one side and the cheapest hotels within walking distance. The temples are about a 20-minute walk away, past the banks and post office. It is an attractive sultry little place, utterly sleepy except when the tours are passing through, where swathes of turban are de rigeur for men and you see women wearing traditional Nubian black net dresses decorated with weaving. The setting on the banks of Lake Nasser is beautiful, with heart-shattering rocks meeting the sapphire water, enhanced by the many green gardens dotted around and the single-storey whitewashed dwellings. It's true there are no beds at rock-bottom prices (though if you want to spoil yourself, the Eskaleh could be the place to do it) but you have to accept that you are going be shelling out to see the temples anyway. Altogether, the African atmosphere, dearth of independent travellers, and chance of seeing the temples in total isolation makes Abu Simbel an excellent overnight stop.

Burckhardt the explorer

The Anglo-Swiss geographer and explorer, Johann (John) Ludwig Burckhardt was born in Lausanne, Switzerland on 24 November 1784. He studied in London and Cambridge and between 1806 and 1809 lived in Syria, where he learnt Arabic and became a follower of Islam, taking the Muslim name Ibrahim Ibn Abd Allah. He left Syria, en route for Cairo and the Fezzan (Libya) from where he was to attempt to cross the Sahara. Local Bedouin spoke of the ruins of a 'lost city' in the mountains. Knowing that the legendary lost city of Petra was in the vicinity of Aaron's tomb on Jebel Harun he persuaded his guides of a desire to sacrifice a goat in honour of Aaron at his tomb. His scheme succeeded and on 22 August 1812 he was guided through the Siq and into the valley where he saw the Al-Khazneh and the Urn Tomb – enough to recognize the City of Petra. When he arrived in Cairo he could find no immediate transport to Fezzan so instead he journeyed up the Nile and discovered the Temple of Ramses II at Abu Simbel. He next travelled to Saudi Arabia, visiting Mecca. He returned to Cairo where he died on 15 October 1817, before he was able to complete his journey.

Ins and outs

Getting there EgyptAir runs daily flights during the winter high season from Cairo via Luxor to Abu Simbel. Direct from Aswan during the summer when the season slumps there are still at least two flights per day and three during the high season. Book a ticket as early as possible, especially in the peak season. Most tickets are sold on the assumption that you will return the same day but it is possible to include overnight stopovers. Seats on the left-hand side of the aircraft usually offer the best views as it circles the temples before landing at Abu Simbel. There are free buses from Abu Simbel airport to the site of the temples.

It is possible to visit Abu Simbel by road (unaccompanied by a convoy) on the public buses which depart from the main Aswan bus station (3.5 km north of town) supposedly three times per day; you can't buy tickets in advance. Don't take the later buses unless you intend to stay the night.

The Temples of Abu Simbel

ⓘ T097-3400 766/3400 325/6, daily 0500-1730 winter, 0500-1800 summer, E£95, students E£53.50, photography inside the temples is strictly prohibited. Sound and Light show, E£75 no student discount, lasts 35 mins, first show starts 2000 in summer (1-3 shows, more on Fri), 1800 in winter (1-2 shows), headphones provide commentary in all languages though you have to turn them up very loud to block out the main commentary. If you have come independently, go early to the first Sound and Light show for sunset. You won't be able to go inside the temples, but can marvel at the outside before the show starts. The following morning, head to the temples for dawn. It's pretty much guaranteed that you will be alone, save for Ramses, Nefertari and the custodians, for at least an hour – and as sunrise colours the colossi it takes your breath away. With the waters of Lake Nasser dark, still and silent before them, pink light slowly creeps up over the feet of the great pharaoh and his queen. The majority of tourists come for a couple of hours via plane or as part of the road convoy, and arrive in a stampede which is best avoided.

The two temples, which were rediscovered in 1813 completely buried by sand, were built by the most egotistical pharaoh of them all, Ramses II (1304-1237 BC) during the 19th

Dynasty of the New Kingdom. Although he built a smaller temple for his queen, Nefertari, it is the four gigantic statues of himself carved out of the mountainside that dominate Abu Simbel. It was intended that his magnificent and unblinking stare would be the first thing that travellers, visitors and enemies alike, saw as they entered Egypt from the south. Behind the statues is Ramses II's Temple of the Sun, which was originally built to venerate Amun and Re-Harakhte but really is dominated by, and dedicated to, the pharaoh-god Ramses II himself.

Although it had become the highlight of the trip for the relatively few intrepid travellers who ventured so far south, it was not until the monuments were threatened by the rising waters of Lake Nasser that international attention focused on Abu Simbel. UNESCO financed and organized the ambitious, costly (US$40 million) and ultimately successful 1964-1968 operation, to reassemble the monuments 61 m above and 210 m behind their original site. Despite its magnificence and beauty, for many visitors to Abu Simbel there is a slight tinge of disappointment because of the combined sense of familiarity and artificiality. Yet the sheer audacity of Ramses' egoism and the scale of the feat of saving the temple from the rising waters of the lake make the trip worthwhile.

Ramses II's Temple of the Sun The entrance steps lead up to a terrace, with alternate statuettes of the king and a falcon to mark the edge, where the imposing façade of the main temple (35 m wide by 30 m high) is dominated by the four-seated **Colossi of Ramses II** wearing the double crown. Each figure was originally 21 m high but the second from the left lost its top during an earthquake in 27 BC. There are smaller statues of the members of the royal family standing at Ramses' rather crudely sculptured feet, which contrast with his ornately chiselled and beautiful faces above. Graffiti, written by Greek mercenaries about their expeditions into Nubia, can be seen on the left leg of the damaged statue but it seems everyone who visited in the 1800s left their mark in the tablets of signatures – even his knee-caps haven't escaped.

The sides of the huge thrones at the entrance to the temple are decorated with the Nile gods entwining lotus and papyrus, the plants representing Upper and Lower Egypt around the hieroglyph 'to unite'. Below are reliefs showing Egypt's vanquished foes, the **Nine Bows of Bound Nubians** on the south side **(5)** and **Bound Asiatics** to the north side **(6)**. The colour and clarity of these larger-than-life fettered prisoners is quite confronting, their differing hairstyles and earrings denote their origins. Lining the façade, above the heads of Ramses, is a row of 22 baboons smiling at the sunrise. A **marriage stela (7)** commemorates the union of Ramses II with Ma'at-Her- Neferure, daughter of the Hittite king.

At the entrance into the temple's rock **Hypostyle Hall** is a door bearing Ramses II's cartouche. Entered the temple you are met by eight striking statues of Ramses, 10 m high and clad in a short kilt typical of the Nubian Osiride form, carved into the eight enormous square pillars supporting the roof. The four statues on the right bear the double crown and those on the left the white crown of Upper Egypt, and the first couple of statues have had their beards inscribed with yet more 19th-century graffiti. On the pillars, Ramses presents **flowers to Min and incense to Isis (8)**, **wine to Horus and flowers to Mut (9)**, **flowers to Thoth and bread to Anubis (10)**, while **Re-Harakhte receives wine (11)**. The hall's ceiling is crowded with vultures in the central aisle and star spangled elsewhere. The reliefs on the walls are colourful and well preserved. The north wall is the most dramatic with four different scenes depicting the **Battle of Kadesh** against the Hittites in 1300 BC **(12, 13)** which, despite what these illustrations might imply, was not an unqualified

Ramses II's Temple of the Sun

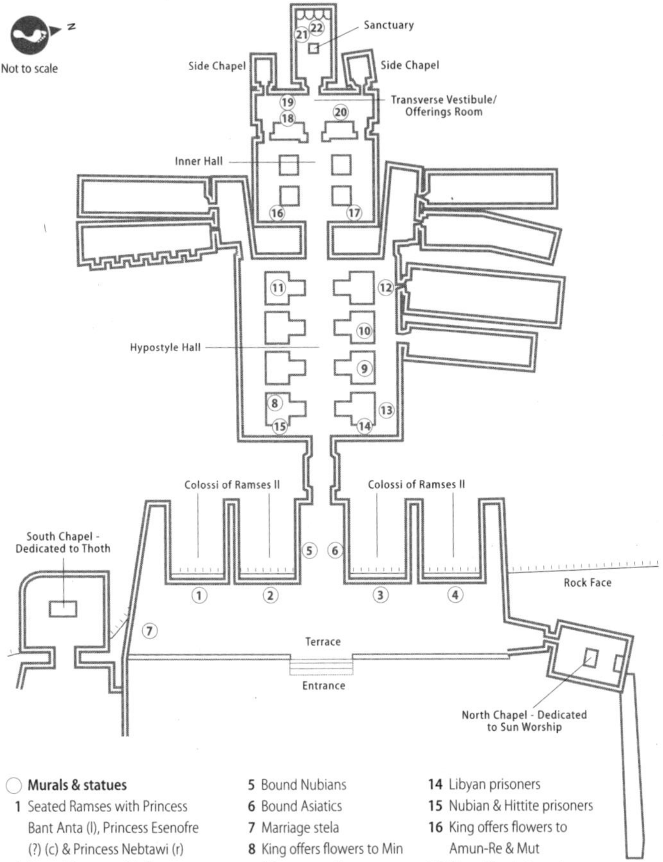

◯ **Murals & statues**

1 Seated Ramses with Princess Bant Anta (l), Princess Esenofre (?) (c) & Princess Nebtawi (r)
2 Seated Ramses with Queen Nefertari (l), Prince Amenhirkhopshef (c) & Ramses' mother Queen Muttuya
3 Seated Ramses with Princess Beketmut (l), Prince Ramessesu (c) & Queen Nefertari (r)
4 Seated Ramses with Queen Mother Muttuya (l), Princess Merytamun (c) & Queen Nefertari (r)
5 Bound Nubians
6 Bound Asiatics
7 Marriage stela
8 King offers flowers to Min & incense to Isis
9 King offers wine to Horus & flowers to Mut
10 King offers flowers to Thoth & bread to Anubis
11 King offers wine to Re-Harakhte
12-13 Battle of Kadesh - recruits arriving, encampment, town of Kadesh, enemy chariots
14 Libyan prisoners
15 Nubian & Hittite prisoners
16 King offers flowers to Amun-Re & Mut
17 King offers lettuces to Min & Isis
18 King offers wine to Min
19 King offers incense to a ram-headed Amun-Re
20 King offers bread to Atum
21 King before barque of Amun anoints Min
22 Four (damaged) statues (l-r) of Ptah, Amun-Re, Ramses II & Re-Harakhte

A bit of Nubian lingo

Hello *Raigri*
How are you? *Er meena bu?*
Good *A denma*
Thank you *Gas si raykum*
Goodbye *Inna fee ya-der*
Hot *Joogri*
Cold *Od*
Come here *In day gerta*
Beautiful *A sheerma*

Egyptian success. The depictions of chariots and camps are particularly revealing of ancient battle methods (it seems lions were involved) but, more interestingly, Ramses's double arm lancing a Libyan may have been an ancient attempt at animation. The slaughter of whole bundles of **prisoners**, generally small in size and with their faces shown in supplication, is a common theme **(14, 15)**. The side chambers, branching off from the hall, were probably originally used to store vases, temple linen, cult objects and Nubian gifts. Their walls are lined with reliefs of sacrifices and offerings being made by Ramses to the major gods, including Amun.

The **Inner Hall** has four columns depicting the Pharaoh participating in rituals before the deities. On the far left, Ramses can be seen before Amun (**16**) while on the right he makes an offering of lettuces, considered an aphrodisiac (**17**). In both these scenes a deified Ramses II has been inserted at a later date. Two sandstone sphinxes, which originally stood at the entrance to the hall, are now in London's British Museum.

Further in and in front of the inner sanctuary is the **Transverse Vestibule** where offerings of wine, fruits and flowers were made. The **Sanctuary** itself, which was originally cased in gold, has an altar to Ramses at its centre, behind which are now statues of Ptah, Amun-Re, Ramses II and Re-Harakhte, unfortunately mutilated. Ramses is deified with his patron gods. Before the temple's relocation the dawn sunrays would shine on all but Ptah (who was linked with death-cults), on 22 February and 22 October. Despite what your guide will say there is no scholastic evidence to connect these two dates with Ramses' birthday and coronation day. A sacred *barque* (boat) would have rested on the altar and the walls beside the door portray the barque of Amun and Ramses. The adjoining side chapels were not decorated.

Temple of Queen Nefertari Although dedicated to the goddess Hathor of Abshek, like that of her husband, the queen's temple virtually deifies the human queen Nefertari. Unsurprisingly it is much smaller than that of Ramses II but is nevertheless both imposing and very, very beautiful. It is cut entirely from the rock and penetrates about 24 m from the rock face. The external façade is 12 m high and lined with three colossi 11.5 m high on either side of the entrance. Nefertari stands with her husband while their children cluster in pairs at their knees. To show the importance of Queen Nefertari her statues are of similar size to those of her husband. Just within the entrance are the cartouches of Ramses and Nefertari. The simple **Hall** has six square pillars, on the aisle side of each is depicted a Hathor head and sistrum sounding box while the other sides have figures of the king and queen making offerings to the gods. Some reliefs in the hall are rather gruesome – the walls backing the entrance show the pharaoh slaying his Nubian and Libyan enemies, who beg for mercy while Nefertari and the god Amun look on. Others show the royal couple engaging in rituals. Note her diaphanous skirts and their assortment of intricate crowns, which are exquisite.

Three corridors lead from the rear of the hall into the **Vestibule**, the central one passing directly into the **Sanctuary**. The back walls of the Vestibule portray reliefs of Ramses and

Nefertari offering wine and flowers to Khnum and Re-Harakhte on the right and to Horus and Amun on the left. Vultures protect the Queen's cartouche on the door above the sanctuary, which is dominated by the figure of Hathor in the form of a cow watching over Ramses. On the left wall, Nefertari can be seen offering incense to Mut and Hathor while on the opposite side Ramses worships the deified images of himself and Nefertari.

Temple of Queen Nefertari

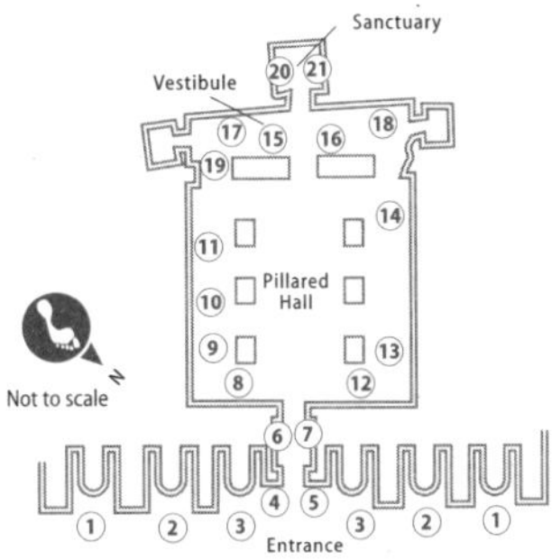

Murals & statues

1 Ramses II with Princes Meryatum & Meryre
2 Queen Nefertari shown as Hathor with Princesses Merytamun & Henwati
3 Ramses II with Princes Amunhikhopshef & Rahrirwemenef
4 Lintel where King offers wine to Amun-Re
5 King offers incense to Horus
6 King offers flowers to Hathor
7 Nefertari offers flowers to Isis
8 Ramses II smites Nubian prisoner before Amun-Re
9 Ramses II receives necklace from Hathor
10 Ramses II crowned by Horus & Seth
11 Nefertari offers flowers & musical instrument to Anukis
12 Ramses II smites Libyan prisoner before Horus
13 Ramses II with offerings
14 Nefertari before Hathor of Dendera
15 Nefertari between Hathor & Isis
16 Ramses II & Nefertari give flowers to Tawere
17 Ramses II offers wine to Horus & Anu
18 Ramses II offers wine to Re-Harakhte & Queen offers flowers to Khnum
19 Nefertari's cartouche between vultures
20 Nefertari offers incense to Mut & Hathor
21 Ramses II worships deified image of himself & Nefertari

Lower Nubia listings

For Sleeping and Eating price codes and other relevant information, see pages 26-31.

Sleeping

Abu Simbel *p330*

L Seti Abu Simbel, T097-340 0720-2, www.setifirst.com. Call the Cairo office, T02-2736 0890-5 or T(+202) 19780 for the best price. This is the fanciest place to stay in Abu Simbel. There are all the 5-star amenities although rooms are a little jaded, but splendid views of Lake Nasser go some way to compensate as do the 2 terraced pools set in verdant gardens. Upstairs rooms are better. Breakfast not included, discounts at the discretion of the General Manager.

A Eskaleh, T097-340 1288, T012-368 0521, F097-340 1143, www.eskaleh.net. Built in the style of a traditional Nubian house, with furniture fashioned from date palms, rough stone floors, domes and terracotta-coloured walls, this little guesthouse is a delight. And though the bathrooms aren't in keeping with the rustic-style building, they are modern and sparkling. The 3 larger, more expensive rooms (doubles US$90) have more space and terraces surrounded by flowers, some have mud-brick lattice windows, all have mosquito nets, a/c, and free internet for guests. The terrace at the front overlooks the lake and vegetable garden, and there are occasional Nubian music nights. Accepts major credit cards.

D Abu Simbel Tourist Village, T097-340 0092, Homely salmon-pink rooms all have private bath, most have a/c (doubles E£150). There's a good view of Lake Nasser from the little garden and management is kind and friendly. It's a 10-min walk from the bus stop on the edge of the village, about 2 km from the temple.

D Nobaleh Ramsis Hotel, T097-340 0106, T097-340 1118. The cheapest option in town with huge high-ceilinged rooms at E£125. Rooms are cool and comfortable but spartan, with TV, a/c and fridge. No breakfast and you might expect a higher standard of bathroom for the price and there are no views. 2 km from the temples, but close to the bus stop, and big discounts negotiable if you call ahead. With prior warning, the manager Yassin may be able to arrange a boat to take you out on the lake.

Camping

Sometimes the **Abu Simbel Village** and the **Nefertari Abu Simbel** permit camping on their grounds, but call ahead to be sure.

Cruises

LL MS Eugenie, bookings through **Belle Epoque Travel**, 17 Sharia Tunis, New Maadi, Cairo, T02-2516 9653, www.eugenie.com.eg. Constructed in 1993 in the style of a Mississippi paddle steamer, 52 a/c cabins with balcony, 2 suites, pre-Revolution decor, 2 bars, 2 large saloons, 2 sundecks, pool, jaccuzi, health club, excellent food and no enforced entertainment. Memorable features include a private sunset tour of Abu Simbel followed by a candlelit dinner on board for which the temples are specially lit.

Eating

Abu Simbel *p330*

Despite Abu Simbel's position in the middle of the desert and the fact most supplies come from Aswan, there is no problem getting a good meal.

Good *felafel* is served in the market, from a stall down the street between **Restaurant Ganoub El-Wadi** and **Wadi El-Nil** café. Wadi El-Nil café is a good spot to people watch under a tree as you sip a tea. Best of all, the correct prices are laminated onto each tabletop.

You can get an alcoholic drink at the **Eskaleh**, **Seti Abu Simbel** and **Nefertari** hotels, albeit an expensive one.

Eskaleh, call ahead to enjoy an excellent 3-course dinner either on the terrace outside or in the lovely dining room among the decorative basketware, woven mats and Nubian artefacts. Vegetables and salads grown in the garden, beer and wine are available (expensive), meals are around E£75 per person.

Fahd, upstairs from **Ganoub El-Wadi**, serves basic stewed veg, meat, rice and salad. Ask the price first, as it is very much negotiable (E£15 or above, depending if you eat meat) and veggies should be wary of scraps of meat in the potato stews.

Ganoub El-Wadi, offers simply served fish, freshly plucked from the lake. No need to quibble about prices.

Il Rahman, this is where tour bus drivers go to eat while their passengers visit the temples. A herby, crispy fish fillet with rice will cost you a mere E£20. Delicious fresh rice pudding from the fridge is E£2. On the opposite side of the road from the other restaurants, keep them to your left and walk towards the temples. Il Rahman is just down the road back to Aswan on the left opposite a now defunct fountain.

Koshari El-Arabi, serves generous portions of decent koshari.

Activities and tours

Abu Simbel *p330*

Boat trips

If there are quite a few of you, hire a boat to visit some of the many mesmerizing islands, see part of Lake Nasser's 8000-km stretch of shore and of course view the temple from the water. You could even see crocodiles sunbathing, water monitors and golden jackals. Yassin at the **Nobaleh Ramsis Hotel**, T097-340 0106, can arrange a boat for a half day holding up to 20 people for E£500;

he needs at least 24 hrs' advance warning in order to get permission from the authorities. For information on *felucca* trips, see page 300.

Cruise boats on Lake Nasser

Since the construction of the High Dam the upper part of the Nile has been effectively cut off to navigation from the lower reaches. The only solution to getting a good vessel on the lake was to set up a shipyard and build one designed for these deeper waters. The most relaxing way to tour Lower Nubian antiquities is aboard one of the elegant cruise boats. Pampered by the luxurious surroundings, high-calibre guides and excellent service, tourists can sit back and appreciate the sheer vastness of desert and lake, a sharp contrast to the lush scenery and teeming villages of the Nile Valley. Few more tranquil places exist. The boat's passengers have the monuments almost to themselves. Cruises usually last 3 nights/4 days or 4 nights/5 days starting either in Aswan or Abu Simbel. Some boats have 7-day itineraries going from Aswan to Abu Simbel and back again.

Other cruise boats on Lake Nasser with 5-star rating are: *Kasr Ibrim*, also owned by **Belle Epoque**, www.kasribrim.com,eg, see above, 65 rooms of an equally excellent standard but this time with 1930s art deco styling. *MS Nubian Sea* has 50 cabins and suites, and serves excellent food; *MS Prince Abbas*, owned by Movenpick hotels, www.moevenpick-hotels.com, and fully refitted to a high spec, 65 standard cabins, 18 junior suites and 4 royal suites.

See also **Lake Nasser Adventure** (see page 337) who run cruises in very small boats, which are quite unique.

Fishing

For fishermen and birdwatchers, there are a few companies that specialize in nature and adventure safaris on Lake Nasser. Fishing is particularly good here, considered big-game fishing, as the damming of the river has created the perfect environment for Nile perch to grow to immense proportions, see box, page 326. Nights are spent under the stars, camping in one of the inlets or aboard a mother ship, and days are spent on a small boat under a searing sun wrestling with the beasts beneath.

The African Angler, T097-230 9748, www.african-angler.net, are a good company to go with. They have highly trained local staff and boats specifically designed for fishing on Lake Nasser. Check their website for the latest prices.

Lake Nasser Adventure, www.lakenasser adventure.com, offer fishing trips sleeping in small boats for 1-3 people, which means complete freedom from any schedule, or via fast boats from a central mother ship. They also organize unique desert cruises, visiting not only temples but allowing time for desert treks and swimming on two boats sleeping up to 14. For complete luxury, the new *Nubiana* takes a max of 8 people on either fishing or desert adventures. 15% discounts between Jun and Sep.

Organized trips

Travel agencies and hotels in Aswan all run daily trips to Abu Simbel. Most reputable agencies generally transport their passengers in an a/c coach and may include a tour guide. They can also book day trips via plane.

For people on a budget, hotels offer 2 basic trips incorporating Abu Simbel (the short, E£60-70 and the long, E£70-80). The short trip picks you up from your hotel at 0330-0400 in the morning, transports you to the **temple** and gets you back by 1300. The long trip stops at the **High Dam**, **Unfinished Obelisk**, and **Philae Temple** on the way back and finishes around 1530. It's tempting to stick it all in 1 day, but the long trip feels very long. Price usually only includes transport in a minivan – some with and some without a/c. If visiting in summer, it is worth the extra few pounds to ensure you have a/c. Admission fees not included.

Both tours usually join the convoy that departs at 0400 in the morning and arrives at the temples around 0800. You only have about an hour to look around before being bussed back to Aswan or on to the next stop on your tour, which can be frustrating. Bring at least some of the food and water you'll need for the morning as prices at Abu Simbel are staggeringly high and remember there are no toilet stops between Aswan and Abu Simbel.

Transport

Abu Simbel *p330*

Bus

Buses leave Abu Simbel from outside Wadi El-Nil Café for **Aswan** at 0600, 1300 and sometimes 1600, E£25, 4 hrs.

Microbuses leave when full costing E£16 and these are marginally quicker. Ask people hanging around Wadi El-Nil to point you in the right direction, you might have to wait a while and scout for passengers.

Directory

Abu Simbel *p330*

Banks 3 banks, Sat-Thu 0830-1400, Bank Du Caire and Bank Misr. **Internet** Café Net, 3rd block back in the *souk*, daily 1000-2400, E£5 per hr. **Medical services** Pharmacy: By the turning to the Seti Hotel, and in the village opposite the *souk*. **Post office** On the way to the temple past the turning to the Seti Hotel, Sat-Thu 0730-1430.

Alexandria & the Mediterranean Coast

Contents

Footprint features

Border crossings

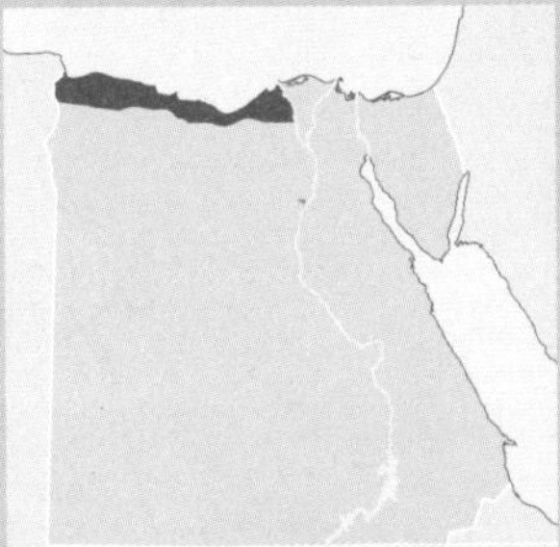

At a glance

Getting around Train is most comfortable from Cairo. Bus or taxi along the coast.

Time required 2 days in Alexandria; as long as you want at a beach resort.

Weather Between Nov and Mar it is very windy and cold at night.

When not to go Summer is packed with Egyptian holiday-makers – hotels get booked up.

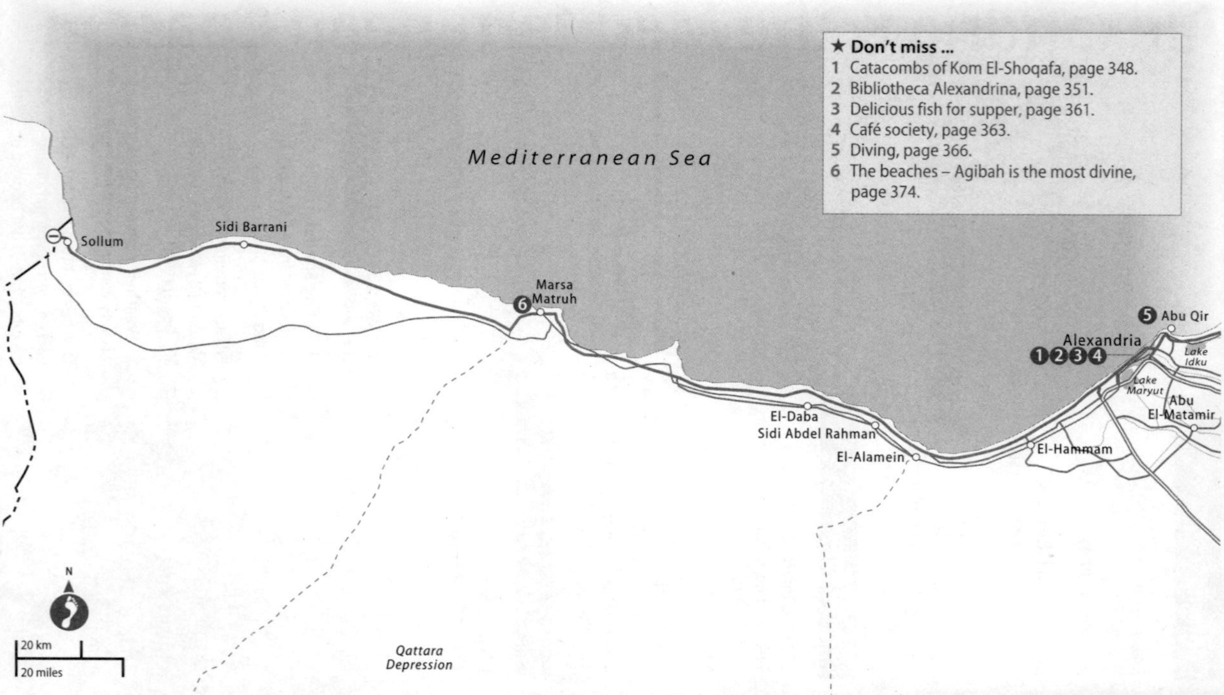
★ Don't miss ...
1 Catacombs of Kom El-Shoqafa, page 348.
2 Bibliotheca Alexandrina, page 351.
3 Delicious fish for supper, page 361.
4 Café society, page 363.
5 Diving, page 366.
6 The beaches – Agibah is the most divine, page 374.
Mediterranean Sea
Sollum
Sidi Barrani
Marsa Matruh
Abu Qir
Alexandria
Lake Idku
Lake Maryut
Abu El-Matamir
El-Daba
Sidi Abdel Rahman
El-Hammam
El-Alamein
Qattara Depression
N
20 km
20 miles

Some 20 km long but only 3 km wide, Alexandria (or *Iskanderiya*, as it is known colloquially) is an emphatic waterfront city, swept by Mediterranean breezes and tangible nostalgia for its legendary past. Though the glory days are long gone and age has made weary the city's face, the modern metropolis is still a fascinating place and is lately experiencing something of a cultural renaissance. The stupendous Bibliotheca Alexandrina is just the beginning – beautiful old museums have been restored and most nights you can enjoy a theatrical, musical or cultural event. About five million people speak at least five different languages and live along a seashore on the edge of east and west, creating a world that is in between. Where else can you indulge in a glass of French wine and some Greek souvalaki followed by a *sheesha* and Italian espresso with the call to prayer and Lebanese pop music in the background?

Heading west from Alexandria, the Mediterranean Coast stretches 500 km to the Libyan border, encompassing ever-expanding beach resorts, to the poignant cemeteries of El-Alamein, site of the huge Second World War battle, which have a power and intensity that time cannot diminish. The government are targeting this area for residential developments, but still striking are the vast extents of coast unmarked by towns or tourism, which create a sense of isolation as you skim the edge of sea and sand towards Marsa Matruh. Here is the turn-off point for Siwa, which draws most travellers onward, although the electric azure of the sea at Agibah beach might tempt you stop awhile prior to being enveloped in the dust of the desert. With domestic tourism making up the majority of visitors, the beach culture on the north coast is considerably more conservative than that of the Red Sea and women may find that outside of the larger resorts with private beaches, hassles abound.

Alexandria

➔ *Colour map 2, A1.* *Population: 3,700,000.*

Alexandria is mythical: old stage for historical characters like Alexander the Great and Cleopatra; former site of one of the world's seven ancient wonders, the legendary Pharos lighthouse; and home of the old library, once the container of all knowledge available on earth. For an area so rich in ancient history, perhaps what's first striking is how little remains above ground. With book-burning patriarchs and earth-shattering quakes, much of Alex's splendid past has been burnt to a crisp, toppled into the sea or buried under the earth. Although tantalizing new archaeological discoveries are frequently revealed when foundations are dug for modern developments, excavations are all but impossible with millions of people thriving in the towering apartment blocks that cover the historic city. Still, there's plenty to see and do and aura of the fabled Alex of yesteryear is slowly revealed as you succumb to her subtle charms. Colonial architecture along the Corniche and around the Orabi and Tahrir midans, the erstwhile antique shops of Al-Attarine, the hectic souks around Karmouz and the civilized retreats of the eastern suburbs all make for absorbing ambles. The new Bibliotheca Alexandrina opened in October 2002, putting the city back on the global map and kick-starting a cultural renaissance. The last few years have seen an influx of musicians and artists, hinting at the beginning of a third Golden Age. If you scuba-dive, it's possible to explore ancient royal remains that have been submerged in the surrounding sea as well as remnants of Napoleon's ill-fated fleet. There are also excellent museums, the creepy Catacombs of Shoqafa, and scores of wonderful seafood restaurants and charming old-world cafés and bars that offer a window onto the city's multifaceted personality. ▸▸ *For listings, see pages 359-368.*

1 **Greater Alexandria**

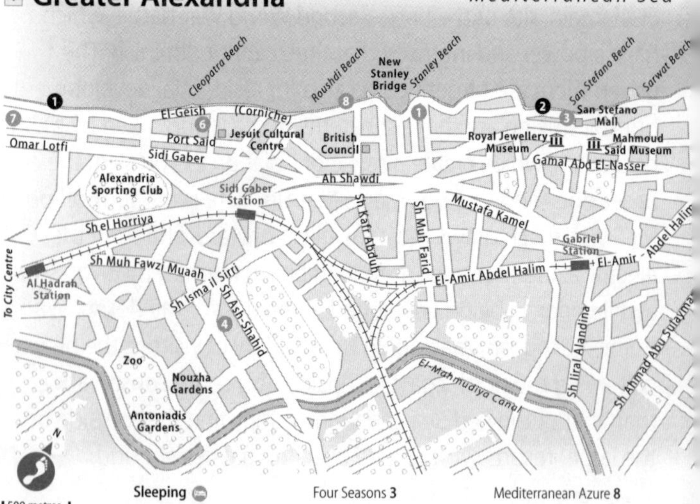

500 metres
500 yards

Sleeping
Dovil **1**
El-Salamlek Palace **2**
Four Seasons **3**
Hilton Green Plaza **4**
Ma'amura Palace **5**
Mediterranean Azure **8**
Nobel **6**
Youth Hostel **7**

Ins and outs

Getting there El Nouzha airport, about 10 km from the town centre, is due to be renovated between 2011-2013. International and domestic flights will therefore use Borg Al-Arab airport, about an hour out of the city. Intercity buses to Alexandria all terminate at the new bus station in Muharram Bey, from where a taxi costs E£10-15 to central destinations. There are at least 12 trains daily from Cairo to the main Misr station. Service taxis stop either near Misr or at Midan Orabi, both fairly central. ▸▸ *See Transport, page 366.*

Getting around Alexandria is a thin ribbon-like city whose residential areas are still largely bound by the El-Mahmudiya canal and Lake Maryut. At the city's western end is the El-Anfushi peninsula, which divides the giant functional Western Harbour and the beautiful sweeping curve of the Eastern Harbour and its Corniche. To the east is a series of beaches that stretch to the Montazah Palace and on to Ma'mura beach and eventually Abu Qir, site of Nelson's 1798 victory over the French fleet. The city's main downtown area, its main transport terminals and many of the hotels are in the blocks around Midan Sa'ad Zaghloul in El-Manshiya, just inland from the Eastern Harbour. There is a useful tram service around the city, constant microbuses traverse the Corniche, and cheap taxis abound. Considering its size and that the population more than doubles in the summer, Alexandria is remarkably easy to navigate.

Information **The main office** ⓘ *southwest corner of Midan Sa'ad Zaghloul, T03-485 1556, daily 0800-1800, 0900-1600 during Ramadan*, is short on facts and maps, but can provide a copy of the Egyptian Tourist Authority '*Alexandria's Ultimate Guide*' which is useful. There is an equally hopeless office at the **Misr Railway Station** ⓘ *T03-392 5985, open daily*

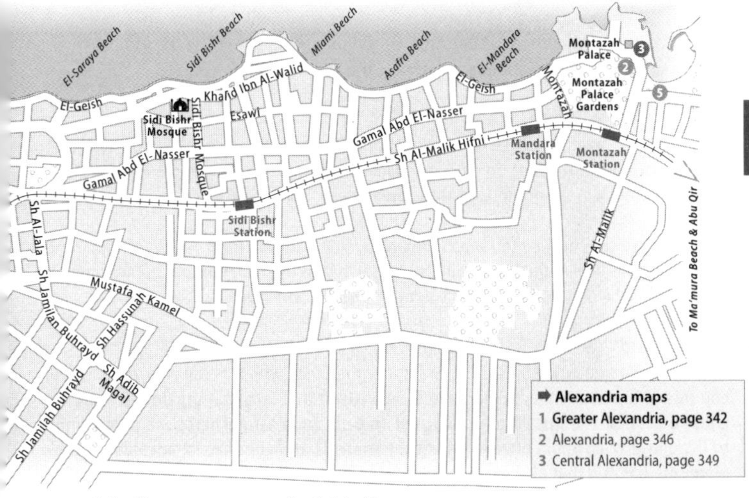

Eating
Mozzarella/Orchid **3**
Racoda **1**

Bars & clubs
Dolphin Nightclub **3**

Seeing the light – Ancient Alexandria

The Mouseion, from which the word *museum* is derived, meaning 'Temple of the Muses', was a vast centre of learning standing at the main crossroads of the city. It was commissioned by Ptolemy I, Soter and the important library was collected under the sponsorship of Ptolemy II, Philadelphus. As well as an observatory, laboratories, lodgings and a refectory for hundreds of scholars, it housed the famous library, Bibliotheca Alexandrina, which by Caesar's day contained nearly a million papyrus volumes. Obviously the material on a scroll of papyrus was shorter than a modern book but nevertheless the amount of information was outstanding. There is no evidence that it was destroyed by the Christians mobs – or by any other group – it is more likely that it gradually declined over a period of time due to lack of support.

The fire from the immense Lighthouse of Pharos could be seen from 55 km across the open sea. It was 135 m high and stood at the mouth of the Eastern Harbour where Sultan Qaitbay's fort now stands. The first storey was square, the second octagonal and the third circular, topped by the lantern. At the very top stood a statue of Poseidon, god of the sea, trident in hand.

It was still in use at the time of the Muslim invasion over 900 years after its construction and was mentioned by Ibn Battuta in 1326 (more than 1600 years after its construction) as being a fortress.

The idea for the lighthouse may have come from Alexander the Great but it was actually built in 279 BC by Sostratus, an Asiatic Greek, during the reign of Ptolemy II (284-246 BC). According to popular myth an immense mirror lens made it possible to view ships far out at sea while the fuel to feed the fire is said to have been hydraulically lifted to the top of the lighthouse. Upkeep was a serious problem. Ibn Tulun attempted some repairs but the great earthquakes of 1100 and 1307 destroyed the ancient foundations and the stones lay abandoned until the Ottoman Sultan Qaitbay decided to build the fort on the site in AD 1479.

0800-1800. For practical advice visit **Misr Tours** ⓘ *on Sharia Sa'ad Zaghloul, T03-480 9617*. The **Tourist Police** ⓘ *Midan Sa'ad Zaghloul, above the tourist information, T03-487 3378*, also has a branch in the grounds of **Montazah Palace** ⓘ *T03-547 3814*.

Best time to visit The Mediterranean climate diverges radically from the rest of Egypt. The northern winds deliver quite a chill in the winter, just as they offer respite in the summer. Alexandria is the only place in Egypt you may need a jacket in July.

Background

Having conquered Egypt by 332 BC, Alexander the Great, who was still only 25 years old, commissioned his architect Deinocrates to construct a new capital city on the coast. He chose a site near the small fishing village of Rhakotis as its natural harbour and proximity to his native Macedonia offered significant strategic and commercial advantages over Memphis. It is said that Alexander sprinkled flour on the ground to mark out a street plan, and took it as an ominous omen when a flock of unruly birds disturbed his scatterings. However, what emerged was the first Egyptian city to be built to the Greek design, with two major roads running north–south and east–west intersecting in the city centre and

Ptolemy history in brief

Following the death of Alexander the Great, Ptolemy, governor of Egypt soon gained control of the country. He took the title of king and founded a dynasty that lasted from 323-30 BC. There were 14 monarchs in all, ending with Cleopatra's son but the first three members of this dynasty were the most important.

Ptolemy I, 367-283 BC, known as Ptolemy Soter (saviour) was a great soldier with administrative ability who built roads and canals, founded the famous Library of Alexandria, wrote a scholarly account of Alexander's campaigns and abdicated aged 82 in favour of Ptolemy II 309-246 BC, surnamed Philadelphus, a cultivated man whose court has been compared to that of Louis XIV at Versailles. He was not a soldier but supported Rome against her foes. Ptolemy III 281-221 BC, like his grandfather, was a vigorous warrior and supreme controller of the eastern Mediterranean who reopened the war against the Seleucids. He was known as a just ruler especially noted for his leniency towards Egyptian religion and customs.

The later members of the dynasty were described as decadent and dissolute, due largely to the increasingly incestuous convention of the king marrying his own sister.

the rest of the town built around them in rectangular blocks, as can be seen in almost any modern North American city. A causeway linking the city to the island of **Pharos** created two huge harbours and Alexandria became a major port.

Alexander never saw his city. He travelled to Asia after instructing his architects and eight years later he was dead after allegedly drinking from a poison-laced chalice. The priests at Memphis refused him burial, so his body was sent to Alexandria instead, though the final location of his tomb has never been ascertained. After Alexander's death his whole empire was divided amongst his various generals. Ptolemy I Soter (323-282 BC) started the Ptolemaic Dynasty (323-30 BC) in Egypt, and Alexandria became a major centre of Hellenistic culture, attracting many of the great and good, acquiring significant social, historical, and commercial importance throughout the Graeco-Roman period.

The Greeks integrated well with the Egyptians and created a new hybrid religion known as the cult of Serapis. Cleopatra VII (51-30 BC), the last of the Ptolemies, seduced first Julius Caesar and then his successor Mark Antony in order to retain her crown. Mark Antony and Cleopatra held sway in Egypt for 14 years until they were deposed by Octavian who became the Emperor Augustus.

Tradition has it that the Gospel was first preached in Alexandria by Saint Mark in AD 62. Whatever the accuracy of this date, Christianity was certainly established around this time and Alexandria remained the centre of its theology for three centuries. However, its presence was still sufficiently threatening to the Muslim conquerors three centuries later to make them move their administration and theological capital inland to Cairo. Although Alexandria was still important as a centre of trade its decline as a city was inevitable when the power base, along with the customary baggage of wealth, learning and culture went south.

With the 16th-century discovery of America and the sea route around Africa to India and the Orient, which made the land route via Egypt virtually redundant, Alexandria lost its former magnificence. The Dutch traveller Cornielle Le Bruyn, in 1702, found the city "almost wholly ruinated ... and having but a few houses inhabited". Indeed, the decline

2 Alexandria

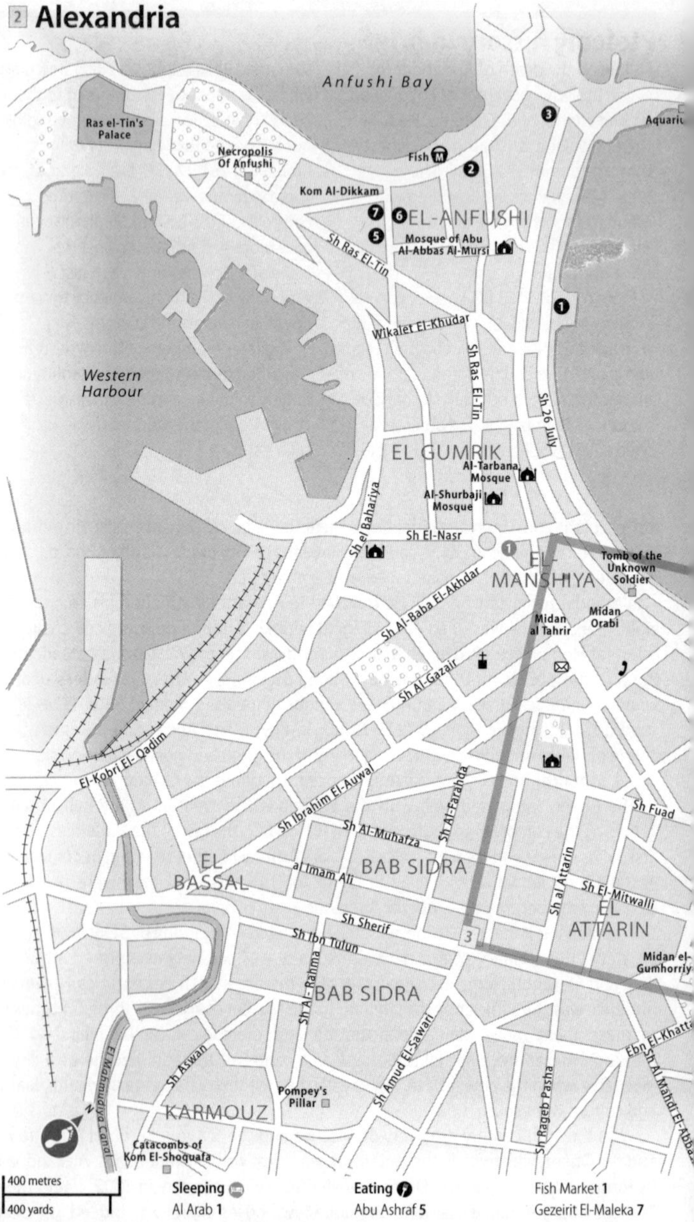
Anfushi Bay
Ras el-Tin's Palace
Necropolis Of Anfushi
Kom Al-Dikkam
Fish
Aquariu
EL-ANFUSHI
Mosque of Abu Al-Abbas Al-Mursi
Sh Ras El-Tin
Wikalet El-Khudar
Western Harbour
Sh Ras El-Tin
Sh 26 July
EL GUMRIK
Al-Tarbana Mosque
Al-Shurbaji Mosque
Sh el Bahariya
Sh El-Nasr
EL-MANSHIYA
Tomb of the Unknown Soldier
Sh Al-Baba El-Akhdar
Midan al Tahrir
Midan Orabi
Sh Al-Gazair
El-Kobri El-Qadim
Sh Ibrahim El-Auwal
Sh Al-Farahda
Sh Fuad
Sh Al-Muhafza
EL BASSAL
al Imam Ali
BAB SIDRA
Sh al Attarin
Sh El-Mitwalli
EL ATTARIN
Sh Sherif
Sh Ibn Tulun
Midan el-Gumhorriya
BAB SIDRA
Sh Al-Rahma
Ebn El-Khatta
Sh Al Mahdi El-Abbas
Sh Amud El-Sawari
Sh Aswan
El Mahmudiya Canal
Sh Rageb Pasha
Pompey's Pillar
KARMOUZ
Catacombs of Kom El-Shoquafa
N
400 metres
400 yards
Sleeping
Al Arab 1
Eating
Abu Ashraf 5
Fish Market 1
Gezeirit El-Maleka 7

Alexandria maps
1 Greater Alexandria, page 342
2 Alexandria, page 346
3 Central Alexandria, page 349

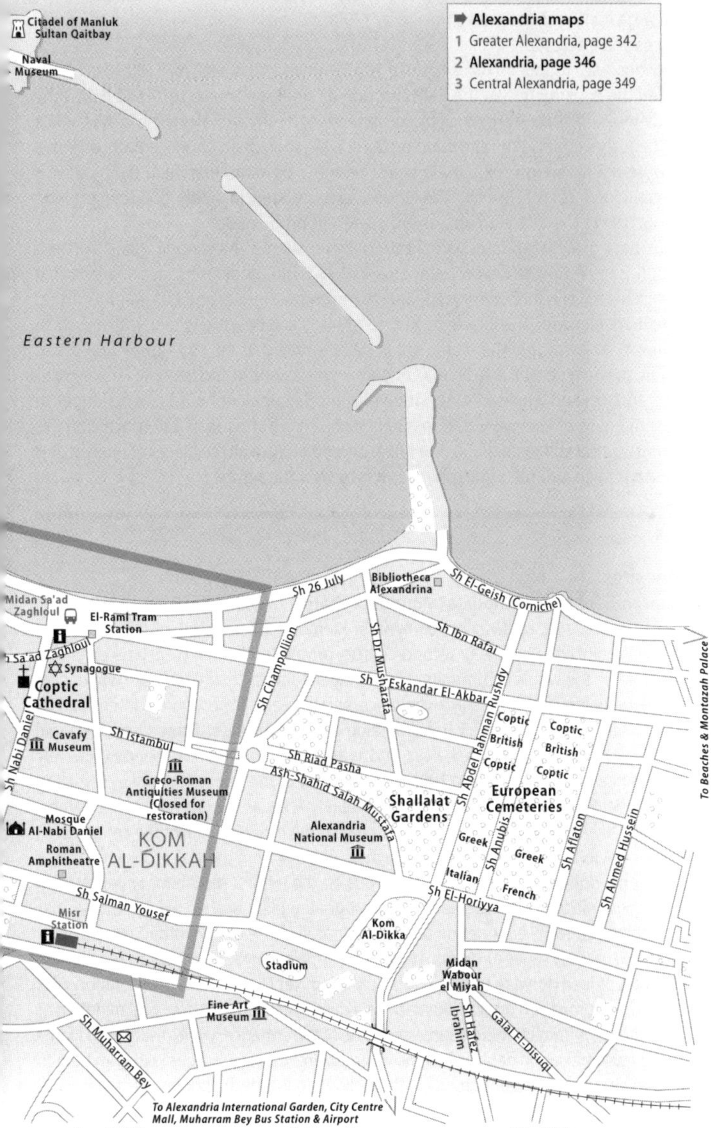

Grand Café **1**
Hosni **6**
Kaddoura **3**
Samakmak **2**
Tikka Grill 1
White & Blue **4**

during the Ottoman period was so great that while Cairo continued to flourish, the population of Alexandria fell to a mere 5000 people by the end of the 18th century. It was easy enough for Napoleon to take the city in 1798, and thus began a new influx of foreign influences and interests.

A saviour was found in the shape of Mohammed (Mehmet) Ali (1805-1848). He organized the construction of the **El-Mahmudiya Canal** starting in 1819 and linked the Nile and Alexandria's Western Harbour, reconnecting the city with the rest of Egypt, while simultaneously irrigating the surrounding land, which had been badly neglected. With a trade route open, foreign trade grew apace with the Egyptian merchant fleet and was later maintained by the British. The British also invested in many building projects including, true to the Victorian obsession, a seafront promenade.

Population growth and industrialization have altered Alexandria since Nasser's revolution (see History of Egypt, page 552) in 1952. The 35 different nationalities that prospered here were soon dispersed, and the ethnic, religious and cultural mesh that once defined Alexandria unravelled. Yet, today it is a modern city still with much to recommend it. Although the outer areas have suffered from too rapid rural-urban migration, the busy central area is small enough to walk around and become familiar with the main squares and landmarks. Although Alexandria's opulent heritage is no longer so obvious, the aura of the town that inspired such literary classics as Lawrence Durrell's *Alexandria Quartet* still remains. So don't rush immediately to all the places of interest. It is as important to absorb the atmosphere as it is to view the sights.

Sights

Ancient sites

The **Catacombs of Kom El-Shoqafa (Mounds of Shards)** ⓘ *T03-484 5800, daily 0830-1630, E£35, E£20 for students, cameras not allowed*, in Karmouz, where many of the houses are 120-200 years old, were originally second-century private tombs that were later extended in order to serve the whole community. Wandering around the half-dark maze where over 300 bodies were interred is quite an experience, and the eerie atmosphere is intensified by the ornate serpents and Medusa heads lurking above doorways. Three styles of burial occurred here – in sarcophagi, on shelves, and as ashes in urns. They have been extensively excavated since their rediscovery in 1900 – another case of the stumbling donkey revealing a hidden underground world. A large spiral staircase serves as the entrance to the tombs, the third and lowest of which is flooded, and corpses were lowered down the central shaft of this stairwell to be entombed below. The main passage from the stairs runs into a large rotunda with a domed roof. Branching from this on the left is a triclinium, or banqueting room, for those visiting the deceased. The short granite pillar pushed away in the corner once supported a central banqueting table. The caracalla leads off the rotunda to the right, an older and spacious series of rooms where bones (mainly horses rather than human) are displayed. Steps lead down to the main tomb, which mixes Graeco-Roman decoration with Egyptian – in columns and on wall illustrations – demonstrating the successful mingling of the two cultures. A Roman noble guards each side of the entrance, while Anubis and Horus attend the mummification depicted on the walls within. Further passages lead from here to several creepy galleries lined with loculi, the hollows in which the bodies were placed. In places red paint can be found below the niches bearing the name of those encased within. Back above ground is a Hypogeum containing over 30 murals, the beautifully decorated Tigran tomb and the surrounding area is scattered with sphinxes and sarcophagi.

On exiting the catacombs, cross one block in front and turn right down a crowded alley for a short walk through a vibrant vegetable *souk* leading to **Pompey's Pillar** ⓘ *Sharia Ahmed Al-Sawari Kamous, daily 0900-1600, E£20, students E£15*. This most famous icon of Alexandria is a 27-m-high and 9-m-thick column of red Aswan granite topped by an impressive Corinthian capital. In previous centuries, it was clearly seen in its 'solitary splendour' by ships coming into harbour, but nowadays is immersed in an area of cloth markets and blocks of flats. See the *Impressions of Alexandria* exhibition in the Bibliotheca to appreciate how early travellers saw the pillar, when it dominated the landscape to become a symbol of the city. Still a rather bizarre spectacle, its origins are the subject of speculation. It certainly does not originate from Pompey, and is thought to have come from the Serapis Temple (40 km to the west) and to have been erected in AD 300 in honour of Diocletian (AD 284-305). It may have supported his statue. Extensive archaeological excavations surround the site. See the three granite sphinxes among a jumble of columns and Coptic crosses and some underground cisterns to the west of the ridge.

3 Central Alexandria

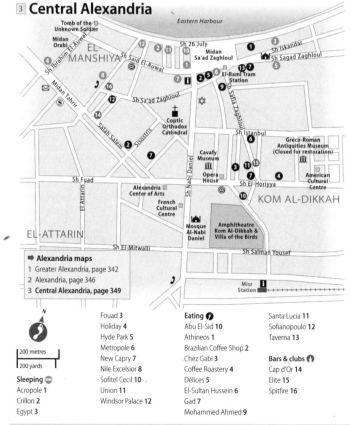

Sleeping
Acropole **1**
Crillon **2**
Egypt **3**
Fouad **3**
Holiday **4**
Hyde Park **5**
Metropole **6**
New Capry **7**
Nile Excelsior **8**
Sofitel Cecil **10**
Union **11**
Windsor Palace **12**

Eating
Abu El-Sid **10**
Athineos **1**
Brazilian Coffee Shop **2**
Chez Gabi **3**
Coffee Roastery **4**
Délices **5**
El-Sultan Hussein **6**
Gad **7**
Mohammed Ahmed **9**
Santa Lucia **11**
Sofianopoulo **12**
Taverna **13**

Bars & clubs
Cap d'Or **14**
Elite **15**
Spitfire **16**

At the very end of the peninsula, in a most imposing position, stands the **Citadel of the Mamluk Sultan Qaitbay** ⓘ *daily 0900-1600, E£25, students E£15, cameras free. Can be reached by No 15 tram from El-Raml (25 pt) or a minibus along the Corniche (50 pt).* It was built in 1479 by Sultan Qaitbay (1468-1496) on the ancient site of, and probably with the stones of, the Lighthouse of Pharos and stands at the far end of the Eastern Harbour as one of a series of coastal forts. A recent restoration has left the entire structure pristine and glowing like lit alabaster, and has opened up floors previously closed to the public. The Citadel is approached up a wide causeway, from which you can pick out the antique granite and marble columns incorporated in the fabric of the west-facing wall. Three sides of the enclosed courtyard were given over to storage and accommodation for animals and troops. The north-facing wall has emplacements for a score of cannon, some still in situ, and the higher look-out tower gives a commanding view over the Mediterranean. The keep houses a small mosque which, unusually for the Delta region, is built in the shape of a cross. The entrance to this mosque is through a huge gateway flanked by pillars of red Aswan granite. Nearby a complex cistern stored water in case of siege. The fort's greatest attraction is the view from the battlements back over the bay

Citadel of Qaitbay

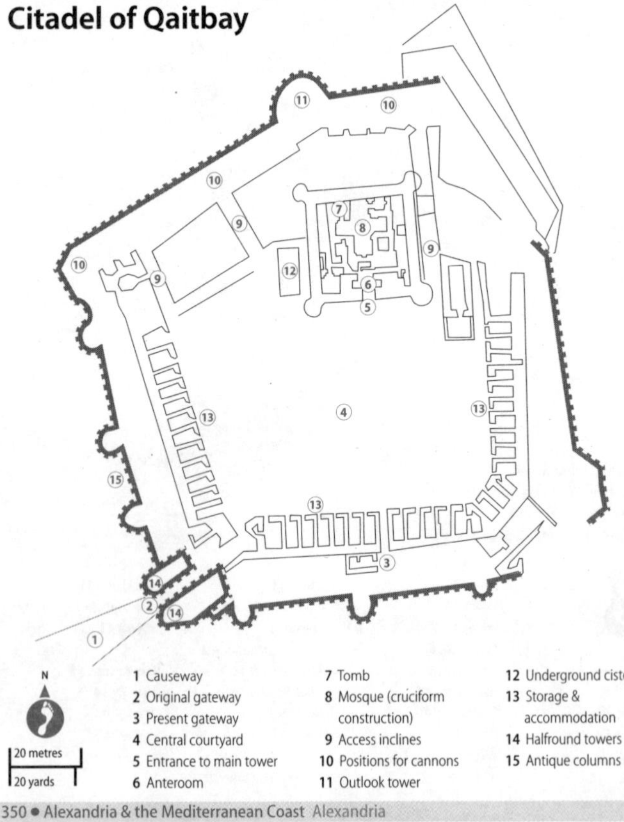

1 Causeway
2 Original gateway
3 Present gateway
4 Central courtyard
5 Entrance to main tower
6 Anteroom
7 Tomb
8 Mosque (cruciform construction)
9 Access inclines
10 Positions for cannons
11 Outlook tower
12 Underground cistern
13 Storage & accommodation
14 Halfround towers
15 Antique columns in walls

toward Alexandria, and these walls are a popular spot for courting couples. Occasionally the citadel is used as a stunning venue for evening dance and music performances. Look out for posters giving details.

The **Necropolis of Anfushi** ⓘ *daily 0900-1430, E£20, E£10 for students, from El-Raml Station trams 15 or 25 toward Ras El-Tin will drop you next to the necropolis,* were first discovered in 1901. These are second- and third-century tombs in which there are some Roman additions. Of the five tombs only three are fit for examination, and the site is rather neglected and might disappoint. The complex is cut into the limestone, which is painted to represent alabaster and marble. You enter the two main tombs down flights of steps. The right-hand stairway is decorated at the turn with scenes of Horus, Isis and Anubis. Below, the right-hand room bears Greek graffiti and naval scenes while the left chamber is more colourful with scenes of deities and a chequer-board pattern above. Inside the second group, the right-hand vestibule has low benches and leads to a chamber while the layout of the left room was modified in the Roman period to house a series of sarcophagi.

North of Misr railway station is the **Kom Al-Dikkah (Hill of Rubble)** ⓘ *daily 0900-1630, E£20, students E£15, camera/video free, tripod E£20,* thought to be the ancient site of the Paneion ('Park of Pan', a hilly pleasure garden), which has been under excavation since 1959. When building began on an apartment block, uncovered instead was a small semicircular 700- to 800-seat **Roman Amphitheatre** with 12 rows of seats faced with Italian marble focussing on a columned stage that has the remains of its mosaic flooring. Some of the seats still show their numbers. A residential quarter with Roman baths from the third century is currently being excavated to the north. This in turn has uncovered the wonderful **Villa of the Birds** ⓘ *separate ticket E£15, student E£8,* an exquisite mosaic on nine panels worth the extra fee for its extraordinary colours. Currently a small area of the site is set aside as an open-air museum showing statues rescued from under the water near Qaitbay.

Bibliotheca Alexandrina

ⓘ *T03-483 9999, www.bibalex.org, Sat-Thu 1100-1900, Fri 1500-1900 (closes at 1400 during Ramadan), E£10, E£5 for students, includes access to the main library, 2 permanent exhibitions and use of the internet (excluding Hotmail and GMail). Tickets are bought at the main booth, on Sharia Port Said a short walk away, where all bags have to be checked in. The Antiquities Museum and Manuscript Museum both cost an extra E£20, students E£10 (tickets purchased inside the library), or a complete ticket costs E£45 (from the main booth). The Planetarium has shows inside a 100-seat sphere for E£10-20, depending on schedule. It's best to visit the Bibliotheca in the afternoon, after the morning and post-lunch rushes, and allow about 4 hrs to see everything.*

Bibliotheca Alexandrina, a 10-minute walk along the Corniche east of El-Raml station, is a striking concrete sun-disc design that rises by the Mediterranean symbolizing the dawn and rise of knowledge that has no end. It took a couple of millennia, but the new Bibliotheca was finally inaugurated in October 2002, a stone's throw away from the site of the ancient library (see box, page 344). The effort, funded by Egypt and other Arab countries, cost US$220 million and is almost a total success story. It boasts the largest open reading room in the world, an inspiring area cleverly lit by windows shaped like eyelids, which allow a perfect intensity and quantity of light for up to 2000 readers. At present it only holds a million books (though there is room for eight million) and there isn't yet a checkout system. An ongoing project is digitizing one million books on Egypt, including the *Description de l'Egypte*, which allows you to zoom in on the amazing details

Western artists in Egypt

A great entourage of scientists, writers and artists accompanied the French occupation of Egypt in 1798, which continued until 1802, opening this hitherto largely protected Islamic country up to a new audience.

The Orientalist artists and writers of the 19th century were confronted in Egypt, and elsewhere in North Africa, with sights and scenes of what appeared to be a startlingly different culture. They recorded what they saw for an audience at home that was eager to catch glimpses of these unknown lands. The *Impressions of Alexandria* exhibition in the Bibliotheca displays many historical (and, at times, fanciful) paintings and drawings of Alexandria as it appeared to these new arrivals to the land. France was the military power in Egypt and much of the Maghreb and it was from here that inspiration came to many of the great French artists – though to indulge their art and their own senses rather than to convey impressions of exotic lands. Some artists such as Baron Gros and Jean-Augustine-Dominique Ingres never actually got as far as Egypt but nonetheless produced fine paintings of the Napoleonic campaigns (viz *The Battle of Nazareth* by Gros).

In addition to the French, the British imperial mission in 19th-century Egypt brought its own harvest of 'Orientalist' works of art. John Frederick Lewis (1805-1875) spent 10 years in Egypt and was a prolific British painter of watercolours of ancient monuments such as Edfu, Upper Egypt and scenes of contemporary Cairo life such as *A Turkish School in the Vicinity of Cairo*.

David Roberts (1796-1864) was another British master of the sketch and oil painting who voyaged along the Nile in 1839, see page 311. His sketches, reproduced as lithographs, are still popular and provide a wonderful catalogue of the major Nilotic sites in the mid-19th century. *Temple at Dendereh* and *The Island of Philae* are fine examples of his work.

Latecomers to Egypt were William Holman Hunt (1827-1910), who was a founder member of the Pre-Raphaelite Brotherhood and who visited Egypt in 1854-1856. His paintings were enlightened by his view of the archaeological sites of Egypt and the Levant, with notable pieces such as *The Great Pyramid* and *Entrance to the Temple of Amun*.

In the 20th century a German modern artist, Paul Klee (1879-1940), was influenced by his travels in Egypt in 1928-1929, from which he took not merely symbols into his paintings but ideas of a holistic universe. His *Legend of the Nile* encapsulated his Egyptian experiences in a single modern picture in pastel.

captured. The premises are also a hub for cultural activities – check their website for a current programme. On the curved wall near the ticket office 4200 jumbled letters from 140 languages symbolize the blending of cultures which the treasures housed in Bibliotheca represent.

Start a visit with the free 20-minute guided tour, available in English, French, Italian and Spanish, which finishes by two excellent permanent exhibitions. **Impressions of Alexandria** features the collection of Mohammed Awad, the contemporary architect, and encompasses photos, drawings and maps of Alexandria's past, including plates from Description de l'Egypte. The text is unusually informative and a lost world is revealed in the beautiful illustrations – although some 1882 sketches of 'typical' Egyptians show how little has changed. **The World of Shadi Abdel Salam**, famed film-maker/renaissance man, contains gorgeously elaborate sketches of set and costume designs that bring the daily life and ceremonies of the pharaohs alive, as well as personal effects and photos. One of his films or documentaries is shown daily at 1430 (or they will screen one especially for you if you're keen, ask at the office at the rear). The adjacent **Manuscripts Museum** holds a facsimile (the original is in Vienna) of the only surviving papyrus from the ancient library, along with Korans inlaid with gold leaf and a New Testament in Arabic. Also on site is the **Archaeological Museum**, containing well-presented antiquities, some of which are from the Graeco-Roman Museum. Finally, there is **Culturama**, a free interactive experience of Egypt's history. It requires five people to run, and is worth doing. Immediately to the west of the Bibliotheca a two-storey food court has sprung up with several cafés providing rooftop seating so you can sip a coffee while enjoying a world-class view over the Bibliotheca and the Mediterranean. There is also a San Giovanni-run café next to the main entrance to the Bibliotheca.

Graeco-Roman Antiquities Museum

ⓘ *5 Sharia El-Mathaf. The museum has been closed for restoration for years and there is still no definite date set for reopening: check the current status with the tourist office on Midan Saad Zaghloul.*

Housed in an impressive building, when the museum reopens it will showcase its fabulous collection of around 40,000 relics from the Graeco-Roman period, mainly taken from local tombs, dating from about 300 BC to AD 300. The most significant cult (even recognized officially by Rome) was that of Serapis, a hybrid of the Greek god Dionysus and the Nile god Osiris. Serapis was depicted as a bull and is directly associated with the ancient Egyptian cult of the Apis bull (see Deities, page 596). One of the museums treasures is a magnificent Apis sculpture in black granite, the inscription dates it at AD 117-138.

Bear in mind that the numbering system of the rooms may well have changed, but highlights to look out for are an example of a Fayoum portrait in **Room 8** (see Fayoum portraits box, page 168) and the mummified crocodile and other pieces from the Temple of Pnepheros, all connected with the crocodile worship practised there, in **Room 9**. **Room 11** illustrates how the mixture of Greek and Egyptian influences produced some interesting sculptures excavated from Athribus near Benha in the Central Delta. On the fragments of tomb paintings in **Room 15** is a *saqiya* or water-wheel with jars to collect and lift the water (see section on the Nile and man, page 575). The Hellenistic sculptures in **Rooms 16-16A** are some of the most worthwhile exhibits in the museum. Look particularly at the Persian god, the lion-headed Mithras; the giant eagle from the Aegean; the graceful figure of Aphrodite and the carefully executed male and female torsos. There are six marble sarcophagi in **Room 17**, most with intricate carvings and one with scenes from the Greek myths, keeping company with what is claimed to be the largest statue ever carved in porphyry (even though it has no head). The tiny Tanagra terracotta figures from Greece displayed in **Room 18a** were associated with burials of young people and provide interesting detail about the dress and fashions of the time. Local Alexandrian excavations provide the displays in **Rooms 19-21**. Look particularly at the figures of the happy gods Bes and Min (see page 596).

Rooms 1-5 are devoted to Coptic artefacts. There are objects relating to St Menas' Monastery (see page 370), including numerous pilgrims' flasks. The textiles have delightful designs – the Copts were recognized as fine weavers. Take time to examine the larger items displayed in the garden, some of the statues are very fine. There are rock-cut tombs in the South Garden and the parts of the Temple of Pnepheros in the North Garden.

Alexander the Great – Greek King of Egypt

Alexander the Great and his army entered Egypt in November 332 BC. He made a sacrifice to Apis in Memphis, taking at that time the twin crowns of Lower and Upper Egypt. He remained in Egypt for some months setting up control of the Egyptian army and founding the city of Alexandria on the coast of the northwest of the Nile Delta. In the spring of 331 BC he marched along the Mediterranean coast to Paraetonium (present-day Marsa Matruh) and thence through the Western Desert to Siwa.

His visit to Siwa was to consult the oracle of Zeus-Amun. The Temple of the Oracle at Siwa (see page 530) is situated to the west of Shali, the new town, at the old site of Aghurmi. There are elaborate stories of Alexander's visit to the oracle temple of Amun but what is clear is that he was received by the priests at Siwa as a pharoah and had a private audience at the oracle. His concern was his expedition against his enemies, the Persians, but he gave no word to his followers on the outcome though in a letter to his mother he promised to tell all when he saw her again (which he never did). Much later it was reported that Alexander was saluted by the oracle as the son of Zeus, which effectively led to his deification and assured him of success in Asia. Certainly, Alexander retained a deep belief in the powers of the god Amun and a flow of gifts continued to come during Alexander's lifetime to the temple priests at Siwa.

He went on in 331 BC to attack Babylon and by 330 BC had control of the Persian empire and thereafter moved his armies into Central Asia and in 327 BC to India. Within 10 years he was master of the known world. He died unchallenged in this role aged 33 on 13 June 323 BC. He was buried in the Egyptian city of Alexandria. (See also box, page 533.)

Alexandria National Museum

ⓘ *110 Tariq Al-Horiyya, T03-483 5519, www.alexmusuem.gov.eg, daily 0900-1400.*

As the Graeco-Roman Museum remains indefinitely closed, this splendid new museum has neatly stepped into the breach. Artefacts are delightfully and properly presented inside an Italianate villa with a small garden, and a visit is a must. The history of the city is revealed chronologically on three levels. The basement contains relics from the pharaonic period, with many finds from Saqqara; look out for the busts of two foreign prisoners in smooth black granite, bearing sad expressions of resignation. There is also a fine sandstone head of Akhenaton, the rebel pharaoh. All pieces have been well chosen and are in an excellent state of repair, beautifully lit to highlight the detail on statues' clothing and hair braiding. The ground floor covers the Hellenistic age of Alexandria, and particularly striking is the white marble statue of local deity Serapis, larger than life, curly-locked and bearded. A huge mosaic with Medusa's head at the centre, discovered during excavations for a cinema, dominates one wall, and some finds from the underwater excavations at Abu Qir include an opaque bronze mirror and delicate jewellery that would have adorned a bride. Upstairs is a collection of Islamic and Coptic artefacts, and a chance for a close inspection of the lamps (or, as they are labelled, 'lambs') that hang in mosques and brightly painted glass bangles that have lost none of their lustre since the 10th century. The skillful weaving of both the Copts and Persians is clearly demonstrated. All in all, it is an excellent museum to visit and of a size that's not too overwhelming.

Other museums and sights

The **Cavafy Museum** ⓘ *4 Sharia Sharm El-Sheikh, open Tue-Sun 1000-1500 (Sun and Thu until 1700), E£15.* Lying to the east of Sharia Nabi Daniel in an alley just north of Tariq El-Horiyya. It is marked with a plaque, ask around for *Al-Mathaf Cavafis*. This is an atmospheric little museum housed in the building where the great Alexandrian poet Constantine Cavafy spent the last 25 years of his life, until his death in 1933. Two of the rooms have been arranged with his household furniture and a rare collection of his books and manuscripts, giving an idea of the place when he was in occupation. It's one of those quaint dusty places that Alex does so well.

The **Royal Jewellery Museum** ⓘ *21 Sharia Ahmed Yehia Pasha, Gleem, T03-582 8348 (behind the governor's residence), daily 0900-1415 and 1700-1815, E£30, students E£15. Has toilets and a small gift shop. Take a tram to El-Founoun El-Gamila from Midan Raml.* This wonderfully restored enormous cream villa (in an area crammed with beautiful villas in varying states of disrepair) originally belonged to Fatma El-Zahra, granddaughter of Mohammed Ali, and was one of King Farouk's palaces. It now houses a glittering collection of treasures on two floors. Apart from the jewels, statues and paintings on display, the mansion itself is of equal interest, containing 10 stained-glass doors and many stained-glass windows depicting romantic scenes of 18th century Europeans. The parquet floors have intricate foliate inlays and the ceiling lamps are works of art. The two bathrooms, cordoned off but on view to the public, are an inspiration. In the ladies, the tiles depict 1930s nymphs surrounded by flamingos, peacocks and other elegant birds, while the gents is decorated with Gallic fishermen and borders of seagulls. The items in the collection considered the most important include: Princess Shivakiar's platinum crown inlaid with diamonds and pearls; Queen Farida's Boucheron tiara encrusted with diamonds and other pieces of jewellery to match; and King Farouk's exquisite Indian chess set enamelled and inlaid with diamonds (note the miniature paintings on the base of each piece). This list is just the beginning of the catalogue.

Mahmoud Said Museum ⓘ *6 Sharia Mohammed Said, Ganaclis, T03-582 1688, open Tue-Sun 1000-1800, E£20, students E£10. Check with the tourist office on Midan Saad Zaghloul before heading out there as the museum was recently closed for restoration. Take a tram from Midan Raml, 25 mins, to San Stefano or Ganaclis, or a minibus along the Corniche (50 pt).* A beautiful, intimate collection opened in 2000 to celebrate Said, a pioneer of Egyptian modern art. Set in the artist's former home, a suburban villa that makes a peaceful haven, the museum features a wide array of Said's work. Sultry nudes and his portrayals of women echo Orientalist works in their vivid use of colour, while portraits of the artist's family and friends are more sombre. An interesting depiction of the inauguration of the Suez Canal and a 1937 scene of the Corniche at night allow a glimpse of Egypt past, and the artist's paintbrushes, easel and some personal effects are displayed in the foyer. Upstairs are pictures by Seif and Adham Wanely, contemporaries of Said, although these are frustratingly undated; downstairs there is a modern art museum with well-presented lively works that are also worth a quick viewing.

The **Museum of Fine Art** ⓘ *6 Sharia Manesce, near Alexandria Stadium, T03-393 6616, www.fineart.gov.eg, Tue-Sun 1000-1300, 1500-2000 on special exhibit days, free.* This airy well-lit space used to have a permanent exhibition of 20th-century Egyptian painting, now housed in the Mahmoud Said Museum basement, while the upper floor is dedicated to temporary exhibitions that are sometimes excellently presented, depending on who is curating them. The nearby ateliers are worth checking out (closed Sun) to see Alexandria's artists at work. Ask at the museum for directions.

How plump is the planet?

Eratosthenes (276-194 BC) lived in Alexandria and was the chief librarian at the Great Library. He was an eminent astrologer cataloguing 675 stars as well as a mathematician – but his fame came from measuring the circumference of the Earth.

At Aswan on the Tropic of Cancer at noon on midsummer's day the sun is directly overhead and casts no shadow. Eratosthenes, who was in Alexandria, measured the shadow cast there and was able to work out the angle of the sun's rays on the same day at the same time. Using information gathered from travellers he had previously concluded that the distance from Aswan to Alexandria was about 800 km. He used these two facts to calculate the circumference of the earth as 40,000 km, an error of only 75 km. He went on to work out the distance from the Earth to the Sun and the Earth to the Moon. His calculation of the angle of tilt of the axis of the Earth at 23° 51'14" was truly amazing in its accuracy.

The **Marine Life Museum** and **Aquarium** ⓘ *daily 0800-1500, 0800-2300 in summer, E£5,* near Qaitbay's Fort house, have a rare collection of fish and marine life. The walls of the quirky Marine Life Museum are decorated with plates from the *Description de l'Egypte*, there are gaudy marine dioramas and the narrow museum is dominated by a fin whale skeleton. The museum nestles under the Citadel. If you prefer your marine animals alive then the Aquarium is just opposite. The **Naval Museum** ⓘ *Sat-Thu 0900-1500,* nearby contains artefacts from Roman and Napoleonic sea battles that are likely to appeal more to specialists than to the casual tourist. Nearby on the way to Ras El-Tin is a small fish market where you can buy fish and have it grilled on the spot. This leaves the problem of where to eat it but there are numerous coffee shops around only too happy for you to sit and eat if you buy a drink from them afterwards. Slightly further round the bay, just opposite Samakmak, boats are still being built by hand on the shore. Visitors are welcome to wander in and watch the builders at work and there is even a shop selling hand-crafted model boats.

Mosques and religious buildings

Inland from the peninsula towards the city centre is the old Ottoman area of Anfushi and some of the most important mosques including the **Mosque of Abu Al-Abbas Al-Mursi** ⓘ *just off the Corniche; all mosques are open from dawn until the last prayer of the day, which is held approximately 1½ hrs after sunset.* Ahmed Abu Al-Abbas Al-Mursi (1219-1287) was an Andalusian who came to Alexandria to join and eventually lead the Shadhali brotherhood. He is the 'patron saint' of Alexandria's fishermen and sailors. His mosque and tomb were rebuilt in 1943 and the current layout is octagonal with Italian granite supporting the roof arches, four domes decorated with floral motifs and a slender 73-m minaret rising in tiers that gives the modern mosque a pleasing weightless aspect. This is one of Alexandria's foremost religious buildings and largest mosque and is well worth a visit. Trams 15 or 25 from El-Raml station will take you there directly, as will a microbus, or it's not far to walk. Note that women are only permitted entry into a room at the back of the mosque and both men and women should dress conservatively.

On Sharia Al-Nabi Daniel is the **Mosque Al-Nabi Daniel**. Although popular myth claims that it houses the remains of the prophet Daniel it actually contains the tomb of a venerated Sufi sheikh called Mohammed Danyal Al-Maridi who died in 1497. Excavation works around the tomb have revealed another tomb from a 10th- or 12th-century Muslim cemetery and for a time it was also thought that this was the site of the Great Soma Temple erected over the tomb of Alexander the Great. Current thinking does not agree, although it is established at least that it is the site of a pagan temple.

In the Ottoman part of the city is the hanging mosque of **Al-Tarbana** on Sharia Farnasa to the east of Sharia Al-Shahid. It has undergone major alterations since it was built in 1685 by Hajji Ibrahim Tarbana. The minaret is supported by two elegant antique columns that stand above the entrance while a further eight columns support the ornamental ceiling. The original Delta-style façade is almost completely obscured by plastering. Nearby to the southeast is the **Al-Shurbaji Mosque**, built in 1757, with an internal layout similar to that of the Al-Tarbana. There have been many modifications and the original minaret is thought to have been destroyed in the British bombardment of 1882, but the *mihrab* is still decorated with the original Kufi inscriptions. It is a peaceful enclave amid the energetic *souk*.

The **Attarine Mosque**, on Mesijd Al-Attarine, dates from the 14th century and stands on the site of the once famous Mosque of a Thousand Columns. It was from here that Napoleon removed the seven-tonne sarcophagus that's now displayed in the British Museum in London.

From the sea, turn left off Sharia Saad Zaghloul onto Sharia Kinesa El-Aqbatto to the **Coptic Orthodox Cathedral**.This recent establishment (1950-1987), presented as a large arched vault, is a fine example of ecclesiastical architecture. It is dedicated to five saints, in particular St Mark whose head is reputed to be buried at this site together with the remains of early patriarchs of the Egyptian church including St Menas (see page 370).

Nearby, and over 145 years old, is the main **Synagogue** ⓘ *69 Sharia Nabi Daniel, Sun-Thu 0900-1300 (allegedly)*. The previous building was destroyed by Napoleon. The synagogue, which serves the tiny community of Jews remaining in Alexandria, is not normally open to the public and the security guards are quite off-putting: but with gentle, polite persistence one might be able to get through into the ornate building. Ask to see some of the 50 ancient 500-1000-year-old Torah scrolls held in worked silver cases in the arc – they are fascinating.

Palaces

To the east of downtown Alexandria lie 17 km of beaches stretching to the beautiful gardens of **Montazah Palace** ⓘ *see below, 1-day passes can be purchased at the gate for E£5, catch a minibus along the Corniche (E£1)*. The palace, a mix of Ottoman and Florentine architectural elements, is now a state guesthouse and closed to the public. It was constructed in the 19th century by the visionary Mohammed Ali as a palace for the engineers who built the barrages that are so important for the irrigation of the Delta. It was later inhabited by King Farouk. The original construction had been halted, and was completed later in the century, on a grander scale, by Sir Colin Scott-Moncrieff.

Further west along the peninsula are formal gardens and then **Ras El-Tin's Palace** (Cape of Figs Palace), which overlooks the Western harbour. It is now the Admiralty Headquarters and is unfortunately closed to the public. It was built so that Mohammed Ali (1805-1848) could review his fleet and was reconstructed in the European Turkish style by Fouad I (1917-1936) to serve as the government's summer seat. It was therefore ironic that his son King Farouk signed his abdication at the palace on 26 July 1952 before boarding a yacht bound for exile in Italy. It can be viewed from the outside.

Beaches

The public beach along the Corniche varies between pleasant and rubbish-strewn, and it is unlikely that you will want to swim here (women certainly would cause a stir). **Stanley Beach** is among the most popular in town and there are all necessary facilities nearby. To the east is the beach at **Montazah Gardens** (see above) and another at Ma'amoura. **Abu Qir**, a small fishing village further east again offers a pleasant beach and the opportunity to sample extremely fresh fish and shellfish.

Gardens and Cemeteries

The **Antoniadis Gardens** ⓘ *near the zoo, daily 0800-1830 winter, 0900-2000 summer, E£2*, was originally owned by a wealthy Greek family and the house is now used for meetings of state. The gardens contain beautiful arrangements of trees and flowerbeds as well as several Greek marble statues. The **Montazah Palace Gardens** ⓘ *open 24 hrs, entrance E£5*, cover almost 160 ha. These formal gardens are a welcome respite from the bustle of the city and stunning on a clear day, the lush greenery being the perfect spot for a picnic. There are lots of cafés and restaurants adjacent to the sea and the beautiful beach makes this the most popular garden in Alex. **Nouzha Gardens and Zoo** ⓘ *Sharia Smouha, open daily 0830-1630 winter, 0830-1730 summer, 25 pt, you can get there directly by taking tram 10 from St Catherine's Square*, has many interesting birds and animals in the zoo. Adjacent gardens have picnic areas. **Shallalat Gardens** ⓘ *closest to the city centre, open 24 hrs, free*, are lovely in parts and have varying levels, rockeries and waterways. **Alexandria International Garden** ⓘ *open daily 0800-sunset, 50-75 pt depending on day of the week*. At the entrance of the Desert Road lies 52 ha of gardens that provide recreational and cultural activities such as water sports. The garden also contains models of famous Alexandria tourist attractions and sites.

The **European Cemeteries** ⓘ *Sharia Anubis, Al-Shatby, Sat-Thu 0900-1500, closed public holidays, free*. The series of cemeteries on either side of Sharia Anubis provide order and peace and are an interesting, if melancholic, diversion. From the sea, the older cemeteries are on the right and the overspill continued onto the left of the street. As well as the Coptic Orthodox enclave (still very much in use) there are Greek (opening times erratic), Italian, French (derelict), Armenian (closed), Jewish and British graveyards. The old Greek mausoleums are greatly embellished and highly atmospheric, while the Italian are adorned with weeping angels and black and white photos of the deceased from the early half of the last century. Alexandria's Catholics are still interred here in modern-day loculi, resembling row upon row of giant concrete filing cabinets. Though the British Protestant cemetery is suitably ascetic, there is a poignant worm-eaten comments book dating back to 1917, in which you can trace the dying out of the last generation of Alexandria's European residents in the 1980s and 1990s. Most of the cemeteries are extremely well-maintained by teams of gardeners. Beautiful drawings by the artist Dessin de Marine Estrangin of the Greek cemetery are displayed in the stairwell at the French Cultural Centre.

Canopus

To the east and 5 km along Ma'mura Bay is Canopus. It bears few traces of the Delta's chief market that flourished before the development of Alexandria and was best known for its **Temple of Serapis**. Canopic jars were produced here, see box, page 234. The motivation for building a city in the area was the Canopic branch of the Nile, which has long since dried up. The city is claimed to have been built by Menelaeus' pilot Canopus on his return from the Trojan wars who was venerated by the local population after his death from a snakebite. Today little remains of the site. The destruction is a recent phenomenon, apparently mainly caused by British occupation during the First and Second World Wars. The ancient remains that have survived, including several statues of Ramses II, are now in the Graeco-Roman Museum in Alexandria. Two abandoned forts to the east of Canopus can be explored.

Further east from Canopus, submerged under the waters of the Mediterranean sea and 2 m of silt are the remains of the ancient cities of **Herakleion**, the main port of entry into Egypt before Alexandria was founded, and **Menouthius**, the centre for the cult of Isis. Recent elaborate excavations have verified the position and extent of these lost cities and produced some fascinating artefacts.

Alexandria listings

For Sleeping and Eating price codes and other relevant information, see pages 26-31.

Sleeping

Alexandria *p342, maps p342, p346 and p349*
Alexandria is Egypt's 2nd largest city and as a major domestic resort for Egyptian tourists, it boasts hotels to suit every budget and taste. The quality of hotel varies considerably in the **C-D** price range, so always ask to see the room first. Besides the main downtown hotels there are others east along the coast toward the exclusive El-Montazah area and beyond. All hotels, whether in the centre or on the Corniche, tend to suffer from traffic noise – day and night.

LL El-Salamlek Palace Hotel & Casino, Montazah Gardens, T03-547 7999, www.sangiovanni.com. Built like an Alpine chalet for the Khedive's Austrian mistress, the Salamlek definitely has class as well as history. Also used as a royal guesthouse/study by King Farouk, it remains exclusive and has retained some of the original furnishing in the suites. It offers all amenities save a pool and benefits greatly from the luxuriant garden location.

LL Four Seasons, 399 Sharia El Geish, San Stefano, T03-581 8000, www.fourseasons.com/alexandria. With silent and plush public areas, rooms with stunning sea views and impeccably trained staff, this is undoubtedly the most luxurious hotel in Alex. Rooms are perfect down to the finest detail, the spa is divine, the gym 24-hr. The dining experience is top class and includes the **Byblos** Lebanese restaurant; **Fish by the sea** (summer only); and great Italian food (see Eating, page 362). Needless to say, it's exceedingly expensive.

LL Hilton Green Plaza, 14th of May Bridge, Somouha, T03-420 9120. Despite the name, the rooms overlook nothing green and the best view is onto the food court, with umpteen restaurant outlets and coffee shops. The complex, fairly new to the scene, fast became young Alexandrians' favourite evening hang-out with its proliferation of stores, food and movie theatres. No need to worry about the noise, all rooms are perfectly soundproofed.

LL Mediterranean Azur, Sharia El-Geish, Rushdi, T03-522 6001, www.azur.travel. An unusual hotel for Alex in being low-rise and directly on the sea, with an arc of posh chalets arranged around a curve of beach. Modern marble foyer and rooms that are attractively fitted out with quality fittings and amenities, all have balcony/terrace (2nd level has better views), there's a Mediterranean restaurant, separate fish restaurant, disco and health club. 2 large clean pools, plus another for kids.

LL-L Sofitel Cecil, 16 Midan Sa'ad Zaghloul, T03-487 7173, www.sofitel.com. Right in the centre of town in the former European quarter, the architecture and ambience harks back to the glory days, though the rooms couldn't strictly be classed 5 star. Past guests include Winston Churchill, Noel Coward, Lawrence Durrell, Agatha Christie, Al Capone and Mohammed Ali Clay. The creaking wire-cage lift won't fail to transport you to centuries past and it will always be 'the' historical place to stay in Alex.

L Metropole, 52 Sharia Sa'ad Zaghloul, T03-486 1465, www.paradiseinnegypt.com. A centrally located landmark hotel established in 1902 and renovated in dramatic fashion. Wonderful Graeco-Roman decor, there's plenty of marble and atmosphere, plus the suites have jacuzzis.
L-AL Windsor Palace, 17 Sharia El-Shohada, T03-480 8123, www.paradiseinnegypt.com. Glorious sea and harbour views from the refurbished rooms, the Windsor is similar to the **Cecil** in its feeling of recent antiquity, but has a more regal air. Worth looking online for a good deal
B Egypt Hotel, 3rd floor, 1 Sharia Degla, El-Raml Station, T03-481 4483. Rooms have been revamped in modern Egyptian style, thus losing some character but gaining TV, fridge and a/c. Breakfast included.
B Ma'amura Palace, El-Ma'amura, T03-547 3450. 75 rooms and suites, good standard, decent views, in the exclusive El-Ma'amura area east of the Montazah Palace. Access to a clean beach, free for guests. A classic place to stay in Ma'amoura. Several Egyptian movies have shot honeymoon scenes in the hotel.
C Dovil Hotel, 274 Sharia El-Geish, Stanley, T03-545 4805. 41 recently renovated clean rooms, overlooking a spectacular view of the new Stanley Bridge across the Stanley Bay. From the hotel roof terrace, you can spot the contents of a military museum not open to the public that includes gigantic ruins pulled out of the sea. Simple, comfortable, breakfast included, recommended.
C Nobel Hotel, 152 Sharia El-Geish, Cleopatra, T03-546 4845. Small but cosy rooms with clean bedding, towels and private baths. Nice sea view from small balconies and very friendly staff. Some rooms have a/c, breakfast included, popular fish restaurant and bar downstairs.
C-D Crillon Hotel, 3rd floor, 5 Sharia Adib Ishak, T03-480 0330. Faded but clean rooms are large and old-fashioned, most have wooden floors and gigantic furniture, the staff are very pleasant and true character has been retained. The reception resembles a museum and there's a choice of either a sea view from the balcony or a private bath – but not both. Breakfast included. 2 tiny singles for E£55.
C-D Union Hotel, 164 Sharia 26th July, Mahatta El-Raml, T03-480 7312. It is still about the best value in town, but over-popularity has resulted in a decline in attitude (some of the staff are very offhand). However, most rooms are spacious and clean and there's a wide price range, depending on how good a view of the sea you desire. Try to book sea-fronting rooms in advance (however, they will probably tell you to ring at 1100 on the day of arrival), though the cheaper side rooms with shared baths have more appealing decor and side sea-views. The shared bathrooms are clean and though each shower has its quirks there is a good hot water supply. Stella is served for a reasonable E£10, breakfast included (but not if you are in the cheapest rooms).
D Holiday, 6 Midan Orabi, El-Manshiya, T03-480 3517. Doubles with intimate bathrooms, price includes breakfast. Not a bad back-up in an interesting part of town, plus views are excellent, high over Midan Orabi with side views of the sea past the Tomb of the Unknown Soldier.
D New Capry, 23 El-Mina El-Sharkia, Midan Saad Zaghloul, T03-480 9310, F480 9703. A mixed bag of 32 rooms that have been modernised in an Arab style, cheaper with a shared (clean) bathroom. Some rooms overlook Midan Saad Zaghloul and the restaurant is good (and cheap) with views over the rooftops, breakfast included. Popular with Egyptian couples, so book ahead.
D Nile Excelsior Hotel, 16 Sharia Borsa Kadema, Manshiya, T03-480 0799. TV, breakfast, fridge, hot water, laundry. Clean uninspiring rooms, some with a sea view window or small balcony streetside, in a good location.
D-E Acropole, 27 Sharia El-Ghorfa Al Togariyya, Midan Saad Zaghloul, T03-480 5980, acropole-hotel@hotmail.com. Clean rooms for a variety of prices depending on

amenities and whether or not there is a view of the Midan. Most have fans, some have fridges/TVs, some have private bathrooms (very much in the room). Popular among city-thriving travellers on a budget, free Wi-Fi, management very pleasant. Breakfast (included) is served in a cheerful space.

E Fouad Hotel, 2nd floor, 1 Sharia Degla, El-Raml Station, T03-487 0684, T03-487 9117. Freshly painted, charming well-lit rooms with a breathtaking sea view of the Eastern Harbour. Located in a historical building. Great value if you don't mind sharing a bathroom, breakfast can be provided.

F Hyde Park Hotel, 8th floor, 21 Sharia Amin Fikri, El-Raml Station, T03-4875 6667. Large rooms are a bit scruffy, but cheap (doubles E£60), with great views and clean sheets. Staff are kindly and if you can get a room overlooking the historic Qua'id Ibrahim Mosque and square, it may be worth the stay. No breakfast.

G Al Arab Hotel, 36 Sharia El-Nasr, El-Manshiya, T03-480 4868. A bit rough, very local, but cheap. For E£25, you can get a bed with clean sheets. All rooms open out to a terrace with a panoramic view of the main port and busy streets. The place has a curious charm to it, but not much else. There's no sign in English, so get yourself to Midan Orabi then ask around.

G Youth hostel, 32 Sharia Port Said, 2 km northeast of city centre, Shatbi, T03-592 5459. E£11 for a dorm bed, a good place to make friends with Egyptian students and always bustling. 3-bed rooms for E£50. Meals available or use of kitchen. Currently accommodation is being offered at 13, Sharia Port Said (on the 1st floor – look for the green triangle) while the main building is being renovated.

Eating

Alexandria *p342, maps p342, p346 and p349*

For an ultra-cheap, totally authentic breakfast experience try one of the *fuul* carts in the street. Alexandria is justly famed for its *fuul* and there are numerous carts dotted around the city from early morning. As they are so popular the food is always fresh and hot. A bowl of beans and bread is standard. You can add lemon, chilli, salads and onion as you please. A good choice if you are sick of Continental breakfasts. Sharia El Mina El-Sharkeya round the corner from the tourist information office usually has 3 or 4 carts in it; handy if you are staying on the Corniche.

TTT Abu Ashraf, 28 Sharia Safar Pacha, Bahari, T03-481 6597. Down the street from **Gezeirit El-Maleka** (see below), the menu and quality of food is comparable, but Abu Ashraf is more famous. The Crown Prince of Denmark is an annual regular.

TTT Abu El Sid, 39 Sharia El-Horiyya, T03-392 9609. Open 1300-0100 daily. Recently opened in the building that housed historic Pastroudis, gone are the charming art deco fittings that inspired Durrell's *Alexandria Quartet*. But the chic Orientalist decor is nevertheless appealing and the purely Egyptian food excellent, as one would expect from this exclusive chain. Sheesha and alcohol on the menu.

TTT Al Farouk, **El-Salamlek Hotel**, Montaza Gardens, T03-547 7999. Egyptian dishes and seafood served in elegant palatial surroundings. Older, experienced waiters provide attentive and classy service.

TTT Fish Market, on the Corniche near Abul Abbas Al-Mursi Mosque, T03-480 5119. Open 1300-1300. Spectacular views overlooking the harbour, this place is always packed and deservedly so. Though it's become a mecca for foreign and local tourists alike, there is no denying the quality and size of the portions, and their salads are still some of the best around. Choose your fish from the iced offerings and enjoy it with a chilled drink.

TTT Kala, **Four Seasons**, 399 Sharia El-Geish, T03-581 8001. Kala stands out for its Fri brunch (E£230 after tax). Every continent is represented and exquisitely presented at this mind-boggling buffet, where you could happily spend all afternoon grazing and still not manage to sample all that's on offer. Definitely worth the treat.

TTT Racoda, Sharia El-Geish, Al-Shatby. A sparkling affair on the Corniche, locals are now saying it's the best place for fish in town. The swanky interior is reflected in the price. A few mins in a taxi from Midan Saad Zaghoul.

₸₸₸ **Samakmak**, 42 Sharia Ras El-Tin, El Anfoushi, T03-481 1560. Open 1000-0200. Italian decor but mainly Egyptian seafood dishes, highly recommended. Good salads come first, then try oven-cooked calamari with butterfly sauce. Cosy inviting atmosphere, though there are no sea views. After lunch go for a wander through the fascinating boat-building area on the beach opposite.

₸₸₸ **Santa Lucia**, 40 Sharia Safeya Zaghloul, T03-486 0332. Open 0900-0100. This darkened venue (on the tour bus circuit) now mixes its continents, so in addition to the famed French cuisine there are takes on Indian and Thai dishes. Not an entirely welcome change, a visit here is more about the history and memories. This is where the classic song *Mustafa Ya Moustafa* made its debut, and there is still nightly piano music.

₸₸₸ **Stefano's**, **Four Seasons**, 399 Sharia El-Geish, T03-581 8001. Probably the best Italian food in Egypt, a diverse menu of antipasto leads into wonderful risottos or pasta, and plenty of meat dishes. The decor is pleasing too, Romanesque with urns, mosaic floors and decorated with a warm palette of reds and pinks.

₸₸₸-₸₸ **China House**, **Sofitel Cecil**, T03-487 7173. The food is authentic enough in this Egypt-wide chain, but it's really the view that is special from the roof of the **Cecil** (though eating outside is really only pleasurable in summer). There is another branch next to San Stefano Mall with dark walls and big brass lamps over the tables, they also do Thai and sushi (12% discount on deliveries), 12 Sharia Mohammed Afeefy, T03-583 9334.

₸₸₸-₸₸ **Mozzarella/Orchid**, Glass House, Sharia El-Geish, San Stefano, T010-883 6615. Daily 0900-0200. Smart and contemporary interior plus outdoor seating by the sea, this dual restaurant is relaxed and popular. **Mozzarella** has an extensive menu of quasi-Italian dishes plus salads/paninis at reasonable prices (E£20-60). **Orchid** is a bit more costly for excellent Thai food (the chef is from Thailand), they also have a sushi menu. Recommended.

₸₸ **Chez Gabi**, 22 Sharia El-Horiyya, next to the Opera House, T03-487 4404. Open Tue-Sun 1300-0030. Good Italian cuisine amid diffused lighting with some trattoria style consisting of much exposed brickwork, old typewriters and artefacts. The first place to introduce pizzas to Egypt in 1979. **Café Royal** bar adjoins. It's down a little alley off Sharia Horiyya.

₸₸ **Gezeirit El-Maleka**, 46-48 Sharia Safar Pacha, Bahari, T03-483 1243. One of the best and most laid-back seafood restaurants in all of Alexandria. For less than E£60 you can have a sample of every item on the menu. Drop the etiquette and comfortably use fingers to pick at the crab and clams. Bustles with people from all walks of life, no sign in English, you'll need to ask around. Highly recommended.

₸₸ **Hosni**, Sharia Safar Pacha, T03-481 2350, opposite **Gezeirit El-Maleka** and under the same management. By far the best grill in the city. An authentic Egyptian haven for carnivores, great value for the price – again no English signage.

₸₸ **Kaddoura**, 33 Sharia Beirum El-Tonsi, T03-480 0405. This has long been *the* seafood place, and although some of the charm has faded with commercial expansion and re-marbling of the premises, the experience is still top-notch. Portions are vast (you're unlikely to want rice), salads are fresh, there's no menu but expect to pay about E£25-50 for a half kilo of fish done Egyptian-style (topped with onion, spices and tomato).

₸₸ **Seagull**, Sharia El-Agami, T03-445 5575. Beachside Egyptian seafood restaurant that is a local landmark. Excellent food and highly recommended, but way out of town in the western industrial area.

₸₸ **Tikka Grill**, on the Corniche in the same building as **Fish Market**, T03-480 5114-9. Open 1300-1300. View overlooking Eastern Harbour. Beautifully presented, spicy Indian grill with salad bar, tender chicken kebabs are great plus more unusual meats such as quail and veal. Serves alcohol.

₸₸ **White and Blue**, **Hellenic Nautical Club**, El-Anfushi, just before Fort Qaitbay, T03-480

2690. Perfect views from the terrace of fishing vessels, the Corniche and the Bibliotheca make this a special location, and the food is excellent too. Hot and cold *mezza*, unusual salads, Mediterranean meat mains and the usual fish selection from the iced display are served by attentive staff. Or just enjoy some *retsina* and enjoy the ambiance. Advisable to book a terrace table anytime, but essential on a Fri.

¥¥-¥ **Taverna**, at El-Raml station, T03-487 8591. Open 0730-0200. Friendly and cheap for Egyptian-style pizzas, pies, meals and sandwiches (fried shrimp is delicious). Very tasty but heavy on oil – it's not a healthy option. There's a cosy restaurant upstairs or you can get takeaway/home delivery.

¥ **Gad**, 1 El-Raml Station, and at Tariq El-Horiyya and Sharia Mohammed Azmy. The original Egyptian stand-up fast-food chain, serves great *fuul* and *ta'amiya* as well as *fiteer* and all the other standard meaty local specialties. Reliably good, clean and cheap.

¥ **Mohammed Ahmed**, 17 Sharia Shakkor Pasha, near El-Raml station, T03-487 3576. Open 0600-2400. A cheap and delicious Egyptian dining experience and a haven for vegetarians.

¥ **Sultana**, next to **Gad** by El-Raml Station (no English sign). Open 0800-1330. You have to eat ice cream in Alex, and this excellent place makes the cones fresh by the minute and has lots of divine flavours to choose from, though mango is the one that sells out.

Cafés

Café society in Alex can't be faulted, whether in a classy period establishment, in one of the thriving *ahwas* noisy with the sound of clattering dominos or at a trendy latte-stop full of students.

Other seaside cafés and *ahwas* are scattered along the Corniche often less than 50 m apart and they are all noisy.

Athineos, by the El-Raml station. An all-time Alexandrian classic, established more than a century ago by a Greek. The old decor remains in the café section.

Brazilian Coffee Shop, 44 Sharia Sa'ad Zaghloul. Open 0730-2200. This very old coffee roaster and stand-up joint has been over-modernized and now has upstairs seating. The branch on Sharia Sisostris, which had retained its period atmosphere and is purported to have the 1st coffee machine in Egypt, is the more appealing of the 2 venues.

Coffee Roastery, Sharia Fouad. If you're longing for a piece of home, this is the best Western-style coffee shop near the city centre and the best branch of the chain. Choose from an extensive menu of coffee, snacks and all sorts of funky fruit drinks. It's a trendy place for the youth to hang out and is hence quite pricey.

Délices, 46 Sa'ad Zaghloul. French-style coffee shop and patisserie. Serves over 40 different pastries in a high-ceilinged, spacious area. Although it's an Alexandria classic, the decor has become a little tacky – but it does have Wi-Fi and alcohol.

El Kobissi On the Corniche just near Kaddoura and marked by flags and palm trees swathed in fairy lights this juice bar is a cut above all the others in town Their fruit salad will set you back US$4 but it is a work of art. Wealthy Egyptians sip their juice in their cars by the kerb. You can sit in a comfy chair and watch life on the Corniche go by.

El-Sultan Hussein, intersection of Sharia El-Sultan Hussein and Sharia Safiya Zaghloul. A typical Egyptian *ahwa* with *sheesha*, backgammon, hot and cold drinks. Spacious and open to the pavement.

Grand Café, El-Kashafa Building, Bahari. Another Western-style café, pleasantly open-air and close to the sea. More of an evening hang-out.

Jungle, Sharia Acasia, behind the Alexandria International Garden. Open-air night café with lots of greenery and jungle-like decor. There is a beautiful swan lake in the middle of the place. Offers *sheesha*, Egyptian food and drinks.

Sofianopoulo, 18 Sharia Sa'ad Zaghloul. Stand-up coffee shop and roaster, pumping the scent of cardamom and coffee out onto the street. Similar to Brazilian coffee shop but manages to retain more of the ambiance of yesteryear. A real gem.

Trianon Le Salon, east end of Midan Sa'ad Zaghloul under **Hotel Metropole**, T03-486 8539. Yet another of Alexandria's classics. Patches of the old elegance remain. Good place for breakfast, they also serve alcohol.

Bars and clubs

Alexandria *p342, maps p342, p346 and p349*
Most of the large hotels have some evening entertainment, though not with the style of the capital. A couple of bars remain that are real relics of Alex's international past and are good places to soak up some atmosphere.
Café Royal, 22 Sharia El-Horiyya, next door to **Chez Gabi Restaurant**, T03-487 4404. Dingy pub atmosphere appeals to some, it's OK for a quiet drink after a night at the Opera House.
Cap d'Or, 4 Sharia Adib, T03-487 5177. Open 1200-0200. Enter the past in this rare survivor of Alexandria's heyday. Dominated by a huge 1919 antique marble bar, the art nouveau interior is covered with mirrors, bottles and memorabilia while the music vies with the sound of the mosque outside. Though the food is only passable (chiefly shrimp or calamari) and you might have to query the bill, it's worth it to imbibe the atmosphere and cold beer.
Dolphin Nightclub, **Helnan Palestine Hotel**, Montazah Gardens, T03-547 3500. Open 2300-0400. Features live singing and belly-dancing.
Elite, 43 Sharia Safia Zaghloul, T03-486 3592. Open 0900-2400. Pleasant little restaurant/bar of checkered table cloths with blue and white art on the walls to match. A great place for loners longing for a quaint reading spot, or for people in search of a quiet place to converse over a beer. The food's not bad and the menu is extensive, and it's nice to be able to look out open windows on the world passing by.
Spitfire, 7 rue de L'Ancienne Bourse, off Sharia Saad Zaghloul. Open 1200-0100. It's a smoky darkened classic, with the prices posted on the wall along with 1001 pieces of bric-a-brac. Lone women might feel a little conspicuous, although there is no real threat. Enquire if their T-shirts are available (they rarely are).

Entertainment

Alexandria *p342, maps p342, p346 and p349*
Look out for the *Alex Agenda*, a free monthly mini-guide that has a calendar of cultural and other events and lists restaurants.

Cinemas

Alexandria has kept some gorgeous art deco cinemas that unfortunately only show Arabic films or terrible American ones; it is better to visit a large mall or join a cine-club to catch a decent movie.
Amir, 42 Tariq El-Horiyya, **Metro**, 26 Sharia Safia Zaghloul, and **Rialto**, 31 Tariq El-Horiyya, are all beautiful environments and you might get lucky with a Hollywood film.
Alexandria Center of Arts, 1 Tariq El-Horiyya, T03-495 6633, shows foreign or Egyptian films at 1800 on Mon.
American Cultural Center, 3 Sharia Pharana St, T03-486 1009, occasionally shows movies.
French Cultural Centre, 30 Sharia El-Nabi Daniel, T03-391 8952, shows arty films.
Jesuit Cultural Centre, 298 Port Said St, near Midan Cleopatra, T03-542 3553, www.jesuit.co.nr, has a cine-club every Sat at 1830 showing quality movies (6-month membership requires 2 photos and E£6).

There are **Renaissance** cinemas inside **Zahran Mall**, T03-424 0844, and **San Stefano Mall**, T03-585 5088, but better is the huge new complex at **City Center Mall**, T03-397 0156, about a E£15 taxi ride away. At the **Green Plaza Mall**, 14th May Bridge, T03-532 5745, there are 6 massive screens but, again, it's a bit of a haul from the city centre.

Concerts and theatre

Alexandria Center of Arts, 1 Tariq El-Horiyya, T03-495 6633, Sat-Thu 1000-2200. Stages free art exhibitions, concerts and theatre in a bustling venue that was the old club of Mohammed Ali.

Alexandria Conference Centre, in the Bibliotheca, has frequent events, and some big names have started to arrive, with ballet, concerts and theatre all catered for. Check www.bibalex.com for details, or you can pick up a free monthly bulletin with the schedule of concerts, visiting exhibitions and public seminars from the entrance of the conference building.
American Center, 2 Sharia Phara'ana, T03-485 2840/1. Open Sun-Thu 0900-2200. Library membership E£5 per year, free internet (Sun-Thu 1000-1500), cultural programmes/ film screenings advertised on site.
El-Anfushi Cultural Centre Theatre, T03-480 4805 and **El-Salam Theatre**, Sharia El-Geish, Mustafa Kamel, T03-543 6543, have performances in Arabic.
French Cultural Centre, 30 Sharia El-Nabi Daniel, T03-391 8952. Sun-Thu 0900-2200. Has regular concerts and theatre in very pleasant surroundings.
Goethe Institute, www.goethe.de/ alexandria. Open Sun-Thu 0900-1500. Library, film screenings and occasional concerts/bands.
Jesuit Culture Centre, 298 Port Said St, near Midan Cleopatra, T03-542 3553, www.jesuit.co.nr. Has regular Arabic music and theatre performances at 2000 in the Garage venue or (in summer) the cooler Italian theatre. Centre open 1300-1900, except Sun. Take a minibus along the Cornice to Cleopatra then walk inland, or tram from El-Raml.
Opera House, 22 Tariq Al-Horiyya, T03-486 5106. Plays, concerts and ballets in the plush interior of the **Sayed Darwish Theatre**.
Puppet's Theatre, Sharia El-Geish, Mustafa Kamel, T03-543 6543.

❂ Festivals and events

Alexandria *p342, maps p342, p346 and p349*
Feb International Book Fair.
Mar International Marathon and the International Yacht Regatta.
26 Jul Alexandria National Day.
Sep International Movie Festival.
Nov (every 2 years) World Alexandria Festival.

O Shopping

Alexandria *p342, maps p342, p346 and p349*
Alexandria has a wide range of shops but lacks the famous *souks* of Cairo. Leather goods including shoes are of good quality and good value. Look also for silk and cotton material and clothes. **Zan'it El-Sittat** in El-Manshiya is a historical shopping spot with a hodge-podge of sewing accessories and cheap beauty items. The **fish market** on Anfushi Bay teems with people and fish, go early when the catch comes in. There is also a shop selling model boats there.

Among the many malls are: **San Stefano Mall**, behind the Four Seasons; **Mena**, Sharia Bilouz, Ibrahimia; **Green Plaza Mall**, at the Hilton Green Plaza Hotel; and the huge new **City Center Mall**, by the Cairo Desert Rd, T03-397 0007-9, which has international clothing outlets.

For fresh fruits and vegetables have a meander around El-Manshiya Sq. Grocery stores are scattered all around the city and are easy to spot. For Western-style supermarkets, there's a **Metro** in the San Stefano Mall and another branch in Cleopatra just after the Cleopatra Tunnel. **City Centre Mall** has the vast **Carrefour** French-owned supermarket, quite an exciting addition for Alexandrians.

Bookshops

Book Centre, 49 Sharia Sa'ad Zaghloul, T03-487 2925. Has the best choice of books in English, French and German.
L'Autre Rive, in the grounds of the French Cultural Centre, 30 Sharia El-Nabi Daniel, T03-497 4151. Open Sun-Thu 1000-2000, Sat 1030-1830. French books (plus a few English titles about Egypt), also sells cards, prints and a few nice handicrafts.
Maarouf 1st floor, San Stefano mall, T03-469 0024, www.maaroufbookshop.com. Open 1100-2300 (Fri from 1200). A small selection

of fiction in English plus books on Egypt. Sells the useful Alexandria Key map.

Monehaat Al Maaref, 44 Saad Zaghloul. Has a small range of English classics and nice coffee-table books.

There's also a row of second-hand bookstalls on Sharia Nabi Daniel, just south of Tariq El-Horriyya, opposite the French Cultural Centre.

Activities and tours

Alexandria *p342, maps p342, p346 and p349*

Beach and water-sports facilities are available at all major hotels. Non-residents can, with permission and a not-always-requested modest fee, use pools at major hotels like the **Sheraton Montazah** and the **Maritim Jolie Ville**. For general sports you could also try:

Alexandria Sporting Club, T03-543 3627/8/9. Golf, tennis, bowling and horse riding but you may need to befriend a member to be able to get in.

Diving and water sports

Alexandra Dive, 24 Sharia 26th July, near Tikka Grill in El-Anfushi, T03-483 2045, T010-666 6514, www.alexandra-dive.com. Organize diving around the ruins of Cleopatra's Empire, a Second World War plane wreck and some 2000 monumental pieces. A 2-dive package from 1000-1400, lunch and water included, costs US$110. It's necessary to book a day in advance, but check the currents and visibility before committing, as the currents and undertow of the Mediterranean can be quite strong. They also rent boats – from small rowing boats (E£20 per half hr) to huge yachts for 20 people (E£2000 for a full day) and can take you fishing (E£25 per person).

Alexandria Yacht Club, adjacent to Qaitbay's Fort, T03-480 2563. Open daily from 0900. Gives sailing lessons (you will need to take membership) and holds an annual regatta in Nov, boats available for hire.

Horse racing

Racing Club, Sharia 14th May, Semouha Club, T03-427 4656.

Tour operators

Atlantic Tours, 40 Sharia Safeya Zaghloul, T03-487 0314, offer fights and tours throughout Egypt.

El Gabry Tours, 23 Sharia Tariq El-Horiyya, T03-482 5956.

Mena Tours, 28 Sharia El-Ghorfa El-Togaria, next to the **Sofitel Hotel**, T03-480 8407, www.mena-tours.net. Long-established Egypt-wide company.

Misr Tours, 28 Sharia Sa'ad Zaghloul, T03-480 8776.

North African Shipping Co, 29 Sharia Ghorfa Torgaria, T03-484 0500, www.nascotours.com.

Thomas Cook, 15 Midan Sa'ad Zaghloul, T03-484 7830, www.thomascookegypt.com.

Transport

Alexandria *p342, maps p342, p346 and p349*

Air

Nouzha airport, T03-425 3996/425 0527 southeast of the city off the main Delta road to Cairo on land reclaimed from Lake Maryut, has 3 flights per week to **Cairo**; 2 per week to **Hurghada** and **Sharm El-Sheikh** (Mon and Fri). **Borg Al-Arab** airport, 1 hr out of the city, T03-459 1486, has flights to **Athens**, **Frankfurt** and many cities in the Gulf.

Note Considering the time wasted at airports and the travel time to and from, it is certainly as quick, and much, much cheaper to travel by bus or train to Cairo.

Airline offices El-Nozha Airport, T03-427 1036, T03-427 2021. **Air France and KLM**, 6 Sharia El-Horiyya, T03-486 8547/8, open Sat-Thu 0800-1630. **EgyptAir**, 19 Midan Sa'ad Zaghloul, T03-486 5701. **Lufthansa**, 9 Sharia Talaat Harb, T03-486 2607, open 0900-1630. **Olympic Airlines**, 19 Midan Sa'ad Zaghloul, T03-482 1014.

Bus

Local Public buses are the most used form of transport by Alexandrians. Tickets cost 25 pt to E£1, depending on how far you ride. They are almost always crowded and are difficult to negotiate. A better option are microbuses, a slightly less rugged way to travel inside the city and you are guaranteed a seat. Journeys along the Corniche are 50 pt-E£1 depending how far, just flag down one of the many passing by. Other microbus hubs are Midan El-Khartoum, Misr railway station and Midan Orabi. Advertise your destination and someone will direct you to the right bus.

Long distance All **West Delta**, T03-480 9685, and **Superjet**, T03-428 9092, buses now arrive and depart from the **Moharram Bey** terminal (in Arabic *El-Mowaf Gedida* or the new terminal) on the outskirts of the city and not from Sidi Gaber as in the past. A taxi costs E£10-15 from downtown to the terminal. The platforms and system are chaotic at present, but Delta buses are serviced from the offices nearest to the entrance and Superjet offices are towards the middle of the station. **West Delta** and **Superjet** buses leave every hour to **Cairo** from 0600-0100, 3 hrs. Tickets cost E£23-27, depending on departure time, for an additional E£12 you can be dropped off at Cairo International Airport. Other destinations are **Siwa**: **West Delta**, 0730, 1100, 1300, 9 hrs, E£27-30. **Marsa Matruh**: **West Delta**, hourly service from 0700-2000, 4 hrs, E£22-25. **Salloum**: **West Delta**, several per day from 0730-0130, E£27. **Port Said**: **West Delta**, 0600, 0800, 1100, 1600, 1800, E£22-25. **Ismailia**: **West Delta**, 0700 and 1400, 4 hrs, E£25. **Suez**: **West Delta**, 0630, 0900, 1430, 1700, 5 hrs, E£25. **Safaga**: 0730 and 1830, via **Ras Ghareb** (E£75), **Zafarana** (E£75) and **Hurghada** (E£80) then **Safaga**, about 9 hrs (E£85). Superjet buses also run to **Libya** 3 times a week, for E£260, and **Saudi Arabia** and **Jordan**. The **Superjet** office at Moharram Bey can provide schedules, T010-2582289, should you wish to take on such a journey overland. **GoBus**, T19567, run buses to **Cairo** from behind Sidi Gaber train station (where they have an office), as well as from Muharrem Bey.

Car hire

Avis, Sofitel Cecil, T03-485 7400. Open 0800-2000. A/c car hire for around E£260 per day including tax and insurance

Taxis

Local Black and yellow taxis can be caught throughout the city. Taxi rides in Alexandria are cheaper than in Cairo, expect to pay around E£5 for a 10-min ride, E£10 for 20 mins, etc. To book a taxi, call **City Cab**, T16516.

Long distance Service taxis depart from **Moharram Bey terminal**, on the outskirts of town. Accessible by minibus from the Corniche (75 pt), Midan El-Gumhoriyya (50 pt) or taxi (E£5-10) the terminal serves all North Coast tourist destinations. Drivers call out their destinations. Vehicles leave when they are full. There is an element of order among the chaos. Counting from the gate: Stand 1 **Cairo** (E£25); 2 **Suez**; 3 **Salloum** (E£25) and **Marsa Matruh** (E£16); 4 **El-Alamein** (E£6.50); 5 **il Hamam**; 6 **Borg El-Arab** then **Abu Mina** (in Arabic- Deir Mari Mina) (E£4), **Rashid** and **Wadi Natrun**. Be warned that although getting to these destinations is very simple and often more convenient and cheaper than the bus, getting back can be harder especially in winter. If you want to visit Abu Mina as a day trip from Alexandria you may need to pay for a taxi to a bus station if there is no sign of a service taxi when you are ready to return or hitch. There are other service taxis to Cairo from near Sidi Gaber railway station throughout the night, leaving when full, listen for the men shouting 'Misr' by the coffee shop to the left of the station, E£25. They also go from just outside Misr railway station.

Train

Alexandria has 2 train stations. The main **Misr Station**, T03-427 4423, is in the city centre. **Sidi Gaber Station** is to the east, about a 15-min taxi ride from El-Raml tram station. Trains to and from Cairo stop at both stations. To **Cairo**, there are many slow non-a/c trains each day, stopping everywhere en route. Tourists, however, will be directed to the 1st- and 2nd-class a/c ticket office to the left of platform 1. The **Espani** train is direct and fast, departing 0700, 0815, 1100, 1500, 1930 and 2215 (2 hrs 40 mins). The **Faransawi** makes 3 stops, departing 0600, 1000, 1300, 1530, 2000, extra trains during summer on Thu, Fri, Sat at 2030 and 2130 (1st: E£46; 2nd: E£29; 3 hrs). It is possible to book advance tickets in Alexandria for the sleeper trains from Cairo to **Luxor/Aswan**, which leave from Giza daily at 2000 and 2110, US$60 per person for an actual bed in a cabin. From Jun-Sep there is a west-bound train to **El-Alamein** and **Marsa Matruh**, leaving at 0600, but you're better off taking the bus.

Tram

Local Trams go from El-Raml station just to the east of Midan Sa'ad Zaghloul. A cheap way (25 pt) to cut long distances across the city and a scenic way to travel if you can afford the time. They run from dawn until 2400. Popular tram routes are: No 15 from El-Raml Station to **Ras El-Tin**; No 25 from Sidi Gaber to **El-Raml Station** and Ras El-Tin; Nos 1 and 2 from El Raml east to Victoria, No 3 from St Catherine's Sq to **Moharram Bey**; No 10 from St Catherine's Sq to **El-Nozha**; No 16 from St Catherine's Sq to **Karmouz**.

Directory

Alexandria *p342, maps p342, p346 and p349*

Banks Central branches of **Bank of Alexandria** at 59 Sharia Sa'ad Zaghloul and 6 Sharia Salah Salam, open Sun-Thu 0830-1400. **Bank Misr**, 9 and 18 Sharia Talaat Harb. **Banque du Caire**, 16 Sharia Sisostris and 5 Sharia Salah Salam. All have cash machines, and further ATMs are easy to spot all over the city. Foreign banks include: **American Express**, 10 Sharia Beatrice Lumumba, T03-395 0918; **Citibank**, 95 Borg El-Silsila, El-Azarieta, T03- 4875236; **NSGB**, 240 Sharia El-Geish, Roshdi, T03-545 2352; **Thomas Cook**, 15 Midan Sa'ad Zaghloul, T03-484 7830, for changing TCs. **Embassies and consulates** **Denmark**, 20 Sharia Peatrice Lumumba, T03-490 6000. **France**, 2 Midan Orabi, T03-487 8477. **Germany**, 5 Sharia Kafr Abdu, Roushdi, T03-486 7503. **Netherlands**, Sharia Mohamed Mas'oud, T03-422 4877. **Spain**, 101 Sharia El-Horiyya, T03-393 9185. **UK**, 3 Sharia Mena, Rushdi, T03-546 7001. **Immigration** **Passport Office**: 25 Sharia Talaat Harb, T03-484 7873, for renewing visas (same day, much less stressful and crowded than the Mugama in Cairo, take 1 photo and photocopy of passport), on the 1st floor, open Sat-Thu 0800-1400. **Internet** Cyber cafés are cheap at around E£3-4 per hr. A convenient place is **MG Net**, 10 Sharia Shohada, with f ast connection and plenty of computers. **Language courses** Regular Arabic Course at the **Arabi Center for Arabic Studies**, 6 Roman Museum St, T/F03-485 8843, www.arabi-center.com. **Medical services** **Egyptian-British Hospital**, Sharia Mohamed Baha' El-Deen El-Ghatwari, Semouha, T03-420 7230. **German Hospital**, 56 Sharia Abd El-Salam Arif, T03-584 1806, www.germanhospital.net. **Somouha Medical Centre**, Sharia 14 May, Semouha, T03-427 2652. **University Hospital**, Kolleyet El-Tib St, T03-486 1861. **Post office** The main post office is next to Misr Station, in the new building to the right of the entrance, open Sat-Thu 0800-2000, T03-496 0088. There's also a convenient office at El-Raml tram station, open till 2100, and at Sidi Gaber train station, T03-546 5169. **DHL**, 14 Sharia Omar Lutfi, Sporting, T03-427 1148. **FedEx**, Sharia 281 El-Horiyya, Sporting, T03-427 2312. **Telephone** There are **Menatel** telephones on every street, cards can be purchased from supermarkets, pharmacies and kiosks for denominations of E£5, E£10, E£20. International calls can be made from the telecom exchange at El-Raml Station, open 24 hrs, and the telecom office opposite Misr Station. International calls from hotels are trouble free but are slightly more expensive. Calls are always cheaper after 2000.

West to Libya

→ *Colour map 1, A2/3.*

From Alexandria, the Mediterranean Coast stretches 500 km west to the Libyan border passing through El-Alamein, Alexandria's local beach resorts of El-Agami and Hannoville, and the new beach resorts of Maraqia, Marabilla, Sidi Abdel Rahman and Marsa Matruh (from where a road leads inland to the Siwa oasis, see page 528), before finally arriving at the Libyan border near Salloum. For the first 30 km a series of developments, more attractive to stay in than to look at, lie between the road and the sea. » *For listings, see pages 375-378.*

Beach resorts west of Alexandria

El-Agami and Hannoville

About 20-25 km west of Alexandria are these two beach resorts, popular with wealthy Egyptians, which tend to be packed during weekends, especially in the summer. They can be reached easily and cheaply from Alexandria by bus, service taxi, or microbus, which leave El-Gumhoriyya and Moharram Bey station every 10-30 minutes.

Abu Sir

Abu Sir, 43 km from Alexandria, is halfway between Alexandria and El-Alamein. Here the important but neglected archaeological site of **Taposiris Magna** dating back to the 27th Dynasty stands to the south of the road. Remains include a necropolis, two temples, a 10th-century church and the lighthouse. In the Ptolemaic period a string of beacons lit up the coast from Pharos in Alexandria to Cyrenaica in Libya. The **Borg Al-Arab** (Arab Tower) just to the east of Abu Sir, is the sole survivor. The 17-m-high lighthouse has the same three-tier construction as Pharos but is just a tenth of the size. The cylindrical top collapsed but it still gives an accurate impression of the appearance, if not the scale, of the Wonder at Pharos. The ancient temple dedicated to Osiris was of Ptolemaic design except for the gate at the east, which had a more traditional pharaonic structure. The series of colonnades are thought to resemble Karnak temple.

A second temple was discovered here at the beginning of the century by Italian archaeologists. Dedicated to the ibis, the sacred bird of Egypt, this was hewn out of the rock and is well enough preserved for the illustrations of birds and animals on the walls to be quite clear today. There is much concern, however, about the continuing deterioration of the buildings due to erosion; the dampness and salt in the atmosphere being harsh enough to make some places of critical concern.

The mound has been excavated – following the discovery during the Second World War of an engraving – and it is here that the necropolis is buried, parts dated as Graeco-Roman and others going back to the 27th Dynasty. All the sarcophagi found here were anthropoidal in shape. Abu Sir was once an important coastal town, surrounded by great walls that have long since crumbled, so now only the gates remain. From the top there is a beautiful view over the Maryut marshes to the sea.

Abu Mina

Abu Mina, 48 km southwest from Alexandria and about 15 km inland from Abu Sir, beyond the new town of Mobarak, was once the most important destination in the east for Christian pilgrims, thanks to **Deir Mari Mina**, one of the largest Coptic monasteries.

St Menas, an Egyptian-born Roman legionary, was martyred in Asia Minor in AD 296 for refusing to renounce Christ. He had rather a bad time: legend has it that first they tore off the soles of his feet, then poked out his eyes before pulling out his tongue. None of these assaults prevented him from standing up to address the crowd. In the end the Emperor himself struck the fatal blow and the body was placed in a lead coffin and sunk out at sea. The coffin was washed ashore, discovered by passing Bedouins and loaded on to a camel. He was buried here when the camel carrying his coffin would go no further. When miracles occurred at the site of his tomb the news travelled across Christendom, via the camel trains, that the tomb of Abu Mina and the Holy Waters nearby could cure sickness and suffering, and his sanctity was assured. Successive emperors built temples and basilicas around the shrine but when the waters dried up in the 12th century the town fell into decay. Excavations have revealed the remains of the basilicas and shrines and much of the surrounding pilgrim town. Most pilgrims left carrying a small amount of healing water in a small clay bottle – marked with the image of a St Menas and two kneeling camels. Saint Menas' day is now celebrated on 11 November. Pope Kyrollos started a new monastery in 1959 and it rises like a white marble mirage above the arid desert. There is a church dedicated to the Virgin Mary and a cathedral where St Menas himself now rests having been transported from the original old monastery. The semi-excavated ruins of the older monastery are 3 km away and can be visited. Most of the artefacts found here are now in a museum in Frankfurt. There is a simple wooden church which is still used by the 120 monks on certain holy days and contains relics of St Menas. The new monastery has a refectory which dispenses free *fuul*, bread and super-sweet tea to all visitors. Ask at the gate to see if one of the English-speaking monks is on-site. If they are they will be happy to spend time telling you the story of St Menas and his gory demise.

El-Alamein → *For listings, see pages 375-378. Colour map 1, A3.*

El-Alamein, 106 km west of Alexandria, owes its fame to what was, until the 1967 Arab-Israeli war, the largest tank battle in history. In July 1942, the Allies under Britain's Field Marshal Montgomery halted the German-Italian advance towards the Nile and – in British eyes, if not in those of the Soviet troops at Stalingrad – turned the course of the Second World War. Winston Churchill later wrote, not entirely accurately, "Before Alamein we never had a victory. After Alamein we never had a defeat". (See box, page 373.)

Ins and outs

El-Alamein is roughly an hour's journey from Alexandria. From Alexandria, you can hop on any bus or service taxi bound for Marsa Matruh (or a service taxi direct to El-Alamein itself in summer) and disembark near the War Museum at El-Alamein. This is up a side road shortly after a blue sign over the road saying 'Marsa Matruh 184 km'. If you are in a vehicle bound for Marsa Matruh then it is a good idea to start telling the driver that you want to get out soon when you see the 184 km sign. (Other roadside distance signs are out of sync on this stretch of road. The distances on adjacent signs can differ by as much as 5 km.) There is a Greek memorial with Egyptian and Greek flags at the bottom of the side road. El-Alamein-bound vehicles usually turn round here anyway. The side road which is where you will find the War Museum, Commonwealth Cemetery as well as several cafés and shops runs parallel and to the south of the main coastal highway for about 3 km before rejoining it. To get back to Alexandria or carry on to Marsa Matruh, you'll have to flag down a vehicle, as there's no bona fide station or depot in town. Alternatively, you can hire a taxi in Alex. A car from a tour company, plus guide and lunch, costs around US$50 per person. If you plan to visit the German and Italian cemeteries over 10 km further along the road it is advisable to have some sort of transport arranged unless you are prepared to walk or hitch. Make sure you have plenty of water if you decide to walk. There is very little public transport along this stretch of road and no cafés or shops at all after you pass Max 24 just after the War Museum.

Sights

El-Alamein was the site of the battle between Germany's Afrika Korps and the Allied Eighth Army that turned the Second World War in the Allies' favour. It is the closest that the Axis forces got to the Nile Valley. The results of the encounter can be seen adjacent to the town in the huge **war cemeteries** (about 11,000 were killed and 60,000 wounded). The Greek war memorial is passed first. The **Commonwealth cemetery** ⓘ *daily 0700-1630 but books of remembrance not available Fri, free*, lies to the east of the town to the south of the road. The silent lines of over 7000 white headstones commemorating those who fought and died supporting the Allied cause produce an intensely sobering effect. 'Gone but not forgotten', 17-year-old Sikhs and New Zealanders lie among Malays, Kenyans and endless rows of others far from home. Despite the sombre surroundings, the gardens here encourage migrant birds – and birdwatchers. The **German cemetery** lies about 8 km to the west of the town between the road and the sea. German and Egyptian flags and a sombre black gate mark the entrance then it's a 1-km walk up to the cemetery. Here, in a sand-coloured building resembling a castle, there are 4200 graves in a single vault with stark, simple black metal statuary. The man with the key will see you coming, he lives nearby. The **Italian cemetery**, the only one in North Africa, lies a further 4 km west of the town on the sea side. The white memorial tower is dedicated to 4800 Italian soldiers, sailors and airmen. Just walk in. There is also a small museum. All signage is in Italian but the photos and maps are self-explanatory. There are well-maintained toilets at all the cemeteries. You may need to ask for a key.

A **museum** ⓘ *daily 0900-1500, E£20, E£10 for students,* to the west of the settlement contains maps of the campaign and some of the uniforms and weaponry used in Egypt by both sides. A clever map/model display with lights and commentary (choose your language) explains the North Africa campaign. There is also information here about the war between Egypt and Israel in 1973.

Note El-Alamein has a fairly good beach but heed the danger signs for unexploded mines. Large parts of the coast and the desert are fenced off because they are still littered with them. Use common sense and keep to the main roads and beaches.

Marsa Matruh → *For listings, see pages 375-378. Colour map 1, A2.* *Population: 25,000.*

Marsa Matruh (290 km northeast of Siwa, 288 km west of Alexandria and 512 km northwest of Cairo), has been transformed from a sleepy village (noted for sponge fishing) and minor port into a popular, low-grade, summer resort for domestic tourists. Despite the government's attempts, it has not – and is unlikely to be – turned into the new mass tourist Mediterranean beach destination for European package tours. Although there are some good beaches and the Mediterranean really is astonishingly luminescent in this area, the little town with a population of around 25,000 has none of the holiday facilities and nightlife that tourists expect. It's very much a town where travellers merely break their journey on the way to Siwa – expect to endure a surprising and irritating degree of attention for a place so unfrequented.

Ins and outs

Getting around Marsa Matruh's streets are on a grid pattern with most of the hotels being on the streets behind and parallel to the Corniche. Buses and service taxis stop at the main station, 2 km south of the Corniche. Taxis to the town centre cost E£5-8, shared pickups cost 50 pt. The airport is a taxi ride to the south of town, though flights only operate in the summer. Getting around town is easy, it's small enough to walk. For places a bit out of the way, such as Rommel's Beach, hire a taxi for around E£5. ▸▸ *See Transport, page 377.*

Information There's a **tourist office** ⓘ *corner of Sharia Iskanderiya and the Corniche, T046-493 1841, Sat-Thu, 0900-1530.* Staff speak English and are reasonably well informed about accommodation and surrounding sites.

Sights

There are really only two reasons for visiting Marsa Matruh: either to travel to the magnificent desert oasis at Siwa (see page 528) or to rest en route to Libya. Most of the area's much-advertised beaches are a severe disappointment. Except for the **Beau Site** and the adjacent **Riviera Beach Chalets** hotels' private beaches, all other beaches in town are public. Western women who choose to swim – in either clothes or swimwear – are

Marsa Matruh

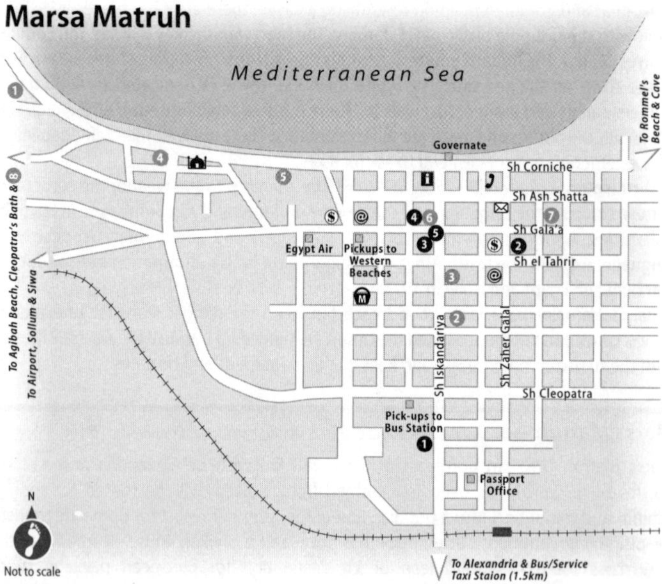

Sleeping
Beau Site **1**
Cleopatra St Giovanni **8**
Ghazala **2**
Hamada **3**
Negresco **4**
Reem **5**
Riviera Palace **6**
Rommel House **7**

Eating
Abdu Kofta **2**
Abu Rabi **1**
Hammo Al-Temsah & Abo El Araby **2**
Kamana **4**
Panayotis **3**
Sahara Grill **5**

The Desert War 1940-1943

Italy, the colonial power in Libya at the outbreak of the Second World War, invaded Egypt in the closing weeks of 1940 thus beginning a long period of fighting between the Axis powers and Great Britain in North Africa. Italian, and later German, strategic plans were the displacement of Great Britain from Egypt, the destruction of Britain's imperial communications links through Suez, and the opening up of the Middle East oilfields to Axis penetration. The local Arab and Berber peoples of North Africa played a remarkably small role in events. The damage and disruption of the war were considerable and their negative effects (see box, 'Mine peril', page 26) persisted for many years after the end of hostilities.

The Italians were soon expelled from Egypt and much of eastern Libya but were powerfully reinforced in Tripolitania in February 1941 by the arrival of German troops and armour that rapidly drove the British back to the Egyptian frontier by April. The German formations were led by General Rommel with skill and audacity. Air power favoured the joint German-Italian armies in the earlier part of the campaign. Rommel's eastward advance was slowed by the protracted resistance of the garrisons, first Australian then British and Polish, at Tobruk. Meanwhile, the main armies fought pitched battles around the Libyan–Egyptian border until Rommel withdrew temporarily in December 1941. He used his improved lines of communication in the west to prepare a counter attack and pushed east again as far as Gazala, near to Derna, in January and February 1942 and, after a pause, into Tobruk and deep into Egypt in June, though his advance was finally held at El-Alamein after a fierce battle. Rommel made a final attempt at Alam Halfa east of El-Alamein to push aside British and Commonwealth forces and break through to the Nile Valley in August 1942 but failed in the face of strong defensive effort and his own growing losses of men and equipment.

The balance in the desert war changed in mid-1942 as the allies gradually won superiority in the air and had more freedom of movement at sea. The Germans and Italians began increasingly to suffer from shortages of equipment, while the health of Field Marshal Rommel gave rise to concern. On the allied side, General Montgomery took over leadership of allied forces and began a build-up of the Eighth Army sufficient to overwhelm the well-trained and experienced Afrika Korps. Montgomery opened his attack at El-Alamein on 23 October 1942 and after 11 days of hard fighting the Axis army was beaten back and retreated by rapid stages to the west to make a last, unsuccessful, stand in Tunisian territory.

bound to experience problems from both voyeurs and exhibitionists who are more used to seeing fully clothed Egyptian women swimming and sunbathing. However, the town is quite clean and modern, if a little soulless. The Corniche has been repaved and palm trees planted, and the attempt to solve the litter problem on the beaches closest to town is making noticeable progress although this is still an issue and even if you just paddle you should watch out for broken glass or crushed drinks cans.

The beaches in the town's bay are protected by two sand spits that will eventually meet and form a lagoon. Lido Beach and Mubarak Beach curve around the bay to the west

Border essentials: Egypt–Libya

Sollum–Al-Bardia

There are many buses (E£12) and service taxis from Marsa Matruh to Sollum each day, the journey takes three to four hours. **Hotel Al-Ahram** is for those who get stuck. The border is 12 km west of Sollum and service taxis, E£5, are available. Service taxis go to Al Bardia. The bus from here goes to Benghazi. If you plan to drive in a private car, come armed with passport and car papers, as you will be stopped at numerous checkpoints en route.

Visas for Libya Not readily available at the border and best obtained in Cairo. They cost US$100 and are valid for three months, but must be used within 45 days.

of the town while in the other direction Rommel's Beach and its small military museum in a cave hewn in the rock, are beyond the small port almost facing the town on the landward side of the east spit. **The Rommel Museum** ⓘ *daily 0900-1500,* gives details of this famous field marshal in the Second World War campaign and the gloomy cave was his actual headquarters. Offshore from the beach is a red buoy, 25 m beyond that is a sunken German U-boat, which can be seen if you have suitable gear.

The better and cleaner beaches are those to the west of the town: among them is **Cleopatra's Bath** (7 km), where Cleo supposedly soaked in a rock engulfed by Mediterranean turquoise, a sort of natural tub. Surrounded by cliffs, the sea gets deep very suddenly. **Cleopatra St Giovanni** (see page 375), the nicest and newest hotel in town, recently opened its doors here. There's also **El-Obeid beach** (20 km) with beautiful white sand that resembles sugar and **Agibah beach** (28 km), the most striking of all, is surrounded by dramatic rock formations and totally undeveloped. It's aptly named – *Agibah*, 'a wonder', and is worth visiting out of season.

Marsa Matruh to Salloum

This last 215 km of road to Libya has little to recommend it. There are some new developments and sundry Bedouin settlements. Sidi Barrani was the site of fierce battles during the Desert Campaign of the Second World War. There is a hotel here, slightly to the west of town, between the petrol station and a mosque just south of the main highway if you happen to get stuck. **Salloum**, the ancient port of Banaris, is the border town with Libya. The **British and Commonwealth cemetery** ⓘ *Sat-Thu, 0800-1430*, at the eastern side of the town has 2060 war graves. If you visit the cemetery you will most likely meet the delightful gardener, Issa. His family have looked after the cemetery since it opened in 1946. He will offer you delicious Libyan tea and access to a clean toilet. It's almost worth the trip to Salloum just to meet him. Apart from the cemetery there are a smattering of very basic cafés around the bus station, a bank with an ATM, three hotels of varying standards, a post office and then the road to Libya.

West to Libya listings

For Sleeping and Eating price codes and other relevant information, see pages 26-31.

Sleeping

El-Alamein *p370*

As there is only 1 hotel in El-Alamein itself, we recommend making the day trip from Alexandria or if stopping en route to Siwa, try **D Max 24**, just past the museum, T012-310 0006, which is convenient but overpriced. It's really more of a café than a hotel. A single room without breakfast is E£100. Double E£150.

The following hotels are some distance from El-Alamein:

AL El-Alamein, Sidi Abdel Rahman, El-Dabaa Centre, west of El-Alamein, T046-468 0140. 209 rooms and villas with own seaside barbecue, very good standard, located on the beautiful white sands of the isolated upmarket resort of Sidi Abdel Rahman about 25 km west of El-Alamein, early reservations essential, open Apr-Nov. Prices have been reduced slightly but rooms and general facilities are not really up to price standard.

AL Jaz Almaza Beach Resort, Km 37, on the road to El-Alamein, T046-439 0000, www.solymar-hotels.com. Another reliable Solymar, it's the only hotel with a pool near Matruh, 40 km away. All the top-class facilities you require plus the Mediterranean could not be more gloriously blue from here. Worth looking online for a deal.

Camping

There are no specific campsites but the El-Alamein Hotel has a tourist camp equipped with all necessary services.

Marsa Matruh *p371, map p372*

Considering Matruh is the prime beach destination on the Mediterranean Coast, there are relatively few nice places to stay. Most hotels are overpriced for what's on offer, and except for the newest of the bunch, are growing rough at the edges. Still, during the domestic tourist season that peaks in Jul and Aug, it's wise to make reservations if you are particular about where you want to stay. Many hotels close in winter; the ones listed below are open all year round.

LL-L Cleopatra St Giovanni, Cleopatra Beach, 7 km west of town, T046-494 7600, www.sangiovanni.com. Beautiful private beach, rooms are lovely on 3 levels. Rate includes half board with open buffet, bar, disco, live band on beach in the evenings, coffee shop, fully equipped health club, jet skis for rent.

L-AL Beau Site, Sharia El-Shatee, 1 km west of Sharia Iskandariya on the Corniche, T046-493 2066. Fully equipped rooms have a view of a splendid blue lagoon and the biggest private beach in town. The food is excellent. Rates include buffet breakfast (half board in summer). Probably the nicest place to stay in Matruh. Day guests can use the beach for E£40/50 in winter/summer. They have a sister hotel at Cleopatra Beach that is only open in the summer.

L-AL Riviera Beach Chalet, Sharia El-Shatee, next to Beau Site, T046-493 8818. Rates include breakfast. Beautifully clean rooms have basic cooking facilities as well as a/c, immaculate bathrooms and a swing chair on the porch. There is a smallish private beach and a lush garden area. Day guests can use the beach for E£15/45 in winter/summer but it is small. Staff are very friendly here.

AL-A New Lido El-Corniche, T046-493 4515. A good choice if you are travelling in a group or as a family. They have clean apartments with 2 bedrooms (4 beds), balconies, sea view, kitchen, bathroom and fan. Right on the Corniche with an internet café and pool hall underneath.

AL-A Riviera Palace, Sharia Gala'a, Market Area, T/F046-493 3045 and T046-493 0472. With fresh white paint and a vaguely nautical theme (the foyer is designed to look like a ship with port holes and railings), this hotel has airy rooms with all the extras. A downtown 3-star hotel, good restaurant and pleasant café, no alcohol. Popularity with tour groups sometimes makes rooms unavailable during summer months, big discounts out of season.

AL-B Negresco, 6 El-Corniche, T046-493 4492. Clean rooms with a/c, TV and fridge. A decent hotel with good views, but like most hotels in the area, considerably overpriced. Breakfast buffet included. Open year round, discounted to E£350 in winter.

A-D Reem, El-Corniche, T046-493 3605. Unspectacular but clean, airy rooms, all with sea view and balcony. Good value in winter, compared to the real budget choices. Breakfast included.

B-C Arous Il Bahr 19 El-Corniche, T046-493 4420. Spotlessly clean rooms all have bathrooms, a/c and sea views.

D Rommel House, Sharia Gala'a, T046-493 5466. Large rooms with large balconies and bathrooms, plus fans, TV and fridge. Nothing special, breakfast included. Prices are reduced slightly in winter.

G Ghazala, Sharia Alum Rum, T046-493 3519. Extremely run down, due to the charming manager's advancing years. Bathrooms, which don't have hot water, are grim but the fairly clean rooms have a wash basin, E£15 for a dorm, E£25 for a private room.

G Hamada, 32 Sharia Iskandriya at Sharia Tahrir, T046-493 3300. The most popular stop for backpackers. Shared bathrooms have hot water but private ones don't, both cost the same. It's quite clean and the staff pleasant. Be aware that the airier, larger front rooms are incredibly noisy at night.

Camping

It's possible to camp for free on the beaches in the town of Marsa Matruh but it's essential to obtain permission from the tourist police first since the beaches are patrolled by armed officers at night. Camping without permission is risky.

Salloun *p374*

E Hotel Sert On the main road just after the cemetery, T046-480 1113. This is the newest and most expensive hotel in Salloum. A single room with bathroom and fan is E£90 without breakfast. It is very clean but the rooms disappointingly don't have a sea view. There is also a restaurant and coffee shop here. These are more geared to tourists than the ones in town. If your budget won't stretch to the Sert then there is a decent, clean hotel right at the bus station.

G El Gezira. There's no phone. Rooms have fans, shared baths are spotless and there is hot water.

G Wahada El Arabi, down a side street between the main road and the sea, 3 blocks east of the bus station, the sign is in English, , no phone. Here E£5 will get you a bed in a grubby room. The shared bathrooms don't have hot water but there is a pleasant roof terrace overlooking the sea and the staff are very friendly. Single women should probably avoid this one.

Eating

Marsa Matruh *p371, map p372*

Besides the hotel restaurants, most notably the **Beau Site** and **Riviera Palace**, there are a few cheap downtown restaurants around the intersection of Sharia Iskandariya and Sharia Gala'a. The best option for cheap eats in winter is probably Sharia Omar Mokhtar, west of Sharia Iskandariya between the Hamada and Ghazala hotels. (To the east of Sharia Iskandariya it is called Sharia Gol Gamal.) Here you can find several fish shops where you can get fish grilled on the spot and restaurants offering chicken or *fuul*. There are also a couple of fruit and veg stalls around here and, of course, coffee shops. Best of all, on the central reservation of Sharia Tahrir, right outside the Hotel Hamada after the dusk prayers a magical stall appears serving delicious, piping hot, freshly-prepared *bileela*, a starchy-porridge type dish. Utterly delicious and warming.

🍴🍴 **Abdu Kofta**, Sharia Tahrir at Sharia Zaher Galal. Serves decent *kofta* and kebab. A good place to experience authentic Egyptian *molokhiyya*, the slimy green soup. Check prices when you order.

🍴🍴 **Hammo Al-Temsah Seafood** and, opposite, **Abo El Araby**, Sharia Zaher Galal. Both serve up deliciously spiced grilled and fried fish and prawns. Open late and recently refurbished.

🍴🍴 **Kamana** and almost opposite **Sahara Grill**, Sharia Zaher Galal just east of Sharia Iskandariya. Both serve standard kebab, chicken and kofta with salad and bread. Negotiate the price before sitting down.

🍴🍴 **Restaurant Panayotis**, Sharia Iskandariya. An old-time restaurant on the scene, opened by a Greek family a few generations back. They only serve food during the summer months, but always have cheap beer.

🍴 **Abu Rabi**, Sharia Iskandariya. No seating, but serves all the Egyptian favourites from dawn until late.

Along the Corniche between **Hotel Reem** and the **Negresco** are all the standard chain restaurants; **KFC**, **Hardees**, **Chicken Tikka** but they all close down in winter. There is another cluster of cafés on the corner by the mosque on the Corniche which stay open into the winter but can't be relied on to provide a meal.

Entertainment

Marsa Matruh *p371, map p372*

There are nightclubs and bars in the larger hotels and discotheques at the **Beau Site**, **Cleopatra**, **St Giovanni** and **Radi** hotels, in summer. Marsa Matruh also has a couple of open-air cinemas (closed in winter) and a local circus. One of the cinemas is just near the tourist information office and the other is on the Corniche just east of **Hotel Arous Il Bahr**. Though they only cater to Arabic-speaking audiences the atmosphere and the popcorn may make it a fun experience.

Transport

Marsa Matruh *p371, map p372*

Air

In the summer, **EgyptAir**, Sharia Galaa, T046-493 6572, offers 3 flights a week between Marsa Matruh and **Cairo**. At present, they fly on Sun, Thu and Fri, but check with the tourist office or EgyptAir office to be sure. There are also weekly charter flights in the summer, currently operated by **Thomson** (www.thomson.co.uk), from London Gatwick and Manchester in the UK.

Bus

Local transport to the beaches of **Cleopatra**, **El-Obeid** and **Agibah** leave every 30 mins during daylight from Midan Al-Gala'a during summer. **West Delta Buses**, T046-490 5079, have buses to **Alexandria** every hour from 0700-2400 plus a few during the night (3½ hrs, E£15-26, depending on schedule). Buses to Alexandria can drop you off at **Sidi Abdel Rahman** or **El-Alamein**. To **Cairo**, there are a/c buses at 0730, 1030, 1200, 1530, 2000 and 0200 (8 hrs, E£40-46). It's wise to book your seat in advance. To **Siwa**, there are 4 buses daily leaving at 0730, 1330, 1600 and 1800 (4 hrs, E£12). Occasional buses leave for Salloum each day usually at around 1500 (E£12, 3-4 hrs). In summer, **Superjet** have buses to Alexandria at 1430, and to Cairo at 1100 and 1500.

Taxis and pickups

The more distant beaches to the west can be reached in summer by the service taxis, microbus or pickups that shuttle back and forth (0800-sunset) from Midan El-Gala'a. E£3-5, depending on how far you go. To get back to town, just flag one down from the street. Service taxis are quicker and cheaper but less comfortable than the express buses to **Alexandria**. Taxis to **Siwa** (4 hrs), E£12, leave early morning or in the afternoon to avoid the midday heat. It is difficult but not impossible to take one of the service taxis, which carry Egyptian expatriate workers, to the **Libyan border** (230 km east of Marsa Matruh) via **Sidi Barrani** (150 km) and **Salloum** (220 km) but it is essential to have a Libyan visa, see box, page 374.

Train

There are sleeper trains that run from 15 Jun to 15 Sep between Marsa Matruh and **Cairo**, via **Alexandria**. They leave Matruh for Cairo on Sun, Tue and Thu at 2300 (approx 7 hrs). Railway Station, T046-493 3036.

Directory

Marsa Matruh *p371, map p372*

Banks Banque Misr, on Sharia Galaa and National Bank of Egypt, across the street from EgyptAir, Sat-Thu, 0900-1430 and 1800-2000, both have ATM.

Immigration Passport Office: T046-493 5351. **Internet** Easy to find, try Fr3on at the western end of Sharia Galaa, 1st floor, open 24 hrs, E£2 per hr, or **Speed Net**, Sharia El Tahrir near Hamada Hotel.

Post office Sharia Ash-Shatta, east of Sharia Iskandariya, Sat-Thu, 0900-1500.

Telephone 24-hr telephones opposite the post office.

Suez Canal Zone

Contents

Footprint features

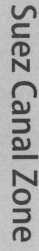

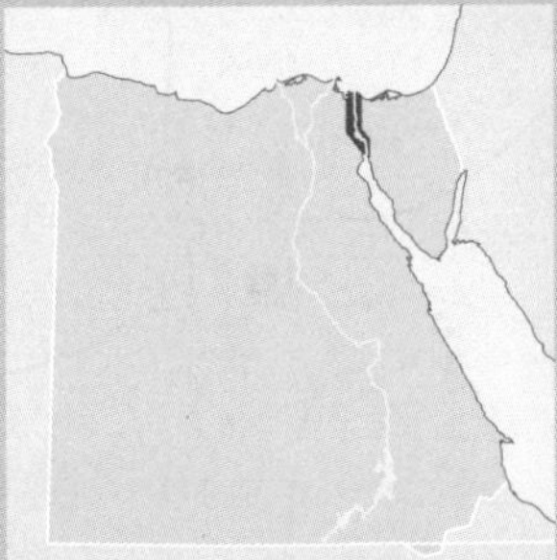

At a glance

Getting around Trains are slow, buses and micros are frequent and faster.

Time required 3-4 days to visit Ismailia and Port Said.

Weather Pleasant and balmy most of the year, though summer is very hot.

When not to go There's no real time to avoid, but if you dislike crazy crowds don't go to Port Said during the Limbo festival in spring.

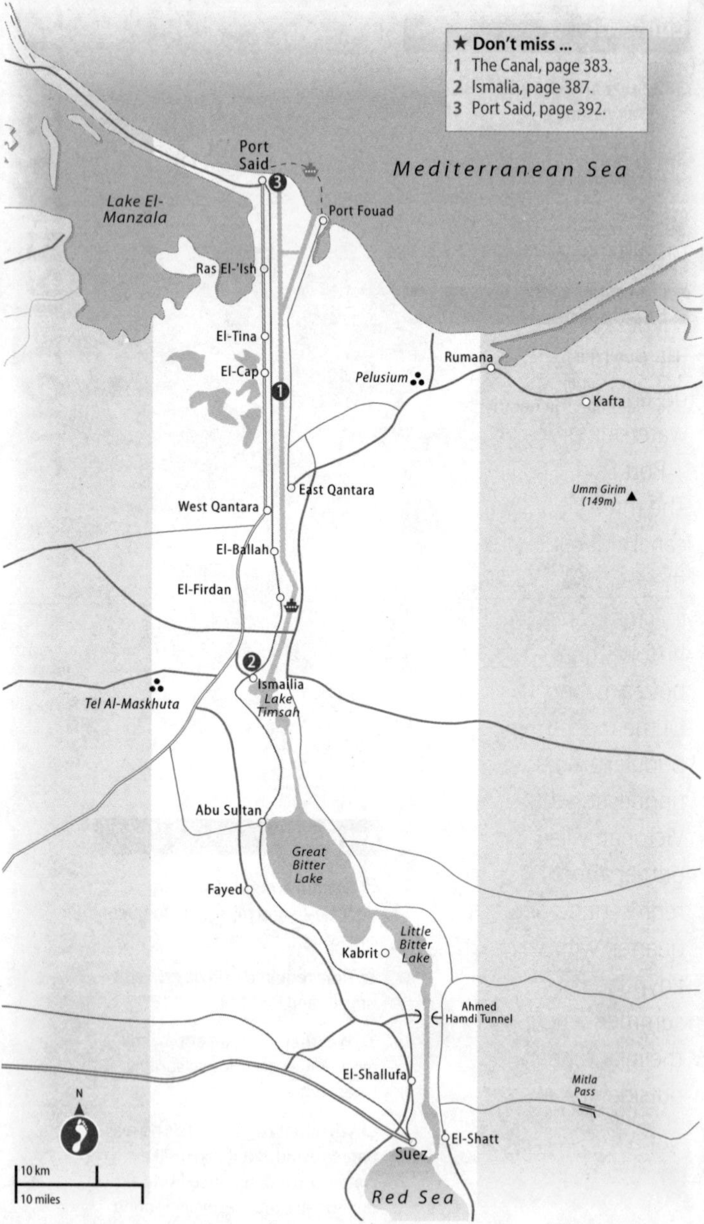
★ Don't miss ...
1 The Canal, page 383.
2 Ismalia, page 387.
3 Port Said, page 392.
Mediterranean Sea
Port Said
Port Fouad
Lake El-Manzala
Ras El-'Ish
El-Tina
El-Cap
Rumana
Pelusium
Kafta
East Qantara
West Qantara
Umm Girim (149m)
El-Ballah
El-Firdan
Ismailia
Lake Timsah
Tel Al-Maskhuta
Abu Sultan
Great Bitter Lake
Fayed
Little Bitter Lake
Kabrit
Ahmed Hamdi Tunnel
El-Shallufa
Mitla Pass
El-Shatt
Suez
Red Sea
N
10 km
10 miles

Although the Suez Canal Zone is not a primary destination for most visitors to Egypt, for enthusiasts of great engineering feats or travellers with time, the detour to Ismailia or Port Said is memorable. We may live in an age where we're less inclined to be impressed by something as mundane as a canal but, seen in context, the Suez Canal was as great a triumph of engineering in the 19th century as the Pyramids were in their day. As one of the world's most heavily trafficked shipping lanes, the canal is among Egypt's greatest riches and is still the greatest navigation route in the world. Convoys of vessels glide along it as if floating on the desert. Viewed from the comfort of a hotel window or the waterside promenade in Port Said, they are fascinating to watch.

Port Said, Ismailia and Suez collectively make up the Canal Zone. The three cities essentially grew up with the construction of the canal alongside the British colonial presence that hung about until the 1956 war. Soon after, the region's proximity to Israel resulted in a temporary mass departure. With such a dramatic and distinct history, the area has a feel that sets it apart from much of Egypt, but each city has managed to retain its own separate character. Of the triad, Ismailia, with a sleepy romantic town centre more popular among local honeymooners than foreign tourists, is unquestionably the prettiest. Streets are lined with well-kept Victorian villas and gardens brim with flowers. Port Said is a much grittier, more decrepit place with remnants of colonial architecture representing almost every European nationality, an old 'native quarter' with endless *souks*, and a local music scene to spice up Egyptian nights. The canal cities are particularly inviting in the summer, where the cool waterside breezes offer respite from the inland heat, and all three cities offer the best fish restaurants outside of Alexandria.

Suez and around

→ Colour map 2, B4. Population: 490,000.

Suez's (Es-Suesi) friendly demeanour compensates in part for what it lacks in looks. The city was badly hit by an Israeli siege in 1973 and though the mess has been cleaned up, with the aid of funds from the Gulf countries, and mines have been cleared, Suez is still a litter-blown town, more of a transit spot than a destination. The only canal city to have ancient roots, during the Ptolemaic period Suez was known as Klysma and in the Middle Ages the walled city, then known as Qulzum, became prosperous thanks to the burgeoning spice trade and the many pilgrims bound for Mecca. In the 15th century it became a naval base and the opening of the Suez Canal in 1869 ensured the city's survival and development. Today it is one of Egypt's largest ports and an important industrial centre producing cement, fertilizers and petrochemicals using domestic oil from the offshore fields in the Gulf of Suez. It was, until recently, the chief departure point for hajj *pilgrims but, since the* El-Salam Boccaccio 98 *ferry sank in February 2006, with the loss of over 1000 lives, the ferry services now chiefly run from Safaga and Hurghada.* ▸▸ *For listings, see pages 384-386.*

Ins and outs

Getting around Buses and service taxis arrive at the new bus station on the Suez–Cairo road, about 6 km from the town centre. Taxis to the town centre cost around E£10, or you can take a microbus for 50 pt from the microbus hub, which is a 10-minute walk from the bus station. The train station is just over 1 km from the Arba'in market, off the main Sharia El-Geish that leads to most hotels and becomes the causeway to Port Tawfiq. Microbuses run around the centre and across to Port Tawfiq for 25 pt. ▸▸ *See Transport, page 386.*

Information The **tourist office** ⓘ *the canal on Sharia Sa'ad Zaghloul, T062-319 1141, officially open 0800-2000, although the conspicuous absence of tourists means they are more likely to be open 1000-1800, Fri 1000-1400,* have useful maps of the city and helpful staff. **Tourist Police** ⓘ *T063-319 3543.*

The City

Some of the streets are too dirty to enjoy walking through but the coastal quarter and the garden in the newly reclaimed area east of the stadium are spruced up and relatively free of litter. Take some time to wander around **Port Tawfiq** where the European influence is strikingly apparent, with neat privet hedges, wide pavements and delightfully quaint colonial houses (commandeered by important Canal Authority employees) and the magnificent Governor's House. Sharia Canal is the perfect vantage point for up-close encounters with the immense tankers that glide past, their hulls painted with Chinese, Danish and other names, the traffic flowing in one direction only each day. Look out for the monument made of four captured US-made Israeli tanks on the northern edge of the peninsula. In the evening, a stroll along Sharia El-Geish across the causeway towards Port Tawfiq can be delightful. For a bit more bustle and a taste of contemporary Suez, the **Souk Arba'in**, west of the centre, is a straggling maze of vendors and stalls in which it's worth searching out the fish market to get a fresh grilled snack. The market gets going at 0700.

Suez Canal

Since its completion in 1869 the Suez Canal, which at 167 km is the third longest in the world, has enabled ships to pass from the Mediterranean to the Indian Ocean via the Red Sea without sailing around the continent. There had been many previous attempts to build a canal including those during the 26th Dynasty by Necho II (610-595 BC) and the Persian Emperor Darius I (521-486 BC). Napoleon's engineers vetoed their own plan to build the canal after calculating (incorrectly) that the sea level in the Red Sea was 10 m lower than in the Mediterranean. Although it was the British who discovered their error in the 1840s, it was Ferdinand de Lesseps, a young French vice-consul in Egypt, who finally persuaded the Khedive Said Pasha (1854-1863), son of Mohammed Ali Pasha, to begin work at the north end of the canal in 1859. Thousands of workers died moving over 97 million cubic metres of earth, before its completion in 1869 during the rule of his successor the Khedive Ismail.

The lavish opening ceremony on 17 November 1869 was attended by many European dignitaries and a party of tourists organized by Thomas Cook, but things soon began to go wrong. Given Britain's constant opposition to the project, it was ironic that it was to her that the bankrupt Ismail was forced to sell his 44% holding in the Suez Canal Company for £4 million (the amount loaned to Disraeli's government by the Rothschild bankers), before the much more enthusiastic French could make an offer. The canal soon produced very significant profits which were being remitted to Britain rather than being ploughed back into Egypt and in the 1920s and 1930s the strategically vital Canal Zone was one of the world's largest military bases.

Since 1945 the canal has been the subject of both important political disputes and serious armed conflicts. Britain reluctantly agreed to remove its troops in 1954 but refused to give a larger share of the revenues to Egypt. The West vetoed World Bank loans to help finance the construction of the Aswan Dam because of the Soviet Union's offer to rearm Egypt after its 1948 defeat by Israel. In reply Colonel Gamal Abdel Nasser nationalized the Suez Canal on 26 July 1956. Britain and France used the pretext of an agreed and pre-planned Israeli invasion of Sinai in October 1956 in an attempt to reoccupy the Canal Zone but were forced to withdraw when the US, wanting to break Britain's stranglehold on the Middle East and get a slice of the action in the region itself, threatened to destabilize the British economy.

The Six Day War with Israel in 1967 caused new damage to the recently rebuilt canal cities and the canal was blocked by sunken ships. Egyptian forces briefly broke through the Israeli's Bar-Lev Line on the east bank of the canal during the Yom Kippur War of October 1973 before being forced back and it was not until 1982 that the Israelis withdrew from the East Bank and the canal reopened.

With access to the canal denied, super-tankers were built to carry vast quantities of crude oil around Africa. These huge vessels are unable to pass through the canal which, in order to face fierce competition from other routes, is now being widened.

Suez Canal in numbers

- About 7% of all sea-transported trade goes through the canal. 39% is shipped to and from the Far East; 35% is shipped between the Red Sea and Arabian Gulf ports; 20% shipped to or from India and Southeast Asia
- Total length of canal: 193 km
- Canal depth: 21 m
- From Port Said to Ismailia: 78.5 km
- Width at water level: 300-365 m
- Navigable width: 180-205 m
- Maximum permissible draught for ships: 17.68 m

Suez and around listings

For Sleeping and Eating price codes and other relevant information, see pages 26-31.

Sleeping

Suez *p382, map p385*

There's plenty of accommodation in Suez, but hotels are often overpriced; cheaper ones get busy and you may have to shop around.

AL Green House, Sharia Port Said, T062-319 1553, greenhouse-suez@hotmail.com. Slightly fading rooms with balconies have a/c, minibar, satellite TV and Gulf views. Like most of the hotels in Suez, the majority of the guests are Egyptians and oil company workers. No bar, but restaurant, *sheesha*, garden and tiny pool (covered in winter). Breakfast buffet included and prices are negotiable.

AL-A Summer Palace, Port Tawfiq, T062-322 1287, www.summer-palace.5u.com. Clean, bright rooms with new furniture have a motel feel and look out onto one of 3 pools. A bit overpriced, the 6 suites are a better deal for what you get. Beers (E£15 for a can) can be had on the terrace with Gulf views or in the bar with billiards, the restaurant is good (Port Tawfiq doesn't have many options) and the staff pleasant. Breakfast included.

A Red Sea Hotel, 13 Sharia Riad, Port Tawfiq, T/F062-319 0190, www.redseahotel.com. This friendly place has clean comfortable rooms with the amenities you would expect for the price. Wood panelling in the public areas give an art deco feel. Ask for a side-view room, from when you can see both the canal and the Gulf from the balcony. Good restaurant, no alcohol, open 24 hrs, has awesome panoramas of the canal. Breakfast included, Wi-Fi available.

E-F Arafat Hotel, Port Tawfiq, T062-319 7992. The cheapest option in the port area, although it's nothing to write home about and you will struggle to find reasonably priced food around here after dark. Some rooms have private bath.

E-F Medena Hotel, 45 Sharia Talat Harb, T062-322 4056. A friendly little place in the thick of things, small garish rooms are crammed with furniture but very clean.

E-F Hotel Sina, 21 Sharia Banque Masr, T062-333 4181. Centrally located, budget hotel though not especially clean. Rooms have fans and TVs. Some have private baths, while shared baths are bearable. Expect noise from the muezzin. It's often full.

F Star Hotel, 17 Sharia Banque Masr, T062-322 8737. Another decent budget hotel that's a bit cheaper than the **Sina** nearby. Rooms are varied in quality and cleanliness. All have fans, some come with private bath.

F Sharia Tariq El-Horiyya Youth Hostel, near sports stadium in front of Hawgag village, T062-319 9069. Women are only permitted to stay in the family rooms (3 beds per room, E£20 per person). Dorm beds for men are E£10. Lockout from 2400-0800. Kitchen available, often noisy.

Eating

Suez *p382, map p385*

Except for seafood, options are limited in Suez. Standard stall food abounds around Sharia Talaat Harb. Around the Arba'in Market you can buy fish and get it grilled nearby for rock-bottom prices, cost depending on weight.

Al-Khalifa, is a particularly good fish restaurant in the town centre where you can pick your own from the day's catch.

Red Sea Hotel, has lots of fish and pasta on the menu – worth considering for the views from the top floor of the hotel.

The Sweet Spot, serves up good *shawerma*.

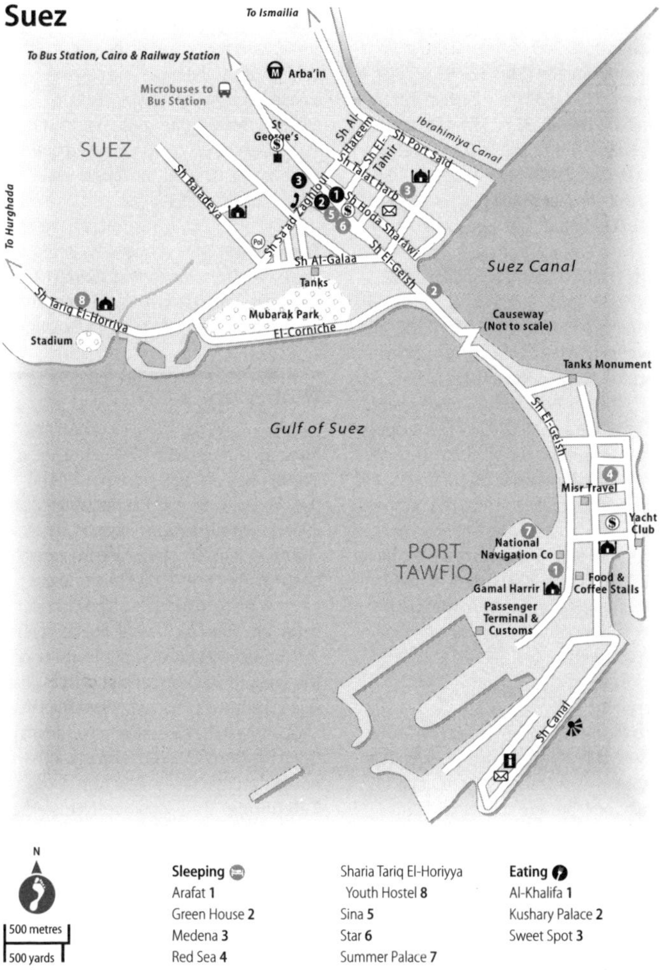

Kushary Palace, on Sharia Saad Zaghloul, round the corner from the Sina and Star hotels. For good *kushary*.

Transport

Suez *p382, map p385*

Bus

East Delta buses, T062-366 4854, leave the terminal (5 km west of the city) every 30 mins between 0600-2000 to/from **Cairo's Turgoman Station** (2 hrs, E£7.50-8.50). Between 0700-1530 there are buses every 30 mins to **Ismailia** (1 hr, E£4-4.50) and to **Port Said** at 0700, 0900, 1100, 1430 and 1530 (2-3 hrs, E£10). Many buses go from 0500-2300 to **Hurghada** (5-6 hrs, E£36-38) via **Ain Sukhna**. It's also possible to head straight to the Sinai from Suez. There are 5 buses daily to **Sharm El-Sheikh** (0830, 1100, 1330, 1500 1800, 5 hrs, E£30), the 1100 bus carries on to **Dahab** (6-7 hrs, E£35) and **Nuweiba** (7-8 hrs, E£35). There is also a bus direct to **Taba** and **Nuweiba** at 1500 (5-6 hrs, E£35). There is 1 bus daily that goes direct to **St Catherine's** at 1400 (4 hrs, E£25). **Upper Egypt** buses, T062-366 4258, have 4 buses daily to **Alexandria** at 0700, 0900, 1430 and 1700 (4-5 hrs, E£25), the morning ones make stops in the Delta but the afternoon ones are direct. They also have 3 buses daily to **Luxor** at 0500, 1700 and 2000 (10 hrs, E£55/61), the 0500 and 1700 carry on to **Aswan** (12 hrs, E£56/66), prices vary depending on the time you depart.

Ferry

Since the El-Salaam ferry disaster in 2006, the vast bulk of ferry services now run from Safaga to Saudi Arabia as bureaucratic hurdles now prevent companies from operating out of Suez. Virtually no passenger ships dock here now. Contact the port, T062-319 1085/6, to see if any ferries are departing for Jeddah, or the **National Navigation Co**, 42 Sharia El-Geish, Port Tawfiq, T062-319 8849, have boats every 3-4 days to Yemboa in Saudi. Bear in mind that the Saudi Arabian Consulate in Port Tawfiq, next to the tourist office, no longer issue visas (available in Cairo only).

Taxi

Service taxis travel to all of the same destinations as the buses and costs are comparable. Though service taxis are speedier, they are often not as comfortable as the a/c buses and will not depart until full. There are plenty of private taxis to run around town for E£3-5.

Train

There are 6 trains run to/from **Cairo** en route to/from **Ismailia** daily, but they're hot and slow. You're better off opting for the bus.

Directory

Suez *p382, map p385*

Banks Bank of Alexandria has an ATM, as does Barclays and BNP Paribas, all on Sharia El-Geish. **Immigration** Passport office: for visa extensions, on Sharia Tariq El-Horiyya, open Sat-Thu 0800-1500. There is also a passport office at the gate of the port. **Internet** There are several internet cafés in town, open 24 hrs, concentrated around the Sina and Star hotels. **Post office** Sharia Hoda Sharawi, 1 block away from Sharia El-Geish, near the causeway to Port Tawfiq. Open Sat-Thu 0800-2000. Also a branch next the tourist office in Port Tawfiq. **Telephone** The telephone office is on Sharia Sa'ad Zaghloul.

Ismailia

➔ *Colour map 2, B4. Population: 285,000.*

Ismailia, 120 km east of Cairo, 90 km north of Suez and 85 km south of Port Said, is the most immediately attractive of the three main Canal Zone cities. Named after Ismail Pasha, Khedive of Egypt, it was built as a depot by the Suez Canal Company in 1861 on the west shore of Lake Timsah (Crocodile Lake), one of Egypt's largest lakes covering 14 sq km. The town is divided by the railway track: the attractive and tranquil Garden City built for the company's European employees to the south; the poorly constructed apartment blocks, financed with Gulf money, to the north. The Sweetwater Canal was dug from its source in Lake Timsah to provide fresh water during the construction of the Suez Canal, and the calm water and sandy beaches of the lake make Ismailia a popular destination for Egyptian honeymooners. The rare desert-weary traveller who ventures here will find the orchard gardens and trees a delight, and the immaculate villas and tranquil boulevards a pleasure to stroll around. There are some excellent fish restaurants in which to while away the evening and a relaxing day can be spent sitting on the beach at the Mercure Forsan Island Hotel watching boats bob by. If you are after high excitement, Ismailia is not the place, but it's certainly ideal for a couple of days of hassle-free downtime. ⏩ *For listings, see pages 386-391.*

Ins and outs

Getting there and around Ismailia's bus station is a few kilometres from town on the ring road across the street from the Suez Canal University, connected to Cairo by frequent buses and services from Turgoman bus station. A taxi to the city centre costs around E£5. The train station is in the centre of town. Sharia Ahmed Orabi, outside the station, runs straight down to the lake. Most hotels are found in close proximity to the train station, while the good fish restaurants are mainly along the bridge south of the Garden City area. ⏩ *See Transport, page 391.*

With its wide tree-shaded pavements, grid-pattern signed streets, and functional traffic rules, Ismailia is a breeze to navigate and most sights can be reached on foot. In summer it's possible to hire a horse-drawn carriage to see the sights. For destinations a bit further away, bicycles can be hired from the streets off Mohammed Ali Quay. Bright orange taxis shouldn't cost more than E£3-5 to get anywhere in town.

Information **Tourist office** ⓘ *T064-332 1078, open Sat-Thu 0900-1400*, is a bit of a trek from the town centre, upstairs in the Mahefezah building, the district authority head office. Hotels in town are often a better source of information.

Sights

The **Ismailia Museum** ⓘ *Sat-Thu 0900-1600, Fri 0900-1100 and 1300-1600, 0900-1500 during Ramadan, E£15, E£5 students,* (established 1932), is in the east of Garden City. This manageably small museum contains some minor ancient Egyptian pieces, including delicate bronze figurines of the Gods, animals and reptiles. There are also several finely painted funerary masks from the Ptolemaic period. However, it is the staggeringly complete fourth-century mosaic (which warns of the evils of wine) illustrating myths from Greek and Roman folklore that is the crowning glory. Note the marble pharaonic-style sarcophagus with a Graeco-Roman head spookily supplanted on it. The museum is an interesting half hour's diversion and worth a visit. Permission is necessary from the museum to visit the Garden of Stelae nearby which holds a few pharaonic remnants, mainly from the period of Ramses II, but they are not wildly impressive and can be seen from the street.

A number of minor sights, although comparatively unimportant, are worth visiting while in town. Next to the Sweetwater Canal is the **House of Ferdinand de Lesseps**, which was at one time a quirky museum but is now functioning as a government guest house and is closed to the public. His private carriage is mounted nearby, at the southern end of Sharia Orabi, while many of his personal possessions and his diaries remain inside, but you'll need permission from the Suez Canal Authority in order to visit.

Ismailia

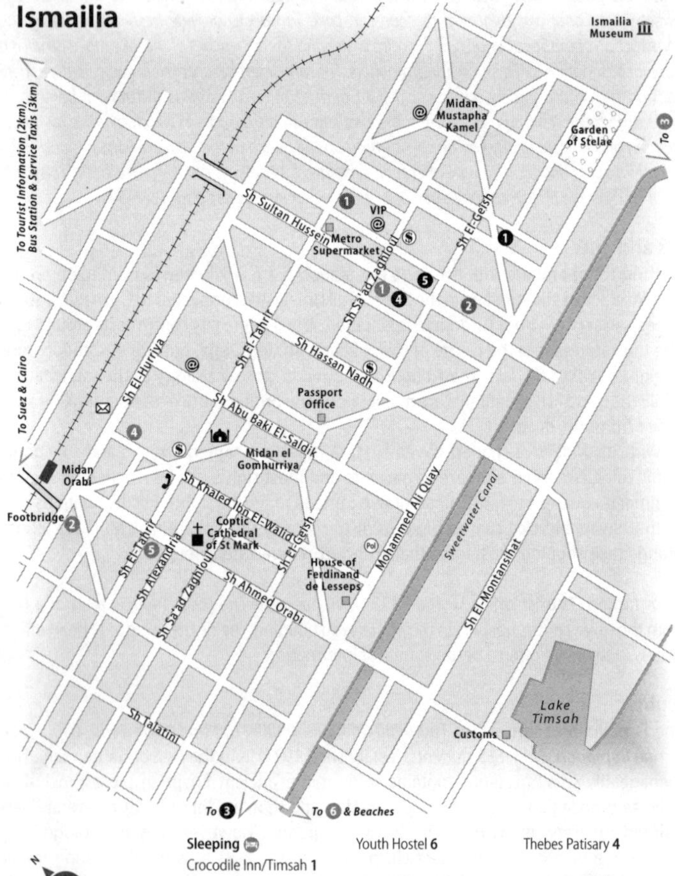

Sleeping
Crocodile Inn/Timsah **1**
Isis **2**
Mercure Forsan Island **3**
New Palace **4**
Travellers' Hotel **5**
Youth Hostel **6**

Eating
El-Mastkay Coffee Shop **1**
Hassan Abu Ali **3**
Nefertiti **5**
Thebes Patisary **4**

Bars & clubs
George's **2**
King Edward **1**

A few kilometres east of the city is a ferry across the Suez Canal to Sinai and the **Bar-Lev Line**, an impressive 25-m-high embankment built by the occupying Israelis to stall any Egyptian advance across the canal and into Sinai (and now enhanced with a large 'Welcome to Egypt' sign). Although Egyptian forces managed to break through the line at the beginning of the October 1973 war, by using the element of total surprise and high pressure water hoses, the Israeli counter-attack across the Great Bitter Lakes virtually succeeded in surrounding the Egyptian army and, under pressure from the superpowers, both sides were forced to the negotiating table. An unusual memorial of 6 October 1973 – a fixed bayonet – is located on the east bank of the canal near the ferry crossing. At the time of research, the car ferry was undergoing maintenance, but foot passengers could still cross (free) to visit the pleasant coffee shops on the east bank. It's worth a visit to the canal in any case to see the immense ships passing through, in amazing contrast to any tiny fishing boat rowing along. A taxi from the city should cost E£5, but foreigners will struggle to get this price. Also some 7 km south of Ismailia on the west bank is the memorial to the unknown soldier, recalling the First World War.

There are some pleasant public beaches around **Lake Timsah** (such as Fairuz Beach, just past the Youth Hostel, E£8, open 0900-2300) and picnicking is popular in Mahalla Park between Lake Timsah and the Sweetwater Canal. However, foreign women might feel conspicuous swimming in the public beaches, and it is well recommended to use the lovely private beach and pool on Forsan Island for the day, see below. In Garden City is the **Coptic Catholic church of St Mark** built in 1930 to a unique architectural design and the **El-Rahman mosque**, to the west of town, was constructed post-1973.

Ismailia listings

For Sleeping and Eating price codes and other relevant information, see pages 26-31.

Sleeping

Ismailia *p387, map p388*
Many hotels are growing weary and are in dire need of remodelling. Nonetheless, with a bit of perseverance, you'll find a room that is comfortable enough to lay your head.

AL-A Mercure Forsan Island, T064-391 6316, www.mercure.com. The best hotel in Ismailia, located on the lush Forsan Island, appears as an unattractive tower block but the back rooms have wonderful views of Crocodile Lake. There are also 5 suites, but the standard rooms are equally nice and all have balconies. The private beach and pool are very appealing, there's a fitness centre, a good restaurant with an open buffet, and a pleasant bar. Beach, pool, football pitch and tennis are available to non-residents for day-use – excellent value at E£100 including lunch.

C Crocodile Inn/Timsah Hotel, 179 Sharia Sa'ad Zaghloul, T064-391 2555. The nicest place to stay in the town centre. Rooms are clean, comfortable, and with bath, TV and a/c. They have a colonial feel with bright white paint and wooden furniture; look at several as the top floor have great balconies and views. Staff speak reasonable English and are friendly. Breakfast included. Singles E£150, doubles E£250.

D New Palace, Midan Orabi, T064-391 6327. A remodelled hotel, which sadly means the loss of most period fittings, but it's still a classy old building. Slightly cheaper rooms at the back are cramped, it's worth paying more for one of the large 4 front-facing rooms with balcony over-looking the Midan. All are clean if slightly shabby, with TV, fridge and decent private baths – check the a/c works. They also have a cheaper single room (E£90) on the top floor with a shared bath, though they are reluctant to let lone women stay there.

Breakfast included, or do without to get a cheaper price.

E Isis, 28 Sharia Abdul Sherif, Midan Orabi, T064-392 2821. Way past its prime, tiles are missing from the floor, stuffing pokes out the chairs, the bathrooms leave a lot to be desired but all rooms have a balcony. It's a passable budget option and hosts local tour groups, thus is often full. Doubles E£75, no breakfast.

G Travellers' Hotel (also known as **Hotel des Voyageurs**), 22 Sharia Ahmed Orabi. Atmospheric old colonial-style hotel from the outside but dirty and lacking in all amenities inside. Terrifying shared baths, no fans, or breakfast, but clean sheets. There is a quaint local *ahwa* downstairs, though, and the location is right if you're on a very tight budget and want to be in town.

G Youth Hostel, Timsah Lake, T064-392 2850. Considering alternative budget options, the hostel is high standard and although it's 2 km south of the centre, there are a couple of great fish restaurants and a host of coffee shops nearby and taxis are only E£2-3 to town. Dorms with 6 beds are peeling but clean with private bath (a bargain at E£11), or sprucer doubles are great value at E£21/35 per person with fan or a/c (you get the room to yourself, unless it's holiday time). The place feels local, with families gathering around the lounge areas and there's a 'beach/garden' out the back by the lake. Breakfast included, parking available, no lock-out, very kind and helpful management. Reception open 0800-0100.

Eating

Ismailia *p387, map p388*

TTT-TT George's Restaurant and Bar, 11 Sharia Sultan Hussein. Open 1200-0100. Known for its food and steaks but best for its stylish bar cluttered with memorabilia – quite possibly the nicest bar in Egypt. All sorts of strays collect in the dark-wood interior where dim lighting and many mirrors enhance the period atmosphere. It's been here since 1950.

TTT-TT Fish Land, past the **Youth Hostel** south of town, T064-391 8433. Open 1300-0300. Large colourful indoor restaurant, plus pagoda-style building and outdoor seating, serving up wonderful fish for E£35-60, and all other marine life including eels. Shrimps come at a price but there are bargain deals such as fish *kofta* (E£15-20), salads E£5, alcohol available.

TT El Nour, just past **Fish Land**, T018-222 1118. Open 1300-0200. More excellent fish to savour; perhaps the environment is not as appealing as **Fish Land** but the set meals are immense with 4 types of fish/shrimp dish, plus salad and rice starting from E£45. Kindly staff will translate the Arabic menu. No alcohol, but an extra special sheesha tofah is worth the E£15.

TT Mulberry Farm, Was Feyan, for a different kind of experience, if you want to see some of the famed orchards surrounding Ismailia, British **Anne Mahmoud** (T010-113 0921, annemahmoud@hotmail.com) welcomes visitors to her idyllic garden on the edge of Was Feyan village, about 15 km west of the city. For E£70 per person, Anne will provide a delicious lunch (vegetables come from the garden) and allow you to relax among the flowers, egrets and mango trees for the day. Great for families, you can also arrange B&B; it's essential to call ahead, if only to get the complex instructions to her house. About E£35 for a taxi from town.

TT-T Hassan Abu Ali, Sharia Mohamed Ali, 2 km southwest of town, the taxi drivers all know it and the journey costs E£3-4. Spread over several floors (all a different colour), they serve fish in all its forms to eat in or take away. Seafood soups are enormous (you won't need anything else), the salads and *mezza* truly excellent, and the fish is done to perfection. It's busy day and night.

TT-T Nefertiti Restaurant, Sharia Sultan Hussein, T064-391 0494. Open 1000-2200. Family-owned with a very friendly and welcoming air, specializes in seafood (E£20-40) though there's also pasta which is incredibly cheap. No alcohol.

El-Mestkawy Coffee Shop, just off Sharia El-Geish (look for the gawdy awning as the sign is far from obvious). A great corner location with plenty of seating on the pavement looking out onto dilapidating wooden balconies and curious passersby.
Souk El-Talatini fish market, a E£3 taxi ride from town. Lots of stalls where you can snack (or feast) on the day's catch.
Thebes Patisary, Sharia Sultan Hussein. Open 0900-0200. Super cheap bakery with Arabic sweets as well as decent Western pastries, safe ice-cream, cappuccino is E£4.50, most bakery items are E£1, there's a/c if you need it.

Bars

Ismailia *p387, map p388*
George's, Sharia Sultan Hussein. See Eating, above, if you like a drink then George's is a must.
King Edward, Sharia El-Tahrir. Opens at 2200. The best thing you can say about this seedy drinking hole is that it is open until 0600. Though it can attract an interesting clientele, the multiple mirrors and whacky striped walls do little to detract from the saturated stench of tobacco smoke. Strictly for drinking, there's no food. There are, however, donkeys to entertain you.

Festivals and events

Ismailia *p387, map p388*
Apr The El-Limbo Festival takes place a week before Coptic Easter. Now best seen in Port Said as the police seem to crack down on festivities in Ismailia.
Aug/Sep The International Folklore Arts Festival, when the streets play host to local and international dance troupes.
Sep The International Festival of Documentary Films in the Mercure Hotel.

Transport

Ismailia *p387, map p388*
Bus
East Delta, T064-320 1513, buses and service taxis leave from the bus station on the ring road 3 km north of town. There are hourly buses to **Suez** (from 0630-1800, E£5, 1-1½ hrs); and **Port Said** (from 0630-1700, E£5-6, 1 hr); **Cairo** (every 30 mins, 0630-2000, E£8-9, 2 hrs); **Alexandria** (0700 and 1430, E£30, 4 hrs); 1 bus to **El-Arish** at 0800 (E£10, 3 hrs); **Sharm El-Sheikh** at 1100, 1430, 1630, 1830 and 2230 (6 hrs, E£40). The 2230 carries on to **Dahab** (E£60, 8 hrs) and a bus goes to **Nuweiba** at 1000 (E£75, 6 hrs). A bus for **Tanta** leaves at 1400 (E£10) but for **Delta** destinations and **El-Arish** service taxis/Peugeots/stretch Mercedes are a better bet, which depart when full 24/7 from the bus station compound.

Train
There are 7 daily trains to **Cairo** between 0500-2045 (3-4 hrs, 2nd class/3rd class E£10/5). There are 2 trains to **Alexandria** (4 ½ hrs, E£22/12) via **Tanta** at 0845 and 1935. To **Port Said** there are 9 trains between 0845-2125 (1¼ hrs, E£10/4). Buses are much the quicker option, however.

Directory

Ismailia *p387, map p388*
Banks The National Bank of Egypt on Midan Orabi, ATM. **Immigration** Passport office is on Midan El-Gomhuriyya, open Sat-Thu 0900-1400. **Internet** Internet costs E£2 per hr in Ismailia. VIP Net have a fast connection, open 1100-0200. **Medical services** Suez Canal University Hospital. **Post office** Beside the railway station, open Sat-Thu 0800-2000.

Port Said

→ *Colour map 2, A4. Population: 538,000.*

Port Said (pronounced 'Bur Sayeed') with its grand promenades, dilapidated wooden-balconied five-storey buildings, air of seedy colonialism and perpetual Mediterranean breeze is something of a gem. In 1975, when it was declared a duty-free zone, it began to rival Alexandria (it's Egypt's second largest port and fourth largest city) as a leading domestic tourist destination – a place where cheap shopping and beach lounging could be combined. At the time of writing, predictions are that the government will remove the Extended Free Zone although, being Egypt, this is threatened on a yearly basis without ever actually happening. The appeal for most foreign visitors is strolling along the waterfront while giant supertankers glide past; come nightfall, the riding lights of container vessels mark the line of their movement. There are remarkably few 'tourist sights' but the colonial port architecture, busy souqs, excellent fish restaurants and lively cafés have appeal for many visitors. ▸▸ *For listings, see pages 394-398.*

Ins and outs

Getting there Port Said is 225 km from Cairo and 85 km north of Ismailia. Most visitors arrive either at the new bus terminal/service taxi depot 3 km west of town or at the railway station near the Arsenal Basin. The city's main streets are Sharia Filistine (Palestine) along the waterfront, and the parallel Sharia El-Gumhoriyya. From the train station, it's a short walk to the Corniche and centre; from the bus station, a taxi to the waterfront costs E£5, or you can negotiate the microbuses into the centre. **Note** As this is still a duty-free zone, have passports ready to enter and leave as they are sometimes requested. Do not be perturbed by the mayhem you might witness on exiting Port Said when the customs checks root out would-be smugglers; it's not uncommon for half your fellow passengers to be thrown out of a service taxi with accompanying beatings. ▸▸ *See Transport, page 398.*

Getting around It is easy to walk around the main streets near the canal, taxis are cheap and microbuses ply the Corniche and main thoroughfares (35 pt). Port Fouad is a free ferry ride away.

Information **Tourist office** ⓘ *43 Sharia Filistine, T066-336 3743/323 5289, supposedly open Sat-Thu 0800-2000, but better to go between 0900-1400*, has good city maps but are short on facts.

Sights

The city was founded in 1859 as a harbour and named after Said Pasha (1854-1863) who began the construction of the canal. Like the other Canal Zone cities there is less to see compared with the major tourist destinations but there are several landmark buildings of note. The three dusty green domes of the **Suez Canal Authority Building** on Sharia Mostafah Kamal are the quintessential symbol of Port Said, though off-limits to the public. The light is best on the buildings along the canal promenade in the morning when the now-shabby façade of the Simon Arzt department store, built in 1923 (one of two identical buildings – the other being in Naples), is flushed by the sun. The imposing ochre-coloured **lighthouse** was the first single concrete structure on the planet and functioned from 1868, the year before the canal opened, until the early 1990s. There is a free ferry (10 minutes) to **Port Fouad** and its yacht basin on the eastern side of the Suez Canal, and thus part of Asia. It retains much of the colonial feel, with quiet residential streets of 1920s villas, green spaces, flower-filled gardens and a popular beach. The musical soul of the city remains strong, rooted in Sufi and other traditions; internationally acclaimed bands play the *simsimiya* and *damma* in beach cafés in Port Fouad on some week nights.

The **Port Said National Museum** ⓘ *Sharia Filistine, has been closed for as long as anyone can remember and the building is totally gutted before restoration begins; no date has been set for re-opening*. Check with the tourist office to see if this has changed, as there's a fine collection of sarcophagi, statues, and two well-preserved pharaonic mummies. The coach used by Khedive Ismail during the inauguration ceremonies of the Suez Canal in 1869 is also here, and worthy of note is a hand-worked shroud and a tunic decorated with images of the apostles.

The **Military Museum** ⓘ *Sharia 23 July near the Corniche, Sat-Thu 0800-1500, E£10*, displays exhibits from the various conflicts fought along the length of the Suez Canal. These include not only the 1956 Suez crisis with some very lurid paintings and dioramas (look for the headless figures in the scene of Nasser at Al-Azhar), but also the successive wars with Israel. The 1973 storming of the Bar-Lev line receives pride of place and is on display in a separate room.

Port Said

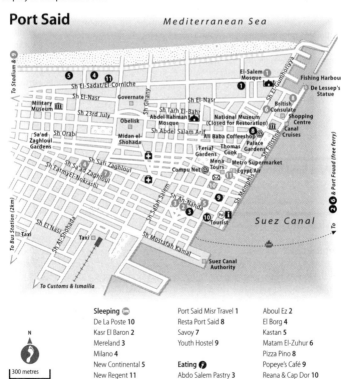

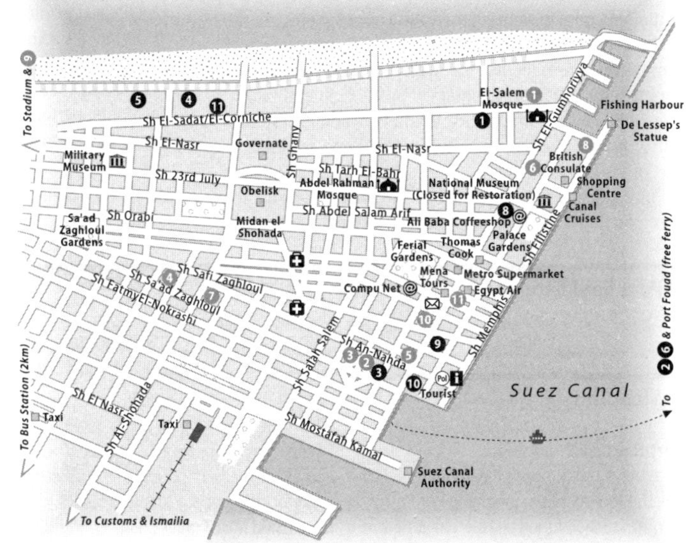

Sleeping
De La Poste **10**
Kasr El Baron **2**
Mereland **3**
Milano **4**
New Continental **5**
New Regent **11**
Panorama **6**
Port Said Misr Travel **1**
Resta Port Said **8**
Savoy **7**
Youth Hostel **9**

Eating
Abdo Salem Pastry **3**
Abou Essam **1**
Aboul Ez **2**
El Borg **4**
Kastan **5**
Matam El-Zuhur **6**
Pizza Pino **8**
Popeye's Café **9**
Reana & Cap Dor **10**
Shawky **11**

The base of the **statue of Ferdinand de Lesseps** stands on the quay by the canal he constructed. The statue was pulled down by nationalists in 1956 – no way to treat the person who brought prosperity to the region! It is now in Suez Canal House awaiting resurrection after the French restored it in the 1990s. However, local feeling is against this remounting and the symbolism it embodies, and there is talk of it being moved to Ismailia. The size of the plinth gives some indication of the immensity of the figure who once stood here – look out for old photographs around town of the statue *in situ* to appreciate how the man once dominated the promenade.

Canal cruising If there are enough people (minimum of 20), cruises along the canal leave from Sharia Filistine, in front of the National Museum. The trip lasts for 1½ hours and costs about E£80 per person, including a soft drink. Call T012-245 5910 to see if a cruise is taking place.

Beaches There is public access to the Mediterranean all along the Corniche and chairs and umbrellas are for hire every few hundred metres. However, this is not a place where Western women can bathe inconspicuously. The Misr Travel and Resta hotels allow day use of their pool and facilities (see Sleeping, page 394), which is a much less stressful option, while the lively cafés on both side of the Corniche are a good mix of Egyptian and continental both in terms of menu and atmosphere.

Cemeteries These lie to the west of town. Apart from the Muslim and Christian cemeteries, there is one maintained by the Commonwealth War Graves Commission with over 1000 graves from the First World War, and nearby is the British Protestant cemetery with around 250 graves. They are worth visiting and easily accessible by minibus from the start of the Corniche.

Port Said is also the access point for **Lake El-Manzala**, an excellent spot for fishing and watching migrating birds and those that overwinter on the shores.

Port Said listings

For Sleeping and Eating price codes and other relevant information, see pages 26-31.

Sleeping

Port Said *p392, map p393*

A couple of classic hotels have shut down of late, but the city has a good range of accommodation fitting all categories. Bear in mind that hotels directly on the beach get booked out on Fri. Breakfast is included, unless otherwise stated.

LL-L Resta Port Said, Sharia Sultan Hussein, T066-332 5511, www.restahotels.com. More intimate than the nearby **Misr Travel** (both in size and atmosphere) the Resta is good quality with brightly decorated rooms and expensive suites. It has no beach but offers stellar views of the canal from all rooms. 3 restaurants with international cuisine and **Pete's Pub**, free Wi-Fi in public areas and 24-hr cyber café. It's a bit pricey, however, for what it is – look for a deal online. There's a small but pleasant pool; non-guests can use it for E£60 per day (drink included).

L Port Said Misr Travel, Sharia El-Corniche, T066-332 0890-7, ps-res@portsaid-hotel.com. Port Said's poshest hotel has sizable rooms with city or canal views, plus some garden chalets. Although splendidly located around the convergence of canal and sea, it is pretty generic and leaves some visitors wanting. However, the large plain pool costs E£75 for outside guests (drink and sandwich included) and there's a 'private' beach. Nightclub, health club, tennis, squash and bowling.

C **New Continental**, 30 Sharia El-Gumhoriyya, T066-322 5024, F066-333 8088. Pleasantly decorated big rooms have little balconies, some with excellent views of the Suez Canal Authority building and ships on the water. A little peeling in places and pillows a bit lumpy, but a/c, fridge, TV for E£180 per double.

C **New Regent Hotel**, Sharia Mohamed Mahmoud, T066-323 5000. It's a concrete slab squeezed between period buildings just off El-Gumhoriyya, but rooms are nicely lit and subtly decorated, and have all the facilities you would expect for the price (single US$35, double US$45). Those at the front have balconies. However, bathrooms are a bit cramped (though that seems to be the norm for most hotels in Port Said).

C **Panorama Hotel**, Sharia El-Gumhoriyya, T066-332 5101-2. Rooms come with a/c, TV and fridge. They feel fresh, with nice lighting, and have good balcony views, it's just the bathrooms that disappoint. The 10th-floor restaurant has panoramas that live up to the name and dinner is suitably priced at E£35.

D **Kasr El Baron Hotel**, corner of Sharia Ramses and Sharia Digla, T066-323 2300. A good location, balconies overlook lots of action in the *souk* and plenty of decrepit classic buildings. Rooms are clean and amply furnished with TV, fridge and fan. Private bath is much preferable, and the doubles with shared bath are cheap enough to make it a better choice than some other bottom-end hotels.

D **Savoy**, Sharia Mohammed Ali, T/F066-333 0057. Spacious square rooms of white/cream tones, with carpets, TV, fridge and a/c. Freshly painted walls if the surfaces are scuffed. Small balconies. Located mid-way between the canal and *souks*. A decent choice for E£150 per double.

E **De La Poste**, 42 Sharia El-Gumhoriyya, T066-322 4048. The façade remains gloriously period, and although renovation has rendered the interior featureless it does mean bathrooms are smarter, mattresses new and pillows soft. All rooms have a/c, fan, TV and fridge; it's worth paying a bit more for a front balcony if you don't mind the noise. 'Internal' rooms have windows onto walls, but have the benefit of being significantly quieter as well as cheaper. Definitely the most distinctive of the budget options, the location is perfect and the pavement café downstairs attracts old-timers. Breakfast not included.

E-F **Milano Hotel**, corner of sharias Safiya Zaghoul and Damanhour, T066-324 6292. In an art deco building, painted green and white inside and out, this is an excellent choice if you want something near the characterful Togary market, devoid of foreigners, and don't mind being a microbus ride away from the canal promenade. 3-bed rooms without bath and balcony are E£55, or E£85 with (price per room not number of occupants). TV, fridge, a/c, no breakfast.

F **Mereland Hotel**, on an alley between Sharia An-Nahda and Sharia Saad Zaghloul, T066-322 7020. All rooms have balconies, it's basic-backpacker but clean enough and relatively recently painted. Doubles with shared bath are E£42 or with inside bath E£67, no breakfast, on a quieter laneway yet central to the markets and near the canal.

F **Youth Hostel**, Sharia El-Amin and El-Corniche (near sports stadium), T066-322 8702. E£11 per bed in a 6- or 7-person dorm, sharing a busy bathroom, breakfast included. Much preferable are the family rooms, E£16 per person (even if you are alone), which have comfy beds, private bath and fans. Very cheap hot meals available when large groups are staying, internet café E£1 per hr, laundry next door; 2 km out of town, but micros run from round the corner. It gets a bit rowdy.

Eating

Port Said *p392, map p393*

There are numerous restaurants serving fairly decent if unspectacular Western food. For cheap Egyptian eats you will have to delve into the bazaar areas. Most notable, though, is the seafood and (weirdly) the Korean restaurant. And make sure you eat a shrimp or calamari sandwich from one of the takeaways.

¥¥¥-¥¥ **Abou Essam**, Sharia El-Corniche, near the Helnan, T066-323 2776. Open 1330-2230. This plate-glass enclave serves excellent fish and the airy interior is curiously pleasant with its fake trellises and shiny spotless surfaces.

¥¥¥-¥¥ **El Borg Restaurant**, on the seafront, T066-332 3442. With flags everywhere, is the best fish place in town – some say it's the best in all Egypt. You'll have to queue for a table on Fri. The seafood soup comes recommended, but it's all good.

¥¥ **Kastan Restaurant**, Sharia El-Corniche T066-323 5242. Open 24 hrs in season, otherwise until about 0300. Specializes in shellfish, but it also has every other kind of fish imaginable cooked in all possible ways.

¥¥ **Pizza Pino**, Sharia El-Gumhoriyya, T066-323 9949, a fashionable place to eat though the decor is more homely than cutting edge, great for tasty Italian fare and desserts, always packed in the evenings and open till 0300. Lit up like a beacon on 2 floors, you can't miss it. Shame they feel the need to have TVs playing pop everywhere.

¥¥ **Reana**, 5 Sharia El-Gumhoriyya, T012-490 9223. Open 1200-2300, Wed 1630-2300. This Port Said institution has been serving large helpings of Korean and Chinese food for the last 30 years, since owner Chon Man Pak arrived from Korea. It's a relaxing environment of brown laminate walls and ceiling softened by red tablecloths and paper lanterns. There's always a good mix of customers, and it's conveniently located above the **Cecil** bar should you wish to carry on drinking after dining. A chance to eat pork if you're having cravings, and (of course) free *kimchee* to start. Not so great for vegetarians, though they go out of their way to improvise with bean curd. 1980s Western music plays lightly in the background.

¥¥-¥ **Popeye's Café**, Sharia El-Gumhoriyya. Open 1030-0100. Serves a good coffee under awnings on the colonnaded street, though pleasant and popular at night also. Inside there's a mish-mash of kitsch memorabilia, marble-tops and photos, and the Western-orientated food is passable and relatively cheap. *Sheeshas* are good and a steal at the price.

¥ **Abdo Salem Pastry**, 9 Sharia Saad Zaghoul, T066-322 1078. Does fine *fittrs* in enormous portions, plus lots of sticky sweets. Takeaway only.

¥ **Shawky**, 3 branches, the most worthwhile being in the midst of Souk Toghary, off Sharia Saad Zaghoul. Open 1000-0200. Any taxi driver will take you. The only place for *kushary*.

In Port Fouad, there are 2 excellent local fast-food places (¥) to indulge in some of Egypt's best *shorba' aads* (lentil soup): **Matam El-Zuhur** on Sharia Ghaziya is open 24 hrs and run by friendly Hag Ismail, while **Aboul Ez** has famed salads/sandwiches. Both have indoor and outdoor seating; neither have English signage, but any local will be able to point you in the right direction.

Bars and clubs

Port Said *p392, map p393*

Port Said is relatively free and easy when it comes to drinking and there are a couple of OK bars that are always busy with locals, expats and any foreigners passing through.

Cap Dor, Sharias Al Nahda and Ghomiriyya, T066-324 8448. Purely functional and no longer serves food, but it does have cheap beer to drink in or take away.

Cecil, Sharia Ghomiriyya. Primrose yellow walls and weird murals don't detract from the pleasure of having a beer while viewing the goings-on outside on the street through the tinted windows. The main place in town to meet other travellers and soak up a bit of atmosphere alongside the Stella (E£10). **Port Said Misr Travel Hotel** has belly-dancing in the club most nights until late. **Matam Ritz**, Sharia Saad Zaghloul, T066-322 1014. Open 1100-0100. Serve passable *gambari* (shrimps) and cans of beer. Few people come to sit in the gloom of the dark wood interior these days, which means the staff are always pleased to see you.

Entertainment

Port Said *p392, map p393*

Cinema

The ultra-modern **cinema**, T066-325 4718, at the **Grand Albatross Hotel** on the Corniche, shows the best English-language films for E£10-12.

Concerts

The **El-Nigma** café, on the beach in Port Fouad, holds weekly concerts every Wed, from about 2100 for 2-3 hrs. Here you can see the long-standing musical tradition of Port Said in its full expression, and if you're lucky the **El-Tanbura** band will be in town, mainstays of the scene since the 1970s. A dozen men playing small harp-like *simsimiyas* might not sound like much but they can get pretty energetic, and members of the audience are free to get up and sing and dance (which they do). On Tue nights, **Albatross** coffee shop plays host to Tahral Bahr, another local band, newer on the scene but starting to get a bit of a following.

Festivals and events

Port Said *p392, map p393*

Apr The **El-Limbo Festival** takes place a week before Coptic Easter. This festival originated in the 19th century when effigies of a despised local governor, Limbo Bey, were burnt in protest. Festivities have been toned down in recent years; no longer do 4-storey-high bonfires rage in the streets and general bedlam ensue. It's a more controlled affair, with a large stage erected on the Corniche on which mannequins are set up (extremely realistic and well made, taking months to prepare) representing a current event or political issue. In 2008, the theme was the bread crisis, in the past it's been footballers when El-Masri, the local team, have not performed to the soccer-mad locals' expectations. Things can still get a bit out of hand, and Port Said is the best place to witness this commemoration now that the Ismailia authorities have pretty much quashed any 'doll-burning' there. The festival lasts for 2 days and begins the night before Sham El-Nessim, the stage is on the intersection of the Corniche and Sharia Ghany.

Shopping

Port Said *p392, map p393*

Many shops still offer an array of imported goods at fairly competitive prices. Items of Egyptian origin that may be of interest include: oriental dresses and fine scarves; silver and gold jewellery; leatherwork; and paintings on papyrus. Remember that it is not permitted to take alcohol out of Port Said. **Sharia El-Toghary** is organized like a typical Egyptian market and sells a wide variety of goods. In fact, you can buy pretty much anything here from quality jeans for about E£60 to spare car parts. Even if you're not interested in consumerism, the shaky old buildings held together with paint and crowded narrow alleys of the old quarter are an exhilarating experience. The second-hand clothes market has been moved to the Balah district on the outskirts of town. **Sharia Filistine** has a European-style shopping centre equipped with parking, restaurant and café, and a range of imported goods though don't get too excited. There is a large and well-stocked **Metro** supermarket on Ferial Gardens.

Activities and tours

Port Said *p392, map p393*

Sports clubs

Fishing Club, north end of Sharia El-Gumhoriyya, T066-323 6870. (Places to fish include: Al-Jameel bridge, Hagar Said, Lake el Manzala, Al-Tafri'a and Port Fouad bridge.) There's a National Fishing Competition each Oct.

Yacht Club, Sharia El-Tirsana/El Baharia, across canal in Port Fouad, T066-324 0926.

Tour operators

EgyptAir, Sharia El-Gumhoriyya, T066-322 4129.

Mena Tours, Sharia El-Gumhoriyya, T066-322 5742, are helpful and speak English.

Misr Travel, Sharia Filistine, T066-322 6735, open 0900-1900.

Thomas Cook, 43 Sharia El-Gumhoriyya, T066-322 7559.

Transport

Port Said *p392, map p393*

Bus

East Delta buses, T066-372 9883, depart hourly from the bus station to **Cairo** (2½ hrs, E£16.50) from 0600-2200; **Superjet** go to **Cairo** at 0700, 0900, 1100, 1630 and 2000 (E£22). There are also regular service to **Alexandria** (7 per day, 3½-4 hrs, E£22-25). To get to **El-Arish**, head to **Ismailia** or **Qantara**. From Suez, there's no shortage of Sinai-bound buses and service taxis. A bus leaves at 1700 daily to **Luxor** (E£60, 20 hrs), via **Hurgharda** (E£45, 6 hrs) and **Safaga** (E£50, 7 hrs). It's wise to book your tickets in advance.

Ferry

Free ferries cross continuously to **Port Fouad**, which is a smarter suburb of Port Said that was founded in 1920s. The journey takes less than 10 mins

Service taxi

Regular and frighteningly quick service taxis run to **Cairo** and **Alexandria** from the depot on Sharia El-Sbah, near the railway station. Service taxis also offer frequent service to other destinations in the Delta, the Canal Zone, and across the canal to **El-Arish**. From the mowaf Dumyat, a few kilometres north of the city, services run to **Dumyat, Mansoura, Tanta** and other Delta destinations.

Train

There are 5 slow and dirty trains a day to and from **Cairo** via **Ismailia** (4-5 hrs, E£5-18 depending on class). Buses and service taxis are a faster and more frequent option.

Directory

Port Said *p392, map p393*

Banks Bank of Alexandria, Central Bank, Bank of Cairo or Thomas Cook all on Sharia El-Gumhoriyya, open 0900-1800. **Immigration** Passport office: 4th floor, Governate Building, Sharia 23rd July, Sat-Thu 0800-1400, T066-322 6720. **Internet** is hard to come by in Port Said. Compu Net by Ferial Gardens will ask a ridiculous E£15 per hr (you can haggle down to E£10) for a slow connection. Otherwise, Ali Baba coffeeshop on Sharia Memphis has Wi-Fi. **Medical services** Al-Suliman Hospital, Sharia 23rd July, T066-323 0220, is the most trustworthy. **Post office** Main post office, open daily 0800-2000, is on the corner of Ferial Gardens near the bus station.

Sinai

Contents

Footprint features

Border crossings

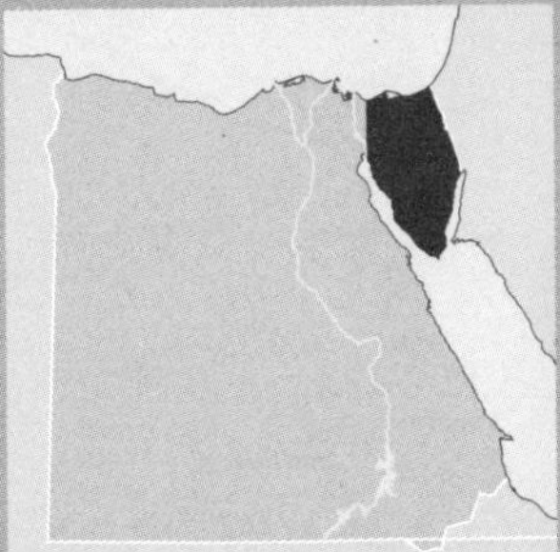

At a glance

Getting around Buses around the interior and between coastal resorts; ferries to Jordan and Hurghada.

Time required If you want to do trekking *and* relax on a beach (especially if you're a diver), you'll need at least 2 weeks.

Weather Sunny in winter but nights are freezing in the mountains. You'll need to take a dip in the sea to cool off in summer.

When not to go If trekking, it's really only the cold winter nights (mid-Oct to Mar) that you may want to avoid.

★ Don't miss …
1 Diving in Ras Mohammed National Park, page 407.
2 Dahab, page 410.
3 Bedouin culture, pages 436 and 442.
4 Mount Sinai, page 448.
5 Desert trekking, page 452.
Mediterranean Sea
GAZA
WEST BANK
ISRAEL
JORDAN
SAUDI ARABIA
Port Said
Port Fouad
Ras El-'Ish
El-Tina
El-Cap
Suez Canal
Pelusium
Rumana
Bir Al-Abd
Lake Bardweel
El-Arish
Rafah
Oruba
Lahfan
El-Maqdaba
Abu Aweigila
Misfaq
Al-Mazar
Katia
Jebel El-Amrar (319m)
Risan Aneiza (368m)
East Qantara
El-Ballah
El-Firdan
Ismailia
Abu Sultan
Khatmia Pass
El-Ousaima
Bir Hasana
Great Bitter Lake
Fayed
Bir Gifgafa
Kabrit
Giddi Pass
Bir El-Thamada
El-Shallufa
Ahmed Hamdi Tunnel
Suez
El-Shatt
Mitla Pass
Nakhi
Ayoun Moussa
Ain-Sudr
Ras en Naqb
Eilat
Taba
Aqaba
Gez Fara'un
Aïn Sukhana
Ras Sudr
El-Thamad
Sinai Peninsula
Coloured Canyon
Za'afarana
Monastery of St Paul
Monastery of St Anthony
To Port Sudan & Jeddah
Abu Zenima
Aïn Furtaga
Nuweiba
Gulf of Aqaba
Oasis of Feiran
Watiya Pass
Red Sea Mountains
Gulf of Suez
Mount Sinai (2285m)
St Catherine's Monastery
Dahab
Abu Durba
Mount Catherine (2637m)
Ras Gharib
El Tur
Jebel Gharib (1757m)
Mount Sabbagh (2266m)
Nabq
Ras Nasrani
Tiran Island
Naama Bay
Straits of Tiran
Sharm El-Sheikh
Ras Mohammed
Ras Mohammed National Park
Red Sea
El-Gouna
N
40 km
40 miles

Sinai is a mysterious land: utterly stark, wildly beautiful and intensely dramatic. Formed by a literal collision of continents, the austere and unforgiving mountains of the interior plummet down to meet golden beaches before melting into the coral gardens of the Red Sea. As the gateway between Africa and Asia via the Suez Canal, the peninsula has been a source of major contention in recent history. It was occupied by Israel after the war of 1967 and returned to Egypt in 1982 with the signing of the Camp David Accords. Continued turbulence in the region has had an impact on tourism, but an ideal climate, the plethora of high-class resorts and backpacker havens, plus the unique natural wonders of the land and the sea keep luring tourists back.

It has been said that the triangular wedge of earth, home to just 340,000 people, is but "24,000 square miles of nothing". Yet with its mystical past, dazzling seas and layers of desolate, majestic peaks, travellers fast come to find that in 'nothing' there is so much. The southern coastal region features some of the best diving in the world. Scuba classes are affordable and the beaches are inviting. Ras Mohammed National Park, at the peninsula's southern tip, is a sanctuary to every species of life that thrives in the Red Sea and a fantasy world for divers and snorkellers. Sinai's rugged interior, too, is magical: where sun and wind and water have converged to paint pictures in the rock and carve jagged peaks that fade endlessly into the horizon in a million shades of pink. Trekkers and pilgrims journey from afar to scramble up the splendid face of Mount Sinai, gaze at the rising sun and marvel at the sacred spot where Moses received the Ten Commandments. The opportunity for a hike through the mountains of the interior should be seized upon before everyone realizes that this is one of the earth's last unspoilt places, proffering isolation and an intimacy with nature that Bedouin have been experiencing for centuries.

Background

Since the beginning of civilization, the Sinai has been one of the most important crossroads to human expansion. Millennia ago, the Pharaohs created a path through the peninsula connecting Egypt to Jerusalem. For the Pharaohs, Sinai served as an easily protected barrier allowing ancient Egypt to blossom unthreatened. Later in the third century BC, it was the stage for the Israelites' exodus out of Egypt. The Romans and Nabateans used an east–west desert route that later became the *Darb El-Hajj*, or the pilgrim's way, to Mecca. In modern times, Sinai's role as a crossroads grew even more pronounced with the completion of the Suez Canal. The strategic significance of this desert wedge and the many people that lay claim to it still yield clashes in the region, most recently in a wave of terrorist attacks by Islamist groups targeting foreign tourists. A series of bombs in Taba in 2004 killed 34 people, then horrific blasts in Sharm El-Sheikh in July 2005 claimed 89 lives, mainly Egyptian, to become the deadliest terrorist attack in the county's history. Dahab witnessed a further terror attack in 2006. Not surprisingly, a security crackdown ensued – but although tourist numbers decreased dramatically for a time, foreigners are now flocking back to Sharm El-Sheikh and development continues at a furious pace. It is the coastline north of Dahab, in the past lively with Israeli backpackers, that has really suffered and many of the pristine beaches now lie empty but for sagging palm-reed huts. It remains to be seen whether the shark attacks in December 2010 off Sharm El-Sheikh, which resulted in the death of a German tourist, will have a lasting impact on visitor numbers.

While most backpackers and more rugged travellers journey overland from Cairo or Israel, or by ship from Hurghada or Jordan, many now fly to Sinai direct via Sharm El-Sheikh airport. And although tourism is generating jobs and bringing in lots of foreign currency, the hasty pace of development in Sinai is of great concern to many. Since the peninsula was returned to Egypt in the early 1980s, South Sinai alone has seen the onslaught of almost 25,000 hotel rooms. The waste of perpetual construction coupled with the overload of tourists and careless divers is resulting in the rapid deterioration of Sinai's main tourist asset: the rich life of the surrounding seas. Add to this the government's North Sinai Agricultural Development Project – a multibillion dollar effort intending to relocate three million Nile Valley residents by 2017. Key to the project is the building of the Salaam canal, a huge and almost finished undertaking that will transport recycled waste water and Nile water through the north of Sinai. How it will impact on the enchantment of Sinai and its Bedouin inhabitants has yet to be determined.

Warning Never allow your driver to stray off the tracks in the desert because in the National Parks it is illegal and because many areas still have mines. Maps of mined areas are unreliable, mines are moved in flood waters and remain hidden. This is a general warning for all desert-border areas of Egypt and the Western Desert but is especially pertinent to Sinai.

Sinai's Protected Areas

With the Red Sea surpassing the antiquities as Egypt's prime tourist attraction, authorities are taking measures to protect the asset that is at the heart of the industry. This protection has taken the form of a network of protected areas along the coast from **Ras Mohammed National Park** (see page 407), **Nabq Managed Resource Protected Area** (see page 409), **Ras Abu Galum Managed Resource Protected Area** (see page 434) to the **Taba Managed Resource Protected Area** (see page 438), and **St Catherine's National Park** (see page 445), which covers a huge swathe of the southern mountains.

With more and more tourists and developments keen to witness the unspeakable beauty of this land, the presence and sustainability of the National Parks is increasingly essential to the region's survival.

West Coast

→ *Colour map 2, B4-C5.*

The west coast of Sinai on the Gulf of Suez is far less attractive than the Gulf of Aqaba coast. It has been spoilt by the oil industry which, while being one of Egypt's sources of foreign exchange, has transformed this region into a mass of oil rigs and gas flares and made it unsuitable for another foreign exchange earner – tourism. However, the best windsurfing in Egypt draws people to Ras Sudr and a couple of short safaris into the interior are feasible from here or from Abu Zneima, removing the need to go all the way to St Catherine's for an inland adventure. ▸▸ *For listings, see page 404.*

Ras Sudr

Near the northern end of the Gulf of Suez, Ras Sudr, 190 km from Cairo and 250 km from St Catherine, is both an oil company town and the site of a noxious oil refinery, and also a year-round destination for middle-class Egyptian tourists. Incessant gusts of wind throughout the day all year round make it *the* spot for windsurfing and kitesurfing. **Moon Beach** offers internationally acclaimed windsurfing opportunities and makes a good weekend break from Cairo less than three hours away.

Nearby sites include **Ain Moussa** – the springs of Moses mentioned in the Bible – and the place where the Hebrews rested after their exodus from Egypt and God provided honey dew and quails. Situated 3 km from Ras Sudr, the pool is at the foot of a small mountain where hot water springs spew out water at 26°C. There's also **Hammamat Pharaoun**, 50 km south of Ras Sudr on a 494-m mountain that rises like a natural pyramid. Some Bedouins call it *Jebel Hammam Firaun Malun*, 'the Mountain of the Baths of the Cursed Pharaoh', believing it was here the King of Egypt drowned in the Red Sea with his army when he was pursuing Moses and his people. A very hot sulphur spring spews out of the mountain at 72°C and flows to the sea. Bedouins have visited these baths for centuries to cure rheumatism. You can bathe in the steamy waters, or in the sea where they fall.

Further to the south is **Serabit El-Khadim** which, in the pharaonic period, was an area well known for the mining of the semi-precious stone turquoise and also copper. Here are the ruins of the 12th Dynasty Temple of Hathor erected for the 'Lady of Turquoise', with a small chapel to Sopdu, who was guardian of the desert ways. It's possible to arrange a tour to Serabit from Sharm El-Sheikh or Dahab, however, it is an adventure to arrange things yourself from this area. South of Ras Sudr, you will find a small port community called Abu Zenima from where it is possible to organize excursions to the lonely turquoise mines of Maghara and the temple a few kilometres further south. Bring lots of water. A reasonable amount to pay a guide is E£80 per day – not including food – and E£80 per camel, then reckon on a further E£80 to cover administration costs and fees.

El-Tur

During the third and fourth centuries El-Tur was an important Christian centre with a monastery (now in ruins) built by Justinian. But now, although it is the administrative capital of south Sinai, the seedy and dilapidated coastal town, 108 km from Sharm El-Sheikh and 170 km from Suez, has little to recommend it. It is, however, an easy and fairly efficient place to renew visas and saves a trip to Cairo. The Mugamma building is on the main road, and a visa usually takes about two hours to process if you go in the morning.

If you do end up here, have a look at the **Fortress of El-Tur**, built by Sultan Selim I in AD 1520 and the **Temple of Serabit Al-Khadim**, which stands on a small hill to the north of the town. To the east of the town are several caves such as **Cave of Hathor**, built during the reign of King Snefru, and **Cave of Souidu**, the God of War.

West Coast listings

For Sleeping and Eating price codes and other relevant information, see pages 26-31.

Sleeping

Ras Sudr *p403*

L-AL Albatross Amira Resort & Spa, 25 km from Ras Sudr city, T017-242 4239, www.pickalbatros.com. Rather an ugly pink expanse of pink building, nevertheless the pool is huge and there are good windsurfing facilities. Rooms are clean and new, but bear in mind that (at the time of writing) alcohol is not available.

B Moon Beach Resort, about 40 km south of Ras Sudr, T02-3760 4050, www.moonbeachretreat.com. All bungalows have a/c and a fridge, plus there are some pricier villas. On site there is a restaurant, bar, water sports and acclaimed on-site windsurfing school with British instructors (T010-581 0088), and a kite surfing beach is a drive away. Yoga is also practised, for those of a gentler persuasion. B&B is available but as there is nowhere else to eat, it's advisable to take dinner as well. Recommended.

El Tur *p403*

C Delmoun, T069-377 1060. 75 rooms with a/c, private bath, breakfast included, not on the beach, best choice in the town centre. Singles E£107, doubles E£237.

Eating

Ras Sudr *p403*

There are a few *fuul*, *taameyya* and *koshari* restaurants in town but only the restaurants in the hotels are recommended.

Transport

Ras Sudr *p403*

Bus

The daily buses between **Suez** and **Sharm El-Sheikh** stop at Rus Sudr. If you want to go to a hotel or resort further on down the road, tell the driver and he will drop you in front.

El Tur *p403*

Bus

There are buses to **Cairo** at 1015, 1145, 1345, and 1615, and frequent services to **Sharm El-Sheikh**.

Sharm El-Sheikh to Dahab

➔ *Colour map 3, A/B6.*

The east coast of Sinai from Ras Mohammed to Taba boasts the most attractive shoreline coral reefs in the northern hemisphere. The climate, tempered by the sea, varies from pleasant in winter to hot but bearable in summer. To the east lie beaches, rugged cliffs and views to Saudi Arabia and Jordan; the west holds the barren interior. ▸▸ *For listings, see pages 412-433.*

Sharm El-Sheikh ➔ *For listings, see pages 412-433. Colour map 3, B6.*

Known by locals and regulars simply as 'Sharm', this name misleadingly encompasses both the town of Sharm El-Sheikh and the resort of Na'ama Bay (6 km further north). The area has developed very rapidly in recent years becoming an international resort destination, at once glamorous and gaudy. Besides the wide sandy beaches and pristine blue sea, Sharm offers a spectacular and exceedingly popular diving area. There is over 60 km of rainbow-coloured vibrant reef teeming with hundreds of different underwater species, dramatic drop-offs and breathtaking formations unparalleled anywhere else in the diving world. The rich rugged interior is also accessible through countless tour operators eager to share the wonder of their desert with nomads of a newer and richer sort. As the region is increasingly brimming over with Western tourists, local people are accustomed to their ways; and, as a result, there is significantly less hassle on the beaches. Sharm is one of the few areas in Egypt where bikinis, beer and booty-shaking are completely the norm.

Ins and outs

Getting there Most travellers landing at Sharm El-Sheikh airport are already booked on a package tour. Independent travellers can take a private taxi (around E£30-100, depending how hard you haggle) 10 km to Na'ama and 17 km to Sharm. Alternatively, get a service taxi (E£5) or microbus (E£3) from the further side of the main road outside the airport. **East Delta Bus** buses from Cairo (470 km) to Sharm via Suez (336 km) leave from Turgoman Station, and also call at Abassiya and Al-Maza terminals. Buses terminate at the new bus station halfway between Sharm El-Sheikh and Na'ama Bay. From there, you can take a taxi (E£15-20) or take a microbus from the entrance to the bus station on to Habada (E£2, from 0630-2400). Ferries from Hurghada arrive at Sharm El-Sheikh port, from where you'll need a taxi. ▸▸ *See Transport, page 432.*

Getting around Take a microbus or taxi to travel between Sharm town and Na'ama Bay (E£2). Microbuses also run up and down the hill between Hadaba and the Old Market area in Sharm. In Na'ama, the micro effectively gets you across the bay but walking around is easy, as the area is quite compact. Getting to the bus station requires either micro or taxi. Most of the major hotels in Sharm offer shuttle buses to Na'ama Bay for free or for a nominal sum.

Information There is a barren tourist office in Hadaba that is not worth the effort of visiting, but all the major hotels can provide detailed tourist information. Useful free publications include *Sinai Weekly*, *Mix* and, in particular, *The Book* ⓘ *Viva Mall, Salem (Peace) Rd between Hadaba and Naama, T069-920 5583, T014-400 4401, www.thebook-sharm.com, open 1000-1800*, where staff provide tourist information and are very helpful. They also can issue you with a Gold Card, which is free and gives discounts in shops and restaurants in Sharm and Dahab. Useful numbers include: **Tourist Police** ⓘ *Na'ama Bay, T069-3660311*; **Ambulance** ⓘ *T069-920 5270-2*; and **Search and Rescue** ⓘ *T012-313 4158.*

Sharm El-Sheikh

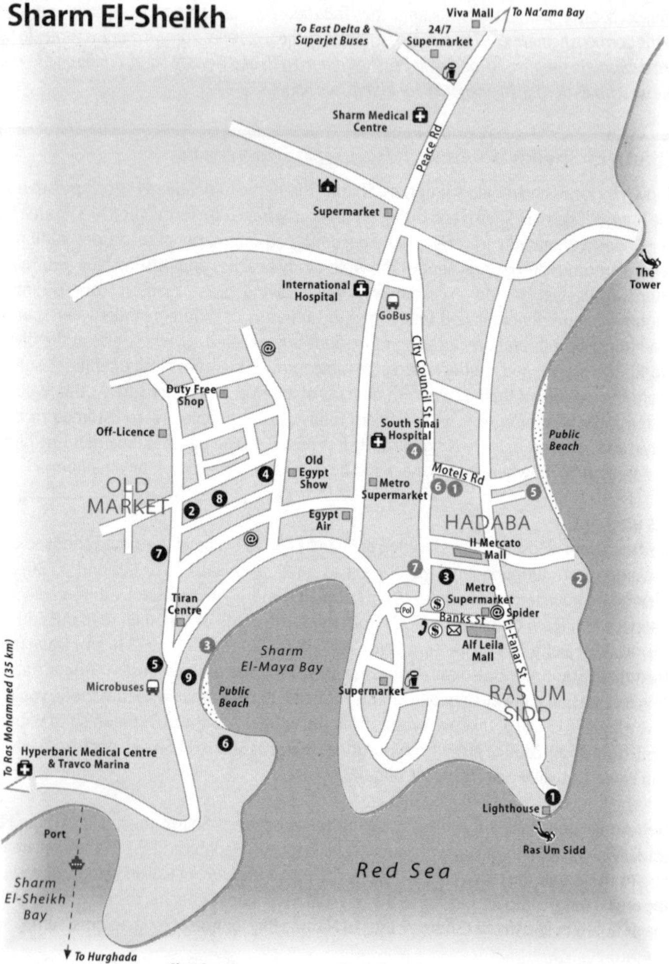

Sleeping
Amar Sina **1**
Iberotel Grand Sharm **2**
Iberotel Palace **3**
Luna Sharm **4**
Ritz Carlton **5**
Sun Rise **6**
Youth Hostel **7**

Eating
El-Fanar **1**
El Masrien **2**
Fisherman's **4**
Koshary el Sheik **5**
Safsafa **7**
Sinai Star **8**
Sports Café **3**
Terrazzina Beach **9**
Terrazzina Too **6**

Sharm El-Sheikh town

The town of Sharm El-Sheikh, which existed pre-1967 as a closed military zone, was used by the Israelis. The small community, still dubbed by some 'Old' Sharm, is rapidly shedding its dilapidated image while managing to retain a relatively authentic Egyptian vibe. These days you can snack cheaply on a kebab or be refreshed at a juice stall, yet rest assured every tourist requirement will be met at a modern, attractively landscaped hotel. In the Old Market there are few scars left from the decimation caused by the bombs that killed 17 people in July 2005; the area has bounced back and souvenir stalls, supermarkets and unpretentious restaurants teem day and night with a mix of Egyptians and foreigners. Cushions and rag-rugs festoon the cafés and fairy lighting is *de rigeur* along the pedestrianized strip.

Many high-quality hotels are now springing up around Hadaba, the hilltop neighbourhood between the town and resort area. While many of these cater to East European holidaymakers on package deals, there are a couple of decent mid-range places available and it's also home to an international community of dive instructors attracted by cheaper property prices and the proximity to Ras Um Sidd, a spectacular shore diving spot. Attempts to prettify Hadaba's wide wastelands are being made as palm trees are planted along sterile highways and new buildings are settling into the landscape. While friendly little communities form around the clusters of mini-markets, coffee shops and dive centres, the Il Mercato centre – a grandiose Italianate outdoor – is a surreal reminder of the aspirations at work in Sharm.

Na'ama Bay → *See map page 408.*

Purely a tourist resort, Na'ama Bay, or 'God's blessing' in Arabic, is generally considered to be more attractive than Sharm town and Egyptians are immensely proud of their 'Red Sea Riviera'. Famed for its smooth sandy beach and peaceful Corniche, huge choice of international hotels and some of the best diving opportunities in the world, Na'ama is rivalling the ancient wonders of the Nile to be the leading tourist attraction in Egypt. Relative to other locales in the Sinai, Na'ama Bay caters to tourists with money to spend. The majority of visitors are on package tours from their home countries, which often include diving opportunities in addition to airfare and accommodation, at very reasonable rates. But for a true taste of Egypt, Na'ama is lacking. In fact there is little or no indigenous Egyptian life to be found and the vast majority of hotel workers come not from Sinai but from elsewhere in Egypt. Life here has been sanitized and simplified, and the result is a plastic version of Egypt by the sea. However, saying that, it can be a pleasant change to stroll down pedestrianized streets lit by faux-Islamic lanterns, where virtually every building is low-rise and no rubbish blows in the breeze. If respite and leisure are what you seek, spectacular views across the clear blue waters of the Red Sea to the mountains of Saudi Arabia make Na'ama Bay an inviting place for relaxation, partying and playing in sea and sand. You don't have to be interested in diving but it helps, as outside of the sea and surrounding desert peaks, there is very little to see. Bedouin villages that may be of interest are more accessible from Dahab. » *For diving and other activities, see page 424.*

Ras Mohammed National Park → *See map page 409.*

ⓘ *The national park, €US$5 plus €US$5 per car, is open from sunrise to sunset, as is the visitor centre, which includes a restaurant, audio-visual presentations, first aid, shops and toilets. There are colour-coded signs that lead visitors to the various attractions. Also crude*

Na'ama Bay

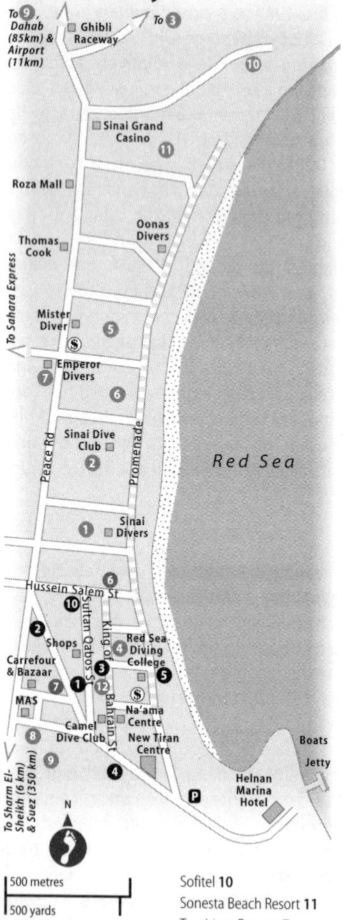

Sleeping
Camel Hotel & Dive **12**
Eden **9**
Ghazala Beach **1**
Hilton Fayrouz Village **2**
Hyatt Regency Sharm **3**
Kahramana **10**
Kanabesh **4**
Marriott Beach Resort **5**
Naama Inn **8**
Novotel **6**
Sharks Bay Umbi **9**
Sofitel **10**
Sonesta Beach Resort **11**
Tropicana Rosetta **7**

Eating
Abou El Sid **1**
Cilantro **3**
Koshary **2**
Hard Rock Cafe **1**
Little Buddha **4**
Viva **5**

Bars & clubs
Drinkies **6**
Tavern **7**

toilets between Main Beach and Observatory Beach. Bring your own water bottles from Sharm El-Sheikh. Taxis to Ras Mohammed from Sharm El-Sheikh cost E£100 for 1 way but it is advisable to keep the taxi for the day – around E£150-200 – as there are no taxis at Ras Mohammed. Vehicles pass through UN checkposts. Passports are scrutinized at the Egyptian checkpoint where Israelis or any non-Egyptians who come in through Taba may experience delays. Note that Ras Mohammed is beyond the Sinai-only visa jurisdiction, so you will need a full Egyptian tourist visa to enter.

Ras Mohammed National Park, Egypt's first, was designated in 1983 and subsequently expanded in 1989. A terrestrial and marine area covering 480 sq km, just 30 minutes from the mania of Sharm, the park offers an underwater spectacle unsurpassed anywhere on the planet. Ras Mohammed is a small peninsula that juts out from Sinai's most southerly tip and is the point where the waters of the shallow (95 m) Gulf of Suez meet the deep waters (1800 m maximum) of the Gulf of Aqaba. The strong currents have resulted in a truly extraordinary ecosystem that encompasses virtually every life form thriving in the Red Sea. Besides the huge variety of brightly coloured fish that live on the coral reef, deep water species like sharks, tuna and barracuda also come to feed. Two of the reefs in the Straits of Tiran are the permanent residences of Hawksbill turtles and there are also turtle nesting beaches within the restricted areas of the park. With more than 20 acclaimed sites, the diving in Ras Mohammed is internationally renowned. (To ensure care of the area, authorities are limiting the number of dive boats coming in so try to book ahead. If you would rather dive from shore, plan to bring a diving guide and your own gear with you). The beaches around the marine gardens are also beautiful. There are some clean shallow sheltered coves perfect for snorkelling as well as more exposed stretches where wind and strong currents necessitate caution. Particularly good fossil reefs dating back 15,000 years can be found all around Ras Mohammed but are especially vivid around the mangrove channel and the visitor centre.

Ras Mohammed is remarkable too for its rare northerly mangroves that lie in a shallow channel at the tip of the peninsula, in an area with many rock pools and crevices in the fossil reef that shelter shrimp, among other stranger creatures. The famous Hidden Bay confuses visitors, because it appears and disappears with the changing tide. The Saline or Solar Lake is interesting for its range of salt-loving plants and bird watchers will also find this a delightful spot. In late summer months, thousands of white stork stop over to rest during their annual migration to East Africa. The park is also an important area for four heron species – grey, goliath, reef and greenback – as well as gulls, terns and ospreys.

Although much of the land appears to be barren and hostile it is in fact home to a variety of life, from insects to small mammals, Nubian ibex and desert foxes. The foxes are often seen near the main beaches and cubs can be spotted at sunset in late spring. They are harmless if approached but should not be fed.

Note Don't come here looking for isolation – there are over 50,000 visitors annually. Some visitors are upset by the number of boats containing inexperienced snorkellers, which scare away marine life. Come on a boat if you are a diver, so you can arrive as the sun comes up and beat the crowds – then your first dive can be enjoyed in relative solitude.

Ras Mohammed National Park

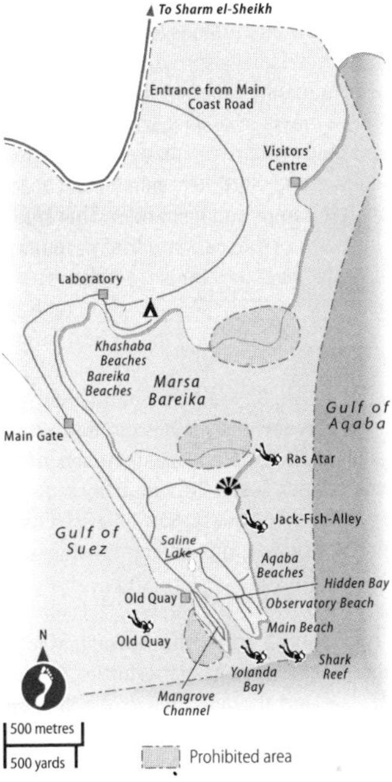

Nabq Managed Resource Protected Area

ⓘ *Entrance E£$5, taxis from Sharm are E£100 for 1-way but it is advisable to keep the taxi for a half-day at around E£200, most hotels organize day trips.*

Nabq Managed Resource Protected Area, 35 km north of Sharm El-Sheikh, is also an outstanding area (designated in 1992) of dense mangroves – not only the largest mangrove forest in Sinai but the most northerly in the world. The area covers over 600 sq km around Wadi Kid, at the edge of which are rare sand dune habitats and a swathe of *arak* bushes, still sold in bundles in the village markets and used for brushing teeth. The presence of the mangroves has allowed multiple ecosystems to develop, sheltering more than 130 plant species and a diverse selection of wildlife. Storks, herons, ospreys and raptors are quite common (the area is recommended for birdwatchers); mammals like foxes, ibex and gazelles are more rare. The hyrax, a small rodent-like mammal which is actually the closest living relative to the elephant, can be found here in Wadi Khereiza. The area's sandy bottom make it a great place for swimming and the diving is good although there is risk of sediment and the reefs lie at some distance meaning that diving is better from a boat and not from the shore.

A small Bedouin settlement, **Ghargana**, lies on the coast where the tribesmen continue to fish in a traditional manner. Here are some teashops and cafés where tourists are welcome. Another Bedouin village, **Kherieza**, is inland from the main coastal valley Wadi Kid. The parks make a sincere effort to involve the Bedouin in their work and to protect their traditional lifestyle, currently under much pressure from the rapid development in the area. Near the settlement is a more modern establishment, a shrimp farm that supplies much of the produce for the hotels and restaurants in Sharm El-Sheikh.

Though popular with safari groups, Nabq is significantly less crowded than Ras Mohammed, but the beaches are decidedly inferior and it is generally much windier.

Dahab → *For listings, see pages 412-433. Colour map 3, A6.*

Dahab, meaning 'gold' in Arabic, still manages to shimmer despite the march of progress. Once known for its laxness with regard to marijuana, unfathomably cheap accommodation and food, and a super-chilled backpacker vibe, people used to come here to get stoned, go diving, and kick back – for weeks at a time. Though the place is still Dahab, things have changed. The Sinai tourist authority, with the hope of bringing in more money and the tourists who have it, have initiated a 'Sharm-ifying' of the area and required many establishments to trade off their beach-front cushions and Bedouin-style seating areas for 'proper' tables and chairs. Fancier hotels have sprouted up, offering a wider range of accommodation for a wider range of humanity, wooden stalls have turned into marble-fronted shops, and everywhere offers a massage or a jacuzzi. The changes haven't impacted on the entire bay, though, and many proprietors have been creative and managed to retain the former flavour. Newcomers and old-timers will still find beach cafés, bazaars and mosques amid crumbling concrete camps and palm trees. Thankfully, despite the influx of construction and tourism, the magic of the sea, sun and stars remains unsoiled. Dahab is still a gem of a place where time dissolves into tea and smoke and the ever-changing colours of the surrounding peaks.

Ins and outs

Getting there Dahab is 98 km north of Sharm El-Sheikh, 82 km from Sharm El-Sheikh airport, 133 km from Taba and 570 km from Cairo. Very few daily buses run north from Sharm El-Sheikh and south from Taba and Nuweiba, service (shared) taxis leave when full, or private taxis can be hired from the main towns in Sinai. East Delta runs daily buses to Dahab from Cairo through Suez and Sharm. Buses arrive in the bus station in Dahab City in the south. To get to Assalah, a pickup taxi (which will be waiting) will transport you for around E£5-10 depending on how many people are with you.

Getting around Dahab can be divided into two distinct areas: the Bedouin village, **Assalah**, and the administrative 'city' of Dahab about 3 km south. Assalah is further divided into three parts: the actual village where locals live and the adjacent tourist areas of **Masbat** and **Mashraba** where travellers hang out. There are also a few self-contained resorts on the water just south of Dahab City in an area known as the **Laguna**. Walking is really the best way to get around, but there is no shortage of pickups and taxis. A taxi costs E£10 from one section of town to the other, pickups are a bit cheaper, depending on the number of passengers. You can always bargain or wait for another ride to come along. ▸▸ *See Transport, page 432.*

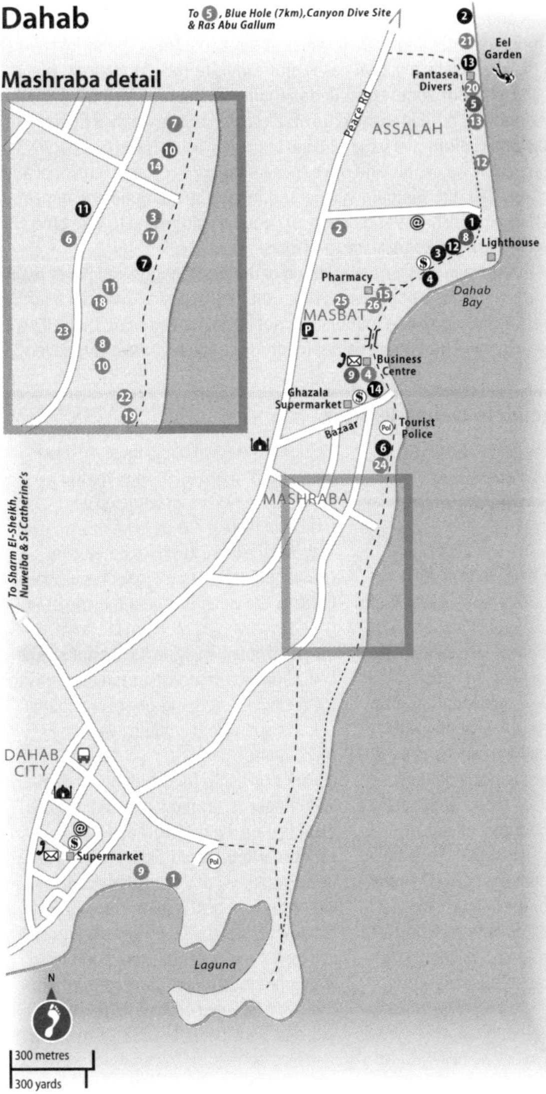

Sleeping
Accor Coralia Club **1**
Alaska **25**
Alf Leila **2**
Bamboo House **4**
Bedouin Lodge **3**
Bedouin Moon **5**
Bishbishi **6**
Blue Beach Club **20**
Christina **8**
Dive Urge **21**
Dolphin **7**
El Salem **24**
Fighting Kangaroo **26**
Ghazala **22**
Hilton Dahab Resort **9**
Inmo **10**
Jasmine Pension **11**
Jowhara **23**
Marine Garden Bedouin Camp/ Sinbad Camp **12**
Mirage Village **13**
Nesima **14**
Seven Heaven **15**
Sphinx & New Sphinx **17**
Star of Dahab **18**
Sunsplash Camp **19**

Eating
Aqua Marine Creperie **6**
Carm Inn **3**
Dahab **11**
Eel Garden Stars **2**
El Dorado **13**
Friends **4**
Jays **12**
Kitchen **14**
Lakhbatita **7**
Nirvana **1**

Bars & clubs
Furry Cup **5**
Rush **9**
Mojito **10**
Yallah **8**

Sights

The changes to Dahab have brought some benefits. The town is still very cheap and significantly cleaner. A boardwalk has replaced the dust path connecting the jumbled mass of beach restaurants, camps and safari centres. There is abundant access to the necessities of modern life – internet, banking, post, telephones. The tourist restaurants are, for the most part, very clean and many of the bathrooms actually have toilet paper. With more bona fide safari companies emerging, Dahab serves as a notable set-off point for serious desert trekking to explore Sinai's mystical oases and exquisite rock formations, but it's primarily a diving and chill-out zone. Local Bedouin offer camel trips into their nearby villages; visitors will doubtless be invited for a cup of spiced Bedouin tea in their homes. The protected area of **Ras Abu Gallum** (see page 434) lies to the north and **Nabq** (see page 409) to the south. Both are easily accessible and offer enchanting tastes of Sinai terrestrial and aquatic wilderness. **Assalah**, the Bedouin village and its nearby surroundings remain a good place to experience the richness and beauty of Bedouin culture and to take time out (or in) for as long as life allows. » *For Activities and tours, see page 429.*

Note Smoking pot in the open is essentially a thing of the past (though you never really know what is burning on the coals of a *sheesha* pipe) and tourist police maintain a subtle but persistent presence. Since growing marijuana is not illegal for Bedouins, but selling it is, it's still around. Bear in mind that the penalties for drug use and possession are severe.

Sharm El-Sheikh to Dahab listings

For Sleeping and Eating price codes and other relevant information, see pages 26-31.

Sleeping

Sharm El-Sheikh *p405, map p406*

For the budget-conscious backpacker, Sharm and Na'ama have little to offer in the way of affordable accommodation except for the EYHA. The majority of sleeping options are at least 4-star and the few cheaper places that do exist are overpriced for what they offer. Rooms are significantly less expensive if they are booked as part of a package or tour.

The town of Sharm El-Sheikh encompasses several neighbourhoods that offer accommodation ranging from the average to the elegant. Most hotels are located in either **Ras Um Sidd**, close to the famous dive site and lighthouse, or the residential clifftop area known as **Hadaba** (meaning 'hilltop'), which contains many middle-of-the-road hotels that may be cheaper but are, for the most part, nothing special. Though most of these places have shuttles to private beaches and are well equipped with many amenities including their own pools, there are much better deals to be had so shop around a bit. When the season is not saturated with tourists or there is war brewing nearby, you may find the more luxurious hotels offer competitive rates. Have a look online. **Sharm El-Maya**, the waterfront area encompassing the downtown part of Sharm El-Sheikh, has a couple of hotels enjoying the advantages of beachfront accommodation and proximity to the traditional shopping area of Old Sharm.

In the spring and autumn, when the tourist season peaks, it is advisable to make advance bookings for the higher-end hotels and budget accommodation, as both extremes are the first to fill up.

LL Ritz Carlton, Ras Um Sidd, T069-366 1919, www.ritzcarlton.com/sharmelsheikh. The 1st Ritz on the continent is still the most de luxe hotel in Sharm and has every amenity imaginable and then some. All 88 sea-view rooms were refurbished in 2010, also garden-view rooms, beach access, award-winning restaurants – each with a different theme, **La Luna Italian** is a must – athletic facilities, diving centre, luxurious spa and candle-lit evenings gazing out to sea.

AL Iberotel Palace, Sharm El-Maya bay, T069-366 1111, www.iberotel-eg.com. Sparkling 2-tier pool among lush foliage and bougainvillea, adjacent sandy beach and a quick stroll to the Old Market.

AL Iberotel Grand Sharm, 1 km from Ras Um Sidd, T069-366 3800, www.iberotel-eg.com. On a coral beach equipped with floating jetty to facilitate entry into water. Pools, restaurants, disco and athletic facilities. Good snorkelling, dive centre, and beautiful views of the sea and Tiran Island.

A Luna Sharm, City Council St, Hadaba, T069-366 5650, www.lunasharm.com. This place bustles with Brits and the poolside music is somewhat loud, but it's known for its friendliness, capable staff and community atmosphere. Price includes breakfast, and half- and full-board are available.

B Sun Rise Hotel, Hadaba, Motels Rd T/F069-366 1725. A good mid-range option, so book ahead as it gets busy. Clean, fresh rooms and a decent-sized pool surrounded by flowers. Restaurants, shuttle bus to beach and **Sinai Rose** diving centre is adjacent. Half-board available.

B-C Amar Sina, Hadaba, Motels Rd, T069-360 0777, www.minasegypt.com. Moorish architecture with dusky domes and kitsch courtyard spaces make this a good choice in Hadaba. Each room is different, there's a decent pool and jacuzzi. **Colona Dive Club** is reputable and particularly popular with Scandinavians.

F Youth Hostel, Hadaba, near the police station, T069-366 0317, sharm.bookings@egyptyha.com. The cheapest place to stay in Sharm by a long shot, beds in 3-bed dorms are E£55 per person, doubles E£60, for single person occupancy E£115, includes breakfast. Rooms are better upstairs with balcony, the view from the back is good, however many rooms have an unpleasant odour and plumbing can be hit and miss. Open 24 hrs. Often full during Egyptian holidays, it's recommended to book via email.

Na'ama Bay *p407, map p408*

The number of hotels in Na'ama Bay continues to grow. The longer established ones extend back from the boardwalk to the main road and some offer marginally cheaper rooms across the Peace highway. Almost every hotel has its own tourist office offering water sports equipment, diving information and desert safaris. Stretching north from Na'ama is a string of resort enclaves, all the way to the protected area of Nabq. Again, the best deals to be had are through tour companies before you arrive. Accommodation for the budget conscious in Na'ama Bay is close to nil, the nearest is in Shark's Bay or at a couple of mid-range places that chiefly accommodate divers. Breakfast is included at all the places listed below.

LL Ghazala Beach, centrally located on the bay plus a sister hotel across the highway, www.redseahotels.com. This old-timer in Na'ama was the tragic scene of one of the 2005 bombs; after renovations, no physical scars remain save for strong security. Rooms are either apartment style in the main building or in cabanas in the garden (preferable). An assortment of restaurants indoors and out represent different cuisines, bars offer happy hours (**Beir Wagen** has Swiss cuisine), huge central pool plus separate and peaceful 'relax pool' for adults only, instant access to beach and all facilities.

LL Hyatt Regency Sharm, T069-360 1234, www.sharmelsheikh.regency.hyatt.com. Beautiful hotel with exquisite gardens overlooking the sea. Beach is coral laden, not ideal for swimming, but pools are fabulous. Disabled rooms, plush public lounges and a lot of marble. Excellent Thai restaurant, some say it's the best place to eat in the bay.

LL Sonesta Beach Resort & Casino, at the northern edge of Na'ama Bay, T069-360 0725, www.sonesta.com/SharmResort. Overlooking the bay, it's a good place to enjoy an evening drink or stay in one of the cool collection of white domes in extensive gardens. Attractive and spacious, the hotel has 7 pools (some heated and some not), dive centre, shops and boutique. The 520 split-level rooms are decorated in Bedouin style with either balcony or patio. Selection of cuisine, including **La Gondola** Italian and **Tandoori** Indian restaurants, several cafés and bars, children's club (5-12 years – runs daily 1000-1600), tennis, squash, spa, 24-hr babysitting service.

LL-L Sofitel, T069-360 0081, www.sofitel.com. A sophisticated hotel with large pool, diving centre and the Near Coral Gardens just off shore. Health club, sauna, jacuzzi, Turkish bath and massage, table tennis, archery (pay locally) and mountain bikes for hire. Shows and entertainment provided by in-house professional team. The Indian restaurant is superb and the inspiring view of the Arabian mountains makes it an excellent place for an evening cocktail.

L Camel Hotel, King of Bahrain St, T069-360 0700, www.cameldive.com. Comfortable and convenient, book ahead as space is limited to 38 rooms. Camel keeps expanding and improving, and as well as the **Roof** bar (the place for late-night drinking among the diving fraternity) there's now the excellent **Tandoori** restaurant and a good Italian. Rooms are large, very clean and nicely (if boringly) decorated, with terraces/balconies, TV and fridge. Disabled rooms available. Free Wi-Fi.

L Hilton Fayrouz, centrally located, T069-600136, www.hilton.co.uk /fayrouz. One of the oldest and most picturesque hotels in Na'ama Bay, it offers double bungalow rooms in lush gardens, with the largest private beach, a playground for children, several bars with happy hours, excellent food, cyber café and Wi-Fi, 1st-class water sports (and dive centre), yacht, glass-bottom boat, pool, tennis, minigolf, beach volleyball, horse riding, massage, aerobics, disco, games room.

L Marriott Beach Resort, T069-360 0190, www.marriott.com. Spacious, modern hotel has recently expanded with additional rooms across the Peace highway, large free-form pool, connected by wooden bridges and surrounded by sun terrace and gardens, spectacular waterfall in the central courtyard. In standard Marriott fashion, it offers all amenities including water-sports equipment rental, dive centre and a health club. Particularly popular with wealthy Egyptians.

L Novotel, T069-360 0172, www.novotel.com. Extremely large yet surprisingly appealing hotel, rooms with terrace or balcony among landscaped gardens, choice of good restaurants, tennis, pool that often plays loud music, attractive stretch of private beach .

L-AL Tropicana Rosetta Hotel, across Peace Rd, T069-360 1888, www.tropicanahotels.com. Best known for the excellent **Emperor's Divers**, it offers comfortable accommodation with satellite, a/c, good Egyptian restaurant, **Shades/Night Magic** disco, mall, laundry and cyber café.

AL Kanabesh Hotel, T069-360 0184, www.kanabeshvillage.com. A more modest option with rather old-fashioned a/c rooms in pleasant grounds, lots of loungers on the roof, right next the private beach with a great choice of restaurants that aren't overpriced. Quieter than most places though it's in the thick of things.

A Eden Rock, T069-360 2250-4, www.edenrockhotel.net. Perched on the cliff overlooking Na'ama Bay, this is a smart boutique hotel with a great pool area and a private beach. Amazing views, good bar area, something a bit different for Sharm. Walking up and down the cliff when it's hot is the only annoyance.

A Kahramana, T069-360 1071-5, www.balbaagroup.com. Fresh, white, bright, good value and hence very popular, this hotel has sizeable rooms all with balcony or terrace (nicest by the pool if you don't mind noise), plus 10 suites. There are 3 bars, including swish 'Fly' lounge bar on the roof as well as a nice Italian restaurant, kids' club and full services including dive centre, A 3-min walk to the beach.

A Oonas Hotel, T069-360 0581, www.oonasdiveclub.com. Very decent, if small, rooms all with balconies (plus 4 suites), in a great position at the northern end of the bay. There's a large private beach, loungers on the hillside and a garden. Predominantly home to divers, but super-friendly to all-comers, the restaurant is reasonably priced and the **Razala**

rooftop bar is just right for a quiet sunset and *sheesha* moment. Show your *Footprint Handbook* for a 10% discount on hotel, diving and courses.

B Naama Inn, T069-360 0801/5, www.naamainn.com. Decent sized rooms with new showers, not all have terraces, small pool, attractively landscaped, private beach a short walk away. About the cheapest you can find in Na'ama, popular with Egyptians, no alcohol served, free Wi-Fi. Dive school attached.

B-D Sharks Bay Umbi Diving Village, 6 km north of Na'ama Bay, 10 mins (E£20) from airport by taxi, T069-360 0942, www.sharksbay.com. 3 levels of accommodation, ranging from basic bamboo huts with clean communal showers (hot water) to the domed Bedouin-style chalets on the hillside. There's an excellent restaurant in a tent by the beach where the speciality is, unsurprisingly, seafood. Coral garden for snorkelling is directly off the beach and the very popular dive centre (run by Bedouin and international staff) offers affordable courses and equipment. Camel, jeep and desert safaris are available if you get bored with the view of Tiran Island.

Ras Mohammed National Park

p407, map p409

It is possible to camp (**D**) in designated sites inside the national park, but it is camping of the rugged sort, with no showers. It costs about E£100 to be dropped off from Sharm by taxi and there is an entrance fee of E£5 per person with an additional E£5 fee for cars. Bring everything you will need including water, as it may not be available. Also note that the park is beyond the jurisdiction of the Sinai-only visa, so plan to come here only if you have obtained a tourist visa that covers all of Egypt, and bring your passport.

Dahab *p410, map p411*

Note A good website, where you can book cheap hotel deals online, is www.dahab.net.

Nowadays Dahab offers something for everyone. There are a few high-end resorts near Dahab City and the lagoon, these are quite self-contained and intentionally separate from the Bedouin village. Their prices fluctuate depending on the season. There's a range of comfortable middle-price options in Assalah; for US$50, expect a/c, a pool, and all the usual 4-star amenities.

Assalah is still a budget traveller's dream, with a few camps offering bungalows and concrete box rooms for less than US$6, or a dorm bed for US$3. For about US$10 per night, you can find a comfortable double room with fan and private bath. Along the beachfront there are dozens of 'campgrounds' varying from slightly run down to exceedingly pleasant. Camp quality varies though all, or parts of all, have electricity, sit-down toilets, hot water, fans and usually a/c. For the sake of security, opt for padlocked rooms or bring your own lock. It's tough to find a bamboo hut these days as most camps now have concrete rooms, expect to pay E£20-40 per person per night. If you want the private bath and maybe fan or a/c, the price varies from E£40-100 per night depending on extras. Many camps offer a discounted breakfast, some only have hot water in winter. Think about what's important to you, keep in mind mosquitoes and peeping toms and look around. Don't drink the tap water – it's brackish and hard. Prices in Dahab for everything are always negotiable and better deals can be made in the low season. If you plan to stay a month or more, say so in advance and many camps will give you a good deal.

Dahab town

L-AL Hilton Dahab Resort, near the laguna, T069-364 0310, www.hilton.com/worldwideresorts. A fully self-contained resort of whitewashed rooms with domes and seductive hammocks on their terraces. Large diving centre (see www.sinaidivers.com), excellent windsurfing and aquasports centre, tennis, central pool (swimming is not permitted in the decorative lower levels!). Travel agent organizes excursions into desert, 3 good restaurants and **Coconut Bar** on the rooftop. It's the snazziest hotel in Dahab though quite isolated from the pulse of Assalah. Off-season, there are bargains to be had when rooms can go down to US$120 per couple, see www.hotels4you.com.

AL Accor Coralia Club, on the lagoon, T069-364 0301, www.accorhotels.com. Attractive bungalow rooms spaced out among lush gardens, good for kite and windsurfers (there are both German and British schools operating from the beach). Superior rooms are newly done out (kitsch Moroccan style) with huge sea-facing balconies, the cheaper garden-view rooms get booked up fast. 2 restaurants, bar, pool (no shallow end), ATM, tennis courts, massage, bicycle hire, volley ball, horse riding, safari and desert trips, diving centre, non-residents can enjoy the pool (but not other facilities) for E£50.

Mashraba

Most camps and hotels in this area have views across the Gulf of Aqaba. Mashraba tends to be quieter and more popular with families and couples. Unlike Masbat, most establishments here have been able to retain the old-style Bedouin seating areas and flavour. All the places below include breakfast in the price, unless otherwise stated.

A Christina, T069-364 0390, www.christinahotels.com. A mid-range mid-sized hotel, with a larger than average pool and well-established garden making the grounds feel quite lush, There's a rooftop restaurant on the sea. A variety of rooms including cheaper ones across the road, away from the sea.

A Nesima Hotel, T069-364 0320, www.nesima-resort.com. One of the nicest places to stay in Assalah, and certainly in Mashraba. Rooms are classy yet cosy, with domed ceilings (even in the bathrooms), some with wheelchair access, some with breathtaking views across the Gulf. There's an elegant restaurant, poolside bar and a popular night-time bar with happy hours and live football. The dive centre is well-established and there's beach and reef access.

B-D Inmo Hotel, T069-364 0370-1, www.inmodivers.de. One of the 1st hotels in Dahab, this is a quality place owned by a German-Egyptian couple. 4 categories of room, all unique, range from chic and luxurious with private terrace to clean 'backpacker'- basic with shared bath. Some rooms are in elevated wooden chalets. Has a sweet little pool area, children's play area, all-round good atmosphere and fills up fast (particularly rooms with balconies on the seafront) so book ahead. Primarily known as a divers' hotel, they also organize desert safaris with local Bedouin guides.

B-D Sphinx and **New Sphinx**, T069-364 0458, www.sphinxdahab.com/www.sphinx-hotels-dive.com. 2 hotels next door to each other with the same owner, they are fairly similar but the original **Sphinx** has just been newly remodelled so try there first. Both are very acceptable, with pools and dive centre. The beachside restaurant, **Funny Mummy** is surrounded by palms and thick with fairy lights, with a roof-top area, which makes an agreeable venue for dining, plus there's a bar.

C Star of Dahab, T069-364 0130. Has reef access and a beach with traditional seating where one can truly gaze at the stars of Dahab. Rooms are all pine and fresh paint with big balconies looking out to the sea. A good breakfast is included.

D Ghazala, T069-364 2414, www.ghazaladahab.com. Domed ceiling rooms, blue and white bedspreads, good value at E£100 per double with fan or a/c E£140. Arranged in 2 facing rows across a central aisle, giving a cosy homely feel but noisy if other guests are hanging out.

D-E Dolphin, T069-364 0258, www.dolphincamp.net. One of very few places that still has some huts made of wicker (shared bathrooms) as well as concrete options (some with private bath), very clean and well maintained though landscaping is minimal and a few plants would be welcome. Conveniently and centrally located while maintaining a peaceful air, there's a good restaurant out front and breakfast is included in the price.

D-E Jowhara, Mashraba St, T069-364 0079, www.jewelofdahab.com, www.bedouin experience.com. Friendly Bedouin place that's been going 25 years, with recently updated large rooms that are especially clean and fresh. Great value, particularly for standard fan rooms (single E£50, double E£70, triple E£100). Surprisingly quiet though on the main road (away from beach), around a garden with palm trees, nice new café. Desert trips easily arranged. Very pleasant and helpful management.

D-E Sunsplash Camp, T069-364 0932, www.sunsplash-divers.com. This long-standing camp, chiefly catering to divers from Germany and returning guests, has moved with the times and the wicker huts are spotless, most now have bathrooms, a/c and heat, and there's a hotch-potch of wooden rooms at the front. Once peacefully located on the edge of Mashraba, the camp is now crowded by new-builds but you can still, within a few strides, snorkel the house reef. Anita, the owner, speaks English, German and Arabic and organizes trips into the desert away from the crowds. Look for the quirky bright blue wooden huts by the boardwalk, which cost E£80.

D-F El Salem, www.elsalemdahab.com. Arranged around the original Bedouin stone house, El Salem has some bare basic rooms for E£50 a double (just beds) and quaintly decorated rooms at the front with a yoga theme (E£85), shared bathrooms. For an en suite the price goes up, but all is negotiable. Yoga 4 times per week and a hippy vibe.

E Bedouin Lodge, T069-364 1125, www.bedouin-lodge-dahab.com. Popular and well-established with freshly decorated rooms (with fan E£80, with a/c E£100 per double) and an unpretentious atmosphere; many guests here are divers. Good views of the sea from the pricier rooms, cosy restaurant is especially inviting at night when lit by candles, and serves some Bedouin dishes, plus beer and sheesha. Bedouin-run and family-friendly. camel, snorkelling and jeep trips arranged.

E Jasmine Pension, T069-364 0852, www.jasminepension.com. Small but well-appointed rooms, some with sea view, are good value in this newish hotel. Staff are friendly without being overwhelming, and they're willing to strike a bargain. The relaxing restaurant is a good spot to start the day, serving decent coffee, excellent juices, lassies and generous breakfasts.

E-F Bishbishi, T069-364 0727, www.bish bishi.com. Although located across the road from the beach, this camp has become a mecca for backpackers as the owner, 'King' Jimmy, succeeds in reviving some of the essence of old Dahab. Rooms are arranged around a garden attractively planted with date palms, there's a cushioned slouching area and plenty of seating, book-swap, bikes (E£40 per day), safaris and trips pretty much anywhere arranged, snorkelling equipment (E£10) and a good menu that's cheaper than most. The range of 40 rooms, with/out attached showers, fans or a/c, are very clean and characterful, with comfortable beds, doubles range from E£50-130. A particularly safe camp for women travelling solo, and there's a real mix of nationalities.

Masbat

Masbat is where most of the action lies. Bars, restaurants blaring Arabic pop, tourist bazaars, hawkers selling everything and nothing and dazzling fairy lighting all loom large. However, most accommodation stretches quite a way back from the promenade and is possible to search out tranquillity.

A Alf Leila, El Fanar St, T069-364 0595, www.alfleilahotel.com. Dahab goes boutique in this gorgeous Arabic-style B&B. The 8 rooms are individually designed and themed, using rich colours and Islamic motifs. Sadly it's next to the main road rather than the beach (10 mins' walk) but some might feel that's a good thing. Fabulous German bakery on the ground floor.

C Bamboo House, T069-364 0263, www.bamboohouse-dahab.com. More attractive inside than out, this hotel in the midst of things has only 7 rooms meaning it's a good idea to call ahead. All rooms have satellite TV, fridge and a/c. Breakfast included.

C-E Alaska, T069-364 1004, www.dahab escape.com, This well-run operation has simple rooms that are spotlessly clean, as are the en suites. On 2 levels, they are more expensive with a/c and balcony, doubles range from E£90-180. Friendly staff, free Wi-Fi, safaris and trips easily arranged. Recommended.

D-G Seven Heaven, T069-364 0080, www.sevenheavenhotel.com. Deceptively large camp in the centre of things, very popular with Japanese divers, they have a huge variety of rooms for all backpacker budgets. Top-end with private bath, a/c or heat and a balcony are actually unattractive, but a great deal are the E£40 rooftop rooms with views (shared bath) while a bed in the a/c dorm is E£20. All rooms include fan and screens on windows, but the shared bathrooms could be cleaner. Internet E£5 per hr, Wi-Fi access is not free, laundry, 10% off rooms for divers, and loads of trips on offer to virtually anywhere.

E Fighting Kangaroo, T069-364 2747, sbulti@gmail.com. Homely, low-rise little 'camp' with plain but clean rooms, very good value (hence often full). Shrubs, creepers and a quiet atmosphere, without hoards of divers. Communal fridge and kitchen for guests' use, safaris/trips are competitively priced.

Assalah

The shoreline north of the lighthouse is dotted with an array of accommodation ranging from cheap camps to more comfortable middle-of-the-road accommodation, all with sea access and loungers on the 'beach' .The vibe turns a bit hippy and New Age as you wander north. Inland lies the non-touristy village where Bedouin, other Egyptians and long-time foreign implants live.

A-B Blue Beach Club, T069-364 0411, www.bluebeachclub.com. There's some tasteful styling in this comfortable hotel, with Arabic lamps and blue glass casting a cool light in the rooms. Pay more for with sea views, though the extension across the road (mountain views) actually has nicer rooms with brand new fixtures and fittings. All have a terrace or balcony. Yoga, diving, horseriding and, of course, massage are on offer.

A-C Dive Urge, T069-364 0957, www.dive-urge.com. An intimate place with 10 well-maintained rooms arranged around a flowery garden. Some have sea views, others have domed ceilings, quirky shapes, pine furniture and bright Mediterranean colours. The beach area has chairs and tables, nearby access to the Eel Garden and on-site dive centre. Run by a British-Egyptian couple plus helpful staff.

C Mirage Village, T069-364 0341, www.mirage.com.eg. Comfortable rooms have some nice touches and decor is muted though rather brown/beige, with fridge, a/c, newly tiled bathrooms and floors. Fine views and beach access, away from the bright lights, a more mature and peaceful air pervades, breakfast included.

E-G Marine Garden Bedouin Camp, T069-364 0211, www.marinegardencamp.com, and **Sinbad**, T069-364 1005, next door both retain the feel of a proper old-school camp. Rooms are simple and spartan, but with clean linen, around well-raked courtyards decorated with the odd mural. Plenty of seating/cushions and hanging out space, use of the kitchen, attracts long-stayers. Rooms at Marine Garden are E£60/80 without/with bath, while Sinbad's cheapest are tiny rooms with shared bath (hot water) at E£35/45 single/double, larger E£50/65, plus some rooms with bath at E£85.

Assalah to the Blue Hole

B Bedouin Moon, T069-364 0695. Beautiful Bedouin-owned and run hotel situated solemnly amid mountains and sandy beach. Rooms have private bath and domed ceilings, a/c, more expensive for a sea view. Highly acclaimed dive centre, Reef 2000, attached. Excellent restaurant. A few kilometres north of Masbat, good place to stay if you're here for the diving and peace.

Eating

Sharm El-Sheikh *p405, map p406*

In addition to the standard buffet-style hotel offerings, there are several good restaurants in town that are frequented by both local and foreign tourists. These days, it's hard to hunt out genuine, cheap local eateries serving *fuul* and *ta'ameyya* sandwiches; easier to spot are *kushari* and *kofta* stalls.

TTT **El-Fanar**, at Ras Um Sidd lighthouse, T069-366 2218, www.elfanar.net. Under Italian management, serves excellent, albeit pricey, food with a variety of wines. The atmosphere is majestic, open-aired, with a stunning view of the sea and mountains of Ras Mohammed. There is live music most evenings. A fantastic place for sunset.

TT **El Masrien**, Old Market area, T069-366 2904 (home deliveries), www.el-masrien.com. Always packed with Egyptian families feasting as well as a sprinkling of tourists, this institution has plenty for vegetarians alongside its famed skewered meats. Noisy indoor seating as well as plenty of outdoor table space. The most popular place to eat in the Old Market. Soon to open a branch in Nabq.

TT **Fisherman's**, Old Market area. Primarily another seafood joint, but in addition serves up some Western, Russian and Egyptian dishes. Enjoy a beer (they ask for E£20 but will go down to E£15) amidst fairy lighting.

TT **Safsafa**, market area. Delicious seafood, only 10 tables, no alcohol, meals starting at around E£35. Has a counterpart in Na'ama Bay – but this is the original and people in the know say it's better, as well as cheaper.

TT **Sinai Star**, on the pedestrianized street, T069-366 0323. Open 1100-0100. Offers excellent grilled fish in generous portions. Prices have increased over the years, but it's still better value than most others and has outdoor seating and a cave-effect interior. They don't serve beer but you can bring your own from the off-licence next door.

TT **Terrazzina Beach**, next to **Iberotel Palace**, T069-366 5046. Enjoy fresh and excellent seafood with your toes in the sand, then chill in the Dahab-style area with a *sheesha*. It costs E£50 if you wish to lounge on their patch of beach from 0900-1900.

TT **Terrazzina Too**, Harbour Rd, Sharm El-Maya, 300 m further along the bay from **Terrazzina Beach**, T010-1477 577, www.terrazzina.com. Table seating over the water or Bedouin-style cushions, this specialist fish restaurant has daily offers (fish or seafood meals plus a beer for US$9-15), fish is imported daily from Alexandria, and they also do Italian food. Entry to the beach is E£100 Sun-Thu (includes towel, mattresses, umbrellas). On Fri, when a beach party goes from 1300-2100, it's E£150, on Sat when the party is 2300-0400 it's E£120 (includes a beer or soft drink). A good mix of nationalities, watersports also on offer.

TT-T **Sports Café**, Horus Mall, Habada, T014-400 4552. Open 1000-0300. Handy café, near the Il Mercato Mall, with free Wi-Fi. Western and Egyptian food is tasty and the menu quite varied, and they do excellent *sheesha tufah*. Screens show sporting events, and there's outdoor seating. No alcohol.

T **Koshary el Sheik**, near the microbus stand opposite the Tiran Centre, is cheap and tasty for koshary and other Egyptian staples.

Na'ama Bay *p407, map p408*

TTT **Abou El Sid**, in front of the Naama Centre, T069-360 3910. Not as magical an environment as the original venue in Cairo, but the fabulous Egyptian/Oriental cuisine matches up.

TTT **Hard Rock Café**, next door to **Abou El Sid**, T069-360 2664, www.hardrock.com/sharm. Regular Hard Rock offerings and atmosphere, good nachos and Mexican/Southern cooking (mains E£35-90), children's menu, opens at 1200, the bar gets kicking after midnight and the disco keeps going until very late.

TTT **Little Buddha**, **Tropitel Na'ama Bay Hotel**, T069-360 1030, www.littlebuddha-sharm.com. Sushi and Asian fusion cuisine in sophisticated surroundings, worth a splash. Hard to see what you're eating in the dim lighting, and best to go early otherwise the music and crowds will certainly distract

¥¥¥ Rangoli, at the **Sofitel**, T069-360 0081. Excellent Indian in a splendid setting with a stunning view out to sea. But arrive early (open 1900) as after 2100 the animation team gets loud and ruins any chance of romance.
¥¥¥ Sala Thai, Hyatt Regency, T069-360 1234. Offers authentic and delicious cuisine, either on terraces overlooking the sea or in the wood-carved interior. Pretty special.
¥¥ Al Dente, Novotel Hotel. The pasta dishes are great and the menu ambitious, in a relaxed and attractive waterfront setting.
¥¥ Cilantro, T16313, this reliable café has branches at the **Hilton Fayrouz** and on the Sanafir Promenade. It feels overpriced but it is good for light meals and good coffee.
¥¥ Peking, Sanafir Hotel. An Asian restaurant that has undergone many incarnations since its original inception to become something of an Egyptian institution. Serves decent, though not necessarily authentic, Chinese food. Part of the Peking chain that has several branches in Cairo.
¥¥ Tam Tam, Ghazala Hotel. Has long been known for excellent Egyptian and Lebanese food and has a large selection of salads – both local and conventional – in a pleasant beachfront location. There are regular folkloric shows in the evenings.
¥¥ Viva Beach, on the promenade, www.viva.sharmnet.com. Open 0900-0200. Beachside restaurant where E£30 gets you a lounger, towel and loud music for the day (but don't expect sophistication). Meals are generous, adjacent **50 Bar** has karaoke and sports while **Lavita** roof bar has DJs (house and r'n'b) and gets messy later on.

Except for fast food, there are no cheap eats in Na'ama. The most-rock bottom is the imaginatively named **¥ Koshary**, on Sultan Qabos St, where a rather average *kushary* comes in at E£5-8.

Dahab *p410, map p411*

The traditional places to eat and chill out have always been the beachside cafés, on bright coloured cushions or close-to-the-ground chairs. Menus are quite similar from café to café though each place offers a different atmosphere, and many have blazing fires on a windy night. If you're looking for a buffet meal or high-end indoor eating experience, check out the restaurants at the **Hilton** or next-door **Swiss Inn**. Most hotels open their buffet dinners to non-residents.

Mashraba

¥¥¥-¥¥ Lakhbatita, on the promenade in Mashraba, T069-364 1306. Offering a wide array of authentic Italian dishes and world cuisines. Romantic atmosphere indoors, which is interestingly decorated with doors and dusty oddments from the Delta. Newly decorated outdoor seating area a metre from the sea, but not as busy as it once was.
¥¥¥-¥¥ The Kitchen, T019-595 9764, www.thekitchendahab.com. Indian, Chinese, Thai and sushi cuisine in a glossy setting on 3 levels (a/c or open air), nicely lit and atmospheric, food is OK value with mains starting from E£35 and going up to E£75 for some of the seafood. Can bring your own alcohol.
¥¥ Aqua Marine Creperie, on the promenade. Open from 0900. Savoury (steak!) or sweet (E£15-30) crêpes with good combos of ingredients, Italian coffee, good juices (E£15).
¥¥ Dolphin Café, next to **Dolphin Camp** in Mashraba. In addition to solid breakfast fare, the dinner menu includes Indian and vegetarian dishes for under US$5, Bedouin-style seating, good samosas and curries – a refreshing respite from the normal Dahab fare (the naan is a little less authentic).
¥¥ Jasmine Pension, T069-364 0852, www.jasminepension.com. A laid-back restaurant on the water's edge with a menu that contains few surprises, but the Dahab standards are better than average and the prices reasonable. Definitely a good choice, particularly popular at breakfast time.
¥¥ Nesima Hotel, T069-364 0320. The restaurant serves alcohol and delicious food and is surprisingly inexpensive. The atmosphere can feel intimate, if you choose the right seat.

¥¥ Dahab Restaurant, T069-364 0118. Good for simple Egyptian fare, such as roast chicken meals, *koftas*, and veg/beans, all served with rice, *tahina* and salad.

Masbat

Bedouin seating in this area has given way to low tables and chairs in most restaurants. Beyond the bridge is a string of gaudily lit but attractive seafront restaurants, which all have similar prices and similar menus. Some might employ more pushy touts than others, but generally they are lively and friendly places where you're likely to end up at some point. Smaller, more eclectic eateries tend to be on the other side of the promenade away from the sea.

¥¥¥-¥¥ Blue Beach, 1st floor above at Seven Heaven. This Thai place might look un-prepossessing, but the dishes are wonderfully authentic as the owner comes from Thailand; always busy with local expats in the know. Chicken forms the core of the menu and makes a refreshing change from fish. Vegetarians are also well catered for, however, with soya as well as vegetable options available. Recommended.

¥¥¥-¥¥ Carm Inn, T069-364 1300. This chi-chi place lives up to its name, Bedouin Arabic for 'small oasis and place of bounty'. Delectable dishes from all over the globe, including India and Indonesia, with inventive vegetarian options, are served in an softly lit grotto among palm trees. Highly recommended.

¥¥¥-¥¥ Friends, T069-364 0232. Has a very pleasant atmosphere and keeps a more Egyptian style to its decor. Beach-side setting, good music, excellent service and extensive salad bar. The food is consistently good and the fresh juice isn't watered down or sugared up. Free Wi-Fi.

¥¥ Jays, at the northern end of Masbat, T069-364 1228. Great food with an extensive menu, always a veggie option, fresh menu every night, tasty desserts. Atmosphere is pleasant with Bedouin-style seating and palm trees.

¥¥ Nirvana, Masbat. Lots of folk enjoying their beach area with recliners during the day, and night it's a fine place to eat decent Indian dishes. Veg/meat thali is E£100/120, main dishes (E£40-65) come with raita, rice, bread and salad.

¥¥-¥ Leila's German Bakery, at Alf Leila B&B, El Fanar St, Masbat, T069-364 0594. This is a really quality place to indulge any cravings for Western delights such as black-forest gateau, apple strudel and sinful pastries.

Assalah

¥¥¥-¥¥ El Dorado, T069-364 1027, www.eldoradodahab.com. Wed-Mon. Italian-managed restaurant and café serves up authentic meals, particularly good pasta isn't cheap (E£65-75), though yummy pizzas are good value (E£45-50) and there are some meat delicacies (E£70-100). The beach area has attractively laid-out loungers beneath woven parasols, with great access to the Eel Garden.

¥¥¥-¥¥ Eel Garden Stars, friendly restaurant in quiet pristine setting, with excellent access to snorkelling. Lots of crêpes, expensive breakfasts but generous portions, excellent food, try the fried aubergines. BBQ night on Fri at 1900.

Bars and clubs

Na'ama Bay *p407, map p408*

Nightlife in Sharm largely centres around Na'ama Bay, with the exception of a couple of places in Nabq and the **Soho Square** complex near the airport, where you can visit the **Ice Bar** (made entirely of ice) for a shot of frozen vodka.

Bus Stop, King of Bahrain St. Open until the wee hours with lots of noise, screened football,pool tournaments, karaoke and r'n'b nights. Pick up a flyer to see what's on.

Camel Bar/The Roof, **Camel Hotel**, T069-360 0700. Open 1700-0200, earlier if there's major sporting event on TV. Buzzing most evenings. A funky and happening spot with typical bar fare, good music and reasonably priced drinks. Very popular with divers and beer enthusiasts, young and old. The Roof bar is a bit more chilled.

Fly, **Kahramana Hotel** roof, T014-666 9266, Bar-lounge with cocktails. It's a good pre-clubbing venue from 1900-0200.
Hard Rock Café, in front of the Naama Centre, T069-360 2664, www.hardrock.com/sharm. With a family-friendly atmosphere in the early evening, the bar starts raging later alongside dance music in typical Hard Rock fashion.
Little Buddha, **Na'ama Bay Hotel**, T069-360 1030. Definitely the most stylish place around, with a cooler crowd sprawled on the comfy seats or grooving through the subtle lighting. The party gets started around 2330 and entry is free.
Pacha, www.pachasharm.com. A vast venue what was the Sanafir hotel, with Ministry of Sound nights at weekends, House Nation on Thu, Ladies Night is Mon and Tue night is Cherry Drops Pool Party. Whatever night, the tunes are pumping.
Pataya, T014-533 3118, Nabq. Wed is foam party night, starting 2300, on the beach.
Rawsha, **Oonas Dive Club**, Open 1700-0100. Rooftop bar that's relaxing and chilled with great sunset potential. Not so busy because it's a bit of a walk along the bay. Sheesha available.
Tavern Bar, www.thetavernbar.com. One for the regulars, this perennially popular place shows football on a large screen and serves up a lot of steaks.

For a more traditional evening, there are plentiful cafés and *ahwas* offering *sheesha*, Arabic music, tea, coffee and often beer lining the 2 main pedestrianized streets. Several off-licences mean you can have a cheaper beer on your balcony.

Dahab *p410, map p411*

Nightlife mainly revolves around the restaurants and hotel bars along the promenade that are open until people leave, plus a couple of places where people get dancing later on.
Furry Cup, **Blue Beach Club**, Assalah, T069-364 0411. Open 1200-late. The closest thing to a real pub, equipped with TV showing football, attracts the British/expat community in the main. There's a happy hour from 1800-2000 and also a beach bar.
Mojito, off the promenade in Mashraba, has a Mexican restaurant on the beach, a sports bar and Dahab's only 'club' at the rear. Party night 4 times a week (in high season), starts in the bar at 2200 and then moves into the club from 2400-0500, entrance free though drinks are pricey.
Nesima Hotel bar, Mashraba. Popular, particularly with divers, and has a happy hour from 1900-2100. There is a DJ on some evenings.
Rush, Masbat. Retains a slightly more refined air at a cool location near the bridge, playing a mix of decent tunes. Nice garden environment.
Yallah Bar, at the northern end of Masbat, always attracts a crowd of drinkers of an evening. There's a beach seating/loungers (very popular during the day) or indoor bar with upstairs area that is a good spots to watch the world go by. Happy hour 1800-2200.

Entertainment

Sharm El-Sheikh to Dahab *p405, map p406, p408 and p411*

Casinos

Na'ama Bay has several late-night casinos based mainly in the hotels. Oldest among them is the **Maritim Jolie Ville's Casino Royale**, open 24 hrs, while the immense **Sinai Grand Casino** on Peace Road presents further temptation. Bring your passport if you intend to gamble.

Shows

Oriental floorshows and bellydancers are largely confined to the major hotels but another (free) option is the Old Egypt show, 2100-2400 nightly, by the market in Sharm El-Maya. The waterfalls and theatrically lit cliff become quite attractive in the half-light and the atmosphere is jovial.

Shopping

Sharm El-Sheikh *p405, map p406*
Souvenirs are significantly cheaper in Old Sharm than in Na'ama Bay. The best-stocked supermarkets in town are: **24/7**, just off Peace Rd near Viva Mall, Hay El-Nour – you'll need a taxi or minibus; and **Metro** supermarket opposite EgyptAir at the bottom of the hill near the old market. There is a duty-free shop in the Old Market, where a tax-free allowance is valid for the 2 days following your arrival.

The Tiran Centre in Sharm El-Maya bay offers upscale shops and chain restaurants. In Hadaba, the **Il Mercato** mall is saturated with all things Western and all to the tune of piped soft-rock music. The nearby **Alf Leila** centre attempts a more rustic feel and sells all the standard souvenirs among some open-air hang-outs for a beer or *sheesha*.

Na'ama Bay *p407, map p408*
Most shops in Na'ama Bay are linked to the hotels and are well stocked with provisions for beach lounging or diving and snorkelling accessories. Tourist shops abound, selling T-shirts, perfume bottles, *sheesha* pipes, Bedouin jewellery and the rest. There are duty-free shops, where a tax-free allowance is valid for the 2 days following your arrival.

There's also a plethora of shopping strips that offer more conventional stores. The **Na'ama Centre**, on the northern side of Na'ama Bay, is overflowing with fashion and jewellery shops as well as chain restaurants.

You can hire an underwater camera at most diving centres. There are several digital stores (which also develop photos) scattered throughout Na'ama Bay.

Bookshops
Bookshops in **Maritim Jolie Ville**, **Ghazala** and **Fayrouz Hilton** hotels.

Dahab *p410, map p411*
There are several supermarkets, which are open 0730-2400. They stock all the basics including bottled water and toilet paper. Fresh **fruit and vegetables** are harder to come by. **Ghazala supermarket**, near the police station is well equipped with most of the essentials.

Necklaces, tie-dyes, skirts and bags etc, the hallmark souvenirs of Dahab, are available in the small bazaars on the main bay and by the taxi drop-off. Don't shop when the Sharm El-Sheikh tourists are in town – everything doubles in price. Barter hard. You'll find **spice stalls**, **carpet sellers**, **lamp shops** and **music shops** blaring the latest Arabic hits and offering a wide range of Western and traditional music.

Activities and tours

Na'ama Bay *p407, map p408*

Bowling
MAS, just up the hill opposite **Hard Rock Café**, T069-360 2220.

City tours
Very dense day trips are on offer to **Cairo** for around US$150-275 (depending on whether travelling via bus or plane) and **Luxor** (0600-2130) for about US$275. If you're trying to cram Egypt into your beach experience, you may want to explore this option, but a hectic and exhausting day does only allow the merest glimpse of Egypt proper. Day trips are organized by **Sun N Fun** (see page 429), as well as the **Sonesta Beach Resort** (see page 413), among others.

Desert safaris
It is possible to book day trips and tours to see parts of Sinai's breathtaking desert interior. Most hotels in Na'ama Bay offer a sort of desert safari, but for the most part they're intended for tourists who want to look through the window of an a/c bus and the experience can be shared with quite a crowd. A tour to **St Catherine's Monastery** (10 hrs), which may include a trek to the summit of **Mount Sinai** and a visit to a Bedouin village costs from US$40-100 depending on content

Responsible diving

There has been a great deal of unnecessary damage caused to the coral reefs around the coast. Divers taking trophies, anchors being dropped onto the living corals, rubbish being thrown into the water. The regulatory bodies set up to prevent this damage to the environment have had little effect – it is up to those who delight in this area to preserve it for the future.

Code of responsibility for reef divers:

1. Check you have the correct weights. As the Red Sea is a semi-enclosed basin it has a greater salt content than the open ocean. The extra salinity requires heavy weights, thus buoyancy checks are essential.
2. Avoid all contact with coral. These living creatures can be damaged by the slightest touch. Many reef fish are inedible or poisonous – but the reef needs them to survive.
3. Remove nothing from the reef. Shells and pieces of coral are an integral part of the reef. In Egypt this is taken so seriously that boat captains can lose their license if either shells or pieces or coral are brought on board.
4. Always move with care. Careless finning stirs the sand and can smother and kill the softer corals.
5. Do not feed the fish. Introducing an unnatural imbalance to the food chain can be fatal and is thus prohibited.
6. Be mindful in caves. Air bubbles trapped in caves can kill the marine creatures who extract their oxygen from the water.
7. Do not purchase souvenirs of marine origin. Aid conservation, do not encourage trade in dead marine objects, which is illegal in Egypt.

and number of people. For US$50, a jeep will transport you to **Wadi Ain Kid**, a lush canyon filled with fruit trees and funky rock formations just 40 km north of Na'ama. Or for about US$60, you can visit the enchanting **Coloured Canyon** and take the hour-long hike to its depths. If you're interested in a more extensive, authentic and rugged desert experience, a better plan is to set off with a real Bedouin guide from Dahab or Nuweiba.

Diving

Water sports in general, and diving in particular, are the main attractions in south Sinai. The reefs off the Gulf of Aqaba coast are some of the best in the world with incomparable coral reefs and colourful marine life. The waters are warm year round, currents are relatively benign and visibility is consistently good. Most divers from Europe book a package before they leave, including diving courses and safaris in combination with accommodation and airfare. This is usually the most economical way to go. If you are an independent traveller, there is no shortage of dive centres available to accommodate you. Most of Sinai's main dive centres are based in Na'ama Bay but organize day-long offshore dive trips to all of the region's major reefs. Many also book week-long live-aboard safaris that traverse the wonders of the Red Sea. Dive centres generally organize all transport to and from Sharm. All offer courses ranging from the beginner's Open Water to instructor level. A standard Open Water course costs €300-390 and takes 4-5 days. Often the certification requires an extra fee of €30, and the manual is about €30. PADI is the most common certificate granted and a world-known diving accreditation. Do your research before you

Diving

SHAUN TIERNEY/SEAFOCUS.COM

Introduction

Diving in the Red Sea is one of those 'must-do' activities. At 2250 km long and up to 380 km wide, this body of water is a lifeline for its bordering countries. Harsh mountain ranges descend to a flat coastal strip then down to a deep-water trough 2000 m deep. The northern end is enclosed – or was until the building of the Suez Canal – while the southern opening into the Indian Ocean is extremely shallow, preventing deep ocean currents entering the gulf. The surrounding deserts and extreme temperatures create the highest salinity in any open sea, yet it sustains one of the world's most impressive coral reef systems with an unrivalled biological set-up.

All the nations that rim the Red Sea have the potential for great diving and most have good dive facilities, although some are still developing. However, nowhere does it quite like Egypt. With 1450 km of coastline, coastal resorts are highly sophisticated and there are more than enough dive centres to cater to the million or more divers who descend on this coast year after year.

Conditions and dive styles vary little from top to bottom of the coast. Visibility is almost always good, there are currents on open dives and calm dives closer to shore. The reefs themselves are a healthy mix of hard and soft corals that support creatures of all sizes, although to see the larger ones you do need to head away from shore. Water temperatures vary from a tropical 28-29ºC in the summer to a more temperate 20ºC in the middle of winter.

SHAUN TIERNEY/SEAFOCUS.COM

Abu Dabab Bay, Marsa Alam.

Sharm El-Sheikh » *page 405*

Diving in Egypt's northern region centres around the town of Sharm El-Sheikh. This area is home to Egypt's first marine park – Ras Mohammed National Park – and the Straights of Tiran, which are an easy distance for day trips from the town and harbour. Despite the numbers of boats, operators and divers, this is an area of unparalleled beauty. Reefs are like rainbows and swarms of orange and blue anthias pepper colourful corals.

A little further south are the Straights of Gubal, the entrance to the Suez Canal, where wreck diving is fantastic. The most famous is the *HMS Thistlegorm*, a British cargo vessel that was bombed during the Second World War. Now she is like a deserted shop, with holds full of motorbikes, engines and even toilets that never reached their destination. Live-aboards that travel out from Sharm often include the *Thistlegorm* on their itineraries as well as reefs further afield.

Travelling north from Sharm, there are two more towns, the port of Nuweiba and Dahab, where more hotels and dive centres have set up. This area is good for those who like a quieter life – numbers on land and in the water are fewer here than at the better-known resorts, yet the diving is still as impressive with clouds of fish engulfing divers just moments from the shore.

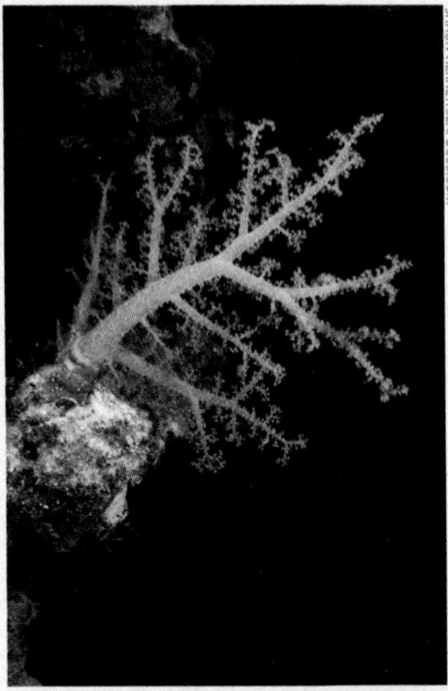
SHAUN TIERNEY/SEAFOCUS.COM

SHAUN TIERNEY/SEAFOCUS.COM

Top: Soft corals on the wall at Ras Mohammed.
Bottom: Blue-spotted ray on the sand.

Ras Mohammed » *page 407*

Off the very southern tip of Ras Mohammed are several dives loosely known as 'Ras'. The actual sites mostly referred to are the twin peaks of Shark Reef and Jolanda. Their joint status derives from dives usually starting on one and finishing on the other. A submerged sea mound is separated from the mainland by a shallow channel and rising from it are the two peaks, themselves linked by a saddle. The dive starts off as a drift at Shark Reef where a wall drops dramatically into the blue. You float past swarming orange and blue anthias and over colourful soft corals feeding in the current. Reef sharks (black and whitetips) are often seen, less often are hammerheads. Next, you pass over the saddle, then it's on to the coral gardens at Jolanda. You may spot a few cargo remains from the freighter of the same name but the wreck itself dropped into the deep during a storm in the 1980s. The dive finally ends in the shallows beyond Jolanda. Giant Napoleon wrasse are sometimes seen here and approach divers inquisitively.

Hurghada » page 468

SHAUN TIERNEY/SEAFOCUS.COM

Opposite Sharm, but on the other side of the Straights of Gubal, is Hurghada, once a small Bedouin encampment and now Egypt's biggest beach resort. There are a phenomenal number of dive centres here, so you will never struggle to find someone to take you diving. And it must be said, there are a lot of divers too, which in the past meant local reefs suffered from over-diving. However, in 1992 a group of operators formed a conservation group that organized mooring buoys and protective schemes. The reefs are now safeguarded under the same rules as Ras Mohammed and are regenerating well.

Hurghada is ideally located to access points north, like the wrecks of Gubal or newly developed El-Gouna, and is the starting point for many live-aboard trips. Some head south to the shipping port of Safaga which has lent its name to another small resort. Quieter than Hurghada, the reefs here are in good condition. Panorama Reef is a joyful discovery, full of crusty hard corals and curious turtles. A recent addition to the dive list is the controversial wreck of the *Salem Express*. In 1991, this passenger ferry was heavily overloaded with pilgrims returning from Mecca to Safaga. She was only a few hours short of home when she hit the reef at Sha'b Shear and sank with a huge loss of life. Ten years on you can dive over what remains. Many people feel that she should be left in peace, but she is majestic in her demise and should be dived with all due respect.

An overnight sail from Hurghada port are the spectacular Brothers Islands. Closed to divers for several years, they are now open but access is regulated. The Brothers are renowned for serious pelagics and hefty currents, so it's not a destination for novices. These reefs are overwhelmed by soft coral rainbows and water so clear it doesn't seem to exist.

Little Brother » page 487

The dramatic underwater pinnacle that is Little Brother is said to have some ripping currents, but arrive on a calm day and you won't believe what you are seeing. Entering at the point of the island is almost a shock. The visibility goes on forever, and then a bit further. You forget to breathe as you can see so far down the water column and even at 40 m (where you shouldn't really be), you can see the boat on the surface as if it is beside you. Soft corals sweep across a steep wall and look like some glorious Gauguin painting. Masses of colourful anthias flit amongst monstrous gorgonias. One moment you are mobbed by Moorish idols, the next by a school of butterflies. But you must keep an eye on the blue as that is where the sharks will be. And yes! a flash of silver out in the channel reveals a majestic scalloped hammerhead.

SHAUN TIERNEY/SEAFOCUS.COM

SHAUN TIERNEY/SEAFOCUS.COM

SHAUN TIERNEY/SEAFOCUS.COM

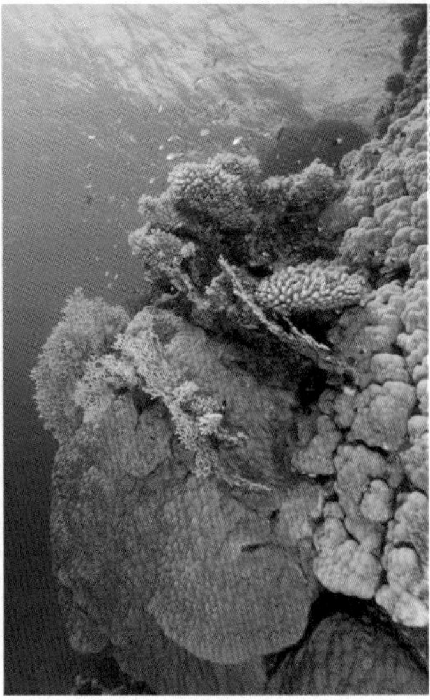

SHAUN TIERNEY/SEAFOCUS.COM

Top left: The walls on Little Brother are coated in soft corals that attract many fish.
Top right: A giant moray eel prowling an Hurghada reef.
Bottom left: Clownfish are common residents of the reef at Ras Mohammed.
Bottom right: Hard corals form steep walls in Marsa Alam.

SHAUN TIERNEY/SEAFOCUS.COM

Marsa Alam » page 481

With a new international airport at Marsa Alam, reefs that were once only accessible by live-aboard can now be reached from the hotels and dive centres at El-Quesir and Marsa Alam. Daedelus and Zabargad reefs, Fury Shoals and St Johns were once just daydreams for most; now there are clusters of resorts in Marsa Alam town, the beautiful bay at Abu Dabab and even some near Hamata, which is about as far south as you can go before you meet the Sudanese border.

Surprisingly, diving here is a little different to the north. There are coastal mangroves and seagrass areas, and the hard corals systems are the best in Egypt. Splendid formations, which form mazes and caverns, are in almost perfect condition.

SHAUN TIERNEY/SEAFOCUS.COM

Top: Turtle feeding in Abu Dabab Bay. **Bottom:** The wreck at Abu Galawa Soraya.

SHAUN TIERNEY/SEAFOCUS.COM

SHAUN TIERNEY/SEAFOCUS.COM

SHAUN TIERNEY/SEAFOCUS.COM

SHAUN TIERNEY/SEAFOCUS.COM

Red Sea reefs have a range of dive sites from caverns to walls. Shallow sandy reefs host a variety of fish life.

Elphinstone Reef » *page 488*

This rather long, oval-shaped reef is a Red Sea legend: its reputation is well deserved, although partly built on how rarely you actually get to dive it. If the currents are too strong or in the wrong direction, you are out of luck; if the wind is up you may not even get from the shore to the reef. But if you are there when the conditions are right, you may see some of the pelagics – such as Oceanic whitetips – that make it famous. And if not, there is so much life in this one small place that only a grand cynic would fail to be impressed. Dives start at depth to see if there are any large animals beneath the plateau and are usually rewarded by dancing schools of chevron barracuda and glimpses of various reef sharks. Ascent then takes you along one side or the other, depending on the day, and on to the most magnificent wall of soft corals and black corals. There are a lot of fish here too, not just the obligatory anthias, but masses of coral trout, some pipefish, jacks in the blue, butterflies and angels, and tangs. You could list fish for ages, but suffice to say, it is all very, very lively.

SHAUN TIERNEY/SEAFOCUS.COM

commit to a dive school, as some are safer and more reputable than others. Be aware that some dive schools try to cram the open-water course into as little as 2 or 3 days. Though it may be cheaper, we do not recommend it. Most large hotels have their own dive centres, the following is a list of some good choices.

Camel Dive Club, centrally located in Na'ama Bay, T069-360 0700, www.cameldive.com. One of the longest established dive centres in Na'ama, slick and friendly service with a 3.5-m training pool. Popular bar inside the dive club area and internet café. Appeals to young cosmopolitan crowd. There is a hotel with 38 rooms in the dive club – comfortable and convenient if you're here to dive, but not cheap. Lots of daily dive trips. Caters to disabled divers.

Sinai dive sites

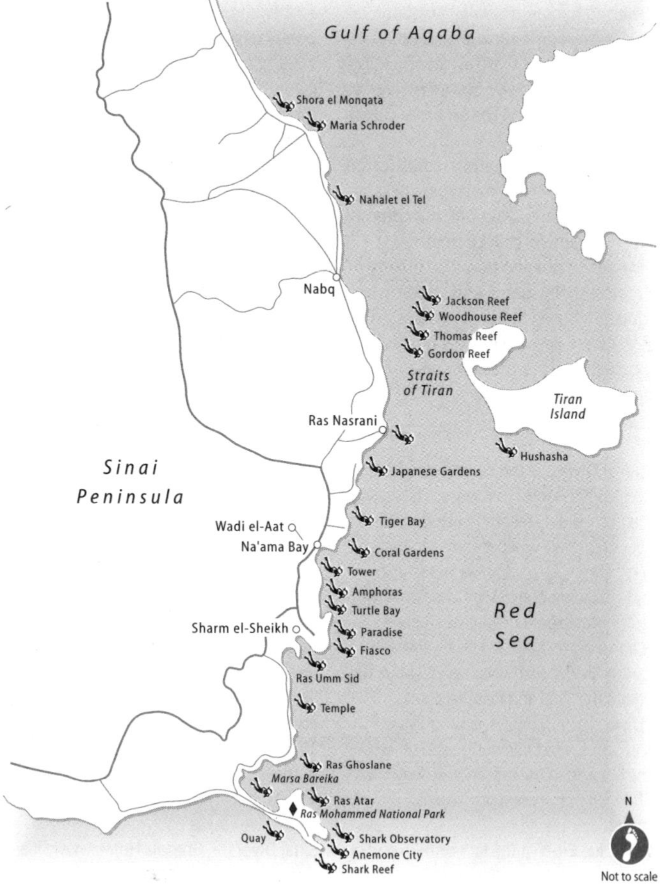

Wrecked ships

Satellite images indicate over 180 wrecks on the bed of the Red Sea. By far the most wrecks are to be found around the dangerous Straits of Gubal at the mouth of the Gulf of Suez. Access is easiest from Hurghada or Sharm El-Sheikh.

Thistlegorm was a 126-m-long, 5000-tonne English cargo ship that was damaged on 6 October 1941 by a long-range German bomber and sank without firing a defensive shot or delivering her goods to the awaiting British troops fighting in the North Africa campaign. Nine of the crew lost their lives. She lies on the massive Sha'ab Ali reef, on the northern edge of the Straits of Gubal, under 30 m of water just as she went down, complete with an incredible cargo of armaments. There are jeeps, trucks, motorbikes, tanks, train cars, a locomotive and an 'explosive' collection of ammunition ranging from rifle bullets to mortar shells, along with uniforms and regulation boots. She was 'discovered' by Jacques Cousteau in 1956 but visits by casual divers to this war grave only began in the late 1990s.

Dunraven, an 8-m sail-equipped steam ship has been lying on the reef of Sha'ab Mahmood just south of Beacon rock since 1876. She is now covered with soft corals and sponges and each year looks more attractive. She lies bottom up with the bow 15 m and the stern (propeller still in place) 28 m below the surface, her journey from Bombay to Newcastle-upon-Tyne incomplete. This English merchant ship carrying a cargo of spices and exotic timber is now home to lion fish and other colourful inhabitants.

Carnatic, once a 90-m luxurious Greek steamship, is a sad tale. With a passenger list numbering 230 and a cargo of gold reported to be then worth £40,000, she hit the reef at Shab Abu Nuas on 13 September 1869. The conditions were calm, the ship remained upright and life for the passengers remained as normal until the vessel snapped in two without warning. Survivors were taken to Shadwan island but 27 people were drowned. £32,000 worth of gold was rescued, but where is the rest? Perhaps it is still there waiting for a lucky diver. The

Emperor Divers, at the Rosetta Hotel on Peace Rd, T069-360 1734, www.emperordivers.com. Highly recommended and known for being sticklers when it comes to safety. A good choice for an open-water course (handy nursery pool) as well as being hugely popular with experienced divers. Offers free transport to/from any hotel, and also organizes live-aboards. Has several branches covering the Sinai and Red Sea coasts.

Mr Diver, T069-360 3796, www.misterdiver.com. A reputable outfit, with offices in the Marriott in Na'ama and the Pyramisa in Shark's Bay, popular with Italians, competitively priced.

Oonas Dive Club, at the far northern end of Na'ama Bay, T069-360 1501, www.oonasdiveclub.com. Mainly European instructors and divers. Pretty much the cheapest for PADI courses, unusual in that 1st dives are actually in the sea in a buoyed-off area. Overseas bookings that include flights can be made online. Mention your *Footprint Handbook* to receive a 10% discount.

Red Sea Diving College, Sultana Building, on the beachfront, T069-360 0145, www.redseacollege.com. PADI 5-star fully equipped IDC centre. Opened 1991, at least 10 multilingual PADI instructors from a good purpose-built facility. Like **Oonas**, it's one of the cheaper and more reputable places to take a dive course.

Sinai Divers, in Ghazala Hotel, www.sinaidivers.com. Claims to be the largest diving abundance of sponges and corals and the favourable light conditions make this popular for underwater photography.

Giannis D was another Greek vessel, 99 m long and full of cargo. She ran aground on the reef at Shab Abu Nuas on 19 April 1983 and later broke in two and sank. The shallowest remains are just 8m under the surface allowing easy access to the bridge and the engine room in the stern. Giannis D, now covered with soft corals, is considered one of the best wreck dives.

Aida II was sunk in 1957 to the northwest of Big Brother Island. The stern section of this supply ship, all that now remains, is encrusted with hard and soft corals and is gradually becoming part of the reef that caused it to sink. At between 30 m and 70 m it makes an interesting dive, but only for the experienced diver, and the schools of barracuda add to the interest.

Chrisoula K was a 106 m Greek cargo ship carrying Italian tiles that struck the northwest corner of Shab Abu Nuas reef at full speed. The wreck remains upright but at an angle with the bow nearer the surface. The hull and much of the superstructure can be visited with safety but the badly damaged bow section should be avoided in rough weather. (Adjacent to the Chrisoula K is an unnamed wreck sloping down from the lighthouse.)

Other wrecks Off El-Quseir, at **Brothers Islands**, are two wrecks. One is an unnamed freighter at the depth of about 80 m with its stern firmly wedged into the sea bed. There are strong currents and viewing the corals on this wreck is only for experienced divers. Further offshore, between **Golbal Island and Tawila** lies a British 4000-tonne steamer that was sunk on 8 October 1941 (see date for *Thistlegorm*, above). The cargo of coals being carried from Cardiff remains with the wreck, which lies at a depth of 50 m, with the deck at 30 m and the funnel at 18 m. Hurghada port has its own wreck, an Egyptian minesweeper sunk in 1973 during the Arab-Israeli war, by friendly fire. It is at a depth of 28 m.

centre in Na'ama Bay, certainly one of the most established. Germans and Brits make up a large part of their clientele. Book in advance in the winter high season. Consistently runs week-long live-aboard boats of a high spec, in addition to lots of daily dive trips and the full range of PADI-certified courses (around €350). They also have branches in Dahab, Taba and Marsa Alam.

Live-aboards Live-aboards are boats that offer accommodation and diving on week-long expeditions. There is a huge variety of boats to choose from, ranging from the tolerable to the luxurious. They sleep anything from 8 to 20 people and all include a dive instructor, dive master and cook. The main advantage of live-aboards is that they cover all the same dive sites as the daily boats but tend to hit them at different times, which means a lot less people in the water and a more intimate diving experience. Another advantage is that divers need not swim very far to dive because the boat is already above the site. A few days offshore also gives divers an opportunity to travel to more remote sites like the waters around Gubal Island. Most visitors to Sharm book a live-aboard in advance with a tour company from their home country but it's also possible to book with a local diving centre. Booking ahead is advisable as these boats tend to fill up fast and have very specific departure/arrival times. Individual travellers should enquire with specific diving centres to find a suitable safari.

Dive sites Against all the odds of decades past, Ras Mohammed and the surrounding reefs are still among the world's top dive sites. The diving opportunities around Sharm are so varied and rich, you'd need a book to highlight them all. The guide that most local dive masters use is Alberto Siliotti's *Sharm El-Sheikh Diving Guide*, which is available in dive shops.

The following is a list of some key sites:

Amphoras/Mercury Unnamed Turkish wreck with a cargo of mercury still evident, on the sandy floor at 25 m. This is a relatively easy dive.

Na'ama Bay Despite the incessant construction and traffic, Na'ama is still teeming with life. There's great snorkelling right off the shore and a lot of people do their introductory dive courses here where shore diving is still possible.

Ras Nasrani A dramatic reef wall dotted with caves. There are 2 spots worthy of note: **The Light**, a 40-m drop-off, with large pelagic fish; and **The Point**, with hard coral boulders. Be mindful of the currents.

Ras Umm Sidd Local site in front of the light tower, within walking distance from Sharm El-Sheikh, abundant with soft corals and fan corals. In summer, with the colliding currents, there is an abundance of pelagics (ocean-going fish) passing.

Shark Bay About 10 km north of Na'ama Bay, this site offers a smooth slope shore entry. It's ideal for beginners and 1st-time night divers. There's a good restaurant, dive centre and simple accommodation. The dive site has a reputation for manta rays.

Ras Mohammed In efforts to preserve this pristine marine garden that offers some of the best snorkelling and diving in the world, access to some areas is restricted and there are limits on the number of boats that can approach. The sheer volume of soft corals, of incredible shapes and colours, are worth the trip in itself. Of the 20 dive sites in the park, **Shark Reef** is worthy of note. Hanging on the southernmost tip of the Sinai Peninsula, currents split along the site resulting in a hugely varied spectacle of life. Depending on the season, you'll see whatever you could see in the Red Sea: sharks, turtles, thousands of schools of fish, a wonderland. **Yolanda**, another popular dive site in Ras Mohammed, is a sea-bottomed wreck from the early 1980s that resulted in countless toilets sprawled around the ocean floor. It is nothing short of surreal to wander amid the wonders of the sea and a bunch of porcelain toilets.

Straits of Tiran Popular with more experienced divers, the straits of Tiran include **Jackson**, **Woodhouse**, **Thomas** and **Gordon** reefs. There are fantastical coral walls, both of hard and soft coral, extremely lively with fish, while in the deeper waters the chance of seeing a dolphin pod is high. The currents can be strong so this area is not advisable for novices. The residue of a few wrecks including *Sangria* and *Laura* are scattered about the strait. Sharks are common. Jackson reef has a 70-m drop-off. There are also coral reefs at 10-15 m, with many large pelagic fish. **Hushasha**, southwest off the island of Tiran is shallow with a sandy floor and sea grass.

The Tower Steep wall, 60 m, large caves with colourful array of fish. The Tower has been so over-dived in recent years that the spot has lost some of its old splendour, but the wall and colours are still impressive.

Go-karts

Ghibli Raceway, near the Hyatt Regency on the road to the airport, T069-360 3939, www.ghibliraceway.com. It's really fun and really expensive. US$20-35 buys you 10 mins on the track, open 1200-0100.

Horse riding

Sofitel, T069-360 0081. Has good stables and relatively healthy horses that can be hired per hour or per day. They also offer overnight desert trips on horseback.

Ice-skating

Soho Square, near the airport, has a fair-sized ice-rink where a session costs E£90.

Motorcycles and quad bikes

Although you can't hire a motorbike to get about town, you can play on a track with **Sahara Express**, info@ktmegypt.com, behind the Marriott on the far side of Peace Rd. They also have quad bikes, as do **Sun N Fun**, T069-360 1623, www.sunnfunsinai.com where they can be rented by the hour (about US$35) or for short desert rides (accompaniment by a local is a legal requirement).

Snorkelling

A cheaper, easier, and less bulky way to enjoy the magic of the sea is by hiring or investing in a snorkel. Equipment can be rented at diving centres and purchased in many beachfront stores. For more remote snorkelling spots, **The Coral Gardens** north of Na'ama Bay, are accessed from the main Peace highway. Look for easy entry into the water so you won't have to splice your feet and kill the coral on your way in. Access is significantly easier during high tide. In the shallows, you will find a vast array of wondrous creatures, corals that open and close, fish that kiss your goggles, exquisite rainbow colours and patterns. Nearby **Ras Um Sidd** is another exquisite place to mill out in the blue with its extreme and diverse drop-offs where currents collide and bring in a wide array of fish. **Ras Mohammed**, too, is a splendid place to snorkel with warm waters and sheltered coves offering homes to over 1000 different kinds of sea life. Check weather conditions carefully before tagging onto a dive boat, as choppy seas and strong currents can make the experience risky, and there is unlikely to be any supervision.

Tour operators

There are travel agents attached to almost all the major hotels, as well as independent ones that can book transport, hotels, sightseeing, desert trips and other excursions. Some better known and reputable agents are:

Spring Tours, Hadaba, T069-366 4427, www.springtours.com.

Sun N Fun, Na'ama Bay, T069-360 1623, www.sunnfunsinai.com.

Thomas Cook, in Gafy Mall (Peace Rd) Na'ama Bay, T069-360 1808. Helpful with travel arrangements to other cities, reserves tickets on the ferry to Hurghada.

Travco, Banks Rd, Hadaba, T069-366 0764, www.travco.com. One of Egypt's biggest agents, offering a wide range of day trips throughout Sinai.

Water sports

In addition to snorkelling and diving, there are countless other ways to enjoy the sea. Glass-bottom boats are offered from most hotels along Na'ama Bay's boardwalk, and there are trips to nearby coral reefs (a popular destination is Tiran Island; snorkelling in the lagoon is a must). You can also rent windsurf boards, hobicats and masks and fins. **Colona watersports,** at the Regency Plaza Resort in Nabq, www.colonawatersports.com, offer kiteboarding, and in 4 days you can become a qualified IKO Level II kiteboarder. Jet skis were banned in Sharm a few years back when 2 Italian tourists died as a result of another tourist's carelessness.

Dahab *p410, map p411*

Desert safaris

Dahab is a good place to set off for the interior by camel or jeep. You can venture inland on a camel with a Bedouin for a few hours, enjoy a cup of tea, and come back to civilization, or you can go for days or weeks at a time to trek around the Sinai, explore the surrounding oases, and dine under diamond-studded skies on coal-cooked grub and fresh Bedouin bread. Like most things, the going rate varies depending on the season, but expect to pay about E£40 per hr for a camel ride and about E£50 per hr for a horse led by a beach-wandering guide. For day-long safaris with food included, it's E£300 or more per day. Popular destinations on camel include **Wadi Gnay** a nearby oasis with a few palms and a brackish spring; **Nabq**, inbetween Dahab and Sharm, a protectorate area that offers the largest mangrove forest in Sinai (see page 409). By jeep, for E£200 per person, you can see the

Coloured Canyon, a beautiful rift with spectacular rock formations covered with swirls and streaks of countless shades of pink, silver, orange and even gold. The trip generally includes the hr-long trek down the canyon. Due to its increasing popularity, be forewarned that it can be quite crowded. Note that from Nuweiba there is cheaper and easier access. **The White Canyon**, often included on day-long jeep trips with the Coloured Canyon, has cloud-white smooth rocks you can hike up. Virtually all the camps and large hotels can either organize the short safaris to nearby attractions or point you in the right direction. Overnight trips and more extensive safaris cost around E£380 per day. The following are a few notable safari companies based in Dahab that may be bit more expensive, but are safe, experienced and well equipped to organize long-distance journeys into remote areas.

Best Friends Safari, T018-298 9716, www.bestfriendssafari.com. The owner, Ahmed, is a vibrant, friendly man who knows the desert well and has worked with local Bedouin for years. He will help you create the trip you want.

Embah Safari,near the Lighthouse, Masbat, T069-364 1690, www.embah.com. Committed to eco-tourism and employing local Bedouin expertise, Embah provide tailor-made excursions for days or weeks at a time and offer educational, adventure, marine and desert safaris. An extremely professional, safe and respectable choice. Also have daily departures, booking ahead is advisable.

Nomad Safari, on the promenade, Mashraba, www.nomadsafarisinai.com. Trips to all around South Sinai and further, with emphasis on Bedouin experiences. Also offer rock-climbing.

Diving

Some of the best diving in Dahab is accessible by land. There are more than 40 diving centres in and around Assalah that rent equipment and run PADI diving courses. Not all are considered to be safe. Accidents used to occur on a daily basis and every year there were a number of deaths. Standards have improved of late, but ask around before choosing a dive centre and ensure whoever you choose to study or dive with is PADI certified, reputable and experienced. See also the box on responsible diving on page 424.

There are many stunningly beautiful and interesting dive sites close to Dahab that are generally less crowded than Sharm El-Sheikh and Hurghada, and since most are shore dives, they don't require the added expense of a boat, which keeps the prices down a bit and allows greater flexibility as divers are not tied to the departure times of boats. The downside is that everything you will see is on a smaller scale, including the marine life. Following is a list of recommended centres, but remember that managers and instructors do change and with them so may the quality of the centre. Prices range from €40-60 for 1 day's diving with full equipment. PADI Open Water courses are in the region of €250-300, plus €30 for the manual. Some dive centres don't include the US$30 certificate fee in the cost of the course so enquire. Most of the centres have instructors catering for a number of languages, including English, French and German.

Big Blue, Assalah, T069-364 0045, www.bigbluedahab.com. Well-regarded operation, provides underwater camera for use on last day of the PADI course.

Desert Divers, Masbat, T069-364 0500, www.desert-divers.com. The only Bedouin-owned dive operation in Dahab, long-established and recommended. Also offers freediving and camel/diving safaris, which trek through rugged lands to reach isolated dive spots.

Fantasea, at the northern end of Masbat bay, near the lighthouse, T069-364 1195, www.fantaseadiving.net. Also rent out windsurf boards.

Inmo, Inmo Hotel and Dive Centre, T069-364 0370-1, www.inmodivers.de. Established since 1988, people keep coming back here.

Nesima, **Nesima Hotel**, Mashraba, T069-3640 0320, www.nesima-resort.com. Reputable dive centre.
Penguin, Mashraba, T069-364 0117, www.penguindivers.com. Has some very cheap on-the-spot offers on PADI courses (€180 plus €32 for manual) and day dives (€18).
Poseidon Divers, Crazy Camel Camp, Peace Rd, Mashraba, T069-364 0091, www.poseidondivers.com.
Red Sea Research, www.redsearesearch.org. This non-profit enterprise teaches skills used in marine research projects (eg gathering data, conservation techniques), geared towards gap year or marine science students.
Reef 2000, **Bedouin Moon Hotel**, between Dahab and Blue Hole, T069-364 0087, www.reef2000.org. Catering mainly for the British and German markets. Offers camel safari to Ras Abu Ghallum, includes food and 2 dives, €100.

Dive sites

North from the lighthouse:
Eel Garden A 15-min walk north of lighthouse, off Assalah, the shallow coral reef is especially good for snorkelling and a safe spot for beginner divers. There's a sandy bottom with a garden of eels, swaying like flowers in the currents as they wait for fish. However, for half the year the currents and winds make diving impossible here – this gives the coral an important break.
The Canyon Opposite **Canyon Dive Centre** a few kilometres north of Dahab. Accessible from the shore, you snorkel along the reef through a narrow break before diving into the canyon. A popular spot for more experienced divers, it bottoms out at 50 m.
The Blue Hole 7 km north of Dahab, the most famous – and infamous – dive in the area. The hole is over 80 m deep and just a few metres from the shore. About 60 m down, there's an arched passageway to the other side of the hole. Attempting to go through it is strongly discouraged. Every year there are stories of advanced divers who die from nitrogen narcosis or carelessness while attempting this dive. At 60 m, you can't see anything anyway, the majesty and life of the place is closer to the surface. Be advised that the Blue Hole is difficult, dangerous and only for very experienced divers.
The Bells Just north of the Blue Hole, along a coral cliff that leads to the hole. A good place to snorkel. Rich with coral and large fish.
South from the lighthouse:
The Islands An enchanting and pristine site just south of Dahab near the Laguna. Close to town and easily accessible from shore. Offers multiple routes in a maze of pathways through delicate pinnacles of coral and rainbow-coloured fish. Light and bright, the experience is a hazy and surreal dream.

A bit further out than the aforementioned sites lies **Ras Abu Gallum** (see page 434), a majestic and remote protectorate area that shelters some of the richest marine life in Sinai. Beginning about 15 km north of Dahab, this stretch of 30 km is only accessible by camel. There are 3 main dive sites with virgin reefs and a wide array of marine life. Most of the listed dive centres lead day-long trips to Ras Abu Galum that include camel transport and 2 dives. Costs range from €60-130 depending on season, number of dives and if you need gear.

Some dive centres in Dahab lead trips to the *Thistlegorm*. Enquire at **Inmo** or **Fantasea** (see above).

Kitesurfing and windsurfing

A consistently strong and steady breeze makes Dahab among the top places to windsurf in Sinai. Several of the high-end hotels, including the **Hilton** and the **Coralia** with its perfect private windsurfing beach, offer surfing schools with introductory classes up to 3-day courses. In Assalah, **Fantasea Dive Centre** rents boards.

Quad bikes

A few places offer quad biking, try **RAM**, on the main road in Mashraba, T012-700 8017, AymanBassyouny@hotmail.com, who offer trips for around E£150-200 for 2 hrs or **Sinai Experts**, in the Hilton hotel.

Snorkelling

Amazing opportunities for snorkelling abound right off the coast of Assalah. Though a coral reef follows the rim of the entire bay, the best spots are right in front of the lighthouse and further south along the reefs of Mashraba. Be aware that despite the reef's proximity to the shore, the currents can be very strong. All the sites listed under Diving are excellent snorkelling areas, particularly popular are Ras Abu Gallum, the Eel Garden and the Blue Hole. All dive centres in Dahab rent snorkel, mask and fins for around E£30 per day. You can also rent them directly at the Blue Hole.

Transport

Sharm El-Sheikh *p405, map p406*

Air

Sharm El-Sheikh International Airport, T069-362 3304/5, is 10 km north of Na'ama Bay with direct flights to and from an increasing number of European cities. Most European charter flights and British Airways leave from the newer Terminal 1 while British charter flights leave from Terminal 2, but check as it's a 5-10 min walk between the two. At least 2 internal flights daily with EgyptAir to **Cairo**, 3 per week to **Hurghada**, 4 per week to **Luxor**, and 4 per week to **Alexandria**.

Airline offices EgyptAir, Sharm Old Market, open 0900-2100, T069-366 1058; www.egyptair.com.

Bus

The East Delta bus station, T069-366 0660, has recently relocated to Hay El-Nour, halfway between Hadaba and Na'ama Bay. Microbuses aren't direct from Habada/Old Sharm/Na'ama, you will have to change on Peace Rd by the Mobil petrol station. At least 12 buses daily to **Cairo**, running from 0730 in the morning until 0100. Costing E£60-70, the trip is 6-8 hrs. Other destinations include: **Suez** (E£30-35, 5-6 hrs); **Dahab**, at 0900, 1430 and 1700 (E£12, 1½ hrs), of which the 0900 and 1700 go on to **Nuweiba** (E£25, 2½ hrs) and the 1030 carries on to **Taba** (E£35, 3½ hrs). East Delta also run 1 bus daily to **Luxor** at 1800 (E£100, 12-14 hrs) and **Alexandria** at 0900 (E£90, 9 hrs). As the schedules are constantly changing, it's best to check departure times. Superjet T069-366 1622, have slightly more comfortable buses with toilets, 7 per day to **Cairo** between 1030 and 2330 (E£70) one of which carries on to **Alexandria** at 1500 (E£90). **Cairo** is also served by Go Bus on Peace Road opposite Delta Sharm Resort.

Car hire

Shahd Limosine, Kalila Centre, Na'ama Bay, T069-360 3066.

Note Drivers beware: there is only 1 petrol station on the 81-km route between Dahab and Sharm El-Sheikh.

Sea

Ferry To **Hurghada**, T069-360 0936, T012-636 0094, 5 per week on Sat, Mon, Tue and Thu at 1700 and Wed at 1800 (from Hurghada to **Sharm El-Sheikh**, same days at 0930, or 0430 on Wed), takes 2 hrs, costs about E£250/US$45, 1 way, E£450 return. To secure a spot, make reservations a day in advance at a hotel or private travel agent like Thomas Cook, T069-360 1808. Ferry leaves from the Sharm marina, T069-366 0313.

Private vessels Visas may be obtained for boats and crews from Egyptian consulates in country of origin. It is possible but more hassle to get one in Sharm El-Sheikh. It is as well to give clear advance (at least 1 week) notification of your intention to berth in the port. The Port Commander must be notified upon arrival. The course of the vessel, in national waters, must be filed and approved by the Port Authority.

Dahab *p410, map p411*

Bus

The East Delta bus station, T069-364 1808, is on the northern side of Dahab City. There are 4 daily buses to **Cairo** at 0900, 1230, 1500 and

2200 (E£90, 8-9 hrs) via **Sharm El-Sheikh** (E£11-16, 1½ hrs), plus a further 8 buses go to Sharm between 0800-2230. 2 buses go north to **Nuweiba** at 1030 and 1830 (E£11, 1 hr) of which the 1030 carries on to **Taba** (E£25, 3 hrs) and will drop you off at beach camps on the way. 2 buses go to **Ismailia** at 1000 and 2230. There's a gruelling bus to **Luxor** every day at 1600 (E£120, 14-15 hrs) which also stops at **Hurghada**. For **St Catherine's** you will have to join a minibus tour from Dahab (E£80-100, departs 2300), or for a drop-off in St Catherine's it's E£60 if you haggle. Bus schedules are posted around most camps. Overnight buses tend to be more expensive.

Car hire

Can be arranged at the Dahab Hilton.

Taxi

Service taxis Faster than the bus, another way to get around from city to city is to wait a service (pronounced *servees*) taxi, which leave when full from next to the bus station. **Taxis** A necessary expense for getting between Dahab City and the beaches. Tourists are usually charged more than Egyptians. To and from the bus station costs E£5. If you join others or take a pickups it's cheaper. To the Blue Hole, E£50 – the driver will wait and bring you back. If you are travelling en masse or can team up with some other wanderers, it is also a good way to get to St Catherine's or other places further afield.

❶ Directory

Sharm El-Sheikh *p405, map p406*

Banks There are several banks in Hadaba on Banks St, plus ATMs at the malls and large hotels. In Sharm El-Maya, there are ATMs in the market area and the Tiran Centre. In Na'ama Bay, there are also several Egyptian banks as well as HSBC (King of Bahrain St). ATMs are plentiful around the malls and in all hotels. Thomas Cook, T069-360 1808/9, in the Gafy Mall, offer TCs, cash advances on visa and other banking services. Big hotels exchange money at the standard rate. **Internet** Tiba Net in Sharm Old Market offers a speedy connection for E£5 and is open 1300-0100. Internet cafés are scattered around Na'ama Bay and are much more expensive at E£20 per hr. **Medical services** Sharm El-Sheikh International Hospital, 24-hr emergency room, T069-366 0984, midway between Sharm and Na'ama Bay, looks like a pyramid. Hyperbaric Centre, at the Travco Marina in Sharm El-Maya, T069-366 0922, for decompression emergencies T012-212 4292. South Sinai Hospital, Kennedy Mall, Peace Rd, T069-920 5790/4, T012-000 3533/44, open 24 hrs. For non-emergency cases, Sharm Medical Centre on Peace Rd, T069-366 1744, or there are doctors on call at the larger hotels. There are vast numbers of pharmacies, clearly signed, all over Sharm and Na'ama and larger hotels have them on site. **Post office** At the top of the hill in Hadaba, T069-366 0518, Sat-Thu 0800-2000. All the major hotels have mail services. **Telephone** The main telephone exchange is in Hadaba on the cliff, open 24 hrs. In Sharm and Na'ama Bay, sim cards are widely available.

Dahab *p410, map p411*

Banks Bank of Egypt in Dahab town accepts TCs and ATM cards. In the northern part of the Masbat there is a National Bank of Egypt that accepts TCs, exchanges money and has an ATM, 1030-2100. Gazala supermarket has a handy ATM outside, or there is bank opposite, open from 0930-2130. **Internet** is widely available, the going rate is E£5-6 per hr. **Post office** In Dahab town centre, Sat-Thu 0830-1500. In Masbat, you will also find a phone and post shop, clearly signed, near the bridge that sells stamps and will deliver your mail. **Telephone** Office in Dahab City.

East coast north of Dahab

As the Gulf of Aqaba narrows, sprawling coastal resorts are replaced by intimate camps and the mountains of Saudi Arabia loom ever closer across the tranquil sea. Nuweiba, from where ferries leave for Jordan, has plenty of mellow places that provide a real escape from humanity while still having all amenities to hand. Venturing further north, civilization peters out and simple Bedouin getaways mingle with the occasional tourist village along a dazzling stretch of coast. The road leads to the border town of Taba, in Egyptian hands since 1989, and chiefly of interest as an entry point to Israel. *▸▸ For listings, see pages 439-444.*

Ras Abu Gallum

Getting there From the Blue Hole, you can hire a camel (E£80) for the hour's journey along a magical track skirting the coast. You can also walk from the Blue Hole (bear in mind there is no shade), or simply arrange a car-and-camel trip in advance from Dahab. It is also possible to arrive from Nuweiba, to the north, by 4WD, which takes nearly two hours. The first 30 minutes, from Nuweiba to the sizeable Bedouin village of Bir Zehir, is on paved road, but after that the track is rough and corrugated.

In addition to the pristine marine gardens at Ras Abu Gallum, another protectorate area designated in 1992, the coast between Dahab and Nuweiba holds some of the most striking above-ground scenery in Sinai. High mountains and long winding valleys run right down to the sea. Although the Protectorate is valued mainly for its rare plant life, the diving here is also superb. It should be noted, however, that access to the underwater cave network at Ras Mamlah is strictly forbidden. Many divers have died here and their bodies remain unrecovered.

Most people come to dive, but the snorkelling along the reef is some of Sinai's best (bring equipment). Ras Abu Gallum remains a majestic tranquil spot with a welcoming Bedouin community and glorious beaches, but it is not unspoiled by the camel trains of tourists trudging through. Lying on the very edge of the sea, the Bedouin village itself is rather scruffy and made largely from plywood. There are several huts on the beach where you can stay, a shop, a couple of restaurants and tea-shops. There is also a solar-powered information centre, plus plenty of bright-eyed Bedouin children who will ask you to buy their jewellery. However, to find complete peace and magic you only have to go a couple of kilometres further north to the **Blue Lagoon** (45 minutes' walk, note that there is another little Bedouin encampment between Ras and the Lagoon). There, the most perfectly aquamarine sea filters into a lagoon set off by blindingly white sand and a reef lies just offshore (with excellent snorkelling when the sea is calm). A couple of idyllic camps await (see Sleeping, page 439).

Nuweiba → *For listings, see pages 439-444. Colour map 5, B6.*

Nuweiba lies 67 km north of Dahab and 64 km south of the Israeli border at Taba on a dazzlingly beautiful stretch of coast. Nuweiba's 'moshav', or cooperative village, used to be a major destination for Israeli tourists during the occupation but has long since been surpassed by Na'ama Bay as the Sinai's primary resort destination. The diving here might be rather tame in comparison to Sharm, but Nuweiba has many splendid sandy beaches with comfortable hotels that tend to be cheaper and are in closer proximity to Israel, Jordan and the wonders of the desert interior.

The town is divided into three distinct areas: the 'city', the port to the south, and the Bedouin village of Tarabeen to the north. Sadly, all three areas (and indeed many of the hotels and small camps along the coast up to Taba) have an eerie ghost-town feel since the second Intifada and, at the time of writing, continued tension means Israeli tourists are conspicuously absent from all but the camps closest to the border. Neglect is much in evidence, as the skeletons of unfinished bungalows and old bamboo huts disintegrate and plastic bags wash up on stretches of Nuweiba's gorgeous coast. But if complete peace and freedom from hassle are what you desire, there are still plenty of cosy camps on clean white sand to be found, and Nuweiba has a natural advantage over most of Dahab in that you can swim straight off the beach and snorkel out to some colourful reefs. Aside from winding down and floating in the Red Sea, it is also a much better place to get to meet Bedouin people and give something back to Sinai by organizing a tailor-made trip into the interior in the company of some locals to see the spectacular wadis and mountain villages.

Ins and outs

Getting around Nuweiba port is the set-off point for the ferry across the gulf to Aqaba. All the buses arrive at Nuweiba port and some continue on to the town centre or vice versa. You can ask the bus driver to drop you off at your chosen camp along the coast north of Nuweiba. From the port you can take a taxi that will deliver you directly to town or the village. Taxis in these parts have an unspoken camaraderie and tend to charge foreigners inflated prices for transport. Standard fare from the port to town centre is E£10-20, from the port to Tarabeen, E£20-30, and from Tarabeen to the town centre E£10. Any jeep or pickup cruising past will offer you 'taxi' and prices become more negotiable. Bargain hard and keep a sense of humour. ▸▸ *See Transport, page 399.*

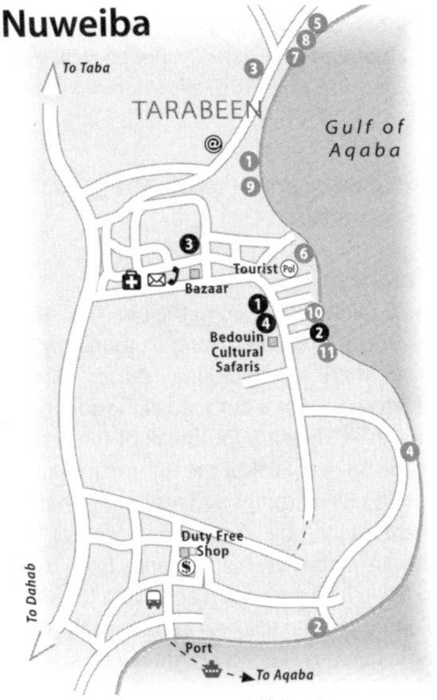

Not to scale

Sleeping
Amon Yahro **11**
Blue Bus **1**
El Waha Village **10**
Helnan Nuweiba **6**
La Sirene **4**
Mondial Village **3**
Nakhil Inn **5**
Nuweiba Hilton Coral Village **2**
Petra Camp **7**
Sababa Camp **8**
Soft Beach **9**

Eating
Cleopatra **1**
Dr Shishkabab **3**
Habiba Village **2**
Hang Kang **4**

Sights

Lounging on the beach, swimming and snorkelling, and playing backgammon, billiards or dominoes are about all one does in Nuweiba itself. The wild dolphin, Oleen, which befriended Abdullah, a local deaf Bedouin, and became a rather dubious tourist attraction for a while, is no longer seen these days. There are plenty of enterprising local Bedouin who organize camel treks and jeep safaris into the magnificent interior for day trips and more

Border essentials: Egypt–Jordan

ZOLL DOUANE

Nuweiba–Aqaba

From Nuweiba Port there are two ferries to **Aqaba** in Jordan that leave at the same time, supposedly 1400, every day except Thursday. The slow ferry takes three to four hours (barring potential obstacles), while the fast one (more expensive, comfortable and less crowded) about 1½ hours. On a Thursday, only the slow ferry is in operation. Times, however, can be erratic. Foreigners must pay in US$, US$60-65 for the slow boat, and US$70-90 for the fast boat (depending on class). The fast ferry is frequently cancelled due to bad weather; if this happens you can always travel overland via Eilat to Aqaba. Arrive at least two hours early to secure tickets for either ferry. To confirm departure time, which may change, call the port, T069-352 0216, or the Coral Hilton, T069-352 0320. The ticket office next to Nuweiba Port is open daily from 0800-1500 and 2000-2200.

Visas One-month Jordanian visas are issued on board, with charges varying according to nationality, but generally around US$15 (payable in dollars or dinars). There is also a US$10 departure tax.

extensive overnight safaris. Many visitors also make short trips to Petra in Jordan via the ferry to Aqaba.

Tarabeen

A 20-minute walk along the beach north of Nuweiba city lies the Bedouin settlement of Tarabeen, sprawled along a stunningly beautiful bay. Reminiscent of Dahab a decade back, there are traditional 'camps', Bedouin-style restaurants and a couple of hotels scattered about a dirt road alongside mini bazaars where shopping is relaxed and easy. However, since the outbreak of the first Intifada in late September 2000, Israelis, who made up over 80% of the tourism around Nuweiba, have virtually stopped coming. As a result, several camps and restaurants have closed, trash is washing up on the shores, and there is a tangible air of sadness in parts. Yet many camps are keeping standards up while the authorities are have recently been trying to smarten the beachfront up, and it's easy to fall in love with the place. From the shore you can see the mountains of Saudi Arabia painted pink on the near horizon as the Gulf of Aqaba narrows towards the north, and as night falls tiny clusters of lights come on in villages across the water – it is utterly magical.

Nuweiba to Taba

Along the striking stretch of shore between Nuweiba and Taba where rugged red mountains twist and turn and pour down to the sea, there are several scatterings of Bedouin camps and tourist villages that offer respite and serenity away from the more trafficky resorts of the south. They all are accessible via bus or service taxi; simply ask the driver to drop you by the roadside at your desired destination. Some camps are dilapidated forgone attempts falling apart at the seams, others are gems and sensitive to their environs. Notable is **Ras Al-Shaitan**, which means 'Devil's Head', an area named for a peculiar rock formation by the beach, 12 km north of Nuweiba. Here, a string of camps on the beach under an amazing virgin Sinai sky are kept busy by Israeli tourists, and there is excellent snorkelling just 20 m offshore. A downside is that the beach is stony in

Taba tug of war

Taba is an enclave of land of no more than 1 sq km on the Gulf of Aqaba seized by the Israelis in the war of 1956 but, unlike the rest of Sinai, not returned to Egypt. Assuming that the Taba strip would be forever Israeli, an international hotel complex was built there (now the Taba Hilton). In 1986 agitation by Egypt for a final settlement of the international border at Taba led the dispute being put to arbitration.

This revealed that the border post at Ras Taba, one of 14 put in place after the 1906 Anglo-Turkish agreement, had been moved by the Israeli side.

In one of the oddest of cases concerning the delimitation of an international border, it was found that the Israeli army had cut away part of the hill at Ras Taba to enable Israeli artillery to have a good sweep of the Sinai coast road as it approached the port of Eilat. At the same time the Israeli military engineers removed the border post that rested on the top of Ras Taba. This gave the Israeli government the excuse to claim that, despite Israeli maps to the contrary, the old border had always run south of the Taba strip. In 1989 the arbitrators returned Taba to Egypt, though it remains virtually an enclave with border posts on all sides.

comparison to other places. **Basata**, meaning 'simplicity' in Arabic, is 23 km north of Nuweiba and the eco-lodge here is one of Sinai's most popular get-aways for good reason – the beach is divine and ambiance perfect. Three kilometres north of Basata and 30 km south of Taba is **Bir Sweir**, where a 2-km-long swathe of soft sandy beach has numerous cheap camps all offering decent facilities (due to its popularity with young Israelis), a reef excellent for snorkelling, and the sun sets on the mountains of Saudi Arabia turning the sea pink. **Taba Heights**, a tourist development just 9 km southwest of Taba, is a newly built 'resort village' comprising of hotels, restaurants, shops and a marina attracting European visitors directly to Taba airport 20 km away. To date, several huge high-end hotels with hundreds of rooms have been built and enjoy 5 km of beach, pools, health clubs, a golf course, casinos and all other five-star amenities, with more luxury hotels under construction. There is a good watersports centre here, whose diving, windsurfing, canoes, etc can be used by travellers who are staying at the smaller camps to the south.

Taba → *For listings, see pages 439-444. Colour map 5, B6.*

This town has a special place in the hearts of most Egyptians because, although it is only tiny, it was the last piece of territory that was occupied by the Israelis. The fact that the luxury Sonesta hotel, one of Israel's best and most popular hotels, was in the Taba enclave no doubt complicated the dispute. Despite having to pay compensation to the Sonesta's owners, before handing the hotel over to the Hilton group to manage and despite the very small size of the area in dispute, Cairo had been determined to retrieve every centimetre of Egyptian land and was satisfied by the outcome.

Taba is unusual, an international border town between an empty desert and the bright lights of Eilat. The coastline is beautiful but exceedingly windy. Besides hotels there is little else in the tiny enclave except barracks and facilities for the border guards and customs officials. Having won Taba back from Israel, the government is now concentrating on development of the tourist industry in the region and is building power stations and other infrastructural facilities to support the planned influx.

Border essentials: Egypt–Israel

Taba–Eilat

Although the checkpoints are always open it is better to cross between 0700-2100. Also avoid crossing on Fridays, just before the Israeli Sabbath when almost all businesses close and transport ceases, and Saturdays altogether. Free three-month Israeli entry visas are available for most Western tourists. Once on the Israeli side of the border you can catch a service taxi or number 15 bus into Eilat.

Note Make sure that your entry card and not your passport are stamped because an Israeli stamp, and even an Egyptian entry stamp from Taba, may disqualify you from entering some Arab countries.

Ins and outs

Getting there and around The easiest way to reach Taba, 390 km from Cairo and 260 km from Sharm El-Sheikh, is via the airport, which has both domestic and international charter flights. Some tourists arrive via Israel's Eilat airport, which is only 15 km across the border. Guests of the Taba Hilton and Nelson Village, see page 441, do not have to pay Israeli departure tax. These hotels will provide a pass to allow free movement through the border during your time of stay.

Sights

Sightseeing in Taba is limited to visits across the Israeli border to Eilat, trips to the beautiful interior, or boats to **Pharaoh's Island**, where lie the ruins of Salah Al-Din's fortress (the most important Islamic remains in Sinai). The fortress was originally built in 1115 by the Crusaders to guard the head of the Gulf of Aqaba and protect pilgrims travelling between Jerusalem and St Catherine's monastery. It was also used to levy taxes on Arab merchants travelling to and from Aqaba. Salah Al-Din took it over in 1171 but abandoned it in the face of European attacks 12 years later. The island is a short boat ride (400 m) from the Salah-el-Din Hotel and the hotel also organizes snorkelling trips around the island's surrounding reefs, but beware – the currents can be strong.

Taba Managed Resource Protected Area is the newest and largest in the network of coastal and inland protected areas (designated in January 1998). It lies south and west of Taba and includes the Coloured Canyon. There is a wealth of ancient writings and carvings on rock walls in the area that span the history of Sinai, the crossroads between Asia and Africa. The scripts include Arabic, Semitic, Greek, Nabatean and other, unknown, languages.

East coast north of Dahab listings

For Sleeping and Eating price codes and other relevant information, see pages 26-31.

Sleeping

Ras Abu Gallum and the Blue Lagoon *p434*

In the Bedouin village at Ras Abu Gallum there are about 10 modest huts on the beach right next to the sea that can be rented for E£20 per person per night. There are a few squat toilets, but no running water or electricity. Water and other basic necessities are available at inflated prices and there are a couple of restaurants/tea-shops.

At the **Blue Lagoon** there are a couple of small camps, with *hooshas* (huts) that are a step above those at Ras Abu Gallum, with rag-rugs, palm trunk seating areas and good restaurants. But it's the location – quite simply other-worldly in its pristine beauty – that makes the effort of getting here worthwhile:

F Laguna Camp, has some good huts, a couple of which sit on a spit of land that extends far into the blue waters, while next door **Selim's Camp** nestles by the Bedouin fishing boats on the lagoon. Both places can provide meals (fish E£60).

Nuweiba *p434, map p435*

Nuweiba has a few higher-spec hotels on the shoreline between the town centre and port. There is also a range of comfortable camps and simple hotels in Tarabeen, the most attractive clusters being at the northern and southern points of the beach now that the central area has become rather dilapidated. See also the listings below for a scattering of magical tourist settlements along the coast between Nuweiba and Tarabeen that offer more remote, tranquil accommodation.

L-AL Nuweiba Hilton Coral Village, on the beach just north of the port, T069-352 0320, www1.hilton.com. Choice of restaurants, water sports, camel and horse riding, safaris, bicycles, squash, tennis, children's facilities, 2 heated pools, bank, internet access, travel agency, disco. A stylish resort, very relaxing, ideal for recuperating, rather isolated from rest of Sinai resorts. Excellent snorkelling is a 15-min walk away. **Aquasport Dive and Watersport Centre** on the beach, one of the best diving centres in Nuweiba.

AL-D Helnan Nuweiba, T069-350 0401, www.helnan.com. Cosy chalet-style rooms with all the extras, private beach, dive centre, tennis, beach volleyball, small gym and a sizable pool. It's worth shelling out that bit extra for well-kept grounds, comfy loungers under wicker parasols, and to be somewhere that's fairly bustling (by Nuweiban standards). Half board available. There's also a large cluster of huts

B-C La Sirene, T069-350 0701, www.lasirenehotel.com. Becoming a bit run down, but rooms are spacious with tasteful decor– all have their own balcony and some have a huge rooftop terrace. No pool, but excellent snorkelling on the coral reef, dive centre is open sporadically.

D-E El Waha Village, T069-350 0420, www.elwahavillage.com. Double rooms in old-fashioned chalets for US$20 (add US$5 for breakfast) with a/c, fridge and TV, or camping on the beach for E£15. It has an air of dereliction, but is kept clean by the pleasant staff.

G Amon Yahro, T016-685 2600. Clean huts with attractive seating areas for hanging out, cheap at E£30. Their little patch of beach is very well maintained (around the edges the rubbish is encroaching).

There's a handful of basic hotels next to the port costing around E£60-90 per night, should you get stranded waiting for the ferry. During the *Hajj* these are always full, but then so is the ferry.

Tarabeen *p436, map p435*

Tarabeen offers a range of possibilities. For E£20, you can still get a hut in one of the basic camps. They are quite comparable in quality, though some have cleaner bathrooms and offer extras like hot water, fans and mosquito nets. For E£50, you can expect to find a room with a/c and private bath.

B Nakhil Inn, T069-350 0879. A tasteful well-run hotel at the northern tip of the bay, on a spotless private beach with direct access to good snorkelling on the reef (free masks). Rooms are spacious with huge windows (the nicest have a mezzanine with views of the sea from the bed), bar, free Wi-Fi, indoor (with fireplace) and outdoor restaurant, desert excursions, dive centre (closed off-season, but offers trips to Ras Abu Galum when open). Unquestionably the nicest place to stay in Tarabeen. Breakfast included.

F Mondial Village, T012-796 3385, mondialvillage@yahoo.com. Stone-built rooms with hot showers en suite, a/c and large clean beds. Food is cheap in a typically laid-back hang-out with a pool table, doubles cost E£50 or E£70 with breakfast, they have beer.

F Soft Beach, T010-364 7586, www.softbeachcamp.com. Managers Kamal and Christine have made the south end of Tarabeen the place to be again. A range of bamboo huts share a good shower block (loo paper), hammocks sway in the breeze and the beach area is swept daily. The reliable menu is a bit pricier, desert trips are easy to arrange – E£200 for 1 person, cost goes down as numbers go up. However, they do get annoyed when you eat your meals at other camps.

G Blue Bus, T010-988 3854, www.bluebus.de. This camp remains the best laid out in town, with a small cluster of huts (clean linen) nestling by a dune by a sandy stretch of beach, and decked out with cushions and rugs in the chill-out spaces. Doubles E£30.

G Petra Camp, T069-350 0086. Run by a young Bedouin lawyer, this place is well-managed and the staff are sweet, offers clean, comfortable huts among a palm garden, decent shared bathrooms with hot water, good food (cheaper than other camps) served as you recline by the water's edge. Guests are consistently happy. Rooms are E£20-40, and there's (slow) internet for E£20 per hr.

G Sababa Camp, T016-183 5517, www.sababacamp.com. An old timer in Tarabeen, huts have doors painted with yin yangs and oms by hippies of yesteryear, as well as fans, mosquito nets, electric outlets and sheets on the beds, bathrooms are clean and the water hot. The restaurant and beach seating is an attractive place to chill out. Desert excursions are offered.

Nuweiba to Taba *p436*

Ras Shaitan

C-E Castle Beach, next to Ayaash (below), T012-739 8495. A bit more comfortable with tasteful bungalows that have electricity and their own terrace. Sheets and towels can also be provided. The bathrooms are cleaned every few hours, restaurant is excellent but more expensive than most. Desert trips with experienced guides available. Generally busy.

E-F Ayaash's Camp (also known simply as 'Ras Shaitan'), T010-525 9109. This is the 1st camp from Nuweiba and lies directly in front of the 'head'. Accommodation is extremely simple, scattered about the hills and shore, some are only a few metres from the waterline. There is no hot water or electricity. Desert safaris are available and it's possible to rent snorkel and fins to explore the reef offshore. There's also a busy restaurant that often is the gathering spot for late-night jam sessions.

F Seven Heaven, Ras Shaitan, www.sevenheavenhotel.com. Friendly family place, of the same dynasty who own places of the same name in Dahab and Luxor. 36 chalets use outside bathrooms, more comfort offered than your basic *hoosha* with beds, mirrors and 2 generators.

Basata

B-D Basata Ecolodge, 23 km north of Nuweiba, T069-350 0480/1, www.basata.com. German-educated owner Sherif El-Ghamrawy has created a genuinely environmentally conscious retreat. There is only candlelight in the 18 simple, clean beachfront huts, plus there are 10 domed villas with private bathrooms. Camping is permitted and very popular. There are some steadfast rules – no drugs or alcohol (in public) and no late-night noise, nudity, or sleeping in the common area. The result is a respectable, family-friendly environment. The kitchen runs on an honour system where guests are invited to take what they want and write it down, but if doing your own cooking doesn't appeal, pizzas and bread are baked fresh daily (minimum charge E£50 per day). Fabulous (optional) communal dinners are served to lodge guests every evening. The beach is perfect and there's a good reef for snorkelling offshore. Sherif organizes desert treks and tours for groups and individuals. It's wise to book ahead, as the huts are often reserved months in advance – especially during national holidays. Israelis will be told it's full, even when it isn't.

Bir Sweir

Breakfasts are not included (usually E£30) and mains are from E£40-80, including the famed *'maglooba'*.

C Sally Land Tourist Village, T069-922 0007, www.sallylandresort.com. Tastefully planned khan-like stone chalets with crenulated roofs and domes are pleasantly white and dark wood inside, on a large stretch of beach, though there are few guests unless the German-Egyptian owners have a group booked. Prices are half-board.

F Alexandria, Bir Sweir, T012-166 1042/T010-618 7041, www.alexandriabeach.com. The most international of all Bir Sweir's camps, with a mix of Europeans and Israelis plus kindly Sudanese staff, is also one of the largest and most popular. Huts are large with 2-4 beds (E£35 per person), the food is homely, shrubs and colourful rugs adorn the area, and they will get you beer. At the southern end of the beach.

F Al Tarek, Bir Sweir, T052-635 1449/012-108 1189, www.altarek-sinai.com. About the cutest huts on the beach at Bir Sweir, with curved rush roofs and shady terraces out the front, are laid out with care and thought to privacy. The lovely manager plays Arabic music in the sociable restaurant. E£30 per person.

F Diana Beach, Bir Sweir, T012-405 0964. Popular place, with good fish meals from the busy kitchen, attractively set out huts and lots of space. Possibly Sinai's best hammock is to be found next to the sea here, E£25 per person.

F Sun Sweir, T018-562 8410. Sweet water showers are a big plus, this smaller camp has 25 huts with lights inside (some with beds, others mattresses). It is open all year round, and especially recommended for the excellent food.

G Paradise Sweir, Bir Sweir, T052-500 1622, www.paradisesinai.com. At the northern end of the beach, this is about the cheapest camp at E£15 per person. Scruffy public areas, but the huts are quite sweet, there's a pool table, lots of Israelis and local Bedouin hanging out, generally bustling.

Taba *p437*

The huge resort hotels at Taba Heights, which include the Hyatt, Marriott, Sofitel and Intercontinental, have all the 5-star trimmings and are chiefly booked from abroad.

L-AL Taba Hilton and Nelson Village, T069-353 0140, www.hiltonworldresorts.com. The reliable, high-rise Hilton has dominated the area for years, right on the Israeli border. Private beach looks onto the tip of the Gulf of Aqaba, 2 pools, tennis courts, acceptable restaurants and bars, plus a nightclub and casino. Snorkelling, quad bikes into the desert and trips to Pharaoh's Island are among the activities on offer. There is an excellent coral reef just off the shore and a diving and watersports centre. Nelson Village is an extension of the hotel and they share facilities. It's more sensitively designed using natural materials and set in pleasing gardens.

AL Tobya Boutique Hotel, T069-353 0275, www.tobyaboutiquehotel.com. Though it doesn't meet all the credentials of a boutique retreat, it is the most quirky choice in town, 2 km south of the border. It is worth knowing that outside guests can use the 2 pools and private beach for the day, should you be stranded for a few hours in Taba. Prices are half-board.

Eating

Nuweiba *p434, map p435*

ΨΨ **Cleopatra**, T069-350 0503, in front of Nuweiba Village. Open 0900-2300. Simple fish, meats and salads are freshly prepared and served under flashing fairy lighting.

ΨΨ **Dr Shishkabab**, in town centre. Open late. Has lost some of its acclaim in recent years but still serves up a cheap shish kabab and other traditional grub; the soups and Egyptian staples are definitely recommended.

ΨΨ **Habiba Village**, T069-350 0770, www.sinai4you.com/habiba. Open until midnight. Beachside restaurant that cooks up fresh Bedouin bread, good fish, and has an 'Italian Corner'. Can get busy from midday as it caters to tourists on day trips from Sharm enjoying the buffet.

ΨΨ **Hang Kang**, Mazara Rd, in front of the Helnan hotel. Open 1000-2200. A notable Asian restaurant that has been around for years, serving up surprisingly good Chinese and Korean feasts (mains E£35-75). Hot and sour soup is a winner, plus there are numerous pork dishes, alcohol served.

Tarabeen *p436, map p435*

All the camps and hotels have eating spots bang next to the sea offering similar food at similar prices.

ΨΨ **Blue Bus**, a popular restaurant with a pleasant beach area to enjoy mid-priced pizzas, pastas and fish. Excellent juices.

ΨΨ **Sababa Camp**, extensive menu including pizzas, pastas and good fresh fish.

Nuweiba to Taba *p436*

ΨΨΨ **Castle Zaman**, Taba-Nuweiba Rd, just north of **Basata Ecolodge**, T069-350 1234/ 018-214 0591, www.castlezaman.com. Open 1200-2230. Set on a hill 1.5 km north of Basata Ecolodge, the owner has spent years perfecting every detail of this dream place, and diners come from afar for the famed slow-cooked meat and seafood specialities, €40 a head (vegetarian version available, but for the same price; book in advance). Alternatively, an entrance charge of E£100 per person allows use of the exquisite pool and private beach for the day, and is redeemable against sunset drinks as the lights start twinkling across the water in the villages of Saudi Arabia. A 'treasure room' has attractive gifts, there's a sauna, and the hilltop setting is divine. Recommended.

Taba *p437*

ΨΨΨ **Taba Hilton**, has several restaurants serving varying cuisines, all are expensive but of a high standard.

There is a coffee shop in the bazaar opposite the bus station that serves tasty cheap Egyptian staples from about 0600, should you get stranded.

Activities and tours

Nuweiba *p434, map p435*

Besides diving and desert safaris, sports equipment and facilities are only available at the large hotels. **The Hilton** rents jetskis and kayaks.

Desert safaris

Desert safaris and excursions are widely available from Nuweiba and the nearby camps and tourist villages. Virtually every hotel and camp has connections with experienced Bedouin that know the desert like the back of their hands. There are countless majestic spots in the Sinai interior, some much more frequented than others. Most visited is the **Coloured Canyon**, a stunning site even in the midst of tour buses. From Nuweiba, you should be able to find a ride in a jeep for E£150-200. Other striking spots often included on camel and jeep safaris are **Ain Um Ahmed**, a large fertile palm-laden oasis fed by the snowmelts from far-off peaks; the impressive **White Canyon**; and **Wadi Ghazala**, a valley where gazelle are known to graze. Easily accessible in a half-day jeep safari (E£300-350) is **Ain Khudra**, or 'green spring', a magical and tranquil destination where a few families live. There are 3 tea-shops here when travellers can stay overnight, and the setting in a white and gold wadi is memorable.

The cost is fairly consistent – by camel it's E£120 per person for a day safari, E£180 per night, including food. Costs generally do not include water, so plan to bring all you need. For a big adventure, some locals organize camel safaris for 2- to 10-day expeditions into the interiors. Trips might include the mountain plateaux of Gebel El-Guna, passing through little-visited wadis where the wind has carved the coloured sandstone into supernatural forms and awesome white sand dunes startle the eye. If you can't find a Bedouin guide that feels good, **Abanoub Travel**, T069-352 0201, www.abanoub.com, is a reputable tour company that has organized safe camel and jeep safaris for years. They're at the pricier end of the spectrum.

Diving

Nuweiba is known more for sandy beaches than diving, but, because its waters are quiet and clear, it makes a suitable spot for beginners. There are some good snorkelling areas offshore, the most famous is the **Stone House**, just south of town. There are a few dive centres around, all of which offer trips to nearby sites that are more impressive than the few reefs off Nuweiba shores.

SCUBA Divers, based in La Sirene, T069-350 0705. Contact them in advance to check whether an international certified instructor is present on site to teach beginners' courses, as now that Nuweiba is so quiet he's not consistently in town. However, diving and snorkelling gear are always available to rent.

Sinai Diving Centre, at the **Helnan Hotel**, T069-3500 401, www.helnan.com, have a well-maintained and efficient centre in the grounds of the hotel.

Transport

Nuweiba *p434, map p435*

Bus

T069-520 3701. Departure times from Nuweiba frequently change so ask at any hotel or camp to confirm times. A bus leaves for **Cairo** at 0900 and 1500 (E£70, 7 hrs). **Sharm El-Sheikh** (E£16, 3 hrs) buses go via **Dahab** (E£11, 1 hr) and leave at 0600 and 1600. A bus goes to **Suez** only at 0600 (E£29), or the 0630 for Sharm carries on to Suez though it's much slower. Buses all depart from the terminal at the port. For **St Catherine's**, you must go to Dahab, and arrange transport there.

Microbuses offer cheaper and sometimes quicker transport. They operate on a leave-when-full policy and travel north and south along the main highway as well as to **Cairo**. Check prices before setting off, but you shouldn't pay more than E£70 to go to Cairo.

Ferry

Two ferries to **Jordan** leave from Nuweiba Port at 1400 on Fri-Wed, one is fast and the other slow; on Thu only the slow boat makes the trip. Visas for Jordan are available on board – see box, page 436, for further details.

Taxis

Service taxis With passengers sharing the cost of the journey, service taxis are available from Nuweiba port to **Taba** and other towns in the region. Taxis around Nuweiba are pricy as it's a captive market – from Tarabeen about E£10 to Nuweiba City and E£20 to the port.

Taba *p437*

Air

Taba Airport, www.taba-heights.co.uk/airport, 18 km inland from Taba, has flights to **Cairo** on Sun and Thu and international charter flights bringing tourists to Taba Heights. There's an EgyptAir office in Taba, but it opens sporadically due to lack of demand. Eilat airport (15 km from Taba) has direct daily flights to major European cities. (No problem at Egyptian border but customs officials at the airport are very thorough).

Bus

East Delta Bus Co, T069-353 0250, runs daily buses to **Cairo** at 1030 and 1630 (6-7 hrs, E£65), **Sharm El-Sheikh** (4 hrs, E£30) via **Dahab** (3 hrs, E£25) and **Nuweiba** (1 hr, E£11) at 0500 and 1500. There is no direct bus to **St Catherine's**; you have to go to Dahab and join a microbus tour.

Taxis

Service taxis driven by local Bedouin regularly transport visitors to **Nuweiba**, **Dahab** and **Sharm**. They are more frequent, more comfortable, and quicker than buses – but more expensive. Assuming the car is full, expect to pay around E£30 per person to **Tarabeen** and **Nuweiba**, E£50 to **Dahab** and E£80 to **Sharm El-Sheikh**.

Directory

Nuweiba *p434, map p435*

Banks Both the Helnan and the Hilton have ATMs. There are also 3 banks with ATMs near the port, the one opposite the bus station is reliable. **Internet** Wi-Fi is available in the Hilton and in Tarabeen there is an internet café on the opposite side of the road to Blue Bus camp, for E£3 per hr. Gamal Camp in the centre of Tarabeen charges for E£20 for a poor connection. **Post office** In Nuweiba City, near the hospital, open Sat-Thu 0800-1500. **Telephone** Just down from the post office, near the bazaar, open 24 hrs.

Taba *p437*

Banks Bank Misr, on the Egyptian side of the border. The Taba Hilton also has a bank that is always open and changes Israeli money. **Post office** Taba Hilton sends mail via adjacent Eilat rather than distant Cairo. **Telephone** is past the bus station on the way to the border, but is not open 24 hrs.

The interior

→ *Colour map 2, B/C 6.*

The largest single protected area in Sinai is St Catherine's National Park (designated in 1987), which covers a roughly triangular area of the mountains south from St Catherine's Monastery. This Greek orthodox monastery at the base of Mount Sinai has attracted pilgrims and visitors for centuries and despite its location in the heart of the Sinai wilderness, it's one of the most important tourist sites in the country. The park also contains ibex, gazelle and hyena, hyrax, leopards and possibly cheetahs. It's a relatively untouched region and a safari across the desert plateaux, past dusty acacias and across dry riverbeds, can be done by foot, camel or jeep. A few intrepid trekkers weave between the ragged shards of the high mountains, surprised by the lush gardens hidden in valleys and dazzled by the ochre glow of the landscape against the blue sky. Bedouin have been recruited as guides and community guards to help the rangers patrol this immense expanse of land and noticeable progress is apparent, particularly in clearing the area of rubbish and providing information and nature trails. Another peak nearby (Egypt's highest) with some great hiking potential and a monastery is Mount Catherine and further west is the welcome flash of green that is Wadi Feiran. ▸▸ *For listings, see pages 450-453.*

St Catherine → *For listings, see pages 450-453.*

Ins and outs

Getting there The road journey from Dahab to St Catherine, which is generally good with little traffic, takes about 1½ hours. However, there is no public transport so you will have to join a tour or hire a taxi for the journey (about E£180). On the way, at the top of a very steep hill there is a breathtaking view over the desert. The coaches and taxis stop here and Bedouins attempt to sell fossils, sand-roses and other souvenirs. While all of the organized tours to St Catherine stop at the monastery itself, the bus service from Cairo stops in the small village of St Catherine about 2 km from the monastery.

Information **St Catherine's National Park visitor centre** ⓘ *T069-347 0032, it is supposed to be open Mon-Thu and Sat 0830-1300, but is frequently locked*, is on the main road before the turning to the monastery. Has information on shorter walks, and a few books and maps of the area, and excellent information on the tribes, ecology and history of the region. Alternatively access walking tours and maps online at www.touregypt.net/walkingtours. A useful and inspiring website is www.st-katherine.net, for information on trekking, Bedouin culture and the St Catherine's region in general.

The **Tourist Police** ⓘ *T069-347 0046*, are in St Catherine's, main square, opposite the bus station.

Best time to visit St Catherine is very cold in winter with a metre of snow a few times a year, and snow sometimes until March, but it is very hot in summer.

St Catherine's Monastery

ⓘ *Cairo office T02-248 28513. Mon-Thu and Sat 0900-1130, Fri 1045-1145, closed Sun and public holidays, free. (Only Orthodox Christians are allowed to attend the long Sun service.) Visitors to the inside of the monastery must dress modestly, no shorts or bare arms are permitted. Although an official tour guide, who will explain the history and symbolism of each part of the monastery, is a bonus he is not essential if you buy the guidebook in the small bookshop near the entrance.*

The **Burning Bush**, through which God is said to have spoken to Moses, holds religious significance for Jews, Christians and Muslims and in AD 337 Empress Helena, mother of Constantine, decreed that a sanctuary was to be built around what was thought to be the site of the bush. This became a refuge for an increasing number of hermits and pilgrims who traversed the wilderness of the Sinai Valley over the following centuries. Israeli pilgrims are few and far between these days, but the monastery has long been unique in that here the three great monotheistic religions have come together peaceably, without clashes. A rather unimpressive. overgrown evergreen bush, which is claimed to be a transplanted descendant of the Burning Bush, grows in the courtyard inside the monastery, and there is an almost continual photo-call going on beneath its thorny branches.

Between AD 537 and 562, Emperor Justinian expanded the site considerably by building fortifications and providing soldiers to protect the residents and adding the Church of the Virgin and the Basilica of the Transfiguration. The monastery and its community which then, as today, was controlled by the Byzantine Church were tolerated by the subsequent Muslim conquerors. The number of pilgrims dwindled until a body, claimed to be that of the Egyptian-born St Catherine, was 'discovered' in the 10th century and was brought to the monastery. This attracted many pilgrims during the period of Crusader occupation (1099-1270). The numbers of both pilgrims and monks, who are now restricted to Greeks

St Catherine's Monastery

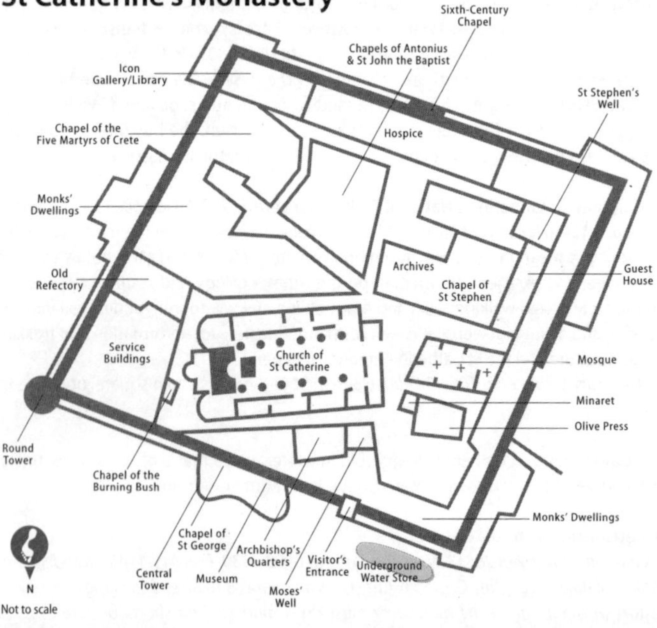

mainly from the Mount Athos area, subsequently waxed and waned until today there are only 25 monks, although the thousands of international pilgrims and tourists actually make the monastery unbearably crowded in the high season.

The site The ancient gate on the western face has been walled up (but the funnel above, for pouring oil on unwary attackers, remains) and now visitors enter through a newer door in the north wall. The outer wall, constructed of local granite by Justinian's builders, is 2- to 3-m thick and the height, which varies due to the uneven topography, is never less than 10 m and in places reaches 20 m. The southern face has some interesting raised Christian symbols.

West of the church is a small 11th-century **mosque** which, originally a guesthouse, was converted apparently in order to placate the Muslim invaders and to encourage them to tolerate the monastery. The detached minaret that faces the church is 10 m high. Significantly, however, the church steeple is considerably taller.

Beyond the entrance is the white rectangular minaret of a Fatimid mosque, built in 1106 as a shelter for pilgrims on the way to Mecca, the keys of which are held by the local Jabaliya tribe. On special occasions the mosque is in use, and Bedouins work in the monastery alongside the monks. The highlight of the walled monastery, which includes the monks' quarters, refectory, library and gardens (not open to the public), is the highly decorative and incense-perfumed **Church of the Transfiguration**. The church was built of granite in the shape of a basilica between AD 542-551, in memory of Emperor Justinian's wife. Its 12 enormous pillars, each a single piece of granite, are free-standing and decorated with beautiful icons representing the saints that are venerated in each of the 12 months of the year. A candle is lit below the relevant icon on each saint's day. Examine the capitals for their Christian symbols. The walls, pillars and cedar-wood doors of the church are all original – by comparison, the 11th-century doors made by the Crusaders seem almost new! The ancient roof is hidden above a more recent (18th-century) ceiling with reliefs of animals and plants. Above them the inscription (in Greek) reads, "This is the gate to the Lord; the righteous shall enter into it." The hanging oil lanterns and swinging incense burners, plus Greek monks lit by shafts of sunlight, do something to detract from the camera-wielding masses shuffling through (even though photography is forbidden). The iconostasis is dated at 1612. In the apse is the chief delight of this building – a magnificent mosaic illustrating the Transfiguration. It is the earliest and one of the finest mosaics of the Eastern Church. The theme is taken from St Matthew's Gospel. Christ is in the centre with Moses and Elijah at each side and Peter, James and John at his feet. Around these are further figures identified as the 12 apostles, the 12 prophets, the abbot at the time of the mosaic's construction and John of Climax, the deacon. The three-tiered bell tower at the western end of the church was built in 1871. There are nine bells, each of a different size. They came as a gift from Russia and are used only for special services. The original wooden bell, older than the metal bells, is used daily.

The **Library** houses some of the monastery's most extraordinary treasures, unfortunately (but not surprisingly) it is closed to the general public. It has an almost unrivalled collection of precious Greek, Arabic, Syriac, Georgian, Armenian Coptic, Ethiopian and Slavonic manuscripts, reputedly second only to that of the Vatican. There are over 6000 books and over 3000 manuscripts, mostly in Greek, including the famous Codex Syriacus, a fifth-century translation of the gospels.

The monastery's small, but excellent, refurbished **museum** ⓘ *E£25, students E£20, visit after 1000 when the initial crush has died down,* contains a collection of the gifts presented to the monastery over the centuries. The treasures were randomly scattered throughout the monastery until their accumulated worth was calculated by Friar Pachomius who then carefully gathered and preserved them in one place. Many interesting items have been lost over the ages, but it is fascinating to trace the routes of the pilgrims and of monks who sought alms through these treasures from cities as far-flung as Moscow and Calcutta. Also on display are a few of the monastery's 2000 priceless icons, a uniquely complete series with examples from every period, and a small selection of illuminated manuscripts from the library.

Because the monastery's **cemetery** in the gardens was so small, a custom developed of storing the overflow of monks' skeletons in the crypt of the Chapel of St Tryphon. This serves as the ossuary of the **Charnel House** that was in the monastery gardens. When a monk died his body was buried in the cemetery in the place of the oldest body, which was then removed to the Charnel House. The remains of the archbishops are kept separate in special niches. There's usually a queue to view this rather macabre room full of skeletons and skulls.

The monastery gardens are small. All the soil was carried here by the monks, who also constructed the water tanks for irrigation. It contains olive and apricot trees, plums and cherries with vegetables growing between. Immediately to the right of the monastery's main entrance at **Kleber's Tower**, which is about 15 m high and 3 m thick, is **Moses' Well**, which it is claimed has never dried up. It is supposed to be where the 40-year-old Moses, fleeing from Egypt, met one of Jethro's seven daughters whom he subsequently married.

Mount Sinai

If you've journeyed this far, attempt a climb up Mount Sinai (Jebel Musa), 2285 m, where, according to Muslim, Jewish and Christian tradition, Moses received the tablets of Law known as the Ten Commandments. The view is particularly spectacular at sunset and sunrise, when the mountain ranges are lit pink and gold. However, the vast majority make the traipse up for sunrise, setting off at an ungodly hour in the cold and dark to find it all but impossible to secure a good spot amidst the mass of blanket-wrapped forms at the summit. Those with limited time do this so as combine it with a visit the monastery (which is only open in the mornings). However, if you have a couple of days, it is better to start the ascent at about 1600 (an hour earlier in winter) in order to arrive at sunset. And, if you walk up via the more challenging steps, frequent solitary interludes can indeed feel spiritual and the passionate pilgrims met on the way only serve to intensify the experience. The 3700 steps, accessed from immediately behind the Monastery, are the shortest route (1½ to two hours), tough going and very difficult in the dark. Take a torch. The steps take you past the sixth-century **Elijah's Gate** and the **Shrive Gate** where pilgrims used to confess their sins to a priest before continuing their hike. You are supposed to take a guide with you, which police try to enforce, which is E£85 (you can negotiate this down). The path is less crowded and dirty than the other route, which is easier but indirect (about 2½ hours) and can be done on camel – there are plenty for hire behind the monastery for about E£100. Either way, the last 700 steps have to be done on foot and take another 30 minutes. Although there are refreshment stalls on the way up, getting more expensive nearer the summit, it is advisable to take at least two litres of water per person if making the ascent during the day. The stiff walk is quite rough and stout shoes and warm clothing are essential. On Mount Sinai is a chapel where services are performed on some Sundays by the monks and a mosque where a sheep is sacrificed once a year. Sleeping near the top is possible (see Sleeping, page 451) and blankets and mattresses are available for hire (E£10) around the summit.

Blazing bushes and Catherine Wheels

Mount Sinai marked the halfway point of the flight of the Jews from Egypt to the 'promised land'. Moses was clearly an inspirational leader for the incident of the burning bush led him to return to Egypt to lead his people to the land of milk and honey. But despite calling down from God the 10 plagues (frogs, lice, locusts, hail and fire among them), he failed to persuade the Pharaoh to release them from their slave labour. Finally the 80-year-old Moses asked God to strike the Egyptians with the passover when the Jews marked their houses with lamb's blood and were spared the massacre of all first-born children. As a result, the Pharoah banished the 600,000 Israelite men, women and children from Egypt. Their epic journey is related in the Book of Exodus in the Bible. They were pursued by the Egyptians (drowned after the Red Sea divided to allow the Israelites across), faced starvation (rescued with manna from heaven) and thirst (saved when a spring flowed from a rock Moses had struck with his staff) and defeated an attack by the Amaleks.

On Mount Sinai, Moses received the wisdom of the Ten Commandments, which have formed the code of practice for human behaviour for centuries.

The supposed site of the burning bush was developed into a monastery and in the 10th century named after Saint Catherine. According to legend Saint Catherine, who was born in AD 294 and was from a noble family in Alexandria, was a Christian convert who was martyred in the early fourth century for refusing to renounce her faith. She converted hundreds of people to Christianity and accused Emperor Maxentius of idolatry. When he tried to have her broken it was claimed that she shattered the spiked (Catherine) wheel by touching it, so Maxentius resorted to having her beheaded in Alexandria. After her execution her body vanished and according to legend was transported by angels to the top of Egypt's highest mountain, now named after her. Three centuries later this body was 'discovered', brought down from the mountain and placed in a golden casket in the church where it remains to this day.

Mount Catherine

At 2642 m Mount Catherine, or Jebel Katrinah, is Egypt's highest peak. It is about 6 km south of Mount Sinai and a five- to six-hour exhausting, but rewarding, climb. It is supposedly compulsory to take a guide, although it is possible to avoid detection and hike alone. Again, there are two routes up, one via the settlement of Arbayin (where you can see hyrax) that is longer but easier, and an steeper alternative route that has the appeal of being more natural. En route you pass the deserted **Monastery of the Forty Martyrs**. The path up to the summit was constructed by the monks who laid the granite staircase up Mount Sinai. On the summit there is a small chapel dedicated to St Catherine with water, a two-room hut for overnight pilgrims or trekkers, and a meteorological station.

Surrounding sights

About 50 km west of St Catherine lies **Wadi Feiran** ⓘ *accessible by taxi from St Catherine for E£120, or get off the Cairo bus (from El Tor or from St Catherine's)*, a fertile winding valley filled with palms and wells. Some say this is where Moses left his people when he went to collect the Ten Commandments. Hence, a **monastery** dedicated to Moses lies at the valley's centre ⓘ *T069-385 0071/2, open Mon-Sat 0900-1200, entrance free; if you wish to visit in the afternoon, pay a E£100 fee. Overnight guests welcome, see page 451*, where five Greek Orthodox nuns live and work. Visitors are admitted to view the two churches within the compound, decorated with icons and an iconostasis carved in Greece. The ruins of the original fourth century monastery are found adjacent to the complex, on a raised mound by the road. A kilometre or so further on from the monastery, in the direction of St Catherine's, are the lush wadi gardens where there are a couple of camps in which travellers can stay. There are several good and challenging hikes nearby. These, and longer treks, can be arranged with local guides on arrival. Wadi Feiran is a good destination for independent travellers, who wish to be flexible and don't want to be bound by any schedule. A reasonable amount to pay a guide is E£80 per day – not including food – and E£80 per camel, then another E£80 to cover administration costs and fees. A couple of kilometres along the road beyond the gardens is the Bedouin village of Wadi Feiran, though there is not much here to detain travellers save a couple of shops.

The interior listings

For Sleeping and Eating price codes and other relevant information, see pages 26-31.

Sleeping

St Catherine *p445*

Apart from the Monastery Guesthouse, most hotels and camps lie 2-3 km away from the monastery in the village of St Catherine, along 2 parallel main roads. Taxis between the village and monastery cost E£10.

AL-A St Catherine Village, Wadi El-Raha ('Valley of Repose'), T/F069-3470324-6, www.misrsinatitours.com. Every room has a view of the monastery in the distance up the valley. Twin-bed chalets of local stone, supposedly in the shape of a Bedouin tent, have been tastefully done out each with a lovely reception area and terrace. Often full in high season. 2 larger villas are available for US$110 per night.

B Daniela, T069-347 0379, www.daniela-hotels.com. Fairly spacious comfortable stone chalets, some with TV, all with heaters, are an easy walk from the village. The restaurant is reliable and tasty, serves Stella for E£15, and provides a good packed lunch for climbing mountains.

B Monastery Guesthouse, T069-347 0353. It's not cheap, but if you can afford it, spend a night at the guesthouse. Being able to wander around the outer walls whenever the mood takes you (and in relative isolation) is the best way to appreciate the monastery. Plus the orchards and gardens are beautiful and restful, the rooms attractive and warm. Cost includes half board, triple and quadruple rooms are also available. It's wise to reserve ahead at all times, but especially during the common pilgrimage months of Apr and Aug. If you want to go for lunch or dinner, give 24 hrs' advance warning, and if you can't actually stay here then a drink in the courtyard coffee shop is next best thing (alcohol is served), open 0700 until late (except on Fri/Sat nights, when it closes at 2100 to reopen 2400-0300).

C El Wadi El-Mouquduss, T069-347 0225. Next to the **Daniela**, it's uninspiring from the outside but not bad value at E£250 half board or E£180 B&B for a double. Nice bathrooms, good heaters, some rooms have balconies (which look down on a murky pool), most have TV (or enquire about their cheaper more basic rooms). The buffets are good, with 10 types of salad as well as the usual meat/rice /veg combo (lunch E£30, dinner E£40).

D-F El-Karm Ecolodge, Wadi Gharbah, T069-347 0032/3, www.ecolodges.sahara safaris.org/alkarm. Manager Jameel Ataya can be contacted on his mobile, T010-132 4693, but only speaks Arabic (though if you leave a message in English someone will get back to you). Alternatively, contact **Bedouin Camp** in St Catherine's for help with reservations, T069-347 0457. Deep in the heart of the south Sinai mountains, accessible by 4WD from El Tarfa village, a lift from St Catherine's is E£130-150 or if you get off the bus at El Tarfa (west of St Catherine's), Jameel can arrange a pick-up from there for the last 30 mins along a bumpy track, E£50. The eco-lodge is fully managed and operated by the Jabaliya tribe with the aim of preserving the traditions of Bedouin culture. Old ruins have been rebuilt to create 8 simple stone rooms that sleep 3-7 people. The setting and isolation are splendid, the walking superb, and a visit here is a special experience. Room only is E£50 per person, E£120 full board. Camping is E£30, use of the kitchen E£10. Though there are blankets, it's a good idea to bring your own sleeping bag (certainly in winter). You can arrange half- or full-day treks from here, or visit the Nabatean ruins nearby, or the dry waterfall at Seida Nughra is a 2-hr walk away. El-Karm feels like the ultimate getaway: it is rare to be somewhere so isolated and untouristed and yet still have a bed to retire to and delicious food.

E-G Bedouin Camp, Al-Milga, T069-347 0457, T010-641 3575, www.sheikmousa.com, near the bus stop, uphill past the square and petrol station. Basic but clean concrete rooms have blankets and screen doors (essential in summer). Dorm beds available, all share a bathroom with hot water and there's space to put up tents. The washing machine is a real bonus. This is the place to come to organize a trekking excursion to the high mountains.

F-G Farag Fox Desert Camp, between the monastery and town centre, T069-347 0344, T010-698 7807. The cheapest choice in town is a good choice. Nestling by an olive orchard, clean, attractive huts with plenty of blankets are E£30 per person and decent shared baths have hot water (E£40 with private bath). You can camp down here for E£10 per tent, or there are a couple of alluring stone-walled gardens 10-20 mins' walk up the valley, with fresh water supply, where you can meditate in complete isolation under the stars (they can provide tents/blankets). Otherwise evenings are spent lolling around in the Bedouin tent drinking free tea around the fire, while candles twinkle on the rocks surrounding the camp. It's run by 2 local Bedouin brothers who also organize trips through the desert plateaus (as opposed to trekking in the high mountains), costing around E£175-200 per person depending upon the size of the group.

Camping

Apart from the great camping spots at Fox Camp (above), most visitors spend the night on Mt Sinai to see the sunrise. The altitude makes for sub-zero night-time temperatures for much of the year – a torch, good sleeping bag and warm clothing are absolutely essential. It is possible to rent blankets and mattresses around the summit for E£10.

Wadi Feiran *p449*

A-B Holy Monastery of the Prophet Moses, T069-385 0071/2, sinai.oasisfaran@yahoo.gr. Hidden within the walled compound of a monastery, guestrooms are spotless and comfortable (if simple). The price includes a good breakfast and dinner, and there are some cheaper rooms which share bathrooms. Palms, frangipani and the historic churches all make for a special stay.

F Greenland , T018-463 2465. Located in the Feiran gardens and identified by a sign next to the road offering tea, the 'Garden of Flowers' has sleeping space under a Bedouin shade on rag-rugs surrounded by blossoming bougainvillea, herb gardens and date palms. There is electricity. Adjacent are 2 other camps (**Beit Al-Shar** and **Holy Oasis**) offering similarly basic accommodation.

Eating

St Catherine *p445*

The hotels all provide a very similar buffet lunch (E£25-30) and dinner (E£30-50) of rice, macaroni, meat, chicken and veg, plus soup at dinner time, as do the camps. There are a couple of virtually identical restaurants in the village, again serving the standard fare but for around E£15, but these sometimes close as early as 1900. The **Monastery Guesthouse** also provides decent meals at the reasonable cost of E£25, though they need a day's warning. For a change, there is an OK *koshary* place to the left of the post office. For *tamaya*, go to the stall next to the bank.

O Shopping

St Catherine *p445*

Fansina, T069-347 0155/010-186 5120, past **Fox Camp** on the left on the way into the village. Open Sat-Thu 1000-1500. Local Bedouin businesswoman Selima works with over 450 women from tribes all over South Sinai to produce gifts and textiles, including *galabiyas* and intricate beadwork trinkets, all at fixed prices. Articles incorporate ancestral designs that would have adorned practical items (such as the bags girls took out when herding goats, or pouches made for nomadic husbands to carry their sugar and tea). Her new premises opened early 2008, the cool interior and shady outdoor area are inviting, Selima herself is quite an inspiration.

There are a couple of gifts shops at the monastery, the better one is in front of the guesthouse. In the village, provisions can be bought at **Supermarket Katreen**, plus a couple of other small grocery stores, bakery, bazaar and petrol station.

Activities and tours

St Catherine *p445*

Trekking

Besides the well-trampled peaks of Mt Sinai and to a lesser extent, Mt St Catherine, trekking opportunities in Central and South Sinai abound. Information about day treks are available at the **St Catherine's National Park Visitor Centre** and online at www.touregypt.net/walkingtours. To explore in depth any of the surrounding peaks you must have a Bedouin guide. Trekking alone is impossible (as well as dangerous) and you will be prevented from doing so. The absolutely perfect month, temperature-wise, is May. During Jul and Aug it is unbearably hot all day, and you have to be pretty hardy to consider a trek in the winter months, though if you're very well-prepared the chilly nights are just about manageable.

Safaris that visit the desert areas, wadis and lower peaks are generally arranged in Nuweiba or Dahab, or through **Farag Fox Safaris** in St Catherine's, T069-347 0344, using guides from the tribes that inhabit these areas. If you are embarking on a long safari that visits more than one territory, you will transfer between camels and guides to those of another tribe (but retain a head guide from the original party) so that you are always in the hands of those who know the region best. Presuming that you are satisfied with your guide and the experience, you may wish to tip (E£80-100 is an acceptable amount).

Some highlights of the area include: **Galt El-Azraq**, a striking and beautiful 7-m-deep spring-fed crystal-clear pool nestled in the rock, an arduous 1-day walk so most people chose to do it as a 2-day trek from St Catherine's. **Wadi Shaqq** is a large canyon beyond Jebel Katrinah, with beautiful *bustans* (orchards) and a hermit's cell and monastery. There are some Bedouin buildings here (some still inhabited) and others that are set up for trekkers with composite toilets, a shower and rock-cut rooms. **Jebel Umm Shomar** is the second tallest peak in Egypt, from where there are staggering views as far as the coastal sandy plains of **El-Tur**. Hikes to/from here visit tiny Bedouin settlements, lush wadis with immense boulders among the date palms, and Byzantine ruins. It's possible to walk from St Catherine's to El-Tur in 3-5 days, via Umm Shomar. **Wadi Nugra** is a rocky valley with a rain-fed 20-m-high waterfall that trickles off mossy boulders into pools perfect for cooling off, in between Nuweiba and St Catherine's, a 3-day trek from St Catherine's. **Sheikh Awad's Tomb** is a picturesque oasis containing the holy man's shrine, a well and a small Bedouin community, a 3-day trek from St Catherine's. Another destination is the unfinished palace of **Abbas Pasha** at 4-hour climb to a summit that affords some of the best views of the high mountains and distant lowlands; a circular trek starting from St Catherine's takes 5 days. **The Blue Valley** is a bizarre sprawl of desert 12 km from St Catherine interspersed with boulders painted blue by a Belgian artist in the late 1970s. Claims as to why he did it vary, there's a common saying in Arabic, "There will be peace with Israel when the sky meets the desert", an impossibility, of course. So the artist, in an attempt to make real the impossible, met with both Prime Minister Rabin and President Sadat to offer his idea in the name of peace, and painted the rock blue to bring the sky to the desert. A noble tale, or was he trying to replicate landscape artists before him? Who knows ... ask your guide for his version of the story.

Most treks tend to be circular, starting and finishing at the same point, although an A–B route is possible (from St Catherine's to El-Tur, for example). Also, many of the areas mentioned above can be linked together to form longer hikes of 15 days or more.

Mountain Tours, T069-347 0457, headed up by Sheikh Mousa, is good for those who don't like to plan too much in advance. Sheikh Mousa will take your passport, and secure the necessary permit, guide, camels, food and equipment. Tell him how much time you have and what you want to see and he'll help create an itinerary. Cost is €30 per person per day, everything included, for a group of at least 3 (more than €50 for 1 person). You may wish to bring water-purification tablets if drinking spring water is a concern.

Sheikh Sina Bedouin Treks, T069-347 0880, www.sheikhsina.com, are good for multiple-day treks. They work alongside Sheikh Mousa and the local community to further the empowerment of the Bedouin tribes. A rotating system of guides and cameleers ensures that each family has a turn benefiting from the tours and an emphasis is placed on sustainable tourism. Guides speak English, French and German and have been trained in first-aid, which could be vital up here.

Transport

St Catherine *p445*

Bus

There are direct buses for the 8-hr journey between St Catherine and **Cairo** at 0600 and occasionally at 1300 (E£60) via **Suez**, and supposedly one to **Dahab** (1300, E£25) though this, more often than not, simply doesn't run. Check at the bus station for the latest schedules.

Taxis

Service taxis If a microbus has come from **Dahab** the night before, it will return from St Catherine at 1100, departing from next to the mosque (E£40 1-way or E£50 return). Micros leave when full between 0600-1300 for **Suez**, E£20-30, or E£350 to hire the whole vehicle. Travellers can share the cost of hiring a 7-seat service taxi to **Dahab** (E£200-250 per car), **Sharm El-Sheikh** (E£300-450), **Nuweiba** (E£200), or other towns in the peninsula.

Directory

St Catherine *p445*

Banks Bank Misr branch on the main street in St Catherine town is open daily from 0830-1400 and 1830-2030, only changes cash and not TCs. It is rumoured that the monastery will soon have an ATM. **Medical services** Next to the tourist police opposite the bus station, not recommended, make the journey to Sharm if you can. **Post office** Opposite the bank in town, open Sat-Thu 0800-1500. **Telephone** There is an international telephone exchange in town open from 0800-2400 near the post office.

Northern Sinai

→ *Colour map 2, A5/6.*

The vast majority of tourists coming to Sinai only visit the Gulf of Aqaba coastline and St Catherine's Monastery, and this is for good reason. Although the northern part of the peninsula has a number of attractions both in El-Arish and along the 210-km Mediterranean coastline stretching from Port Said to the border at Rafah, these are low-key in comparison to the temptations of the Red Sea and interior. Distinctly different in feel from the red rugged south, Northern Sinai has softer charms, with palm-fringed beaches and creamy sand dunes that melt into Mediterranean lagoons. Birdwatchers will find fulfilment in the Zaranik Protectorate Reserve, while El-Arish appeals to those who like to mix a taste of the beach with a gritty dash of Bedouin culture. As the situation on the Rafah border grows ever more tense, very few travellers make it this far – either as a destination or en route to Israel. » *For listings, see pages 457-458.*

Ins and outs

Getting there The road east from Ismailia crosses the Suez Canal Bridge, also known as the Japanese–Egyptian Friendship Bridge, which rises bizarrely out of the desert and affords brief views down the length of the canal. Coming from Suez further south, the road goes through the Ahmed Hamdi Tunnel.

Pelusium and Lake Bardweel

The road to El-Arish passes through some wild-looking towns, next to huge dunes and goat-herders roaming among the scrub, and past small enclaves of nomadic settlements. About 40 km along the road from Qantara to El-Arish there is a signpost for **Pelusium** ⓘ *daily 0900-1600.* The road is surfaced until it crosses a small canal. Turn left on to the next (unsurfaced) road. This road is not passable after rain – be prepared to walk from the tarmac. If you have your own transport and official permission you can visit these Roman ruins, also known as Tel El-Farame. The site covers a wide area, littered with ancient rubble, stone, bricks and columns, of which the highlight is the partially uncovered amphitheatre. The city was situated on a now dry tributary of the Nile and guarded access from the east and acted as a customs post. It is mentioned in the Bible as 'the stronghold of Egypt'. The Persians came through here and both Pompey and Baldwin I ended their days here in tragic circumstances.

Lake Bardweel (66,500 ha) is important for fish such as mullet and seabass as well as migratory birds but access to the shore is often difficult. At the eastern end is the **Zaranik Protectorate** where over 200 species of migrating bird have been recorded. This area is of such significance that it has been preserved as a wetland under the auspices of UNESCO. Take the track north at the hamlet of Al-Sabeka (the sign says keep to the road but forgets to mention the landmines).

El-Arish → *For listings, see pages 457-458. Colour map 2, A6.*

This town, 180 km east of the Suez Canal, is the governorate capital of North Sinai and used to be noted for its 30 km of palm-lined fine white-sand beach. El-Arish means palm huts in Arabic, of which you won't see many these days as – like so many other places along the coast of Sinai – concrete has become the dominant feature. Still, it's a quiet, bumbling sort of place, good for family getaways or groups of friends who may wish to rent somewhere on the beach and enjoy one another's company and not much else. The Bedouins of Northern Sinai weave beautiful fabrics and rugs, which are brightly displayed at the sprawling weekly *souk*. The new museum is a tragically empty edifice, beautifully laid out and lit, with exquisite pharaonic, Islamic, Coptic and Bedouin displays. Al-Nakheel to the east is the best beach at El-Arish with famous but depleted palm trees extending the length of the shoreline. Also very noticeable in El-Arish is the high proportion of limbless beggars, victims of landmines.

Ins and outs

Getting around The town consists of two main streets, Sharia Fouad Abu Zakry, which runs along the beach, and Sharia 23rd July, which runs perpendicular to the beach and finishes up at Midan Baladiya. The bus and long-distance service taxi stations are 2 km west of the town centre, a E£5 ride from most hotels. From Midan Baladiya it is a 2- to 3-km walk or minibus ride (50 pt) to Fouad Abu Zakry and the beach.

Information There is an almost useless **Egyptian General Authority for the Promotion of Tourism office** ⓘ *T068-336 3743, Sat-Thu 0900-1400*, in the same office as the **Tourist Police** ⓘ *T068-335 9490*, on Sharia Fouad Abu Zakry. The main **police station** is on Sharia El-Geish on the way to Rafah.

Sights

The **El-Arish Museum** ⓘ *on the Rafah road, T068-3324 105, Sat-Thu 0900-1330, E£5 in a taxi or 50 pt by micro, tickets E£20, students E£10, cameras E£20, it might be worth paying to take a camera in, as the lighting throws up dramatic shadows and reliefs on the pharaonic exhibits*. This huge temple-like edifice, built to cope with stampedes of visitors of which there are virtually none, is overstaffed to a spectacular degree even by Egyptian standards. Opened in April 2008, it is an almost perfect museum experience except for the fact that the labelling fails to inform you where any of the items originate from – but if you have made it as far as El-Arish, this is not to be missed. The first couple of rooms display majestic pharaonic pieces, with helpful diagrammatic murals to illustrate how the reliefs fitted into temple friezes; worthy of note are the displays dedicated to Hathor in her various guises, sometimes represented as a cow and other times as a human with a cow's ears. The Islamic collection incorporates an intricate *mashrabiya* window with stained-glass panels and immense draperies from the *Ka'ba*, as from 1223-1962 a factory in Cairo was the main manufacturer of the embroidered cloth that covers the holiest place of Islam. As well as an array of Coptic icons, there is a small coin room where accompanying text actually manages to make the minting techniques and politics of ancient currencies interesting. Further on, in the basement, the heritage of Sinai is brought to life through a beautiful collection of chunky jewellery, vicious swords and daggers, adornments for camels, and the most heavily embroidered *gallabiyas* imaginable. Cumbersome *borga* veils, heavy with chains, tassels, hundreds of coins, seeds, beads and embroidery remind you what an extraordinary culture still inhabits this land.

The Thursday Bedouin market (*Souk El-Khamees*), in the oldest part of town, is best reached from Midan Baladiya, just follow the crowds. If you are in El-Arish on a Thursday, it's a good notion to visit the museum to see the Bedouin designs and handiwork before moving on to the weekly market to haggle over newly crafted versions of any designs that took your fancy. You'll need to get up early as mornings are most fun among the endless piles of aubergines, T-shirts, crockery and condiments all laid out on the ground. Prices for Bedouin trinkets are reasonable and the dress of the women who have journeyed here to sell goods is not a million miles away from that on display in the museum. **El-Arish Fortress** is on a plateau to the southwest of the town on the remains of an ancient pharaonic castle. Beside the pieces of aqueduct, and hidden behind wooden walls (absolutely no entry) where excavations are taking place, are the ruins of the fort rebuilt by the Turk Sultan Sulayman Al Qanouni in 1560 and demolished in the First World War by British bombardment. There is a small zoo, east of town opposite the museum, but it's not worth the visit. Between Abi-Sakl to the west and the zoo to the east is the harbour, used mainly by fishing vessels (fishing permits may be granted). The village of Kilometre 21 hosts a camel-racing festival in August/September each year, which attracts competitors from Libya and the Gulf countries. Otherwise pastimes in El-Arish tend to revolve around the beach.

The **Zaranik Protectorate** ⓘ *around 30 km east of town, US$5 per person and US$5 per car*, encompasses the eastern shore of Lake Bardaweel and extends north to the sea. It is a wildlife haven protected since the mid-1980s. In September, thousands of birds (up to 270 different species, including flamingo) stop here en route from Europe to Africa. It's also an important turtle site. At the entrance of the protectorate, there is an informative visitor centre that shows films. It costs E£25-30 to get here in a taxi from El-Arish (it is not possible to get off the bus by the turn-off to the park and walk, it's too far from the main highway). There are several campsites for US$10 per person per night and there are 10 (new) double rooms available. It's best to bring your own food and use their kitchen, and there's a washing machine, fridge, binoculars and telescopes for guests' use. To arrange a visit – one day's notice is requested – call Mr Saat (director of the protectorate) on T010-544 2641.

Border crossing to Palestine and Israel

It is no longer possible to cross to Israel/Gaza at the Rafah and all travellers now use the Taba border crossing (see box, page 438).

Northern Sinai listings

For Sleeping and Eating price codes and other relevant information, see pages 26-31.

Sleeping

El-Arish *p454*

During the Jul-Sep high season it may be difficult to find a room on the beach without pre-booking. During the winter most hotels are quiet and some shut down, but the ones listed below are open whatever the season. In the town centre there are a few acceptable budget options, should you just need to crash for a night.

L Swiss Inn Resort, Sharia Fouad Abu Zakry, T068-335 1321. Previously the **Oberoi**, some of the brass, marble and wood remains in public areas, while rooms have huge beds and sea views. Recreation facilities include health spa, tennis courts, a large saltwater pool and another (more attractive) freshwater one. There's a well-stocked bar and beer is also available at the coffee shop, where outside guests congregate. High season is US$180 half board, otherwise it's a bargain at E£25 to use the pool and lovely private beach for the day.

D Greenland Beach, Sharia Fouad Abu Zakry, T068-336 0601. Recently repainted in lurid yellows with peach tiled floors, some rooms have views of the sea (and of rooftops) and the bathrooms are decent. However, single female travellers would do best to avoid staying here. No breakfast.

E Macca Hotel (no English sign) on Sharia Al-Salam, a side street off the northern end of Sharia 23 July, T068-335 2632, F068-335 2632. Mercifully free from traffic noise, the **Macca** is bustly and bright and staff are friendly and effective. All in all, it is a good choice and rooms have balconies and baths. The restaurant is cheap and decent, breakfast is included, doubles E£105 singles E£75.

E Moon Light, Sharia Fouad Abu Zakry. A funny faded peeling kind of a place, with chalet rooms around a scruffy garden. The beach is a few steps away but is rather littered, yet it is often busy, has the potential to be fun if you're in a group, and is cheap. The cafeteria has drinks but no food.

F Safa Hotel, Sharia 23 July, T068-335 3798. Best of the bottom-rung choices in town with a variety of rooms in different configurations spread over several floors. Freshly painted and most rooms are bright – although they don't have the cleanest linens or bathrooms in the world. On arrival, you can ask for clean sheets and towels, and the staff try their best. No breakfast.

Camping

Camping is permitted in the Zaranik Protectorate, US$5 a night. It may be possible to camp on the beach if you can get permission from the police.

Eating

El-Arish *p454*

Besides the hotels and a series of stalls by the beach that sell *fuul* and other standards, there are a few cheap restaurants and *ahwas* (with *sheesha*) in and around Midan Baladiya.

ΨΨ **Basata**, in the western part of town. Offers a pleasant atmosphere with good seafood, geared more towards tourists.

Ψ **Batebat**, diagonally opposite Aziz, focuses on meat. Good *tagens*, *koftas* and chicken.

Ψ **Sammar** and **Aziz** on Sharia Tahrir just north of Midan Baladiya, serve up good cheap grilled food with a variety of salads.

Ψ **Tahrir Fuul** stand, near Aziz, no English sign just ask around, churns out excellent *fuul* sandwiches. Or try the narrow *souk* street, just north of Aziz restaurant, where there is another local joint on the left that has an excellent array of salads and sandwich fillings and a small seating area inside.

Entertainment

El-Arish *p454*

Nightlife in El-Arish thrives around the cafés of Midan Baladiya, where no matter the night, you will find people puffing on *sheesha* pipes, sipping tea and playing backgammon. El-Arish is a rather conservative community and there aren't many places that serve alcohol. The safest bet is the Swiss Inn, which has a well-stocked bar and a pleasant outside coffee shop that serves beer.

Shopping

El Arish *p454*

There are some rather sleazy tourist shops on Sharia 23 July but for quality items it is better to bargain at the Bedouin market.

Transport

El Arish *p454*

Bus

East Delta Bus Co, T068-332 5931 run several daily buses between El-Arish and **Cairo** (4-5 hrs, E£26-32), and 1 per day to **Ismailia** and **Qantara**, where you have to change for **Port Said**. The bus terminal is a couple of kilometres east of Midan Baladiya, accessible by microbus.

Taxis

Service taxis to/from Midan Koulali Terminal in **Cairo** (5 hrs, E£30): Midan El-Gomhoriyya in **Ismailia** (3 hrs, E£15) or by the Suez Canal in **Qantara** (2½ hrs, E£12). To get to **Port Said** there is a free ferry across the canal from East to West Qantara, from where you can either board another service or a train. Taxis to **Cairo** leave early morning.

Minibuses run back and forth from the *souk* to the beach and around town (50 pt), as do 1970s 'stretch' Mercedes.

Directory

El Arish *p454*

Banks Bank of Alexandria; Misr Bank; National Bank of Egypt, are available in town; the main hotels will also change money. **Internet** E£1-2 per hr, try Big Star Net opposite Sinai Sun hotel on Sharia 23rd July, 1200-2400, or Hadeer Net, opposite the Moon Light hotel on the Corniche. **Medical services** Mubarak International Hospital, T068-332 4018/9, should be your 1st choice, otherwise El-Arish General Hospital, Sharia El-Geish, T068-336 1077. **Post office** The post office, open 0800-2100, and the international **telephone exchange** are close together, off Sharia 23 July between the Sinai Sun Hotel and Midan Baladiya.

Red Sea & the Eastern Desert

Contents

Footprint features

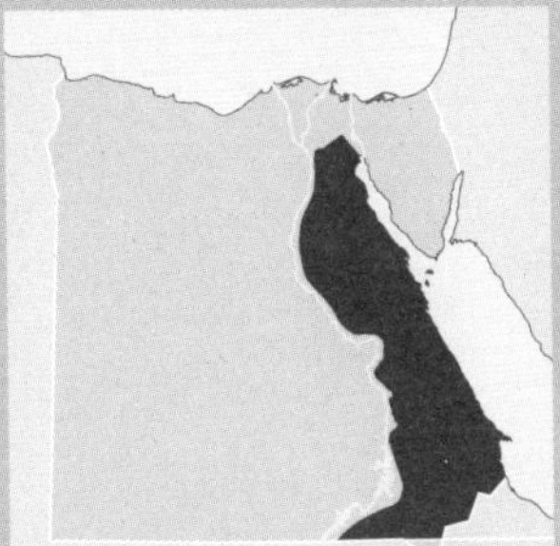

At a glance

Getting around Buses and service taxis between the main towns, then taxis to the resorts. There are flights to Marsa Alam. Catamarans cross the Gulf of Suez from Hurghada to Sharm El-Sheikh.

Time required At least a week if you're planning on both diving and desert exploration.

Weather Searingly hot between May and mid-Sep.

When not to go If you want to do an extended desert excursion, avoid summer as tours do not run during this time.

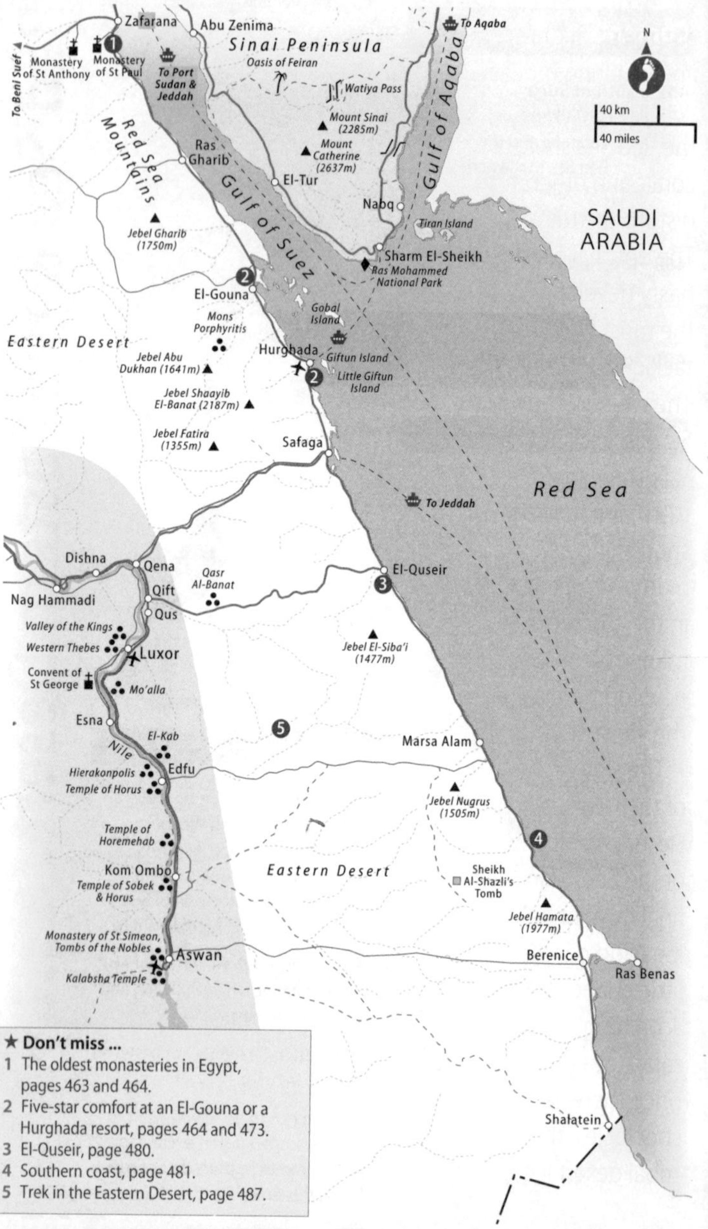

★ **Don't miss ...**

1 The oldest monasteries in Egypt, pages 463 and 464.
2 Five-star comfort at an El-Gouna or a Hurghada resort, pages 464 and 473.
3 El-Quseir, page 480.
4 Southern coast, page 481.
5 Trek in the Eastern Desert, page 487.

Birthplace of Christian monasticism 16 centuries ago, the isolated and inspiring monasteries of St Anthony and St Paul herald the way into this contradictory swathe of Egypt. The eastern rim of the Red Sea shelters a thriving expanse of brilliantly coloured fish, corals and other marine life. With no rivers flowing into the sea to disturb the translucent waters, the corals blossom unimpeded. The optimal conditions for such water delights has resulted in hasty development as epitomized by the sprawl of Hurghada, the most visited coastal resort town in Egypt, now reviled for its tackiness but still a good place to cut loose if you crave a party. The shoreline is also famous for its wind, drawing kitesurfers to Safaga, acclaimed for its first-class facilities.

Further south lies the beguiling port of El-Quseir, at one time the main departure point for all *hajj* pilgrims. Days are spent snorkelling at a nearby beach or visiting the ruined fortress, and nights are spent around campfires under a sea of stars. Thankfully, in the south the government is striving to protect the wealth of marine life insisting on eco-friendly practices for all new tourist developments, thus some attractive camps and eco-lodges dot the coast around Marsa Alam.

The slowly widening major fault line running along the length of the Red Sea created the dramatic mountains of the Eastern Desert, a belt stretching for about 1250 km from the southern tip of the Suez Canal. These mountainous desert expanses are the final frontier before Saharan Africa and deep in their folds thrive ibex and gazelle, while nomadic tribes live a traditional lifestyle little changed in 6000 years. Most visitors traverse or overlook the scorching, virtually uninhabited region to get to the coast, and a safari into the interior is a quest that involves effort and time. But once there, jagged charcoal peaks and wondrous astronomical spectacles, the scattering of Roman era ruins and encounters with tribal desert life are gifts to the soul.

South of Suez

➔ *Colour map 2, B/C4-3, A4.*

The Red Sea coast stretches down from Suez towards Hurghada, encompassing the resorts and enclaves around Ain Soukna and becoming progressively more beautiful and unspoilt as it extends further south. Inland from Zafarana, the Red Sea monasteries are Egypt's oldest and attract thousands of Coptic pilgrims to the desert hinterland. The plush and extensive resorts of El-Gouna, built on a succession of islands, tempt wealthy Cairenes and Western package tourists with their good diving and high-class dining. El-Gouna often feels more like Europe than it does Egypt, and is easily connected to the capital by twice-weekly flights or a five-hour bus ride.
⏩ *For listings, see pages 465-467.*

Aïn Sukhna ➔ *For listings, see pages 465-467.*

Only two hours from Cairo, on the Red Sea about 60 km south of Suez, the shoreline of Aïn Sukhna is a popular getaway for middle class and wealthy Cairenes seeking respite from the chaos of the capital. Although it lacks the breadth of sea life that thrives further south, and the horizon is perpetually dotted with huge oil tankers, it still retains the beauty of a Red Sea shoreline and makes a convenient beach stop for anyone based in Cairo if time is limited. It's supposed to be a region of hot springs, hence its name (which does literally mean 'hot springs'), but the appeal centres much more around the sandy beaches and resort culture. The location of Sukhna also makes it a popular spot for birdwatchers, as it's on the raptor migration route. There are no budget hotels, just several resorts, most offering water sports, snorkelling, fishing and lots of restaurants, pools and other activities. If you want solitude, avoid Sukhna on the weekends.

Zafarana and the Red Sea monasteries ➔ *Colour map 3, A3.*

From Ain Sukhna, an ugly swathe of construction stretches almost the entire distance to Zafarana, 62 km south on H44 at the junction to Beni Suef. The most noticeable feature to the north of the town is a wind farm with hundreds of towering turbines. For travellers, the small community of Zafarana is really just an access point to the two isolated monasteries of St Anthony's and St Paul's, and where there is an acceptable hotel that independent travellers can utilise if intending to visit both the monasteries. St Anthony's and St Paul's lie hidden in the folds of the Red Sea mountains, and are the oldest in Egypt. Pilgrim tours to these monasteries are organized by the **Coptic Patriarch** ⓘ *22 Sharia Ramsis, Abbassiya, Cairo T02-2591 7360*, and foreign tourists are welcome to join. No-one (save for young men who are considering the monastic life) is allowed to stay at St Anthony's, while St Paul's is less likely to leave you bed-less in the desert (although this may involve sleeping by the gatehouse).

Ins and outs

Getting there Day tours to the monasteries are offered by a number of Hurghada travel agents including **Misr Travel**, see page 478. Otherwise a group can negotiate a single price with a local taxi from Hurghada, Suez or Cairo. Provided it is not too hot and you take enough water it is also possible to get part way to St Anthony's by service taxi, from Beni Suef or Zafarana. Service taxis leave from the road behind the NPCO petrol station. A blue and white sign 35 km from Zafarana indicates the monastery, from where there are still 15 km more to go on foot, unless you manage to hitch a lift. You could hire a vehicle from Zafarana to take you for about E£50. For St Pauls, the Hurghada to Cairo/Suez bus can drop you at the turn-off, approximately 24 km south of Zafarana, which is indicated with blue and white signs. From here, the road leads about 12 km up a slight incline but, again, you may well be able to hitch a ride. Be aware that trying to visit either of the monasteries in one day by public transport/hitching and walking is a tall order, and it would be foolish to attempt both unless you are intending to stay in Zafarana at the end of the day. It's a tough 30-km trek over a plateau between the two monasteries, and this should never be embarked upon without a guide. This can be arranged in Zafarana with local Bedouin; try asking the manager of the Sahara Inn to assist you. Note that St Paul's only opens on Fridays, Saturdays and Sundays during the fasting period from 25 November to 7 January, and that St Anthony's only opens on Fridays, Saturdays and Sundays during the fasting time of Lent (55 days) from about mid-February to mid-April, depending on the Coptic calendar.

St Anthony's Monastery

ⓘ *Daily 0400-1645 except during Lent (Feb to mid-Apr) when it only opens Fri, Sat and Sun. A monk who is fluent in your language will be assigned to give a tour.*

Known locally as Deir Amba Antonyus this is the more important of the two monasteries for Coptic pilgrims, and attracts more foreign visitors than St Paul's to admire its extraordinary and bright wall paintings. The Christian monastic tradition has its origin in the community that established itself here in the fourth century, and the daily rituals still observed have hardly changed in the last 16 centuries.

The 'father of monasticism' St Anthony (AD 251-356) was born in the small village of **Koma Al-Arus**. He became a hermit after he was orphaned at 18 just before the height of the persecution against the Christians by Emperor Diocletian (AD 284-305). By AD 313 not only was Christianity tolerated but it had also been corrupted by its adoption as the state religion. This led to increasing numbers of hermits following Anthony's example and seeking isolation in desert retreats (see St Catherine's monastery, page 445 and El-Fayoum, page 166). After his death, at the reported age of 105, the location of his grave was kept secret but a small chapel was erected that became the foundation of the monastery.

In the course of its history it has been subject to attacks from the Bedouin tribes in the eighth and ninth centuries and the Nasir Al-Dawla who destroyed it in the 11th century. It was restored in the 12th century by monks from throughout the Coptic world, only to be badly damaged again in the 15th century when the monks were massacred by rebellious servants. Syrian monks were sent to rebuild it in the mid-16th century and it was subsequently inhabited by a mixture of Coptic, Ethiopian and Syrian monks. Its importance rose and many 17th- to 19th-century Coptic patriarchs were chosen from among its monks; by the 18th century it was receiving increasing numbers of European visitors. The result is that the five-church monastery has developed into an enormous complex containing all the commodities of a village. There is a free canteen and a couple of souvenir shops. The outer walls, some sections of which can be walked along, span 2 km. Around 120 monks now reside within the complex.

St Anthony's Church, parts of which date back to the 13th century, is the oldest church in the complex. Relatively recent cleaning and restoration has revealed the fabulous colours of paintings covering each and every wall, previously preserved under centuries of soot and grime. While inside, try to identify the apostles in the picture on the south wall. The faces of the camels, horses and martyrs which are depicted are strikingly natural. Tradition always held that the relics of St Anthony lay beneath the altar, and a recent survey has confirmed that there is indeed a tomb below. There are four other churches in the complex. **St Mark's Church** dates from 1766 and is reputed to contain the relics of St Mark the Evangelist in a chest on the north wall, though this is normally closed to foreign visitors. You will also be shown the ancient **refectory**, containing a sixth-century stone table and the spring that St Anthony discovered which still provides all the monastery's water needs today.

The **Cave of St Anthony**, 276 m above and 2 km northeast of the monastery, is a steep walk but the view alone from the terrace in front of the cave, 690 m above the Red Sea, justifies the climb. From the monastery, a 15-minute walk along a gravel road leads to the modern Church of the Christ and the Resurrection, from where steps lead up for a painful 30- to 45-minute climb to the cave. The cave, where St Anthony is supposed to have spent the last 25 years of his life, consists of a tunnel (which is a tight squeeze) leading to a dark chamber. The decorations on the walls are medieval graffiti often complemented by more recent additions in the shape of supplications stuck into the cracks of the walls by visiting pilgrims. Take water, a hat and a torch with you for this mini-expedition, and be warned it is quite a tough walk with no shade. Shoes should be left outside the entrance to the cave.

St Paul's Monastery

ⓘ *Daily 0530-1700 except during Lent and between 25 Nov and 7 Jan, when the monastery only opens on Fri, Sat and Sun.*

The smaller Monastery of St Paul was built around the cave where St Paul the Theban (AD 228-348) spent his life. Although the dates do not actually match, he is supposed to have fled the persecution of **Decius** (AD 249-251) and arrived in the eastern desert from Alexandria at the age of 16. He is the earliest hermit on record and was visited by St Anthony to whom he gave a tunic of palm leaves. St Paul apparently acknowledged him as his spiritual superior and St Anthony's Monastery has always overshadowed that of St Paul both theologically and architecturally. It is now home to a community of around 90 monks.

The larger of the two churches is dedicated to St Michael and there are two sanctuaries. The south one is dedicated to St John the Baptist where a strange 18th-century gilded icon depicts the saint's head on a dish. The **Church of St Paul** contains the actual cave where he lived and what are claimed to be his relics, which were preserved during the many raids on the monastery. The worst of these was in 1484, when Bedouin tribes massacred the entire population of monks and occupied the monastery for the following 80 years. Things are rather more tranquil now, though the tour buses of Coptic pilgrims can cause a bit of a stir.

El-Gouna → *For listings, see pages 465-467. Colour map 3, B5.*

The upmarket resort of El-Gouna is just 25 km (30 minutes in a taxi) north of Hurghada but a million miles away in terms of ambiance and aesthetics. It attracts a far more sedate foreign crowd, mainly families and couples, plus wealthy Egyptians who come to their private villas on weekends and public holidays. All the hotel developments and villas have been constructed in a Nubian/Arabesque style and are dotted across a series of beautiful islands interlinked by seawater lagoons. There are also many uninhabited islands and coral reefs that are exposed only at low tide. With its collection of chic restaurants and cosy inns overlooking a harbour brimming with colourful sails, a stroll down the boardwalk is a delight. Shuttle buses run from the hotels to the heart of El-Gouna, where an immaculate square is surrounded by tasteful shops and sophisticated restaurants and the pedestrianized cobbled streets are lit by pottery lanterns. It doesn't look or feel like anywhere else in Egypt, and for many travellers the effect is too plastic and surreal to warrant an extended stay (there are no budget hotels in town anyway), but for a special evening out away from the tacky bustle of Hurghada, El-Gouna certainly delivers quality and class. The **information office** ⓘ *open 0900-2300*, can provide good maps and information about the area, or check www.elgouna.com. Useful telephone numbers: **emergency** ⓘ *T065-358 0011*; **hyperbaric chamber** ⓘ *T012-218 7550*.

▸▸ *For diving information for the Red Sea, see pages 24 and 426.*

South of Suez listings

For Sleeping and Eating price codes and other relevant information, see pages 26-31.

Sleeping

Zafarana *p462*

E Sahara Inn, T012-2363 445/6. This decent if simple hotel has 4 large rooms in the new wing sharing a spacious terrace, with TV, a/c and hot water in the clean white rooms. There are also 8 rooms in the older wing with fans, bathrooms and TV but no balcony. The kind manager will negotiate on price. Breakfast is not included. The restaurant is tourist-friendly.

El-Gouna *p464*

Almost all hotels in El-Gouna are top-class and rather beautiful, both design and location-wise. Although they are totally self-contained with all the facilities you could desire, unlike some of the big resorts along this coast the nightlife of the town is easily accessible and you are not confined to your hotel for an evening's entertainment. Any accommodation in El-Gouna can be booked online at www.elgouna.com.

LL-L Movenpick, 30 km from airport, T065-354 4501, www.moevenpick-hotels.com. Built from terracotta, in gardens with tropical plants and palms framed by the desert behind and the lagoon in front. There are 4 pools, health club, a selection of bars and restaurants including **El-Sayadin** on the beach and a great Thai restaurant, and children's club. **Angsana Spa** is one of Egypt's most luxurious.

AL Captain's Inn, T065-358 0170. Cosy and comfy rooms overlooking Abu Tig Marina, free shuttle buses run to the lagoon. Use of the next door hotel's pool.

A Dawar El-Omda, central El-Gouna, T065-358 0063-6, www.dawarelomda-elgouna.com. A smaller hotel, with comfortable rooms furnished in traditional Egyptian style although they are slightly showing their age. The hotel's name literally means 'Omda's home' (chief's home) and the design resembles an Egyptian community leader's house. The pool is delightful, frequent boats run to Zaytona beach and the outside restaurant/bar is the perfect place for an evening drink among soft lamplight and flowering trees. Some of the cheapest beds in El-Gouna, surprisingly.

Eating

Zafarana *p462*

🍴🍴 **Sahara Inn**. The cleanest and most tourist-orientated place to eat between Cairo and Hurghada, with pizza, fish and alcohol available.

🍴 **Horus Cafeteria**, near the police checkpoint on the road north to Cairo. Decent Egyptian meals and breakfast are available on the large terrace of this local haunt, and the toilets are acceptable. No English sign.

El-Gouna *p464*

Among the most upmarket of resorts in Egypt, dining well in El-Gouna takes little effort. Restaurants tend to congregate around each other, making menu perusing easy.

YYY **Biergarten**, Kafr El-Gouna, varied menu from *wurst* and *sauerkraut* to spaghetti. Dancing on Wed.

YYY **Bleu Bleu**, Abu Tig Marina, T065-549702-4. Unquestionably El-Gouna's most elegant restaurant, the French cuisine is superb and set in lovely environs.

YYY **El-Sayadin**, Movenpick Hotel, T065-354 4501. Truly excellent fish in an amazing beachside setting, plus some Oriental delicacies.

YYY **Kiki's**, Kafr El-Gouna. A wide selection of authentic Italian food (Italian-owned), there's intimate indoor seating or the outdoor terrace overlooking the lagoon.

YYY-YY **Club House**, www.elgounaclub house.com, opposite Dawar El-Omda. Try the lunch selection of Italian-inspired food, freshly prepared. As the population of El-Gouna is largely Coptic, they have developed a good range of vegetarian dishes to fit in with the frequent fasting. It's also a friendly and bustling place for a drink by the pool.

YY **Tamr Henna**, T065-358 0521. Mixture of Turkish, Egyptian and Italian dishes, there's something for everyone, it's also the best place to have a *sheesha* and people-watch in the main square. There's also an a/c interior.

Bars and nightclubs

El-Gouna *p464*

Besides the standard hotel bars, there are several funky places to go for a drink:

Barten, at the end of the marina. Intimate bar with modern decor highlighted by red lights and minimal furniture. Popular with young trendy Cairenes.

Mangroovy Beach Bar, special seafood dinners with dancing round the bonfire on Sun and Wed. Access by shuttle bus.

Sand Bar, Kafr El-Gouna. Small in size but with a lively atmosphere, cheap draught beer, good selection of wine and tasty bar snacks, cold beer and loud music, very popular with divers.

Activities and tours

El-Gouna *p464*

Orange Concept, www.theorangeconcept.com, are a high-standard Dutch venture who offer wakeboarding, waterskiing, parasailing, etc, for all ages and levels of experience.

Also above the water's surface there is **horse riding**, **tennis** and an international grade 18-hole **golf course**.

The El-Gouna tourist information office, Downtown, can organize afternoon trips into the nearby desert to sip tea with the local Bedouin and watch the sunset.

Diving

This location provides for the visitor flora and fauna not normally found any further north and gives opportunity for day boats to reach dives normally accessed only by live-aboards. Dives may include the 2 wreck sites as well as the coral gardens and pinnacles. Diving Clubs are all top-notch in terms of safety and eco-consciousness, but are some of the most expensive in Egypt. They also have good snorkelling day trips, mainly to the Dolphin House, Gobal Island or Tawila Island. Among many are:

Blue Brothers Diving Centre, Ocean View Hotel, Abu Tig Marina, T012-321 8025, www.bluebrothersdiving.de.

TGI Diving, Marine Sporting Club, www.tgidiving.com. Open Water course €439 all-in, single day with 2 dives €65.

Transport

Aïn Sukhna *p462*

Bus

Buses bound for **Hurghada** will stop if you request them to (though you may have to pay the full Hurghada-bound fare). The frequent buses to/from **Suez** are E£10 and take 1 hr. There are also plenty of microbuses running along the coast between **Suez** and **Hurghada**, just hitch a ride, if there's a seat, they'll stop. Since there's no real bus stop in Sukhna, the police checkpoint south of the Portrait Hotel is a good place to wait if you're trying to get back to Suez or **Cairo**.

El-Gouna *p464*

Air

Hurghada airport is just 20 km away, with frequent flights from **Cairo** and elsewhere. Taxis from Hurghada airport cost E£60-80, depending on your bargaining skills.

Bus

Local Shuttle buses around El-Gouna cost E£5 for daily ticket and E£15 weekly ticket. Recently imported are some exotic buses from Pakistan to add real colour to the shuttle system, and tuk-tuks run around town for E£5. **Long distance** There are several buses commuting between El-Gouna and **Cairo** daily, run by **GoBus** (previously the El-Gouna Transportation Company). Buses bound for El-Gouna leave from the Ramses Hilton in central Cairo and Nasr City at 0730, 1345 and 0045. It's essential to buy your ticket in advance. The ticket booth is next to the **Superjet** sale's counter at Maspiro Mall on the museum side of the Ramses Hilton. Buses bound for **Cairo** leave from Gouna at 0930, 1400, 1630, 1930, 0030. Tickets are E£85-100. Buses to **Hurghada** leave every 20 mins from 0700-2400, E£5. The **High Jet Company** have cheaper less luxurious buses, E£55-65.

Taxi

Taxis running between El-Gouna and **Hurghada** cost E£60-90.

Directory

El-Gouna *p464*

Banks There are 7 banks, open Sun-Thu 0900-1400. **Internet** Café near Tamr Henna; ProLink club at Abu Tig Marina. **Medical services** El-Gouna Hospital, is world class, T065-3580 012-17, www.elgounahospital.com. There are 3 pharmacies generally open 0900-2100. **Post office** Central, open Sat-Thu from 0900-2000.

Hurghada

→ *Colour map 3, B5. Phone code 065.*

People generally end up in Hurghada, 506 km southeast of Cairo, 395 km south of Suez and 269 km northeast of Luxor, for one of three reasons: they've landed an absurdly cheap package tour, they're a diver, or they're stopping off en route between the Sinai and the Nile Valley. In fact, the city is viewed in an ever more disparaging light as increasing numbers of Eastern European package tourists swamp it year-round. Twenty years ago the town centre consisted of one ahwa *where fishermen would congregate and a couple of stores; nowadays, hotel developments stretch for 25 km down the coast and the booming real-estate business means there is furious (and hideous) construction of apartment blocks inland. In some ways it is an ideal location for a new tourist development: it is in a virtually uninhabited region, a long way from the Islamic fundamentalist strongholds; the hotels and holiday villages that have been built are largely self-contained, with the exception of fresh water, which is supplied from the Nile Valley; and they employ workers from the major cities. Unfortunately, the area has been developed too quickly since the first constructions in 1992 and frequently without adequate planning controls. However, the beauty of the sea and surrounding mountains is indisputable, some parts of town feel Egyptian in a way that sanitized Na'ama Bay fails to, and (despite the heavy tourist presence) plenty of folk are genuinely friendly and anything goes.* ▸▸ *For listings, see pages 473-479.*

Ins and outs

Getting there and around Most visitors arrive at Hurghada from the airport, 6 km southwest of the town centre. A taxi to/from town costs E£30-40. Arriving at either bus station (with **Superjet** or **Upper Egypt Bus Co**) you will need to take a short minibus ride unless you plan to stay at the hotels near the Upper Egypt Station. Expect to pay 50 pt-E£1 and possibly 50 pt-E£1 for baggage, especially if it takes up seating. Public transport will drop you in Dahar centre, from where there are microbuses on to Sigala, and then it's another change to get to the Resort Strip.

Dahar is the base for most locals and backpacking travellers, where cheap eats and budget accommodation are found. Two kilometres south, the area known as **Sigala** begins, satiated with mid-range hotels inland and more expensive ones by the seaside. The 'heart' of package-tour Hurghada, the area is filled with restaurants, dive clubs, cafés and nightlife haunts, although this was originally the old fishing village of which just a few old buildings linger on.

Although it is easy to walk around the relatively compact downtown of Dahar it is necessary, when trying to get to the port or the holiday villages to the south of town, to take cheap local buses and minibuses or the town's taxis, which are supposed to use their meters (starting at E£3). Alternatively cars and bicycles can be hired from some of the hotels. Ferries to Sharm El-Sheikh and Duba depart from the port at Sigala's northern tip. Further south, high-end 5-star resorts wind down the coast back to back with no end in sight. The road continues south all the way to the Sudanese border. ▸▸ *See Transport, page 478.*

Information The **tourist office** ⓘ *near the Marine Sports Club, Sharia Bank Misr, Resort Strip, T065-346 3221, open daily 0830-2000.* Also useful are some free publications called the *Red Sea Bulletin* and *In My Pocket Hurghada*, which can be picked up in hotels and restaurants. **Tourist Police** ⓘ *T065-346 3300.*

Sights

Hurghada (in Arabic, *Al-Ghardaka*) lures visitors with its promise of clear skies, stellar water sports facilities and easy access to diving. A few hotels have coral gardens actually on their site and there are plenty of coral islands offshore from which to study the hidden life below the warm blue waters. However, travellers merely passing through between the Nile Valley and the Sinai will easily be able to fill time, find a cheap hotel with use of a pool, and have a big night out for not too much money. The *souk* gets even livelier on a Friday with Egyptian shoppers and vendors filling the pavements with their wares. The noise and jostle of people, bikes, cars, bright tacky souvenirs, tired white donkeys,

1 Hurghada

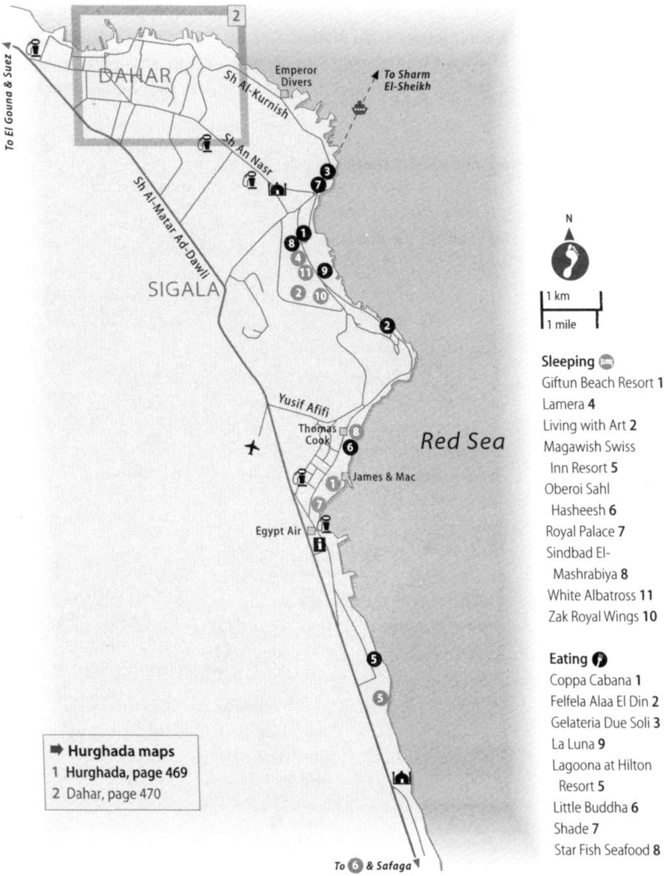

galabiyas and veils alongside scantily clad Russian tourists, the smell of *sheesha* pipes, herbs, dead chickens and bad drains assaults all the senses.

If you want to observe a bit of the real life of Hurghada residents, take a stroll around the 'Egyptian areas' in Dahar behind the **Three Corners Empire Hotel** or near 'Ugly Mountain' behind Sharia Abdel Aziz (from which there are great views, sunsets are especially spectacular in the autumn). The housing is pretty crumbly and the streets strewn with litter. Here you will find traditionally dressed women staying at home and scruffy children playing in the streets, boys are bold and loud and girls in *hijabs* wander from school in demure, giggly groups. The old harbour area is an interesting stroll as well, with bright coloured fishing vessels, a vibrant dry dock and small shops catering to locals. There's been a bit of a move to clean up these areas because of the tourists but you can still get a glance of life as it really is in the rest of Egypt.

The **Marine Museum** ⓘ *daily 0800-2000, E£10 for the museum and its adjacent aquarium*, is about 6 km to the north of the town centre and is associated with the National Institute of Oceanography and Fisheries. A good place to begin learning about the marine life of the area with stuffed examples of coral reef fish, shark, manta rays and associated birdlife as well as samples of coral and shells. The **Aquarium** ⓘ *daily*

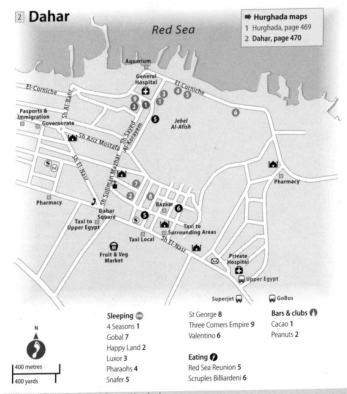

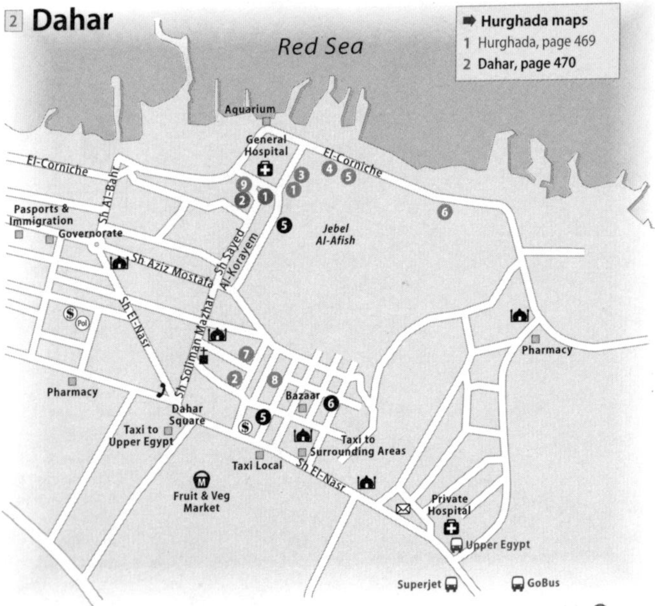

N

400 metres

400 yards

Sleeping
4 Seasons **1**
Gobal **7**
Happy Land **2**
Luxor **3**
Pharaohs **4**
Snafer **5**
St George **8**
Three Corners Empire **9**
Valentino **6**

Eating
Red Sea Reunion **5**
Scruples Billiardeni **6**

Bars & clubs
Cacao **1**
Peanuts **2**

0900-2200, E£10, on Sharia El-Corniche near the hospital, is quite small but has live specimens in well-marked tanks. It may be worth a visit if you are not a diver, though a glass-bottomed boat is much more of an experience for E£50.

Dive sites

Among the best dive sites are **Um Gamar**, 1½ hours north, a plateau of beautiful soft and hard corals with a good drop-off and cave. Also has a kingdom of poisonous snakes. Dives are made onto a slope that drops gradually from 15 m to 76 m. **Sha'ab Al-Erg** is 1½ hours north. There's a coral plateau including table coral and, if you are lucky, manta rays and dolphins. At the **Careless Reef** you may see shark. There is a spectacular drop-off and ergs. This site is for advanced divers only, due to the currents. The island stands over three columns of rare corals resting originally on a 10- to 15-m surface. **Giftun Islands** are close to Hurghada and thus very popular, and fast deteriorating. Fortunately they possess a number of reefs still teeming with plenty of fish including moray eels. **El-Fanadir**, is a popular site close to Hurghada with a pretty reef wall and drop-off with nice soft corals. **Sha'ab Abu Ramada**, 40 minutes south, with a good drop-off, has lots of fish and coral. Usually a drift dive. The corals shapes are unique: round and brain-like. Nearby **Gota Abu Ramada**, is nicknamed the 'Aquarium' due to the abundance of marine life among the mountainous coral garden, including butterfly fish, snappers, and banner fish. Further afield are a series of islands including **Shadwan**, **Tawlah** and **Gubal**, around which there are chances of seeing pelagic fish and dolphins.

Hurghada islands, reefs & dive sites

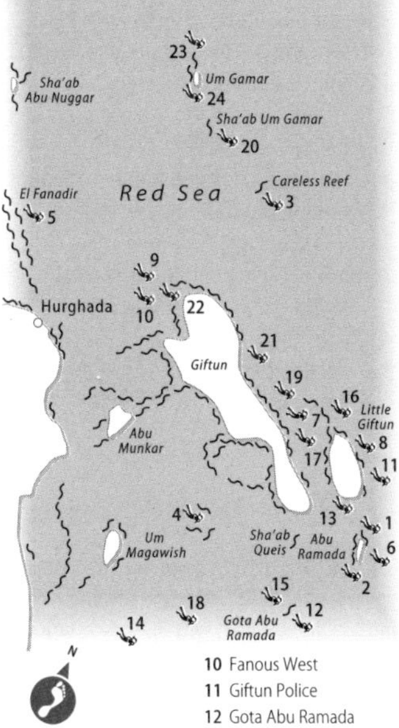

Not to scale

Dive sites

1 Abu Ramada North
2 Abu Ramada South (The Aquarium)
3 Careless Reef
4 El Aruk
5 El Fanadir
6 Erg Abu Ramada
7 Erg Sabina
8 Erg Somaya
9 Fanous East
10 Fanous West
11 Giftun Police
12 Gota Abu Ramada
13 Little Giftun
14 Sha'ab Disha
15 Sha'ab Eshta
16 Sha'ab Farasha
17 Sha'ab Sabina
18 Sha'ab Tiffany
19 Sha'ab Torf
20 Sha'ab Rur
21 Stone Beach
22 Turtle Bay
23 Um Gamar North
24 Um Gamar South

Beaches and etiquette

There are **public beaches** ⓘ *E£7-10, depending on services*, in Dahar near the Three Corners Empire, around the Port at Sigala and after the V-junction on Sharia Sheraton Sigala. At all three, and in particular the first two it is unacceptable to wear a bathing costume or less. Women sit in a proper manner on upright chairs and if they do venture into the sea, they are fully clothed. Men can wear shorts.

If you are not staying at a hotel with beach access, the only option is to pay to use one of the resorts' beaches. This costs between E£50-100 daily.

Diving in Hurghada – tales and tips

- If you want to take any qualifications make sure your instructor can speak your mother tongue. You can't be safe if you cannot understand the instructor. 'We all speak the same language underwater', is a sign you should be looking elsewhere. Be careful in choosing your dive centre – safety, environmental impact and price should be on your agenda. Bargain-basement prices could mean that short cuts are being made.
- Make sure you are insured to dive.
- Fly-by-night operators do exist. Always be on your guard. Go to an approved operator and watch out for scams, eg non-PADI centres flying PADI flags.
- The best options are those centres that have regular guests on dive holidays flying in from abroad.
- Common tricks include: cheap deals, making you feel guilty or rude if you refuse, sudden loss of understanding of your language, free desert/restaurant trips, offers of marriage! Also talk of donations to the decompression chamber, Sinai National Parks and Giftun Islands – these are virtually all compulsory and it is the diver that pays. (The government has introduced a US$1 a day charge for the decompression chamber and a US$2 tax for the Giftun Island Reef.)
- HEPCA (Hurghada Environmental Protection and Conservation Association), www.hepca.com, is concerned about environmental destruction. It organizes cleanups at various Red Sea sites. Some dive centres are members, but this is not necessarily a guarantee of safety.
- Membership of the Red Sea Diving and Watersport Association and the Egyptian Underwater Sports Association is not proof of safety either. Membership is a requirement of law.
- Contact PADI, BSAC, CMAS and SSI while at home for advice.
- Check whether dive centres will pick you up or if you will have to arrange your own transport.

Excursions from Hurghada

By boat A recommended trip is to **Mahmya Island**, about one hour off the coast of Hurghada, which has a gorgeous beach, some good snorkelling and a restaurant. It's also possible to take a trip further afield to Tobia Island, in Safaga Bay, with its sandy lagoons and untouched (for how long?) corals surrounded by turquoise water. There's also a sea cruise via Shedwan Island, the Gulf of Suez, and even Ras Mohammed (see page 407). The trip takes at least six hours and costs about E£250 – check with local travel guides. These trips do not run every day, but according to demand.

By land Day trips visit the Roman ruins of **Mons Claudianus** near Jebel Fatira (1355 m), the largest and best-preserved site in the Eastern Desert. There's evidence here of Roman military presence, a penal colony, a Roman road and columns as well as a Roman settlement with houses, stable and the fortress of Om Dikhal. It's also a quarry and you can see the remains of the cells used to house the workers/prisoners who quarried the stone, some of which made its way to Rome in barges where it formed the pillars in the portico of the Pantheon.

Mons Porphyritis, 55 km northwest of Hurghada at the foot of Jebel Abu Dukhan (1641 m), has some ruinous remains of a Roman temple to Serapis and ancient quarries for porphyry, a popular stone used for sarcophagi and facing walls. To visit the two Roman sites, you will need to hire a car for at least a half-day.

Hurghada listings

For Sleeping and Eating price codes and other relevant information, see pages 26-31.

Sleeping

Hurghada *p468, maps p469 and p470*
There are as many officially registered hotels in Hurghada as there are non-registered ones – and new ones springing up all the time. Although most visitors pre-book their accommodation as part of a package with their flight there should be no problem, except perhaps during the winter high season, for independent travellers to find a room. Like everywhere in Egypt, prices change, sometimes drastically, depending on the number of tourists, so treat these prices as variable. Single female travellers should be on guard when staying at budget hotels.

LL Oberoi Sahl Hasheesh, Sahl Hasheesh, T065-344 0777, www.oberoihotels.com. Truly luxurious and utterly exclusive, miles away from the mass tourism of Hurghada in both mood and geography, this is the top choice for those who can afford it. An all-suite resort, built in the domed Moorish style, all columns, arches and striped facades, from the sunken marble baths you can see the sea or the walled gardens. The pools are sublime as is the private beach, and the spa receives high praise.

L Magawish Swiss Inn Resort, Resort Strip, T065-346 4620-9, www.swissinn.net. 425 rooms, good standard, private bay and beach to south of port, offers all the normal facilities plus a wide range of water sports and children's activities.

AL Living With Art, the German Consulate, 465 El-Gabal El-Shamali, Sigala, T065-344 5734, T012-211 8338, www.livingwithart.biz. 18 modern apartments of varying sizes and layouts, all uniquely decorated, with large bathrooms, several balconies, warm lighting and decor and specially designed wrought-iron furniture. From the rooftop (with bar, spa, jacuzzi, pergolas and loungers) there are amazing views down the hill over town and sea. Karin is a simply wonderful cook, evenings are spent drinking German beer in her homely kitchen, and you'll forget you are in Hurghada the moment you enter the tranquil courtyard of bougainvillea. And at €50 per person half-board, it is excellent value for such a unique place.

AL Royal Palace Hotel, Sigala, T065-346 3660, www.royalpalacehotel.com. 120 rooms, private beach, 3 restaurants, good food. With a good diving centre and easy access to the beach for disabled people, this is one of the most reliable hotels in Hurghada, despite being slightly tacky.

AL Sindbad El-Mashrabiya, Resort Strip, T065-344 3330/2, www.sindbad-group.com. A pleasant Moorish-style hotel with 3 pools, plenty of excellent watersport facilities and its own private beach. This is where the yellow Sindbad Submarine trips are based.

A Giftun Beach Resort, Sharia Youseff Afifi, Resort Strip, T065-346 3040, www.giftun beachresort.com. Comfortable bungalows set in a vast private sandy beach, 8 km from town at the start of the resort strip. Pool, squash, tennis and all watersports are free except diving (James & Mac dive centre on site is recommended), windsurfing and tennis lessons. Main restaurant provides buffet meals and there are bars and discos. A good choice.

A The Three Corners Empire Hotel, Sharia Sayed Korrayem, Dahar, T065-354 9200/9, www.threecorners.com. Part of the Triton hotels chain, this domineering block in Dahar is always busy with package tourists and is a reliable mid-range choice. There's an unspectacular pool, plenty of bars and bazaars and a handy location in the thick of Downtown.

C Luxor Hotel, Sharia Mustashfa, Dahar, T065-354 2877, www.luxorhotel-eg.com.

Relatively new place, rooms here are more comfortable than most in this price range and bathrooms clean. Set back from the main road, it's a quiet if anonymous choice. There's a small front terrace, and discounts for longer stays. Guests can use the beach/pool a nearby hotel.

C Zak Royal Wings Hotel, Sigala, T065-344 6012, www.zakhotel.com. All rooms have views on to the small central swimming pool and the standard amenities you would expect for the price. Everything is painted white giving an almost Mediterranean air, the **Rossi** restaurant serves decent Italian food, adjacent **Papas Bar** is famed, and the location set back from the road is in its favour. A small and pleasant hotel.

C-D White Albatros, 162 Sharia Sheraton, Sigala, T065-344 2519, walbatros53@hotmail.com. Very clean hotel in the upper range of the budget category, and worth paying the extra for cheerful white rooms with green paintwork and decent bathrooms. British management, rooms with bath. Fridge, TV, a/c and balconies on the upper floors have seaviews. Popular with long-staying guests, there's a nice rooftop with loungers and downstairs coffee shop.

D Lamera Hotel, Sharia Sheraton, Sigala, T065-344 2075. Large clean rooms are nothing special and paintwork is grubby, but it's a convenient location mid-way along Sigala's main drag. Rooms have all the amenities you'd expect, TV, fridge, a/c, and there is access to a beach (about 10 mins' walk). Get a room high up at the front for sea views.

D Valentino Hotel, Sharia El-Corniche, Dahar, T010-620 2182. Small, friendly and spotless this is a good choice that has mid-range facilities for almost budget prices. Freshly painted rooms (a/c, satellite TV) and public spaces. There's a popular and laid-back terrace coffee shop (with alcohol) and a cute restaurant for breakfast. Staff are very polite.

E Snafer Hotel, off Sharia Sayed al-Korayem, Dahar, T/F065-354 0260, snafer_hurghada_hotel@hotmail.com. Decent-sized plain rooms all have fridge, a/c and balcony. The large soft beds and clean white linen are a real mark up from most of the budget places, as are the bathrooms, and compensate for a slightly higher price. There's no lift, which is a bit of a killer for the upper rooms (some of which have sea views). For breakfast pay E£10.

E 4 Seasons Hotel, off Sharia Sayed al-Korayem, Dahar, T/F065-354 4201, T012-7143 917, forseasonhurghda@hotmail.com. Rooms are clean if scruffy, all with balconies, fans or a/c, some bathrooms are very poky. Use of the pool at the **Geisum Village** is a bonus, as is the roof terrace. Recommended among others in the budget category, has a more backpacker vibe and runs cheap snorkelling trips to Giftun Island. Breakfast included.

E-F Pharaohs, off Sharia Sayed El-Korayem, Dahar. Rooms vary in quality, best are on top floor where a sea view is available. A little gloomy but close to the action and has a small garden at the front. Breakfast costs E£10.

F St George Hotel, off Sharia El-Nasr, Dahar, T065-354 8246. Rooms are certainly musty, gloomy and shabby, but have clean sheets, fans, and there's a roof view. Only the rooms with shared bath have balconies, while the Christian family that own it are kind.

G Gobal, Sharia Sheikh Sabak, Dahar, T065-354 6623. Small very cheap rooms, all with bathrooms outside, are do-able if you're on a real budget. You won't see any other foreigners here, sheets are clean and staff pleasant.

Eating

Hurghada *p468, maps p469 and p470*

Good restaurants in Hurghada are as plentiful as good hotels. Many of the cheaper ones are in Dahar, with a few in Sigala. If you feel extravagant head to the new Marina Blvd area for great Thai, Spanish and other international cuisine. A bigger beach and pool have been created here, and with the absence of cars it's a relaxing spot during the day – perfect for children – and then comes alive at night.

TTT Lagoona, at **Hilton Resort**, T065-346 5036. Open daily 1930-2330. A fish restaurant and international dishes. Open aspect gives breathtaking views.

🍴🍴🍴 **Little Buddha**, next to **Sindbad Club**, Village Rd, Resort Strip, T065-345 0120, www.littlebuddha-hurghada.com. Cocktails, great sushi and Pacific cuisine can be sampled on the 1st-floor seating area under the gaze of a giant gold Buddha. Food served from 1600. Turns into a club later on.

🍴🍴🍴 **Shade**, Marina Blvd, Sigala. Swedish-owned, this restaurant-bar has a Norwegian chef and everything on the menu is grilled and fresh. The salmon steak is tremendous, frequented by Hurghada's ex-pats.

🍴🍴🍴-🍴🍴 **La Luna**, Sharia Sheraton, Sigala, T065-344 8691-3. Generic Italian restaurant making an attempt at contemporary decor, some out-door seating, and very popular for its excellent pizzas and vast menu. They are open 24 hrs.

🍴🍴🍴-🍴🍴 **Scruples Billiardeni**, Sharia Abdel Azizi Mostafa, Dahar, T065-354 4796, www.scruples-reasea.com. Open 0900-0100. Classy it ain't, but if you fancy a steak or vaguely French cooking in an unpretentious place, head here. The outdoor chairs by a market square also make a good location for a beer.

🍴🍴 **Cacao Bar**, Sharia Sayed al-Korayem/ Hospital St, Dahar, T012-6184 861. Pretty good Italian food, the pizzas are recommended. It's also a popular drinking hole, see page 476, open 24 hrs.

🍴🍴 **El-Joker Fish Restaurant**, Midan Sheraton, Sigala, T065-344 3146. Has a long-standing reputation. Pick your own fish, pay by weight, or choose from the extensive menu of 'meals'. A no-frills kind of fish joint, don't be put off by the exterior, the environment improves as you ascend the stairs.

🍴🍴 **Felfela Alaa El Din**, Sharia Sheraton, Dahar T065-344 2411. Offers modestly priced authentic Egyptian food, overlooking the sea, a little out of the town centre, north of the resort strip, but worth it for the view and the food.

🍴🍴 **Red Sea Reunion**, Sharia Sayed al-Korayem/ Hospital St, Dahar, T012-719 6267, www.redsearunion.com. In its heyday, this was about the only restaurant with a rooftop terrace and hence always packed out. Not so now, but the rooftop remains relaxing and pleasant both day and night, offering Italian, Indian, fish and steaks. They have Nubian music on Wed nights, and a relatively low-key DJ on other nights, and the staff are genuinely friendly. Free Wi-Fi.

🍴🍴 **Rossi Pizzeria**, **Zak Wings Hotel**, Sharia Sheraton, Sigala, T065-344 7676. Traditional Italian cuisine and sandwiches with a decent salad bar.

🍴🍴 **Star Fish Seafood Restaurant**, Sharia Sheraton, Sigala, T065-344 3751. Open 1200-0100. Excellent value for grilled, fried or baked fish, fabulous shrimps and the salads are some of the best around for only E£3. A large clean functional place, busy at all hours, they also home deliver. There is a new branch in the Senzo Mall.

🍴 For passable *koshari*, try the joint on Sharia El-Nassr to the left of the Upper Egypt bus station.

Ahwas and cafés

Authentic local *ahwas* are in Dahar. There are a number by the small mosque in the centre. Strictly speaking they're generally patronized by local men only, but with so many foreigners around, few take offence if visitors enjoy a sheesha or a cup of tea and gaze at the world on the streets around you. There are also numerous tourist cafés including those mentioned here as restaurants and bars. Try the sugar cane juice E£1, fresh orange E£5, or whatever fruit is in season, at the best juice shop in Hurghada on Sharia Sayyed, next to **Supermarket Rashidy**.

Coppa Cabana, Sharia Sheraton, Sigala, T012-796 3653. Gorgeous home-made Italian ice cream, plus coffee that's the real-deal, this cute corner café never disappoints. They also have a new place at the Marina Blvd, **Gelateria Due Soli**. It is more about the gelati than the coffee.

Miramar, Mohamady Hwedak St, T065-345 0920. An upmarket coffee shop frequented more by wealthy Egyptians than package tourists. Dark red interiors with striped Moorish arches, Orientalist prints on the walls, and comfy indoor and terrace seating, you soon forget the ugly main road outside when puffing on one of the best *sheeshas* in town.

Bars and nightclubs

Hurghada *p468, maps p469 and p470*
At the last count there were over 100 bars in Hurghada. As a major tourist resort there is less worry about offending Islamic sensibilities. As a result, besides the main hotel restaurants, which feature discos and serve alcohol, there are a few clubs in town. There are plenty of belly-dancing shows at all the big hotels on a nightly basis, mostly performed by Russian women.

Cacao Bar, Sharia Sayed al-Korayem/Hospital St, Dahar, T012-6184 861. Open 24 hrs and always has a few drinkers whatever the time, happy hours daily from 1500-1800, free Wi-Fi, and occasional live music. The pizzas aren't bad, either.

HedKandi, Marina Blvd. A chilled-out vibe by the sea, during the day it's a pleasant spot to relax on the beach then it transforms at night-time into a rocking disco, plus they have excellent full-moon parties.

Little Buddha, next to **Sindbad Resort**, Village Rd, Resort Strip, T065-345 0120, www.littlebuddha-hurghada.com. Open 2330-0400. The coolest place to go out and many rate it as the best club in Hurghada.

Ministry of Sound, Papas Beach Club, T016-883 3550, www.ministryofsound egypt.com, Sigala. A proper night out, with good music, and the place is usually packed. Resident and guest DJs from Europe, as you'd expect from the Ministry the music gets everyone going 7 nights a week.

Peanuts Bar, Sharia, Dahar. Open from 1200-0200. Copious amounts of peanuts available to supplement copious amounts of beer, a happening spot with package tourists from the nearby Three Corners. Free Wi-Fi and sports events shown on big screens.

Shopping

Hurghada *p468, maps p469 and p470*
Hurghada has very few local shops although all of the major hotels and holiday villages have shopping arcades that cater for tourists' requirements. Souvenir stands are plentiful. T-shirts, towels, carpets, jewellery, scarabs, *sheesha* pipes, papyrus, pyramids, stuffed camels – the list is endless. If buying gold or silver make sure it's stamped and you get a certificate of authenticity. Remember trade in coral and some animals and fish is illegal. Herbs here are much cheaper than at home, but if your travels will take you beyond Hurghada, better deals exist elsewhere. Duty-free goods can be bought at the Pyramid at the roundabout in Sigala and next to the **Royal Palace** and **Ambassador** hotels. Bear in mind that passport stamps for duty- free are only valid for 2 days. There is a **Metro** supermarket on Sharia Sheraton and Sharia An-Nasr and **Abu Ashara supermarket** on Sharia Sheraton, both are well stocked. The local fruit and vegetable market is near Al-Dahar Sq, beyond Sharia El-Nasr. If you are travelling further south this is your last chance to stock up on products such as moisturizer, tampons, contact lens solution and hair conditioner.

Bookshops

Al Ahram, in Esplanada Mall, south of Sigala. Open 0900-2200.

Pyramid Bookshop, in Jasmine Village. With international newspapers.

Red Sea Bookstores, Zabargad Mall, Sharia Al-Hadaba, www.redseabookstores.com. Open 1100-2300. Has the best selection of books in Hurghada.

Activities and tours

Hurghada *p468, maps p469, p470 and p471*

Boat trips

All-day boat excursions go to Giftun Island, in the bay, which has a nice beach and good snorkelling even though it gets overcrowded.

Who sells sea shells?

The answer is nobody should sell shells because nobody wants to buy.

The sale of shells and coral is illegal, and large fines and long prison sentences can result if you are successfully prosecuted. Removing anything living or dead from the water in Protected Areas is forbidden. Fishermen are banned from these areas. Continuing to plunder the marine environment will cause permanent damage.

The Environmental Protection Association, along with operators of dive centres and hotels are desperately trying to educate visitors. Unfortunately, they know they have a better chance of persuading the tourists not to buy than the locals not to sell.

It's easy to join a boat from any of the cheap hotels or from the marina for €25, expect your tour to include a fish barbecue. To just visit the island for a couple of hours is €15. For around €400, you can rent a private boat from the port or the athletic marine club for a day.

Some tour operators and hotels, including: **Flying Dolphin Sea Trips**, **Nefertiti Diving Centre** and **Sunshine Sea Trips**, also organize longer boat trips including 3-day trips to Gobal Island, overnight excursions to Giftun, and expeditions to the deeper reefs such as the House of Sharks (20 km south) where experienced divers can see hammerheads, tiger sharks and other exotic marine life.

To view the underwater world and keep dry there is the Finnish-built a/c 44-seater **Sindbad Submarine**, T065-344 4688, offering a 2-hr roundtrip including about 50 mins underwater. Should be booked the day before. Transfer by boat 30 mins, out to submarine, which goes down to 22 m with diver in front attracting fish with food (not a recommended procedure). Trips everyday leaving from 1000-1200. Price US$50 for adults and US$25 for children under 12.

Sailing boats are available in Hurghada too. Catamarans and toppers are best found at the windsurf schools. Glass-bottomed boats are available at most hotels for about E£50 per hr per person.

Desert trips

It's become easy to arrange day trips to the desert from most tour operators/hotels, to get a sense of the endless expanses surrounding the city and a chance to have a bit of a Bedouin 'camp' experience. Expect to pay about €35 for a quad bike, €25 per person for a place in a jeep, or €50-60 for 2 people in a buggy.

Diving

Though the terribly rapid development of tourist sites and the excessive underwater traffic from thoughtless divers keen to take a piece of the Red Sea home has yielded tragic destruction in the reefs around Hurghada, the area still boasts some of the best diving in the world. The waters are warm year-round, visibility is always good, and currents are mild. In addition to a wide variety of coral, vast schools of sparkling tiny fish and large pelagic swimmers along the seabed's deep walls, you may have the chance to swim with dolphins, hammerheads and manta rays.

Below is a selection of the better diving clubs. All teach accredited dive courses and offer live-aboard safaris to nearby sites, daily and extended trips. Shop around a bit before you commit, make sure you can get on with your dive instructor and that s/he speaks your language. Choose with care, check the qualifications, see what safety precautions are in place. Cheap may not be best.

Colona Divers, in **Magawish Swiss Inn Resort**, Resort Strip, T010-213 8409, www.colona.com.

Diver's Lodge, at **Intercontinental Resort**, Resort Strip, T065-346 5100, www.divers-lodge.com.

Emperor Divers, Hilton Plaza, T065-344 4854, www.emperordivers.com, with branches all over the Red Sea they come highly recommended.
James and Mac, Giftun Beach Resort, T065-346 2141, www.james-mac.com. Good reputation.

Fishing
An International Fishing Festival takes place every Feb. Spear fishing is illegal in the Red Sea.
Marine Sports Club, next to the Grand Hotel, T065-346 3004.

Snorkelling
Boats with motors to tow or for fishing or snorkelling are for hire. **Three Corners, Shedwan** and **Coral Beach** hotels all have house reefs, but the best reefs are offshore. With a tour, a day's snorkelling, including lunch, costs from €25-40. Good snorkelling sites include Giftun Islands, Fanadir, Um Gamar, and Mahmya island.

Tour operators and travel agents
Besides the independent travel agents there is at least one in each major hotel. With the Nile Valley only a few hours away, many travel agencies organize day-long tours to Luxor that depart Hurghada in the early morning convoy and return in the evening.
Misr Travel, Sigala, T065-344 2131.
Thomas Cook, 3 Sharia El-Nasr, Dahar, T065-354 1870. Main office for tourist facilities. Also a branch with financial services in Sigala, at 8 Sharia Sheraton.

Windsurfing
Windsurfing is particularly good thanks to the gusty winds, usually 4-8 on Beaufort Scale. Many hotels offer equipment but much of it is outdated. The best equipment is found at centres offering windsurf holiday packages. Ensure your choice of centre has a rescue boat that works.
Happy Surf, www.happy-surf.de have branches at the **Hilton Plaza** and **Sofitel** (German-run). Expect to pay about €150 per hr, more for kiteboards.
Planet Windsurf, www.planetwindsurf.com, British-based company; also do kiteboarding.

Transport

Hurghada *p468, maps p469 and p470*

Air
International flights go to and from all over Europe. There are 2 or 3 daily flights from Hurghada to **Cairo**. Flights also go direct to **Aswan**, **Sharm El-Sheikh** and **Alexandria**. Times and numbers of flights change daily so it is best to visit **EgyptAir** in person or go online, as the phones are rarely answered. Flights to Cairo and Sharm El-Sheikh are approximately E£300.

Airlines EgyptAir, www.egyptair.com, in the square with the new mosque and a branch on Sharia Sheraton, T065-346 3034-7. Open 0800-2000.

Bus
Local Minibus and microbuses make regular circuits of Dahar. A ride from Dahar to Sigala should cost E£1.
Long distance The main bus station is on Sharia El-Nassr in Dahar from where **Upper Egypt** buses leave. Further down the street to the south are the **GoBus** and **Superjet** offices. **High Jet**, T065-344 9700, have an office near the police station in Sigala.

Upper Egypt, T065-354 7582, runs regular daily buses north to **Suez** (every hr, 0600-2400; 5 hrs; E£35) and **Cairo** (11 per day; 6-7 hrs, between E£50-70 depending on time of departure). There are 6 buses per day southeast to **Luxor** (5 hrs; E£30), via **Qena**, 2 of which carry on to **Aswan** (8 hrs). Buses to **El-Quesir** (2 hrs, E£25) via **Safaga** (E£5-7) leave at 0100, 0300, 0500 and 2000, carrying on to **Marsa Alam** (4 hrs, E£35) and **Shalatein** (E£50, 9 hrs).

Superjet, Sharia Al-Nasr, T065-355 3499, runs 4 daily buses to **Cairo** at 1200, 1430, 1700 and 2400 (6 hrs, E£70); the 1430 goes on to **Alexandria** (9 hrs, E£90).

GoBus (previously called El-Gouna Transport), Sharia Al-Nasr, T065-355 6199, T19567, runs 17 daily buses to **Cairo** (via **El-Gouna**) 6 hrs, E£45-150 depending on class of bus (the 1430 is cheapest).

Many of the buses to and from Cairo are genuinely 'lux', with a/c and plastic still covering the seats, and therefore more expensive. It's wise to check schedules south to Marsa Alam as they fluctuate seasonally, and a good idea to book a ticket a day in advance if you are going to Luxor, Aswan or Alexandria.

Car

Most car rental agencies are scattered around Sharia Sheraton.

Ferry

High speed a/c ferry to **Sharm El-Sheikh** on the Sinai Peninsula (1½ hrs, though weather can impact duration), booking is essential from Red Sea Jet, office on the Sharia Sheraton in front of Pacha resort, T065-344 9481/2, or through a travel agent such as Thomas Cook, Sharia El Nasr, Dahar, T065-354 1870, or Spring Tours, Sharia Sheraton, Sigala, T065-344 2150. 1-way fare costs E£250, return E£450. Ferries leave Hurghada for Sharm El-Sheikh at 0900 on Sat, Tue and Thu and at 0400 on Mon. They depart from Sharm El-Sheikh back to Hurghada on the same days at 1700, or 1800 on Mon.

There are also 3 weekly ferry services to **Duba**, in Saudi Arabia (3 hrs, departs 1000 but you should be in the port at 0800, E£325, more if you have a car). Contact Sheriff Tours, at Sand Beach, T065-345 5147, to book a ticket or for more information.

Taxi

Local Minimum charge E£5-10 within Dahar. To get to **Sigala** from Dahar, E£15-20. **Long distance** Service taxis operate to destinations south, north and west, although as a foreigner you may have to be insistent to join those travelling to the Nile Valley or south to Marsa Alam (lone travellers or couples stand a better chance). You need to go to the service taxi station across the roundabout from the Telephone Centrale. Service taxi fares are approx E£5 to **Safaga** (1 hr), E£20 to **Marsa Alam** (3 hrs), E£50 to **Cairo** (5-7 hrs), E£25 to **Suez** (4 hrs). You may have to wait some time for the car to fill up (7 people, microbus 14). If you're in a rush, you can pay for empty seats in order to leave sooner. For long distances, fares and travel times are less than the bus but it's more dangerous as drivers often speed quite fearlessly.

Directory

Hurghada *p468, maps p469 and p470*

Banks CIB, T065-344 8412; Bank of Alexandria, T065-354 9575; Banque Misr, Sharia El-Nasr, T065-354 6624; HSBC, Sharia Sheraton, T065-344 0741. Banks open from Sun-Thu 0900-1300, 1800-2100, Fri and Sat 0900-1330. Money transfers can be arranged through Thomas Cook, Sharia El-Nasr, Dahar, T065-354 1870, and Western Union, Sharia Sheraton, Sigala, T065-344 2771. **Immigration** Passports and Immigration Office: north of the town on Sharia El-Nasr, open Sat-Thu 0800-1400, T065-354 6727. **Internet** Internet cafés are abundant in Dahar and generally cost a minimum of E£3 per hr for a fast connection. Plenty of restaurants also have Wi-Fi. **Medical services** International Hospital, El-Ahya, T065-355 3785, El-Salam hospital, Sigala, T065-354 8785-7, and the General Hospital on Sharia Aziz Mostafa, T065-354 6740. The best hospital is in El-Gouna, El-Gouna Hospital, T065-3580012-7, www.elgounahospital.com.eg, where there is also a decompression chamber; decompression chamber also in Hurghada at the Naval Hospital, T065-344 9150. **Post office** Main branch on Sharia El-Nasr, open Sat-Thu 0800-2100. **Telephone** Outside of the hotels, Telephone Centrales are on the main roundabout of Sharia El-Nasr, in Dahar, and on Sharia Sheraton and Midan Shedwan, in Sigala.

South of Hurghada

➔ Colour map 3, B5-C6.

Until the 1980s, the coast south of Hurghada was virtually untouched by tourism and a wealth of coral reefs and islands lay undisturbed but by the adventurous few. Recent years have seen a boom in hotel building, and large resorts pepper the coast between El-Quseir and Marsa Alam as an airport brings in package tourists mainly from Germany and Italy. Yet the port of El-Quseir remains a peaceful little place, with accommodation suiting backpackers and a unique atmosphere, while south of Marsa Alam restrictions imposed to protect the environment mean that new hotels have to be eco-friendly and hence there are some truly stunning getaways if you have the time and the money. The interior of the Eastern Desert remains one of Egypt's least explored areas, hiding ancient tribes and scattered ruins in the mountainous expanses stretching towards Sudan. *➤➤ For listings, see pages 483-490.*

Safaga

Safaga stands 567 km from Cairo, 65 km (45 minutes by taxi) south of Hurghada's airport, where the coastal road meets the main road across the Eastern Desert to Qena. Though the town isn't particularly beautiful, it has this stretch of the Red Sea's usual attractions: diving, snorkelling and perhaps the most famous wind on the coast. The stiff breezes that favoured the trading vessels along these shores now provide excellent conditions for kite- and windsurfing, generally cross-shore in the morning and side-shore in the early afternoon. The Windsurfing World Championships have been held here in the past. There are a few large resort hotels in Safaga, and the proximity of the beautiful sandbank island of Tobia and the lagoon at Ras Abu Soma give the option of easy day-trips. Safaga has also gained a reputation as a health tourism destination, with many psorisis and arthritis sufferers journeying from afar to roast in the mineral-enriched black sands. With such geological riches, the area does not rely totally on tourism. It has local phosphate mines that export the mineral overseas.

Most travellers simply pass through in a convoy on their way between Hurghada and the Nile Valley. Outside of the sea, there is very little to visit other than a small fort that overlooks the town and offers good views.

El-Quseir

Further south is El-Quseir, 650 km from Cairo and 140 km south of Hurghada, an old Roman encampment and once a busy port. Far enough away from the hoards of package tourists in Hurghada and Safaga, and without any mega-resorts such as are found on the stretch of coast south to Marsa Alam, the small sleepy town has managed to retain a lot of its ancient charm. Coral-block houses with creaky wooden balconies are dotted around the old village by the seafront, people are incredibly friendly and move at a slower pace. The surroundings are still pristine and the nearby snorkelling and diving superb, but the town's real charm lies in the unspoilt continuity of real life – something that's missing from other more user-friendly beach retreats in Sinai and the Red Sea. The sense of history and sea-trade, the tangible presence of Islam (heightened by the noise of 33 mosques) and the narrow pastel-toned streets make it feel like an Egyptian version of Zanzibar. But considerably smaller and with fewer tourists.

The name 'Quseir' means 'short' as this was the starting point both of the shortest sea-route to Mecca and the shortest way to the Nile Valley, five days away overland by camel. Located in a small inlet sheltered by a coral reef, the modern road inland from El-Quseir to Qift, just south of Qena, follows an ancient pharaonic route that is lined with forts, built at a time when almost 100 small but very rich gold mines operated in the region. It was from El-Quseir that Queen Hatshepsut departed on her famous expedition to the Land of Punt and throughout the pharaonic era there was trade with Africa in wild animals, to supply the pharaohs with elephants during times of warfare. This was also once the most important Muslim port on the Red Sea. In the 10th century it was superseded first by Aydhab, which is the ancient name for the Halaib in the currently disputed triangle on the Egyptian/Sudanese border, and then by Suez after the canal was opened in 1869. Now the port's main function revolves around the export of phosphates. The 16th-century fortress of Sultan Selim (rebuilt by the French in 1798) still dominates the town centre and creates a mystique that no other Red Sea village quite has.

Sights The partly ruined **fortress** ⓘ *E£15, students E£8, 0800-1700 daily except during Fri prayers, incorporates an excellent visitor centre,* was built in 1571 by Sultan Selim to protect the Nile Valley from attacks from the sea and to shield pilgrims bound for Mecca from Bedouin raids. The devoted left their camels and horses at the fort while they made the *hajj*. There was conflict here at the end of the 18th century – during the French campaign, and then again between the British Indian Army coming in from Bombay and the Egyptian campaign to the Arabian Peninsula headed by Ibrahim Pasha in 1816. (See box on Mohammed Ali and family, page 551.) The central watchtower affords good views of the surprisingly high mountain ranges to the south, which contain the mineral wealth of the area; from here the sea and mountains were surveyed for invaders.

Other buildings from this earlier period include the mosques of Al-Faroah, Abdel-Rehim Al-Qenay and Al-Sanussi and the fabulous derelict granary just behind the old police station. There are also a significant number of tombs, mainly near the fortress and Corniche, of holy men who died en route to Mecca, which are still considered important by the town's inhabitants. To the north of town, the compound of the old Italian phosphate mining works contains derelict warehouses, an ornate modern church and a tiny crumbling 'museum' containing a few mouldering stuffed animals, reptiles and birds (someone will appear with the key). Nearby is a small but colourful fruit and vegetable market.

Wadi Hammamat About 100 km along en route to Qift, Wadi Hammamat has some 200 examples of pharaonic graffiti – hieroglyphic inscriptions – in the cliff, including the names of Pepi, Sesostris, Seti, Cambyses and Darius. The inscriptions lie along an ancient trade route where remains of old wells and watch towers are also detectable.

Marsa Shagra

This remote bay, 113 km south of El-Quseir and 13 km north of Marsa Alam, has transformed into a small village celebrated by divers. There is an extensive underwater cave system to explore, and some outstanding coral formations. It's also near a group of striking offshore reefs with great sloping walls, the mysterious **Elphinstone Reef** among them, where in its dark depths some say lie the remains of an unknown pharaoh. (See page 488).

Marsa Alam

Once merely a tiny fishing village 130 km south of El-Quseir, Marsa Alam is developing fast, with a new mall being built to the south of town. Nevertheless, the surrounding area (if not the town itself) remains a gem of the southern coast. Marsa Alam is also a way station between the Nile Valley and the Red Sea since a road through the Eastern desert connects it to Edfu, 250 km to the west. The small harbour is nestled in a beautiful area where the coast is lined with mangrove swamps that encourage rich bird and marine life. These mangroves are protected and all new developments are supposed to be eco-conscious in order to ensure the preservation of the fragile environment. There is nowhere to stay in the town itself, and the coast north to El-Quseir is dotted with Disney-esque resorts that make an astonishing spectacle lit up at night. Independent travellers are usually heading south of Marsa Alam to one of the smaller camps at Tondoba Bay, Marsa Nakari, Wadi Lahami or Wadi Gimal. It is not a particularly welcoming town and has no discernible centre, save for the bus station. There is also very little public transport and most of the resorts or camps are spread along the coast. A taxi is needed to get around, and it is best to try not to arrive late at night without a reservation somewhere. ▸▸ *For dive sites, see page 488.*

Berenice

A very ancient city named by Ptolemy II, Berenice became a trading port around 275 BC. The ruined temple of **Semiramis** is near the modern town. Inland there are remains of the emerald mines of Wadi Sakait that were worked from pharaonic to Roman times. Berenice is noted for both quantity and quality of fish and having a climate reputed to promote good health. The coast is lined with mangrove swamps and there are some beautiful coves that are completely isolated. However, it is extremely unlikely you would be able to visit the town as the police are particularly uncooperative here. The nearest you will probably get is on a live-aboard dive boat.

Offshore is the **Zabargad**, a most unusual volcanic island. Evidence of its origin is found in the (olive-green) olivine mined as a semi-precious gem stone. Mining has been active here on and off since 1500 BC. **Peridot Hill** (named after another semi-precious stone) offers breathtaking views of the surrounding area. A wonderful place to watch the dolphins and, in season, the migrating birds. Once off limits to visitors, Zabargad Island has finally been declared a Protected Marine Park by the Egyptian government. Sometimes a permit is required for this area, though a bit of *baksheesh* to the right people can often grant access. It is still relatively untouristed and safari boats spend three to four days exploring the dive sites and surrounds.

Excursions inland There is one interesting excursion possible from here into the interior, but a guide is essential. The tomb and mosque of **Sidi Abul Hassan Al-Shazli** lies some distance inland. The buildings are modern, being last restored on the instructions of King Farouk after his visit in 1947. The road is a distance of 110 km southwards off the main road west towards Edfu. Al-Shazli (1196-1258) was an influential Sufi sheikh originally from the northwest of Africa but who spent much of his life in Egypt. He had a large and important following and was noted for his piety and unselfishness. He travelled annually to Mecca, for which Marsa Alam was convenient. His *moulid* is popular despite the isolation of the site, attracting around 20,000 devotees. Events stretch over the 10 days before Eid Al-Adha, and if you are in the area at this time it's the ultimate *moulid* experience, however the road is officially closed to foreigners and you will need a lot of willpower and some luck to get through.

Shalatein

The last outpost before Sudan, 100 km south of Berenice, Shalatein is not easily accessible for independent travellers as the political situation remains sensitive due to the disputed border area and thus the police are rather twitchy. For two months in 2010, the town was inexplicably closed to all foreigners and now getting here on public transport is almost 'mission impossible' through the numerous police check-posts. The vast majority of visitors come on a day trip from the big hotels in either Marsa Alam or El-Quseir. Shalatein is very spread out, with a split between modern governmental/military buildings and the shanty town-like market area to the south. Homes and businesses are generally made of plywood, painted pale blue and green, peopled by white-clad men and invisible women. The few concrete constructions include a basic hotel and a domineering restaurant serving tour groups that pass through. The reason for visiting is the exceptional daily camel market that brings Sudanese herders to mingle with the Bashari, Ababda and Rashaida tribespeople who make up the main population of the town. The market is busiest on a Thursday when local traders are frantically wheeling and dealing before the weekend; consequently, Fridays are the least active time to visit (although the market does still operate), while most of the tourist groups come on Tuesday or Wednesday. While the Rashaida migrated from Saudi Arabia around 200 years ago, the Bashari belong to the nomadic Beja tribe who have been wandering the Red Sea hills for 6000 years, not answering to any central government until the early 1990s. Both tribes wear their traditional clothes like a uniform, Rashaida men in mauve *galabiyas* and the women in dark red dresses laden with jewellery, whilst Bashari men twist a fine length of cotton 4-7 m long around their heads to form a massive turban called an *ema*. Camels are traded between the locals and the squatting Sudanese who wear long knives and carry a camel whip and wooden bowl for watering their beasts; thousands of euro can be passed over the sand during these transactions. The current going price for a camel is E£6000-7000. Aside from the animal market, wooden stalls sell a huge variety of produce and products, intermingled among these are a few selling 'souvenirs' such as the silver, pottery, shields and swords that are still used in the daily routines of the tribespeople. An organized trip here is pricey, at around €80, but as it is presently the only easy way to visit this remarkable town it's money well spent.

South of Hurghada listings

For Sleeping and Eating price codes and other relevant information, see pages 26-31.

Sleeping

Safaga *p480*

LL La Residence des Cascades, 48 km, Safaga Rd, T065-354 2333, www.residencedescascades.com. On the Soma Bay peninsula, renowned for the golf course (in which it stands) as much as for its Thalassotherapy centre, this hotel is wonderfully plush and has endless leisure facilities, as well as spectacular views and surroundings. Go online for the best prices.

L-AL Menaville Resort, about 5 km north of Safaga port, T065-326 0064-7, www.menaville.com. A good 4-star choice. Chalets and villas in gardens, by pool or adjacent to the very good beach, all rooms a/c, telephone, minibar and terrace or balcony. Shops, bank, laundry, clinic. 24-hr café, cycle hire, billiards, table tennis. Has own dive centre, www.menadive.com, with private jetty. Unlimited shore diving from hotel reef and boat dives available with all equipment for hire.

El-Quseir *p480*

There are a couple of excellent budget and mid-range options in El-Quseir that make for a memorable visit. Hotels in town don't have pools, but you can use the perfect beach at Rocky Valley Beach Camp, 14 km north, for E£20 per day, which includes a soft drink.

AL-A Movenpick Resort, El-Quadim Bay, 5 km north of El-Quseir, T065-333 2100, www.moevenpick-hotels.com. Unbeatable value (book online) and one of the coastline's most stunning hotels with a coral reef running the entire length of the private beach. You can almost snorkel from your room. Moorish style, environmentally conscious, lovely gardens and beach, large pool, 3 restaurants of which **Orangerie** is recommended. Masses of activities on offer and Subex Dive Centre, see page 487.

A Flamenco Beach & Resort, 7 km north of town, T065-335 0200-9, www.flamenco hotels.com. High-class resort on a beautiful stretch of beach, bustling but relaxed atmosphere, good food, and a couple of lovely pools. Generic architecture and room design, but worth checking online as you can score some great deals, especially in summer. Mainly Italian and German guests, snorkelling off the end of the pier.

B-G Rocky Valley Beach Camp, Abu Sawatir, T065-333 5247, T010-653 2964, www.rocky valleydiverscamp.com. Probably the best eco-camp on the entire stretch of eastern coast, 10 pristine and tasteful huts with comfy beds are dotted up the hillside, with stunning views to the sea below. Some have private bathrooms, others share hot showers. There's good snorkelling and diving straight off the beach, where there's a café, simple huts (€5 per night, bring a sleeping bag), shade and loungers. It's candlelit at night (the generator goes on for a few hours every day) and they throw a great party by firelight if you're up for it. Has own dive centre, and perfect host Hassan El Assy also runs trips to the Eastern desert (see below). The only irritation is that the road runs between the camp and the beach, though that is usually the case with any camp along this coast. A taxi costs E£20 from the bus station.

C-D Al Quseir Hotel, Sharia Port Said, T065-333 2301. At the northern end of the harbour, this hotel of just 6 rooms in an old merchant's house is atmospheric and unusual, expect exposed brick walls and wonky stairs. Large rooms have little furniture (bed, wardrobe, sink, fan and a/c) but the wooden floors and ceilings and old doors with Islamic details make them special. On each floor there are 3 rooms that share 2 spacious bathrooms and, although relatively expensive for a real budget traveller, it's a place you won't forget. Breakfast is included and they are prepared to negotiate on price.

C-D Roots Camp, Abu Sawatir, T010-212 3414. Next door to **Rocky Valley Beach Camp** and not as attractively sited nor as welcoming, but it is cheaper and enjoys the same stretch of sand. Clean new wooden chalets have a/c and private bath, plus older palm/stone huts with floor-standing fans share bathrooms, all are simply furnished with natural tones. Bedouin seating area, beer E£15, plans for a dive centre, currently the area is a bit of a building site.

E-F Sea Princess Hotel, south of town next to the petrol station, T065-333 1880. The only budget option in El-Quseir, the majority of rooms resemble prison cells and share rather grubby bathrooms (singles E£30, doubles E£50). However, there are 3 newer pricier rooms on the 2nd floor with en suite and a/c, much more acceptable though with hard beds and pillows. You're better off paying a bit more in the **Al Quseir Hotel** if you want to be in town. Staff don't speak much English but are pleasant.

Marsa Shagra *p481*

Though several establishments have sprouted up in these parts in recent years, the oldest among them is still at the top, both for its comfort, facilities and experience, as well for its environmental sensitivity.

LL-AL Ecolodge Shagra Village, reservations in Cairo T02-2337 1833, in Shagra, T012-244 9073, T012-244 9075 www.redsea-divingsafari.com. Set back from the beach to the west of the coast road (so as not to spoil the view), the construction in local red sandstone is very sympathetic. A central domed area containing all the main facilities is surrounded by chalets, huts and tents with lots of space. All are spotlessly clean and very comfortable but only the chalets have private bath. There is no pool or bar, but the bay boasts a stunning beach with a fantastic house reef, good for shore dives and snorkelling. However, it is not in the isolated seclusion you might expect, as there are a cluster of resorts all around. The owner, Hossam Helmi, is a pioneer in the area, and one of the foremost environmentalists on the coast. He's also a diving enthusiast and knows the surrounding seas better than most. Extensive diving day-long safaris are organized from the hotel. 2 offshore dives cost €35 per person all inclusive.

Marsa Alam *p481*

Hossam Helmi (see Marsa Shagra above) has 2 other high-end camps, each with their own bay and live-aboards.

LL-AL Marsa Nakari, 18 km south of Marsa Alam, offers chalets, huts and tents.

L-AL Wadi Lahami, 142 km south of Marsa Alam has chalets and tents. Diving safaris are organized with a 3-day live-aboard programme at €85 per person per day all inclusive (food and dive gear). They also have kite- and windsurfing facilities at Wadi Lahami. Reservations to both camps are made through the Cairo office, T02-2337 1833.

AL-A Shams Alam, reservation office in Cairo, T02-2417 0046, www.shamshotels.com. A comfortable resort, 50 km south of Marsa Alam, though the food is not highly rated. Accommodation is in pale pink bungalow-like complexes with domed roofs. There's a nice private sandy beach with a bar and windsurfing, and a rather small freshwater pool with a bar. The **Wadi Gamal Dive Centre** nearby specializes in diving safaris to more remote reefs in the south and is recommended. Price includes half board.

Also recently sprung up is a stretch of old-style camps in Tondoba Bay, 14 km south of Marsa Alam. The camps are a 5- to 10-min walk from a wide expanse of beach and are vaguely eco-orientated, however they are generally quite expensive (compared to equivalents in Dahab, say). Call ahead and try to negotiate a deal as it's definitely a peaceful, friendly place to hang out for a couple of days even if you're not into diving. When hiring a taxi from the bus station in Marsa Alam, ask for '*Kilo Arbatarsha*' if the driver seems unsure where Tondoba is, and it should cost no more than E£25.

A Aquarius, T010-646 0408, www.aquariusredsea.com. By far the most aesthetically pleasing of the camps, 18 circular rush peaked huts all have acacias planted outside, white linen, draped sail-effect interiors, camel wool blankets and rugs (but no fan, windows, or en suite). There are also larger bungalows with rustic furniture, bathrooms, fans – though the quirkiness of the huts might be more appealing. Either way, the rooms on the higher ground are breezier and the best choice. Electricity switched off 2400-0600 and 0900-1600. Full board the only option. Their **Aquarius Dive Centre** is fully equipped.

A-B Bedouin Valley, T02-2632 6665, T012-218 1427, www.southredsea.net. Cobbled stone chalets have wooden floors, proper furniture and tiled bathrooms with towels, plus there are standing fans. In landscaped rockery gardens, there's a *sheesha* corner for starlit chilling and in- and outdoor restaurants, but no alcohol. **South Red Sea** dive centre on the beach.

B-C Deep South, T012-450 1296, best views as on the highest ground and there's a cute wicker pub on site. Rooms are quite basic with beds and wardrobes being the only furniture, no fans, and all decorated with murals – some more lurid than others – giving a hippy-ish vibe. Clean, tiled shared bathrooms adjoin the open-air restaurant. New larger chalets have private baths. The food is highly recommended.

D Emy Camp, T012-771 6023. The cheapest option in Tondoba are these simple, but sizable, white concrete chalets. All have fans, tiled floors, big beds and shared bath (though 6 huts are being constructed with private bath). Samir and Sara are laid-back and lovely hosts, he used to sing in a rock band and ensures that there are always tunes playing. Meals are generous and tasty with an Oriental slant. Diving can be arranged.

Camping

A-B Fustat Wadi El Gemal, 45 km south of Marsa Alam, T012-240 5132, www.wadielgemal.com. A remote location 7 km inside one of Egypt's most beautiful and culturally fascinating national parks, this place makes a great base for anyone who has seen enough of the beach and wants to get back to nature. Striking tents (*'Fustat'* means 'tented camp') some with en suites, have very comfortable beds, or huts of traditionally woven palms are dotted around the austere desert landscape. Activities include trekking and camel trips (they also have camel wagons) and it's a chance to learn about tribal culture and the desert environment. The main dining tent, stylishly lit by a chandelier with huge bolster cushions to recline on, serves up great food and the breakfast is truly memorable. There's also a small bazaar selling handicrafts.

Shalatein *p482*

Should you manage to negotiate the transport difficulties and police check-points, there is a bearable hotel in Shalatein located right next to the market:

F-G El Haramin, T016-653 1178. Large rooms cost E£40 without bath, or E£50 with private bath, both have a/c and fans. Cleanliness is not a high point, but rooms have balconies and clean sheets are provided on request. The location is ideal, with the camel market and eating options a short walk away.

Eating

Safaga *p480*

As Safaga is significantly less touristed than nearby Hurghada, most restaurants are confined to the hotels, as are the bars and discos. There are some cheap cafeterias selling standard grilled fare along the main drag, Sharia Al-Gomhuriyya.

El-Quseir *p480*

Eating out in El-Quseir can be a delicious experience, particularly if you like fish. For standard food like *fuul* and *taamiyya*, look around the main market street. Any of the coffee shops lining the beach are cheap fun places to hang out in the evenings with decent *sheesha* and traditional drinks, but you might want to agree the price first.

Al Quseir Hotel, T065-333 2301, has a good chef who (with advance warning) can put on a real spread with your choice of meat/fish/veggies for around E£70. The price goes down the bigger the group.

El Ferdous Restaurant, at the north end of the harbour just before **Al Quseir Hotel**, is a great little fish restaurant with very reasonable prices. Choose between a clean a/c interior or seating on the beach. Fish is about E£35 per kilo, prawns E£140 or local grilled squid E£90. This is where the locals go for a treat, highly recommended.

Marianne Restaurant, on the Corniche, T065-333 4386. Open 0800-2400. A more varied menu including Italian dishes, kebabs, and of course fish and calamari. Meals come with rice and salads, vegetarians are catered for, drinks moderately priced, and they sell cans of Saqqara for E£15. The upstairs balcony laden with bougainvillea and pottery urns is the best place to dine, otherwise there is beach seating, but note that the toilets leave a lot to be desired.

Rocky Valley Beach Camp, T065-333 5247, T010-6532964, www.rockyvalleydivers camp.com. Call in the morning and you can state your preference for dinner, fabulous fresh fish and shrimps cooked on the grill, plus great salad, and beer is usually available. If you're lucky the delightful staff will get singing and dancing round the campfire later on, or you can just recline on cushions and watch for shooting stars as you digest.

Koshary El Mina, Corniche. This restaurant at the north end of the Corniche is more popular for its kebabs than its *koshari*.

Marsa Alam *p481*
Choices in the small village are very limited. Outside of the hotels and camps, there's really only one local café that's clean enough to warrant a recommendation. It's at the entrance to town on the right side of the main road, across from the port. Order whatever's on the stove.

Shalatein *p482*
There are a few local eateries in the market area serving meals for E£10-20, and in the camel *souk* itself there is a popular little shack that does good Egyptian breakfasts for rock-bottom prices. Otherwise, the 3-storey orange Ristorante Basma Genoub, T010-777 2184, on the main road near the market, open 1000-2400, does meals of camel meat, salad, rice and veg for E£50 including a soft drink. The 2nd floor with a domed ceiling and kitsch decor is the nicest.

Festivals and events

Marsa Alam *p481*
Oct/Nov Characters of Egypt Festival, this 3-day festival in Wadi El-Gemal National Park celebrates the different desert tribes of Egypt with traditional dancing, sports, music and camel racing. It is held in the spectacular wadi, where hundreds of participants and spectators can camp for the duration, see www.wadielgemal.com for details.

Activities and tours

Safaga *p480*
Diving
The best dive sites around Safaga are Panorama, where a sloping hill leads to a dramatic drop-off and sharks and mantas often linger; and Abu Qifan, a remote and pristine site that leaves behind the traffic of Hurghada live-aboards. The prolific marine life is an underwater photographer's dream. There are frequent sightings of dolphin, ray, barracuda, reef and leopard shark. All dive centres in Safaga organize day trips and half-day to the nearby sites. A standard PADI Open Water course, all inclusive, costs €350-380.
Barakuda, at Lotus Bay, 5 km north of Safaga, T065-326 0049, www.barakuda-diving.com, have several centres around the Red Sea and a live-aboard.
MenaDive, T065-326 0060, www.menadive.com, are a well-established eco-conscious operation running out of the Menaville Hotel.

El-Quseir *p480*
Desert trips
Rocky Valley Tours, Sharia Port Said, just south of the Corniche, T065-333 5247, www.rockyvalleydiverscamp.com. Sat-Thu 1000-1500 and 1800-2300. Organize a range of short jeep safaris into the Eastern Mountains, some with a geological bent, for around €35 per night including Bedouin BBQ. 1-day hiking, half-day camel safaris to the village of Oum Hamid or trips to the camel market at Shalatein (€80) are also available. Pretty flexible and comparatively cheap.

Diving
Shallow dives Off the shore at Movenpick's Subex Dive Centre, www.subex.org (very professional and eco-conscious, but extremely expensive) is El-Qadima Bay with a variety of topography and fauna; about 10 km further south is the more sheltered El-Kaf.
Deep dives The islands Big Brother and Little Brother are about 1 km apart, 67 km off the shore northeast of El-Quseir. They were off limits for a few years until authorities developed a protection plan. They reopened in the late 1990s as part of a newly decreed Protected Marine Area. 2 exposed parts of the same reef, the Brothers offer what some say is the best diving in the Red Sea. Divers pilgrimage to make the plunge, and special permission is required as the area is strictly regulated. Access is by live-aboard. The walls are a vertical 900 m. On Big Brother, the larger island, there's a stone lighthouse constructed

by the British in 1883 (and still working). To the northwest of Big Brother are 2 wrecks. The unnamed cargo vessel with its shattered bow can be reached at 5 m (and then deeper as it is at an incline). The other wreck is **Aida II** (see box, page 426). The strong currents around Little Brother are home to vast fan corals and caves, and sharks are of various sorts are often seen. Along with stunning corals, these 2 dives offer an impressive range of fish.

Rocky Valley Beach Camp, Abu Sawatir, 14 km north of El-Quseir, have a good little set-up and run PADI Open Water courses for €310, including manual and certification, and 2 dives per day for €35. There is a reef off the beach for shore diving and they also rent snorkelling masks and fins for E£15 per day.

Marsa Shagra *p481*

Desert trips

Though most venture this far south for the underwater splendours, the desolate majesty of the desert is the ideal place for reflection and respite above ground. Hotels can help you organize jeep and horseback safaris into the surrounding mountains to visit nearby oases and a number of ghost cities created when the mines were abandoned. More in-depth exploration of the wadis, tribal villages and desert habitat is becoming possible.

Red Sea Desert Adventures, T012-230 9142, www.redseadesertadventures.com. Can organize anything from a day trek to a 2-week expedition visiting some extraordinary sites, many of which have yet to be fully uncovered. The season lasts from Oct-Mar; longer safaris require a minimum of 5 people and need to be booked at least a month in advance. Standard day-packages might include land-sailing, quad-riding, star-gazing camels and dancing performances (see the website for details of these).

Marsa Alam *p481*

Desert trips

Fustat Wadi El Gemal, T012-240 5132, www.wadielgemal.com. Wadi Gemal is a protected area south of Marsa Alam, and this eco-conscious set-up runs half-day camel safaris (€35 with a delicious dinner) or night safaris (€85) as well as day/night hiking trips, Much better is to immerse yourself for a few days in the enclave of the National Park. This provides a rare opportunity to trek into the Valley of the Camels or Wadi Sakhit, with a local Beja guide, for a day or few. Not only does this mean the chance of seeing ibex, gazelles and migratory birds but the scenery is stunning and savannah-like, and historical sites can be explored on the way. They also do 4WD trips for a minimum of 4 people.

Diving

At the **Abu Dabab** dive site, dugongs are seen on most days in the sea-grass, hence it is very popular. Too popular in fact, as the propellers of boats and hundreds of divers daily are causing stress to the ponderous beasts, who do not necessarily like being followed as they are trying to feed. Turtles, guitar sharks and rays are also frequent visitors. **Elphinstone Reef**, also known as Sharks' House as it's rare not to see one of 7 species, including tigers and hammerheads, 12 km off shore, only for experienced divers due to the depth; **Daedalus Reef**, 60/96 km off shore; **Sha'ab Samadai**, the Dolphin House, 5 km southeast in Marsa Alam National Park, comes with a 100% guarantee of seeing spinner dolphins. Entrance fees apply to the crescent-shaped reef and numbers are restricted to 100 divers and 100 snorkellers per day. There is also a no-human zone as efforts are made to protect the pod (which is very unusual in that it stays at the reef rather than the open ocean, as spinners typically do). Divers cannot enter the lagoon but can dive around the outside of the reef, where there are caves and pinnacles of soft and hard coral; **Dolphine Reef**, 15 km to the northwest of Ras Banas; **Zabargad Island**, 45 km southeast of Berenice. Dive sites near Berenice are only accessible on live-aboard dive boats.

All the big resorts around Marsa Alam have their own dive centres, and there are 3 smaller outfits and a decompression chamber at Tondoba Bay, 14 km south of Marsa Alam, where there is a house reef. The following are both reputable and offer Open Water courses:

Aquarius, T010-646 0408, www.aquariusredsea.com.

Blue Heaven Holidays, T017-805 8885, www.blueheavenholidays.com. Offer a unique opportunity in Egypt for divers to get involved in reef conservation and monitoring efforts alongside marine scientists. It's a chance to enhance your own environmental knowledge while collecting valuable data that will aid the protection of the southern reefs. Visit their website to see when the next surveys are being undertaken.

South Red Sea Enterprises, T02-2635 2406, www.southredsea.net.

Wadi Gimal Diving Centre, T012-244 4931, wadigamal@shamshotels.com, 45 km south of Marsa Alam. Offer a wide variety of dive trips to unspoilt areas of the southern Red Sea including live-aboards.

Transport

Safaga *p480*

Bus

Buses via **Hurghada** (E£10) to **Suez** (E£20-40) every 1-2 hrs of which 5 go on to **Cairo** (7-8 hrs, around E£50). Buses to **Qena** (E£12-15), **Luxor** (E£25) and **Aswan** (E£30-35) 4-5 times a day. Buses to **El-Quesir** (2 hrs, E£8) and **Marsa Alam** (3 hrs, E£15) leave at 0600, 1600, 1900, 2100, 0200.

Ferry

Safaga is now one of the main departure points for vessels to Saudia Arabia since operations have virtually ceased from Suez. Sea passenger boats leave here for **Duba** daily. During the *hajj* there are passenger boats to **Jeddah** (not advised). Check at the port.

Taxi

Service taxis follow all the bus routes – change at **Suez** for **Cairo**. Prices are comparable to bus costs, but the journeys tend to be a bit faster (and more terrifying).

El-Quseir *p480*

Air

There is an international airport 70 km south of town that also serves **Marsa Alam**. Package tourists also fly in via **Hurghada**, 80 km north.

Bus

The bus station is about 2 km inland; frequent microbuses run from town along the Corniche continuing on to the bus station. Check all times and destinations as schedules change often. There buses to **Cairo** (8 hrs, E£85) via **Safaga** and **Hurghada** (2 hrs, E£15) at 0500, 1200 and 2000; 2 pass through **Suez** at 0500 and 2330 (6 hrs, E£25). There is 1 daily bus to **Qift** that departs at 0500. From there, you can easily find a bus or train to **Luxor** (1 hr) and **Aswan** (4 hrs). As with other cities on the coast, independent travellers bound for the Nile Valley on public buses are generally OK (ie won't get kicked off) if there are only 4 or less on board. There are also supposedly 4 buses per day to **Marsa Alam** (E£10, 2 hrs) and beyond at 0500, 0800, 1400, and 2130.

Service taxi

Service taxis and microbuses leave from a compound next to the bus terminal. They run throughout the day (on a leave-when-full basis; you can be waiting a while), and are reluctant to take foreigners. However, be insistent, as despite what drivers believe, the police do not fine services that take foreign passengers. You may, however, have to pay double the local fare to secure a ride. To **Marsa Alam**, E£10, 2 hrs; to **Qena**, E£12, 2 hrs; to **Safaga** 1½ hrs, E£5.50; to **Hurghada**, E£10, 2hrs; to **Qift**, E£16, 3 hrs. Change at **Suez** for **Cairo**.

Marsa Alam *p481*

Air

There is an international airport 60 km north of Marsa Alam that also serves **El-Quseir**.

Bus

To get out of Marsa Alam, ask the locals about the latest schedules once you get to town, as things change with the winds. At present, from Marsa Alam to **Cairo**, there are buses that stop in **Safaga** and **Hurghada** at 1000, 1500 1800 and 2000 (E£65); otherwise it's easy to catch a ride to Hurghada and transfer. Crossing the road to **Edfu** from Marsa Alam is difficult for tourists, as many drivers are wary of the 3 check points on the way, but if you want to try and trust the unspoken 4 tourists or less rule, the public bus heads west around 2400 and takes 4 hrs and carries on to **Aswan**, E£16, 3 hrs.

Taxi

Service taxis (Peugeot-style) run up and down the coast regularly, on a leave-when-full basis. They are comparable in price to the buses, but faster and more frequent, though again drivers can be obstructive to tourists. There are infrequent services throughout the day to **El- Quseir** (E£10, 2 hrs), where more northbound and westbound services/buses depart from.

Shalatein *p482*

Bus

Buses leave from the *souk*, near the Ristorante Basma, and go via the bus station in town, to **Cairo** at 0700, 1430 and 1700 (E£85) via **Hurghada** and towns in between. To **Qena** at 0900 and 1100.

Directory

Safaga *p480*

Banks Banque Misr, El-Quseir–Hurghada Rd.

El-Quseir *p480*

Banks Bank Misr on Sharia 10th Ramadan, road heading north out of town, plus mini-banks in the resorts. **Internet** Casper Net, Arab League St/Sharia Gamat al-Dowal el-Arabiya, T010-2292627, 1.5 km north of town centre, E£3 per hr for fast connection, 1000-0400, Fri from 1300. **Post office** on the main road heading north out of town, Sat-Thu 0830-2000.

Marsa Alam *p481*

South of the central T-junction there's a small settlement with a pharmacy, supermarket and telephone. All the big resorts have modern communications, shops and medical supplies

Western Desert

Contents

Footprint features

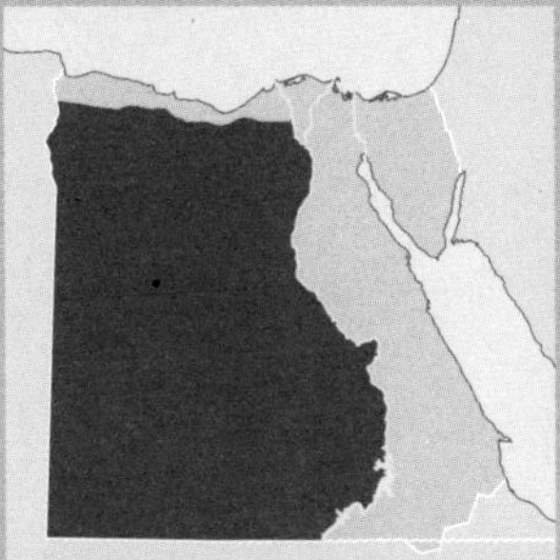

At a glance

Getting around Buses between the oases; jeeps or camels as part of a safari trip.

Time required To visit all the oases in one big desert loop, with a couple of nights camping, you'll want at least 10 days.

Weather Freezing cold winter nights, blistering hot summer days. Best times are Mar-May and Sep-Nov.

When not to go During Ramadan, safari trips are curtailed. Likewise, in summer few excursions are organized as it's simply too hot. Apr carries a risk of sandstorms.

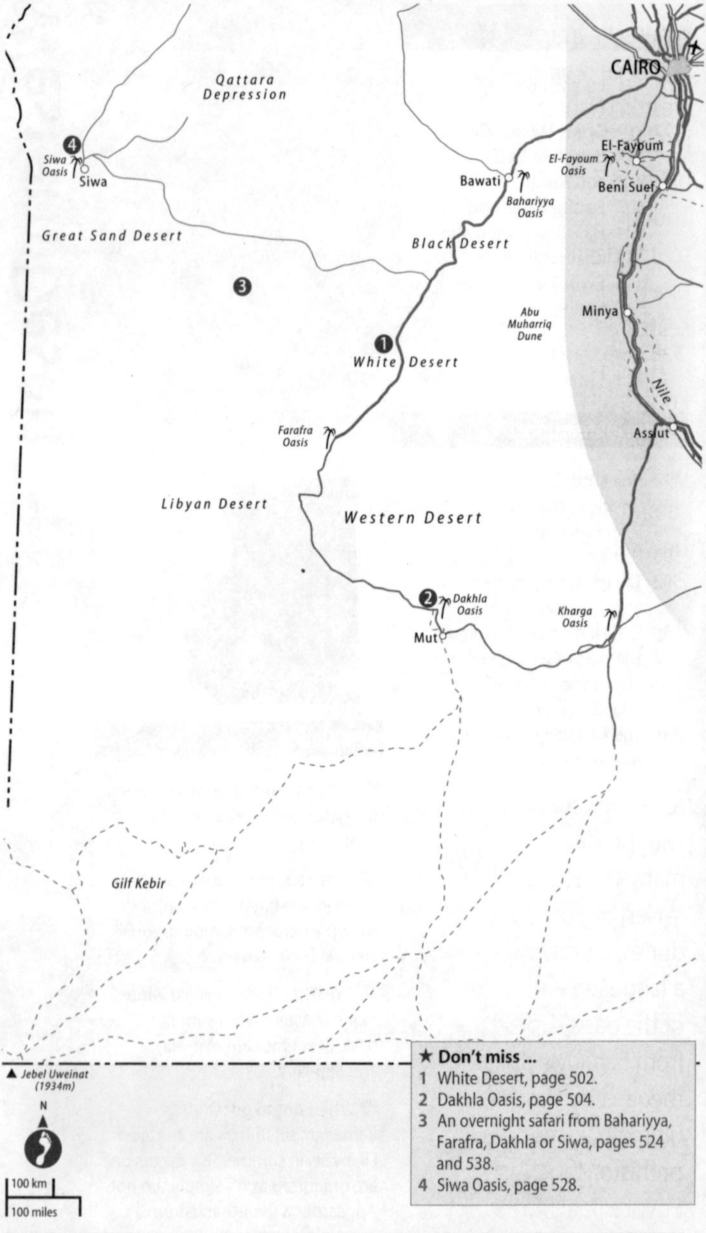

★ Don't miss ...

1 White Desert, page 502.
2 Dakhla Oasis, page 504.
3 An overnight safari from Bahariyya, Farafra, Dakhla or Siwa, pages 524 and 538.
4 Siwa Oasis, page 528.

Wherever you are in Egypt, the desert is never far away. Its presence is tangible, omnipotent, mystical. Spanning from the western banks of the Nile to Libya and extending south all the way to Sudan, the Western Desert constitutes more than two-thirds of Egypt's total area and supports less than 2% of its population. Though more accessible than ever before, the region is still not a tourist destination, it is a traveller's destination, and only travellers of a particular sort are drawn to this captivating land: those in search adventure filled with beauty, challenge and insight.

There are four major oases that make up what has come to be known as the Great Desert Circuit. Nearest to Cairo is Bahariyya, an easy set-off point for safaris into the Black Desert and awash with peaceful camps from where day hikes up dramatic mountains or meanders through timeless palm plantations bewitch those who linger. Farafra, a remote and quiet village clutching on to tradition, lies on the doorstep of the White Desert, a psychedelic wonderland of luminescent rock sculpted by the wind to resemble minarets and mushrooms. Dakhla, with its soft pink sands and enchanting medieval settlements, has a palpably warm demeanour in which it is easy to lose the sense of being on a tourist trail. And although the government's New Valley reconstruction project of the 1970s and 1980s infiltrated Kharga with hordes of Delta workers and concrete structures, here lie many of the desert's chief archaeological treasures.

Nestling on the Libyan border, Siwa, brimming with rolling dunes, crumbling temples, fields of palms, bubbling springs and a language and culture all its own, personifies the enchantment of the oasis experience. It's possible to link Siwa to the inner oases from Bahariyya more easily now than in the past, and go for a mega-circuit of the desert via the Darb El-Siwa road. And for the ultimate adventure, the immense plateau of the Gilf Kebir with its prehistoric rock art is a two-week safari across the Uweinat Desert, Egypt's final frontier.

Ins and outs

Getting there and around

Travel around the main oases is straightforward and unimpeded. Coming from Cairo, the natural choice feels like an anti-clockwise journey around the circuit beginning by going into the desert past the Pyramids at Giza and on to **Bahariyya**. Alternatively, a clockwise exploration can start in **Kharga** coming either from Luxor (via private taxi) or Assiut by bus. It's also become easier to incorporate far-flung **Siwa** (see page 528) into the loop, via the much-improved (but still fairly rugged) track known as the **Darb El-Siwa**, which crosses the Great Sand Sea between Siwa and Bahariyya. Permits are required to traverse this road, obtained at either end for US$5 per person plus an E£11 fee, and usually take a day to process. A 4WD is essential, as sand dunes have blocked the road at points and there are frequent corrugations. Vehicles start in a convoy with a military escort (although they tend to split off en route). There are numerous police checkpoints, and if you don't have a local guide/driver accompanying you these will prove troublesome. Although it is relatively expensive to hire a vehicle (E£1400-1500 per car) it avoids losing days back-tracking to Cairo and is an intense and isolating experience that enables a satisfyingly complete circuit of the oases. The tourist information offices at either end can advise on obtaining permissions (in Siwa, they may even process it for you) and put you in touch with others who want to make the trip if you wish to save costs. Overnight camping is not permitted when traversing this route (safaris have to be organized separately if you wish to explore the area more lengthily) thus the journey is around six to eight hours, depending on detours made.

The main four oases are well connected to each other and to Cairo via public transport in both directions. **Upper Egypt Travel** (see page 149) runs several air-conditioned buses daily plus there are also microbuses circulating, so finding a ride is rarely a problem. If you intend to travel by coach, though, it is wise to buy your ticket at least a day in advance to ensure a seat. Also bear in mind that public transport in the remote oases can be less consistent and reliable than other parts of the country so double check all schedules and call upon a bit more patience than usual. If you lack the time, or the inclination, for all this you can fly direct from Cairo to New Valley Airport at Kharga, where it's possible to get a taste of the desert, but you will be missing far more. It may be true that Kharga has more interesting monuments than some of its neighbours, but the desert itself is the star of this area and Kharga, with its sprawling modern town, is undoubtedly a disappointment to some.

If you are interested in an extended desert expedition, it is essential to plan ahead. Organized safaris to the Gilf Kebir, especially, need to be booked months in advance plus the season is fairly short, it being way too hot from May to August and freezing at night from December to February. Security precautions taken by the Egyptian authorities mean you will have to be accompanied by armed guards for more remote parts of your journey. If you are self-driving, be prepared to provide food and all essentials for the escort. They cause no problems though the effectiveness of their protection is questionable.

Self-driving The key to safe travel in desert regions is reliable and well-equipped transport. For the motorist, motorcyclist or pedal cyclist there are ground rules which, if followed, will help to reduce risks. In normal circumstances travellers will remain on tarmacked roads and for this need only a well-prepared 2WD vehicle. Choose a machine that's known for its reliability and for which spares can be easily obtained. In Egypt Peugeot and Mercedes are found with adequate spares and servicing facilities. If you have a different type of car/truck, make sure that you take spares with you or have the means of

Driving in the desert

- If you can get a guide, who perhaps wants a lift to your precise destination, use him.
- Set out early in the morning after first light, rest during the heat of the day and use the cool of the evening for further travel.
- Never travel at night or when there is a sandstorm brewing or in progress.
- Always travel with at least two vehicles – and remain in close, visual contact.
- Do not cross open flat desert in case the going changes without warning and your vehicle beds deeply into soft sand or a gully.
- Well-maintained corrugated road surfaces can be taken at modest pace but rocky surfaces should be treated with great care to prevent undue wear on tyres.
- Sand seas are a challenge for drivers – ensure your navigation lines are clear so that weaving between dunes does not disorientate the navigator.
- Especially in windy conditions, sight lines can vanish, leaving crews with little knowledge of where they are. Cresting dunes from dip slope to scarp needs care to ensure that the vehicle does not either bog down or overturn.
- Keep off salt flats after rain and floods especially in the winter and spring when water tables can rise and make the going hazardous in soft mud.
- Even when on marked and maintained tracks, beware of approaching traffic.

getting spares sent out. Bear in mind that transport of spares to and from rural Egypt might take a tediously long time. Petrol/benzene/gas is available everywhere, diesel is equally well distributed except in the smallest of southern settlements. 4WD transport is useful even for the traveller who normally remains on the tarmacked highway. Emergencies, diversions and unscheduled visits to off-the-road sites become less of a problem with all-terrain vehicles. Off the road, 4WD is essential, normally with two vehicles travelling together. A great variety of 4WD vehicles are in use in the region; Toyota and Land Rover are probably found the most widely.

Vehicles going into any desert area should have the following basic equipment: full toolkit, vehicle maintenance handbook and supplementary tools such as clamps, files, wire, spare-parts kit supplied by car manufacturer, jump leads, spare tyre/s, battery driven tyre pump, tyre levers, tyre-repair kit, hydraulic jack, jack-handle extension, base plate for jack, spare fuel can/s, spare water container/s and cool bags.

For those going off the tarmacked roads other items to include are: Foot-tyre pump, heavy-duty hydraulic or air jack, power winch, sand channels, safety rockets, comprehensive first-aid kit, radio/telephone, emergency rations kit, matches, Benghazi burner (a double-skinned water boiler), maps, compasses, GPS, latest road information and guides to navigation by the sun and stars.

Permits Currently permits are not required for the White Desert (though there is an entry fee of US$5 usually included in the cost of a tour). Even for overnight safaris from Siwa, Farafra and Dakhla permits are technically required but are a formality – obtainable overnight. The same goes for the journey on the Siwa to Bahariyya road. Overnighting in the desert on this route requires pre-planning, however, as does any significant detours from the main roads and extended travel on less-frequented routes – you will need to organize permits in advance. Any reputable travel agent will obtain the necessary

Safety checklist

- On extensive desert treks and expeditions, allow time to acclimatize to full desert conditions. Conserve your energy at first rather than acting as if you were still in a temperate climate. Most people take a week or more to adjust to heat conditions here.
- Stay out of direct sunlight whenever possible, especially once the sun is high. Whenever you can, do what the locals do and move from shade to shade.
- Wear natural-fibre clothes to protect your skin from the sun, particularly your head and neck. Use a high Sun Protection Factor (SPF) cream, preferably at least SPF15 (94%) to minimize the effects of UV.
- Drink good-quality water regularly. It is estimated that 15 litres per day are needed by a healthy person to avoid water deficiency in desert conditions, even if there is no actual feeling of thirst. The majority of ailments arising in the desert relate to water deficiency and so it is worth the small effort of regular drinking of water.
- Be prepared for cold nights by having some warm clothes to hand.
- Stay in your quarters or vehicle if there is a sandstorm.
- Deserts and stomach upsets have a habit of going hand in hand. Choose hot, cooked meals in preference to cold meats and tired salads. Peel all fruit and uncooked fresh vegetables. Do not eat milk-based items or drink untreated water unless you are absolutely sure of its good quality.
- Sleep off the ground if you can. There are very few natural dangers in the desert but scorpions, spiders and snakes are present (though rarely fatal) and are best avoided.

permission to travel on your behalf, for a fee and with one-month's warning, but if you are self-driving it might take longer for your application to be processed. Obtaining a permit requires two photocopies of the important pages of your passport and the Egyptian entry stamp, two passport photos and an outline of your trip itinerary. Permits must be obtained in Cairo (it is not possible to arrange them on arrival in any of the oases towns) from the 26th Group Military, in front of Cinema Tiba, Raba' El Adawiya in Nasr City.

Safety When planning a trip never underestimate the potential dangers of the desert. Driving conditions have improved significantly over the years, but there are still relatively few places to stop for petrol, food or water so fill up on all essentials before beginning your excursion. There are no service stations between towns. You need the right type of vehicle, and the necessary driving skills to handle it in this terrain. Make sure you take enough cash with you, credit cards will not do and you will only find ATMs in Dakhla and Kharga.

The Sahara is extremely varied in its topography and climate. Each day has a large range of temperature, often of more than 20°C, with the world's highest temperatures recorded here at over 55°C, and the nights sometimes below freezing. With this in mind, it is essential that you come to the desert prepared. In addition to light clothing of natural fibres, bring sufficient layers for the cooler nights. Also essential on any desert trek or expedition are: a first-aid kit, hat, whistle, torch, rehydration packets, high energy foods, and extra water.

In the desert border areas of Egypt, **unexploded mines** are a hidden danger. Maps of mined areas are unreliable, some were never marked. Always obey the precautionary signs. Floods can move mines considerable distances from the original site. Be warned – people do die.

The Great Desert Circuit

→ *Colour map 1, B3/4.*

The Great Desert Circuit became accessible in the 1980s, when a road was built linking the oases of Bahariyya, Farafra, Dakhla and Kharga. These are all situated on a long-dead branch of the Nile, and depend for their livelihood on the massive fossil water reservoirs beneath the Libyan Desert. The area was designated the 'New Valley' in 1958 with a scheme to tap this subterranean water source and relocate landless peasants from the overcrowded Nile Valley and Delta. » *For listings, see pages 517-527.*

Bahariyya Oasis and Bawati → *For listings, see pages 517-527. Colour map 1, A3.*

Ins and outs

Getting there and around The journey to Bahariyya Oasis from Cairo, 310 km west of the Pyramids of Giza along Route 341, takes five to six hours by bus, with one stop en route, four to five hours by service taxi or four hours in a 4WD. Beware if arriving by bus as there is intense competition, and sometimes ugly rivalry, among hotel and safari touts and you may be bombarded when disembarking. If this happens, head to the tourist office and the manager will contact your chosen camp so they can come and collect you. From Siwa, it is possible to hire a vehicle and driver to make the journey along the rough road through the Great Sand Sea, arriving in Bahariyya six to eight hours later.

Bicycles are a good way to get around Bahariyya. Several camps can provide them, or ask around for Mohamed Ali who rents a few bikes from his shop on the Farafra Road, E£10 per day.

Bahariyya Oasis

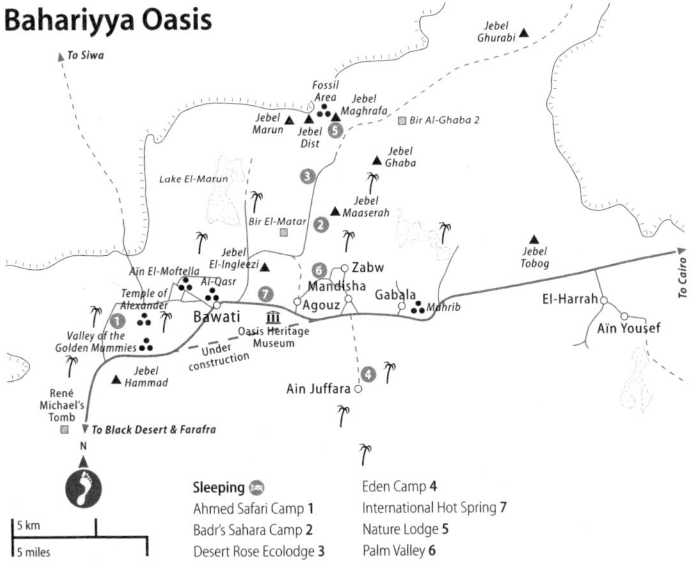

Information The official **Egyptian Tourist Authority (ETA) office** ⓘ *T02-3847 3035/9, open Sat-Thu, 0830-1500*, is in the government building on the main street near the Popular Restaurant (which is also a good source of information). The manager, Mohamed Abd El-Kader, is also contactable on his mobile at any time, T012-373 6567. The **Tourist Police** ⓘ *T02-3847 3900/2*, are 1 km east of town on the Cairo road.

Background

The closest oasis to Cairo in distance and the furthest in historical time, Bahariyya dates back to the Middle Kingdom and it was the thriving commercial heart of the great caravan routes from the time of the 26th Dynasty. Millions of years before the pharaohs, dinosaurs tramped through forests, swamps and saltwater, leaving their bones to be discovered in 1914 in the area around Jebel Dist. At 2000 sq km and with about 35,000 inhabitants, it is the smallest of the four depressions. The farmed areas, producing dates, olives and wheat, have been passed down through generations of small landowners, and the oasis' fortunes have waxed and waned in tandem with the availability of ground water. Throughout their history, the people of the oasis have prevaricated between independence and cooperation with the ruling regime. In the last few centuries they have cooperated fully with any government but still maintain a slightly independent stance, although they are very welcoming to visitors.

Bawati

Bawati is the oasis' main settlement, where a slightly Wild-West ambiance and mass of unfinished construction do much to obscure its immediate charms. But though the town centre is far from aesthetically pleasing, the outlying camps are delightfully restful and desert dunes and mountains are never far away. The remains of Bawati's sister village, **Al-Qasr** are to the west of town, beneath which lies Bahariyya's ancient capital. Here you will see stones from a 26th Dynasty (664-525 BC) temple reused for house building and the remains of a Roman triumphal arch that stayed intact until the 19th century. Bawati and its environs are good for walking, whether just strolling around the old town and nearby peaceful plantations, or undertaking a more strenuous hike up one of the surrounding peaks. There is a circular walk worth taking along the main road and the oasis road through the gardens, by **Aïn Bishmu**, the Roman springs, where the hot water is used for bathing and washing clothes. Cultivation of fruit – apricots, dates, figs and melons – takes place in these gardens. The women who work in the gardens also contribute to the household finances by selling embroidered goods. The hill to the southwest of the town is known as the '**Ridge of the Chicken Merchant**' as here in underground passages are small recesses, which are the burial sites of a great many mummified ibis and hawks, dating from the 26th Dynasty and clearly relating to worship of Thoth and Horus.

Excellent sunsets and views of the oasis are to be had from the top of **Jebel El-Ingleezi**, 'English Mountain' (also known as Jebel Williams after the officer stationed here), where the ruins of a First World War fortress controlled by the British are found. It's an easy walk (or jeep ride) to the top. **Jebel Dist**, the pyramid mountain 17 km north of town, presents a challenging climb to gain spectacular views of 100,000 palm trees (coming down is tough as the surface is gravely). The area around the mountain and nearby **Jebel Maghrafa** is famed for the discovery of dinosaur remains in the early part of the 20th century and again in 2001; fossils of all descriptions are found here in abundance. Also of interest here may be the Naghi family's **camel breeding farm** ⓘ *on the slopes of Jebel Dist, T012-368*

2070, enquire at the tourist office or through Ashraf Lotfi, T012-165 3037, who owns nearby Nature Lodge, if language difficulties arise. You can see how camels are bred and buy camel wool blankets and products. **Jebel Ghurabi** ⓘ *30 km north of town, requires 4WD*, is a dream location in the midst of beautiful sand dunes: it's a good, short excursion that cannot fail to impress.

Other small settlements in the vicinity are all worth visiting to see how these sturdy people combat the elements and to get a taste of real oasis life. Once on the floor of the depression (coming from Cairo) take the track to the south of the road that continues beyond **El-Harrah** (rock cut tombs) and its ponds, used by the locals for duck breeding, to the gardens around the spring of **Aïn Yousef**. Further west along the main road the ruins of **Muhrib** are out of bounds at present but a tarmacked road opposite on the right leads to **Gabala** where the encroaching sands have been spreading over the oasis gardens for the last 20 years and have covered the rest of the road. Approaching closer to Bawati, again on the right, are the villages of **Mandisha** and **Zabw**, also fighting a losing battle against the encroaching sand. The last turn right before Bawati leads to **Agouz**. A guide from the village is an asset when visiting these small settlements.

Sights At the time of writing, the following sights in Bahariyya are officially open to the public: the Temple of Alexander, Aïn El-Moftella, the tombs of Zad-Amun ef-Ankh, Banentiu and Amenhotep Huy and the Antiquities Inspectorate 'museum' that houses the

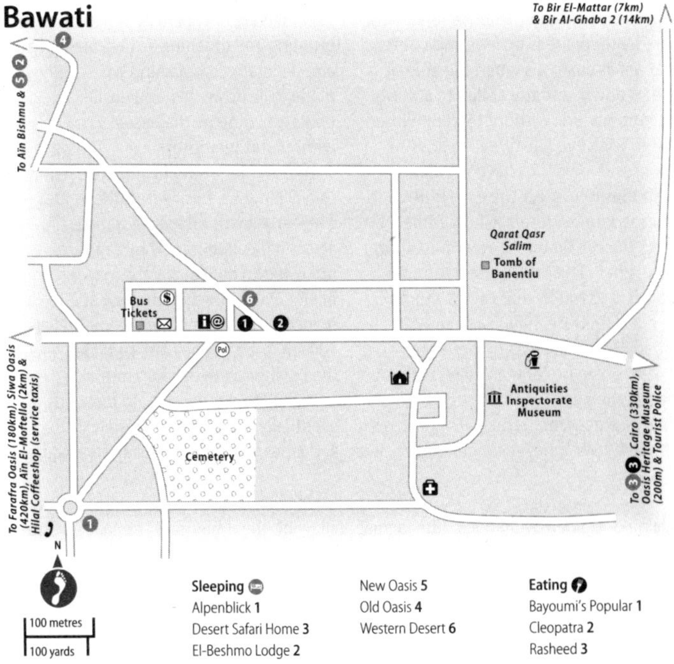

Camels

There are two kinds of camel, *Camelus dromedarius*, the Arabian camel with one hump and *Camelus bactrianus*, the Bactrian which has two. Arabian camels, introduced into North Africa in the fifth century BC, though only as domestic animals, are about 3 m long and about 2 m high at the shoulder. They can be white or black.

Interesting physical characteristics that allow these animals to survive in the desert include hairs inside the ear opening as well as the ability to close the nostrils between breaths, both preventing sand infiltration; thick eyebrows to shade the eyes from the sun's glare; a pad of skin between the two large toes on each foot forming a broad, tough 'slipper' that spreads the animal's weight over a larger area and prevents sinking in the loose sand; large bare leathery areas on legs and chest that act as cushions when the animal kneels down; and the ability to survive for long periods without food or without water. Each eye has three eyelids, the upper and lower lids have very long eyelashes to protect the eyes from sand whipped up by desert winds, while a third, thinner lid blinks away dust from the eyeball. The skin inside a camel's mouth is so tough that cactus thorns do not penetrate, hence a camel can eat anything, 'even its owner's tent'.

Camels can go for many days without food as the hump can store up to 35 kg of fat as emergency rations. They can go without water for even longer, depending on the weather and the kind of food available. As camels do not sweat but instead function at a higher body temperature without brain damage, their demands of fluid are less. At a waterhole they drink only enough to balance their body moisture content.

Less pleasant camel characteristics include a most unpredictable nature, especially in the mating season, which includes nasty habits like using its long sharp teeth to bite people and other camels, viciously kicking with the back legs, spitting and being generally awkward. When a camel stands up it moves in a series of violent jerks as it straightens first its hind legs then its front legs. When a camel walks, it moves both the legs at one side at the same time, giving a very rolling motion.

Camels are unwilling beasts of burden, grunting and groaning as they are loaded and generally complaining when being made to lie down or stand up. Once underway though, they usually move without further protest.

These large, strong beasts are used to pull ploughs, turn water wheels and carry large loads for long distances across difficult terrain. They can carry up to 400 kg but usually the load is nearer 200 kg. Despite moving at a mere 6-7 km an hour, camels can travel 100 km in a day. They also provide their owners with hair for cloth, rich milk and cheese, dried dung fuel and eventually meat, bones for utensils and hides for shoes, bags and tenting.

acclaimed Golden Mummies (the actual Valley of the Mummies remains officially off-limits). One ticket (E£45, students E£25) purchased in the Antiquities Inspectorate's makeshift museum covers admission to all sights; note that it is valid for one day only. (Without your own transport getting between the various sites included in the ticket will take two to three hours.) Cameras require an additional ticket, E£25 (or hefty *baksheesh* inside the tombs).

Museums The **Antiquities Inspectorate Museum** ⓘ *daily 0800-1600*, known to some as the Bawati museum, and to others as the Mummy Hall, shelters some of the finds from surrounding ruins. Among the 10 on display are are five of the acclaimed 'golden mummies', so dubbed for their gilded coffins (see box, page 502), badly displayed yet still extraordinary for their lifelike representation of the deceased, complete with curly locks and long eyelashes. The **Oasis Heritage Museum** ⓘ *opening times erratic, E£5 donation requested*, highlights the artwork of Mahmoud Eed, a local self-taught Bedouin artist. Clearly inspired by the old-timer, Badr of Farafra, Eed moulds clay to depict his experience of life in the oasis. The museum also houses dioramas that offer a view of daily life in Bahariyya. At the store, you will find beautiful embroidered dresses and locally made silver jewellery.

Tombs and temples ⓘ *All are allegedly open 0800-1600 (1700 in summer)*. In Bawati village, nestled on the small hill of Qarat Qasr Salim, are the tombs of **Banentiu**, a wealthy merchant and **Zad-Amun ef-Ankh** , his father, both from the 26th Dynasty. A steep descent leads to Banentiu's hypostyle hall where the four columns, unusual in that they are square, are painted on all sides with deities while the ceiling presents a fantastic winged sun-disk motif. In both tombs the decorations remain intensely colourful and clearly portray the gods at work carrying out the mortuary rituals.

The **Tomb of Amenhotep-Huy**, mayor of Bahariyya oasis in the 18th to 19th Dynasty, rests on a ridge called Qarat Hilwa, a few kilometres northwest of town. It's quite hard to spot without a guide and, though not visually remarkable, is the most ancient tomb in area.

The **Temple of Aïn El-Moftella**, 2 km west of town, was built in the 26th Dynasty during the reigns of Kings Apries and Amasis (Ahmose II). The temple has four ruined chapels protected with a new roof, decorated with scenes depicting the king presenting offerings to 18 different gods.

The **Temple of Alexander the Great**, at Al-Qasr Allam built in 332 BC and occupied perhaps until the 12th century AD, stands at the northern end of the site where the golden mummies were discovered. The temple is unique in being built to honour a living person and was begun after Alexander visited Bahariyya on his way back from consulting the Oracle in Siwa. Behind the temple the priests' houses were built. The administrator lived to the east of the building and in front were 45 storerooms made of mud brick where a small statue of the priest Re was found. The temple itself is constructed of local sandstone. A granite altar over 1 m in height was erected to the south of the entrance, inscribed with Alexander's name and now on view in the museum in Cairo. In the inner sanctuary Alexander, with the mayor who built the temple, is shown in bas-relief making offerings to Amun-Re and other gods.

One of the delights of visiting Bawati is a soak in one of its sulphury steaming **hot springs** ⓘ *women swimming should wear an opaque loose-fitting T-shirt over a bathing suit*. A couple of camps have springs nearby (see Sleeping, page 517), or try **Bir El-Mattar**, 7 km northeast of Bawiti, though it is not particularly beautiful as the cool water pours out of a viaduct into a small cement pool. Men bathe here by day, and women by night. **Bir Al-Ghaba 2**, 7 km further down the road, is extremely hot. **Bir Sigam**, 7 km east of town on the Cairo road, is definitely the best place to bathe in Bahariyya. Locals often splash around here when the sun's out, but come night, men and women travellers can soak undisturbed in stunning moonlit environs.

The golden mummies of Bahariyya Oasis

It is widely reported that the find of these mummies in 1996 was in fact made almost four years earlier and that in that time the discovery was supressed to allow some 'private' excavations. Be that as it may, these golden mummies are as exciting a find as Tutankhamen's Tomb. It seems this cemetery was in use from the construction of Alexander's Temple to the fourth century AD. The mummies are all different – individual men, women and children. The mask and upper bodies of many were coated with gold, others decorated with painted scenes. Each mummy has, unusually, a painted smile.

It will be some time before this site is open to the public and then it is unlikely that the mummies will be on view. In the meantime five mummies are on display in the Antiquities Inspectorate museum.

There are three kinds of mummy: the first is wrapped in linen without a sarcophagus; the second is laid to rest in a pottery coffin; and the third is characterized by its decorations – pasteboard made of linen or papyrus, from the head to the waist on which artists have depicted scenes, or those wearing gilded masks and often surrounded by funerary artefacts.

Bahariyya to Farafra

Just 12 km beyond the outskirts of Bawati is the **Runi shrine of Rene Michael**, the Swiss explorer who lived in the village for seven years, rediscovered the area and was so enchanted by the beauty of the place that he wanted to be buried here in the desert. Beyond lies the **Black Desert**, the pebbles of dolerite darkening the land, and the road begins to rise out of the Bahariyya depression through a bright rainbow canyon. On the plateau are numerous erosion features known locally as 'lions'. Of special note are the small mountains of calcite. One, just 10 m to the left of the road, is called Jebel El-Izza or **Crystal Mountain**, more like a big hill and with a flower-like growth of crystal formations sprouting forth around the small arch in the centre. The road cuts through the escarpment and descends towards the Farafra depression. Of the flat topped outliers, two are particularly prominent to the east of the road, and are known as the **Twin Peaks**.

Beyond is the fabled **White Desert** (Sahara Al-Beida) the reason why most tourists have come so far. By moonlight, the eerie wind-sculpted landscape has been compared to the Arctic wasteland, and sunrise here is the highlight of many trips. The luminescent glow of the white rock, whipped by the wind into peaky meringues, against the drifting sands is truly other-worldly. These strange shaped rocks have caught the imagination of countless travellers – intrigued by them and inspired by them. Geologists will delight in the huge calcite crystals, the chalk fossils and the accumulations of pyrites. To the north of Jebel Gunna a road goes west to **Aïn Della** (Spring of the Shade).

Farafra Oasis → *For listings, see pages 517-527. Colour map 1, B3.*

Farafra offers a good starting point for safaris into the nearby White Desert and a thorough taste of oasis life, much unfettered by the onslaught of tourism. It is the smallest and most isolated of the oases in the Western Desert though the deep depression in which it lies suggests that it was once larger. The village of **Qasr El-Farafra** was based around a large 116-room mud-brick fort or castle (*qasr*) from which it got its name. This was used by the villagers when they were under attack until it collapsed in 1958.

The inhabitants of Farafra, who spawn mainly from two extended families, have been involved in trade and contact with the Nile Valley since earliest times. Until quite recently, residents in Farafra numbered less than 5000, before a wave of *Saidis* (Upper Egyptians), migrated to the isolated oasis to exploit the vacant fertile land. Now there are more than 15,000 people living peacefully together, though the separation of quiet-natured Farafrans and more animated Saidis is apparent in the local *ahwas*.

Sights

There are no ancient sites to visit in this oasis and the nearby desert landscapes are the real draw of this region for most travellers. However, the village is a lovely slow-moving place, with dusty tree-lined roads and traditional, decorated houses. Steamy hot springs, and mellow and welcoming locals make it a relaxing stop between sights and safaris. The old district of Qasr El-Farafra has narrow alleys and houses of sun-dried bricks, and on Thursday nights Sufis still observe a *zikr* at Sheikh Marzuk's shrine. The adjacent palm gardens give the opportunity for a delightful rustic wander and add to the time-warp appeal of the little town. The local market on Thursday mornings brings out brightly clad women, just ask *'fein el-souq?'* to be directed to the right spot.

Farafra

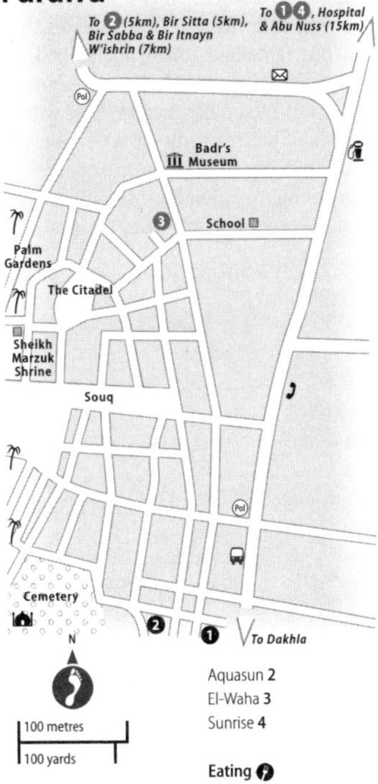

Sleeping
Al-Badawiya **1**
Aquasun **2**
El-Waha **3**
Sunrise **4**

Eating
Hussein's **1**
Samir's **2**

Badr's Museum ⓘ *E£10 entrance includes a brochure and 2 postcards of Badr's work; usually open 0900-1400 (or until sunset during busy seasons), if not, enquire in the coffee shop next door and someone will lead you to Badr, T012-170 4710*, is dedicated to the work of Badr, the first of several oasis artists who has been invited to share his work, spirit and culture in galleries around the world. Badr built the museum, a work of art in itself, with his own hands. Set up like a traditional Farafran home, the rooms are overflowing with sculptures, sand paintings and watercolours. Badr's art is filled with sadness, depth and longing. It's mythic, surreal and an earnest reflection of life in the desert and among the people of Farafra. If you're lucky, you'll meet Badr's brother Gamal, a superb *urghul* (traditional flute) player who accompanies a band of impressive local musicians. Ask Badr if he's playing at any weddings or celebrations during your visit.

Bir Sitta, next to the Aquasun Hotel and **Bir Sabba** nearby are steaming hot springs 5 km out of town, where 38 °C baths are enjoyed by both locals and tourists. Taxis there and back cost around E£20-30 with waiting time. In the same direction, about 7 km out of town, **Bir Itnayn w'ishrin** is even better, being more isolated, deeper and surrounded by lush farmland. A moonlight soak here is guaranteed to be in solitude, with the only visible lights being the stars.

The lake of **Abu Nuss** is about 15 km north of Farafra and despite the weeds taking over large areas it is an attractive spot and home to plenty of birdlife. The rocky bottom prevents the deep water from getting too murky and a cooling dip is wonderful in the heat of summer. It's also a good place for sunset, with the background of the desert plateau, white mountains and vivid vegetation contrasting with the silent waters.

Dakhla Oasis and Mut → *For listings, see pages 517-527. Colour map 1, B3.*

Moving on southeast from Farafra, the much larger Dakhla Oasis, with a population of around 75,000 in 14 settlements, sprouts up after 310 km. Buses make the journey in three to four hours; cars in three hours. The first 100 km of the journey are through unoccupied oases and open areas of sand that in places extend over the road. Beyond, the sand dunes increase in size. As you come upon the oasis, primary colours explode. A million shades of pink in the cliffs meld with bright golden sand dunes, wide blue sky and the lushest fields in all the oases.

Known as the pink oasis, Dakhla is a magical place that has managed to dodge the extreme urbanization of nearby Kharga. The people are among the friendliest and most sincere in all of Egypt. They welcome travellers with curiosity and hospitality as they openly share their traditional way of life that has remained much unchanged for centuries. With the capital Mut, at the centre, there are some notable ancient sights to both the east and west. The old town of Al Qasr is incredibly picturesque, with a well-preserved mud-brick maze of narrow streets and houses some of which are still occupied, surrounded by green cultivation and rolling dunes. Dakhla is also a good place to venture into the desert for star-gazing and overnight exploration. Like Bahariyya, there's no shortage of eager guides who will organize everything from a day's hop around the sights to an 11-day camel trek to Farafra.

Dakhla Oasis

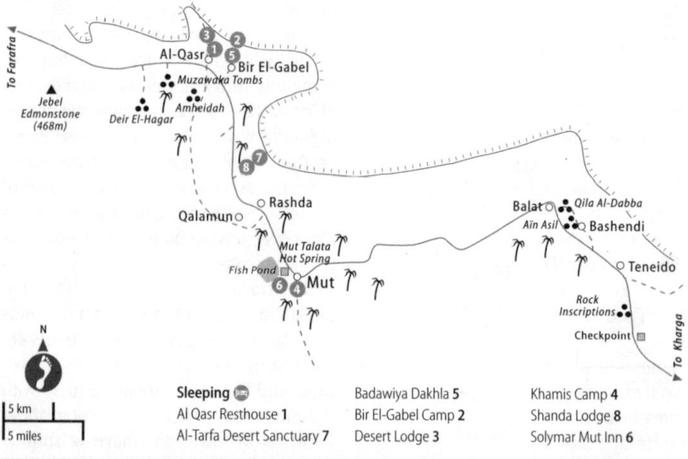

Sleeping
Al Qasr Resthouse **1**
Al-Tarfa Desert Sanctuary **7**
Badawiya Dakhla **5**
Bir El-Gabel Camp **2**
Desert Lodge **3**
Khamis Camp **4**
Shanda Lodge **8**
Solymar Mut Inn **6**

Sights in Western Dakhla

Deir El-Hagar ⓘ *E£20, students E£10, 0800-1700, expect to have to offer* baksheesh *to guards (E£3-5)*, a small sandstone temple built during Nero's reign (AD 54-68) to honour the triad of Theban gods: Amun Re, Mut and Khonsu. The site, surrounded by a wall intended to deflect drifting sand, is well preserved – due, ironically, to being enveloped by sand for much of its recent history. Without your own transport, getting here requires a bit of effort. It's easiest to hire a taxi/minibus from Al-Qasr (8 km, E£25-30 round trip, including a visit to Muzawaka, see below) or hire a bicycle from Al-Qasr Resthouse (E£5), go 5 km along road to Farafra before taking a left turn, signed, and follow the track through a village and on to the temple.

The temple consists of a two-columned court and a hypostyle court with four columns, a vestibule and a sanctuary. Each of the columns in the hypostyle hall has inscriptions to Emperor Titus, the columns in the sanctuary to Domitian, Vespasian and Nero. There are some interesting bas-reliefs and inscriptions representing religious life, and traces of paint remain. Notice the smoke-covered columns near the sanctuary, thought to be residue of ancient rituals. Ask the guard to point out the Coptic graffiti, a clear indicator that the temple was later used as a church. Also inscribed on the temple walls and columns are the names of numerous 19th-century travellers, the most famous being Gerhard Rohlfs, the German explorer. It is an isolated and mystical spot, and you will probably be the only visitor here to enjoy the temple in peace.

The main tombs at the Roman period **Muzawaka Tombs (Hill of Decoration)** have been officially closed for years, awaiting restoration that has yet to begin. Vividly painted with myths relating to the afterlife, the tombs of **Petosiris** (AD 54-84) and his wife **Sadosiris** contain all the elements of the ancient traditions but rendered in the Graeco-Roman style. However, the site is still worth a visit, as a bit of *baksheesh* (E£3-5) will yield an unbelievable viewing of mummies – the closest you'll ever get. Notice the hands of the males rest by their sides while the hands of the females cover their genitalia. There is one tomb with the skeleton of a child that is frequented by local women wanting to conceive. Without your own vehicle, you can get here by taxi from Al-Qasr (see above) or take a public pickup (50 pt) and ask to be dropped off at the dirt road leading to the tombs (signed), or it's an easy 5 km by bike. It's also possible to walk from Al-Qasr in less than half an hour across the sands.

Al-Qasr

ⓘ *32 km north of Mut, if you're coming from Farafra, you can ask to be let off here; from Mut, take a pickup for E£1.25.*

This old Islamic settlement, built upon the foundation of an older Roman settlement, is Dakhla's fortified medieval capital. Wandering around the enchanting ancient town gives a taste of the timelessness of oasis life, and travellers who are disappointed by the dereliction of the shali in Siwa might find their imaginations more fuelled by the rambling labyrinth of Al-Qasr. The narrow alleys of the old quarter, covered as protection from the sand and sun, contain constant reminders of the antiquity of the area. Ancient wooden lintels at doorways are decorated with carved inscriptions from the Koran and date back to AD 1519. There are still a few inhabited houses (residents will urge you inside for a glass of *shai* or *tamarind*), but newcomers are no longer permitted to settle in the old buildings. A guard will greet you if you enter via the main street, signed from the main highway (to avoid being accompanied, enter via one of the smaller alleys found east or west of the centre) and expect a bit of *baksheesh* (E£5-10). In return, he will let you inside the house of

It must have been a mirage

For a fascinating optical illusion try the mirage, a feature of all romantic travellers' adventures in the desert. Most commonly they occur in hot desert regions where the distant and most welcome pool of water perhaps reflecting swaying palm trees turns out, much to the disappointment of the thirsty traveller, to be another area of parched sand.

A mirage is caused by the bending of rays of light as they pass through different layers of air that vary in temperature and density. The rays of light that come to the eye directly from the swaying palm fronds are interpreted by the brain in their correct position. Those rays that travel nearer to the hot ground surface move faster through the warmer, less dense air as they meet less resistance. They change their direction as they travel, bending closer to the ground. The brain, however, assumes the rays have travelled in a direct line and records the blue sky as a pool of water and the trees as reflections. The illusion, perhaps overused by film producers and novelists, is of wide expanses of inviting, shimmering 'water'.

The rays are misinterpreted by the brain but they do exist so the mirage can be photographed. That does not, alas, make the water available to quench your thirst.

Abu Nafri and direct you to the beautifully restored **Ayyubid madrasa**, which served as both a school of *sharia'a* (Islamic law) and a courtroom. Look for the holding cells (separate for men and women) and more permanent jail inside, and the recesses for lamps and books. Climb to the roof for a spectacular view, but take a guide to steer you away from several areas that are too weak to walk upon. Just outside the *madresa* is the place where those who were found guilty by the court were hanged.

The **Nasr El-Din mosque** is marked by a three-storey minaret that doubled as a lookout tower, 21 m high, rebuilt in the 19th century. Climbing the minaret will cost an additional E£5-10 in *baksheesh*. The serene tomb of Sheikh Nasr El-Din is inside the old mosque, decorated with verses from the Koran around the interior in deep red paint. Also make sure you see the ancient corn mill (made of acacia wood and a huge palm trunk, it would have been turned by an ox), and the olive oil press where the scent of olives still lingers. It is worth visiting the small but informative **Ethnographic Museum** ⓘ *daily 0800-1700, except during Fri prayers, E£5,* founded by Alia Hussein, a premier anthropologist of the oases. Photographs and crafts from all the oases are on display and labelled. There is also a steel mill still in use and a nearby pottery factory where you can witness a family making mud bricks and *zirs* (water-coolers) in the same manner they have for centuries.

Beyond Al-Qasr, the road turns south toward the ruined city of **Amheidah** where tombs dating from 22nd century BC are being excavated although there is not much to view as yet. The road continues onward to Mut via the Mamluk hilltop village of **Qalamun**, where there are striking views of the area from among the ruins of the old city and many twisty streets to meander through, although be prepared for children to get boisterous at the sight of a tourist. Go there before there is nothing left, as the ruined mud-brick fortress has been much damaged by rain and increased access to and use of water in the still-inhabited houses is destroying the foundations. A short distance further on this side road is the **Magic Spring** (Bir El-Bayada), a popular destination for locals and tourists as the warm water bubbling up from underground makes for an enjoyable bathe. An attractive café (plus toilet) make it a good place to stop and rest.

Mut

Although set in a beautiful landscape bursting with life, Mut (pronounced *moot*), Dakhla's capital, is not immediately appealing. However, the old ochre-coloured remains of the citadel and its surrounding alleyways are in stark contrast to the wide roads, traffic lights and roundabouts of the sprawling modern town. It is both a lively and laid-back place with a wide range of inhabitants from as far away as Nubia, Sudan, and Libya, all living

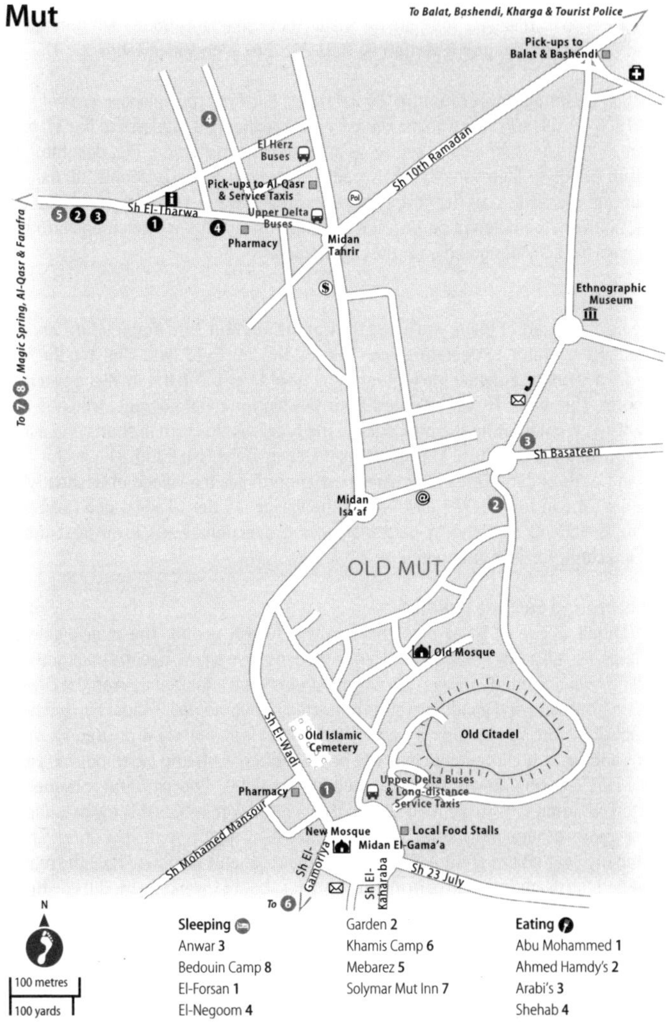

peacefully together. With a more extensive choice of food and accommodation, and easier transport links to onward destinations, Mut attracts more overnight guests than nearby Al-Qasr.

Information The **tourist office** ⓘ *T/F092-821686, T012-179 6467, Sun-Thu 0800-1400 and evenings from 1800-2100 (all day during busy periods)*, is near Midan Tahrir on the road to Al-Qasr. Manager Omar Ahmed is well informed about the area and can help organize trips into the desert. He can be contacted on his mobile at any time, including Friday. The **Tourist Police** ⓘ *T092-782 1687*, are on Sharia 10th Ramadan, about 1 km northeast of Midan Tahrir. The main **police station** ⓘ *T092-782 1500*, is on Midan Tahrir.

Sights The **Ethnographic Museum** ⓘ *rarely open, but if you call manager Ibrahim Kamel on T018-574 0789 he'll come with the key to let you in; entrance is supposed to be E£3, but he will drop strong hints for a tip*, is set out as an ancient Islamic house. This delightful little museum brings to life everyday items traditionally used by oasis people. Ibrahim will explain the mechanism of deer-traps and the cunning wooden lock system utilized on doors, highlight the different purposes of colourful woven mats and ceremonial clothing, and reveal the activities going on in the clay dioramas.

Around Mut

In the northern part of town, you'll find the **hot springs Mut 3** (in Arabic, *Mut Talata*) on the left. Here, water temperatures can reach 43°C. For E£10, you can use the large (orange) pool in the **Solymar Inn** for the day, or have a free dip in the smaller one outside the hotel. The water is rust coloured from the high mineral content, which is a bit off-putting. Women using the pool outside the hotel should swim in shorts and a loose fitting opaque T-shirt. After 1 km are the lakes known as the **Fish Pond**, a haven for water fowl and oasis birdlife. Three kilometres further north lies the village of **Rashda** where there are Roman ruins at the east end of the village. As the villagers don't call them Roman, or indeed anything in particular, asking directions leads to a great deal of amusing confusion and disagreement.

Sights around Eastern Dakhla

The tranquil village of **Balat** dates back to the Turkish period. The mauve-coloured dwellings are still partly inhabited and fertile gardens have palms, banana trees and vines dangling over ancient doorways. The narrow streets were intended to keep the city cool and safe from sand and winds as well as protected from potential invaders on horse and camelback by forcing impending warriors to fight on foot. Pottery urns used for drying onions and herbs are integrated into sun-baked rooftop walls and ingenious mud-brick stoves illustrate how meals were prepared in past times. Two peaceful mosques still function, whirring fans suspended among the mud-brick pillars, and the atmosphere is almost more otherworldly than Al-Qasr. A 'warden' might spot you entering and accompany your visit, pointing out old lintels, the ingenious wooden locks, the mayor's house and the dilapidated old corn mill in return for about E£5 *baksheesh*. Outside the old village, there is a good bakery and a few places to get refreshments and tea. The village is accessible via infrequent pickup from Mut, E£1.50, or a private taxi to the village, nearby sites and Bashendi will cost E£80-100 for four hours.

Nearby, **Qila Al-Dabba** ⓘ *0800-1700, entrance E£25, students E£15*, the ancient necropolis of Balat offers visitors a look at mud-brick *mastabas* that mark the tombs of sixth-Dynasty governors. Two have been extensively excavated by a group of French archaeologists that continue to work on the site a few months every year. Inside the tomb of Khentika you can see faint-coloured reliefs of daily life and images of the governor and his wife. His mummy was found here, but has been relocated to the Cairo museum, while his beautiful funeral stele and other treasures lie in Kharga Museum. The tomb of Ima-Pepi contains a decorated sarcophagus and is worth a peek if you have made the trip out here.

About 1.5 km east of the Necropolis, the French have also been working for more than 20 years at **Aïn Asil** ⓘ *your ticket to Qila Al-Dabba will allow you access to the Aïn Asil ruins,* an Old Kingdom settlement that was abandoned around Ptolemaic times. Excavations thus far have uncovered the remains of a fort and farming community.

Bashendi, on a huge arch at its entrance, describes itself as a 'model' village. It's a working community, not quite as picturesque as nearby Balat, but quaint enough with narrow streets, mud houses and lots of smiling children that excitedly ask for pens. (Riders on the Paris–Dakar route introduced this concept to the children on their frequent stops to the village where they often distribute pens and T-shirts.) Someone will produce a key to see the internal decorations of the Roman period second century Tomb of **Kitnes** ⓘ *entrance is an overpriced E£20, but a bit of* baksheesh *will facilitate a quick viewing*. The original funerary reliefs depict Kitnes meeting the gods Min, Seth and Shu. Smoke from past ceremonies stains the ceiling and the surrounds are littered with sarcophagi. The Tomb of **Bash Endi** (name derived from a medieval Sheikh from India known as Pasha Hindi) consists of a Roman base and a much more recent Islamic dome. Notice the handprints covering the walls. Local women believe that three hands on the walls of a sheikh's tomb can lift the black magic that prevents them from conceiving. The acoustics in Bashendi's tomb are remarkable. If you're not alone, have your companion whisper in the far left corner of the tomb and put your ear around the near right corner to hear.

Dakhla to Kharga

The journey from Dakhla to Kharga, 195 km in an easterly direction, takes over three hours. Immediately beyond **Teneida**, and its tombs on the left of the road, is a checkpoint. Look out now for the sandstone outcrops very near the road. On the closest, to the south, are a number of **rock inscriptions** – some purporting to be very old. Note the rock formations in the area, a particularly striking one resembles a sitting camel. This area marks the intersection of two ancient caravan routes, one between Dakhla and Kharga; the other connecting Teneida to the Darb El-Arbaeen (Forty Days Road).

Kharga Oasis

→ *For listings, see pages 517-527. Colour map 1, B4.*

Pre-industrial Kharga was very different from the city here today. At that time the water level was considerably higher and the route was vital for the caravan trade. The New Valley scheme has converted this attractive oasis into a modern concrete town thereby removing almost all traces of its former charm. Nevertheless, a few spectacular historical sites are within easy access, and the city has been beautified somewhat by the liberal planting of trees and an effective clean-up campaign. Kharga Museum houses many treasures from the surrounding area and beyond, while smaller villages and the soft peachy sand-scapes on the outskirts of town make for good half-day outings. Like other oases, everything shuts down during the heat of the day and siesta is almost compulsory. The security situation has relaxed considerably since 2007; independent travellers are no longer accompanied by a policeman (except sometimes late in the evening) and can move around freely unlike before.

Information Tourist office ⓘ *T/F092-792 1205/6, Sun-Thu 0800-1400 and most evenings 1800-2100*, opposite Kharga Oasis Hotel. Mohsen Abd Al-Moneam, T010-180 6127, speaks good English and will be keen to help arrange tours around the oasis. The **Tourist Police** ⓘ *T092-792 1367*, are next door to the tourist office.

Sights

Al-Wadi Al-Gadeed Antiquities Museum ⓘ *Sharia Gamal Abdel Nasser, daily 0800-1700, closed for Fri noon prayer, E£30 for foreigners, E£15 students*, Though poorly labelled it is a fabulous museum that showcases artefacts found throughout the oases and really puts things in context if you are coming on from Dakhla. The ground floor displays alabaster, granite and basalt perfume bottles and vessels of all shapes, tones and sizes, immaculately preserved. In particular look at the mournful golden mummy mask from Labeka, the painted sphinxes and linen-wrapped mummified rams with vibrantly spotted stucco. Nearby stand life-like marble feet in Graeco-Roman sandals and children's toy boats and animals fashioned from clay. Upstairs, hundreds of bangles made of glass, palm-leaf, brass and lacquer mingle with ceramic tiles and glass from Cairo's Islamic Art Museum, and Mohamed Ali's tableware rescued from Manial Palace. Coptic wooden friezes and weavings complete the collection. The almost total lack of visitors means staff will have to go ahead of you switching on lights, and you will doubtless have the place to yourself. If you visit alone you will almost certainly meet the director, Mahmoud Youssef, who will invite you for tea to practise his English and try to sell you postcards and a CD of the museum's collection. He has a wealth of knowledge about the local sites.

To get to the **Temple of Nadoura** go north from town and turn right at the triumphal arch. This sandstone temple was built by Antonius Pius in AD 138 and later used as a fortress by the Ottomans. Though the temple is in ruins (and only a few inscriptions remain) a walk to its mount gives a splendid view of the Temple of Hibis and the surrounding desert. It's an excellent place to take in the setting sun.

The **Temple of Hibis**, 2 km to the north of the town, is dedicated to Amun and was begun in 510 BC at the beginning of the Persian occupation under Darius and completed under Nectanebo II. This imposing temple is dedicated to the triad of Theban gods, Amun Re, Mut and Khonsu. At the time of writing, the inner areas were closed for restoration, after a botched attempt to move the temple to higher ground resulted in the majority of the stone blocks being badly damaged. From the outer to the inner gate is an avenue of sphinxes and the walk up to the temple through the remains of pylons is still impressive. the ornamentation and designs within the temple are mainly animals, showing vultures, dogs and serpents intertwined with Persian and Egyptian deities. To get there, you can take a pickup to the end of town and walk the remaining 2 km, or flag down a microbus/service taxi en route and ask them to drop you at the temple (*ma'abad*).

The **Necropolis of El-Baqawat** ⓘ *winter 0830-1700, summer 0800-1700, E£30, students E£15*, was once so far from civilization that hermits came for the seclusion it offered. Now, about 500 baked brick tombs, originating from an early Christian burial site and dating from the third to the seventh centuries, lie crumbling in the desert. It is a deeply evocative site and, if you are fortunate, you may escape being guided to wander at will and explore the small chapels covering 263 of the tombs. The most interesting features of the burial ground are the vivid wall paintings of biblical scenes in the Chapel of Peace and the Chapel of the

Exodus. Some are fairly crudely executed and others were defaced by the ancient Greeks. The chapels are known by the illustrations they contain, which are mainly of Old Testament scenes depicting Adam and Eve, the Exodus (note the Pharaoh's soldiers pursuing Moses on foot and by camel), Daniel in the lion's den, Noah's Ark, Abraham and Isaac. (Look out for Jonah being vomited out of the whale's stomach.) From the New Testament, the Virgin Mary and St Paul feature most often. Takla Hamanout, an Ethiopian

Kharga

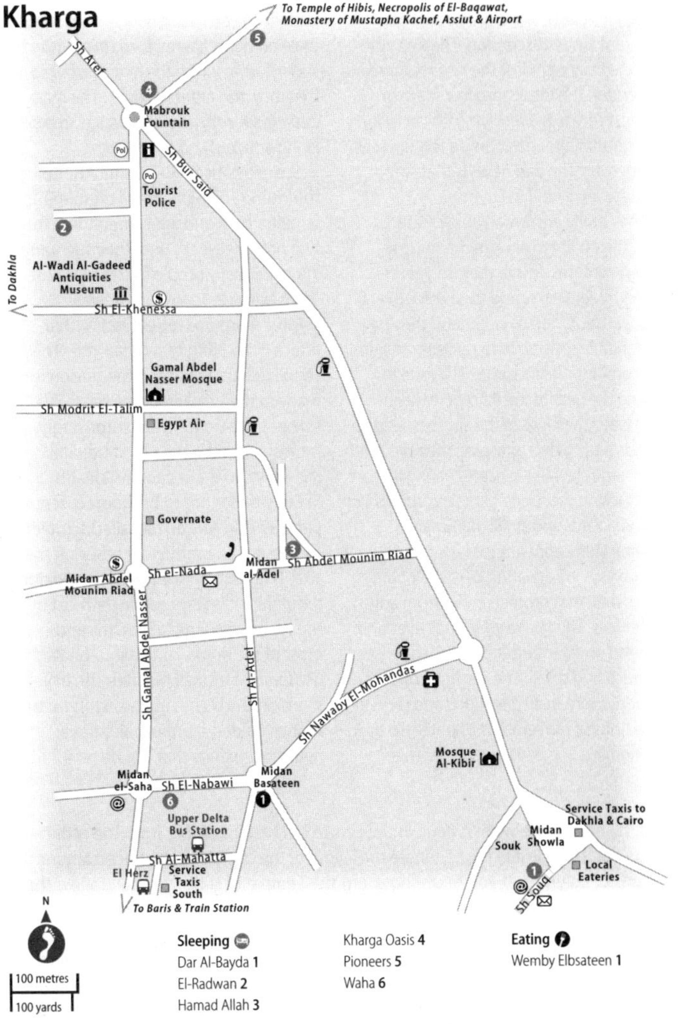

Scorpions – a sting in the tail

Scorpions really deserve a better press. They are fascinating creatures, provided they do not lurk in your shoe or shelter in your clothes.

Scorpions are not insects. They belong to the class Arachnida as do spiders and daddy longlegs. There are about 750 different kinds of scorpion. The average size is a cosy 6 cm but the largest, *Pandinus imperator*, the black emperor scorpion of West Africa, is a terrifying 20 cm long. The good news is that only a few are really dangerous. The bad news is that some of these are found in Egypt.

They really are remarkable creatures with the ability to endure the hottest desert climates, revive themselves after being frozen in ice, and survive for over a year without food or water and they have a remarkable resistance to nuclear radiation.

Scorpions are nocturnal. They shelter during the heat of the day and to keep cool wave their legs in the air. They feed on insects and spiders, grasping their prey with their large claw-like pincers, tearing it apart and sucking the juices. Larger scorpions can devour lizards and small mammals.

Their shiny appearance is due to an impervious wax coating over their hard outer shell that protects them from any water loss. They have very small eyes and depend on their better developed senses of touch and smell. The sensitive bristles on the legs point in all directions and pick up vibrations of movements of potential prey or enemies. This sensitivity gives them ample warning to avoid being seen by heavy-footed humans.

The oft-reported 'courtship dance' before mating is merely repeated instinctive actions. The grasping of claws and the jerky 'dance' movements from side to side are a prelude to copulation during which the male produces spermatozoa in a drop of sticky fluid to which the female is led so that they may enter her body. The male departs speedily after the 'dance' to avoid being attacked and devoured.

Scorpions bear live young. After birth, the young scorpions crawl on to the female's back and are carried there for two or three weeks until their first moult. They gradually drop off after that time and have to fend for themselves.

Most scorpions retreat rather than attack. They sting in self-defence. The sting is a hard spine and the poison is made in the swelling at the base. The sole of the bare foot, not surprisingly, is most often the site of a sting, and the advice in the section on Health in Essentials is not to be ignored, see page 39. The African fat-tailed scorpion (we do not recommend measuring the size) is described as aggressive and quick-tempered. It is responsible for most of the reported stings to humans and most of the human fatalities. The *Buthus occitanus*, the small Mediterranean yellow scorpion, and *Leirus quinquestriatus*, the African golden scorpion, also have neurotoxic stings that can be fatal.

saint, is shown here with St Paul. In the centre is a basilica dating from the fifth century AD, one of the oldest in Egypt, where the layout of the church can be traced amongst the remains of columns. If you're on foot from the Temple of Hibis, you can follow the dirt track from through a palm grove into the desert. By vehicle, just continue on the road to Assiut, you'll find the entrance on the left less than 1 km north of the temple.

Cliffs, speckled with tombs, dominate the area. Follow these north from the necropolis to the mud-brick ruins of the **Monastery of Mustapha Kachef** (Mustapha the taxman), which makes good use of the lofty position. Five stories high, the arched passageways and chambers are filling up with sand, and from the ramparts you can gaze at the ruins of a small church on the desert plain below.

South of Kharga

ⓘ *Service taxis and covered pickups operate along the main road, but infrequently, and walking between the sites and villages requires effort to say the least. Hiring a taxi for a day costs around E£150, or a 4-hr trip is E£60-70. Bargain hard.*

There is a track east of Kharga that goes south through peach-coloured desert and contrasting green orchards to Bir Gennah village. Here are **No 3 spring**, where a peaceful bathe can be had in temperate waters (pumps are switched off at night) and a deserted village covered by sand dunes. The villagers have had to relocate to New Gennah, a few kilometres away across the main road. **Qasr El-Ghuweita** ⓘ *20 km along the road to Darfur, 0800-1700, E£30, students E£15,* is a 25th Dynasty temple dedicated to Amun, Mut and Khonsu atop an imposing hill with glorious views. Surrounded by a massive mud-brick wall, the interior has graceful columns with lotus capitals and an exquisite lower band of processional reliefs. Stairs to the left of the sanctum lead onto the roof, where those who don't suffer from vertigo can take a daring walk along the walls to see the columns from above. **Qasr Zayan** ⓘ *5 km further, 0800-1700, E£30, students E£15* is a Ptolemaic and Roman Temple, again to Amun, and back on the main road, **Bulaq** village has wells/springs with temperatures reaching 39°C and a primitive resthouse and campsite. On the way back to Kharga from here (if you are not carrying on to Dush), a left turn by the vast petroleum cylinders will take you to New Gennah, where five families live among the date palms on the edge of another huge dune that threatens to engulf their new abode. Sunset from the dune, when the sky and sand take on an unearthly glow, is a magical experience. Carrying on south from Bulaq brings you to **Qasr Dush** southeast of **Baris** ⓘ *0800-1700, E£35, students E£17*, with a Roman Temple dedicated to the Gods Serapis and Isis; there's also a mud-brick Turkish fortress, an ancient church and some Coptic pottery. The road to Luxor (another 225 km) turns off at Jala.

North of Kharga

To the north excursions can be made to **Aïn Umm Dabadib** with ruins of ancient settlements and a Roman castle; **Qasr El-Labeka**, one of the largest forts in this oasis, boasting Roman tombs and a temple from where many of the most exquisite pieces in Kharga Museum were unearthed; and **El-Deir** where walls and towers still stand. A 4WD is needed for excursions to Aïn Umm Dabadib.

Excursion to Gilf Kebir → *Colour map 1, C2.*

The immense flat-topped plateau of the Gilf Kebir (Great Barrier) lurks in the southwest corner of Egypt about 720 km from the Nile and 960 km from the Mediterranean – about 500 km from the nearest post office, petrol station or coffee shop. It spreads over 7770 sq km, a vast shelf the size of Switzerland, split by a narrow ridge of land into a northern and a southern section. The table of the Gilf itself is gravelly and largely featureless, with huge slabs of basalt in places, but the edges of the plateau are a different story: penetrated by huge sand wadis and enormous dune systems that in places rise 300 m to meet the level of the plateau. Amid this most awesome of natural settings is what is unquestionably one of the richest storehouses of prehistoric rock art in the world. **The Cave of the Swimmers** is the most famous, but recent discoveries have revealed many other incredible sites dating back more than 7000 years, and there is certainly much more to be explored.

Intrepid visitors that come here have to travel across mind-blowing expanses of sand to reach the dune-filled and deserted wadis scarring the plateau of the desolate Gilf. Yet it was not always so, as rock paintings left by Neolithic tribes, the mystique of the lost oasis of Zerzura, and theories that it was once a station on a pharaonic donkey-caravan route from the Nile to Kufra in Libya all attest to an active past. Utterly hostile, virtually rainless, at times blisteringly hot, at others freezing cold, the Gilf was named and fixed on maps only as recently as 1926 by Prince Kamal El-Din, a son of King Fuad. Now a whole new generation of travellers is enduring – and enjoying – the rigours of desert life to view the plethora of Neolithic and pre-Dynastic sites and admire the spectacular and beautifully wild scenery. An undeniable and deepening attraction to the desert is felt by all who come here, as expressed by the legendary desert explorer Hassanein Bey in his 1925 book *The Lost Oases*, "The desert is terrible and it is merciless, but to the desert all those who once have known it must return."

Ins and outs

Getting there From Farafra, a tarmac road takes you to the oasis of **Abu Minquar** from where you head across the **Great Sand Sea** to the northern edge of the Gilf. Safaris taking this route may well camp at **Regenfeld** (Rainfield), so dubbed by the 19th-century German explorer Gerhard Rohlfs. The story goes that in 1874, when Rohlfs was trying to cross the Great Sand Sea to Kufra in Libya, he found his camel train desperately short of water and many days away from any known human habitation. Saved by a miraculous rainstorm (which happens about every decade in the desert) Rohlfs was able to refill his supplies and was saved. He built a cairn to commemorate his deliverance that still remains, much added to, and an empty bottle stuffed with messages, which doesn't.

Another route starts at Mut, in Dakhla Oasis, and traverses the **Darb El-Tafawi**. A minor road goes as far as **Abu Ballas**, an isolated hill to the south of the Great Sand Sea, more than halfway to the Gilf Kebir. Here, a vast number of giant clay pots were rediscovered in 1918. The ones remaining are almost all broken, and most of the others have been purloined by souvenir gatherers over the years. As Almasy first tantalizingly suggested, it could be a staging post on a donkey-caravan route to Kufra used by the pharaohs, one of a chain of nearly 30 staging posts that Carlo Bergman has since discovered (in 2000) covering the 350-km trail from Dakhla to the Gilf Kebir. Weight to this argument is further given by hieroglyphic rock inscriptions found some 200 km southwest of Dakhla, one of which attests to the ancient Egyptians 'meeting with the oasis dwellers' to the west. The site of the main inscriptions is being kept a secret, as modern day rock-artists have already defaced the engravings on the more accessible sites.

Safety A journey to the Gilf Kebir should never be undertaken lightly. It requires a minimum of 10 days, more if you carry on to Siwa across the Great Sand Sea. Self-drivers will have to overcome a few bureaucratic hurdles. Expeditions are entirely self-supporting and permits are required. (For more information on self-driving, see page 494). Given the complexity of the arrangements, by far the easiest way is to organize a trip is through an experienced agency, who will need at least a month's advance warning. In fact, it's best to book as far in advance as possible, as increased accessibility and interest in the Gilf means demand is high, plus the season is short due to extreme heat in summer and bitter cold in winter. See page 525 for some recommended agencies. Organized expeditions include a minimum of two vehicles, drivers, a guide, at least one cook, an army officer, fuel, GPS and all safety and other equipment. It can be cold at night, so check what sleeping equipment is provided and make sure to supplement it if you feel the cold. Most of the day will be spent in a car, not surprisingly with such distances involved, but lunch stops aim to take in an interesting feature and night camps usually are very scenic.

The fragile environment of the Gilf is easily damaged, and the new wave of desert travellers can't fail to have a detrimental impact. Ancient vessels and pottery have already been damaged by reckless drivers before any proper archaeological surveys have been done. Most rubbish is either burnt or buried, but make sure you speak up if you feel unsuitable garbage is being left behind. It is on everyone's conscience to keep their impact to an absolute minimum, and to try to ensure others are doing the same.

Note Eleven Western tourists and eight Egyptians were kidnapped in the border region in 2008 and the area remains sensitive. » *Contact one of the Farafra-based tour agencies on page 525 to check the current situation.*

Background

The story of exploration in the Gilf Kebir and Great Sand Sea is as remarkable as the phenomenal natural wonders and prehistory that the colourful characters discovered there. In 1932, members of the so-called Zerzura Club led by Almasy and Clayton set out in search of the lost, perhaps mythical, oasis of Zerzura in this most hostile of landscapes. An expedition was undertaken to investigate the Gilf from the air, from where they saw several wadis rich with vegetation that were used by nomads for grazing. So in 1933, they mounted an overland expedition to see if these valleys were indeed Zerzura. What they found, in addition to three wadis that fitted the descriptions of Wilkinson's notes of 1835, was a wealth of prehistoric rock art and trade items that are now thought to show links shared by pharaonic cultures and these ancient inhabitants. Had it not been immortalized by the book and film of *The English Patient*, the Gilf might have remained unknown to all but the most adventurous archaeologists and modern-day explorers.

Hassanein Bey was the first to locate the huge massif of **Jebel Uweinat**, on the borders of Egypt, Libya and Sudan. He came from Kufra in 1923 on foot, and inspired other (motorized) explorers to attempt to find a route from Egypt. Currently, Jebel Uweinat is not being included on safari itineraries to the region as it is a sensitive zone and is effectively a no-man's land on the Egyptian, Sudanese and Libyan borders. This means the astounding rock art of **Kharkur Talh** is off the agenda at present.

Silica Glass Field

The Silica Glass Field, north of the Gilf Kebir towards Siwa Oasis, is signalled by a group of cairns. The origin of the pale green opalescent stone is a puzzle, with theories for the existence of the compacted sediments ranging from prehistoric volcanic activity to an extra-terrestrial impact that melted the sand. In any case, it is a fascinating place to scour around for interesting shapes and formations of the opaque stuff, with some bits even appearing to have been carved into Neolithic tools. (The area is now protected and the removal of any glass is forbidden). The glass field also lends weight to the theory that the pharaohs traded as far west as this, as it has been revealed that an emerald-like gem in a piece of Tutankamun's jewellery is actually silica glass.

The Northern Gilf

The Northern Gilf Kebir is being eroded into islands and cones by the white sands of the Great Sand Sea. Dunes spill up and over the walls of wadis, making an incredible spectacle as they clash together and battle their way to the top. The Northern Gilf is famed more for being the believed site of the Zerzura oasis and for its dramatic scenery than it is for its rock art sites, which are few in number. Considering that three large wadis here are quite vegetated it is peculiar that seemingly so few prehistoric people decorated the mountain, but there is no adequate hypothesis as to why not.

On the eastern side, the black mountains of the Gilf are banked with stunning dunes of red sand, hence the name **Wadi Hamra** (Red Valley). Clayton was the first to arrive in 1931 when he found plenty of trees (still the case) and the curved-horned goat-antelope known as Barbary sheep (now rare). The rock engravings in Wadi Hamra are thought to predate those of Wadi Sora and Karkur Talh and depict wild animals including rhinoceros and giraffes, rendered in quite a crude style. It's amazing to think that this desert once was a savannah that supported such beasts. The massive **Wadi Abd al-Malik** runs north–south through the Northern Gilf, stretching almost its entire length. It is here that in 1938 the explorer Peel found a small grotto, in the eastern fork of the wadi, where both walls are painted with depictions of dark red and white cattle. Acacia grow here, and when the explorers first arrived they found the sites of Tebu grass huts and remains of baskets.

The Southern Gilf

On the eastern side of the Southern Gilf there are several more wadis, including **Wadi Dayyiq** where you can see the remnants of an ancient manufacturing plant where Neolithic people crafted tools from rocks, and the chiselled blades and arrows still lie scattered over a wide area. Also on this side of the Gilf is the narrow pass known as **Al-Aqaba**, the Difficult, from which you can ascend from the desert floor onto the plateau itself to cross the scarp, as did the adventurers of the 1930s. It is not easy today, so for them it must have really warranted the name. Though Almasy thought his friends from the Long Range Desert Group mined this pass during the war, it is used by travellers today without incident despite rumours that the Egyptian Army, in order to thwart the Libyan smugglers whose tracks criss-cross the desert, have mined it themselves. Along the northwest edge of the scarp, valley after valley can be seen from the top, with dazzling views of the Libyan plain below.

Deep into the Gilf, **Wadi al-Bakht** (Valley of Luck) is littered with the evidence of the ancient communities that lived here. First explored in 1938, this whole area, including the dune face, is littered with coloured pottery, bones, grinding stones and the bizarre shells of ostrich eggs. **Wadi Wasa**, the Wide Valley, is somewhere expeditions often camp for the night. The drama of the islands and mini-wadis that converge in the expansive valley makes it one of the most visually astounding sights in the whole region. Shaw's Cave, above Wadi Wasa, was discovered in 1936 and contains paintings of cattle and a homestead along the rear of the recess.

An absolute highlight of the Gilf Kebir is the **Foggini-Mestikawi Cave** about 40 km north of Wadi Sura, only discovered in 2002 and probably the most extraordinary rock art site in the Sahara. It's a short scrabble up the cliff to a recess covered with literally hundreds of rock paintings, all wonderfully preserved. As well as domestic cattle, these paintings portray the beasts of the savannah – lions, giraffes on the hoof and ostriches – mingling among human figures, with the yellow, orange, black and white hues still amazingly fresh.

Wadi Sura, named by Almasy who came here in 1933 (although Clayton saw it first, two years earlier, he is not credited with finding the rock art), means Picture Valley in Arabic. Though it is not strictly a wadi, being more of an offshoot of the main Gilf, it is certainly hyped for the pictures that lie in the shallow hollows of the cliffs, which include the most famous Cave of the Swimmers. Inside the cave are scores of figures, and no doubt there were once far more, plus pictures of dogs, cattle, giraffes and ostriches. The swimmers themselves are rather sylph-like compared to the chunky upright men, and some seem to be diving. They are intriguing not just for their simple beauty, but also because they imply that once this desiccated landscape contained a lake. It's said that early visitors (and possibly more recent ones) sprinkled the paintings with water to bring out their colour. This, in addition to their exposure to the elements, means some people are surprised by the poor condition of the paintings (as well as shocked at the fact they are not actually in a deep cave).

About 15 m south is the **Cave of the Archers**, where about 20 unclothed figures, painted dark red and white, carry bows and hunt skinny-legged cattle. The men have no hands or feet, and just splodges for heads, and are painted in a style coined 'balanced exaggeration' by Hans Winkler who was part of the 1938 Monod expedition. Their shoulders are broad and they have triangular torsos and tapering legs, while white bands adorn their bodies quite clearly against their umber skin.

The Great Desert Circuit listings

For Sleeping and Eating price codes and other relevant information, see pages 26-31.

Sleeping

Bahariyya Oasis and Bawati *p497, maps p497 and p499*
New camps and mid-range hotels are sprouting up more quickly than ever. Some are idyllic getaways on the edge of the desert – good bases for exploring the local area – and provide free pick-ups and drop-offs to town. Camp accommodation tends to be in wicker or concrete huts, rather than tents. All include breakfast and most offer half- and full-board options. Many camps have fires of an evening, or you can lounge in a Bedouin tent drinking endless miniature cups of tea. Tours into the desert and transport to nearby springs and sights can easily be organized from all hotels and camps.

L-AL International Hot Spring Hotel, on the outskirts east of Bawati, T02-3847 3014, www.whitedeserttours.com. This German/Japanese-managed spa has slightly institutional, absolutely spotless rooms with private bath, a/c and heaters (the chalets at the back are the best). Built around a hot spring, there's massage, sauna and a health centre on site. Half-board is part of the deal, call in advance if you just wish to come for lunch/dinner/ beer. If you don't have your own transport full-board may be the best bet, as the town is 3 km away. Prices decrease in the summer. Bedouin music accompanies dinner for groups of 50-plus and the restaurant has infra-red heaters for chilly winter mornings. There are easy walks to the English mountain behind for excellent views and Peter is a warm and welcoming host. See www.whitedeserttours.com for info on safaris, motorbike and self-drive desert adventures.

A Palm Valley, a few kilometres out of town in Agouz, T02-3849 6271. Spacious comfy rooms, some with a/c. Restaurant offers half- and full-board. A small palm garden adds to the appeal, and there is a great view of nearby Jebel Ingleezi.

A-C Old Oasis Hotel, near the Bishmu springs, T02-3847 3028.

www.oldoasissafari.com. A wide range of rooms: plush spacious ones upstairs enjoy views of the crumbling old town; older ones are shabbier but pristine and are next to the shady garden with pleasant seating areas among the rockeries. There's a spring-fed pool, which means it is popular with tour groups, especially in summer.

B Desert Rose Ecolodge, T02-3984 0861, www.desertrose-ecolodge.com. About 10 km north of Bawati in the peaceful neighbourhood of Bir Al-Matar, has delightful new chalets built using natural materials. Traditional stone floors and wooden windows, rush and palm trunk ceilings, 4-poster beds with nets, and clay lanterns to cast a welcoming glow. The restaurant uses organic produce from the garden and vegetarians are well catered for. If you show your *Footprint Handbook*, owner Mohamed Tahoun will give you a 15% discount.

B Western Desert Hotel, T012-301 2155, info@westerndeserthotel.com. Located just near **Bayoumi's Popular Restaurant** this brand-new hotel lacks character but is handily located for the museum and bus stop. Clean, fresh rooms have a/c and bathrooms.

B-D Nature Lodge, T012-165 3037, www.khaset-xp.com, www.sandslodges.com, about 15 km north of Bawati in Bir Al-Ghaba, near the Pyramid Mountain. Spotless simple huts, lit by candles, are attractively spaced about a flourishing garden of bougainvillea. Huts share a bath, but are much more pleasant than the 2 chalets with private bath. The chef is a master craftsman, using organic ingredients from the garden, and food is served Bedouin-style inside or on wicker tables and chairs outside. Bicycles are available and good walks to Jebel Dist, the surreal pyramid-shaped mountain you can see from camp. Owner Ashraf Lotfi is a charming man, providing genuine hospitality, He has created a peaceful retreat that people keep coming back to. Tailor-made tours throughout the Western Desert are recommended. There's no alcohol for sale, but you can chill any supplies in their fridge.

C-E Alpenblick Hotel, T02-3847 2184, T011-582 3356, alpenblick.hotel@yahoo.com. The 1st hotel in Bahariyya, an old favourite for backpackers although it's been spruced up and the more expensive rooms upstairs have a/c, TV and good bathrooms. Includes breakfast of large helpings of bread, use of the kitchen, and though the restaurant is soulless there are plans for a rooftop coffee shop. The courtyard has shady areas. Staff are friendly and the location is ideal for those arriving by bus and visiting the museum but it's not a place to linger.

C-E Eden Camp, 10 km south of Bawati, T02-3847 3727, T012-731 1876, www.edengardentours.com. A peaceful, litter-free camp in a small palm garden by a hot spring. The orange-brown mineral-rich water of the pool is the perfect place to relax under the stars. Cosy huts (watch your head on the doorframe) share excellent baths, 2 a/c rooms with private bath available, as well as space to sleep under the stars. Prices are half-board and a hot-water urn dispenses water for tea and coffee all day. A perfect place to stay if you're looking for some mellow lounging in the desert, or just come to enjoy dinner and beer by the fireside. There are good sunsets from the nearby jebel, and transport into town is free. Talaat has been taking safaris into the desert for many years.

C-E El-Beshmo Lodge, T02-3847 3500, www.elbeshmolodge.com. On the road to Bishmu this sparklingly clean hotel has 23 basic rooms set around a courtyard. There is a secluded (orange) pool. All but 5 rooms have private bath. Tasty meals are available for E£35.

D-E Ahmed Safari Camp, 5 km outside of town within walking distance to a hot spring and close to Alexander's temple, T02-3847 2770, www.ahmedsafari camp.com.
A popular and long-standing camp in the area, offers space to pitch a tent (E£20, breakfast included), and a variety of rooms (the newer ones are far superior, domed ceilings incorporate Stella bottles to cast a green glow). A 15-bed dorm is planned. There are a couple of split-level family rooms

which sleep up to 8, and generally the camp is good value for money. Free transport to Bawati, 2 bikes available. Food from the organic garden and a swimming pool in summer. Long- and short-range tours are available including a daily tour to the White Desert.

D-E New Oasis, T02-3847 3030, T012-123 3418. On the road to Bishmu, provides slightly shabby accommodation with a view over the surrounding palms. All rooms have private baths, some with a/c. Worth looking at a few to get the best value. New rooms and a pool are being built. There are free bikes available and oranges grow on the terrace. Friendly staff can help to arrange tours.

D-F Desert Safari Home, T02-3847 1321, www.desert-safari-home.com. Clean rooms with good bathrooms around a flowery courtyard, where you can get a beer. Insist on seeing the cheaper rooms, there are also dorm beds that they will be reluctant to tell you about. It's on the eastern edge of town, but walkable from the centre.

F Badr's Sahara Camp, T010-745 9591, 3 km north of Bawati, is a good budget choice, with huts in rows beside shady central seating areas. Spectacular views of the oasis and lush foliage add to the appeal. Concrete and reed huts are both simple but clean. Decent shared bathrooms, a Bedouin tent for communal dinners, free pickup from the bus station. Desert safaris are easily arranged.

Farafra Oasis *p502, map p503*

AL-A Aquasun, a quiet option 5 km from town, T012-211 8632. Stylish a/c rooms have satellite TV and surround a bougainvillea-filled garden of chirping birds. Next to Bir Sitta hot spring and with an indoor pool that is filled for guests. Rates are half board. Hitch a pickup to town for E£2 or hire a taxi, E£10-15.

A-C Al-Badawiya Hotel, T092-751 0060, T02-2526 0994, www.badawiya.com. Attractive domed architecture, plenty of comfy social areas to sit and relax (in and out), flowery shady courtyards and a clean pool have ensured it's the most popular choice in town. Older rooms are either large split-level doubles or twin beds on one level, with bath, a/c and TV. They also have newer, plusher suites, some of which have fireplaces and all of which have fabulous bathrooms that are total heaven after a night in the desert. A great selection of oasis handicrafts are for sale, breakfast costs extra.

C-E Sunrise Hotel, 1 km north of town, T012-720 0387, T010-708 1506, www.sunrise4safari.com. Very clean doubles mimic the style of **Al-Badawiya** but without the high-spec fixtures and fittings. However, the simple restaurant is attractive, vegetables are grown in the garden, and the staff are friendly and helpful.

E-F El-Waha Hotel, the only real budget option, 300 m north of town near the Badr museum, T012-720 0387, T010-708 1506. Run by the same people as the **Sunrise Hotel**. Clean rooms have private baths with hot water, some have balconies but with views over a school yard. Cheaper rooms share a mosquito-filled bathroom, or you can sleep on the roof for E£10.

Dakhla Oasis and Mut *p504, maps p504 and p507*

There's quite a range of accommodation in Dakhla, from the 5-star €300 a night **El-Tarfa** to the basic but delightful **Al-Qasr Resthouse**. Many hotels and camps rent bicycles and will gladly arrange a tour of the area for you or desert safaris further afield. 'Camps' in this area usually offer a place to pitch a tent, as well as simple bungalow accommodation. Most hotels are found in Mut, but Al-Qasr is an infinitely more appealing place to stay despite limited accommodation options.

LL Al-Tarfa Desert Sanctuary, situated half-way between Al-Qasr and Mut, T/F092-910 5007/8, www.altarfa.travel. A sumptuous, exclusive mud-brick lodge and spa complex billing itself as Egypt's 1st eco-luxury lodge, Al-Tarfa boasts panoramic views of the surrounding palms and cliffs. Some of the tastefully appointed suites have a private pool but for those less fortunate there is a stunningly clear blue pool with full bar and sunbathing deck. All of the 20 beautifully presented rooms have a/c. Gourmet meals are served in a variety of locations around the lodge. Rates are full board. Horses are available to explore the surrounding area. A range of massage treatments are offered in the spa along with a sauna, steam room, plunge pool and gym.

LL Shanda Lodge, www.shandalodge.com, 30 stylish, brand-new, mud-brick suites and 20 rooms each with their own balcony. Situated between Al-Qasr and Mut, to reach the lodge you drive up a track passing donkey carts and welcoming children. Has yet to develop any character but the location is wonderful.

LL-L Desert Lodge, on the hill behind Al-Qasr, T092-787 7062, T02-2690 5240, www.desertlodge.net. Built in the traditional style with tiny wooden windows, flat roofs and daub, the large attractive rooms have balconies either overlooking the town or onto the mountains. Only a few rooms have a/c. There's a relaxing warm spring, a spa, easy access to hill walks, and an inviting air of elegance throughout. Price includes half board; the food and service is of a high standard and dinner here is strongly recommended (call ahead). They have an art/calligraphy studio and organize walks to collect stones to grind to make paints from, just as in Pharaonic times.

L-AL Solymar Mut Inn, 3 km on the road north of Mut, by the hot spring Mut 3, T/F092-792 7982/3, T092-782 1530, www.solymar.com. Operated by the same management as **Pioneers** in Kharga, rooms are functional and have front terraces with fans either around the very orange pool, or in a separate 'villa'. Quality huts are available, but are expensive and rather near the road. The restaurant offers a pleasant ambiance and there's a bar with the widest selection in town. Tour groups stay here for the pool fed by the rich spring, however since it's open to non-guests for E£10 all day, use it and find another place to sleep. There's a 25% discount in the summer.

L-A Badawiya Dakhla, Bir Al-Gabel, Al-Qasr, T092-772 7451/2, www.badawiya.com. 2 km east of Al-Qasr, with domed chalets built in the traditional adobe style circling a mini-mountain. The 48 rooms and 2 suites are tastefully fitted out to a high standard, with awesome views from their terraces over the fields to the dunes and mountains. The pool is divine, and the staff considerate and kind. Managed by the long-established **Badawiya Expedition Travel** in Farafra, safaris from here are slickly organized.

C-E Bedouin Camp, near El-Douhous about 7 km before Mut, T092-785 0480. Clean concrete rooms with bath, on a hill-top overlooking the valley. One of very few places run by local Bedouin, it's a good place to come for peaceful days and evening campfires, and to arrange good-value, well-run camel safaris. Breakfast is included and the new restaurant is attractive, even if the rooms are not especially so.

D El-Negoom, Mut, T092-782 0014. All rooms are clean and bright, with balconies. Configurations and amenities vary widely, so view a selection. Rooms overlooking the lush garden of fruit trees are a good option. Rooms available with a/c and private bath or without. There's a new pool. Breakfast is included, the restaurant also serves a lunch buffet and dinner (E£40). 15% discount in summer. Staff are friendly and kind.

D Mebarez Hotel, Sharia El-Tharwa, Mut, T/F092-782 1524. Clean, carpeted double rooms with fridge, some with TV. Breakfast included. Management is friendly but the atmosphere a bit drab. The lobby is blissfully cool. Popular with package tours. In the summer, there's a small pool available, 25% discount in summer. Sparkling restaurant serves a good dinner (E£40, phone ahead if you're not a guest).

D-E El-Forsan Hotel, near Midan Gama'a, Mut, T092-782 1343. Management very straightforward and helpful, rooms are clean and spacious with a range of options. There are also a few chalet-style rooms out the back, which are popular. Dinner costs E£30 and is more varied than most. Single women might feel uncomfortable, especially if using the shared bathroom. A good location if getting a service taxi in the morning.

D-F Bir El-Gabel Camp, the turn off is 2 km east of Al Qasr but make sure you get driven up the long driveway, T092-772 6600, T012-106 8227. Simple rooms with nets, towels, clean linen and breakfast come with or without private bath. Camping in the garden is E£50 per tent and a good dinner costs E£30. A small, deep spring-fed pool is behind the hotel and they can arrange hot sand baths nearby. The setting on the edge of both farmland and desert, with views of the nearby ridge, is glorious.

F Al-Qasr Resthouse, on the main road in the centre of Al-Qasr, T092-772 6013. Friendly Mohammed offers 4 very simple but reliable rooms, with portable fans, with clean shared bath for E£10/15 per person, without/with breakfast; camping on the roof is also possible (mattress provided, E£4). Guests generally stay longer than they expected, the atmosphere is so warm and the town so appealing. The resthouse has a telephone and tasty meals are served on the roof, plus there's ice cream and beer. It's a good place to go if you want any information on transport in the area, or to hire a bicycle (E£5).

F Anwar Hotel, in the centre of Mut between the old and new parts of town, T092-782 0070. Desert_lover40@yahoo.com Rooms are comfortable, all with fans and some with a/c. Only 1 has a private bath and shared baths are grubby. Breakfast included and restaurant downstairs has all the regular dishes and a *felafel* stand. Beer available, bicycles E£15 per day. They offer tours on motorbikes as well as the usual jeep or camel excursions. Single women may get unwanted attention from staff.

F Garden Hotel, in the centre of town, T092-782 1577. Decent but basic rooms have fans and clean sheets, and there are good views from the roof. A bit shabbier than other budget options, but the cheapest central hotel. Dorms can get stuffy and shared bathrooms are a bit grubby. The manager, Mohamed Ali, goes out of his way to please. You can get bikes and beer here, both E£10 each. There's a washing machine available for use for E£5.

Camping

Apart from camps listed above that have space for tents, **F Khamis Camp**, is 2 km south of Mut, T092-782 1577, run by the Garden Hotel. You can pitch a tent E£5 per night, or rent a hut for E£15. It's a quiet and remote site, surrounded by sand dunes with a nearby hot spring, but very badly maintained. The unreliable restaurant will necessitate a frequent hike to town for food.

Kharga Oasis *p509, map p511*

L Pioneers, on road out to Assiut, T/F092-792 9751/2/3, www.solymar.com. Clean, comfortable and everything works, even the satellite TV, rooms are laid out like any Western hotel. There's a well-maintained, mid-sized swimming pool open to non-guests for E£80, a view of verdant palm groves at the back and from the roof you can see the Temple of Nadoura. There's also a well-stocked bar (beer E£35 including taxes) and a good, albeit soulless, restaurant. Prices are half board.

B-C El-Kharga Hotel, Sharia Gamal Abdel Nasser,T092-792 4940, kharga.hotel@gmail.com. Built in 1960 (the main building is very much of its time), rooms in the main block are spotless, large, with nice balconies. Newer rooms, vaguely in the oasis tradition are in the palm garden at the rear. The restaurant is unspectacular, but reasonably priced and they have beer, call ahead if not a guest at the hotel.

D Dar Al-Bayda, Midan Showla, T092-929 9393. Most rooms have fans, TV and bathroom, but it's overpriced for what it offers and public areas are dirty. Only worth staying here if you are getting an early service taxi in the morning.

D-E Hamad Allah Hotel, off Sharia Abdel Moneim Riad, T092-792 0538. Shabby, but spacious, carpeted rooms have fridge, TV and blank balconies. A/c works, essential if you're in Kharga in summertime. Decent restaurant with set menu prices, as well as a bar and garden. Solo female travellers may feel uncomfortable here.

E El-Radwan, off Sharia Gamal Abdel Nasser, behind the museum, T092-792 1716. A very good choice at the lower end of the spectrum, clean rooms have fridge, a/c, satellite TV and inoffensive bathrooms. Some have balconies. Fresh lilac paint pervades throughout and staff are pleasant. A bit far away from any restaurants. Rooms overlooking the social club opposite can be very noisy if there is a function going on.

F-G Waha, Sharia El-Nabawi, T092-792 0393. The cheapest choice in town and a favourite overnight spot for drivers and budget travellers, Waha is cramped but comfortable enough. Rooms have fans and sheets are clean. Some have balconies. The shared bathrooms are very grubby and the hot water supply is erratic. Staff are friendly and helpful, don't be put off by the dark and sinister lobby.

Camping

Ayoun El-Wadi, near Bulaq village, 25 km south. A pleasant camping spot, with use of facilities, for E£20 per night.

El-Kharga Hotel, see above. Use of hotel facilities is permitted, E£25 per night.

Eating

Bahariyya Oasis and Bawati *p497, maps p497 and p499*

Most hotels and camps serve up a decent breakfast (included in the price of an overnight stay) and can provide full or half board. It's worth eating at your chosen camp as in town there are only a few small shops and cheap places to eat.

Bayoumi's Popular Restaurant. Truly the most popular gathering spot in town with tasty simple meals (though no menu) for E£20-25 (negotiate the price of everything – even drinks – first), decent bathrooms, and an owner who is full of information. It's also about the only option in town where you can publicly indulge in a beer.

Cleopatra. 0600-2400. Decent salads, chicken and stewed veg dishes for E£2-12 and is a safe bet.

Rasheed Restaurant, on the main street near the Oasis Heritage Museum. Good for sweets, *sheesha* and reliable basic meals.

Farafra Oasis *p502, map p503*

Except for the snazzier restaurants in **Al-Badawiya**, **Aquasun** and **Sunrise** hotels (all of which you should call in advance), there are local eateries in the town centre.

Hussein's Restaurant serves *fuul*, grilled chicken, omelette or tinned tuna with chips or bread and Coca Cola or tea, E£15-25.

Samir's, follow the smoke to find it. Serves the standard *fuul* and *taamiyya* as well as grilled chicken and kebab with salad and bread. Meals are E£10-15 (depending whether or not you eat meat) inside there are sit-down tables or Bedouin seating under the whirl of the fans.

Ahwas and cafés

For *sheesha*, tea and coffee, there are a couple of options, a bustling *ahwa* by the 'bus stop' that is popular among *Saidi* immigrants and a quieter more local *ahwa* near the Badr museum. There is a small bakery and a few stores that sell all the basics, including a couple of pharmacies.

Dakhla Oasis and Mut *p504, maps p504 and p507*

Most restaurants offer the exact same food and few have menus. Lunch or dinner in Dakhla usually consists of salad, soup, rice, and some kind of vegetable and meat, the cost for a meal ranges from E£15-35. Bear in mind that most places are shut by 2200. It's worth establishing the price of the meal before you eat it.

On Sharia Es-Sawra El-Khadra is a row of 3 restaurants owned by 3 brothers: **Ahmed Hamdy's**, is definitely the best and most popular with tourists and locals alike. In addition to the regular dishes, they serve up delicious fresh juice. Nearby, find **Abu Mohammed**, which is overpriced and not very good, but he serves beer. In between the 2 is **Arabi's**, a better choice and he also has beer. **Shehab**, close to Midan Tahrir, is thronged with locals enjoying the meat-oriented menu.

Felafel is available in front of Anwar's, and there are a couple of *fuul* stalls on Midan El-Gama'a. Fruit can be found at the market in Midan Tahrir.

Kharga Oasis *p509, map p511*
Besides the hotels and the few local cafés the choice is limited. The area around Midan Basateen has the most local eating options. For fruit or *felafel* and *fuul*, try the *souk* near Midan Showla.

Pioneers, see Sleeping. Offers an extensive evening buffet for E£80.

Wemby Elbsateen, on Midan Basateen, T092-793 7105. Recently had a refurb and raised the prices, to locals' horror, but it serves standard meats, chicken, good soup, and some tasty bean dishes in clean surroundings.

Good ice cream from the parlour beneath Al-Waha Hotel, near Midan Basateen.

Bars and clubs

Bahariyya Oasis and Bawati *p497, maps p497 and p499*
Bedouin Music and Teahouse, in Agouz, T02-3847 2431. Abd El-Sadik Badromani recites poetry and plays delightful traditional music on his *simsimaya*, a classic Bedouin string instrument. He started inviting people into his home years ago but with increased traffic, he has since created a large Bedouin-style area just outside his house to host visitors. If you want to go, ask anyone for Badromani, it's a 2-km walk from Bawati and every taxi driver knows his place. Starting times are 2000 (winter) or 2100 (summer). He also serves tea, coffee, and beer.

Otherwise in Bahariyya, drinking is confined to a couple of the hotels and camps, or **Popular Restaurant**.

Dakhla Oasis and Mut *p504, maps p504 and p507*
For beer, try **Meberez**, the **Solymar Inn** or **Abu Mohamed**. There is also a store that sells Stella near the Anwar Hotel. In Al-Qasr ask at the **Al-Qasr Resthouse**.

Kharga Oasis *p509, map p511*
The **Pioneer** has a well-stocked bar, or try the **Hamad Allah Hotel**.

Shopping

Bahariyya Oasis and Bawati *p497, maps p497 and p499*
There is not much in the way of quality shopping in Bahariyya, but the **Girls Handicraft Workshop** just off the road to Farafra, T02-3847 1485, open1000-1300, is a Japanese venture working with local women to produce traditional designs embroidered on bags, *galabiyyas*, coasters, etc.

Also on the road to Farafra, between Bayoumi's Popular restaurant and the Hilal café is the **NGO Desert Lovers** shop, offering a range of traditional textiles and hand-crafted souvenirs.

There are also several handicrafts stalls around the hub of **Popular Restaurant**, selling camel-hair blankets, a few pieces of jewellery and *galabiyyas* embroidered with Bedouin designs.

Farafra Oasis *p502, map p503*
Shopping in Farafra has been revolutionized by the **Al-Hayah** workshop behind Al-Badawiya Hotel, www.al-hayah.org, open 0800-1330, which employs around 30 local women and has revived traditional crafts in the town. Al-Hayah also trains local men up

as desert guides and aims to preserve the area's natural attractions. It's interesting to visit the pretty building and see the women at work, and prices are extremely reasonable. Basketware woven from coils of palm leaves go for E£10-30, Bedouin rugs in rich reds E£90-500 (some take up to a month on the hand-looms) and camel hair ones between E£100-120; black *galabiyyas* with colourful designs are E£100-150 and there are many mittens and woollens, of course, for E£20-40.

It's also worth checking out the famous **Dr Socks** who has made quite a lucrative business cycling around town selling camel socks and other goods. He can be found at Badr's Museum and Al-Badawiya Hotel (where there is also a handicrafts shop). **Farafra Handicrafts Bazaar** can be found opposite Badr's Museum.

Dakhla Oasis and Mut *p504, maps p504 and p507*

There are a number of handicraft shops selling local basketware and jewellery near the entrance to Al-Qasr's ancient Islamic settlement.

Activities and tours

Many safaris now seem to transport all the comforts of a hotel into the desert, with chairs, tables, chefs and campbeds. It's preferable to seek out companies that use local guides, not only for their skills and knowledge of the area (and so you can experience true Bedouin cooking and hospitality), but also to provide employment to the people of the oases. If you are happy with your guide, it's common courtesy to tip, reckon on around E£30 per day.

Bahariyya Oasis and Bawati *p497, maps p497 and p499*

In Bahariyya there are over 100 people working as guides of the Western Desert, so standards are pretty variable. The recently established NGO **Desert Lovers** is aiming to provide proper training regarding environmental awareness, geology and first aid to guides and drivers. Licences will be issued to those who have completed the course. The NGO will also be running 2 free clean-up trips per year into the desert – contact Ashraf Lotfi at **Nature Lodge**, T012-165 3037, for further information.

Every hotel and camp can organize safaris, ranging from an afternoon trip to multi-week adventures. Most common are jeep tours, though increasingly more opt to explore by camel or on foot. The most popular safari takes 2-3 days and includes the **Black Desert**, **Crystal Mountain**, and the **White Desert**. Depending on the quality you are seeking, prices vary significantly. For a jeep filled with 6, expect to pay about US$35-40 or E£170-200 per person per day. For intrepid expeditions, such as to the **Gilf Kebir**, don't make saving money the deciding factor: your personal safety in the hands of a reliable outfit should be more of a priority. In addition to safaris organized through the hotels, the tourist office can arrange desert trips for reasonable prices. There are also a few particularly reputable freelance tour guides:

Hamuda Kilani, T012-756 5643. One of the foremost guides in the area, incredibly knowledgeable about the Western Desert, speaks good English and French. Great sense of humour and takes care of his clients. Specializes in walking trips.

Lotfi Abd-el-Sayad, T02-3847 3500, www.beshmolodge.com. A kind character and a safe, experienced desert driver and tour guide, a classic on the safari scene.

Yahia Kandil, T012-321 6790, www.desertshipsafari.com. Has been organizing 1- to 3-week trips for over 20 years.

Farafra Oasis *p502, map p503*

Tours and excursions into the surrounding desert are organized by all local hotels. (**El-Waha** offers the cheapest deals, although the quality is questionable.)

Badawiya Expedition Travel, T02-2526 0994, www.badawiya.com, has been around the longest and is managed by the 3 local Bedouin brothers. They can organize pretty much any trip, ranging from 1 to 40 nights by jeep or camel, and serve quality dinners cooked on a campfire every night. They also run 3 trips every year to clean up the White Desert for 5 days, which are hugely popular. They have 2 Cairo offices: 22 Sharia Talaat Harb, Downtown, T02-2575 8076 and 42 Road 104, Maadi Cairo, T02-2526 0994.
Khaset Expeditions, Farafra, www.khaset-xp.com, are an Egyptian-French partnership who also run recommended trips to the Gilf Kebir.

Dakhla Oasis and Mut *p504, maps p504 and p507*

Dakhla might not boast a great sand sea or a white desert, but the rolling dunes and mountainous backdrops are all the more magnificent when there are no other campfires in sight. **Al-Qasr Resthouse** will help organize trips by camel for E£130-170 per person per night, for up to 5 nights, or a jeep for E£400 per day. Omar Ahmad, T012-1796467, who manages the tourist office in Mut, arranges overnight safaris by jeep or camel for £150-200 per person and also 4- to 5-hr tours around Dakhla, taking in Al-Qasr, Al-Gedida, Qalamun and some dunes, for E£75-100 per person (depending on the size of group). **Badawiya Expedition Travel** (see above) can arrange longer adventure tours into the surrounding desert.

For something a bit different, Arabi Helmy of **Arabi's Restaurant** in Mut, T092-782 1180, T010-9001968, can arrange for a healing oil and mud massage followed by immersion into a hot sand bath (€50 with overnight camping and dinner in the desert, €30 for healing alone). Meditation retreats are available through **Hathor Chalet**, adjacent to **Bir El-Gabel Camp**, 4 km east of Al-Qasr, T0049-(0)9123 6533. The loneliness of the desert plains 10 km north of Mut are an ideal location for restoring the soul and finding perfect solitude, while the charming chalet provides accommodation and use of a kitchen. Large groups can stay at the nearby **Bir El-Gabel Camp**, where meals are also provided.

Kharga Oasis *p509, map p511*

To organize a desert trip, contact Mohsen Abd Al-Moneam on T010-180 6127, or at the ETA office on Sharia Gamel Abdel Nasser. He can help organize short safaris of 1 or 2 nights in the sand dunes around the Kharga oasis.

Transport

Bahariyya Oasis and Bawati *p497, maps p497 and p499*

Bus

Buses from Bawati to **Cairo** leave daily at 0630, 1000 and 1500, it's recommended to book a day in advance (4-5 hrs, E£25). Cairo-bound buses coming through from **Farafra** leave Bawati around 1200 and 2400 daily. You can't reserve tickets but if there's space, you can hop on. Buses leave for **Farafra** (3 hrs) and on to **Dakhla** (6 hrs) at 1200 and 2330. The ticket kiosk (T02-3847 3610, 0600-1500 and 2030-2330) where buses arrive and depart, is next to the tourist office and only sells tickets for journeys originating in Bawati. Otherwise pay on the bus if you can get a seat.

Taxi

From outside the Hilal coffee shop, several service taxis and microbuses leave for **Cairo** daily as soon as they're full (E£25), but not after midnight; microbuses delivering workers to **Farafra** sometimes pass through and will pick people up if there's room. The cost of a private service to Farafra is around E£200-225. See page 494 for information on travelling to Siwa via the Darb El-Siwa road.

Farafra Oasis *p502, map p503*

Bus

Buses and service taxis congregate around the Tamawy *ahwa*. 2 daily a/c buses to **Cairo** (8-10 hrs, E£45) via **Bahariyya** (2-3 hrs, E£20) are supposed to leave at 1000 and 2200. Tickets must be purchased on board. The night bus originates in Dakhla and is often full so arrive early. There are 2 daily buses to **Dakhla** (4-5 hrs, E£25) that leave daily around 1400 and 0200. Buses also pick up from Al-Badawiya Hotel, by arrangement with the staff who will flag them down for you. Check the latest timetables at any hotel or *ahwa*, especially as times vary between summer and winter. Microbuses to **Dakhla** and **Bahariyya** leave when full, generally quite early in the morning, fare E£17. Rarely to **Cairo**.

Dakhla Oasis and Mut *p504, maps p504 and p507*

Air

Dakhla has an airport, but services have been suspended due to a lack of demand. This doesn't look like it will change soon, but check with the tourist office to find out the latest information.

Bus

El Herz on Sharia Tamir north of Midan Tahrir, Mut, T092-782 4915, 0700-2200, have 1 service per day to **Cairo** at 1900 (E£44, 10-11 hrs) via **Kharga** (E£15, 2 hrs). **Upper Delta** have 2 ticket offices open 0600-2200 (buses pick up from both) one on Midan Tahrir, T092-782 4921 and another downtown on Midan El-Gama'a, T092-782 4366. They run 2 buses daily from Mut to **Cairo** (E£70, 11-12 hrs) via **Kharga** (E£15, 2-3 hrs), bypassing Assiut, at 1900 and 2000; and 2 buses to **Cairo** (E£75, 12-13 hrs) via **Farafra** (E£25, 3-4 hrs) and **Bahariyya** (7-8 hrs, E£50), daily at 0600 and 1700 (1800 in summer), taking 12-13 hrs. Buy a ticket at least the day before to ensure a seat. All Cairo-bound buses should have a/c. There are additional daily buses that stop in **Kharga** and only go as far as **Assiut** (E£30, 6 hrs) at 0600 and 2200. Many of these prices are tourist prices and are about E£10 more than a local would pay, there is very little you can do about it. Presently, there are no direct buses to **Luxor**. You can either take a bus to Assiut and change there or hire a microbus or car.

Taxi

Local Service taxis, usually in the form of shared covered pickup trucks, connect Midan Tahrir to **Al-Qasr** (E£1.25). Services for **Balat** and **Bashendi** leave from the depot near the hospital. It's easiest to find a ride in the early morning and services are few and far between on Fri and Sat.

Long distance There are also service taxis from Midan Gama'a to the above destinations for about the same cost as the buses. They are a bit less comfortable, but can be a good option if the buses are full or if you want to leave at an unscheduled time. Easiest to find them in the morning and early evening, they can take a while to fill up. To hire a car/ minibus direct to **Luxor** costs around E£700-800 and takes 5 hrs on the new road.

Kharga Oasis *p509, map p511*

Air

There is 1 direct flight to/from **Cairo** every week on Sun leaving Cairo at 0800 and returning from Kharga at 1500; and a flight on Wed via **Assiut**. Flight time is 50 mins and costs around US$150 each way. The airport, T092-792 0457, is 5 km northeast of town. The flights are operated by the Ministry for Petroleum, T092-792 1611, T012-007 3125.

Bus

Buses leave from Sharia Al-Mahatta, south of the town centre off Sharia Gamal Abdel Nasser. **El Herz**, T092-792 1435, have 2 buses daily to **Cairo** at 1600 and 2230 (E£50, 8-10 hrs, book a seat in advance) and 1 to **Dakhla** coming from Cairo at 1900 (E£10, 3-4 hrs). **Upper Delta**, T092-793 4587, go to **Cairo**,2 each day departing at 2200 and 2300 (E£41, though you will probably be charged tourist rates of E£51). They also have 3 buses daily to **Dakhla**, 1400, 2300, 0400 (3-4 hrs, E£10) with a/c, coming from **Cairo**. To go to **Luxor** or if you miss the direct bus to Cairo, your best bet is to travel via **Assiut**, 4 daily buses at 0700, 0900, 1100 and 1300, 4-5 hrs, E£10) and catch a train or bus from there. Or hire a private car.

Taxi

Service taxis and microbuses from Midan Showla are about the same cost as the bus and sometimes quicker, though they don't leave until they're full. Easiest to find rides out of town in the morning (0600-1000) and evening (1700-2200) when it's cooler. Most popular destinations include **Assiut** (2 hrs, E£10) and **Dakhla** (2 hrs, E£10) Minibuses south to **Baris** (1 hr, E£5) are caught from a side street near the new bus station. You can also hitch a ride to nearby sights if a service taxi is en route. Covered pickups and microbuses shuffle people from one side of town to the other for 25 pt. Private taxis around town are E£2-3. A private taxi to Luxor along the new road not yet used by public transport costs E£250-350, depending on your bargaining skills and the season.

Train

The weekly **Luxor** train has not run for a year or more due to sand encroaching on the track. Check with the tourist office to see if the situation has been rectified.

Directory

Bahariyya Oasis and Bawati *p497, maps p497 and p499*

Banks National Bank, changes cash but doesn't deal with credit cards or traveller's cheques, no ATM, Sun-Thu, 0800-1500, T02-3847 2200. **Internet** MN Net, on main rd left of Popular Restaurant, E£10 per hr. **Medical services** There are many doctors, if you need one, ask at the Popular Restaurant or any hotel. There's a small hospital on the road to Cairo, T02-3847 2390. There's a pharmacy near Popular Restaurant, open daily from 0800-0100. **Telephone** For international calls, you're best off trying the International Hotsprings Hotel.

Farafra Oasis *p502, map p503*

Banks No bank, though you may find some local folks who will buy dollars. **Medical services** Hospital, T092-751 0047, 1.5 km out of town toward Bahariyya.

Dakhla Oasis and Mut *p504, maps p504 and p507*

Banks Misr Bank, near Midan Tahrir, open Sun-Thu 0830-1400 and 1800-2100, has ATM. **Internet** Available at the Forsan Hotel, E£10 per hr, and at Midonet, near Gardens Hotel, E£4 per hr. **Medical services** General Hospital, T092-782 1555. **Telephone** Telecom, open 24 hrs, on Sharia 10th Ramadan. International calls can also be made from the tourist office.

Kharga Oasis *p509, map p511*

Banks Bank du Caire has ATM, open Sun-Thu 0800-1400. The Solymar Hotel also has ATM. **Internet** Networking & Internet on Midan el-Saha, open 1000-0200, E£2 per hr. **Medical services** General Hospital, T092-921500. **Post office** Sharia El-Nada and another south of Midan Showla, Sat-Thu, 0800-2100.

Siwa Oasis

➔ *Colour map 1, A2. Population: 27,000.*

In the northeastern corner of the Western Desert sprouts the Siwa Oasis, a place like no other. Less than 60 km from the Libyan border, isolated for centuries by hundreds of kilometres of rolling sand dunes, Siwa was inaccessible by car until an asphalt road was built in the early 1980s connecting it to Marsa Matruh. The 300-km road winds through desert oblivion and suddenly gives way to a striking shroud of green. About 82 km long east–west and 20 km north–south at its widest point, the oasis, 18 m below sea level, shelters 30,000 date palms, 70,000 olive trees and hundreds of bubbling springs. Despite its seclusion, Siwa has long drawn in visitors from afar, captivated by its singular culture and beauty. In the early 20th century, the oasis lured one or two tourists a month. Now, some 8000-10,000 tourists visit every year.

South from Siwa the Sudanese border lies across 700 km of desert. Of this, 400 km is The Great Sand Sea, which, like a frozen storm with waves 100 m high, casts rolling dunes in every direction. Legend tells of a lost oasis and true adventurers still come in search. Perhaps the descendants of Cambyses live on ... (see box, page 531). ▸▸ *For listings, see pages 535-539.*

Ins and outs

Getting there It is possible to approach Siwa from Bahariyya but a reliable 4WD vehicle is essential. The trip takes between six to eight hours, depending on stops, and the cost for the car is E£1400. Enquire at the tourist office at either end of the route if you want to make the 420-km journey. There is a daily bus direct from Cairo, leaving at 1945 from Turgoman station, nine hours, otherwise you will have to change in Alexandria. ▸▸ *See Transport, page 538.*

Getting around You can easily cycle, or hire a *karetta*. A couple of places rent motorbikes, though the sandy roads necessitate a bit of experience and a great deal of concentration. Safaris to the outlying villages and springs require a jeep, and trips are easily arranged through most hotels, restaurants and shops.

Information **Tourist office** ⓘ *at the entrance of town, west of the new mosque, T046-460 1338, official hours are 0900-1400, 1600-2000.* Mahdi Hweiti, an articulate and knowledgeable Siwi native, has a wealth of information about the oasis and can arrange tours to nearby sites and help anyone who wants to make a more epic desert venture. Documentaries on the region in several languages are available. Even if you stop by after hours, Mahdi is often hanging out around his office, or can be contacted on his mobile, T010-546 1992.

The **Tourist Police** ⓘ *T046-460 2047*, now have a department in the police station, open 24 hours.

Note With its customs unchanged for centuries, untarnished by the world around, a heightened sensitivity is called for when visiting Siwa. You will quickly see how modestly many Siwan women dress, covered from head to toe in a shawl with black fabric covering their faces – and women visitors are requested to keep legs and upper arms covered. Women travellers should further be aware that walking alone is still regarded as odd behaviour by oasis dwellers, as only a small percentage of married Siwan women even venture out the home and then only to visit family and friends. Also bear in mind that it is unacceptable to take photographs of Siwan women. Alcohol and affection are forbidden in public.

Background

Siwans, currently numbering 27,000, have always been fiercely independent; the oasis only officially became part of Egypt in the 19th century. It has been inhabited, with reliance on the 200 and more fresh, salt, warm and cold springs, since Palaeolithic times. The economy is based on agriculture, dates (the Sa'idi date is preferred for eating) and olives, the date palms bearing fruit in 10 years and the olives in five. Water supply is from natural springs; no pumping is necessary but the springs are capped to provide some control as, ironically, surplus water is a serious problem. Quarrying, transport, trade (and smuggling) are also important and there is an increasing revenue from tourism but labour costs are high as labourers have to be brought in and need food and accommodation.

The people of Siwa are extraordinary, retaining customs and traditions from centuries past, as well as their own language, Siwi, a Berber dialect with Algerian roots. The old script can still be seen embroidered down the centre of ceremonial scarves and clothes, but the ability to decipher it has been lost and the symbols are now used merely as decoration. Traditional Siwan music and singing is haunting and beautiful, incorporating the *muzmar*, two bamboo pipes that produce five notes by blowing through two mobile reeds and the *shababa*, an iron pipe, 70 cm long with six holes akin to a recorder.

The Oscar-winning film *The English Patient* drew attention to this area. With increased tourism, the building of an Olympic Pool and stadium that seats 20,000 and the upsurge of luxury hotels, there are plans afoot to open the adjacent military airport that guards the nearby Libyan border to commercial traffic. This could increase the visitors, currently about 150 a week, to vast numbers to be accommodated in planned luxury tourist villages and almost certainly damage the very essence of this remote area. Locals dread the day. Visit before it's too late.

Sights

Siwa deserves some time – to appreciate the oasis in all its splendour, moving slowly is essential. There are hot and cold springs to swim in, ancient tombs housing beautiful paintings, and the temple of the Oracle that has attracted pilgrims for centuries

Siwa Oasis

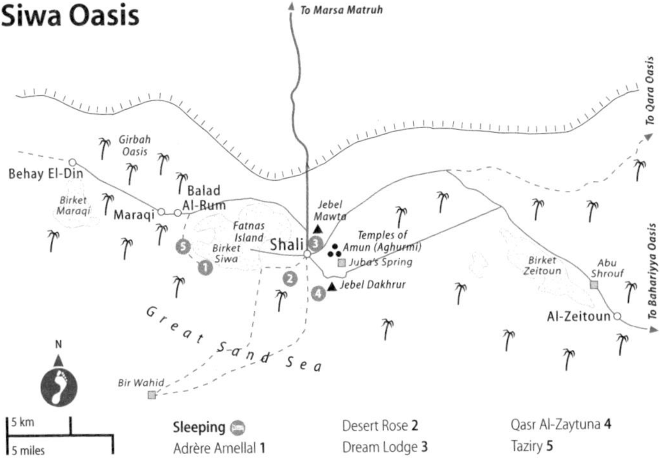

Sleeping
Adrère Amellal **1**
Desert Rose **2**
Dream Lodge **3**
Qasr Al-Zaytuna **4**
Taziry **5**

(Alexander the Great, among them). Much of the pleasure lies in simply wandering around the sultry town or biking through dusty palm groves and no visit would be complete without at least one night in the desert, underneath far too many stars to count and blanketed by the silence of the Great Sand Sea. The Siwans' low-key nature is a further refreshing respite from the hustlers of other heavily trafficked destinations.

The main settlement was medieval **Shali**, straddling two low hills within the depression, but now abandoned. The ruins of the old town established in 1203 are still impressive and the minaret of the 17th-century mosque (which is in use) remains. In parts, the walls and alleyways are being reconstructed and despite the ravages of time and rain many buildings are still surprisingly high, but generally a wander through Shali is like traversing a giant sandcastle. The mud-brick walls and towers are floodlit at night, a splendid sight. Stretching away from the base of the old city, new stone dwellings, mainly single storey, have been constructed. They are certainly not so attractive but probably much more comfortable. Until recently, Siwans painted their houses in celebration of portentous events such as weddings, and a pale blue tint saturated the town. Now, the ornamental daubs and patterns around doors and windows have faded away as all new buildings are required by regional government to be a traditional mud-brick colour to merge in with the desert surrounds. The new mosque of Fuad I, a solidly built structure of stone in the pleasant style of the late 19th-early 20th century, is the natural centre of the new town. Adjacent to it is the tomb of Sidi Soliman, a local saint, where you might be lucky enough to witness a Sufi *zikr* on Thursday nights, although this practice is beginning to die out. There is one traditional **olive press** remaining in Siwa, on the eastern edge of Shali, driven by donkey power and in operation only at the end of the olive season around December/January. Arrangements to visit can be made at the tourist office.

The **House of Siwa Museum** ⓘ *Sun-Thu 0900-1500, admission E£5*, showcases artefacts, clothing and decorations used until very recently in the houses of the oasis. The building was made using traditional techniques and materials.

Around Siwa

Birket Siwa salt lake and **Fatnas Island**, 5 km southwest of town, is a popular mini-excursion from Siwa. The walk is pleasant, but a little too long if it's hot. A bike ride is better, or you can hire a *karetta* (donkey cart) for around E£15-20 to take you, wait an hour, and bring you back. If you are planning to visit to watch the sunset it is not recommended to walk back alone, as the darkness that descends is absolute.

Unfortunately, a government irrigation effort in the middle of the lake has resulted in a significant receding of water and the death of the famed leaning palm. Fatnas (or Fantasy Island as its known in tourist lingo) has managed to retain much of its beauty, however, and is always a good spot for a picnic. There is a cold spring-fed pool, perfect for swimming in (women should wear opaque T-shirt and shorts), and a small coffee shop that offers *sheesha* and soft drinks. The sunsets overlooking White Mountain and the surrounding *mesas* are spectacular. Camping is possible, inquire with Omran, the kind man who runs the café. Take precautions against the many mosquitoes.

The temples, spring and mountain described below can be linked into an easy half-day circular bike ride, plus the few hotels and attractive camps exploiting the peace and isolation around the edge of Jebel Dakrur provide an opportunity to stop for lunch. An alternative idea is to rent a *karetta* (donkey cart) for the day. The boys who drive them may even take you to visit their home. There are two temples dedicated to Amun near the deserted village of Aghurmi 3 km east of Shali. The **Temple of the Oracle** ⓘ *0900-1700,*

The Oracle of Amun

It was The Oracle of Amun that brought Siwa to the attention of the world, from the 26th Dynasty (664-525 BC) onward. Alexander the Great is known to have consulted the Oracle in 331 BC after wresting control of the country from its Persian rulers in order to ask it if, as he suspected, he was indeed the son of Zeus. His arrival with a large party of friends and an even larger number of soldiers must have caused quite a stir in sleepy Siwa. Unfortunately, posterity does not record the Oracle's response. Nearly 200 years earlier, Egypt's Persian ruler Cambyses (525-522 BC) is said to have carelessly lost an army of 50,000 men who were dispatched from Aïn Dalla near the Farafra Oasis to Siwa in order to destroy the Oracle. The army was simply never seen again having been either buried by a sandstorm or snatched by aliens.

E£25, students E£15 (see box, above) is built on a large rock amid the remains of the village. It dates back to the 26th Dynasty and, though crudely restored by German archaeologists, rambling around the ruins in the footsteps of Alexander cannot fail to leave an impact. There are spectacular views of the nearby Temple of Umm 'Ubayda, Jebel Mawta and across the palm groves to the shimmering salt lakes. The site of the second temple, **Umm 'Ubayda** from the 30th Dynasty is marked by an area of fallen blocks in which one wall – all that survived the 1877 earthquake – is left standing, carefully inscribed and with blue and green hues still visible.

Juba's Spring (also called Cleopatra's Pool although it has nothing at all to do with the lady) was mentioned by Herodotus. It is supposed to change temperature during the day but in reality the change is due to the relative difference between air temperature and the temperature of the person dipping in. Women are advised to swim in a long T-shirt and shorts, though the constant presence of a policeman keeps the area hassle-free. You're likely to find the pool empty most of the day, though Fridays are more crowded. The cute adjacent café makes it a good rest point on a bike ride, even if you don't fancy getting in the rather algae-infested water.

Wedding Spring is used by Siwan's as part of their wedding ceremony. A beautiful, clear blue spring with bubbles swirling up from the depths it can be a welcome place to break a bike ride. It is about 1 km along the road to Aghurmi on the left.

Jebel Dakhrur, the 'mountain' that sprouts up in three mounds about 4 km southeast of town, is the site of Siwa's annual **Siayha festival** in October (see Festivals and events, page 537). The summit awards stunning views of the oasis all around and is worth climbing. The salt lake shimmers amid a blanket of palms, with the Great Sand Sea abruptly encroaching on the edge. In July and August around midday when it's hot enough to cook a chicken outside, sufferers come from afar to be buried in the **hot sands** (sand bath: *hammam ramal*) around Jebel Dakhrur with the hopes of alleviating their arthritis, rheumatism and even impotence.

Jebel Mawta ⓘ *E£25, students E£15, 0900-1800, no photographs allowed inside*, or Mountain of the Dead is a conical hill about 1.5 km north from the centre of Shali. It is honeycombed with tombs from 26th Dynasty to the Roman period, varying from small chambers to large composite excavations complete with columns and wall paintings. Anything worth stealing has long since been removed. During 1940 many items were 'sold' to the visiting troops by Siwans who had moved into the tombs for security. Of the tombs open to visitors that of Si-Amun, a rich local merchant, is the most striking, with wall paintings of him and his family, of Nut the goddess of the sky, and a very recognizable maple tree. Others that are open include the Tomb of Mesu-Isis, the Tomb of the crocodile and the Tomb of Niperpathot (for which the custodian will bring a key), which is in relatively poor condition. There are panoramic views towards the Great Sand Sea from the top of the hill.

Among the most beautiful spots to visit around Siwa is **Bir Wahid**, an enchanting hot spring set amid silky dunes and a lush garden, about 12 km off road from town (permits required). It is no longer possible to camp here, and sadly rubbish has begun to accumulate now that the Bedouin man who used to be permanently based at the spring has had to move on. Most safari guides will stop en route at one of the natural sweet water cold pools, perfect for swimming. In the vicinity, there are plenty of opportunities to climb dunes and rocky summits, search for fossils or go sand-surfing.

Out to the east from Siwa is **Birket Zeitoun**, a huge saltwater lake, visible from the summit of Jebel Dakhrur and quite a desolate place due largely to its high salinity. Still, its

Siwa Town (Shali)

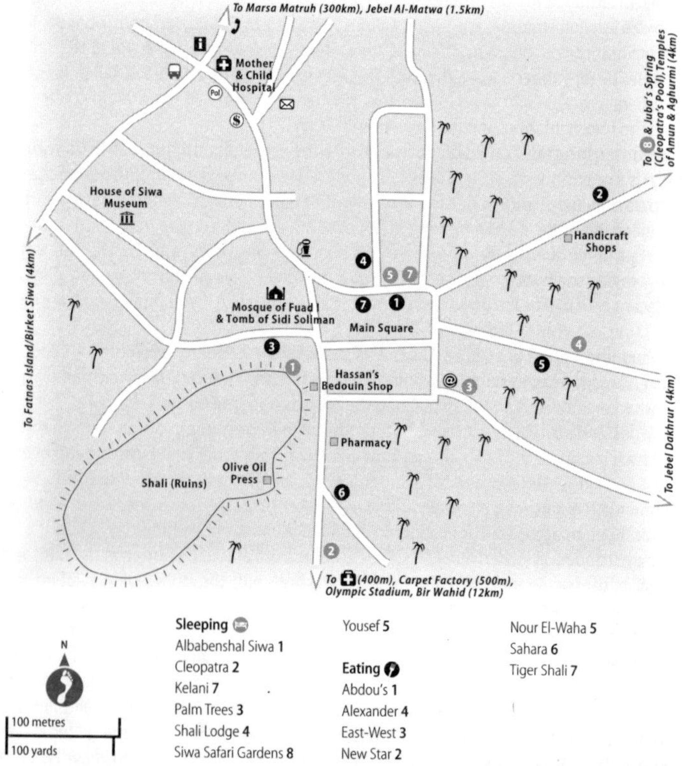

Sleeping
Albabenshal Siwa **1**
Cleopatra **2**
Kelani **7**
Palm Trees **3**
Shali Lodge **4**
Siwa Safari Gardens **8**
Yousef **5**

Eating
Abdou's **1**
Alexander **4**
East-West **3**
New Star **2**
Nour El-Waha **5**
Sahara **6**
Tiger Shali **7**

A long lost tomb?

First it was, then it probably wasn't, and now it definitely isn't – the long lost tomb of Alexander the Great. The announcement in 1991 by Greek archaeologist, Liani Souvaltzi, that she had uncovered (at Balad Al-Rum in Maraki, Siwa) possibly the most important archaeological find since that of Tutankhamen's tomb created a storm of controversy. Her claim centred around a 50-m above-ground 'tomb' that Souvaltzi says bears the same markings as that of Alexander's father, King Philip of Macedonia, including his royal symbol, an eight-pointed star. Just 18 m away, lay an entrance to a tunnel guarded by two royal lion statues and three stelae. The inscriptions found, she claimed, describe Alexander's poisoning and funeral procession to Siwa.

The find, if authentic, would have rewritten history. According to ancient texts, the conqueror expressed a wish to be buried in Siwa where he had been deified in 331 BC, but was finally laid to rest in Alexandria. A team of Greek experts, who flew out immediately to assess the find, concluded that there was 'no evidence' of Alexander's tomb: the inscriptions were from the late Roman rather than earlier Hellenistic period, and the 'royal' eight-pointed star was a common theme in Macedonian monuments. Meanwhile, the burial chamber, at 76 cm wide, is too narrow for a sarcophagus to pass through. The Supreme Council of Antiquities distanced themselves from the media furor that was unleashed by Souvaltzi's claims and have since declared that the tomb is categorically not that of Alexander the Great and forbidden her from ever working in Egypt again. Excavations have been halted and Souvaltzi on her last visit was reportedly horrified at the damage and disruption to the site, from where the stone blocks of the Doric temple have been removed en masse to a depository. Souvaltzi's declaration that she is mystically guided by saints in her search for the tomb of Alexander has done little to persuade the archaeological community of the validity of her investigations.

silvery water and salty edges offer a stunning reflection of a sunset. Near the edge of the lake, some 37 km southwest of town, the beautiful spring **Abu Shrouf** bubbles up invitingly. The water is a deep shade of blue and so clean you can see the bottom and schools of little fish. It's undisputedly the nicest pool around, and often empty, save the female donkeys that are supposedly confined to the area for mating. Whenever a local loses his donkey, the first question asked is,'have you been to Abu Shrouf?' Going to Abu Shrouf is also a widely known euphemism for 'did you have sex?' Lone women travellers, be cautious if a man invites you to accompany him alone to the spring. Further south along the lake, there is a small Bedouin village and the ruins of **Al-Zeitoun**, an old community that once tended the lushest gardens in the oasis until an Italian bombing raid in 1940 led to its abandonment. There the dwindling remains of a small temple and an age-old circular olive press are worth a look, as well as a nearby hill dotted with old Roman tombs.

West of the town, the road skirts the northern edge of Birket Siwa, along a honey-toned rockface speckled by the square pockets of hundreds of tombs, to the cluster of settlements known as **Maraqi**. It was here, near the village of Balad El-Rum, that Greek archaeologists claimed to have discovered the tomb of Alexander the Great under the remains of a Doric Temple, see box, above. After about 35 km the tarmac peters out at

The 'sacred aunt' of the Arabs – the date palm

Egypt produces about half a million tonnes of dates each year, though only a small portion of the total is made up of top-quality dessert fruit. Even so, dates are an important part of the Egyptian rural diet and each year some 62,000 tonnes of dates are produced from scattered palmeries in the Delta and valley areas, though principally in the commercial plantations of the true desert or the oases such as Siwa. The date palm is among the longest established orchard trees in Egypt and was a favoured symbol on monuments from pre-dynastic times.

The prophet Mohammed called on the Islamic faithful to protect the date palm, which he called their 'sacred aunt' because of its many uses as a food, building material and provider of shade. The Swedish naturalist Carl Linnaeus paid homage to the beauty and generosity of the palm tree when he classified it in the order of Principes, 'The Order of Princes'. The green and yellow foliage of the date palm is also a fine decoration in the otherwise vegetation-less squares and avenues of many Egyptian cities. In the western oases of Egypt, the palm is the tree of life, its fruit, leaves and wood the basis of the local economy. The Latin name of the date palm, *Phoenix dactylifera*, can be translated as 'the Phoenician tree with fruit resembling fingers'.

For the oasis dwellers, the date is so precious that they have a name for each stage of its growth. Trees may produce up to 100 kg of dates annually for a whole century. However, in order to do this, it needs manure and a lot of water, anything up to 300 litres a day.

The palm tree provides many essentials for its owner. The trunks are used to support roofs of houses, strengthen walls and in slices are used to make doors. One or two trunks make an adequate bridge over an irrigation channel, and with pieces cut out can be used as steps. The fibres on the trunk are removed and used as stuffing for saddles while the base of the palm frond, stripped of its leafy part, makes a beater for washing clothes and a trowel for the mason. Palm fronds are used to make baskets and a variety of mats such as the famous *margunah* or covered basket of Siwa. Midribs have enough strength to be used to make crates and furniture. Leaf bases are used for fuel and fibre for packing. The sap is drained and consumed as a rough but intoxicating beer known as *laghbi*or. This practice is banned for Muslims, who are forbidden alcohol and in any case drawing the sap can also kill the tree and is therefore discouraged by the authorities. The flesh of the fruit, which is rich in sugar and vitamins is eaten by man and the stone is eaten by camels (date stones can even be ground and used to supplement coffee). Best quality fresh dates are a delicacy for the rich. Dried and pressed dates stay edible for long periods and can be taken on journeys or used to sustain the nomads in their wanderings. The almighty date is also first to pass the lips and break the daily fast during Ramadan.

the Bedouin village of Behay Al-Din on the shore of **Birket Maraqi**, where you can swim in the salty water. The ridge here is scattered with the fossils of shells and sea creatures, and not only has splendid views of the lake and mesas but is a marvellous vantage point from which to watch a sunset turn the world of cream-coloured sand to rose-pink.

Qara Oasis, reached from either Marsa Matruh or Siwa, this is the only other place where Siwi is still spoken. Permission is needed to visit the oasis and overnighting there is not allowed. Although situated between Matruh and Siwa (the turn off is near to Bir Nus resthouse) it is currently far easier to arrange a trip there from Siwa due to the plethora of tour operators who have 4WDs. If you are alone it is best to ask around all the safari offices around the square and you may find a group to join. A 4WD for the day will cost about E£1400-1500 and can take four to six people depending on the seating layout. A day's notice is needed to obtain the necessary permission.

Siwa Oasis listings

For Sleeping and Eating price codes and other relevant information, see pages 26-31.

Sleeping

Siwa Oasis *p528, maps p529 and p532*
The range and quality of accommodation in Siwa has increased tremendously over the last few years, to the point where it is now as famed for its exquisite eco-lodges as it is the enchanting surroundings. Budget travellers can still find a bed for a bargain, although this is the place to splash out a bit and find real tranquillity in one of the mid-range retreats edged by desert, especially as the town square is invariably noisy. It is also possible to rent a room for longer stays (or just a day or 2) at the **Nour El-Waha** and **New Star** restaurants, both of which have a couple of lovely rooms of a high standard in their palm gardens. For stays of a month or more, try the owner of the **Dream Lodge** who has apartments for rent in town or ask Mahdi at the information office about other long-stay options.

LL Adrère Amellal, 16 km west of town at the foot of, and built into, White Mountain. Reservations must be made through the Cairo office, T02-2736 7879, info@eqi.eg.com. This extraordinary mud-brick complex melds beautifully into the surrounding landscape and the views overlooking Birket Lake are breathtaking. There is no electricity, only medieval-esque candles and 1000 oil lamps. The rooms are sublime, made by locals with local materials (palm and olive wood, salt, kharsif, and rocks from nearby mounts) while decor is muted creams, beiges and whites. The pool is magical, there is a library composed entirely of translucent blocks of salt, and each dining area is more heavenly than the last. The price includes full board and access to the 24-hr bar, plus daily safaris to Bir Wahed and other sites (only horse riding is extra). Unfortunately, non-guests have to be invited by a resident in order to enjoy more than just a look round.

AL Taziry, T02-3337 0842, www.taziry.com. Similar in feel to the **Amellal**, this eco-lodge lies at the foot of the Red Mountain with glorious views of the White Mountain and lake. Rooms have a bit more colour in the furnishings and fittings, which might be a good thing depending on taste, and again there is no electricity to detract from the starlit nights. It's a bit more affordable at US$145 (per room) and in low season that drops even lower.

A Albabenshal Siwa, T046-460 1499, T010-361 4140. This latest enterprise by the owner of **Adrère Amellal** incorporates old walls of the Shali to create an astonishingly serene and special environment. Austere rooms are discerningly decorated, huge beds have camel-wool blankets and crisp duvets, salt lamps cast a mellow glow, and palm trunks and natural materials complete the rustic look. The 11 rooms are all different and spacious, with TV and fan, or braziers in winter. There's free Wi-Fi. Sensational breakfast included, on one of the roof terraces – be sure to try the olive jam.

A-B Shali Lodge, Midan El-Souk, 200 m east of the town centre, T046-460 1299. This idyllic retreat is most people's 1st choice so it's often booked up. Built in the traditional Siwan style with mud bricks and palm-wood ceilings and furniture, the gorgeous rooms are spacious and spotless, decorated with local Bedouin crafts and rugs. Unlike the eco-lodge, Shali has electricity, satellite TV, fans and natural heaters in the winter. A pool is being built. The restaurant features some of the best food in town, set on the breezy roof among the fronds of date palms. Breakfast included.

B-C Siwa Safari Gardens, on the road to Aghurmi, just before the Wedding Spring, T046-460 2801/2, T012-405 8074, www.siwagardens.com. Traditionally built, tasteful rooms set around a tranquil, lush garden with an immaculately maintained pool. Efficiently and lovingly run by a German-Egyptian couple. Prices are for half board.

B-C Qasr Al-Zaytuna, on the road to Dakhrur, T046-460 0037. Under new management and due to reopen, very tasteful soft-toned rooms have hardwood floors and high ceilings. There is a suite available with a decent kitchen. Very close to Jebel Dakrur, a good place to stay for anyone interested in sand baths or being away from what little action there is in town. There's also a pool, peaceful garden and restaurant.

C Desert Rose, 3 km south of town, T012-440 8164. In a mystical setting on the edge of the Great Sand Sea, 8 rooms and 5 bungalows are found in total peace and seclusion. Breakfast is inclusive and meals are available (E£35), which could be worthwhile as bikes struggle with the bumpy, sandy track. Call ahead to check Ali is there to welcome you or to be collected.

C Dream Lodge, near Jebel Al-Mawta, T046-460 0272, gamalsiwa@gmail.com. Hidden away on the north of town, this friendly place has 8 rooms around an intimate garden and central pool. Though not strictly 'traditional', rooms have character, some with domed ceiling, others mud-brick walls and wicker furniture, TV and fridge. All are spotless and have little verandas, it's only the bathrooms that are disappointingly small. There is a circular Siwan sitting room, communal barbeque and fire, and use of the kitchen. Extremely peaceful and relaxing, breakfast included, meals available.

E-F Cleopatra, 200 m south of the town centre, T/F046-460 0421. Not a bad budget option and quieter than most. The slightly pricier chalets are spotless with tiled floors, private bath and fan, but bring a mosquito net. The old branch is cheaper and worn around the edges. Staff are friendly and helpful.

E-F Palm Trees, T046-460 1703, T012-046 6652. There's a range of accommodation from bungalows with fans and private bath to the slightly scruffier old rooms in the main building. An old-timer on the scene, **Palm Trees** remains a backpacker's favourite and the garden makes a great spot to meet other travellers. Check out sunset over Shali from the rooftop.

F Kelani Hotel, in the main square, T012-403 9218, T012-105 7977. The Kelani offers clean simple rooms with or without bath. It can be noisy but the views of the Shali from the roof are great. Friendly staff.

F Yousef, in the main square, T046-460 2565. Rooms are simple but clean and cheerfully painted. All have fans and some include private bathroom and balcony. Located right on the square, which makes it noisy at times. The view from the roof is excellent and it's a good budget choice. Youssef himself is very friendly and helpful.

Camping

This is a sensitive area close to the Libyan border, so despite the good relations, don't camp without permission from the tourist office. Some people camp out by the hot spring behind Jebel Dakhrur and it's possible to camp on Fatnas Island, see page 530. West of Siwa by 35 km is the Bedouin village of Behay El-Din where you can stay in a tent on the ridge with views of Birket Maraki, contact hospitable Omar Edris Abu Zahra on T010-611 8139; if language difficulties arise, ask Mahdi at the tourist office to help out with translation. Mahdi can also give you more leads on camping in the desert.

Eating

Siwa Oasis *p528, maps p529 and p532*
As far as the oases go, there's quite a range of good grub in Siwa. Most restaurants are scattered around the town centre and serve up fairly comparable food, for comparable prices (all cheap).

¥¥¥-¥¥ **Albabenshal**, on the edge of the ruins. The standard of food is excellent, the views magnificent especially at night and the breeze welcome.

¥¥¥-¥¥ **Kenooz Siwa**, on the roof at Shali Lodge, see Sleeping, above. It's still quite modestly priced, and the atmosphere is inviting, with a choice of outdoor and inside seating. The menu is diverse and features delicious vegetarian dishes, or various crêpe and couscous meals.

¥¥ **Nour El-Waha**, across the lane from the Shali Lodge, has a quaint candlelit atmosphere, good food, *sheesha* (E£7) and lots of backgammon. It's also pure pleasure to relax here during the day, when sunlight filters through the swishing palms.

¥ **Abdou's**, the longest standing of all the eateries is cheerful and welcoming, though lacking in intimate atmosphere. The kebab is especially good and it's always reassuringly busy.

¥ **Alexander Restaurant**, north of the square, good for Egyptian standards.

¥ **East-West Restaurant**, near the bus station (open the earliest). Has a few tables outside and serves the most authentic curry around.

¥ **New Star**, set in a shady palm garden this place serves up simple, well-cooked fare.

¥ **Palm Trees** in the garden of the hotel. Run by the same team as Abdou's; tasty, reliable meals are served in a relaxing, peaceful setting.

¥ **Sahara**, tucked away just south of the square on the way to Cleopatra Hotel, this relative newcomer has a big fire, colourful cushions and *sheesha tufah*.

¥ **Tiger Shali**, upstairs next to Abdou's, newer on the scene and has the most generous portions in town (meals come with a fresh salad), is very cheap and well worth giving a go.

Festivals and events

Siwa Oasis *p528, maps p529 and p532*
Oct Siayha Festival, just before the date harvest during full moon, on the rock of Jebel Dakrur. It lasts 3 days and over 10,000 local people (but not married Siwan women) come together to celebrate friendship with prayers and sing religious songs. The elements of Sufism are strong and *zikrs* are performed nightly. A truly exceptional event that welcomes visitors. Book accommodation in advance if you intend to come.

Shopping

Siwa Oasis *p528, maps p529 and p532*
Handicraft shops have sprung up all over Siwa, selling both local merchandise and items from all over Egypt. There are carpets woven from local wool, in thick bright stripes of red, yellow and blue and traditional wedding gowns in black – which are equally eye-catching but less popular as a purchase, they go for between E£400-800. Embroidered blue blankets, worn by Siwan women, cost around E£80-200, depending on size and quality. The intricate wedding scarves, stitched with red and green, are around E£350 (using modern materials) or E£600 (with shells). Original old Siwan silver jewellery has long been purloined, but there are some good copies – try the small shops just before New Star restaurant for an attractive selection of traditional designs. Salt lamps are becoming a popular purchase, small ones go for about E£50 and large ones E£250. For Bedouin items, Hassan's Bedouin shop (no English sign) on the west of the square, sells attractive goods made in Sidi Barani on the north coast. There's also a carpet factory in town that employs 250

women who weave intricate patterns and are very welcoming to visitors. The local market every Fri, in the street to the left of the tourist office is bustling, especially in the morning. If you want to buy some Siwan music, ask Mahdi at the tourist office to source a CD by local artist Mohamed Romar for you, costing around E£30. Opposite Abdou's restaurant is **Nahardeen** herbal medicine shop. Here you can watch them mixing and grinding herbs to treat a wide variety of ailments. The Albabenshal Hotel has a lovely shop selling edible Siwan products in beautiful, minimalist packaging.

Bookshops

Fathy Malim Bookshop. English and French books available. Fathy has published a couple of informative books on Siwan culture, available at his shop and other outlets in town.

Activities and tours

Siwa Oasis *p528, maps p529 and p532*

Safaris

Most hotels will help you organize day-long or overnight safaris around the oasis. Rates fluctuate quite a bit. Day-long excursions generally cost around E£100-140 per person, including a guide. Overnight trips including food cost E£170-250 per person. Check carefully what you are being offered. Some drivers will take you to a makeshift camp set up in the desert while others will take you for a real sleepout. Be clear about what you would prefer then check what your driver is offering. Also, if possible try to see the vehicle you will be going in before you pay. Safaris to Bahariyya via the White Desert can be arranged, they generally take 2 nights and 3 days, expect to pay E£1000 per day for a jeep. If you are alone it is best to ask around all the safari offices round the square to find a group to share costs with.Bear in mind that some safari leaders are more reputable than others, those listed below are recommended.

Abdullah Baghi is an extremely articulate English speaker with fascinating tales. He was personally honoured for his commitment to his community by Kofi Anan and he now leads trips. Ask for him around the **Shali Lodge** or the **Cleopatra Hotel**.

Ali, T010-304 1191, also based at the **Shali Lodge** in the mornings and his handicrafts shop in the main square in the afternoons, organizes safaris.

Mahdi at the tourist office also leads trips. He's especially fond of showing visitors around the nearby antiquities; his wealth of knowledge makes the visits meaningful.

Sand-boarding

Several shops rent out sandboards for E£30 (wood) or E£50 (plastic) per day, though you may get boards included as part of a safari trip.

Transport

Siwa Oasis *p528, maps p529 and p532*

Bus

The bus station (open 24 hrs) and taxi halt are next to the tourist office at the entrance of town. There are 5 a/c **West Delta buses** daily to **Marsa Matruh** (0700, 1000, 1300, 1500 (winter) or 1700 (summer), 2200, E£17), 3 of which carry on to **Alexandria** (0700, 1000, 2200, E£35). There is 1 bus direct to **Cairo** at 2000, E£60, 9 hrs. Buy your tickets at least 2 hrs in advance. If travelling on the 0700 or the Cairo bus, buy them the night before to ensure you have a seat. Minibuses for Marsa Matruh leave when full from in front of the new mosque, and also cost E£17.

For the 420-km journey direct to **Bahariyya** across the desert road, it's E£1400 per vehicle for the 6- to 8-hr trip, max 4 people. The majority of vehicles crossing are jeeps (4WD is essential), which leave in convoy from the military intelligence office at 0700. Permits need to be sorted out a day in advance (you'll lose a day with Fri) through your driver, US$£5 per person plus an E£11 admin fee.

Donkey carts

Donkey carts, or *karettas* as they are called here, are for hire everywhere. Expect to pay around E£20-25 for a quick round-trip journey to nearby sites like the Temple of Amun or Fatnas Island. For long waits, pay an additional E£10, more at night. A ride from the bus station to a hotel in town shouldn't cost more than E£5.They can also be hired as a gentle way to see all the sights. Expect to pay at least E£80 for this but remember that you will be helping to sustain an important element of Siwan culture.

Taxi

Service taxis bound for the coast leave daily, generally around mid-morning and late afternoon. For longer distances, there are service pickup trucks that will shuffle visitors around the oasis. They are generally found in front of the tourist office. You'll find the most options in the early morning.

❻ Directory

Siwa Oasis *p528, maps p529 and p532*
Banks Bank du Caire, just north of the town centre, changes money but there's no ATM, Sun-Thu 0830-1400, T046-460 0748. Most hotels will buy euro and dollars.
Internet There are a few internet cafés scattered around the town centre, the going rate at present is E£9-10 per hr.
Post office Located near the tourist office, 0830-2100. **Telephone** Central phone station open 24 hrs, near the tourist office. It's also possible to use the phones at most hotels.

Background

Contents

Footprint features

History

The River Nile has been the key influence on life in Egypt since the beginning of civilization. This vast supply of sweet water permitted the creation of a society that produced the many wonders of ancient Egypt. Today, no less than in the past, modern Egypt depends on the river to support its huge population. The Nile is Egypt's lifeblood.

The Sahara began to desiccate some 10,000 years ago and divided the Caucasoid populations of North Africa from the Negroid populations of West and Equatorial Africa. The original agricultural mode of production that had been the basis of settlement there was gradually replaced by nomadic pastoralism which, by around 4000 BC, had become the preserve of two groups, the Libyan-Berbers in the east part and the ancestors of the modern Touareg in the west. North African populations, all classified as part of the Hamito-Semitic group which stretched east into Arabia, soon became sub-divided into the Berbers in the west, the Egyptians in the east and the Nilo-Saharians and Kushites to the south, in what today is Sudan.

The key to the development of a complex civilization lay in the water and soils of the Nile Valley. By 3000 BC, the Nile was supporting a dense sedentary agricultural society which produced a surplus and increasingly allowed socio-economic specialization. This evolved into a system of absolute divine monarchy when the original two kingdoms were amalgamated by the victory of King Menes of Upper Egypt who then became the first pharaoh. Pharaonic Egypt was limited by an inadequate resource base, being especially deficient in timber. Although it was forced to trade, particularly with the Levant (Eastern Mediterranean), it never became a major seafaring nation. Equally, the growing desertification of Libya meant that its influence never extended west. Instead, the Egyptian Empire sought control up the Nile Valley, towards Kush (or Nubia) which it conquered as far south as the Fourth Cataract (between Khartoum and Wadi Halfa in Sudan) by 1500 BC. It also expanded east into the Levant, until it was restrained by the expanding civilizations of the Fertile Crescent (the arc of territory lying between the rain-fed east Mediterranean coastlands/Syria/Mesopotamia) after 2300 BC.

By 1000 BC, Pharaonic Egypt was being pressured from all sides. The Hyksos (the shepherd kings of Egypt – 2000-1700 BC – who migrated to Egypt from Asia) threatened the Delta from the Mediterranean, whilst the Lebu from Libya also began to settle there. They eventually created the 21st (Sheshonnaq) Dynasty of the New Kingdom in 912 BC which, for a short time, extended its power east as far as Jerusalem. In the seventh century BC, however, Egypt was conquered by its Kushitic imitators to the south in the Nubian Kingdom under King Piankhy who founded the 25th Pharaonic Dynasty.

The Nubians were expelled some years later by the Assyrians, but their conquest marked the end of the greatness of Pharaonic Egypt. Thereafter, Egypt was to be a dependency of more powerful states in the Middle East or the Mediterranean. The rulers of Nubian Kush in their turn, having been expelled from Egypt, looked south from their new capital at Meroe – to which they had moved as a result of the subsequent Persian conquest of Egypt in 525 BC and later Persian attempts to conquer Kush. Kush became, instead, the vehicle of transmission of iron-working technology and of Egyptian concepts of divine political organization southwards as well.

Pharaonic Egypt → *For dates see box, page 544.*

About 3100 BC, King Menes succeeded in uniting Upper and Lower Egypt into a single kingdom. His new capital at Memphis, about 15 km to the south of modern-day Cairo, was deliberately located on the border of Upper and Lower Egypt. Despite this, the rivalry between the two parts of Egypt continued until the end of the Early Dynastic Period.

The **Old Kingdom** began with the Third Dynasty and ushered in a major period of achievement. A series of strong and able rulers established a highly centralized government. The 'Great House', *per-aha* from which the word pharaoh is derived, controlled all trade routes and markets. The calendar was introduced and the sun god Re was the most revered deity. Until then it was common practice for leaders to be buried in underground mausoleums (*mastabas*).

In the 27th century BC King Zoser and his chief architect Imohotep constructed the first step pyramid in Saqqara, the huge necropolis across the river from Memphis, and pyramids became the principal method of royal burial for the pharaohs during the next millennium. The scale of organization required to mobilize the resources and manpower to build these phenomenal pyramids is testimony to the level of sophistication of this period. The three Fourth Dynasty giant pyramids of Cheops, Chephren and Mycerinus erected on the Giza plateau still awe the world today.

By the end of the Old Kingdom, the absolute power of the pharaohs had declined. Local leaders ruled their own *nomes* (provinces) and a second capital emerged at Heracleopolis. Few great monuments were built in this very unstable **First Intermediate Period**.

During the 11th Dynasty Menutuhotep II reunited the country and created a new capital at Thebes (Luxor). Remains from this era, the Middle Kingdom, demonstrate its prosperity.

During the five dynasties of the **Second Intermediate Period**, central authority again disintegrated and Egypt was controlled briefly by Asiatic kings known as the Hyksos, who introduced horses and chariots to Egypt.

The **New Kingdom**, spanning the 18th to 20th Dynasties and based at Thebes, ushered in a period of unparalleled wealth and power. During these 400 years the kingdom prospered and expeditions led to the creation of a huge empire. Military campaigns in Western Asia by Tuthmosis III, now known as the Napoleon of Ancient Egypt, brought Palestine, Syna and Nubia into the empire and their wealth and cheap labour poured into Thebes. The temple complex of Karnak and the Valley of the Kings are but two of the astounding remains of the era. During this period Akhenaten renounced the traditional gods in favour of a monotheistic religion based on the sun god Re but his boy-king successor Tutankhamen immediately reverted to the former religion and its principal god Amun. After the military dictatorship of Horemheb, a general who seized the throne, royal power was restored by Ramses I. Ramses II, a most prestigious builder, reigned for 67 years. Following the death of Ramses III, the last great pharaoh, effective power moved increasingly into the hands of the Amun priests and the empire declined. The pharaohs' power was diminished through intra-dynastic strife, decline in political grip on the levers of power and loss of control of day-to-day administration.

During the **Late Dynastic Period** the succession of dynasties, some ruled by Nubians and Persians, became so weak that **Alexander the Great** had little difficulty in seizing the country. Although he did not spend long in Egypt his new capital city of Alexandria, where he is believed to be buried, still flourishes. His empire was divided among his generals and Ptolemy established the **Ptolemaic Dynasty** which ended with the reign of Cleopatra VII, the last of the Ptolemies before Egypt became a province of the Roman Empire.

Dynasties in Egypt up to 30 BC *(only includes rules mentioned in text)*

Early Dynastic (3100-2686 BC)
First Dynasty (3100-2890 BC; Memphis)
Menes
Second Dynasty (2890-2686 BC)
The Old Kingdom (2686-2181 BC)
Third Dynasty (2686-2613 BC)
King Zoser (2667-2648 BC; Step Pyramid, Saqqara)
Huni
Fourth Dynasty (2613-2494 BC; Pyramids of Giza)
Snefru
Cheops (Khufu)
Chephren (Khafre)
Mycerinus (Menkaure)
Shepseskaf
Fifth Dynasty (2494-2345 BC)
Unas
Sixth Dynasty (2345-2181 BC)
South Saqqara Necropolis
Teti
Pepi I
Pepi II
First Intermediate (2181-2050 BC)
Seventh Dynasty (2181-2173 BC)
Middle Kingdom (2050-1786 BC)
Eleventh Dynasty (2050-1991 BC)
King Menutuhotep II (Creation of Thebes; Luxor)
Twelfth Dynasty (1991-1786 BC)
Amenemhat I (1991-1961 BC)
Senusert I (1971-1928 BC)
Senusert II (1897-1878 BC)
Amenemhat III (1842-1797 BC)
Queen Sobek-Nefru (1789-1786 BC)
Second Intermediate (1786-1567 BC)
Fifteenth Dynasty (1674-1567 BC; capital Avaris)
New Kingdom (1567-1085 BC; Thebes)
Eighteenth Dynasty (1567-1320 BC; Temples of Luxor and Karnak)
Amenhotep (1546-1526 BC)
Tuthmosis I (1525-1512 BC)
Tuthmosis I (1512-1504 BC)
Tuthmosis IV (1425-1417 BC)
Amenhotep III (1417-1379 BC)
Amenhotep IV (Akhenaten; 1379-1362 BC)
Tutankhamen (1361-1352 BC)
Ay (1352-1348 BC)
Horemheb (1348-1320 BC)
Nineteenth Dynasty (1320-1200 BC)
Ramses I (1320-1318 BC)
Seti I (1318-1304 BC)
Ramses II (1304-1237 BC)
Seti II (1216-1210 BC)
Siptah (1210-1204 BC)
Tawosert (1204-1200 BC)
Twentieth Dynasty (1200-1085 BC)
Sethnakht (1200-1198 BC)
Ramses III (1198-1166 BC)
Ramses IV (1166-1160 BC)
Ramses V (1160-1156 BC)
Ramses VI (1156-1148 BC)
Ramses VII (1148-1141 BC)
Ramses IX (1140-1123 BC)
Ramses XI (1114-1085 BC)
Late Dynastic (1085-332 BC)
Twenty-second Dynasty (945-715 BC)
Twenty-fifth Dynasty (747-656 BC)
Shabaka (716-702 BC)
Twenty-sixth Dynasty (664-525 BC)
Necho II (610-596 BC)
Twenty-seventh Dynasty (525-404 BC; Persian occupation)
Cambyses (525-522 BC)
Darius I (521-486 BC)
Thirtieth Dynasty (380-343 BC)
Nectanebo I (380-362 BC)
Nectanebo II (360-343 BC)
Late (332-30 BC; Macedonian Kings, capital Alexandria)
Alexander III (The Great; 332-323 BC)
Philip Arrhidaeus (323-317 BC)
Ptolemaic Era (323-30 BC)
Ptolemy I (Soter 323-282 BC)
Ptolemy II (282-246 BC)
Ptolemy III (246-222 BC; Edfu Temple)
Ptolemy IV (222-205 BC)
Ptolemy V (205-180 BC; Kom-Ombo Temple)
Ptolemy VII (180-145 BC)
Ptolemy VIII (170-145 BC)
Ptolemy IX (170-116 BC)

The Three Crowns of Egypt

The king was a reincarnation of a god – Re, Aten, Amun or Horus. He was addressed by the god as "my living image upon earth".

A king was recognized on illustrations by his garments and paraphernalia. The most important of these was his crown. The earliest kings wore the white bulbous crown of Upper Egypt. The red crown of Lower Egypt was even more distinctive with a high back and forward-thrusting coil. A king wearing the double crown was thought to symbolize his control over all Egypt.

The ultimate sign of kingship, however, was the uraeus on his forehead, a rearing cobra with an inflated hood – generally in gold.

Other items of importance associated with kingship included the hand-held crook and flail and the false plaited beard.

The division of power between Rome and Constantinople resulted in the virtual abandonment of Egypt. Egypt's autonomy led to the development of the Coptic church, which was independent from both the Byzantines and the Romans, and whose calendar dates from AD 284 when thousands were massacred by the Roman emperor Diocletian.

Greeks and Phoenicians

In North Africa, Egypt's failure to expand westward permitted other developments to occur. The coastal area became the arena for competition between those Mediterranean civilizations which had acquired a naval capacity – the Greeks and the Phoenicians. Indeed, this became the future pattern and resulted in the history of the region being described in the terms of its conquerors.

We do know, however, that the Greek and Phoenician settlements on the coast provoked a response from the nomadic communities of the desert such as the Garamantes around the Fezzan in Libya. These communities appear to have specialized in warfare based on charioteering and they began to raid the new coastal settlements. At the same time, they also controlled trans-Saharan commerce – one of the major reasons why the Phoenicians, at least, were so interested in North Africa. As a result, they also engaged in trade with the new coastal communities, particularly those created by the Phoenicians. Other invasions also took place, this time of northeast Africa from southern Arabia, bringing Arab tribes into Africa. The new Arab invaders spread rapidly into modern Ethiopia and Eritrea.

The Greeks had begun to colonize the Egyptian and eastern Libyan coastline as part of their attempt to control Egyptian maritime trade. Greeks and Phoenicians competed for control of the old coastal areas in Libya and eventually created an uneasy division of the region between themselves. The Greeks took over Egypt after the creation of the Ptolemaic Kingdom on the death of Alexander the Great in 323 BC and incorporated Cyrenaica (in Libya) into the new kingdom. The Phoenicians, by now being harried in their original Lebanese home base of Tyre by the Assyrians and Persians, created a new and powerful maritime commercial empire based at Carthage (in Tunisia), with outlying colonies to the west, right round to the Atlantic coast at Lixus (Larache).

Isis and Osiris

Myths have always played an important part in the religion of ancient Egypt and it is not possible to separate myths from religious rituals. The story of Isis and Osiris, a central Egyptian myths was written on papyrus some 5000-6000 years ago.

According to the story, Osiris was the son of Geb, the earth god, and was therefore descended from the sun god Re. He was known to have been a great and good king and was particularly concerned with agricultural techniques, growing crops to provide the essentials: bread, beer and wine. He ruled wisely and when he travelled abroad Isis, his sister and wife, most competently took charge.

His brother Seth was filled with jealously and hatred for Osiris and was determined to be rid of him. This he did with the help of the Queen of Ethiopia and another 72 conspirators. Seth had constructed a most magnificent chest, which exactly fitted the measurements of Osiris. At a feast all the guests tried the chest for size and when Osiris took his turn the conspirators nailed down the lid and sealed it with boiling lead.

The sealed chest was carried to the banks of the Nile and thrown into the river where it floated out to sea and came to land at Byblos in Syria. There a tamarisk tree grew up immediately and enclosed the chest. The size of this magnificent new tree caught the eye of the king of Byblos, Melcarthus, who had it cut down to make a pillar to support the roof of his palace.

Isis, distressed by the disappearance of her husband's body and aware that without funeral rites he could never rest in eternity, went out to search for him. It took some time to trace the route to Byblos, find the chest still encased in the trunk of the tree but now supporting a main room in the king's palace and even longer to persuade them to part with that pillar and the chest.

She made her way back to Egypt with the body of Osiris still in the chest. Here she was a little careless for, leaving the chest hidden but unguarded, she went off to be reunited with her young son. By some mischance Seth, hunting by the light of the moon, stumbled on the chest. He immediately recognized the container and in his rage cut the body into 14 separate pieces.

Seth, determined to rid himself of his brother once and for all took the pieces and scattered them through all the tribes of Egypt. Undaunted, Isis set out again, this time in a papyrus boat, to retrieve the separate pieces which she did with the help of her sister Nephthys, the gods Thoth and Anubis and some magic. At every place she found a part of her husband she set up a shrine. The severed parts were brought together and Osiris was restored to eternal life.

Horus, the son of Isis and Osiris, was brought up in secret to protect him from harm. When he reached manhood he swore to avenge the wrong done to his father and mother. Another myth describes his victory over Seth, after one or two setbacks, and how he was declared by the tribunal of gods to be Osiris's rightful heir.

The Roman Empire

Control of Egypt and North Africa passed on once again, this time to the rapidly expanding city-state of Rome. Control of the Ptolemaic Kingdom of Egypt passed to Rome because of Roman interest in its agricultural produce and Egypt became a province of Rome in 30 BC.

Coptic monasteries

The difficult problem of border security for Roman administrators was solved by creating the limes, a border region along the desert edge which was settled with former legionaries as a militarized agriculturalist population. Thus, although the border region was permeable to trade, resistance to tribal incursion could be rapidly mobilized from the resident population, while regular forces were brought to the scene. The limes spread west from Egypt as far as the Moroccan Atlantic coast.

Christianity

Egyptian Christianity became the major focus of the development of Christian doctrine. The Coptic Church became the main proponent of Monophysitism (the belief that there is only one nature in the person of Jesus Christ (ie that he is not a three-in-one-being) after the Council of Chalcedon in AD 451; Donatism (direct giving, official largesse) dominated Numidia (an area approximately the size of present-day Algeria). At the same time, official Christianity in Egypt – the Melkite Church (Christians adhering to the rulings of the Council of Chalcedon that there are two natures to the person of Christ and who are known as 'monarchists' or 'supporters of the Byzantine emperor') – combined with the Coptic Church to convert areas to the south of Egypt to Christianity. See also page 571.

The Jews in Egypt

Jewish involvement in Egyptian affairs has long historical roots. Twelve tribes of Israel were forced by famine to migrate to Egypt where they remained as an under-privileged minority until led out by Moses in the 13th century BC, eventually to move to Canaan in today's Palestine. During the period of dominance of Egypt by Greek and Roman cultures, the Jews became scattered around the lands of the respective empires in the Diaspora. At that time Egypt was a major destination for the Jews in exile. It is estimated that as many as one million Jews lived in Egypt, with important centres of Jewish activity in Alexandria (see page 357), Leontopolis (north of Cairo in the eastern delta) and even in Lower Egypt as far south as Elephantine Island.

The Jewish population in Egypt declined with the passing of the Hellenistic tradition and the imposition of a less tolerant Roman government. During the Islamic era, the Jews, though subject to some social constraints and dealt with separately for tax purposes, thrived as traders and bankers in addition to their role as skilled craftsmen in the *souks*. Occasional violence occurred against the Jews, who tended to be associated in the Egyptian popular mind with the foreign community and thus attacked at times of anti-British or anti-French riots in the major cities, as for example in 1882, 1919, 1921 and 1924. In general, however, it was true that Jews in Egypt fared far better and were more tolerated than Jews in some countries of Europe.

This all changed dramatically with the rise of Zionism in the period from 1890 and the return of Jews to Palestine. Even before the Second World War the scale of Jewish migration to Palestine provoked fears in the Egyptian body politic and there were serious riots against the Jews in eight cities, most importantly in Alexandria and Cairo in 1938-39. Foundation of the State of Israel in 1948 brought an inevitable outbreak of rioting in which the Jews were a principal target. The Arab-Israeli wars of 1948, 1957, 1968 and 1973 added to the problem. Some 29,500 Jews left Egypt for Israel in the years 1949-1972 alone, in the latter years in official expulsions. As a result of the flight to Israel and migration elsewhere, the Jewish population in Egypt has fallen from approximately 75,000 in 1948 to around 100 in 2008, the majority of whom live in Alexandria.

A return of diplomatic relations between Egypt and Israel after President Anwar Sadat's visit to Jerusalem in 1977 improved official links and economic contacts between the two sides (albeit put in jeopardy by Israel's break of faith with the peace process in 1997), but the Jews have never returned as a community to Egypt.

The Islamic Period

In AD 642, 10 years after the death of the Prophet Mohammed, Arab armies, acting as the vanguard of Islam, conquered Egypt. To secure his conquest, the Arab commander, Amr Ibin Al-As, immediately decided to move west into Cyrenaica (part of Libya) where the local Berber population submitted to the new invaders. Despite a constant pattern of disturbance, the Arab conquerors of Egypt and their successors did not ignore the potential of the region to the south. Nubia was invaded in AD 641-642 and again 10 years later. Arab merchants and, later, Bedouin tribes from Arabia, were able to move freely throughout the south. However, until AD 665, no real attempt was actually made to complete the conquest, largely because of internal problems within the new world of Islam.

The Muslim seizure of Egypt was, despite the introduction of Islam, broadly welcomed by the Copts in preference to remaining under the Byzantine yoke. Islam slowly prevailed, as did the introduction of Arabic as the official language, although there remained a significant Coptic minority. Cairo became the seat of government and emerged as a new Islamic city. While the seeds of Islam strengthened and blossomed there were centuries of political instability which led to the creation of countless dynasties, mainly ruled by foreign Muslim empires. The new faith was only fleetingly threatened when the Christian Crusader armies attacked Cairo and were repelled by Salah Al-Din (AD 1171-1193).

The Great Dynasties and their successors

The Fatimids The first of the great dynasties that was to determine the future of North Africa did not, however, originate inside the region. Instead it used North Africa as a stepping stone towards its ambitions of taking over the Muslim world and imposing its own variant of Shi'a Islam. North Africa, because of its radical and egalitarian Islamic traditions, appears to have been the ideal starting point. The group concerned were the Isma'ilis who split off from the main body of Shi'a Muslims in AD 765.

The Fatimids took control over what had been *Aghlabid Ifriquiya*, founding a new capital at Mahdia in AD 912. Fatimid attention was concentrated on Egypt and, in AD 913-914, a Fatimid army temporarily occupied Alexandria. The Fatimids also developed a naval force and their conquest of Sicily in the mid-10th century provided them with a very useful base for attacks on Egypt.

After suppressing a Kharejite-Sunni rebellion in Ifriquiya between AD 943 and AD 947, the Fatimids were ready to plan the final conquest of Egypt. This took place in AD 969 when the Fatimid general, Jawhar, succeeded in subduing the country. The Fatimids moved their capital to Egypt, where they founded a new urban centre, Al-Qahira (from which the modern name, Cairo, is derived) next to the old Roman fortress of Babylon and the original Arab settlement of Fustat.

The Fatimids' main concern was to take control of the Middle East. This meant that Fatimid interest in North Africa would wane and leave an autonomous Emirate there which continued to recognize the authority of the Fatimids, although it abandoned support for Shi'a Islamic doctrine.

Hillalian invasions Despite Fatimid concerns in the Middle East, the caliph in Cairo decided to return North Africa to Fatimid control. Lacking the means to do this himself, he used instead two tribes recently displaced from Syria and at that time residing in the Nile Delta – the Banu Sulaim and the Banu Hillal – as his troops. The invasions took place slowly over a period of around 50 years, starting in AD 1050 or 1051, and probably involved no more than 50,000 individuals.

The Hillalian invasions were a major and cataclysmic event in North Africa's history. They destroyed organized political power in the region and broke up the political link between Muslim North Africa and the Middle East. They also damaged the trading economy of the region. More than any other event, the Hillalian invasions also ensured that Arabic eventually became the majority language of the region.

Egypt after the Fatimids Fatimid power in Egypt did not endure for long. They were forced to rely on a slave army recruited from the Turks of Central Asia and from the Sudanese. They found it increasingly difficult to control these forces and, eventually, became their victims. In 1073 AD, the commander of the Fatimid army in Syria, which had been recalled to restore order in Egypt, took power and the Fatimid caliph was left only with the prestige of his office.

What remained of the Fatimid Empire was now left virtually defenceless towards the east and the Seljuk Turks, who were already moving west, soon took advantage of this weakness. They were spurred on by the growth of Crusader power in the Levant and, after this threat had been contained, Egypt soon fell under their sway. Control of Egypt passed to Salah Ad-Din Ibn Ayyubi in AD 1169 and for the next 80 years the Ayyubids ruled in Cairo until they in their turn were displaced by their Mamluk slaves.

The Mamluks The Mamluks were a class of Turkish slave-soldiers. The first Mamluk Dynasty, the Bahri Mamluks, were excellent administrators and soldiers. They expanded their control of the Levant and the Hijaz and extended their influence into Nubia. They cleared the Crusaders out of the Levant and checked the Mongol advance into the Middle East in the 1250s. They also improved Egypt's economy and developed its trading links with Europe and Asia. Indeed, the fact that the Mamluks were able to control and profit from the growing European trade with the Far East via Egypt was a major factor in their economic success.

In AD 1382, the Bahri Mamluks were displaced from power by the Burgi Mamluks. Their control of Egypt was a period of instability and decline. The Ottoman Turks, in a swift campaign in 1516-1517, eliminated them and turned Egypt into a province of the Ottoman Empire.

The Ottomans in North Africa

The Ottoman Occupation

The Ottomans emerged with some strength from the northwest heartlands of Anatolia in the 15th century. By 1453 they controlled the lands of the former Byzantine Empire and 65 years later took over Syria and Egypt before expanding deep into Europe, Africa and the Arab Middle East. The Syrian and Egyptian districts became economically and strategically important parts of the empire with their large populations, fertile arable lands and trade links.

Egypt was a valued part of the Ottoman Empire, ownership of which provided the Sublime Porte (the Ottoman Court at Constantinople) with control over the Nile Valley, the east Mediterranean and North Africa. Power was exercised through governors appointed from Constantinople, but over the centuries an Egyptian, mainly Mamluk (of Caucasian origin) elite imposed itself as the principal political force within the country and detached the area from the direct control of the Ottomans. In most areas of the empire, the ability of the sultan to influence events diminished with distance from the main garrison towns and a great deal of independent action was open to local rulers and tribal chiefs outside the larger towns.

The great benefit of the Ottoman Empire was its operation as an open economic community with freedom of movement for citizens and goods. Traders exploited the Ottoman monopoly of land routes from the Mediterranean to Asia to handle the spice, gold and silk from the East, manufactures from Europe and the slave and gold traffic from Africa. Ottoman tolerance of Christian and Jewish populations led in Palestine/Syria to the growth of large settlements of non-Muslims. Arabic continued as the local language and Islamic culture was much reinforced. Elaborate mosques were added to the already

Mohammed Ali and his successors

Mohammed Ali, the founder of the Khedival Dynasty, was born in Macedonia in 1769, came to Egypt in 1800 as an officer in the Turkish army, and was made governor under the nominal control of the Ottoman Sultan in 1805. He remained in post as a vigorous and development-orientated ruler until 1848. He died in 1849, having initiated the modernization of Egypt and the creation of a national identity, and is buried in the eponymous mosque in the Citadel in Cairo.

Ibrahim Pasha, eldest son of Mohammed Ali, was trained as a political leader as well as a soldier. He acted very successfully as his father's right-hand man but in his own right ruled for just four months in 1848. (See his imposing statue erected in Midan Opera by his son.)

Abbas Pasha (1848-1854) was the son of Mohammed Ali's third son, Tusun. He organized the laying of a railway from Cairo to Alexandria with British support and encouragement. In other respects, however, he was reactionary, closing schools of advanced studies and slowing down the modernization process.

Sa'id Pasha (1854-1863), second son of Mohammed Ali, served as an admiral in the Egyptian fleet and gave permission for the Suez Canal to be constructed. Sadly a large foreign debt was left as a legacy to his successor.

Khedive Ismail (1863-1879), son of Ibrahim Pasha, was considered one of the great builders of modern Egypt, being responsible for the building of the Suez Canal, the Opera House, Ras El-Tin Palace and Abdin Palace. He was a man of great energy and vision. He expanded Egyptian influence in the south and east but eventually led the country deeper into debt and into subservience to the French and British.

Khedive Tawfik (1879-1892) was the son of Ismail, during whose reign Egypt's financial problems led to foreign takeover and, finally, the beginning of the British occupation in 1882. Manial Palace, his dwelling in Cairo, houses an important museum (see page 111).

Khedive Abbas Hilmi II (1892-1914), son of Tawfik, was noted for his interest in preservation and conservation of the country's ancient monuments. His attempts to develop a nationalist political movement came to nothing. He was deposed by the British in 1914.

Sultan Hussain Kamal (1914-1917) was the second son of the Khedive Ismail. He owed his throne to the British and, despite the hardships of the war period, he ruled without challenging British power in Egypt.

King Fuad (1917-1936) was another son of the Khedive Ismail, though much more an Egyptian nationalist than his brother Hussain Kamal. Egypt became more politically active and was given a form of independence in 1922 as a constitutional monarchy. However, Fuad was unable to create a political role for himself and was caught up in the political battles between the British and the nationalist politicians.

King Farouk (1936-1952) was Fuad's son and the penultimate Khedival ruler of Egypt. Like his father, he became unable to manage an increasingly radical nationalist community in Egypt, and the British occupiers were distracted by the demands of the Second World War and its legacies of change. Farouk had few political friends and he was forced to abdicate in 1952 in the face of the revolution by the Young Officers led by Gemal Abdel Nasser. Farouk's infant son, Fuad II, was nominally successor to the throne but lost all rights in the new constitution of 1953.

diverse architectural heritage. Outside the larger towns, however, pastoralism, farming and parochial affairs remained the major occupation of the people and cultural and other changes were slow to occur.

Until the late 18th century the Ottoman Empire was wealthy, its armies and fleets dominant throughout the region, but after that date a marked decline set in. European powers began to play a role in politics and trade at the expense of the sultan. The empire began to disintegrate. During the 19th century Egypt under the Khedives, the famous Mohammed Ali and his successor Ismail, were only nominally under the sultan's control. Egypt adopted Western ideas and technology from Europe and achieved some improvements in agricultural productivity. The cost was ultimate financial and political dominance by the French and British in this part of the empire. In Palestine, too, colonial interventions by the French in Syria and Lebanon reduced Ottoman control so that by the time of the First World War the collapse of the Ottoman Empire was complete and the former provinces emerged as modern states, often under a European colonial umbrella.

Egypt and Sudan

In Egypt, the Ottoman administration soon found itself struggling against the unreconstructed remnants of Mamluk society, with the province frequently splitting into two units, each controlled by a different section of the Mamluk Dynasty. By 1786, the Ottomans had destroyed the Mamluk factions and restored central control. In 1798, Napoleon's army conquered Egypt, delivering a profound cultural shock to the Muslim world by demonstrating, in the most graphic manner, the technological superiority of Europe. In 1805 Mohammed Ali was appointed governor and lost no time in breaking away from the Ottoman Empire to found a new dynasty, the **Khedivate**, which remained in power for nearly 150 years.

Mohammed Ali sought to modernize Egypt and to expand its power. He brought in European military advisors, destroyed the remnants of the old political elite in Egypt and instituted wide-ranging economic reforms. In the Sudan, Mohammed Ali's Egypt was more successful; after the initial invasion in 1820, some 40 years were spent consolidating Egyptian rule, although, in 1881, the experiment failed (see box, page 551).

By that time, Egypt itself had succumbed to the financial pressures of its modernization programme. Borrowings from Europe began, with the inevitable consequence of unrepayable debt. In addition, Britain realized the potential importance of Egypt for access to its Indian Empire, particularly after the Suez Canal was opened in 1869. A debt administration was instituted in 1875, under joint British and French control. In 1881, a nationalist officers' rebellion against what they saw as excessive European influence in the Khedivate, provoked a British takeover which lasted until 1922. Following British military commander General Gordon's death in Khartoum and the consequent British campaign against the Mahdist state in the Sudan, which culminated in the Battle of Omdurman in 1898, Britain instituted an Anglo-Egyptian condominium over Sudan.

Colonialism

The British occupation of Egypt introduced a regime which, as the well-known historian Ira Lapidus said, "managed the Egyptian economy efficiently but in the imperial interest". Railways were built and widespread irrigation was introduced; the population virtually doubled in 35 years; private property was increasingly concentrated in the hands of a new elite; and the foreign debt was repaid. Industrialization was, however, neglected and Egypt became increasingly dependent on cotton exports for revenue.

Social and political relations were not so smooth. The British occupation of Egypt coincided with a wave of Islamic revivalism. At the same time, a secular nationalist tradition was developing in Egypt which crystallized into a political movement at the end of the 19th century and was stimulated by Egyptian resentment at British demands on Egypt during the First World War.

At the beginning of the First World War, the potential vulnerability of the Suez Canal (see box, page 383) and the strategic implications of the Turkish-German alliance led Britain to increase its control over Egypt by declaring it a protectorate. This led to the emergence, over the following 20 years, of both Arab and Egyptian nationalist movements which eventually procured nominal independence for Egypt in 1936, although Britain reserved the right to protect the Suez Canal and defend Egypt. By the end of the Second World War, this complex political system had outlived its usefulness and in 1950 Egypt unilaterally abolished the Canal Zone Treaty.

In 1952 the constraints of the British mandates, and the frustration following the defeat in the 1948 Arab-Israeli war, led to the emergence of a new class of young army officers who staged a bloodless coup overthrowing King Farouk and ousting the remaining British troops. The new leader, Colonel Gamal Abdel Nasser, inherited a politically fragmented and economically weak state burdened with an ever-increasing demographic problem.

When the World Bank, at the behest of the USA, refused to help finance the construction of the new Aswan High Dam in 1956, Nasser nationalized the Suez Canal in order to raise the necessary revenues. This sent shock waves throughout the world and led to the Suez Crisis in which an Anglo-French force invaded and temporarily occupied the Canal Zone. Nasser's dreams of development were hampered by Egyptian/Israeli tensions including the shattering Egyptian defeat in the 1967 war. He died in 1970 and was succeeded by Anwar Sadat. Sadat was aware that Egypt could not sustain the economic burdens of continual conflict with Israel so, despite the partially successful October 1973 war which restored Egyptian military pride, he sought peace with his neighbour. In 1977 he made a historic trip to Jerusalem and laid the foundations for the 1979 Camp David Peace Accords which enabled Egypt to concentrate on her own economic development and firmly allied Egypt with the USA. While he was applauded abroad he was considered a traitor in the eyes of the Arab world and Egypt was diplomatically isolated. His assassination by Islamic fundamentalists in October 1981 brought vice-president Hosni Mubarak to power.

Modern Egypt

Government

Egypt became a republic in 1952 with a presidential system of government. For nearly 30 years, president Hosni Mubarak had effective control of the armed forces and the cabinet and could convene or dissolve the single tier People's Assembly virtually at will. He was also head of the ruling National Democratic Party (NDP) and was the principal influence on cabinent membership. Despite efforts to introduce an element of democracy into government with general elections for the People's Assembly the Assembly was still seen as a puppet organization for the regime. Regional government is carried out through four groups of administrations – the governorates for the Desert, Lower Egypt, Upper Egypt and the urban areas. Sub-districts operate from regional capitals and separately for the cities of Port Said, Alexandria, Cairo and Suez. There have been generally fruitless attempts to reform the civil service but, with almost a third of the work force in public administration and defence, progress has been slow. Travellers should not have high expectations of officials and official agencies, though there are some institutions, mainly military, which function well. Personal influence has always been a key element in making the system work. Public dissatisfaction with the lack of any real democracy, coupled with hatred of inherent corruption and widespread economic hardships, errupted in January 2011. Mass anti-government protests broke out across Egypt, centring on Midan Tahrir in Cairo, resulting in the overthrow of the regime and the ousting of President Mubarak on 11 February. At the time of going to press, an interim military regime is in control and will govern by martial law for at least six months until elections are held. It remains to be seen what path towards democracy Egypt will take after this revolution.

There still exist major dissident groups whose activities have in the past affected travellers. The Muslim Brotherhood – a form of fundamentalist Islamic organization (see also box, page 571) – has flourished in Egypt for many years. The Muslim Brotherhood is the leading opposition group but has been officially banned since 1954. However, by running as independent candidates, they won nearly a quarter of seats in the National Assembly in 2005. The more extreme splinter groups, which have resorted to terrorism, have been pursued by state agencies. In addition to attacking members of the government, often successfully, the extremists are opposed to corrupt foreign influences, of which the excesses of the tourist industry, including the country's belly dancers, are seen as a key part. Opposition groups have been suppressed by severe laws such as the detention regulations and by an ever-present security service, the *mokhabarat*.

Heritage

Egypt's natural assets in the form of skills and fabric are at risk. There is now a clear need for the advanced industrialized countries to understand the basis of Islamic science and technology. Certainly this would help to bridge the growing cultural divide between themselves and their more numerous neighbours to the east. In particular, appreciation is required of the way in which Islamic culture has matured over the long-term, so that the valuable skills and technologies of Egypt are not discarded for short-term gains. The pace of 21st-century modernizations might all too quickly sweep away the remains and the folk memories associated with traditional culture.

Egypt fact file

Official name	Gumhuriyah Misr Al-Arabiyah (Arab Republic of Egypt)
National flag	Equal horizontal bands of red, white and black with a central emblem of Salah Al-Din's golden eagle clutching a panel bearing the country's name in its claws.
Official language	Arabic
Official religion	Islam
Statistics	Population: 80 million. Work force: 21.9 million. Religion: Muslim (mainly Sunni) 90%, Christian 10%. Infant mortality rate: 20.5/1000. Fertility rate: 3.1%. Overall life expectancy: 71. Literacy in 15-24 year olds: 86.8%.

Source: UNDP Human Development Report 2008

There is also a risk that rapid technological change forced on a developing Egypt by the industrialized nations could lead to the indigenous technology being unnecessarily discarded instead of being used and, in the future, being deployed with advantage. The urgency of the problem of conservation or rescue of traditional Islamic technologies is acute. War and strife are depleting physical assets such as buildings and other works. Quite apart from man-made disasters, the processes of weathering on mud brick, from which many Islamic traditional constructions are made, is considerable. The comparatively recent abandonment of traditional villages, old mosques and underground water cisterns in Egypt has exposed traditional technology/material culture to destruction by natural erosion.

Agriculture

Agriculture is the basis of the Egyptian economy accounting for 16% of total national output and 31% of employment. Despite very rapid urbanization, farming and the rural community remains at the cultural heart of the country. Current land patterns show the vital importance of the Nile Valley and Delta because the rest of the country is little better than wasteland. Unfortunately even this very limited arable area is being reduced by the encroachment of Cairo and other urban areas.

Traditional agriculture

The great mass of Egyptian farmland is under traditional forms of agriculture and worked by the *fellahin*, the Egyptian peasantry. Farming is based on use of the waters of the River Nile for irrigation which are now available, theoretically, throughout the year from Lake Nasser. There has been a gradual increase in production of commercial crops but self- sufficiency is an important aim of small farmers. Wheat, rice, vegetables and fodder are the main crops, the latter to support the considerable number of draught (3.18 million buffalo), transport (two million asses and 200,000 camels) and other animals (3.23 million cattle, 3.3 million goats, 4.41 million sheep and 87 million chickens) kept mainly on farms. It is estimated that six million people are engaged directly in the traditional farming sector.

Land tenure

Until the 1952 land reforms, 1% of Egypt's landowners possessed 90% of the farming land. The reform stripped the former royal house of its lands and the state took the estates of the great families who had controlled rural Egypt. In their place the revolutionary authorities established centrally controlled cooperatives which substituted civil servants for the former landlords, a move which did little to alter the agricultural system or indeed benefit the peasants. At the present time the peasantry is either landless or has tiny fragments of land which are mainly uneconomic. The average availability of land per cultivator is put at 0.35 ha. Attempts to reclaim land in the desert regions using underground water, newly constructed canals and high technology irrigation systems have, of yet, been of marginal use in resolving Egypt's shortage of agricultural land.

Modern agriculture

Modern farming is principally a matter of the operations of the centrally managed cooperatives on reformed land and the activities of the mixed farms on recently reclaimed land in the rimlands of the delta and the newlands in the desert interiors. The cooperatives, which are still largely government managed, have been turned over to commercial crops for the most part – cotton, sugar cane, maize and rice, some destined for export. The newland farms specialize in exploiting the opportunities for early cropping for the supply of fruit and vegetables to the European market. The new farms stand out in the landscape with their contemporary buildings and rectangular field patterns.

Economic plans, potential and problems

Egypt's economic potential is hindered by the paucity of its natural resources which, besides oil and natural gas produced in large enough quantities to meet domestic demand and some exports, are limited to iron, phosphate and a few other non- hydrocarbon minerals. Another difficulty for Egypt is its meagre area of fertile land and reliance on the waters of the Nile. The growth of irrigation and hydroelectric schemes in the Upper Nile countries is putting the country's water supply at risk and there is no substitute. Industrialization has some scope for expansion but the past record here is not encouraging.

A further challenge for Egypt is that economic growth needs to exceed its 2.1% annual population increase. For some years Egypt has depended on predominantly US and European foreign aid, which still accounts for up to 50% of food supplies needed annually from abroad that enable Egypt to feed itself.

Ultimately it seems that Egypt will have to continue to rely on its current principal sources of foreign exchange – oil, tourism, Suez Canal fees, and expatriate remittances – for its economic salvation. Unfortunately all four are to varying degrees dependent on stable political conditions in Egypt and the rest of the Middle East, which has not been the case.

Energy

At the heart of the modern economy is the **petroleum** sector. The oilfield areas are widely distributed among the Suez/Sinai zone to the east and the more recently discovered Western Desert fields. Crude sales abroad account for about half of all exports.

Natural gas resources are even more significant than oil and several oil companies and governmental organizations are working to further tap into the resource, a cleaner burning fuel that is increasingly important given the state of the environment and the fact that the Aswan High Dam now supplies less than 13% of the country's total electricity use.

Industry

Since the 1952 revolution, there has been a growing tendency to turn to industrialization as a means of achieving faster economic growth and providing for the needs of an expanding population. Most industries were then state-owned, carried very large work forces and were inefficient. The country did, nonetheless, lay the basis for iron and steel, automobile and petrochemical sectors. Industry was concentrated around Cairo and its outliers such as Helwan. In recent years Egypt has industrialized steadily through a growth of small, private- and/or foreign-funded plants producing consumer goods, textiles, arms and processed foodstuffs. Egypt compares well with industrial growth in emerging markets to other developing economies. However, the country is a long way from achieving its ideal of being the manufacturing centre for the Arab world.

Tourism

Another primary source of foreign currency, tourism directly employs one million people in Egypt, in addition to all the income tourists bring in outside of their hotels and restaurants. With almost 13% of Egypt's workforce kept employed by spending visitors, the perpetual wavering of the industry has weighed heavy on the state of the economy. The 1997 Luxor massacre was the first serious blow, resulting in a drop from 4.5 million visitors in 1996 to less than 3.5 million the following year. It recovered only to slump again after 9/11 and the Al-Aqsa *Intifada*. The War on Iraq resulted in another serious setback, as did the Sinai bombings in 2004-2005. Doubtless the current political upheaval, with the overthrow of President Mubarak and an uncertain political path in the future, will have a great impact on tourism during 2011-2012. However, people do always come back to Egypt, and any future government will want to secure the revenue gained from tourism. Optimism remains high that the tourist industry will not suffer too greatly as Egypt finds her path to democracy.

Culture

Architecture

The development of the Egyptian architectural tradition is both complex in so far as many influences affected it over the country's long history and discontinuous because of alien invasions and the impact of internal economic decline. In Egypt, even more than in other states of the Middle East, the extant pre-Islamic heritage in architecture is considerable – readily visible in the pyramids, temples and tombs throughout the length of country. The Egyptian showcase reflects almost all styles from the dawn of history because Egypt lay at the crossroads of the known world for so long, across the rich and desirable nodal point of African, Mediterranean, European, Turkic, Arab and Persian influences. Even after the coming of Islam, Egypt experienced a diversity of architectural styles, as dynasty succeeded dynasty bringing new fusions of imported and local building techniques. In Egypt, Orthodox Islamic, Shi'ite, Ottoman and many other ruling elites brought in their own ideas of the function and design of public/religious buildings, often together with the craftsmen to construct them, but always interacting with local architectural traditions in a way that gave innovative results in mosques and other great building projects.

In Egypt there are not only local variations on the Islamic theme but also continuities in existing vernacular building styles and Coptic church architecture of the Graeco-Roman basilica models, as at St Barbara (see page 108).

The transition from felt to stone

It must be remembered that the early Islamic conquerors were soldiers and often migrant pastoralists in lifestyle. The nomadic tradition, for all its emphasis on a minimum of light, transportable materials has, over time, produced exciting artefacts in the form of tents, particularly the black tent which survive still in the desert outposts of Egypt. Immediately after the conquest of Egypt by Amr Ibn Al-As in the seventh century, the Islamic armies used the existing Egypto-Roman stock of citadels, forts and housing at Fustat, which enabled some of the historical legacy of the area to survive.

Rapid development in Islamic technologies

But is was the remarkably rapid development of science and technology in the construction of Islamic buildings (especially the *mesjid al-jami* – Friday Mosque – from a primitive model in Medina built by Mohammed in AD 622) to the building of the original city of Baghdad on the instructions of Caliph Al-Mansur in the eighth century and the contemporary expansion of Cairo. Notable in this growth of technology was the codification of knowledge by the great ninth-century engineer Al-Karaji, who laid down the scientific principles on which urban water supply works should be undertaken. In the same way, the sciences developed by the Islamic surveyors of the 11th century such as Al-Biruni were also important. It is worth recalling the architectural excitement of the technological and material innovations that stirred invention and development in Egypt in the early Islamic period.

The mosque

At the heart of Islamic architecture is the mosque. The elaboration of Islamic architecture centring on the mosque took place despite the men of the Arab conquest being essentially unlettered nomads and warriors. To redress the shortcomings of the Arab armies, their rulers imported skilled architects, masons and tile workers from established centres of excellence in the empire – Persians, Armenians and others. Together these itinerant teams of artisans and their Islamic patrons developed a wonderful and distinct style of building form and decoration which are among the great legacies of Islam, especially in its early innovative period.

The mosque was the first and main vehicle of spectacular Islamic architecture, because it was a form based initially on the prayer building constructed by the Prophet himself and was important in enabling Muslims to conform with a need to pray together on Friday. In the Madinah mosque the worshippers faced north towards the holy city of Jerusalem but changes brought about in the first century after the death of Mohammed saw the *qibla* – direction of prayer – moved to face Mecca.

Key parts of mosques While all mosques vary in detail of layout and decoration, the basic floor plan remains more or less uniform. Enduring elements early mosques include the **entrance**, normally large and ornate, in the north wall, and the **mihrab**, or niche in the *qibla* wall, which indicates the direction of Mecca and hence the direction in which to pray. The main prayer hall is the **sahn**, which can be a simple square, though more often it has (usually four) arcaded porticoes, the longest and most decorated of which is the sanctuary or *liwan*. The **minbar**, or pulpit, is sited to the right of the *mihrab* and opposite the lectern from which readings are made from the Koran. The **maqsurah**, normally made as a wooden grill, in the sanctuary protects the officiating *imam* from the congregation. The **koubba**, or dome, which was adopted as a roof form in the Dome of the Rock at Jerusalem, from whence Mohammed ascended to heaven. An outer courtyard or **ziyada** is generally found or a recess with flowing water or water jugs where people gather and perform their ritual ablutions before prayer. In the teaching mosques the **liwan** or specially created cloisters or side rooms served as classrooms or hospital sick-rooms.

As the caliphate extended and grew wealthy, so the architecture of the main Friday mosques, made for mass worship by the faithful on the holy day, became more magnificent as exemplified in the Great Mosque of Damascus, built in the eighth century AD, which also had a square **ma'dhana**, or minaret outside the main building for the **muezzin** to call people to prayer. In addition to the great mosques used for public prayer on holy days, there are local mosques of plain construction, many with architectural modifications to suit regional conditions of climate, culture and the availability of building materials in Egypt. The basic layout even here is uniform, though the ornamentation and wealth in carpets in the **sahn** many well vary.

Understanding the mosque

The non-Muslim traveller in Egypt is allowed into nearly all mosques, albeit with some restrictions on times for public access. To make sense of a visit to a mosque, the following principles and guidelines might be useful. Remember that the mosque serves as a centre for congregational worship in Islam. The word *mosque* implies a place of prostration and this is borne out in the plan of every mosque. The architecture of mosques, like that of traditional Christian churches, was designed to induce quiet and contemplation, above the noise and bustle of everyday life – to induce a subjection of the individual to Allah.

Muslims pay particular attention to this solemn sanctity of the mosque. Behaviour is muted and decorous at all times, particularly during services, of which the main ones are Friday Prayers. Women are not forbidden from taking part in public services at the mosque but very rarely do so.

The Egyptian contribution to the mosque

Egyptian mosques in particular show great variety of decoration and some differences in ground plan. Even to the untutored eye, five principal styles of mosque can be seen in most Egyptian cities; Fatimid (967-1171), Ayyubid (1171-1250), Mamluk (1250-1516), Ottoman (1516-1905) and modern (1905-present).

The Fatimids left as their monument the great Mosque of Al-Azhar in Cairo, square in plan with a roofed sanctuary on twin-pillared colonnades. There were two side cloisters.

The Ayyubid buildings After the overthrow of the Fatimids by Salah Al-Din (1171 AD) a new mosque style grew up in Egypt, reflecting the mosque as a major public building by scale and ornamentation. A good example of this style is the Madresa of Sultan Al-Salih Ayyub. Unlike all previous mosques, it provided a separate teaching room for the four great schools of Orthodox Islam in a pair of mosques, each with a double *liwan*. Look out for the windows at ground level and for the discordance between the alignment of the adjacent street and the *liwans*, resulting from the need to set the *qibla* facing Mecca.

Legacy of the Mamluks The legacy of the Mamluks includes the Madresa of Sultan Hassan, built in 1356-1360. It is an Islamic building on a giant scale with the tallest minaret in Cairo. Architecturally, it is also distinct for its simplicity and for the separate *liwans*, entrances to which are all offset from the magnificent *sahn*.

The Ottoman intervention The Ottomans ruled for many years (16th-19th century) during which Egypt experienced a flood of new architectural ideas – the use of light as a motif, and the deployment of slender pillars, arches and minarets of Turkish origin. The Mosque of Suleyman Pasha dated to 1528 was the first Ottoman mosque to be built in Cairo exhibiting these features, that of Mohammed Ali Pasha was one of the last, with its tall octagonal minaret and fine Ottoman dome.

The modern period The modern period is represented by the Al-Rifai Mosque, completed in 1911, which blends Mamluk with contemporary architecture and by the standard village mosque, small, block built, neat but uninspired.

Features of the mosque

Each architectural feature of the mosque has undergone development and change. For example, the minaret (*ma'dhana*) evolved to provide a high point from which the prayer leader (*muezzin*) could call (*adhan*) the faithful to their devotions five times each day. Construction of minarets to give a vantage point for the *muezzin* began in Damascus at the end of the seventh century AD. The earliest minaret that has survived is the one at the Great Mosque in Kairouan, Tunisia, built in the eighth century. The minaret of the Ibn Tulun Mosque in Cairo with its external spiral staircase is dated to 876-879. There is some belief by scholars that the three-part form of the Egyptian minaret was taken from the 135-m Lighthouse of Pharos at Alexandria, of which the extant Abu Sir lighthouse 43 km west of Alexandria is a small-scale copy.

The minarets of the Egyptian mosque are quite distinct despite reflecting influences from elsewhere in the Islamic world. There is great variety in the shape and architectural effects of Egyptian minarets as may be seen from the illustration of three fine minarets in Cairo. The minaret of the Ibn Tulun Mosque has the only original standing minaret tower with an external spiral staircase in Africa and an octagonal third section while the minaret of Sanjar Al-Gawli Madresa carries an extended square base with short and delicate second and third sections. In contrast, the splendid early 15th-century minaret of the Sultan Al-Barquq mausoleum displays great variety as it evolves from square to modified cruciform to circular to octagonal. Yet there is an underlying general tendency for the Egyptian minaret to have three separate levels including a base of square section, overlain by a multifaced column usually octagonal in shape surmounted by a circular tower, itself terminating in an elaborate miniature pavilion. The finial is provided by a small gilded spire carrying a crescent.

The original brick-built minarets in Egypt used finely worked panelling and line work as on the Ottoman minaret of Sultan Hassan near the Cairo Citadel. The passage of time saw the expensive kiln brick medium dropped in favour of stone and finally rough random stone covered with a plaster rendering. These painted towers have been augmented in the recent past both in Egypt and other Muslim countries by what has become a standard modern equivalent, reproduced in new urban and country settlements, alike. It is plain and repetitive – scarcely a description of the more traditional and characterful minarets – but serves its purpose (see box, page 88), and remains a principal topographic marker in the Egyptian landscape.

Madresas – Islamic colleges

Closely linked to the mosque in both religious and architectural form is the *madresa*, a college of higher education in which Islamic teachings lead the syllabus. The institution originated in Persia and developed in the West in the 13th century. The construction of places of advanced learning was a response by orthodox Sunni Islam to the growth of Shi'ite colleges but they soon became important centres in their own right as bastions of orthodox Islamic beliefs. Subjects other than theology were taught at the *madresa* but only in a limited form and in ways that made them adjuncts to Sunni teachings and acceptable to a very conservative religious hierarchy. Unfortunately, therefore, the *madresa* became associated with a rather uninspired and traditional academic routine in which enquiry and new concepts were often excluded. Muslim scholars believe that knowledge and its transmission sadly fell into the hands of the least academic members of the theological establishment. The poor standards of science, politics, arts and ethics associated with the Arab world in the period since the 13th century is put down by some Arab academics to the lack of innovation and experiment in the *madresa*, a situation which has only very recently begun to break down in Sunni Islam. It can, however, be argued that formal Islam needed firm basic teachings in the face of rapidly expanding popular Islam and its extravagant Sufi beliefs.

The shortcomings of the *madresa* in creative teaching terms were in part compensated for by the development of the college buildings themselves. The Egyptian style before the beginning of the 10th century was based on norms borrowed from Syria and Iraq but after that time was mainly modelled on a more Mediterranean tradition with use of a high domed roof as in the mosque of Al-Guyushi in the military area above Sharia Al-Muqqatam in Cairo. The small courtyard is separated from the *sahn* by a vaulted transect. The Al-Azhar Mosque complex in old Cairo began life as a principal congregational mosque but become a great teaching university for Islam, much added to and altered and thus at the apex of the *madresa* form. Other fine architectural works can be seen at the Sultan Barquq Madresa in Cairo with its marbled entry and wonderful four-liwan courtyard and the Madresa of Tatar Al-Higaziya with its ribbed stone dome.

Madresas were until quite recently widely used for student accommodation and teaching. Visitor entry is restricted to specific times but fairly free access is allowed to the building. The rise in awareness of Islam among the young signalled by the high tide of Islamism in Egypt has given the *madresa* an added political interest and social vitality in recent years.

Mausoleums – a very Egyptian celebration of death

One of Cairo's most eye-catching features, visible even as the traveller comes into the centre of town on the Heliopolis road from the airport, is the City of the Dead, where 15th-century tombs and later additions offer an unparalleled range of Islamic funerary architecture. There are also some separate tomb-temples of the Islamic period which are now parts of larger mosque and *madresa* complexes such as the finely worked Tombs of Amir Salar and Sangar a-Gawli in Sharia Saliba.

The private house

Although there was some inertia in the architectural style/practices and building techniques in Islamic Egypt, aided by the Ottoman imperial practice of adopting local building types without change, the private houses belonging to great families and powerful personages showed much individuality alongside strong elements of continuity. All houses had a central courtyard or *waset al-dar*, with perhaps a columned area, fountain, water basin and even trees, which was reached indirectly through a corridor from the street. The house entrance was usually via a studded door to a lobby or pair of small rooms designed to ensure that no-one from the street could either view or easily enter the inner courtyard or rooms. Around the central courtyard were clustered all the principal rooms, including in large houses a collection of family rooms set around a main living space or an area to give family privacy to visitors. These groups of rooms had a small courtyard and may be seen as the successors to the peri-styles of Graeco-Roman houses in North Africa or to the Perso-Ottoman *haivans*. Libraries were important in the houses of public figures, while some great houses had internal *hammam* or bath areas.

Naturally, there was a large staff and housing for it in establishments of this kind to service the kitchen, the daily needs of the resident family and the transport/guard functions necessary for a public figure. The harem was kept distant from the public rooms and often near the baths. Kitchens, stores, water well/storage, stables and accommodation for servants took up considerable space. Egyptian great houses of the 18th and 19th centuries rarely had a developed upper storey, though roof areas were accessed by stairways and used for laundry, the drying of fruits and for water gathering for the cistern below. Open space within the house was often generous in scale. A fine example of the classical Egyptian house can be seen at the House of Zaynab Khatun in Sharia Mohammed 'Abduh near the Al-Azhar Mosque. This building was first laid out in 1468 for Mithqal Al-Suduni, a minister of Sultan Jaqmaqis, and has Ottoman additions. It was restored in the 1950s and is open to the public. There are many fine historic houses in various states of repair in Cairo which are rarely seen by visitors simply because they are overshadowed by so many wonderfully attractive public buildings. As a sample of early housing, visit the **Gayer-Anderson Museum** entered from the southeast corner of the Ahmed Ibn Tulun. The museum is in what are two restored houses of the 16th century and 17th century, with a number of fine features such as a screened balcony (*mashrabiyyah*) and marbled sitting room. Sadly many of the older grand houses in diverse styles borrowed from France, Greece and Italy of the 18th and

19th century have been demolished and few examples remain for which there is public access. In Ismailia look out the house of de Lesseps on Mohammed Ali Quay as an example of 'colonial period' housing.

In lower-class dwellings this same formula was repeated but on a smaller scale and without the baths and libraries. Today, many larger houses are laid out using an offset entry system just like the older Islamic houses, though few modern dwellings benefit from total family privacy, thick walling, a generous central courtyard and ornamental gardens. Finding mud-brick for construction purposes is getting difficult as a result of prohibitions on brick-making, so that low-rise houses are roughly constructed in cement blocks. Increasingly, better-off Egyptians are in any case abandoning the traditional house for apartments in tower blocks.

Art and crafts

Jewellery

The dynamic history of the region has produced imaginative traditional designs mixed with foreign elements leading to a range of decoration few regions in the world can rival. Influences from the Phoenicians, Greeks and Romans, Arabs and Andalusians have each contributed subtly to the immense range of jewellery found in Egypt.

Although some urban dwellers have adopted Western attitudes to dress and decoration, at times of festivals and especially for marriage ceremonies, traditional dress and elaborate jewellery that has changed little since the Middle Ages is still worn. The increase of tourism, while in some cases destroying traditional values, is in fact promoting and preserving crafts, especially jewellery making, by providing an eager and lucrative market for ornaments that was rapidly declining. Unfortunately, with the changes of cultural values, changes in fashion and style also occur and unfortunately large quantities of old, exquisite silver jewellery have been destroyed to provide raw materials for new pieces.

There is a division of tastes and wealth between towns where gold is favoured and the countryside where silver predominates. Basically, traditional styles continue to be popular and jewellery tends to become more traditional the further south one goes. A general shift can be discerned away from silver towards gold, as it is now believed to be a better investment. According to Islamic law, silver is the only pure metal recommended by the Prophet Mohammed. For the majority of Muslims this sanction is felt to apply only to men who do not, as a rule, wear any jewellery other than a silver wedding ring or seal ring.

Despite a whole field of inspiration being forbidden to Muslim jewellers, that of the human form, they developed the art of decorating jewellery in ways that eventually merged to become a distinctive 'Islamic' style. Using floral (arabesque), animal, geometric and calligraphic motifs fashioned on gold and silver with precious and semi-precious gems, coral and pearls they worked their magic.

Every town has its own jewellery *souk*. There is almost always a distinction between the goldsmiths and the silversmiths and there are also shops, designated in Egypt by a brass camel over the door, which produce jewellery in brass or gold plate on brass for the cheap end of the market.

The tourist industry keeps whole sections of the jewellery business in work producing designs which have a historical base: predominantly the scarab, the ankh (the symbol of eternal life), the Eye of Horus, Nefertiti's head and hieroglyphic cartouches. The jewellery

The talisman

The use of amulets and other charms was well developed in ancient Egypt when magic charms were worn like jewellery or put into the wrappings round a mummy – to ward off evil. Among the most sought-after charms was the Eye of Horus or the *ankh*, the cross of life. Protective necklaces were particularly treasured and among the beads would be small carvings of animals representing gods – a hawk for Horus, or a baboon for Thoth. In the same way stelae (marker stones) or house charms stood at the door begging the gods to protect the family from danger.

The 'evil eye' is a powerful force in the contemporary local societies of Egypt and North Africa. It is believed that certain people have the power to damage their victims, sometimes inadvertently. Women are thought to be among the most malignant of possessors of the 'evil eye', a factor associated with the 'impurities' of the menstrual cycle. Even a camera can be considered as an alien agent carrying an 'evil eye' – so only take photographs of people where they are comfortable with the idea and be exceptionally careful about showing a camera at weddings or, more importantly, funerals. Envy too is a component of the 'evil eye' and most conversations where any praise of a person or object is concerned will include a *mashallah* or 'what god wills' as protection against the evil spirits that surround humankind.

Major victims of the 'evil eye' are the young, females and the weak. Vulnerability is seen to be worst in marriage, pregnancy and childbirth, so that women in particular must shelter themselves from it. Uttering the name of 'Allah' is a good defence, alternatively amulets are used, a practice originating from the wearing of quotations from the Koran written on strips of cloth which were bound into a leather case and then strapped to the arm. The amulet developed as a form in its own right, made of beads, pearls, horn or stone brought back from a pilgrimage. Amulets also have the power to heal as well as to protect against the occult. In Egypt today, medicine, superstition and ornament combine to give an array of amulets worn both everyday and for specific use.

spans the entire range of taste and quality from the very cheap mass-produced pendants to finely crafted very expensive pieces. Jewellers also sell a great number of silver items, at the cheaper end of the tourist market, as 'ethnic' jewellery. Gold and silver jewellery is usually sold by weight and, although there might be an additional charge for more intricate craftmanship, this means the buyer must judge quality very carefully.

The earring is by far the most popular and convenient ornament. It appears in an infinite variety of styles with the crescent moon shape being the most common. This is closely followed by the bracelet or bangle which is also very much part of a woman's everyday wardrobe.

Most of the jewellery is worn both as an adornment and as an indication of social status or rank. It generally has some symbolic meaning or acts as a charm. Jewellery is usually steeped in tradition and is often received in rites of passage like puberty, betrothal and marriage. Women receive most of their jewellery upon marriage. This is usually regarded as their sole property and is security against personal disaster.

Many of the symbols recurrent in jewellery have meanings or qualities which are thought to be imparted to the wearer. Most of the discs appearing in the jewellery represent the moon which is considered to be the embodiment of perfect beauty and femininity. The greatest compliment is to liken a woman to the full moon. Both the moon and the fish are considered as fertility symbols. The crescent is the symbol of Islam but its use actually predates Islam. It is the most common symbol throughout the region and acquires greater Islamic significance with the addition of a star inside. Other symbols frequently seen are the palm and the moving lizard both of which signify life and the snake which signifies respect.

Amulets are thought to give the wearer protection from the unknown, calamities and threats. They are also reckoned to be curative and to have power over human concerns such as longevity, health, wealth, sex and luck. Women and children wear amulets more frequently as their resistance to evil is considered to be weaker than that of a man.

The most popular amulets are the *Hirz*, the Eye and the *Khamsa* or hand. The *Hirz* is a silver box containing verses of the Koran. Egypt in particular has a preoccupation with the Eye as an amulet to ward off the 'evil eye', usually modelled on the Eye of Horus which, as with most symbols in Ancient Egyptian jewellery, has always had mystical connotations. The *Khamsa* is by far the most widespread of the amulets, coming in a multitude of sizes and designs of a stylized hand. This hand represents the 'Hand of Fatima', Mohammed's favourite daughter. Koranic inscriptions also form a large section of favoured pendants and are usually executed in gold and also heavily encrusted with diamonds and other precious stones.

Coins or *mahboub* form the basis of most traditional jewellery, from the veils of the Bedouins of the Nile Delta to the bodices of the women from the Egyptian oases. Spectacular ensembles are worn at festivals and wedding ceremonies. Each area, village or tribe has its own unique and extraordinary dress of which jewellery, be it huge amber beads as in Sudan or hundreds of coins, forms a fundamental part.

Among the more interesting items are anklets called *khul khal*, worn in pairs and found in a great variety of styles. In Egypt they are mostly of solid silver fringed with tiny bells. Fine examples are expensive due to their weight. They are losing popularity among the younger generation as they are cumbersome to wear with shoes and because of their undertones of subservience and slavery. It is still possible to see them being worn by married women in the more remote villages of Egypt.

Today the main jewellery bazaar is Cairo's Khan El-Khalili (see page 75). Jewellers in all main cities sell modern versions of traditional jewellery.

Dress

Dress traditions in Egypt are a striking and colourful evidence of a rich cultural heritage. Here, as in all societies, dress is a powerful form of cultural expression, a visual symbol which reveals a wealth of information about the wearer. Dress also reflects historical evolution and the cumulative effects of religious, ethnic and geographical factors on a society.

The many influences which have shaped Middle Eastern history have produced an equally diverse dress culture in which elements from antiquity, the Islamic world and Europe are found. The heritage from earlier times is a rich blending of decorative motifs and drapery. Carthaginian material culture drew upon local traditions of colourful geometric ornament, which is still seen in Berber clothing and textiles, and luxury goods from Egypt. Greek and Roman fashions have survived in the striking dress of the inhabitants of the deserts and mountains. The Arabs introduced a different dress tradition, influenced by the styles of Egypt and Syria. Here the main features were loose flowing robes and cloaks, wrapped turbans and headcoverings which combined a graceful line, comfort and modest concealment. The establishment of Islamic cities encouraged a diverse range of professions and occupations – civil and religious authorities, merchants, craftsmen – all with their distinctive dress. Within cities such as Cairo specialist trades in textiles, leather and jewellery supported dress production. Widening political and commercial relations stimulated new elements in dress.

The Ottoman Turks introduced another feature into city dress, in the form of jackets, trousers and robes of flamboyant cut and lavishly embroidered decoration. Finally European fashion, with emphasis on tailored suits and dresses entered the scene. The intricate pattern of mixed dress styles reflects an adjustment to economic and social change.

The widest range is seen in urban environments where European styles mingle with interpretations of local dress and the clothing of regional migrants. Men have adopted European dress to varying degrees. The wardrobes of civil servants, professional and business men include well-cut sober European suits worn with shirts, ties and smart shoes. Seasonal variations include fabrics of lighter weight and colour and short-sleeved shirts and 'safari' jackets.

Men's city dress alternates between European and local garments according to taste and situation. Traditional dress is based on a flexible combination of loose flowing garments and wraps which gives considerable scope for individuality. One of the most versatile garments is the *gallabiyya*, an ankle-length robe with long straight sleeves and a neat pointed hood, made in fabrics ranging from fine wool and cotton in dark and light colours to rough plain and striped homespun yarn. Elegant versions in white may be beautifully cut and sewn and edged with plaited silk braid. A modern casual version has short sleeves and a V-shaped neck and is made of poly-cotton fabric in a range of plain colours. Professional men may change from a suit into a *gallabiyya* at home, while working class men may wear a plain or striped *gallabiyya* in the street over European shirt and trousers.

A handsome and dignified garment worn by high-ranking state and religious officials is the *kaftan*, another long robe with very wide sleeves and a round neck. The cut and detail, such as the use of very fine braid around the neck and sleeves and along the seams, are more formal than those of the *gallabiyya*. The modern *kaftan* has narrower sleeves and is worn in public by men of an older and more conservative generation. Traditional dress may be completed with the addition of drapery. Examples include the *selham* or *burnous*, a wide semicircular cloak with a pointed hood and the *ksa*, a length of heavy white woollen cloth which is skilfully folded and wrapped around the head and body in a style resembling that of the classical Roman toga.

Headcoverings are a revealing indication of status and personal choice. A close-fitting red wool felt pillbox cap, a *fez*, *tarboosh* or *chechia*, with a black tassle is rarely seen in Egypt now. The distinctive, often checked, headsquare (*kiffiyeh*) of the Bedouin is secured by a heavy double coil (*igal*) of black wool. The ends of the cloth may hang loose or be wrapped around the face and neck for protection against heat or cold. The more traditional loose turban of a length of usually white, less commonly brown, cotton is widespread in Egypt, worn by a wide selection of the working men.

Women's town dress is also a mixture of traditional and modern European forms and depends on wealth, status and personal taste. In the larger cities where women are employed in business and professions, European clothes (modest long-sleeved blouses and long skirts) are worn, accessorized with scarves and jewellery.

However, traditional dress is remarkably enduring among women of all classes. The most important garments are the *kaftan* and *gallabiyya* of the same basic cut and shape as those for men. The *kaftan*, as worn in the past by wealthy women, was a sumptuous garment of exaggerated proportions made of rich velvet or brocaded silk embroidered with intricate designs in gold thread. The modern *kaftan* is usually made of brightly coloured and patterned lightweight fabric and edged with plaited braid. The shape is simple and unstructured with a deep slit at each side from waist to hem. Variations can be found in texture and colour of fabric, changes in proportions of sleeves and length of side slits. The *kaftan* in its many variations is always worn as indoor dress and can suit all occasions. A light shawl may be draped around the neck and the hair tied up with a patterned scarf. Women who normally wear European dress to work often change into a *kaftan* at home. Very chic versions, combined with modern hairstyles and accessories, are worn as evening wear at private and official functions.

Literature

Early Egyptian literary roots

Champollion's and his academic successors' work on the ancient languages of the pharaonic period have opened up official state and private stores of written materials on which work still remains to be done. The pre-Islamic Egyptian tradition was preserved through to the present day to an extent in Coptic liturgies and there is hope for a renaissance in a broader literature now that Coptic is again being taught in religious schools.

Arabic has been the overwhelmingly most important language in Egypt since the 17th century. Classical Arabic had been perfected long before the Prophet Mohammed but its use in the Koran, the oldest existing book in Arabic, has made it the basis of Muslim texts and liturgies, and of the Arabic exemplified in the literatures of the several Arab nations. Among the very earliest of Arabic writing is a tablet dated AD 512 found at Zabad in Syria. A considerable body of oral literature in Arabic is also known to have existed before that time – mainly poetry. In the early centuries of Islam, there was a flowering of religious, philosophical and scientific texts that in translation had an impact well beyond the boundaries of the Muslim world.

Egypt as a literary powerhouse

Cairo in the 19th century witnessed a remarkable expansion of literary activity under internal pressures of embryonic nationalism and the impact of Western cultural and scientific influences in the so-called 'modernist' movement. Expansion was greatly assisted by the exploitation of machine printing presses. Poetry, biography and history became the staple element in Arabic literature of the 20th century. There was also an explosion of interest in political affairs as literacy spread and anti-colonial attitudes deepened. New literary forms were adopted such as the novel, the most influential of which was *Zaynab* by Husayn Haykal published in 1914 dealing with human relations and the pastoral theme.

In the 21st century the book stands and book shops in Egypt carry a growing weight of publications. Much is ephemeral, a great number of school and university text books are translated from Western languages but there is also a good proportion of writing by Arab authors. The international success of Naguib Mahfouz's novels is an indicator of the strength of contemporary Egyptian literature. Among the most influential women writers is Nawwal El-Saadawi, who is revered among leading female writers as a feminist and political radical. Her book *Woman at Point Zero* is available in English and many other languages. She operates under constraint of the censor in Egypt. Look out for books by Ahdaf Soueif, who, although Egyptian, writes in the English language. Her best known work is *In the Eye of the Sun*, a novel based on her own upbringing in Cairo.

Reflections of Egyptian literature in the West

Of course, the number of non-Arab Arabic readers is limited and most educated people outside the Muslim world come into contact with Egyptian literature in translation; the novels of Nobel Prize winner Naguib Mahfouz are a case in point. Mahfouz ran foul of the conservative religious establishment in Egypt and was very badly hurt in 1994 by an Islamist assassin responding to a judgment issued against him by a fundamentalist cleric. He wrote less from that time until his death in 2006, but much of his work remains to be published in translation.

There were also foreign residents in Egypt who were authors of international standing and who brought Egyptian society and environment to the attention of an external audience. Notable in English was Lawrence Durrell with his *Alexandria Quartet*, a series of novels that take as their subject the Alexandria of the expatriate Europeans. Lesser known is Constantine Cavafy (1863-1933), a poet whose home can be visited in Sharia Sharm El-Sheikh in central Alexandria.

Egyptian popular music

Egypt is the recording centre of the Arab world, although Lebanon is beginning to become a rival once more. Egyptian popular music dates back to pharaonic times, but it is influenced much more by the country's Arab and Islamic heritage. While Western music is popular with the cosmopolitan upper class, the vast majority of Egyptians prefer their own indigenous sounds. Arabic music is based on quarter notes rather than the Western half-tone scale.

Classical Arabic music is the traditional music of the upper class with its roots in the court music of the Ottoman empire. Sung in classical Arabic, it is highly operatic, poetic and stylized in form. It is characterized by a soloist backed by mass ranks of violinists and cellists and a large male choir. Its most famous singer by far, and the Arab world's first singing superstar, was Umm Kalthoum (see box, page 112) who died in 1975. During her five-hour concerts, her endless melodic variations could ensure that one song lasted up to two hours.

This tradition was lightened and popularized in the 1960s by Abdul Halim Hafez, the other 'great' of Egyptian music, whose romantic croonings in colloquial Arabic also dominated the Arab musical scene.

By contrast, **Shaabi**, or 'popular' music, is that of the working classes, particularly the urban poor. Like Algerian Rai, it has retained a traditional form but through stars such as Ahmed Adawia or more recently Shaaban Abd Al-Reim – who was catapulted into fame with his song *I Hate Israel* – it broke convention by speaking in plain and often raunchy language about politics and the problems of society.

Al-Musika Al-Shababeya or 'youth music' is highly popular with the middle and upper classes and is sometimes imitated in the *Shaabi*. First appearing in the late 1970s, it is a mixture of Arabic and Western influences, taking typical Arabic singing and Arabic instruments such as the *dof* drum and *oud* lute and underpinning this with a Western beat. The seminal album is Mohamed Mounir's *Shababik* (Windows) which, in partnership with Yehia Khalil, revolutionized Egyptian pop music in 1981 by introducing thoughtful lyrics, harmonies and a jazz-rock influence into still authentically Arabic music. In the late 1980s Hamid Al-Shaeri pioneered the offshoot **al-Jil** or '(new) generation' wave of sound whose fast handclap dance style glories in its self-proclaimed Egyptian-ness. It spawned a clutch of stars such as Amr Diab and Hisham Abbas but its disco style and safe lyrics brought criticism that Egyptian pop music had become stagnant and repetitive. Amr Diab remains a massive star, however, and still enjoyed international success with his 2002 hit 'Akhtar Wahed' and is in huge demand at society weddings. Since 2000, concerts and live bands have become ever more prominent in the music scene and one of the most popular in Cairo now are Wust El Balad, who mix rock, folklore and reggae into the standard pop formula. Shababeya music also has some female stars, the most notorious of which is Ruby whose raunchy lyrics and style have caused her videos to be banned on Egyptian TV.

Much less popular is Egyptian ethnic music, although it has its adherents particularly in the countryside. Of particular note are **simsimmeya** music, named after its dominant guitar-like stringed instrument, which comes from Ismailia and around the Suez Canal zone; **Saiyidi** or Upper Egyptian music, the rhythms of which are based on the wooden horn, *mismar saiyidi*, and two-sided drum *nahrasan*; the **Delta Fellahi** or peasant music which is calmer and less sharp; and **Nubian** music, which possesses a more African feel, and, unlike Arabic music, uses the pentatonic scale. The pre-eminent Nubian folkloric singer is Hanza Alaa Eddin, who counts among his admirers Peter Gabriel and The Grateful Dead.

Recordings of Egyptian music are available in all cities from small roadside kiosks (often bootleg), market stalls, or record shops. For Saidi and Nubian albums, you'll find the largest selection in Upper Egypt around Aswan and Luxor.

People

Egypt has a population of around 80 million, more than 90% of which is concentrated in the Nile Valley and Delta. Average densities are put at 65 people per sq km but in Cairo and the irrigated lands densities of many thousands per square kilometre are recorded. The growth rate of Egypt's population remains a sensitive matter given the difficulties of the government in providing jobs and feeding the people. In the 1970s the annual rate of increase was tailing off at 2.1% per year but there was a spurt again in the mid-1980s to 2.9% per year. However, it fell again in the 1990s to 1.9% and during the years 1996-2006 the rate remained fairly stable at 2.1%. The population at this latter rate will double every 37 years. In the recent past there were high levels of emigration to the oil-exporting states of the Persian Gulf. Meanwhile, the crude death rate has fallen over the last 25 years and life expectancy has gone up to male 67 and female 69, thus adding to the growth of the population size.

The population is youthful with 36% under the age of 15, 58% in the working age group 15-59, and 6% over 60. Literacy is high at 54%, with males at 64% being better placed than women at 39% literate.

Racial origins

Egyptians living in the Nile Valley between Aswan and the sea have ancient origins. It is speculated that the people of the Nile Valley were of Berber origin with some Arab and Negroid admixtures. The people of the Delta had a slightly different early history and thus had distinct racial origins in which Armedoid and Arab elements were fused with the other peoples of the Nile Valley. Other racial additions were made from invasions from Libya, then from the desert lands of Arabia and Persia in the east, and finally the Mediterranean connections which are most graphically illustrated by the Alexandrine conquest and the Roman establishment in northern Egypt. Today Egyptians see themselves as having common racial and cultural origins which increasingly are not identified absolutely with the Arabs and Arab nationalism as a whole.

Religion

The practice of Islam: living by the Prophet

Islam is an Arabic word meaning 'submission to God'. As Muslims often point out, it is not just a religion but a total way of life. The main Islamic scripture is the *Koran* or *Quran*, the name being taken from the Arabic *al-qur'an* (the recitation). The Koran is divided into 114 *sura*, or 'units'. It is for Muslims the infallible word of God revealed to the Prophet Mohammed.

The practice of Islam is based upon five central tenets, known as the Pillars of Islam: *Shahada* (profession of faith), *Salat* (worship), *Zakat* (charity), *saum* (fasting) and *Hajj* (pilgrimage). The mosque is the centre of religious activity. The two most important mosque officials are the *imam* (leader) and the *khatib* (preacher) who delivers the Friday sermon.

The *Shahada* is the confession, and lies at the core of any Muslim's faith. It involves reciting, sincerely, two statements: 'There is no god, but God', and 'Mohammed is the Messenger [Prophet] of God'. A Muslim will do this at every *Salat*. This is the prayer ritual which is performed five times a day, including sunrise, midday and sunset. There is also the important Friday noon worship. The Salat is performed by a Muslim bowing and then prostrating himself in the direction of Mecca (*qibla*). In hotel rooms throughout the Muslim world there is nearly always a little arrow, painted on the ceiling – or sometimes inside a wardrobe – indicating the direction of Mecca and labelled '*qibla*'. The faithful are called to worship by a mosque official. Beforehand, a worshipper must wash to ensure ritual purity.

A third essential element of Islam is *Zakat* – charity or alms-giving. A Muslim is supposed to give up his 'surplus' (according to the Koran); through time this took on the form of a tax levied according to the wealth of the family. Good Muslims are expected to contribute a tithe to the Muslim community.

The fourth pillar of Islam is *saum* or fasting. The daytime month-long fast of Ramadan is a time of contemplation, worship and piety – the Islamic equivalent of Lent. Muslims are expected to read 1/30th of the Koran each night. Muslims who are ill or on a journey have dispensation from fasting, but otherwise they are only permitted to eat during the night until 'so much of the dawn appears that a white thread can be distinguished from a black one'.

The *Hajj* or pilgrimmage to the holy city of Mecca in Saudi Arabia is required of all Muslims once in their lifetime if they can afford to make the journey and are physically able to do so. It is restricted to a certain time of the year, beginning on the eighth day of the Muslim month of *Dhu-l-Hijja*. Men who have been on the *Hajj* are given the title *Haji*, and women *Hajjah*.

The Koran also advises on a number of other practices and customs, in particular the prohibitions on usury, the eating of pork, the taking of alcohol, and gambling. The

Fundamentalism

Islam has been marked over the course of history by the emergence of rigorous revivalist movements. Most have sought a return of the faithful to the fundamentals of Islam – the basic doctrines of the Prophet Mohammed – uncluttered by the interpretations of later Islamic jurists and commentators. Behind the movements was the general idea that Muslims should go back to the simple basics of their religion. Some, like the Wahhabi movement in Saudi Arabia were puritan in concept, demanding plain lives and an adherence to the tenets of Islam in all daily aspects of life. Others imposed a rigorous schedule of ritual in prayer and avoidance of the 'unclean' in public life.

In the last 100 years there has been a growing tendency in the Islamic world for revivalist movements to be reactions to political, military and cultural setbacks experienced at the hands of the Western industrialized world. The aim of the reformers has been to make good the disadvantage and backwardness of the Muslim states when contrasted with the powerful countries of Europe, America and the Far East. The matter is varied and complex, but the clear linkage between an increasingly dominant Western culture and economy and the growth of reactive Islamic movements is inescapable.

In Egypt, the Muslim Brotherhood was an early form of revivalist movement of this kind. Founded by a schoolteacher in 1928, it initially tried to take Islam back to its roots and therefore to its perceived strengths but was later taken over by extremists who used its organization for political ends. It developed as a clandestine political group and harnessed religious fervour to political objectives, including the assassination of political enemies. The Muslim Brotherhood remains Egypt's main Islamic political movement, though in a more moderate form, and now holds a quarter of seats in the National Assembly. Harsh government crackdowns on the Brotherhood have the potential to undermine the liberal concept of Islam that is entrenched in Egyptian society (and has so far stopped more radical groups such as Al-Qaida winning over large sections of the population), leaving it susceptible to the assault of Wahhabism on 'prurient' cultural pastimes. This lack of any understanding between the government and the Islamist opposition gives Egypt's political system an unneeded air of fragility. Politically, the Egyptian government has struggled to find ways either to repress or co-opt extreme Islamist movements which have been responsible for the murder of, and injury to Egyptians and foreign tourists. Attacks on the state by the Islamists have diminished but remain a serious issue and one that is unlikely to completely go away at present.

application of the Islamic dress code varies. It is least used in the larger towns and more closely followed in the rural areas.

Christians in Egypt

The Copts take their name from a corruption of the Greek word *aigupioi* for Egyptian. They were concentrated in the region from Girga to Assiut and had a community in Old Cairo until recently. Nowadays many have moved to the metropolitan area of Cairo and its suburbs. The number of Christians of all kinds in contemporary Egypt is put officially at 3.5 million but is thought to be much larger in reality (at around six million), of which the

Islamic dietary laws

Islam has important rules governing what things may be eaten by the faithful. The Koran specifically forbids the eating of the flesh of swine and the drinking of wine. Other rules dictate how an animal may be slaughtered in proper Islamic manner and ban the consumption of meat from any carcass of an animal that perished other than in the approved way. Any food made of animal's blood such as black pudding or boudin is strictly excluded from the diet of a good Muslim. Non-muslim visitors are not included in these controls and international food is provided in all quality hotels.

The ban on wine has been interpreted as a total outlawing of all alcohol. In practice, local traditions have led to relaxations of the ban. Some areas, such as much of Turkey forbade Muslims from trading in alcohol but not necessarily from drinking it. Indeed sufi poets used wine as a metaphor for liberty and the ecstasy of truth – and perhaps often as a real stimulant to freedom of the soul! As the poet Hafez wrote:

"From monkish cell and lying garb released,
Oh heart of mine,
Where is the Tavern fane, the Tavern priest,
Where is the wine?"

In Egypt Sufism, it was a road to spiritual understanding, but the tradition of wine imbibing was never well developed here. Wine is produced in Egypt though the quality varies round the 'only fair' standard.

Fasting is a pillar of Islam, as originally of Judaism and Christianity. It demands that Muslims desist from eating, drinking and smoking for the month of Ramadan during the hours of daylight. The Ramadan fast, always followed by the faithful in Libya and Egypt, is now rigorously enforced by social influence.

Travellers are unlikely to be disconcerted by Islamic taboos on food and during Ramadan meals will be provided at normal times. However, the Ramadan fast can be very inconvenient for the uninitiated Western traveller. Quite apart from a rising tide of irascibility in some of the Egyptian population, the break of fast in the evening may result in reduced and more erratic service in transport, hotels and restaurants. The holidays that follow the fast have a similar impact as most local people meet with their extended families and leave their places of work for several days.

majority (4.4 million) are of the Coptic Church. There are also some 90,000 members of the Alexandrian rite, affiliated to Rome and quite separate from the Coptic Church proper.

The Coptic language is no longer spoken. It originated from the language spoken in Egypt in the early Christian era, at that time written in Greek characters. Although there were regional variations in the Coptic language, by the fifth century AD they had merged into a universal form throughout Egypt. The language has been in disuse since the sixth century as a working language though it survived in use in religious rituals. Arabic is the language of the Coptic church services.

The Coptic Church is very old – for it is believed that St Mark, author of the gospel, preached in Egypt during the time of Emperor Nero and founded a church in Alexandria. He is considered the first patriarch. The Coptic Church is close in belief and form to the Armenian, Ethiopian and Syrian Orthodox rites and differs from Rome which believes in the dual nature of Christ and God while the Copts believe in the unity of the two. The Arab invasion of Egypt in the seventh century put the Coptic Church under siege and made it a minority religion in the country. It survived, however, despite some persecution.

The Coptic Church is led by the patriarch of Alexandria and all Egypt from Cairo with 12 bishops. The Church runs a series of Coptic churches and monasteries throughout the country and has a foundation in Jerusalem. The Copts are heirs to a rich Christian literature going back to the third century AD. Egyptian governments have normally recognized the historical and religious importance of the Coptic community by giving cabinet posts to at least one of its members. The appointment of Boutros Boutros Ghali as Secretary General of the United Nations in January 1992 did much to highlight the strength of the Coptic role in Egypt.

Religious practices in the Coptic church Baptism of infants takes place when the child is about six weeks old, with three immersions in consecrated water in the plunge bath. Confirmation takes place at the same time. Men and women are segregated during church services (to left and right) and while men must remove their shoes before moving through the screen from the nave to the altar, women are forbidden to enter that part of the church.

The most important celebration in the church's calendar is Holy Week, culminating on Easter Day. This is preceded by a fasting time of 55 days during which no animal products may be eaten, nor wine nor coffee drunk. Like the Muslims no food or drink is permitted between sunrise and sunset. Holy Week is a time of special prayers beginning with a mass on Palm Sunday, after which family graves are visited. On Good Friday altars are draped with black and many candlelight processions take place at dawn – commemorating the entry of Jesus into Jerusalem. Easter Sunday is a day of celebration. Christmas is preceded by 43 days of fasting, ending on 6 January (Christmas Eve) with a midnight service and a celebratory meal. Christmas Day, after church, is a time for visiting relations and friends.

Land and environment

Geography

Egypt lies at the crossroads of Africa and the Middle East as well as having extensive borders on the Mediterranean and Red Sea. The narrow green ribbon of the Nile cuts its way from south to north through the seemingly endless desert. There is an additional 2000 km of Red Sea where offshore the area is fringed with teeming coral reefs. And to complete these rich offerings is the Mediterranean Sea coast. The overall area of the country is 1,002,000 sq km, which is over twice the size of Morocco.

Egypt's location in northeast Africa gives it great strategic importance arising from its position at the junction of the land routes joining Africa to the Near and Middle East and the sea routes from the Atlantic/Mediterranean and the Indian Ocean/Red Sea. Its borders abut in the north onto the Mediterranean coast and for much of the east onto the Red Sea. These two coastal reaches are separated by the isthmus of Suez, a 150-km land bridge linking the eastern outliers of the Nile Delta with Sinai. The international frontier with Israel runs northwest across the Sinai Peninsula from the Taba strip at the head of the Gulf of Aqaba to the coastal plain of the Negev with a deviation to take account of the Gaza strip. The border area is clearly marked and the area is monitored by UN forces. Offshore in the Gulf of Aqaba care is needed not to stray across undemarcated frontiers because the Israelis are particularly sensitive about the possibility of terrorists crossing by sea from the three neighbouring Arab countries just over the water.

Egypt's 1000-km southern border is with Sudan. There is a dispute over ownership of land and economic rights in the Halaib area immediately adjacent to the Red Sea which travellers should avoid. Egypt's 1300-km-long border with Libya on the west is one where there have always been periodic tensions. Nomads often smuggle goods across the border in the area between Siwa/Al-Jaghbub and the coastline in the territory of Ulad Ali tribe. The only official crossing point is in the north on the coast road near Sollum. There is some dispute in the Egyptian-Libyan offshore zone about the alignment of the boundary but this does not currently affect either land or sea transport.

Main regions

Egypt's two largest life-sustaining regions, the Delta and the Nile Valley are both clustered close to its water supplies. The Delta lies north of Cairo and is a vast, low, flat triangle of land through which the tributaries of the Nile pass to the sea. South of Cairo the Nile is contained within a rich and fertile but narrow 2-3 km incised valley which eventually reaches Lake Nasser which is a 425-km ribbon of water extending up to and beyond the border with Sudan. The Delta and the Nile Valley contain almost 99% of the country's cultivated land and approximately the same proportion of the population. East of the Nile Valley is the Eastern Desert and the narrow Red Sea coastline. To the east of the Delta lies the formerly isolated Sinai Peninsula which now has international airports and harbours and is traversed by major roads. West of the River Nile is the Libyan Desert which is usually referred to as Egypt's Western Desert. It is broken up by the occurrence of the Al-Uweinat Heights in the southwest which extend in an elongated plateau towards the lowlands of Dakhla Oasis, which has larger parallel formations in the north as the Qattara and Siwa depressions which, together with Dakhla, form the eastern edge of the Sirtican embayment. The long coastal plain between Alexandria and Marsa Matruh gets narrower towards the west as it approaches the Libyan frontier in the Gulf of Sollum.

Egypt is a country of lowlands and low-lying plateaux of which 60% is less than 400 m above sea-level. The few areas of high relief are the Al-Uweinat Heights in the southwest and in the Eastern Desert adjacent to the Red Sea coast where mountains rise to over 1000 m. The highest mountain in the country is Jebel Katrina next to St Catherine's Monastery (see page 449) which reaches 2228 m at its summit.

Egypt has the River Nile as its only but vital river. The total annual flow down the Nile, from the Blue Nile and River Atbara which both start in the Ethiopian highlands and the White Nile which begins in East Africa's Lake Victoria, is normally 55 cu km. Under the 1959 Nile Waters Agreement, Egypt is entitled to take 37 cu km but, because Sudan so far does not use its full allocation, has been able to take more. There is now growing pressure in all the upstream states for more water and another water crisis is looming.

Egypt has undertaken extensive engineering projects on the River Nile over the centuries which reached a peak with work by the British authorities in the 19th and early 20th centuries. In the modern period the Aswan High Dam, which was designed to give Egypt both water-storage facilities and hydroelectric power for its new industries, was built with Russian assistance in the 1960s. In fact the low level of the River Nile in the late 1980s led to a major crisis and precipitated a crash programme to build power stations dependent on locally produced natural gas.

The construction of the Aswan High Dam also reduced the deposition of silt on Egyptian farmlands in the Nile Valley and the Delta. This has necessitated the use of large quantities of fertilizer and led to a decline in the offshore fishing production. Despite some initial success in the search for sub-surface water reservoirs under the deserts, the River Nile remains the very lifeblood of Egypt. There are no other perennial streams, although *wadis* run elsewhere after heavy rain as brief but dangerous spates.

The Nile and man

The River Nile runs for 6435 km and drains one-fifth of the entire African continent. It rises as the White Nile in Lake Victoria close to Jinja in Uganda and flows as the Victoria Nile through the tropics to Lake Albert. The Nile then begins its course through Sudan as the Bahr El-Jebel eventually reaching the central plains of Sudan and becoming sluggish and ponding up during the annual flood in the marshy papyrus swamps of the *Sudd* (Arabic for 'dam'). The Sobat, which takes its source in the Ethiopian Highlands, is an important water supply for the White Nile system. It joins the Blue Nile at Khartoum. The Blue Nile drains an area deep in the Ethiopian Highlands and, like the Atbara which also joins from the east bank, provides run-off from the Northeast African monsoon. Between Khartoum and Aswan the river passes over six cataracts. The cataracts are wide rapids which make navigation impossible, the steepest of the cataracts, the sixth, is at Sababka 80 km north of Khartoum.

The River Nile in Egypt is entrenched in a narrow valley below the surrounding land and has only one cataract at Aswan. In its last 325 km before entering its Delta the River Nile tends to keep to the east bank with the main cultivated zone of the valley on the west bank. Most irrigation requires water to be lifted from the river by traditional means such as the *saqiya*, *shadoof* or by mechanical pumps.

The Nile Delta is the heartland of Egypt. It covers a great silt plain built up by the river over centuries. The Delta stretches 160 km from the vicinity of Cairo north to the Mediterranean coast and 250 km across the Mediterranean end of the wedge. The main distributaries in the Delta are the Western Rosetta and Eastern Damietta 'mouths', which are the axes of intensive irrigation networks.

The flow of the River Nile has been influenced by fluctuations in rainfall in the countries where the river has its sources. It is possible that long-term climatic change is involved, indicating that the flow in the river might never recover to the average of 84 cu km in the period 1900-1959 from the 1984-1987 level of less than 52 cu km. The water flow during floods has always varied, as we know from inscriptions in pharaonic times, but recent trends are worrying for the states that rely on the river.

Division of Nile waters is governed by the international agreements of 1929 and 1959, which ultimately gave 48 cu km to Egypt and 4 cu km to Sudan but the arrangement involved only Egypt and Sudan and excluded Ethiopia and the East African states. Argument over allocation of Nile waters continues, with Egypt's rights as the downstream state most at risk. Egyptian governments have felt so strongly on the issue of maintaining their share of Nile waters that they have threatened to go to war if the traditional division was changed against Egyptian interests. A master plan for the future use of Nile waters seems to be a distant prospect.

Finding the source of the River Nile

The ancient Egyptians believed that the waters of the River Nile came from a mystical paradise of plenty. Early exploration by the Greeks and Romans established that the Nile ran at least from the site of modern-day Khartoum. In the 17th century a steady stream of European explorers and adventurers began seeking the source of the Nile. Most notable was James Bruce, a Scotsman who in 1769 began a trip which led him to the head waters of the Blue Nile. He was followed by the Englishmen Richard Burton, John Speke and James Grant, who traced the Nile back to the Lake Victoria connection and, finally, Sir S W Baker, who went further south to Lake Albert. Full mapping of the Nile Basin went on until the 1960s. The 1980s film *Mountains of the Moon* captures the discovery of the source of the Nile.

Traditional irrigation in Egypt

In Egypt a basic problem for farmers was lifting water from the River Nile up the river banks which enclosed it. Simple systems of lifting water included windlasses and pulleys were used initially to enable humans or animals pull up leather bags full of river water. Some mechanization followed in which flow-turned wheels were used. These were driven by the current of the river and had pots or wooden containers to carry the water to be deposited at a higher level as at El-Fayoum. In much of the country where irrigation canals have little or no flow an animal powered wheel is exploited. Perhaps the classic and oldest water lifting device in Egypt is the *shadoof*, a weighted beam which is swung into the water by its operator and swung up and on to land with the help of a counter balance on the other end of the beam. In recent times water has been led to the fields by diesel and electric pumps.

The water supply system of Egypt has been much improved. Even before the construction of the Aswan Dam and the later High Dam much had been done to improve the water storage and flow control of the River Nile. Below the river works at Aswan is the Esna barrage, a masonry dam which acts as an enormous weir to raise the height of the River Nile so that water can be led off in side channels to serve the lands lying under the canal. Downstream at Assiut a diversion dam was constructed to send water throughout the year into the existing Ismail Pasha Canal. A second diversion dam was built at Nag Hammadi between Assiut and Esna. In the Delta, the replacement Mohammed Ali barrage was erected on the Rosetta branch. Other dams exist at Edfina and at Sennar in Egypt and Jebel Awlia in Sudan.

The use of the River Nile for navigation has been limited by the narrow, gorge-like nature of some stretches of the upper valley, by the Sudd of Sudan and the existence of the six cataracts in the riverbed downstream of Khartoum. In Egypt the River Nile unites the country and local and long-distance craft ply the waterway on a scheduled basis. A large fleet of passenger vessels transport tourists on the Nile from Luxor to Aswan to serve the great monuments of ancient Egypt (see Nile Cruisers, page 250).

Feluccas

One of the most splendid sights on the river is the local *feluccas* under sail. The *felucca* is a lanteen-rigged sailing vessel for inshore or river work. It has very shallow draught so that it can safely cross shoals and can be easily rowed if the wind is absent or unfavourable. Most *feluccas*, once for transporting produce up and down the Nile, are now available for hire by tourists by the hour or the day for a suitably bargained price which will depend on the season and other factors.

The *felucca* is much smaller and less magnificent than the Nile boats of the ancient Egyptians. These ancient craft developed from bundles of papyrus reeds, woven or bound together to make a buoyant crescent-shaped hull for carrying light loads. Later in the Old Kingdom wood was the principal raw material for constructing larger vessels whose shape followed that of the papyrus craft. Most wood was imported to make a keelless craft with a sail and steering gear made up paddles at the stern. By the Middle Kingdom boats took on a more crescent-shaped silhouette, while a cabin was added to the deck immediately before the stern deck. In the New Kingdom boats on the River Nile were longer and more sophisticated, with deckhouses sited round the mast and ceremonial daises both stern and aft. The sail on the New Kingdom vessels was rigged between top and bottom spars and was much wider than earlier types of sail. An example of an Old Kingdom (fourth Dynasty) boat was found at the Great Pyramid at Giza. It was 43.6 m long and when found was still unbuilt kit. The ship was made to be constructed with boards bound to ribs and to carry a small deckhouse and a single steering paddle.

Climate

Egypt is a desert country. Even its frontage to the Mediterranean offers only a modest tempering of Saharan conditions in the vicinity of the coast in the Alexandria region. Here rainfall is at a maximum with an average of 188 mm per year with summer maximum temperatures averaging 30°C and diurnal ranges rarely more than 10°C. Moving inland brings a rapid decline in rainfall. Cairo, some 150 km from the sea, has an annual average rainfall of 25 mm, a maximum temperature of 35°C and average diurnal ranges of temperature of up to 15°C. Progression southwards brings even greater extremes. At Aswan rainfall drops away to 1 mm per year and average maximum temperatures rise to 37°C with a diurnal range of as much as 18°C. The profound aridity of Egypt outside the Nile Valley makes it absolute desert for the most part, relieved only where water occurs such as the oases of the Western Desert.

Flora and fauna

In the desert environment, annual plants have a very short life span, growing, blooming and seeding in a few short days, covering the ground, when moisture content permits, with a patchy carpet of low-lying blooms. Desert perennials are sparse, tough and spiny with deep root systems. Desert animals are rarely seen, being generally nocturnal and/or underground dwellers to avoid the heat. With water from the River Nile, an oasis or precipitation in the south, the plants are tropical and subtropical and the wildlife becomes more obvious in the form of small and medium-sized mammals like rats and the Egyptian mongoose. Bird life proliferates by the water, with roosting egrets, herons, kingfishers and hoopoes all very common. The birds of prey range in size from kestrels to black kites and Egyptian vultures. The number of Nile fish is decreasing but the coasts continue to teem with fish.

Although predominantly desert there are many sub-regions. The northern coast of Egypt is influenced by the Mediterranean but the scrub vegetation soon gives way to semi desert; the Nile Delta area includes coastal wetlands and salt marsh; inland lakes and reservoirs provide saltwater and freshwater sites for migrating and resident birds. The limited areas of arable agriculture along the narrow Nile Valley and in the extensive Delta contrast with the vast expanses of scrub. The mountain ranges of Sinai provide their own climate, delaying flowering and shortening the growing season. Even the desert areas which cover so much of this region provide contrasts, the sands (*erg*), gravels (*reg*) and rock (*hammada*) being interspersed with the occasional flourishing oasis. The Red Sea provides a colourful and unusual selection of sea creatures.

Many of the habitats mentioned above are under threat, either from pollution, urbanization, desertification or advanced farming techniques. Fortunately the conservation movement is gaining pace and many National Parks and Nature Reserves have been created and programmes of environmental education set up. However, regrettably, wildlife is still regarded as a resource to be exploited, either for food or sport.

In desert regions, wildlife faces the problem of adapting to drought and the accompanying heat. The periods without rain may vary from four months on the shores of the Mediterranean to several years in some parts of the Sahara. Plants and animals have, therefore, evolved numerous methods of coping with drought and water loss. Some plants have extensive root systems; others have hard, shiny leaves or an oily surface to reduce water loss through transpiration. Plants such as the broom have small, sparse leaves, relying on stems and thorns to attract sunlight and produce food. Animals such as the addax and gazelle obtain all their moisture requirements from vegetation and never need to drink, while the ostrich can survive on saline water. Where rain is a rare occurrence, plants and animals have developed a short life cycle combined with years of dormancy. When rain does arrive, the desert can burst into life, with plants seeding, flowering and dispersing within a few weeks or even days. Rain will also stimulate the hatching of eggs which have lain dormant for years. Many animals in the desert areas are nocturnal, taking advantage of the cooler night temperatures, their tracks and footprints being revealed in the morning. Another adaptation is provided by the sandfish, which is a type of skink (lizard) which 'swims' through the sand in the cooler depths during the day. Perhaps the most remarkable example of adaptation is shown by the camel. Apart from its spreading feet which enable it to walk on sand, the camel is able to adjust its body temperature to prevent sweating, reduce urination fluid loss and store body fat to provide food for up to six months.

Mammals

Mammals have a difficult existence throughout the area, due to human disturbance and the fact that the species is not well adapted to drought. Many have, therefore, become nocturnal and their presence may only be indicated by droppings and tracks. Mammals

Papyrus

This word was the name given to the plant *Cyperus papyrus* which grew alongside the Nile. Later it was also given to the writing material made from the plant. Papyrus is a straight, tall, reed-like plant. Its leafless, triangular stems rise to 5 m above the water being as 'thick as a man's arm' at their lower part. It is topped by drooping spikelets of insipid flowers and long, thin leaves like soft ribs of an umbrella.

To produce writing paper the pith from the stem was cut into narrow strips and arranged in alternate layers at right angles to each other. The sheets were pressed together and dried in the sun, the natural juice of the plant making the pieces stick together. The sheets were pasted together to form rolls which varied in length. An example in the British Museum is 30-m long. On the inner side of the roll the fibres went across and the writing usually went the same way as the fibres. Paper made this way was cheap. The Egyptians are recorded as using it soon after 3000 BC and the Greeks around 500 BC.

The more slender stalks were woven into baskets (Miriam made a basket for Moses out of papyrus before she hid him in the same plants by the water's edge) and the thicker ones were tied into bundles and used to construct cheap, light boats, the earliest craft on the Nile. Isis went to search for the several parts of Osiris, see page 546), in a papyrus boat. The fibre used to make ropes, matting, awnings, sails and the pith, in addition to its important use for paper, was actually used as food by the less fortunate. The dried root of the papyrus plant was used as fuel and being a harder substance, the manufacture of utensils. The papyrus plant no longer grows in Egypt but can be found in the Sudan.

represented here include the red fox which is common in the Delta, the sand fox, a lighter coloured hare, the shrew and two species of hedgehog, the long-eared and the desert. The appealing large-eyed and large-eared desert fox or fennec is less common and is often illegally trapped for sale. Despite widespread hunting, wild boar survive. Hyenas and jackals still thrive particularly in Sinai, while wild cats are also found in Sinai and the Delta. The leopard, formerly common in North Africa, is now extremely rare, but is occasionally seen in some isolated regions in Sinai, often to the panic of the local people.

There are three species of gazelle, all well adapted to desert conditions; the dorcas gazelle preferring the Western Desert, the mountain gazelle inhabiting locations above 2000 m in Sinai and the desert gazelle locating in the *reg* of the northern Sahara. The latter is often hunted by horse or vehicle, its only defence being its speed. There are over 30 species of bat in the area, all but one – the Egyptian Fruit bat – being insectivorous. Recent ringing has shown that bats will migrate according to the season and to exploit changing food sources. Many species of bat have declined disastrously in recent years due to the increased use of insecticides and disturbance of roosting sites.

Rodents are well represented. They include the common house rat and the large-eyed Sand rat, the gerbil and the long-tailed jerboa which leaps like a tiny kangaroo. Many gerbils and jerboas, sadly, are found for sale in pet shops in Europe.

Weasels are common in the Delta region, and even in urban areas such as Cairo, where they keep down the numbers of rats and mice. The snake-eating Egyptian mongoose with a distinctive tuft on the end of its tail is frequently sighted but sightings of porcupines are rare and then only in the far south. The ibex too is only found in the south.

Prickly pears or barbary figs

Opuntia Vulgaris is the Latin name for the prickly pear cactus, with its large, flat, spined leaves, which is used for boundary hedges or less commonly shelter belts to deflect wind from delicate plants.

The attractive flowers of yellow or cyclamen occur on the rim of the leaves from May onwards and provide a bright splash of colour. If your visit occurs in July or August do not hesitate to try the fruit of the barbary fig. Obtain them ready peeled from roadside sellers and certainly do not pick them yourself as they are protected by a multitude of fine spines, almost invisible to the naked eye, which can only be removed by an expert.

Warning – consume these fruits in moderation as more than two or three can cause constipation!

Reptiles and amphibians

The crocodile, treated as a sacred animal by the Egyptians (see El-Fayoum) who kept them in tanks by their temples, is no longer found north of the Aswan Dam. A few remain in Lake Nasser and in Sudan. Tortoises are widespread. Terrapins are less common. Both tortoises and terrapins are taken in large numbers for the pet trade. There are over 30 species of lizard in the area, the most common being the wall lizard, which often lives close to houses. Sand racers are frequently seen on dunes, while sand fish and sand swimmers take advantage of deep sand to avoid predators and find cooler temperatures in the desert *reg*. Spiny lizards have distinctive enlarged spiked scales round their tails. The *waran* (or Egyptian monitor) can grow to over a metre in length. Geckoes are plump, soft-skinned, nocturnal lizards with adhesive pads on their toes and are frequently noted running up the walls in houses. The chameleon is a reptile with a prehensile tail and a long sticky tongue for catching insects. Although basically green, it can change colour to match its surroundings.

Snakes are essentially legless lizards. There are some 30 species in Egypt but only vipers are dangerous. These can be identified by their triangular heads, short plump bodies and zig-zag markings. The horned sand-viper lies just below the surface of sand, with its horns projecting, waiting for prey. The saw-scaled carpet viper, which is of variegated dark camouflage colours, is twice the size but don't stay to measure, it is considered the most dangerous snake in Egypt. The Sinai or desert cobra, up to 2 m long, was the symbol of Lower Egypt. It too is deadly. Sand boas stay underground most of the time. Most snakes will instinctively avoid contact with human beings and will only strike if disturbed or threatened. For what to do if you are bitten by a snake, see Health, page 39.

River, lake and marine life

There are over 190 varieties of fish in the River Nile, the most common being the Nile bolti with coarse scales and spiny fins and the Nile perch, frequently well over 1.5 m in length. Bolti are also found in Lake Nasser. Other fish include the inedible puffer fish, lungfish (which can survive in the mud when the waters recede), grey mullet and catfish which are a popular catch for domestic consumption but some species can give off strong electric shocks. Decline in fish numbers is blamed on pollution, over-fishing and change of environment due to the construction of the Aswan Dam. Marine fish such as sole and mullet have been introduced into Lake Qaroun, which is becoming increasingly saline.

The Mediterranean Sea has insufficient nutrients to support large numbers of fish. The numerous small fishing boats with their small mesh nets seriously over-exploit the existing stock. The catch is similar to the North Atlantic – hake, sole, red mullet, turbot, whiting. Sardines occur off the Nile Delta but in much reduced quantities due to pollution. Tuna, more common to the west, are caught off Libya too. Grey mullet is fished in and off the Nile Delta while sponges, lobsters and shellfish are also harvested.

The fish of the Mediterranean pale into insignificance against 800 species of tropical fish in the Red Sea not to mention tiger and hammerhead sharks, moray eels, slender barracudas and manta rays. Here, while sport and commercial fishermen chase after tuna, bonita and dolphin, scuba divers pay to explore the fringing coral reefs and view the paint box selection of angel, butterfly and parrot fish and carefully avoid the ugly scorpion fish and the even more repulsive stone fish.

Insects

There are a number of insects that travellers might not wish to encounter – bedbugs, lice, fleas, cockroaches, sand flies, house flies, mosquitoes, wasps and ants. By contrast there are large beautiful dragonflies which hover over the river, the destructive locusts fortunately rarely in swarms, and the fascinating black dung beetles, the sacred scarab of the Egyptians, which roll and bury balls of animal dung as food for their larvae. Scorpions, not insects, are all too common in Egypt. See box, page 512.

Birds

The bird life in the region is increased in number and interest by birds of passage. There are four categories of bird. Firstly, there are 150 species of **resident bird**, such as the crested lark and the Sardinian warbler. Resident birds are found mainly in the fertile strip of the Nile Valley and in the Nile Delta. There are surprisingly few in the oases. Secondly, there are the **summer visitors**, such as the swift and swallow, which spend the winter months south of the equator. **Winter visitors**, on the other hand, breed in Northern Europe but come south to escape the worst of the winter and include many varieties of owl, wader and wildfowl. **Passage migrants** fly through the area northwards in spring and then return southwards in increased numbers after breeding in the autumn. Small birds tend to migrate on a broad front, often crossing the desert and the Mediterranean Sea without stopping. Such migrants include the whitethroat, plus less common species such as the nightjar and wryneck. Larger birds, including eagles, storks and vultures, must adopt a different strategy, as they depend on soaring, rather than sustained flight. They rely on thermals created over land, so must opt for short sea crossings following the Nile Valley, Turkey and the Bosphorus.

There are a number of typical **habitats** with their own assemblage of birds. The Mediterranean itself has a poor selection of sea birds, although the rare Audouin's gull always excites twitchers. Oceanic birds such as gannets and shearwaters, however, overwinter here. The Red Sea coast hosts the indigenous white-eyed gull and white-cheeked tern, migrant pelicans, gregarious flamingos and, near Hurghada, brown boobies. Ospreys breed on the nearby Isle of Tiran.

Wetland areas attract numerous varieties of the heron family such as the night heron and squacco heron, while spoonbill, ibis and both little and cattle egrets are common. Waders such as the avocet and black-winged stilt are also typical wetland birds. The species are augmented in winter by a vast collection of wildfowl. Resident ducks, however, are confined to specialities such as the white-headed duck, marbled teal and Ferruginous duck. On roadsides, the crested lark is frequently seen, while overhead wires often contain corn buntings, with their jangling song, and the blue-cheeked and green bee-eaters. Mountain areas are ideal for searching out raptors. There are numerous varieties of eagle, including Bonelli's, booted, short-toed and golden. Of the vultures, the griffon is the most widely encountered. The black kite is more catholic in its choice of habitat, but the Montagu's harrier prefers open farmland.

The desert and steppe areas have their own specialist resident birds which have developed survival strategies. Raptors include the long-legged buzzard and the lanner, which prefer mountain areas. The Arabian rock pigeon of Sinai is a protected species. Among the ground-habitat birds are the houbara bustard and the cream-coloured courser. Duponts lark is also reluctant to fly, except during its spectacular courtship display. The trumpeter finch is frequently seen at oases, while the insectivorous desert wheatear is a typical bird of the *erg* and *reg* regions.

Special mention must be made of the Nile Valley. Essentially a linear oasis stretching for hundreds of kilometres, it provides outstanding birdwatching, particularly from the slow-moving cruise boats, which are literally 'floating hides'. Apart from the wide range of herons and egrets, specialities include the African skimmer, Egyptian geese, pied kingfisher and white pelican. Even the tombs and monuments are rewarding for the ornithologist, yielding Sakar falcons, Levant sparrowhawks and the black-shouldered kite.

Birdwatching locations

Lake Burullus A good location for Delta birds – thousands of wigeon, coot and whiskered tern and other water birds. Access can be difficult.

Lake El-Manzala (in the Eastern Delta with access from Port Said) It is an important overwintering area for water/shore birds.

Lake Bardweel (on the north Sinai coast) Well known for migratory birds in their thousands, especially in the autumn, and in particular water birds, ducks and herons. Shore birds too like avocet and flamingo can been seen here.

Wadi El-Natrun Here in the shallow lagoons may be found Kittlitz's plover and blue-cheeked bee-eaters, but don't expect an instant sighting.

Near Cairo Near the airport at Gabel Asfar the recycling plant provides a mixed habitat with opportunities to see painted snipe, Senegal coucal and the white-breasted kingfisher. The Egyptian nightjar may be heard but is unlikely to be seen. Cairo Zoo, Giza is recommended for the song birds in the gardens. In cities, or any settlement for that matter, the black kite acts as a scavenger. Near Cairo, at the Pyramids, look out for the Pharaoh eagle owl.

Suez This is the perfect place for observing migratory birds; raptors in particular which pass over in their thousands, also gulls, waders and terns. Look for the greater sand plover and broad-billed sandpiper also white-eyed gull and lesser-crested tern more often associated with the Red Sea. All these resident and migratory birds are attracted by the mud flats and conditions in Suez Basin.

Taba region Residents include Namaqua dove, little green bee-eater, mourning, hooded and white-crowned black wheatears. Migrants include olivaceous and orphean warblers. White-cheeked and bridle tern can be seen off the coast between Taba and Sharm El-Sheikh.

Mount Sinai Look for Verreaux's eagle which nest in this area. Residents include lammergeier, Sinai rosefinch frequently sighted near St Catherine's Monastery, barbary falcon, sand partridge, little green bee-eater, rock martin, desert and hoopoe larks, scrub warbler, white-crowned black and hooded wheatears, blackstart, Tristram's grackle, brown- necked raven and house bunting. There are special migrants to be observed such as masked and red-backed shrikes, olive-tree and orphean warblers. Look also for Hulme's tawny owl.

Tip of Sinai (around Ras Mohammed) The Nabq protected area is recommended. Mark up sooty falcon seen on the cliffs nest here, Lichtenstein's sandgrouse further inland near the recycling plant, white-eyed gull, bridled tern, white-cheeked and lesser-crested tern (less common are brown booby and crested tern). Osprey nest in this region too. Migratory birds include white storks. There is a white stork sanctuary near Sharm El-Sheikh.

El-Fayoum oasis Noted for water birds and waders. It has been associated with duck hunting from ancient times. Overwintering duck, coot and grebe gather here in great numbers. Lake Qaroun in El-Fayoum oasis is a saltwater lake and the area is now protected. In winter it's covered with water fowl. On the north shores of the lake falcons and hawks quarter the ground and in the trees see the green bee-eater, bulbul and grey shrike. Note too lapwing, swallow and Senegal thick-knee. Shore birds include sandpiper, curlew, coot and grebe.

Red Sea (off Hurghada) A rich habitat supporting 15 species of breeding bird, both water birds and sea birds. Brown booby, western reef egret, white-eyed and sooty gulls, crested, lesser crested and white-cheeked terns, red-billed tropicbird, bridled tern are on the list. The islands in the Red Sea provide a safer habitat for the birds. Such is Isle of Tiran, approach only by boat, not to land. Osprey nest here, in places quite common. Sooty (a few) and white-eyed gulls (more common) are found on the uninhabited islands further south.

Around Luxor Look for black-shouldered kite, black kite, Egyptian vulture, Senegal thick-knee, purple gallinule with perhaps a painted snipe or a Nile Valley sunbird on Crocodile Island where Hotel Movenpick has made an effort to protect the environment for these birds. On the other side of the River Nile in the Valleys of the Kings and Queens are rock martin, trumpeter finch, little green bee-eater. Desert birds found anywhere in desert are represented here by hoopoe and bar-tailed larks.

Dakhla Oasis The surface of the large lake called the Fishpond is almost obscured by birds, mainly avocet, stilt and coot.

Aswan One of the best places for herons and kingfishers, best viewed from the river itself. Pied kingfishers and Egyptian geese are common. At Aswan try Saluga Island, which is a protected area.

Abu Simbel This is important due to its southerly location. After viewing the monuments take time to look for rarities including long-tailed cormorant, pink-backed pelican, yellow-billed stork, African skimmer, pink-headed dove and African pied wagtail.

Jebel Elba In the very southeast corner of Egypt Jebel Elba has samples of sub-Saharan birds – Verreaux's eagles, pink-headed doves and perhaps even ostrich. However, this region cannot be visited without a permit, which is not likely to be forthcoming.

Books

Ancient Egypt

Murnane, William J *The Penguin Guide to Ancient Egypt* (1983, Penguin Books). A comprehensive book detailing the monuments and culture of Ancient Egypt. There are loads of illustrations and descriptions of almost every major monument in the country.

Quirke, S and Spencer J (eds) *The British Museum Book of Ancient Egypt*. An accessible and solid general overview of Ancient Egypt, with glossy pictures highlighting the museum's impressive collection.

The Shire Egyptology series (Shire Publications Ltd, Princes Risborough, Bucks, UK). A fascinating series including *Egyptian Coffins, Mummies, Pyramids and Household Animals, Temples, Tools & Weapons*.

Tyldestey, Joyce *Daughters of Isis: Women of Ancient Egypt* (1994, Penguin Books). "Egypt was undoubtedly the best place to have been born a woman in the whole of the Ancient World." Drawing upon archaeological, historical and ethnographical evidence, this book tells why and offers an engaging account of women's daily life in Egypt.

Area-specific guidebooks

Blottiere, Alain *Siwa; the Oasis* (2000, Harpocrates). A nice little book that's not too dense. Gives a good account of the legends, ancient history and modern-day life of Siwa through a personalized narrative.

Fakhry, Ahmed *Siwa Oasis* (1973, AUC Press). An extensive look at the life, history and monuments of Siwa from the premier Egyptian archaeologist of the Western Desert. Also look for Fakhry's *Bahariyah and Farafra* (2003, AUC Press) where he highlights his explorations into the oases.

Gazio, Pierre *The Fayoum; An Historical Explanation* (2007, Harpocrates). Beautiful photographs and a thoroughly interesting insight into the history of the Fayoum. You could spend a week there with the help of this book.

Ghisotti and Carletti *The Red Sea Diving Guide*. Written by Italians but translated into several languages, the colourful guide includes 3D diagrams of reefs and illustrations of more than 100 species of fish.

Haag, Michael *Alexandria; City of Memory* (2004, Yale University Press). A portrait of Alex in the early 20th century, it's especially good on bringing the literary figures who lived in the city to life.

Hassanein Bey, AM *The Lost Oases* (AUC Press). Fascinating re-edition of the great desert explorers' travails in the Western Desert, first published in 1925.

Hewison, R. Neil *The Fayoum; History and Guide* (2008, AUC Press). Good for practical information as well as history, this little guide takes you along some interesting detours.

Vivian, Cassandra *The Western Desert of Egypt – An Explorer's Handbook* (2007, AUC Press). The most comprehensive guide to the Western Desert, includes maps, GPS coordinates, and loads of historical, ecological and cultural information. This book is essential to any extensive exploration of the oases. Revised in 2007.

Williams, Caroline *Monuments in Cairo – The Practical Guide* (2008, AUC Press). The most up-to-date and comprehensive guide to Islamic Cairo. Includes detailed walking tours, maps and historical accounts, and explanations of all the important buildings and mosques, just recently revised.

Fiction

Al-Aswany, Alaa *The Yacoubian Building* (2004, AUC Press). This novel is set in an actual building on Sharia Talaat Harb, it's quite racy and very enlightening about all levels of Egyptian society. It caused a big stir in the Arabic world when first published. There is a film of the same name.

Follet, Ken *The Key to Rebecca* (Pan Books, 1980). A pulse-racing adventure story set during the Second World War teams up a young Jewish girl and a stalwart hero to stop the Nazis unlocking the secrets of Cairo.

Hassan Oddoul, Haggag *Nights of Musk* (2007, AUC Press). Stories from Old Nubia, before and after the flood, capturing the essence of a culture that is being swept away.

Ondaatje, Michael *The English Patient* (McClelland and Stewart, 1992). Passionately evokes the mystery and beauty of the desert and stimulates an interest in the lives of explorers.

Soueif, Ahdaf *The Map of Love* (Anchor, 2000). A family saga mixing the history of modern Egypt and a 19th-century love story.

Thomas, Rosie *Iris and Ruby*. Light-hearted poolside reading about the relationship between a teenage runaway to Egypt and her grandmother, who reminisces about her life in Cairo during the Second World War.

History, culture and society

Abu Lughod, Lila *Veiled Sentiments: Honour and Poetry in a Bedouin Society*. A sensitive anthropological study of the Awlad Ali tribe in the Western Desert that puts forth an insightful account of Bedouin culture.

Atiya, Nayra *Khul-Khaal – Five Egyptian Women Tell Their Stories*. Compelling accounts from five women of varying socio-economic and cultural backgrounds. Offers tremendous insight into the lives of contemporary Egyptian women.

El-Sadawi, Nawal *The Hidden Face of Eve*. Written by the renowned Egyptian feminist, the book details the situation of Arab women and speaks directly of female genital mutilation, divorce and prostitution. It is banned in Egypt.

Murphy, Caryle *Passion for Islam – Shaping the Modern Middle East: The Egyptian Experience* (2002, Scribner). An accessible and fascinating account of Islam and its ever-changing role in Egypt. Offers a thorough introduction to those interested in understanding the motivation and fuel behind Islamist movements, especially amid the current political climate.

Rodenbeck, Max *Cairo: the City Victorious*. Written by the Economist's Egypt correspondent, this accessible and impressively researched book details 5000 years of Cairo's great history and offers keen insight into the nature of Egyptians past and present.

Maps and town plans

Cairo Maps: A Practical Guide (2008, AUC Press). Accurate, easy-to-use, well-indexed booklet covering all Cairo and Giza. Small enough to easily carry around with you.

Michelin Map No 154 covers Egypt. The **Oxford** Map of Egypt (OUP) is very good. Sinai, printed in Switzerland by **Kümmerly and Frey**, gives most of the sites.

Look out for the excellent maps produced by **SPARE** – Society for the Preservation of Architectural Resources of Egypt – with detailed information of The Citadel, Islamic Cairo and Khan El-Khalili.

Several maps of the whole of Egypt and of the major towns are available from the Egyptian Survey Authority, 1 Sharia Abdel Salam Aref, Dokki, Cairo, open Sun-Thu 0830-1500, T02-37484904. www.portal.esa.gov.eg/Portal.

Travel accounts

Duff Gordon, Lucie *A Passage to Egypt* (2007, Tauris & Co Ltd). This unconventional Victorian left her husband and children in England to travel to Egypt for health reasons, but never went home. She became immersed in Egyptian society of the late 1800s and this account of her life, based on correspondence with her family, is utterly absorbing.

Edwards, Amelia B *A Thousand Miles up the Nile* (1877, Century Publishing, London). Engaging detailed travel account highlighting a journey up the Nile, extensive writing on ruins as well as people, in the voice of a 19th-century woman novelist who, after this trip, became an authority in Egyptology.

Flaubert, Gustav *Flaubert in Egypt* (Penguin). A collection of personal writings that highlight more of Flaubert's jaunts through brothels and bathhouses rather than an exploration of the monuments. An entertaining and often hilarious read.

Pick, Christopher *Egypt: A Traveller's Anthology*. An interesting collection of writings from a diverse group of 19th- and early 20th-century writers – Gustav Flaubert, Mark Twain and EM Forster among them.

Sattin, Anthony *The Pharaoh's Shadow*. A travel account that embraces both modern and ancient Egypt, weaving an interesting tale that illuminates links and continuities between the two worlds.

Sattin, Anthony *Winter on the Nile* (2010, Hutchinson). Gustave Flaubert and Florence Nightingale both journeyed down the Nile in the 19th century, at the same time and yet never meeting. This excellent book reveals their separate voyages of self-discovery, and also brings their world of untouched landscapes, monuments and temples vividly to life.

Sonnini, CS *Travels in Upper and Lower Egypt*. Famed naturalist and traveller, the Frenchman visited Egypt in 1777. The English translation of his accounts was published in 1799.

Wildlife

Boulos, Loutfy *Flora of Egypt* (1999, AUC Press). Premier guide to plant life in Egypt, encyclopedic in scope and including over 500 drawings and pictures.

Hoath, Richard *Natural Selection – A Year of Egypt's Wildlife* (1992, AUC Press). Engaging text recounting Egypt's wide array of life throughout the varied regions and seasons, includes animal sketches by the author. Richard Hoath also writes a column on wildlife for the monthly *Egypt Today*.

Khalil, Rafik and Aly, Dina *Egypt's Natural Heritage* (2000). A beautiful hardcover picture book offering documentation of Egypt's wildlife and scenery through images and descriptive text.

Lane, Edward W *An Account of the Manners and Customs of the Modern Egyptians* (AUC Press). First published in 1836, this seminal account has never been out of print.

Miles, John *Pharaohs' Birds* (1998, AUC Press). Detailed guide of ancient and present-day birds in Egypt, including possible safaris for avid birdwatchers.

Footnotes

Contents

Basic Egyptian Arabic for travellers

It is impossible to indicate precisely in the Latin script how Arabic should be pronounced so we have opted for a very simplified transliteration that will give the user a sporting chance of uttering something that can be understood by an Egyptian.

Greetings and farewells

Hello	*ahlan wasahlan/ assalamu aleikum*
Goodbye	*ma'a el salama*
How are you?	*Izayak?* (m); *Izayik?* (f)
Fine	*kwayis* (m) *kwayissa* (f)
See you tomorrow	*Ashoofak bokra* (m) *Ashoofik bokra* (f)
Thank God	*il hamdullil'allah*

Basics

Excuse me	*law samaht*
Can you help me?	*Mumkin tisa'idny?* (m) *Mumkin tisa'ideeny* (f)
Do you speak English?	*Bitikalim ingleezy?* (m) *Bitikalimy ingleezy?* (f)
I don't speak Arabic	*Ma bakalimsh 'araby*
Do you have a problem?	*Fee mushkilla?*
Good	*kweyyis*
Bad	*mish kweyyis, wahish*
I/you	*ana/inta* (m); *inty* (f)
He/she	*howwa/heyya*
Yes	*aiwa/na'am*
No	*ia'a*
No problem	*mafeesh mushkilla*
Please	*min fadlak* (m) *min fadlik* (f)
Thank you	*shukran*
You're welcome	*'afwan*
God willing	*Insha'allah*
What?	*Eih?*
Where?	*Fein?*
Where's the bathroom	*Fein el hamam?*
Who?	*Meen?*
Why?	*Leih?*
How?	*Izay?*
How much?	*Bikam?*

Numbers

0	*sifr*
1	*wahad*
2	*etneen*
3	*talaata*
4	*arba*
5	*khamsa*
6	*sitta*
7	*saba'a*
8	*tamenia*
9	*tissa*
10	*ashra*
11	*hidashar*
12	*itnashar*
13	*talatashar*
14	*arbatashar*
15	*khamstashar*
16	*sittashar*
17	*sabatashar*
18	*tamantashar*
19	*tissatashar*
20	*'ayshreen*
30	*talaateen*
40	*arba'een*
50	*khamseen*
60	*sitteen*
70	*saba'een*
80	*tmaneen*
90	*tissa'een*
100	*mia*
200	*miteen*
300	*tolto mia*
1000	*alf*

Dates and time

Morning	*el sobh*
Afternoon	*ba'd el dohr*
Evening	*masa'*

Hour	*sa'a*
Day	*yom*
Night	*bil leil*
Month	*shahr*
Year	*sana*
Early	*badry*
Late	*mit'akhar*
Today	*inaharda*
Tomorrow	*bokra*
Yesterday	*imbarah*
Everyday	*kol yom*
What time is it?	*E'sa'a kam?*
When?	*Imta?*

Days of week

Monday	*el itnein*
Tuesday	*el talaat*
Wednesday	*el arba'*
Thursday	*el khamees*
Friday	*el goma'*
Saturday	*el sapt*
Sunday	*el had*

Travel and transport

Airport	*el matar*
Plane	*tayara*
Boat	*markib*
Ferry	*'abara*
Bus	*otobees*
Bus station	*mahatit otobees*
Bus stop	*maw'if otobees*
Car	*'arabiya*
Petrol	*benzeen*
Tyre	*'agala*
Train	*atr*
Train station	*mahatit atr*
Carriage	*karetta; calesh*
Camel	*gamal*
Donkey	*homar*
Horse	*hosan*
Ticket office	*maktab e'tazakir*
Tourist office	*makta e'siyaha*
I want to go…	*a'yiz arooh* (m) *a'yiza arooh* (f)
Does this go to…	*da beerooh*
City	*madeena*
Village	*kareeya*
Street	*shari'*
Map	*khareeta*
Passport	*gawaz safar*
Police	*bolice*

Directions

Where is the…	*fein el…*
How many kilometres is ...	*kem kilometers el ...*
Left	*shimal*
Right	*yimeen*
After	*ba'ad*
Before	*'abl*
Straight	*doghry; ala tool*
Near	*gamb*
Far	*bi'eed*
Slow down	*bishweish*
Speed up	*bisora'*
There	*hinak*
Here is fine	*hina kwayis*

Money and shopping

25 piasters/a quarter pound	*robe' gineih*
Bank	*benk*
Bookstore	*maktaba*
Carpet	*sigada*
Cheap	*rikhees*
Do you accept visa?	*Mumkin visa?*
Do you have...	*'andak ...* (m); *andik ...* (f)
Exchange	*sirafa*
Expensive	*ghaly*
Gold	*dahab*
Half a pound	*nos gineih*
How many?	*kem?*
How much?	*bikem?*
Jewellery	*seegha*
Market	*souk*
Newspaper in English	*gareeda ingleeziya*
One pound	*gineih*
Silver	*fada*
That's too much	*kiteer awy*
Where can I buy...	*fin ashtiry...*

Food and drink

Beer	*beera*
Bread	*'aysh*
Chicken	*firakh*
Coffee	*'ahwa*
Coffee shop	*'Ahwa*
Dessert	*helw*
Drink	*ishrab*
Eggs	*beid*
Fava beans	*fu'ul*
Felafel	*ta'ameyya*
Fish	*samak*
Food	*akul*
Fruit	*fak ha*
I would like...	*a'yiz* (m); *a'yza* (f)
Juice	*'aseer*
Meat	*lahma*
Milk	*laban*
Pepper	*filfil*
Restaurant	*mata'am*
Rice	*roz*
Salad	*salata*
Salt	*malh*
Soup	*shorba*
Sugar	*sucar*
The check please	*el hisab law samaht* (m) *samahty* (f)
Tea	*shay*
Tip	*baksheesh*
Vegetables	*khodar*
Vegetarian	*nabaty*
Water	*maya*
Water pipe	*shisha/sheesha*
Wine	*nibeet*

Accommodation

Air conditioning	*takeef*
Can I see a room?	*Mumkin ashoof owda?*
Fan	*marwaha*
Hotel	*fondoq*
How much is a room?	*Bikam el owda?*
Is breakfast included?	*Fi iftar?*
Is there a bathroom?	*Fi hamam?*
Room	*oda*
Shower	*doush*

Health

Aspirin	*aspireen*
Diarrhea	*is hal*
Doctor	*dok-tor*
Fever	*sokhoniya*
Hospital	*mostashfa*
I feel sick	*ana 'ayan* (m) *ana 'ayanna* (f)
I have a headache	*'andy sod'a*
I have a stomache ache	*'andy maghas*
I'm allergic to	*'andy hasasiya*
Medicine	*dawa*
Pharmacy	*saydaliya*

Useful words

Church	*kineesa*
Clean	*nadeef*
Cold	*bard*
Desert	*sahara*
Dirty	*wisikh*
Hot	*har*
Less	*a'al*
More	*aktar*
Mosque	*gami'*
Mountain	*gabal*
Museum	*el mathaf*
River	*nahr*
Sandstorm	*khamaseen*
Sea	*bahr*
Summer	*seif*
Valley	*wadi*
Winter	*shita*

Dodging touts

You'll get hassled less and respected more if you learn a bit of Arabic.

no thank you!	*La'a shocrun*
I told you no!	*U'ltilak la'a*
I don't want; I'm not interested	*Mish ay-yez* (m) *mish ay-zza* (f)
enough	*Bess*
finished, that's it	*Khalas*
'when the apricots bloom' (ie 'in your dreams')!	*F'il mish mish*

Who's who in Ancient Egypt

Kings and queens

Akhenaten

Amenhotep IV, who later took the name of Akhenaten, ruled for 15 years around 1379-1352 BC. He is remembered for the religious revolution he effected.

The authority of the priests of Amun-Re, the Sun God, the chief god of the Egyptians, had grown so great it almost rivalled that of the pharaohs. The pharaoh was regarded as the son of Amun-Re and was bound by strict religious ritual, part of a theological system understood clearly only by the priests, wherein lay their power.

Meanwhile a small religious cult was developing with the god Aten (a manifestation of the old sun-god Re of Memphis) at the centre, the sole god. This new cult appealed to the young prince and after he succeeded his father he changed his name to Akhenaten meaning 'it is well with the Aten' and moved his capital from Thebes to an entirely new city identified with the modern Tell El-Amarna, though no trace remains (see page 201).

This idea of the sole god was new in Egypt, new in the world, and Akhenaten is known as the first real monotheist. There is no evidence that the new religion appealed to the mass of the people for while the king was deeply involved in his worship his empire fell into decay.

The new religious ideas were expressed in carvings. While the pharaoh as the son of god could not be portrayed and the queen rarely appeared at all in reliefs and statues, Akhenaten changed all the conventions and his artists represented him, and his wife and family, as they were, riding in chariots, bestowing gifts to his followers, even kissing.

When Akhenaten died at the age of 41, his half brother, Tutankhaton, a young boy, succeeded him. The Court returned to Thebes, the priests of Amen returned to power, the king changed his name to Tutankhamen (see page 593) and everything possible was done to wipe out Akhenaten's 'heretical' religion.

Cheops

Cheops or Khufu was an Old Kingdom pharaoh, the second king of the fourth Dynasty succeeding his father Snefru. His mother was Queen Hetepheres. He reigned between 2549 BC and 2526 BC. He is well known as the builder of the Great Pyramid of Giza (see page 117). He is recorded as having had four wives. Three names are given – Merityetes, Hen-utsen and Nefert-kau, one of whom was his sister/half-sister, and one queen is unnamed. For Merityetes and Hen-utsen there are smaller pyramids built beside his own.

Herodotus records his reign and that of his son Chephren (Khafre) as a century of misery and oppression under wicked and tyrannical kings but in Egyptian history he is considered to have been a wise ruler. Nevertheless, there certainly was misery. He shut all the temples and forbade the people to make sacrifices. At the same time he forced them to give up their livelihoods and assist in the construction of the pyramid being part of the team of a hundred thousand men who worked a three month shift. The preliminaries and actual construction took over 20 years. Part of the preparation was the construction of the oldest known paved road. Its purpose was to allow the huge granite facing blocks for his pyramid to be dragged and rolled to the site. Small fragments of the road exist today.

Cleopatra 69-30 BC

In 51 BC at the death of her father Ptolemy XIII she became joint ruler of Egypt with her younger brother. Three years later she was ousted from the throne but reinstated by Julius Caesar. It is related that while Julius Caesar was seated in a room in the citadel in Alexandria two slaves entered bearing a magnificent carpet. 'Cleopatra, Queen of Egypt, begs you to accept this gift' said one and as the carpet unrolls out sprang the 19-year-old Cleopatra. Dazzled at the sight of such loveliness, so the tale goes, the stern warrior fell in with all her plans, helping her subdue her enemies and permanently dispose of her brother.

When the daggers of the conspirators at Rome removed Caesar's protection she turned her charms on Mark Antony. Called to his presence to answer charges of assisting his enemies she came, not as a penitent but in a barge of beaten gold, lying under a gold embroidered canopy and fanned by 'pretty dimpled boys'. This certainly caught his attention and conveniently forgetting his wife and duties in Rome he became her willing slave. While Cleopatra had visions of ruling in Rome as Antony's consort his enemies at Rome prevailed on the Senate to declare war on such a dangerous woman. The battle was fought at Actium in 31 BC but Cleopatra slipped away with her ships at the first opportunity leaving Antony to follow her as a hunted fugitive.

Cleopatra attempted to charm Octavian, Antony's conqueror, but he was made of sterner stuff and proof against her wiles. Antony killed himself and Cleopatra, proud and queenly to the last chose to die by the bite of a poisonous asp (an unsubstantiated fact), rather than be taken to Rome in chains. Certainly an eventful life for a woman who never reached her 40th birthday.

Hatshepsut

She was the first great woman in history living about 1503-1482 BC in the 18th Dynasty. She had immense power, adopted the full title of a pharaoh and was dressed in the full regalia down to the kilt and the false beard. She ruled for about 21 years.

She was the daughter of Tuthmosis I and Queen Ahmose and was married to her half brother Tuthmosis II who came to rule Egypt in 1512 at the death of his father. He was not very strong and at his death Hatshepsut, who had had no sons of her own, became the regent of his young son Tuthmosis III, son of a minor wife/woman in the harem. She took effective control of the government while pretending to be only the prince's regent and Tuthmosis III was made a priest of the god Amun.

Around 1503 she gave up all pretence of being subservient to her stepson and had herself crowned as pharaoh. To have reached this position and to retain it indicates the support of a number of faithful and influential officials in her government. Her steward Senenmut was well known and may have been the father of her daughter Neferure.

Determined to expand commercially she despatched (with Amun's blessing, she said) an impressive expedition to Punt on the African coast (now part of Somalia) from which were brought gold, ebony, animal skins, live baboons, processed myrrh and live myrrh trees to decorate her temple and that of Amun in Karnak. Tributes also flooded in from Libya, Nubia and the nearer parts of Asia.

In the name of/to honour the god Amun-Re (the main god of the region and her adopted 'father') she set about a huge reconstruction programme repairing damage caused to earlier temples and building new ones. The chapels to the Thebian Triad behind the Great Pylon of Ramses II at Luxor were built by Hatshepsut and Tuthmosis III. She renovated The Great Temple of Amun, at Karnak where she introduced four huge (30 m+) obelisks made of Aswan granite. At Beni Hasan she built a rock cut temple known as Speos

Artemidos but her finest achievement was her own beautiful temple on Luxor's West Bank cut into the rock at three different levels.

The wall reliefs in the temple fortified her position of importance, her divine birth which is a very complicated set of scenes involving the god Amun, her mother and herself as a baby; her selection as pharaoh by Hathor; her coronation by Hathor and Seth watched over by her real father, Tuthmosis I.

Her expedition to the exotic land of Punt is depicted in very great detail with pictures of the scenery (stilt houses) and selected incidents from the voyages (some baboons escaping up the rigging). Items brought back are offered to Amun in another relief. She even had depicted the huge barges used to transport the four obelisks she had erected for her adopted father (Amun) in Karnak.

To continue her position as a pharaoh even after her death she had her tomb cut in the Valley of the Kings. It was the longest and deepest in the valley.

Late in his reign Tuthmosis III turned against the memory of Hatshepsut and had all her images in the reliefs erased and replaced with figures of himself or the two preceding male pharaohs. In many places her cartouches have been rewritten too. Unfortunately he had all her statues destroyed.

Ramses III

Ramses III reigned from 1198-66 BC, in the 20th Dynasty, which was noted for the beginning of the great decline of Egypt. He was not part of the decline, however, and was considered a worthy monarch. He excelled himself in the earlier part of his reign with victories on land and victories at sea vanquishing the Cretans and the Carians. On land he used the military colonies established by previous rulers such as Ramses II and Seti I to conduct his missions further into Asia. He had little trouble subduing the tribes far into Asia but had problems nearer at home – having to fight to hold his position as pharaoh. A group of invaders made up of Libyans, Sardinians and Italians managed to advance as far as Memphis in the eighth year of his reign but their defeat put him in a much stronger position internally.

Having had his fill of expeditions to foreign parts and no doubt having returned with sufficient booty to have made the trips worthwhile and make him a very wealthy monarch he paid off his troops and set about adding to and constructing temples and other monumental works. Of particular note are the buildings at Medinet Habu (see page 278). Here there is a magnificent temple with the walls covered in reliefs depicting the engagements on land and sea in which he had been so successful. Even the gate is inscribed with reliefs showing the despatch of prisoners and where a neat design on the pylons shows a cartouche of each vanquished country surmounted by a human head and with bound arms. This is a valuable historical record of Egypt and the surrounding lands at this time.

In brief he restored law and order within Egypt and provided some security from outside aggression. He revived commercial prosperity. His attentions to the temples of Thebes, Memphis and Heliopolis certainly enriched Egyptian architecture. He was, however, unable to turn the slow ebb of his country's grandeur that was said to be suffering from 'fundamental decadence'.

He was assassinated. Four sons, all bearing the his name, succeeded him but their reigns were not distinguished and the decline of Egypt was hastened.

Tutankhamen

Pharaoh of the New Kingdom, 18th Dynasty, Tutankhamen reigned from 1361-1352 BC. He was the son of Amenhotep III and probably his chief queen Tiy and was married to

Akhenaten's daughter. He was too young to rule without a regent. He died in the ninth year of his reign at about 18 years of age, leaving no surviving children, his regent Ay succeeded him by marrying his widow.

He was originally called Tutankhaton but changed his name to Tutankhamen to distance himself from Atun and the cult of Atun worship of his half brother Amenhotep IV (Akhenaten). He moved his capital back to Memphis and to eradicate the effects of the rule of his predecessor he restored the temples and the status of the old gods and their priests. His greatest claim to fame was his intact tomb discovered by Howard Carter in 1922, details of which are given on page 265.

Tuthmosis I – the trend setter

He was an 18th-Dynasty pharaoh who ruled from around 1525-1512 BC. He is noted for his expansion of the Egyptian Empire south into Nubia and east into present day Syria. He led a river-bourne expedition into Nubia to beyond the fourth Cataract (he was after the gold there) and set up a number of defensive forts along the route. His foray across the Euphrates was part of his campaign against the Hyksos who caused many problems for the Egyptians. Tuthmosis I used the Euphrates as the border over which he did not intend these enemies to cross.

He is also noted for the building and renovation works he contracted at Karnak. Much of the inner temple of Amun at Karnak is attributed to him. In particular the sandstone fourth Pylon in front of which one of his obelisks still stands, and the limestone fifth Pylon that marked the centre of the temple at the time, and behind which was the original position of the sanctuary of Tuthmosis I.

He was born in the era when burial in a pyramid was 'out of vogue' and being buried in a secret tomb in the rocks of the surrounding hillside was just coming 'in'. It is suggested that his tomb was the first in the Valley of the Kings and he certainly set a trend. Even so his red quartzite sarcophagus was found in the tomb of his daughter Queen Hatshepsut and is now in the museum in Cairo.

Zoser

This was a king of the Old Kingdom, the second king of the 3rd Dynasty. It is hard to piece together his history. He succeeded his brother and perhaps reigned for 19 years between 2667-2648 BC. Two of his daughters were called Intkaes and Hetephernebti, their names taken from steales in the complex.

His funerary complex at Saqqara (see page 159) is an example of some of the world's most ancient architecture and it was all, not only the Step Pyramid, but also the huge enclosure wall and the subsidiary temples and structures, designed by Zoser, under the charge of his talented architect/chancellor/physician Imhotep. This building was important being the first large scale building to be made completely of stone. In addition it was of an unusual stepped design. Many of the buildings in the surrounding complex were never intended for use but were replicas of the buildings used by the pharaoh on earth so that he could use them in eternity. Eventually he was buried under his Step Pyramid. So what was the other tomb for in the complex? Perhaps it was for his entrails as it was too small for a royal person?

He made Memphis his capital, giving impetus to the growth in importance of this town, which eventually became the political and cultural centre.

Travellers interested in seeing his likeness must visit room 48 in the museum in Cairo. It has the huge seated figure of King Zoser taken from the complex.

Deities

There were hundreds of gods and goddesses worshipped by the ancient Egyptians. Over time some grew in favour and others became less important. In addition each district of the country had its own deities. It is useful to have an idea of their role in ancient Egypt and to recognize them on the wall paintings and carvings. They could be represented in more than one way, being different aspects of the same god.

Aker

An earth god often shown with the head of a lion, Aker guarded the east and west gates of the afterworld.

Amun

He was first worshipped as a local deity in Khmun in Middle Egypt in Hermopolis and later when his cult reached Thebes his importance spread to all of Egypt. He was believed to be the creator of all things, to order time and the seasons. When he sailed over the heavens he controlled the wind and the direction of the clouds. His name means 'the hidden' or 'unseen one'. At times he was identified with the sun-god Re, hence Amun-Re, and as Amun-Min was the god of fertility. He was often drawn as a human form with twisted ram horns and two tall feathers as a headdress, a sceptre/crook in one hand and a ceremonial flail in the other, an erect phallus and a black pointed beard.

The sacred animals with which he was identified were the ram and the goose (the Great Cackler). As the ram-headed god he renewed the life in the souls of the departed. He was part of the Thebian Triad with Mut, his wife, and Khonsu, his adopted son.

Anubis

This god was responsible for the ritual of embalming and looking after the place where the mummification was done. Indeed he was reputed to have invented embalming, his first attempt of this art being on the corpse of Osiris. When Anubis was drawn on the wall on either side of a tomb's entrance the mummy would be protected. He helped Isis to restore life to Osiris. He was also included in scenes weighing the dead person's heart/soul against the 'feather of truth', which was the only way to enter the next world. In the earlier dynasties of the Old Kingdom he held an important position as lord of the dead but was later overshadowed by Osiris. Later he was better known simply as a conductor of souls. He was closely associated with Middle Egypt and bits of Upper Egypt. He was depicted as a recumbent black dog/fox/jackal or a jackal-headed god. On any illustration the ears of the creature were alertly pricked up and slightly forward. The association with a fox/jackal was the number of jackals that were to found in the cemeteries. Sometimes he was shown seated on a pylon.

Anukis

This was the wife of Khnum and the mother of Sartis, the third member of the Elephantine Triad. She was the goddess of the first cataract area and was depicted wearing a high crown of feathers and carrying a sceptre of papyrus plant.

Apis Bulls

The sacred bulls of Memphis were black bulls with a white triangle on the forehead and a crescent shape on the flank. A sacred bull was believed to contain the spirit of Ptah, lived in a palace and was guest of honour at state functions. When it died it was mummified and buried at the tomb of the Serapeum at Saqqara and a new younger bull, its reincarnation, took its place. It was sometimes represented with a sun disc between its horns.

Apophis

This was a symbol of unrest and chaos in the form of a large serpent. It was kept under control by the stronger powers of good, in particular the cat-goddess Bastet and by Sekhmet the fierce lioness god.

Aten

He was the sun-god depicted as the solar disc emitting bright rays that often terminated in human hands. For a time, under Akhenaton, worship of Aten was the state religion. He was considered the one true god. After the demise of Akhenaton he disappeared into obscurity.

Atum

This was one of the first forms of the sun-creator god. He was originally just a local deity of Heliopolis but joined with Re, as Atum-Re, he became more popular. Re took the part of the sun at the zenith and Atum that of the setting sun when it goes to the underworld. As this he was represented as a man, sometimes an old man, indicating the dying of the day.

Bastet

The famous cat goddess of the Delta region was the daughter of Re. She represented the power of the sun to ripen crops and was considered to be virile, strong and agile. Her home city was Bubastis (see page 183) but her fame spread widely. She was initially a goddess of the home but in the religion of the New Kingdom she became associated with the lioness war goddess. She was regarded as a friendly deity – the goddess of joy.

She was represented as a woman with a cat's head, carried an ancient percussion instrument, the sistrum, in her right hand, a breast plate in her left hand and had a small bag hung over her left arm. Numerous small cat figures were used in the home for worship or as amulets. Mummified cats (votive offerings) were buried in a vast cemetery at Bubastis. She was loosely connected with Mut and Sekhmet.

Bes

This was a strange creature, the god of dancing, merriment and music, and capable of playing many musical instruments. He was always portrayed as a jolly dwarf with a large head, a round face, round ears, goggle eyes, protruding tongue, sprouting lion's whiskers, which later became stylized as a fancy collar, under a tall headdress of feathers. He had short bow legs and a bushy tail. He was one of the few gods drawn front face on rather than in profile.

It is suggested his hideousness was to drive away evil spirits and hence pain and sorrow. As the guardian of women and children he kept the house free from snakes and evil spirits. He was portrayed on vases, mirrors, perfume jars and other toilet articles and even on the pillows of mummies. He was frequently represented in birth houses as the guardian of women in childbirth.

Buto

This deity, also known as Wadjet, was a cobra goddess whose fame spread from the Delta to all of Lower Egypt. She was known as the green goddess (the colour of papyrus) and was said to be responsible for the burning heat of the sun.

Geb/Shu/Nut

These members of the Heliopolitan ennead, are frequently depicted together. Geb (god of the earth), son of Shu (god of the air or emptiness), was married to his sister Nut (goddess of the sky). The sun-god Re was displeased with this association although most gods seem to marry their sisters and ordered Shu to keep the two apart. Hence all three are represented together with Shu between Geb's green recumbent form and Nut arching in the sky.

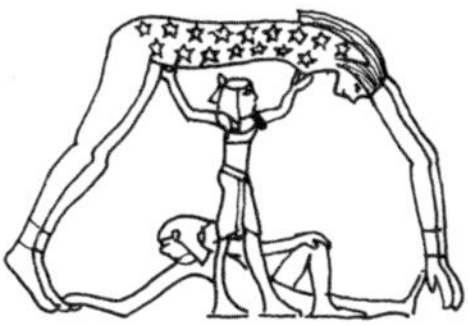

Geb

As explained, this was the god of the earth, the physical support of the world. Along with his sister/wife Nut he was part of the second generation ennead of Heliopolis. He was usually drawn as a man without any distinguishing characteristics though he sometimes had the head of a goose which was distinguishing enough. He could be also be depicted as a bull in contrast to Nut's cow. His recumbent form mentioned above represented the hills and valleys and the green colour the plants growing there.

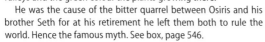

He was the cause of the bitter quarrel between Osiris and his brother Seth for at his retirement he left them both to rule the world. Hence the famous myth. See box, page 546.

Hapi/Hapy

He was the god who lived next to the river because he controlled the level of Nile and was responsible for the floods. He was even responsible for the dew that fell at night. He was represented as a bearded man with a female breast wearing a bunch of papyrus on his head and carrying offerings or leading a sacrifice. There was an association here with Apis.

There was another god Hapi who was one of the sons of Horus, the baboon headed guardian of the Canopic jar of the lungs.

Harpokrates

This was the name given to Horus as a child. In illustrations he was a naked child with a finger in his mouth. The side lock of hair he wore is an indication of youth.

Hathor

This was the goddess of the sky who was also known as the golden one. Her name means 'castle of the sky-god Horus'. She was a goddess of festivity, love and dance. The original centre of her cult was Dendara and her importance spread to Thebes and Memphis. With the increase in her fame and contrary to her earlier nature she became known as a goddess of the dead and the region of the dead. She was believed to have been responsible for nearly destroying all mankind. See myths, page 218. On illustrations she was represented as a cow, a cow-headed woman or a woman with a headdress of a disc between two horns and large cow-like ears.

Heh

This lesser known god can be seen kneeling holding a palm branch notched with the number of the years in a king's life.

Heqet

This was a frog goddess who sometimes assisted at childbirth.

Horus

Horus was a very important god, the falcon-headed sky god. Horus means 'he who is far above' and the hawk fits this image. Hence he was depicted as hawk-headed or even a full hawk often wearing the double crown of Egypt. The hawk's eyes are thought of as the sun and the moon. Horus' left eye was damaged in his conflict with Seth and this was thought to indicate the waxing and waning of the moon. He probably originated in the Delta region and the cult spread to all of Egypt. It was only later that he became associated with Isis and Osiris as their son.

Imhotep

He was a man, one of two mortals (the other was Amenhotep) who were totally deified. He was recorded as the designer of the first temple at Edfu and the official architect of Zoser's step pyramid. When he was later deified it was as a god of healing and made the honorary son of Ptah. He was known, not as a temple builder, but, as a patron of scribes, a healer, a sage and a magician, and was worshipped as a god of medicine. He was considered to have been a physician of considerable skill.

At the time of the Persian conquest he was elevated to the position of a deity. His cult reached its peak in Greaco-Roman times where his temples at Memphis and on the island of Philae in the Nile were often crowded with unhealthy people who slept there hoping that a cure for their problems would be revealed to them in their dreams. He was depicted on wall illustrations as a seated man holding an open papyrus.

Isis

She was one of the most important ancient Egyptian goddesses, the most popular goddess in Egypt from around AD 650 right up to the introduction of Christianity. Originally the cult was in Lower Egypt but it spread to embrace eventually the whole of Egypt and parts of Nubia. Her name means 'throne' and because the word throne is feminine it was depicted by a woman's figure. This made her the mother of the king who

sat on the throne. She receives a number of mentions as the grieving widow of Osiris. She was also the sister of Osiris, Seth and Nephthys.

She was held in high esteem as the perfect wife and mother and became the goddess of protection. She was also an enchantress, using her power to bring Osiris back to life again. She was represented as a woman with the hieroglyph sign for a throne on her head, an orb or sun between two horns, and was generally sitting nursing her son Horus, or seen also kneeling at a coffin of Osiris. Her ability to give life to the dead meant she was the chief deity at all funerals.

There are temples to her at Dendara, on Philae and in the Nile Delta. Several temples were dedicated to her in Alexandria where she was the patroness of seafarers. She was guardian of the Canopic jar that held the viscera.

Khepri

He was the sun-god represented as a scarab beetle with a sun disc. As the scarab beetle rolls a ball of dung around so the Egyptians thought this was how the sun was moved. They thought the scarab possessed remarkable powers and used it as an amulet. See box, page 162.

Khnum

He was represented on wall drawings as a man with a ram's head with long twisted horns. The Egyptians believed he made the first man by moulding him in clay from the Nile on a potter's wheel. Over time his area of responsibility changed. He lived at the first cataract on the Nile where he presided over all the cataracts of the Nile. He had the authority to decide whether or not the god Hapi 'rose' and the Nile flooded. He was associated with temples at Elephantine and Esna.

Khonsu

He was regarded as the son of Amun and Mut. The three made up the Thebian Triad. He had the ability to cast a range of spells, dispel demons and act as an oracle. He travelled through the sky at night and sometimes assisted the scribe of the gods. As the moon god he was usually represented as a man wearing a disc of the full moon and horns on his head or the head of a falcon. He had a single lock of hair to show his youth.

Ma'at

This well loved deity was the goddess of order, truth and justice. She was the daughter of the sun-god Re and Thoth the goddess of wisdom. She can be seen at the ceremony of judgement, the balancing of the heart of the deceased against a feather. The scale was balanced by Ma'at or her ideogram, the single ostrich feather as a test of truthfulness. The priests with her were judges. She often appears, confusingly, as two identical goddesses, a case of double judgement. She was very popular with the other gods. She was also depicted on wall paintings in the solar barque.

Mertseger

This was the goddess of the west, a cobra goddess from Thebes. She was said to punish those who did not come up to scratch with illness or even death.

Min

This was the god of sexual prowess, of fertility and of good harvests. He was depicted bearded, wearing a crown of two feathers, phallus erect, a ceremonial flail in his raised right hand and a ribbon from his headdress reaching down to the ground at the back. He was worshipped at Luxor. His feast day was an important festival often associated with wild orgies. He was worshipped too as the guardian of travellers as he protected the routes to the Red Sea and in the Eastern Desert. The lettuce was his sacred plant.

Montu

The war god Montu who rose to importance in the 11th Dynasty protected the king in battle. He has a temple to the north of the main temple in Karnak. His image was hawk-headed with a sun disc between two plumes.

Mut

She was originally a very ancient vulture goddess of Thebes but during the 18th Dynasty was married to the god Amun and with their adopted son Khonsu made up the Thebian Triad. The marriage of Amun and Mut was a reason for great annual celebrations in Thebes. Her role as mistress of the heavens or as sky goddess often had her appearing as a cow, standing behind her husband as he rose from the primeval sea Nu to his place in the heavens. More often she was represented with a double crown of Egypt on her head, a vulture's head or lioness' head on her forehead. Another role was as a great divine mother. She has a temple south of the main temple at Karnak.

Nefertum

He was one of the Memphis deities most often associated with perfumes. He was represented as a man with a lotus flower on his head.

Neith

The goddess of weaving, war and hunting, among other things. She was also protector of the dead and the Canopic jars. She wore a red crown of Lower Egypt and a shield on her head (sometimes held in her hand), held two crossed arrows and an ankh in her hand. She was connected with Sobek and was worshipped at Memphis, Esna and Fayoum.

Nekhbet

In her more important guise she was the vulture or serpent goddess, protectress of Upper Egypt and especially of its rulers. She was generally depicted with spreading wings held over the pharaoh while grasping in her claw the royal ring or other emblems. She always appeared as a woman, sometimes with a vulture's head and always wearing a white crown. Her special colour was white, in contrast to her counterpart Buto (red) who was the goddess of Lower Egypt. In another aspect she was worshipped as goddess of the Nile and consort of the river god. She was associated too with Mut.

Nephthys

Her name was translated as 'lady of the house'. She was the sister of Seth, Osiris and Isis. She was married to Seth. She had no children by her husband but a son, Anubis, by Osiris. She wears the hieroglyphs of her name on her head. She was one of the protector guardians of the Canopic jars and a goddess of the dead.

Nut

She was goddess of the sky, the vault of the heavens. She was wife/sister of Geb. The Egyptians believed that on five special days preceding the new year she gave birth on successive days to the deities Osiris, Horus, Seth, Isis and Nephthys. This was cause for great celebrations. She was usually depicted as a naked woman arched over Shu who supported her with upraised arms. She was also represented wearing a water pot or pear shaped vessel on her head, this being the hieroglyph of her name. Sometimes she was depicted as a cow, so that she could carry the sun-god Re on her back to the sky. The cow was usually spangled with stars to represent the night sky. It was supposed that the cow swallowed the sun that journeyed through her body during the night to emerge at sunrise. This was also considered a symbol of resurrection.

Osiris

This was one of the most important gods in ancient Egypt, the god of the dead, the god of the underworld and the god of plenty. He had the power to control the vegetation (particularly cereals because he began his career as a corn deity) that sprouted after the annual flooding of the Nile. He originated in the Delta at Busiris and it is suggested that he was once a real ruler. His importance spread to the whole of Egypt.

Annual celebrations included the moulding of a clay body in the shape of Osiris, filled with soil and containing seeds. This was moistened with water from the Nile and the sprouting grain symbolized the strength of Osiris. One of the main celebrations in the Temple at Abydos was associated with Osiris and it was fashionable to be buried or have a memorial on the processional road to Abydos and so absorb the blessing of Osiris. There are temples dedicated to Osiris at Edfu and on Bigah Island opposite Philae.

According to ancient Egyptian custom when a king and later any person died he became Osiris and thus through him mankind had some hope of resurrection. The Apis bull at Memphis also represented Osiris. The names Osiris-apis and Sarapis are derived from this.

He was shown as a mummy with his arm crossed over his breast, one hand holding a royal crook the other a ceremonial flail. These crook and flail sceptres on his portraits and statues showed he was god of the underworld. He wore a narrow plaited beard and the white crown of Upper Egypt and two red feathers.

Ptah

He was originally the local deity of the capital Memphis and his importance eventually spread over the whole of Egypt. He was very popular at Thebes and Abydos. He was worshipped as the creator of the gods of the Memphite theology. Ptah was the husband of Sekhmet and father of Nefertum. Only later was he associated with Osiris. He was the patron of craftsmen, especially sculptors. He was renowned for his skill as an engineer, stonemason, metal worker and artist.

He was always shown in human form, mummified or swathed in a winding sheet, with a clean shaven human head. He would be holding a staff and wearing an amulet. The Apis bull had its stall in the great temple of Ptah in Memphis.

Qebehsenuf

The falcon headed guardian of the Canopic jar of the intestines was the son of Horus.

Re

This was the sun-god of Heliopolis and the supreme judge. He was the main god at the time of the New Kingdom. His importance was great. His cult centre was Heliopolis and the cult reached the zenith in the fifth Dynasty when he had become the official god of the pharaohs and every king was both the son of Re and Re incarnate.

Re was the god who symbolized the sun. He appeared in many aspects and was portrayed in many different ways. He was found in conjunction with other gods Re-Horakhte, Amun-Re, Min-Re etc. As Amun-Re (Amun was the god from Thebes) he was king of the gods and responsible for the pharaoh on military campaigns where he handed the scimitar of conquest to the great warriors. Re was king and father of the gods and the creator of mankind. It was believed that after death, the pharaoh in his barge joined Re in the heavens.

He was thought to travel across the sky each day in his solar boat and during the night make his passage in the underworld in another boat. He was represented as man with a hawk or falcon's head wearing a sun disc or if dead with a ram's head.

Sekhmet

This was another aspect of the goddess Hathor. Sekhmet the consort of Ptah was a fierce goddess of war and the destroyer of the enemies of her father the sun-god Re. She was usually depicted as a lioness or as a woman with a lion's head on which was placed the solar disc and the uraeus. She was also the goddess who was associated with pestilence, and could bring disease and death to mankind but her task also was to do the healing and her priests were often doctors. She was said to have chained the serpent Apophis.

Selket

This was one of the four goddesses who protected the sources of the Nile. As the guardian of the dead she was portrayed often with a scorpion on her head. She was put in charge of the bound serpent Apophis in the underworld.

Seshat

Seshat was shown as a woman with a seven-point star on her head, and dressed in a panther skin. She was the goddess of writing and of recording the years. She carried a palm leaf on which she wrote her records.

Seth

Seth did not begin with such bad press. He was in favour in the 19th Dynasty especially in the Eastern Delta around Tanis but by the Late Period he was considered evil and on some monuments his image was effaced. By the Christian era he was firmly in place as the devil. The Egyptians thought Seth who was the brother of Osiris, Isis and Nephthys tried to prevent the sun from rising each dawn. As such an enemy of mankind they represented him as a huge serpent-dragon. He was sometimes depicted as a hippopotamus and sometimes took the form of a crocodile as he did to avoid the avenging Horus. More often he was depicted as an unidentified animal, a greyhound, dog, pig, ass, okapi, anteater or a man with the head of an animal. The head had an unusual long down curved snout and the ears were upstanding and square-tipped. The eyes were slanting and the tail long and forked. He was also seen in drawings standing at the prow of the sun-god's boat.

Shu

He and his twin sister and wife Tefnut were created by the sun-god Re by his own power without the aid of a woman. They were the first couple of the ennead of Heliopolis. He was father of Geb the earth god and Nut the sky goddess. He was the representation of air and emptiness, of light and space, the supporter of the sky.

He was portrayed in human form with the hieroglyph of his name, an ostrich feather on his head. Often he was drawn separating Geb and Nut, for their union was not approved of by Re.

Sobek

He was known as the crocodile god, protector of reptiles and of kings. Crocodile gods were common in Fayoum, mainly at the time of the Middle Kingdom and also at Esna and Kom Ombo. Live crocodiles at the temples were believed to be this god incarnate and accordingly were treated very well. These sacred crocodiles were pampered and bejewelled and kept in a lake before the temples. After death they were mummified. Confusingly he was usually depicted with Amun's crown of rams' horns and feathers.

Taweret
This upright pregnant hippopotamus had pendant human breasts, lion's paws and a crocodile's tail. Sometimes she wore the horns of Hathor with a solar disc. She was also known as Apet/Opet. She was the goddess of childbirth and attended both royal births and the daily rebirth of the sun. She was a goddess at Esna.

Tefnut
She was the wife/sister of Shu, the lion-headed goddess of moisture and dew, one of the Heliopolitan ennead.

Thoth
His cult originated in the Nile Delta and wa s then mainly centred in Upper Egypt. He was held to be the inventor of writing, founder of social order, creator of languages, patron of scribes, interpreter and adviser to the gods, and representative of the sun-god Re on earth. He gave the Egyptians knowledge of medicine and mathematics. He possessed a book in which all the wisdom of the world was recorded. In another aspect he was known as the moon god. He was also associated with the birth of the earth.

Thoth protected Isis during her pregnancy and healed the injury to Horus inflicted by Seth. He too was depicted in the feather/heart weighing judgement ceremonies of the diseased and as the scribe reported the results to Osiris. His sacred animals were the ibis and the baboon. Numerous mummified bodies of these two animals were found in cemeteries in Hermopolis and Thebes. He was usually represented as a human with an ibis' head. The curved beak of the ibis was like the crescent moon so the two were connected and the ibis became the symbol of the moon god Thoth.

Wepwawet
He was the jackal-headed god of Middle Egypt, especially popular in the Assiut region. He was know as 'the opener of the ways'.

Glossary

A

Abbasids Muslim Dynasty ruled from Baghdad 750-1258

Agora Market/meeting place

Aïd/Eïd Festival

Aïn Spring

Almohads Islamic Empire in North Africa 1130-1269

Amir Mamluk military officer

Amulet Object with magical power of protection

Ankh Symbol of life

Apis bull A sacred bull worshipped as the living image of Ptah

Arabesque Geometric pattern with flowers and foliage used in Islamic designs

B

Bab City gate

Bahri North/northern

Baladiyah Municipality

Baksheesh Money as alms, tip or bribe

Baraka Blessing

Barbary Name of North Africa 16th-19th centuries

Basha See Pasha

Basilica Imposing Roman building, with aisles, later used for worship

Bazaar Market

Bedouin Nomadic desert Arab

Beni Sons of (tribe)

Berber Indigenous tribe of North Africa

Bey Governor (Ottoman)

Borj Fort

Burnous Man's cloak with hood – tradional wear

C

Caid Official

Calèche Horse-drawn carriage

Canopic jars Four jars used to store the internal organs of the mummified deceased

Capital Top section of a column

Caravanserai Lodgings for travellers and animals around a courtyard

Cartouche Oval ring containing a king's name in hieroglyphics

Chechia Man's small red felt hat

Chotts Low-lying salt lakes

Colossus Gigantic statue

D

Dar House

Darj w ktaf Carved geometric motif of intersecting arcs with super-imposed rectangles

Deglet Nur High quality translucent date

Delu Water-lifting device at head of well

Dey Commander (of janissaries)

Dikka Raised platform in mosque for Koramic readings

Djemma Main or Friday mosque

Djin Spirit

Dólmenes Prehistoric cave

Dour Village settlement

E

Eïd See Aïd

Eïn See Aïn

Erg Sand dune desert

F

Faqirs Muslim who has taken a vow of poverty

Fatimids Muslim dynasty AD 909-1171 claiming descent from Mohammed's daughter Fatimah

Fatwa Islamic district

Fellaheen Peasants

Felucca Sailing boat on Nile

Fondouk/Funduq Lodgings for goods and animals around a courtyard

Forum Central open space in Roman town

Fuul Fava beans

G

Gallabiyya Outer garment with sleeves and a hood – often striped

Garrigue Poor quality Mediterranean scrubland

Gymnasium Roman school for mind and body

H

Haikal Altar area

Hallal Meat from animals killed in accordance with Islamic law

Hamada Stone desert
Hammam Bath house
Harem Women's quarters
Harira Soup
Hypogeum The part of the building below ground, underground chamber

I

Iconostasis Wooden screen supporting icons
Imam Muslim religious leader

J

Jabal See Jebel
Jami' Mosque
Janissaries Elite Ottoman soldiery
Jarapas Rough cloth made with rags
Jebel Mountain
Jihad Holy war by Muslims against non-believers

K

Ka Spirit
Khedivate The realm of Mohammed Ali and his successors
Kilim Woven carpet
Kif Hashish
Kissaria Covered market
Koubba Dome on tomb of holy man
Kufic Earliest style of Arabic script
Kuttab Korami school for young boys or orphans

L

Lintel Piece of stone over a doorway
Liwan Vaulted arcade
Loculus Small compartment or cell, recess

M

Mahboub Coins worn as jewellery
Malekite Section of Sunni Islam
Malqaf Wind vent
Maquis Mediterranean scrubland – often aromatic
Marabout Muslim holy man/his tomb
Maristan Hospital
Mashrabiyya Wooden screen
Mastaba Tomb
Mausoleum Large tomb building
Medresa School usually attached to a mosque
Médina Old walled town, residential quarter
Mellah Jewish quarter of old town
Menzel House
Mihrab Recess in wall of mosque indicating direction of Mecca
Minaret Tower of mosque from which the muezzin calls the faithful to prayer
Minbar Pulpit in a mosque
Mosque Muslim place of worship
Moulid Religious festival – Prophet's birthday
Moussem Religious gathering
Muezzin Priest who calls the faithful to prayer
Mullah Muslim religious teacher
Murabtin Dependent tribe

N

Necropolis Cemetery
Noas Shrine or chapel
Nome District or province

O

Oasis Watered desert gardens
Obelisk Tapering monolithic shaft of stone with pyramidal apex
Ostraca Inscribed rock flakes and potsherds
Ottoman Muslim Empire based in Turkey 13th-20th centuries
Ouled Tribe
Outrepassé Horse-shoe shaped arch

P

Papyrus (papyri) Papers used by Ancient Egyptians
Pasha Governor
Phoenicians Important trading nation based in eastern Mediterranean from 1100 BC
Pilaster Square column partly built into, partly projecting from, the wall
Pisé Sun-baked clay used for building
Piste Unsurfaced road
Pylon Gateway of Egyptian temple
Pyramidion A small pyramid shaped cap stone for the apex of a pyramid

Q

Qarafah Graveyard
Qibla Mosque wall in direction of Mecca

R

Rabbi Head of Jewish community
Ramadan Muslim month of fasting

Reg Rock desert
Ribat Fortified monastery
Riwaq Arcaded aisle

S

Sabil Public water fountain
Sabkha Dry salt lake
Saggia Water canal
Sahel Coast/coastal plain
Sahn Courtyard
Salat Worship
Saqiya Water wheel
Sarcophagus Decorated stone coffin
Sebkha See Sabkha
Semi-columnar Flat on one side and rounded on the other
Serais Lodging for men and animals
Serir Sand desert
Shadoof Water lifting device
Shahada Profession of faith
Shawabti Statuette buried with deceased, designed to work in the hereafter for its owner
Shergui Hot, dry desert wind
Sidi Saint
Souk Traditional market
Stalactite An ornamental arrangement of multi-tiered niches, like a honeycomb, found in domes and portrals
Stele Inscribed pillar used as gravestone
Suani Small, walled irrigated traditional garden
Sufi Muslim mystic
Sunni Orthodox Muslims

T

Tagine/tajine Meat stew
Taifa Sub-tribe
Tariqa Brotherhood/Order
Thòlos Round building, dome, cupola
Triclinium A room with benches on three sides
Troglodyte Underground/cave dweller

U

Uraeus Rearing cobra symbol, sign of kingship

V

Vandals Ruling empire in North Africa 429-534 AD
Vizier Governor

W

Wadi Water course, usually dry
Waqf Endowed land
Wikala Merchants' hostel
Wilaya/wilayat Governorate/district

Z

Zaouia/zawia/zawiya Shrine/Sennusi centre
Zellij Geometrical mosaic pattern made from pieces of glazed tiles
Zeriba House of straw/grass

Index → *Entries in bold refer to maps.*

D

E

F

G

M

U

V

W

Y

Z

Credits

Footprint credits

Project editor: Nicola Gibbs
Layout and production: Emma Bryers
Cover and colour section: Pepi Bluck
Maps: Kevin Feeney
Proofreader: Ria Gane

Managing Director: Andy Riddle
Commercial Director: Patrick Dawson
Publisher: Alan Murphy
Publishing Managers: Felicity Laughton, Nicola Gibbs
Digital Editors: Jo Williams, Jen Haddington, Tom Mellors
Marketing and PR: Liz Harper
Advertising: Renu Sibal
Finance and administration: Elizabeth Taylor

Photography credits

Front cover: Bas relief at Thebes Necropolis, Paule Seux / hemis.fr
Back cover: Qurna, painted house, Paule Seux / hemis.fr

P1: Chad Ehlers / photolibrary.com
P2-3: Carl Hiebert / photolibrary.com
P6-7: Bildagentur-online / McPhoto/Alamy
P8: RCB Shooter / Shutterstock

Printed in India by Nutech Print Services.

Every effort has been made to ensure that the facts in this guidebook are accurate. However, travellers should still obtain advice from consulates, airlines etc about travel and visa requirements before travelling. The authors and publishers cannot accept responsibility for any loss, injury or inconvenience however caused.

Publishing information

Footprint Egypt
6th edition

May 2011

ISBN: 978 1 907263 40 8
CIP DATA: A catalogue record for this book is available from the British Library

Published by Footprint
6 Riverside Court
Lower Bristol Road
Bath BA2 3DZ, UK
T +44 (0)1225 469141
F +44 (0)1225 469461
footprinttravelguides.com

Distributed in the USA by Globe Pequot Press, Guilford, Connecticut

Acknowledgements

First, my great thanks to Debra Winters for all her research, hard work and enthusiasm in covering the Western Desert and Aswan – and also for being such an excellent travel companion. Neither would this project have been possible without the help and knowledge shared by Jeff Allen, Saad Ali, Jane and Mike Betts, Katharine Bowerman, Kevin Eisenstadt, Hassan El Assy, Annemarie Hickman, Hakeem Hussein, Mahdi Hweiti, Mohamed at El-Qasr Resthouse, Sara Kayser, Ashraf Lotfi, Walid Ramadan, Eran Shaham, Mohamed Tahun, Anne Tiernan, Sam Ward and Claudia Wiens. I thank you all so very much.

Thank you also to everyone at Footprint, especially Nicola Gibbs and Alan Murphy.